D1434778

Corporation Tax

2013-2014

Your book is fully updated online. Make sure you have your login details!

Your key benefits

Memo Online – a regularly updated service that features the entire contents of the book:

- fully searchable and always up to date giving you peace of mind

- store information, create notes and set up alerts to suit your own needs

Multi-user version – enabling more than one person to access the service at the same time (option available on request at www.flmemo.co.uk/requestlogin.php)

Email updates – alerting you to the latest news and fully integrated in the online service

Indicator has joined forces with **FL Memo**

Abbreviations

The following abbreviations are used in *Corporation Tax Memo*:

ACSOP	Approved Company Share Option Plan	FII	Franked Investment Income
ACT	Advance Corporation Tax	FRS	Financial Reporting Standard
AGM	Annual General Meeting	FRSSE	Financial Reporting Standard for Smaller Entities
AIA	Annual Investment Allowance		
AIM	Alternative Investment Market	FSA	Financial Services Authority
ARD	Accounting Reference Date	FSMA 2000	Financial Services and Markets Act 2000
Art	Article		
ARTG	Appeals, Reviews and Tribunals Guidance	FYA	First Year Allowance
		GAAP	Generally Accepted Accounting Principles
ASB	Accounting Standards Board		
BIM	Business Income Manual	GREIT	Guidance on Real Estate Investment Trusts Manual
BIS	Department for Business, Innovation and Skills		
		HMRC	H.M. Revenue and Customs
BS	British Standard	IA	Initial Allowance
CAA 2001	Capital Allowances Act 2001	IA 1986	Insolvency Act 1986
CA 1985	Companies Act 1985	IAS	International Accounting Standard
CA 2006	Companies Act 2006	IASB	International Accounting Standards Board
CASC	Community Amateur Sports Club		
CFC	Controlled Foreign Company	ICAEW	Institute of Chartered Accountants in England and Wales
CFM	Corporate Finance Manual		
CG	Capital Gains Manual	ICTA 1988	Income and Corporation Taxes Act 1988
CG group	Capital Gains Group		
CH	Compliance Handbook Manual	IFRS	International Financial Reporting Standards
CIHC	Close Investment Holding Company		
CIOT	Chartered Institute of Taxation	INTM	International Manual
CIR	Commissioners of Inland Revenue	IPTM	Insurance Policyholder Taxation Manual
CIRD	Corporate Intangibles Research and Development manual		
		IR35	Personal Service Company Rules
CITM	Community Investment Tax Relief Manual	IRC	Inland Revenue Commissioners
		ITA 2007	Income Tax Act 2007
Co	Company	ITEPA 2003	Income Tax (Earnings and Pensions) Act 2003
CTA 2009	Corporation Tax Act 2009		
CTA 2010	Corporation Tax Act 2010	ITTOIA 2005	Income Tax (Trading and Other Income) Act 2005
CTM	Company Tax Manual		
CTSA	Corporation Tax Self Assessment	LIFFE	London International Financial Futures and Options Exchange
CVS	Corporate Venturing Scheme		
DMBM	Debt Management and Banking Manual	LIFO	Last In First Out
		LLP	Limited Liability Partnership
DOTAS	Disclosure of Tax Avoidance Schemes	LTA 1987	Landlord and Tenant Act 1987
DTI	Department of Trade and Industry	Ltd	Limited
DWP	Department for Work and Pensions	MCT	Mainstream Corporation Tax
EBT	Employee Benefit Trust	MSC	Managed Service Company
EC	European Community	NBCG	Non-statutory Business Clearance Guidance
ECJ	European Court of Justice		
EEC	European Economic Community	NIC	National Insurance Contributions
EIS	Enterprise Investment Scheme	OECD	Organisation for Economic Cooperation and Development
EM	Enquiry Manual		
ESC	Extra Statutory Concession	OEIC	Open Ended Investment Company
ESOP	Employee Stock Ownership Plan	OFM	Offshore Fund Manual
ESOT	Employee Share Ownership Trust	Para	Paragraph
EU	European Union	PAYE	Pay As You Earn/PAYE Manual
FA	Finance Act	PCTCT	Profits Chargeable to Corporation Tax
FHL	Furnished Holiday Letting	PE	Permanent Establishment
FIFO	First In First Out	PID	Property Income Distributions

PIM	Property Income Manual	SRSOS	Savings Related Share Option Scheme
plc	Public Limited Company	SSE	Substantial Shareholding Exemption
PLR	Potential Lost Revenue	SSAP	Statement of Standard Accounting
PR	Press Release		Practice
QCB	Qualifying Corporate Bond	TB	Tax Bulletin
R&D	Research and Development	TCGA 1992	Taxation of Chargeable Gains Act 1992
RE	Relief Instructions Manual	Tech	ICAEW Technical Release
Reg	Regulation	TIOPA	Taxation (International and Other
REIT	Real Estate Investment Trust	2010	Provisions Act) 2010
RPI	Retail Prices Index	TMA 1970	Taxes Management Act 1970
s	Section	TSEM	Trusts, Settlements and Estates Manual
SACM	Self-Assessment Claims Manual	TWDV	Tax Written Down Value
SCE	Societas Co-operative Europaea	UITF	Urgent Issues Task Force
Sch	Schedule	UK	United Kingdom
SDLT	Stamp Duty Land Tax	VAT	Value Added Tax
SE	Societas Europaea	VCM	Venture Capital Schemes Manual
SI	Statutory Instrument	VCT	Venture Capital Trust
SP	Statement of Practice	WDA	Writing Down Allowance
SIP	Share Incentive Plan	YMCA	Young Men's Christian Association

Contents

Preface

Corporation Tax Memo 2013-2014 is the **latest addition** to the FL Memo range, bringing you a new, comprehensive coverage of this subject in the distinctive FL Memo style.

Corporation tax is both a cost and area of risk to all companies, which needs to be controlled and reduced (where possible). The tax evolves on almost a daily basis not only via legislative changes, but also as a result of case law, HMRC Briefs and other official material.

The material in *Corporation Tax Memo* is fully updated to reflect changes in law and practice up to 1 September 2013, but, as with all our Memo publications, we will keep you **updated regarding changes** as they happen throughout the year via our:
- full **online service**, with integrated updates;
- **fortnightly emails** detailing developments or points of interest; and
- full analysis of the **Budget** report and other significant developments.

Corporation Tax Memo 2013-2014 is unique in its style, with the full complexities of corporation tax explained in language you can understand, reliably written by our experienced in-house tax professionals. The **precise text** is founded on statute, case law and other official materials, with legislative and other references given throughout. The book is also packed with **worked examples** and practical tips to enhance the expert commentary.

Corporation Tax Memo 2013-2014 is **easy to navigate**, progressing from section plan through chapter outline to specific paragraph, which means you can easily find the answer to your particular query. Each section is devoted to a separate area of corporation tax, comprehensively indexed and fully cross-referenced to related topics. The appendix contains many tables of numerical and factual data, in addition to a complete table of cases.

Indicator-FL Memo Ltd
October 2013

PART 1

Scope

Scope
Summary

The numbers cross-refer to paragraphs.

Basic principles

A. Purpose

Initially, companies used to be subject to the same taxation system as individuals, paying income tax on the profits which they made. In 1965, this was changed so that companies paid tax under their own specific system. Successive amendments were made over the following years before the framework of the current system was introduced in 1999, along with the addition of self-assessment for corporation tax.   **1000**

One of the **major reasons** for the imposition of corporation tax stemmed from the differences which arose between the unincorporated traders (around which the tax system had grown) and the new corporate entity which had an identity which was separate from that of its owners. A company's ability to retain funds and distribute them to individual shareholders initially resulted in a level of double taxation, with profits being taxed once in the company, and then again when distributed. To counter this, an imputation system was introduced which allowed a measure of credit to an individual for tax paid by the company. This system still exists today (see *Tax Memo* for details on the taxation of dividends for individual shareholders).

Successive amendments have attempted to keep pace with the changing nature of companies' operations e.g. as more companies have established operations abroad, or to combat avoidance schemes. In some cases, changes have been made to incentivise certain types of corporate behaviour, such as encouraging expenditure on research and development.

The imposition of corporation tax is seen as a fundamental necessity in terms of what it provides toward government spending. In 2011/12, according to the Office for National Statistics, the government raised over £42,000 million from corporation tax.   **1005**

B. Sources of authority

Primary legislation

Although corporation tax has to be renewed every year via the Finance Act, the majority of the provisions relating to it reside in existing legislation. The most relevant pieces of legislation are: **1035**
– Taxes Management Act 1970;

- Income and Corporation Taxes Act 1988;
- Taxation of Chargeable Gains Act 1992;
- Finance Act 1998;
- Capital Allowances Act 2001;
- Corporation Tax Act 2009; and
- Corporation Tax Act 2010.

When the **legislation needs to be amended**, or where new legislation is introduced, this will generally be done by way of changing one of the main statutes. However, in some cases, the legislation will remain in the Finance Act itself. For instance, the Finance Act 1998 introduced the self-assessment rules for companies, and this is where those rules remain.

Secondary legislation

1040   A number of **statutory instruments and regulations** are made by the Government without the need for full parliamentary approval. When making primary legislation, i.e. Acts of Parliament, the Government reserves the power to make minor adjustments to the legislation so that these can be enacted far more quickly than legislation passing through the normal parliamentary process. Such uses have included the ability to extend or restrict the availability of certain schemes such as:
- the introduction of enhanced capital allowances for "green" expenditure; or
- changing elements of the loan relationship rules in order to keep up to date with revised accounting standards.

Other sources

1045   There are a wide number of non-statutory materials which either have the force of law, or are persuasive guidance in its interpretation.

Material	Detail
UK case law	There is a significant catalogue of decisions made in previous cases which form precedent for lower courts These precedents are, in effect, law made by the courts, typically in making interpretations of the legislation, although sometimes it stretches further than this In some situations, decisions in non-tax cases may be binding on a court where the decision is on a common definition
European cases	Cases decided in Europe are increasingly affecting domestic corporation tax rules For example, cases relating to losses in groups with overseas companies, and controlled foreign companies have forced the UK Government to make significant changes to domestic legislation to comply with its obligations under European law
Statements of practice	These are issued by HMRC stating their interpretation of the law, and how they will apply it in given circumstances
Extra-statutory concessions	These are areas where discretion given to HMRC under the legislation is exercised in favour of the taxpayer After a court decision, however, these are now being examined on an individual basis to see if the particular concession is outside the discretion given to HMRC and, where appropriate, are either being repealed or embodied in legislation
Press releases	HMRC publish these for a number of purposes, including: - to announce measures which are to be introduced in a forthcoming Finance Act but are intended to come into effect prior to the Act being passed; and - to give HMRC's view on a topical matter

Material	Detail
HMRC manuals	These consist of the internal guidance given to HMRC staff, including details on procedures and checks that should be made on returns These are very useful for practitioners when ascertaining areas of risk, and how HMRC will approach certain matters However, certain parts of the guidance are not available to the public under the Freedom of Information Act 2000
Accounting standards	As the starting point for any corporation tax calculation is the profit shown in the accounts, accounting standards are of fundamental importance in the process A number of tax cases over the years have been decided based purely upon prevailing accountancy practice at the time

C. Administration

Enforcement

The **responsibility** to apply the legislation and collect tax rests with the Commissioners for Her Majesty's Revenue and Customs (HMRC). This body was created in 2005 after the merger of the Inland Revenue and HM Customs and Excise. They process the necessary returns, make assessments, deal with claims made, apply allowances, carry out enquiries and collect tax due.

1075

Generally speaking, a company will be **allocated a tax office** based on its geographical location. However, there are a number of specialist offices which deal with certain sectors such as oil companies or charities. There is also a continuing evolution within HMRC which is reducing the number of offices, resulting in changes to the way in which enquiries, in particular, are being handled. However, with the requirement for online filing, this is unlikely to affect most companies in their day to day dealings with HMRC.

Large business offices Over the past few years, HMRC have been attempting to forge closer links with businesses, and have introduced large business offices in order to deal with the tax affairs of the **largest companies** in the UK. Each of the companies covered by a large business office (LBO) is allocated to one of 17 business sectors, and has a customer relationship manager (CRM) assigned to them. It is this single point of contact which the company will use for queries about all taxes relating to the company. HMRC believe that this will allow the CRM to be able to gain a better knowledge of the business of the company, and so assist it more efficiently. The CRM is also able to work with the company to identify where there may be compliance risks and address them accordingly.

1080

Company's responsibilities

Since 1999, a system of self-assessment has applied to corporation tax. This means that the company is responsible for the calculation of its own tax liabilities. It must submit its calculations, along with accounts and specified returns, to HMRC by a due date. These are simply checked for arithmetical issues at this point and the return is accepted as correct. However, HMRC have a time period during which they can enquire into the return. Although a number of these are chosen randomly, each return undergoes a risk assessment so that certain returns can be targeted.

1085

CHAPTER 2

Who is liable?

A. Entities affected

Basic principles

2000   Although it is largely believed that corporation tax only applies to companies, this is incorrect. A company is **defined** as any body corporate or unincorporated association. As such, this **includes** all companies and may affect:
– companies limited by shares or guarantee;
– unlimited companies;
– companies registered under the Industrial and Provident Societies Acts;
– building societies registered under the Building Societies Acts;
– trading or investment companies;
– foreign-based companies with a permanent establishment in the UK (¶2055);
– co-operatives;
– charities (¶86000+) or community amateur sports clubs (¶86270+), where elements of their income may be subject to tax, including companies owned by charities; and
– clubs and associations, and other unincorporated associations. These are generally accepted as "two or more persons bound together for one or more common undertakings, each having mutual duties and obligations, in an organisation which has rules which identify in whom control of it and its funds rest and on what terms, and which can be joined or left at will". *Conservative & Unionist Central Office v Burrell* [1982]

Corporation tax will **not extend to** the following:
– sole traders, or partnerships between individuals;
– limited liability partnerships;
– local authorities and local authority associations;
– investment clubs; or
– health service bodies.

B. Residence issues

2030   The residence of a company is critically important as it will determine the extent to which UK corporation tax will be applied.

Determining a company's residence

There are two **methods** of determining a company's residence status. If either of these give the UK as the place of residence, all of the company's profits will be subject to UK corporation tax. A company will be considered resident in the UK if it is either:
– incorporated in the UK (although it may be considered not resident where it is dual resident and a double tax convention applies to deem the company as resident in the other state (¶90050+); or
– its central management and control takes place in the UK.

2035
ss 13–18
CTA 2009

Central management and control

The test of central management and control, and the fact that exercising this in the UK would make a company UK resident, is not laid down in statute but is well established through various court decisions. There is no single test or single factor which determines the situation, and as such, each case must be examined based on its own facts.

In examining the situation, it is the highest form of control that is taken into account, as opposed to the day to day business decisions. Ordinarily, this will be where the board meetings of the company take place. However, it should not automatically be assumed that this approach will be accepted by HMRC.

2040

> EXAMPLE
> 1. The sole shareholder of a Dutch incorporated company appointed himself as co-director of the company. Although not considered to be resident in the UK, he spent significant amounts of time in the UK and worked in London. During his employment he arranged a transaction for the Dutch company, involving the purchase and sale of shares. His fellow director was resident in the Netherlands.
> The Dutch resident director prepared board minutes regarding the arrangement, but the tribunal found that these were sufficiently flawed in their explanation of the actual agreements finally entered into that the person carrying out the work of the company (both on the day to day level and board level) was the director located in the UK, and that this work was carried out whilst he was in the UK. The tribunal stated that the director's activities went much further than "ministerial matters or matters of good housekeeping" to the extent that they were concerned with "policy, strategic and management matters", and that this included "decision-making" in relation to the company's business.
> This continued after the UK-based director resigned, and although the board decisions were minuted in the Netherlands, it was clear that the remaining director was exercising no discretion and blindly following the shareholders' decisions. As such, it was considered that the central management and control of the company was performed in the UK, making the company UK resident. *Laerstate BV* [2009]
> 2. A South African diamond mine was owned by a company registered there. Its head office was also located in South Africa with the shareholders meeting there as well. The diamonds were sold via a London syndicate. Although its directors met in both South Africa and London, the majority of the directors were resident in London.
> It was held that, as a matter of fact, the company's worldwide activities were controlled from the UK. *De Beers Consolidated Mines Ltd v Howe* [1906]

It is not common practice for HMRC to argue that the central management and control of a **subsidiary** is where the parent company is located. However, they will make this assertion where the parent simply assumes control of the board of the subsidiary company.

2045

> EXAMPLE A company incorporated in the US was owned by its parent based in the UK. Its Articles of Association stated that any ordinary meetings of the shareholders would take place in the US, but any extraordinary general meetings must take place in the UK. A minority of the directors were resident in the US, and they were to run the company on a day to day basis. However, all extraordinary board meetings had to take place in the UK and this was the only type of meeting at which policy could be affected. The majority of the directors were based in the UK and also served on the board of the parent company. This, coupled with the fact that policy decisions could only be made in the UK, led the court to decide that the subsidiary was in fact controlled from the UK, and as such, resident here. *American Thread Co v Joyce* [1913]

Effect of residence

2050
s5 CTA 2009

The determination of a company's residence is vital in ensuring that the correct sources of income or gains are subjected to tax in the UK. The following table outlines the extent of taxation on the profits and gains arising, depending on a company's residence status and the origin of the profits or gains.

Company's status	UK profits	UK gains	Overseas profits and gains
Resident in UK	y	y	y
Non-resident but having permanent establishment (PE) in UK	Arising from PE trade only [1]	On assets used in PE only	Not taxed
Non-UK resident	n [2]	n	n

Note:
1. The profits arising from the UK PE will be subject to corporation tax as if it is a separate entity from the company itself.
2. If a non-UK resident company generates other income in the UK, this will be subject to income tax at the basic rate.

Permanent establishment

2055
ss 1141-1144
CTA 2010

A permanent establishment (PE) can either be:
– a **fixed place of business** from which the business of the company is at least partly carried on. This may include its place of management, a branch, an office, factory, building site or similar; or
– an **agent acting** for the company who has, and regularly exercises, authority in acting for the company.

A company will **not be deemed** to have a PE in the UK where:
– an independent agent acts in the ordinary course of business on their behalf; or
– the activities undertaken by an agent, or at a fixed place of business, are only considered to be auxiliary or preparatory to the activity of the business as a whole. This may include using facilities for the storage of goods belonging to the company, or the purchasing of goods for the company.
For further details, see ¶92140+.

CHAPTER 3

What is liable?

A. Chargeable profits

The **starting point** for assessing the profits of a company is the statutory accounts. These will generally be prepared in terms of the various Companies Acts. However, since a number of bodies which are subject to corporation tax are not subject to the Companies Acts, the **legislation states** that the profits of any trade must be computed based on generally accepted accounting standards. This means that the profits should be accounted for in accordance with either UK GAAP or IAS (¶11055+).

3000
s 46 CTA 2009

The **income and expenses** are then **split** according to the source of the income, as different rules apply to different sources of income. The categorisation of income is listed below.

3005

Type of income	¶¶
Trading income	¶14000+
Property income	¶10000+
Profits from non-trading loan relationships	¶16350+
Income from overseas	¶90000+
Distributions received (and income received after deduction of tax)	¶18295+
Chargeable gains	¶30000+
Miscellaneous income	¶21050+

Further, if the company has **two or more trades**, these should also be separated for computational purposes as a number of provisions are restricted based on the trade. For instance, losses made in one trade and carried forward can only be used against profits of that same trade in later periods. Each trade will also require the preparation of a capital allowances computation (¶25110+).

Once the various rules have been applied to each source, the resulting totals are then aggregated before the company's profits are subjected to tax. The **basic format** is as follows:

3010

	£
Trading income	x
Loan relationship gains	x
Overseas income	x
Miscellaneous income	x
Income from land and property	x
Income received under deduction of tax and taxable distributions	x
Chargeable gains	x
	x
Less: Payments qualifying for charitable donations relief	(x)
Profit chargeable to corporation tax	x
Corporation tax thereon @ x %	x.xx
Less: Income tax suffered at source	(x.xx)
Net corporation tax payable	x.xx

B. Chargeable periods

3040 Corporation tax is charged by reference to accounting periods of a company, but the **rates are set** based on financial years (FY). **Financial years** start on 1 April and run through to 31 March of the following year. They are denoted by the year in which they start, for instance, FY13 runs from 1 April 2013 to 31 March 2014.

An accounting period is not the same as a **period of account**. A period of account is the period for which a company prepares its accounts. Generally speaking, for a continuing business where the accounting reference date does not change, the chargeable period will be the 12 month period matching the period for which it prepares statutory accounts. After an accounting period ends, a new one automatically begins.

Start of an accounting period

3045
s 9 CTA 2009

A company's **first accounting period** commences when it first comes within the charge to corporation tax. This could be when the company:
– commences to trade;
– opens an interest-bearing bank account;
– becomes resident in the UK; or
– makes a disposal of an asset resulting in a chargeable gain or allowable loss at a time that would not otherwise be in a chargeable period.

Subsequent accounting periods will start on the day following the end of the last one, unless the company is no longer within the charge to corporation tax.

> EXAMPLE A company agreed to sell its trade and assets to a fellow group company, with the purchase price left outstanding on loan. There was no provision in the sale agreement for interest to be charged on the outstanding loan. At the same time, the two companies entered into an agency agreement so that the vendor continued trading but on the purchaser's behalf. There was no provision for the company to be remunerated for its work as agent.
> It was decided that the trade, and therefore the accounting period, ceased when the trade was sold. As there was no source of income arising, the company was no longer within the charge to corporation tax, and so no new period began.
> Some time later, a sum was deposited in an interest-bearing account, and this triggered the start of a new accounting period. *Walker v Centaur Clothes Group Ltd* [2000]

End of an accounting period

An accounting period will be deemed to end at the **first of any of the following**:
- 12 months passing since the start of the period;
- the company's period end date passes (known as its accounting reference date);
- the end of a period for which the company does not make up accounts;
- the company starting or ceasing to trade;
- the company ceasing to be chargeable to UK corporation tax, for instance either by cessation of trade (or all of its trades if there are more than one) or by becoming non-resident; or
- entering, or coming out of, administration.

Where a company has **more than one trade**, and uses more than one accounting date, it can choose which will be used for the purposes of corporation tax. However, HMRC may override this choice if they believe another of the dates is more appropriate.

> <u>MEMO POINTS</u>   In some cases, such as where a company has not made any returns or prepared accounts, the start and end of an accounting period may be **unascertainable**. In this case, HMRC will make assessments based on what they believe the periods to be, and can amend these should more information come to light.

3050
s 10 CTA 2009

s 11 CTA 2009;
CTM01530

s 12(8) ICTA 1988;
CTM01550

Annual variations in accounting date

In some cases a company may make up **accounts to a specific day** rather than date, for instance, the last Saturday in August. This practice can be quite common, particularly amongst clubs and associations. HMRC will accept these accounts as being for a year, provided the date to which they are made up does not vary from the mean date by more than 4 days. The **mean date** is calculated as being the middle date between the latest and earliest that the accounting date would be.

In order **to receive this treatment**, the company must agree that:
- each period is to be treated as a 12 month period, and that all assessments are based on the 12 months to the mean date; and
- for all other corporation tax purposes, the accounts are treated as being made up for the 12 months to the mean date.

> <u>EXAMPLE</u>   A Ltd makes up its accounts to the Saturday nearest 31 July each year, and has formally agreed to 31 July as its mean date. A Ltd makes up accounts from Sunday 29 July 2012 to Saturday 3 August 2013. This will be treated as the return for the year to 31 July 2013.

3055
CTM01560

Period of account exceeding 12 months

It is possible that a company will **not prepare accounts** for a period that **matches** its chargeable period for corporation tax purposes.

> <u>EXAMPLE</u>   B Ltd decides to change its accounting reference date from 31 December to 30 June. In order to do so, the company prepares a set of accounts for the year to 31 December 2011, and then accounts for the 18 month period to 30 June 2013. Its accounting periods for tax will be the:
> - year ended 31 December 2011, based on the normal rules;
> - year ended 31 December 2012, based on 12 months after the commencement of the period; and
> - 6 month period running from 1 January 2013 to 30 June 2013, being the start of the next accounting period up to the company's accounting reference date.

3060
s 52 CTA 2009

Where the period of account **does not coincide** with the accounting periods that are determined under the rules at ¶3045 and ¶3050, there is no requirement to re-draft the accounts. A series of rules allows the company to **attribute** the profits from the longer period across the accounting periods. Each accounting period requires a computation and return.

Trading income   In the case of trading income, the rules allow a **time apportionment** to be made (to avoid the need to prepare a new set of accounts). The apportionment must be

3065
CTM01405

made based on the number of days falling into each period before any deductions for capital allowances.

> EXAMPLE Following on from the example in ¶3060, in the 18 month period to 30 June 2013, B Ltd showed adjusted profits for tax purposes before capital allowances of £250,000. This will be apportioned as follows based on 547 days in the longer period of account:
>
> | Chargeable period | Days in chargeable period | Profit apportioned £ |
> |---|---|---|
> | 1 Jan 2012 – 31 Dec 2012 | 366 | 167,276 |
> | 1 Jan 2013 – 30 Jun 2013 | 181 | 82,724 |

Where HMRC believe that using the time apportionment method leads to an **inappropriate result**, they may apportion profits in a more suitable manner.

> EXAMPLE C Ltd produced a set of accounts for a 5 3/4 year period, and apportioned the profits into 6 chargeable periods based on a time apportionment method. It was decided that this resulted in an inappropriate split of the profit. A different apportionment method was used instead, based on when a number of property deals were concluded. *Marshall Hus & Partners Ltd v Bolton* [1981]

Comment   This case was decided prior to a slight change in wording in 2009. At the time of the decision the wording said profits "shall" be split based on the number of days. From 2009 this was changed to "must". This slight change in wording may influence the position.

3070
ss 210, 1307
CTA 2009

Other income and deductions   The following table indicates how other types of income or deductions should be allocated between accounting periods. Where **time apportionment** is applicable, the method described for trading income should be used.

Type of income/deductions	Basis of allocation
Non-trading loan relationship credits and debits	Where possible, allocate to accounting period in which item accrues Otherwise, time apportion
Overseas income	Overseas trades: time apportion Other sources: allocate to accounting period in which income arises
Miscellaneous income	Time apportion
Income from land and property	Time apportion
Chargeable gains	Accounting period in which disposal occurs
Charitable donations	Accounting period in which paid
Capital allowances	Calculate separately for each accounting period

PART 2

Business activities

Business activities
Summary

The numbers cross-refer to paragraphs.

CHAPTER 1

Trading

Most of the time, it will be obvious whether a company is carrying on a trade. Indeed, the question of whether a trade exists is essentially one of fact. For this purpose, a professional activity is treated the same as trading.

5000

However, it may be less clear cut when unusual activities are undertaken, or losses are sustained without any future prospect of a profit.

If a trade is not present, it is necessary to consider whether any investment activity is undertaken (¶6000+), or whether the company is actually dormant (¶7000+).

SECTION 1

Definition

Although statute only says that the term "trade" includes any venture in the nature of trade, this actually has a very wide scope, which would include:

5050
s 1119 CTA 2010

– an isolated transaction *CIR v Fraser* [1942]; or

– a speculative adventure that yields an unexpected profit. *Wisdom v Chamberlain* [1968]

Trade must be used in its ordinary dictionary sense. *Smith Barry v Cordy* [1946]

It is often used to denote operations of a commercial character by which a trader provides some kind of goods and/or services to customers for reward. *Ransom v Higgs* [1974]

Whether the trade is intended to be **profitable**, or indeed ever makes a profit, is usually irrelevant (¶5330+).

Comment   Before the law was rewritten, statute referred to every trade, manufacture, adventure or concern in the nature of trade.

Profession

5055

Statute does not define profession, but the term **indicates** an occupation requiring intellectual skill e.g. an architect, or a controlled manual skill e.g. a sculptor. Incorporated firms of lawyers, accountants, surveyors etc will therefore be liable to corporation tax in the same way as a normal trading company.

s 35 CTA 2009

Comment   The rewritten law does not mention profession as it was deemed unlikely that a company would be carrying on a profession or vocation.

Influence of case law

5060
BIM20051

HMRC state that the following **conclusions** can be drawn from case law:
– trade cannot be precisely defined;
– certain characteristics can be identified which are normally those of a trade; and
– other characteristics can be found which preclude a profit from being that of a trade.

Case law is a fruitful source of principle, although care should be taken when comparing facts between a particular situation and settled case law, as there will inevitably be distinguishing factors which may lead to a different conclusion.

SECTION 2

Badges of trade

5110
BIM20201

The approach of the courts has been to examine the facts and look for the presence, or absence, of common features or characteristics of trade i.e. badges of trade. Some of these badges tend to be more pertinent to individuals who may be trading rather than companies, but they are included here for completeness. These factors were codified by a Royal Commission in 1955, and since then other elements have also become important, which are included in the table below.

It is not necessary to show that all the badges are present for an activity to be a trade.

Comment   **Intention** to trade is usually not admitted by a person who disputes the tax treatment of a transaction. It is important to differentiate between the intention to trade, and the intention to seek a profit from a transaction (¶5330+). Intention can be ignored where the facts and circumstances behind a transaction support one contention far more than the other, whether this be to the advantage or disadvantage of the taxpayer. Indeed, HMRC prefer to decide a case on its merits, based on the badges of trade, without having to rely on the stated or inferred intention of the taxpayer. The only time when intention is of paramount importance is when the facts are inconclusive, or where a transaction is undertaken with a dual motive (e.g. land acquired to accommodate an existing trade, but also with a view to development and resale).

Summary

5115

Badge	Detail	¶¶
Nature of the asset	Is it of a type normally sold for profit?	¶5145+
Period of ownership	Shorter period usually indicates trading	¶5190
Frequency and number of transactions	Repeated transactions support the existence of a trade	¶5210+
Changes made to the asset	Repaired or improved to maximise sale proceeds?	¶5250+
How was the sale carried out	Sold in a way typical of trading?	¶5285+

Badge	Detail	¶¶
Profit-seeking motive	An intention to make a profit supports trading, but by itself is not conclusive	¶5330+
Method of acquisition	Acquired as a gift or inheritance?	¶5375
Source of finance	Was borrowing necessary, or were other assets sold	¶5395
Existence of similar trading transactions	Does the scope of existing trade extend to new transactions	¶5415
Mutual trading	Trading with company members	¶5435

1. Nature of the asset

The nature of the asset can be of great importance when considering whether a trade exists, as some assets are clearly only bought to sell on (e.g. in a case featuring toilet rolls). On the other hand, others are unlikely to be the subject of a trading transaction because there is a **presumption** (although not a certainty) that they are bought either:
– for investment and perhaps exploited for income (e.g. shares);
– for personal enjoyment e.g. a painting, where any profit made on eventual sale is a welcome by-product of ownership rather than an end in itself; or
– as capital assets for an existing trade e.g. a printing press.

5145
BIM20245

> MEMO POINTS 1. The **number of items acquired** may indicate a trading situation. HMRC caution that other badges of trade should be present irrespective of the number of items.
> 2. **Land** can be held for investment or as trading stock, and therefore the nature of land is of no help in deciding whether a trade exists.

BIM20265

> EXAMPLE
> 1. A man with various business interests (including lending money and owning a cinema company) was offered the chance to acquire over 1 million toilet rolls in a single purchase whilst in Berlin. Back in the UK, he sold the whole lot in a single sale transaction.
> It was held that the sale amounted to an adventure in the nature of trade. *Rutledge v CIR* [1929]
>
> 2. A woodsman, with no prior experience of the whisky trade, bought whisky in bond for £407. A couple of years later, he sold it for £1,131. In the interim, the consignment was never delivered to him, and he did not advertise in order to make the sale.
> It was held that the transaction was an adventure in the nature of trade. *CIR v Fraser* [1942]

Income-producing

If an asset is **exploited for** income e.g. rent or dividends, then this would initially indicate an investment.

5150
BIM20250

If, however, **expenses** are incurred in relation to the asset e.g. interest on borrowings, and as a result no profit is made (or indeed a loss is sustained) whilst the asset is owned, this would nullify the income-producing advantage (other than to reduce the cost of holding the asset). In such a case, any positive financial benefit could only be crystallised once the asset was sold. Whilst this is not necessarily indicative of trading, it does mean that the income derived from the asset cannot be a factor which implies an intention to hold the asset purely as an investment.

> EXAMPLE A solicitor purchased a farm and surrounding land, with the majority of the cost funded by a mortgage. The rental income only covered half of the mortgage interest.
> The solicitor submitted plans for development, although he did not undertake further work himself, nor did he advertise any plots for sale. As a result of third parties approaching him to make a deal, he managed to sell over 20 building plots over a period of 5 years.
> It was held that the solicitor was carrying on a trade rather than holding a long term investment. *Cooke v Haddock* [1960]

Value

5155
BIM20250

Assets are often held until they **appreciate** in value, perhaps as an alternative to income yield. However, if an asset is sold within a short time scale, has no aesthetic value, and produces no income, this may indicate trading.

> EXAMPLE An actor was worried about the possible devaluation of the pound. He therefore decided to buy silver bullion which was linked to the US$, and had enjoyed a steady value over the past 3 years. Due to market fluctuations, the actor made a large profit on various bullion transactions, although he stated that this was not his intention. Some of the transactions necessitated heavy borrowing, with high interest charges, which could only be repaid by selling the bullion.
>
> It was held that the transactions were an adventure in the nature of trade because the bullion itself served no use, did not produce any income, and the intention had been to hedge against devaluation. *Wisdom v Chamberlain* [1968]

Financial assets

5160
BIM20250

Transactions in financial assets, such as shares, options, and bonds do not of themselves indicate trading, although of course if this activity is undertaken within a financial trade such as banking, then there is no doubt as to how the transactions should be treated.

Such assets are normally held for investment purposes, either for income production or capital growth.

Selling these assets after a short period of ownership might be classed as speculation akin to gambling, which does not amount to trading. If there is a cohesive strategy which determines when to buy and sell, this could be to satisfy either a trading or investment objective. Other factors should therefore be reviewed in order to settle the question.

HMRC treat **derivatives** and other transactions, which mirror the risks and rewards of share ownership, in the same way as the actual assets themselves.

> EXAMPLE A fruit and vegetable importing company started making stock market deals after suffering a downturn, employing new people as a consequence and maintaining proper accounts. Stocks were held for a period of less than 1 year. The directors were advised that this activity was within the scope of the company's Memorandum of Association. Unfortunately the deals resulted in losses. The issue was whether this amounted to a trade of dealing in shares or mere speculation.
>
> It was held that a trade was being carried on, as the company obviously intended to resell the stocks, rather than hold them for the longer term. *Lewis Emmanuel v White* [1965]

---

2. Period of ownership

5190
BIM20310

Trading in its most basic form requires a turnover of assets in order to realise a profit. If many years have elapsed between purchase and sale, this would hardly suggest such an intention, although certain assets obviously require a lengthy maturity time e.g. whisky.

The **longer the period** of ownership of an asset, the more this suggests no intention to trade. Although there may be a vague wish to realise any appreciation in value some time in the future, the main intention is to hold on to the asset.

Making a contract to sell before the purchase even takes place is also a clear indicator of trading. *Johnston v Heath* [1970]

It has been held that this particular badge cannot be decisive by itself. *Marson v Morton and Others* [1986]

> EXAMPLE
> 1. An employee of a building company earned a relatively modest salary (just over £500 p.a.), but was offered the chance to acquire land (with planning permission already granted) for £15,000. He did not have sufficient means to make the acquisition, but approached various purchasers. He made a contract to sell on the land for £25,000 with one prospective acquirer. About a week after this contract was signed, he contracted to buy the land from his employer.
>
> Despite this being an isolated transaction, it was held that the purchase and sale was an adventure in the nature of trade. *Johnston v Heath* [1970]

2. The shareholders of a potato merchant company were advised by an estate agent to acquire some land with planning permission for £65,000. Their intention was to make a medium-term investment. In the event, they sold the land for £100,000 to a company in which the agent had an interest, after only 3 months. They had had no involvement in the sale themselves, as the agent dealt with the timing and pricing issues.
It was held that the land had been held as an investment. The key question was whether the company was investing money or doing a deal. *Marson v Morton and Others* [1986]

---

3. Frequency and number of transactions

A **single isolated transaction** can amount to the carrying on of a trade, although it would be unusual. HMRC state that the test, undertaken by looking at all of the badges of trade, is whether the operations involved in the transaction are of the same kind, and carried on in the same way, as those which are typical of ordinary admitted trading in the line of business in which the transaction was carried out. *CIR v Livingston and Others* [1926]; *CIR v Fraser* [1942]; *Rutledge v CIR* [1929] (¶5145)

5210
BIM20230

EXAMPLE Three unconnected individuals (a ship repairer, a blacksmith and a fishmonger) purchased a cargo ship in order to convert it into a steam-drifter. This required much modification, and the ship repairer and blacksmith worked on the project themselves. The ship was then sold at a profit.
It was held that this was an adventure in the nature of trade. *CIR v Livingston and Others* [1926]

Series of operations

The **systematic repetition** of a transaction indicates trading. A series of operations may therefore amount to the carrying on of a trade, especially if the effect is habitual and continuous. The decision really depends on the frequency e.g. the more transactions of the same type, the more likely it is that a trade exists. Rather than looking at each transaction in isolation, the effect of the items as a whole should be considered.

5215

EXAMPLE During a boom in the local cotton spinning trade, a director of a spinning company joined a syndicate in order to acquire a cotton mill and then strip it of its assets. The venture was very successful, and was repeated another three times.
It was held that, taken individually, each transaction would not have been a trade, but collectively they constituted a trade. *Pickford v Quirke* [1927]

Note:
This conclusion does not apply to share dealing.

Treatment of earlier transactions

The question then becomes whether the nature of an earlier transaction can be **influenced by** later ones i.e. the first transaction may itself have been treated as non-trading (had others not occurred subsequently). If the first transaction becomes part of a pattern, it too can be treated as trading.

5220

EXAMPLE A taxpayer started a driving school which was profitable, and a year later he transferred it to a newly formed company in return for cash and shares. Within 4 years, he had repeated this process in respect of a further 29 driving schools. He stated that the transfers were made to protect the business.
It was held that all of the transfers constituted an adventure in the nature of trade, with the later transactions influencing the correct treatment of the first. *Leach v Pogson* [1962]

---

4. Changes made to the asset

The following modifications are typical of trading:
- processing;
- manufacturing; or
- an adaptation to make the item more readily marketable.

5250
BIM20275

In all such situations, **money is expended** in order to heighten the profit achieved on sale. *CIR v Livingston and Others* [1926]

However, the **nature and scale** of the expenditure may be such that no trade is indicated, and the costs would be incurred by anyone owning the asset e.g. repairs to restore functionality, insurance against loss, or routine maintenance.

5255   If assets are broken down **into smaller lots** to facilitate a sale, this may amount to trading.

> EXAMPLE
>
> 1. Two taxpayers acquired a cotton spinning plant with the intention of making a quick sale. Unfortunately they ended up having to sell it in five lots over the following 2 years.
> It was held that the only reasonable conclusion on the evidence was that the transaction was an adventure in the nature of trade. *Edwards v Bairstow & Harrison* [1955]
>
> 2. Three taxpayers, who worked for three different firms, formed a syndicate to purchase brandy speculatively from the Cape Government for resale. Purchases were made through an agent who sold a certain amount on commission. The remainder was delivered to the UK, where it was blended with other brandy, recast, and then resold in lots on the syndicate's behalf.
> It was held that this activity amounted to a trade. *Cape Brandy Syndicate v CIR* [1921]

---

5. How was the sale carried out?

5285
BIM20280

If the **tasks involved** in selling an asset mirror those of a trader in the same line of business, it is likely that the taxpayer is carrying on a trade. *CIR v Livingston and Others* [1926] (¶5210); *CIR v Fraser* [1942] (¶5145)

Supplementary work

5290
BIM20285

If supplementary work, such as advertising or employing sales people, is undertaken to secure a sale, this would indicate trading.

> EXAMPLE   A taxpayer, who usually traded in agricultural machinery, purchased a huge stock of surplus government aeroplane linen. The terms of the contract required him to take delivery of the whole amount over the next 6 months. He began advertising the linen to the public, which required a sales office and sales people. He maintained a separate bank account for the business, and kept the usual accounting records. He managed to sell the whole consignment in small lots, amounting to over 4,000 orders.
> It was held that this activity could only be trading. *Martin v Lowry* [1926]

Formation of company

5295
BIM20290

If a company is formed **explicitly for the purpose** of a transaction, this would support trading.

> EXAMPLE
>
> 1. A company was formed for the purpose of acquiring land rich in copper. Over the next 2 years, the land was sold, in two lots, to another company, with the consideration being shares of the purchaser. A profit of over £275,000 was made on the transactions.
> It was held that the purchase and resale of the land constituted a trade. *Californian Copper Syndicate (Limited and Reduced) v Harris* [1904]
>
> 2. A company was formed for the purpose of purchasing land in order to plant and grow rubber trees. There was an intention to sell the land eventually. Insufficient funds meant that the land was sold to another company much earlier than intended, before any rubber could be processed or sold.
> It was held that no trade existed, and the sale was merely the crystallisation of a capital profit. *Tebrau (Johore) Rubber Syndicate Ltd v Farmer* [1910]

Reasons for sale

5300
BIM20295

The reasons behind the sale should be examined, as an emergency sale (e.g. to realise much needed funds to pay off creditors or tax arrears), or a once in a lifetime windfall, would not indicate that the purchase was ever made with an eventual profit in mind. Of course it is possible for a change in intention to occur. *West v Phillips* [1958]; *Mitchell Bros v Tomlinson* [1957]

> EXAMPLE
> 1. A builder stopped constructing new buildings during the Second World War, but still owned 2,495 houses, of which only 287 were for resale (the remainder being let). He began to sell both types of house after the war, as severe statutory changes to the rental market meant that the rental income was no longer a match for his tax arrears and mortgage costs.
> It was held that the houses for resale remained trading stock of the building business, so that any profit should be treated as trading income. The sales of the rental properties were outside the scope of the trade, and therefore were not taxable. *West v Phillips* [1958]
>
> 2. Two taxpayers started building homes in the 1930s with the intention of letting them. Being successful, they let further houses in order to produce income for their retirement. As in the case above, the rental conditions after the war meant that it was no longer economic to retain the houses, and they were sold off as and when the opportunity arose.
> It was held that they had carried on a trade of buying and selling property. *Mitchell Bros v Tomlinson* [1957]

---

6. Profit-seeking motive

This is only one factor to be considered along with all the other relevant elements. However, where the other badges do not give a decisive view, motive may tip the balance one way or the other. The **person's stated intention** must be compared to other evidence, and the activity must be looked at in the round. *Rutledge v CIR* [1929]

5330

Some **assets** are more likely to be held as investments. Although a profit may be expected on eventual disposal due to an appreciation in value, the main point of holding investments is usually to derive income, or to enjoy their inherent aesthetic value.

Shares may be bought with the intention of making a profit, but can also be investment vehicles. Speculative trading, which resulted in losses, was held to be more of an investment activity. *Salt v Chamberlain* [1979]

> EXAMPLE A taxpayer who had his own system of predicting which shares would rise in value made various purchases and sales of shares on the Stock Exchange. Unfortunately he made losses.
> It was held that this activity did not amount to a trade. *Salt v Chamberlain* [1979]
>
> **Note:**
> Contrast this decision with that in *Lewis Emmanuel v White* (¶5160), the difference being that the Lewis case involved a company rather than an individual.

Not main purpose

A trade may be carried on, even though there is no intention to make a profit.

5335

For example, a recreation ground provided for a town was not intended to be profitable, but was held to amount to a trade. *CIR v The Stonehaven Recreation Ground Trustees* [1929]

Supporting activities for non-profit making ventures may themselves be trades. For example, a profitable restaurant was run alongside education classes and leisure facilities, both of which did not break even. It was held that the restaurant was a trade, despite the fact that it would be carried on even if it made a loss. *Grove v YMCA* [1903] Once such a trade has been identified, it is important to exclude income and expenditure attributable to non-commercial operations from the computation of trading profit. The manner in which profits from a trading activity are applied does not have any bearing in deciding whether that activity amounts to a trade.

For mutual trading, see ¶5435.

> EXAMPLE A recreation ground (including tennis courts and bowling green) was managed by trustees. To use the ground, a daily ticket or season ticket had to be held. The monies raised by the ticket sales were used for the management and improvement of the ground.
> It was held that a trade existed. *CIR v The Stonehaven Recreation Ground Trustees* [1929]

Fiscal motive

5340   If the sole purpose behind a transaction is to **obtain a tax advantage**, e.g. sustain a loss to set against other taxable income, this does not amount to trading, even where certain characteristics of trading are present. It is essential to have a commercial objective. *Overseas Containers (Finance) Ltd v Stoker* [1989] (¶5345)

Where a fiscal purpose is present but there are elements of commerciality i.e. the tax advantage is a by-product of the transaction, it may still be treated as trading.

Groups

5345   There has been conflicting **case law** in this area which has either supported the idea of looking at the purpose of a transaction from a group context, or from the individual company's perspective. *Overseas Containers (Finance) Ltd v Stoker* [1989]; *New Angel Court Ltd v Adam* [2004]

BIM20105   **HMRC** now state that the transaction should be considered from the perspective of the individual company, even in a group context.

> EXAMPLE
> 1. Company A was formed by four shipbuilders, and five container ships were ordered from a German shipyard. The consideration was payable in instalments in Deutschmarks, and this was financed by German loans. A subsidiary company (Company B) was formed to deal with the financial side of the transactions, and it took over the German loans, lending the same amount of money in sterling to Company A. Company B took out further German loans in respect of two more ships, and lent the same amount in sterling.
> As sterling devalued, heavy exchange losses were sustained by Company B, which were only partly offset by the interest charged on the sterling loans, leaving a shortfall of over £14m.
> It was held that the formation of Company B served no commercial purpose, and its purpose was to obtain a fiscal advantage by converting the exchange loss into a trading loss. Therefore, looking at the arrangement purely from Company B's perspective, no trade was carried on. *Overseas Containers (Finance) Ltd v Stoker* [1989]
>
> 2. Company C acquired nine investment properties from other group companies but treated them as trading stock in its own accounts. In the next 4 months, it managed to sell eight of the properties. It was held that Company C had indeed acquired the properties as trading stock due to the fact that its existing trade was property dealing, and there had always been the intention to resell with a view to making a profit. *New Angel Court Ltd v Adam* [2004]

---

7. Method of acquisition

5375   The circumstances behind the acquisition may indicate whether a trading intention existed initially, as an asset may be acquired via:
a. a **gift or inheritance**, in which case HMRC must show that the asset became trading stock before the sale i.e. a supervening trade subsequently arose. *Taylor v Good* [1974] Of course the taxpayer may wish to infer a trade in order to crystallise a loss; or
b. purchase, when the market involved in the acquisition may indicate whether the acquisition is for resale, for private use, or for investment.

In **a.** above, it must be proved that the taxpayer **formed an intention to trade** before the asset was sold, and it is also important to ascertain at what date this intention occurred. This may be evidenced by work done to the asset. There may be capital gains tax implications at the date when the appropriation to trading stock occurred, and this would have a knock-on effect on the allowable cost of the asset for the purposes of calculating any trading profit or loss.

BIM20315   **HMRC** state that they will only pursue a supervening trade for profitable transactions if the amounts involved are substantial, and there is evidence of a clear change of intention.

> EXAMPLE   A taxpayer acquired a large house in the country, which had historic connections with his family and needed substantial renovation, at auction for just over £5,000. Having entered the auction on a whim, he was surprised at his success, and initially discussed residing there with his wife, who was against the idea mainly because of the condition of the house. He therefore applied

for planning permission to demolish the house, and build 90 new homes on the land. Permission was obtained some years later, and in the interim he received unsolicited offers from developers. As a result, he sold the land for just over £54,000.

It was held that this activity was not an adventure in the nature of trade as the original purchase did not have a trading motive, and the remaining transactions undertaken to ensure a profitable sale were not sufficient to substantiate a trade. *Taylor v Good* [1974]

8. Source of finance

If an asset is purchased with **funds from an existing trade**, and the trade would need those funds in the short to medium term, it is likely that the sale of the asset would form part of that trade, and this would have been the intention on its acquisition.

5395
BIM20305

However, the asset may only be **replacing another investment**, and in such a case would not form part of an existing trade.

EXAMPLE A builder purchased a lease and constructed some shops, two of which were leased to his wife and taken out of the business accounts altogether. Twenty years later, the shops were sold at a profit. Meanwhile, the builder had also acquired a dwelling for his foreman, and this was sold 9 years later. The proceeds from all three sales were paid into the business.

It was held that all of the properties were investments, and so the sales were not within the scope of the existing trade. *Harvey v Caulcott* [1952]

9. Existence of similar trading transactions

In this case, a trade already exists, and the issue is whether the **scope of that trade** encompasses certain transactions.

5415
BIM20270

If there is a **similarity** between the new transactions and those which are unquestionably part of the trade, this would strongly indicate that all of the transactions should be treated as trading.

Of course, where **completely different** transactions are undertaken, it is more difficult to make a connection. *CIR v Fraser* [1942] (¶5145); *Marson v Morton and Others* [1986] (¶5190)

10. Mutual trading

A person cannot derive a taxable profit from trading with himself, and this applies not only to companies, but also to individuals and groups of people. Where the customers are the same group of people as the traders, no taxable profit will result. A **key feature** of mutual trading is the presence of a common fund belonging to the members which is used entirely for their benefit. Any profit is therefore simply treated as a surplus of members' contributions, and can be returned to the contributors without charge. The mutuality principle applies only to trading profits of the organisation. It is not essential for the activities to be **exclusively mutual**. *Carlisle and Silloth Golf Club v Smith* [1913]

5435
BIM24001

MEMO POINTS 1. Any **distributions** made on the **liquidation** of a mutual company to contributors, who previously received a trading deduction for their contributions, are taxed as trading profits.

2. A **company trading with its shareholders** does not necessarily satisfy the conditions for the mutuality principle to apply. *Liverpool Corn Trade Association Ltd v Monks* [1926]

EXAMPLE

1. A golf club was obliged by the terms of a lease to allow the public to use the course on the payment of a fee.

It was held that income derived from the public was trading income. *Carlisle and Silloth Golf Club v Smith* [1913]

2. A company was set up to provide a corn exchange and other benefits for people in the corn trade. In return, subscribers:
– purchased a share;

– paid an annual subscription;
– paid an entrance fee to the exchange; and
– paid extra fees for specific facilities.
It was held that the company was carrying on a trade. *Liverpool Corn Trade Association Ltd v Monks* [1926]

SECTION 3

Specified activities

5485 This section looks at betting and illegal activities. For the scope of a typical trade, and what is included in trading income, see ¶10105.

Betting and gambling

5490
BIM22015

Betting and gambling do not constitute trading. *Graham v Green* [1925] This would include professional gamblers who devise their own system of placing bets.

On the other hand, **exploitation of gamblers** i.e. providing an establishment in which to gamble, or being a bookmaker, is an adventure in the nature of trade. A bookmaker, who is defined as someone carrying on an activity where the odds are in his favour, must include, within his trading income, any winnings or losses from placing his own bets.

BIM22016

    ⌐MEMO POINTS⌐   1. For this purpose, a bet is **defined as** a contract between two persons, concerning a future uncertain event, and one shall win from the other a sum of money depending on the outcome of that event.
2. **Spread betting** is usually not a trade, which means there is no relief for losses, and no tax on profits.

5495
BIM22019

Exceptionally, a bet may be within the scope of an existing trade. Examples would include:
– a bet used to hedge a loan interest rate; and
– the owner of a gambling establishment taking part in a card game on the premises with members of the club and winning most of the time. *Burdge v Pyne* [1968]

However, where a vocation affords the opportunity to make a bet on the outcome of a game (e.g. golf), this has been held not to be a trade. This is on the basis that the bets do not arise from the playing services, and that there is no organisation to support the view that a business of betting is carried on. *Down v Compston* [1937]

Illegal activities

5500
BIM22005

Whether a trade exists is not affected by whether the activities, either in whole or in part, are illegal. The usual badges of trade need to be applied, and in particular a **commercial element** must exist. Pure crime (e.g. blackmail or burglary) does not involve the commercial acquisition and supply of goods or services.

There is specific case law in the following situations:

Situation	Trade?	Reference
Burglary	No	*J P Harrison (Watford) Ltd v Griffiths* [1962] *Lindsay, Woodward & Hiscox v CIR* [1932]
Smuggling alcohol for sale	Yes	*Lindsay, Woodward & Hiscox v CIR* [1932]
Operating illegal gaming machines	Yes	*Mann v Nash* [1932]
Drug dealing	Yes	*Lindsay, Woodward & Hiscox v CIR* [1932]
Receiving stolen goods	Possibly	*Partridge v Mallandine* [1886]
Prostitution	Yes	*IRC v Aken* [1990]

CHAPTER 2

Investment business

If a company has an investment business, whether exclusively or as a hybrid (i.e. in conjunc-   **6000**
tion with an accompanying trade), this has implications for the deductibility of expenses
and other reliefs. Investments commonly comprise shares in other companies or property.

SECTION 1

Definition

Since 1 April 2004, **two key terms** have applied: **6050**
− an investment company, in relation to losses in unlisted shares which can be relieved   CTM08040
against income; and
− a company with investment business, which is relevant as regards the deductibility of
management expenses.

> MEMO POINTS   1. For details of:
> − **management expenses**, see ¶17620+;
> − **other reliefs** applicable to an investment company, see ¶37230+; and
> − **close investment holding companies**, see ¶75945+.
> 2. UK resident investment companies which have **overseas activities** can elect for a designated
> currency to be used for tax purposes, other than the functional currency used in the accounts
> (¶17210).

A. Investment company

An investment company is a company: **6080**
− whose **business consists** wholly or mainly of making investments (¶6120); and   CTM08040
− where the **principal part of its income** is derived from those investments.

Note that the company's purpose is not a relevant factor.

The definition specifically includes authorised investment trusts, unit trusts, open-ended investment companies and savings banks (excluding trustee savings banks).

Income

6085
CTM08030

The principal part of the income should be measured over a **representative period**. For this purpose, such a period may extend for longer than a year depending on the nature of the income. *FPH Finance Trust Ltd v CIR* [1944]; *MacNiven v Westmoreland Investments Ltd* [1997]

> EXAMPLE
>
> 1. A company dealing in shares, A Ltd, had previously been treated as a trading company, but during a period of 15 months it only received investment income as it made substantial trading losses. It went into voluntary liquidation immediately afterwards.
> It was held that A Ltd was not an investment company, because its activities were directed to earning profits from its dealings in stocks and shares. The income derived from the stocks and shares in which it dealt (i.e. dividends and interest) was incidental. *FPH Finance Trust Ltd v CIR* [1944]
>
> 2. B Ltd, a property holding company, had been treated as an investment company for many years, but after selling the last property, there was a 2 year gap until another was purchased. The issue was whether B Ltd ceased to be an investment company during that time.
> It was held that there had been no change to B Ltd's business when looking at a period of activity longer than simply the 3 relevant years, and therefore it was an investment company throughout. *MacNiven v Westmoreland Investments Ltd* [1997]

B. Company with investment business

6115
s 1218 CTA 2009;
CTM08040

Statute defines such a company as one whose business consists wholly or partly of making investments. **All companies** can therefore potentially qualify, provided that they have a business which fits this definition.

Comment   This relaxation of the rules permits hybrid companies to claim relief for management expenses.

Making investments

6120
CTM08050

HMRC state that the company's business (in the sense of its occupation) must consist of making investments, and this is a question of fact.

"Making" can **mean** simply investing and holding, so it would be possible for a company making just one investment to have an investment business. *CIR v Tyre Investment Trust Ltd* [1924]

A housing society was held to have a business even though its **purpose** was to provide affordable housing for those in need. *Medway Housing Society Ltd v Cook* [1996]

> EXAMPLE
>
> 1. C Ltd was formed principally to acquire the shares in two foreign companies and sell them on to a UK company, D Ltd. C Ltd purchased other investments, selling only one holding, and taking an active interest in the affairs of the two foreign companies.
> C Ltd contended that it was a holding company, and was not carrying on a trade or business.
> It was held that the principal business of C Ltd consisted of making investments. *CIR v Tyre Investment Trust Ltd* [1924]
>
> 2. A housing society was formed to acquire the housing stock of a local authority. It charged rent below market value, and this was mainly paid through housing benefit. Undertakings were given to both existing and new tenants to limit future rent increases. A business plan, necessary to obtain loans to finance the purchase of the housing stock, projected a profit over a period of time.
> It was held that the society was an investment company because:
> − "investment" meant the laying out of monies in anticipation of a profitable capital or income return. In this respect, the business plan was evidence that the purchase of the housing stock was intended to result in a profit over time;

– the fact that profit was to be ploughed back to finance the society's objects, and not to be distributed to members, was irrelevant; and

– the very business of the society was the provision of affordable housing in return for below market value rent, but nevertheless at a level which produced a profit. *Medway Housing Society Ltd v Cook* [1996]

Business

Business has been **defined** as an "active occupation or profession continuously carried on". *CIR v Marine Steam Turbine Co Ltd* [1919] It should be noted that a later case clarified that no emphasis should be put on "active", as this would limit the scope of business too much, and the purpose for which a company was set up was of overriding importance (¶7100). *CIR v The Korean Syndicate Ltd* [1921]

6125
CTM08050

SECTION 2

Particular situations

A. Holding companies

HMRC consider that there are **four categories** of holding or parent companies, as follows:

6175
CTM08060

Description	Investment company	Company with investment business
Carry on the mainstream trading activities of the group	x	x
Income consists only of dividends, interest, and rents from subsidiaries	✓	✓
Income additionally includes management charges paid by subsidiaries	✓[1]	✓
Hybrid companies	x	✓
Note: 1. The company might be carrying on a trade of providing management services (i.e. on an organised basis in return for reward), in which case it would not qualify as an investment company. If the company is only recharging costs to subsidiaries with no profit element, then it is unlikely that there is a trade.		

Intermediate holding companies

An intermediate company may either be:

– a device through which dividends are passed, incurring no expenses itself, and therefore unlikely to have a business; or

– incurring significant expenditure whilst receiving income from the subsidiaries.

The **key issue** in each case is whether there is a separate business at all, and if there is, whether that is wholly or partly making investments.

Expenditure incurred may relate to the businesses or trades of other group companies, in which case it will not qualify as management expenses for the intermediate holding company, unless it is recharged in the future. For further details of management expenses, see ¶17620+.

6180
CTM08060

CTM08180

B. Ceasing to trade

6210
CTM08070

The term investment company or investment business would not normally encompass the situation where a trading company ceases to trade, and is then left with **deposits** earning some interest either before liquidation or until a new trade commences. *Carpet Agencies Ltd v CIR* [1958]; *E Y L Trading Co Ltd v CIR* [1962] It is necessary for such a company to retain a business, and for that business to be mainly or partly the making of investments. Otherwise, the company will be dormant (¶7050+).

However, HMRC do concede that, depending on the particular facts, a company which has an **intention** to make investments, and has significant deposits for a period of time, may qualify as a company with investment business (¶7110+).

> [EXAMPLE]
> 1. E Ltd ceased to trade as a carpet dealer but continued to hold investments, comprising a trade investment, Defence Bond, and loans to connected companies. For certain reasons liquidation was delayed. The issue was whether E Ltd had become an investment company once the trade ceased. E Ltd argued it had carried on two businesses – trading as well as holding investments.
> This contention was rejected and it was held that E Ltd was not an investment company. The period after the cessation of trade amounted to a state of flux during which the directors were making a decision as to the future activities of the company. The company still remained a carpet dealer. *Carpet Agencies Ltd v CIR* [1958]
>
> 2. F Ltd ceased to trade and sold the entire business, including a company shareholding. The directors then resolved that the company should become an investment company. However, the only asset held by F Ltd was cash received from the sale of the business.
> It was held that F Ltd had not become an investment company, because the resolution was not sufficient – there had to be a holding of investments, and cash was inadequate for this purpose. *E Y L Trading Co Ltd v CIR* [1962]

6215
CTM08080

Exceptionally, it may be possible for a company in **liquidation** to be an investment company, or a company with investment business, especially if the company had such a business prior to the commencement of its winding up.

CHAPTER 3

Dormant companies

A dormant company has no trade or business. Such a company will not be within the tax system until it begins some kind of business activity. This means that it does not file tax returns, and is not included as an associated company in relation to any other company. There are, however, accounting requirements which must be observed.

7000

SECTION 1

Scope

The status of dormancy is not usually difficult to ascertain. The absence of a trade is not definitive, as the company may be carrying on an investment business (¶6000+).

7050

Comment   A company may be dormant for a number of **reasons**, for example:
– to protect a company name;
– to hold an asset or intellectual property (for example, as nominee); or
– as a property management company set up as a vehicle to own the headlease or freehold of a property.

1. Definition

There is no comprehensive statutory definition of the word "business" for tax purposes, and reliance is placed on case law.

7080
s 1169 CA 2006

For **accounting purposes**, a company is considered to be dormant during any financial year in which it has no significant accounting transactions, **unless** it is regulated by the FSA or is an insurance company.

In practice, this means that the company must not have entered a transaction in its accounting records except:
- as a result of subscriber shares being issued;
- a fee paid to Companies House for a change of name;
- a fee paid to Companies House for reregistration from private company to public or vice versa;
- a penalty paid to Companies House for failing to deliver accounts on time; or
- a fee paid to Companies House with the company's annual return.

For the accounting requirements for dormant companies, see ¶7265+.

---

2. Case law

7100

There has been limited case law on whether a company is considered dormant i.e. whether it has a business or not. The word "business" tends to suit its meaning to the context in which it is found. *Town Investments Ltd v Department of the Environment* [1978]

CTM03590

HMRC state that a readily identifiable business is a much wider concept than trade, so a reduced level of activity is sufficient. The absence of income is not necessarily a determining factor. The holding of assets (particularly if they are capable of producing income or gains), or the laying out of expenses may be evidence of a business.

> EXAMPLE
> 1. A Ltd was formed to hold patents which related to the invention of the steam turbine. The inventor granted the company a licence in return for royalty payments relating to the sale of each new machine. A Ltd went into liquidation 3 years later. Its assets were transferred to another company, B Ltd, in return for cash, shares in B Ltd, and a royalty fee.
> As the royalty fees due to A Ltd were substantial, the winding up was aborted. Subsequently, A Ltd just received royalties and paid dividends to its shareholders. It had no staff or offices, and B Ltd was responsible for company secretarial work.
> It was held that A Ltd was not carrying on a trade or business. *CIR v Marine Steam Turbine Co Ltd* [1919]
>
> 2. C Ltd was formed for the purpose of acquiring concessions and rights, turning them to account, and investing any related cash which was surplus to requirements. Partial rights to a gold mine in Korea were acquired, and 3 years later these rights were assigned under an agreement in return for a percentage of profits gained from the mining operation.
> For the period under review, C Ltd received bank interest and the royalties, distributed dividends to its shareholders, and paid premiums on a sinking fund policy.
> It was held that C Ltd was carrying on a business, as it was carrying out the purpose for which it had come into existence i.e. acquiring concessions and turning them to account. *CIR v The Korean Syndicate Ltd* [1921]

Property letting

7105

There have been several cases dealing with the question of whether the letting of property amounts to a business.

> EXAMPLE
> 1. D Ltd was incorporated in 1960 for the purpose of carrying on a tobacco business, although the Memorandum of Association covered a wide range of activities, including the granting of rights in relation to the land and property of the company. Land was acquired, upon which a factory and bonded warehouse were constructed. By 1964, the tobacco business closed due to continuing losses, and the properties were rented out to third parties. The company tried to set off its trading losses against the rental income. This was disputed on the basis that no business was being carried on once the tobacco trade ceased.
> It was held that the rents were received in the course of carrying on the business of putting D Ltd's property to profitable use by letting it out for rent. If a company was formed for the purpose of making profits for its shareholders, then any gainful use to which it put its assets amounted to the carrying on of a business. Although the carrying on of business generally requires some activity, this may be intermittent, with long intervals of inactivity also occurring. *American Leaf Blending Co Sdn Bhd v Director-General of Inland Revenue* [1978]

2. To avoid French legal consequences, E Ltd was incorporated to acquire a French holiday property. Mr A held 75% of the shares, and he provided the funding for the acquisition. No rent was paid to E Ltd, and only Mr A and his family used the property, paying all the bills themselves. The property was not acquired for investment purposes, and was not for sale.
It was held that E Ltd was not carrying on a business. Indeed the Special Commissioner said, "Anything less like the carrying on of a business by a company is hard to imagine." *John M Harris (Design Partnership) Ltd v Lee* [1997]

3. F Ltd was incorporated for the purpose of carrying on an investment business. F Ltd owned and let a freehold residential property, received dividends from shareholdings in other companies, made an interest-bearing loan to a connected company, and received interest on a bank deposit.
It was held that any one of these activities would amount to the carrying on of a business. *Land Management Ltd v Fox* [2002]

4. G Ltd, whose Memorandum of Association included the granting of rights in relation to property, traded for many years from a property which it owned in Glasgow. It was a member of a group. In 1966, it vacated the property, moving the trade to rented premises, and let out the original property to the same tenant for the next 40 years. In 1995, the trade ceased completely. An agent was appointed to:
– collect the rent due on the property (valued at £90,000 in 1999);
– arrange a rent review every 3 years; and
– ensure appropriate insurance cover was maintained (paid for by the tenant).
G Ltd was also owed over £1.2 million (on which no interest was paid) by a group company. G Ltd had no staff (other than the two directors), no bank account of its own, and no payments were made by G Ltd (either in the form of salary or dividends).
It was held that G Ltd was not carrying on a business. It was simply letting out former trading premises without any active participation or management, and these premises formed a small part of G Ltd's assets. It had never intended to acquire the property as an investment. *HMRC v Salaried Persons Postal Loans Ltd* [2006]

Bank deposits

A further issue concerns the **receipt of bank interest** on deposits, and whether this renders a company active.

7110

EXAMPLE H Ltd ceased trading after only 5 months and placed its accumulated profits in a bank deposit account on which it received bank interest. The bank account was the sole asset of H Ltd. It was held that this was an exceptional instance where the company was not carrying on a business. It had been set up to trade, and when that trade ceased, its surplus funds were not actively managed but simply left on deposit. *Jowett v O'Neill & Brennan Construction Ltd* [1998]

HMRC state that when a company claims that the receipt of bank interest is not a business, the facts should be carefully considered. If the facts are similar to those in the Brennan case and there is no evidence, either of active management of the monies invested, or that the situation has been contrived for the avoidance of tax, then it may be accepted that the company is dormant.

7115
CTM03591

However, a **close company** which simply holds a bank deposit account will fall within the definition of a close investment holding company (¶75945+), and will be liable to corporation tax at the full rate.

3. Holding companies

HMRC accept that a non-trading holding company is dormant provided that, throughout the accounting period, the following **criteria** apply:
– it has no assets other than shares in its 51% subsidiaries (¶65505); and
– it is not entitled to any deduction for any outgoings, and it has no income or gains other than dividends which it has distributed in full to its shareholders.

7145
s 26 CTA 2010

If one or more of these **conditions are not met**, the company may still be dormant, depending on the particular facts in the light of the principles outlined above.

SECTION 2

Implications

7195   Dormancy has implications for:
- communicating with HMRC;
- any associated companies; and
- transfer pricing adjustments.

Communication with HMRC

7200   Form CT204 is sent to the company periodically (at least every 5 years) to **review** whether the company has traded or carried on any other activity in the period, and also to enquire about the future. This would include the receipt of any income or the disposal of any assets.

7205   **Members' clubs and similar organisations** which exist primarily for recreational and other non-commercial purposes may, at HMRC's discretion, be treated as dormant even though they receive small amounts of investment income.

However, the following entities are **excluded** from this concession:
- a privately owned club run by its members as a commercial enterprise for personal profit;
- a housing association or registered social landlord;
- a trade association;
- a thrift fund;
- a holiday club;
- a friendly society; or
- a company which is a subsidiary of, or wholly owned by, a charity.

The treatment applies where the **annual corporation tax liability** is not expected to exceed £100, and the club is run exclusively for the benefit of its own members. For each year of dormancy, the body must have no anticipated allowable trading losses, no chargeable assets likely to be disposed of, and no anticipated payments subject to deduction of tax at source. This will be subject to a review at least every 5 years.

> MEMO POINTS   1. The concessional treatment is also extended to **non-profit making flat management companies** which pay no dividends and make no other distributions of profit, and which are liable to income tax deducted at source on investment income received (not exceeding £1,000 p.a.) on sinking funds.
> 2. For **further details**, see flmemo.co.uk/ctm7205

Associated companies

7210   Corporation tax is chargeable on a company's profits for an accounting period by reference to the prevailing **tax rates and thresholds**.

To prevent profitable companies from splitting into several smaller companies to take advantage of lower tax rates, special rules apply where a company has one or more associated companies (¶40180+). These rules ensure that the bands for determining the rate of tax are divided equally between all the associated companies.

Normally, a company is associated with another company if one controls the other, or both are controlled by a third party. Dormant companies are, however, excluded from being associated companies and this therefore reduces the corporation tax payable by the rest of the group.

Transfer pricing

7215   To prevent the manipulation of internal pricing structures, provisions exist whereby transactions between organisations must be computed on an arm's length basis. This is known as transfer pricing.

For accounting periods beginning on or after 1 April 2004, the transfer pricing provisions (¶70000+) **do not apply** to companies which:

– were dormant throughout the accounting period ending on 31 March 2004, or, if there is no such accounting period, the 3 month period ending on that date; and
– have continued to be dormant at all times since the end of that period (apart from any transfer pricing adjustments).

SECTION 3

Accounting requirements

A dormant company is not exempt from the normal requirements to prepare, issue and file financial statements, even though it has had no financial activity and can show no financial results. With limited exception, accounts must be filed even where the company has been dormant for a number of years, or where it has never traded.

7265

The **criteria** under which a company can **claim dormant status** correspond broadly with those for tax purposes, i.e. there should be no accounting transactions in the financial period, with the exception of those in ¶7080 which are expressly permitted.

7270
s 1169 CA 2006

On the other hand, care must be taken to ensure that the company's dormant status is not **compromised by incidental transactions** such as:
– bank charges;
– interest received on bank and other balances;
– movement on inter-company accounts;
– sundry expenses; or
– write offs.

It is important to remember that the concept of **materiality** does not apply in considering whether or not a company is dormant, because any transaction, irrespective of value, could determine whether or not the company can be classified as dormant.

1. Exemption from audit

From an accounting point of view, one of the most significant implications for dormant companies is that the majority of them are exempted from the obligation to have their financial statements audited. Some are automatically exempted, whilst others qualify for this status only if they meet additional criteria.

7300

There is a specific **requirement to have an audit** in respect of a company which at any time during the year was a banking company, an authorised insurance company or an authorised person under Part 4 of the Financial Services and Markets Act 2000.

s 481 CA 2006

In addition, any **shareholder** (or group of shareholders) holding not less than 10% of the company's issued share capital may require the company to be audited notwithstanding any exemption it would otherwise enjoy. Thus, even if a company would be automatically exempt, this exemption would fall away if the requisite number of shareholders wished it. They would achieve their objective by lodging a notice during the financial year in question, but not later than 1 month before the end of the year.

Automatic exemption

A dormant company is automatically exempt if it:
a. has been dormant since formation; or
b. was dormant since the end of the previous financial year, and meets the following criteria to be considered a small company:
– either its individual financial statements for the year were entitled to the exemption available to small companies, or would have been had it not been a public company or a member of a so-called "ineligible group"; and
– it was not required to prepare group financial statements for the year.

7305
s 480 CA 2006

> ⎯MEMO POINTS⎯ 1. The exemption criteria for **small companies** are that at least two of the following conditions must be met:
> – the annual turnover is £6.5m or less;
> – the balance sheet total is £3.26m or less; or
> – the average number of employees is 50 or fewer.
> 2. An **ineligible group** under the 2006 Companies Act is one in which any of the members is a public company or a body corporate (other than a company) whose shares are admitted to trading on a regulated market in an EEA state. Note that under the 1985 Companies Act, the ineligibility was extended to bodies corporate anywhere in the world which had the power to offer their shares or debentures to the public, even if the body corporate had never exercised that power.

Small companies

7310   In order to qualify for the exemption, the company must be both dormant and a small company (¶7305). If the company has **traded in previous years**, then in order to qualify as small in a particular year it must meet the qualifying criteria in that financial year and in the preceding one.

Where a company has not been dormant since formation but **subsequently seeks dormant status**, it must pass the test that it was permitted to prepare small company financial statements for the previous financial year. The following examples illustrate how the test is applied.

> ⎡EXAMPLE⎤
> 1. If A Ltd was a small company with a December year end, and it became dormant during 20X1, it could elect to dispense with an audit in 20X2.
>
> 2. If B Ltd first met the criteria for classification as a small company in 20X1, it would become entitled to prepare small company financial statements in respect of 20X2. This results from the requirement to meet the small company criteria 2 years in succession. B Ltd may dispense with an audit in 20X3.
>
> 3. If C Ltd was not a small company in 20X1, the earliest date at which it could elect to dispense with the audit would be 20X4 because it would not be able to prepare small company accounts until 20X3.

7315   The directors of the company can **claim exemption** from audit, on the grounds that the company is dormant, by signing a statement to this effect on the face of the balance sheet.

Companies not meeting small company criteria

7320   There is a relaxation of the normal "small company" rules in respect of dormant **public companies** and **members of ineligible groups** which are dormant. As long as these companies meet the size criteria to be a small company, their status as a public company (or their membership of an ineligible group) will not prevent them from taking advantage of the audit exemption available to other dormant companies. However, the requirements regarding documents to be filed at Companies House and/or distributed to members will differ slightly, as follows.

Private companies		Public companies
File at Companies House	Distribute to members	File at Companies House and distribute to members
Abbreviated[1] balance sheet Notes to the accounts	Directors' report Profit and loss account (where the company traded in the previous financial year)	Balance sheet Directors' report Notes to the accounts Profit and loss account (where the company traded in the previous financial year)
Note: 1. For small and medium-sized companies, the Companies Act offers a special dispensation to submit **abbreviated accounts** – essentially a simplified set of accounts, drawn up solely for this purpose. For further details, refer to *Accountancy and Financial Reporting Memo*.		

2. Financial statements

Typically, a dormant set of accounts will **include** a balance sheet and related accounting policies and notes – in compliance with the Companies Act – although these will inevitably be relatively brief.

7350

However, in respect of the first year in which a company is dormant (i.e., where it had traded in the previous financial year), a profit and loss account showing the comparative figures is required. A statement of recognised gains and losses may also be required for the same purpose (¶11490+).

> MEMO POINTS 1. In some cases a dormant company can submit **Form DCA** (Dormant Company Accounts) to Companies House, although this is not suitable for all dormant companies (especially those which have **become dormant** in the current financial year, but which have residual balances on the balance sheet relating to earlier periods). The form has been designed for those companies seeking only to issue shares to the initial subscribers to the Memorandum of Association. The form cannot be used for recording other transactions. The completion of this form does not eliminate the need to prepare accounts for shareholders.
> 2. If a company has been dormant **since incorporation**, Form DCA can also be used where any fees or penalties are paid by a third party without any right of reimbursement.

The annual accounts must be **delivered to Companies House** in accordance with the normal rules, i.e., within 10 months of a company's accounting reference date (ARD) for a private company and 7 months for a public company. Should these be filed late, a dormant company, just as any other, will be penalised.

7355

> MEMO POINTS Generally, the ARD is the last day of the financial year (i.e., the period starting on the day after the end of the previous financial year or, in the case of a new company, on the day of incorporation). A company's first ARD is set on incorporation but can subsequently be changed.

Where a dormant company's accounts are not audited, the balance sheet must contain a **statement by the directors**, in a position above the signature(s) of the director(s), stating that:
– the company was dormant throughout the financial year, and so is entitled to claim exemption from audit under the Companies Act 2006;
– the members have not requested that the company have its accounts for the respective financial period audited; and
– the directors recognise their responsibilities for ensuring the company keeps adequate accounting records, and for preparing accounts which give a true and fair view of the company at the end of the financial period in accordance with the requirements of the Companies Act.

7360

Comment The directors' statement replaces, on the grounds of dormancy, the requirement to pass a special resolution to claim exemption from appointing auditors.

3. Ending of dormant status

As a general rule, a company forfeits its status as dormant when it:
– resumes trading;
– engages in transactions which require an accounting entry; or
– otherwise ceases to fulfil the conditions required for dormant status.

7390

As a **consequence**, the audit exemptions may also cease, unless the company continues to satisfy the audit exemption criteria for small companies.

When a company loses its dormant status it is not required to **notify** the Registrar of Companies.

7395

PART 3

Chargeable profits

Chargeable profits
Summary

The numbers cross-refer to paragraphs.

CHAPTER 8 **Sundry items including anti-avoidance**

Overview

10000

A company which is chargeable to corporation tax may have more than one source of income (and related expenses). The total profits chargeable to corporation tax must be determined.

Chargeable profits (or losses) are computed separately for each source of income. For the calculation of the tax liability, see ¶40010.

Pro-forma

10050

The following pro-forma summarises the main items of income and gains that may be received by a company, and the deductions that are then available.

> MEMO POINTS   1. **Dividends received** from UK companies are usually ignored in the profit computation (unless the company deals in shares, when dividends are treated as trading income). However, dividends received are included in **franked investment income** when calculating the company's tax liability (¶40115+).
> 2. **Dividends paid** are distributions of post-tax profit to shareholders (¶18000+).
> 3. In an extended period of account, the **timing** of the tax charge depends on whether the income is assessed on a receipts basis or an accruals basis (¶3040+).

10055

Item	£	¶¶
Income and gains[1]		
Profits from trade	x	¶10105
Interest and loan relationships	x	¶10110
Property income	x	¶10115
Income from foreign possessions	x	¶10120
Other income not included in any of the above	x	¶10125
Chargeable gains	x	¶10130
	x	
Less: Deductions		
Loss relief (amount of relief depends on source of loss)	(x)	¶10160
Management expenses	(x)	¶10165
Qualifying charitable donations	(x)	¶10170
Profits chargeable to corporation tax	x	
Note:		
1. The figures to be included are the net income remaining once the related expenses have been deducted.		

SECTION 2

Summary of income and expenditure

A. Income and gains

Profits from a trade

10105   It is important to be clear about the **scope** of the trade, and indeed to identify whether there is more than one trade.

All **receipts** which derive from the trading activity should be included, usually following the accounting treatment adopted in the company's financial statements (¶11000).

Expenses are only deductible if incurred wholly and exclusively for the purpose of the trade (¶14540). Moreover, only revenue expenditure is relevant, so capital expenditure (¶13000) is ignored (although capital allowances (¶25000), which are the tax equivalent of depreciation, may be available as a deduction).

For further details, see ¶11000+.

Interest and loan relationships

10110   Interest received and paid outside the activity of the trade is taxed under the loan relationship rules, as are most income or expenses relating to a **money debt**. There is no distinction between income arising in the UK or overseas.

For further details, see ¶16000+.

Property income

10115   Income derived from the **exploitation of land or property** in the UK is normally assessed as property income. This specifically includes income from the following sources:
– licences to occupy or use land;

– ground rents; and
– the granting of a right to an individual to use a caravan or houseboat in one particular location.

Exceptionally, property income may be either exempt, or taxed as trading income.

For further details, see ¶19000+.

MEMO POINTS   1. **Exempt income** includes income derived from the occupation of commercially managed woodlands or real estate investment trusts.
2. Income arising from the following sources is taxed as **trading income**:
– farming or market gardening;
– mining, quarrying, fishing etc;
– tied property;
– easements; and
– the running of guest houses and hotels.

Income from foreign possessions

Overseas income, from whatever source, is taxable as income from foreign possessions.   **10120**
This **includes**:
– income from overseas property letting (¶19575);
– foreign dividends (¶90290); and
– profits of foreign trades which have no UK element (¶90000+).

Profits from letting and trading are calculated using the same rules as for UK letting and trades.

Interest, however, is included within the loan relationship rules (¶10110).

Where **tax is suffered** in the country of origin, double taxation relief may be available (¶90480).

If income **cannot be remitted** to the UK, relief may also be available (¶90210).

Other income

This category is a catch-all for revenue receipts which do not fall within any of the above   **10125**
provisions.

In particular, the following are assessed under this title:
– assessments to recover tax repaid in error;
– certain commission income;
– income arising after the cessation of the trade; and
– income charged under anti-avoidance rules such as tax advantages from transactions in securities, and gains from life policies and offshore funds.

For further details, see ¶21050+.

Chargeable gains

UK resident companies are subject to corporation tax on all gains arising from the sale of   **10130**
chargeable assets, **regardless of the location of the asset**. The gain is assessed in the accounting period in which the **date of disposal** falls.

Where the allowable expenditure exceeds the disposal proceeds, a loss will result (¶37000).

An exemption is available for substantial shareholdings (¶32090) in other trading companies.

For further details, see ¶30000+.

B. Deductions

Loss relief

There are complex rules which apply to losses and how they can be relieved. Each type of   **10160**
income category may result in a loss, and usually the loss can be set against income in the

same category or carried forward. Certain categories can be set against income generally, carried back or surrendered to other group companies (if applicable) (¶35000+).

Capital losses (those resulting from the disposal of a capital asset at a loss) may either be set off against other current chargeable gains, or carried forward against future gains (¶37000+).

Management expenses

10165   Companies with an investment business (¶6115) can obtain relief for the **revenue** expenses of managing their investments (¶17620). As with trading expenses, there are several categories of expense which are disallowed.

Where **expenses exceed investment income**, the excess can be relieved by either carrying it forward or surrendering it to other group companies.

Charitable donations

10170   Charitable donations may be made either in monetary form (¶22085) or as a gift of qualifying investments (¶22245). Certain donations may qualify as a current year trading deduction or can be group relieved. There is no mechanism to carry forward excess donations.

CHAPTER 2

Accounting profits

The starting point for calculating the chargeable profits of a company is the accounting profit   **11000**
or loss before tax as shown in the financial statements. It is therefore important to fully
understand how the accounts have been compiled and, in particular, which accounting
policies and principles have been applied.

SECTION 1

Why are accounts important?

11050
BIM31019

The **computation** of chargeable profits requires a two stage process:
a. prepare accounts under GAAP (Generally Accepted Accounting Practice); and
b. carry out any tax adjustments which are required by law i.e. either as a result of a specific rule (e.g. certain expenses are disallowable) or the application of a general tax requirement (e.g. that only revenue expenditure is deducted against profits).

As the tax computation takes the accounting profit/loss before tax as its **basis**, the accounting treatment of all the company's transactions has a bearing on the final tax liability. In recent years, considerable reliance has been placed on the accounting entries to determine the tax treatment, unless there is a specific requirement to the contrary.

Comment   Certain UK tax rules rely exclusively on the accounting treatment to determine the taxable amounts e.g. intangible fixed assets.

Financial information

11055
s 46 CTA 2009

Statute now requires that **trading profits** must be prepared in accordance with GAAP (i.e. an accounting basis which intends to give a true and fair view), subject to any specific tax adjustment required by law. The full amount of profits must be assessed, so if the accounts do not include these for any reason, an adjustment would be required.

UK based companies use one of three possible **GAAP** regimes: UK GAAP, International GAAP, or a special regime for smaller companies called the FRSSE (Financial Reporting Standards for Smaller Entities – see ¶11180). GAAP is derived from various sources, most importantly Company Law and the Standards, Statements and various other pronouncements issued by the Financial Reporting Council, which is the independent regulator responsible for promoting high quality financial reporting and corporate governance in the UK.

Accounts are deemed to be prepared under GAAP even when this is not in fact true. *Gallagher v Jones* [1994]; *Tapemaze Ltd v Melluish* [2000]

> ⌐MEMO POINTS┐   1. **Barristers and advocates** do not have to comply with the accounting require-ments in the first years of practice.
> 2. **Lloyds underwriters** and life insurance companies, as well as certain financial institutions, have special rules.

11060

In particular circumstances, accountancy can give a **wrong result** for tax purposes, where the accounts:
– are based on an analysis of the facts that is wrong in law. *CIR v Gardner Mountain & D' Abrumenil Ltd* [1947];
– are found to be based on factual assumptions which are insufficiently reliable. *Owen v Southern Railway of Peru Ltd* [1956]; or
– are simply inconsistent with the true facts. *BSC Footwear Ltd v Ridgway* [1971]

HMRC would expect adjustments to be made in order to calculate the taxable profit.

11065

The other issue to bear in mind is that accounting **principles are not static**. Current account-ancy is increasingly more codified and standardised. Indeed, HMRC admit that there has been considerably less need in recent years for judicial intervention to determine the correct accountancy treatment.

Case law

11070
BIM31019

In recent years, the courts have emphasised that taxable profits must not be computed on a **basis** divorced from the principles of commercial accountancy. *Gallagher v Jones* [1994]

However, HMRC state that on the occasions where the commercial accounts take an **unrealistically conservative view**, there may be a debate about whether an alternative commercially acceptable treatment would be available, and whether this would satisfy the basic underlying concepts of accounting, such as **matching**, **recognition**, and **prudence**. Of course, accountancy is not an exact science, and there can be disagreement between accountants as to the best way of treating particular transactions or issues.

EXAMPLE

1. Two taxpayers leased boats under an agreement that provided for an initial period of 2 years, in terms of which an upfront payment was to be made, followed by 17 monthly payments. The remaining 5 months of the initial period were to be rent free. At the end of the 2 years, the boats could be leased for a further 21 year period at a peppercorn rate of £5 p.a. The taxpayers sought to deduct the payments as and when they were made, rather than spreading them equally over the 2 year period.
It was held that the accounts were very misleading, and that expenditure did not necessarily become deductible in the period in which it was incurred. *Gallagher v Jones* [1994]

2. A 1994 case (before the implementation of FRS 12 concerning provisions) considered whether a provision for the future overhaul of jet aircraft was deductible.
It was held that the accounts were prepared in accordance with accepted principles of commercial accountancy at the time (for the current treatment of provisions see ¶11885+). *Johnston v Britannia Airways* [1994]

3. A partnership of architects transferred the business to a company in 1975. The nature of the practice meant that there were many long term contracts during which instalment payments were received. Revenue was recognised on an earned basis, with work in progress containing a conservative view of future profits, which, of course, was an estimate. At the time of the business transfer, over £5m of instalment payments were excluded from profit on the uncompleted contracts. Final accounts for the period were submitted to HMRC in 1979, and during the intervening 4 years, the contracts concluded giving complete information as to the final profit achieved. HMRC argued that the estimates of profits should be amended to reflect subsequent events.
It was held that the accounts as prepared had been drawn up on the correct principles of commercial accounting and that profits should not be anticipated if they had not yet been earned. *Symons v Lord Llewelyn-Davies' Personal Representatives and others* [1983]

HMRC state that where there is an **accepted rule** of commercial accountancy that:
– applies to the situation;
– is not one of two or more equally applicable rules; and
– is consistent with the established facts and is not inappropriate to determine the true profits, then it must be followed unless there is specific legislation to the contrary. *Gallagher v Jones* [1994]

11075
BIM35201

SECTION 2

Duty to prepare accounts

A. Accounting records

It is incumbent upon the directors of all companies to make sure that adequate financial records are kept. These records must be **sufficient** to show and explain the company's transactions and be capable of being used as a basis for the preparation of financial statements in respect of each period of account.

11125
s 386 CA 2006

In practice, there are no hard and fast rules as to the exact **form and content** of these records, the only specification being that they should contain day to day entries of income and expenditure, and provide a record of the company's assets and liabilities (¶45130).

Retention period

Accounting records must be kept for the following periods, depending on the **type of company**, from the date on which they are made:
– for a private company, 3 years; and
– for a public company, 6 years.

11130
s 388 CA 2006

11135   For **tax purposes**, however, the retention period is generally longer in respect of both private and public companies (¶45190+).

Location

11140   Accounting records must be kept at the company's registered office (or another location which, in the view of the directors, is appropriate) and should be **available** at all times for inspection by officers of the company.

B. Types of accounts

11170
s 394 CA 2006

Further to their duty to keep accounting records, the directors of all companies registered under the Companies Act are required to **prepare** annual financial statements in respect of each period of account and these are to include a balance sheet, a profit and loss account, and additional information by way of notes to the accounts.

These statements must present a true and fair view (¶11390+) of the state of the company's affairs.

These statements should **comply with**:
– the statutory requirements of the Companies Act as to form and content; and
– accounting standards and UITF abstracts.

> MEMO POINTS   1. These accounting standards are called **Financial Reporting Standards** (FRS).
> 2. **UITF** stands for Urgent Issues Task Force, and abstracts are published as a proactive response to current issues arising, as bringing new accounting standards into force can be a lengthy process.

Unlisted companies

11175
s 395 CA 2006

Unlisted UK companies have the **choice** of preparing their financial statements in accordance with UK GAAP or under International Financial Reporting Standards (IFRS). IFRS include standards and statements issued by the International Accounting Standards Board (IASB).

Comment   Generally, the main reason for a UK company to choose International GAAP is because it is part of a group with parents, subsidiaries or fellow subsidiaries outside the UK.

11180   **Small and medium sized companies** (which are estimated to represent more than 95% of all companies) may opt to prepare abbreviated versions of their financial statements (different requirements apply depending on whether the company is small or medium sized).

In addition, in the UK the Financial Reporting Standard for Smaller Entities (FRSSE) provides an accounting framework for smaller companies. Entities that choose to adopt the FRSSE are exempt from the provisions of other accounting standards – unless consolidated accounts are being prepared. An international version of the FRSSE (IFRS for SMEs) was published in July 2009 by the IASB.

> MEMO POINTS   Eligibility requirements for companies wishing to adopt the FRSSE:
> 1. A **small company** must meet at least two of the following **criteria**:
> – annual turnover is £6.5m or less;
> – the balance sheet total is £3.26m or less; or
> – the average number of employees is 50 or less.
> 2. A **medium company** must meet at least two of the following **criteria**:
> – annual turnover is £25.9m or less;
> – the balance sheet total is £12.9m or less; or
> – the average number of employees is 250 or less.

Groups

11185   In regard to groups and group accounts, the **ultimate parent company** must produce consolidated financial statements that include all of its subsidiaries. Such accounts incorporate in full the information contained in the individual accounts of the constituent undertakings of the group as if it were a single undertaking, with certain consolidation adjustments.

Although a combined liability for taxation will be shown, it is important to remember that UK corporation tax is calculated on the basis of individual companies and therefore, from a tax perspective, group accounts are simply an aggregation of balances.

Listed companies must use IFRS for the group accounts.

SECTION 3

Accounting standards

Accounting standards in the UK are set by the Financial Reporting Council (FRC) and these apply to entities in the UK and Ireland that have not chosen to use IFRS.   **11235**

The FRC has adopted a strategy of convergence with international standards.

Accounting standards are principles-based; in other words they establish **broad rules** as well as dictating **specific treatments**.

Summary

The most important accounting standards and topics from a tax perspective, inasmuch as their guidance will be persuasive in arriving at taxable profits, are discussed below.   **11240**

Topics	Reference	¶¶
Accounting policies, estimation techniques and measurement bases	FRS 18	¶11270+
Financial performance, extraordinary items, and prior year adjustments	FRS 3	¶11490+
Post balance sheet events	FRS 21	¶11550+
Revenue recognition and the substance of transactions	FRS 5, Application Note G	¶11595+
Stock valuation	SSAP 9, UITF 40	¶11645+
Provisions and contingent liabilities	FRS 12	¶11855+
VAT	SSAP 5	¶11985+

In addition, deferred tax is discussed at ¶11800+.

A. Accounting policies

In short, FRS 18 defines accounting policies, the estimation techniques used in implementing these policies, and the bases used for financial measurement. Accounting policies should be consistent with company law, accounting standards and UITF abstracts.   **11270**

1. Scope

Accounting policies are those principles, conventions, rules and practices adopted by an entity to specify how the **effects of transactions** are to be reflected in its financial statements. For example, a particular policy may specify whether a balance should be recognised as an   **11300** asset or a loss, the basis on which it is to be measured, and where in the balance sheet or profit and loss account it is to be presented.

---

2. Governing principles

11320

Both the Companies Act and the accounting standards require company financial statements to be prepared according to the following basic principles:
- going concern;
- accruals basis;
- consistency;
- prudence; and
- separate valuation of assets and liabilities.

The Act allows companies to depart from these only if there are special reasons to do so. Both the Act and FRS 18 require the notes to the financial statements to give details of the departure, the reasons for it, and its effect on the accounts.

BIM31032

HMRC state that FRS 18 treats going concern and accruals as critical to the selection of accounting policies. Consistency and prudence are desirable rather than fundamental aspects of financial information.

Going concern

11325
FRS 18 (23)

As a general rule, a company is both required and **presumed** to prepare its financial statements on the basis that it is continuing with its operations as a going concern, **unless** there are compelling questions to the contrary, such as:
- it has ceased trading or is in the process of liquidation; or
- its directors have no realistic alternative but to cease trading or to liquidate the entity.

Accruals basis

11330
FRS 18 (27)

The accruals basis of accounting states that **revenue and costs** should be **recognised** as they are earned or accrued rather than when their cash value is received or paid.

As a result, the effects of transactions are recognised when they **occur** and they are **recorded** in the accounting records and reported in the financial statements of the periods to which they relate.

Certain **exceptions** apply for tax purposes e.g. pension contributions (¶14890+) and late salary payments (¶14615).

Consistency

11335

Accounting policies must be applied consistently from one reporting period to another. This requirement not only facilitates a logical means of **comparison** with an entity's **previous financial periods**, but also allows the results of **different entities** to be compared.

Prudence

11340

The concept of prudence dictates, essentially, giving the most cautious **representation** of financial events. For example, if a company foresees a particular loss in the forthcoming year, it should be taken into account immediately. To some extent, this may seem to run counter to the accruals concept (which would say that an event should be recognised during the period when it occurs) but there is an equally valid argument that says that where such a loss is foreseen, the facts giving rise to such an opinion have in fact occurred. For example, if a business purchases stock for £1,200 but then because of a sudden slump in the market, it becomes apparent that the realistic resale value is only £900, the stock should be valued at £900 in the accounts. This will result in a loss of £300 which, in accordance with the concept of prudence, is recognised immediately.

Prudence requires accounting policies to take account of **uncertainty** about the existence of assets, liabilities, gains and losses, or the amount at which they should be measured. There is, however, no need to exercise prudence where there is no uncertainty. HMRC state that prudence should not be used as a reason to create, for example, hidden reserves or excessive provisions, deliberately understating assets or gains, or deliberately overstating liabilities or losses.

BIM31032

---

3. Selecting the most appropriate policies

The most appropriate accounting policies should be selected on the basis of the following four **criteria**: relevance, reliability, comparability and understandability.

11370
FRS 18 (17),
(30);
BIM31032

There is obviously a need to balance these objectives with each other, and also to balance the costs of providing financial information with the likely benefit to the users of that information.

Criteria	Details
Relevance	Relevant information is information provided in a timely manner to assist readers in evaluating both their previous conclusions and their future decisions
Reliability	Reliable information faithfully represents (or can reasonably be relied on to represent) that which it is intended to represent, is free from bias or error, is in all material aspects complete and, where conditions are uncertain, is prudent (¶11855+)
Comparability	In the selection of accounting policies, directors should consider whether they are widely used in the industry; where an entity's policies deviate, the directors should be able to show why this is not only desirable but also results in an enhanced level of presentation for users
Understandability	The information provided by financial statements must be capable of being appreciated and understood by users who have a reasonable knowledge of business, economic activities and accounting, and who are willing to study the information with reasonable diligence An appropriate accounting policy will enable such users to perceive the significance of the information given

---

4. True and fair view

Entities should adopt accounting policies that enable their financial statements to give a true and fair view. These accounting policies should be consistent with the requirements of accounting standards, UITF Abstracts and the Companies Act.

11390
FRS 18 (14)

However, in certain circumstances, strict compliance may result in the unusual (and unexpected) situation in which readers are not given a **proper appreciation** of a company's financial statements e.g. if additional information beyond the normal scope is necessary to explain an unusual transaction. In such a case, supplying the additional information will satisfy the true and fair requirement.

11395

Materiality

Materiality is the judgement made by the preparers of accounts about whether an item should be reflected in those accounts to give a true and fair view. It involves a judgement of what information should be included, and is a threshold quality so that the information provided is relevant and important, and is not swamped by unnecessary detail (which would impair understandability).

11400
BIM31045

An item would be material to the statements if its **misstatement or omission** might reasonably be expected to influence the economic decisions of the users of the statements.

BIM31047

HMRC admit that some entries in accounts depend on the estimates and judgement made by the preparers of the accounts, and will therefore lie within a range of values. As all information should be free from deliberate or systematic error, this should prevent materiality judgements being skewed in a particular direction. Ultimately, however, the factual accuracy of any item in accounts is a matter for the tribunal (¶54335+) to decide.

Override

11405

FRS 18 (15)

In special circumstances, the accounting treatment required by the Act might not result in a true and fair view even if additional information is given. In this event, the company is **obliged** to depart from the relevant provisions to the extent necessary to give a true and fair view, and consequently follow an accounting treatment that is not in accord with the Act. This situation – in which a company deliberately disregards a Companies Act requirement – is known as the true and fair override. It may be used in **special circumstances only**, such as where a company finds itself, in relation to a specific issue, in a situation that other companies facing the same issue would not be in.

---

5. Estimation techniques

11435

Estimation techniques are methods adopted by an entity to arrive at estimated money amounts for assets, liabilities, gains and losses. Examples are methods of depreciation (e.g., straight line or reducing balance), and the different methods to estimate the proportion of trade debts that may not be recoverable.

---

6. Measurement bases

11455

Measurement bases refer to the way in which **monetary attributes** of assets, liabilities, losses and gains are measured. For example, an asset may be measured in various ways: historical cost (the amount paid for it) or current value. Generally, accounting standards or company law will prescribe which measurement basis is to be used for particular items, but sometimes these are open to choice. Whether prescribed or selected, however, measurement bases are a matter of accounting policy.

Changing bases

11460

Where a company switches **from one basis to another** (e.g. it previously reported certain assets on the historical cost basis but now reports them on their disposal value), this represents a change in accounting policy. A change in accounting policy necessarily gives rise to a **prior period adjustment** (in other words, a restatement of, or modification to, an amount relating to the prior period), thus preserving comparability and consistency.

Where, however, a company **changes a method of measuring** a monetary amount, this is not a matter of accounting policy. Continuing the example above, the company, in measuring the disposal value of its assets, can do so by reference to prices quoted in advertisements, previous experience in disposing of assets, or even on the basis of an actual offer received from a prospective purchaser of the assets. This is therefore a change in estimation technique, and not a change in accounting policy.

B. Reporting financial performance

11490

FRS 3, which introduced changes to the profit and loss account when it was first issued, has particular relevance from a taxation perspective because it determines the starting point for the corporation tax computation.

FRS 3 requires that all gains and losses recognised in the financial statements should be included in the profit and loss account or the statement of total recognised gains and losses.

> MEMO POINTS The purpose of the **statement of total recognised gains and losses** is to show the extent to which shareholders' funds have increased or decreased during the year from all gains and losses. Because not all of these will necessarily have flowed through the profit and loss account, they need to be captured and disclosed elsewhere in full.

Disclosure of information

Any special circumstances that affect any liability for taxation (or credit) for the financial year concerned, or potentially any future period, should be disclosed by way of note. These disclosures must be given whether **in respect of** profits, income or capital gains, as well as any special circumstances. An example would be the effect on the tax charge of any losses, whether utilised in the current year or carried forward.

11495

Similarly, the effects of a fundamental change in the basis of taxation should always be shown.

Where there has been an **extraordinary item**, the concept of consistency requires that the tax effects should also be treated as extraordinary even if the item itself and its tax effects are recognised in different periods of account. An example of this situation is seen where the tax relief in respect of an extraordinary loss is utilised in a later period.

11500
FRS 3 (22)

Prior period adjustments

Another area of concern dealt with by FRS 3 is that of prior period adjustments, which sometimes leads to confusion as to if, and when, such an adjustment is required.

11505
FRS 3 (60)

The **general rule** is that prior period adjustments arise from either:
– the need to correct a fundamental error (i.e. an error so significant that it affects the validity of the financial statements and raises doubt as to the "true and fair view"); or
– changes in accounting policies.

Care must be taken to differentiate between changes in accounting policies and **changes in estimation techniques** as the latter do not give rise to prior period adjustments.

The following table gives examples of both types of change, and the appropriate accounting treatment:

11510

Transaction	Change in:		Make prior year adjustment
	Accounting policy	Estimation technique	
Company becomes member of a group and has to change (some of) its accounting policies to match those used by the group	y	n	y
Company changes its method of depreciating a class of fixed assets from reducing balance to straight line	n	y	n
Company previously charged interest incurred in connection with the construction of a fixed asset, but now elects to capitalise it in accordance with FRS 15	y	n	y
Company adjusts its provision for bad debts	n	y	n
Company changes its revenue recognition practices	y	n	y

In respect of transactions requiring a prior year adjustment, as well as fundamental errors, corrections must be made by restating prior periods and adjusting the opening balance of retained profits. In addition, a note explaining the circumstances that gave rise to the adjustment must be given.

11515

> EXAMPLE
>
> **Note x (to Balance sheet)**
> **Profit and loss account**
>
> | | £ |
> |---|---|
> | At beginning of year – as previously stated | 100,000 |
> | Prior year adjustment | 35,000 |
> | At beginning of year – as restated | 135,000 |
> | Profit for the year | 20,000 |
> | At end of year | 155,000 |
>
> **Prior year adjustment**
> During the previous financial year, interest on loans amounting to £35,000 – used to finance costs of construction of tangible fixed assets – were charged to the profit and loss account. In the current year, the directors decided it would be more appropriate to include these interest costs in the cost of the tangible fixed asset. As this amounts to a change of accounting policy, the interest amount in respect of the previous year has been disclosed as a prior period adjustment.

11520

BIM34070

For tax purposes, prior period adjustments are **included in the tax computation** in the year of change, unless a **fundamental error** has occurred, in which event previous tax returns should actually be amended.

A **positive adjustment** arising from a change of accounting policy is chargeable as a receipt of the trade arising on the first day of the first period of account when the policy takes effect. Similarly, a **negative adjustment** is allowed as a deduction in computing profits as an expense arising on the first day of the first period of account of the new accounting policy.

C. Events after the balance sheet date

11550

Events that occur between the balance sheet date (i.e. the date on which the period of account under review ends) and the date on which the financial statements are authorised for issue, are known as post balance sheet events. FRS 21 specifies the accounting treatment to be adopted.

Smaller companies reporting under FRSSE need not comply with FRS 21. Listed entities are obliged to follow IFRS and therefore apply IAS 10.

There are **two categories** of post balance sheet events – these are termed adjusting and non-adjusting events.

Adjusting events

11555
FRS 21 (8)

Adjusting events refer to circumstances that existed **at the balance sheet date**, in respect of which information came to light only afterwards, thus requiring a **revision of the amount recorded** in the financial statements.

One example of an adjusting event might be the outcome of a court case that confirmed that the entity did in fact have a present obligation at the balance sheet date, even if at the time the liability was not apparent. Another example could be the discovery of fraud or error, the result being that the financial statements are incorrect.

BIM31040

Where **work in progress** is ascertained some time after the balance sheet date, the **review** undertaken at that time will reflect events up to that time, and it would be unusual for a subsequent review to be needed. HMRC state that common sense should determine whether subsequent material events are likely to occur after the time of the initial review.

Non-adjusting events

11560
FRS 21 (3)

Non-adjusting events are those that provide evidence of conditions that arose only **after the balance sheet date**. As these circumstances did not exist at the time, the entity does not make an adjustment to amounts recognised in the financial statements. Nevertheless, it may be appropriate to draw the attention of users of the financial statements to the facts, and this is done by way of a note.

Examples of a non-adjusting event might be the announcement of a plan to discontinue an operation or dispose of a subsidiary. Failure to recognise the effect of such an event on the financial statements could create **going concern** implications i.e. there could be doubt as to true and fair presentation or even the appropriateness of presuming the company to be a going concern. An entity's financial statements should not be prepared on the going concern basis if, after the balance sheet date, the directors intend to cease trading or are of the opinion that there is no alternative but to do so.

Disclosure

The following table summarises the disclosure requirements:

11565

Rule which applies	Adjusting events	Non-adjusting events
General rule (FRS 21)	All adjusting post balance sheet events must be reflected in the financial statements. Separate disclosure of adjusting events by way of a note is not a specific requirement of the standard	Non-adjusting events should be disclosed by way of a note to the accounts, and should explain the nature of the event and an estimate of the financial effect. If this is not possible, a statement to that effect should be added. Where applicable, any taxation implications should be separately disclosed
Companies Act requirement	Although the Act does not make any distinction between adjusting and non-adjusting events, it requires the directors' report to include particulars of materially adjusting events affecting the company that have occurred since the year end	

D. Revenue recognition

Whilst there is no specific standard for recognising revenue under UK GAAP, the topic receives some treatment in FRS 5, "Reporting the substance of transactions" and Application Note G, which was issued as an amendment to it. Additional guidance has also been given in the form of UITF 40 in relation to service contracts.

11595

Importance

The importance of revenue recognition from a tax perspective derives from the general principle that the reporting of revenue for accounting purposes is followed for tax purposes as well. Because a reporting entity's financial statements should both report and reflect the substance of the transactions into which it has entered, the provisions of FRS 5 were crafted to ensure that the commercial effect of a company's transactions – as opposed to their strictly legal form – is reported in its financial statements.

11600
FRS 5 (14)

Comment Sometimes the tax treatment of transactions follows their legal form, which could be significantly different from the accounting treatment.

Overview

The relationship between the accounting standard, abstract and Application Note is set out in the table below.

11605

Standard	Scope
FRS 5, Reporting the Substance of Transactions	Principal standard on revenue recognition
Application Note G	General principles of revenue recognition
UITF 40	Additional guidance – accounting for revenue on service contracts (¶11760+)

Summary

11610 The basic principles of revenue recognition are summarised in the following table:

Condition	Accounting treatment
Revenue recognition	Seller recognises revenue under a contract with a customer when it obtains the right to consideration[1] in exchange for performance of the contract[2]
Recognising contractual performance	Goods: in accordance with delivery terms
	Services: period over which service provided (e.g. cleaning contract) Must consider what specific activities constitute performance of a contract
Contracts comprising mixture of goods and services	Must consider the terms of the contract, e.g. does the performance of the contract consist of clearly identifiable stages? If so, are these stages separable?
Contract consists of separable stages	1. Is each stage "an end product"?
	2. What benefit does the customer gain at each stage of completion?
	3. Where does the balance of risk lie at each stage of the contract?
Seller receives payment in advance from customer	The seller should recognise a liability equal to the payment received, representing its contractual obligation When the seller obtains the right to consideration through performance of the contract, the liability should be reduced, with the reduction simultaneously reported as turnover
Partial right to consideration	The seller should recognise turnover only to the extent that it has obtained the right to consideration through its performance
Fair value	Revenue should be measured at fair value of the right to consideration[3], normally the contract price, net of discounts, VAT and similar sales taxes
Time value of money	Where material to reported revenue, the revenue recognised should be the present value of expected cash inflows The unwinding of the discount should be credited to finance income as this is a gain from a financing transaction
	Subsequent adjustments to a debtor to reflect time value of money or credit risk should not be included within turnover

Note:
1. **Right to consideration** is defined as a seller's right to the amount received or receivable in exchange for performance of a contract.
2. **Performance** is the fulfilment of the seller's contractual obligations to the customer through the supply of goods and services.
3. **Fair value** is the amount at which goods and services can be exchanged in an arm's length transaction between informed and willing parties.

Assets and liabilities

11615
BIM31050

FRS 5 allows an item to be recognised in the balance sheet where:
– it can be measured with sufficient reliability; and
– there is sufficient evidence of its existence.

Assets are **defined** as rights or other access to future economic benefits controlled by a company as a result of past transactions or events. Liabilities are defined as an entity's obligations to transfer economic benefits to others as a result of past transactions or events.

The **importance** of these economic definitions is their effect on the timing of the recognition of profits.

> [MEMO POINTS] **Future benefits** would include the right to use the asset and to enjoy the proceeds on its disposal or realisation.

E. Stock

Stocks on hand for resale at the end of the period of account are of special importance for the obvious reason that their valuation affects not only the balance sheet, but also the computation of trading profit for the year. Unsold stock at the year end is shown as an asset in the balance sheet and a trading receipt in the profit and loss account (like income). Opening stock and any purchases are deducted as an expense. The valuation of stock can therefore have a significant impact on the trading profit.

11645

1. Overview

All reporting entities whose financial statements are designed to show a true and fair view are subject to the provisions of SSAP 9, "Stocks and long-term contracts". Stocks can be **classified** in various ways e.g. raw materials, consumable stores, semi-finished goods (work in progress), finished goods, and goods purchased for resale (trading stock). A business may hold a combination of these, each one potentially requiring different valuation methods.

In addition, **long term contracts** i.e. those that fall into two or more periods of account, include stocks and inventories that need to be accounted for according to specific rules.

11675

2. Valuation

Stock is normally valued at the lower of cost and net realisable value.

The **key issues** in the valuation of stocks are as follows:

11695
SSAP 9 (21), (26)

Valuation method	Detail
Historical cost	Stocks are valued for inclusion in the balance sheet at historical cost i.e. purchase price or cost of production If prices change whilst stock is still held, items should be valued on a FIFO basis (first in, first out), rather than LIFO basis (last in, first out)
Net realisable value (NRV)	If it appears that the amount that can realistically be realised (i.e. market value) is lower than historical cost, the stock should be written down to, and stated at, the NRV When making this comparison of cost with NRV, each line of stock should be considered individually and not in aggregate
Replacement cost	Stock may also be stated in the financial statements at replacement cost but only if this is lower than the net realisable value This approach is not often followed in practice
Alternative accounting rules	Where a company adopts the alternative accounting rules[1], stock may be stated at the lower of current replacement cost and net realisable value, with any permanent diminution in value (e.g. on obsolescence) provided for This method is not often used in practice

Valuation method	Detail
Adjustments and write-downs	Adjustments may be required to stock items e.g. where there are transfers to/from stock from/to fixed assets, or on the cessation of trading
Adjustments for tax purposes	Accounting profits (and therefore stock valuation) may need to be adjusted for the following: – appropriations of stock (¶11710); and – cessation of trading (¶11715)
Note: 1. For further details see *Accountancy and Financial Reporting Memo*.	

11700
BIM33115

In many cases it is impractical, if not impossible, to value **each item individually**. HMRC will generally accept any method of valuing stock which meets the requirements of an accepted accounting practice and faithfully reflects the facts.

Basis of valuation changes

11705
BIM34005,
33190

If the basis of stock valuation changes, any **accrued profit (or expense)** is taxable in the year when it is recognised in the accounts i.e. backdating does not apply, even though the change in valuation may relate to prior periods. *Pearce v Woodall Duckham Ltd* [1978]

A recent instance of such a change involves the treatment of **depreciation** when it is included as part of unsold stock at the year end. Although depreciation is normally added back to the accounting profit because it is not an allowable expense for tax purposes, where the depreciation charge is carried forward in stock to the next period of account, it does not need to be added back because it has not reduced the profit for the current year. *HMRC v William Grant & Sons Distillers Ltd*; *Small (Inspector of Taxes) v Mars UK Ltd* [2007] Companies that need to change their stock value to reflect this case law would have to make a one-off adjustment to opening stock (which would in effect be a prior year adjustment – see ¶11505).

Appropriations

11710
s 157 CTA 2009;
s 161 TCGA 1992

Where assets are appropriated **from trading stock** for any purpose (or retained by the trader on cessation of trade), the market value of the stock is included as a receipt for tax purposes and the trader will be treated as having acquired the asset at market value.

A similar provision applies where fixed assets are appropriated **to trading stock** when the asset is deemed to be sold at market value and stock acquired at that same price. However, where this would result in either a chargeable gain or allowable capital loss, the trader may make an election which, in effect, treats the gain (or loss) as part of the trading profit. This is achieved by reducing the market value included in stock by the amount of the gain (or increasing it if the result is a loss). The election must be made within 2 years of the end of the accounting period in which the asset was appropriated.

For transfers between group companies see ¶67130+.

Cessation of trade

11715
ss 162–165
CTA 2009

On the cessation of a trade, market value applies **unless** a transfer of stock is made to a connected party. If several assets are sold together, including stock, a just and reasonable apportionment of the consideration should be made.

ss 166–167
CTA 2009

A transfer **to a connected party** who is intending to trade in the UK is also valued at market value, unless this is greater than both cost and the price agreed between the parties. In this latter case, a joint election can be made, within 2 years of the accounting period end, to substitute the greater of cost and the agreed price. The election cannot apply to work in progress.

s 168 CTA 2009

  MEMO POINTS   For this purpose, a party is **connected** with another where either:
– the relationship falls within any of the situations in ¶31375;
– one is a partnership in which the other has a right to a share;

– one is a company which the other can control (¶75310+); or
– both are companies which are controlled (¶75310+) by another person.

EXAMPLE Mr A ceases his trade and transfers it to a company owned by him, A Ltd.
The agreed consideration for the stock (which cost £35,000) is £50,000. If sold to a third party, the stock would be valued at £60,000.
The default value for the stock will be £60,000, but A Ltd and Mr A can jointly elect to reduce this value to £50,000.

3. Long term contracts and work in progress

Work in progress may or may not contain a proportion of overhead expenses. *Ostime v Duple Motor Bodies* [1961] This obviously has an effect on valuation.

11745
SSAP 9 (22)

With respect to long term contracts, the **choice of accounting treatment** will have a significant impact on the entity's reported results for the period – for both financial reporting and tax purposes. Long term contracts can take various **forms**, such as:
– the design, manufacture or construction of a single asset (e.g. civil engineering contract);
– the provision of a service (e.g. catering contract); or
– a combination of assets and services that make up a single project (e.g. refurbishment of a chain of retail outlets).

For a long term contract to exist, it must extend over more than one period of account, and its effect on the accounts must be material.

Forms of contracts

The most common types of long term contracts are fixed-price or cost-plus contracts.

11750

With a **fixed-price contract**, the contract price is by definition known in advance. From year to year, the amount to be taken into account as turnover is independent of the issue of how much profit should recognised.

On the other hand, under a **cost plus contract**, an agreed profit percentage is applied after all legitimate costs have been authorised. At the year end, this percentage is applied to determine the appropriate turnover figure. Such costs as have been incurred (including those not yet approved) should be used to derive the profit or loss to date on the contract. Where there are known additional costs yet to be incurred, even those that will not be approved under the contract, they must be provided for once they are identified.

Summary of treatment

The general rules for the accounting treatment of contracts can be summarised as follows:
1. Where the **outcome** of the contract can be **assessed with reasonable certainty**, even if it is not complete, that part of the profit attributable to the work performed at the accounting date should be included in the profit and loss account for the year.
2. Where the **outcome** of the project is **less than certain**, or losses are envisaged, then a different accounting treatment is required.
3. Where it is **not possible** at any stage in the contract to **assess the degree of profit** with any certainty, turnover and costs recognised should be equal, the effect being not to recognise any profit on that contract. This is common practice in the early stages of long projects.
4. Where it can be foreseen that a **loss will be made**, full provision should be made.

11755

Service contracts

As regards service contracts, UITF 40 applies to all companies, including those using the FRSSE, for all accounting periods ending on or after 22 June 2005.

11760

The key elements of UITF 40 are as follows:
1. If a single contract may be divided into separate clearly **identifiable stages**, it may be appropriate to account for them as separate transactions.

2. Where a contract for services falls into **separate periods of account**, it should be accounted for as a long term contract.

3. Where the substance of a contract is that the seller's **obligations are performed over time**, revenue should be recognised as contract activity progresses, to reflect the seller's partial performance of the contract. The revenue recognised should reflect the accrual of the right to consideration as the contract activity progresses.

4. If the substance of the contract is that a **right to consideration does not arise until the occurrence of a critical event**, revenue should not be recognised until the event occurs.

5. The **accounting policy** should be applied consistently to all similar contracts and from one accounting year to the next.

11765
Sch 15 FA 2006

Spreading relief The use of UITF 40 represents a change of accounting policy, which in turn requires the **restatement of opening balances** (i.e. work in progress) on the balance sheet for accounting periods ending on or before 22 June 2005. The extra profit which arose as a result is called adjustment income (taxed as miscellaneous income), and can be spread over a maximum of 6 years as follows:

Year	Charged to tax
1 – 3	Lower of: – 1/3 of the original adjustment income; and – 1/6 of the business profits[1] for that year
4 – 5	Lower of: – amount remaining untaxed (if any); – 1/3 of the original adjustment income; and – 1/6 of the business profits[1] for that year
6	Any balance outstanding

Note:
1. The **business profits** are the profits as computed for tax purposes, excluding any capital allowances, and before the adjustment income is taken into account.

EXAMPLE B Ltd changed its policy to comply with UITF 40 for the first time in Year 1. This resulted in an increase in profits of £150,000. The adjustment income is calculated as follows:

Year	Profits £	Adjustment income	
		£	Calculation method
1	240,000	40,000	1/6 of business profits
2	360,000	50,000	1/3 of adjustment income
3	180,000	30,000	1/6 of business profits
4	240,000	30,000	amount outstanding
5	270,000	n/a	n/a
6	300,000	n/a	n/a

11770

MEMO POINTS 1. If an accounting period ends by reason of the company **ceasing to be within the charge to corporation tax** or the commencement of winding up proceedings, the whole of the remaining untaxed adjustment income will be taxed. If ceasing a particular business, but still within the charge to corporation tax, the spreading relief continues.

2. The 1/3 limit is proportionately reduced for **short periods of account** (i.e. less than 12 months), but the whole adjustment income can still be spread over 6 years, irrespective of how many accounting periods are included in the 6 year period.

3. It is possible for an **adjustment expense** to arise rather than a profit, and this can be treated in the same way as adjustment income.

4. An election can be made to **bring forward the adjustment income** so that more of it is taxed earlier than would otherwise be required. Such an election must be made before the first anniversary of the normal filing date for the accounting period in question, and must show how much adjustment income is to be taxed. In future years, the original adjustment income is treated as being reduced by the amount charged early.

F. Deferred tax

Taxable profits are rarely, if ever, the same as accounting profits because the criteria for recognising items of income and expenses are different for the two purposes. Certain items can be taxable, or tax deductible, at a different time to when they are recognised for accounting purposes, or in some cases may not be recognised or allowed at all. The consequent tax adjustments made to the accounting profit distort the resulting tax charge shown in the accounts.

11800
FRS 19 (2)

Accruals concept

At the most basic level, deferred tax is the estimated **amount** of tax that will arise from the gap (i.e., timing difference) between accounting and taxable profits.

11805
FRS 19 (7)

Applying the accruals concept, the tax charge shown in the accounts should take account of all tax consequences of income and expenses disclosed in the current period, even though those consequences may only be recognised in a later period.

A **distinction** must, however, be made between differences in the accounting and tax treatment which are permanent, and those which relate to timing only.

11810

1. **Permanent differences** arise when there are items recognised in the financial statements that will never be brought into charge to tax, or allowed as a tax deductible expense. For example, certain entertainment expenses will never be allowed as a tax deductible expense, and this difference will never resolve in the future. Such differences are irrelevant for the purposes of the deferred tax calculation.

2. **Timing differences** arise when an item is taxable or deductible in a different period to that in which it is recognised in the accounts. They are said to "originate" when they first arise, and "reverse" when they resolve in a later period. The rationale adopted by FRS 19, "Deferred Tax", is to apply the liability method, which broadly means that tax is provided for on timing differences only, in an amount that is estimated to be the liability for tax payable at some point in the future. In order to help remove the distortions to the tax charge, a provision for a deferred tax liability or a deferred tax asset is created.

Summary

The following table summarises the deferred tax treatment of certain common items:

11815

Item	Type of difference	Deferred taxation adjustment required?	Detail
Disallowable expenditure	Permanent	n	
Deferred expenditure	Timing	y	Where expenditure is allowed for tax in the year that it is incurred, but for accounting purposes there is a delay in recognition, a deferred tax liability will arise Examples include capitalised interest costs, and expense prepayments
Accelerated capital allowances	Timing	y	See ¶11820
Unrelieved tax loss	Timing	y	Where set-off is not available, and the losses are carried forward, deferred tax comes into play, because the losses may lead to an eventual tax reduction or even refund when they are set off This constitutes a timing difference The use of capital losses is more restricted, so deferred tax is rarely provided for

Item	Type of difference	Deferred taxation adjustment required?	Detail
Unpaid pension contributions	Timing	y	For accounting purposes, contributions to pension schemes are recognised on the accruals basis whilst the rule for tax purposes is that contributions paid wholly and exclusively for the purposes of the business to registered schemes are allowed in the period in which they are made (i.e. cash basis) Where there have been special payments to a pension fund (such as lump sum payments to make up a shortfall), tax relief may be spread (¶14980+), which further diverges from the accounting treatment
Revaluation gain	Timing	y	Normally revaluation gains do not give rise to a deferred tax adjustment By exception, deferred tax is provided if: – the revaluation gain is recognised in the profit and loss account (such as for marked-to-market gains revalued to fair value); or – there is a binding agreement to sell the asset at the balance sheet date and the resulting profit or loss has been recognised
Intra-group profits on stock reversed on consolidation	Timing	y	Whilst the individual tax charges of each group member will be aggregated in the group's consolidated accounts, the tax effect of consolidation adjustments must also be included Such adjustments give rise to timing differences for the group which must be recognised by deferred tax Examples would include: – alignment of accounting policies; and – elimination of intra-group transactions
Unremitted income from group undertakings	Timing	y	Where tax could be payable on the future receipt of past earnings of a subsidiary, associate or joint venture (taking account of any double taxation relief), deferred tax should be recognised to the extent that: – dividends have been accrued as receivable; or – a binding agreement has been entered into so that past earnings will be distributed in the future

Accelerated capital allowances

11820
FRS 19 (9)

Deferred tax is often relevant in respect of capital allowances, which are the tax deductible equivalent of depreciation (which is not tax deductible).

An asset is commonly depreciated at a slower rate in the financial statements i.e. the capital allowances claimed in the tax computation have the effect of writing off the asset more quickly. Although this gives rise to an initial tax advantage, this timing difference will slowly erode over time, and ultimately resolve when the asset is sold, because an adjustment will be made in the tax computation to reverse the excess capital allowances previously given to the extent of the proceeds received.

> MEMO POINTS 1. For details of accounting for **fixed assets**, and in particular depreciation, see ¶25050+.
> 2. For **details** of capital allowances see ¶25120.
> 3. Even where an asset is **not depreciated**, deferred tax should still be provided on the timing difference that arises when capital allowances are claimed. e.g. an investment property.
> 4. Where **capital allowances are retained** by the company even when the asset is sold for a profit e.g. business property renovation allowances which cannot be withdrawn once a set period of ownership has elapsed, a different treatment applies. From acquisition, deferred tax should still be recognised on such an asset, as the company should not anticipate holding the asset for the requisite period. After the period has expired, however, the allowances claimed become a permanent difference and the deferred tax that has previously been recognised should be reversed.

> EXAMPLE C Ltd purchases plant for £10,000 on 1 January 20X1 which qualifies for capital allowances on a 20% reducing balance basis, and is depreciated at 15% per annum on a straight line basis. The company has a 31 December year end.
> The following timing differences will arise up to 31 December 20X3:

	20X1 £	20X2 £	20X3 £	Total £
Depreciation charge	1,500	1,500	1,500	4,500
Capital allowances	2,000	1,600	1,280	4,880
Timing differences: Originating/ (reversing)	500	100	(220)	380

> In 20X4, the plant is sold for £6,000, when the net book value is £5,500, giving an accounting profit on disposal of £500. For tax purposes, the maximum capital allowances which should have been given are only £4,000 (10,000 – 6,000), so a balancing charge of £880 is required.

	20X4 £
Profit on disposal	(500)
Balancing charge	880
Timing differences: Originating/(reversing)	(380)

Measurement

11825
FRS 19 (37)

Deferred tax is measured using the average tax rates that are expected to apply when the timing differences reverse, based on the tax rates that have been enacted, or substantively enacted, by the balance sheet. In practice, current tax rates are often used, as they are invariably the only rates that have been enacted.

If future profits are expected to increase, it is prudent to use the mainstream rate of corporation tax.

> MEMO POINTS 1. The IASB has stated that **substantial enactment** occurs when any future steps in the enactment process will not change the outcome. In the UK, this means when the House of Commons passes a resolution under the Provisional Collection of Taxes Act 1968.
> 2. To reflect the **time value** of money, it is possible to discount a deferred tax liability, although this is not usually undertaken due to the increased complexity of calculation. For details see *Accountancy and Financial Reporting Memo*.
> 3. The basic rule is that a **deferred tax asset** may only be recognised if there is sufficient evidence that it is likely to be recoverable at the balance sheet date. In practice it is rare to recognise a deferred tax asset.

> EXAMPLE Continuing the example at ¶11820, an average tax rate of 26% applies throughout the period. The associated deferred tax balances would be:

	20X1 £	20X2 £	20X3 £	20X4 £
Timing difference	500	100	(220)	(380)
Tax rate	26%	26%	26%	26%
Deferred tax liability increase/(decrease)	130	26	(57)	(99)
Deferred tax liability	130	156	99	0

G. Dealing with uncertainty

11855   In general, an entity's balance sheet must reflect all the assets and liabilities that are known to exist at the balance sheet date. However, for various reasons, it may be unclear **whether an obligation actually exists**. And, even where the existence of an obligation is known, there may still be some uncertainty regarding its measurement (in financial terms) or the timing of the payment required to discharge it.

Both the Companies Act and GAAP require that the obligation be classified either as a **provision** or as a **contingent liability**, depending on the circumstances.

1. Provisions

11885
FRS 12 (2)

Provisions are **defined** in FRS 12 as liabilities of uncertain timing or amount. Though the FRS clearly regards provisions as a type of liability, it considers them separately from other liabilities because of the element of uncertainty surrounding them.

Scope

11890
FRS 12 (3)

A number of specific provisions fall **outside** the scope of the standard as follows:
– financial instruments carried at fair value;
– provisions for executory contracts (i.e. contracts in which both parties have not fully performed their obligations) unless the contract is "onerous" (i.e. a contract in which the unavoidable costs of meeting the obligations imposed by it exceed the economic benefits anticipated from it);
– insurance companies; and
– provisions specifically covered by other accounting standards (e.g. provisions for pensions or deferred taxation).

Recognition

11895
FRS 12 (14)

FRS 12 states that a provision should be recognised as a liability in the financial statements when **all** of the following **criteria** are met:
– an entity has a present obligation as a result of a past event;
– it is probable that a transfer of economic benefits will be required to settle the obligation; and
– a reliable estimate can be made of the obligation.

FRS 12 (15)

<u>MEMO POINTS</u>   1. Before a **present obligation** can exist, an obligating event must have taken place i.e. one that results in the entity having no realistic alternative but to settle the obligation created. The obligations will be legal (i.e. enforceable by law) or constructive (i.e. it creates a valid expectation in the other party that the entity will settle the obligation).

FRS 12 (18)

2. Only those obligations arising from **past events** and existing independently of an entity's future actions are recognised as provisions.

3. The obligation to **transfer economic benefits** is an integral component of the definition of a liability. Similarly, in determining whether a provision in respect of a liability should be recognised, there must be a probability that such a transfer will take place. For this purpose, an occurrence is regarded as "probable" if it is more likely than not to occur (i.e. a probability greater than 50%). FRS 12 (23)

4. The use of **estimates** is an essential part of the preparation of financial statements. Provisions, by their nature, are more uncertain than most other balance sheet items. Companies are normally able, in respect of likely situations, to determine a range of possible outcomes and make a sufficiently reliable estimate of the obligation that will arise. Instances in which a liability is known to exist but no reliable estimate can be made are unusual. However, where this does happen, the liability cannot be recognised as a provision but, instead, must be disclosed as a contingent liability (¶11945+). FRS 12 (25),(26)

The **amount** to be recognised as a provision should be the best estimate of the expenditure required to settle the present obligation at the balance sheet date. This requirement holds even where it would not be possible to settle it at the balance sheet date, but only at some future date. **11900**
FRS 12 (36)

> MEMO POINTS   1. Where the effect of the **time value of money** is material, the amount of a provision should be the present value of the future expenditures expected to settle the obligation. The discount rate used should be a pre-tax rate that reflects current market assessments of: FRS 12 (45)
> – the time value of money; and
> – the risks specific to the liability.
> For further details of discounting see *Accountancy and Financial Reporting Memo*.
> 2. Where **future events**, such as changes in legislation and technology, are expected to affect the amount required to settle an obligation, the provision should be adjusted to reflect these events. However, this treatment can be applied only if there is sufficient objective evidence that the changes will occur. Gains expected to be made on the disposal of assets should not be taken into account in measuring a provision even if the expected disposal is closely linked to the event that gives rise to the provision. FRS 12 (51), (54)
> 3. Where a company is able to look to a **third party to reimburse** either part or all of the amount required to settle a provision, it should reduce the amount of the provision accordingly, but only if the company: FRS 12 (56)
> – would not be liable for the costs even if the third party failed to pay them; or
> – will be liable for the full amount of the costs not reimbursed, but the reimbursement is virtually certain to be received when the company discharges the obligation.

The following are examples of situations that may require provisions to be made: **11905**

Transaction	Make provision?
1. Company has an accounting date of 30 June. During July it learns that it is obliged to incur clean-up costs for environmental damage that had been caused before 30 June	Yes (the company has a present obligation)
2. Company makes a decision that, in future, it intends to incur costs in respect of environmental damage it expects to cause as a result of future operations	No (there is no present obligation)
3. Company has an accounting date of 31 December. On 15 December, the board decides to close down an unprofitable division. This decision was not communicated to any of those affected, and no other steps were taken to implement the decision	No (Under FRS 12 decision does not give rise to a constructive obligation unless it has been communicated to those affected by it in a way that raises a valid expectation in them that the entity will discharge its responsibilities)
4. Same situation as 3. above except that the board had agreed a detailed closure plan by the accounting date, and details were communicated to customers and employees	Yes

Official view

11910
BIM46510

HMRC state that a provision made in accounts will be **allowable** for tax purposes only if it:
- is in respect of allowable revenue expenditure and not, for example, in respect of capital expenditure; *RTZ Oil & Gas Ltd v Elliss* [1987]
- is in accordance with UK GAAP;
- does not conflict with any statutory rule governing the time at which expenditure is allowed; and
- is estimated with sufficient accuracy.

11915
BIM46535,
46545

Examples of allowable and disallowed provisions are shown in the following table:

Situation	Tax treatment	Reference
Cost of work under a warranty which a trader gives on the sale of merchandise (or under consumer protection legislation)	Allowed	
Liabilities under onerous contracts as soon as a net loss is foreseen e.g. rent payable on vacated properties	Allowed	*Herbert Smith v Honour* [1999]
Commission refundable by an insurance intermediary on the lapse of a policy where the commission is recognised as income at the inception of the policy	Allowed	
Cost of rectification work by builders, including retentions up to the level that these have been recognised as income within accounts	Allowed	
Operating losses that will or may arise from obligations entered into subsequent to the balance sheet date	Disallowed	*Meat Traders Ltd v Cushing* [1997] FRS 12 (68)
Restructuring provisions where the business has a detailed formal plan for restructuring and has created a valid expectation in those affected that it will carry it out[1]	Allowed	FRS 12 (75) FRS 12 (88)
Provisions where the only event that might require them is an unpublished decision of the directors	Disallowed	
Provisions for future expenditure required by legislation where the business could avoid the obligation by changing its method of operation e.g. by stopping doing whatever is affected by the legislation	Disallowed	
Provisions for future repairs of plant and machinery owned by the business	Disallowed	See ¶25000+ for expenditure relating to fixed assets
Provision for future repairs where the asset is held under an operating lease that contains a repairing obligation e.g. tenants' repairing leases of property	Allowed	FRS 12 (14) FRS 12 (22)
Note: 1. The detailed formal plan should set out: – the business or part of the business affected; – the location; – the location, number and function of the employees who will lose their jobs; – the costs; and – the date of implementation. A provision should cover only those costs necessarily incurred to undertake the restructuring, and not any relating to the ongoing activities of the company.		

2. Contingencies

Contingent **liabilities** are even less certain than provisions; they become certain only on the occurrence of some future event – in other words they are, at best, possible future liabilities.

11945

Scope

FRS 12 **defines** a contingent liability as:
a. a possible obligation that arises from past events and whose existence will be confirmed only by the occurrence or non-occurrence of one or more uncertain future events not wholly within the entity's control; or
b. a present obligation that arises from past events but cannot be recognised because:
– it is not probable that a transfer of economic benefits will be required to settle the obligation; or
– the amount of the obligation cannot be measured with sufficient reliability.
Examples of contingent liabilities include:
– guarantees given by a company in respect of possible defective goods; or
– the outcome of a legal dispute, where it is not clear if a present obligation on the part of the company actually exists (one example may be a legal action brought by an employee).

11950
FRS 12 (2)

Accounting treatment

Contingent liabilities are not recognised in financial statements (in other words, no monetary adjustment is made in the accounts), but they should be **disclosed** by way of a note, as follows:
– brief description of the nature of the contingent liability;
– estimate of its financial effect;
– indication of the uncertainties that exist; and
– the possibility of any reimbursement.

Similarly, **contingent assets** are not recognised in the accounts, but are disclosed only if an economic inflow is probable

11955
FRS 12 (28),
(91)

H. VAT

Income and expenditure should be stated net of VAT as the accounts should reflect the role of the company as a collector of VAT only.

11985
SSAP 5

By exception, VAT is included within **expenditure** where it cannot be reclaimed in the following situations:
– the company is not registered for VAT;
– some or all of the activities of the company may be exempt for VAT purposes, which affects the recoverability of input VAT; and
– certain types of expenditure, such as business entertaining, incur VAT which cannot be recovered.

Turnover should always be stated net of VAT. If a company wishes to show turnover inclusive of VAT, then the VAT element must be shown as a deduction to arrive at the turnover figure net of VAT charged.

Small business schemes

The following table summarises the treatment of VAT in relation to the small business VAT simplification schemes.

For further details see *VAT Memo*.

11990

Scheme	Taxable[1] turnover threshold (£)	Description	Accounting issues
Cash accounting	1.35m	VAT is not payable or refundable until income is received and expenses are paid	Balance shown as due to/from HMRC in the accounts will not agree to the amount shown on the relevant VAT return, even if the financial year end and VAT year end coincide
Annual accounting	1.35m	Allows only one VAT return a year to be submitted, and VAT payments can be made in instalments based on the previous year's liability	Balance shown as due to/from HMRC in the accounts will not agree to the amount shown on the VAT return
Flat rate scheme	150,000	Ignores all the usual VAT rules A set percentage (dependent on trade sector) is applied to turnover which becomes the amount due to HMRC	The amount payable is the only entry in the balance sheet VAT account, and is deducted from turnover All expenses are shown gross, with the exception of capital assets costing more than £2,000, when input VAT can still be recovered

Note:
1. In this context, assuming the company was VAT registered, taxable means that the turnover would be subject to VAT (at whatever rate) i.e. not exempt.

CHAPTER 3

Capital or revenue

As only revenue expenditure is deductible from the taxable profits, the dividing line between capital and revenue is crucial to a company's tax computation. The amounts involved may make a huge difference in the bottom line profit and the tax payable.

13000

SECTION 1

Why is there a distinction?

By statute, corporation tax is chargeable only on revenue income and chargeable gains. For the most part, capital expenditure is not deductible from income when computing chargeable profits. However, other reliefs may be available (¶25000), and in certain cases, a deduction for capital expenditure is specifically allowed by statute (for example, the costs of raising loan finance).

13050
ss 2, 93 CTA 2009

It is therefore vital to identify all capital expenditure in order to ensure that the computation is compliant with the law.

Similarly, capital income is not taxable as trading income, and may escape tax altogether, depending on the circumstances.

Comment Capital expenditure in the hands of one taxpayer is not necessarily a capital receipt in the hands of the recipient. For example. if a tractor is sold by a dealer from his trading stock, the proceeds will be a revenue receipt, even though the tractor is acquired as a capital asset by the farmer.

Accounting treatment

Accountancy practice and tax law are not fully aligned on the treatment of capital items. The most common example of this **divergence** is the accountant's use of depreciation for

13055

tangible fixed assets, which is not deductible in the tax computation. In tax matters, tax law must always take precedence.

The main concern of the accountant is to match expenditure with related income: that is, to determine when expenditure is consumed in earning profits. This may not accord with the tax treatment of that expenditure.

Statutory treatment

13060
s 53 CTA 2009

The only statutory provision is that in calculating the profits of a trade, no deduction is allowed for items of a capital nature.

BIM35110

   ⌐MEMO POINTS⌐ Under s 74 ICTA 1988, the following expenditure was specifically **prohibited from deduction**:
– any capital withdrawn from, or any sum employed or intended to be employed as capital in, the trade (excluding interest payments); and
– any capital employed in improvements to premises occupied for the purposes of the trade.
Although this section has been repealed, HMRC appear to consider that its principles are still applicable.

Importance of case law

13065
BIM35005

There is no statutory rule for determining which expenses are of a revenue nature and can be deducted in computing profits. It has therefore fallen to the courts to arrive at principles governing the computation of trading profits. The courts usually start from the principles of commercial accounting – that is, setting expenditure necessary to earn profits against the related receipts – but such principles are not definitive for tax purposes. *Beauchamp v FW Woolworth plc* [1989]

> ⌐EXAMPLE⌐ A Ltd took out two loans totalling 100m Swiss francs, both for 5 year terms. On repayment, an exchange loss of £11.4m was suffered.
> It was held that the loss was not deductible against profits because the loans increased the capital employed in the trade. The loss was incurred in connection with a capital transaction and therefore was not an allowable deduction. *Beauchamp v FW Woolworth plc* [1989]

13070

Unfortunately, there is no single definitive **test** that will determine the issue in all circumstances. Instead there is a large body of case law, which has at least reduced uncertainty in the majority of situations (although it has produced conflicting interpretations in some).

In each individual case it is essential to establish the relevant **facts** as they applied at the time the expenditure was incurred or income received. Certain factors may be more important or relevant in certain situations, and no single factor is likely to be decisive.

HMRC have released an online toolkit to assist in deciding between capital and revenue treatment, which can be found at flmemo.co.uk/ctm13070

SECTION 2

Receipts

13120

Capital income relates to the company's long term survival, and may include compensation for loss of premises or other large scale receipts which are not attributable to the normal trade or company activity.

Unless specifically brought into charge by statute, **revenue income** must be in the form of money or money's worth to be taxable. *Tennant v Smith* [1892]

It there is any doubt as to the tax treatment, it is likely that the receipt will be taxable.

Summary

13125

Situation	¶¶
Desisting from trading	¶13130
Exclusivity agreements	¶13135
Compensation	¶13145
Inability to use asset	¶13150
Payment in lieu of profits	¶13155
Unallocated receipts	¶13160

Desisting from trading

A payment received in return for restricting trading operations may or may not be capital, as the following cases illustrate.

13130

> EXAMPLE
>
> 1. B Ltd, a manufacturer of magnesium, agreed with a major chemical company, C Ltd, not to produce chlorine, but instead to purchase it from C Ltd. In return, C Ltd agreed to pay £x per ton of caustic soda (formed during the chlorine production process) which B Ltd would have made had it produced chlorine itself.
> It was held that the payments relating to the caustic soda were trading receipts of B Ltd, as they represented compensation for profits lost by not producing chlorine. *Thompson v Magnesium Elektron Ltd* [1944]
>
> 2. A famous actor agreed not to appear in any film other than *Henry V* for a period of 18 months. In return, the film company paid him £15,000.
> It was held that the payment was not trading income (it did not relate to the actor's vocation), and was therefore to be treated as capital. (It might have been taxable as a receipt in return for a service provided, but this argument was not pursued before the court.) *Higgs v Olivier* [1952]

Exclusivity agreements

Exclusivity agreements **provide for** a company to purchase goods from a particular supplier for a number of years. In return, the company receives a lump sum payment or a loan. In the latter case, a portion of the loan amount is waived periodically so that if the contract runs its full course, none of it is repayable.

13135
BIM40301

Whether a receipt under an exclusivity agreement is revenue or capital depends upon the **purpose** for which it is paid, so where the company:
– uses the sum to meet capital expenditure as designated by the supplier, it may be accepted that the receipt is capital in nature; or
– is free to spend the lump sum as it chooses, the lump sum should be regarded as a trade receipt even if the sum was in fact used to meet capital expenditure.

13140
BIM40305

Loans are only taxable when a repayment is waived: that is, when the contingency concerning the repayment is resolved. In this case, the tax treatment will follow the accountancy treatment.

For the treatment of the payer in this situation, see ¶13280.

Compensation

A sum which is referable to **trading operations** will normally be regarded by HMRC as a trade receipt even where the payer's legal liability is never established. This is also the case where a non-business entity would be entitled to the same compensation.

13145
BIM40105

Damages will only be capital where they relate to a **damaged or destroyed asset** of the company.

Inability to use asset The tax treatment of a payment received will **depend on** whether the asset's unavailability is permanent or temporary.

13150

> EXAMPLE
>
> 1. A manufacturer of fireclay goods owned a fireclay bed which unfortunately ran underneath a railway track. For obvious safety reasons, the bed could not be exploited, and so the Railway Company paid related compensation.
> It was held that the compensation was a capital receipt for the permanent loss of a capital asset. *Glenboig Union Fireclay Co Ltd v CIR* [1930]
>
> 2. A steamship was booked in for an overhaul by a specified date. Unfortunately, the repairs took longer than anticipated, and damages were paid to the owners based on their loss of profit arising from the unavailability of the ship.
> It was held that the damages were a trading receipt because the asset was only temporarily unavailable. *Burmah Steamship Co Ltd v CIR* [1922]

13155   **Payments received in lieu of profits**   These will **normally** be trading receipts, **unless** the loss of profits is so detrimental that the whole existence of the company is put at stake.

> EXAMPLE
>
> 1. Before the First World War, D Ltd, a UK company, was party to a profit-sharing agreement with a Dutch competitor, E Ltd. The related income and expenditure were attributable to D Ltd's trade. During the war, the agreement had to be suspended, and afterwards, the companies were unable to come to a compromise over the amounts owed. D Ltd was therefore paid £450,000 as damages to terminate the agreement.
> It was held that the payment was capital because the terminated agreement was a structural part of D Ltd's profit-making apparatus. *Van den Berghs Ltd v Clark* [1935]
>
> 2. F Ltd agreed to appoint an agent in Scotland under a contract which was supposed to run for 3 years. In the event, it was terminated by F Ltd prematurely, and the agent received related damages.
> It was held that the damages could not be regarded as capital, because the similar contracts under which the agency worked were a temporary and variable element in the business. *Kelsall Parsons & Co v CIR* [1938]

Unallocated receipts

13160   Unallocated receipts (i.e. those with no designation as to how they should be spent) will be trading income.

Industrial development grants are taxable as income unless they are for specific capital expenditure, cover a corporation tax liability, or are taken into account elsewhere in the tax computation.

> EXAMPLE   G Ltd received an interest relief grant from the Department of Trade which was intended to safeguard employment. However, G Ltd had complete freedom in the use of the money. The amount of £47,000 was calculated to cover the compound interest which would arise on a loan of £200,000 over 7 years.
> It was held that, on the facts of the case, such an undifferentiated receipt (which was not earmarked either for capital or revenue) was a trading receipt. *Ryan v Crabtree Denims Ltd* [1987]

SECTION 3

Expenditure

13210   **Capital** expenditure provides the profit-making structure within which the business is conducted. The items acquired are therefore retained for long term use in the business. Capital expenditure is the opposite of revenue expenditure, and commonly includes:
– intangible assets (e.g. goodwill); and
– tangible assets, such as buildings, machinery and plant.

Broadly, capital expenditure is not allowable as a deduction against profits unless there is a specific statutory allowance.

Note that abortive expenditure is treated exactly the same as if the event leading to the change in plan had not occurred. *ECC Quarries Ltd v Watkis* [1975]

Revenue expenditure denotes the day to day running costs of a business. These are the costs incurred when making a profit or loss. Common examples include the purchase of stock, and the costs of employing staff.

In general, revenue expenditure is tax deductible.

13215

Classifying expenditure

The boundary between revenue and capital expenditure is often a grey area rather than a sharp dividing line. It has been said, "In this area at least, where no decision can be said to be right or wrong, the only safe rule is to go by precedent. So the thing to do is to search through the cases and see whether the instant problem has come up before. If so, go by it. If not, go by the nearest you can find." *Heather v P E Consulting Group Ltd* [1972]

13220
BIM35910

There is no definitive list of items which are capital or revenue. However, over time, the following **criteria** have emerged from case law and are taken into account by HMRC:

13225
BIM35010

1. Whether expenditure is capital is a question of law, be it a specific provision of tax statute, commercial law or trust law which is definitive.
2. The accountancy treatment, even in accounts prepared under GAAP, may be informative but it cannot be decisive.
3. Perpetual expenditure (a series of payments with no terminal date in view) is unlikely to be capital.
4. The main determining factor is the effect of the expenditure, rather than its purpose. Hence related documentation may be informative, but cannot of itself resolve the issue.
5. Capital expenditure will usually result in the acquisition, disposal or modification of an identifiable capital asset, either tangible or intangible.
6. Capital expenditure will usually produce an enduring result.
7. The nature of the asset concerned may be important. If it is not part of the company's trade to deal in such assets, the expenditure is likely to be capital.

EXAMPLE

1. Due to loss of staff to competitors, A Ltd decided to set up a pension scheme in order to secure long service from valued employees. An initial large payment to the scheme was required from A Ltd to enable the existing staff's past years of service to be taken into account.
It was held that this payment constituted capital expenditure, the reasoning being that, "When an expenditure is made, not only once and for all, but with a view to bringing into existence an asset or advantage for the enduring benefit of a trade, I think that there is very good reason (in the absence of special circumstances leading to an opposite conclusion) for treating such expenditure as properly attributable not to revenue but to capital." *British Insulated and Helsby Cables Ltd v Atherton* [1925]

Note:
Later cases have tended to focus on the effect of the expenditure rather than the motive behind it.

2. Access (a credit card company) entered into an agreement with Eurocard for the use of Access cards at all Eurocard retail outlets. The owner of Eurocard held the Interbank licence in the UK. Access paid the owner £75,000 to terminate that licence and cease to trade.
It was held that the payment was made by Access to:
– obtain the sole UK Interbank licence; and
– protect goodwill by ensuring the closure of a competitor.
As such, the payment could only be capital. *Walker v The Joint Credit Card Co Ltd* [1982]

A. Key factors

Summary

13255
BIM35901

Issue	¶¶
Recurring payments	¶13260
What was obtained	¶13265
Acquisition, improvement or disposal	¶13270
Identifiable asset	¶13275
Expenditure on intangibles	¶13280

Recurring payments

13260   Recurring expenditure on the acquisition of assets, such as the employee car pool, is capital. This is also the case where the acquisition is achieved through **instalment** payments, although HMRC's view is that there may be a fine line between the payment of a capital sum by instalments, and revenue payments for the use of an asset such as finance lease rental payments (¶82000).

Conversely, a **single payment** may not always be capital, such as a golden handshake to a departing employee which will still be a revenue expense.

What was obtained

13265   Although some historical cases looked at the motive behind the expenditure, the **modern approach** is to identify what was actually obtained or achieved by the expenditure in question.

> EXAMPLE
> 1. B Ltd leased a motorway service area from the Government under a long term agreement. Part of the rent payable was based on B Ltd's gross takings. As tobacco duty increased, so did the rent. Therefore B Ltd renegotiated the lease, paying a lump sum in return for excluding tobacco duty from gross takings for the purposes of the rent calculation.
> It was held that the payment was once-and-for-all expenditure on a capital asset to make it more advantageous. *Tucker v Granada Motorway Services Ltd* [1979]
>
> 2. C Ltd rented trading premises. The landlord informed C Ltd that the rent would increase from £5,000 p.a. to £12,500 p.a., even though a market rent would have been £7,500 p.a. C Ltd instructed an agent to serve a counter-notice on the landlord in order to reduce the rent demand. However, the agent failed to do this, and a settlement was reached with the landlord to pay £11,500 p.a. The agent paid damages of £14,000 to C Ltd.
> It was held that the compensation was paid in recognition of the increased revenue cost (i.e. rent) that C Ltd would have to incur, and therefore it was a trading receipt. *Donald Fisher (Ealing) Ltd v Spencer* [1989]

Acquisition, improvement or disposal

13270
BIM35605

For expenditure to be capital, it must be spent on the:
- acquisition (*Rolfe v Wimpey Waste Management Ltd* [1989]);
- improvement (*Tucker v Granada Motorway Services Ltd* [1979] (¶13265)); or
- disposal (*Mallett v The Staveley Coal & Iron Co Ltd* [1928]);

of a capital asset.

It is not sufficient that it was paid **in connection with** the acquisition, improvement or disposal of the asset. For example, a restaurant may hope to maintain the goodwill of customers by paying its staff well, but staff costs would not thereby amount to a capital asset.

> **EXAMPLE**
> 1. D Ltd purchased several sites for the purpose of waste tipping. In claiming a revenue deduction, D Ltd stated that it had acquired the land in order to use the airspace above it as "consumable tipping space".
> It was held that the expenditure related not to airspace, but to an interest in land, which by its nature could only be a capital asset. *Rolfe v Wimpey Waste Management Ltd* [1989]
>
> 2. E Ltd, a colliery company, mined coal from beds which were leased from two landowners. It agreed to make lump sum payments in order to surrender the leases which still had a lengthy term to run.
> It was held that the payments were capital because they were made in order to rid E Ltd of unwanted capital assets. *Mallett v The Staveley Coal & Iron Co Ltd* [1928]

Identifiable asset

A capital asset must have its own identity: in other words, it is necessary to specify on what the expenditure is incurred. *Tucker v Granada Motorway Services Ltd* [1979]   **13275**

Note that even a tangible asset may have a very **limited economic life**. HMRC accept that where that life is less than 12 months, the expenditure should be treated as revenue.

Expenditure on intangibles

The key question with intangibles is whether the identifiable asset is of a sufficiently substantial and enduring nature to count as capital.   **13280**

HMRC's view is that expenditure on **licences** which are well defined in law is likely to be capital if the rights endure for at least 2 years.

Expenditure on **commercial advantages** will only be capital if the payment secures a permanent advantage (such as the closing down of a potentially damaging competitor). *Walker v The Joint Credit Card Co Ltd* [1982] (¶13225) Expenditure on the temporary closure of a competitor has been held to be revenue. *CIR v Nchanga Copper Mines* [1964]

Expenditure on the acquisition or cancellation of **trade agreements** will normally be revenue in nature. *Vodafone Cellular & Others v Shaw* [1997] However, if the agreement is of such importance that the business would be extinguished by its loss, the expenditure may be capital. *Van den Berghs Ltd v Clark* [1935] (¶13155).

> **EXAMPLE**
> 1. F Ltd entered into exclusivity agreements with a number of petrol retailers with the following terms:
> – F Ltd agreed to reimburse the retailers for the costs of decoration, and the resiting and maintenance of petrol pumps; and
> – the retailer agreed to buy for resale only F Ltd's brand of petrol.
> Initially the agreements had a term of less than 1 year, but due to action by competitors, the terms were extended to 5 years or more, and advance payment was made by F Ltd in respect of each retailer's estimated expenditure.
> It was held that the payments were made to preserve goodwill, and were therefore paid wholly and exclusively for the purposes of the trade. No capital assets of an enduring nature were created. *Bolam v Regent Oil Co Ltd* [1956]
>
> 2. A petrol company, G Ltd, entered into agreements where it paid a lump sum, based on the amount of petrol expected to be sold, to certain retailers. The contract terms were as follows:
> – the retailer leased his petrol station to G Ltd at a nominal rent; and
> – G Ltd sublet the station back to the retailer at a nominal rent for the same period less 3 days, with terms which bound the retailer to take all his petrol supplies from G Ltd.
> It was held that the payments were premiums for leases and made for the acquisition of an interest in land. Since G Ltd did not deal in land, the payments had to be capital in nature. *Strick v Regent Oil Co Ltd* [1965]

B. Some common situations

Repairs, alterations and improvements

13310
BIM46900

A distinction must be made between repairs, which are a revenue expense, and alterations or improvements, which are capital.

The courts have relied upon the concept of the **entirety** of an asset. If the entirety is replaced, then the expenditure is capital. If a lesser amount is replaced, the expenditure is likely to be a repair. The decision obviously depends on the facts of each case.

PIM2020

Comment HMRC accept that the boundary between repairs and improvements will necessarily change with the passage of time to reflect **technological advances**. So the replacement of a part of the entirety with the nearest modern equivalent is allowable as a repair. A common example is double-glazing, where HMRC now accept that replacing single-glazed windows by double-glazed equivalents counts as allowable expenditure on repairs.

BIM46904

The cheaper option may still be capital, so the **cost** is really irrelevant.

> EXAMPLE
>
> 1. A colliery company built a pithead chimney, and several years later it became unsafe. It was therefore demolished, with another one constructed nearby.
> It was held that the construction of a new chimney was capital expenditure, as the entire asset was replaced. *O'Grady v Bullcroft Main Collieries Ltd* [1932]
>
> 2. In contrast, the replacement of a factory chimney was held to be a revenue expense, because the new chimney, like the old, was a subsidiary part of the whole factory. *Samuel Jones & Co (Devondale) Ltd v CIR* [1951]
>
> 3. A football club demolished a wooden and steel spectators' stand because of safety concerns. The replacement stand was made of concrete, nearer the football pitch, and had offices etc behind the seats which had not been there before. The crowd capacity was the same.
> It was held that the new stand was capital as it was a distinct and separate asset. See also ¶25370. *Brown v Burnley Football & Athletic Co Ltd* [1980]

13315
BIM35450

Where a company **acquires an asset in need of repair**, the expenditure may be treated as capital where either:
– the asset could not be used until the repairs had been carried out; or
– the purchase price was reduced to reflect the poor state of the asset, although a decrease in respect of normal wear and tear would not necessarily imply a capital expense.

Where a **lease** is taken on, and the lessee agrees to reinstate the property to a good state of repair, this may also be capital (although see ¶19205 for premiums paid).

HMRC consider that if the expenditure would have been treated as revenue had the asset's ownership not changed, it is still revenue when incurred by the new owner.

> EXAMPLE
>
> 1. H Ltd purchased a second-hand ship which was known to be in a deteriorated state (also reflected in the price paid). A survey was completed some months later (after it had undertaken one voyage), the results of which required A Ltd to undertake expensive repairs to make the ship seaworthy.
> It was held that a small portion of the expenditure was deductible as the cost of repairs arising during the period of ownership, but the bulk of the expenditure represented the cost of making the ship seaworthy at all. This would be disallowed because it was properly part of the capital cost of acquisition. *Law Shipping Co Ltd v CIR* [1923]
>
> 2. A cinema company acquired new cinemas which needed repair and redecoration because building work had been prohibited during the recent Second World War. It was still possible to operate the cinemas in their current state (which was no worse than other cinemas owned by competitors), and the acquisition price had not been lowered at all.
> It was held that the whole of the expenditure was allowable as a trading expense, as the cinemas remained usable despite their state of disrepair. *Odeon Associated Theatres Ltd v Jones* [1971]

Computer software

The treatment of computer software really **depends on** its longevity within the particular business. Where the software has a transient existence, and upgrade versions are purchased regularly, the expenditure is more likely to be a revenue item.

13320
BIM35810

Situation	Detail	Tax treatment
Software acquired under licence	Regular payments made	Revenue expense to be recognised in accordance with the correct accounting practice
	Lump sum paid	If software is expected to have a useful economic life of: – less than 2 years, HMRC will accept that the expenditure is revenue (to be recognised over the life of the software); or – at least 2 years, it will be a capital asset, where it will fall within either the intangibles regime (¶28135) or capital allowances rules (¶25405)
Hardware and software licence purchased as a package		Apportion expenditure between: – hardware which will be eligible for capital allowances (¶25330); and – software, which will then be subject to the rules above
Software developed in-house	Development is part of a major new project	Capital
	Piecemeal improvement of a computer system that is already in use	Revenue

HMRC's view is that the cost of a **website** is analogous to that of a shop window. The cost of constructing such a window (setting up the website) is capital, whereas the cost of periodically changing the display (maintaining the website) is revenue.

13325
BIM35870

CHAPTER 4

Trading income and expenditure

A trading company's profit and loss account is likely to include items which must be treated differently for tax purposes. It is therefore essential to identify which items should be treated as trading income or expenditure, and then ascertain whether all income is taxable and which expenses are deductible. **14000**

Depending on the nature of the company's activities, certain types of income and expenditure (such as property income or loan relationships) may need to be separated out in the tax computation due to specific rules which apply to them.

For the treatment of income and expenses relating to periods before commencement, and after cessation, of the trade, see ¶60105 and ¶61130 respectively.

SECTION 1

Scope of the trade

Once it has been established that a trade exists (¶5000+), the scope of that trade must be determined to ensure that all relevant income and expenditure is correctly included in the computation. In many situations, the scope will not be of concern, as it will be obvious that virtually all income and expenditure relates to trading income, except for items which are prescribed a different tax treatment. However, the scope may be crucial when sundry or one-off income is received, or the divide between capital and revenue items (¶13000+) is not clear. **14050**

A. Within the existing trade?

As the scope of a trade is a question of fact, ostensibly similar cases have been decided very differently. **14080**

Realisation of assets

The realisation of assets may be within a trade or a capital receipt. **14085**

> EXAMPLE
>
> 1. A company was formed for the purpose of acquiring patents and exploiting them for monetary gain e.g. by granting licenses. It sold three patents outright, and the issue was whether this resulted in trading income.
> It was held that its trade did not include dealing in patent rights, and the sales were therefore capital disposals. *Collins v The Firth-Brearley Stainless Steel Syndicate Ltd* [1925]
>
> 2. A company was formed for the general purpose of acquiring patents, licences and concessions, and turn them to account. Its Memorandum of Association contained the power to sell and dispose of property.
> The company acquired an interest in the patent relating to a turbine pump and also acquired interests in foreign patents relating to the same invention. Under licence agreements granted by the company, the pump manufacturers had the option to acquire the whole of the foreign patent rights, and this was exercised in certain cases for a further payment.
> It was held that the profits on sale were trading profits as the possibility of the sale of the foreign patents had been foreseen as part of the company's normal trading arrangements. *The Rees Roturbo Development Syndicate Ltd v Ducker* [1928]

Sale of assets used in the trade

If assets are used in the trade **before being sold**, they may become trading assets rather than fixed assets of the company. **14090**

> EXAMPLE
> 1. A company constructed railway wagons and then sold them or hired them out. The wagons for hire were capitalised in the accounts and depreciated. Wagon manufacture was prohibited during the First World War,, and so the value of existing wagons increased. The company therefore decided to sell all its wagons at a large profit. The two key issues were: whether the company carried on two trades (one of sales and one of hire), and whether the sale of the previously hired-out wagons represented a capital profit.
> It was held that the profit was a trading receipt of a single trade which consisted of the manufacture of, and making a profit from, wagons. The company manufactured and traded in wagons, and the subsequent exploitation of the manufactured product was a matter of domestic business. *The Gloucester Railway Carriage and Wagon Co Ltd v CIR* [1925]
>
> 2. Amongst other activities, a company operated a passenger boat service. In 1939, the boats were requisitioned by the Admiralty. During the Second World War, the company carried on and extended its other activities of shipbuilding and repairing. After the war, some boats were returned by, and others bought from, the Admiralty in order to recommence the passenger service. Some of the newly-purchased boats, which had been used for the passenger service, were later sold.
> It was held that the sales were trading receipts. The boats never became fixed assets of a separate passenger business, but were used in a wider single business of building, repairing and selling ships, and of passenger-carrying. *J Bolson & Son Ltd v Farrelly* [1953]

Acquisition of an opportunity to trade

14095   When acquiring mines or other **sites to be exploited**, a distinction must be made between a capital acquisition and stock purchase.

> EXAMPLE
> 1. A company manufactured nitrates and iodine from mineral deposits found on land that it owned. The question was whether the cost of the mineral bed and the extraction represented a revenue cost of raw materials, or a capital expense.
> It was held that the costs were capital. The company claimed that its trade was one of converting the minerals into a marketable commodity. The courts took the view that the company had made a capital investment in the mineral bed and then worked it as a mining concern. *Alianza Company Ltd v Bell* [1905]
>
> 2. A company sold gold extracted from tailings (the residual left after gold is extracted from mined ore) after subjecting the material to a treatment process. The issue was whether the acquisition of rights in dumps of tailings represented deductible purchase costs.
> In contrast to *Alianza* above, it was held that the tailings did indeed represent raw materials which had already been mined, so the costs were deductible. *Golden Horse Shoe (New) Ltd v Thurgood* [1934]

B. Situations involving land

Lettings

14125   **Rent** is usually assessable as the income of a separate property business (¶19000+). By exception, the following types of income are treated as a trading income:
– wayleaves (¶19175);
– temporary letting (up to 3 years) of surplus business accommodation, provided that part of it is still used for the taxpayer's trade (¶19170); and
– income from tied premises (when goods are sold by another person at premises owned by the taxpayer).

14130
BIM 22001
Income from **furnished lettings** is rarely trading income, unless the landlord remains in occupation and provides additional services such as those of a bed and breakfast, hotel or guesthouse.
Furnished holiday lettings are usually treated as a trade: see ¶19410.

Farming and market gardening

For corporation tax purposes, farming and market gardening are trades. All farming activity in the UK by the same company is treated as a **single trade**.

For the special computational rules which relate to farming, see ¶84000+.

14135
s 36 CTA 2009

Mining and quarrying

Income (including related rental income) **derived** from the following is taxable as trading income:
- mines;
- quarries;
- gravel and sand pits;
- brickfields;
- ironworks;
- gas works;
- canals and railways; and
- fairs, tolls and fishing rights.

14140
s 39 CTA 2009

Woodlands

The occupation of woodlands for a **commercial purpose** (with a view to the realisation of profits) is not a trade and is ignored for corporation tax purposes.

14145
s 37 CTA 2009

Oil industry

Oil **extraction** and the **exploitation of oil rights** are treated as a separate trade. All related profits are ring-fenced from any other trade that the company may be carrying on.

14150
ss 274, 279
CTA 2010

SECTION 2

Adjustment of profits

The following pro-forma shows how the accounting profit/loss must be adjusted in order to obtain the taxable trading figure.

14200

14205

Adjustment	Example	£
Accounting profit		x
Add: Expenditure not allowed	Depreciation	x
	Entertaining	x
Add: Income not shown in accounts but assessable[1]	Intangible asset credit	x
Less: Income not assessed as trading income	Income taxable as different type of income, such as rent or interest	(x)
	Items not taxed as income such as capital receipts	(x)
Less: Expenditure not in accounts	Share scheme deduction	(x)
	Pension contributions paid	(x)
Less: Capital allowances (¶25120)		(x)
Trading profits		x
Note: 1. This would rarely occur where accounts are prepared under GAAP (¶11055).		

SECTION 3

Trading income

14255   Capital profits and repayment supplement (¶48375) are **excluded** from trading income. For details of the capital and revenue divide, which includes compensation, see ¶13000. Loan relationships are dealt with at ¶16050.

Summary

14260

Topic	¶¶
Gratuitous receipts	¶14290
Deposits	¶14330
Government subsidies	¶14360
Insurance proceeds	¶14390
Commission	¶14420
Reverse premiums	¶14455

A. Gratuitous receipts

14290   Depending on the circumstances, an unexpected gift may not be taxable.

Past service given

14295   Usually receipts relating to past service are taxable, particularly where the **remuneration** for that service was initially **inadequate**. However, unsolicited receipts may not relate to the trade.

EXAMPLE
1. A firm of accountants agreed not to accept re-election as auditors. Subsequently, they received a lump sum of over £2,000 for loss of the office.
It was held that the sum did not represent consideration for past services. It was therefore not taxable. *Walker v Carnaby Harrower* [1969]

2. An insurance broker ceased to act for a client because of a change of ownership. The broker was paid £1,000 for each of the next 5 years.
It was held that the payments were gifts, being wholly unsolicited and unexpected. Although paid in respect of the previous long relationship between the companies, the broker's past service had not been inadequately remunerated. There was also no implication that the relationship may be resumed in the future. *Simpson v Reynolds & Co (Insurances) Ltd* [1975]

3. A company ran licensed catering establishments under 13 tied tenancy agreements from another company. Certain of these agreements were terminated at the choice of the lessor, who made ex gratia payments to the company.
It was held that the payments were not trading receipts, being wholly unsolicited and unexpected. The payments were made, in part, to maintain goodwill between the parties. *Murray v Goodhews* [1978]

4. A firm of estate agents arranged an acquisition of a site which the client was to develop. Normally, the agent would have been appointed as letting agent once the development was complete. However, the site was soon sold so the estate agents did not receive any letting business. The agents complained to the client, who agreed to pay them a lump sum.
It was held that the lump sum was taxable as a trading receipt because, firstly, although the payment was voluntary, it had been solicited by the agents; and secondly, the initial agency work relating to the site acquisition had not been adequately remunerated. *McGowan v Brown & Cousins* [1977]

Settlement of disputes

Payments relating to the settlement of disputes are unlikely to be **voluntary**, and hence will be taxable on the recipient.

14300

> EXAMPLE
>
> **1.** A Ltd made hats and had a large contract with a major retailer, B Ltd. Unfortunately, B Ltd decided to stop selling hats, but did offer help in setting up production for other clothing merchandise. A couple of years later, B Ltd ceased all trade with A Ltd, and offered £5,000 as an ex gratia payment which was rejected. A Ltd then took legal action and received £22,500 in full settlement. It was held that the sum was taxable as a trading receipt as it was not made voluntarily, and it related to the loss of trading opportunities since A Ltd was very reliant on B Ltd for its business. *Creed v H & M Levison Ltd* [1981]
>
> **2.** C Ltd rented trading premises. The landlord informed C Ltd that the rent would increase from £5,000 p.a. to £12,500 p.a., even though a market rent would have been only £7,500 p.a. C Ltd instructed an agent to serve a counter-notice on the landlord in order to reduce the rent demand. However, the agent failed to do this, and a settlement was reached with the landlord to pay £11,500 p.a. The agent paid compensation of £14,000 to C Ltd.
> It was held that the compensation was paid in recognition of the increased revenue costs (rent) that C Ltd would have to incur, not because of a change in the nature of the lease. It was therefore a trading receipt. *Donald Fisher (Ealing) Ltd v Spencer* [1989]

B. Deposits and overpayments

Money paid by customers as a deposit will only become trading income if it would have been treated as such when first received. A **distinction** must be made between:
– monies received on behalf of clients which are unclaimed, usually as a result of a mistake by the customer; and
– deposits retained when an order falls through.

14330

> EXAMPLE
>
> **1.** A racehorse auctioneer only sent proceeds of sale by post when he received a written order from the vendor customer. Once 6 years had elapsed, any unclaimed balances were appropriated by the auctioneer.
> It was held that the unclaimed balances were not assessable as receipts of the business as they remained the property of the customers. The balances could not become a trade receipt on appropriation. *Morley v Tattersall* [1938]
>
> **2.** A tailor accepted orders for bespoke suits on receipt of a deposit. If the suit was not made, the deposit was appropriated by the company.
> It was held that the deposits were taxable as trading receipts. *Elson v Price Taylors Ltd* [1962]
>
> **3.** A company received payments from its customers in error over a period of years. In some cases, these payments were not repaid to the customer, nor offset against any other liability of the customer. Such payments were transferred to its balance sheet after the payments had been unreconciled for 6 months.
> Upon preparation of the accounts for the year, these payments were then released to the company's profit and loss account as income. This action did not affect the legal position, which meant that if a customer could show that overpayment had occurred, the sum would be refunded, even after the sum had been released to the profit and loss account.
> The company's position was that the payments were not trading receipts, as they did not relate to a service that had been provided. It also argued that, whilst the payments had been appropriated by it, as it was allowed in law to do, it was never legally entitled to the payments.
> It was held that the payments were trading receipts, as:
> – the company was trading and the receipts related to a business relationship between the company and its customer, even though the sums were received in error; and
> – there did not have to exist any legal entitlement to receive the sums for them to be trading receipts (and in any event the company was entitled to receive and keep the sums until a claim for repayment was made). *Pertemps Recruitment Partnership Ltd v HMRC* [2011]

C. Government subsidies

14360
s 102 CTA 2009

The receipt of an **Industrial Development** grant (under the grant for business investment scheme) is a trading receipt unless it is either:
– for designated capital expenditure;
– compensation for the loss of a capital asset; or
– to cover a corporation tax payment.
Subsidies relating to **employment costs** are also taxable as trading receipts.

D. Insurance proceeds

14390
s 103 CTA 2009

Where a company has already made a **deduction for a loss or expense**, and then receives an insurance payout to cover the cost, the insurance monies will be taxable up to the level of the amount previously deducted.

For key man insurance, see ¶14715.

E. Commission

14420
SP 4/97

Commission is taxable as a receipt of the business, even where it is **passed on to the customer** (for example, as a reduction in regular insurance or pension policy premiums), provided the company had an enforceable legal right to receive that commission which was subsequently given up in favour of the customer. However, where the company neither receives the commission nor has any such entitlement to it, there will be no taxable receipt.

Commission passed on to a customer as an inducement to enter into a transaction is deductible if it is laid out wholly and exclusively (¶14540) for the purpose of the trade.

14425

Commission **received as a consequence of carrying on a trade** is treated as a trading receipt. Examples might include:
– insurance commission to which an accountant becomes entitled in the course of his profession;
– commission received in respect of business insurance contracts (so if the premium paid has been reduced by the commission, the company should only deduct the net cost); or
– a cash-back receipt on a company car (which will reduce the cost of the car for the purposes of capital allowances).

F. Reverse premiums

14455
s 96 CTA 2009;
BIM 41075

A reverse premium is **defined** as a payment received by way of inducement to enter into a property transaction, where:
– the company becomes entitled to an estate or interest in, or a right in or over, land; and
– the payment is made by the grantor or his nominee.
Normally, such a payment occurs when a landlord is trying to obtain a new tenant.
Note that the following are **excluded** from these rules:
– the sale consideration in sale and leaseback transactions (¶19505), where the asset remains on the balance sheet, and the transaction is effectively one of refinancing;

– contributions towards capital expenditure (which is therefore not taxable on the tenant, but allows the landlord to claim capital allowances); and
– payments to an individual who is going to reside in the property as his only or main residence.

> MEMO POINTS 1. For this purpose, the terms **company** and grantor include any person connected with them (¶31375).
> 2. The **grantor** is the person who grants the rights in the land.
> 3. A **payment** could be in the form of a benefit (such as a contribution to the tenant's costs), but must be an outlay of money, such as a lump sum or the write off of a loan. A rent-free or reduced-rent period therefore does not count as a reverse premium.

A reverse premium is taxable as a revenue receipt. So where the property is **occupied for the purposes of a trade**, it will be a trading receipt; otherwise it is treated as property income (¶19000).

14460
s 98 CTA 2009;
UIIF 28

In accordance with GAAP, the reverse premium may be **spread** on a straight-line basis over the period of the lease (or up to the first rent review if shorter). However, spreading is not applicable if at least two parties to the lease are connected with each other (¶31375), and the terms of the lease are not at arm's length. In this case, the whole premium is taxable in the period of account when the property transaction occurs (or when a trade commences, if later).

SECTION 4

Trading expenses

Most expenses incurred by a trading company are likely to be deductible. However, a computation usually has at least one or two adjustments reflecting:
– disallowed expenditure which fails the wholly and exclusively test (¶14540), or for which a deduction is prohibited by statute; and/or
– expenditure for which the tax rules differ from the accounting treatment.

14510

> MEMO POINTS

With effect from 20 December 2012, in determining whether a deduction is allowable in cases involving tax avoidance arrangements, a prohibitive rule will have priority over a permissive rule. This means that no deduction will be due if a prohibitive rule applies, even if a deduction would otherwise be due under a permissive rule. The stated purpose is to prevent the artificial creation of business losses.

s 51 CTA 2009

A. Wholly and exclusively

There is a **general prohibition** on the deduction of an expense which is not incurred wholly and exclusively for the purpose of the company's trade.

14540
s 54 CTA 2009

In broad terms, this means that:
– the expense must not be too remote from the trade; and
– there must be no duality of purpose (that is, the only reason for incurring the expenditure is to benefit the trade and earn profits).

> EXAMPLE
> 1. The chimney of a pub fell in, injuring a guest. The company who owned the pub paid damages of £1,490.
> It was held that the damages were not deductible as "it was not enough that the disbursement is made in the course of, or arises out of, or is connected with, the trade, or is made out of the profits

of the trade. It must be made for the purpose of earning the profits." This is sometimes expressed by saying that "purpose is everything", but it should be noted that this is an old case and the law has undergone considerable development since it was decided.*Strong & Co of Romsey Ltd v Woodifield* [1906]

2. A company won a tax appeal relating to the deduction of remuneration paid to an employee. It incurred significant legal expenses for which it claimed a deduction.

It was held that "neither the cost of ascertaining taxable profit, nor the cost of disputing it with the authorities, is money spent to enable the trader to earn profit in his trade." So the claim was dismissed. *Smith's Potato Estates Ltd v Bolland* [1948]

3. A construction company (C Ltd) paid in excess of £70,000 a year (more than half of its advertising budget) to M Ltd, a motor sports company which took part in rallying. There was no written agreement for the sponsorship. C Ltd's sole shareholder and director was an experienced rally driver who had competed in races organised by M Ltd (although not in cars that were sponsored by his own company). C Ltd's banner was displayed on several of M Ltd's cars. C Ltd's turnover had increased by 76% in 3 years.

It was held that there was no evidence to support a commercial rationale behind the sponsorship, nor had any review been undertaken of its supposed positive effect. These facts, coupled with the C Ltd's evasive response to HMRC's enquiry, meant that there was held to be a dual purpose to the expenditure. *Protec International Ltd v HMRC* [2010]

Private use

14545   In a company setting, there is no scope for the company to have private use of assets or services.

Where a **director** has private use of a company asset, the associated costs would relate to the trade as employee remuneration, but the director would be assessable on the benefit as employment income (see *Tax Memo* for details).

Dual motive

14550   **Basic requirements of living**, such as feeding or clothing oneself, have undermined many cases in which a deduction has been claimed. (See also ¶14630.)

> EXAMPLE
> 1. A self-employed carpenter, who usually worked from home, claimed a deduction for the cost of eating lunch in a café when working on site.
> It was held that as the taxpayer had to eat in order to live (but did not have to eat in order to work), no deduction could be given. (There was another problem in this case because only the excess cost had been claimed, which meant that the exclusivity rule was not met either). *Caillebotte v Quinn* [1975]
>
> 2. A female barrister purchased black clothes and shoes to wear in court, as this "uniform" was required by her profession.
> It was held that although she had bought the clothes in order to carry out her professional duties, there was still a dual purpose because of the requirements of warmth and decency. The conscious motive of the taxpayer was only one factor to be taken into account. *Mallalieu v Drummond* [1983]
>
> 3. A From time to time, the staff and partners in a large firm of chartered accountants were asked to relocate between offices. The firm contributed towards removal costs and other expenses incurred. In a particular instance, the firm contributed towards the costs of two partners.
> It was held that the removal expenditure was incurred to allow the partners to set up their private residences. Hence the expenditure was not wholly and exclusively for the purposes of the partnership's trade. *MacKinlay v Arthur Young McClelland Moores & Co* [1989]

14555   Protecting a company from **destruction** was held to be wholly and exclusively for the purpose of the trade.

> EXAMPLE   A stockbroker was fined by the ruling Council of the Stock Exchange for breaches of its rules. The stockbroker claimed a deduction against profits for the fines, and for his legal fees.
> It was held that the fines could not be deducted, as this would dilute the punishment. However, the legal costs were deductible, because everyone has the right to a defence. *McKnight v Sheppard* [1999]

B. Common expenses in the accounts

Summary

14585

Area	Specific expense	Deductible?	¶¶	Reference
Staff costs	Employer's NIC	✓		s 1302 CTA 2009
	Remuneration unpaid for more than 9 months after accounting period end	x	¶14615	s 1288 CTA 2009
	Excessive remuneration	x	¶14620	
	Training and welfare costs	✓	¶14625	ss 73 – 75 CTA 2009
	Travel and subsistence costs of employees on business trips	✓	¶14630	BIM 47705
	Incentive schemes based on performance which are formally communicated to employees, genuinely earned and there is an obligation on the employer to provide the award	✓		BIM 45080, 47010
	Reasonable rewards provided in relation to a formal suggestion scheme	✓		BIM 47015
	Removal costs to relocate employee including: – payments under schemes which guarantee the sale price of the employee's former home; and – costs incurred on the purchase and subsequent sale of the employee's home by the employer, so long as the house is purchased at a fair valuation, is immediately placed on the market, and is sold as quickly as possible without being used by the company in the meantime	✓		BIM 42531
	Security costs for employees where safety is threatened wholly or mainly due to company's particular trade	✓		BIM 47301
	Termination payments including statutory redundancy Excludes certain payments connected with cessation of trade	✓	¶14635	ss 76 – 79 CTA 2009;
	Payment for a restrictive covenant which is taxable on employee and made to protect the trade	✓		s 69 CTA 2009
Repairs	Replacement of subsidiary part of asset	✓	¶13310	
	Replacement of asset or substantial part of asset	x		
	Initial repairs to put asset into functioning state	x		
	Initial repairs but asset already usable	✓		

Area	Specific expense	Deductible?	¶¶	Reference
Depreciation	Depreciation relating to purchased assets and those bought via hire purchase	x	¶25050+	
	Profit or loss on disposal of such assets	x		
	Depreciation of assets acquired under finance leases	✓	¶82115	
Computer software	Including website costs	Varies	¶13320	
Financial	Bank interest incurred for business purposes	✓		s 297 CTA 2009
	Interest on late tax (including PAYE and NIC, and tax under the construction industry scheme), VAT and penalties	x		s 1303 CTA 2009
	Incidental costs of obtaining loan finance	✓	¶16000+	
	Foreign exchange gains and losses	Varies		BIM 45875
	Guarantee payments	Varies		BIM 45301
Professional fees	Legal fees relating to capital items (may qualify as costs for capital gains purposes or for capital allowances)	x		BIM 46405
	Legal fees relating to revenue items e.g. debt collection, employment contracts, trade agreements	✓		
	Compliance costs incurred in relation to the requirements of Companies House and Stock Exchange e.g. share register upkeep, costs of AGM, Stock Exchange quotation	✓		BIM 42510
	Business accounts preparation	✓		BIM 46450
	Costs of tax appeal irrespective of outcome Costs relating to a VAT dispute concerning the liability of supplies may be allowable where the VAT returns have been correct, or any inaccuracy relates to arithmetical errors only	x		BIM 37840, 46455
	Accountancy fees incurred during a tax enquiry Accountancy fee protection insurance	Varies	¶14685	
	Valuation fees relating to accounts or Companies House requirements	✓		BIM 42540
Insurance	To cover loss and damage to company assets e.g. stock and premises	✓		BIM 45501, 45505
	To cover risk of fire, or temporary loss of profits due to unforeseen events	✓		BIM 45510
	To cover professional negligence of company and employees	✓		BIM 45515, 45520
	Key man insurance other than when a condition of company obtaining finance	✓	¶14715	BIM 45525, 45530

Area	Specific expense	Deductible?	¶¶	Reference
Donations and contributions	Contribution to an approved local enterprise agency	✓		ss 82 – 86 CTA 2009; BIM 47610
	Contribution to training and enterprise council	✓		
	Contribution to Urban Regeneration company	✓		
	Salary of an employee who is seconded to a charity	✓		s 70 CTA 2009
	Small donation to local charity e.g. where company could claim as part of promotion or advertising cost For Gift Aid see ¶22055 See also gifts below	✓		BIM 45072
	Donation to political party other than when trying to protect the company's existence	x		BIM 42528; *Morgan v Tate and Lyle Ltd* [1954]
Gifts	Food, drink or tobacco or vouchers given to customers unless just a sample of company product made available to public	x		s 1300 CTA 2009
	Other goods costing less than £50 per donee p.a. and prominently marked with company name	✓		
	Part of sales promotion where customer is required to do something in return i.e. not really a gift	✓		
	Gifts to charities, designated education establishments, the Historic Buildings and Monuments Commission for England, the Trustees of the National Heritage Memorial Fund, or the National Endowment for Science, Technology and the Arts	✓		
	Gifts of trading stock and goods[1] to charities, a designated educational establishment (¶26100), or community amateur sports clubs (¶86270) Market value of any benefit received in return by the company is taxable	✓		ss 105 – 108 CTA 2009
Subscriptions	For trade purpose (excludes political subscriptions) e.g. to a professional body Where the company has a direct trade connection with a charity or its objects, the allowance of a relatively small annual subscription may be accepted	✓		BIM 47405

Area	Specific expense	Deductible?	¶¶	Reference
Entertaining	Staff entertaining and gifts not just for benefit of shareholders/directors If employee takes client out for a meal, whole cost is disallowed unless expense allowance given to employee	✓		s 1299 CTA 2009
	Customer entertaining, unless company's trade is to provide entertainment for a fee (e.g. a restaurant) Where entertaining is provided under an obligation that requires the other party to provide something of value in return, this will not normally fall within the definition of business entertaining	x		s 1298 CTA 2009; BIM 45010; *Celtic Football and Athletic Club Ltd v C & E* [1983]
	Sponsorship involving hospitality	x		
	Training for employees which includes some hospitality	✓		
Advertising	Advertising of company's products which does not fall to be treated as entertaining or sponsorship involving hospitality (see above)	✓		BIM 42550
	Event to attract potential customers, costs including room hire and entertainment	Room hire deductible, entertainment disallowed		*Netlogic Consulting Ltd v HMRC* [2005]
Leases	Lease premium for property used for trading purposes	✓	¶14735	ss 62, 63 CTA 2009; BIM 46251, 46255
	Running costs of property e.g. rent, business rates, council tax, ground rents or feu duties, and the cost of insurance (both building and contents)	✓		BIM 46801, 46810
	Renewal of short lease (i.e. less than 50 years) with landlord's consent – connected professional fees which are allowed on de minimis grounds Otherwise, such costs are capital	✓		BIM 46420
	Leasing of plant		¶82000	
	Hire of vehicles	in part	¶14760	ss 56 – 58 CTA 2009
Misdeme-anours	Payments which relate to a crime e.g. bribes and ransoms unless not criminal in UK	x		s 1304 CTA 2009
	Penalties resulting from failure to comply with tax rules (including VAT)	x		s 1303 CTA 2009; BIM 31610
	Losses arising from theft by director	x		*Bamford v ATA Advertising Ltd* [1972]
	Fines (not parking)	x		BIM 42515
	Parking fine of employee paid by employer	✓		
	Parking fine relating to company cars	x		
	Penalties for breach of trading standards	x		BIM 42515 *CIR v Alexander von Glehn & Co Ltd* [1920]

Area	Specific expense	Deductible?	¶¶	Reference
Other	Bad debts incurred in the trade and recognised as impairment losses in the accounts i.e. based on objective evidence[2]	✓		s 55 CTA 2009
	Damages paid if not capital	✓	¶13265	
	Removal expenses (not for expansion) of company	✓		BIM 42530
	Research and development costs which are revenue items	✓	¶78000	s 87 CTA 2009
	Payments to Export Credit Guarantee Department	✓		s 91 CTA 2009
	Waste disposal sites – preparation and restoration costs which do not qualify for capital allowances	✓	¶14820	ss 142 – 145 CTA 2009

Note:
1. A gift of medical supplies or equipment from trading stock for humanitarian use by a **non-UK charity** will also be deductible, including the cost of transportation etc. The market value of any benefit received by the company will be taxable.
2. Historically, there used to be a distinction between the movements on a specific **bad debt** provision (which was allowed) and a general bad debt provision (which was disallowed). Following the implementation of IAS 39, this distinction no longer applies, and any entry for bad debts in the financial statements must be recognised as an impairment loss which will be deductible in the tax computation.

1. Staff issues

Unpaid remuneration

If remuneration remains unpaid more than 9 months after the accounting period end, it is **disallowed** in that accounting period. A deduction is then allowed in the accounting period of payment. It follows that remuneration which is never paid is never deducted.

14615
ss 1288, 1289
CTA 2009

If the CTSA **return** is filed before 9 months have elapsed and, at the date of filing, the remuneration remains unpaid, no deduction can be claimed. If the remuneration is subsequently paid (before the 9 month deadline), the return can be amended accordingly.

MEMO POINTS   1. Remuneration is **defined** as an amount treated as earnings by either an employee or office holder (a director or company secretary).
2. For this purpose remuneration is **paid** when it is treated as received by the employee: that is, when he becomes liable to PAYE and NIC on it (or would do if it were not exempt). For this purpose, the following rules apply:
a. earnings for **employees other than directors** are treated as received when:
– the payment of earnings is made; or
– if earlier, the employee becomes entitled to the payment; and
b. for **directors**, earnings (whether arising from the directorship or a different role) are treated as received on the earliest of the following dates:
– when the payment of earnings is made;
– when the director becomes entitled to the payment;
– when sums on account of earnings are credited in the company accounts or records (regardless of whether the director has the right to draw the money);
– where the amount of earnings for a period has already been determined, the date on which the period of account ends; or
– where the period of account has already ended, the date when the amount of earnings for a period is determined.
3. It is common for a **general accrual** to be made for directors' bonuses in the draft accounts, which is then approved at the annual general meeting. For the accrual to be recognised for accounting purposes (and, therefore, for corporation tax purposes), it is important that the company has at least a constructive obligation at the balance sheet date to pay extra remuneration to the directors, and this should be appropriately minuted as a board resolution. See ¶11885 for more details concerning provisions.

Excessive remuneration

14620   A company is usually contractually committed to paying remuneration to its employees. However, excessive remuneration paid to persons **connected to shareholders** may be disallowed, unless it can be shown that the rate is at arm's length. This is a question of fact.

> ⌐MEMO POINTS⌐   For **employee benefit trusts**, see ¶15035.

> ⌐EXAMPLE⌐   A firm paid commission (based on the company's profits) to the two sons of its proprietor. Initially the rate of commission was 5%. It rose to 10% for the next 3 years, and then to 33% (because the proprietor was suffering from ill-health, which meant more responsibility was taken on by the sons). It was held that a commercial commission rate was 10%, and any amounts paid in excess of that should be disallowed. *Stott and Ingham v Trehearne* [1924]

Training and welfare costs

14625   The following costs incurred by a company in respect of an employee are deductible.

Cost	Conditions	Reference
Subsidised or free lunches	Made available to all employees	BIM 47070
Opportunity to participate in sport		
General training costs	For staff development which is wholly and exclusively to benefit the trade	
Counselling on termination of employment (including related travel expenses)	All of the following criteria must be satisfied: **a.** the employee must have been employed (either full time or part time) for a 2 year period ending either when the counselling begins, or when the employment ends; **b.** the only or main purpose of the counselling is to enable the employee to adjust to losing his job or find some other method of earning income (including self-employment); **c.** the counselling is generally available to employees or a particular class of employee; and **d.** the counselling consists of the giving of advice, imparting skills, or providing normal office facilities or equipment	s 73 CTA 2009
Retraining courses (and related travel costs) of up to 2 years' duration allowing the employee to retrain for a new career	All of the following criteria must be satisfied: **a.** the employee begins the course while employed by the employer or within the period of 1 year after the employment ceases; **b.** the employee ceases to be employed by the employer before 2 years have elapsed from the end of the course and is not re-employed by the employer within the following 2 years; and **c.** the training is generally available to all employees or a particular class of employee If either **a.** or **b.** above are not met (e.g. the employee is re-employed), the employer must give notice to HMRC within 60 days in order that corporation tax relating to the erroneous deduction can be repaid	ss 74, 75 CTA 2009

Travel costs

14630   HMRC follow case law in stating that subsistence costs (such as food and drink) are not
BIM 47705   deductible as everyone must eat to live. However, extra costs may be incurred wholly for

business purposes where a **business involves a lot of travel**, or where **occasional business trips** are required outside the normal pattern of work. In these cases, modest expenses incurred may be deducted.

Where an **overnight stay** is required, the hotel accommodation and reasonable costs of overnight subsistence (meals) are deductible, whether or not included on the same invoice.

Redundancy and payments on termination

Where a termination is contemplated, it is usually in the interests of the business to get rid of the employee, either because of financial constraints or the individual's misfit with the organisation.

14635
ss 76 – 79
CTA 2009
BIM 38300 +

The related costs will normally be deductible, **except** where:
– the termination is linked to the cessation of trade when more complex rules apply; or
– an ex gratia payment is made to a director or employed shareholder, particularly following a change of ownership of the company.

> EXAMPLE A company wanted to retire a director who had been appointed for life. In order to avoid adverse publicity, a settlement was reached which resulted in a payment of £19,200 made over 5 years.
> It was held that this sum was deductible. *Mitchell v B W Noble Ltd* [1927]

Cessation of trade Non-statutory redundancy payments up to a **limit** of 3 times the gross statutory payment are deductible. See *Employment Memo* for details of statutory redundancy.
Outplacement counselling (¶14625) is also deductible.

14640
s 79 CTA 2009

Ex gratia payments The deductibility of ex gratia payments made to a **director or shareholder** may be challenged on the basis that the payment is more properly treated as either a distribution or consideration for share capital following a change of ownership. This arises from the probable duality of purpose behind such payments. *James Snook & Co Ltd v Blasdale* [1952]

14645

2. Professional fees

Professional fees are a common source of disallowable expenditure. The make-up of this expense heading in the accounts must be carefully analysed in order to ensure all necessary adjustments are made in the tax computation. The table at ¶14585 gives a summary of the more commonly contentious issues.

14675

Legal fees relating to capital items

Typical disallowed legal fees include those relating to the following:
– equity finance, including the purchase of own shares, and also taking over another company;
– investments and loans to other companies which fall outside the lender's trade;
– forming and registering a company, or changing a company's status e.g. from limited to unlimited status or to a plc;
– defending against a petition by shareholders to wind up a company;
– licences governing the use of the company's fixed assets or which are capital in their own right; and
– leases of plant and machinery and leases of business premises.

For further details of the capital/revenue divide, see ¶13210.

14680
BIM 46415

Fees relating to enquiries

Additional accountancy fees arising from the opening of an HMRC enquiry will **not be allowed** if the enquiry reveals discrepancies that are the result of careless or deliberate behaviour (¶52575) and this results in additional liabilities.

14685
EM 3981

However, where there is:
– no addition to profits; or
– an adjustment, but only to the year under enquiry, and it arises other than from the careless or deliberate behaviour of the company,
the additional accountancy fees will be **allowable**.

BIM 46452

The cost of **insurance against fees** incurred in relation to enquiries will only be allowed when the additional fees covered would themselves have been allowable. For example, if the policy allows the company to claim for expenses incurred where careless or deliberate behaviour is involved it will not be allowable. It is not permissible to apportion fees into allowable and disallowable amounts. It is irrelevant whether or not any claim is made on the policy in an accounting period.

3. Key man insurance

14715
BIM 45525

Key man insurance **premiums** will be allowable if both of the following conditions are met:
– the sole purpose of taking out the insurance is to cover the loss of trading income that may result from the absence of the key person, and not a capital loss; and
– in the case of life insurance policies, they are term insurance, providing cover only against the risk that one or more of the lives insured dies within the term of the policy, with no other benefits. The insurance term should not extend beyond the period of the employee's usefulness to the company.

Premiums relating to the following are **disallowed**:
– endowment policies on the life of a key person taken out as a condition for providing long-term finance (the premiums are not regarded as "incidental" to obtaining the finance);
– whole life or endowment policies; and
– critical illness or accident policies with an investment content. *Earl Howe v CIR* [1919]

BIM 45530

⌐ MEMO POINTS ⌐ 1. HMRC give the following as examples of where the **sole purpose test** is not met:
– where the policy is in respect of directors who are major shareholders but not other employees; or
– if benefits under the policy exceed the usual employee benefits which are typically offered to employees of equivalent status in similar companies.
2. Generally, where the premiums are deductible, any **receipts** under the policy will be taxable. However, there is no guarantee that where the premiums are disallowed that any receipts will escape tax.

4. Leases

a. Property used for trade purposes

14735
ss 62, 63 CTA 2009;
BIM 46255

If a company is occupying premises for a trade purpose under a lease, and pays a **premium**, the taxable income of the landlord (¶19205) is spread over the lease term in order to calculate the deduction.

> ⌐EXAMPLE⌐ A Ltd grants a 21 year lease of a property to H Ltd for a premium of £400,000 and a rent of £10,000 p.a. B Ltd occupies only 2/3rds of the premises for trading purposes.
> To work out the deduction available to B Ltd, the taxable income for A Ltd must first be calculated (see ¶19215) which works out to be £160,000. (400,000 x (21 – 1) / 50))
> So B Ltd can claim a deduction of £7,619 in relation to the premium, in addition to the annual rent of £10,000. (160,000 x 1/21)

⌐ MEMO POINTS ⌐ 1. For rules governing the **deemed length of the lease**, see ¶19210.
2. If the premises are only **partly used** for a trading purpose, the cost must be apportioned.
3. The deduction is available to a **successor tenant** where the original tenant has assigned the lease to another party.

s 4 CAA 2001

4. Where the tenant is entitled to claim **capital allowances** on the fixtures in the property (¶26230), any amount of the premium deducted under the rule above must be excluded from the amount on which capital allowances are claimed.

Where a trader provides **residential premises for an employee**, a deduction may be allowed for:
– any rent paid by the trader; and
– council tax, repairs and insurance,
to the extent that such expenses exceed any amounts made good by the employee.

14740
BIM 46820

If rent paid by the employee exceeds the employer's costs, the profit should be assessed as property income.

The **benefit in kind** charge on the employee must include the value of any lease premium where the lease term does not exceed 10 years, and was entered into, or extended, on or after 22 April 2009. For full details of benefits in kind, see *Tax Memo*.

---

b. Hire of vehicles

Unless an appropriate election has been made, the treatment of vehicle hire costs changed for agreements entered into after 31 March 2009, so that the **date of the agreement will be crucial** to the correct tax treatment.

14760
ss 56 – 58A
CTA 2009

In brief, the older rules distinguish between vehicles on the basis of cost, while the more recent provisions look at the carbon dioxide emission levels of cars.

> MEMO POINTS   1. For this purpose, an agreement is regarded as **entered into** on the date after which the hirer or lessee is entitled to exercise its right to use the vehicle under the lease.
> 2. Where the agreement includes arrangements for the provision of a **replacement car** when the first car is not available, the first car and any replacement car are treated as if they were the same car.

Agreements entered into before 1 April 2009

There is a restriction on the deductible expenditure relating to hired vehicles (including cars and motorcycles) if the **retail price** when new **exceeds £12,000**.

14765
BIM 47715

However, the following situations are **excluded**:
a. a vehicle primarily suited for carrying goods;
b. a vehicle of a type not commonly used as a private vehicle and unsuitable for such use;
c. a qualifying hire car, meaning one provided wholly or mainly for hire to the public in the ordinary course of a trade and either:
– hired to the disabled; or
– not normally hired to the same person for 30 or more consecutive days, or 90 or more days in total in any 12 month period;
d. an electrically powered car but not motorcycles;
e. a car (but not a motorcycle) with low carbon dioxide emissions (no more than 120gm per km); or
f. payments under a hire purchase agreement where either:
– ownership passes automatically at the end of the contract; or
– the price payable to acquire the car at the end of the contract is not more than 1% of the retail price when new (where the hirer decides to exercise a purchase option contained in the hire agreement).

> MEMO POINTS   1. For this purpose, **new** cars are unused and not second-hand. HMRC will treat a car as new even if it has been driven a limited number of miles for the purposes of testing, delivery, test driving by a potential purchaser, or used as a demonstration car.
> 2. The **retail price** should either be the actual price paid by the lessor for the car when new or, where the lessee does not have this information, the manufacturer's list of suggested retail prices net of any discount generally available. In either case, the price includes extras, delivery and VAT.

The **allowable deduction** for the rent of the car is restricted to:

14770
BIM 47717

$$\text{Expenditure} \times \frac{(\pounds12,000 + P)}{2P}$$

where:
P is the retail price of the car when new. The **expenditure** includes the rental payment along with any unrelieved VAT, but excludes identified maintenance costs.

Any **rebates** received at the end of the lease will be similarly restricted when calculating the taxable amount.

> EXAMPLE   C Ltd rents a car which has a retail price when new of £20,000. The rental charge is £3,000 p.a.
> The deductible rent is limited to £2,400. (3,000 × (12,000 + 20,000)/40,000)
> This is actually 80% of the cost.
> When the lease ends, C Ltd is entitled to a rebate of £1,000. Only £800 is taxable. (1,000 @ 80%)

Agreements entered into from 1 April 2009

14775
s 57 CTA 2009

Scope   There is a restriction on the deductible expenditure relating to hired cars which do not meet specified commercial or environmental criteria.

For the purposes of the restriction, a **car** means a mechanically propelled road vehicle:
– other than a motorcycle (defined as a mechanically propelled vehicle with fewer than four wheels and with an unladen weight of up to 410 kg);
– other than one primarily suited for the carrying of goods; or
– of a type not commonly used as a private vehicle and unsuitable for such use (although how the company actually uses it is irrelevant).

Comment   **Motorcycles** are no longer subject to a restriction, as they are excluded from being cars for corporation tax purposes from 1 April 2009. Contrast this to their treatment before 1 April 2009 (¶14765).

14780

Excluded cars   The restriction rules do not apply to expenditure on the hiring of a car which satisfies any of the following criteria:
– a car that was first registered before 1 March 2001;
– a car that has low carbon dioxide emissions of 130g/km or less;
– a car that is electrically propelled; or
– a qualifying hire car.

> MEMO POINTS   1. The carbon dioxide limit was 160g/km **before 1 April 2013**.
> 2. The **emissions figure** is shown on the vehicle registration document or can be obtained from flmemo.co.uk/tm14780.
> 3. Where **more than one emission figure is given**, the CO_2 emissions (combined) figure is used.
> 4. **Bi-fuel** cars will have emissions figures for each type of fuel, and in this case, the lowest figure is taken.

s 57(2) CTA 2009
> 5. A **qualifying hire car** is one which is either:
> – hired under a hire purchase agreement where there is either no option to purchase, or the purchase price is less than 1% of the retail price of the car when new; or
> – leased under a long funding lease (¶82215), as separate rules apply.

14785
s 58A CTA 2009

Intermediate lessors and short-term hire   Where either of the following conditions shown in the table below are met, and no arrangements exist for the purpose of avoiding tax, the hire charge will not be restricted.

Situation	Details
Short-term hiring in	Company hires car for 45 consecutive days[1] or less
Long-term hiring out	Company hires car which is then leased to another party for more than 45 consecutive days[1,2,3]

Note:
1. For this purpose, **periods of hire** are added together if there is a gap of 14 days or less between them. So a period of consecutive days (the main period) is linked to a period of consecutive days:
– that ends not more than 14 days before the main period begins;
– that begins not more than 14 days after the main period ends; and
– which is linked to another linked period (one that ends or begins not more than 14 days after a linked period begins or ends).
2. Where a company sublets the same car for **periods of varying length** (some which are less than 45 days and some are more, either to the same or different customers), a just and reasonable apportionment of the related expenses must be made.
3. If the lessee is an **employee or officer** of the company, or of a connected person (¶31375), the restriction still applies. This is also the case where the lessee makes any car (not just the hired car) available to an employee or officer of the company at any time during any periods of hire under arrangements involving the company or a connected person.

EXAMPLE

1. D Ltd hires a car from E Ltd from 1 May to 9 June for £30 per day. The period of hire is 40 days, so the hire is short-term, and there is no restriction on the deduction of £1,200. (30 x 40)

2. F Ltd hires a car with emissions of 140g/km from G Ltd for a period of 3 years, at an annual cost of £2,500. F Ltd then sublets the car to H Ltd for 3 years, receiving annual income of £3,000. As both periods exceed 45 days, F Ltd has no restriction on its hire charge of £2,500 because it sublets the car.
As H Ltd does not sublet the car, and the hire period exceeds 45 days, it must restrict the hire charge.

3. A Ltd hires a car with emissions of 170g/km from B Ltd for a period of 4 years, at an annual cost of £4,000. Although A Ltd sublets the car, none of the rental periods involved exceed 45 days.
A Ltd is therefore subject to the restriction.

4. C Ltd hires a car for 20 days from 1 July to 20 July (the main period), and also hires it for other periods as shown below:

BIM 47755

Period	Linked?	Explanation
1 June to 14 June	n	Ends more than 14 days before 1 July
1 August to 8 August	y	Begins less than 14 days after 20 July
16 August to 15 September	y	Begins less than 14 days after 8 August

The total period which relates to the July hire is as follows:

Dates	Number of days
1 July to 20 July	20
1 August to 8 August	8
16 August to 15 September	31
Total	59

So C Ltd must apply the restriction to the hire expenses for all of the periods except for the costs relating to the period from 1 June to 14 June.

5. D Ltd has 30 cars which it has leased for 6 months. Only 10 of the cars have carbon dioxide emissions which exceed 130g/km, and the details are as follows:

BIM 47760

Number of cars	Details	Restriction applies?
2	Sublet for more than 45 days	n
5	Short-term and never let out for more than 45 days	y
3	Used for both short term hire and longer lets	See note 1

Note:
1. The company must consider each of these cars individually and calculate (on a just and reasonable basis) the proportion of the total period each car was sublet for less than 45 days, and apply the restriction to that proportion of the rental expenses for that car.

Calculation The **disallowed part** of the hire charge is 15%.

For this purpose, the hire **expenditure includes** the rental payment along with any unrelievable VAT, but **excludes** identified maintenance costs.

Any **rebates** received at the end of the lease will be similarly restricted when calculating the taxable amount.

14790
s 56 CTA 2009;
BIM 47740

MEMO POINTS   Where **connected persons** (¶31375) incur expenses on the hiring of the same car for the same period, the restriction only applies to the expenses incurred by one of them. Where only one of the agreements is a commercial one (agreed at arm's length), the restriction falls on the lessee of that agreement. If all of the leases involved are commercial, the restriction is applied to the expenses incurred by the first one in the chain of hire arrangements.

s 58B CTA 2009

EXAMPLE

1. E Ltd hires a car for 3 years. The car has carbon dioxide emissions of 138g/km and the business pays a rent of £6,000 per year.
The business must restrict the deduction claimed for the car rentals by £900. (6,000 × 15%)

2. F Ltd is a parent company to G Ltd and H Ltd. As F Ltd has a better credit rating, it contracts with a leasing company to hire 100 cars which it will then sublet to the subsidiaries.

> F Ltd is a commercial lessee and as this is the only commercial lease, F Ltd must restrict the hire charges in its tax computation.
> Even if F Ltd sublets the cars on a commercial basis, it is still the first commercial lessee in the chain, and so it would still have to apply the restriction.

---

5. Waste disposal sites

14820   Although preparation and restoration costs incurred on waste disposal sites would be normally treated as capital, statute makes specific provision for the deductibility of these expenses against trading profits.

Site preparation costs

14825
ss 142–144
CTA 2009

Excluding the cost of the site itself, costs will be deductible as long as the following **conditions** are met:
– they do not qualify for capital allowances;
– the company holds a waste disposal licence when beginning to dispose of waste into the site; and
– the relief is claimed.

The **amount** of relief is:

$$(A - B) \times \frac{C}{C + D}$$

where:
– A is the cumulative expenditure incurred up to the end of the period of account;
– B is the amount of expenditure already relieved;
– C is the volume of waste disposed of into the site during the period of account; and
– D is the remaining capacity of the site for further deposits at the end of the accounting period.

> EXAMPLE   G Ltd's trade is waste disposal, and it has a December year end. It acquires a site on 1 April.
> Preparation costs and waste deposits for the first two years (ending 31 December) are as follows:
>
> | Year | Costs £ | Waste deposited m^3 | Capacity remaining m^3 |
> |------|---------|------------------|---------------------|
> | 1 | 50,000 | 100,000 | 500,000 |
> | 2 | 30,000 | 60,000 | 440,000 |
>
> So for Year 1, the formula is applied as follows:
>
> $$50,000 \times \frac{100,000}{100,000 + 500,000}$$
>
> So the deduction for Year 1 is £8,333.
>
> For Year 2, the deduction is £8,600. $(50,000 + 30,000 - 8,333) \times \dfrac{60,000}{60,000 + 440,000}$

> MEMO POINTS   1. Any **pre-trading costs** are deemed to be incurred on the first day of trading.
> 2. If there is a **change of ownership** of a site, the purchaser stands in place of the vendor when applying the formula.

Restoration costs

14830
s 145 CTA 2009

Restoration costs are deductible **so long as** they do not qualify for capital allowances, and they are incurred as a condition of any relevant licence or planning permission.

> MEMO POINTS   1. Where the payment is to a **connected person** on or after 21 March 2012 relief is not allowed until the work is completed.
> 2. For payments on or after 21 March 2012 relief is **denied** if the main purpose, or one of the main purposes, of an arrangement involving the company is to secure a deduction under these provisions.

C. Expenditure not in the accounts

Summary

14860

Situation	Detail	¶¶
Pension contributions	Adjustment to profits	¶14910
	Disallowed contributions	¶14930
	Large increase in contributions	¶14980
Provision of shares to employees	Employee benefit trusts	¶15035
	Setting up approved schemes	¶15075
	Share incentive plans	¶15095
	Shares given directly to employees	¶15120
Deemed earnings payment	Personal service company rules	¶77060
	Managed service company rules	¶77140

1. Pension contributions

An employer will pay contributions gross, and obtain tax relief by setting them against trading income. Generally, contributions to **registered pension schemes** paid wholly and exclusively for the purposes of the business are allowed in the period in which they are made, regardless of when they are deducted in the accounts. However, larger contributions are subject to special rules.

14890

There is no corporation tax deduction for payments into an **employer financed retirement benefit scheme** (a non-contributory scheme), because a deduction is only available when benefits are distributed out of the fund. The amount of the deduction is the lower of the contribution and the distribution for the period. The disguised remuneration rules (¶15050) apply to any scheme of this type, including when a company merely makes provision to set aside cash to purchase a pension for an employee.

s 246(2) FA 2004

a. Adjustment to profits

As the accounting treatment is not followed for tax purposes, the employer's tax computation must be adjusted as follows:
– add back the pension expense as shown in the profit and loss account; and
– deduct contributions actually paid to registered pension schemes in the period (up to the amount permitted under the tax rules).

14910

b. Disallowed contributions

There are two situations where contributions made may still be disallowed permanently:
– where the wholly and exclusively rule denies the deduction. This is only likely to occur where either the payments are made for a non-trade purpose (for instance as part of an **excessive remuneration package**), or as part of arrangements for **ceasing business** where there is no pre-existing contractual obligation to make the payments; and
– where an **asset-backed contribution** is made.

14930

MEMO POINTS   For sponsoring employers of **multi-employer schemes**, the levels of contributions are set for the scheme as a whole. HMRC's view is that if the amount paid to the group pension

BIM 46020

scheme is apportioned between the employing companies on a reasonable basis, then the wholly and exclusively rule will have been met.

Excessive remuneration package

14935
BIM 46035

HMRC's view is that it is the amount of the overall remuneration package (not just the amount of the pension contribution) which should be compared to the **value of the work** undertaken by that individual (particularly a controlling director or shareholder).

Contributions may vary depending on whether the pension scheme is sufficiently funded.

The wholly and exclusively rule will be met where the director, close friend, or family member is paid on a basis commensurate with **employees who are unconnected** with the business and perform duties of similar value. This can be difficult in small companies where only shareholders are directors. A wider comparison will then typically be sought.

Where the facts show that a definite part of the contribution is not wholly and exclusively paid out for the purposes of the trade, only that part is disallowed.

Ceasing business

14940
BIM 46040

On ceasing to trade, a company may either be under:
– a **contractual obligation** to make contributions to the pension scheme, in which case the contributions will be deductible; or
– **no contractual obligation**, when the contributions will not be deductible if they were made for non-business purposes, although if made to preserve reputation and morale, a deduction can be claimed.

> EXAMPLE
>
> 1. A company had a policy of granting pensions on retirement for its employees. When its business ceased it promised to do similar for its remaining employees. It was held that the payments were made not for the purposes of the trade but in order to cease trading. They were therefore not allowable. *CIR v Anglo Brewing Co Ltd* [1925]
>
> 2. A member of a printing group was to close its business but the parent company knew that without further payments to employees whose employment was being terminated the business of the group as a whole would be affected. It was held that the extra payments made were allowable as they were to facilitate orderly trading, albeit not by the company that was closing down. *O'Keefe v Southport Printers Ltd* [1984]

Asset-backed contributions

14945
ss 196B – 196L
FA 2004

Finance Act 2012 introduced a number of new provisions relating to the making of asset-backed pension contributions for contributions on or after 22 February 2012. The Government saw that in certain cases relief was being received in a manner and amount that was beyond what was originally intended.

> MEMO POINTS While there are **transitional** rules for arrangements entered into prior to 29 November 2012, and then for contributions on or after that date and up to 22 February 2012, this section covers only the current rules.

14950

A **simple asset-backed contribution** involves the company agreeing to make a contribution to its pension fund. The pension fund agrees to purchase an asset with a predicted income stream from the company. The purchase will typically be for a fixed period although this is not a prerequisite. It is then agreed that the debts arising, one from the agreement to make a contribution and the other from making the purchase, are offset so no debts remain. It is the date of this agreement that is considered to be the date on which the pension contribution is made.

14955

The **upfront contribution** (that is the amount originally agreed as being made to the pension fund) will **not be allowable** if the arrangement is not considered to be an acceptable structured finance arrangement, and two further conditions apply.

The first condition is that under the arrangement:
- the borrower receives in any period money or other asset forming an advance from the lender;
- the borrower (or someone connected to them) disposes of an asset (the "security") to the lender (or someone connected with them);
- as a result of the asset transfer the lender is entitled to receive payments in respect of the security;
- the borrower is an employer (or connected to them); and
- the advance, or at least part of it, is paid or provided by the lender from the employer's contributions.

The second condition is that it is reasonable to assume that any of the payments made in the arrangement are calculated on the basis that at least some of the original advance represents a loan which is to be repaid by any of the other payments. This condition is essentially the situation that the legislation is intended to counter.

> MEMO POINTS   There are a number of **highly complex schemes** involving multiple employers in a group or using partnerships to secure relief beyond the amount intended by the legislation. The rules apply equally to these.

Acceptable structured finance agreement

There are a number of conditions that an arrangement must satisfy if it is to be considered to be acceptable and ensure that the upfront pension contribution does not fall to be disallowed.   **14960**

1. Following GAAP (¶11055), the **borrower's accounts** must show a financial liability in respect of the advance, and this should occur in the accounts for the period in which the advance is received. The arrangement should also be a structured finance arrangement (¶21915). This recorded financial liability should be reduced to nil by the end of the payment period by the payments to the lender.

2. The **lender** must be the trustees of the pension scheme (or the person managing it) and must make the advance directly to the borrower: that is, the pension fund makes the advance out of the employer's contribution. The advance, and the liability recorded in the borrower's accounts, should match the employer's contribution.

3. In a simple arrangement, at the time the **advance** is made:
- it should be the lender who is entitled to the regular payments referred to in ¶14950.
- the payments should arise at times that have been fixed and fall at intervals of no more than a year, with the first payment being due no more than a year after the advance is paid;
- the payments should be received within 3 months of the due date;
- each payment should become part of the scheme's funds when received;
- the payments are to be the same in terms of amount;
- the total amount of the payments should not be less than the amount of the employer's contributions; and
- all payments should be expected to be received within 25 years of the date the contribution is made.

As these conditions have to be satisfied at the time the advance is made, the arrangement must be clear about what the pension fund will receive over the course of the arrangement. This means that stacking the payments towards the end of the agreement, or any contingency on payments, will ensure that the arrangement will not be considered acceptable.

4. There should be **no "commitment"** given in relation to the payments. This means no undertaking must be given by the employer, anyone connected with the employer, or someone chosen to represent the employer (except for the trustees of the pension scheme) as to the destination of the funds once they are received by the pension fund.

c. Large increase in contributions

Spreading of deductions may be required where there is an increase of more than 210% in the level of employer contributions from one period to the next. Although there is **no overall**   **14980**
s 197 FA 2004

limit on the contributions that an employer may make, the tax relief may be spread so that part of the contribution is treated as paid in a later accounting period. Spreading is not required if **no contribution was made in the previous year** (that is, the pension scheme is new).

Otherwise, the contributions must be spread if:
– the current period's contribution exceeds 210% of the previous period's contribution; and
– the amount exceeding 110% of that paid previously is £500,000 or more.

> ⌐MEMO POINTS⌐ 1. If the current and previous **periods are not the same length**, the previous period's contribution should be adjusted when making the comparison.
> 2. If the employer **operates more than one pension scheme**, each scheme is looked at separately, so the total of employer contributions made to all schemes is not relevant.
> 3. Where the company ceases trading in the period of payment, or one of the periods in which a payment would be spread to, the company would not receive any relief for the contribution without special rules. These rules allow the company to make the choice to either receive relief for the remaining unrelieved contribution in its final accounting period or allocate the excess on a day basis from the date of the start of the accounting period in which the contribution was made to the date on which trading ceased.

14985 The **excess payment** (the amount by which the current year's contribution exceeds 110% of the previous year's contribution) is spread as follows:

Amount of excess contributions (£)	Spread over [1]
< 500,000	n/a
500,000 to 1 million	2 years
1 million to 2 million	3 years
> 2 million	4 years

Note:
1. Payments are spread evenly over the periods. If an accounting period is less than 12 months, the deduction is restricted accordingly.

⌐EXAMPLE⌐
1. A Ltd pays £100,000 to the pension scheme in Year 1, and pays £600,000 in Year 2.
The amount of £600,000 exceeds 210% of £100,000. (£210,000)
However, the excess payment itself is only £490,000. (600,000 – (110 % × 100,000))
So the spreading rules do not apply and relief will be obtained in full in the year of payment.

2. B Ltd pays £100,000 to its pension scheme in Year 1, and then £620,000 in Year 2.
The amount of £620,000 exceeds £210,000 (which is 210% of £100,000).
The excess is £510,000. (620,000 – (110% × 100,000))
Therefore this excess contribution must be spread forward over 2 years, giving the following deductions:

Year	Deduction (£)	Calculation
1	100,000	Contribution paid
2	365,000	110,000 + (510,000 × 50%)
3	255,000	510,000 × 50%
	720,000	

2. Provision of shares to employees

15015 Staff are often rewarded with shares in the employer company, as this can be an effective way of retaining and motivating key employees.

The employer may choose to set up an employee share scheme trust which creates an artificial trading market, as well as being a vehicle in which to store shares.

The entries in the profit and loss account have no meaning for tax purposes, so any accounting deduction must be added back.

a. Employee benefit trusts

An employee benefit trust (EBT) is a trust set up for the benefit of employees as a vehicle for **employers to provide benefits** on a discretionary basis. The employer appoints trustees, and the running of the trust is determined by the trust deed.

15035
BIM 44500

An EBT is often set up in conjunction with an employee share ownership scheme, to provide a market place for the shares (known as employee share ownership trusts (ESOTs) or employee share ownership plan (ESOP) trusts).

HMRC view EBTs, especially general purpose EBTs which are not used for any of the functions in ¶15040 below, as potential devices for avoiding income tax and NIC.

Company payments to EBTs which have no link to employment will not be deductible, although if there is a subsequent event which means the employees becomes taxable on an amount, a corporation tax deduction will be available.

Comment   Historically, EBTs were used to provide employees with loans, but following case law and subsequent anti-avoidance provisions (including the new disguised remuneration rules (¶15050)), this has become untenable. *MacDonald v Dextra Accessories Ltd* [2005]

Setting up

Payments made to set up the trust are treated as capital expenditure, and are, therefore, not deductible, **unless** the trust exists for any of the following purposes:
– share-related benefits under employee share schemes set up to give employees a stake in the employer company;
– pension and other benefits under retirement benefit schemes;
– accident benefits; or
– healthcare benefits. *Heather v P E Consulting Group Ltd* [1972]

15040
BIM 44535

Contributions to the trust

Two **criteria** must be satisfied in order for contributions to be deductible:
a. the payment is not capital (determined using the principles outlined from ¶13210+); and
b. it is made wholly and exclusively for the purposes of the trade. *Mawsley Machinery Ltd v Robinson* [1998]

15045
ss 1290 – 1296
CTA 2009

The employer must make payment to the scheme manager, and the corporation tax **deduction will occur** when the employees become taxable on a benefit provided. The deduction will be delayed when benefits are provided more than 9 months after the accounting period end. Of course, any amount unrelieved can be deducted in a subsequent period once the benefits are actually provided.

> MEMO POINTS   For this purpose, **employees become taxable** when any of the following conditions are satisfied:
> – the benefit gives rise to both a tax and NIC charge (including where the disguised remuneration rules apply (¶15050+), in which case the earnings arise when the relevant step is taken, or at the start of the employment where the step predates the employee's commencement date);
> – such charges would arise if the employee was resident in the UK and the employment duties were performed in the UK;
> – the benefit is made in connection with the termination of employment; or
> – the benefit relates to an employer financed retirement benefits scheme.
> However, deemed income arising from the provision of employee shareholder shares (¶15130) does not constitute a taxable benefit for these purposes.

s 1292 CTA 2009

Disguised remuneration

There is an immediate income tax and NIC charge if a relevant third person takes steps to allocate or earmark cash or assets, or make them available by way of loan or distribution, to an employee. A typical scenario involves an EBT.

15050

ss 554B – 554D
ITEPA 2003

[MEMO POINTS] 1. A **relevant third person** excludes group companies, unless the arrangement intends to avoid tax. So loans can be made by group companies to employees e.g. to fund the acquisition of shares.

2. A **relevant step** is any of the following:
– a third party earmarks cash or assets for the benefit of an employee, with a view to a later relevant step being taken either by the third party or any other person, which may be entirely discretionary;
– a third party takes steps to pay money or transfer an asset to an employee, a person linked to or nominated by an employee, or within a class of people nominated by an employee; or
– without transferring the property in an asset to an employee etc, a third party makes the asset available so the benefit is the same as if the property had been transferred outright.

15055

s 554J ITEPA 2003

There is an **exemption** from the disguised remuneration rules for all approved share schemes, and the provision of key man and convertible shares.

HMRC FAQs

HMRC have confirmed that a company can make payments to an EBT without triggering an income tax charge so long as they are intended to fund the **acquisition of shares** which are to be allocated to employees in future.

Where shares are set aside and their allocation is **contingent on a future event** e.g. the attainment of particular performance targets, this will not be immediately taxable on the employee so long as:
– the payment of shares is subject to conditions which, if not met, will mean that there will be no possibility of the employee (or a person linked with the employee or chosen by the employee) receiving the shares or retaining any form of current or future entitlement to the amount they do not receive; and
– the arrangement specifies a date for the vesting of the shares, which can be a maximum of 10 years from the date of grant.

If a **loan** is made to an employee by an EBT, an immediate income tax charge will arise even if the loan is subsequently repaid. No refund of the tax will be made.

---

b. Setting up approved schemes

15075

ss 987, 999
CTA 2009

The incidental costs of running an employee share scheme are deductible as revenue expenditure.

In general, the costs of **setting up** employee share schemes and employee share ownership trusts are considered to be capital, and not deductible for corporation tax. This includes the initial amount settled to bring the trust into existence. However, costs incurred in setting up the following types of approved employee share scheme are given a statutory deduction as a trading expense:

Type of scheme	Restrictions	Reference
Share incentive plan (SIP)	No deduction is allowed if, before approval[1], an employee acquires rights under the plan, or the trustees acquire shares for the purposes of the plan; see also ¶15095+	s 697 CTA 2009
Savings-related share option scheme (SAYE) or Company share option plan (CSOP)	No deduction is allowed if, before approval[1], an employee or director acquires rights under the scheme	s 999 CTA 2009
Qualifying employee share ownership trust	Depends on when the trust is established[2]	s 1000 CTA 2009
Note 1. If approval is given more than 9 months after the end of the accounting period in which the expenses are incurred, the deduction is given for the period in which the approval is given. 2. If the trust is established more than 9 months after the end of the accounting period in which the expenses are incurred, the deduction is given for the period in which the trust is established. For this purpose, a trust is established when the deed under which it is established is executed.		

MEMO POINTS 1. **Approved company share option plans** (CSOPs) are discretionary, so the options may be granted to employees on a selective basis rather than to the workforce as a whole. There will generally be no income tax charge on the grant or exercise of the options, nor on the subsequent increase in value of the shares. Capital gains tax on the eventual disposal of the shares is usually the only tax charge for the employee. The shares which are used to form part of a CSOP must be fully paid up, irredeemable ordinary shares in the company setting up the scheme or a company which controls it. The aggregate market value of shares over which an individual may hold unexercised rights under the scheme must not exceed £30,000. The subscription price must not be manifestly less than the market value of shares at the time when the rights are acquired. If exercised at least 3 but no more than 10 years after grant, there will be no income tax charge.

2. A **company savings-related share option scheme** allows employees to acquire shares using the funds retained in a savings scheme for a period of between 3 and 7 years. Providing the scheme is approved, the grant of the share options will be tax free, as will the increase in value of the shares between the grant of the option and its exercise. Interest and bonuses paid in relation to the funds in the scheme are also exempt from tax. The shares which are used to form part of an SRSOS must be fully paid up, irredeemable ordinary shares in the company setting up the scheme, or a company which controls it. The scheme rules must permit contributions between a minimum of £10 and a maximum of £250 per month. The price must not be manifestly less than 80% of the market value of shares at the time when the rights are acquired.

3. Only expenses that qualify under a **statutory provision** are deductible. In particular, this excludes deductions recognised under GAAP, following a change in accounting standards, even when share options were not exercised. The statutory deduction is given instead of, not in addition to, the accounting deduction.

ss 1038 – 1038A
CTA 2009

4. The **disguised remuneration** rules (¶15050) do not apply to approved share schemes.

c. Share incentive plans

Only appropriate to quoted companies, share incentive plans (SIPs) allow shares worth up to £7,500 per annum to be passed to a trust on behalf of each employee without giving rise to an income tax charge. The shares are then transferred to the employee once a specified period of between 3 and 5 years has elapsed.

15095
BIM 44255

Broadly, the scheme allows for four different categories of shares:

Category	Details
Free	Up to £3,000 p.a. appropriated to the employee by the employer
Partnership	Purchased by the employee through deductions from salary – maximum value £1,500 p.a.
Matching	May be offered by the company if partnership shares purchased – maximum ratio 2 matching shares for each partnership share
Dividend	Purchased with up to £1,500 p.a. of dividends reinvested on behalf of the employee

A scheme may contain free and/or partnership shares, and the award of free shares may depend on performance targets being met.

In addition to set up costs, the following costs incurred in connection with an SIP are **deductible**:

15100
ss 988 – 998
CTA 2009

– running costs;
– payments to the trustees of an SIP to acquire shares;
– cost of the free and matching shares awarded to employees (equal to the market value of the shares at the time they were acquired by the trustees. This deduction can only be made in the period of account in which the shares are awarded to the employees); and
– the excess of market value over the amount paid by the employee in relation to partnership shares.

However, **no deduction** is available for:
- shares awarded to non-PAYE individuals;
- shares awarded to employees which have previously been awarded but forfeited, and for which the company has previously claimed a deduction;
- shares already provided to this or another trust in relation to which a deduction has previously been given;
- expenses in providing dividend shares; or
- shares which are liable to depreciate substantially for reasons that do not generally apply to the company's shares.

d. Shares given directly to employees

15120

ss 1006 – 1013
CTA 2009;
BIM 44250

A corporation tax deduction can be claimed for the costs of providing shares directly to employees (rather than through a share scheme trust). Under these provisions there is no requirement for complex arrangements using trusts. The basic idea is that the corporation tax deduction is given at the same time as the employee is chargeable to income tax.

Comment   Any deduction available under the **share incentive plan** rules is given in priority to this statutory corporation tax deduction.

Qualifying conditions

15125

To qualify, the following conditions must be met **at the time** that the shares are awarded (or the options to acquire the shares are exercised):

Condition relates to	Requirement	Reference
Reason for share/option acquisition	Due to a person's employment, so that shares may be awarded to ex-employees, directors, ex-directors, and relatives of employees or directors	s 1007 CTA 2009
Issuer of shares/grantor of options	The company granting the shares (or options) must be one whose business is within the charge to UK corporation tax[1, 2] The company must be either: - the employing company; - the parent of the employing company[3]; - a member of a consortium that owns the employing company; - a member of the same consortium as the employing company or its parent which is a member of the same commercial association[4] as another company owned by the consortium; or - a qualifying successor company (where the original grant was an option)	s 1008 CTA 2009
Type of shares	Must be ordinary, fully paid up, non-redeemable shares and either: - listed on a recognised stock exchange (¶95320) or under the control of a company whose shares are listed on a recognised stock exchange; or - unlisted in a company that is not under the control of any other company	s 1008 CTA 2009
Employee	Must be subject to UK tax for the award of the shares or options (or would be if he were resident in the UK and his duties were performed in the UK)[5]	s 1009 CTA 2009

Note:
1. This also applies to companies that would be within the charge to corporation tax but for the fact that an election has been made in respect of the profits of its overseas permanent establishment (¶90160).
2. For a **grant of an option** to acquire shares, this condition needs to be satisfied at the time that the option is granted, whereas the other conditions need to be satisfied at the time that the option is exercised. Following a company takeover, any qualifying options can be transferred to the new company, which will then be eligible for the corporation tax deduction (assuming all the other conditions are met by the new company) i.e. the new options stand in the shoes of the old options.
3. A company is a **parent company** if it owns 51% of the share capital of the subsidiary (¶65505).
4. A **commercial association** of companies is a number of companies carrying on businesses of such a nature that they may be reasonably considered to make up a single composite undertaking.
5. The employee is deemed to be taxable in the UK even though the shares or options are awarded via the **enterprise management incentive scheme, savings-related share option scheme or approved company share option plan.**

Relief

A tax deduction is given to the company in the **accounting period** in which the employee acquires a beneficial interest in the shares.

15130
ss 1010, 1013
CTA 2009

The **amount** of the relief is equal to:
– the difference between the market value of the shares at the time of acquisition and the amount paid or payable by the employee (or another) for the shares. This deduction is, therefore, equal to the amount that is subject to income tax on the employee; and
– other expenses relating directly to the provision of the shares (**excluding** establishment and administration of the share scheme in addition to the financing costs (including interest, fees, commission, stamp duty) for which there is a separate relief (¶15075)).

For share options, any amount paid by the employee in respect of grant and exercise is taken into account.

There is **no relief** for the deemed income of up to £2,000 arising to an employee who receives shares under an employee shareholder agreement.

> MEMO POINTS Under an **employee shareholder agreement**, an employee can be given shares in exchange for the surrender of various rights arising under employment legislation. The first £2,000 worth of shares is deemed income and is not subject to income tax or NIC as earnings. The employer must pay for legal advice up to a "reasonable" level, irrespective of whether the employee or job applicant finally elects to become an employee shareholder, and this cost is deductible.

> EXAMPLE C Ltd grants options relating to 10,000 shares to Mr D when they are worth £1 each, and Mr D is required to pay this amount as consideration. Three years later, the shares are worth £5 each and Mr D exercises his options.
>
> | | £ |
> |---|---|
> | Value on exercise | 50,000 |
> | Consideration paid | (10,000) |
> | Corporation tax deduction in accounting period when options exercised | 40,000 |

Convertible shares

Broadly, a convertible share is a share which contains the **right** to change into another type of share at some time in the future. This type of share is often seen in management buy-out situations, where conversion is dependent on the achievement of performance targets. The following are **examples** of convertible shares:
– the holder has an immediate or conditional entitlement to convert them into other shares;
– an arrangement has been entered into which will create an entitlement to convert on the occurrence of certain events; and
– the conversion will occur on the happening of an event outside the control of the holder.

15135
ss 1011 – 1013
CTA 2009

The basic principle is that the corporation tax relief is determined by the deemed taxable income of the employee.

> MEMO POINTS There is **no relief** for the deemed income of up to £2,000 arising to an employee who receives shares under an employee shareholder agreement I¶15130).

15140
BIM 44400

The corporation tax deduction for convertible shares is available as follows:

Event	Amount of relief (the deemed employment income)	When relief is given
Award of the shares	Usually only the value attributable to the unconverted part of the share[1]	In the accounting period in which the recipient acquires a beneficial interest in the shares
Acquisition as a result of the exercise of an option	Difference between the market value of the shares at the date on which the option is exercised and the amount paid for the shares (including the cost of the option, if any) plus any employer's NIC which was relieved in arriving at that income If the option is granted under the EMI scheme, the corporation tax relief is equal to the market value of the share when the option is exercised (depending on whether the employee has made a restricted value election[2]) less any amounts paid by the employee, ignoring any discount given to the employee	
Conversion of the shares whilst still owned by the employee	Increase in market value between the old share (as if it was not convertible) and the new share, less any consideration paid for the entitlement to convert[3] If new shares do not qualify for relief (¶15125), no deduction available to company on conversion	
Disposal of the shares for consideration while they are still convertible	Disposal proceeds less the market value of the shares (as if they were not convertible) less any consideration paid for the entitlement to convert[3]	
Right to convert is extinguished in return for consideration	Consideration received[3]	
Receipt of a benefit in connection with the entitlement to convert	Amount of money or money's worth received[3]	
Death of employee	Amount that constitutes employment income on the assumption that there was a deemed chargeable event at the date of death (i.e. conversion, disposal whilst still convertible, or right of conversion extinguished)	In the accounting period in which the employee dies

Note:
1. Unless the shares are part of an anti-avoidance transaction, when the full value is taxed (including the right to convert in future).
2. It is possible for the employee and employer to jointly elect to ignore outstanding restrictions and tax the receipt of the share on its unrestricted value.
3. Ignore any income tax relief for employer's NIC met by the employee and also ignore the rules relating to restricted securities with artificially depressed market value.

EXAMPLE   Mr E is given 1,000 convertible A shares by F Ltd on 1 May 2008, which have the right to convert into ordinary shares five years later. F Ltd has a December year end.
On acquisition, the market values are as follows:

	£
Shares with conversion rights	1,100
Shares without conversion rights	1,000

So F Ltd obtains a deduction of £1,000 in the year ended 31 December 2008.

> Mr E still holds the shares on conversion and pays £200 for the right to convert, when the relative market values are as follows:
>
> | | £ |
> |---|---|
> | Shares with conversion rights | 2,500 |
> | Shares without conversion rights | 2,000 |
>
> So F Ltd obtains a deduction of £300 in the year ended 31 December 2013. (2,500 – 2,000 – 200)

Restricted shares

Shares which are restricted in any way will have a lower market **value** than equivalent unrestricted shares. However, if an employee pays full unrestricted value for the shares on acquisition, no income tax charge will arise, and hence the company can ignore all of the following rules.

15145
s 1011 CTA 2009

Certain shares which can be **forfeited within 5 years** of acquisition are exempt from the rules for restricted shares unless an election is made.

Examples of restrictions include:
– forfeiture or compulsory sale if an employee leaves the employer, except in the case of misconduct;
– restricted dividend, voting or other rights;
– redeemable shares; or
– restrictions on the right to dispose of the shares excluding the usual pre-emption rights found in the Articles of Association which apply to all the company's shares, as long there is no clause which requires such shares to be sold for less than market value.

Unpaid or partly paid shares, which may be subject to forfeit if a future call is not paid, are not usually restricted shares.

> MEMO POINTS   It is possible for the employee and employer to jointly **elect** to ignore outstanding restrictions and tax the receipt of the share on its unrestricted value. See *Tax Memo* for details.

An income tax charge will arise **on acquisition**, when the taxable amount is the restricted value received.

15150

A further income tax charge occurs on the happening of a **chargeable event**, taken as a proportion of the unrestricted value immediately after the event as follows:

$$\frac{\text{Unrestricted value on acquisition} - \text{Deductible amount}}{\text{Unrestricted value on acquisition}} \times \text{Unrestricted value after event}$$

where the deductible amount is the sum of the:
– consideration given for the shares;
– amounts already charged to income tax; and
– expenses incurred in relation to the shares.

> MEMO POINTS   A **chargeable event** is one of the following:
> – the shares ceasing to be restricted whilst still owned by the employee (employees are commonly required to remain with an employer for a minimum time before restrictions are lifted);
> – any restriction affecting the shares is varied or removed while still owned by the employee; or
> – the shares are sold while still restricted.

The company can obtain a corporation tax deduction as follows:

15155

Event	Amount of relief (the deemed employment income)	When relief is given
Award of the shares	Restricted value received	In the accounting period in which the recipient acquires a beneficial interest in the shares
Lifting or variation of restrictions	Amount that constitutes employment income plus any employer's NIC which was relieved in arriving at that income	
Selling shares with restrictions still attached		
Death of employee while shares still restricted	Amount that constitutes employment income on the assumption that shares had been sold immediately before death	In the accounting period in which the employee dies

EXAMPLE   Mr A is given 1,000 shares, which cannot be sold for the next 3 years, by B Ltd on 1 May 2010. B Ltd has a December year end.
On acquisition, the market values are as follows:

	£
Unrestricted shares	1,000
Restricted shares – reduces value by 20%	800

So B Ltd obtains a deduction of £800 in the year ended 31 December 2010.
On 1 May 2013, the shares are no longer subject to forfeit, and their value is now £2,000.
Using the formula, B Ltd obtains a deduction of £400 in the year ended 31 December 2013.
$((1,000 - 800)/1,000) \times 2,000)$

CHAPTER 5

Financial income and expenditure

16000   The following issues relate to corporate finance (the raising of funds and management of money) and are dealt with in this chapter:

Topic	Definition	¶¶
Loan relationships	Profits and losses such as interest and expenses, arising from the lending and borrowing of money	¶16050
Derivative contracts	Profits and losses arising on various types of financial instruments such as futures, forwards, options, and swaps	¶16775
Foreign exchange	Profits and losses arising from translating foreign transactions, assets and liabilities into sterling	¶17135
Management expenses	Expenses of running an investment business	¶17620

MEMO POINTS   1. The **accounting treatment** of these items can be critical to the tax consequences. Note that for accounting periods beginning on or after 1 January 2015, companies that have not yet adopted IFRS will be required to make a choice between a new EU-IFRS or a new UK GAAP. This will particularly affect the treatment of loan relationships and derivatives.
2. Details of the **debt cap** rules, which affect the financing costs of an international group, are covered at ¶70530+.

SECTION 1

Loan relationships

16050   A company needs money not only to fund the commencement and expansion of its business, but also to meet its working capital requirements. Whilst equity can be relied upon for a certain level of funding, almost every company borrows money, usually in the form of an overdraft or bank loan on which interest will be payable.

Investment of surplus funds will often result in interest earned or some other type of income.

A. Scope

16080   Transactions resulting from the borrowing and lending of money fall to be taxed within the **loan relationships** regime.

Interest, expenses, and all other similar types of profits, gains and losses are generally taxed in a manner based on how they are reflected in the accounts, although several overriding rules exist (particularly in relation to connected parties).

Excluded situations

16085
CFM 30130, 31010

The following items are **not within the loan relationships regime**:
– trading debts (debts for the supply of goods and services, including those between group companies). However, if the creditor company lends money to the debtor company so that it has the funds to repay the debt (either by book entry or by cash changing hands), there will be a new agreement between the parties which will be a loan relationship;
– ordinary and preference shares (¶18245);
– distributions, except where amounts that would otherwise be treated as distributions are taxable as loan relationships (e.g. returns on alternative finance and certain amounts payable by building societies);

- leasing or hire purchase arrangements;
- rents;
- interest due on quarterly instalments of corporation tax;
- payments made as a result of guaranteeing another person's liabilities (but see ¶16095); and
- amounts taxable or receivable under life assurance policies.

> ☐ MEMO POINTS ☐ A **grant** may be a loan relationship where its terms require repayment, unless certain conditions are met, and interest is payable in the meantime. However, a grant which has no such conditions attached cannot be a loan relationship.

Entities

The loan relationship rules apply to companies **within the charge to UK corporation tax**, including companies that are members of partnerships. No distinction is drawn between trading and non-trading companies, although a loan relationship will be taxed differently depending on whether it is for a trading or non-trading purpose.

16090

Non-resident companies come within the rules only if they are trading in the UK through a permanent establishment (¶92140); but see also ¶16480 regarding the termination of a loan.

The rules also apply to those unincorporated associations which are subject to corporation tax.

Definitions

A loan relationship is defined as:
- a money debt (¶16100);
- which results from a transaction for the lending of money (¶16110).

16095
s 302 CTA 2009

There must be a legal **obligation** on the borrower to repay. This means that a contract is not enforceable until it is completed when the vendor has a right to receive consideration. Similarly, some debt does not become enforceable until a future date. An equity shareholder has no right to repayment of his shares, and so does not enter into a loan relationship with the company.

The **value** of the debt may be fixed or fluctuate.

> ☐ MEMO POINTS ☐ 1. The **guaranteeing** of a third party debt is not lending money, so no loan relationship exists between the guarantor and the lender. However, a loan relationship may exist between the guarantor and the borrower where the guarantor has the right to reclaim amounts it has paid from the borrower (known as the subrogation principle). If the borrower does not refund the guarantor, relief may be available so long as the guarantor and borrower are not connected.
> 2. All **discounts** fall to be taxed as a loan relationship credit for the creditor, so long as the discount is not treated as a trading receipt and is not within the alternative finance arrangement provisions.

s 480 CTA 2009

Money debt

A money debt is one which is to be **settled** in any of the following ways:
- by payment of money (in any currency);
- by transfer of a right of settlement under a debt which is itself a money debt; or
- by the issue or transfer of any shares in any company.

16100
s 303 CTA 2009

If either party to the transaction has the option to settle the debt in some other way, it is ignored, and a loan relationship is still deemed to exist.

> EXAMPLE
> 1. A Ltd made a loan of £20,000 to B Ltd which sells computers.
> A Ltd agrees to the debt being repaid in kind i.e. by accepting a new server system from B Ltd.
> This is still a money debt even though it was settled in a way other than cash.
>
> 2. C Ltd loans D Ltd £20,000. D Ltd has already loaned E Ltd £20,000.
> On the due date, D Ltd arranges for E Ltd to repay the money direct to C Ltd.
> This is still a money debt because it was settled by the transfer of rights to another money debt.
>
> 3. F Ltd loans G Ltd £20,000. The terms of the debt give G Ltd the option to issue shares instead of making a cash repayment.
> This is still a money debt, because it is possible for the debt to be discharged via cash.

16105
CFM 31030

Where repayment is **contingent** on an event, this is still likely to be a debt, particularly where it has the hallmarks of a loan: for example, it is evidenced by a debt instrument, carries interest, ranks above share capital in a liquidation, and is treated as a loan for accounting purposes. *Smart v Lincolnshire Sugar Ltd* [1937]

However, HMRC say that in their view no debt exists in the extreme case where someone has only a contingent right to an unascertainable sum that may become payable at an unknown future date. *Marren v Ingles* [1980]

Transaction for the lending of money

16110
CFM 30150

This **includes**:
- overdrafts and bank loans;
- intercompany and directors' loans (not where goods or services are supplied);
- mortgages; and
- bank deposits, and building society shares and deposits.

s 303(3) CTA 2009

The issue of a **debt instrument** for the purpose of representing security for a money debt will also result in a loan relationship, including:
- company bonds, loan notes and debentures;
- Eurobonds;
- bills of exchange;
- commercial paper;
- certificates of deposit;
- gilts and government stock; and
- funding bonds.

> EXAMPLE A Ltd buys a property from B Ltd for £800,000, paying £200,000 initially.
> If:
> – the remainder is left unpaid (by mutual agreement), there has been no lending of money so it is not a loan relationship; or
> – B Ltd issues loan notes for the remaining £600,000 to A Ltd, this is evidence of a transaction for the lending of money, and so a loan relationship exists.

16115
s 481 CTA 2009

In the following circumstances, the loan relationship rules apply when there is **no lending** but there is still a money debt:
- interest arising on a late paid trading debt;
- interest on late paid or repaid tax (excluding late paid income tax or capital gains tax);
- judgement debts;
- late payment interest or exchange differences on completion, for example on land or share sales;
- repo price differentials; and
- imputed interest under the transfer pricing rules (¶70000+).

See also the situations in ¶16120 below.

> MEMO POINTS In this case, the only **amounts to be taxed** under the loan relationship rules are:
> – interest;
> – exchange gains and losses;
> – profits, but not losses, on a related transaction for the transfer of the right to receive interest;
> – impairment losses on business payments and the reversal of those impairment losses (for this purpose, a business payment is one which would be taxed on the recipient either as a receipt of a trade or property business); and
> – a release debit brought into account by the creditor, or a profit brought into account by the debtor, where a trade or property business debt is released.

Interest-like returns

16120
CFM 31080, 40140

Sometimes a lender receives a return that is economically equivalent to interest, although it is not technically interest in the eyes of the law. The most common example would be the return from redeemable, cumulative fixed rate preference shares.

The following table summarises these other situations where loan relationships may arise:

Situation	Details	Reference
Shares accounted for as liabilities under GAAP (see *Accountancy and Financial Reporting Memo* for further details) such as redeemable fixed rate preference shares	All of the following criteria are met: – the companies are not connected (¶31375); – the shares are not publicly issued or do not have the same terms as shares already issued to the public; – the shares are held for an unallowable purpose i.e. where the main purpose of the arrangement is to secure a tax advantage; and – the return on the shares is equivalent to interest[1]	s 521B CTA 2009, CFM 45500
Disguised interest	Applies to arrangements made on or after 22 April 2009 producing returns which are economically equivalent to interest[1] No loan relationship where either: – there is no tax avoidance purpose[2]; – the return is already taxable under some other provision; or – the arrangement involves only excluded shares[3]	s 486B CTA 2009, CFM 42000
Alternative finance arrangements (for example, Sharia-compliant transactions) which provide a return that economically amounts to interest	See ¶16125+	s 509 CTA 2009, CFM 44000
Manufactured interest (amounts which economically represent interest)	The arrangement giving rise to the manufactured interest is treated as a quasi-loan relationship, so payments and receipts are subject to the loan relationship rules	s 539 CTA 2009
Repos[4], where the legal ownership of securities is temporarily transferred while the economic ownership is retained by the original owner Interest or dividends received by the temporary owner and which are reimbursed to the original owner in the form of manufactured payments	Where a company has disposed of its rights or liabilities relating to securities, it must still recognise amounts in respect of the relationship in its accounts prepared under GAAP These amounts are taxable under the loan relationship rules	s 542 CTA 2009, CFM 46010

Note:
1. A return will be **economically equivalent to interest** where:
– it is based on the time value of an amount of money;
– the rate is comparable to a commercial rate; and
– it is predictable (i.e. not a result of chance).
2. A company that is not a party to an arrangement for a tax avoidance purpose can still irrevocably **elect** that the disguised interest rules apply to a return. This would be beneficial where a greater tax burden would otherwise result.
3. Excluded shares are those held by the company in either:
– a connected company (¶16560+);
– a joint venture company (i.e. where the company, together with another person, controls a company, and the test at ¶90605 is met); or
– a controlled foreign company (¶90590+).
This prevents the disguised interest rules applying when an interest-like return arises to a company purely as a result of an increase in the value of any share that it holds in a group company.
4. Most **repos** are two party agreements under which one party sells securities to another for cash, and repurchases the same or equivalent securities at a later date.
The repurchase price will normally be equal to:
– the original sale price (which will be just below the market value of the securities); plus
– an increment equivalent to interest on a loan of the same amount for the period of the repo.
An agreement may reduce the repurchase price in lieu of interest due to the original owner (i.e. because no interest payments are made during the period of the repo). The reduction is treated as a manufactured payment.

[EXAMPLE]
1. C Ltd subscribes for 200,000 £1 redeemable, cumulative, fixed rate preference shares in D Ltd. The shares are guaranteed by D Ltd's parent company.

The terms of the share are as follows:
– a fixed dividend of £10,000 each year which accumulates if D Ltd is unable to pay;
– priority over ordinary shares on D Ltd's liquidation; and
– full repayment on redemption.
As these shares have all the hallmarks of a debt, they create a loan relationship.

2. E Ltd purchases an asset for £100,000 from F Ltd, and agrees to sell the asset back to F Ltd for £115,000 in 3 years' time.
If the return of 5% per annum is reasonably comparable to a commercial rate of interest, then this transaction provides an interest-like return in a manner that would not, without any special rules, be taxed as interest.

Alternative financial arrangements

16125   Alternative financial arrangements have been developed by the financial services industry to cater for those who want to avoid the receipt or payment of interest (because, for example, such payments are prohibited by Sharia law). These rules are not **limited** to Sharia compliant products but also apply to any finance arrangement that falls within their terms.

For all arrangements except investment bonds, **one of the parties** involved must be a financial institution.

s 502 CTA 2009   MEMO POINTS   A **financial institution** is defined as:
– a bank or a building society;
– a wholly owned subsidiary of a bank or building society;
– a person licensed under the Consumer Credit Act to carry on a consumer credit business or consumer hire business;
– a person authorised in an overseas jurisdiction to receive deposits or other repayable funds from the public and to grant credits for its own account; or
– an issuer of alternative finance investment bonds.

16130   For tax purposes, any profit element attributable to the financial arrangements is treated as
s 510 CTA 2009   interest by both the payer and the recipient (although for financing purposes, the profit element continues to be treated as a finance return, not interest).

For the purposes of the loan relationship rules, the **amount of the money debt** depends on the type of product as follows.

Type of product	Details	Amount of loan	Reference
Purchase and resale (Murabahah)	A financial institution buys an asset for onward sale at a profit to the borrower, and all or part of the sale price is deferred Borrower sells the asset to access the cash and pays back the institution over a period of time Alternative to borrowing using a conventional loan or mortgage	First purchase price of the asset paid by institution	ss 503, 511 CTA 2009, CFM 44050
Diminishing shared ownership (Musharaka)	Partnership-style arrangement whereby a financial institution acquires a beneficial interest in an asset together with the eventual owner who: – makes a number of payments to the institution which reimburses it for its share of the asset plus a mark up; and – has exclusive rights to the benefit of the asset to which the arrangement applies, including any income, profit or gain that is attributable to the asset Therefore, where the asset increases in value over the period of the arrangement, the eventual owner is entitled to the whole of that increase Alternative to borrowing using a conventional loan or mortgage	Amount paid by the institution for its acquisition of its beneficial interest in the asset	ss 504, 512 CTA 2009, CFM 44070

Type of product	Details	Amount of loan	Reference
Deposit arrangement (Mudarabah)	A company deposits money with a financial institution, which then invests it as it sees fit and shares any profit it makes with the company Similar to a conventional bank deposit account	Amount deposited by the company with the financial institution	ss 505, 513 CTA 2009, CFM 44090
Profit share agency (Wakala)	A company appoints a financial institution as its agent, who invests money given to it by the company in its own business or in third party businesses The company is entitled to a specified amount of the profits resulting from the use of the money by the agent The agent is entitled to any profit in excess of the specified amount Similar to a conventional bank deposit account	Amount provided by the company to the agent	ss 506, 513 CTA 2009, CFM 44100
Investment bonds (Sukuk[1])	Economically equivalent to a marketable security issued by banks, companies or governments to raise finance, and held by financial institutions, pension funds or other corporate or non-corporate investors Most bonds function like conventional debt securities i.e. the investor is assured of an interest-like return and repayment of capital	Amount of the loan which is shown in the accounts prepared under GAAP	ss 507, 513 CTA 2009, CFM 44120

Note
1. The singular is sakk.

B. Amounts

All of the profits and losses relating to loan relationships are subject to corporation tax as income and expenses respectively, no matter whether the company treats them as revenue or as capital. The only **exception** to this is where the worldwide debt cap operates to exempt the income (¶70530+), or where the company is in receipt of exempt income because the EEA payer cannot obtain a domestic deduction.

16160
s 299 TIOPA 2010

The taxable amounts usually reflect the figures in the accounts, although it can become more complicated when exchange movements are involved.

1. Accounting practice

The gains and losses that are included in a corporation tax computation essentially mirror those that are computed for accounts purposes, **providing** an acceptable method has been adopted (in effect, either UK or International GAAP).

16190
s 307 CTA 2009

Most taxable items will **appear in** the company's profit and loss account, but, where appropriate, items in the statement of total recognised gains and losses (or statement of changes in equity where IAS apply) should also be taken into account.

s 308 CTA 2009

All **prior period adjustments** (¶11505+), unless arising from a fundamental error which requires an amended tax return to be filed, should be taken into account for tax purposes.

s 309 CTA 2009;
CFM 33110

ss 311, 312, 455A
CTA 2009;
CFM 39200 +

s 321 CTA 2009;
CFM 33170

[MEMO POINTS]   1. Since 1 January 2005, listed companies are required to use **international accounting standards** (IAS), for the preparation of consolidated accounts (other companies can choose to adopt IAS). To ensure that companies are not unfairly discriminated against when they adopt IAS, special provisions apply to ensure that companies moving to IAS will be treated in a similar manner to those preparing accounts under UK GAAP. The differences are detailed where appropriate. In the rest of this section, references to companies adopting IAS will also include those companies that prepare their accounts under UK GAAP, but adopt FRS 26.

2. Where the accounts **do not comply with GAAP**, the company will still be taxed on the amounts which would have been shown had GAAP compliant accounts been prepared. For example, amounts may be incorrectly debited or credited in an earlier period when they should be included in the accounts for a later period. The later loan relationships computations should be prepared on the basis that correct accounting was used for the earlier period. This is the case even if, viewed in isolation, the accounts for the later period might be said to be in accordance with GAAP.

3. There is an override where **not all profits are recognised in the accounts** (which may happen where IAS are followed and an asset or liability is derecognised). For example, where a credit is not recognised or is offset (such as an interest receipt being offset by an equal and opposite dividend payment), the credit is still brought into account for tax purposes.

Further, as certain tax avoidance schemes have attempted to **exploit this asymmetry** between the accounting and tax regimes, for accounting periods ending after 6 December 2010, where a company is **party to tax avoidance arrangements** (in addition to being a party to a creditor loan relationship):
– all amounts derecognised are still taxable; and
– losses arising from derecognition (other than an actual disposal) are not allowable as a tax deduction.

4. If a debit or credit relating to a loan relationship is **recognised in equity or shareholders' funds** (for example, because of the accounting principle of substance over form), the amount should still be taxed because it is the legal form which is important. However, the timing of the debit or the credit should follow the accounting treatment. For example, where interest paid by the company is treated as a dividend and accounted for on a due and payable basis rather than being accrued, it would be taxed on the due and payable basis.

GAAP

16195   The accounting **options** available to companies depend on whether they are listed or choose to apply fair value accounting:

Comment   In 2005, the methods of accounting for financial instruments were changed under FRS 26. However, in practice, **small companies** using the FRSSE will often not have changed their accounting regime, and so the amortised cost basis will basically give the same results as the old accruals method. See also note 1 at ¶16000 for future developments.

Type of company	Accounting standards which apply	Overview of requirements [1]	Method of accounting
Listed Unlisted and applying fair value accounting	FRS 26, FRS 29 (as well as presentation and disclosure requirements of FRS 25 and FRS 29)	There are four ways of accounting as follows:	
		a. financial assets or liabilities at fair value through profit or loss – assets and liabilities which are either classified as held for trading or are designated by the entity as at fair value through profit or loss upon initial recognition	Fair value
		b. held-to-maturity investments – non-derivative financial assets, with fixed or determinable payments and fixed maturity, that an entity has the positive intention and ability to hold to maturity other than those that: – the entity designates as at fair value through profit or loss upon initial recognition; – the entity designates as available for sale; and – meet the definition of loans and receivables	Amortised cost basis

Type of company	Accounting standards which apply	Overview of requirements [1]	Method of accounting
		c. loans and receivables – non-derivative financial assets with fixed or determinable payments that are not quoted in an active market, other than those: – that the entity intends to sell, immediately or in the near term, and those that are designated as at fair value through profit and loss upon initial recognition; – that are designated as available for sale upon initial recognition; or – for which the holder may not recover substantially all of its initial investment, other than because of credit deterioration, which must be classified as available for sale	Amortised cost basis
		d. available-for-sale financial assets – non-derivative assets that are designated as available for sale, and are not classified as financial assets at fair value through profit or loss, held-to-maturity investments or loans and receivables	Fair value with gains and losses recognised immediately in the statement of total recognised gains and losses [2]
Other unlisted companies not applying the FRSSE	FRS 4, FRS 13 (as well as presentation and disclosure requirements of FRS 25 and FRS 29)	Immediately after issue, debt should be recorded at the amount of net proceeds of the issue i.e. the fair value after deducting issue costs At the end of each accounting period, the amount of the debt is increased by the finance costs for the period and reduced by any payments made in respect of the debt (e.g. interest and any capital payments)	Amortised cost basis
Small companies	FRSSE		

Note:
1. **Full details** of the accounting requirements are given in *Accountancy and Financial Reporting Memo*.
2. The statement of total recognised gains and losses is a primary statement whose purpose is to show the extent to which shareholders' funds have increased or decreased during the year from all gains and losses, whether realised or not. (Some gains may be recognised in one period but realised in another.) Because not all gains and losses will necessarily have flowed through the profit and loss account, to satisfy the requirements of full and proper disclosure, they must be captured and reflected elsewhere.

Measurement

Unless the loan relationship involves connected companies (¶16560+), either of the following methods is acceptable:

16200
s 313 CTA 2009

a. fair value accounting, which requires assets or liabilities to be shown in the company's balance sheet at their fair value (the amount that an independent third party would pay for a debt asset, or the amount that the company would have to pay to a third party to release the debt liability in the profit and loss account). Measurement takes place on acquisition, at each period end, and on disposal; or
b. amortised cost base accounting, which requires the loan asset or liability to be shown in the balance sheet at cost as adjusted for:
– amortisation of any discount or premium, fees for borrowing/lending etc.; and
– any impairment (bad debt), releases or repayments.

MEMO POINTS 1. Where **one of these methods has not been adopted**, the taxable profit or loss must be recomputed using an acceptable basis. Any brought forward amounts are also similarly recomputed if they were not prepared on an acceptable basis.
2. Where a company **changes from GAAP to IAS**, no debits or credits that arise as a result should fall out of account for tax purposes. The main issue would be a difference in the carry forward figure of a loan from the earlier accounting period, and the brought forward figure in the next

SI 2004/3271
reg 3A;
ss 316–319
CTA 2009

CFM 36000 +

accounting period. However, any difference in the carrying value of an asset or liability between the period of change and the previous period can be spread equally over 10 years.
3. When a **company is a partner** of a partnership which is involved in a loan relationship, no account is taken of debits or credits in relation to the loan relationship when calculating the profits of the firm for corporation tax purposes. The credits and debits are determined separately for each company partner, and each must bring into account a share of the debits and credits corresponding to its profit share ratio (¶85370+).

2. Fairly represents

16230
s 307 CTA 2009;
CFM 33020

The credits and debits, when taken together, must fairly represent the company's profits and losses from its loan relationships.

However, certain amounts are dealt with separately under the tax rules, being either ignored or restricted (¶16235).

> ▭ *MEMO POINTS*   1. This rule takes **precedence** over the requirement for GAAP (which is similar to the true and fair override which applies when preparing accounts in general).
> 2. The phrase **taken together** implies that credits and debits are regarded as individual positive or negative entries in the company's accounts, rather than looking at net amounts representing profits and losses.

Exceptions

16235
CFM 33180

The following items are **not brought into account** for tax purposes, or are **restricted**, even where they appear in accounts prepared under GAAP:
– a close company releases or writes off a loan to a participator (¶16540);
– debts are released as part of certain insolvency arrangements, or where there is a debt-for-equity swap (¶16440);
– debits result from the revaluation of debt assets unless fair value accounting applies (¶16240);
– the loan is for an unallowable purpose (¶16500+) or not undertaken at arm's length (¶16510);
– a government investment in a company is written off; or
– losses are imported.

CFM 33240;
s 92 CTA 2010

> ▭ *MEMO POINTS*   1. Under **PFI or government contracts**, a debt may be written off. In this case, no credit arises under the loan relationship rules, because the company's allowable losses will be restricted by the amount released.

s 327 CTA 2009;
CFM 33250

> 2. A **loss is disallowed** if it arises on a loan relationship which is **not subject to UK corporation tax**. For example, the company may have been non-UK resident, or if trading through a UK branch, the loan relationship may not have been held for the purposes of the branch. Only companies using the **amortised cost basis** are affected. Even where the loan relationship is subsequently transferred or sold to another party, any loss must still be restricted.
> If a company purchases an overseas company which has losses arising on loan relationships, those losses will not be available for group relief.

16240
s 324 CTA 2009;
CFM 33210

Revaluation   If a company is a creditor in a loan relationship using the **amortised cost basis**, any general bad debt provision or write down of the loan to the lower of cost or market value will not result in a debit for tax purposes. Only an impairment loss (¶16435) or formal debt release will be recognised.

s 325 CTA 2009

> ▭ *MEMO POINTS*   1. This rule does not affect companies using **fair value** accounting.
> 2. If such a provision or write down is **reversed**, no credit is taxable either.

Summary

16245
s 307 CTA 2009

The following items are **brought into account** under the loan relationship provisions:
a. all interest under the loan relationships (including any interest imputed under the transfer pricing regulations (¶70000+));
b. all profits, gains and losses (including those of a capital nature) arising to the company from the loan relationship;
c. all charges and expenses incurred directly under, or for the purposes of, the company's loan relationships or related transactions; and

d. exchange movements on loan relationship assets (unless they are recognised in the company's statement of recognised gains and losses or statement of changes in equity or matched (¶17415+)).

Where the company uses an **effective interest rate** method, interest, discount and expenses may all be spread over the life of the loan relationship, and it may be that only a single figure appears in the profit and loss account. However, for the purposes of these rules, interest has its own special significance.

Interest

As there is **no statutory definition** of interest, the following case law principles must be relied upon for identifying it:

16250
CFM 33030

– a principal sum must exist (money has been advanced) *Re Euro Hotel (Belgravia) Ltd* [1975];
– interest is the return or compensation for the use of that money which belongs to, or is owed to, another person (because he himself is deprived of its use), and can only arise by virtue of a legal right *Westminster Bank v Riches* [1947]; and
– a voluntary payment cannot be interest, even if it is paid in lieu of interest. *Seaham Harbour Company v Crook* [1931]

The **legal substance** of a payment is of paramount importance (rather than the terminology used in any documentation).

In particular, the items at ¶16120 are included as interest on a loan relationship.

However, interest that is taxed as a **distribution** (for example, a payment dependent on the results of the debtor company), will not be allowed as a loan relationship debit. Loan relationship credits which arise in these circumstances will not be taxed unless they are created by tax avoidance arrangements.

s 465 CTA 2009

Other profits, gains and losses

Other profits and losses on a loan relationship (other than interest and expenses) can **arise** from:

16255
CFM 33050

– the contract terms;
– the accounting treatment; or
– a related transaction (¶16260).

These profits and losses can **include** the following:
– results from ceasing to be a party to the loan relationship (¶16480);
– the results from a debt release;
– changes in the fair value (where the loan relationship is accounted for under fair value accounting);
– impairment losses and their reversal (¶16435+); and
– discounts or premiums.

> EXAMPLE G Ltd owns a security with a nominal value of £50,000. The company paid £46,000 for it (a discount of £4,000), and sells it for £44,000. The loss on sale is £6,000.
> The discount of £4,000 is a credit, and the loss on sale of £6,000 is a debit.

Related transactions A related transaction is any **transfer of a loan relationship**: that is, the acquisition or disposal of any of the rights or liabilities under that relationship. Common examples would be the sale, novation, gift, surrender or release of a debt.

16260
ss 304, 305
CTA 2009

Either the borrower or lender may transfer his obligations under such an arrangement.

> MEMO POINTS 1. The **creation** of a loan relationship is not an acquisition for this purpose. Only the transfer of an existing loan relationship can be an acquisition.
> 2. A **novation** involves substituting a new debt for the original debt but keeping the same lender. It requires agreement of all parties involved in the original debt agreement and commonly occurs in corporate restructuring or takeovers.
> 3. Transfers involving **repos** and stock loans are not treated as related transactions.
> 4. A company that **formally waives** a debt, releasing the debtor from its obligation to pay, is disposing of its rights under the loan relationship, and this is a related transaction.

CFM 31130

5. A debt **write-off** is not a related transaction because the debt is not extinguished. Instead the impairment loss rules apply (¶16435+).

Charges and expenses

16265
s 307 CTA 2009;
CFM 33060

Only charges and expenses **directly** incurred in respect of the items in the following table are allowed.

So **indirect** costs, such as key man insurance premiums and the cost of general investment advice, are not treated as loan relationship debits.

s 329 CTA 2009;

⬒MEMO POINTS⬓ 1. **Abortive expenditure** is allowed if it would have been allowed had the loan actually come into existence.
2. **Guarantee fees** will only be allowed if the loan would not have been advanced without the provision of the guarantee. If this is not the case, relief may be available under the normal trading expense rules, if the expenditure is incurred wholly and exclusively for the purposes of the trade (¶14540+).

s 330 CTA 2009

2. **Pre-trading expenditure** incurred during the 7 years prior to commencement of trade may be treated as a trading debit for the first trading period if it would have been a trading debit if incurred post commencement. The company must elect for this treatment to apply within 2 years from the end of the first accounting period (¶60120).

Situation	Examples
Bringing a loan relationship into existence	Arrangement fees
	Fee or commission for a loan guarantee
	BIS fees for investing surplus cash in a liquidation
Entering into, or giving effect to, a related transaction[1]	Broker's fees on purchase or sale of existing securities
	Legal fees on the transfer of a security
Making payments under a loan relationship or related transaction[1]	Cost of making interest payments
	Early redemption penalties
Taking steps to ensure receipt of payments due under a loan relationship or related transaction[1]	Solicitor's fees incurred in pursuing a debt defaulter
Note: 1. For details of what comprises a related transaction, see ¶16260.	

C. Computation

16295

Once the amounts involved have been established, the treatment of credits and debits (i.e. income and expenditure) arising on loan relationship contracts depends upon whether the items arise in respect of **trading or non-trading transactions**.

Held for the purpose of the trade?

16300
s 298 CTA 2009;
BIM 40805

Many companies will **borrow money** or incur debt for the purpose of the trade: for example, to acquire property or plant, or to expand the business.

However, a much smaller class of company will **lend money** as part of its trade, usually as a bank, insurer or financial trader. Interest and dividends rank as trading receipts only when it is an integral part of the company's business operations to employ capital to produce such income. So, for example, if money is invested in order to be available for the purpose of the company's trade in future years, this does not turn the company into a lender. *Nuclear Electric plc v Bradley* [1996]

1. Trading transactions

Trading debits and credits are included in the computation of profits either as income or expenses. Most of the time, **no adjustment** to trading profits is required. However, if amounts have been capitalised on the balance sheet, they should still be taxed as part of trading profits. The loan relationship rules override the wholly and exclusively basis (¶14540+).

16330
s 297 CTA 2009

> EXAMPLE A Ltd is a small manufacturing company which takes out a loan for £200,000 to fund the acquisition of new machinery. The interest rate is 7% p.a., and the company pays a fee of £2,000 at the start of the loan, as well as additional legal costs of £500. The amortised cost basis of accounting is used.
> As the loan has been taken out for the purposes of the company's trade, it is a trading loan relationship, and no adjustment to the accounting profits is required.

2. Non-trading transactions

A non-trading loan relationship arises when the contract is not entered into for the purpose of a trade.

16350

Common situations where a non-trading relationship arises are:
- bank interest on cash accounts;
- interest on late paid tax;
- an investment company; and
- a property business (either UK or overseas).

Overview

Non-trading items are **pooled**. If the resulting net position is a:
a. credit (income), it is assessable as a non-trading loan relationship credit in the accounting period when it arises; or
b. debit, it is known as a non-trading loan relationship deficit, which can be:
- carried forward against non-trading profits of later accounting periods;
- set off against profits of any kind of the current period;
- set off against non-trading loan relationship credits arising in a period ending within the previous 12 months; or
- surrendered as group relief.

16355
ss 299 – 301
CTA 2009

Carry forward of deficit

In the absence of a claim to relieve the deficit in any other way, it is carried forward by default, and automatically **set against** the company's non-trading profits of future years. The deficit is treated as a deficit of the subsequent accounting period, but it is not aggregated with any other debits or credits of that period.

16360
s 457 CTA 2009

The company can limit the **amount** of deficit which is to be relieved in any particular future period by making a claim within 2 years of the end of the accounting period within which the deficit would otherwise be used. The claim must specify the amount which is not to be set off. Any remaining unrelieved deficit is carried forward until it is utilised.

s 458 CTA 2009

> MEMO POINTS 1. For this purpose, **non-trading profits** are those against which a trading loss cannot be relieved, such as profits from loan relationships, chargeable gains, property income and miscellaneous income.
> 2. It may be **beneficial** to make a claim where a company wishes to preserve entitlement to double tax relief.
> 3. For the restriction which may apply on a **change of ownership**, see ¶60370.

> EXAMPLE B Ltd has overseas income of £100,000 which has suffered overseas tax of £23,000, and property income of £30,000. It has a non-trading loan relationship deficit brought forward of £150,000. Although it would be possible to entirely wipe out the profits for this accounting period, this would waste the double tax relief available on the overseas income. B Ltd therefore makes a claim to

except £120,000 from being set off, and that amount is carried forward to the next accounting period. (150,000 – 30,000)

	£	£
Overseas income	100,000	
Property income	30,000	
		130,000
Non-trading loan deficit (restricted by claim)		(30,000)
PCTCT		100,000
CT (FY2013) @ 23%		23,000
Tax credit relief		(23,000)
CT payable		Nil

Set off against current period profits

16365
ss 459, 461
CTA 2009;
CFM 32060

Provided the company is not a charity, the whole or part of a non-trading loan relationships deficit can be set off against profits of the current accounting period. A claim must be made within 2 years of the end of that accounting period. Note that only the deficit arising in the current period can be set off in this way, so any deficit brought forward is not relevant.

The deficit can be set off against all types of **profits**, trading or non-trading, but the profits concerned must be clearly identified in the claim.

The **order of set off** is as follows:

	£	£
Trading profits	X	
Trading losses b/f	(X)	
		X
Current period deficit		(X)
		X
Property income		X
Property losses		(X)
Current period trade losses		(X)
Trade losses carried back from a later period		(X)
Non-trading loan deficit carried back from a later period		(X)
PCTCT		X

> **EXAMPLE** C Ltd has trading income of £300,000, overseas income of £80,000 which has suffered overseas tax of £11,500, and property income of £40,000. It has a current period non-trading deficit of £400,000.
> C Ltd makes a claim to offset £370,000 of the deficit, leaving £30,000 to carry forward.
>
> | | Trading £ | Property £ | Overseas £ | Total £ |
> |---|---|---|---|---|
> | Overseas income | 300,000 | 40,000 | 80,000 | 420,000 |
> | Non-trading loan relationship deficit | (300,000) | (40,000) | (30,000) | (370,000) |
> | PCTCT | - | - | 50,000 | 50,000 |
> | CT (FY2013) @ 23% | | | 11,500 | 11,500 |
> | Tax credit relief | | | (11,500) | (11,500) |
> | CT payable | | | Nil | Nil |

Carry back of deficit

16370
ss 459, 462, 463
CTA 2009

CFM 32070

Provided the company is not a charity, it can make a claim to carry back a non-trading deficit to the preceding 12 month period. The deficit is **set against** non-trading profits arising from loan relationships that are otherwise unrelieved.

The **amount** that must be claimed is the **lower of**:
a. the deficit remaining after any amount surrendered as group relief and after any claim for a current period set off (¶16365); and

b. the profits available for relief in the preceding 12 months: that is, the non-trading profits arising from loan relationships and derivative contracts after any amounts claimed that relate to the following:
– deficits of the same period;
– losses or deficits from an earlier period (that is, a period before the accounting period of the deficit which is to be carried back);
– trading losses set against profits of the same or preceding year; and
– charitable donations.

If the company has an **investment business** (¶6000+), capital allowances and management expenses also reduce the profits available for offset.

MEMO POINTS   1. If there is **more than one accounting period**, the later period gets relief before the earlier period.
2. If an **accounting period begins before** the start of the 12 month period, profits must be apportioned.

EXAMPLE D Ltd has the following results:

	Year 5 £	Year 6 £	Year 7 £
Trading profits	300,000	350,000	150,000
Trading loss brought forward	(50,000)		
Property income	20,000	21,000	21,000
Chargeable gains			80,000
Loan relationship credits	10,000	20,000	10,000
Loan relationship debits	(12,000)	(10,000)	(300,000)

First the net position of the loan relationships must be determined:

	Year 5 £	Year 6 £	Year 7 £
Loan relationship credits	10,000	20,000	10,000
Loan relationship debits	(12,000)	(10,000)	(300,000)
Net position	(2,000)	10,000	(290,000)

In Year 5, the deficit could be set against any type of profits after relief for trading losses has been claimed, but D Ltd chooses instead to carry it forward.
In Year 6, the deficit carried forward from Year 5 is set off against the property income.
In Year 7, the deficit wipes out all profits in that year, and £39,000 is available for carry back to Year 6. However only £8,000 of profits are available for set off in Year 6, being the loan relationship credit less the deficit brought forward from Year 5. (10,000 – 2,000)

	Year 5 £	Year 6 £	Year 7 £
Trading profits as relieved by losses	250,000	350,000	150,000
Property income	20,000	21,000	21,000
Net loan relationship credits	-	10,000	-
Chargeable gains	-	-	80,000
	270,000	381,000	251,000
Carried forward deficit	-	(2,000)	-
Current period deficit claim	-	-	(251,000)
	270,000	379,000	Nil
Carry back deficit claim	-	(8,000)	-
PCTCT	270,000	371,000	Nil

Deficit memorandum

	Year 5 £	Year 7 £
Net deficit	2,000	290,000
Current period claim	-	(251,000)
	-	39,000
Carry forward – set off	(2,000)	-
Carry back claim	-	(8,000)
	Nil	31,000

So a deficit of £31,000 is available to carry forward against non-trading profits of future periods.

Group relief

16375
s 99 CTA 2010;
CFM 32090

A group or consortium claim for non-trading loan relationship deficits falls within the general rules for group relief (¶66050+), and requires a 75% holding in each group company (whether direct or indirect). There is no requirement for the **surrendering company** to utilise any of the deficit before the group relief is claimed.

A restriction may apply to **impairment losses** (¶16435) when consortium relief is involved. However, there is no such restriction on group relief because no impairment losses are allowed on loans between group members (they are connected companies).

> ⬛ MEMO POINTS   1. For this purpose, non-trading loan relationship deficits include debits on **derivative** contracts.
> 2. If a company is receiving group relief from a **consortium member**, see ¶16445+.

> ⬛ EXAMPLE   E Ltd is a member of the EFG group and has the following results:
>
> | | Year 9 £ | Year 10 £ | Year 11 £ |
> |---|---|---|---|
> | Trading income | 4,000 | 20,000 | 30,000 |
> | Net loan relationship credits | | 8,000 | |
> | Net loan relationship debits | (10,000) | | (5,000) |
>
> In Year 9, E Ltd could surrender its deficit to another group member, make a claim to set it off against its trading income or carry it forward.
> Assuming that E Ltd claims the current year set-off, it then has £6,000 unrelieved.
> In Year 11, the deficit of £5,000 could be group relieved, set off against current year income, or carried back. However, the amount to be carried back is limited to £2,000 because the unrelieved deficit of £6,000 brought forward has priority. (8,000 – 6,000)

D. Special situations

Summary

16405

Situation	¶¶
Impairment losses and debt releases	¶16435+
Termination of a loan relationship	¶16480
Unallowable purpose	¶16500+
Close companies	¶16540
Connected parties	¶16560+
Transfers between groups	¶69405+

1. Impairment losses (bad debts)

16435
s 307 CTA 2009;
CFM 33220

Accounting standards require that at each balance sheet date, companies must assess financial assets and trade debts for recoverability and impairment. Any impairment losses or reversals are recognised in the profit and loss account and taxed as a corresponding debit or credit, unless the parties to the loan relationship are connected (¶16630).

A **provision** is not an allowable impairment loss unless it is based on objective evidence of an event or circumstance that will reduce future cash flows, and the reduction can be reliably estimated (¶11895+).

However, impairment losses are not restricted to cases where the creditor feels default is probable (or has in fact occurred), but can extend to situations where there is data indicating that the **estimated future cash flows** from a group of assets will decrease.

> **EXAMPLE**   F Ltd has statistical evidence that a rise in mortgage rates correlates with an increase in credit default by its customers. In Year 1, mortgage rates increase and F Ltd recognises an impairment loss. This loss will be allowable for tax purposes, even though it cannot be attributed to individual customers.

Debt releases

In the rare circumstance where a creditor releases a debtor from the obligation to pay, **any amounts credited** in the accounts are usually taxable as a loan relationship credit unless the parties are connected (¶16630). However, no taxable income will arise where the **debtor uses** the amortised cost basis and any of the following situations apply as shown in the table below.

16440
s 322 CTA 2009;
CFM 33190

Comment   Under a debt release, a creditor company has formally agreed to waive all or part of the debt, usually signing a deed of waiver. So legally the debtor owes nothing to the creditor.

Situation	Details	Reference
Release is part of a **statutory insolvency arrangement**[1]	A statutory insolvency arrangement is where the debtor company is released from its liabilities under any of the following arrangements with its creditors, and this allows the debtor company to continue trading and avoid liquidation: – a voluntary arrangement under the Insolvency Act 1986, Schedule 4 or 5 to the Bankruptcy (Scotland) Act 1985 or the Insolvency (Northern Ireland) Order 1989; – a compromise or arrangement under Part 26 of the Companies Act 2006 or the Northern Ireland equivalent (substituted with effect from 6 April 2008); or – any similar arrangement under the domestic law of an overseas state	s 323 CTA 2009
Debtor meets **insolvency conditions** and the debtor is not connected (¶16560+) to the creditor	The insolvency conditions[1] are met if the debtor is either: – in liquidation; – in administration; – in administrative receivership; – subject to the appointment of a provisional liquidator under s 135 Insolvency Act 1986 or the Northern Ireland equivalent; or – in any of the above situations under the domestic law of an overseas state	s 323 CTA 2009
Release is in consideration of ordinary shares issued by the debtor i.e. a **debt-equity swap** Excludes a release of relevant rights where a company acquires the impaired debt of a connected company (¶16650+)	Ordinary share capital means any share capital apart from fixed rate preference shares Most debt/equity swaps will represent a bargain at arm's length, although the equity will currently be worth less than the debt which it replaces (however, as the debtor can continue to trade, the creditor may enjoy an appreciation in value over time)[2] The difference in value is credited to the share premium account unless IAS has been adopted, when the difference is recognised in the income statement No loan relationship credit arises where the creditor is given option to acquire shares (which would probably be exercised) or where there is a delay between the debt release and the equity issue As a loan is being converted into shares, this has chargeable gains implications[3]	s 322(4) CTA 2009, CFM 33200

Note:
1. For **details** of insolvency, see *Company Law Memo*.
2. Whether the **consideration** for the debt release is actually shares will be determined on the facts of each case. In particular, the disregard will not apply if the creditor has no interest in being a shareholder in the debtor company and is releasing the debt gratuitously, whilst the shares are issued with the purpose of obtaining a tax advantage for the debtor company. For example, where a £100,000 loan is released for 1,000 shares worth less than £10,000 and the creditor then sells the shares almost immediately to existing shareholders, it is likely that HMRC would mount a challenge.
3. A loan relationship is treated as a **qualifying corporate bond** (QCB). When a QCB is exchanged for a non-QCB, there is a disposal of the QCB and any credit or debit must be brought into account.

Consortia

16445
ss 364–371
CTA 2009;
CFM 35610

As a consortium company and its members are not treated as connected companies, an impairment loss may be recognised on any loan relationship between them.

However, the debit resulting from an impaired loan to a consortium company is **restricted** when a consortium member (or another member of its group) also claims consortium relief. Broadly, the impairment debit is restricted to the **higher of** the impairment loss or the consortium relief claim. The consortium and group members are looked at collectively, taking into account all loan relationships involving the consortium company and its members, and all consortium relief claimed from the consortium company.

> MEMO POINTS 1. A **consortium company** is a:
> – trading company owned directly by the consortium; or
> – trading company that is a 90% subsidiary of a holding company owned directly by the consortium; or
> – holding company owned directly by the consortium.
> For full details, see ¶65350+.
> 2. The **creditor** may be a consortium member or a member of its group.
> 3. The **debtor** may be the consortium company or, where relevant, its subsidiary.

s 366 CTA 2009

> 4. Where a **debt is released**, this should result in a loan relationship credit being recognised by the consortium company, in which case no restriction to the member's loan relationship debit is necessary.

16450

The provisions apply as shown in the following table. Where **two or more companies are affected** by a restriction on impairment losses or reduction of taxable credits on a recovery, apportionment applies.

Situation	Details	Reference	See example
Current period impairment debits	Reduced by any amount of consortium relief claimed in the same group accounting period [1] Net consortium debit [2] cannot be reduced below nil	s 365 CTA 2009	1, 2
Impairment recoveries	A corresponding reduction is made for any subsequent impairment recoveries by the amount of any restrictions already made This ensures that where there has been a previous restriction of the amount of impairment losses, the otherwise taxable recovery is reduced or eliminated	s 367 CTA 2009	3
Current period consortium relief	Claim is limited by any excess impairment debits from earlier periods which have not already been reduced by prior consortium relief claims However, only the amount by which the consortium relief claim exceeds the impairment debits of the same period is restricted	s 368 CTA 2009	4
Current period consortium relief exceeds current period impairment debits	Where consortium relief exceeds impairment debits, it is carried forward, and potentially restricts future impairment loss debits (so a consortium relief claimant cannot avoid the restriction just by deferring the impairment loss to another accounting period)	s 369 CTA 2009	5

Note:
1. A **group accounting period** is any accounting period of the consortium member or a corresponding period of a group member where:
– those two accounting periods coincide;
– the accounting period of the member covers more than half the accounting period of the group member; or
– the accounting period of the member includes part of the accounting period of the group member but the remaining part does not fall within any accounting period of the member.
2. The **net consortium debit** is the excess of the impairment debits over impairment credits (i.e. when an impairment provision is reversed) for the group.

EXAMPLE

1. Reduction of impairment loss

A Ltd is a consortium company owned 50% by B Ltd and 50% by X Ltd.
B Ltd is a member of a 75% group, involving C Ltd and D Ltd.
X Ltd is also a member of a 75% group, involving Y Ltd and Z Ltd.

B Group

The following amounts are loaned to A Ltd:

Lender Details

	£	£
B Ltd	100,000	
Impairment loss recognised		(50,000)
C Ltd	30,000	
D Ltd	60,000	
Net consortium debit		(50,000)

The net consortium debit is £50,000 (being the impairment loss which is not recognised as a loan relationship credit by A Ltd).

The B Group claimed consortium relief of £51,000, and so the impairment debit is reduced to nil, because the consortium relief exceeds the net consortium debit. (£51,000 compared to £50,000)

X Group

Y Ltd made a loan of £100,000 to A Ltd but has recognised an impairment loss of £60,000. So the net consortium debit for the X Group is £60,000.

The X Group claimed consortium relief of £51,000, and so the impairment loss is reduced to £9,000. (60,000 – 51,000)

2. Apportionment where more than one company has an impairment loss

If X Ltd in example 1 also made a loan of £100,000 to A Ltd in the same year, and recognised an impairment loss of £30,000, then the total net consortium debit for the X Group would be £90,000. (60,000 + 30,000)

The consortium relief claimed is £51,000, which means the impairment losses are reduced to £39,000. (90,000 – 51,000)

These need to be apportioned between X Ltd and Y Ltd so that each company obtains an impairment debit as follows:

		£
X Ltd	$\dfrac{30,000 \times 39,000}{90,000}$	13,000
Y Ltd	$\dfrac{60,000 \times 39,000}{90,000}$	26,000
		39,000

3. Recovery of debt in future year

In Year 1, F Ltd (a consortium member) recognises an impairment loss of £50,000 on a loan to G Ltd (a consortium company). In the same year, consortium relief of £55,000 is surrendered from G Ltd to F Ltd.

In Year 2, £40,000 of the debt is recovered from G Ltd.

The tax treatment will be as follows:

Year 1: The impairment loss is reduced to nil and consortium relief is given on the full amount of the £55,000.

Year 2: The £40,000 will be set against the previously disallowed impairment loss and consequently will not be a taxable receipt for F Ltd. The balance of £10,000 can be carried forward for offset against future recoveries. (50,000 – 40,000)

4. Excess impairment loss from earlier period

Instead of the situation in example 3. above, assume that this time F Ltd recognises an impairment loss for Year 1 of £40,000, and consortium relief of £15,000 is surrendered from G Ltd to F Ltd.

In Year 2, F Ltd recognises a further impairment loss of £20,000 and consortium relief of £30,000 is surrendered from G Ltd to F Ltd.

The tax treatment will be as follows:

Year 1: The impairment loss is reduced to £25,000 and consortium relief given on the £15,000. (40,000 – 15,000)

Year 2: The impairment loss is reduced to nil by set off against the consortium relief. The consortium relief is reduced to £20,000 by set off against the impairment loss of the prior year. The reduction

is only £10,000 because this is the amount left after setting consortium relief against the current year impairment loss. (30,000 – 20,000)
So £15,000 of excess impairment loss is carried forward to limit future consortium relief claims.

5. Excess group relief carried forward
Taking F Ltd and G Ltd again, this time F Ltd recognises an impairment loss of £100,000 in Year 1, and consortium relief of £32,000 is surrendered from G Ltd to F Ltd.
In Year 2, G Ltd surrenders £130,000 of consortium relief.
In Year 3, F Ltd recognises a further impairment loss of £70,000, but G Ltd does not surrender any losses.
The tax treatment will be as follows:
Year 1: The impairment loss is reduced to £68,000 and consortium relief given on the £32,000.
Year 2: The consortium relief is reduced to £62,000 by set off against the impairment loss of the prior year. (130,000 – 68,000)
Year 3: Although there is no current year consortium relief claim, consortium relief of £62,000 has been carried forward from Year 2, which reduces F Ltd's impairment debit to £8,000. (70,000 – 62,000)

---

2. Termination of a loan relationship

16480   A company may cease to be a party to a loan relationship because of any of the following reasons:

Reason	Tax consequences	Reference
Ceasing to be party to a loan relationship (by sale or novation) and consideration deferred or contingent	Company brings in debits and credits in the accounting periods following disposal as if the loan relationship still existed Tax treatment depends on the circumstances in the accounting period before disposal: if the loan was held for a non-trading purpose, the debits and credits will be treated as arising from a non-trading loan relationship	s 331 CTA 2009, CFM 33280
Ceasing to be UK resident or loan relationship transferred to non-UK part of the company	Deemed disposal of all a company's loan relationships at their fair value immediately before ceasing to be UK resident, and immediate reacquisition at the same value Resulting credits or debits are brought into account under the normal rules unless the main purpose of the company migration is tax avoidance when any debits may be disallowed (¶16500)	ss 333, 334 CTA 2009, CFM 33300
Repos and stock lending where a company has ceased to be party to a loan relationship but continues to recognise amounts in respect of that relationship in determining its profit or loss	The credits and debits are accounted for under the loan relationship rules	s 332 CTA 2009, CFM 33290

EXAMPLE   A Ltd manufactures cruise ships, and issues debt securities to B Ltd which are redeemable on the completion of a new ship. In the meantime, B Ltd sells the securities to C Ltd, but the full consideration will be dependent on the amount paid out by A Ltd.
B Ltd will continue to recognise income when it is no longer a party to the loan relationship, and the tax treatment of that income will depend on what would have happened had the consideration been received at the date of sale.

---

3. Unallowable purpose

16500
ss 441, 442
CTA 2009

There is an anti-avoidance rule which disallows debits which can, on a just and reasonable apportionment, be **attributed to** a loan relationship or related transaction (¶16260) which has an unallowable purpose i.e. a non-business purpose or a main purpose of securing a tax advantage.

Further, transactions which are not carried out at arm's length are subject to a separate rule.

The table below shows how the unallowable purpose **rule is applied** by HMRC:

16505
CFM 38180, 38190

Situation	Unallowable purposes	Allowable purposes
A company is able to obtain relief for the same expenditure or loss on the borrowing in more than one jurisdiction	If it has uncommercial features, or where relief might be available more than once on the same costs (taking the overall position of a company or group into account)	Commercial transaction No double relief claimed
Borrowing from an exempt body (e.g. a pension fund)	Uncommercial arrangements	Even if connected with borrower so long as commercial transaction
Borrowing to fund a repurchase of its shares	Structuring the arrangement so as to obtain a tax advantage for any person	Amount borrowed is limited by market forces No tax advantage motive
Borrowing from a third party by one group member which is then lent to other UK resident group members	Arrangement obtains more than one deduction for the costs of the borrowing (loans are not taken out for purely commercial reasons) Lending company does not expect to make a pre-tax profit (e.g. lending at a rate lower than the cost of the third party borrowing)	Borrowing undertaken for the commercial purposes of the group Group only obtains one deduction for the costs of the loan
Where a debit in one group company is matched by an equal and opposite credit (which is fully taxed) in another group company for the same loan relationship	Funding is used to obtain an advantage (e.g. where the credit is set off by losses or management expenses which could not otherwise be relieved)	No tax advantage is obtained
Write off of a loan	If the loan was not taken out for a commercial purpose (e.g. the company made an interest-free loan to a director's polo club funded by third party borrowing – no costs associated with either loan would be allowed as a loan relationship debit unless there was also a commercial motive (such as advertising) when a just and reasonable apportionment should be made)	Commercial transaction
Transactions or arrangements which have the main purpose of securing loan relationship debits for repayments of loan principal	Convoluted arrangements where a loan is taken out by a group member from a third party, but payments are made to the third party by another group member which effectively reduces the amount borrowed by the group, but the borrowing company can still obtain a loan relationship debit for the original loan	n/a

Transactions not at arm's length

16510
s 444 CTA 2009;
CFM 38400

With certain exceptions, where any disposal or acquisition of a loan relationship is not undertaken at arm's length, any debits or credits brought into account (either **at the time** of the transaction or in the future) are ignored for tax purposes. Instead, the company must calculate the credits and debits as though the transaction had been carried out at arm's length. Note that the general transfer pricing provisions take precedence over this rule.

The **exceptions** are as follows:
– when the loan relationship is initially created (although the general transfer pricing provisions may require an adjustment (¶70655+));
– when a company buys a debt at undervalue (although the vendor will be required to make an adjustment); and
– intra-group transactions (¶69405+).

---

4. Close companies

16540
s 321A CTA 2009;
CFM 33180

No loan relationship debit will arise where a close company **releases or writes off** a loan, or any part of a loan, made to a participator on or after 24 March 2010.

For details of loans to participators, see ¶75575+.

Comment   **Directors' loans** are often overdrawn which can result in a penalty tax for the company (¶75750+). A loan write off by the company is one way of avoiding this penalty tax, and in the past, this had the added advantage of obtaining a loan relationship debit. Dividends may now be a more attractive method of clearing an overdrawn loan, although a write-off may still be more tax efficient than salary or bonus payments.

> ☐ *MEMO POINTS*   1. Broadly, a close company is one which is **controlled** by five or fewer shareholders or by any number of its directors.
> 2. A **participator** is any person having an interest in the capital or income of the company, specifically including a person who:
> – possesses or is entitled to acquire issued share capital or voting rights in the company;
> – is a loan creditor of the company;
> – possesses or is entitled to acquire a right to receive or participate in distributions of the company, or in any amounts payable by the company (in cash or kind) to loan creditors by way of premium or redemption; or
> – is entitled to secure that income or assets (whether present or future) of the company will be applied directly or indirectly for their benefit.
> 3. Relief for **interest paid late** (more than 12 months after the end of the accounting period) may be delayed when a close company is the debtor in a loan relationship and the creditor is a participator or associate (¶16610).
> 4. There is a special rule which applies to **deeply discounted securities** (¶16695) issued by close companies.

---

5. Connected parties

16560
CFM 35020

The loan relationship rules have specific requirements in relation to connected companies as shown in the following table. The definition of connected depends on the particular requirement.

s 466 CTA 2009

> ☐ *MEMO POINTS*   1. Companies are **defined** as connected if, during the accounting period, one has control of the other, or both are under the control of the same person. The relationship between a consortium owned company and a consortium member does not constitute a connected party relationship for this purpose.

s 472 CTA 2009

> 2. **Control** requires either:
> – a person to have the power to secure that the affairs of the company are conducted in accordance with his wishes by means of holding shares or the possession of voting power (in the company or any other company); or
> – powers conferred by the Articles of Association or any other document.
> 3. Where a **company is a partner** and the partnership is involved in a loan relationship with the company, see ¶85455.

Situation	Definition of connected	¶¶
Required to use amortised cost basis	A company has control of the other, or both are under the control of the same person, at any time during the accounting period	¶16580+
Restricted relief for late paid interest	As above plus: – one company holding a major interest in another; – participation under the close company rules; and – a connection with an occupational pension scheme	¶16605+
Restricted relief for impairment losses	As for amortised cost basis	¶16630+
Relief for discounted securities postponed	As for amortised cost basis	¶16685+
Group relief for non-trading deficits	75% group i.e. holding company has 75% interest in all group companies, whether held directly or indirectly	¶16375

MEMO POINTS The **former anti-avoidance provisions** in this area, relating to non-commercial rates of return and so-called hybrid securities, were repealed with effect from 18 July 2011. They were replaced by the group mismatch scheme provisions (¶69490+).

a. Calculating the amounts

Subject to one exception (¶16585), if two companies are connected, both must use the amortised cost basis for computing the tax consequences of their loan relationship, irrespective of the accounting methods used in their financial statements.

16580
ss 348, 349
CTA 2009

This also applies where the connected party stands in the position of creditor or debtor by way of a series of loan relationships. Note that there can still be a series of loan relationships where **partnerships or individuals** are involved.

EXAMPLE
1. A Ltd controls B Ltd. C Ltd is not connected to either company.
If A Ltd lends £20,000 to C Ltd, and C Ltd lends £20,000 to B Ltd, this results in a loan relationship between connected companies (i.e. A Ltd and B Ltd through C Ltd).

2. D Ltd controls G Ltd. D Ltd lends £10,000 to Mr E, who lends it to Mr F, who lends it to G Ltd. Although Mr E and Mr F cannot be parties to a loan relationship, if a company were to hypothetically replace them, a loan relationship would exist in respect of each money debt.
Therefore G Ltd is indirectly a debtor to D Ltd's loan, and a loan relationship involving connected parties exists.

Financial traders

The only **exception** arises when the creditor in a loan relationship is a financial trader. The creditor may compute its tax position using the fair value basis if the following conditions are satisfied:

16585
s 469 CTA 2009

a. the company must buy and sell debt assets as an integral part of its trade (or, in the case of an insurance company, its basic life assurance and general annuity business);
b. the company must have bought that particular debt as part of that trade;
c. the debt must be listed on a recognised stock exchange (¶95320) at the end of the period, or be a security redeemable within 12 months of issue;
d. similar debt assets must be beneficially owned by third parties (similar means they are treated as the same kind by a recognised stock exchange, or would be so treated if listed); and
e. third parties must beneficially own at least 70% of the company's debt assets (although there is a relaxation for a total of 3 months in every accounting period, which reflects the

fact that a company may be connected to a securities dealer who takes a while to offload the company's loan stock).

b. Late paid interest

16605
ss 373, 379
CTA 2009

Most companies involved in a **loan relationship with another company** will not be affected by this rule as it only takes effect where a company creditor is located in a tax haven.

Interest is normally recognised as a loan relationship debit on an accruals basis, and not when it is paid. Connected parties could therefore obtain relief for debits without ever becoming taxable on the corresponding credits, particularly where the **creditor is an individual** (including a partnership comprising some individuals), a **pension scheme or trust**.

If interest is paid late (not paid within 12 months of the end of the accounting period in which it accrues) and no loan relationship credit is brought into account by the creditor, the loan relationship debit is postponed until payment is made.

CFM 35830

⌐ MEMO POINTS ¬   1. Payment may be made by **book entry** (for example, to the intercompany account) provided the paying company has enough funds available and the recipient is free to draw on those funds unconditionally.
2. A loan relationship **credit is brought into account** when it is recognised for tax purposes: for example, when. the credit is chargeable but is relieved by debits or group relief, or an impairment loss has been adjusted for. It is not necessary for tax to be paid in order for the credit to be brought into account.
3. The late interest rule also applies where the connected party stands in the position of creditor or debtor by way of a **series of loan relationships**.

⌐ EXAMPLE ¬   A Ltd owns 35% of B Ltd, and C Ltd owns the remaining shares. A Ltd has loaned £10,000 at an interest rate of 8% to B Ltd. B Ltd is unable to make the interest payments and A Ltd provides for an impairment loss against the interest.
As A Ltd does not control B Ltd the impairment loss is allowable. A Ltd is still recognising the interest due to it even though the debit arising from the impairment cancels out the credit from the interest. So B Ltd can still obtain a loan relationship debit on the interest as it accrues.

Scope

16610
ss 374 – 378
CTA 2009

Subject to the **overriding requirement** that any company creditor has to be resident or effectively managed in a non-qualifying territory for the late interest rule to apply, the following situations could be affected:
– the creditor is a close company participator (or connected to a participator);
– the lender is a company and either it has a major interest in the borrower or the borrower has a major interest in it; or
– the lender is the trustee of a retirement scheme and the borrowing company is either the scheme employer, or is connected to, or has a major interest in, the scheme employer.

s 374 CTA 2009

⌐ MEMO POINTS ¬   1. A **non-qualifying territory** means a country with which the UK does not have a double tax agreement containing a non-discrimination clause (one under which nationals of both states must be treated equally in relation to tax). **Residence** in a qualifying territory is determined under that territory's domestic laws.

s 375 CTA 2009

2. Except where collective investment schemes are involved, the close company rule takes effect when the **debtor company is a close company** (¶75050+) and the creditor is any of the following:
a. a participator (¶75355+) in the debtor company, including any loan creditor of the company (however, a person is not a participator if they are only a loan creditor, having no other rights or interest);
b. an associate (¶75390+) of a person who is a participator;
c. a company which is controlled by a participator of the debtor company (or in which he has a major interest);
d. a person who controls a company which is a participator of the debtor company; or
e. the associates or controlled companies of the person in **d**. above.

s 376 CTA 2009

The late paid interest rule has **no effect** where all of the following criteria are satisfied:
– the debtor company is a small or medium sized enterprise (¶70050+);

– the creditor is not resident in a non-qualifying territory i.e. a country with which the UK does not have a double tax agreement containing a non-discrimination clause; and either
– the debtor company is only close because of rights being attributed to another of the partners in a collective investment scheme limited partnership; or
– the creditor is a collective investment scheme limited partnership (or would be if it was not a company).

This exclusion means that venture capital investors can loan money to companies which they also invest in.

3. A **collective investment scheme** is any arrangement made or offered by an investment manager under which the contributions, or payments, made by the investors are pooled and managed with a view to obtaining profits and income.

4. The **major interest** rule affects situations where A and B together control C, with each having a 40% or greater interest. The interests of A and B would include those of any companies connected with them (companies controlled or under common control).

s 473 CTA 2009

EXAMPLE

1. Mr D lends £200,000 to E Ltd, a close company.
If Mr D is not a shareholder in E Ltd, he is not connected to the company.
However, if Mr D only owns one ordinary share of the 3,000 issued, he is a participator and is connected.

2. Mr F lends £200,000 to H Ltd, a wholly owned subsidiary of another company, G Ltd. Mr F owns one ordinary share of the 3,000 issued in G Ltd.
Mr F is a participator in H Ltd whether or not G Ltd is close.

3. A plc and B plc are both listed, and each has a 45% interest in C Ltd, with D Inc holding the remaining 10% of the shares. Each shareholder lends £50,000 to C Ltd.
C Ltd is not a close company because it is controlled by non-close companies.
A plc and B plc both have a major interest in C Ltd.
Although D Inc together with either A plc or B plc controls C Ltd, it does not have a 40% interest, and so it is not connected to C Ltd.

4. The EFG partnership lends £50,000 to H Ltd, a wholly owned company, and interest of £5,000 p.a. is payable. H Ltd defaults on the interest payment and a delay of more than 12 months after the accounting period end occurs.
The partnership is comprised of:

	Profit share ratio
Mr E	10%
F Ltd	42%
G Ltd	48%

H Ltd is not controlled by either F Ltd or G Ltd, but it is a close company.
F Ltd and G Ltd both have a major interest in H Ltd.
However, F Ltd and G Ltd are both UK resident, and so there is no restriction on the debit resulting from the interest due to those companies.
Mr E, being an individual, is not within the loan relationship rules, and so the interest due on his portion of the loan will not result in a debit. For this purpose, Mr E is deemed to have lent H Ltd £5,000, and so H Ltd's loan relationship debit will be restricted by £500 until payment is made. (5,000 @ 10%)

5. A Ltd is a subsidiary of B Ltd, and has an occupational pension scheme for its employees. B Ltd borrows £50,000 from the scheme.
As A Ltd and B Ltd are connected (because B Ltd controls A Ltd) the late interest rule would apply to the loan.

---

c. Impairment losses and debt releases

Subject to certain exceptions, where a loan to a connected debtor goes bad, and the creditor company either recognises an impairment loss or releases the connected debtor from the loan, no loan relationship debit is available to the creditor company, and no credit is taxable on the debtor company. This rule primarily exists to prevent double relief for the same economic loss as well as encouraging equity funding of subsidiaries.

Note that exchange gains or losses are not affected by this rule.

16630
s 353 CTA 2009

s 354 CTA 2009

The **exceptions** (¶16635+) are:
- debt-equity swaps;
- insolvent creditors; and
- deemed releases taxable on the debtor when an impaired loan is acquired or the parties become connected.

Where a company makes a loan to an **unconnected party**, it will receive the usual relief for impairment losses. If the **companies subsequently become connected**, there is no relief for impairment losses that arise in:
- the accounting period in which the two companies become connected; or
- in subsequent periods.

There is no requirement to write back the relief already given. If debts which were impaired or written off before connection are recovered, this will result in a taxable loan relationship credit. (See also the deemed release rules at ¶16650+.)

> ⬛ MEMO POINTS ⬛   1. An impairment loss is essentially just a bad debt, **defined** as a debit relating to an irrecoverable amount of the loan.
>
> s 360 CTA 2009   2. Where no debit was allowed for an **impairment** loss, its **reversal** (when the bad debt becomes recoverable again) does not result in a credit.
>
> s 355 CTA 2009   3. Where the creditor and debtor **cease to be connected** (for example, following the a sale of a company), the usual rules apply from the start of the accounting period after the connection is broken. A loan relationship debit can thus be recognised for any impairment loss arising since the companies became unconnected. However, no relief is available for any impairment loss or release of a debt that relates back to the time when the companies were connected.
>
> 4. If the creditor **sells the debt** while connected with the debtor, thereby realising the loss, no loan relationship debit arises (the same rules apply as if the loan relationship still existed between the connected companies).
>
> 5. There are special rules for **consortium companies** (¶16445).

Debt-equity swaps

16635
s 356 CTA 2009

Where a **debtor is in difficulties**, a creditor may accept shares in the debtor instead of a repayment. This can result in the debtor and creditor becoming connected.

Where the following **conditions** are met, any impairment loss in connection with the debt-equity swap is allowed in the accounting period when it occurs:
- the creditor must treat the liability as discharged;
- the debt is swapped for ordinary shares (any share capital apart from fixed rate preference shares) in the debtor; and
- the creditor was not connected to the debtor before the swap took place.

No **further debits** relating to impairment losses involving that debtor company can be recognised by the creditor company, because the companies are now connected.

> ⬛ EXAMPLE ⬛
> 1. A Ltd loans £20,000 to B Ltd, an unconnected company. After 2 years, B Ltd is unable to repay the loan, and A Ltd agrees to swap £5,000 of the loan for 60% of the shares in B Ltd and release the remaining £15,000.
> As A Ltd and B Ltd are unconnected before the swap, A Ltd obtains a loan relationship debit of £15,000 for the debt release.
>
> 2. If A Ltd instead swapped £3,000 of the loan for a 20% shareholding and released £4,000, this would not result in A Ltd and B Ltd becoming connected. So the release would obtain relief.
> In the next accounting period, A Ltd then agrees to a further swap involving £4,000 of the loan for a 40% shareholding and £3,000 is released. The companies do become connected as A Ltd now controls 60% of B Ltd. A Ltd obtains a loan relationship debit of £3,000 but any subsequent release will not obtain relief.

Insolvent creditors

16640
s 357 CTA 2009;
CFM 35410

If the creditor becomes insolvent, impairment relief is still available for any **amounts accruing after** the date of the proceedings, whether or not the creditor continues to be connected to the debtor company. Impairment loss relief is not available before that date.

To be insolvent, the creditor must be:
- in insolvent liquidation;
- in insolvent administration;
- in insolvent administrative receivership;
- subject to the appointment of a provisional liquidator under section 135 Insolvency Act 1986 or the Northern Ireland equivalent; or
- in equivalent circumstances to any of the above under the domestic law of an overseas state.

If a creditor obtains a loan relationship debit for impairment in the above circumstances, no credit is assessed on the **debtor** provided the liability is released during a period in which the amortised cost basis is used.

s 359 CTA 2009

Insolvent debtors

Insolvency may **break the connection** between the creditor and the debtor, in which case any debt release is not taxable by virtue of the usual rules applying to insolvent debtors (¶16440).

16645
ss 322, 358
CTA 2009

Where the **connection remains**, the release will not result in a credit under the usual rules for connected companies.

Deemed releases

There are two cases in which the debtor is taxable on a loan relationship credit when either:
- a **connected creditor** acquires impaired debt to which the debtor is party (¶16660); or
- **unconnected parties** to an impaired debt become connected (¶16655).

16650
s 362 CTA 2009

> MEMO POINTS **Arrangements** are entered into with the main purpose of reducing the amount of the deemed release calculated in accordance with either ¶16655 or ¶16660. Such a scheme is statutorily effective if entered into on or after 27 February 2012. This rule also applies to arrangements entered into before 27 February 2012 if the deemed release would have occurred on or after that date.

s 363A CTA 2009

Companies becoming connected Where there is a difference between the values recognised in respect of the debt in the accounts of the debtor and creditor, there will be a deemed release of all or part of the loan on the date that the parties become connected. This results in a tax charge on the debtor, whether or not the creditor recognises a corresponding impairment adjustment.

16655
s 362 CTA 2009

The amount of the deemed release on the debtor is given by the following formula:

Amount of the debt shown in debtor's accounts – Carrying value of the debt in the creditor's accounts

where:
a. the **debt in the debtor's accounts** is calculated as if a period of account had ended just before the companies became connected; and
b. the **carrying value in the creditor's accounts** will reflect either:
- the book value (calculated using the amortised basis of accounting) at the end of the period of account before the companies became connected; or
- where the creditor acquired the debt after that date, the consideration given for the debt's acquisition.

> MEMO POINTS 1. The rules were slightly different for companies which became connected **on or before 31 March 2012**. For details, see *Corporation Tax Memo 2012-2013*.

> EXAMPLE 1. C Ltd and D Ltd are unconnected. C Ltd owns £1m worth of bonds issued by D Ltd and accounts for them at fair value. D Ltd recognises the bonds under the amortised cost basis at £1m in its accounts.
> C Ltd has a calendar year accounting period, and at 31 December 2013, the fair value of the bonds was £800,000.
> C Ltd and D Ltd become connected on 1 July 2014.

C Ltd must now account for the loan relationship on an amortised cost basis, as the companies are connected, and at 31 December 2013 this would have resulted in a value of (say) £750,000. Therefore, C Ltd must recognise a debit of £50,000. (800,000 – 750,000)
Further, the pre-connection carrying values in C Ltd and D Ltd must be compared: £1m cost in D Ltd as at 1 July 2014 compared to £750,000 cost in C Ltd (being the value of the asset on an amortised cost basis on the last day of the period of account ending immediately before the one in which the companies became connected).
D Ltd must therefore recognise a deemed release of £250,000. (1,000,000 – 750,000)
2. If C Ltd only acquires the bonds on 1 February 2014 (i.e. after 31 December 2013) for (say) £700,000, the deemed release will be £300,000. (1,000,000 – 700,000)

16660
s 361 CTA 2009

Acquisition of impaired debt at an undervalue　When a connected creditor acquires impaired debt to which the debtor is party (either because it was already connected to the debtor, or it acquired shares in the debtor at the same time as acquiring the loan), the debtor will be taxable on the undervalue unless any of the **exceptions** shown in the table below apply (all of which require the acquisition to be an arm's length transaction).

Exception	Details	Reference
Corporate rescue	Both the following conditions must be met: **a.** there has been a **change in the ownership of the debtor** company at any time in the period beginning 12 months before, and ending 60 days after, the date of the acquisition; and **b.** it is reasonable to assume that, but for the change in ownership: – the debtor company would have met one of the insolvency conditions (¶16440)[1]; and – the acquisition of the creditor loan relationship would not have been made	s 361A CTA 2009, CFM 35540
Debt-for-debt exception[2] – requires like for like exchange	Applies if either condition below is met: **a.** the acquisition involves a creditor loan relationship that is **represented by a security** (the old security) where; – the creditor issues a new security of its own in exchange for the old security[3]; and – the new security has the same nominal value as the old security and, at the time of the acquisition, has substantially the same market value as the old security; or **b.** the acquisition involves a creditor loan relationship that is **represented by an asset other than a security** (the old unsecured loan) where: – the creditor issues a new unsecured loan in exchange for the debtor company's old unsecured loan; and – the amount of the new unsecured loan and its terms are substantially the same as those of the old unsecured loan	s 361B CTA 2009, CFM 35550
Equity-for-debt exception	The **consideration for the debt** is: – an issue of the creditor's own ordinary shares; – an issue of the ordinary shares of another connected company; or – an entitlement to shares in the creditor or connected company	s 361C CTA 2009, CFM 35560

Note:
1. HMRC accept that this condition is satisfied where insolvency is avoided not only by the change in ownership but also by steps taken following the change in ownership. They also accept the situation where the company has evidence that the insolvency conditions would be met but the company has not publicly acknowledged its potential insolvency because of confidential discussions required with lenders and auditors.
2. HMRC accept that this will include cases where:
– the issuer of the new security/loan agrees to pay any accrued but unpaid interest on the old security/loan when it acquires it; or
– a proportion of the old debt is released in exchange for new debt, and a proportion in consideration of the issue of shares.
3. Minor differences in the terms of the old and the new security (or unsecured loan), such as interest and repayment, will not prevent application of the exception.

Actual release of the debt Any **subsequent** release of the debt (known as a release of relevant rights) will result in taxable income for the debtor, unless the equity-for-debt exception applied (or could have applied where the circumstances met more than one exception). The amount of the credit is the discount at which the creditor acquired the debt, less any amounts taxed on the creditor in respect of the discount.

16665
s 358 CTA 2009

d. Deeply discounted securities

Broadly, a deeply discounted security is one where the **difference between the issue price and redemption amount** exceeds or might exceed:
– 0.5% of the redemption price for each year of the term of the debt, where the term is less than 30 years, or
– 15% of the redemption price where the loan period is 30 years or more.

16685
CFM 37200 +

However, the following are **excluded** from being a deeply discounted security:
– company shares;
– gilt-edged securities which are not strips;
– excluded indexed securities (those where the redemption value is linked to the value of capital gains tax chargeable assets);
– life assurance policies; and
– capital redemption policies.

> EXAMPLE E Ltd issues loan notes with a face value of £12,000. The issue price is £10,000 and the notes will redeem in 5 years' time.
> The difference between the issue price and the redemption amount is £2,000.
> This is more than 0.5% of the redemption price over 5 years, so the loan notes are deeply discounted securities. (12,000 × 0.5% × 5 = 300)

Consequences

Mirroring the late interest rules, where such a security is **beneficially owned by** a connected company which is based or effectively managed in a tax haven (otherwise known as a non-qualifying territory (¶16610)), and the full amount of credit is not recognised under the loan relationship rules for any accounting period, the debtor's relief for the discount will be deferred until the security is redeemed.

16690
s 407 CTA 2009

This rule also applies where the creditor holds securities indirectly through a **series of loan relationships**.

s 412 CTA 2009

> EXAMPLE F Ltd issues a security for £40,000 to G Ltd, an unconnected UK company. The security will be redeemed for £60,000 in 4 years. G Ltd then issues a security for the same amount, with an identical return, to H SA, a non-resident subsidiary of G Ltd.
> The rules treat H SA as the creditor for the security issued by F Ltd.

Close companies

Subject to the overriding requirement that any creditor company holding the security has to be resident or effectively managed in a tax haven, the same rule applies to close companies (except where collective investment schemes (¶16610) are involved).

16695
s 409 CTA 2009

Relief for the discount will be deferred if the full amount of credit is not recognised under the loan relationship rules for any accounting period, and **deeply discounted securities are issued to**:
a. a participator (¶75355+), including any loan creditor of the company;
b. an associate (¶75390+) of a participator;
c. a company which is controlled by a participator;
d. a person who controls a company which is a participator; or
e. the associates or controlled companies of the person in **d**. above.

Where the security is held by a participator (or his associate, etc.) for only part of an accounting period, the deferred amount is apportioned on a time basis.

s 410 CTA 2009

> ⌐MEMO POINTS⌐   1. A person is **not a participator** if he is only a loan creditor, having no other rights or interest, or is a bank which acquired the security only through its ordinary banking business.
> 2. Where the following conditions are met (involving **collective investment schemes**), no deferral applies i.e. the debtor recognises a loan relationship debit as normal:
> **a.** the issuing company is a small or medium-sized enterprise (¶70050+);
> **b.** the creditor is resident in a country with which the UK does not have a double tax agreement containing a non-discrimination clause; and
> **c.** either:
> – the issuing company is only close because of rights being attributed to another of the partners in a collective investment scheme limited partnership; or
> – the creditor is a collective investment scheme limited partnership (or would be if it was not a company).

e. Anti-avoidance provisions

16715   Until 18 July 2011, specific anti-avoidance provisions applied to the following situations:
– a company entered into a loan relationship and received a non-commercial return on its investment, but a connected company received a benefit; and
– a security which carried rights to acquire shares in a company was held (directly or indirectly through a series of loan relationships) by a connected company, and the debits recognised by the debtor company exceeded the credits recognised by the creditor company in a corresponding accounting period.

As result of the group mismatch scheme provisions (¶69490+), these rules were repealed with effect from 19 July 2011. For details of their former operation, see *Corporation Tax Memo 2012-2013*.

SECTION 2

Derivatives

16775   Derivatives are often used to limit a company's exposure to certain risks such as those arising from fluctuating interest rates, exchange rates, and commodity prices. In addition, larger companies and banks use derivatives for speculation, investment and trading purposes.

Comment   Owner managed businesses may use derivatives from time to time, and this commentary is designed with their needs in mind.

A. Scope

1. Definitions

16805
s 576 CTA 2009
Broadly, a derivative is a financial instrument whose value derives from an underlying asset, and the derivatives tax regime covers virtually all of them.

However, certain instruments may be **excluded** from being taxed under the derivatives regime where their underlying subject matter consists of any of the following, and certain criteria are met:
– intangible fixed assets;

– shares; and
– the rights of unit holders under a unit trust.

Exclusions

The excluded underlying subject matter is detailed in the following table:

16810

ss 590, 593
CTA 2009;
CFM 50580

> MEMO POINTS   Where the **underlying subject matter** consists:
> – **wholly** of an excluded asset, it will not be treated as a derivative for tax purposes; or
> – **partly** of an excluded asset, then the derivative will be split into two notional contracts if it is an option or future (using a just and reasonable apportionment), or come wholly within the derivatives regime where it is a contract for differences (¶16830).
> For this purpose, any matter which is **minor or of subordinate value** is ignored (HMRC state that 5% or less fulfils this criteria).

Matter	Details	Reference
Intangible fixed assets	Options and futures involving intangible fixed assets are excluded, as any profits and losses are dealt with under the intangible fixed assets regime (¶28135+) For this purpose, an intangible fixed asset is one accepted as such for accountancy purposes e.g. goodwill, patents, know-how, trade marks, registered designs, computer software and telecommunications rights	s 589 CTA 2009
Shares which give an entitlement to receive distributions (excluding shares in an open ended investment company[1])	Shares which are not designed to give an interest-like return (¶16120) or treated like debt The derivative must fall within one of the following categories: **a.** a quoted option to subscribe for shares, where the contract was entered into for non-trade purposes or the company is either a mutual trading company or carrying on a life assurance business; **b.** an option or future over shares (other than an embedded derivative) which could constitute a substantial shareholding (¶16965), and the contract was entered into for non-trade purposes; **c.** an approved derivative held by a life assurance business; **d.** equity derivatives (other than embedded derivatives) that hedge[2] assets or liabilities and the contract is entered into for non-trade purposes or by a mutual trading company; or **e.** equity derivatives that hedge[2] convertible or asset-linked securities	ss 591, 710 CTA 2009
Rights of unit holders	Units in a unit trust which are not treated for tax purposes as being creditor relationships	s 589 CTA 2009

Note:
1. An **open ended investment company** is broadly defined as a company that invests in other companies, but has no limit on the number of its own listed shares that it can make available for sale.
2. To **hedge** means to limit the company's exposure to changes in the value of an item which could make the company's profits particularly volatile.

Criteria to be satisfied

If not excluded by ¶16810 above, both of the following conditions must be satisfied for the derivative to fall within the derivatives tax regime:

16815

Condition	Details	Reference
Must be a relevant contract	Either a future (¶16820), option (¶16825) or contract for differences (¶16830) Includes embedded derivatives[1]	s 577 CTA 2009

Condition	Details	Reference
Must be treated as a derivative in the accounts	Under rules of FRS 25 and FRS 26 or any replacement accounting standard[2] which states that a derivative is a financial instrument or other contract which: – is settled at a future date; – requires no outlay or a minimal initial net investment; and – has a value that changes in response to a change in an underlying variable However, the following also fall to be treated as derivatives: **a.** where the underlying subject matter is a commodity[3]; or **b.** a contract for differences (¶16830) whose underlying subject matter is either: – land (wherever situated); – tangible movable property (other than commodities which are tangible assets); – intangible fixed assets; – weather conditions; or – creditworthiness	s 579 CTA 2009

Note:
1. Where a financial instrument is **bifurcated** (i.e. the accounts separate out the host contract and the derivative e.g. a loan relationship and derivative), the characteristics of the embedded derivative will determine whether it is an option, future or contract for differences.
2. Where a company is **not using these standards** (e.g. because a small company is using the FRSSE or a company is using IAS), one should imagine that it does.
3. **Commodity** is not defined and so the term is given its usual dictionary meaning i.e. an item that is bought and sold, especially a raw material or manufactured item. Common examples include agricultural products such as wheat and soya beans, metals, oil products and electricity.

Futures

16820
s 581 CTA 2009

A future (or a forward) is an arrangement between two parties to buy or sell a particular asset at an agreed price some time in the future. Both parties are **obliged** to carry out the transaction.

A contract described as a future, which can only be **cash settled** (without the delivery of any property), is regarded for tax purposes as a contract for differences (¶16830).

The **underlying subject matter** of a future is the property which would fall to be delivered at the date and price agreed when the contract was made, assuming the future is allowed to run to fruition.

> *MEMO POINTS* 1. The **price** may not be static i.e. it may be based on as yet unknown market indices or exchange rates.
> 2. The **purchaser** of a future is obligated to purchase the specified asset and this is known as a long position.
> 3. The **vendor** is obligated to sell the asset and this is known as a short position.

Options

16825
s 580 CTA 2009

An option affords the holder the security of knowing that he can trade an asset at a certain price, while retaining the chance to make a profit from favourable market conditions. The holder can allow the option allowed to **lapse**, as there is no obligation to exercise it.

The grantee of the option pays an amount **on grant** (known as the premium) regardless of whether the option is ever exercised.

The **underlying subject matter** of an option is the property to be delivered on its exercise.

> *MEMO POINTS* 1. A **call** option is the right to buy.
> 2. A **put** option is a right to sell.
> 3. Where a contract is described as an option, but can only be **cash settled**, this is regarded for tax purposes as a contract for differences ¶16830.
> 4. The term "option" includes a **warrant**, which is an instrument entitling the holder to subscribe for shares in a company or assets representing a loan relationship of a company.

Contract for differences

A contract for differences is intended to make a profit or avoid a loss **by reference to** fluctuations in either:
- the value or price of property referred to in the contract; or
- an index or other factor designated in the contract.

16830
s 582 CTA 2009

The following are **excluded** from being a contract for differences:
- an insurance contract;
- a capital redemption policy;
- an indemnity contract;
- a guarantee;
- a warranty; or
- a loan relationship.

A **swap**, which is an exchange of something such as interest rates or currencies (such as swapping a floating interest rate for a fixed interest rate), is treated for tax purposes as a contract for differences.

2. Entities

The derivative rules apply to companies within the charge to corporation tax, including unincorporated associations.

16860

Company partners of a **partnership** are chargeable on their share of the profits or losses of derivatives held by the partnership.

B. Calculation

Profits and losses relating to derivatives (including most exchange gains and losses) are subject to corporation tax as income and expenses respectively, no matter whether the company treats them as revenue or as capital.

16890

The derivative rules take priority over other corporation tax rules, except where a contract could be treated as a loan relationship when the loan relationship rules take precedence.

1. Amounts

As with loan relationships, the gains and losses that are included in a corporation tax computation essentially mirror those that are computed for accounts purposes, providing an acceptable **accounting method** has been adopted i.e. UK or International GAAP.

16920
s 597 CTA 2009

The following choices are available:
- UK GAAP excluding FRS26 and associated standards;
- FRS 26, which requires fair value accounting (¶16200);
- FRSSE; or
- IAS 39 (which also requires fair value accounting).

> MEMO POINTS 1. Note that for accounting periods beginning on or after 1 January 2015, companies that have not yet adopted IFRS will be required to make a **choice** between a new EU-IFRS or a new UK GAAP. This may affect the way in which such a company treats derivatives.
> 2. Where the accounts do **not comply with GAAP**, the company will still be taxed on the amounts which would have been shown had GAAP compliant accounts been prepared.
> 3. Credits or debits which are **disclosed in reserves**, e.g. the statement of total recognised gains and losses, are also brought into account.
> 4. Where a company **changes from GAAP to IAS**, no debits or credits that arise as a result should fall out of account for tax purposes.

s 599 CTA 2009

ss 599A, 599B,
698A CTA 2009

5. All **prior period adjustments** (¶11505+), unless arising from a fundamental error which requires an amended tax return to be filed, should be taken into account for tax purposes.

6. There is an overriding exception where **not all profits are recognised in the accounts** (which may happen where IAS are followed and an asset or liability is derecognised). For example, where a credit is not recognised or is offset (such as an interest receipt being offset by an equal and opposite dividend payment), the credit is still brought into account for tax purposes.

Further, as certain tax avoidance schemes have attempted to **exploit this asymmetry** between the accounting and tax regimes, for accounting periods ending after 6 December 2010, where a company is **party to tax avoidance arrangements** (in addition to being a party to a derivative contract):

– all amounts derecognised are still taxable; and

– losses arising from derecognition (other than an actual disposal) are not allowed as a tax deduction.

16925
s 595 CTA 2009

The credits and debits, when taken together, must fairly represent the company's profits and losses from its derivatives.

For this purpose, the following items are **brought into account**:

a. all profits, gains and losses (including those of a capital nature) arising to the company from the derivative;

b. all charges and expenses incurred under, or for the purposes of, the company's derivatives or related transactions; and

c. exchange movements on derivatives (unless they are recognised in the company's statement of recognised gains and losses or statement of changes in equity, or matched (¶17415+)).

s 596 CTA 2009

MEMO POINTS   1. A **related transaction** means any disposal or acquisition of rights or liabilities under the contract e.g. a sale, gift, surrender or release.

CFM 51090

2. In HMRC's view there are four categories of **expenses**:

a. bringing a derivative contract into existence, such as bank commission for an interest rate swap, or a premium payable for an option;

b. entering into, or giving effect to, a related transaction, such as the costs of delivering an asset where a contract is settled by physical delivery;

c. making a payment under a derivative contract or related transaction, such as bank charges for making swap payments; and

d. pursuing payments due under a derivative contract or related transaction e.g. solicitors' fees for enforcing rights under a derivative contract.

s 607 CTA 2009

Expenditure is not allowable if it is not directly related to a specific derivative transaction. However, **abortive** expenditure which is incurred in connection with entering into a derivative contract, and would be allowable, is deductible whether or not the company ultimately enters into the contract or related transaction.

2. Inclusion in computation

16955

The resulting debits and credits are brought into account in the same way as loan relationships (¶16970), although certain exceptions apply as detailed below.

Exceptions

16960

In the following situations, non-trading credits and debits are calculated in the normal way, but are brought into account as chargeable gains or allowable losses.

For all exceptions the following **criteria** must be met:

a. the contract is not held for trading purposes (unless the company is a mutual trading company, or holds the contract for the purposes of life assurance business); and

b. the company is not an excluded body (i.e. an authorised unit trust, an investment trust, an open ended investment company or a venture capital trust).

Exception	Detail	Reference
Contracts relating to land or tangible moveable property excluding commodities	Credits and debits on the derivative are brought into account as capital gains or allowable losses	s 643 CTA 2009, CFM 55090

Exception	Detail	Reference
Property based total return swaps (in which changes in the value of properties, or a property index, are swapped for an interest rate)	The following conditions must be met: **a.** the contract must be a contract for differences; **b.** the contract must designate one or more indices; **c.** at least one of the indices must be an index of changes in the value of land; and **d.** the underlying subject matter must also include interest rates The contract is split into a capital element and the income element, with the capital portion computed as: R% × N where: – N is the notional principal amount of the contract; and – R % is the percentage change (if any) in the capital value index for the accounting period	s 650 CTA 2009, CFM 55100
Post 1 January 2005 equity options embedded into convertible or exchangeable securities (creditor relationships only)	The following conditions must be met: **a.** the underlying subject matter must be qualifying ordinary shares[1] or mandatorily convertible preference shares[2]; **b.** the company must bifurcate the hybrid security in its accounts, or have elected to be treated as if it did; and **c.** the conversion shares must not have a pre-determined cash value The tax treatment is as follows: – profits or losses arising from the embedded equity option are charged as capital gains or allowable losses; – the conversion of a convertible security is not treated as a disposal; and – the base cost is adjusted so that there is no double charging of gains or losses when the shares are eventually disposed of	ss 645, 646, 670 CTA 2009, CFM 55200
Post 1 January 2005 exactly tracking contracts for differences that are embedded in a share-linked security (creditor relationships only)	The following conditions must be met: **a.** the underlying subject matter must be qualifying ordinary shares[1] or mandatorily convertible preference shares[2]; and **b.** the contract must be an exactly tracking contract i.e. it must match the change in value of the underlying asset from the date of issue to redemption, as shown by the following formula: D = R% × C where: – D is the amount received on redemption; – R% is the percentage change in the underlying assets or index; and – C is the original cost of the security The tax treatment is as follows: – any profits or losses arising on the embedded derivative are treated as chargeable gains or allowable losses; and – the base cost of the security is adjusted so that there is no double counting of gains or losses	ss 648, 672 CTA 2009, CFM 55290

Note:
1. These are any shares in a company except those carrying a right to a fixed rate dividend but no other rights to share in profits, and the company must either be listed on a recognised stock exchange (¶95320), a holding company or a trading company (meaning a company carrying on trading activities, and whose activities do not include, to a substantial extent, activities other than trading activities).
2. These must be converted into, or exchanged for, qualifying ordinary shares within 24 hours of being acquired.

16965
s 641 CTA 2009

Gains and losses If an embedded derivative is shown at **fair value** at each balance sheet date, there will be a credit or debit for each accounting period. These credits and debits are aggregated and netted off to give either an annual chargeable gain or allowable loss. This is in addition to the gain or loss sustained at the end of the contract.

s 663 CTA 2009

In certain circumstances, **losses** arising can be carried back to any accounting period which falls wholly or partly within the period of 24 months ending immediately before the start of the loss period. Relief must be given as far as possible for the later period before carry back to the earlier period. The company must make a claim to carry back either the whole loss or a part of it within 2 years from the end of the loss period.

> MEMO POINTS If the **substantial shareholding exemption** (¶32090+) would apply to an embedded derivative if it was exercised in the accounting period, then the gain or loss is ignored. Broadly, the exemption applies when a trading company or group holds at least 10% of the ordinary share capital of another trading company (or member of a trading group), and both the holding and trading activities were sustained for a continuous 12 month period beginning not more than 2 years prior to the disposal.

Purpose of derivative

16970
ss 573, 574
CTA 2009;
CFM 51030

Where a derivative contract is entered into for the purposes of a **trade**, the credits and debits are treated respectively as trading receipts and trading expenses. Commonly, this would arise with a bank or financial trader, but any company may use derivatives to support its trading operations. HMRC give the example of a manufacturer using a commodity derivative to hedge raw material prices.

Otherwise, derivatives are treated as **non-trading** loan relationship credits or debits (being aggregated with credits and debits arising from the company's loan relationships) and all the rules relating to the taxation of credits and relief of deficits (¶16350+) apply.

> MEMO POINTS 1. If a company enters into a derivative contract for **both trade and non-trade purposes**, the resulting credits and debits should be apportioned.
> 2. A **property company** is not carrying on a trade for this purpose.

s 691 – 692
CTA 2009

> 3. A derivative entered into for an **unallowable** purpose (that is, a non-commercial purpose (¶16500+)) will result in debits which can only be set off against credits from the same contract (excluding credits resulting from exchange gains).

C. Special situations

Summary

17000

Topic	¶¶
Embedded derivatives	¶17030+
Hedging	¶17075+
Groups	¶69550+

1. Embedded derivatives

17030

An embedded derivative may be part of a contract incorporating a loan relationship or some other kind of instrument. FRS 26 and International GAAP require embedded derivatives to be **bifurcated**: that is, to be accounted for separately from the host contract.

Contract not including loan relationship

Where an embedded derivative is **separated** from a contract other than a loan relationship (for example, a lease) in the financial statements, the separation is ignored for tax purposes (so an amortised cost basis is used to compute the profits and losses arising on the whole contract) **unless**:
– an election is made before the end of the first accounting period in which the contract is bifurcated (so long as the contract is not one of long term insurance or the underlying subject matter is not commodities);
– the underlying subject matter of the embedded derivative consists of shares in a company, when the embedded derivative is a chargeable asset for capital gains whilst the host contract is treated as a loan relationship; or
– the embedded derivative is used to hedge an asset or liability (¶17075+).

17035
ss 584, 586, 617
CTA 2009

s 592 CTA 2009

Contract including loan relationship

Hybrid instruments containing a loan relationship and derivative element are split for the purposes of measurement and disclosure in the financial statements, and this **separation** applies for tax purposes too. The most common examples are convertible and exchangeable securities.

17040
ss 415, 585
CTA 2009

The **derivative element** will be treated as an option, future or contract for differences depending on its particular characteristics.

However, the following contracts are **treated differently**:

17045

Contract	Details	Reference
Options to acquire shares which are separated from a creditor relationship	See the post 1 January 2005 equity options embedded into convertible or exchangeable securities in ¶16960	ss 645 – 647 CTA 2009
Options to acquire shares that are separated from a debtor relationship	When the holder exercises the option, the issuer fulfils its obligation by paying the holder the cash equivalent of the conversion or exchange shares The issuer is treated as making a chargeable gain or allowable loss in the terminal period	s 654 CTA 2009, CFM 55430
Contracts for differences that are separated from a creditor relationship and are linked to movements in the value of shares	See the post 1 January 2005 exactly tracking contracts for differences that are embedded in a share-linked security in ¶16960	s 648 CTA 2009
Contracts for differences that are separated from a debtor relationship and are linked to movements in the value of shares	Contract must satisfy the same conditions as for the post 1 January 2005 exactly tracking contracts for differences that are embedded in a share-linked security shown at ¶16960 When the debtor relationship ceases, a normal capital gain or allowable loss will result as the embedded derivative is treated as an asset For this purpose: – the disposal proceeds are the proceeds from the issue of the whole security; and – the cost is the amount to discharge the obligations of the whole security	s 658 CTA 2009, CFM 55470

2. Hedging

To hedge means to limit the company's exposure to changes in value of an item which could make the company's profits particularly volatile.

For hedging of exchange risk using a derivative contract, see ¶17505.

17075

Accounting methods

17080   A company which is preparing its financial statements under **FRS 26 or IAS** will be required to account for any derivative contracts on a fair value basis.

In contrast, companies **not using these accounting standards** will account for the derivative "off balance sheet" so that the combined contract (the derivative plus the hedged item) is accounted for as a single item, usually on an accruals basis

17085   To level the playing field for all companies, **changes in the fair value** of a derivative which is used as a hedge can be disregarded in the following circumstances, unless the company elects otherwise (either at the inception of the contract or when starting to apply these accounting standards for the first time):

Situation	Details	Reference
A currency contract is used to hedge a forecast transaction or a firm commitment	So long as: – there is a hedging relationship[1] between the contract (or part of it) and the forecast transaction or firm commitment; and	SI 2004/3256 regs 6, 7, 10, CFM 57080
A commodity contract or a debt contract (one not including interest rates in any way) is used to hedge a forecast transaction or a firm commitment	– any changes in fair value arising on the hedged item are not brought into account for corporation tax purposes, profits or losses arising in respect of the currency contract (including any transitional adjustments and prior year adjustments) are broadly recognised on the same basis as those of the hedged item (i.e. under GAAP) Company can opt out of these rules by either: – continuing to apply their accounting treatment to the taxation of the derivative contract; or – adopting a reg 9A election[2]	SI 2004/3256 regs 6, 8, 10, CFM 57200
A contract whose underlying subject matter includes interest rates is used to hedge an underlying transaction	For this purpose, the contract could be an interest rate swap, forward rate agreement, an interest rate future, or a swap contract where payment falls to be made by reference to an interest rate or an index relating to income or retail prices So long as: – there is a hedging relationship[1] between the contract (or part of it) and the hedged item; and – any changes in fair value arising on the hedged item are not brought into account for corporation tax purposes, profits or losses arising in respect of the interest rate contract (including any transitional adjustments and prior year adjustments) are recognised on an appropriate accruals basis[3] (broadly on the same basis as profits and losses of the hedged item) Company can opt out of this rule by making a reg 9A election[2] although this cannot apply where the hedged item is accounted for on an amortised cost basis or involves connected party debt	SI 2004/3256 reg 9, CFM 57300
A currency forward to hedge the proceeds of a rights issue or open offer of shares	Shares are issued in a currency other than the company's functional currency (¶17205) Resulting profits or losses that arise on the forward contract are not taxable, unless profits are distributed to shareholders when the exchange gain is taxed in the accounting period when the distribution is made	SI 2004/3256 regs 7A, 10A, CFM 57140

Situation	Details	Reference
A derivative contract whose underlying subject matter includes currency is used to hedge an investment in shares, ships or aircraft	See ¶17505	SI 2004/3256 regs 3-5

Note:
1. A **hedging relationship** exists where the derivative contract is either:
a. designated as a hedge in the company's accounts; or
b. intended to act as a hedge of the company's exposure to either:
– changes in fair value of a hedged item; or
– variable cash flows resulting from the hedged item which could affect the company's profit or loss.
2. A company may make a **reg 9A election** when a contract has been treated as a cash flow hedge in the accounts. This means that changes in fair value which are recognised in the statement of recognised gains and losses (or the IAS equivalent) are only brought into account for tax purposes when they are transferred to the profit and loss account or are included in the carrying value of an asset or liability i.e. the accounting treatment is followed for tax purposes.
3. An **appropriate accruals basis** means that
a. the contract is shown in the company's accounts at cost as adjusted for any cumulative amortisation of any premium or other amount needing to be recognised;
b. credits and debits reflect the amounts of any payments under the contract and an effective interest rate method (¶16245) is used in respect of the interest;
c. exchange gains and losses are recognised as a result of the translation of the contract at the balance sheet date; and
d. profits or losses, which arise as a result of the contract coming to a premature end, are amortised and brought into account over the unexpired term of the hedged item.

SECTION 3

Foreign exchange

Foreign exchange risks and differences affect many companies. For example, a company may trade outside the UK, borrow or lend in a foreign currency, or invest in assets which are denominated in a foreign currency, such as shares in an overseas subsidiary.. In most cases, there is no adjustment required for exchange gains and losses. **17135**

However, companies may need to consider the following topics:
a. the requirement that a company's corporation tax computation be completed in sterling, so where a company prepares its accounts in another currency, or operates in a third currency, the results must be translated. This also affects a holding company or company with branches overseas, when the foreign results are consolidated into the UK accounts;
b. foreign exchange gains and losses are now included in either the loan relationships regime or the derivatives regime, although there are exceptions for long term loans; and
c. the use by a company of foreign currency liabilities to hedge the exchange rate risk of foreign currency assets (for example, its net investment in an overseas subsidiary), the matching of assets and liabilities is permitted.

Definition

An exchange gain or loss arises when the value of an asset or liability valued in one currency is compared with its value in another currency at two different times. **17140**
ss 475, 705
CTA 2009

> EXAMPLE In June, a British company purchases plant and equipment from a Dutch company for €255,000. The sterling exchange rate is £1 = €1.20.
> The purchase price is due for settlement 2 months later and is recorded as a liability in the accounts at £212,500. (255,000/1.20)
> In August, the euro exchange rate has moved to £1 = €1.10, resulting in a liability of £231,818. (255,000/1.10)
> The resulting exchange loss of £19,318 is shown in the profit and loss account. (231,818 – 212,500)

A. Figures in the accounts

17170   Corporation tax is a sterling tax and so **all the entries on a corporation tax return must be in sterling**. In addition to the rules for the current period computation, losses carried forward and carried back have their own rules.

1. General principles

17200
s 5 CTA 2010

Under both UK GAAP and International GAAP, a company can operate in one currency (its functional currency) and compile its accounts in another. As a result, a company's income and chargeable gains must be translated into sterling where another currency would otherwise be used.

> ⬚MEMO POINTS⬚   Where a company has a **branch** operating in a different functional currency, the results of that branch are translated into the company's accounts currency. The balance sheet of the foreign currency branch is also retranslated each year. Any exchange differences arising on the retranslation will be taken to reserves and disregarded for tax purposes.

Non-investment companies

17205
CFM 64140

For companies which are not investment companies (¶17210), the following rules apply:

Situation	Functional currency [1]	Currency used for accounts	Action	Reference
UK resident company operating in sterling and preparing accounts in another currency	Sterling	Other	Calculate profits and losses as if company used sterling for its accounts using appropriate rate (¶17215)	s 6 CTA 2010
UK resident company operating in currency other than sterling and preparing accounts in a third currency	Not sterling	Other – not sterling and not the same as functional currency	Method to translate into sterling laid down as follows: **a.** calculate profits or losses in the functional currency [2] (ignoring any exchange gain or loss when translating from functional to accounts currency); then **b.** translate those figures into sterling using appropriate rate	s 7 CTA 2010
UK resident company operating in currency other than sterling and preparing accounts in same currency	Not sterling	Same as functional currency	Use sterling to calculate profits or losses by: **a.** calculating profits or losses in the accounts currency; then **b.** translating those figures into sterling using appropriate rate	s 8 CTA 2010
Non-UK resident company preparing accounts for UK permanent establishment in currency other than sterling	Not sterling	Same as functional currency		s 9 CTA 2010

Note:
1. **Functional currency** is the currency of the primary economic environment in which the company operates.
2. The legislation now refers to the **relevant currency** in order to include the case of an investment company (¶17210), but for a trading company its relevant currency is its functional currency.

Investment companies

Where certain criteria are met, UK resident investment companies can elect for a **designated currency** to be used for tax purposes, other than the functional currency used in the accounts. This would enable such companies to limit their exposure to foreign exchange fluctuations for tax purposes.

17210
ss 6(1A), 7(1A)
CTA 2010

If no election is made, the usual rules in ¶17205 apply.

For this purpose, an investment company is **defined** as a company whose:
– business consists wholly or mainly in the making of investments (¶6000+); and
– income is principally derived from those investments.

One of the following **criteria** must be satisfied, either:
a. a significant proportion (undefined) of the company's assets and liabilities are denominated in the designated currency; or
b. the currency is the functional currency of the ultimate parent company of the group to which the company belongs.

s 9A CTA 2010

The **election** will take effect from the beginning of the first period of account following that in which it is made (so there will be a gap when the election has no effect), and endure until either another election is made or a revocation event occurs.

s 9B CTA 2010

As a **consequence** of the election, any foreign exchange gains or losses that arise in the first period of account under a new functional currency from a loan relationship (or derivative contract) held by the investment company are not to be brought into account. This applies both where the change takes place due to a:
– change of functional currency for accounting purposes; or
– change in the designated currency.

ss 328(2A), 606(2A)
CTA 2009

> MEMO POINTS 1. This election is not available for **partnerships**.
> 2. A **newly incorporated company** can make an election at any time in the period beginning with the date of the company's incorporation and ending immediately before its first accounting period, although where the criteria above are not met at the beginning of the first accounting period, the election is void. A successful election would take effect from the date of incorporation.
> 3. A **revocation event** is one of the following:
> – the company no longer meets one of the criteria **a.** or **b.** above; or
> – at the beginning of its first accounting period, a newly incorporated company meets the criteria regarding a significant proportion of its assets and liabilities being denominated in the elective currency, but later in the accounting period that is not the case.
> 4. It is possible to make an election in respect of a **controlled foreign company** (¶90555+).

Appropriate exchange rate

Where profits are to be translated into sterling, the company has a **choice** of using:
a. the average exchange rate for the accounting period; or
b. for a single transaction, an appropriate spot exchange rate; or
c. for a series of transactions, a rate derived on a just and reasonable basis from appropriate spot rates for those transactions.

17215
s 11 CTA 2010

Computational adjustments such as capital allowances and disallowed expenditure should all be calculated in the foreign currency, and deducted from the company's profits before translation occurs.

Capital gains are calculated in sterling, except that from 1 September 2013 special rules apply to disposals of shares, ships or aircraft: see ¶17220.

> MEMO POINTS 1. Where the tax legislation refers to a **specific sterling amount** (for example, the pre April 2009 capital allowance limit for expensive cars of £12,000), this should be translated into the functional currency at rates **b** or **c** above (as appropriate).
> 2. As part of the standard **capital gains** computation (that is, unless ¶17220 applies) each of the following must be translated using the appropriate spot rate for the date of the event in question:
> – the original cost of the asset;
> – any improvement expenditure, acquisition or disposal expenses; and
> – the disposal proceeds.

s 10 CTA 2010

CFM 64180

EXAMPLE

1. Functional currency and accounts currency are different
C Ltd trades in the UK but prepares its accounts in euros.
The sterling accounting records show a profit of £1 million. The financial statements will show an exchange gain or loss when translating this result into euros.
For tax purposes, the profit of £1 million is used, thereby ignoring any exchange difference, and other computational adjustments such as capital allowances etc must be computed in sterling.

2. Functional currency and accounts currency are the same but not sterling
The UK branch of a US company has accounts which show the following:

	US$	US$
Income		250,000
Expenses including:		(130,000)
Entertaining	8,000	
Depreciation	22,000	
Profits		120,000
Capital allowances		20,000

The entertaining and depreciation must be disallowed so that the profit before capital allowances is US$150,000. (120,000 + 8,000 + 22,000)
The taxable profits are therefore US$130,000 after deducting capital allowances. (150,000 – 20,000)
This is translated into sterling using the average exchange rate for the year of (say) £1: US$1.6, giving a profit for UK tax purposes of £81,250.

17220
s 9C CTA 2010;
SI 2013/1815

From 1 September 2013, capital gains computations on **disposals of shares, ships or aircraft** are subject to special rules if at any time during the period of ownership, the company's **relevant currency was not sterling**.

The gain or loss on disposal is first computed using the company's relevant currency. The result of the computation is then converted into sterling using the spot rate at the date of disposal.

MEMO POINTS   1. The **relevant currency** is the company's functional currency, unless it is an investment company with a designated currency (¶17210) which is different from its functional currency. In such a case, its relevant currency is that designated currency.
2. **Shares** includes an interest in shares.
3. The **period of ownership** begins on the date of acquisition (or, if earlier, the first date on which allowable expenditure was incurred on the asset) and ends on the date of disposal.
4. If the company incurs allowable expenditure, or disposes of the asset for consideration, which is **not in its relevant currency**, the expenditure or consideration must first be translated into the relevant currency using the spot rate for the day of the event in question.
5. If the company has **changed its relevant currency** during the period of ownership, items dating from before the change must be translated into the relevant currency which applied after the change, using the spot rate for the day of the change. Translations required under memo point **4** above are performed before translations under this rule.

2. Losses

17245
s 11 CTA 2010

Unless a company changes the currency in which it computes its taxable profits and losses, any non-sterling losses will be carried forward or back in the currency in which they originated.

The exchange rate used for translating carried forward or back losses into sterling is now the same as that used to translate the profits during the period of offset (¶17205).

MEMO POINTS   1. For the special rules which deal with the situation when a company has losses that originated in one currency but are **offset against profits computed in a different currency**, see ¶17265.
2. Where a company has **losses that originated in sterling** but are offset against profits computed in a non-sterling currency, see ¶17265.

Carried back

For this purpose, the following **types** of losses are included:
- trading losses; and
- non-trading deficits from loan relationships.

17250
s 17 CTA 2010

Carried forward

For this purpose, the following **types** of losses are included:
- trading losses;
- non-trading deficits from loan relationships;
- management expenses;
- non-trading losses on intangible fixed assets;
- UK property business losses;
- overseas property business losses;
- patent income – relief for expenses; and
- losses from miscellaneous transactions.

17255
s 17 CTA 2010

Simple case – no change in functional currency

When the company continues to use the same functional currency throughout, the loss is held in its currency of origin until set off. It is only **translated** into sterling **when** it is set against profits, and the same **exchange rate** is therefore used for both the loss and the profits.

17260
ss 12, 13 CTA 2010;
CFM 64370, 64400

EXAMPLE
1. **Carry back**
D Ltd uses US dollars as its functional currency, and has the following results

	Year 6 US$	Year 7 US$
Trading profits	20,000	10,000
Non-trading loan relationship	3,000	(15,000)
Average exchange rate	1: 1.6	1: 1.4

In Year 7, D Ltd claims to set off US$10,000 of the non-trading loan relationship deficit against current year trading income, which leaves US$5,000. This remaining deficit is not translated into sterling until it is utilised.
D Ltd then carries US$3,000 back to set against the non-trading loan relationship credit in Year 6. Note that the loss is not translated to sterling first.
The remaining profits of US$20,000 in Year 6 are translated into sterling at 1: 1.6 which gives a PCTCT of £12,500.

2. **Carry forward**
E Ltd uses US dollars as its functional currency, and has the following results

	Year 8 US$	Year 9 US$
Trading (losses)/profits	(50,000)	30,000
Average exchange rate	1: 1.5	1: 1.2

There is no requirement to translate the Year 8 loss into sterling when it arises.
When the loss is offset against the trading profits of Year 9, US$30,000 of profit is reduced to nil by the loss.
This leaves US$20,000 of trading loss to carry forward to future accounting periods.

Change in functional currency

Where the company changes its functional currency, this presents a problem as losses will be in one currency whilst profits will be in another. To get round this, the loss is translated into the functional currency of the company when it is offset, and then the usual rules of ¶17260 apply.

Where losses are:
– **carried back**, the spot rate on the last day of the last accounting period with the previous operating currency is used; or

17265
ss 12, 13 CTA 2010

– **carried forward**, the spot rate on the first day of the first accounting period with the new operating currency is used.

> EXAMPLE
> **1. Carry back**
> F Ltd has a calendar year accounting period.
> In Year 6, F Ltd has a functional currency of US dollars and makes a taxable trading profit of US$60,000.
> In Year 7, F Ltd changes to euros, and makes a loss of €80,000.
> The spot rate on the last day of Year 6 between US$ and the euro is 1: 1.20.
> F Ltd wants to carry back enough losses to extinguish the profits in Year 6. The euro losses need first to be translated into US dollars by using the spot rate on the last day of Year 6. This means that €72,000 must be translated into dollars to give relief of US$60,000. (72,000/1.20 = 60,000) €8,000 of losses are carried forward. (80,000 – 72,000)
>
> **2. Carry forward**
> G Ltd has a calendar year accounting period.
> In Year 10, G Ltd has a functional currency of US dollars and makes a trading loss of US$60,000.
> In Year 11, G Ltd changes to sterling, making a trading profit of £15,000 in that year, and in Year 12, a further trading profit of £30,000.
> The spot rate on 1 January of Year 11 between US$ and sterling is 1: 1.2
> The dollar losses need to be translated into sterling by using the spot rate on the first day of Year 11, which gives losses of £50,000. (60,000/1.2)
> This offsets the profits in both Year 11 and Year 12, leaving £5,000 of losses to carry forward. (50,000 – 15,000 – 30,000)

B. Loan relationships and derivatives

17295   Exchange differences may arise on amounts payable in a foreign currency and any outstanding capital balance held in a foreign currency.

When the company becomes a party to a contract, the foreign currency loan relationship or derivative is translated into the functional currency used for the company's accounting records, and then subsequently revalued at each balance sheet date.

> MEMO POINTS   For **investment companies**, see also ¶17210.

1. Scope

17325
s 483 CTA 2009;
CFM 61070

Any foreign cash held by the company is treated as a money debt. Similarly, exchange differences on a provision made in the accounts relating to future liabilities of a trade or property business (both UK and overseas) will be treated as a loan relationship debit or credit.

> EXAMPLE A Ltd has invested US$105,000 in a US dollar bank account. At the beginning of the accounting period, the account is worth £75,000 and at the end it is worth £70,000. So A Ltd has suffered an exchange loss of £5,000 which is included as a loan relationship debit. (75,000 – 70,000)
> Interest is received once a year, and under GAAP, US$800 was accrued at the end of the last accounting period which was translated at 1: 1.4 to give £571. When the interest is received, the exchange rate has moved to 1: 1.5 which translates to only £533. So there is an exchange loss of £38, which again is treated as a loan relationship debit. (571 – 533)

Exclusions

17330
s 486 CTA 2009

Where an exchange difference arises on interest relating to **UK tax**, this is ignored for the purposes of the tax computation i.e. any loss is not deductible but any gain is not taxable.

Similarly, any exchange difference is ignored on **foreign tax** unless the tax is allowed as a deduction rather than a credit under the double taxation rules (¶90505).

Any exchange differences arising on **non-deductible items** (such as entertaining) are also ignored, although exchange gains and losses on capital items are recognised as loan relationship debits and credits.

Exchange rate

Accounting practice requires that a foreign currency transaction be translated into the company's functional currency at the spot rate on the day it occurs. Where **multiple transactions** occur, it is reasonable to use an average rate for a week or month.

17335
ss 307, 696
CTA 2009

Then, at each **balance sheet date**, monetary items are translated into the functional currency at the closing rate.

The **source** of exchange rates is not prescribed.

Non-monetary assets

Normally, only monetary assets and liabilities are retranslated at each accounting date.

17340
CFM 61110

Non-monetary assets are **translated only** when they are acquired or created, unless they are matched with a foreign liability.

---

2. Computation

Depending on the type of asset or liability involved, most exchange gains and losses fall within the usual rules for loan relationships and derivatives so that the **key issue** is whether the transaction has been entered into for the purposes of a trade (¶16295+).

17370

> MEMO POINTS   1. The following **anti-avoidance** provisions within the loan relationships and derivatives regimes apply to exchange differences as with any other debit or credit:
> – the unallowable purpose rule (¶16500); and
> – the treatment of a debtor relationship as a distribution (¶16250).
> 2. If a transaction is **not at arm's length**, and in particular where a loan (or part of it) would not have been advanced had the transaction been on commercial terms, any related exchange difference is ignored for tax purposes.

s 447 CTA 2009

Summary

The following table highlights those instances where special rules apply:

17375

Situation	Details	Reference
Fair value accounting	See ¶17380+	SI 2005/3422, CFM 61160
Loan relationship between connected parties	Exchange gains and losses are still recognised even where a debit for an impairment loss is denied (¶16630)	ss 352, 354, 360 CTA 2009, CFM 61130
Exchange differences taken to reserves	Exchange gains and losses are ignored when taken to reserves (e.g. statement of total recognised gains and losses or equity) in the following circumstances: **a.** exchange differences arising on a loan by a company to a foreign subsidiary or a hedged asset, when the exchange differences are only brought into account on disposal of the investment or asset (¶17415); and **b.** the whole exchange difference arising on the translation of part of a company's business from one currency to another when the closing rate/net investment method is used for accounting purposes (e.g. an overseas branch)	s 328(3) CTA 2009, SI 2002/1970 reg 13(2A) CFM 61140

Situation	Details	Reference
Exchange differences on certain shares	Exchange differences on shares held by a company are only recognised when the shares are disposed of, except when: – shares denominated in a foreign currency are treated as creditor loan relationships (¶16120) so they must be accounted for on a fair value basis which would include exchange differences; or – the shares are part of a repo agreement which falls within the loan relationships regime, when the exchange differences are recognised as loan relationship debits and credits	CFM 61150

Fair value accounting

17380

ss 308, 597
CTA 2009;
SI 2005/3422;
CFM 61160

The exchange difference is bundled up with all the **other factors** which make up a transaction's fair value.

In the following cases, a fair value profit or loss can be **divided** up into an exchange difference and a residual profit or loss, both of which are then treated as separate debits and credits:
– a loan relationship asset is accounted for as an available for sale asset (¶16195);
– a loan relationship asset or liability is accounted for at fair value through the profit and loss account; or
– the asset or liability is the hedged item in a designated fair value hedge which is protecting the company against exchange risk (either exclusively or in conjunction with other risks).

> MEMO POINTS   1. When the company **uses IAS or FRS 26 for the first time**, this division does not apply.
> 2. Where a bond, loan note or similar asset is accounted for as an **available for sale asset** and uses a different currency to that of the company's accounts or operations, the accounting treatment will naturally separate out the exchange difference and disclose it in the profit and loss account.

17385   The **residual amount** is calculated by comparing the fair value and the exchange difference as follows:
– subtracting an exchange gain from a fair value profit;
– adding an exchange loss to a fair value profit;
– subtracting an exchange loss from a fair value loss; or
– adding an exchange gain to a fair value loss.

> EXAMPLE
> 1. B Ltd's accounts show a fair value profit of £200,000 on a currency swap, of which £70,000 is an exchange gain.
> The residual credit is £130,000. (200,000 – 70,000)
>
> 2. C Ltd's accounts show a fair value profit of £80,000 on a currency swap, of which £70,000 is an exchange loss.
> The residual credit is £150,000. (80,000 + 70,000)
>
> 3. D Ltd's accounts show a fair value profit of £50,000 on a currency swap, of which £70,000 is an exchange gain.
> The residual debit is £20,000. (50,000 – 70,000)
>
> 4. E Ltd's accounts show a fair value loss of £150,000 on a currency swap, of which £100,000 is an exchange loss.
> The residual debit is £50,000. (150,000 – 100,000)
>
> 5. F Ltd's accounts show a fair value loss of £100,000 on a currency swap, of which £200,000 is an exchange gain.
> The residual debit is £300,000. (100,000 + 200,000)
>
> 6. G Ltd's accounts show a fair value loss of £40,000 on a currency swap, of which £60,000 is an exchange loss.
> The residual credit is £20,000. (40,000 – 60,000)

C. Matching

Matching describes a situation where a foreign liability is taken on in order to hedge the exchange risk of a foreign asset. As any exchange rate changes will affect the liability's value in exactly the opposite way to the asset's value, the company will not be vulnerable to currency fluctuations i.e. where the rate change decreases the value of the asset, it will also reduce the liability, so the effect of the exchange movement is cancelled out.

17415

Reliance on accounting treatment

Normally, assets such as **shares** in a foreign subsidiary would not be retranslated at each **balance sheet date** as shares are a non-monetary asset. However, a **loan** or similar liability is a monetary asset which would be subject to fresh translation at each year end. Therefore the commercial effect of matching would not be followed through in the financial statements.

17420
CFM 62010

To **overcome this divergence** from commercial reality, **UK GAAP** (excluding FRS 26) allows the exchange differences on assets and liabilities which are matched to be taken to reserves and netted off (known as the offset method).

In contrast, **IAS** and **FRS 26** require most exchange gains and losses to be taken to the profit and loss account, including those relating to a hedged foreign equity investment. To level the playing field for all companies, special rules ensure that these matched exchange differences arising from shares, ships or aircraft are also not liable to tax.

1. UK GAAP

The offset method is generally **applied to** individual investments or borrowings, except where an investment, or a number of investments, have been financed by a particular loan. This means it can also be applied where investments are managed on a pool basis and financed by a basket of different currency loans.

17450

Types of assets

For accounting purposes, matching applies to:
– **shares** in a foreign company (including those used in a repo transaction where they are still shown as an asset on the balance sheet); and
– long term **loans** (including intercompany trading accounts where payment is deferred) which are intended to finance the foreign operation in a way akin to equity.

17455

Criteria

The criteria that must be met for offset to apply are as follows:
a. any exchange gains or losses in any accounting period that **arise on borrowings** may be offset only to the extent of the total exchange differences on the equity investments;
b. the foreign currency borrowings whose gains and losses are used in the offset process should not exceed, in aggregate, the total net realisable **value** of the investments;
c. there must be consistent **application of the accounting treatment** adopted over time (even where a gain would otherwise be realised on the loan); and
d. if the **liability exceeds the asset**, only the exchange difference on the matched part of the liability is taken to reserves, and the remainder goes through the profit and loss account.

17460
SSAP 20

> MEMO POINTS   1. The liability and asset do not have to be denominated in the same **currency**, so long as the arrangement effectively hedges the exchange risk.
> 2. The **liability may predate the asset** (if the loan was taken out before the purchase of the investment) but only the exchange differences arising on the borrowings which were generated during the period when the currency hedge was in place can be offset. Any exchange differences arising beforehand must be taken to the profit and loss account.

3. Similarly, when the **matching comes to an end**, either because the loan is repaid or the asset is sold, the offset method only applies up to the date of cessation.

> EXAMPLE
>
> 1. A Ltd holds shares of US$100,000 in its subsidiary, B Inc, which are matched with a US$100,000 loan.
> At the balance sheet date, there is an exchange gain of £10,000 on the translation of the shares into sterling and an exchange loss of £10,000 on the loan.
> The exchange differences are netted off in reserves.
>
> 2. C Ltd has a loan of US$200,000 which partly hedges a US$400,000 investment.
> At the balance sheet date, the loan is retranslated into sterling which gives an exchange gain of £15,000 i.e. the loan value has decreased. The investment has also decreased in value by £30,000 due to the exchange rate movement.
> C Ltd can take the £30,000 exchange loss and £15,000 exchange gain to reserves and net them off.
>
> 3. D Ltd has a loan of US$600,000 which hedges a US$400,000 investment.
> At the balance sheet date, the loan is retranslated into sterling which gives an exchange gain of £45,000 i.e. the loan value has decreased. The investment has decreased in value by £30,000 due to the exchange rate movement.
> In this case, as the liability exceeds the asset value, only £30,000 of the exchange gain can be taken to reserves and netted off. The remaining £15,000 must go through the profit and loss account and is taxable.
>
> 4. E Ltd has a Hong Kong subsidiary which holds assets in US$. The value of the subsidiary's shares in E Ltd's accounts is HK$400,000. E Ltd decides to hedge its exchange risk by taking out a loan in US$.
> Any exchange differences on the matched asset and liability could still be taken to reserves (even though the currency for each is different) because the hedge is commercially effective.

2. Other GAAP

17490
CFM 62620

When using **IAS or FRS 26**, matching at single company level is not allowed, and so exchange gains and losses are disclosed in the profit statements.

As it is not clear from the accounts whether any assets have been economically matched with liabilities, or how much of the exchange difference on the liability is actually set off by an equal and opposite movement on an asset, there are special tax rules which ignore the accounting treatment under IAS. Instead, the matching treatment is continued, **disregarding** the exchange differences on liabilities whilst they are matched with certain assets, and then bringing them into charge when the asset is disposed of.

Asset matched by loan relationship

17495
SI 2004/3256 reg 3

Debtor loan relationships can be matched with investments which are shares, ships or aircraft where either of the following conditions are met:
a. the debtor loan relationship is in such a currency that the company could reasonably expect to eliminate (or reduce) the economic risk of holding the asset. It is the company's intention which is important here, and there is no requirement for the loan to be in the same currency as the hedged asset. (In this case the debtor loan relationship can only be matched to the extent that it does not exceed the carrying value of the asset); or
b. the shares, ships or aircraft are treated as designated hedges against exchange risks in accordance with IAS 39 or FRS 26.

CFM 62670, 62790

> MEMO POINTS 1. The carrying value of the matched liability on acquisition, or when the asset is acquired (if later), **must not exceed the carrying value of the asset** at the relevant time i.e. a snapshot of the value assessed periodically (at least every 92 days) throughout an accounting period, usually coinciding with the management accounts prepared by the company.

SI 2004/3256
reg 2(3A)

> 2. In response to recent disclosures made to HMRC, companies can only defer foreign exchange differences arising, on a just and reasonable basis, from the **date** that they have a foreign currency loan relationship which is matched with shares, ships or aircraft. This clarification is relevant where an existing loan relationship is matched with a purchase of an asset on or after 6 December 2011.

Creditor loan relationships will be treated as matched against a company's share capital if, in the accounting period immediately preceding the first accounting period commencing on or after 1 January 2005, exchange movements were taken to reserves and matched against exchange movements arising on share capital.

17500
SI 2004/3256
reg 3(6)

Matching using a derivative

A derivative may be used to match shares, ships or aircraft (provided they are not held for trading), where it is either:
a. intended to act as a hedge of the exchange risk on the asset (or part of the asset); or
b. a **designated** fair value hedge.

17505
SI 2004/3256 reg 4

Where the derivative is accounted for at **fair value**, the exchange difference needs to be dissected out from the other factors which influence its value (¶17380).

> MEMO POINTS   1. There is a **limit on the value** of the derivative which can be matched (in a similar way to loan relationships), so that only the carrying value of the asset can be matched. For this purpose, the value of the derivative is defined as the amount of one currency which the company is obligated to pay in return for receiving an amount of a different currency.
> 2. In response to recent disclosures made to HMRC, companies can only defer foreign exchange differences arising, on a just and reasonable basis, from the **date** that a foreign currency derivative is matched with shares, ships or aircraft. This clarification is relevant where an existing derivative contract is matched with a purchase of an asset on or after 6 December 2011.
> 3. Derivatives can also be used to match a **company's own shares** where the company's profit would be exposed to exchange rate movements e.g. where the share capital is accounted for as a liability, such as preference shares, and the accounting rules require exchange rate movements to be taken to the profit and loss account or income statement.

SI 2004/3256
reg 4(1A)

CFM 62850

> EXAMPLE   F Ltd has a US subsidiary which is shown at US$200,000 in its accounts at the beginning of the year. F Ltd takes out a swap at the beginning of the year which means it agrees to sell US$200,000 for £150,000 at the end of the year. For this purpose, the value of the derivative contract is US$200,000, and it is fully matching the value of the shares.
> At the end of the year, the exchange rate is such that US$200,000 is only worth £130,000. So F Ltd has made a profit on its swap of £20,000, which is an exchange gain. This will be disregarded until the shares are disposed of.

Valuation of shares which are matched

A company can elect for the shares against which a debt/currency contract is matched to be valued at the **higher of** the accounts value and the net asset value underlying the share-holding. Where no election is made, the accounts value is always used.

17510
SI 2004/3256
reg 4A

The **election** is irrevocable and any future shares acquired will be affected as well as those held at its inception.

> MEMO POINTS   1. The **time limit** for the election is 30 days after the company first matched shares under condition **a.** in either ¶17495 or ¶17505 above.
> 2. The election must be made in writing, and **state** the name of the company and the length of the review period which it will adopt.
> 3. **Group members** can autonomously decide whether to elect or not.

CFM 62730

For this purpose, **net asset value** is:

17515
CFM 62750, 62760

Value of the assets – Value of the liabilities

where the liabilities are those owned by the investment company, or any company control-led by it, and denominated in the currency whose exchange risk is being hedged.

HMRC state that the **currency denomination** of an asset or liability will normally be defined by the functional currency of the environment of the business operation within which the asset or liability is located.

When an election has been made, the company only needs to **check the shares' value** if the liability is only partially matched and the hedged amount exceeds the book value of the shares. This check is undertaken periodically (at least every 92 days) throughout an account-ing period, usually coinciding with the management accounts prepared by the company.

> ☐ MEMO POINTS   1. For **100% subsidiaries**, underlying net asset value is determined by reference to the assets and liabilities which would appear in a notional consolidated balance sheet of the investment company. In practice, the treatment of the assets and liabilities in the actual group consolidated accounts (whether published or not) will be conclusive.
> 2. For **partly owned investments**, the underlying net asset value is reduced for the following factors:
> – the proportion of the shares held by the taxpayer company; and
> – the rights attached to those shares.
> 3. Where a company has a **branch with a functional currency that differs** from that of the main business operations, the assets and liabilities of that branch are excluded.
> 4. Only by exception would a financial **asset or liability denominated in some other currency** be excluded. Usually such financial assets or liabilities would either have only an immaterial effect or be part of the company's normal business operations.

> ☐ EXAMPLE   A Ltd holds shares in B Inc. B Inc has two subsidiaries, C Inc, located in the US, and D SA, located in France.
> B Inc has a functional currency of US$.
> A Ltd is hedging its exposure to US$, and so must identify the assets and liabilities denominated in US$. The assets and liabilities in D SA will be excluded.

---

3. Bringing amounts back into account

17545
ss 328(3), 606
CTA 2009;
CFM 62230

When an asset is matched with a loan or derivative contract, exchange gains or losses on the liability are initially disregarded for tax purposes.

They are then brought back into account when there is a **disposal** of the asset (other than a no gain/no loss disposal). This would include the case where a creditor loan relationship, which was treated as quasi-equity funding of a subsidiary, is repaid (¶17570).

> ☐ MEMO POINTS   1. When using a **derivative contract** as a net investment hedge, the matching rules apply only to an exchange difference calculated using rates of exchange. When a **forward currency contract** is used, the exchange difference must be split into two parts as follows:
> – an exchange gain or loss computed by reference to spot rates which can be matched; and
> – a residual amount which will consist of a forward premium or forward discount which cannot be matched.
> 2. The disposal of an **asset belonging to a foreign branch** of a company will not result in an exchange gain or loss being taken into account, unless the asset is a long term equity investment (¶17200+).
> 3. Where a disposal is made at **no gain/no loss** (i.e. between companies in a capital gains group (¶65415+)), any matched exchange gain or loss will be calculated on the date of the no gain/no loss disposal, but will not be brought into charge until the asset is subsequently sold.

Type of asset disposed of

17550
SI 2002/1970;
SI 2010/809

The tax consequences depend on the type of asset which has been matched and then disposed of (either wholly or partly), as shown in the table below.

> ☐ MEMO POINTS   1. Disposal is **defined** by the capital gains rules, and so includes deemed disposals such as negligible value claims (¶30090).
> 2. The **timing** of the disposal is also determined by the same rules (¶30125).
> 3. Even if an asset has been **matched for only a short period of time**, the company must retain sufficient records so that any exchange difference can be brought back into account when the asset is eventually disposed of.

Type of asset	Treatment of asset disposal	Treatment of matched exchange difference	¶¶
Shares	Chargeable gain or loss	Part of chargeable gain or loss	¶17565
	Exempt as substantial shareholding (¶32090+)	Exempt	¶17560
Loan[1]	Taxed as income	Taxed as income	¶17570
Ship			
Aircraft			
Note:			
1. In this case, the repayment of the loan would trigger the taxation of the matched exchange difference.			

Quantifying the exchange difference

The exchange difference brought back into charge is that arising in relation to liabilities which were matched with assets during the period of ownership of those assets.

17555
CFM 62350, 62360

From 1 September 2013, if the assets are **shares, ships or aircraft** on which the gain or loss must be computed in the company's relevant currency (¶17220), the gains or losses on matched liabilities must be computed on the same basis.

SI 2013/1843

Otherwise, HMRC state that any method of computation which is **just and reasonable**, and which has regard to the way in which the aggregate exchange difference has been computed in any earlier accounting period, is acceptable.

Where a **single type of asset** has been matched (such as shares in a subsidiary), it is usually quite straightforward to identify the liability which was the matching vehicle, and hence the relevant exchange gains and losses. This is the case even where different liabilities have matched the asset at different times. HMRC's view is that a review of the tax computations for the relevant accounting periods should show which exchange differences have been disregarded previously.

17560
CFM 62370

A company may instead have a **pool of assets**, which are regarded, for tax purposes, as matched by various liabilities and currency contracts in the following order:

SI 2004/3256 reg 5

a. loan relationships, ships or aircraft;

b. shares (excluding foreign business assets) which would give rise to a chargeable gain on disposal; and then

c. shares which are treated as substantial shareholdings (¶32090+) for the purposes of the substantial shareholding exemption (SSE) or assets of a foreign permanent establishment.

> MEMO POINTS   1. For the purposes of deciding where the **SSE** would apply, the shares are always **deemed to have been held** throughout a 12 month period (¶16965), unless there is a subsequent real disposal which fails the 12 month ownership test.
> 2. Where matched assets are denominated in **more than one currency**, the priority rules are applied on a currency-by-currency basis e.g. if a company has assets in euros, and also in dollars, the euro assets are assessed and then the dollar assets. Liabilities can be regarded as hedging an asset even though they may be in different currencies (¶17460).
> 3. An **exchange of shares for QCBs** is treated as a disposal for the purposes of these rules, so a deemed gain or loss is calculated on the basis that the shares had been sold at the date of exchange, and this is then heldover until the disposal of the QCBs.
> 4. A **share-for-share exchange** is not treated as a disposal of the original shares, so no matched exchange differences are brought into charge until the new holding, or part of it, are subsequently disposed of. Similarly, as the new shares stand in the shoes of the original shares, any hedging instruments which were matched to the original shares are deemed to automatically match the new shares.

EXAMPLE   E Ltd is a UK trading company with the following foreign assets on its balance sheet:

	Acquisition cost US$	SSE?
Shares in F Inc, a US trading subsidiary	300,000	y
Shares in G Inc, a non-trading US subsidiary	200,000	n
Long term quasi-equity loan to H Inc, a US subsidiary	100,000	n

E Ltd took out a US loan of US$500,000 to hedge its exchange rate exposure. This will be matched first with the quasi-equity loan, then the non-trading US subsidiary shares, and then the SSE shares.
1. If the quasi-equity loan is repaid, the exchange gain or loss recognised in reserves is brought into charge. However, there will be an opposite exchange difference on the US loan, so no taxable amount arises. In practice, no computation need be completed.
2. If the shares in F Inc are sold, this is subject to the SSE. So again no computation needs to be completed as no tax charge will arise.
3. If the shares in G Inc are sold, these are chargeable to tax. Assuming that E Ltd's relevant currency (¶17220) has always been sterling, the resulting gain must be computed in sterling.

The exchange rate at acquisition (and at the inception of the US loan) was 1.5: 1
On disposal of the shares, the exchange rate is 1.2: 1

		£
Value of matched loan at acquisition	200,000/1.5	133,333
Value of matched loan on disposal	200,000/1.2	(166,667)
Exchange loss		33,334

So the exchange loss brought into charge on disposal of the shares is £33,334 and this reduces the sale proceeds of the shares.

Shares

17565
SI 2002/1970 reg 4

Broadly, the **disposal proceeds** for the shares are adjusted for any exchange difference, so that:
- any gain increases the disposal proceeds;
- a loss reduces them; and
- if the loss exceeds the proceeds, this is treated as additional acquisition expenditure.

If the disposal value is not at arm's length, the arm's length value must be substituted for the proceeds.

SI 2002/1970
regs 7, 8, 14

MEMO POINTS   Where the shares have previously been the subject of **no gain/no loss** transfers, the disposal consideration on the ultimate disposal is adjusted for all exchange differences which have been disregarded i.e. by looking at a capital gains group as one company. Where the rule for disposals post 5 April 2010 would disadvantage a company because the deduction of exchange losses from the proceeds limits the available indexation allowance, the company can elect for the pre 6 April 2010 rules to apply so that the matched exchange difference results in a free-standing loss. However this free-standing loss cannot be transferred to another group company.

EXAMPLE

1. A Ltd acquires shares in an Irish subsidiary in Year 2 for £500,000. In Year 5, these shares are sold for £1 million. The substantial shareholding exemption does not apply.
The exchange risk arising from fluctuations in the euro is hedged through a currency swap, and the accumulated exchange loss is £150,000 which has so far been taken to reserves and disregarded for tax purposes.
The chargeable gain is computed as follows:

	Year 5 £
Disposal proceeds	1,000,000
Exchange loss coming into charge	(150,000)
Revised disposal proceeds	850,000
Acquisition cost	(500,000)
Chargeable gain before indexation	350,000

2. If, instead, A Ltd sells only 40% of the shareholding for (say) £300,000, 40% of the exchange loss is brought back into account, and the acquisition cost is determined by using the usual part disposal formula (¶31130+). If the market value of the remaining shareholding is £500,000, the computation is as follows:

		Year 5 £
Disposal proceeds		300,000
Exchange loss coming into charge	150,000 @ 40%	(60,000)
Revised disposal proceeds		240,000
Acquisition cost	$\frac{300,000}{300,000 + 500,000} \times 500,000$	(187,500)
Chargeable gain before indexation		52,500

3. B Ltd is a UK resident company which acquired its US subsidiary for a payment of US$2 million (which was translated into £1 million at the time). The shares were hedged by a loan of US$2 million, and all exchange differences were disregarded for tax purposes.
Two years later, B Ltd sold its subsidiary to a fellow group member, C Ltd, at no gain/no loss. C Ltd also chose to hedge the investment by means of a currency swap.

Four years later, C Ltd sells the subsidiary's shares for £3 million, and the substantial shareholding exemption does not apply. Both B Ltd and C Ltd have always operated in sterling.
During their respective periods of ownership, B Ltd matched exchange gains of £200,000, and C Ltd matched exchange losses of £300,000. The cumulative matched exchange difference is therefore a loss of £100,000. (200,000 – 300,000)
On the sale of the subsidiary outside the group, the disposal proceeds are reduced by £100,000 to £2,900,000. (3,000,000 – 100,000)

Other assets

For long term quasi-equity loans, **ships and aircraft**, a net gain or loss will be brought into account as a loan relationship credit or debit.

17570
SI 2002/1970 reg 6

In regard to **loans**, there will be two types of exchange difference to consider: first, the difference which has been matched with a liability, and second, the exchange difference on the loan asset itself which has been taken to reserves. All of these exchange differences come into charge when the loan is disposed of by being repaid or transferred to a new creditor (including a group company).

SI 2002/1970 reg 13

SECTION 4

Management expenses

Companies with an investment business (¶6000+) (including hybrid companies and non-resident companies) can obtain relief for the expenses of managing their investments in a very similar way to expenses incurred by trading companies.

17620
s 1219 CTA 2009

There is **no statutory definition** of management expenses.

A. Scope

Unless specifically allowed by statute (¶17730), management expenses must satisfy the following **criteria**:

17650
o 1210 CTA 2000

a. they are not deductible elsewhere in the tax computation (the expenses do not relate to a particular source of income or fall to be treated under a specific tax provision, such as the loan relationship regime);
b. the investments are not held for an unallowable purpose during the accounting period;
c. the expenses relate to the investment business;
d. they are not capital; and
e. they are referable to the accounting period.

> MEMO POINTS Note that in contrast with trading expenses, there is no requirement for the expense to be incurred **wholly and exclusively** for the purpose of the business (¶14540). The statutory criterion is whether the remuneration is an expense of managing the investment business.

Excluded expenditure

However, expenditure relating to the following can never be deducted as management expenses:
– business entertaining;
– rents in excess of a market rent paid under a sale and leaseback of land;
– penalties relating to tax compliance (including VAT); and
– payments constituting a criminal offence including under duress of blackmail.

17655
ss 1298, 1303, 1304 CTA 2009

Anti-avoidance

17660   There are also two anti-avoidance tests which apply:
a. whether investments are held for an allowable purpose; and
b. whether the company is entering into arrangements in order to gain a tax advantage.

17665   **Allowable purpose?**   Investments are deemed to be held for unallowable purposes if they:
s 1220 CTA 2009;
CTM 08225
– are not held for business or commercial purposes; or
– relate to activities outside the charge to corporation tax.

However, merely receiving **non-taxable income** such as dividends, **exempt gains** under the substantial shareholdings rules, or otherwise exempt income or gains from certain kinds of investment vehicle (such as an authorised unit trust), are not regarded as activities outside the scope of corporation tax.

Where necessary, expenses must be **apportioned** on a just and reasonable basis in order to find the allowable amount.

CTM 08220   [MEMO POINTS]   1. HMRC regard investments for **social and recreational purposes** as unallowable unless they relate to employees.
2. Investments relating to **activities outside the charge to corporation tax** cover the following:
a. mutual trading or services provided by a members' club to its members; or
b. where a UK permanent establishment of a non-resident company, such as a branch, pays expenses that do not relate to its own activities. However, investing in a company that is not itself subject to UK corporation tax, such as an overseas subsidiary, is not within this prohibition.

17670   **Arrangements**   Holding investments in connection with any arrangements the main
s 1220 CTA 2009;
CTM 08234
purpose of which is to secure a tax advantage, is also an unallowable purpose. The mere fact that an expense is deductible does not bring this rule into play. What matters is the extent to which **obtaining the deduction** has driven the transaction or agreement: simply choosing a more tax efficient route will not cause the deduction to be automatically disallowed unless a tax advantage was one of the main purposes of any arrangements.

[MEMO POINTS]   1. For this purpose, arrangements are widely **defined** to include any agreement, understanding, scheme, transaction or series of transactions (whether or not legally enforceable).
2. **Tax advantage** is specifically defined to include obtaining or increasing a management expenses deduction, as well as any other tax advantage such as obtaining reliefs, repayments or reductions in tax.

Related to the investment business

17675   For details of how to determine whether a company has an investment business, see ¶6000+.

Expenses allocated to a **property business** are not deductible as expenses of management. They form part of the separate property business calculation.

Expenses which **relate to** both an investment business and **another part of a company's activity** must be apportioned on a just and reasonable basis.

CTM 08060   [MEMO POINTS]   There can often be uncertainty about the precise status of **intermediate holding companies**, and whether they are entitled to claim management expenses as a company with an investment business or as trading expenses in respect of management services. Where a company like this is acting as a group service company, incurring and recharging costs to other group members, it will have a trade. Costs incurred in respect of the management of its investments will be management expenses. Costs will need to be separated appropriately. Where costs have been intermingled but would qualify in a subsidiary, in practice they can be allowed if recharged in future (¶6175+).

Capital or revenue

17680   **Subject to** certain exceptions (¶17730), capital expenses are specifically disallowed.
s 1219(3) CTA 2009
Just because investments are held on capital account or expenses are charged to a "capital" account does not automatically make them disallowable, however. HMRC state that the principles used for trading companies (¶13050+) also apply for companies with investment business.

Changing investments The direct costs of changing investments are not allowable. A **distinction** is therefore made between costs incurred as part of the decision-making process when managing investments, and those incurred directly when implementing the acquisition or disposal of a particular investment. It is irrelevant whether the acquisition or disposal is aborted: it must be assumed that the company's plan is always successful.

17685
CTM 08190, 08260

HMRC's view is that costs arising **prior to a decision being made**, such as reviewing potential acquisitions or disposals, obtaining preliminary reports and business plans, are part of the management of the investments, and therefore allowable. Costs of implementing the decision, such as brokerage fees and stamp duties, are capital costs which are allowed when the investment is sold.

HMRC give the following examples of when a decision would be **evidenced**, in relation to:
- acquisitions, an offer being made to the target company; and
- disposals, marketing the investment to be sold.

HMRC accept, however, that there may not be an absolute cut-off point in time, and that the facts of each case are crucial.

Referable to the accounting period

Unless specific rules apply for recognising amounts for tax purposes (as, for example, with pension contributions), expenses are referable to an accounting period if they are **debited in the accounts** for that period in accordance with GAAP, or would be debited if the accounts were drawn up on that basis.

17690
ss 1224 – 1227
CTA 2009

The **location** of the debit is irrelevant. The expenses could be debited to the profit and loss account, statement of total recognised gains and losses, or (if using International GAAP) the income statement, statement of changes in total equity or other statement of amounts brought into account.

s 1255 CTA 2009

> MEMO POINTS 1. If the **accounting period** for tax purposes **does not match the period of the statutory accounts**, the expenses should be time apportioned unless that would be unjust or unreasonable.
> 2. If **no accounts are prepared** for a period, then expenses will still be deductible provided they would have been debited under UK GAAP had accounts actually been prepared.

> EXAMPLE E Ltd changes its accounting period end from 30 June to 31 December. It prepares accounts for an 18 month period to 31 December. These include the following expenses:
>
> | | £ |
> |---|---|
> | Light and heat | 15,000 |
> | Postage and stationery | 5,400 |
> | Wages and salaries | 60,000 |
>
> The expenses will be allocated to the corporation tax computations as follows:
>
> | | 12 months to 30 June (2/3) £ | 6 months to 31 Dec (1/3) £ |
> |---|---|---|
> | Electricity | 10,000 | 5,000 |
> | Stationery | 3,600 | 1,800 |
> | Salaries | 40,000 | 20,000 |

If an expense **previously deducted is then reversed in the accounts** by crediting it back, the credit is deducted from the management expenses for the period in which it is reversed in the accounts. Any credit in the accounts needs to be analysed between amounts that reverse a deductible expense, and those that are taxable in any event. Only that part of the credit that relates to the original expense should be set against management expenses. The credit cannot be set against management expenses brought forward.

17695
ss 1228 – 1231
CTA 2009

If the **credit exceeds the management expenses**, the excess is taxable as part of total income.

> EXAMPLE F Ltd has management expenses of £12,600 in Year 8.
> In Year 9, the auditors adjust the accounts for over-accrued investment advice of £4,000, so that a credit appears in the accounts. Management expenses (ignoring the credit) are only £3,800.

The corporation tax computation is follows:

	£	£
Management expenses, Year 9	(3,800)	
Reversal of prior expense	3,800	
	Nil	
Included in taxable income, Year 9		200

17700
ss 1249, 1250
CTA 2009

Remuneration, and provision for remuneration, is only deductible on the accounting basis if it is paid (¶14615) within 9 months of the period end. If not paid within 9 months, the remuneration is deductible in the period in which it is paid.

If the corporation tax **return is being prepared before the 9 months have elapsed**, and the remuneration is unpaid at that point, it must be assumed that it will not be paid. If, after submitting the return, the remuneration proves to have been paid within 9 months of the period end, the return can be amended.

CTM 08330

Directors' remuneration may not be fully allowable. Remuneration should be justifiable compared to the services provided and duties performed. Anything in excess might not be regarded by HMRC as an expense of management.

B. Expenses allowed by statute

17730   Unless indicated otherwise, the items below are always deemed to be management expenses and so the following tests can be ignored in relation to them:
a. relating to an investment business;
b. whether the expenses are capital; and
c. whether the investments are held for an allowable purpose (¶17665).
However, any expenses relating to tax avoidance (¶17670) will still not be deductible.

Area of the business	Subject	Details	Reference
Employees	Share ownership	Costs relating to approved share incentive plans [1,2] Where free or matching shares are given to employees (¶15095+), market value of shares is deductible as a management expense	ss 985, 1221 CTA 2009
		Costs for setting up Save As You Earn option schemes and company share option plans [1]	ss 999, 1221 CTA 2009
		Costs of setting up an employee share ownership plan [1]	ss 1000, 1221 CTA 2009
		Where shares or an option to obtain shares is acquired by an employee, the difference between the market value of the share and the consideration received from the employee is deductible as a management expense [2]	ss 1013, 1021, 1221 CTA 2009
	Pensions	Contributions paid to registered pension schemes subject to the spreading rules [2]	s 196 FA 2004, s 1221 CTA 2009

Area of the business	Subject	Details	Reference
	Termination of employment	Statutory redundancy and approved contractual payments for employment termination – to be allocated on a just and reasonable basis if the employee is working on more than the investment business [3]	s 1239 CTA 2009
		Additional redundancy or approved contractual payments up to three times the statutory amount provided all or part of the business has permanently ceased [3]	s 1242 CTA 2009
		Reimbursement to the government for payments it has made under the Employment Rights Act 1996 and equivalent Northern Ireland legislation [2,3]	s 1243 CTA 2009
		Payments for restrictive undertakings which are taxable for the employee [2,3]	s 1234 CTA 2009
		Costs (and travelling expenses) for counselling services for employees whose office or employment ceases provided various conditions are met [3]	s 1237 CTA 2009
	Retraining	Retraining course expenses (and travelling expenses) where the necessary conditions regarding the course and employment are met (for periods ending before 1 April 2009 the employee had to be exempt from tax on the payments) [3]	s 1238 CTA 2009
	Temporary secondment	Salary costs for an employee who is temporarily seconded to a charity or educational establishment	s 1235 CTA 2009
	Payroll deduction agents	Payments made to approved payroll deduction agents to reimburse them for costs incurred by the agent, and the employer's costs in doing so (this relates to charitable giving schemes) [3]	s 1236 CTA 2009
	Relocation	Payments that guarantee the sale price of an employee's home are included, but not the acquisition and disposal of the property itself, which are capital gains items [2,3]	CTM 08360
Assets	Capital allowances	Capital allowances on plant and machinery used in the investment business if they cannot be set against income [3]	s 1233 CTA 2009
	Vehicle hire	Deductions for car hire are restricted (¶14760+) [2,3] Where the agreement was entered into before 1 April 2009, these rules also include the hire of motorcycles	s 1251 CTA 2009
Statutory compliance		Payments to the Export Credit Guarantee Department [3]	s 1245 CTA 2009
		Levies and costs paid under the Financial Services and Markets Act 2000 [3,4]	ss 1246, 1254 CTA 2009
		Administration costs relating to statutory duties such as the shareholders' register, printing the accounts, and costs of an annual meeting [2,3]	CTM 08410

Area of the business	Subject	Details	Reference
Other	Contributions to local enterprise organisations [5] or urban regeneration companies	As reduced by any benefit the company or a connected person receives, if the costs of obtaining that benefit directly would not be deductible [2,3,4]	ss 1244, 1253 CTA 2009
	Overseas dividends	Until 31 December 2013: payment of a manufactured overseas dividend [2] (an amount which relates to an overseas dividend and is paid in connection with the transfer of overseas securities)	ss 790, 791 CTA 2010
	Manufactured dividends	From 1 January 2014: payment of a manufactured dividend [2] (an amount which relates to an dividend and is paid in connection with the transfer of securities) which is taxable on the recipient as trading profits or a distribution from an REIT (¶19635)	ss 814A, 814C CTA 2010

Note:
1. If the plan is not approved by HMRC within 9 months of the accounting period end, the costs are not deductible as management expenses until the accounting period when approval is actually given.
2. These costs are subject to the rules on unallowable purpose, and must be apportioned if not wholly relating to the company's investment business.
3. These costs are subject to the rules on capital expenses.
4. Receipts relating to the following will be taxable:
– any disqualified benefits relating to contributions to local enterprise organisations or urban regeneration companies (if not already taken into account in reducing the deduction for the contribution); and
– certain repayments due under the Financial Services and Markets Act 2000.
5. Local enterprise organisations are local enterprise companies and agencies, training and enterprise councils or business link organisations.

C. Computation

17760
s 1222 CTA 2009

Once the management expenses have been identified and quantified, they must be **reduced by** any non-taxable income received by the investment business. For this purpose, non-taxable income excludes franked investment income (¶18330)).

ss 1219, 1223
CTA 2009

Management expenses are **deducted from** total profits (taxable income and taxable gains) in priority to any other deductions.

MEMO POINTS   1. For the treatment of management expenses when there is a **change of ownership** of the business, see ¶60325+.
2. For a **non-UK resident** company, expenses would be reduced by any non-taxable income derived from certain sources held in the course of its investment business carried on through a UK permanent establishment. Those sources are property or rights used by, or held by, that establishment.

Group relief

17765
s 105 CTA 2010

A group claim for excess management expenses falls within the general rules for group relief (¶66050+), and requires a 75% holding in each group company (whether direct or indirect).

The **amount** of any expenses **available** for group relief is the excess left after the company has utilised the maximum amount of management expenses against its own profits.

It is not possible to surrender management **expenses brought forward** from an earlier accounting period.

EXAMPLE A Ltd and B Ltd are members of the same 75% group. Their results are as follows:

	A Ltd £	B Ltd £
Trading profits		4,000
Chargeable gains	2,500	
Credits from non-trading loan relationships	1,500	7,000
Qualifying charitable donations		(2,000)
	4,000	9,000
Current period management expenses	6,000	
Management expenses brought forward	1,000	

A Ltd's excess management expenses for the year are £2,000. (6,000 – 4,000)
A Ltd's management expenses are utilised as follows:

	£	£
Current period management expenses		6,000
Management expenses brought forward		1,000
		7,000
Less: Deducted against current year profits		(4,000)
Surrendered to B Ltd (limited to current year only)		(2,000)
Management expenses to carry forward		1,000

Excess expenses

Any excess not group-relieved must be carried forward, and treated as management **17770**
expenses of the following period (subject to any reduction in relation to government
investments written off (¶16235)). The excess can be carried forward indefinitely as long the
company retains its investment business.

The excess **carried forward** also includes excess qualifying charitable donations (known as
charges on income for periods ending before 1 April 2010).

EXAMPLE C Ltd's corporation tax computations for Years 8 and 9 are as follows:

Year 8	£	£
Taxable income		14,278
Management expenses		(16,305)
Excess management expenses carried forward		(2,027)

Year 9	£	£
Taxable income		11,576
Management expenses brought forward	2,027	
Management expenses in period	15,158	
Group surrender	(1,847)	
		(15,338)
Excess management expenses carried forward		(3,762)
Non-trading loan relationship deficit carried forward		142

Note:
The maximum amount available for group surrender in Year 9 is £3,582. (15,158 – 11,576)

CHAPTER 6

Distributions

18000 Broadly, a distribution is any payment made by a company which reduces its assets by making a return of profits to the shareholders. Such payments are not deductible for corporation tax purposes, and do not reduce the profits chargeable to corporation tax.

Most distributions received (whether paid by UK or non-UK resident companies) are exempt from the charge to corporation tax.

For details of shadow ACT, which affects companies who paid dividends before 6 April 1999, see ¶41190+.

Comment The distribution legislation is designed to prevent a company giving assets to its shareholders free of tax.

Scope

Distribution implies that a shareholder gains at the company's cost. So the return of share capital, or the issue of share capital, in return for new full value consideration are not occasions when a distribution arises.

18050
s 1000 CTA 2010

The term distribution is widely used but a payment may not be a chargeable distribution for corporation tax purposes. Note that a chargeable distribution may still be exempt. For the rest of this chapter the term distribution is used to mean a payment that is recognised as such for tax purposes.

The following table summarises the current position.

Payment	Included as a distribution for tax purposes	Excluded – not a distribution for tax purposes	Reference	¶¶
Distributions made by a liquidator		✓	s 1030 CTA 2010	¶18085
Distributions of assets prior to dissolution		✓	s 1030A CTA 2010	¶18090
Stock dividends		✓	s 1049 CTA 2010	¶18095
Payments for group relief (provided the payment does not exceed the group relief surrendered)		✓	s 183 CTA 2010	¶66740
Certain purchases by a company of its own shares		✓	s 1033 CTA 2010	¶18560
Dividends (including capital dividends)	✓		s 1000 CTA 2010	¶18125
Transfer of assets [1]	✓		s 1020 CTA 2010	¶18165
Interest on certain securities	✓		ss 1005, 1006 CTA 2010	¶18185
Issue of redeemable share capital or securities [1]	✓		s 1003 CTA 2010	¶18220
A bonus issue following a repayment of share capital	✓		ss 1022, 1023 CTA 2010	¶18240
Provision of benefits to participators in a close company i.e. one which is controlled by up to five members or any number of directors	✓		s 1064 CTA 2010	¶75875
A distribution in a cross-border merger where the company ceases to exist without being wound up		✓	s 1031 CTA 2010	¶18090
Small distributions to members on dissolution of an unincorporated non-trading association		✓	ESC C15	¶18090

Note:
1. Unless there is new consideration provided to the company by the members.

---

1. Exclusions

18080 The following scenarios do not create a distribution for corporation tax purposes:
- distributions by a **liquidator**;
- distributions on **dissolution**, including after a cross-border merger;
- **stock dividends**;
- payments for **group relief** (¶66740); and
- certain **purchases of own shares** involving an unquoted trading company (¶18560).

Liquidation

18085
s 1030 CTA 2010

In addition to the repayment of the nominal share capital, any **amounts** distributed by the liquidator in respect of the share capital do not fall to be treated as a distribution. This could include a payment of dividend arrears. For further detail of liquidations see ¶61295.

Dissolution

18090
ss 1030A, 1030B
CTA 2010;
ss 1000 – 1003
CA 2006

When, rather than following the more formal liquidation route, a company is either:
- being struck off by the Registrar; or
- has made or anticipates making an application to have the company struck off,

then (subject to a number of conditions) any amounts paid out will not be treated as distributions.

Provided the company has secured (or intends to secure) the payment of any sums due to it and intends to satisfy (or has satisfied) all debts owed by it, a payment of no more than £25,000 will not be treated as a distribution. The dissolution must be completed (or all the company's debts paid) within 2 years of the distribution or the exemption will cease to apply.

ESC C15

An **unincorporated association** can choose to treat any distributions as capital payments so long as:
- its prior activities have substantially been of a social or recreational nature;
- no trade or investment business has been carried on; and
- the distribution is not large (not defined).

s 1031 CTA 2010

A distribution made by a company in the course of a **cross-border merger** (¶79840) is deemed to be made by a liquidator so long as it relates to the share capital. This would, therefore, exclude distributions relating to securities.

> _MEMO POINTS_ 1. If there are a **series of payments** made the £25,000 limit applies to the aggregate of all payments.
> 2. Prior to 1 March 2012 a similar relief was available by concession. For details of this see previous editions of _Corporation Tax Memo_.

Stock dividends

18095
s 1049 CTA 2010

A stock dividend is an issue of shares by a UK resident company **resulting from** either a bonus issue or where a member chooses to take shares in lieu of cash. Note that in this case even redeemable shares do not fall to be treated as a distribution.

For the reporting requirements relating to stock dividends see ¶47165.

> _MEMO POINTS_ A **bonus issue** is so named because shares are issued in respect of an existing shareholding without any new consideration being given by the member. However, a bonus issue following a repayment of share capital may be treated as a distribution (¶18240). If selling shares received as a result of a bonus issue see ¶32235.

---

2. Dividends

18125
s 1000(1) CTA 2010

With the **exception** of stock dividends (¶18095), all dividends are treated as distributions.

This **includes**:
- cash dividends;
- dividends in specie; and

– capital dividends (distributions paid out of the surplus arising on the realisation of a capital asset). *IRC v Reid's Trustees* [1949]

However, where a dividend is **waived** no distribution arises. To be effective the member must deliver the waiver to the company before he acquires the right to the dividend. A waiver may cover a single dividend or a series of dividends.

Effective date

A **shareholder acquires the right** to a dividend when it becomes due and payable: that is, when a resolution is made either by the members or directors.

18130

The following table shows when a dividend is deemed to become payable.

Type of dividend	Detail	Become payable	Reference
Interim		When payment actually made	*Lagunas Nitrate Co Ltd v Schroeder & Co and Schmidt* [1901]
Final	Resolved to be paid at a certain date	When members approve it at general meeting	Re *Severn and Wye and Severn Bridge Rly Co* [1896]
	Resolved to be paid at a future date	At future date	*Potel v IRC* [1971]

Reporting

When **drawing a cheque or warrant** to pay a dividend a UK company must send a voucher to the member (or his bank). Failure to do so can result in a penalty of £60 for each voucher, up to a maximum of £600 in respect of any single distribution of dividends.

18135
s 1104 CTA 2010

> MEMO POINTS   1. **Qualifying distributions** (¶18330) vouchers must show the amount of the dividend paid, its date of payment, and the amount of any tax credit.
> 2. Reports of **non-qualifying distributions** must also be made (¶47160).

s 1100 CTA 2010

---

3. Transfer of assets

A transfer of assets or liabilities from a company to its members is treated as a distribution if the **market value** of the benefit received by the member exceeds the consideration paid. This can of course work in reverse, so that where the member receives extra value when transferring an asset to the company, this excess is also a distribution.

18165
s 1020 CTA 2010

If the difference in value is shown in the company's profit and loss account this will be disallowed when computing taxable profits.

> MEMO POINTS   1. For this purpose a **member** is a person whose name is entered in the Register of Members.
> 2. Prior to 17 July 2012 there was an exception (there was no distribution) if the transfer was:
> – in cash or kind between **UK resident** companies (¶2030) under common control, or where one is a 51% subsidiary of the other;
> – of assets (other than cash) or liabilities between **unconnected** UK resident companies, so long as neither is a 51% subsidiary of a non-resident company; and
> – to **employees or directors** who are taxed under the benefits in kind legislation (see *Tax Memo* for further details).

---

4. Interest on securities

Payments of interest by a company at a **rate** in excess of a normal commercial rate (determined by reference to the amount invested) may be treated as a distribution.

18185
ss 1005, 1006
CTA 2010

Such an interest payment needs to be split into two amounts representing the:
– normal commercial rate, which is treated as a loan relationship (¶16160); and
– excess over the normal commercial rate, which is taxed as a distribution.

ss 1007, 1008
CTA 2010

MEMO POINTS Although the **amount invested** is usually the principal secured, some securities are issued at a premium, and this too must be taken into account (a commercial rate of interest is calculated on the sum of the principal and the premium). If securities are issued at a discount, only the discounted amount is taken into account. For this purpose, the **principal secured** is the minimum amount that the holder is entitled to on maturity under the terms of the security's issue.

> EXAMPLE A Ltd borrows £30,000 from B Ltd. The corresponding interest rate is 15%, when a normal commercial rate would be 10%.
> The annual interest charge is £4,500. (30,000 @ 15%)
> Of this, £3,000 is a loan relationship credit, and £1,500 is a distribution. (30,000 @ 10%, 30,000 @ 5%)

Special securities

18190

ss 1015–1017,
1032 CTA 2010

Payments of interest in respect of the following securities (including **secured and unsecured loan stock**) may also be treated as a distribution. However, no distribution will arise where securities are issued to another company within the charge to corporation tax, and the recipient company is not exempt from tax on the interest.

Situation	Detail	Exception
Bonus issues	No consideration given by the recipient	No distribution arises where the bonus securities were issued before 6 April 1965 in relation to shares, or before 6 April 1972 in relation to securities
Securities convertible into shares Securities carrying a right to receive shares or securities	Securities issued after 5 April 1972 carrying a right to receive shares or securities of the company	No distribution arises where the shares received on conversion are listed on a recognised stock exchange (¶95320) or issued on terms comparable with listed securities
Securities carrying interest at a rate dependent upon the level of profits of any part of the business	Includes the case where interest only paid if business makes a profit Irrespective of rate of interest (even if at a commercial rate, interest is still treated as a distribution)	No distribution arises in relation to interest on ratchet loans (interest increases as profits fall and vice versa) paid after 20 March 2000 A return on relevant alternative finance[1] is not treated as a distribution
Securities connected with shares in the company	Securities are connected with shares in a company where the rights attaching to the shares or securities are such that it is necessary or advantageous to own both	
Equity notes held by a company which is associated with, or funded by, the issuing company	Equity notes are, broadly, those where the likely redemption date is more than 50 years after the date of issue[2] Companies are associated if one owns 75% of the other, or both are 75% subsidiaries of a third company	

Note:
1. **Alternative finance** transactions are structured so that activities prohibited under Islamic Sharia law are avoided i.e. gaining wealth by interest, bribery or gambling. For further details see ¶16125.
2. An **equity note** must satisfy any of the tests below (in regard to the principal) so either:
– no redemption date is given;
– the redemption date, or the latest date for redemption, falls more than 50 years after the date of issue;
– the redemption date is after a particular event occurs, and it is probable or certain that the event will occur; or
– the issuing company can secure that there is no specified redemption date and that the redemption date falls more than 50 years after the date of issue.

5. Issue of redeemable share capital or securities

If redeemable share capital is issued and the member does not give the company full value **consideration** in return, a distribution is deemed to arise on the under-value. This also applies to securities issued in the same circumstances.

For this purpose, the **value** of the:
– share capital is the amount of the share capital together with any premium payable on redemption; and
– security is the amount of the principal together with any premium payable on maturity.

18220
ss 1003, 1004
CTA 2010

6. Bonus issue following repayment of share capital

A distribution is deemed to occur when a company:
– repays share capital (**except for** certain types of fixed rate preference shares); and
– subsequently issues bonus shares (shares which are treated as paid up even though the member has not given the company any consideration).

For **non-close companies**, this rule only applies if the bonus issue either:
– is of redeemable shares; or
– occurs within 10 years of the repayment date.

The **value** of the distribution is calculated by taking the total amount of share capital repaid, and deducting any amount which has already been caught under this rule.

18240
ss 1022, 1023
CTA 2010

> ⌐MEMO POINTS⌐ For **close companies**, all bonus issues relating to a share capital repayment are caught: there is no time limit. For this purpose a close company is one under the control of five or fewer persons and not controlled by a non-close company. For further details see ¶75000.

> ⌐EXAMPLE⌐ C Ltd has £100,000 issued ordinary capital and £40,000 redeemable preference shares.
> In Year 1, C Ltd redeems all of the preference share capital.
> In Year 2, a bonus issue of two ordinary shares for every ten held is made, amounting to £20,000.
> In Year 3, a further bonus issue of two ordinary shares for every twelve held is made, amounting to £20,000.
> In Year 4, a further bonus issue of one ordinary share for every fourteen held is made, amounting to £10,000.
>
> C Ltd has made the following distributions:
>
> | Year | Bonus issue £ | Distribution £ | Total distribution £ |
> |------|------|------|------|
> | 1 | - | - | - |
> | 2 | 20,000 | 20,000 | 20,000 |
> | 3 | 20,000 | 20,000 | 40,000 |
> | 4 | 10,000 | - | - |
>
> In Year 4, although a bonus issue of £10,000 occurs, the full amount of the redemption has already been treated as a distribution, so that no further distribution is deemed to arise.

Preference shares

If fully paid up fixed rate dividend preference shares are repaid, the rules in ¶18240 above do not apply, so long as their **terms** do not change until their repayment and either they:
– have been in **issue** at 6 April 1965; or
– were **issued** since 6 April 1965 as fully paid shares wholly for new consideration that was not derived from ordinary shares.

18245
ss 1022, 1023
CTA 2010

> ⌐MEMO POINTS⌐ 1. For this purpose **fixed rate preference shares** are shares which:
> – only carry the right to dividends at a fixed percentage of the nominal value of the shares; and
> – carry rights in respect of dividends and capital that are comparable with quoted fixed dividend shares.
> 2. **New consideration** not derived from ordinary shares means the member gives value to the company other than in the form of:
> – the surrender, transfer or cancellation of ordinary shares of any company;
> – the variation of rights in ordinary shares of any company; or

– consideration derived from a repayment of share capital paid in respect of ordinary shares of any company.

3. **Ordinary shares** are any type of shares except preference shares.

SECTION 2

Distributions received

18295   The treatment of chargeable distributions received depends on the nature of the recipient – broadly, whether the recipient is liable to corporation tax or income tax.

A. Corporate recipients

18325   All distributions received by UK resident companies (whether from UK or non-UK payers) are assumed to be liable to corporation tax as income unless they are either capital distributions or exempt. Most distributions received will be exempt from corporation tax.

However, an issue which potentially affects all companies is that of franked investment income, which is important when computing the tax rate applicable to the company.

Further, the value shifting rules (¶32410) must always be considered where a dividend is paid and then the company is sold.

MEMO POINTS   Distributions received **before 1 July 2009** were taxed differently depending on the residency of the paying company, so that distributions from a company resident:
– in the UK were not chargeable to corporation tax; and
– outside the UK were taxed as overseas income, although a double tax agreement may have reduced or eliminated the tax charge.

Franked investment income

18330
ss 1126, 1136
CTA 2010

Exempt qualifying distributions received by a company are known as franked investment income. Any such distributions received (other than from group companies) must be grossed up by 100/90 and added to PCTCT to calculate the augmented profits (¶40115).

For this purpose, a **qualifying distribution** is defined as any distribution **except** a:
– bonus issue of securities or redeemable shares by a UK company;
– redemption of bonus shares on a winding up; and
– distribution by a company in the form of shares or securities which it received as a distribution from another company.

s 1109 CTA 2010   While a company is entitled to a **tax credit** equal to 1/9th of a qualifying distribution, it can only be reclaimed by a company which receives the distribution as a representative for a person who is liable to income tax.

---

1. Capital distributions

18360
s 931RA CTA 2009;
s 1027A CTA 2010

A capital distribution means a company distribution which is not treated as income for tax purposes in the hands of the recipient. It therefore represents a return of surplus capital (either from paid up share capital or a share premium account).

Where the distribution could be exempt under the rules in ¶18380+ or taxed as a capital sum derived from an asset (¶31165), the exempt distribution rules take priority. However, just because the distribution is exempt income does not mean it cannot be taken into account for the purpose of chargeable gains. For example, the entire proceeds of a share buyback (¶18495) are taxable as a chargeable gain in the hands of a company. *Strand Options & Futures Ltd v Vojak* [2004]

2. Exemptions

Depending on the size of the company, two different regimes apply:
- one for small companies (¶18385); and
- one for other companies (¶18390).

18380

However, the following distributions are **always taxable** in every case:
a. interest payments on certain securities (¶18185 and ¶18190); and
b. where a deduction is allowed outside the UK for the payer of the distribution.

The exemption can also be **disapplied** in any case (so that the distribution becomes taxable) if the company so elects within 2 years of the end of the accounting period in which the distribution is received. This may be relevant where a loss-making company still wants to benefit from the terms of a double tax treaty, and claim relief for foreign tax suffered on an overseas dividend (¶90480).

s 931R CTA 2009

Small companies

A small company is **defined** as one which has:
- fewer than 50 employees; and
- either a turnover or a gross balance sheet total not exceeding €10 million.

18385
s 931S CTA 2009

However, open-ended investment companies, authorised unit trusts, insurance companies and friendly societies are excluded.

Subject to an election to the contrary, a distribution received by a small company will be exempt where both of the following **conditions** are satisfied:
- the payer of the distribution is UK resident (¶2030) or resident in a qualifying territory; and
- the payment is not part of a scheme designed to secure a tax advantage.

> MEMO POINTS 1. A company will only be considered to be **not small** once the criteria have been exceeded for two consecutive periods.
> 2. Where a company is part of a **group**, the limits apply to a group as a whole.
> 3. A **qualifying territory** is a country with which the UK has a double tax agreement containing a non-discrimination clause (i.e. where nationals of both states must be equally treated in relation to tax). However, a paying company who is expressly excluded from one or more terms of a double tax agreement with the UK will not fulfil this criteria e.g. a company which qualifies for domestic tax reliefs in certain countries such as Malta and Cyprus.
> 4. The test for **residency** in a qualifying territory will be determined under the territory's domestic laws.

s 931C CTA 2009;
SI 2009/3314

Other companies

For companies that are not small (¶18385), there are five types of exemption which cover most distributions received by UK resident companies, **subject to** several anti-avoidance rules.

18390
s 931D CTA 2009

Exemption	Criteria	Reference
Distribution from controlled companies	Recipient alone controls (¶75275) the paying company, or recipient together with another person controls the paying company with one of the parties controlling between 40% and 55% of the share capital, rights and voting power Exemption does not apply if distribution is paid: – out of pre-control profits (profits earned before the recipient controlled the company); or – as part of a tax avoidance scheme	ss 931E, 931J CTA 2009
Distribution on non-redeemable ordinary shares	Shares must be true ordinary shares (having no preferential right to dividends or to a company's assets on a winding up) Exemption does not apply where a scheme exists involving quasi-preference or quasi-redeemable shares (that is, the terms of a share have been manipulated in order to fall within this exemption)	ss 931F, 931K CTA 2009

Exemption	Criteria	Reference
Distribution on portfolio holdings of less than 10%	For this purpose, a portfolio holding means less than 10% of: – the issued share capital (or class of share capital where the payer has issued more than one class); – the rights to profits available for distribution; and – the rights to assets on a winding up Interests of connected parties (¶31375) are taken into account, so that in practice the recipient and any connected party must own less than 10% of the paying company	ss 931G, 931L CTA 2009
Dividend derived from relevant profits (profits resulting from non-avoidance transactions)	If a company has profits that are derived from avoidance transactions (where the activity of an overseas company allows a tax deduction in the UK but with no corresponding taxable income), this exemption will not be available until the profits have been distributed as taxable dividends For this purpose, transactions up to 30 June 2008 are deemed to only result in relevant profits	s 931H CTA 2009
Dividend in respect of certain shares accounted for as liabilities under GAAP	Dividends paid when all of the following criteria are met: – the recipient and the paying company are not connected (¶31375); – the relevant shares are treated by the issuing company as a liability for accounting purposes (see *Accountancy and Financial Reporting Memo* for further details); – the shares are not publicly issued; – the shares are not held for an unallowable purpose (¶16500); and – the return on the shares is equivalent to interest For example, certain redeemable preference shares	ss 521C, 931I CTA 2009

18395 **Anti-avoidance rules** Altogether there are eight rules, and those **specific** to a particular exemption are detailed in ¶18390 above.

The rules which **affect any exemption** are as follows (reference to scheme means a tax advantage scheme):

Rule	Details	Reference
Schemes in the nature of loan relationships	Where the following conditions are met: – the recipient and dividend payer companies are connected (¶31375); and – the dividend gives a return reasonably comparable to a commercial rate of interest based on the time value of money This would cover shares with guaranteed returns	s 931M CTA 2009
Schemes involving distributions for which deductions are given	Where a tax deduction is obtained outside the UK	s 931N CTA 2009
Schemes involving payments for distributions	Where the dividend takes the form of an annual payment or where a right to taxable income is forgone in return for a potentially exempt distribution	ss 931O, 1301 CTA 2009
Schemes involving payments not at arm's length	For transactions not already subject to the transfer pricing rules (¶70000), where the dividend payment alters the amount payable for goods and services between two companies	s 931P CTA 2009
Schemes involving diversion of trade income	Where a scheme converts trading income (e.g. for a share dealing company) into distribution income in order to access an exemption This would normally involve another party receiving the distribution instead of the share dealing company	s 931Q CTA 2009

B. Non-corporate recipients

The tax treatment **depends on** whether the distribution is a qualifying distribution or not. The following outlines the tax treatment of individuals. For details of personal representatives and trustees see *Tax Memo*.

18425

Qualifying distributions

Dividend income is taxed as the top slice of an individual's savings income. **Tax is payable** on the amount of the distribution, plus the tax credit, **at the following rates**:

18430
s 397 ITTOIA 2005

Taxable amount 2013/14 (£)	Rate	Known as
0 – 32,010 (basic rate band)	10%	the "dividend ordinary rate"
34,370 – 150,000 (higher rate band)	32.5%	the "dividend upper rate"
Over 150,000 (additional rate band)	37.5%	the "dividend additional rate"

For details of the bands which apply to other tax years, see *Tax Memo*.

A notional **tax credit** is calculated as 1/9th of the net dividend (i.e. 10% of the gross dividend). Tax is charged on the gross amount. UK residents and certain eligible non-residents can deduct tax credits from their income tax liability. A tax credit cannot give rise to a refund (if a distribution is, for example, partly covered by the personal allowance).

18435

MEMO POINTS   The following **non-residents** can claim a tax credit for qualifying distributions:
– citizens of the Republic of Ireland, Commonwealth citizens and nationals of EEA states, who are entitled to, and actually have claimed, personal allowances; and
– residents of an overseas territory with which the UK has a double taxation treaty, which provides for tax credits.

Non-qualifying distributions

Non-qualifying distributions are taxed like qualifying distributions, **except** that there is no tax credit. Therefore, tax is charged on the actual distribution received. Income tax is still treated as having been paid at the 10% dividend rate. This reduces the tax liability, but cannot give rise to a refund.

18440
s 400 ITTOIA 2005

Where the redemption of **bonus shares**, other than on a winding up, gives rise to a higher rate tax liability, the liability will be reduced by the amount of any higher rate tax paid on the original issue of bonus shares (i.e. the non-qualifying distribution). See *Tax Memo* for further details.

Capital distributions

Capital distribution means a distribution from a company which is **not treated as income** for tax purposes in the hands of the recipient.

18445

A UK recipient of a capital distribution is treated as having made a disposal of his shares, and so a chargeable gain arises. See *Tax Memo* for details of capital gains tax.

SECTION 3

Purchases of own shares

In most cases, where a company makes a purchase of own shares and pays more than the capital originally subscribed for the shares, the excess constitutes a distribution.

18495

However, the following exceptions apply so that shares sold back to a company by:
a. corporate shareholders on or after 1 July 2009 are likely to result in a chargeable gain (¶30000), as the transaction will probably be exempt from being taxed as a distribution (¶¶18380); and
b. individual shareholders of unquoted companies may result in a capital payment subject to capital gains tax.

Comment   The main reason why a company would want to purchase its own shares is to allow a shareholder to exit the company when no buyer can be found. Further, a buy-back would increase gearing which may be commercially attractive. Note that stamp duty is payable when form 169 is filed with the Registrar of Companies.

Cancellation of shares

18500
For most buy-backs, the shares purchased must be cancelled so that the company does not regain ownership of the shares.

s 195 FA 2003
However, **listed companies** (including companies listed on AIM) are permitted to purchase their own shares and hold them in "Treasury", and subsequently either cancel or sell them. For tax purposes Treasury shares will be treated as if they do not exist. They will be treated as cancelled when they are purchased into Treasury.

> ⌐MEMO POINTS⌐   Any **subsequent disposal** of Treasury shares by the company to a third party investor is treated as a new share issue, but no venture capital trust (VCT) investment relief (¶80355+) is available to the investor. The company must notify the investor accordingly, at the time of such a subscription, and a copy of this notice must also be sent to HMRC no later than 3 months after the subscription.

A. Distribution treatment in unquoted companies

18530
Unless capital treatment applies, a buy-back is treated as a distribution. The **taxable amount** is the proceeds of the buy-back less the amount originally subscribed for the shares.

In certain circumstances it may be **less beneficial** for the shareholder to receive a capital payment than a distribution. It is imperative that both scenarios are considered in detail so that the shareholder does not suffer tax unnecessarily.

In order for the buy-back to be taxed as a distribution, it is theoretically necessary to **breach** one of the **conditions for capital treatment** (¶18565).

> ⌐MEMO POINTS⌐   A **breach of conditions** can be arranged, for example, by manipulating the loan and share capital to ensure that an individual remains connected with the company following the buy-back. In practice it is usually enough when applying for clearance (¶18720) to inform HMRC that the buy-back is not for the purpose of benefiting the company's trade (¶18615).

> ⌐EXAMPLE⌐   Mr A, a 25% shareholder, is selling his 20,000 shares back to B Ltd for £70,000. Mr A bought his shares for £40,000 from Mr C a couple of years ago. The original subscription price for the shares was £20,000.
> The excess over the subscription price is taxed as a distribution of £50,000 in the hands of Mr A. (70,000 − 20,000)
> A capital loss of £20,000 is realised on the difference between the subscription price and the price Mr A paid to Mr C. (20,000 − 40,000)

B. Capital treatment in unquoted companies

18560
s 1033 CTA 2010
Provided certain conditions are met, a buy-back from an individual shareholder will be treated as a capital disposal.

However, capital treatment will **not apply** where the transaction is carried on either:
− for the avoidance of tax; or
− to enable the vendor to share in the profits of the company without receiving a dividend.

MEMO POINTS   1. The company must pay the total **amount due** for the shares immediately in cash.
2. There will be no corporation tax deduction for **legal and other expenses** relating to the buy-back, even where it is undertaken for the benefit of the trade.
3. For **certainty of tax treatment** relating to a particular transaction, prior clearance can be obtained from HMRC (¶18720).
4. A capital disposal may be **less expensive** for a shareholder if he has capital losses or trading losses to set against the gain, or can claim entrepreneurs' relief. See *Tax Memo* for further details.

CTM 17600

Comment   Care must be taken with **bonus issues** (either before or after the buy-back).

EXAMPLE   If Mr A, in the example in ¶18530 above, had held his shares for 6 years, and all other criteria were met, the capital treatment would apply.
A capital gain of £30,000 would arise (before reliefs and annual exemption), against which Mr A could set any capital losses arising. In particular, entrepreneurs' relief might substantially reduce the gain.

Summary

The following table summarises the criteria which apply.

18565
s 1033 CTA 2010

Element	Criteria	Vendor conditions	Reference	¶¶
Company	UK resident unquoted trading company or holding company of a trading group	Depends on reason for purchase – see below	s 1033 CTA 2010	¶18595
Reason for purchase: either	For the benefit of the trade of the company or that of a 75% subsidiary (¶18615)	UK resident in the year of the buy-back	s 1034 CTA 2010	¶18640
		Has held the shares for 5 years (3 years if the shares were inherited)	s 1035 CTA 2010	¶18645
		If still holding shares after the buy-back, has had his interest substantially reduced	s 1037 CTA 2010	¶18650
		Not connected with the company immediately after the buy-back	s 1042 CTA 2010	¶18660
	To enable inheritance tax to be paid on the death of a shareholder (where undue hardship would otherwise arise)	None	s 1033 CTA 2010	¶18690

1. Company requirement

The company and any parent company (any company which beneficially owns more than 50% of the shares) must be unquoted and UK resident (¶2030). For this purpose AIM shares are unquoted.

18595
ss 1033, 1048
CTA 2010

For details of what constitutes **trading** see ¶5000. Note, however, that trading **excludes** dealing in shares, securities, land or futures.

2. Benefit of the trade

Where relevant, the purchase of the shares must be made wholly or mainly to benefit a trade **carried on** either **by** the company or its 75% subsidiary.

18615

HMRC have published **guidance** on the situations in which they consider a purchase of own shares would be for the benefit of the trade. These primarily relate to the existence of an unwilling shareholder who could disrupt the operation of the business, including:
– outside shareholders who wish to withdraw their equity finance;

SP 2/82;
Tax Bulletin 21

– a controlling shareholder retiring to make way for new management;
– a shareholder fundamentally disagreeing with the way that the company is run;
– personal representatives of a deceased shareholder wishing to realise the value of the shares; and
– a legatee of a deceased shareholder who does not want to hold shares in the company.

The main point is that the buy-back should not be undertaken solely for the shareholder's benefit.

> <u>MEMO POINTS</u>   1. A **75% subsidiary** means that the parent company beneficially owns at least 75% of the ordinary shares. This holding may be direct, or through another company (¶65115).
> 2. HMRC generally require the entire shareholding of an **unwilling shareholder** to be purchased by the company, although they may accept a lower amount in the following situations:
> – insufficient funds are available to purchase the full holding in one tranche; or
> – for sentimental reasons, a retiring controlling shareholder wishes to retain a small stake in the business. In this situation, the vendor's holding (including shares held by his associates) must be substantially reduced (¶18650).
> 3. Where a **company** wishes to buy out a shareholder but has **insufficient funds**, it is not unusual for the departing shareholder to loan part of the proceeds back to the company. Where the issued share capital of the company is low in relation to the company's market value, this may result in the former shareholder being connected with the company. To avoid this, it is acceptable for the company to make a bonus issue to shareholders prior to the purchase of own shares, thus increasing the issued share capital.

3. Vendor criteria

18635   The vendor criteria below only apply where the **purpose** of the buy-back is to benefit the company's trade.

Residence

18640   The vendor must be UK resident in the tax year of the buy-back.
s 1034 CTA 2010

> <u>MEMO POINTS</u>   1. An individual is **resident** for a tax year (year ending 5 April) if he meets any of the following statutory tests relating to that year:
> – he spends at least 183 days in the UK;
> – his main home is in the UK and he spends at least 30 days there;
> – he works full-time in the UK; or
> – he dies when his main home is in the UK and he has a recent history of UK residence.
> There are also tests of non-residence which generally reflect the opposite of the above circumstances, and which he must not meet. Even failing the above tests, an individual can still be UK-resident if he has **sufficient UK ties** of family, work, accommodation and frequent presence, and a recent history of UK residence.
> It is possible for a **split year** to arise when an individual enters or leaves the UK. In that case, he is treated as resident for part of the year, and non-resident for the rest.
> Note that these criteria apply only for **2013/14** and subsequent tax years. For full details of the criteria, see *Tax Memo 2013-2014*, and for earlier years see previous editions of *Corporation Tax Memo*.
> 2. For **2012/13 and earlier tax years**, the individual had also to be ordinarily resident in the UK. This was a broader concept which reflected habitual residence, and has now been subsumed into the statutory criteria for UK residence. For full details, see *Tax Memo 2013-2014*.
> 3. A **trust** residence is determined by the residence of its trustees, as follows::

Residence of trustees[1]	Status of settlor when he provided funds to trust	Residence of trust
All UK-resident	(Irrelevant)	UK-resident
All non-resident	(Irrelevant)	Non-resident
At least one is UK-resident, and another is non-resident	UK-resident or UK-domiciled[2]	UK-resident
	Non-resident and not UK-domiciled[2]	Non-resident

Note:
1. A trustee who is non-resident, but exercises his trusteeship in the course of a business carried on in the UK through a branch, agency or permanent establishment, is treated as UK-resident.
2. Domicile is a link to a jurisdiction, and is not necessarily the same as place of residence or nationality. For further details of trusts and domicile see *Tax Memo*.

Ownership period

The **minimum** ownership period is usually 5 years (measured at the date of sale).

However, if the shares were **inherited** (either under the terms of a will or by the rights of intestacy) the required period is reduced to 3 years, and in this case the ownership period of the deceased and his personal representatives are aggregated.

Where relevant, the previous ownership period of a **spouse** or civil partner is taken into account so long as the relationship still subsists when the buy-back occurs (that is, the couple were living together both at the time of the original transfer and also at the date of the buy-back).

If the vendor has acquired the shares in **different tranches**, the shares repurchased by the company are matched with the earliest acquisitions to give the longest possible period of ownership.

18645
ss 1035, 1036
CTA 2010

EXAMPLE Mr D inherited the following shares in E Ltd:

Year	Number of shares
1	300
2	700
4	800

If Mr D sells 500 shares in Year 3, these are matched with the acquisition in Year 2, following the usual identification rules.
If E Ltd repurchases all of Mr D's shares in Year 7, these are matched with the acquisitions in Year 1 and Year 4, and the remaining 200 shares in Year 2.

Substantial reduction in interest

This means that the shareholder's interest in the company or group (after the purchase of own shares) **must be less than** 75% of his interest immediately before the buy-back. The interests of his associates must also be taken into account, unless it is the associate disposing of shares so that another shareholder can satisfy this test.

18650
s 1037 CTA 2010

If a transaction occurs within 1 year of the buy-back, which would have the effect of failing this test, then this is deemed to be part of an arrangement which then nullifies the capital treatment.

For this purpose interest is **measured** in terms of both share ownership and entitlement to profits.

MEMO POINTS 1. The following are **associates** for this purpose:
– spouses or civil partners living together;
– children aged under 18 and their parents;
– a person connected with a company and that company, and also any company controlled by it (in this case the company is also associated with any other company which that person controls);
– a person who acts under another's instructions in relation to the company and that other person;
– trustees and the trust settlor and his associates;
– trustees and the beneficiary and anyone else who may become beneficially entitled to at least 5% of the trust shares (as measured in value); and
– personal representatives and any person who is or may become beneficially entitled to more than 5% of the shares forming part of the death estate.

ss 1059 – 1061
CTA 2010

2. **Profits** available for distribution by a company are the sum of:
– accumulated realised profits not distributed less accumulated realised losses;
– £100; and
– where relevant, the amount which would be needed to pay all fixed rate distributions in a year.

s 1038 CTA 2010

3. The interest in **shares** (both before and after the buy-back) is measured as follows:

$$\frac{\text{Nominal value of the shares owned by the vendor}}{\text{Nominal value of the issued share capital of the company}}$$

EXAMPLE F Ltd has issued 10,000 shares of £1 each. Mr G has a shareholding of 6,000 shares (i.e. 60%) and sells 4,000 of them back to F Ltd, leaving him with 2,000 shares.
After the buy-back occurs there remain 6,000 shares in issue, with Mr G holding 2,000. This means he now holds 33%.
Mr G has substantially reduced his holding. (60% × 75% = 45% which is more than the remaining 33% shareholding)

18655
s 1039 CTA 2010

Groups   Where the repurchasing company is a member of a group, then the substantial reduction test may become more complex if either of the **scenarios** below apply:
– the vendor still owns shares in a group member after the buy-back; or
– the vendor or his associate owned shares in a group member before the buy-back.

As for a single company, it is the combined interests of the vendor and his associates which are subject to the test.

The interests in the group are **calculated** by:
– looking at each company in turn;
– aggregating the resulting fractions; and
– dividing them by the number of group companies in which the vendor had an interest either before or after the buy-back.

MEMO POINTS   For this purpose a group is **defined** as a company and its 51% subsidiaries (¶18165), including:
– a company that has ceased to be a member of the group, if there are arrangements under which it could rejoin the group; and
– any successor company (or group), which took on a significant part of a business from the purchasing company or group less than 3 years before the date of the buy-back.

EXAMPLE Mr A holds interests in group companies as follows (each of whom have 1,000 issued ordinary share capital of £1):

Company	Number of shares owned
B Ltd	300
C Ltd	50
D Ltd	30
E Ltd	-

Mr A sells his holding in C Ltd back to the company.
Before the purchase, the calculation of interests is as follows:

$$\frac{300}{1,000} + \frac{50}{1,000} + \frac{30}{1,000} + 0 = \frac{380}{1,000} = 38\%$$

This must be divided by three (as this is the number of companies Mr A has an interest in), so this group interest is 12.67%.
After the purchase, the calculation of interests is as follows:

$$\frac{300}{1,000} + 0 + \frac{30}{1,000} + 0 = \frac{330}{1,000} = 33\%$$

This must again be divided by three, so the group interest is 11%.
To have substantially reduced his interest Mr A needs to retain less than 9.503 %. As he still has an 11% share he has not substantially reduced his interest in the group.

Connection to company

18660
s 1042 CTA 2010

Immediately after the share buy-back the vendor must not be connected with the company or any company in the same group.

A person is connected with the company if, immediately following the purchase of own shares, he
a. controls the company (¶75275); or
b. owns, or is entitled to acquire (together with his associates), more than 30% of the:
– voting power;
– issued share capital;

- issued share and loan capital; or
- assets on a winding up.

For this purpose a holding of **loan capital** acquired in the normal course of a money-lending business is disregarded, so long as the lender takes no part in the management of the company

> MEMO POINTS Following the amendment of CA2006 on **30 April 2013**, it is permissible for a company to pay for the shares by instalments. Unpaid future instalments are liabilities of the company, amounting to loans made to it by the vendor of the shares. Such liabilities may need to be taken into account when considering whether the vendor is connected with the company.

SI 2013/999

4. Payment of inheritance tax

In cases of hardship, the proceeds of the buy-back can be used to discharge the inheritance tax liability resulting from a death which would otherwise not be affordable. Payment must be made within 2 years of the death, and substantially all of the proceeds must be used for this purpose although any related capital gains tax liability arising on the share buy-back can also be met out of the same funds.

18690
s 1033 CTA 2010

Note that, in this case only, the **vendor** does not need to fulfil any specific criteria.

5. Administration

Where capital treatment applies, reporting obligations are placed on the company. A clearance procedure also exists to ensure that HMRC will treat a particular set of circumstances as falling within the capital treatment.

18710

Comment It is vital to obtain clearance before proceeding with any particular transaction.

Reporting

The **company** must make a report to HMRC **within** 60 days of paying the proceeds of the buy-back. The report must contain relevant details and explain why the buy-back falls within the rules for capital treatment. This is the case even where prior clearance has been obtained (¶18720).

18715
s 1046 CTA 2010

Any **person** connected to the company, who knows of a **scheme or arrangement** (¶18560) that affects the buy-back, must report the details to HMRC. Again the time limit is 60 days, and this period starts from the day that the person first knows about the buy-back and the scheme.

HMRC have the power to issue a **notice** to the company or anyone connected to it to obtain information as follows:
- a declaration stating whether a scheme exists or has existed; and
- any other information which can be reasonably obtained by the recipient.

Failure to comply with any of these requirements will result in penalties (¶52360).

Clearance

Clearance may be obtained from HMRC confirming whether or not capital treatment applies to a particular transaction.

18720
ss 1044, 1045
CTA 2010;
SP 2/82

An **application** should be made giving full details of the proposed transaction, and HMRC then have 30 days in which to give a decision or request further information. Failure to give full and accurate information would render the clearance, if granted, ineffective. Such a clearance is usually combined with an application relating to transactions in securities (¶21535), and in this case, two copies of the clearance application and enclosures should be sent.

There is no right of **appeal** to the tribunal should HMRC not give clearance.

MEMO POINTS 1. Applications should be **sent to**:
Clearance and Counteraction Team (Anti-Avoidance Group)
SO528
PO Box 194
Bootle
L69 9AA
Email: reconstructions@hmrc.gsi.gov.uk
2. Full **guidance** on the order and presentation of information is given by HMRC in the annex to SP 2/82.

CHAPTER 7

Property income

Income deriving from land or property is treated as a property business for companies, distinguished only by whether the property is located within the UK or overseas. **19000**

All profits and losses from UK properties owned by a company are pooled together for each accounting period and taxed as a single property business. Similarly, all of a company's overseas properties are taxed as a single overseas property business (¶19575).

The Real Estate Investment Trust regime (¶19635), which offers a tax exempt arena for holding property, is available to listed companies only.

For the annual tax on enveloped dwellings, see *Tax Memo 2013-14*.

SECTION 1

Scope

Every activity which a company carries on with a view to generating income from land in the UK forms part of a single property business. **19050**

ss 205, 207
CTA 2009

This includes the **exploitation** of an estate, interest or right in or over land as a source of rents or other receipts.

> ‾MEMO POINTS‾ 1. **Rent** includes any payments by a tenant for work to maintain or repair the premises which are not required by the lease terms.
> 2. **Other receipts** include:
> – payments in respect of a licence to occupy or otherwise use land;
> – payments in respect of the exercise of any other right over land; and
> – rent charges and other annual payments received in respect of, or relating to, the land.
> 3. A right to use a **houseboat or caravan** at only one location is treated as a right deriving from an interest in land.
> 4. Where a company is also a partner in a **partnership** which is carrying on another property business, the two property business of the partnership is treated as distinct and separate from that of the company alone.

Exclusions

19055
ss 38, 39, 208
CTA 2009

The following **activities** do not form part of the company's property business:
a. farming or market gardening carried out in the UK (¶84055);
b. income from any of the following types of concerns:
– mines and quarries;
– ironworks, gasworks, salt springs or works, alum mines or works, waterworks and streams of water;
– canals, inland navigation, docks and drains or levels;
– rights of fishing;
– rights of markets and fairs, tolls, bridges and ferries; and
– railways and other kinds of way; and
c. other commercial occupation of land in the UK (excluding woodlands, which are not taxable).

Note also that the rent-a-room scheme does not apply to companies.

SECTION 2

Properties in the UK

19105

Income and expenses from properties in the UK are **recognised** on an accruals basis (¶11330) using GAAP principles (so, for example, capital items (¶13050) are not included in profits).

As the results are aggregated among all UK properties, there is no requirement to apportion or allocate costs or even income to specific properties for tax purposes.

For property business **losses**, see ¶36205.

> ‾MEMO POINTS‾ For this purpose, the **UK excludes** the Isle of Man and the Channel Islands.

A. Income

19135
ss 210–212
CTA 2009

Income and expenses are generally computed in the same way as profits from a trade (¶14200).

For corporation tax purposes, the following rules are therefore particularly pertinent:
– credits or debits arising from **loan relationships** (¶16050) and **derivative contracts** (¶16775) are taxed separately from the property business;
– **interest received or paid**, and any other similar items must be excluded from the property business profits and included within the tax computation as credits or debits of loan relationships (¶16080) or derivative contracts (¶16775);

– **capital allowances** (¶25110) are available on tangible assets and are deducted from the property business profits (or added to profits, if a balancing charge arises); and
– any **intangible assets** held by the property business are dealt with under the appropriate regime (¶28135), and any resulting credits or debits included within the property business results.

---

1. Exclusions

Income which is taxable as part of a **trade** is obviously excluded from a property business. In particular this excludes:
– tied premises (i.e. goods are sold by another person at premises owned by the taxpayer), where receipts are taxable as part of the trade;
– the operation of a caravan site when a trade is carried on;
– small rental streams from surplus business accommodation (¶19170); and
– certain income from wayleaves (¶19175).

19165
s 213 CTA 2009

Surplus business accommodation

The company may choose to treat income arising from surplus business accommodation as trading income, provided that:
a. the premises are not held as trading stock, and are partly **used** for the trade and partly let;
b. the premises are **temporarily surplus** to requirements, which means:
– it has either been used for the purposes of the trade, or acquired, within the last 3 years;
– it is intended to use the premises for the purposes of the trade at a later date; and
– the accommodation is let, or a licence to occupy is granted, for less than 3 years; and
c. the amount of rental income is relatively small (not defined).

Once the choice is made to tax as trading income, this treatment must be maintained for as long as the conditions are satisfied.

19170
s 44 CTA 2009

Wayleaves

A wayleave is **defined** as an easement, servitude, or right in or over land which is enjoyed in connection with either:
– an electric, telegraph, or telephone wire or cable (this includes a pole, pylon or any other related apparatus); or
– a pipe for the conveyance of anything (this also includes any related apparatus).

19175
s 45 CTA 2009

The company may choose to include the wayleave in its trading profits provided that:
– some or all of the land is **used for carrying on its trade**; and
– **no other items** (rents, similar receipts or expenses) relating to that land are accounted for as part of the company's property business (other than any which relate only to the wayleave itself).

Otherwise, the wayleave is included in the company's property business.

However, the company may choose to tax income relating to UK **electric-line wayleaves** as either:
– trading income (as above); or
– property business income, either as part of an existing UK property business (if it has other rental receipts in the accounting period) or as a stand-alone activity.

ss 277 – 279
CTA 2009

---

2. Lease premiums

Lump sums received for the grant of a **lease of not more than 50 years** are taxable partly as income and partly as a chargeable gain (unless the company is a property dealer, in which case they would be treated as trading income).

19205
s 217 CTA 2009

PIM 1204

The lease may either be **granted by** the freeholder, or as a sublease by the tenant (in which case the sublease tends to expire not later than 1 day before the head lease ceases).

In certain cases (¶19220), a deemed premium may arise.

> MEMO POINTS   1. A premium for a lease **in excess of 50 years** is always a capital receipt.
> 2. A premium or other lump sum paid for the **assignment or sale of a lease**, in which all of the tenant's interest in an existing lease is transferred to another party, is also a capital receipt.
> 3. The **Scottish equivalent** of a premium is a grassum.
> 4. For **reverse premiums** (an incentive payment to attract tenants), see ¶14455. Note that for the landlord, this will be a capital expense unless made by a builder or developer in the course of a trade, or the payment is actually a contribution to the tenant's fixtures when the landlord can claim capital allowances.

Length of the lease

19210
ss 243–245
CTA 2009

Special provisions exist to prevent landlords **manipulating the length of the lease** term so as to gain a tax advantage. HMRC will consider the terms of the lease. If there is a clause in the lease or other agreement which in practice affects the likely termination date of the lease, the lease may be deemed for tax purposes to end at some other date, according to the following rules:

1. If the lease is likely to **terminate before** the expiry of the lease, the lease term will be deemed to end at that earlier date. For example, if a 60 year lease at a commercial rent includes a clause whereby the rent can be doubled after 10 years have expired, it would be likely that the lease term will be treated as ending after the 10 years have expired;

2. If the lease is likely to **continue beyond** the expiry of the lease, the lease will be deemed to end at the later date. For example, a 20 year lease with an excessive rent charged, containing a clause permitting the lease to continue for a further 20 years at a reduced rent, would be likely to be deemed to end after the 40 years have expired; or

3. If a lease of the **same premises** is likely to be granted to the tenant or person connected with him on the expiry of the original lease, the lease term will be deemed to end at the expiry of the further lease. For example, a 10 year lease, granted to Mr B, containing a clause that on expiry a further lease will be granted to Mrs B, is likely to be deemed to end on the expiry of Mrs B's lease.

> EXAMPLE   1. A Ltd grants a 60 year lease at a commercial rent, including a clause whereby the rent can be doubled after 10 years. It is likely that the lease term will be deemed to be only 10 years.
> 2. B Ltd grants a 20 year lease at an excessive rent contains a clause permitting the lease to continue for a further 20 years at a reduced rent. It is likely that the lease term will be deemed to be 40 years.
> 3. A 10 year lease, granted to CLtd, contains a clause that on expiry a further lease will be granted to D Ltd, a fellow group company. It is likely that the lease term will be deemed to end on the expiry of D Ltd's lease

Charge to income

19215
s 217 CTA 2009

The proportion to be charged as income depends on the length of the lease, and is treated as a receipt of the property business for the accounting period in which the lease is granted. The income-tax proportion is given by the following **formula**:

$$P \times \frac{(50 - (Y\text{-}1))}{50}$$

where:
− P is the premium received; and
− Y is the number of complete years of the lease.

s 236 CTA 2009

> MEMO POINTS   1. If a premium is payable in **instalments**, the company can elect to pay the corporation tax in instalments over the shorter of 8 years and the period over which the premium is payable.
> 2. For the deduction available to a **tenant who is subletting**, see ¶19405.
> 3. For the deduction available to a **tenant who uses** the property **for business** purposes, see ¶14735.

> EXAMPLE X Ltd lets a property on a 40 year lease and receives a premium of £20,000.
> The proportion taxed as income is £4,400. $(20,000 \times \frac{(50-39)}{50})$

Deemed premiums

In the following situations, a landlord will be deemed to receive a premium:

19220

Situation	Detail	Reference
Tenant repairing obligations	Where a landlord imposes an obligation on the tenant to undertake improvement work, and forgoes rental or premium income in return, a deemed premium arises The deemed premium is valued as the amount by which the requirement to undertake the improvement work increases the value of the landlord's reversionary interest (valued at the date of the commencement of the lease)	s 218 CTA 2009
Lump sum payments	The following will be taxable as premiums in the usual manner in the year in which the sum is paid: – payments in lieu of rent; – payments for the surrender of the lease; and – payments for the variation or waiver of the lease terms For the purposes of the formula in ¶19215 above: – the premium is the total sum received; and – the duration of the lease is the period from the year the payment was made to the end of the original lease term or, where applicable, the period for which the variation or waiver is effective	ss 219 – 221A CTA 2009
Sale with right to repurchase[1]	A deemed premium arises on a sale with a clause giving the vendor (or a connected person (¶31375)) the right to reacquire the freehold within 50 years For the purposes of the formula in ¶19215 above: – the premium is the amount by which the sale price exceeds the price at which it is to be repurchased; and – the duration of the lease runs from the date of sale to the earliest possible repurchase date.	ss 224, 226 CTA 2009

Sale with right to leaseback[1,2]	A deemed premium arises on a sale with a clause giving the vendor (or a connected person (¶31375)) the right to be granted a leasehold interest in the property within 50 years, unless the leaseback is granted within 1 month of the sale
	For the purposes of the formula in ¶19215 above:
	– the deemed premium is the excess of the original sale price over the sum of:
	  – any lease premium; and
	  – the value at the date of the sale of the freehold of the reversionary interest immediately after the lease has begun to run (it will usually be necessary to agree this value with the District Valuer); and
	– the duration of the lease runs from the date of sale to the earliest possible leaseback date.
		ss 225, 226
		CTA 2009

Assignment of lease at undervalue	Where a short lease is granted at an undervalue and a profit is made on a subsequent assignment of the lease, the assignor will be treated as having received a premium.
	For the purposes of the formula in ¶19215 above:
	– the premium is the smaller of:
	  – the amount forgone by the landlord (the additional amount which the original grantor of the lease could have charged but did not); and
	  – the profit made on the assignment of the lease (any profit made in excess of the amount paid for the original lease or, where applicable, the amount paid for the last assignment); and
	– the duration of the original lease is used
		ss 222, 223
		CTA 2009

Note:
1. Where the sale **contract does not fix the date** of reconveyance or leaseback, and the **price varies** with the date, the calculation is first performed using the lowest possible contractual price. When the reconveyance or leaseback takes place, the calculation can be revised and a repayment claimed. HMRC cannot increase the original charge.
2. There are several **anti-avoidance rules** affecting sale and leaseback transactions (¶19505).

EXAMPLE

1. A Ltd grants a 10 year **tenant repairing lease**, which requires the tenant to undertake specific improvement works. In return, no rent will be charged.
The improvement works increase the value of A Ltd's reversionary interest by £100,000 from the value at the date that the lease commenced.
A Ltd is taxable on the deemed premium of £82,000 in the accounting period in which the lease is granted. ($100,000 \times \frac{(50-9)}{50}$)

2. B Ltd grants a 10 year lease which contains a clause allowing the tenant to pay a **lump sum** of £20,000 in Year 5 in lieu of rent for the remaining term of the lease.
For this purpose, the duration of the lease is 5 years (the period remaining from the original lease term).
B Ltd will be taxable on the deemed premium of £18,400 in the accounting period of receipt.

($20,000 \times \frac{(50-4)}{50}$)

3. C Ltd sold a property in Year 1 for £500,000, with a **right to repurchase** in Year 3 for £475,000. The amount of the deemed premium is £25,000. (500,000 – 475,000)
The duration of the lease is 3 years.

C Ltd will be taxable on an amount of £24,000. ($25,000 \times \frac{(50-2)}{50}$)

4. D Ltd sold a property in Year 1 for £500,000, with a clause giving the company the **right to be granted a lease** of the property in Year 3 for a premium of £100,000.
After liaising with the District Valuer, it was agreed that the value of the reversionary interest was £300,000.
The deemed premium is £100,000. (500,000 – (100,000 + 300,000)

D Ltd will be taxable on an amount of £96,000. ($100,000 \times \frac{(50-2)}{50}$)

5. E Ltd **granted** a 10 year lease in Year 1 to F Ltd. A premium of £50,000 would have represented a market rate, but in fact only £10,000 was charged. The **amount forgone** by the landlord is therefore £40,000. (50,000 – 10,000)
In Year 3, F Ltd **assigns** the lease to G Ltd for £35,000.
F Ltd would be chargeable as follows:

		£	£
Consideration received – smaller of:			
F Ltd's profit; and	35,000 – 10,000	25,000	
Amount forgone		40,000	
			25,000
Deemed premium	$25,000 \times \frac{(50-9)}{50}$		20,500

In Year 5, G Ltd assigns the lease to H Ltd for £50,000. G Ltd would be chargeable as follows:

		£	£
Consideration received – smaller of:			
G Ltd's profit; and	50,000 – 35,000	15,000	
Balance of amount forgone	40,000 – 35,000	5,000	
			5,000
Deemed premium	$5,000 \times \frac{(50-9)}{50}$		4,100

B. Expenses

Expenses are only deductible where they have been incurred wholly and exclusively (¶14540) for the **purposes** of the property business.

> MEMO POINTS 1. Where a rental property is **temporarily empty** (for example, between tenancies), expenditure incurred during a vacant period may still be deducted provided it relates wholly and exclusively to the rental business.
> 2. Capital expenditure on the **construction of a sea wall or embankment** to protect the premises against flooding is deductible as a revenue expense spread over 21 years. This deduction is subject to the condition that the same person is carrying on the property trade and incurring the expense.

19250

Summary

Common deductible expenses include:

19255

Expense	Overview	¶¶
Insurance	Includes costs of insuring vacant properties which are available to let	¶19260
Repairs and maintenance	Excludes any capital costs such as refurbishment or improvements	¶19265
Management fees	Includes rent collection costs	
Advertising	Advertising for new tenants is allowable (for example. newspaper adverts) Excludes permanent advertising costs e.g. expense of permanent boards and signs, and also advertising property to buy and sell	
Rent and rates	Usually deductible	¶19275
Legal and professional fees	Excludes capital legal fees such as those relating to acquiring the property, or to the first letting (or subletting) of the property for more than 1 year	¶19280
Wear and tear allowance	Only available for furnished properties	¶19290

Insurance

Premiums paid in respect of the following **risks** are deductible:
- damage to the fabric of the property;
- damage to the contents; and
- loss of rents (but see ¶13210).

With the exception of insured rents, **amounts recovered** should normally be set against the cost of repairs, although where there is a delay in receiving monies from an insurer, it may be necessary to deduct the expense before crediting the receipt.

Receipts relating to loss of rents will be taxable as income where the premiums were deductible.

19260
PIM 2040

Repairs and maintenance

Costs that are not capital will be deductible. For this purpose, the following issues need to be considered:
a. whether the property has been **improved or altered** by the expenditure, and to what degree (a small improvement which is incidental may count as a repair). Reconstruction or rebuilding is always capital with repairs to retained existing structures counting as revenue. In certain cases, an apportionment of costs incurred will be required;

19265
PIM 2020

b. the availability of capital **allowances** on capital costs (¶25240), and the wear and tear allowance for furnished residential property (¶19290);

c. contributions by the tenant towards repair costs are taxable as income, and it is incorrect to set them off against the costs incurred by the landlord;

d. dilapidations payable by the tenant can be treated as follows, where:

– the landlord subsequently disposes of the property or occupies it, they are likely to be compensation for the poor state of the property and taxed as a capital receipt;

– new tenants are found, they will be compensation for the lower rent yield and hence fill a hole in the landlord's profits; or

– they are a contribution to the repair costs incurred by the landlord, the net expense borne by the landlord is deductible.

> MEMO POINTS   1. HMRC has published a draft version of revised guidance on revenue repairs to property (see flmemo.co.uk/ctm19265). This is meant to be included in the Business Income Manual some time in 2013, together with guidance on the statutory renewals basis (¶19295). HMRC also intends to publish revised guidance on the more complex capital versus revenue aspects of repairs.
> 2. For **grants** received, see ¶13160.
> 3. There are allowances in respect of **energy-saving** work such as installing loft, cavity wall or solid wall insulation, draught proofing or insulation for hot water systems (¶19395).

19270
PIM 2020

Common examples of deductible repairs include the following:

– exterior and interior painting and decorating;
– stone cleaning;
– damp and rot treatment;
– mending broken windows, doors, furniture and machines such as cookers or lifts;
– repointing; and
– replacing roof slates, flashing and gutters.

See also ¶13310.

> EXAMPLE   A Ltd refurbishes a kitchen in a property which is part of its letting business. The following work is undertaken:
> – stripping out and replacement of base units, wall units, sink etc;
> – retiling;
> – work top replacement;
> – repairs to floor coverings;
> – associated replastering; and
> – rewiring.
> If the kitchen is basically replaced with a similar type of kitchen then this is a repair.
> If, however, some further storage is fitted (such as additional cabinets), and/or extra appliances are acquired, that would an improvement and those particular costs would be capital additions.
> If the whole kitchen is improved – for example, the design is customised and the materials and units are of a much higher quality than before – the entire cost would be capital.

Rent and rates

19275
PIM 2025, 2030

Where the company **occupies part of the property** which it also lets out, a proportion of the rent and rates payable by the landlord may be deductible.

If an entire property is available to let, but some **parts are vacant**, it is still acceptable to deduct the total costs.

> MEMO POINTS   1. For this purpose, the **costs include**:
> – business rates;
> – water rates and water service charges; and
> – council tax.
> 2. **Council tax** (or the Scottish equivalent) is a liability which is generally payable by individuals who live in a domestic property. Where the landlord is liable for the charge (such as in the case of empty properties, or multiple occupancy dwellings), it is deductible in the property business.

Legal and professional fees

HMRC give the following **guidance** in respect of legal fees:

19280
PIM 2205

Fees relating to	Detail	Deductible?
Renewal of a lease	If the lease is for less than 50 years	✓
	Exclude any proportion of the costs that relate to the payment of a premium on the renewal of the lease	
Change of tenants	Costs of similar replacement lease excluding any expense relating to the premium	✓
Change of use	Costs are likely to be capital, for example if a long lease replaces a short lease, or a new tenant found after occupation by the landlord	x
Valuation	For insurance purposes	✓
Accountancy charges relating to rental accounts and normal recurring computation of tax liabilities of the property business itself	Excludes tax fees relating to any other matter	✓
Planning	Costs in connection with negotiations under the Town and Country Planning Acts	x
Subscriptions	To associations representing the interests of landlords	✓
Arbitration	Cost of arbitration to determine the rent of a holding	✓
Debt collection	In respect of late rents	✓
	Pursuing debts of a capital nature, such as the proceeds due on the sale of the property	x
Eviction	Of an unsatisfactory tenant in order to relet the property	✓

Furnished residential properties

As no capital allowances can be claimed on **furniture and fittings** provided by the company in a fully furnished residential property which it lets out, there is a choice between either:
– a wear and tear allowance of 10%; or
– the renewals allowance (¶19295).

19285
s 248 CTA 2009

The wear and tear allowance is simple to calculate, and gives an earlier deduction as compared to the renewals allowance.

Once a choice has been made, it must be followed consistently year on year.

> MEMO POINTS   1. For this purpose, a furnished let is **defined** as a lease or other arrangement under which the tenant pays the company, and in return, is entitled to the use of the premises and also to the use of furniture. This includes a caravan or a houseboat.
> 2. Furniture **commonly provided** in such a residence would include:
> – movable furniture or furnishings, such as beds or suites;
> – televisions;
> – fridges and freezers;
> – carpets and floor-coverings;
> – curtains;
> – linen;
> – crockery or cutlery; and
> – other things which a tenant would normally otherwise provide for himself (e.g. white goods).
> If the accommodation is only **partly furnished**, the 10% wear and tear allowance is not due.
> 3. For **furnished holiday lettings**, see ¶19410.
> 4. Note that capital allowances are available for furnished **commercial property** such as offices.

19290
ss 248A – 248C
CTA 2009;
PIM 3200

Wear and tear allowance A deduction of 10% of the net rent is available to recognise the depreciation of furniture provided with the property.

For this purpose, **net rent** is the total rent due for the property less any charges and services that would normally be borne by a tenant. Common examples of these charges are council tax and water rates.

This allowance is not available on furnished holiday lettings (¶19410).

> MEMO POINTS 1. Where the company lets **both furnished and unfurnished** properties, the net rent must only take account of the net rent from the furnished lettings.
> 2. Where relevant, the chargeable amount of a **premium** (¶19215) is included in the net rent.
> 3. Even where the allowance is claimed, the landlord can also deduct the net cost of renewing **fixtures** (which are not usually removable, such as baths or toilets) as revenue repairs to the fabric. The net cost is the purchase price less any proceeds received for the old fixtures.
> 4. From a future date (yet to be announced), the wear and tear allowance is to be **reformed** so that it becomes conditional upon the property's energy efficiency.

> EXAMPLE B Ltd lets a furnished property and has a year end of 31 March.
> The annual rental income was £12,000 to 31 December, and £15,000 thereafter.
> B Ltd incurred the following expenses:
>
> | | | £ |
> |---|---|---|
> | Insurance | | 400 |
> | Ground rent | | 800 |
> | Water rates | | 1,200 |
> | Management fees | 20% of rent | |
>
> B Ltd's property business profits are calculated as follows:
>
> | | | £ | £ |
> |---|---|---|---|
> | Rental income (accruals basis): | | | |
> | 9 months at 12,000 p.a. | 9/12 × 12,000 | 9,000 | |
> | 3 months at 15,000 p.a. | 3/12 × 15,000 | 3,750 | |
> | | | | 12,750 |
> | Expenses: | | | |
> | Insurance | | 400 | |
> | Ground rent | | 800 | |
> | Water rates | | 1,200 | |
> | Management fees | 20% of 12,750 | 2,550 | |
> | Wear and tear | 10% of (12,750 – 1,200) | 1,155 | |
> | | | | (6,105) |
> | UK property profits | | | 6,645 |

19295

Renewals allowance By concession, until 30 March 2013 the landlord also had the option of claiming the net cost of replacing a particular item of furniture etc. (but not the cost of the original purchase). This concession was **withdrawn** by HMRC in relation to expenditure incurred **on or after 1 April 2013**.

The **net cost** was the purchase price less any proceeds received in respect of the original.

If an **exact replica is not acquired**, HMRC's view is that common sense should be used to find the cost of an equivalent replacement.

> MEMO POINTS At the time of writing, HMRC's property income manual had yet to be updated for this change.

> EXAMPLE C Ltd replaced a washing machine in a let residential property, and received £30 scrap value.
> The company acquired a washer-dryer for £500. The comparable cost of the original washing machine would have been £300.
> So C Ltd could claim a deduction of £270. (300 – 30)

C. Special situations

Summary

19325

---

1. Beginning and ending a property business

Starting

When a property business commences, the usual **pre-trading expenditure** rules operate (¶60115).

19355
s 210 CTA 2009;
PIM 2505

For this purpose, the **commencement date** is a question of, fact and would usually be the date that the first property is let.

Ceasing

The **date of cessation** is when the last let property is disposed of, or starts to be used for some other purposes. While there is any property owned by the company still being let, the property business will continue.

19360
PIM 2510

HMRC state that if letting ceases and later recommences it is a question of fact whether there is a new business or a resumption of the old one, and they give the following guidance:

Situation	Indicates cessation?
Company has been trying unsuccessfully to obtain tenants in a period when properties are vacant	n
Property is temporarily unavailable while work on repairs or alterations are carried out	n
More than 3 year gap between the last let of a property and the letting of a newly acquired property	y
Less than 3 year gap, but properties sold, and in the meantime, the proceeds were invested in another type of business venture, before the company acquired another property to let	y
Proceeds from sold properties invested in the bank while locating suitable other property to purchase	n
Property ceases to be let and is put to another use (for example, a director occupies it)	y

19365
ss 280 – 286
CTA 2009

As with a trade, a post cessation **receipt** (¶61130), such as a late insurance payout or debt recovery, is taxable as miscellaneous income (being a sum received after a company permanently ceases to carry on a business and which arises from the previous carrying on of that business).

Post cessation **expenses** (such as debt collection fees) can be set against the receipts, or used against other income (¶61145).

A company can elect to **carry back** any post cessation receipts to the date that the property business ceased.

On ceasing a property business, any unrelieved **losses** (¶36235) will lapse unless:
– the company still has an investment business (¶6115) when the losses can be treated as management expenses (¶17620); or
– there is a temporary period of dormancy before the property business recommences (for example, while the company acquires other properties).

---

2. Specific circumstances

Landlord's energy-saving allowance (LESA)

19395
ss 251 – 253
CTA 2009;
SI 2008/1520

An energy-saving allowance is available for capital expenditure incurred no later than 31 March 2015, to landlords who **install** any of the following **items** (assuming they do not qualify for capital allowances (¶25240)) in any part of a building containing a dwelling house:
– loft insulation or cavity wall insulation;
– solid wall insulation;
– draught-proofing;
– insulation for hot water systems; or
– floor insulation.

The allowance is **not available** in respect of:
– a property in the course of construction;
– furnished holiday lettings;
– where the person incurring the expenditure does not have an interest in the property, even if they are in the course of acquiring an interest; or
– expenditure incurred more than 6 months before the property business commences (¶19355).

CA 11520

> MEMO POINTS   1. For this purpose, a **dwelling house** is defined as a building, or a part of a building, which provides the facilities required for day to day private domestic existence. Where a building contains more than one dwelling house, the common parts (such as stairs and lifts) do not comprise a dwelling house for this purpose.
> 2. **University halls of residence** can be dwelling houses where there are bedrooms with en-suite or communal toileting facilities, and a shared or communal kitchen/diner.
> 3. No specific **claim** is required, just an appropriate entry on the corporation tax return.

19400
PIM 2072

The **maximum amount** of LESA available is £1,500 per dwelling house. Where a single building contains two or more dwellings, the landlord can therefore claim up to £1,500 on each dwelling.

> MEMO POINTS   1. A just and reasonable **apportionment** of the expenditure must be made if:
> – the property is jointly or separately owned, or subject to differing estates or interests;
> – the expenditure is incurred by more than one person;
> – the property contains both residential and commercial units; or
> – the property contains more than one dwelling.
> 2. Any **contribution from any other person** towards the expenditure is to be deducted from the amount that may be claimed, whether or not the contributor will be making a claim.

> EXAMPLE
> 1. D Ltd spends £2,000 installing an energy-saving item in a building containing a let residential property and a shop. The item is equally beneficial to both properties.
> D Ltd can claim a deduction of £1,000.
>
> 2. A building contains two dwellings, E and F. Dwelling E has been allocated costs of £2,000, and dwelling F has been allocated costs of £1,000.

The deductions available are £1,500 for dwelling E, and £1,000 for dwelling F. The excess over the £1,500 limit cannot be transferred to dwelling F.

Grant of sublease

A tenant who sublets a property will be eligible for a deduction in respect of the **premium paid on the headlease**, where the landlord is taxable on a proportion of it as income (assuming the headlease is not in excess of 50 years' duration (¶19205)).

19405
ss 227, 228
CTA 2009

The **amount** of the deduction depends on whether the tenant charges a premium to the subtenant, as shown in the following table.

Situation	Initial deduction	Annual deduction
Premium charged by tenant to subtenant	Premium assessed to income on landlord x Number of years in subleaseNumber of years in headlease	Any excess[1] of initial deduction over premium charged to subtenant
No premium charged to subtenant	None	Premium assessed to income on landlordNumber of years in headlease

Note
1. The initial deduction cannot create a **loss** in the hands of the tenant who sublets the property. Any deduction which exceeds the assessable amount of the sub-premium must be set against the rental income over the period of the sublease. If the sublease is granted part way through an accounting period, the deduction available against rental income must be pro-rated.

MEMO POINTS 1. The premium need not have actually been **paid by** the tenant, provided it was paid by another party who held the same lease at an earlier date. Similarly, the premium may have been **paid to** a previous landlord who granted the headlease. This affects leases which have been assigned.

PIM 2305

2. If the **landlord** is **exempt from tax** (for example, a charity), a deduction is still available for the tenant provided all of the other criteria are met.

PIM 2310

3. Where only **part of the property is sublet**, an apportionment of the landlord's taxable amount should be used. HMRC consider that professional valuation advice on the split may be needed in sizeable or difficult cases.
4. For details of the deduction available where the **tenant uses the property for trading** or vocational purposes, see ¶14735.
5. This calculation applies equally to a **deemed premium** arising on payments made for the variation or waiver of a lease, or an assignment of a lease at an undervalue (¶19220).

EXAMPLE
1. A Ltd grants a 25 year lease on a property to B Ltd for rent of £10,000 p.a. and a premium of £5,000. A Ltd is taxable on a portion of the premium using the formula in ¶19215. This gives £2,600.

$$(5,000 \times \frac{(50-24)}{50})$$

After 2 years, B Ltd sublets the property to C Ltd at a rent of £15,000 p.a. and **no premium**. B Ltd (and its successors if any) can deduct from this rental stream both the rent of £10,000 p.a. payable to A Ltd, and £104 p.a. notional rent relating to the premium it paid to A Ltd. (2,600/25)

2. A Ltd grants a 25 year lease on a property to B Ltd for rent of £10,000 p.a. and a premium of £5,000 (as above). A Ltd is taxable on £2,600 of the premium as income.
B Ltd **sublets** the property to C Ltd for 10 years **for a premium** of £4,000, and annual rent of £12,000. B Ltd is assessed to income of £3,280 on the premium charged to the subtenant.

$$(4,000 \times \frac{(50-9)}{50})$$

The initial deduction in respect of the premium paid on the headlease is calculated as £1,040. (10/25 × 2,600)
So overall B Ltd is taxable on net income of £2,240. (3,280 − 1,040)

3. D Ltd grants E Ltd a 25 year lease of a warehouse for a premium of £50,000 plus annual rent.

D Ltd is taxable on £26,000 of the premium. $(50,000 \times \frac{(50-24)}{50})$

E Ltd sublets to F Ltd under a 15 year lease starting on 1 January for a premium of £20,000. E Ltd has a 31 March year end.

E Ltd is assessed to income of £14,400 on the premium charged to the subtenant. $(20,000 \times \frac{(50-14)}{50})$

E Ltd can claim a deduction of £15,600 in respect of the headlease. $(15/25 \times 26,000)$

This means there is **excess relief** of £1,200. $(15,600 - 14,400)$

The deduction is spread over the period of the sublease i.e. £80 is deducted in each full year. $(1/15 \times 1,200)$

For the first accounting period in which the subletting takes place, only a quarter's deduction is allowed (to reflect the fact that the letting commenced on 1 January).

Furnished holiday lettings

19410
s 264 CTA 2009

Special rules apply when a rental business consists of the letting of furnished holiday accommodation (including caravans), where tenants take on short term lets.

All such property let out by a company is treated as a separate **activity**. A material activity may itself be treated as a trade rather than a property business.

s 264(2A) CTA 2009

Furnished holiday letting treatment also applies to properties within the **European Economic Area** (EEA). This treatment was accepted informally by HMRC for some years, and became statutory for accounting periods beginning on or after 1 April 2011.

19415
ss 265 –, 268A
CTA 2009;
PIM 4100

Scope   The **qualifying criteria** for FHL depends on whether an accounting period begins before or after 1 April 2012, as shown in the following table:

Criteria	Accounting periods beginning	
	Before 1 April 2012	On or after 1 April 2012
Reason for letting	Property must be let on a commercial basis with a view to the realisation of profits (excluding lets to family or friends at nominal rates)	
Available for letting to the public	For at least 140 days during the relevant period[1]	For at least 210 days during the relevant period[1]
Actually let[2]	For at least 70 days during the relevant period[1]	For at least 105 days[3] during the relevant period[1]
Use of furniture	Tenant must be entitled to the use of the furniture	
Long term occupation	Periods of occupation by same tenant exceeding 31 days are ignored (excluding occupation which is a result of exceptional circumstances) when totalling the number of days for each letting condition above If property is occupied for the long term by a tenant for more than 155 days (not necessarily consecutively) in a relevant period[1], then property is not an FHL	

Note:
1. The **relevant period** is usually the company's normal accounting period, however:
– when commencing the furnished holiday let (that is, the accommodation was not let furnished in the 12 month period preceding the accounting period), the relevant period is the 12 months from the date that the letting commenced; and
– on cessation, if the accommodation was let furnished in the previous accounting period, the relevant period is the 12 months ending with the date that the letting ceased.
2. Where the company has **more than one property** which would be treated as furnished holiday lettings but for the 70 or 105 day rule, the number of days actually let can be averaged. However, an averaging election must be made separately for UK properties, and those outside the UK but within the EEA (so, for example, a UK property cannot be averaged with a French property).
3. There is a **period of grace election**, which can be made where the property will fail the 105 day test (only) for up to 2 years, so long as:
– there is a genuine intention to let the property in excess of 105 days (evidenced by actively marketing it);
– the property has already satisfied the FHL criteria in the current accounting period; and
– no averaging election (see above) has been made.
The election must be made in respect of the first year when the 105 day test is failed, within 12 months of the filing date of the relevant CTSA return (¶46110). Note where the 210 day test is failed, no period of grace election is available, as the property cannot be an FHL.

EXAMPLE A Ltd let the following properties in the year ended 31 March 2014:

Property	Days available	Days let	Eligible as furnished holiday let?
1 (existing property)	210	195	Y
2 (existing property)	130	115	N
3 (existing property)	215	85	N (but see below)
4 (acquired 1 June)	220	80 (plus 30 days to 31 May 2014)	Y (see below)
5 (sold 30 June)	35 (plus 175 days in the previous accounting period from 1 July)	5 (plus 55 days in the previous accounting period from 1 July)	N (but see below)

Property 1 – qualifies as it meets both the 210 day and 105 day tests.
Property 2 – does not qualify as it does not meet the 210 day test (averaging is only possible where the 105 day test is not met).
Property 3 – does not qualify as it does not meet the 105 day test, but it may be included in an averaging claim.
Property 4 – the 12 month period commences on 1 June and, as the property was let for a further 30 days after the end of the accounting period, this equates to total days let in the 12 month period of 90 days, therefore satisfying both the 105 and 210 day tests.
Property 5 – the 12 month period ends on 30 June, and taking into account the days let and days available in this 12 month period, it would not qualify as it did not meet the 105 day test, but it may be included in an averaging claim.

Averaging claim:
It is possible to include all four or fewer properties in an averaging claim in order to achieve the desired result. If all four properties are included, the average days let for each property would be:
(195 + 115 + 110 + 60)/4 = 120
meaning that all four properties would qualify as furnished holiday lettings.

Tax advantages   The following table shows the tax advantages of furnished holiday lettings.   **19420**

Comment   Capital allowances claims should not be delayed as it is likely that tighter deadlines will be imposed from 2012 in respect of property fixtures.

Advantage	Detail	Reference
Entitlement to capital allowances	On furniture and furnishings in the let property, and also machinery etc used outside the property (such as vans and tools) If only part of property let as an FHL, the qualifying expenditure should be apportioned If property permanently stops being a FHL, a deemed disposal of the furniture occurs at market value (which would require the company to identify the furniture concerned, and result in a balancing adjustment if there was only one FHL) HMRC's view is that a temporary cessation of the business, arising because not all of the FHL conditions are met, will not cause a deemed disposal No allowances on the land or building No wear and tear allowance (¶19290) available	s 269 CTA 2009, s 17 CAA 2001, PIM 4120
Treated as a trading asset	For the purposes of the substantial shareholdings exemption (¶32090)	

Computation   Once a particular property qualifies within an accounting period, the tax advantages in ¶19420 above apply for the whole of that accounting period, even for lettings **outside the period for which** the furnished holiday lettings **conditions are met**.   **19425**
PIM 4120

The same is true when the property is kept solely for letting as furnished holiday accommodation, but is in fact **closed for part of the year** because there are no customers. The expenses incurred when the property is closed are still deductible, so long as there is no private use.

If the computation results in a **loss**, see ¶36305.

Flat management companies

19430
PIM 1070;
s 42 LTA 1987

A flat management company is often **set up to** manage the common areas of a block of flats. The company is controlled by the occupiers of the flats, and payments are made to it by the tenants in order to ensure that both the routine servicing and longer term repairs are adequately financed. These **payments** are treated as capital under the property legislation, and the company is therefore not taxable on them as income. Instead, the company is deemed to be a trustee of these funds (with an implied power of accumulation), and a trust tax return may need to be completed each year.

TSEM 5710

Any **investment income** received on these funds is treated as trust income although it is taxable at the standard rate rather than the special rate applicable to trusts. Where tax is deducted at source, no further tax will be due.

> ⎡MEMO POINTS⎤ 1. The **funds** are usually designated as a service charge fund and a sinking fund (longer term). The service charge fund should roughly break even each year, while the sinking fund may grow to a substantial amount.
> 2. For details of **trust** taxation, see *Tax Memo*.

TSEM 5750

> 3. For **further details** of flat management companies, and in particular the tax implications of those (such as charities and public bodies) that do not fall within s 42 LTA 1987, see the HMRC Trusts and Estates Manual

Non-resident landlords

19435
s 971 ITA 2007;
SI 1995/2902;
PIM 4800

The non-resident landlords scheme is used for taxing the UK rental income of landlords whose usual place of abode is outside the UK.

The **rental** payable to such a landlord must be **paid** net of tax deducted at basic rate, **unless** the landlord applies to HMRC for the rent to be received gross.

As the landlord's **tax liability** will almost certainly differ from the amount of basic rate tax suffered at source, a self-assessment tax return must be submitted in respect of each tax year.

INTM 370060

> ⎡MEMO POINTS⎤ 1. For this purpose, companies have their **usual place of abode outside the UK** where either:
> – their main office or other place of business is outside the UK; or
> – they are incorporated outside the UK, unless they are regarded as UK resident for tax purposes.
> The UK **branch** of a non-resident company, where that branch is within the charge to UK corporation tax, does not have a usual place of abode outside the UK.
> 2. The **person who must deduct the tax** is usually the letting agent. If there is no agent involved, and the amounts paid to the landlord (including any premium) exceed £5,200 per annum, the tenant must deduct basic rate tax. Other tenants may be asked to deduct tax by HMRC.
> 3. The **deducted tax** is accounted for quarterly (on a calendar year basis), via the submission of a return within 30 days of the quarter end. An annual return must be submitted by 5 July. The landlord must also be given a certificate showing the amount of tax deducted.
> 4. Only an agent can take into account **letting expenses** (¶19250) before calculating the income tax to deduct. Letting expenses incurred directly by the landlord are ignored for this purpose (although they will be deductible when computing the property profits for the purposes of the self-assessment tax return).
> 5. For details of income tax and **self-assessment** returns, see *Tax Memo*.

19440   **Gross rents**   The landlord can receive rent gross by applying to HMRC to join this scheme.

If the **application is approved**, a certificate of exemption will be issued, which can be presented to the payer of the rent. The landlord must then complete a self-assessment tax return and pay income tax under the normal rules (including making payments on account). The certificate will be withdrawn if the criteria for receiving gross payments do not continue to be satisfied, subject to an appeals process.

> ⎡MEMO POINTS⎤ 1. To **apply** to receive rental payments gross, the landlord must complete form NRL1 and satisfy any of the following criteria:
> – the UK tax affairs are up to date;

– the company has never had any UK tax obligations; or
– the company does not expect to be liable to UK tax for the year in which it is making the application. The company must also undertake to comply with all UK tax obligations, such as completing self-assessment tax returns and paying tax on time. An appeal can be made against non approval.
2. **Full details** of the scheme can be found at flmemo.co.uk/ctm1992

3. Anti-avoidance

Summary

19470

Topic	¶¶
Selling off the rental income stream	¶19475
Gains taxed as income	¶19490
Leaseback transactions	¶19505

Selling off the rental income stream

Rent factoring is an arrangement whereby a person obtains a **lump sum payment** (a "finance amount") in return for selling a **rental income stream** (excluding the granting of a lease). The finance amount is, in effect, a loan which is repaid by the regular rental payments, and is calculated to take into account an interest charge over the term of the agreement.

19475

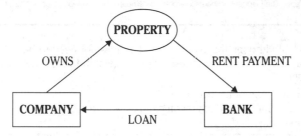

The following arrangements are **excluded** from these rules, however, as they are taxed under other provisions:
– arrangements under which a lease is granted;
– where the finance amount is taken into account in determining trading profits;
– sale and repurchase, and sale and leaseback, arrangements; and
– where the pricing of the arrangement depended on the anticipated availability of capital allowances on the land.

19480

> MEMO POINTS Where a **lease** is artificially interposed over property in what is essentially a rent factoring arrangement, any premium charged for the lease will be taxed under the rent factoring provisions (the premium is effectively a loan against the future income stream). This excludes any arrangement that depends on capital allowances being available to an unconnected third party.

Arrangements **entered into**:
– on or after 6 June 2006 are covered by the rules for structured finance arrangements (¶21915); and
– before 6 June 2006 are dealt with by the former rent factoring provisions, which treat the finance amount as property business income for the chargeable period in which the agreement is made.

19485

ss 43A–43G
ICTA 1988

> EXAMPLE In 2005, A Ltd owns freehold land which it leases to a bank for 51 years for a premium of £1m. The bank immediately grants a 5 year sublease to A Ltd in return for annual rental payments of £220,000, which will total £1.1m. At the end of the 5 year period, the land will revert back to A Ltd.
> In substance, A Ltd has borrowed £1m, which it repays over the 5 year period plus interest of £100,000. As a result of the arrangements, A Ltd becomes entitled to a deduction for the rent payable of £220,000 p.a. which reflects not only interest but also repayment of the capital amount of the loan.

Under the rent factoring rules, the £1m premium received by A Ltd is taxed as income in the period of receipt.
If this arrangement had been entered into after 6 June 2006, see ¶21915.

Gains taxed as income

19490
ss 819, 828, 831
CTA 2010;
BIM 60300

Where a disposal of land situated in the UK (including assets derived from land) results in a chargeable gain, the proceeds may be taxed as sundry income where avoidance is involved and any of the following **conditions** apply:

Condition	Clearance procedure available [1]
The land was acquired with the sole or main objective of making a gain on disposal	y
Development took place in order to realise a gain later on	y
The land was trading stock [2]	n

Note:
1. The following apply to **clearance procedures**:
– the application must be in writing;
– the application must be made to the tax office to which the applicant makes tax returns; and
– the applicant must provide full particulars of the disposal and all the background facts that are relevant otherwise the clearance will be void.
HMRC must respond within 30 days.
2. In the case of a company which holds land as **trading stock**, and disposes of it in the normal course of trade, the rules will not apply. The disposal of shares in a holding company, which owns at least 90% of such a company, is also excluded.

19495
BIM 60320

HMRC's view is that although the avoidance of tax does not need to be deliberate in order for the rules to apply, the simple purchase, improvement and subsequent sale of a property will not be caught.

Two situations which commonly occur are:
– a **diversion** arrangement, in which income or proceeds are diverted to another party, such as an overseas company; and
– a **slice of the action** arrangement, in which part of the consideration for the sale of the land is contingent upon profits derived from future development by the purchaser (when the amount treated as sundry income would be restricted to when the intention to develop was formed)

Comment   In practice, unless there are complex arrangements, only development profit is likely to be attacked under these provisions. Where a clearance procedure is available, it should always be used.

s 816 CTA 2010

    MEMO POINTS   1. For these purposes, **land includes** any buildings or interest in land other than a dwelling house.
2. **Assets derived from land include** shares in a company which owns the land.

s 820 CTA 2010

3. A disposal by an individual or company **connected** (¶31375) with the acquirer or developer of the land may be caught by these provisions.
4. Obtaining **planning consent** does not constitute development.

BIM 60460

    EXAMPLE
1. **Diversion**: an individual entered a contract to sell land to an overseas company at undervalue, and the contract terms allowed the overseas company to sell the land on. In fact, the land was sold on three times, so that the eventual proceeds were split between the individual and three overseas companies (none of which was liable to UK tax on any gains).
It was held that the individual was taxable on the whole of the proceeds given for the land, because he provided the opportunity for the companies to make a tax-free gain by entering into this arrangement. *Sugarwhite v Budd* [1988]

2. **Slice of the action**: trustees granted a lease to a development company, and only received a premium when the development work was finished. The amount of the premium was dependent on the price achieved by the company for each plot of land which it subleased.

It was held that the premium should be taxed as sundry income because the trustees had entered into the arrangement in order to develop the land, and the premium was otherwise a gain of a capital nature. *Page v Lowther* [1983]

In most cases, the **taxable company** is the one which realises the gain. However, where a company provides (either directly, or indirectly through a series of transactions) an opportunity for another person to make a gain, it is the company that is taxable.

19500
s 821 CTA 2010

The **amount taxable** as sundry income is the proceeds that are available for the vendor to enjoy when the gain is realised, less relevant expenses. Normal trading principles apply particularly with reference to reverse premiums and lease premiums generally.

s 822 CTA 2010

> *MEMO POINTS*   1. Where **money is deposited** to cover possible contingencies, the amount of the deposit will not be taxable until it is released.
> 2. Where an amount is taxed as sundry income, it is excluded from any **chargeable gains** computation.

Leaseback transactions

Leaseback transactions (those in which the transferor takes on a lease of the property he has previously transferred) come in two forms:
a. a sale followed by a leaseback; or
b. a lease followed by a leaseback.

19505

Both situations are subject to special tax rules.

> *MEMO POINTS*   1. For sale and **repurchase**, see ¶19220.
> 2. For **lease premiums** generally, see ¶19205.

Sale and leaseback   Broadly, where a company sells land (realising a capital gain) and then leases it back from the buyer, anti-avoidance rules apply if an excessive **rent** is paid.

19510
s 838 CTA 2010;
BIM 61300

This is also the case where any person associated with the company makes the rental payments, or arrangements are made so that there is no leaseback but a **payment akin to rent** is paid.

The purpose is to prevent the company (or its associate) from obtaining advantageous tax relief on the rent paid.

> *MEMO POINTS*   1. The **sale** could involve the following types of transfer:
> – the granting of a lease or any other transaction involving the creation of a new estate or interest in the land;
> – the transfer of a lessee's interest under a lease by surrender or forfeiture; or
> – a transaction or series of transactions affecting land where the owners beforehand and afterwards are not exactly the same.
> 2. For this purpose, a **lease includes**:
> – an underlease, sublease or any tenancy or licence;
> – an agreement for a lease, underlease, sublease, tenancy or licence; and
> – in the case of land outside the UK, any corresponding interest to the above.
> 3. For this purpose, the following situations result in **associated** parties:
> – there are two transactions which are affected by these rules, and the persons involved are acting in concert or the two transactions are in any way reciprocal; or
> – two or more companies participating in a scheme of reconstruction or amalgamation.
> Further, the following parties are associated:
> – an individual is associated with his spouse, his own relatives and their spouses, and also his spouse's relatives (including their spouses);
> – a trustee is associated with the settlor or an associate of the settlor;
> – a person is associated with a body of persons which he or his associates control; and
> – two or more bodies of persons associated with the same person are associated with each other.
> Spouse includes civil partner. Relative means a sibling, ancestor or lineal descendant.

s 835(3) CTA 2010

s 846 CTA 2010

s 847 CTA 2010

s 882 CTA 2010

The corporation tax deduction for the **rental payments** is restricted to a commercial rent. Any unrelieved amount is carried forward, and only set off if there are subsequent underpayments of rent. When the payments under the lease stop, the ability to carry forward also ceases. Hence it is likely that some rental payments will remain unrelieved.

19515
s 840 CTA 2010

When making the comparison with a commercial rent, any part of the payment which relates to **service charges or rates** usually borne by the tenant is excluded.

s 843 CTA 2010

BIM 61305

BIM 61330

MEMO POINTS 1. A **commercial rent** is the rent payable under a replica lease negotiated on the open market at the time the actual lease was created, with the same terms and duration. HMRC will ask the company for an estimate of the commercial rent, supported by any available evidence.

2. The **recipient** is not affected by any adjustment made to the rent payment.

EXAMPLE C Ltd sells a property to D Ltd, and leases it back for 4 years. The rent payable under the lease is £30,000 for Years 1 and 2, £1 in Year 3, and nil in Year 4. The commercial rent would be £15,000 per annum.

C Ltd will be able to set off the rental payments against its trading income as follows:

Year	Unrelieved b/fwd £	Rent payment £	Deduction allowed £	Unrelieved c/fwd £
1	Nil	30,000	15,000	15,000
2	15,000	30,000	15,000	30,000
3	30,000	1	15,000	15,001
4	Nil	Nil	Nil	Nil

As no further rent payments are due after the end of Year 3, the unrelieved amount of £15,001 is lost.

19520
s 850 CTA 2010

Assignment or surrender and leaseback Where a **short lease** (one with less than 50 years to run) is assigned or surrendered, and the company then takes on a **new lease for a term of 15 years or less**, part of the premium received for the surrender will be taxed as income.

The reason is that in substance the premium is a loan, and the rent payable under the new lease represents a repayment of that loan plus interest.

BIM 61340

s 855 CTA 2010

s 859 CTA 2010

MEMO POINTS 1. The rules also catch the situation where a company assigns or surrenders the lease, and an **associated** person pays the increased rent.

2. Where a leaseback is disguised as a lease for more than 15 years (for example, by reducing the rent after part of the lease period), **length of the leaseback** is the period for which the extra rent is payable, or (where the company lessee has the power to end the lease) the earliest possible date for the lease to terminate. For example: a lease of 16 years is assigned in return for another lease of 16 years less 1 day, but an increased rent is only payable for 8 years. In this case, the leaseback is deemed to be for a period of 8 years.

3. **Variations in the terms** of a lease in return for consideration, which result in a greater rent being payable by the company lessee, are also caught by these rules.

19525
s 851 CTA 2010

The **taxable proportion** of the premium is found by using the formula:

$$\frac{16-N}{15}$$

where N is the term of the new lease expressed in years.

If the company has a trade, the income will be assessed as trading income. Otherwise the income will be treated as sundry income.

s 852 CTA 2010

MEMO POINTS Where the **leaseback does not include the whole of the property** originally leased, only a reasonable proportion of the premium is taxed as income.

EXAMPLE E Ltd, a trading company, surrenders the lease on its premises for £12,000, subsequently taking out a new 5 year lease. The amount of the premium taxed as trading income will be £8,800.

$$(12{,}000 \times \frac{(16-5)}{15})$$

SECTION 3

Overseas properties

19575
ss 206, 290
CTA 2009

Broadly, the same computational rules apply to an overseas property business (one in which the property is located outside the UK) as to UK properties.

The two streams of income (UK and overseas) must be kept separate, because of the different loss reliefs which are available (¶36275).

> MEMO POINTS   1. Where the activity overseas would constitute a **trade** (¶5000), those rules take priority over the property income provisions.
> 2. If the company has **more than one property**, the business results are aggregated, except when foreign tax has been suffered on the income before it is received by the company (¶19585).
> 3. An overseas property business is treated as **starting or ceasing** not only when letting commences or terminates, but also when the company comes or ceases to be within the charge to UK corporation tax.

s 289 CTA 2009

Exceptions from UK rules

The rules for taxing post-cessation receipts (¶19365) do not apply to overseas property income. The furnished holiday lettings regime (¶19410) does not apply to any property outside the EEA.

19580
ss 264, 280
CTA 2009

Relief for overseas tax suffered

Where any income has suffered foreign tax, it will be necessary to keep a **separate record** of the income and expenditure for affected property, in order to identify the amount of UK tax attributable to that particular income.

19585
PIM 4705

The set-off of **losses** (including charitable donations, deficits on loan relationships and derivatives, and management expenses) should be done in such a way as to ensure that the least amount of double tax relief is wasted.

For **details** of double taxation relief and foreign tax generally, see ¶90480.

SECTION 4

Real estate investment trusts

A company **listed** on a recognised stock exchange and which carries on a qualifying property rental business may elect for the real estate investment trust (REIT) regime to apply, provided certain conditions are met.

19635

An **unlisted** company may be involved with REITs as a shareholder, in which case, any distribution received (¶19880) is taxed as UK property income provided it derives from tax-exempt profits. The recipient must keep this income separate from other UK property income and overseas property income for the purposes of loss relief.

s 548 CTA 2010

Comment   At the time of writing there were only 27 REITs in the UK, with a total market capitalisation of £27.8 million (http://www.bpf.org.uk/en/reita/reits/uk_reit_list.php). This is thought partly to be due to the stringent conditions attached to the regime. The Treasury held a consultation exercise with the property industry in 2012 with a view to removing some of the barriers, and in particular:
– removing the requirement for any REIT to be listed, so that AIM listed companies could participate;
– introducing an initial period when a start-up REIT could be a close company whilst it grows its business and attracts new investors; and
– enabling institutional investors (¶19710) to set up REITs.
A further consultation on institutional investment has recently been held, and closed on 14 June 2013.
To date the only outcome of the consultations has been to introduce the concept of UK REIT investment profits: see ¶19680.

Summary

A company which opts into this regime pays no corporation tax on qualifying property rental income or chargeable gains.

19640

The provisions apply not only to pure property-owning companies, but also to ordinary trading companies that have a large portfolio of real estate holdings. This is because a REIT can have a mixture of qualifying property rental business income and other income (referred to here as residual taxable income), provided certain conditions are met (¶19705).

The REIT regime applies equally to single companies and groups. Any differences in the rules that apply as a result of a company being in a group are detailed in the relevant sections.

ss 523, 606
CTA 2010

MEMO POINTS A **group** is essentially a 75% CG group (¶65415), with the proviso that the principal company has to be UK resident, although there is no residence restriction on the other members of the group.

A. Scope

1. Definition

19670

ss 519–520
CTA 2010

A property rental business is defined as a UK property business (¶19000) or the overseas equivalent, where certain conditions are met (¶19705).

MEMO POINTS For **groups**, a property rental business includes:
- all the property rental business of UK resident members; and
- the UK property rental business of non-UK resident members.

Exclusions

19675 The following table shows those situations to which the REIT regime cannot apply:

Subject	Detail	Reference
Letting of property	That is only incidental to the company's main purpose of buying property with a view to profit on resale (in other words, a property trade is carried on)	s 604 CTA 2010
	That is temporarily surplus to requirements (meaning it is let for no more than 3 years) and had been used for administrative purposes of the property rental business. The let space itself must be small compared with the space occupied for administrative purposes	
	Services provided to tenants of overseas properties	
	Income arising from structured financial arrangements (¶19485) in which the rental income from property is sold or factored in some way	
	If the property would be regarded under GAAP as owner-occupied, unless the exclusive occupant is a person not connected with the company (or any company in the group)	
Activities	Operating a caravan site	s 605 CTA 2010
	An electric line wayleave	
	The siting of a pipeline for oil, a mast or similar structure for a mobile telephone network, or a wind turbine	
Income from	Dividends from another REIT, unless classified as UK REIT investment profits [1] (¶19680)	
	An interest in a limited liability partnership that is in the process of being wound up	
Note: 1. This classification is only available for accounting periods commencing on or after 17 July 2013.		

UK REIT investment profits

To facilitate investment in one REIT by another, profits distributed to it (¶19725) by the target REIT are considered to be **income from a property rental business** of the investing REIT. The notional property rental business is considered to be separate from the company's actual property rental business.

This means that unlike normal dividends, such income does fall within the REIT regime. The income is referred to as UK REIT investment profits.

This treatment applies only to distributions which an REIT receives in an **accounting period beginning on or after 17 July 2013**. If the recipient is a company in a group REIT, it is the accounting period of the principal company which is applicable for this purpose.

A **distribution** constitutes UK REIT investment profits only if:
– it is a distribution out of exempt profits (¶19885);
– to a shareholder which is itself a UK company REIT (or member of a UK group UK REIT); and either
    – it is made by a UK company REIT in respect of profits or gains (or both) of the property rental business of the company; or
    – it is made by the principal company of a UK group UK REIT in respect of amounts shown in the financial statements (statement of group's property rental business: ¶19710) as profits or gains (or both) of UK members of the group, or of the UK property rental business of non-UK members of the group.

19680
s 549A CTA 2010

---

2. Qualifying conditions

In order to opt into the REIT regime, several conditions must be met:
a. by the company; and
b. in relation to:
– the type of business carried out; and
– the proportion of profits and assets represented by the property rental business.

19705

Company requirements

The company (or principal member of a group) must, throughout each accounting period, comply with the following conditions:

19710
ss 528, 532, 533
CTA 2010

Condition	Detail
UK resident	See ¶2030+
Listed or traded on a recognised stock exchange (¶95320)	Condition must be met by the end of the company's third accounting period as a REIT [1]
Not be close	It is acceptable for the company to be close: – in any accounting period which ends within the first 3 years from the date the company joins the REIT regime [2,3]; – at the start of the first day of the accounting period, provided it reasonably expects to comply with the rules on part of the first day and throughout the rest of the accounting period; or – because of a participator which is an institutional investor [4]
Not be an OEIC	As defined by s 236 FSMA 2000
Only have in issue a maximum of two types of shares	Namely: – one class of ordinary shares (that are listed on a recognised stock exchange [1]; and – non-voting preference shares (which may have the right to convert)

Condition	Detail
Not borrow under terms that entitle the lender to: – receive an excess return on repayments; or – interest which depends on the results of the company's business, the value of its assets or is in excess of a market rate	A loan will not be treated as being dependent on the results of a company's business if the terms simply allow interest charges to go up if profits decline or down if profits improve
Submit financial statements to HMRC[5]	Containing details of income, expenses, profits before tax and assets valued

Note:
1. The relaxation for the first three accounting periods applies only to accounting periods beginning on or after 17 July 2012.
2. Applies to a company which became an REIT on or after 17 July 2012, and to an existing REIT from its first accounting period commencing on or after that date.
3. If an accounting period begins during and ends after the 3 year period, the company must not be close during that part which falls after the 3 year period.
4. Institutional investor is widely defined, but includes a unit trust, an OEIC, a pension scheme, a charity or a registered social landlord. This condition applies only to a company which became an REIT on or after 17 July 2012, and to an existing REIT from its first accounting period commencing on or after that date. Prior to that date the exemption applied only to a participator which was a collective investment scheme.
5. For **groups**, three sets of accounts are required to be prepared for:
– all the property rental business of the group (which will include property rental business operated by non-resident group members);
– the tax exempt part of the property rental business of the group (which will include all the property rental business of UK resident members and the UK property rental business of non-UK resident members); and
– all the other business of the group not already reported.
Where a subsidiary is less than 100% owned, the figures in the statements are reduced to reflect the percentage ownership.

Type of business

19715
ss 529 – 530A
CTA 2010

The company must carry on a business that involves:
a. at least three properties (with no single property having a value in excess of 40% of the total value of the properties involved in the business); and
b. distributing most or all of the profits of its property rental businesses arising in the accounting period, on or before the normal CTSA return filing date (¶46110).

19720   **Properties**   One property is **defined** as being any unit which is designed and fitted out for separate rental.

Properties are to be **valued** in accordance with International Accounting Standards (IAS) and if the IAS standards offer a choice between fair value and cost basis, the fair value should be used.

No account can be taken of any liabilities relating to the properties.

19725   **Distribution of profits**   Profits may be distributed via either cash dividend or stock dividend (shares issued in lieu of cash).

The company **must distribute**:
– 100% of its UK REIT investment profits (¶19680); and
– at least 90% of the profits of its (actual) property rental business.

This is often referred to as a property income distribution (PID) by the company. See below for group PIDs.

The following **criteria** apply when deciding whether the distribution rule has been met:
a. the property rental business profits are calculated under the normal principles (regardless of whether the income arises from UK property or overseas property) on the assumption that:
– all claims for capital allowances are made (there is no need for the company to actually make the claims); and
– account is taken for debits and credits arising on loan relationship and derivative contracts so far as they relate to the property rental business (¶19850);

b. if a REIT is prevented (due to a legal impediment, such as insufficient reserves) from distributing its profits, it need only distribute as much as it legally can;
c. where a distribution has been withheld to avoid the penalty on the 10% rule (¶19860), it will still count towards the 90% distribution;
d. if the company's profits for the period increase after the tax return filed, the company may rectify the position at any time up to 3 months from the last date the return can be amended (¶46300); and
e. if, as a result of the requirement to value a stock dividend at its market value (see note), the amount distributed becomes less than the required amount, the company has an additional 6 months from its filing date to rectify the position.

> MEMO POINTS 1.If the cash equivalent of a stock dividend exceeds the market value of the shares by at least 15%, the market value must be substituted for tax purposes.
> 2. If the company, for whatever reason, **fails to distribute** the required proportion of profits, then the amount not distributed will be taxed at the mainstream rate of corporation tax, calculated using the formula:

ss 564, 565
CTA 2010
SI 2006/2864

$$P - D$$

> where:
> – P is the required distribution percentage of the profits arising in the relevant accounting period; and
> – D is the amount of profits which have actually been distributed by the return filing date.
> The taxable amount cannot be reduced by any loss relief, expense or other type of deduction.
> To **avoid this charge** to tax, the company has 3 months from the date that the tax profits can no longer be altered, in which to declare and pay a dividend to bring them up to the requisite amount.
> 3. For **groups**, the distribution must be made by the principal company (based on all the UK REIT investment profits of the group, and on the profits of all the property rental business of the group including the rental profits of non-UK resident subsidiaries). In addition, the legal impediment let-out on distributions is extended to include restrictions that apply to the distribution of profits by any group member.

Balance of business

The REIT must fulfil the following conditions:
a. At least 75% of its **profits** must be generated from its property rental business and/or from UK REIT investment profits (¶19680). For this purpose, the following items are excluded from tax-exempt profits:
– realised and unrealised capital gains and losses;
– changes in the fair value of hedging derivative contracts; and
– items outside the ordinary course of the company's business.
b. At least 75% of its **assets** must relate to its property rental business and/or shares in other UK REITs. For this purpose:
– the assets are valued (¶19720) at the start of each accounting period; and
– cash balances related to residual activities (¶19810) count towards the 75%.

19730
s 531 CTA 2010

When giving notice to HMRC to enter the REIT regime (¶19795), the company does not have to satisfy the 75% asset test provided it does so from the start of the accounting period.

Properties **leased to other group companies** do not count towards satisfying either of these tests.

> MEMO POINTS 1. For the purpose of the 75% test, cash includes bank deposits and gilts. Cash involved in residual activities only counts towards the 75% limit in accounting periods beginning on or after 17 July 2012.
> 2. **Other UK REITs** means UK REITs that are not part of the same group as the company or group being tested.

B. Operation of the regime

Summary

19760   The tax implications of becoming a REIT can be summarised as follows:

Situation	Tax consequences	¶¶
Entry into the regime[1]	New accounting period starts	¶19800
	Deemed cessation and recommencement of property business	¶19800
Ongoing activities	All profits of any residual taxable trade are taxed at the mainstream rate of corporation tax as the small profits rate does not apply	¶19810
	Profits deriving from the REIT assets and REIT shares are exempt from corporation tax and ringfenced	¶19855
	Dividends can be paid gross in certain circumstances Recipient is taxed on them as property income	¶19880
	Assets disposed of to third parties are exempt from tax	¶19900
	Assets transferred from any taxable activities to the tax exempt property business are treated as taking place at market value For capital allowances purposes the transfer is at tax written down value	¶19900
Leaving the regime	Deemed cessation and recommencement Assets are transferred at market value, although for capital allowances purposes the transfer is at tax written down value	¶19955

Note
1. The former entry charge on a company that became a REIT was abolished on 17 July 2012: see ¶19815..

Anti-avoidance

19765   The **transfer pricing** rules (¶70000) apply to the exempt or residual taxable business of a REIT whether or not it is an SME.

ss 545, 546
CTA 2010

Where HMRC believe a company has tried to obtain a **tax advantage** for the REIT or another person, they can send out a notice to the company to counter the tax advantage (by, for example, cancelling a repayment, raising an assessment etc). In addition, they may assess the company to an additional amount of corporation tax equal to the tax advantage obtained. The company has the right to appeal within 30 days of receipt of the notice.

For this purpose, a tax advantage is **defined** as a relief or increased relief from, or repayment or increased repayment of, tax, or the avoidance or reduction of a charge to tax or an assessment to tax or the avoidance of a possible assessment. (This definition is further extended to include arrangements where the sole or main purpose is to avoid the entry charge.)

1. Becoming a REIT

19795   Companies that wish to join the REIT regime must give **notice** in writing to HMRC before the start of the relevant accounting period. The notice must contain the date that the company wishes the REIT to start.

ss 524, 525
CTA 2010

The notice must also be accompanied by a statement to the effect that the company reasonably expects all the company conditions (¶19710) to be satisfied for the first accounting period.

For **groups**, the principal member needs to give notice to HMRC when entering the regime and the company conditions need only be met by the principal company.

s 523 CTA 2010

Cessation and recommencement

On the date of joining the regime (as specified in the notice), an **accounting period** ends. The company's existing property business (relating to the properties which are to enter the REIT) is deemed to cease (although all other activities of the company are treated as continuing).

19800
ss 536, 537
CTA 2010

A new property rental business within the REIT is deemed to commence at the date of entry.

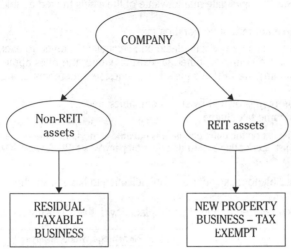

Consequently:
a. any UK property business (or overseas equivalent) which enters the REIT is ring-fenced. This means that tax **losses** arising before the date of entry cannot be carried forward (although see ¶19810);
b. there is a deemed disposal and reacquisition (at market **value**) **of** the **assets** of the old property rental business, which:
– for capital allowances purposes take place at tax written down value, so no balancing allowances or charges will arise;
– for capital gains tax purposes do not result in a chargeable gain (and therefore any loss accruing is not an allowable loss); and
– for any subsequent disposal of the assets transferred into the exempt business, means that the uplifted market value is generally used as the base cost.

19805
GREIT 03015

s 602 CTA 2010

Residual activity

Up to 25% of the company's assets can be non-qualifying for the REIT regime. The tax-exempt and taxable parts of a company's (or group's) activities are treated as two exclusive businesses. Therefore it is not possible for losses to be group relieved between them, or for capital assets to be transferred between them on a no gain/no loss basis.

19810
s 171(2)(da)
TCGA 1992;
s 601 CTA 2010

However, any **losses** brought forward from the period prior to the REIT commencing are still available to set against profits and gains arising from the residual activity while the company is a REIT (and indeed afterwards, should the company cease to be a REIT). In particular, **capital losses** that arose in the pre-entry period continue to be available to be carried forward for use against future chargeable gains in any taxable part of the company's business, subject to the normal capital loss carry forward rules (¶37180).

Entry charge

19815
ss 538, 539
CTA 2010

The former entry charge was **abolished** for any company that became a REIT on or after 17 July 2012.

Prior to that date, notional income was treated as accruing to the REIT on the date of entry to the regime. This taxable amount was calculated as follows:

$$\frac{\text{Market value}}{\text{Tax rate}} \times 2\%$$

where:
– market value was the aggregate market value of the assets treated as sold and reacquired (¶19805); and
– tax rate was the main rate of corporation tax.

s 534(3) CTA 2010

For **groups**, the entry charge was calculated and separately charged to each member of the group. (Where a single company joined an existing group, the rules applied as if it were a single company joining the REIT regime). For non-resident members of a group the charge was:
– based on UK properties owned by such companies; and
– treated as an income tax charge.

GREIT 03025,
03028

MEMO POINTS   The tax on the entry charge was **payable** at the same time as the usual corporation tax due for the first accounting period that the company was a REIT. CTSA instalment payments could apply (¶48095).

19820
s 540 CTA 2010

The company was able to make an irrevocable election to have this notional income **spread** over 4 years

In this case, the 2% referred to above was replaced with the following rates:

Instalment	Percentage which applies
First	0.50%
Second	0.53%
Third	0.56%
Fourth	0.60%

The **first instalment** arose on the date that the REIT regime applied to the company (and the remaining instalments at annual intervals thereafter).

If a company **ceases to be within the REIT regime** before the 4 year period is up, any remaining instalments become due immediately.

---

2. Ongoing activities

Business results

19850
ss 544, 599
CTA 2010

The results of the property rental business are **calculated** under normal principles (¶19135), although the maximum amount of capital allowances are always deducted. Gains or losses arising from the disposal of rental properties are dealt with separately (¶19900).

GREIT 04020

In addition, account is taken for debits and credits arising on **loan relationship and derivative** contracts so far as they relate to the property rental business (although bank interest arising on surplus funds will not be part of the business for this purpose). This includes contracts entered into in order to hedge risks associated with the business, and contracts with embedded derivatives. However, a derivative whose underlying subject matter is either shares in property companies or units in property unit trusts is excluded (¶16805).

19855
s 534 CTA 2010

Profits of the property business are:
a. generally exempt from corporation tax, although a tax charge can be imposed in certain circumstances (¶19860); and

b. ring-fenced, meaning that:
– any **losses** incurred by the exempt business (that is, property losses and non-trading loan relationship deficits) may not be offset against profits of any residual taxable business carried on by the company (and vice versa). Note, however, that the overseas property losses which arise in the exempt business can be set against any exempt business profits; and
– any receipts accruing to the exempt business after entry into the regime in respect of its **"pre-entry" business** are not treated as income of the exempt business. Similarly, the exempt business is distinct from any activity carried on after the company leaves the regime.

For **groups**, the ring-fencing provisions apply to the group as a whole with the result that losses of the exempt part of the business are not available for offset against profits from any taxable part of the group (and vice versa).

ss 541, 542
CTA 2010

Occasions of tax charge

A tax charge will be imposed on a REIT if either:
a. it pays out **distributions to holders of excessive rights** (¶19865), defined as corporate investors that own 10% or more of the company dividends, share capital or voting rights, unless the company has taken reasonable steps to avoid making such a payment; or
b. its **financing cost ratio** (¶19875) is less than 1.25, unless HMRC waive the charge due to unforeseen severe financial hardship.

19860
ss 543, 553
CTA 2010

Distribution to substantial corporate investors The following **formula** gives the additional income that is to be added to the company's income from its residual taxable business and taxed accordingly:

19865
ss 551, 552
2010;
2864

$$(DO \times SO \times \frac{BRT}{MCT}) + (DP \times SP \times \frac{BRT}{MCT})$$

where:
– DO is the total amount of profits of the tax exempt business that are distributed via ordinary shares;
– SO is the lesser of the excessive shareholder's percentage interest and the percentage of the distribution received;
– DP is the total amount of profits of the tax exempt business that are distributed in respect of preference shares;
– SP is the lesser of the excessive shareholder's percentage interest and the percentage of the distribution received in respect of any preference shares held;
– BRT is the basic rate of tax in force at the time of the distribution; and
– MCT is the mainstream rate of corporation tax.

GREIT 02123

The taxable amount resulting from the formula cannot be **reduced** by any loss relief, expense or other type of deduction.

> EXAMPLE D plc is a REIT with 1,000,000 ordinary shares in issue (and no preference shares). Basic rate income tax is 20%, and the corporation tax rate is 23%.
> Z Ltd owns 150,000 shares. D plc declares a dividend of 15p per share and as Z Ltd has sold its right to dividends on 70,000 of the shares to an individual shareholder, the company receives the dividend on the remaining 80,000 (an amount of £12,000).
> Z Ltd is a corporate investor holding more than 10% of the shares, so the dividend triggers a tax charge on D plc.
> DO will be £150,000. (1,000,000 × 15p)
> As Z Ltd's dividend received is less than its shareholding, SO will be 8%.
> The notional income for D plc is £10,434. (150,000 × 8% × 20% /23%)
> The amount of corporation tax due will be £2,400 i.e. the same amount as basic rate income tax on the distribution of £12,000.

On making a distribution to a corporate investor with an interest of 10% or more, the company must **provide the following details** on its usual quarterly return (¶47115):
– the name and address of the recipient;
– the amount of the distribution;

19870
SI 2006/2864 reg 11

- the recipient's interest in the company;
- particulars of the transaction giving rise to the distribution; and
- what the company has done (if anything) to avoid making such a distribution.

19875

s 543 CTA 2010;
GREIT 02200

Financing cost ratio   For each accounting period commencing on or after **17 July 2012** it is necessary to determine whether the financing costs of the tax-exempt property business make its **financing cost ratio less than 1.25**. If it is, corporation tax is chargeable at the mainstream rate on the lesser of:
- the excess financing cost; and
- 20% of the profit of the tax-exempt property business.

To see whether the ratio is less than 1.25, the following **formula** is used:

$$\frac{\text{Tax exempt profits (before capital allowances)}}{\text{Financing costs of tax exempt profits}}$$

The **excess financing cost** means the actual financing costs, less so much of those costs as would make the financing cost ratio equal to 1.25.

For this purpose, the following are included as financing costs:
- interest payable on borrowings;
- amortisation of discounts relating to borrowing;
- finance costs arising under finance leases; and
- costs of alternative finance (¶16125).

> MEMO POINTS   1. When calculating the financing cost ratio for **groups**, the calculation is changed to:
>
> $$\frac{\text{Tax exempt profits of the UK property rental business (before capital allowances)}}{\text{Financing costs of the exempt profits (excluding intra-group funding)}}$$
>
> 2. Exceptionally, HMRC **will waive the charge** where:
> - the company was in severe financial difficulties during the accounting period;
> - the result of the calculation is below 1.25 due to unforeseen circumstances; and
> - the company could not have been expected to take action to avoid the drop in the ratio.
> 3. For **accounting periods commencing before 17 July 2012** the same rules applied, except that:
> - the cap on the chargeable amount at 20% of profits did not apply; and
> - the financing costs to be taken into account also included:
>   - costs of raising finance;
>   - debits or credits arising on derivative contracts in relation to debt finance; and
>   - other costs considered to arise from a financing transaction under GAAP

> EXAMPLE   E plc has tax exempt profits of £95,000, after deducting capital allowances of £5,000. Interest (the financing cost) of £90,000 is payable.
> Applying the formula, the financing cost ratio is only 1.11, which is less than the required level. (100,000/90,000)
> For the ratio to be 1.25, the interest charge would have to be only £80,000.
> The excess interest which causes a breach in the ratio is therefore £10,000, and this is the amount of taxable income. (90,000 – 80,000)

Making distributions

19880

ss 973, 974
ITA 2007;
SI 2006/2867
regs 2, 7

Dividends from the exempt business (PIDs) must be **paid gross** where the company reasonably believes the recipient to be either:
- a UK resident company or permanent establishment; or
- a tax exempt body such as a local authority, health service body, charity etc.

Otherwise, the dividend should be **paid net** of basic rate tax, and a certificate of tax deducted should be provided to the recipient.

Any tax deducted is accounted for on a quarterly return (¶47115), which must be accompanied by a reconciliation statement showing the profits to which the distribution is attributed (¶19885).

Comment   The existence of **substantial corporate investors** (those with shareholding of at least 10%) does not disqualify the company from being an exempt business. Instead, an additional tax charge may be levied on the company (¶19860).

Income from which dividend paid   Dividends are treated as being paid out of the following income, in **order**:

a. UK REIT investment profits (¶19680), in satisfaction of the 100% distribution requirement;

b. rental profits of the exempt business (in satisfaction of the 90% distribution requirement (¶19725));

c. profits which are subject to corporation tax (the company is under no obligation to treat the dividend as paid out of these profits; the amount (if any) identified with the distribution is at the company's discretion). Such payments are paid as a normal dividend, with the usual tax credit attached;

d. other profits of the exempt business for the current or preceding year (to the extent that they are not already identified as having been distributed); and

e. tax exempt gains on disposal of assets of the exempt business (¶19900).

If the above does not exhaust the distribution, the remainder is treated as a normal dividend, with the usual tax credit attached.

A distribution attributed to tax-exempt income (**a**, **c** and **d** above) is referred to as a **property income distribution** (PID) and in the hands of a recipient is generally treated as UK property income.

19885
s 550 CTA 2010;
GREIT 08010

EXAMPLE F plc is a UK REIT and has the following results:	
	£
Distributions from a UK REIT in which it holds shares	5,000
Tax exempt profits	10,000
Tax exempt gains	1,000
Taxable income	1,300
Taxable gains	700

F plc pays an interim distribution of £8,000 in June, and a final distribution of £6,500 in March (after the accounting period has ended).
The interim distribution is paid out as a PID, and so is £6,000 of the final dividend.

	£
UK REIT investment profits to be distributed (100%)	5,000
Tax exempt profits to be distributed (10,000 x 90%)	9,000
Total profits to be distributed	14,000
Interim PID	8,000
Final PID	6,000
	14,000

Thus F plc has satisfied its distribution requirements for the accounting period. If F plc pays the other £500 of dividend as PID as well, that could be attributed to category c (see above) or set towards the distribution requirements for the next accounting period.

Treatment in hands of recipients   Distributions received from a REIT by another REIT in an accounting period (of the recipient) beginning on or after **17 July 2013** are treated as UK REIT investment profits: see ¶19860.

19890
ss 548, 549
CTA 2010

Otherwise, distributions to shareholders are:

– **chargeable to tax** as profits from a UK property business. There is no tax credit attached to this income although basic rate tax may have been deducted at source (¶19880); and

– treated as income of a separate UK property business. This means that **losses** from any other rental business of the shareholder cannot be set off against distributions from the exempt REIT. Distributions from different exempt REITs are, however, treated as income from the same business.

For **groups**, only the principal company can pay out dividends to shareholders. Dividends which are paid out of profits deriving from UK property owned by a non-resident member

ss 519, 520
CTA 2010

of a group are treated in the same way whether they are paid directly from that company or via an intermediate overseas holding company.

Disposals

19895   **Taxable business**   Any gains accruing to the residual taxable part of the business are charged to tax at the **mainstream rate**. The small profits rate is not available.

19900
s 535 CTA 2010

Exempt business   Capital gains accruing to the exempt business are usually not chargeable to corporation tax where the **asset** disposed of was **used**:
– wholly and exclusively for the purposes of the exempt business; or
– partly for the exempt business and partly for any residual taxable business, provided it was not used in the taxable business for a period of more than 1 year in aggregate. (If the period exceeds 1 year, the gain is apportioned on a fair and reasonable basis.)

For disposals on or after 17 July 2012, the gain is not taxable if the disposal was from one member of a group REIT to another member.

s 556 CTA 2010

Otherwise, there will be a taxable gain if an asset was:
– used entirely for the exempt business but is **then sold** in the course of the trade of the residual business (the gain is calculated by using the price the company first paid for the asset as the base cost and ignoring any uplift in this value on the deemed disposal and reacquisition on entry (¶19805)); or
– **developed** with the intention of retaining it as an investment property, but it is then sold within 3 years of completion and the costs of development exceeded 30% of the value of the property on acquisition. Depending on the facts, this may either be as a trading profit or capital gain.

ss 555, 557
CTA 2010

s 556(6) CTA 2010

> ⌐MEMO POINTS¬ 1. Where an **asset is moved from the exempt business to the taxable business (or vice versa)**, the disposal is treated as taking place at market value. For capital allowances purposes, the disposal takes place at tax written down value.
> 2. For **groups**, the relevant capital gains for these provisions are gains of UK resident members and non-UK resident members that have a property rental business in the UK.

19905
s 556(4) CTA 2010

Where the disposal gives rise to a **chargeable gain**, a company which became a REIT before 17 July 2012 may be entitled to reclaim a proportion of the entry charge (¶19815), calculated as follows:

$$\frac{\text{Asset Market Value}}{\text{Aggregate Market Value}} \times \text{Tax paid}$$

where:
– asset market value means the market value of the asset at entry;
– aggregate market value means the aggregate market value of assets treated as sold and reacquired on entry (¶19805); and

GREIT 04055

– tax paid means tax paid on entry, which will be 2% where the charge was paid in one lump sum, or 2.19% where the company is paying the entry charge in instalments (irrespective of whether the gain occurs before the instalments have all been paid).

> ⌐EXAMPLE¬ G plc purchased a property for £80,000. G plc became a REIT 2 years later, when the market value (and fair value) of the property was £100,000, and the value of the remaining properties put into the REIT was £900,000. G plc paid the entry charge of £75,000 in a lump sum.
> The property is developed at a cost of £31,000 and then sold for £250,000 within 3 years. The cost of development exceeds 30% of the fair value of the property at entry to the REIT regime. Therefore the property is deemed to leave the tax-exempt business and become part of the residual taxable business.
> The gain before indexation of is £139,000. (250,000 – 80,000 – 31,000)
> G plc can also claim a repayment of the proportion of the entry charge which relates to the property of £7,500. (100,000/1,000,000 x 75,000)

19910
s 547 CTA 2010

If an asset previously used in the exempt business is sold and the **disposal funds are invested** in any form of interest-producing account (for example, on deposit with a bank), any credits or debits arising are taxed as part of the residual taxable business.

If the disposal took place in an accounting period ending before 17 July 2012, then for 2 years following the disposal, the proceeds of the sale count as an asset of the company for the purposes of the 75/25 split (¶19730), although the income does not.

Where an asset disposed of was **used partly in the exempt trade** and partly not, the proceeds will be apportioned on a just and reasonable basis.

Demergers If a company which is a UK REIT transfers an asset involved in the property rental business to a subsidiary, and that subsidiary is then disposed of to another group, the subsidiary can enter the acquiring REIT group as long as it gives notice of entry to HMRC within 6 months of the date of the asset transfer. In this case, no entry charge is levied.

19915
s 558 CTA 2010

---

3. Ceasing to be a REIT

Termination event

A company will remain within the regime until one of the following termination events occurs:

19945

Terminating event	Detail	Date of leaving the regime	Reference
Notice issued by the company	Voluntary termination	As specified in the company notice[1]	s 571 CTA 2010
Notice issued by HMRC	Expulsion A notice can only be issued by HMRC where any of the following apply: – the minor breach conditions (¶19950) have been exceeded; – the company has been given two notices under the cancellation of tax advantages (¶19765) in a 10 year period beginning on the date the first notice was issued; or – HMRC consider the breach is sufficiently serious to warrant a notice	The end of the accounting period before the one in which the event that triggered the issue of the notice occurs	s 572 CTA 2010
Breach of company conditions (¶19710)	Minor breaches are permitted A breach of the close company condition or listing condition does not result in automatic expulsion from the regime if it is appropriate for this breach to be dealt with through the minor breach provisions	The end of the accounting period prior to the breach	s 578 CTA 2010

Note:
1. The notice must **specify**:
– the date on which the condition was breached (and when it was satisfied again (if applicable));
– the requirement and nature of the breach; and
– what the company has done (if anything) to avoid the breach recurring.
For **groups**, the notice has to be issued to the principal company.

Minor breaches

When considering the minor breach rules the important **factors** are:
– how many breaches have occurred; and
– what conditions have been breached (i.e. just the profitability conditions (¶19730) or the business conditions (¶19715) or a combination of both).

19950
ss 575–577
CTA 2010

The **number** of breaches that are permitted **in a 10 year period** (running from the start of the accounting period in which the first breach occurred) are as follows:

Type of breach	Type permitted
Any of the profitability conditions only	Any or all of the conditions can be breached twice in a 10 year period
Any of the business conditions only	
Combination of any of the profitability and business conditions (multiple breach)	Maximum of four breaches in any 10 year period

EXAMPLE H plc (with a 31 December year end) is a UK REIT, with the following history of breaches:

Breach number	Condition	Type of breach	Date
1	Profitability conditions	75% profit requirement	31 December 2008
2	Profitability conditions	75% asset requirement	31 December 2010
3	Profitability conditions	75% profit requirement	31 December 2011
4	Profitability conditions	75% asset requirement	31 December 2016
5	Business conditions	3 property requirement	31 December 2017

The 10 year period starts on 1 January 2008 and runs until 31 December 2017.
For the first four breaches the multiple breach conditions do not apply (all the breaches are from the same condition). As H plc has only breached each of the two profitability conditions twice it can still remain in the regime.
The fifth breach is of the business conditions so the multiple breach provisions apply. Although H plc has still not breached this particular condition twice, it has overall had five breaches in a 10 year period, so will be expelled from the regime from 31 December 2016, being the end of the accounting period before the last event that triggered the notice.

Effect of cessation

19955
s 579 CTA 2010

Where a company leaves the REIT regime, an **accounting period** comes to an end. Any property rental business still carried on by the company is treated as a new business.

Any **losses** from the tax exempt business cannot be carried forward.

Assets are treated as disposed of and reacquired at market value. For capital allowances purposes the transfer takes place at tax written down value.

MEMO POINTS Where a company (or a group) is **in the regime for less than 10 years** special rules apply as follows, so that where the company:

s 581 CTA 2010

– **leaves voluntarily**, any gains on previously tax exempt assets that are disposed of in the 2 year period from the date of cessation are computed without regard to the uplift in base cost arising from the initial entry into the regime; or

s 582 CTA 2010

– leaves the regime as a result of a **notice by HMRC** or a breach of company conditions, HMRC may determine a different cessation date than that which would normally apply. This is an anti-avoidance measure designed to prevent a REIT from artificially engineering its exit from the regime (by, for example, breaching one of the conditions) to utilise losses.

CHAPTER 8

Sundry items including anti-avoidance

In addition to the rules for the taxation of specific categories of income, there are general **21000** provisions relating to:
– items treated as miscellaneous income;
– income from deceased persons' estates;
– broad anti-avoidance rules (such as those governing certain transactions in securities); and
– charitable donations.

SECTION 1

Miscellaneous income

21050
s 979 CTA 2009

Although most income is classified within one of the main categories (trading, loan relationships, property and so on), some receipts are taxed under the general heading of miscellaneous income.

Before taxing an item within this category, the company should ensure that:
– the item has the qualities of income rather than capital (¶13000);
– it is taxable (it is not outside the scope of corporation tax, such as winnings from gambling, money derived from a hobby or income received as a gift); and
– it should not appear under some specific heading in the tax computation.

A. General principles

Recognition

21080

The general rule is that miscellaneous income is assessed on the profits received during an accounting period.

Where **accounts are prepared for a period in excess of 12 months**, the accounts figures should be apportioned on a daily basis to arrive at the income for each accounting period.

The amount included in the tax computation is the gross amount, regardless of whether **income tax** has been deducted at source. Relief will be available for any income tax suffered on miscellaneous income in accordance with the normal rules (¶41120).

Special rules apply to **patent income** (¶28930).

Losses

21085
s 91 CTA 2010

Relief for losses incurred on transactions which would be assessable under the term miscellaneous income (if profitable) can be obtained by setting the loss against other miscellaneous income for the **same period**, or, if this is not possible, by carrying forward the loss and setting it against **future profits** of any miscellaneous income.

Summary of main provisions

21090

Topic	¶¶
Tax repaid in error	¶21120
Commissions	¶21150+
Anti-avoidance	¶21385+

MEMO POINTS   1. For **post cessation receipts** see ¶61130.

s 610 CTA 2010   2. Other than for charitable recipients a **discretionary payment** made by trustees from a UK resident trust is ignored for corporation tax purposes, so it will not be included in income, and the tax deducted at source will not be available for set off or repayment. For payments from estates see ¶21215.

s 969 CTA 2009   3. Income arising from the **holding of an office** by the company is liable to corporation tax. The taxable amount is calculated with regard to the income tax rules which apply for the tax year in which the accounting period ends (see *Tax Memo* for details of employment income).

s 974 CTA 2009   4. Where **foreign dividend coupons** (those relating to shares outside the UK) are sold, the proceeds are taxed as miscellaneous income.

s 976 CTA 2009   5. **Annual payments** which are not charged to corporation tax under any other provision (and which are not covered by an exemption), are liable to corporation tax as miscellaneous income.

For this purpose annual payments **include** items such as annuities, and are characterised by a legal obligation to pay, and by being treated as income in the hands of the recipient. If a payment forms part of the recipient's trading receipts, it is not treated as an annual payment. The word annual in this respect does not imply a payment once a year, but denotes a quality of recurrence; the obligation must cover a period of more than 1 year to be considered an annual payment.

B. Tax repaid in error

Where there has been an **over repayment** of tax, an assessment can be made to recover tax which HMRC discover has been repaid to the company in error.

21120
Sch 18 paras 52, 53
FA 1998

Such an assessment treats the amount repaid as miscellaneous income, and carries interest from the date on which it was repaid until such time as the company pays the tax.

For further details see ¶48410.

C. Commissions

Commission income can be received following the introduction of a customer to a supplier of goods or services. The tax treatment depends upon whether the company has a trade.

21150
SP 4/97

Trading companies

Where the company who makes the introduction is trading, and regularly receives such commission income, this will be taxed as trading income.

21155

Even where the company arranges for the **customer to receive the commission direct** (by a reduction in insurance premiums for example), it will remain taxable trading income on the company so long as it has an enforceable legal right to the commission which is forgone in favour of the customer. However, where the company does not receive the commission, and has never had any entitlement to it, there will be no taxable receipt.

Non-trading companies

Where the company making the introduction is not trading, the commission will be taxable as miscellaneous income if it arises under an enforceable contract.

21160

Commission passed on

Where the commission is passed on to the customer, a **deduction** will be available if the customer required the commission to be passed on to him as a condition of entering into the transaction. However, where an ordinary retail customer receives a sum for purchasing goods or services, this will not be taxable on him.

21165

SECTION 2

Estate income

On the death of an individual, the property in his estate does not pass directly to the legatees or under the rules of intestacy. The property vests in his personal representatives, who are responsible for collecting the property, settling any outstanding liabilities or obligations, and then distributing the residue.

21215

An estate is therefore akin to a company, in that beneficiaries of the estate cannot access their property or income until it is distributed by the personal representatives. Such distributions can occur both during the administration period and once the administration of the estate is complete.

A. General principles

Income in the estate

21245

The income from the estate will retain its identity in the hands of the beneficiary, and will be taxed at the rate applicable for that source.

s 967 CTA 2009

A company beneficiary is entitled to request a **statement** from the personal representatives detailing the income arising to the company from the estate in a particular accounting period, including any tax treated as borne on that income.

Grossing up

21250

Each source of income is grossed up at the basic **rate** or dividend ordinary rate as appropriate. Payments are deemed to be made first out of income taxable at the basic rate, and then from dividend ordinary rate income.

Payments from the estate

21255

ss 934 – 936
CTA 2009

The treatment of sums paid to beneficiaries during the administration of an estate will **depend on** the beneficiary's interest in the estate, and also whether the estate is a UK one or foreign.

Type of interest	Description	¶¶
Absolute	Once the administration of the estate is complete, the beneficiary will be entitled to both the income and capital in his own right	¶21285
Limited	Entitles the beneficiary to a right to income once the administration of the estate is complete (for example, a life tenancy or an immediate post-death interest)	¶21290
Discretionary	The beneficiary is only entitled to any income of the residue if a discretion is exercised in his favour	¶21295

MEMO POINTS   For this purpose, a **foreign estate** (¶21325) is one where not all of the income is subject to UK tax, or where the personal representatives are not directly assessable e.g. they are all non-resident.

B. UK estates

Absolute interest

21285

ss 937, 938
CTA 2009

Payments made to a beneficiary with an absolute interest are treated as arising in the accounting period in which the payment is made.

However, the amount treated as **taxable income** is **limited** to the amount of the beneficiary's entitlement to the residuary income in each accounting period, up to and including the year of payment. Any excess over the entitlement to residuary income will be treated as a payment of capital.

Where there are **excess estate expenses** over residuary income, they are carried forward and deducted from income of the following period.

> `MEMO POINTS` 1. **Residuary income** for these purposes is defined as the aggregate of estate income excluding specific dispositions and contingent distributions, after deducting interest (other than interest on late inheritance tax) which is charged on the residue.
> 2. When the **administration of the estate ends**, any unrelieved expenses will be set against any remaining income which has not yet been paid out.

Limited interest

Payments made to a beneficiary with a limited interest are treated as arising in the accounting period in which the payment is made.

21290
ss 939, 944
CTA 2009

Amounts that remain payable to the beneficiary **once the administration has been completed** are normally treated as received in the accounting period when completion occurred. However, if the limited interest ceased before the completion of the administration, the income is treated as received by the beneficiary in the accounting period of cessation.

Discretionary interest

Payments made to a beneficiary with an discretionary interest are treated as arising in the accounting period in which the payment is made.

21295
s 940 CTA 2009

C. Foreign estates

If a company receives a payment from a foreign estate which has suffered UK income tax on part of its aggregate income, the corporation tax payable may be reduced. The reduction depends on the type of interest held by the company.

21325

Absolute interest

Where the beneficiary has an absolute interest and submits an appropriate claim, the tax chargeable is reduced by an amount calculated according to the following **formula**:

21330
s 960 CTA 2009

$$T \times \frac{A}{B}$$

where:
- T is the corporation tax charge;
- A is the amount of the estate's income which has borne UK income tax;
- B is the aggregate income of the estate for the relevant tax year.

For this purpose, the **relevant tax year** is the tax year which would apply if the company was within the charge to income tax.

Limited and discretionary interests

Where the beneficiary has a limited or discretionary interest and submits an appropriate claim, the tax chargeable will be reduced by an amount calculated according to the following **formula**:

21335
s 961 CTA 2009

$$T \times \frac{A - C}{B - C}$$

where:
- T is the corporation tax charge;
- A is the amount of the estate's income which has borne UK income tax;
- B is the aggregate income of the estate for the relevant tax year (¶21330); and
- C is the amount of income tax already borne by the aggregate income for the relevant tax year.

SECTION 3

Anti-avoidance

21385 There are anti-avoidance provisions in virtually every area of corporation tax, intended to combat perceived mischief. Provisions relating to particular topics are detailed in appropriate areas of *Corporation Tax Memo*. This section deals with provisions of a wider nature. For the new statutory General Anti-Avoidance Rule, see ¶55000.

Summary

21390

Provisions	¶¶
Tax advantages from transactions in securities	¶21420
Certain transactions involving property	¶19490
Gains from life policies	¶21565
Gains from offshore funds	¶21675
Structured finance arrangements	¶21915

A. Transactions in securities

21420 Transactions involving securities may require a clearance from HMRC (¶21535) in order to be sure of the tax treatment, because anti-avoidance legislation may treat profits (including gains) from securities as income.

Comment These rules are subject to ongoing consultation and may be completely repealed in future.

1. General principles

21450
s 733 CTA 2010

Whenever a company is party to a transaction in securities there may be a risk that HMRC will seek to counteract any corporation tax advantage obtained, if it falls within any of the circumstances shown in the table in ¶21485 below.

s 732 CTA 2010

MEMO POINTS 1. **Corporation tax advantage** means:
– obtaining relief or increased relief from corporation tax;
– becoming entitled to a repayment or increased repayment of corporation tax; or
– avoiding an assessment (or a possible assessment) to tax, or obtaining a reduced assessment.
An advantage may be obtained as a result of a single or multiple transactions in securities.

s 751 CTA 2010

2. **Securities** include unsecured loan notes, debentures, and shares. Where a company is not limited by shares (for example, it is limited by guarantee), securities also include any interests in the company held by its members.
3. **Transactions** in securities include:
– sale, purchase, redemption or transfer of securities;
– issuing or securing the issue of new securities;
– applying or subscribing for new securities; and
– altering the rights attached to securities.
A transaction could also possibly involve the **liquidation** of a company, although by itself it will not be considered a transaction in securities..

EXAMPLE Mr A owns 100% of X Ltd which has £300,000 in its bank accounts representing undistributed profits. Mr A subscribes for shares in Y Ltd, and X Ltd then transfers its trade and assets (except the cash) to this new company. X Ltd is then put into liquidation.

As Mr A will receive a capital receipt instead of taxable income, HMRC would act to cancel this tax advantage.

Exception

To **avoid a counteraction** the company must convince HMRC (i.e. the onus of proof is very much on the company) that obtaining a tax advantage is not the main object (or one of the main objects) of the transaction, and that the transaction is being carried out either:
– for genuine commercial reasons; or
– in the ordinary course of making or managing investments.

21455
s 734 CTA 2010

> MEMO POINTS   **Genuine commercial reasons** include resisting a takeover bid. *IRC v Brebner* [1967] Another case involved an individual who ran his own farm. He sold shares in a private investment company to finance the purchase of a nearby farm, which he wanted to combine with his existing business. It was held that the transaction was undertaken for genuine commercial reasons. *Clark v IRC* [1978]

---

2. Circumstances

Summary

21485
ss 736 – 742
CTA 2010

Circumstance	¶¶
A taxpayer receives an abnormal dividend (one substantially exceeding a normal return on the amount paid for the security), and as a consequence of that transaction, the company receives non-taxable consideration	¶21490
A company receives consideration in connection with the distribution of profits, or realisation of assets, of a close company[1]	¶21495
Non-taxable consideration, in the form of securities issued by a close company, received as part of a transaction involving the transfer of an asset between two close companies[1], or a transaction in securities involving at least two close companies[1]	¶21500
Note: 1. For this purpose, a close company means any unquoted company (unless controlled by a quoted company), and any company under the control of five persons or less.	

Abnormal dividend involved

The **non-taxable consideration** received by the company must represent assets available for distribution, future receipts of the company or trading stock, in a form in which it is not taxed as income.

21490
s 736 CTA 2010;
CTM 36826, 36835

When deciding **whether a dividend** is abnormal, HMRC and the First-tier Tribunal must have regard to the length of time the securities have been held, the terms of the securities (especially if a fixed rate dividend would normally apply), and the previous dividend payment history.

EXAMPLE

1. B Ltd subscribes £10,000 for 10,000 £1 shares in C Ltd.
A week later, C Ltd pays a dividend of £0.10p per share, so B Ltd receives £1,000. This is an abnormal dividend, because the annual equivalent yield would be £52,000 on a £10,000 investment.

2. F Ltd is owned 60% by Mr G (60,000 shares) and 40% by H Ltd (40,000 shares), a company under the control of Mr G. A third party agrees to purchase F Ltd for £20 million, after F Ltd pays a dividend of £10 million. As Mr G waives his dividend rights, the total dividend is paid to H Ltd. H Ltd agrees to sell its 40% shareholding in F Ltd for £2 million (equivalent to £25 per share). Mr G sells his 60% interest for £18 million (equivalent to £150 per share).

If the dividend from F Ltd is considered abnormal, HMRC will counteract the tax advantage received by Mr G (who has received a capital receipt instead of any dividend income which would be liable to income tax) and H Ltd (which has received non-taxable consideration (i.e. the dividend)).

3. A company knew it would make a large profit and created new shares with the right to a very high dividend. These shares were sold to a dealing company, who received the dividend, and then sold the shares at a loss. This loss could be set off against the dividend income, thereby avoiding tax. HMRC counteracted this advantage. *Greenberg v IRC* [1972]

Extraction of funds from a close company

21495
s 737 CTA 2010;
CTM 36840

An **amount** is received which **represents** assets available for distribution, future receipts of the close company, or trading stock, in a form in which it is not taxed as income.

EXAMPLE

1. Miss A owns 100% of X Ltd and Y Ltd, both trading companies. Y Ltd has distributable reserves of £400,000. Miss A decides to sell her shares in X Ltd to Y Ltd at market value. Y Ltd pays her £200,000 for the shares in cash.
Miss A has received cash of £200,000 which is not liable to income tax, and this cash represents distributable profits of Y Ltd. So HMRC will counteract this tax advantage.

2. Mr B owns 100% of Z Ltd, a trading company, which has distributable reserves of £800,000. Mr B wants to avoid income tax and receive a capital sum.
He sets up an employee benefit trust, to which Z Ltd makes a contribution of £800,000. The trust then acquires some of Mr B's shares for £800,000. So Z Ltd has, in effect, financed the acquisition of its own shares instead of paying a dividend.
So HMRC will counteract this tax advantage.

3. A company sold picture frames, one containing a valuable painting. Instead of selling the painting and distributing the proceeds, the following plan was conceived: all other stock was sold, and another company bought the shares in the framing company. So instead of a dividend, the taxpayer received a capital receipt. *IRC v Wiggin* [1979]

Securities received as a result of a close company transaction

21500
s 738 CTA 2010;
CTM 36845

The **consideration represents** assets for distribution of one of the companies.

If the consideration is in the form of **non-redeemable shares**, any tax liability resulting from HMRC's counteraction is deferred until the shares are repaid.

EXAMPLE

1. Mr C owns 100% of X Ltd and Y Ltd. Both companies have distributable reserves of £200,000. Mr C sells his X Ltd shares to Y Ltd. The consideration is 200,000 £1 redeemable preference shares and £30,000 of ordinary shares in Y Ltd.
Instead of receiving a dividend from Y Ltd, Mr C has received shares. As the ordinary shares are non-redeemable, no tax liability from HMRC's counteraction crystallises until the shares are repaid, if ever.

2. A company owned property which was expected to be very profitable when sold. The shareholders exchanged their shares for shares in another company for a large premium. The original company then paid a dividend up to its new parent company.
The shareholders took out interest-free loans from the company, which therefore avoided a tax charge. *Williams v IRC* [1980]

---

3. HMRC counteraction

21530
ss 743–746, 750
CTA 2010

If HMRC intend to counteract a tax advantage, a set procedure is followed whereby the company is informed how the transaction will be taxed, and given the opportunity to appeal.

Counteraction **may include** disallowing a loss, taxing a capital receipt as income, or refusing a repayment of tax.

MEMO POINTS Details of the **procedure** are as follows:
a. a preliminary notice is sent to the company by HMRC;
b. the company may then assert that these rules do not apply, giving reasons by statutory declaration within 30 days of the notice;

c. where HMRC do not agree with the company, the matter is put before the First-tier Tribunal, who will decide whether the counteraction is valid; and
d. where the First-tier Tribunal so decides, HMRC will then serve a notice stating how the transaction will be taxed, against which the company can appeal.

Obtaining clearances

In order to obtain **certainty** on how a transaction will be taxed, it is advisable to apply for clearance in advance that HMRC will not counteract any tax advantage.

21535
ss 748, 749
CTA 2010

Once the written application is received, HMRC have 30 days in which to give clearance or request further information (to which the taxpayer must respond within 30 days or the application will lapse).

When **refusing** an application, HMRC will usually state their reasons. There is no right of appeal against a refusal.

> ▭ MEMO POINTS   1. The **letter requiring clearance** should contain as much information as possible about the transaction, particularly emphasising the reasons why the transaction is not being undertaken just to obtain a tax advantage. Failure to advance full information could render any clearance void.
> 2. Virtually all clearances are dealt with by the same HMRC team (¶95380), requiring only one letter about the transaction to be sent to the following **address**:
> Clearance and Counteraction Team (Anti-Avoidance Group)
> SO528
> PO Box 194
> Bootle
> L69 9AA
> Market sensitive information should be marked for the attention of the Team Leader.
> Clearance applications can also be emailed to: reconstructions@hmrc.gsi.gov.uk,
> 3. **Other clearances** under the following provisions may also be made at the same time as for transactions in securities:
> – demergers;
> – purchase of own shares;
> – acquisition of EIS company shares by a new company;
> – share exchanges;
> – reconstructions; and
> – intangible fixed assets.

SP 3/80

B. Life policies

A company which is a party to an **investment life insurance contract** (otherwise known as a life policy or annuity) is liable to tax under the loan relationship rules (¶16050). Any profit will be treated as a non-trading loan relationship credit, and any loss will be a debit.

21565

Comment   These rules apply for accounting periods beginning on or after 1 April 2008. Previously, gains arising on these types of contracts were taxable under the chargeable event gain provisions which were unnecessarily complicated for companies to apply. There are transitional rules which apply for companies who held contracts before 1 April 2008 (¶21615).

1. Scope

An investment life insurance contract is **defined** as:
– a policy of life insurance which has, or is capable of acquiring, a surrender value;
– a contract for a purchased life annuity; or
– a capital redemption policy.

21595
s 561 CTA 2009

The definition **excludes**:
– investment life insurance contracts under a registered pension scheme (or contracts purchased with sums or assets held for the purposes of such a pension scheme); and

– life insurance policies issued before 14 March 1989 if they have not been subsequently varied.

> ⬜ *MEMO POINTS*   1. A **purchased life annuity** means an annuity:
> – granted for consideration in money or money's worth in the ordinary course of a business of granting annuities on human life; and
> – payable for a term ending at a time ascertainable only by reference to the end of a human life.
> 2. A **capital redemption policy** means a contract made in the course of a capital redemption business.

---

2. Occasions of tax charge

21615
s 562 CTA 2009;
IPTM 3910, 3915

As for other types of loan relationships, the tax treatment of the contract will largely be **determined by** its recognition in the financial statements under GAAP.

However, no tax charge will arise where a lump sum exceeds the surrender value of a contract, and the payout is due to **death or critical illness** i.e. the mortality or morbidity gain is not taxable.

A tax charge will arise in the following circumstances:
– where the contract is **not accounted for at historic cost** (at fair value, current cost or amortised cost basis), in which case an annual charge will apply based on changes in the carrying value of the contract in the company's accounts; and
– if any rights under the contract are **disposed of** (for example, by surrender or assignment) or come to an end (for example, on maturity), in which case relief may be available for tax treated as already paid (¶21635).

s 567 CTA 2009;
IPTM 3930

> ⬜ *MEMO POINTS*   There are **transitional rules** which apply when a company used the chargeable gain event rules **prior to the first accounting period beginning on or after 1 April 2008**. Briefly, at the beginning of the accounting period when the loan relationship rules start to apply (the start date), the company was treated as having surrendered all the rights under the contract for an amount equal to its carrying value in the accounts. In most cases, no gain will arise, especially where historic cost accounting is used.
> Where a **gain does arise**, it only becomes taxable as a non-trading loan relationship credit if the company disposes of all or part of the contract rights (where only part of the rights are disposed of then only the proportion of the gain relating to the rights disposed of are brought into account). There is no tax treated as paid in this situation.
> Two other rules may also apply, depending on whether the company accounts for the contract:

s 568 CTA 2009;
IPTM 3935

> **a.** at fair value and the **cost** of the contract (usually the premiums paid) **exceeds the fair value** of the contract at the start date. In this case, taxable non-trading loan relationship credits will only begin to arise on the contract once the fair value exceeds the cost; and

s 569 CTA 2009;
IPTM 3940

> **b.** on a basis other than fair value, and the **carrying value of the contract exceeds the fair value** at the start date (so a loss would arise if the contract were surrendered). In this situation, no non-trading debits can be brought into account on the contract until they exceed the amount of the loss.

---

3. Tax treated as already paid

21635
s 563 CTA 2009;
IPTM 3920

As an **insurer has already borne** UK tax in relation to the insurance contract, an amount of tax is treated as being paid (at a rate equal to the basic rate of income tax) when a company disposes of its rights under an investment contract.

The tax treated as paid is **set against** the company's corporation tax liability for the accounting period in which the disposal occurs. Any excess cannot be repaid to the company nor set off in any other accounting period.

s 564 CTA 2009

The relief is computed differently, depending on whether or not the company uses fair value accounting.

> ⬜ *MEMO POINTS*   This mechanism is available where the **contract forms part** of the basic life assurance and general annuity business of a UK insurer, other than tax-exempt friendly society business, or is part of a comparable EEA business.

Not using fair value accounting

A **grossing up** system operates, so that the original non-trading loan relationship credit arising from the disposal is increased by the following **fraction**:

$$\frac{AR}{100 - AR}$$

where AR is the corporation tax rate applying to the policyholder's share of income and gains of the insurer, which is currently 20% (equivalent to the basic rate of income tax). The amount of the increase is treated as tax paid.

21640
s 563 CTA 2009

> [EXAMPLE] D Ltd's accounting period ends on 31 December. It took out a policy 5 years ago, paying a premium of £20,000. It surrenders 25% of the policy for £8,000.
> The non-trading loan relationship credit on the disposal is £3,000. (8,000 – (25 % x 20,000)),
> This must be grossed up to give an increased non-trading loan relationship credit of £3,750.
>
> $(3,000 \times \frac{20}{100 - 20})$
>
> The tax treated as paid is £750. (3,750 – 3,000)

Using fair value accounting

Again, the original non-trading loan relationship credit (NTLR credit) arising from the disposal is grossed up, but the following **formula** is used:

$$PC \times \frac{AR}{100 - AR}$$

21645
s 565 CTA 2009;
IPTM 3920

where:
– PC is the profit from contract; and
– AR is the corporation tax rate applying to the policyholder's share of income and gains of the insurer, which is currently 20% (equivalent to the basic rate of income tax).

For this purpose the **profit from the contract** is the amount payable on the related transaction, less the fair value of the contract on the later of:
– the date that the contract was made; and
– the start of the company's first accounting period beginning on or after 1 April 2008.

Where **the disposal is only of part of the rights** only a proportion of the fair value of the contract immediately before the disposal (as represented by the proceeds) is deducted.

IPTM 3925

> [EXAMPLE] E Ltd's accounting period ends on 30 June, and on 15 July it takes out an investment contract with a premium of £20,000, which is also the initial fair value. The fair value at the end of Year 1 is £22,000, and at the end of Year 2 it is £21,500.
> During Year 3, E Ltd surrenders 50% of the rights under the contract policy for £12,000, the fair value immediately before the disposal being £24,000.
> The fair value of the contract at the end of Year 3 is £12,750.
> The tax consequences are as follows:
>
> | Accounting period | Detail | £ |
> | --- | --- | --- |
> | Year 1 | Increase in contract value – NTLR credit (22,000 – 20,000) | 2,000 |
> | Year 2 | Decrease in contract value – NTLR debit (21,500 – 22,000) | (500) |
> | Year 3 | Part disposal[1] | 1,750 |
> | | Tax available for set off | 500 |
> | | Increase in value – NTLR credit[2] | 2,000 |
>
> **Note:**
> 1. The ungrossed up NTLR credit is calculated by deducting 50% of the fair value at the most recent year end from the proceeds, which gives £1,250. (12,000 – (50 % x 21,500))
> The tax treated as paid is calculated by computing the profit from the contract and grossing it up. For this purpose, the profit is calculated by deducting 50% of the original fair value from the proceeds, which gives £2,000. (12,000 – (50 % x 20,000))
>
> The NTLR credit is increased by using the formula, which gives £500. $(2,000 \times \frac{20}{100 - 20})$

So the NTLR credit is £1,750. (1,250 + 500)
The tax treated as paid is £500.
2. The increase in the value of the contract retained is calculated by deducting 50% of the fair value at the end of Year 2 from the fair value at the end of Year 3, which gives £2,000. (12,750 − (50 % x 21,500))

C. Offshore funds

21675
SI 2009/3001
reg 101

To prevent companies avoiding UK tax by investing in offshore funds which accrue income instead of distributing it, a gain arising on the disposal from such a fund may be liable to corporation tax as miscellaneous income. Note that charitable companies and registered pension schemes are exempt from these rules.

1. Scope

What is an offshore fund?

21705
ss 355, 356 TIOPA
2010

An offshore fund cannot be a partnership (including a limited liability partnership).

However, any fund with the following **characteristics** will be an offshore fund:
a. a mutual fund (which includes all unit trust schemes) resident or based outside the UK;
b. that allows participants to participate in:
– the acquisition, holding, management or disposal of the property; or
– profits or income arising from the same activities;
c. but in which the participants do not have day to day control of the management of the property, although they might have a right to be consulted or to give directions about it; and
d. in which a reasonable investor would expect to be able to realise all or part of an investment by calculating the net asset value of the property or by using indexation.

It is the **company investor's responsibility** to know whether it has an investment in an offshore fund.

Priority of tax rules

21710
SI 2009/3001
regs 25, 26, 28

Even where an offshore fund exists, the **following tax regimes take precedence**, so that any related income and gains will be taxable under these rules rather than the offshore funds provisions:
– loan relationships (particularly affecting bond funds (¶21740), and where a normal commercial loan is made to a fund);
– derivative contracts (¶16775), where the holding in the fund is via a financial instrument;
– intangible assets (¶28135);
– controlled foreign companies (¶90555);
– funds held as trading stock, or where a disposal would be taken into account in the profits of a trade;
– chargeable gains in respect of excluded indexed securities (i.e. where the amount payable to redeem the debt is calculated by applying a percentage to the amount of the security. The percentage is the change over the redemption period in an index of certain assets); and
– life policy contracts (¶21565).

2. Types of fund

21740

The tax treatment of income derived from an interest in an offshore fund, and the disposal of that interest, depend upon the nature of the fund as shown in the table below.

Where a fund has an **excess proportion of interest-bearing investments** (broadly more than 60% of the fund's asset value) during the company's accounting period, this is known as a bond fund. In this case, the fund is treated as a creditor loan relationship of the company (¶16160).

The underlying funds in an **umbrella fund** are treated as separate funds, so that the overall arrangements of umbrella funds are disregarded.

s 360 TIOPA 2010

Comment   Offshore funds may fall within the requirements of reporting funds for one accounting period, and be treated as non-reporting for the next. So the company investor must ensure it is aware of the status of the fund for every accounting period.

Fund type	Subcategory	Detail	Tax treatment of disposals	¶¶
Reporting[1]		HMRC approved Participants are taxable on their share of the undistributed fund income	Chargeable gains	¶21760
Non-reporting	Transparent[2]	Participants are taxable on fund income arising on the underlying investments	Chargeable gains	¶21805
	Non-transparent	Participants are taxable on distributions made from the fund	Offshore income gain	¶21815

Note:
1. HMRC publish a **list** of reporting funds, which is updated monthly, at flmemo.co.uk/ctm2366
2. A typical **transparent fund** would be an open-ended investment company. **HMRC** give full **guidance** as to the characteristics of a transparent entity in the International Manual.

INTM 180010

3. Reporting funds

A reporting fund is HMRC approved and the UK participants effectively agree to pay UK tax on the undistributed income of the fund.

21760
SI 2009/3001 reg 92

The fund must make a report to its participants for each reporting period (normally, its period of account) within 6 months from the end of that period.

The report must **declare** the following information:
– the amount distributed to the participants in the period, per unit investment; and
– the excess income (undistributed) of the period (if any), per unit investment.

SI 2009/3001 reg 94

Participants are taxed on the sum of these two amounts.

For companies, other than where a bond fund (¶21740) exists, the whole sum is likely to be exempt from corporation tax so long as the **excess income** would be a dividend were it to be distributed.

SI 2009/3001 reg 98

Disposals

The capital gains tax **definition** of disposal (¶30080) applies for these purposes, particularly regards the timing of disposal, and the matching of disposals with acquisitions (the share pooling rules).

21765
SI 2009/3001
regs 17, 18, 45;
OFM 27500

The disposal of an interest in the fund is treated as a normal chargeable gain, but any **undistributed amounts already taxed** are treated as part of the cost of acquisition (that is, effectively as a deduction). For this purpose the date of acquisition is the fund distribution date.

21770
s 38 TCGA 1992;
SI 2009/3001 reg 99

MEMO POINTS   1. Any **income received** after the interest in the fund is disposed of is treated, for tax purposes, as received immediately before disposal.
2. As **charitable companies** will have been exempt from tax on undistributed funds, the cost of acquisition will not be increased where a gain, which is not crystallised for charitable purposes, arises.

4. Non-reporting funds

21800   These funds have no obligations to HMRC. The tax treatment depends on whether the fund is transparent.

An offshore income gain may arise in relation to a non-reporting fund, and also a fund which has been a non-reporting fund at some time during the period when the company was an investor in the fund.

Transparent funds

21805
OFM 13200

A UK investor in a transparent non-reporting fund is liable to corporation tax on the income of the fund as it arises, less a deduction for the management expenses of the fund. It is of no tax consequence how much of the fund's income is actually distributed. The fund should send a voucher to the investor, detailing the amount and type of income.

SI 2009/3001 reg 16   Where the fund itself is a **participator in a reporting fund** the taxable income will include the relevant proportion of the undistributed income of the reporting fund (¶21760).

21810
SI 2009/3001
reg 29;
OFM 16500

Disposals   Any gain on disposal of an interest in an income transparent offshore fund will not be taxed as an offshore income gain (so the usual chargeable gains rules apply) **unless**:
– at any time during the period of ownership of the interest more than 5% of the value of the offshore fund's assets consisted of interests in other non-reporting funds (ignoring investments in certain other transparent funds); or
– the fund fails to make sufficient information available to participants in the fund to enable them to meet their UK tax obligations.

> ⬚ MEMO POINTS   1. Where the **5% limit is breached**, the fund may apply for reporting fund status in order to avoid an offshore income gain on its investors.
> 2. **Sufficient information** would include details of the income arising to the fund which are attributable to the investor, as well as confirmation as to whether or not the 5% rule has been met.

Non-transparent funds

21815
s 490 CTA 2009

The tax treatment of UK investors in a non-transparent fund depends on whether the fund has corporate form.

Unless the fund is a bond fund (¶21740):
– distributions received **from a corporate entity** (such as an OEIC) will be exempt in the hands of a company investor; and
– investors in a **non-corporate entity** (a foreign unit trust) are taxable on the fund's income (less expenses) when it is allocated to them (irrespective of whether it is distributed). The allocated amount is taxed as miscellaneous income.

21820
SI 2009/3001
regs 32, 33

Disposals   Except for the taxing of gains as income, the usual chargeable gains rules apply to disposals. There is no indexation allowance.

When any offshore income gain arises, the taxable amount is treated as miscellaneous income in the accounting period in which the disposal occurs. The taxable amount is deducted from the proceeds for the purpose of calculating any actual **chargeable gain** (to avoid double charging). In most cases this will eliminate any capital gain.

SI 2009/3001 reg 42   A **loss** is treated as a nil gain for this purpose, although any loss arising under the usual chargeable gains rules is available for relief as a capital loss (¶37000).

s 13 TCGA 1992   UK shareholders of a non-resident company which sustains an offshore income gain may be liable to tax on an appropriate proportion of the gain (¶76040).

21825   The **basic gain** is the proceeds less acquisition cost before any indexation allowance.

There are special provisions in relation to:
– exchanges of securities or interests, including schemes of reconstruction; and
– group transfers at no gain/no loss.

MEMO POINTS 1. When an interest in a non-reporting fund is **exchanged** for an interest in another type of entity (i.e. not a non-reporting fund), a disposal is deemed to occur at market value for the purposes of calculating the offshore income gain. The exchange could be as a result of an exchange of securities or interests, or a scheme of reconstruction.

SI 2009/3001 regs 35 – 37

2. When an interest in an offshore fund is **transferred between group members** the gain arising when the interest is eventually disposed of outside the group ignores any indexation allowance which was available on the intra-group transfer.

SI 2009/3001 reg 40

5. Change of status

If a fund changes from:

21855
SI 2009/3001 reg 100

a. reporting to non-reporting status, the participant may elect (via the corporation tax return) to be treated, for tax purposes, as making a deemed disposal and reacquisition of the interest at market value. This would crystallise the already accrued gains as chargeable gains rather than as income; or

b. non-reporting to reporting status, a similar election can be made to crystallise the accrued gain within the offshore income gains regime. Subsequent gains would then be treated as chargeable gains. If the election is not made any subsequent disposal will still be potentially chargeable as income.

SI 2009/3001 reg 48

6. Transitional rules

As the offshore regime substantially changed from 1 December 2009 there are transitional rules to enable companies to convert to the new set of rules.

21875

Holding in qualifying offshore fund

Where a company held an interest in a qualifying offshore fund under the regime which existed prior to 1 December 2009, this previous status could continue until the fund's period of account ending just before 31 May 2012. Broadly, such a fund had to pursue a full **distribution policy** (distributing at least 85% of the income and UK equivalent profits of the fund for each accounting period), so that no offshore income gain arose on disposal of the interest, and investors are only taxable on the amounts distributed. See earlier editions of *Corporation Tax Memo* for further details.

21880

Where a qualifying offshore fund **then becomes**:
− **a reporting fund** (¶21760), no taxable gain arises; or
− **a non-reporting fund** (¶21800), any subsequent disposal of the interest will be subject to the offshore income gain rules, unless the participator elected (via the corporation tax return) for a deemed disposal at 1 December 2009 so that any gain accrued up to that date was a chargeable gain. For this purpose, the deemed proceeds are the net asset value of the fund attributable to the participator's interest.

SI 2009/3001 Sch 1 para 4

Holding in non-qualifying offshore fund

Where a company held an interest in a non-qualifying offshore fund under the regime which existed prior to 1 December 2009 which then **becomes a reporting fund** (¶21760) the company can elect (via the corporation tax return) for a deemed disposal at 1 December 2009, so that any gain accrued up to that date is taxable as an offshore income gain (¶21820). For this purpose the deemed proceeds are the net asset value of the fund attributable to the participator's interest.

21885
SI 2009/3001 Sch 1 para 5

A company may have acquired rights prior to 1 December 2009 (or after this date where a legally enforceable agreement was entered into before 30 April 2009) which **did not constitute a material interest in an offshore fund, or where the fund was not an offshore fund under the old regime**, so that a chargeable gain would have been expected when disposing of the rights. This tax treatment is preserved, and these are known as protected rights. Where the company acquires further rights in the fund on or after 1 December 2009

SI 2009/3001 regs 30, 43

these are known as non-protected rights. Protected and non-protected rights are treated as separate assets for the purposes of the share pooling provisions (¶32190). The protected rights are always treated as disposed of first.

D. Structured finance arrangements

1. General principles

21915   Structured finance arrangements enable companies to borrow money and obtain effective tax relief both for the interest and the repayment of the principal. The arrangements come in three different guises (formally known as Type 1, Type 2 and Type 3). Type 1 is a simple scheme compared with Types 2 and 3, which are distinguished by their complexity and the involvement of a partnership structure.

These tax rules apply for all amounts arising on or after 6 June 2006, unless the previous rent factoring rules (¶19485) applied to an arrangement entered into before that date.

The rules have no effect on the lender.

s 775 CTA 2010   [MEMO POINTS]   For this purpose, **arrangement** includes any agreement or understanding, whether it is legally enforceable or not.

Exceptions

21920   The structured finance arrangement rules do not apply where:
s 771 CTA 2010   **a.** the **whole of the advance** is:
– charged to tax as an amount of income (being a pure income profit) or brought into account in computing income (being a receipt whichs form part of the profit calculation of a business); or
– brought into account as a disposal receipt for capital allowances purposes (although if a balancing charge is not wholly taxable, this exception is not applicable);
b. the transaction is **accounted for** as:
– a stock lending or repo arrangement;
– an alternative finance arrangement; or
– a loan relationship (although this exception is not applicable if there is no lending involved (¶16115)); or
c. the **asset** transferred is the subject of a sale and finance leaseback, or the arrangement is one in relation to which the lessee's rental deductions are restricted (¶82680). For this purpose it is irrelevant whether the leaseback is a long funding lease.

s 772 CTA 2010   [MEMO POINTS]   In the case of **a.** above, the **charge may fall upon** the company, any connected person (¶31375) or, where relevant, a member of the partnership.

Intention behind the rules

21925   The tax rules **attempt to** level the playing field between different methods of obtaining finance: that is, between a direct loan on the one hand, and on the other a redirection of income relating to an asset which is owned and disposed of (usually temporarily) by the borrower. In the latter arrangement, the income on the asset is still deemed to arise to the borrower, although relief is given for the finance charge.

s 776 CTA 2010;   [MEMO POINTS]   1. For this purpose receiving an **asset or payments in respect of an asset** includes:
CFM 73050   – obtaining the value of, or a benefit from, an asset whether directly or indirectly;
– the discharge, in whole or in part, of any liability; and
– payments in respect of any asset that is substituted for the original asset.
2. **Disposal** takes its meaning from the chargeable gains rules, so it includes (for example) a part disposal or the grant of a lease.

EXAMPLE

1. F Ltd obtains a 5 year loan of £500,000 from a bank secured on a warehouse. Over the 5 year period interest of £30,000 is payable each year, along with £100,000 of the principal, resulting in a total of £650,000 over the loan's term.
Tax relief would be due for the interest payment only.

2. G Ltd holds a property in respect of which annual rental income of £130,000 will arise. The property is transferred to a bank for a 5 year period in return for a lump sum of £500,000. At the end of the period, G Ltd reacquires the property and its rental stream for nil consideration. A total of £650,000 is paid to the bank.
In substance, this arrangement is a loan, because G Ltd retains the risks and rewards of owning the property. Under GAAP, G Ltd will continue to recognise the property in its accounts and will show the lump sum as a financial liability. The rental income will also be shown in the accounts, with £100,000 of each payment reducing the liability, and £30,000 being shown as a finance charge in the profit and loss account.
The only difference between the two examples above is that the income stream of the property is diverted to the lender. G Ltd will not be able to escape tax on this income due to the structured finance arrangement rules.

3. A Ltd and B Ltd are members of a group. A Ltd intends to lease a warehouse to B Ltd, but it needs funds of £800,000 for expansion.
So A Ltd leases the warehouse to the bank for 1 year for a premium of £800,000.
The bank immediately grants a 1 year lease to B Ltd. No premium is payable, and rent of £840,000 is payable (which represents the funding of £800,000 plus interest).
The bank is still treated as receiving payments in respect of the warehouse transferred by A Ltd, even though the payments relate to the sublease. The sublease is a benefit deriving from the warehouse.

2. Simple structures

In substance, these are lending transactions which are secured on certain assets that repay the loan. As such they have the following **characteristics**:
– the borrower receives either money or another asset (termed the advance) from the lender;
– the borrower recognises the advance as a financial liability (in effect a secured loan) in its accounts prepared under GAAP;
– the borrower (or a connected person) transfers an asset to, or for the benefit of, the lender (or a connected person);
– the lender (or a connected person) is entitled to receive payments in respect of the asset; and
– the payments reduce the amount of the financial liability shown in the borrower's accounts.

21955
ss 758, 760
CTA 2010;
CFM 73060

MEMO POINTS 1. For this purpose, the borrower and lender are not **connected persons** simply because of the debt. Apart from that, the usual connected persons definition applies (¶31375).
2. Where the borrower receives an **asset other than money as the advance**, this would usually be easily convertible into cash.
3. The **accounts** in the case of a:
– **group** include the consolidated accounts of the group of which the borrower is a member; and
– **partnership** include the accounts of any member of the partnership.
4. Where the accounts of the borrower are **not drawn up in accordance with GAAP** the rules operate as if they had been.
5. The **asset transferred to the lender** does not have to be income producing at the time of transfer. It will usually be transferred back to the borrower at the end of the repayment term. However, it may be that by then the asset is totally depleted (devoid of value).

ss 758, 774
CTA 2010

Relevant effect

There are only consequences under these rules where the arrangements result in a relevant effect, which is broadly where the **borrower escapes tax** on income or **becomes entitled to a tax deduction**. The amounts involved are usually obvious from the accounts.

21960
ss 759, 761, 762
CTA 2010;
CFM 73090, 73100

There are **three types** of relevant effect as follows:

Type	Detail	Tax consequence
Pure income profit not charged to tax	As a result of the arrangements, an amount of income is not charged to tax on the borrower[1], or where relevant, a connected person	The income is restored to the borrower (or the connected person) and chargeable to tax
Receipts not charged to tax	As a result of the arrangements, receipts[1] which form part of the calculation of a profit (whether of a trade, a property business or some other business) are not charged to tax	The advance is treated as a loan relationship[2] so that relief is available for the finance charge (as shown in the accounts) whenever a payment is made to the lender (which will be treated as part principal and part finance charge) The usual rules relating to unallowable purpose (¶16500) and late interest (¶16605) apply
Entitlement to tax deduction	As a result of the arrangements, the borrower[1] accesses an income deduction e.g. a trading expense, property business expense or any deduction against total profits This happens where the loan is repaid by a newly created expenditure stream for which tax relief is claimed	

Note:
1. Where the borrower is a **partnership** the partnership entity is ignored, so that it is the partners themselves who are considered to see whether the income is charged to tax, brought into account in computing income or there is an entitlement to a deduction.
2. For **corporate partners** of a partnership the interest is attributed in accordance with the partnership shares, and each partner will be subject to the loan relationship rules in relation to that part of the interest.

EXAMPLE

1. C Ltd holds a property in respect of which annual rental income of £130,000 will arise. The property is transferred to a bank for a 5 year period in return for a lump sum of £500,000. At the end of the period C Ltd reacquires the property and its rental stream for nil consideration. A total of £650,000 is paid to the bank.
All the conditions of a simple structure are met, and the arrangement will have a relevant effect if C Ltd escapes tax on the rental income of £130,000 p.a. In this case the income is restored to C Ltd (ignoring the arrangement completely). Further, relief is available for the finance charge of £30,000 p.a.

2. D Ltd owns freehold land which it leases to a bank for 5 years for a premium of £1m.
The bank immediately grants a 5 year sublease to D Ltd in return for annual rental payments of £220,000, which will total £1.1m. At the end of the 5 year period the land will revert back to D Ltd. In substance D Ltd has borrowed £1m, which it repays over the 5 year period plus interest of £100,000. As a result of the arrangements D Ltd becomes entitled to a deduction for the rent payable of £220,000 p.a., which reflects not only interest but also repayment of the capital amount of the loan.
The structured finance arrangement rules mean that there will be no deduction for the rents paid, but there will be a deduction for the interest charge.

Disposals

21965
s 263E TCGA 1992

Where an asset is disposed of by the borrower (or a connected person) to the lender (or a connected person) the disposal is disregarded for chargeable gains purposes, so long as either of the following **conditions** are met:
– only the transferor has the right or obligation to reacquire exactly the same asset at any subsequent time; or
– the asset will subsequently cease to exist at any time, and the lender (or a connected person) will own it from the time of the disposal until the time it subsequently ceases to exist.

Where these conditions are **not met** the disposal will be taxable at market value.

When the transferor **reacquires the asset** the disposal by the lender is also ignored for tax purposes.

3. Complex structures

There are **two types** of complex structures, as summarised in the following table. Again, the effect of the tax rules is to restore taxable income to the borrower, and allow any finance charge as a deduction.

21995
ss 763, 767
CTA 2010

Overview	Conditions
The asset is transferred to the partnership under the arrangement by the transferor partner (who must be a partner after the transaction, but does not have to be beforehand)	The following criteria apply to both types of arrangement: – the partnership receives an advance (¶21955) from the lender;
The asset is already held by the partnership and either: – a new member joins the partnership and takes a profit share in return for a capital contribution that is in substance a loan; or – an existing partner takes an increased share in the profits in return for a capital contribution that is in substance a loan	– the partnership recognises the advance as a financial liability (effectively a secured loan) in its accounts[1] prepared under GAAP; – the lender (or connected person) is either admitted to the partnership or receives an increased share of its profits; – the lender's share of the partnership profits falls to be determined (wholly or partly) by reference to payments in respect of the security; and – those payments reduce the amount of the financial liability shown in the accounts prepared under GAAP
Note: 1. The liability could also be recognised in the transferor partner's **accounts**, or, where the partner is a group member, the consolidated accounts of the group.	

Tax consequences

There are only consequences under these rules where the **arrangements result in** the relevant member of the partnership either:
– escaping tax on an amount of income;
– escaping tax on receipts which form part of the calculation of a profit (whether of a trade, a property business or some other business); or
– becoming entitled to a tax deduction against income.

22000
ss 765, 766, 768, 769 CTA 2010;
CFM 73220

For this purpose the identity of the **relevant member** depends upon whether the asset is:
– transferred to the partnership, in which case it is the transferor partner (only); or
– already held by the partnership, in which case it is all of the partners (excluding the lender) before the change in profit share ratios occurs.

The tax rules operate to reverse the effect of the structured finance arrangement, so that the income is still taxable on the relevant member or, where applicable, the tax deduction is not obtained. However, as for simple structures, relief will be available for finance charges.

> EXAMPLE E Ltd transfers, to a newly formed partnership, an asset that will produce £600,000 of income over the next 5 years. F Ltd joins the partnership by contributing £500,000 as capital and will take 90% of partnership profits over the next 5 years (equating to £540,000 i.e. repayment of the £500,000 with interest). E Ltd will take 3% and G Ltd, the third partner, will take the remaining 7%.
> Assuming all of the criteria for a complex structure are met the transferor partner, E Ltd, is the relevant member and will be taxable on the income of £600,000, with relief for the finance charge shown in its accounts. It will not be taxed on its profit share from the partnership. F Ltd and G Ltd will be taxed on their actual profit shares because they are not relevant members.

Finance charges

Any finance charge that is shown in the **accounts** prepared under GAAP will be treated as interest on a loan. For this purpose the payments to the lender are divided into interest and principal, and treated as paid when the lender actually receives them.

22005

For any corporate partners involved in the scheme, the advance is treated as a loan relationship.

Where the **asset is**:

– **transferred to the partnership**, the interest payable, as shown in the accounts of the partnership or of the transferor partner, is allowed as a tax deduction; or

– **already owned by the partnership**, the interest payable, as shown in the accounts of the partnership or of a relevant member (¶22000), is treated as payable by the partnership. So an appropriate share of the interest charge is deductible by each relevant member.

SECTION 4

Charitable giving

22055
ss 189, 190
CTA 2010

A company which makes a cash donation, or transfers certain assets, to a charity will receive a corporation tax deduction provided that:

– certain qualifying conditions are met; and

– any benefit received by the company in return is relatively modest.

Such a donation is referred to as **Gift Aid**.

> MEMO POINTS   1. An **annuity** or other type of annual payment is likely to be deductible as a management expense (¶17620), unless it comes within the rules for charitable giving.
> 2. Relief for charitable payments used to fall under what was known as the **charges on income** regime, which differentiated between trade charges and non-trade charges.. This distinction is now meaningless.

A. Gift Aid

22085

Subject to the exceptions below, a cash donation made by a company to a charity is deductible from profits.

> MEMO POINTS   1. Any payment which is **intended** to come within Gift Aid **by the donor** is treated as an annual payment (¶21090) by the recipient.
> 2. The **company** donor may be resident or non-resident, but cannot be a charity itself. For this purpose non-resident companies must be trading in the UK through a permanent establishment.
> 3. For this purpose **charity** also includes:

s 202 CTA 2010

> – the National Heritage Memorial Fund;
> – the Historic Buildings and Monuments Commission for England; and
> – a scientific research association, meaning a body which has as its sole object the undertaking of research and development which may lead to, or facilitate, an extension of any class of trade, and is precluded from distributing its profits to its members by its Memorandum of Association.
> 4. The donor company should keep normal accounting **records** regarding the donation, including any acknowledgement in correspondence.

1. Exceptions

22115
ss 189 – 191
CTA 2010

Unless the company is a wholly owned subsidiary of the charity, the following are not treated as Gift Aid donations:

– distributions (¶18050), but ignoring transfers of assets at an undervalue;

– payments conditional upon future repayment or property acquisition (¶22125) by the charity; or

– amounts deductible elsewhere in the tax computation (such as interest subject to the loan relationships regime).

Payments which are **made in return for** a benefit to the donor may also be non-deductible: see ¶22155.

Subsidiaries of charities

If the company donor is a wholly owned subsidiary of a charity the following rules apply:
– **payments** made to the charity will not constitute a distribution (unless they are genuine dividends);
– a **repayment** from the charity to the company will not jeopardise the Gift Aid payment, provided it is only made to correct an overpayment (the company made a donation based on estimated profits and this proved to be too much). The repayment must be made within 12 months of the end of accounting period; and
– the rules about the **timing of donations** (¶22210) are relaxed.

22120
ss 194, 200
CTA 2010

To count as a subsidiary, all of the company's **ordinary share capital** must be owned directly or indirectly by at least one charity. If the company is **limited by guarantee**, all of the members which have entitlement to profits and assets on a winding up must be either a charity or a company owned by a charity.

Property acquisition

No relief will be available if the donation is **contingent on** the charity acquiring property either from the company or a person who is associated with the company, as part of an arrangement.

22125
s 193 CTA 2010

However, if the property is **gifted** to the charity a deduction is still available.

MEMO POINTS   1. There is no specific **definition** of property for this purpose.
2. A person is **associated** with a company if he is connected to either the company or a person who is connected to the company (¶31375).

---

2. Benefits received by the company

A donation is **not deductible** if the donor company(or a person associated with it):
– receives benefits (goods or services) as a direct consequence of the donation; and
– the **value** received within the accounting period exceeds specified limits.

22155
s 195 CTA 2010

For this purpose, benefits **exclude**:
– any corporation tax deduction received by the company as a consequence of the donation; and
– a published acknowledgement of the donation (provided it is not actual advertising of the donor).

MEMO POINTS   1. A person is **associated** with the company where he is connected to the company (¶31375).
2. The benefit may be **provided by** the charity or a third party. However, goods or services which are provided by a third party, but completely unsolicited by either the charity or the donor, do not count as benefits.

Value

In addition to the **limits** shown in the table below, there is an **overriding maximum** of £2,500 which applies to benefits received from the same charity within the same accounting period. If this level is exceeded, all donations to that charity within that accounting period are disqualified.

22160
s 197 CTA 2010

The rules disallowing tax relief for tainted donations (¶22170) do not apply provided these limits are not exceeded.

Amount of each donation	Maximum benefit permitted per donation
0 to £100	25% of donation
£101 to £1,000	£25
£1,000 to £10,000	5% of donation
Over £10,000	£2,500

EXAMPLE

1. A Ltd donates £1,200 to a charity and the directors attend an event at the charity's expense (worth £70) as a consequence.
The maximum permitted benefit is £60. (1,200 @ 5%)
As the benefits received exceed this maximum, the donation does not qualify as a deduction.

2. B Ltd, which has a calendar year accounting period, makes three unconnected donations to a charity as follows:

Date	Amount (£)	Benefits (£)
24 March	200	-
19 June	300	-
22 November	500	50

The donations on 24 March and 19 June both qualify for as no benefits are received.
The last donation results in a benefit which exceeds the limit of £25 so that it does not qualify.

Donations or benefits payable over a period

22165

s 198 CTA 2010

If payments or benefits are received over a period **which is not a year**, their value must be adjusted before making the comparison with the limits in ¶22160 above.

Situation	Convert to annual amount [1]
Benefit relates to a period of less than 12 months	Compute annualised figures for benefit and donation by using: $\dfrac{365}{A}$ where A is the number of days in the period
Payment gives the donor the right to receive benefits at intervals during a period of less than 12 months	
Benefits are part of a series which are receivable at intervals, and the donations are also part of a series which are made at intervals over less than a year	Compute annualised figures for benefit and donation by using: $\dfrac{365}{B}$ where B is the average number of days in the period
One-off benefit is associated with a series of donations made at intervals of less than 12 months	Compute annualised figure for donations by using: $\dfrac{365}{C}$ where C is the average number of days in the period during which the payment is made

Note:
1. Where the period or the intervals are measured in **calendar months**, annualising can be done by reference to calendar months.

EXAMPLE

1. C Ltd makes a single payment of £200 to a charity and in return the director receives a free year's subscription for a magazine which is worth £40.
The subscription relates to a year so that no annualising is required.
The benefit exceeds the limit of £25, so that the donation does not qualify.

2. D Ltd makes a single payment of £100 to a charity and in return the director receives a free 6 months subscription for a magazine which is worth £20.
The subscription is only for 6 months so the donation and benefit must be annualised.

The annual equivalent of the:
- donation is £200 (100 x 12/6); and
- benefit is £40. (20 x 12/6)
The benefit exceeds the limit of £25, so that the donation does not qualify.

3. E Ltd makes a single payment of £120 to a theatre charity and in return the director receives the right to a 2% discount on tickets purchased in the next 6 months, which is worth £10.
The right to the discount only lasts for 6 months and so the donation and benefit must be annualised.
The annual equivalent of the:
- donation is £240 (120 x 12/6); and
- benefit is £20. (10 x 12/6)
As the benefit does not exceed the limit of £25 the donation qualifies.

4. F Ltd makes monthly payments of £20 to a charity by standing order and in return the director receives a free monthly magazine which is worth £3 a time.
Both the donations and benefits relate to intervals of less than 12 months, so they must be annualised.
The annual equivalent of the:
- donation is £240 (20 x 12/1); and
- benefit is £36. (3 x 12/1)
The benefit exceeds the limit of £25 so that the donations do not qualify.

5. G Ltd makes monthly payments of £5 to a charity by standing order and in return the director receives a free gift worth £6 i.e. a one-off benefit.
The donations must be annualised which gives a value of £60. (5 x 12/1)
As the benefit does not exceed the limit of £15 (i.e. 25% of £60) the donations qualify.

Tainted donations

If the limits shown in ¶22160 are **exceeded**:
- a purpose test applies to determine whether a charitable donation is **tainted**; and
- the charity and the donor are jointly and severally liable for penalties and the repaying of excess tax relief.

22170

The **consequence** of a company donor making a tainted donation is the loss of any tax relief which would otherwise have been available on the donation.

s 939F CTA 2010

> ⌐MEMO POINTS⌐ The former **regime for substantial donors** ceased to apply to new donors from 1 April 2011. Charity transactions with donors who were already substantial donors before 1 April 2011 continued to fall under the old rules up to and including 31 March 2013. If a pre-existing substantial donor enters into a transaction caught by the old rules, but that transaction is not tainted under the new rules, then no charge to tax will arise.
> In brief, the old rules deny tax relief to the charity by treating the benefits paid to the donor (which excludes a wholly owned subsidiary) by the charity as non-charitable expenditure (unless undertaken at arm's length for genuine commercial reasons). For this purpose a substantial donation is a cumulative amount of:
> - £25,000 or more in any 12 month period; or
> - £150,000 or more over a 6 year period.
> Substantial donor status applies for the accounting period in which the limit is exceeded, and the following 5 years.

Sch 3 paras 28, 30
FA 2011

ss 502–510
CTA 2010

For this purpose a charitable donation is tainted where it meets all of the following **conditions**:

22175
s 939C CTA 2010

a. the donor is not a qualifying charity-owned company;
b. the donor (including a connected person) enters into arrangements, and it is reasonable to assume from the likely consequences that there would have been no such donation had the arrangements not existed. The timing of the donation is irrelevant: it does not matter whether the arrangements pre-date the donation or vice versa; and
c. the main purpose, or one of the main purposes, of the arrangements is to obtain an advantage for the donor or a connected person, directly or indirectly, from the charity or connected charity. For this purpose, **there is no advantage** if:
- the person by whom the benefit it is obtained applies it for charitable purposes only;
- it is a benefit which is ignored for charitable donations relief (¶22160);

s 939E CTA 2010

– the donation is a gift of qualifying investments and the advantage is a benefit the value of which is taken into account in determining the amount eligible for tax relief (¶22275); or
– the donation is a gift of trading stock for which tax relief would be available (¶14585) and the advantage is a benefit which gives rise to a taxable profit.

MEMO POINTS   1 A **qualifying charity-owned company** is one which:
– is wholly owned by one or more charities, at least one of which (or a charity connected with one of which) is the charity to which the donation is made; and
– it has not previously been under the control of, and does not carry on a trade or business previously carried on by, a person who stands to obtain a financial advantage from the arrangements in question (or a person, other than a charity, who was connected with such a person in the last 4 years).

s 939C(4) CTA 2010   2. A person is **connected** (¶31375) to a donor at any point in a specified period, which begins at the earliest of, and ends at the latest of, any of the following times when:
– the arrangements are entered into;
– the donation is made; or
– the arrangements are first materially implemented.

s 939G CTA 2010   3. A **connected charity** means a charity which is connected with another charity in a matter relating to the structure, administration or control of either charity.

ss 939D(5), 939I CTA 2010   4. **Arrangements** include any scheme, arrangement or understanding of any kind, whether or not legally enforceable, involving a single transaction or multiple transactions. Common examples of such arrangements are:
– the sale or letting of property;
– the provision of services;
– the exchange of property;
– the provision of a loan or any other form of financial assistance; or
– making an investment in a business.

---

3. Computation

22205   A qualifying donation is deductible from profits without grossing up.

Timing

22210   The **usual rule** is that only donations actually paid in the accounting period can be deducted in the tax computation.

s 199 CTA 2010   However, companies which are **wholly owned subsidiaries of at least one charity** may claim relief for payments which are made in the 9 months following the end of the accounting period.

The purpose of this rule is to allow such companies to have the time to determine their taxable profits, which are then reduced to nil by the donation.

MEMO POINTS   The delayed claim need not cover **all** of the donations made in the 9 month period, but no further relief can be given for any remaining profit subsequently paid to the charity outside the 9 month period. The claim must be made within 2 years from the end of the accounting period in which the donation is paid, although HMRC have discretion to extend the time limit.

Interaction with other reliefs

22215   Charitable donations are deducted after all other reliefs except group relief according to the
s 189 CTA 2010; CTM 09100   following pro-forma. A deduction cannot create a **loss**.

Excess charitable donations can be group relieved, but there is no carry forward or carry back mechanism, so once a company's profits have been reduced to nil, any remaining amount not surrendered to a group company is wasted.

The deduction is mandatory, so no **claim** is involved.

MEMO POINTS   Donations can also be set off against tax on apportioned profits of a **controlled foreign company** (¶90555).

	£
Profits	X
Deficits on non-trading loan relationships (¶16355)	(X)
UK property business losses (¶36235)	(X)
Trading losses (¶36080)	(X)
Surplus capital allowances re special leasing (¶82565)	(X)
Charitable donations (limited to reducing profit to nil)	(X)
	X

EXAMPLE A Ltd has the following computation for its current accounting period:

	£
Taxable trading profits	60,000
UK property business profits	15,000
Chargeable gains	20,000
	95,000
Deficit on non-trading loan relationships	(50,000)
Qualifying charitable donations	(10,000)
PCTCT before group relief claim	35,000

A Ltd can therefore accept a group relief surrender of up to £35,000.

B. Transfers of assets

The value of an outright gift of qualifying investments by a non-charitable company to a charity is deductible from taxable profits when a claim is made.

22245
s 203 CTA 2010

MEMO POINTS 1. **Gift** in this context includes a sale at an undervalue.
2. Where a company makes a **gift of trading stock** to a charity see ¶14585. Note that a company cannot claim both types of relief for the same asset.
3. Detailed **HMRC guidance** can be found at flmemo.co.uk/ctm22245

Qualifying investments

The following assets are qualifying investments. Note that a company cannot donate its own shares.

22250
ss 204, 205
CTA 2010

Asset	Details
Shares or securities listed on any recognised stock exchange	Includes London and PLUS-listed in the UK, and any recognised overseas stock exchange
Shares or securities traded on a designated market in the UK	The only such markets are: – the Alternative Investment Market (AIM) of the London Stock Exchange; and – the PLUS-quoted market of PLUS Markets
Units in an Authorised Unit Trust	An authorised unit trust is one in respect of which an order under s 243 FISMA 2000 is in force
Shares in a UK Open Ended Investment Company (OEIC)	The OEIC must be incorporated in the UK under s 236 FSMA 2000
An interest in an offshore fund	The offshore fund must be a mutual fund either: – constituted by a non-resident body corporate; – constituted via other arrangements under the domestic law of another territory which create rights of co-ownership; or – under which property is held on trust for the participants of the offshore fund where the trustees are non-resident
The whole of a beneficial interest in a qualifying interest in land (including buildings)	See ¶22255

22255
s 205 CTA 2010

Land and buildings   A **qualifying interest** means either:
– a freehold interest in land in the UK; or
– a leasehold interest in land in the UK which is a term of years absolute, **excluding** agreements to acquire a freehold interest or agreements for a lease.

s 213 CTA 2010

For this type of asset (only) the charity must give the donor a **certificate** detailing the following:
– a description of the qualifying interest that has been donated;
– the date of the disposal; and
– confirmation that the charity has acquired it.

s 216 CTA 2010

Relief will be **withdrawn** where a disqualifying event occurs during the period running from the date of the disposal until 6 years after the end of the accounting period in which the disposal took place. A disqualifying event occurs if the donor, or a connected person (¶31375), enjoys a right or gains an interest relating to the land otherwise than for full consideration, and not as a result of transfers following death.

s 205(6) CTA2010

⎡MEMO POINTS⎤ 1. The **Scottish** equivalents are:
– the interest of the owner; and
– a tenant's right over or interest in property subject to a lease.
2. An **accompanying** disposal to the charity of any **easement, servitude, right or privilege** relating to the land is a separate transaction for the purposes of this relief.

s 214 CTA 2010

3. Land **owned by more than one person** (either jointly or as tenants in common) must be wholly disposed of to the charity by all of the owners. The relief, where available, will then be apportioned between them.

Qualifying recipients

22260
s 217 CTA 2010

For this purpose, **charity** includes:
– the National Heritage Memorial Fund; and
– the Historic Buildings and Monuments Commission for England.

In contrast to Gift Aid, scientific research associations are not qualifying recipients.

Nature of the disposal

22265
RE 1853

The relief must be claimed for the disposal itself, and cannot apply if the **assets have already been sold**, even if the proceeds are immediately given to the charity.

If the charity requires the company to sell the investments on its behalf as its agent, relief would still be due so long as it is clear that the donor has irrevocably given the qualifying investments to the charity beforehand. Evidence should be retained in this case, such as correspondence showing:
– the charity accepting the company's gift and asking for it to be sold on their behalf;
– the charity requesting that the company passes the sale proceeds to them at the same time as sending the transfer documents; and
– the company giving either all, or the agreed proportion of, the sale proceeds to the charity.

Timing

22270

The deduction is **available** in the accounting period of the disposal.

For this purpose, the **date of disposal** is the day when the whole of the beneficial ownership of an investment passes to the charity as follows:

Type of situation	Date of disposal
General rules:	
Disposal of shares and securities	Date on stock transfer form
Disposal of land	Date that conveyance of property is completed
Grant of lease	Date on which lease granted
Specific situations:	
Disposal made under contract	Date when contract made
Conditional contract	When all conditions are satisfied
Gift made by declaration of trust	When declaration made

Deduction

The **amount** of the deduction is **limited** so that it can only reduce the taxable profits (¶22215) to nil (it cannot create a loss). 22275

The **calculation depends on** whether the transfer is an outright gift or a sale at an undervalue. Note that where market value is required in the paragraphs below, the general valuation rules for chargeable gains apply (¶30410). A post-transaction valuation check is available (¶30430).

Outright gift The following **formula** is used to calculate the deduction: 22280 s 206 CTA 2010

Net advantage of the investment to the charity + Incidental costs of disposal – Consideration received

MEMO POINTS 1. The **net advantage** to the charity depends on whether the transfer is: ss 209 - 212 CTA 2010
– a no ties gift, in which case market value would normally be used except where tax avoidance was involved; or
– subject to an obligation that the charity must fulfil (towards any party, not just the donor), in which case market value (or acquisition cost in certain cases of tax avoidance) is reduced by any liabilities taken on by the charity.
2. **Tax avoidance**, in this situation, means that the asset (or any asset from which the donated asset derives) was **acquired by the donor less than 4 years** before the disposal as part of a scheme or arrangement in order to access or increase this relief. In this case the donor's acquisition cost would be used where this was lower than the market value.
Where the donated asset is **derived from a different asset** the acquisition cost is a just and reasonable proportion of the original asset's cost to the donor, less any amount the donor, or a connected person, receives as part of the scheme they are involved with.
3. **Incidental costs** of disposal include the following, which must be incurred wholly and exclusively for the purposes of the disposal: s 207 CTA 2010
– fees and commission payable to a surveyor, valuer, auctioneer, accountant, agent or legal adviser;
– costs of transfer and conveyance;
– costs of advertising to find a buyer; and
– costs reasonably incurred in making any valuation or apportionment required under this relief.
4. For this purpose, **consideration received** includes the value of any benefits received by the donor (or any connected persons (¶31375)) as a result of the gift.

EXAMPLE

1. B Ltd donates shares in a listed company worth £10,000 to a charity, incurring a broker's fee of £50. In return the directors receive theatre tickets worth £150.
B Ltd can claim a deduction of £9,900. (10,000 + 50 – 150)

2. C Ltd donates securities worth £10,000 to a charity. The charity is under an obligation (for which it received £800) to sell these securities for £1,000 to a third party. C Ltd receives a benefit of £50 from the charity in recognition of the donation.
Although the shares are worth £10,000 on the open market the charity can only receive £1,000 due to the obligation.
So C Ltd can only deduct £950. (1,000 – 50)

3. D Ltd enters into a contrived arrangement which involves purchasing £100,000 of shares in a listed company for £20,000, subject to an option to sell them back to the vendor for £1 in 3 years' time. A week later D Ltd donates the shares to a charity and tries to claim a deduction of £100,000. In fact, D Ltd can only claim a deduction of £20,000, being the acquisition cost of the shares purchased as part of a scheme less than 4 years before they were donated.

Sale at an undervalue The same formula as in ¶22280 above is used, **except** that: 22285 s 206 CTA 2010
– the charity's payment for the asset reduces the net advantage to it; and
– the incidental costs of disposal are limited to the excess of deemed proceeds (assuming a no gain/no loss transfer for chargeable gains purposes (¶31280)) over actual proceeds. If the charity pays an amount greater than the value taken into account for chargeable gains purposes, no entry will be made in the formula for costs of disposal.

EXAMPLE

1. A Ltd sells shares in a listed company worth £5,000 to a charity for £2,500. In return, the charity gives the directors tickets to an event worth £100.
A Ltd can claim a deduction of £2,400. (5,000 – 2,500 – 100)

2. B Ltd sells shares in a listed company to a charity for £2,000 when they are worth £6,000. The incidental costs of disposal are £150. It receives no other benefits from the charity.
B Ltd can claim a deduction of £4,150. (6,000 – 2,000 + 150)

Administration

22290   A **claim** for relief is made on the CTSA return.

Evidence of the donation should be retained, which would include:
– for property, the certificate mentioned at ¶22255; and
– for shares or securities, a dated copy of the transfer form or some other dated document irrevocably giving the qualifying investments to the charity.

PART 4

Holding assets

Holding assets
Summary

The numbers cross-refer to paragraphs.

CHAPTER 1

Acquiring and holding tangible fixed assets

25000   Tangible fixed assets are held by virtually all companies, and deductions are available in the form of capital allowances in respect of most types of asset.

The following categories of assets also attract capital allowances:
– those used in research and development (¶78610+); and
– for expenditure incurred before 1 April 2002, know-how and patents (¶28895+).

For full details of intangible fixed assets see ¶28000+.

SECTION 1

Scope

Accounting classification

25050
FRS 15;
FRSSE; IAS 16

For accounting purposes, tangible fixed assets are assets that have physical substance and are held for **use** either for:
– the production or supply of goods and services;
– rental to others; or
– administrative purposes on a continuing basis in the company's activities.

FRS 15 (62)

Fixed assets fall into a variety of **categories**, each requiring classification in order to determine the appropriate accounting treatment and disclosures. Broadly, each of the following categories comprises tangible fixed assets which have a similar nature, function or use within the business:
– land and buildings;
– plant and machinery;
– fixtures, fittings, tools and equipment; and
– payments on account and assets in the course of construction (which can usually be ignored for tax purposes).

These classifications can be narrowed further to meet the requirements of specific industries.

25055   The concept of **depreciation** is defined as the cost resulting from the wear and tear, consumption or other reduction in the useful economic life of a tangible fixed asset, whether arising from use, passage of time or obsolescence through technological change.

The purpose of depreciation is to charge, to the profit and loss account, a notional sum that reflects the costs of using tangible fixed assets during a particular financial period on a consistent basis. Depreciation is also a measurement of the loss in value of tangible fixed assets over a given time period.

Tangible fixed assets, other than non-depreciable land, should be reviewed at the end of each financial year for **impairment** (¶28065):
– when either no depreciation is charged (deemed immaterial); or
– the asset's useful economic life exceeds 50 years.

FRS 11

Tax classification

For tax purposes, capital expenditure is defined by what it is not, i.e. it **excludes**:
– expenditure which is allowed as a deduction in the calculation of business profits or earnings from an employment or office;
– an amount which would be treated as a business receipt or employment income by the recipient, or where the sale of the asset would be a revenue receipt; and
– annual payments from which income tax should be deducted (¶21090).

25060
s 4 CAA 2001

Most of the time, tangible fixed assets in the accounts will be capital items for tax purposes.

> MEMO POINTS 1. **Number plates** are a useful example of an asset which has both tangible and intangible elements. The physical number plate is a chattel that only becomes plant once it is attached to a car. The right to a particular registration number (i.e. a personalised one) is an intangible asset which cannot qualify for capital allowances.
> 2. Where assets, previously treated as trading stock, are **appropriated to fixed assets** (i.e. where any subsequent profit on sale would be a capital receipt), the original expenditure on acquiring the assets is treated as capital expenditure.

CA 21250

SECTION 2

General principles

Capital allowances are the tax equivalent of depreciation, and enable a company to write off the cost of certain capital assets against taxable income. However, not every depreciated asset will qualify for capital allowances.

25110

Exclusions

The following tangible assets do not currently qualify for capital allowances:

25115

Type of asset	Detail	¶¶
Most commercial buildings	Except those qualifying for either: – research and development allowances; – business premises renovation allowances; or – flat conversion allowances	¶26485+
Residential buildings	Except for rented properties which are furnished holiday lets	¶19410+
	The following tax reliefs are also available: – wear and tear allowance; – renewals allowance (for expenditure prior to 1 April 2013); and – energy-saving allowance	¶19290 ¶19295 ¶19395+
Land	Except where qualifying for either: – mineral extraction allowances; – land remediation relief; or – dredging allowances	¶26890+

Overview of regime

There are **four types** of capital allowance (which are deducted from profits like an expense, and can, in most cases, create or augment a loss) which are shown in the table below.

25120
s 2 CAA 2001;
CA 11101

All assets that qualify are given a writing down allowance (WDA) on an annual basis (although some assets may qualify for a first year allowance (FYA) or initial allowances (IA) in the year of acquisition). Some assets are pooled together and others are dealt with separately. In addition, the annual investment allowance (AIA) is available to cover expenditure up to a certain threshold.

On **disposal** of an asset a balancing allowance (i.e. a deduction against profits) or balancing charge (i.e. an add-back like depreciation) may arise. For this purpose the proceeds are restricted to the original cost of the asset.

> ⌐*MEMO POINTS*¬   1. The **length of the accounting period** is irrelevant for initial allowances, first year allowances and balancing adjustments. However, where the accounting period is shorter than 12 months, the writing down and annual investment allowances are proportionately reduced.
> 2. Where there is a **change of rate** of WDA, or a change in the threshold of the AIA, special rules apply for accounting periods straddling the date of change.
> 3. The following result in a disposal (i.e. **cessation of ownership**) for capital allowances purposes:
> – sale (which is deemed to occur when ownership of the asset passes or, if later, at the time of completion of the contract);
> – loss;
> – destruction; or
> – gift.

Type of allowance	Applies to	Mechanism
Annual investment allowance (AIA)	Plant and machinery	From 1 January 2013, the maximum AIA is £250,000 for a 12-month accounting period
Writing down allowance (WDA)	Plant and machinery Business premises renovations Flat conversions Dredging Mineral extraction	The amount of WDA for an accounting period depends upon the percentage which applies and the length of the accounting period e.g. if the annual rate of WDA is 18%, the rate of WDA for a 6-month accounting period is effectively 9% WDA are calculated using the pool basis A pool may include a single asset or a class of assets Depending on the type of asset, the method used will be either the reducing balance basis or the straight line basis The value in the pool is reduced by the current period WDA and then carried forward for future periods
First year allowance (FYA)	Plant and machinery	Only available in accounting period of acquisition (although there are special rules where VAT adjustments are made under the capital goods scheme (¶25595)) Rates vary depending on latest government initiative (and are currently 100%) Any remaining expenditure then qualifies for WDA in later accounting periods
Initial allowance (IA)	Business premises renovations Flat conversions	Available in the accounting period of acquisition, unless incurred prior to trade (or other activity) commencing when allowance delayed until the activity starts May claim a partial initial allowance

> ⌐EXAMPLE¬   A Ltd has a calendar year accounting period.
> In Year 5, its accounting profits are £100,000. Depreciation is £10,000 and capital allowances are £8,000. There is also a balancing charge of £4,000.

The tax computation proceeds as follows:

	£	£
Profit per accounts		100,000
Add: Depreciation	10,000	
Balancing charge	4,000	
		14,000
Less: Capital allowances		(8,000)
Taxable profits		106,000

Purpose of expenditure

The purpose of the expenditure **depends on** the type of allowances claimed as shown in the following table. By far the most common qualifying expenditure relates to plant and machinery (¶25330+).

25125
s 15 CAA 2001

Type of allowance	Overview	¶¶
Plant and machinery	Must be a qualifying activity such as a trade, managing investments or property business	¶25270+
Business premises renovation	Costs incurred by the company when undertaking works which bring a qualifying building (situated in a disadvantaged area) back into commercial use	¶26550
Flat conversion	Costs of converting disused spaces above commercial premises into dwellings	¶26735+
Land remediation	Remediation costs incurred by the company in making contaminated or derelict land usable	¶27025+
Dredging	Dredging done in the interests of navigation	¶27190+
Mineral extraction	Costs incurred in finding and acquiring a mineral asset	¶27360+

Amount of expenditure

Expenditure includes payment **in the form of** money and the exchange of assets (in which case the market value of the asset will be used).

25130
s 13 CAA 2001

Where an asset is to be used for the qualifying activity, having been **utilised previously** by the company **for some other purpose**, the value used for capital allowance purposes is the lower of cost and market value.

VAT Unless the company is **registered for VAT** and the VAT incurred is recoverable input tax, VAT will be a cost of the asset. The VAT payable on an asset is usually determined by the first use of that asset.

25135
ss 546 – 551
CAA 2001

However, the capital goods scheme makes subsequent adjustments to the VAT where the company is involved in the making of **both exempt supplies and taxable supplies** (at any VAT rate) at any time in the next 5 or 10 years and:
– input tax is incurred on computers, ships, aircraft and certain land and property interests, with the value of the expenditure exceeding a certain limit; and
– those assets are used for business purposes.

Where a capital goods scheme adjustment requires **VAT to be paid** to HMRC, this means that the cost of the asset is increased for the purposes of capital allowances. Conversely, where an amount of **VAT is due from HMRC**, this reduces the asset's cost.

The **timing** of the increase/decrease to the cost of the asset occurs in the accounting period when the VAT adjustment is actually made (i.e. the last day of the VAT period of the return which includes the adjustment). The VAT adjustment is usually made on the second VAT return after the trader's VAT year (e.g. for quarterly traders, this would always be the quarter including September).

MEMO POINTS   1. Where **VAT is assessed** by HMRC without appearing on a VAT return, the additional expenditure is incurred on the date of the VAT assessment.

2. Where the **trade is treated as discontinued**, and some VAT has not been returned or assessed, any additional expenditure is incurred on the date of the discontinuance.

3. For **further details** of the capital goods scheme see *VAT Memo*.

4. There are specific rules for VAT in regard to **first year allowances** (¶25595) and the **annual investment allowance** (¶25960).

EXAMPLE   B Ltd prepares accounts to 30 June but has a VAT year of 31 March. The company acquires a computer in January 2011 at a cost of £200,000 plus VAT of £35,000. B Ltd makes wholly taxable supplies in interval 1 (ending 31 March 2011), but becomes partly exempt in interval 2 (ending 31 March 2012), able to recover only 80% of its input tax.

Assume B Ltd can claim capital allowances of 20% on a reducing balance basis each year, having used up its annual investment allowance on other assets.

The initial input tax recovered will be £35,000, so that the cost of the asset for capital allowances purposes is £200,000.

In interval 2, the adjustment will be £1,400 due to HMRC (20% of 35,000/5), and this will be disclosed on the return for the VAT period ended 30 September 2012. This increase in cost is treated as occurring on 30 September 2012 for capital allowances purposes.

The capital allowances computation up to 30 June 2013 (assuming a constant rate of WDA of 20%) will be as follows:

Year ended		£
30 June 2011	Acquisition	200,000
	Allowance @ 20%	(40,000)
	Value carried forward	160,000
30 June 2012	Value brought forward	160,000
	Allowance @ 20%	(32,000)
	Value carried forward	128,000
30 June 2013	Value brought forward	128,000
	Addition	1,400
		129,400
	Allowance @ 20%	(25,880)
	Value carried forward	103,520

25140
BIM 39528

Foreign currency   With the exception of pre-trading expenditure, foreign currency expenditure is translated into sterling at the **exchange rate** for the date on which it is treated as incurred for capital allowance purposes. So for hire purchase contracts (¶26335+), all qualifying amounts would be translated at the exchange rate for the day on which the asset is brought into use.

If the **date of payment and the date that the expenditure is deemed to be incurred are not the same**, an exchange difference is likely to arise. In this case, any exchange loss should be deducted from the expenditure on which allowances are given.

MEMO POINTS   1. Although **pre-trading expenditure** is treated as incurred on the day on which the trade begins, it should be translated into sterling at the exchange rate for the day on which it is actually incurred.

2. For companies which prepare their **financial statements in a non-sterling currency** see ¶17170+.

Timing of expenditure

25145
s 5 CAA 2001

Subject to one exception, expenditure is incurred on the date on which the **obligation to pay** becomes unconditional, irrespective of when payment is actually made. For hire purchase contracts see ¶26340.

In most cases, the customer is legally bound to pay for goods on delivery, so it is the delivery date when the obligation becomes unconditional, including goods sold subject to reservation of title.

The exception applies when the supplier agrees to a **credit period exceeding 4 months**, when the expenditure is incurred on the payment date.

Where payment is made via **instalments**, each instalment paid after the 4-month time limit is considered separately and treated as incurred on the actual date of payment. Those incurred within the first 4 months of delivery are treated as incurred on the date of delivery.

If the **obligation** to pay an amount of expenditure **is artificially advanced** (i.e. to an earlier accounting period) than would be the case in a normal commercial contract, the actual payment date is when the expenditure is incurred. HMRC state that this anti-avoidance provision would only be applied in cases where the **expenditure involved was substantial**.

CA 11800

EXAMPLE

1. C Ltd acquires a photocopier for £5,000, paying £4,000 on delivery (on 19 June) and £1,000 after a further 6 weeks.
As both instalments are within 4 months of the delivery date, the total expenditure of £5,000 is incurred on 19 June.

2. D Ltd acquires a printing press for £400,000, with delivery timed for 1 April. Under the contract, payment is not required until 6 months have elapsed after delivery i.e. 1 October.
In this case, the expenditure is not incurred until payment is actually legally required on 1 October.

3. If C Ltd, in example 1 above, did not have to pay the balance of £1,000 for 6 months (i.e. until 19 December), it would incur expenditure of £4,000 on 19 June, and £1,000 on 19 December.

4. E Ltd has an accounting period end of 31 August. On 1 August, it orders some plant which will be delivered on 13 September. Under a normal commercial contract, payment would be due on delivery. Instead, the supplier agrees to demand payment on 1 August, but gives E Ltd a 6-week credit period. So E Ltd is able to claim capital allowances in the earlier accounting period as the order date pre-dates the year end.
HMRC may consider this to be avoidance.

MEMO POINTS 1. A **milestone contract** is one where the asset becomes the property of the purchaser as it is being constructed e.g. big building or infrastructure projects. The obligation to pay depends on when the work is certified so, in most cases, the expenditure will be incurred when a portion of the work is certified. However, where part of the asset becomes the property of the purchaser in one accounting period and the work is certified within 1 month of the end of that period, the expenditure is treated as incurred in the earlier accounting period.
2. Any **retention** will not be incurred for capital allowances purposes until the relevant contractual conditions are satisfied.
3. Where expenditure **pre-dates the commencement** of trade (or other activity), the cost is deemed to have been incurred on the first day of trading. There are special rules for FYA (¶25590).
4. For **VAT** and irrecoverable input tax see ¶25135.

25150
s 5(4) CAA 2001

s 12 CAA 2001

Abortive expenditure

Under the usual rules, where **full ownership is never attained**, the purchase is not eligible for capital allowances e.g. where the purchaser withdraws from the supply contract or the supplier defaults.

25155
s 67 CAA 2001;
CA 23350

However, if expenditure is incurred under a **contract**, where, **were it to be fully performed**, ownership of the asset would be achieved, capital allowances can be claimed e.g. a deposit is paid.

If the **contract falls through** before it is fully performed, so that the purchaser ceases to be entitled to the benefit of the contract, the rules in ¶26350 apply.

Claims

Subject to one exception, capital allowances must be claimed **on the CTSA return**, and in the absence of a claim (or if a claim is made out of time), no allowances will be due, which will mean an increased corporation tax charge.

25160
s 3 CAA 2001

A claim may be partial (i.e. it is not obligatory to claim the full entitlement), but the **amount** must be specified.

MEMO POINTS 1. The **exception** is plant and machinery allowances in respect of special leasing (¶82565).

2. Whilst provisional claims are prohibited, it is possible to **alter** (including withdraw) a claim by submitting an amended return (¶46300).

25165
Sch 18 para 82
FA 1998

Subject to enquiry cases, the usual **time limit** for a claim is 12 months after the filing date of the CTSA return, although HMRC may accept later claims where circumstances beyond the company's control prevented it from making a claim on time.

Sch 18 para 83
FA 1998

Where a claim **reduces** the allowances in respect of **another accounting period** (e.g. where returns are submitted out of order), the company has 30 days to submit an amended CTSA return for the other accounting period. If it fails to do so, HMRC can amend the return (against which the company has a right to appeal).

Sch 18 para 82
FA 1998

MEMO POINTS   1. Where there is an HMRC **enquiry** into the return, a claim can be made 30 days after its closure, unless:
– the enquiry is limited to amending or withdrawing a capital allowances claim (¶25160);
– HMRC amended the return after the enquiry, when the company can make a claim 30 days after the notice of the amendment was issued; or
– there is an appeal against an amendment, when a claim can be made 30 days after the appeal is determined.

CA 11140

2. For this purpose, HMRC state that the following **do not constitute circumstances beyond the company's control**:
a. a change of mind;
b. hindsight, showing that a different combination of claims might be advantageous;
c. oversight or error, whether on the part of the company or its advisers;
d. absence or indisposition of an officer or employee of the company unless:
– the absence or illness arose at a critical time, which delayed the making of the claim;
– in the case of absence, there was good reason why the person was unavailable at the critical time; or
– there was no other person who could have made the claim on behalf of the company within the normal time limits.

Categorisation of expenditure

25170

An item of expenditure cannot qualify for more than one type of allowance. So where expenditure would potentially **qualify for multiple allowances**, a choice must be made, which must be applied consistently in later years.

However, a **subsequent purchaser** of such an asset is not bound by the previous owner's decision.

Identity of claimant

25175
s 67 CAA 2001

The **asset** must usually **belong to** the person claiming the allowances i.e. the owner has the ability to give it away.

MEMO POINTS   1. For **fixtures**, see ¶26260.
2. **Employees** can claim capital allowances in respect of assets used for the purposes of employment. Here the test is more stringent, and additionally requires that the asset is used necessarily for the purposes of the employment. This broadly requires that the taxpayer would be unable to perform the duties of his employment without the asset, and thus a claim will be unlikely to succeed where an employee's predecessor had not found it necessary to acquire a similar asset. No capital allowances are available for private cars used for business purposes, but instead a separate claim for mileage allowance can be made (see *Tax Memo*).
3. Capital allowances can be claimed by the lessee of an asset leased under a **long funding lease** (¶82215+).

s 175A CAA 2001

4. Companies providing **services** (i.e. including the provision, operation and maintenance of plant and machinery, with the aim of reducing their clients' **energy** bills) can claim capital allowances for plant and machinery installed on a client's land even where they do not have an interest in that land, so long as:
– both parties submit an election within the usual time limits (¶25165);
– the energy management company, or another connected person, must carry out all (or substantially all) of the operation and maintenance of the plant and machinery;
– the client must have an interest in the land; and
– the plant and machinery must not be for use in a dwelling house (¶25285).

In order for an energy management company to claim a 100% FYA on such expenditure, the assets must also satisfy the conditions in ¶25540.

5. For **sale and leaseback** transactions see ¶82440.

Tenants can claim allowances for assets (which are not fixtures (¶26250+)) that they are obliged to provide under the terms of a lease, for as long as the assets are used in the tenant's business e.g. a shop is let to a tenant who must provide the shelves. When the lease ends, the tenant does not need to bring a disposal value to account. The **lessor** must bring a disposal value into account when a disposal event (¶26090) occurs after the lease ends.

25180
s 70 CAA 2001

Subject to two exceptions, where another party makes a **contribution to the owner's expenditure** (even where the owner becomes entitled to such a contribution after the asset's acquisition date), capital allowances are generally only available on the net cost. Except in respect of dredging allowances (¶27195), it is irrelevant whether the contribution is revenue or capital.

25185
s 532 CAA 2001

The **other party** (i.e. the non-owner) can claim allowances on the amount of the contribution if the asset would have qualified in its hands for either plant and machinery allowances, or mineral extraction allowances, and the two parties are not connected (¶25190).

ss 537, 538, 541
CAA 2001

A non-returnable **grant** or subsidy which specifically relates to the acquisition of capital assets is treated as a contribution for this purpose, even where the receipt or entitlement to the grant is after the expenditure has been incurred. *Cyril Lord Carpets Limited v Schofield* [1966]

MEMO POINTS   1. The two **exceptions**, which mean that capital allowances are available to the owner on the whole cost of the asset, are:
– the receipt of insurance or compensation money for putting an asset out of use (e.g. by demolition or destruction, when no deduction is made to the qualifying expenditure); and
– contributors (other than public bodies) who cannot obtain tax relief i.e. no deduction is available against profits of a trade or similar activity.
2. Where part of the **contribution is repaid**, the owner can claim capital allowances on the amount repaid only if:
– the grant was made by a public body i.e. the Crown, any government or any other public or local authority, or
– the repayment is taxable on the contributor as a balancing adjustment or a revenue receipt.
This concession only applies for repayments made before 1 April 2013.

ss 535, 536
CAA 2001

Connected parties

As with most tax provisions, there are special rules when an asset is transferred between connected parties. The following table summarises all the situations where one party is connected with another.

25190
ss 574, 575, 575A
CAA 2001

Identity of the party/parties	Situations where connected
Two individuals A and B	– A is B's spouse or civil partner; – A is B's relative[1]; – A is the spouse or civil partner of a relative of B; – A is a relative of B's spouse or civil partner; or – A is the spouse or civil partner of a relative of B's spouse or civil partner
Two companies C Ltd and D Ltd	– the same person (Mr G) has control[2] of both companies; – Mr G has control of C Ltd, and individuals connected with Mr G have control of D Ltd; – Mr G has control of C Ltd, and Mr G has control of D Ltd when taking into account the interests of individuals connected him; or – C Ltd and D Ltd are each controlled by a group of two or more persons, and the groups either consist of the same persons, or could be regarded as consisting of the same persons if, in one or more cases, a member of either group were replaced by a person with whom the member is connected

Identity of the party/parties	Situations where connected
A company and a person	The person has control[2] of the company either on his own account or by taking into account the interests of persons connected with him When a company is in liquidation, it is the liquidator who has control of its assets
Two or more persons acting together to control any body corporate (including a company)	Connected with one another and also any person acting on the directions of any of them to secure or exercise control[2] of the company
Member of a partnership[3]	Is connected with: – any other partner in the partnership; – the spouse or civil partner of any other partner; or – a relative[1] of any other partner
Trustee of a settlement[4]	Is connected with: – any settlor of the settlement and anyone connected with him; – a close company whose participators (¶75355+) include the trustees of the settlement (or such a company which would be close were it to be UK resident); – any body corporate controlled[2] by a close company as detailed immediately above; – trustees of any subfunds of the settlement, or where the settlement is itself a subfund of a principal settlement, the trustees of any other subfunds of the same principal settlement

Note:
1. A **relative** is a brother, sister, ancestor or lineal descendant.
2. A person **controls** a company if that person can use the following to ensure that the company conducts its affairs in accordance with their wishes:
– shareholding;
– voting power; or
– powers given to the person by the Articles of Association.
Each of these criteria may apply to the company itself or another company which is able to exercise control of the original company.
3. Control of a **partnership** requires the right to more than one half of the assets or more than one half of the income of the partnership.
4. For the strict **definitions** of settlement, settlor, subfund and principal settlement see *Tax Memo*.

SECTION 3

Plant and machinery

25240

s 11 CAA 2001

In order to qualify for plant and machinery allowances, a company must:
– be carrying on a qualifying activity, and
– incur qualifying expenditure (i.e. capital expenditure (¶13210+) on the provision of plant or machinery wholly or partly for the purposes of the qualifying activity) and as a result of this expenditure, the company owns the asset.

A. Qualifying activity

25270

This is basically all taxable activities **excluding** passive investment.

So long as the expenditure is incurred wholly or partly for the purposes of a qualifying activity carried on by the company, then capital allowances will be available.

Where the company **carries on more than one activity**, capital allowances should be calculated separately for each one (which requires two main pools of general expenditure etc (¶25920)).

Exception

Plant and machinery used for business entertainment (including hospitality or anything incidental to the entertainment) do not qualify for capital allowances, although **excluded** from this prohibition are:
– assets used for staff entertaining, unless provided as part of a larger function involving normal business entertainment; or
– where the company's qualifying activity includes the provision of that asset which is sold, or provided for free, as part of an advertising campaign to the public.

25275
s 269 CAA 2001;
CA 27200

Summary

The qualifying activities for plant and machinery allowances are:
– a trade (¶5000+);
– a UK or overseas property business;
– a furnished holiday letting business (¶19410+);
– a profession or vocation;
– a mine, quarry or canal or other concern giving rise to profits from land charged to tax as a trade;
– management of an investment company;
– a special leasing business; and
– an employment or office (other than divers in the North Sea).

25280
s 15 CAA 2001

Property business

Capital allowances are given separately to a UK property business (¶19105+) and an overseas property business (¶19575+).

25285
ss 16, 35 CAA 2001

For any type of property business (¶19000+), plant etc provided for use in a dwelling house is **excluded** from capital allowances. A block of flats is not a dwelling house for this purpose, although the individual flats are.

Plant serving the **common parts** of a building, which contains at least two dwelling houses, is qualifying expenditure e.g. a lift. Central heating systems which serve the whole building would partially qualify, on the basis that the parts serving the individual dwelling houses should be excluded.

> ‾MEMO POINTS‾ For this purpose a **dwelling house** is **defined** as accommodation which makes available facilities that are required for day to day private domestic existence. So whilst a second home is a dwelling house the following are excluded:
> – hospital;
> – prison;
> – nursing home; or
> – hotel.
> HMRC state that any building, or part of a building, that affords domestic facilities should be treated as a dwelling house.

CA 11520, 20020

Management of an investment business

Where an asset's **revenue costs** (i.e. repairs and running expenses) are treated as management expenses (¶17620+), then the cost of purchasing the asset is qualifying expenditure.

25290
s 18 CAA 2001;
CA 20050

Capital allowances are deducted from income, and any excess remaining then becomes management expenses.

Special leasing

Stand-alone leasing, which does not **form part of another activity**, such as a trade or property business, is called special leasing. The qualifying activity starts and ends on the same dates as the leasing.

25295
ss 19, 35 CAA 2001

Each asset so leased is treated completely separately for the purposes of capital allowances. For further details see ¶82565.

Employment or office

25300
ss 20, 36 CAA 2001

Cars acquired by employees do not qualify for capital allowances.

For **other assets**, the expenditure must be necessarily provided for use in the employment (¶25175).

B. Qualifying expenditure

25330

Plant and machinery is basically all tangible fixed assets (i.e. with a life of at least 2 years) used in the business **excluding**:
– computer software (but see ¶25405); and
– land and buildings.

The **classification** of expenditure into plant or buildings is particularly problematic, as some items included within buildings are deemed to be plant by statute. Although there are now statutory lists of items within each category, there is still a heavy reliance on a vast body of case law (which can be distilled into a few key principles for most purposes).

s 26 CAA 2001

[MEMO POINTS]   1. Where applicable, **demolition** costs (net of any insurance monies or other proceeds) of plant and machinery are added to the qualifying expenditure in the accounting period when demolition occurs, unless the plant is replaced, when the costs are added to the acquisition price.

CA 21220

2. **Animals** can qualify as plant so long as they have an expected life of at least 2 years, and function as apparatus with which the trade is carried on e.g. a guard dog, horses in a riding school, or a circus animal. Farm animals (except for sheep dogs) are excluded, because they are stock items. Where a farmer has made a herd basis election (¶84190+), no capital allowances are available.

How to ascertain whether expenditure qualifies

25335

Reference should be first made to the **exclusions**, which mainly involve buildings and items incorporated in buildings. However, these exclusions are **overridden** in certain instances because there is also a list of specified plant in statute.

CA 21135

Where an item is not mentioned in statute, case law principles should then be applied, although HMRC state that each case turns on its facts, and an item which is plant in one case does not mean that it is plant in another. Indeed, the definition of plant can only be answered in the context of the particular industry concerned, and possibly in light also of the particular circumstances of the individual company's own trade. *CIR v Scottish & Newcastle Breweries Ltd* [1982]

Comment   Knowledge of the trade or activity, and its functional requirements in relation to equipment and apparatus, are vital to support any capital allowances claim.

1. Exclusions

25365
CA 22050

Unless specified as plant by statute (¶25405+), any work done to a building or substantial man-made structure, or works involving the alteration of land, will not constitute an acquisition of plant. However, other types of allowances may be available (¶26485+).

There is no UK case law where a building was held to be plant, but case law does exist for structures being considered plant.

ss 21, 22, 24
CAA 2001

[MEMO POINTS]   1. For this purpose, **land** excludes buildings or other structures, and any asset which is so installed or otherwise fixed to any description of land as to become, in law, part of the land. It does include land covered by water, and any estate, interest, easement, servitude or right in or over land.
2. **Building** includes all of the following types of assets:
a. those incorporated in the building;

b. those which, although not incorporated in the building (usually because they are movable), are of a kind which are normally incorporated into buildings; and
c. any of the following:
– walls, floors, ceilings, doors, gates, shutters, windows and stairs;
– mains services, and systems for either water, electricity or gas;
– waste disposal systems;
– sewerage and drainage systems;
– shafts or other structures in which lifts, hoists, escalators and moving walkways are installed (but see ¶25375); and
– fire safety systems.
3. A substantial man-made **structure** is defined as any of the following:
– a tunnel, bridge, viaduct, aqueduct, embankment or cutting;
– a way, hard standing (such as a pavement), road, railway, tramway, a park for vehicles or containers, or an airstrip or runway;
– an inland navigation, including a canal or basin or a navigable river;
– a dam, reservoir or barrage (including any sluices, gates, generators and other equipment associated with it);
– a dock, harbour, wharf, pier, marina or jetty, or any other structure in or at which vessels may be kept, or merchandise or passengers may be shipped or unshipped; and
– a dike, sea wall, weir or drainage ditch.

Setting vs function

Plant includes whatever apparatus is used by a company for carrying on its business i.e. all goods and chattels (excluding stock), fixed or movable, live or dead, which is kept for permanent employment in the business. *Yarmouth v France* [1887]

25370
s 22 CAA 2001

An item of plant must perform a function in the business rather than providing the setting in which the business is carried on. *Benson v Yard Arm Club Ltd* [1979]

More recently, these principles have been expanded further into **three tests**, looking at whether the item:
a. is used for carrying on the business;
b. comprises stock in trade; or
c. could be the business premises or part of the business premises (note that it is irrelevant how purpose-built the premises may be – they are not plant because they are the premises).
Wimpy International Ltd v Warland; Associated Restaurants Ltd v Warland [1989]

The same case also suggested four general factors to be considered in deciding whether an **item is part of the premises**:
– does the item appear visually to retain a separate identity?
– with what degree of permanence has it been attached to the building?
– to what extent is the structure complete without it (i.e. if the item is an add-on, and the structure or building can function well without it, the item may be plant where it fulfils a separate purpose in the business e.g. atmospheric lighting)?
– to what extent is it intended to be permanent, or alternatively is it likely to be replaced within a short period?

EXAMPLE

1. A fast-food chain claimed capital allowances on the replacement of shop fronts, floor and wall tiles, murals, lighting, new water tanks, suspended ceilings (over the eating areas), staircases and raised floors.
It was held that the items which were acquired in order to create an atmosphere, such as murals, decorative brickwork, special lighting and wall panels, were within the definition of plant, as were the water tanks.
The other expenditure was deemed to be inseparable from the premises in which the trade was carried on, and did not constitute plant. *Wimpy International Ltd v Warland; Associated Restaurants Ltd v Warland* [1989]

2. A company refurbished a number of public houses.
It was held that the following items qualified for allowances as alterations to a building connected with the installation of plant:
– strengthening the floor in order to take the weight of plant and machinery;
– toilet cubicle walls and partitions (although this case is not decisive on this point); and

– an inclined floor in a new cold store which was incidental to the cost of the installation of a drainage channel (but not a non-slip floor or wipe clean floor which had no link to any specific plant).

However, wall panelling that could easily be removed without damage to the building was an unexceptional component of the building, so it was deemed to be part of the building and as such not available for allowances. *J D Wetherspoon plc v HMRC* [2012]

3. A company put down an all-weather horse racing track to extend the opportunity for racing. It was held that the track could not be plant as it was part of the premises on which racing could take place – an asset did not lose its character as part of the premises because it was separately identifiable and of different construction. The track merely enlarged the area of the racecourse. *Lingfield Park 1991 Ltd v Shove* [2004]

4. Another company installed five-a-side synthetic football pitches, comprised of a sand-filled synthetic grass carpet on a stone pitch base. The costs included excavation and infilling. It was held that the carpet could be regarded as both the setting for the business and the means by which that business was carried on i.e. it could have a separate identity from the premises. Therefore the carpet was plant, and the works undertaken constituted the alteration of land for the purpose only of installing the plant. *Anchor International Limited v IRC* [2003]

5. A company which owned a petrol station redeveloped its forecourt and this included a new canopy. This bespoke canopy covered the entire service area, providing adequate lighting and protection from the weather. It was held that the canopy was not plant, since it merely provided shelter and was not "part of the means by which the operation of supplying petrol is performed". *Dixon v Fitch's Garage Ltd* [1976]

6. Due to safety concerns, a stand at a football stadium was demolished, and a new one was constructed which was made of modern concrete, and stood in almost the same position, and had virtually the same capacity, as the previous stand. HMRC agreed that the new seats were plant, but rejected any claim in relation to the stand itself. It was held that the stand was "the setting or place where, rather than the means by which, the trade is carried on". So it could not be plant. *Brown v Burnley Football & Athletic Co Ltd* [1980]

Whole vs piecemeal approach

25375
CA 21160

A system, such as an electrical system, should usually be considered via a piecemeal approach rather than as a whole. *Cole Brothers Ltd. v Phillips* [1980]

In a case involving an access site and wash hall containing car wash equipment, the taxpayer wanted to adopt an entity approach and claimed that the whole site was a single item of plant. It was held that a piecemeal approach should be adopted. *Attwood v Anduff car wash* [1997]

CA 21170

⬚ MEMO POINTS ⬚ 1. HMRC state that an **electrical system** in a building is a single entity of plant only if all of the following conditions are satisfied:
– it is specifically designed and built as a whole;
– it is designed and adapted to meet the particular requirements of the trade;
– the end user items of the electrical installation function as apparatus in the trader's business; and
– the electrical installation is essential for the functioning of the business.
They go on to say that the following are plant:
a. the main switchboard, transformer and associated switchgear, provided that a substantial part of the electrical installation (both the equipment and the ancillary wiring) qualify as plant;
b. a standby generator, and the emergency lighting and power circuits it services;
c. lighting in sales areas (customer areas in banks) if it is specifically designed to encourage the sale of goods on display (even if there is no other lighting); and
d. wiring, control panels and other equipment installed specifically to supply equipment that is plant or machinery.
The same approach should be used for **similar systems** such as cold water, sewerage and gas systems.

s 25 CAA 2001;
CA 21190

2. The direct costs of installing a **lift or escalator** present a similar problem. HMRC state that wiring costs relating to the operation of the lift etc qualify for allowances. Whilst the shaft itself is not plant, costs will qualify where an **existing building** has been altered in order to accommodate it, and the primary purpose of the work is to install the lift (not to make it operate better). HMRC state that where the part of the building housing the installation would be eradicated or abandoned in the event that the lift was removed, that would indicate that the expenditure was wholly for the purpose of the installation of that plant.

2. Statute defined plant

The following items are **always plant** for capital allowances purposes:

25405
s 23 CAA 2001

Item	Detail	Reference
Thermal insulation added to an existing building	¶25730	ss 28, 35 CAA 2001, CA 22220
Computer software	Where an election is made (¶28170), all capital expenditure (¶¶13050+) is plant irrespective of whether there is a physical asset or the software is digitally downloaded For this purpose, software includes computer programs and data, and the right to use it Data stored within computer programs, such as a spreadsheet, is not software	s 71 CAA 2001, CA 22280
Provision or replacement of integral features	¶25410+	ss 33A, 33B CAA 2001
Safety costs at sports grounds	Expenditure incurred up until 31 March 2013 to comply with the terms and conditions of a safety certificate that has been issued under the Safety of Sports Grounds Act 1975, Fire Safety and Safety of Places of Sport Act 1987, or as specified by a local authority Includes installation of a police control room where required by local authority	ss 30 – 32 CAA 2001, CA 22240 – 22260

Integral features

When a company incurs expenditure on the provision or replacement of features, capital allowances are available (albeit at a lower rate (¶25920)).

25410
s 33A CAA 2001;
CA 22320

For this purpose integral features **only include** the following:
– an electrical system (including a lighting system);
– a cold water system i.e. a system for taking water from the point of entry to the building (or structure) and distributing it through the building as required;
– a space or water heating system, a powered system of ventilation, air cooling or air purification; and any floor or ceiling comprised in such a system;
– a lift, an escalator or a moving walkway; or
– external solar shading.

However, capital allowances will not be available for any asset whose principal purpose is to **insulate or enclose the interior** of a building, or to provide interior walls, floors or ceilings which are intended to remain permanently in place. *Hampton v Fortes Autogrill Ltd* [1980]

Comment   Where the assets qualify for allowances under this rule, and also as environmentally beneficial plant (in respect of which FYA are available), the company can claim one allowance only.

MEMO POINTS   1. **Replacement** means that at least 50% of the cost of replacing an integral feature has been incurred, either all at once or within any period of 12 months. This rule is in place to prevent companies from claiming a revenue deduction for what is really capital expenditure on a building. HMRC state that a business will know whether or not a specific integral feature has worn out, and whether or not it plans to replace the whole, or the bulk of it, within the next year. The policy intention is to adopt a "light touch" approach, so that there are no additional requirements, as to lists of expenditure or valuations, for the operation of the replacement rule.
2. An **electrical system** is one which takes electrical power (including lighting) from the point of entry to the building or structure, or generation within the building or structure, and distributes it through the building or structure, as required.
3. The cost of a **ducting system** within the building or structure follows the tax treatment of the system(s) that the ducting supports. Where ducting supports more than one system, the relevant

25415
CA 22340

CA 22330

expenditure should be apportioned on a fair and reasonable basis, and capital allowances will be available on each portion at the applicable rate.

4. Anti-avoidance provisions apply to prevent **expenditure artificially qualifying** as an integral feature by transferring it to a connected party (¶25190) after 1 April 2008.

EXAMPLE

1. A Ltd installs a new permanent false ceiling in its premises, in order to conceal new wiring and service pipes.
B Ltd installs a plenum ceiling in its premises, the principal purpose of which is to function as an integral part of the heating or air conditioning system (i.e. the fourth side of a duct).
Only B Ltd's expenditure is on an integral feature.

2. C Ltd decides to replace the electrical system in its factory. The cost of total replacement is £150,000. The accounting period ends on 30 September. C Ltd pays £60,000 prior to the work commencing on 1 September, and the remaining £90,000 6 months later.
Even though the initial cost of £60,000 only represents 40% of the total replacement cost, it is still classed as capital, as more than 50% of the replacement cost is incurred within a period of a year. If it had not been it could have been expensed as a repair.

3. D Ltd occupies 4 floors of a multi-storey office block for the purposes of its business. D Ltd replaces the wiring etc on the ground floor only.
Broadly, this represents 25% of the cost of replacing the electrics for all four floors. So it does not constitute expenditure on the "replacement" of an integral feature.

Other plant

25420
s 23 CAA 2001 List C;

CA 22030

The items in the following table **must pass the usual case law tests** (¶25330+) to be plant.

Item	Detail	Reference
Machinery (including devices for providing motive power) not within any other item in this list [1]	Includes machines and the working parts of machines Whilst a machine is usually obvious, anything which has a moving part e.g. a door handle, constitutes machinery	CA 21010
Manufacturing or processing equipment, storage equipment (including cold rooms), display equipment, counters, checkouts and similar equipment [1]	Storage equipment includes cold rooms and mezzanine floors which are used for storage	CA 22070 *Hunt v Henry Quick* [1992] *King v Brindisco* [1992]
White goods [1]	Including: – cookers; – washing machines; – dishwashers; – refrigerators and similar equipment; – washbasins and sinks; – baths and showers; – sanitary ware and similar equipment; and – furniture and furnishings	
Hoists [1]	Excludes shafts or other structures in which hoists are installed unless ¶25375 applies	
Sound insulation [1]	Provided mainly to meet the particular requirements of the qualifying activity	
Computer, telecommunication and surveillance systems [1]	Including their wiring or other links	
Refrigeration or cooling equipment [1]		
Fire alarm systems and sprinklers [1]	Including other equipment for extinguishing or containing fires	
Burglar alarm systems [1]		

Item	Detail	Reference
Moveable buildings intended to be moved in the course of the qualifying activity	Excludes prefabricated school buildings and ships used as floating restaurants	*St John's School v Ward* [1974] *Benson v Yard Arm Club Ltd* [1979]
Moveable partition walls [1]	Where intended to be moved in the course of the qualifying activity HMRC state that the walls must need to possess mobility as a matter of commercial necessity	*Jarrold v John Good & Sons Ltd* [1963] *Leeds Permanent Building Society v Proctor* [1982]
Decorative assets provided for the enjoyment of the public in a hotel, restaurant or similar trades [1]	HMRC state that the taxpayer must show that: – the trade involves the creation of atmosphere/ambience and, in effect, the sale of that ambience to its customers; and – the items on which plant or machinery allowances are claimed were specially chosen to create the atmosphere that the taxpayer is trying to sell They give the example of a painting on an accountant's office wall, which is not plant because selling atmosphere is not part of an accountant's business	*CIR v Scottish & Newcastle Breweries Ltd.* [1982] CA 21130
Advertising hoardings, signs, displays and similar assets [1]	If shelters are leased (e.g. a bus shelter) in order to display advertisements, these are plant (although where deemed to be a fixture, the claimant must have an interest in the relevant land (¶26265))	CA 22110
Swimming pools [1]	HMRC state that allowances should be available for the trades of hotelier, caravan park operator, holiday camp operator etc An ornamental pool would be excluded Excludes costs of changing rooms and sun lounges Includes cost of excavation, pool construction and terracing, diving boards, slides and structures on which such boards or slides are mounted If the pool is an indoor pool, the building housing it is not plant	CA 22060
	Includes swimming pool which performed the function of providing pleasurable and safe buoyancy for the swimmer	*Cooke v Beach Station Caravans Ltd* [1974]
Glasshouses	Excludes unheated glasshouse Where constructed so that the required environment (i.e. air, heat, light, irrigation and temperature) for the growing of plants is provided automatically, HMRC guidance says that the following conditions must be satisfied: – the structure and the equipment are designed as one unit to operate as a single entity; – it incorporates extensive computer controlled equipment, without which the structure cannot operate to achieve the optimum artificial growing environment for the particular crops involved; and – the equipment was permanently installed during the construction of the glasshouse	*Grays v Seymours Garden Centre (Horticulture)* [1993]
Cold stores	If a refrigerated building is incapable of an independent existence as a building, then the whole building is potentially plant	CA 22120

Item	Detail	Reference
Caravans provided mainly for holiday lettings[2]	Excludes caravans occupying residential sites (except a caravan provided to a farm employee by a farmer), and also a holiday camp, leisure park, hotel or conference centre HMRC state that a caravan is plant if it does not occupy a fixed site and is regularly moved as part of normal trade usage, even if it is only moved from its summer site to winter quarters For a holiday caravan site (and HMRC state there is no requirement for regular movement), a caravan includes anything that is treated as a caravan for the purposes of either: – the Caravan Sites and Control of Development Act 1960; or – the Caravans Act (Northern Ireland) 1963	CA 22100
The alteration of land for the purpose only of installing plant or machinery	Excludes golf putting greens See ¶25370 for artificial sporting surfaces	*Family Golf Centres Ltd v Thorne* [1998]
The provision of dry docks	Dry dock to transport ships to and from the river	*CIR v Barclay Curle and Co Ltd* [1969]
The provision of any jetty or similar structure provided mainly to carry plant or machinery		
The provision of pipelines or underground ducts or tunnels with a primary purpose of carrying utility conduits		
The provision of towers to support floodlights		
Gas and sewerage systems[1]	Provided mainly to either: – meet the particular requirements of the qualifying activity, or – to serve particular plant or machinery used for the purposes of the qualifying activity So general systems for water, power, waste disposal system and sewerage do not constitute plant	
Reservoir which is part of water treatment system	Either: – incorporated into a water treatment works; or – any service reservoir of treated water for supply within any housing estate or other particular locality	
Silos provided for temporary storage or storage tanks	A grain silo distributed the grain it contained so that it acted as a transit silo rather than a warehouse It was held that the silos were plant because the silos themselves, and their external walls, were part of a complex unit in which every piece was essential to the efficient operation of the trade i.e. akin to a tool	*Schofield v R & H Hall Ltd* [1975]
The provision of slurry pits or silage clamps		
The provision of rails, sleepers and ballast for a railway or tramway		

Item	Detail	Reference
Safes, and strong rooms in bank or building society premises [1]		
Buildings provided for testing aircraft engines run within the buildings		
The provision of structures and other assets for providing the setting for any ride at an amusement park or exhibition		
The provision of fish tanks or fish ponds		
The provision of fixed zoo cages		

Note:
1. As in ¶25410 above, capital allowances will not be available for any asset whose principal purpose is to **insulate or enclose the interior** of a building, or to provide interior walls, floors or ceilings which are intended to remain permanently in place.
2. HMRC have an agreement with the **National Caravan Council** which applies to trades that consist of hiring out caravans or the provision of caravan sites. Under this agreement, the following **qualify** for allowances:
– water supplies (i.e. mains or other apparatus used to convey water to or around sites – and hot water systems);
– electricity supplies (i.e. heavy cables, distributive wiring and general electrical apparatus, and diesel generating apparatus); and
– sanitary fittings, baths and wash basins.
However, the following are **excluded**:
– roads;
– proposed sites for individual caravans;
– buildings erected as sanitary blocks; and
– sewage and drainage pipes installed as public health requirements.

C. Quantifying the amount on which allowances due

Direct costs?

The **boundaries** which apply to qualifying expenditure mean that costs must directly relate to the provision of plant or machinery.

25450
CA 20060

The following costs qualify:
– transport and installation (i.e. costs of getting the asset into place);
– altering buildings incidental to the installation of plant and machinery for the purposes of the trade;
– demolition of existing plant and machinery that is being replaced (if the plant is not replaced, the net cost of the demolition is treated as qualifying expenditure in its own right (¶25330)); and
– moving plant from one site to another and re-erecting it (providing the costs are not revenue expenses).

> MEMO POINTS   1. **Professional fees** (such as fees of architects, consultants and surveyors) are allowed to be included in capital expenditure where separate fee notes are issued, or where costs are separately identified on the fee note in respect of work done in connection with a building and with the provision of plant.
> 2. Although a detailed analysis and attribution of **preliminary costs** (e.g. labour costs for overrun on projects, insurance, security and site costs) to qualifying plant is generally beneficial to the taxpayer, this often entails too much expense, so that apportionment of such costs is usually the only viable option. *J D Wetherspoon plc v HMRC* [2012]
> 3. For **VAT** see ¶25135.

> EXAMPLE
>
> 1. E Ltd borrowed money to fund the construction of an oil rig, and the commitment fees and interest were correctly charged to capital.
> It was held that these items could not qualify for capital allowances because they did not constitute expenditure on the provision of the rig – they were expenditure on obtaining funds with which to acquire the rig. *Ben-Odeco Ltd. v Powlson* [1978]
>
> 2. F plc ordered machinery from a Swiss manufacturing company, with the payments due in instalments. The supplier could not finance the construction of the machinery on its own, and so a bank agreed to lend the necessary funds, as long as the customer company paid its instalments to the bank. Unfortunately, the value of the Swiss franc soared, so that the amount of sterling required to convert into francs increased far beyond the amounts stated in the contract.
> It was held that the additional cost was eligible for allowances. *Van Arkadie v Sterling Coated Materials Ltd* [1983]

Partial ownership of asset

25455
ss 270, 571
CAA 2001

A **part** of an asset will still qualify for capital allowances as if the whole asset was owned. This also applies where a company owns a **share** of an asset, so long as the asset is used for the purposes of a trade.

For **sale and leaseback** transactions see ¶82440.

Connected persons and anti-avoidance

25460
ss 213–224
CAA 2001

When an asset is transferred between connected parties (¶25190) as part of a relevant transaction, no **first year allowances or the annual investment allowance** can be claimed.

For expenditure incurred on or after 1 April 2012, a **relevant transaction** is either:
– a sale of plant or machinery;
– a hire purchase or similar contract;
– an assignment of a hire purchase or similar contract; or
– one which has an avoidance purpose or is part of, or occurs as a result of, a scheme or arrangement with an avoidance purpose.

s 230 CAA 2001

No relevant transaction will occur where plant has been sold to the buyer in the normal course of the seller's business of manufacturing or supplying such plant, and both of the following conditions are satisfied:
– it has never been used before the sale or the making of the contract; and
– the main purpose(s) of the arrangement (or any connected with it) is not to avoid tax.

Where the main purpose of the transaction is the obtaining of a **writing down allowance**, the capital expenditure deemed to be incurred by the new purchaser is either:
– the disposal value that the vendor is required to bring into account on the transaction (¶26085+); or
– if there is no such amount, the lower of the current market value of the plant or machinery or the amount originally incurred by the vendor.

> MEMO POINTS   1. A transaction will have an **avoidance purpose** if the main purpose, or one of the main purposes, of a party in entering into the transaction is to enable any person to obtain a superior plant and machinery allowance than that intended. All advantages which the avoidance is intended to obtain will be cancelled out e.g. a timing advantage and/or excessive allowances.
> 2. In addition to transactions involving connected parties, the following are also affected by this anti-avoidance rule:
> – a **transaction to obtain allowances** i.e. one where it appears that the obtaining of allowances is the sole or main benefit that might be expected to accrue from the transaction, or transactions of which the relevant transaction is one; or
> – a **sale and leaseback**, where the contract was made before 9 October 2007 (¶82680+).
> 3. On 12 August 2011, the Government initially withdrew the relaxation relating to plant sold **in the normal course of the seller's business**, but this was then reinstated, with additional safeguards to challenge avoidance activity.

D. Pooling and available allowances

A pooling system operates for most assets, so that all plant and machinery is put within the main pool, unless the plant is:
- subject to the special rate pool;
- subject to a short life asset election; or
- to be separately identified.

25490

Certain assets qualify for an FYA at 100%, and AIA is available on most plant up to a specified limit (¶25940+).

Summary

25495

Expenditure incurred	Subcategory	Which pool?	Treatment	¶¶
Environmentally friendly assets	Environmentally beneficial plant and machinery	Main	FYA of 100%, and repayable tax credit if makes a loss	¶25525+
	Energy-saving plant and machinery			¶25535+
	Gas refuelling stations		FYA of 100%	¶25560
	Zero-emission goods vehicles			¶25555
Enterprise zone assets	Located in assisted areas			¶25680+
Assets with longer life	Thermal insulation	Special rate	8% WDA	¶25730
	Integral features			¶25410+
	Long life assets – useful economic life > 25 years			¶25735+
Cars	Cars with carbon dioxide emissions not exceeding 95g/km[1]	Main	FYA of 100%	¶25550
	Cars with carbon dioxide emissions > 130g/km[2]	Special rate	8% WDA	¶25790+
	Pre-April 2009 purchases which cost > £12,000	Single asset pool	18% WDA up to £3,000 p.a.	¶25800+
Short life assets		Single asset pool	18% WDA	¶25835+
Fixtures		Possibly main and special rate pool	18% WDA or 8% WDA	¶26230+
Ships		Separate ship pool	18% WDA or 8% WDA	¶26385+
Assets leased out	Long funding leases	Main pool usually	18% WDA	¶82215+
	Other leases where asset used for trade	Main pool usually	18% WDA, possibly FYA	¶82515+
	Other leases where asset not used for trade	Separate pool	18% WDA	¶82565
	Assets leased overseas where lease finalised before 1 April 2006	Depends on type of lease	Protected leases have 18% WDA, others 10% WDA	¶82585+

Note:
1. For expenditure incurred prior to 1 April 1013 this limit was 110g/km.
2. For expenditure incurred prior to 1 April 1013 this limit was 160g/km.

1. Environmentally friendly assets

a. Scope

Environmentally beneficial plant and machinery

25525
ss 45H, 45I
CAA 2001;
SI 2003/2076;
CA 23135

Environmentally beneficial plant and machinery qualifies for an FYA at 100% and also, where the FYA claim results in a loss, a repayable tax credit.

Broadly, the assets that qualify are those which improve water quality and reduce water use. They must not be second-hand, and any equipment falling within the criteria must be certified by the Government.

For details of the **criteria** which need to be met for each type of technology see flmemo.co.uk/ctm25525.

If a **certificate** of environmental benefit is **revoked**, the company should amend any capital allowance claim accordingly.

Class	Subcategory
Cleaning-in-place equipment	Monitoring and control equipment
	Spray devices
Efficient showers	Aerated showerheads
	Automatic shutoff showers
	Flow regulators (removed from 7 August 2013)
	Low flow showerheads
	Thermostatic controlled showers
Efficient taps	Automatic shutoff taps
	Electronic taps
	Low flow screw-down/lever taps
	Spray taps
Efficient toilets	Low flush toilets
	Retrofit WC flushing devices
	Urinal controls
Efficient washing machines	Commercial washing machines
	Industrial washing machines
Flow controllers	Control devices
	Flow limiting devices
Greywater recovery and reuse equipment (from 7 August 2013)	Standardised greywater recovery and reuse units
Leakage detection equipment	Data loggers
	Pressure reducing valve controllers
	Remote meter reading and leak warning devices
Meters and monitoring equipment	Flow meters
	Water management software
Rainwater harvesting equipment	Monitoring and control equipment
	Rainwater filtration equipment
	Rainwater storage vessels
	Rainwater treatment equipment
Small scale slurry and sludge dewatering equipment	Belt press equipment
	Centrifuge equipment
	Filter press equipment

Class	Subcategory
Vehicle wash waste reclaim units	Partial or full reclaim system
Efficient industrial cleaning equipment	Walk-behind scrubber/driers
	Ride-on scrubber/driers
	Steam cleaners
Water management for mechanical seals	Seal water recycling units
	Internal flow regulators
	Monitoring and control units
Water reuse systems	Efficient wastewater recovery and reuse systems

<u>MEMO POINTS</u> 1. These categories are reviewed on an annual basis, subject to satisfactory methods of certification, identification and cost effectiveness. **Additional categories** and technologies may be added to the scheme.

A company (or trade association) can **apply** to DEFRA for such **an addition** by submitting a written proposal (by the summer preceding the next Budget) which shows that:
– the technology is plant and machinery for capital allowances purposes;
– it offers significant water savings or water quality enhancement over current practice;
– support for the technology would increase its market penetration. A major obstacle to the uptake of the product should be price (however, it is accepted that there may be other obstacles, e.g. lack of knowledge or conservatism by end users);
– it is easy for taxpayers to identify whether an individual product is eligible e.g. by providing a list of approved products;
– it meets the Government's other environmental objectives e.g. it should not substitute water use for that of a hazardous chemical; and
– the technology is broadly applicable across as many sectors as possible to avoid conflict with current EC State Aid rules.

There is no limit to the number of times a technology can be proposed.

2. Environmentally beneficial plant and machinery **provided for leasing** only qualifies for 100% FYA if it is provided for leasing as background plant and machinery (¶82275+).

3. When a **new technology is announced** as being a category of environmentally beneficial asset, and expenditure is incurred on that technology before the necessary legislation is put in place, an FYA will be available on that purchase but only on the date that the legislation takes effect.

Where an asset includes **components** that qualify as environmentally beneficial, the certificate issued to the purchaser will state the cost of those components. If that cost exceeds the actual expenditure incurred on the asset, then only the actual expenditure qualifies for a 100% FYA. Where stage payments are made for the asset, each payment is apportioned between the total cost of the asset and the amount relating to the component.

25530
s 45J CAA 2001

EXAMPLE G Ltd purchases a piece of equipment, costing £80,000, that incorporates an item of environmentally beneficial plant which is shown as £20,000 on the certificate.
If G Ltd pays for the equipment with three stage payments of £30,000, £30,000 and £20,000, the proportion of each payment qualifying for a 100% FYA is:

Stage payment	Calculation	£
1	30,000 × 20,000/80,000	7,500
2	30,000 × 20,000/80,000	7,500
3	20,000 × 20,000/80,000	5,000

Energy-saving plant and machinery

Expenditure incurred, in the most part from 1 April 2012 onwards, on the following assets are **excluded** from first year allowances:
– solar panels, where the expenditure must be allocated to the special rate pool (¶25725+); and

25535
ss 45A–45C
CAA 2001

– assets that qualify for tariff payments (either under the Feed-In Tariff scheme or Renewable Heat Incentive), although assets falling within the combined heat and power category will not be excluded until 1 April 2014.

Subject to the exclusions above, each class of technology which is treated as energy-saving plant and machinery must satisfy the conditions set out in the **Energy Technology Criteria List** published by the Carbon Trust (see flmemo.co.uk/ctm25535).

Certain plant may also appear on the **Energy Technology Product List**, although this is not a fully inclusive list.

Class	Subcategory	Listed product?
Air-to-Air Energy Recovery Devices		✓
Automatic Monitoring & Targeting (AMT)	Portable AMT equipment	✓
	Component-based AMT systems	x
Boiler equipment	Automatic boiler blowdown control equipment (until 7 August 2013)	✓
	Biomass boilers and roomheaters	✓
	Burners with controls	✓
	Combustion trim controls (until 2 August 2012)	✓
	Condensate pumping equipment (until 7 August 2013)	✓
	Condensing economisers	✓
	Flue gas economisers	✓
	Gas-fired condensing water heaters	✓
	Heat recovery from condensate and boiler blowdown	✓
	Hot water boilers	✓
	Localised rapid steam generators	✓
	Heating management controllers for wet heating systems	✓
	Retrofit burner control systems	✓
	Sequence controls (until 2 August 2012)	✓
	Steam boilers	✓
Combined heat and power	n/a	x
Compressed air equipment	Energy-saving controls for desiccant air dryers (until 2 August 2012)	✓
	Flow controllers	✓
	Master controllers	✓
	Refrigerated air dryers with energy-saving controls	✓
Heat pumps for space heating	Air source: air-to-water heat pumps	✓
	Air source: gas engine driven split and multi-split heat pumps	✓
	Air source: packaged heat pumps	✓
	Air source: split and multi-split heat pumps	✓
	CO_2 heat pump for domestic water heating (from 7 August 2013)	✓
	Ground source: brine-to-water heat pumps	✓
	Water source: split and multi-split heat pumps	✓
	Heat pump dehumidifiers	✓
	Heat pump driven air curtains	✓

Class	Subcategory	Listed product?
Heating ventilation and air conditioning equipment	Close control air conditioning equipment	✓
	Building environment zone controls	✓
High speed hand air dryers	n/a	✓
Lighting	High efficiency lighting units	x
	Lighting controls	x
	White light emitting diode lighting units	x
Motors and drives	Integrated motor drive units	✓
	Permanent magnet synchronous motors	✓
	Single speed AC induction motors	✓
	Switched reluctance drives (until 7 August 2013)	✓
	Variable speed drives	✓
Pipework insulation	n/a	x
Radiant and warm air heaters	Biomass-fired warm air heaters	✓
	Radiant heating equipment	✓
	Warm air heating equipment	✓
Refrigeration equipment	Absorption and other heat-driven cooling and heating equipment	✓
	Air blast coolers	✓
	Air-cooled condensing units	✓
	Automatic air purgers (until 7 August 2013)	✓
	Automated permanent refrigerant leak detection systems	✓
	Cellar cooling equipment	✓
	Commercial service cabinets	✓
	Curtains, blinds, doors and covers for refrigerated display cabinets	✓
	Evaporative condensers	✓
	Packaged chillers	✓
	Refrigeration compressors	✓
	Refrigeration system controls	✓
	Refrigeration display cabinets	✓
Solar thermal systems	n/a	✓
Uninterruptible power supplies	n/a	✓

Listed products For all products **except** lighting, combined heat and power, component-based AMT systems and pipework insulation, the following **costs** are included in the amount on which an FYA is due:

25540

– the cost of the equipment;
– direct transportation;
– direct installation, including cranage (to lift heavy equipment into place), project management costs and labour, plus any necessary modifications to the site or existing equipment; and
– professional fees, so long as they are directly related to the acquisition and installation of the equipment.

> MEMO POINTS   1. If the **product forms part of a larger piece of equipment**, there is a published claim value available from flmemo.co.uk/ctm25540. If the claim value exceeds the total cost incurred on the equipment containing the qualifying product, only actual expenditure qualifies for a 100% FYA.
> 2. Where **stage payments** are made for the asset, each payment is apportioned between the total cost of the asset and the amount relating to the eligible product. For an example see ¶25530.

CA 23150

3. **Energy services providers** (¶25175) can claim a 100% FYA, as long as the supply of the asset to the client does not simply amount to leasing. Where fixtures are involved, the energy services provider is not required to have an interest in the land to which the asset is fixed.

In all cases, the following criteria must be met:
– the provider makes an election with the client;
– the plant or machinery is not for use in a dwelling house (¶25285); and
– the provider, or a connected person (¶25190), carries out all, or substantially all, of the operation and maintenance of the plant or machinery.

25545   **Unlisted products**   Each of the unlisted products have their own requirements as follows:
– **component-based AMT systems** require a Department of Energy and Climate Change (DECC) Certificate of Energy Efficiency to be issued;
– **combined heat and power equipment** needs both a Combined Heat and Power Quality Assurance (CHPQA) Certificate and a DECC Certificate of Energy Efficiency;
– **lighting** products just require a written confirmation from the manufacturer or supplier that the product is eligible for the claim; and
– **pipework insulation** requires written confirmation from the supplier that the pipework insulation, and any attachments, have been fitted in line with BS5422.

CA 23140

MEMO POINTS   Expenditure, incurred on a technology that is subject to the **issue of a certificate**, can qualify for a 100% FYA even if it was incurred before the certificate was issued, but the claim cannot be made until certification is given.

Low emission cars

25550
s 45D CAA 2001;
CA 23153

A 100% FYA is available on low carbon dioxide cars **until** at least 31 March 2015 so long as the car:
– is unused and not second-hand;
– is first registered on or after 17 April 2002; and
– has CO_2 emissions (¶25790) of not more than 95g/km, or it is an electric car (i.e. its sole means of propulsion is electricity).

For this purpose, a car is **unused** etc even where it has been driven for a limited number of miles for the purposes of testing, delivery, test driven by a potential purchaser, or used as a demonstration car. Where the **full FYA is not claimed**, the balance of the expenditure is placed in the main pool (¶25890).

MEMO POINTS   1. For the **definition** of car see ¶25785.
2. **Leased** cars can also qualify for an FYA (but only for expenditure prior to 1 April 2013).
3. For expenditure incurred **prior to 1 April 2013** the emission limit was 110g/km.

Zero-emission goods vehicles

25555
ss 45DA, 45DB
CAA 2001

Expenditure incurred, on or after 6 April 2010 until 5 April 2015, on unused (i.e. not second-hand) zero-emission goods vehicles will qualify for a 100% FYA.

However, the following **businesses** are **excluded**:
– those that are considered to be in difficulty;
– where State Aid has not been repaid and it has been deemed illegal;
– fisheries and aquaculture businesses; and
– those that manage the waste of others.

There is a **maximum cap** of €85 million, which applies for each undertaking for the entire 5-year period that the FYA is available.

MEMO POINTS   1. A zero-emission goods vehicle is **defined** as a mechanically propelled road vehicle which cannot emit any CO_2 when driven (in any circumstances), and which is of a design primarily suited for the conveyance of goods or burden of any description.
2. An **undertaking** is defined as a stand-alone company, or a company and its partner enterprises and linked enterprises (basically a group). For definitions of these terms, see ¶78300.

EXAMPLE
1. A Ltd is a stand-alone company. In Year 1 it spends €5 million on zero-emission goods vehicles. This means that it still has €80 million available to spend on zero-emission goods vehicles for the remaining 4 years of the scheme.

2. If A Ltd joins a group in Year 2, its own total expenditure is added to that of the group. So if the group had spent €50 million in Year 1, the total going forward would be €55 million.

3. If A Ltd leaves the group in Year 3, the cumulative total incurred by the group affects both the group and A Ltd for future years.
If the group had not spent any more on zero-emission goods vehicles during Year 2, both A Ltd and the group would be deemed to have spent €55 million on qualifying vehicles.

Refuelling stations

Expenditure until 31 March 2015 on new equipment installed at a gas refuelling station to **refuel** vehicles **with** natural gas, biogas or hydrogen fuel, will qualify for a 100% FYA.

25560
s 45E CAA 2001;
CA 23155

For this purpose, the **equipment** could include:
- storage tanks;
- compressors and pumps;
- controls and meters;
- gas connections; and
- filling equipment.

Associated costs, such as transport and installation, are also eligible for allowances.

There is no requirement for the refuelling station to be **used by** cars or by the general public.

---

b. First year allowance

An FYA is only **available** in the accounting period when the asset is acquired, and assumes that the company owns the asset as a result of the expenditure.

25580

There are special rules when:
- VAT is adjusted under the capital goods scheme; and
- expenditure is incurred before the qualifying activity commences.

Comment The availability of FYA has changed over recent years, being at different rates depending on the asset purchased or the size of the company. To a large extent, these allowances have been replaced by the annual investment allowance (¶25940+).

Excluded situations

An FYA is not available in the following situations:
- costs incurred in the accounting period in which the qualifying activity is discontinued;
- where an asset has been received as a gift;
- on cars, other than low emission cars;
- on ships or railway assets (but only for expenditure prior to 1 April 2013);
- on long life assets (¶25735+);
- where an asset is brought into use for the purposes of a qualifying activity, having been acquired for something else;
- where there is a change in the nature or conduct of a business, and the main benefit, or one of the main benefits, that could reasonably be expected from the change is obtaining an FYA.

25585
s 40 CAA 2001,
CA 23110

Generally, there is no FYA on assets to be used **for leasing**, other than where specified in ¶25525 to ¶25550 above.

Where an asset is **partly used for the qualifying activity**, and partly used for some other purpose, the FYA will be apportioned on a just and reasonable basis.

s 205 CAA 2001

Before activity commences

If qualifying expenditure is incurred before the company's activity commences, the actual date of expenditure is important e.g. if an **FYA is withdrawn** by the Government before trading commences, but the asset was purchased before the date of withdrawal, an FYA would still be due.

25590
s 50 CAA 2001

VAT

25595
ss 234–240
CAA 2001;
CA 29230

Additional VAT payable under the capital goods scheme (¶25135) is qualifying expenditure for the FYA (at the same rate as the original expenditure) so long as:
– the asset is still used for the qualifying activity when the VAT is incurred (i.e. it has not been disposed of);
– the availability of the FYA has not been withdrawn in the meantime; and
– the asset is not leased overseas other than by protected leasing (¶82615).

The actual allowance will be recognised in the tax computation in the accounting period when the VAT is actually payable (¶25135).

If an **additional VAT rebate** is received during the ownership of the asset, this is a disposal event (¶26090).

Partial claims

25600
s 52 CAA 2001

An FYA is available in full, even where the accounting period is less than 12 months.

A partial claim may be made (on the corporation tax return), in which case the **balance of the expenditure** will be put into the main pool.

Where indicated on the return, the balance will enter the main pool in the same accounting period as the partial FYA claim.

Comment   A partial claim may be desirable where there is also a disposal from the main pool in the same period which would otherwise result in a balancing charge. Other factors (such as cash flow) are relevant in deciding whether or not to claim the full amount of FYA, and each case should be addressed on its own facts.

EXAMPLE   During the current accounting period, B Ltd purchased machinery costing £20,000, and a low carbon dioxide emitting car costing £15,000.
The balance brought forward on the main pool was £40,000.
If FYA is claimed in full:

	FYA assets	Main pool	Allowance given
	£	£	£
WDV b/fwd	-	40,000	
Addition	15,000	20,000	
FYA	(15,000)		15,000
	-	60,000	
WDA @ 18%		(10,800)	10,800
WDV c/fwd		49,200	
Total allowances			25,800

If FYA is not claimed in full:

	FYA assets	Main pool	Allowance given
	£	£	£
WDV b/fwd	-	40,000	
Addition	15,000	20,000	
FYA claimed	(10,000)		10,000
	5,000		
Addition to main pool	(5,000)	5,000	
		65,000	
WDA @ 18%		(11,700)	11,700
WDV c/fwd		53,300	
Total allowances			21,700

---

c. Repayable first year tax credit

25620
Sch A1 CAA 2001

Where a company **makes a loss**, due to claiming the allowances available on environmentally beneficial plant and machinery (¶25525+) or energy-saving plant and machinery (¶25535+), it may be entitled to a repayable first year tax credit.

Comment This scheme enables loss-making companies to actually benefit from their choice of environmentally friendly assets, otherwise the resulting reduction in tax liabilities would be delayed.

Excluded companies

The following types of companies are excluded:
– co-operative housing associations;
– self-build societies;
– charitable companies; and
– scientific research associations.

25625
Sch A1 para 1
CAA 2001

Applicable expenditure

This scheme is applicable for expenditure incurred on or after 1 April 2008 until at least 31 March 2018.

25630
Sch A1 para 3
CAA 2001

MEMO POINTS 1. Any sums that become due as a result of an additional **VAT** liability (¶25135) will not be eligible for the credit system. However, first year tax credits are not adjusted where there is an additional VAT rebate.
2. The deeming provisions that treat **pre-trading expenditure** as occurring on the first day of trade do not apply for this purpose, so where a trade or activity commenced after 1 April 2008, but the expenditure was incurred before 1 April 2008, no first year tax credit is due.

Surrender

The **amount** of loss that can be surrendered is the amount of the loss arising from the FYA claimed on the qualifying expenditure **less** any amounts that:
– could have been utilised to set off against other profits arising in the same accounting period;
– have been utilised to offset against profits from an earlier period;
– could have been surrendered as group (¶66050+) or consortium relief (¶66475+);
– have been surrendered for another form of credit; and
– reduce the loss a company incurs by virtue of a government investment in the company being written off (¶36015).

25635
Sch A1 para 1
CAA 2001;
CA 23176, 23181

Once the loss is surrendered, it is not available for any other relief. Partial surrenders of the maximum amount are possible.

MEMO POINTS A company may make claims for a first year tax credit and also a **research and development tax credit** (¶78360+) at the same time. In this instance, there is no prescribed order of surrender, although the return will need to be clearly marked as to the amount of each claim.

EXAMPLE
1. C Ltd incurs £200,000 on qualifying plant, and makes a claim for a 100% FYA. As a result, it makes a loss for the year of £50,000.
Its surrenderable loss will be £50,000.
If the loss incurred had been £300,000, the surrenderable loss would have been £200,000.

2. D Ltd makes a loss of £200,000 in its accounting period. It has incurred £150,000 on qualifying energy-saving equipment and £100,000 on qualifying R&D.
The following options are possible when surrendering the loss of £200,000:
– £150,000 FYA and £50,000 R&D;
– £100,000 FYA and £100,000 R&D; or
– anything in between those figures.
However, D Ltd cannot surrender both £150,000 FYA and £100,000 R&D because together they amount to more than the loss of £200,000.

3. E Ltd has a trading loss of £400,000 for its accounting period, with £300,000 being attributable to FYA on energy-saving plant. The company has also received interest of £100,000. It has trading losses brought forward from an earlier period of £150,000. E Ltd has one subsidiary which has property profits of £50,000 for the same accounting period. There is no claim for group relief. E Ltd pays £300,000 PAYE and NIC for the accounting period.
E Ltd's unrelieved loss is £250,000. (400,000 – 100,000 – 50,000)

As this is less than the FYA of £300,000, the surrenderable loss is £250,000, and the company can claim a first year tax credit of £47,500. (250,000 @ 19%)

4. Assuming the same facts as example 3, except E Ltd has two subsidiaries, one with property profits of £50,000, and the other has a trading loss of £100,000.
A claim for group relief is made between the two subsidiaries, so that the property profits are reduced to nil.
E Ltd's unrelieved loss is still £250,000. (400,000 – 100,000 – 50,000)
It is irrelevant that another claim for group relief was made.

Amount of credit

25640
Sch A1 para 2
CAA 2001

The total amount of the repayable credit is 19% of the loss that is surrendered, **up to a maximum** of the greater of £250,000 and the company's total PAYE and NIC liability for payment periods ending during that year.

As with most allowances, the company has the choice of how much it wishes to surrender.

Sch A1 para 17
CAA 2001

☐ *MEMO POINTS*   1. A **payment period** is a period which ends on the fifth day of a month, and in respect of which the company is liable to account for PAYE and NIC to HMRC.
2. When computing the **total PAYE and NIC payable**, any deductions that the company is authorised to make for the following are ignored:
– statutory parental pay; and
– statutory sick pay.
3. The first year tax credit upper limit is not reduced when a company claims an **R&D tax credit**.

Sch A1 para 28
CAA 2001

4. An anti-avoidance rule prevents a company making an **artificially inflated** claim for first year tax credits, where arrangements are entered into wholly or mainly to let a company obtain a tax credit:
– to which it would not otherwise be entitled, or
– which is larger than the one to which it would otherwise be entitled.
Arrangements include any scheme, agreement or understanding, whether or not legally enforceable.

Obtaining payment

25645
s 3(2B), Sch A1
para 18 CAA 2001;
CA 23187

The tax credit must be separately **claimed** on the corporation tax return, and the following information should be submitted with it:
– a list of the plant and machinery that qualifies for an FYA;
– the amount of expenditure incurred;
– the date when it was incurred; and
– where relevant, certificates of energy efficiency or environmental benefit (¶25525, ¶25545).

On the making of a valid claim, payment will be made to the company with the following **restrictions**:
– the credit will be used to settle any outstanding corporation tax liabilities;
– where there are any outstanding PAYE or NIC liabilities in respect of the accounting period, there is no requirement for HMRC to make the payment; and
– HMRC may withhold a payment where the period for which the credit is due is under enquiry. However, they may make a partial payment at their own discretion.

s 826 ICTA 1988

Interest is payable on first year tax credits from the filing date (or date of claim if this is later) until the date that payment is made.

Sch 18 para 52
FA 1998

Subsequent **repayment** by the company will be required in the event of:
– an amended claim which alters the amount of surrendered losses;
– an enquiry into a company tax return concluding that a tax credit claim was excessive;
– a certificate of energy efficiency or environmental benefit being revoked; or
– disposal of the asset within 4 years.

HMRC will issue an assessment to recover the related tax (which is taxed as miscellaneous income (¶21050+)), and interest will run from the date of the original payment of the tax credit until the assessment is paid.

Disposal

Where a company claims a tax credit and, within 4 years from the end of the accounting period in relation to which the credit was paid, disposes of an asset that attracted the FYA, there may be a **clawback** of the credits paid. This will also result in a corresponding increase in the loss carried forward from the accounting period to which the credit related.

25650
Sch A1 para 24
CAA 2001;
CA 23191

However, where the company **still owns plant** qualifying for an FYA which cost at least the amount of loss surrendered for the tax credit, no clawback will occur. The amount of the clawback will also be reduced where the company makes a loss on the disposal.

The clawback may be **implemented** via an amended return (the company has 3 months in which to make HMRC aware that an amendment is necessary) or via an HMRC assessment.

Sch A1 para 27
CAA 2001

The **amount of the clawback** is calculated using the following formula:

Sch A1 para 26
CAA 2001

(Surrendered losses − Cost of retained plant) − (Cost of disposed plant − Disposal value)

If this gives a negative answer, there is no restored loss, and no amendment to the tax credit.

> MEMO POINTS 1. Disposal is **defined** at ¶26090.
> 2. Where there has been a **previous disposal**, any losses already restored are deducted from the result of the formula above.

EXAMPLE
1. In Year 4, F Ltd spends £200,000 on various items of energy-saving plant and claims an FYA on the full amount. It makes a loss of £50,000, which it surrenders for a first year tax credit of £9,500.
In Year 6, F Ltd sells half of this energy-saving plant.
There will be no clawback as F Ltd still owns plant attracting FYA that originally cost £100,000 which is more than the loss surrendered of £50,000.

2. Taking the facts as in example 1 above, but assume that F Ltd sells all of the energy-saving plant for £170,000, so there is no retained plant.
The result of the formula is £20,000. ((50,000 − 0) − (200,000 − 170,000) = 50,000 − 30,000)
So the restored loss is £20,000 (which is available for carry forward from the end of Year 4) and the tax credit clawed back is £3,800. (20,000 @ 19%)
The tax credit relating to the loss on disposal of £30,000 is kept. (200,000 − 170,000)

2. Enterprise zones

Enterprise zones are designated areas which qualify for special advantages, such as simplified planning regulations and discounted business rates, in order to stimulate new building, and also benefit local deprived economies.

25680
s 45K CAA 2001

First year allowance

A 100% FYA (¶25580+) is available for expenditure on certain plant and machinery incurred by UK-resident trading companies between 1 April 2012 and 31 March 2017, which is to be primarily used in zones **located** in designated assisted areas.

25685

There is a **maximum** limit of €125 million for each investment project, which would cover, for example, setting up a new business, expanding an existing business or enabling a fundamental change to a product or production.

s 212U CAA 2001

> MEMO POINTS 1. For this purpose **trading** also includes a mining, transport or similar undertaking.
> 2. The **area** must be "assisted" when the expenditure is actually incurred. An area may be designated assisted with retrospective effect. The following areas have been designated as assisted:
> − Sheffield;
> − Liverpool;
> − Tees Valley;
> − North Eastern;
> − the Black Country;
> − Humber;
> − London Royal Docks;
> − Irvine;

– Nigg;
– Dundee;
– Deeside;
– Ebbw Vale; and
– Haven Waterway.

Exclusions

25690
s 45M CAA 2001

The following exclusions apply:

Criteria	Exclusions
Company activity	Fisheries and aquaculture sectors
	Management of waste of undertakings
	Coal, steel, shipbuilding or synthetic fibres sectors
	Agricultural sector including: – the primary production of agricultural products; – on-farm activities necessary for preparing an animal or plant product for the first sale; and – the first sale of agricultural products by a primary producer to wholesalers, retailers or processors, where that sale does not take place on separate premises reserved for that purpose
Financial health	Companies in financial difficulty
	Companies subject to an outstanding recovery order following a European Commission decision declaring a State Aid illegal
Plant	Second-hand plant
	Replacement expenditure i.e. where the new plant merely replicates the function of plant previously owned [1]
	Expenditure which is taken into account for the purposes of another State Aid grant or relevant payment made towards that expenditure [2]
	A means of transport, or transport equipment for the purposes of a business in the road freight or air transport sectors

Note:
1. Where **part** of the expenditure is **replacement expenditure**, a just and reasonable apportionment should be made.
2. Where the expenditure could qualify for an FYA, but also **another State Aid**, the company will need to consider which is more advantageous. Where the FYA is claimed in one accounting period, and then the company subsequently claims another Aid, the FYA must be withdrawn by submitting an amended CTSA return.

Use

25695
s 45N CAA 2001

Plant, in respect of which an FYA has been claimed, must be primarily used by the company (or a connected person) **for at least** 5 years within the relevant designated assisted area. If this condition is failed, the FYA must be withdrawn, by submitting an amended CTSA return.

s 45L CAA 2001

Anti-avoidance rules will also deny (in all or in part) the FYA where **artificial arrangements** are entered into in order to access the allowance, but the plant is primarily going to be used outside the designated area.

3. Assets with longer life

25725
s 104A CAA 2001

The following assets are included within the special rate pool, so named because it attracts a lower rate of allowance (¶25920), as dictated by statute:
– thermal insulation;
– integral features (¶25410);
– long life assets;
– cushion gas; and
– solar panels (for expenditure incurred on or after 1 April 2012, as other generous tax incentives are available).

Most of these assets are expected to have a longer life span than assets allocated to the main pool.

Note that **cars** with high emission levels (¶25790) are also included within this pool, because the lower rate of allowances is intended to act as a disincentive to making such an acquisition.

Thermal insulation

Expenditure incurred on adding thermal insulation to all **buildings** (apart from dwelling houses (¶25285) for which the energy-saving allowance would be due (¶19395+)) **occupied** for the purpose of a qualifying activity, or let as a property business, is put into the special rate pool, so long as no other tax deduction is available.

25730
s 28 CAA 2001;
CA 22220

Typical examples (where the thermal insulation is a primary purpose) include:
- roof lining;
- double-glazing;
- draught exclusion; and
- cavity wall filling.

Long life assets

Long life assets are **defined** as assets which have an estimated useful economic life as a fixed asset (in any business) in excess of 25 years when new (i.e. unused and not second-hand). Depending on the asset, a monetary limit may apply.

25735
s 91 CAA 2001;
CA 23720

The **expected life** should be estimated by reference to the known facts, at the earlier of when capital allowances are first claimed or when the asset is first brought into use e.g. based on how it will be used, whether it will physically deteriorate, whether it will become obsolete etc.

First use ignores holding the asset as trading stock or its construction.

> MEMO POINTS 1. If an asset has been bought **second-hand**, the use by other owners should be taken into account. This also applies where the asset is likely to be sold in working order.
> 2. The 25-year test should be applied to a whole item of plant or machinery, and not to its **component parts**. So part of an asset cannot be excluded from the long life asset rules.
> 3. A **fixture in a building** or structure may qualify as plant or machinery, in which case it is the life of the fixture itself which is important.
> 4. **Improvements** to an asset should be treated separately, so its useful economic life starts when it is first brought into use and continues until the part representing the improvement is likely to cease to be used.
> 5. Certain **industries have agreements** with HMRC in respect of which assets are to be treated as long life, although the terms are not binding on individual companies e.g. printing presses (which are not usually expected to have a technological life of 25 years) and jet aircraft.

CA 23780

The following are specifically **excluded** from long life asset treatment:
- cars (although see ¶25790 for high emission cars); and
- plant and machinery used wholly or mainly in a building used as an office, showroom, hotel, retail shop or dwelling house.

25740
ss 93 – 96
CAA 2001

> MEMO POINTS 1. HMRC interpret an **office** as meaning a building occupied by managerial staff, or concerned with marketing or administration.
> 2. A **hotel** is an establishment held out by the proprietor as offering food and drink and, if so required, sleeping accommodation, to any traveller presenting himself who appears able and willing to pay a reasonable sum for the services and facilities provided, and who is in a fit state to be received.
> 3. A **retail shop** is defined as a place to enable the public to see and purchase goods or materials by retail, and to serve as a place of exhibition and sale of a shopkeeper's wares.
> 4. **Dwelling** is defined at ¶25285.

The following are always long life assets **irrespective of the level of expenditure**:
- a share in plant and machinery;
- contributions to expenditure on plant and machinery; and
- plant for leasing.

25745
ss 97 – 100
CAA 2001;
CA 23740

Other assets will only be long life assets where the **cumulative spend** by the company on those assets exceeds £100,000 in the particular accounting period (as adjusted for shorter accounting periods and associated companies (¶40185)).

s 103 CAA 2001;
CA 23750

[MEMO POINTS] 1. Where **expenditure** in respect of an asset is **spread over more than one accounting period**, all the expenditure to be incurred under a contract is treated as incurred in the same accounting period as the first instalment when deciding whether the monetary limit is met.

2. Unless coming within one of the exceptions (¶25740), **second-hand assets** will be long life assets if they were treated as such by the previous owner. The additional expenditure incurred when the asset changes hands should be included when deciding whether the monetary limit has been exceeded in respect of other asset purchases. **HMRC** state that they **only expect** a company to establish whether a second-hand asset was treated as long life in the hands of the previous owner where either:

– the asset is of a type that is clearly likely to have been treated as long life; or

– it is reasonable to expect that the information will be readily available to the company e.g. on a sale between connected persons, the sale of a business as a going concern or a sale and leaseback.

HMRC will accept that a second-hand asset is not long life if they have already considered the facts for the previous owner.

3. A second-hand **asset brought into the UK from abroad** will be a long life asset if it was reasonable to expect that the asset would have a useful economic life of at least 25 years when it was new (even if the remaining life when it is imported is less than 25 years).

[EXAMPLE]

1. A Ltd has a calendar year accounting period. In January, the company spends £60,000 on plant which will be leased and which has a useful life of 30 years. In June, the company spends £80,000 on a long life machine.

As the plant is to be leased, there is no expenditure limit, so that the asset is treated as a long life asset. The machine does not exceed the £100,000 limit so that it is not a long life asset.

2. B Ltd has a calendar year accounting period. The company enters into two contracts concerning assets with a useful life of 30 years as follows:

– Contract 1, £200,000 payable in two instalments, £90,000 in Year 2 and £110,000 in Year 3; and

– Contract 2, £90,000 payable in Year 3.

For the purposes of the monetary limit, the whole £200,000 of Contract 1 is treated as incurred in Year 2 so that the limit for that accounting period is exceeded. So both instalments are subject to the long life asset rules.

Contract 2's expenditure of £90,000 is treated as incurred in Year 3 and is below the limit, so the asset is not a long life asset.

3. In Year 5, C Ltd buys a new printer with an expected life of 30 years for £40,000 and a second-hand binder for £50,000. The binder was treated as a long life asset by the previous owner.

Although C Ltd's total expenditure is £90,000, the binder is treated as a long life asset because it was treated as one by the previous owner.

If the printer had cost £60,000, it would also have been treated as a long life asset because the total spend of £110,000 would then have exceeded the monetary limit.

Cushion gas

25750

s 28 FA 2010

Expenditure incurred on the provision of cushion gas, which is to be **used as** plant in a gas storage facility, is treated as special rate expenditure. All new leases of cushion gas effective from 1 April 2010 are treated as funding leases (¶82310).

4. Cars

25780

Cars do not qualify for the annual investment allowance, and only low emission cars (of 95g/km or less) qualify for FYA (¶25550).

This means that most cars will fall within the main pool, unless the emissions are very high (in excess of 130g/km) when the special rate pool applies.

The capital allowances regime for cars changed on 1 April 2009, so that the **date of purchase** will determine how the car attracts allowances.

CA 23540

[MEMO POINTS] 1. For expenditure incurred **prior to 1 April 2013** the low emission level was set at 110g/km and the higher level at 160g/km.

2. Where expenditure was incurred under **an agreement that was entered into after 8 December 2008**, but the car was not made available until 1 August 2009, the expenditure is subject to the post-1 April 2009 rules.

3. Where there is **expenditure on the same car which occurs both before and after 1 April 2009**, the old and new expenditure is treated separately, which may mean that the same car appears in more than one pool. Any disposal proceeds would need to be allocated in the same ratio as the respective acquisition costs.

EXAMPLE D Ltd has a calendar year accounting period. On 30 December 2008, it ordered the following high emission cars:
– Car 1 cost £50,000 with a deposit of £5,000 payable on 30 December 2008, and the remainder payable on the date of delivery of 31 May 2009; and
– Car 2 cost £100,000 under an agreement signed on 30 December 2008, which required a deposit of £75,000 on that date, and the remainder payable on the date of delivery of 31 August 2009.
The deposit for Car 1 is subject to the pre-April 2009 rules (i.e. as an expensive car because the total cost exceeds £12,000), as it is delivered before August 2009. The remaining £45,000 is subject to the post-1 April 2009 rules (i.e. as a high emission car subject to the special rate pool). Car 2 is subject wholly to the post-1 April 2009 rules (i.e. as a high emission car subject to the special rate pool) as it is acquired via an agreement entered into after 8 December 2008, and the car does not have to be delivered until after 1 August 2009.

Scope

For capital allowances purposes, a car is **defined** as a mechanically propelled vehicle **excluding**:
– a motorcycle;
– a vehicle which is constructed in such a way that it is primarily suited for transporting goods of any sort;
– one which is not commonly used as a private vehicle and which is not suitable for use as a private vehicle (although how the company actually uses it is irrelevant);
– a car that it is illegal for the taxpayer to use as a private vehicle;
– cars used by a driving school and fitted with dual control mechanisms;
– emergency vehicles (i.e. a vehicle equipped with a fixed blue flashing light on the roof which can only be used on the road by a fire officer or police officer);
– Hackney carriages; and
– double cab pick-ups with a payload of one tonne or more (i.e. the difference between a vehicle's maximum gross weight and its kerbside weight).

25785
s 268A CAA 2001;
CA 23510

MEMO POINTS **Motorcycles** are excluded from being cars for corporation tax purposes from 1 April 2009. A motor cycle is defined as a mechanically propelled vehicle with less than four wheels, and with an unladen weight of up to 410 kg. **Prior to 1 April 2009** motorcycles were included as cars.

Purchases on or after 1 April 2009

For purchases on or after 1 April 2009, the available capital **allowances depend on** carbon dioxide emissions, so that a car with an emissions level:
– of over 130g/km is put into the special rate pool (¶25920), attracting a WDA of 8% (uncapped);
– between 96g/km and 130g/km is put into the main pool (¶25920), attracting a WDA of 18% (uncapped); and
– of 95g/km or less is eligible for a 100% FYA (¶25550).

25790
ss 45D, 104A,
104AA CAA 2001;
CA 23510

MEMO POINTS 1. The **emissions figure** is shown on the vehicle registration document or can be obtained from flmemo.co.uk/ctm25790.
2. Where **more than one emission figure is given**, the CO_2 emissions (combined) figure is used.
3. **Bi-fuel** cars will have emissions figures for each type of fuel, and in this case, the lower figure is taken.
4. Cars that were **registered before 1 March 2001** are allocated to the main pool regardless of their actual emissions.
5. **Very small manufacturers** may produce cars with unknown emission figures, and in this case the expenditure is allocated to the special rate pool.
6. For cars **acquired before 1 April 2013**, the following thresholds applied so that cars with emissions of:
– over 160g/km were put into the special rate pool;

s 268C CAA 2001

– between 111g/km and 160g/km were put into the main pool; and
– 110g/km or less were eligible for a 100% FYA.

25795

s 104F CAA 2001;
CA 23560

On the **disposal** of a car, there is no balancing adjustment, unless the company is ceasing its qualifying activity.

$\boxed{\text{MEMO POINTS}}$ When a company, whose **activity includes making cars available to other people**, owns high emissions cars and permanently ceases that activity, the balancing allowance on the special rate pool will be restricted, where the following criteria are met:
– another company in the same 75% group (¶65055) carries on a qualifying activity of making cars available to other people within 6 months of the cessation; and
– the balancing allowance arising in the ceasing company's special rate pool is greater than any balancing charges (less balancing allowances) arising in its other pools.
The balancing allowance will be limited to the amount by which balancing charges exceed balancing allowances on those other pools. Any excess balancing allowance remaining is treated as qualifying expenditure for the special rate pool of the group company. The deemed date of this expenditure is usually the day following the cessation of the first company's activities.

Purchases before 1 April 2009

25800

Unless qualifying for an FYA (¶25550) due to low carbon dioxide emissions, the treatment of expenditure incurred before 1 April 2009 depends on whether the car:
– was a qualifying hire car, when the expenditure will remain in the main pool and be subject to the 18% WDA;
– **cost £12,000 or less** when the expenditure will also remain in the main pool attracting a WDA of 18%; or
– **cost more than £12,000** (known as expensive cars), when a separate treatment still applies.

s 82 CAA 2001

$\boxed{\text{MEMO POINTS}}$ 1. A **qualifying hire car** is a car that is provided wholly or mainly for hire to, or the carriage of, members of the public (i.e. excluding connected persons (¶25190)) in the ordinary course of a trade, and satisfies one of the following conditions:
a. it is not normally hired to the same person for 30 or more consecutive days, and the cumulative total in any 12-month period is not 90 or more days;
b. it is provided for hire to a person who uses it in such a way (i.e. commercially) that condition **a.** is satisfied; or

s 268D CAA 2001

c. it is a car provided wholly or mainly for use by a disabled person receiving certain types of disability living allowance or a mobility supplement.
2. For guidance on **determining** whether a car is a **pre 1 April 2009** car see ¶25780.

25805

ss 74 – 76
CAA 2001;
CA 23520

Expensive cars and motorcycles   Until the first accounting period of the company that straddles 1 April 2014, each expensive car (or motorcycle) that was placed in a separate capital allowances pool before 1 April 2009 continues to receive a WDA (at the main pool rate) which is **limited** to £3,000 per year. Where the accounting period is more or less than a year, this restriction is reduced or increased proportionately.

On **disposal** (i.e. sale, permanent loss or destruction), a balancing adjustment will arise (subject to special rules where the car is transferred to a connected person). To calculate the adjustment, the disposal value (¶26085+) is deducted from the brought forward balance before WDA are given. If the result is a negative figure then a balancing charge arises, and if it is positive then a balancing allowance arises.

If such a car is still held at 1 April 2014, the balance on the single asset pool at the end of the accounting period containing this date is transferred to the main pool (i.e. instead of being relieved by a balancing allowance).

s 79 CAA 2001

$\boxed{\text{MEMO POINTS}}$ 1. Where a person makes a **contribution towards the cost** of a car, the £3,000 limit is divided between the person making the contribution and the recipient.
2. Where a car (of any value) is disposed of to a **connected person** (¶25190), or a hire purchase contract is assigned to a connected person, the disposal value of the car (and the corresponding acquisition cost for the purchaser) will be the lesser of its:
– market value; or
– original cost.
This rule does not apply if an election has been made to continue the trade on a change of ownership (¶60445+) or on a company reconstruction (¶79290+).

EXAMPLE

1. During the 8 month period ended 31 March 2010, E Ltd purchases Car 1 for £20,000. For the accounting period ended 31 March 2011, Car 2 is acquired for £15,000. Car 1 is disposed of for £10,000 in the accounting period ended 31 March 2013.

	Car 1 £	Car 2 £	Allowances given £
Period ended 31 March 2010			
Addition	20,000		
WDA (restricted to 8/12 of £3,000)	(2,000)		2,000
Year ended 31 March 2011			
WDV b/fwd	18,000		
Addition		15,000	
WDA (restricted to £3,000)	(3,000)	(3,000)	6,000
Year ended 31 March 2012			
WDV b/fwd	15,000	12,000	
WDA @ 20% (restricted to £3,000)	(3,000)	(2,400)	5,400
Year ended 31 March 2013			
WDV b/fwd	12,000	9,600	
Disposal	(10,000)		
	2,000		
WDA @ 18%	-	(1,728)	1,728
Balancing allowance	(2,000)	-	2,000
	Nil	7,872	3,728

2. F Ltd has a calendar year accounting period, and purchases a car on 1 January 2008 costing £50,000. The transitional period therefore ends on 31 December 2014 (as this is the accounting period which contains 1 April 2014).
The car will be treated as an expensive car until the end of the transitional period, and WDA will be capped at £3,000 p.a. for the 7 years to 31 December 2014.
The unrelieved expenditure at that point is £29,000. (50,000 – (3,000 × 7))
This cost enters the main pool at 1 December 2015 and, for all future accounting periods, the car is treated like any other plant in the main pool (i.e. the WDA is given with no capping).

3. G Ltd buys a car for £155,000 and claims the usual capital allowances. A couple of years later, when the market value of the car has dropped to £120,000, the company sells it to H Ltd (a company under common control) for £40,000.
The anti-avoidance rules apply, so that the market value is substituted for the sale proceeds. G Ltd is treated as selling the car for £120,000, and H Ltd's acquisition cost is also £120,000.
If, instead, the value of the car had appreciated to £165,000, the original cost of £155,000 would have been substituted.

5. Short life assets

As some assets may have a useful life which is far shorter than the period over which they would be written off in the main pool, a company may elect to treat them as short life assets, each having their own pool.

25835

Comment Companies should always make an election where a disposal is likely to result in a balancing allowance.

Exclusions

The following cannot be treated as short life assets:
- cars, except those hired out to disabled persons receiving disability allowance;
- special rate pool assets (¶25725+);
- assets only partly used for the qualifying activity (¶26165+);
- assets that receive a partial depreciation subsidy (¶26210);

25840
s 84 CAA 2001

– ships;
– assets received as a gift, or which did not previously attract allowances;
– assets which have previously been used for long funding leasing (¶82215+);
– assets used for overseas leasing and receiving a 10% WDA (¶82620); and
– assets used for special leasing (¶82565), i.e. leased other than in the course of a trade.

Scope

25845
s 83 CAA 2001

A company must elect for short life asset treatment. Curiously, the **actual or expected life** of the asset is irrelevant.

s 85 CAA 2001

A short life asset **election** must be made in writing and must specify the assets concerned, the expenditure incurred, and the date on which it was incurred. The election, once made, is irrevocable. The normal time limits apply (¶25160+).

    `MEMO POINTS` If a person **incurs expenditure in parts**, the time limit for making the election depends upon the accounting period in which the first part of the expenditure was incurred.

The single pool

25850
ss 86, 87 CAA 2001;
CA 23640

Every short life asset is treated as being in a pool of its own which is separate from the main pool, and allowances are given at the same rate as those in the main pool. WDA are proportionately reduced for accounting periods of less than a year.

If the asset is acquired on or after 1 April 2011 and:
– **disposed of within 8 years** from the end of the accounting period in which the expenditure was incurred, the disposal proceeds are deducted from the brought forward balance on the pool and a balancing adjustment will arise;
– **used for a non-qualifying purpose** within the 8 years (e.g. leasing other than in the course of a trade), it will cease to be a short life asset from the beginning of the accounting period when the change in use occurs, and the balance will be transferred to the main pool; or
– **still owned** and used for the qualifying purpose by the end of the 8-year period, the WDV is transferred to the main pool at the beginning of the next accounting period.

    `MEMO POINTS` For assets **purchased prior to 1 April 2011** the 8-year period above is only 4 years.

`EXAMPLE`
1. A Ltd has a calendar year accounting period. At the beginning of Year 6, the brought forward balance on the main pool is £20,000. In September of Year 6, a short life asset is acquired at a cost of £8,000. The short life asset is sold in Year 8 for £4,000. Assume WDAs are given at a rate of 20% p.a.

	Main pool £	Short life asset pool £	Allowances £
Year 6			
WDV b/fwd	20,000		
Addition	-	8,000	
WDA @ 20%	(4,000)	(1,600)	5,600
Year 7			
WDV b/fwd	16,000	6,400	
WDA @ 20%	(3,200)	(1,280)	4,480
Year 8			
WDV b/fwd	12,800	5,120	
Disposal		(4,000)	
		1,120	
WDA @ 20%	(2,560)	-	2,560
Balancing allowance	-	(1,120)	1,120
	10,240	Nil	3,680

2. The facts are the same as example 1, except that the short life asset was acquired before 1 April 2011 and is still held at the end of Year 10:

	Main pool	Short life asset pool	Allowances
	£	£	£
Year 8			
WDV b/fwd	12,800	5,120	
WDA @ 20%	(2,560)	(1,024)	3,584
Year 9			
WDV b/fwd	10,240	4,096	
WDA @ 20%	(2,048)	(819)	2,867
Year 10			
WDV b/fwd	8,192	3,277	
WDA @ 20%	(1,638)	(655)	2,293
Year 11			
WDV b/fwd	6,554	2,622	
Transfer from SLA pool	2,622	(2,622)	
	9,176		
WDA @ 20%	(1,835)		1,835
	7,341	Nil	

Large numbers of assets

Where assets are held in large numbers, and **separate identification** is either **impossible or impractical**, a modified computation with assets shown in batches will be accepted. Where identification is impossible, the assets must have a similar average useful life.

HMRC will accept any election that gives information about the assets by reference to batches of acquisitions, with their costs aggregated and shown in one amount, so long as the scope of it is clear. **Each batch** will form a separate pool. If disposal proceeds cannot be linked to any particular acquisition, then they should be treated as disposal proceeds of the earliest period for which a short life asset (SLA) pool is in existence.

25855
SP 1/86

CA 23640

EXAMPLE B Ltd runs a restaurant which requires a lot of glassware, which is deemed to have a useful life of only 3 years. The company spends £2,000 on wine glasses in Year 4, and £1,500 in Year 5. B Ltd sells some of the glass for recycling in Year 7 for £50. WDAs are given at a rate of 20% p.a.

	Short life asset pool 1	Short life asset pool 2	Allowances
	£	£	£
Year 4			
Addition	2,000		
WDA @ 20%	(400)		400
Year 5			
WDV b/fwd	1,600		
Addition		1,500	
WDA @ 20%	(320)	(300)	620
Year 6			
WDV b/fwd	1,280	1,200	
WDA @ 20%	(256)	(240)	496
Year 7			
WDV b/fwd	1,024	960	
Disposal	(50)		
WDA @ 20%		(192)	192
Balancing allowance	(974)		974
			1,166
Year 8			
WDV b/fwd	Nil	768	

Disposals at less than market value

25860
ss 88, 89 CAA 2001

If a person sells an SLA at less than market value, the market value is taken as the disposal value **unless**:
– there is **employment income** assessed on the buyer; or
– the asset is sold to a **connected person** (¶25190), and a **joint election** is made to have the sale treated as taking place at the pool value. In this case, the buyer stands in the shoes of the vendor, so that the original 8-year period still applies (in essence the transfer of the asset is completely ignored).

Where a **connected party** transaction occurs and **no election** is made, the cost to the buyer will be the market value of the asset, but the original 8 year period will still apply. The vendor will account for a balancing adjustment on the disposal.

E. How allowances are given

25890
ss 53, 54 CAA 2001;
CA 23210

Expenditure is pooled in order to calculate writing down allowances and balancing adjustments. Basically, each pool works by adding all expenditure together, deducting the value of any disposals, and giving an allowance on the resulting figure.

Each company's activity will have its own assets and therefore its own set of pools.

The pools which may be applicable are:
– main pool;
– special rate pool; and
– single asset pools.

1. Types of pool

25920

All assets enter the main pool **unless** falling within the rules for the special rate pool or being required to be held in a single asset pool.

Type of pool	Assets affected	Tax treatment	¶¶
Single asset	Expensive cars acquired prior to 1 April 2009	The single asset pool has the effect of treating the asset separately The pool operates in the same way as the main pool, except that a balancing allowance could arise on the asset's disposal, and the small pools rule does not apply	¶25805
	Short life assets		¶25835+
	Ships		¶26385+
	Assets used partly for other purposes		¶26165+
	Assets where a partial depreciation subsidy is received		¶26210
	Assets where a company contributes to a third party's asset cost		¶25185
Special rate	Thermal insulation	Rate of WDA is 8% [1] Balancing charge arises where disposal value exceeds pool balance Small pools rule applies	¶25730
	Integral features		¶25410+
	Cars with CO_2 emissions exceeding 130g/km [2]		¶25790+
	Long life assets		¶25735+
	Cushion gas		¶25750

Type of pool	Assets affected	Tax treatment	¶¶
Main pool	Default place for all assets unless required to be placed in another pool	Rate of WDA is 18% [3] Balancing charge arises where disposal value exceeds pool balance Small pools rule applies	

Note:
1. For accounting periods ending before 1 April 2012, the rate was 10%. For the calculation of the hybrid rate which applies for accounting periods straddling this date, see ¶26050.
2. For expenditure incurred prior to 1 April 2013 this was 160g/km.
3. For accounting periods ending before 1 April 2012, the rate was 20%. For the calculation of the hybrid rate which applies for accounting periods straddling this date, see ¶26050.

2. Annual investment allowance

Broadly, the annual investment allowance (AIA) is a capped 100% first year allowance for virtually all plant or machinery expenditure, excluding cars. It is available to all companies (except corporate partnerships) in relation to expenditure incurred on or after 1 April 2008.

25940
s 38A CAA 2001;
CA 23081

Any qualifying **expenditure not covered** by the AIA will attract WDA at the appropriate rate, depending into which pool the expenditure is put.

Excluded situations

The AIA is not available in the following situations:
– where an asset has been received as a **gift**;
– on **cars**;
– costs incurred in the accounting period in which the qualifying **activity is discontinued**;
– where an asset is brought into use for the purposes of a qualifying activity, having been **acquired for some other purpose**, including a long funding lease;
– where there is a **change in the nature** or conduct of a business, and the main benefit, or one of the main benefits, that could reasonably be expected from the change is obtaining an AIA; or
– expenditure incurred wholly for the purposes of a **North Sea ringfence** trade.

25945
s 38B CAA 2001

> EXAMPLE C Ltd is a company that has already used up its AIA for its current accounting period. The company wants to buy some plant for £20,000, and makes a loan to a sole trader who buys it for his new plant operating business, and therefore accesses the AIA. The plant is installed in C Ltd's premises and operated by its employees as subcontractors for the sole trader who charges C Ltd an operating fee. The benefit of the AIA is shared between the parties in the amount of the fee.
> As the sole trader started his trade purely for the advantage of C Ltd (a change in the nature or conduct of a business) in order to access the AIA on its behalf, he has no entitlement.

Anti-avoidance AIAs are not available where:
– a company incurs expenditure on a **relevant transaction** with a **connected person** (¶25190);
– transactions are entered into where either the sole benefit is to obtain an AIA, or where one of the **main purposes** of the arrangement is to obtain an AIA to which the company would not otherwise be entitled; and
– **sale and leaseback** arrangements.
For further details see ¶25460.

25950
ss 214, 216, 217
CAA 2001

Use of asset

Plant or machinery must be **owned** at some point during the accounting period, and acquired for use in the qualifying activity, although it does not have to have **come into use** for the allowance to be available.

25955
CA 23084

If qualifying expenditure is incurred **before** the company's **activity commences**, the actual date of expenditure is important.

s 38A CAA 2001;
CA 23083

VAT

25960
s 236 CAA 2001

Additional VAT payable under the capital goods scheme (¶25135) is qualifying expenditure for the AIA so long as the asset is:
– still used for the qualifying activity when it is incurred (i.e. it has not been disposed of); and
– not leased overseas other than by protected leasing (¶82615).

The actual **allowance will be recognised** in the tax computation in the accounting period when the VAT is actually payable (¶25135).

Where the **original expenditure** was prohibited from qualifying for the AIA due to anti-avoidance provisions, any additional VAT is similarly excluded.

Interaction with other allowances

25965
CA 23084

The AIA complements the other enhanced allowances available such as the:
– 100% FYA for environmentally friendly assets;
– research and development allowances;
– flat conversion allowances; and
– business premises renovation allowances (BPRA).

If **expenditure qualifies for more than one allowance**, the company may choose which allowance to claim, and may allocate allowances in the way that is most beneficial.

> EXAMPLE   D Ltd is an expanding company which incurred the following expenditure in the year to 31 March 2012:
> – £95,000 on converting an empty warehouse in a disadvantaged area into a new retail outlet, which qualifies for BPRA at 100%;
> – £10,000 on environmentally beneficial equipment, qualifying for FYA at 100%;
> – £5,000 on new electrical and central heating systems i.e. integral features, which qualify for 8% WDA; and
> – £50,000 on a new van and other general equipment, qualifying for 18% WDA in the main pool.
> D Ltd can allocate its £25,000 AIA:
> – first to the £5,000 of 10% integral features expenditure; and
> – then the remaining £20,000 to the 18% main pool expenditure,
> which preserves the 100% enhanced allowance for environmentally beneficial expenditure and the 100% allowance for BPRA expenditure.

Cap

25970
s 51A CAA 2001;
CA 23085

The cap applying **from 1 January 2013** is £250,000 per company (although there are restrictions for groups and companies under common control) for a 12-month period. If an accounting period is shorter than a year, the limit is pro-rated accordingly.

s 11 FA 2011

Where an accounting **period straddles** this date, a calculation has to be performed to ascertain the maximum amount. In cases where the period is a number of whole months, HMRC will accept that it is just and reasonable to make the calculation on either a daily or monthly basis. Otherwise, an apportionment made on a daily basis will be required. For the application of this rule to related companies see ¶25985.

> MEMO POINTS   1. The cap has been amended a number of times since its introduction. The following table gives both the historical amounts and the currently legislated future amounts:

Period	Cap (£)
1 April 2008 to 31 March 2010	50,000
1 April 2010 to 31 March 2012	100,000
1 April 2012 to 31 December 2012	25,000
1 January 2013 to 31 December 2014	250,000
From 1 January 2015	25,000

s 51B CAA 2001

2. Where a company carries on **numerous trades and activities**, the company may choose how to allocate the single AIA.

EXAMPLE E Ltd has a calendar year accounting period ending on 31 December 2012. Its total AIA is calculated as follows:

		£
Period to 31 March 2012	3/12 × 100,000	25,000
Period to 31 December 2012	9/12 × 25,000	18,750
Total AIA potentially available for the year		43,750

If E Ltd incurred no qualifying expenditure in the period from 1 January 2012 to 31 March 2012 and spent £30,000 in the remainder of the year, the maximum AIA available would still be £18,750. When the amount of the maximum AIA drops you cannot carry forward unused relief from the earlier part of the period. However, expenditure up to the maximum as calculated could have been covered if it was incurred prior to 31 March 2012.

Of course WDAs would still be available for the expenditure not qualifying for AIA, and in some cases, a short life asset election (¶25835+) could be considered.

As the temporary increase in the allowance is the third maximum to apply inside a 12-month period it is possible that a company will have to perform a more complex calculation.

25792
Sch 1 para 1
FA 2013

EXAMPLE F Ltd has an accounting year ending on 28 February 2013. Its total theoretical AIA is calculated as follows:

		£
1 March 2012 to 31 March 2012	1/12 × 100,000	8,333
1 April 2012 to 31 December 2012	9/12 × 25,000	18,750
1 January 2013 to 28 February 2013	2/12 × 250,000	41,667
Total AIA potentially available for the year		68,750

However, this overall maximum for the period is further broken down for expenditure in each part of the period.

Expenditure between 1 March 2012 and 31 March 2012
A full year's allowance must be calculated based on the fact that the later increase in the allowance did not happen. As such the calculation would be as follows:

Period	Calculation	Amount (£)
1 March 2012 to 31 March 2012	1/12 × 100,000	8,333
1 April 2012 to 28 February 2013	11/12 × 25,000	22,917
		31,250

Expenditure between 1 April 2012 and 31 December 2012
Again no account is to be taken of the increase in the allowance. The calculation for this part of the period is simpler as it is the number of months after 1 April 2012 (the date of reduction) to the end of the accounting period (28 February 2013) at the lower rate. In this case it would be £22,917. (11/12 × 25,000) This amount is then reduced by any amount claimed for the first part of the period that exceeds the limit for that period (£8,333).

Expenditure between 1 January 2013 and 28 February 2013
The maximum that can be claimed for this period is based on the number of months falling after 1 April 2012, calculated as if the two parts to the period were separate.

Period	Calculation	Amount (£)
1 April 2012 to 31 December 2012	9/12 × 25,000	18,750
1 January 2013 to 28 February 2013	2/12 × 250,000	41,667
		60,417

Restrictions on AIA

The AIA will be apportioned on a just and reasonable basis where either:

25975

– an asset is **partly used for the qualifying activity** and partly used for some other purpose; or
– the company receives (or is likely to receive) a **partial depreciation subsidy** (¶26210) in respect of the expenditure.

There are also restrictions where the company is a member of a group or under common control with other entities.

25980

s 1161 CA 2006; ss 51F, 51G, 574 CAA 2001

Related companies A single AIA will be **shared** in the circumstances shown in the table below.

In all cases, the single AIA:
– is available for **qualifying costs** incurred in the accounting period which ends in the particular financial year (i.e. from 1 April to following 31 March); and
– can be **allocated** between the companies as they see fit.

Situation	Detail	Reference
Single group	A group is entitled to a single AIA per financial year A subsidiary company will be considered to be in a group for a financial year where, at the end of its accounting period ending in that financial year, it is under the control of the parent[1]	s 51C CAA 2001
Groups under common control and related	Where, in a financial year: – two or more groups of companies are controlled[2] by the same person; and – a member of one group is related[3] to a member of another group, the AIA is shared amongst all the companies in the groups involved	s 51D CAA 2001
Other related[3] companies under common control[2] who are not members of a group	Companies involved are entitled to a single AIA There is no requirement to consider whether a company is linked to a non-corporate entity (e.g. a sole trader or partnership)	s 51E CAA 2001

Note:
1. Company A is a **parent** of another company B if either:
a. company A holds the majority of B's voting rights exercisable at general meetings outright, or by agreement with other members;
b. company A can remove or appoint directors of B with a majority of votes;
c. company A has the right to direct the financial and operating policies of B, either by contract or under B's constitution; or
d. company A holds an interest in B for the long term with a view to exercising control (usually at least a 20% interest), and:
– actually exercises dominant influence; or
– A and B are managed on a unified basis.
2. **Control** is defined as being able to secure that the affairs of the company are carried out in accordance with someone's wishes, either by way of shareholding or the possession of voting rights in that or another company, or by way of some agreement including the Articles of Association. However, in looking at this, no account is to be taken of the rights of connected parties (¶25190).
A company (including the parent company of a group) is controlled by a person in a financial year if it is controlled by that person at the end of its accounting period ending in that financial year.
3. A company is **related** to another company in a financial year if either or both of the following conditions are met:
– the shared premises condition (¶25990); and/or
– the similar activities condition (¶25995).
Companies can either be related directly or indirectly (by virtue of two companies being related to a third).

EXAMPLE G Ltd draws up its accounts to 30 April each year.
If Z Ltd is a parent of G Ltd for the accounting period ended 30 April 2013, both companies must share the AIA for the financial year ended 31 March 2014.

25985

s 11 FA 2011

Where more than two companies with different accounting periods share an AIA, the maximum AIA that each can claim is **reduced** (but not below nil) by any amounts allocated to another company with the same or later (ending) accounting period.

EXAMPLE The ABCD group has the following accounting periods which straddle 1 April 2012:

Company	Accounting period ending	Maximum AIA £
A	30 April 2012	93,750
B	31 December 2012	43,750
C	31 March 2013	25,000
D	31 March 2013	25,000

The absolute maximum AIA that the companies can share is £93,750.

If Companies C and D between them claim amounts totalling £25,000, then Companies A and B's maximum claim would be reduced by £25,000. If Company B claimed the reduced maximum of £18,750 (43,750 – 25,000), then Company A could only claim the reduced balance of £50,000. (93,750 – 18,750 – 25,000)

The **shared premises condition** is met where two or more companies, under common control, carry on their qualifying activities from the same premises at the end of either company's accounting period which ends in the financial year.

25990
s 51G(5) CAA 2001;
CA 23090

EXAMPLE E Ltd is controlled by Mr F and has an accounting period end of 30 April. In 2012, E Ltd had sole occupancy of its premises at 30 April. On 19 June, A Ltd, another company controlled by Mr F, rents one floor of E Ltd's premises. A Ltd has a calendar year accounting period. So at 31 December 2012, both companies are occupying the same premises.
This means that E Ltd and A Ltd are related for the financial year (ended 31 March 2013), and they will be entitled to a single AIA between them.

The **similar activities condition** is met when two or more companies, under common control, derive more than 50% of their turnover from the same first level of the NACE classification system, being one of the following:
– agriculture, hunting and forestry;
– fishing;
– mining and quarrying;
– manufacturing;
– electricity, gas and water supply;
– construction;
– wholesale and retail trade, repair of motor vehicles, motorcycles and personal and household goods;
– accommodation and food service activities;
– transportation and storage;
– information and communication;
– financial and insurance activities;
– real estate activities;
– professional, scientific and technical activities;
– administrative and support service activities;
– public administration and defence, compulsory social security;
– education;
– health and social work activities;
– arts, entertainment and recreation;
– other service activities;
– activities of households as employers, undifferentiated goods and services producing activities of households for own use; and
– extra-territorial organisations and bodies.

25995
s 51G(6) CAA 2001;
CA 23090

MEMO POINTS 1. **NACE** is a well established statutory industry classification system.
2. Downloads giving **full details of each category** are available from flmemo.co.uk/ctm25995.

Claim

The AIA may only be claimed in the accounting period in which the qualifying expenditure is actually incurred. There is no mechanism to **carry forward** any unused balance to a later accounting period.

Companies have a **choice** as to whether to claim the AIA at all, and whether it is a full or partial claim.

26000
s 51A CAA 2001

Subsequent disposals

Where an asset, in respect of which AIA has been claimed, is subsequently disposed of, any proceeds must be brought into account in the pool or pools the asset was included in.

26005
s 61 CAA 2001;
CA 23086

When a **replacement** is acquired, the AIA will be available against the respective costs, although care should be taken where the balance on the pool is low, as a balancing charge may result.

> EXAMPLE B Ltd, an expanding company, buys a new machine for £20,000 and sells the old machine for £5,000. The balance of unrelieved expenditure in the main pool is nil.
> B Ltd claims £20,000 AIA and has a balancing charge of £5,000.

---

3. Writing down allowances

26035 This allowance is available year on year in **all pools**, and is based on a percentage of the remaining expenditure in the pool at the time that the allowance is applied.

WDA are calculated on a reducing balance basis i.e. the percentage is applied to the remaining balance in the pool. The balance of expenditure carried forward (known as written down value or WDV) is reduced by the allowances given in the year.

Computation

26040 The following pro-forma computation shows how the allowances are given in the pools:

	£	£
Written down value brought forward		x
Expenditure qualifying for AIA	x	
Less: AIA	(x)	
		x
Add: Expenditure not qualifying for FYA		x
Disposal value		(x)
Subject to small pools rule		x
WDA @ x % [1]		(x)
Add: Residue of expenditure qualifying for FYA which is unrelieved[2]		x
Written down value carried forward		x

Note:
1. The rate of allowance depends on the pool.
2. This expenditure is added to a pool in order to access WDA in future periods. Where a 100% FYA is claimed, the residue is nil, but it must still be added in order to account for a balancing adjustment on disposal where necessary.

26045
ss 56, 104D
CAA 2001

The **amount claimed** as an allowance reduces the pool for future periods. It is not necessary to claim the full amount available. Any allowance that is not claimed will result in a larger residue being carried forward.

Where the **accounting period is less than a year** the amount of the allowance will be pro-rated. Although the apportionment should be made on the basis of the number of days in the chargeable period, typically it can be calculated based on the number of months.

> EXAMPLE C Ltd has a written down value brought forward of £20,000 in the main pool. The company has no asset movements during the year and has a 6-month accounting period.
> The maximum WDA that C Ltd can claim is £1,800. (20,000 @ 18% × 6/12)

Rate change

26050
s 10 FA 2011

For accounting periods ending on or after 1 April 2012, the rates of WDA applying to:
- the main pool reduced from 20% to 18%; and
- the special rate pool reduced from 10% to 8%.

Where an **accounting period straddled 1 April 2012**, a hybrid rate had to be calculated. This rate is calculated by time apportioning the rates applicable during the accounting period and adding them together. The percentage is **rounded up** to two decimal places.

EXAMPLE   D Ltd has an accounting year ending on 31 December 2012. Therefore 91 days would fall under the old rate, with the remaining 275 days falling under the new.
The calculation of the hybrid rate is as follows:

WDA rate	Days in period	Calculation	%
20%	91	91/366 × 20%	4.97%
18%	275	275/366 × 18%	13.52%
Hybrid rate			18.49%

Small pool balance

Where the residue in either the main pool or special rate pool is **less than or equal to** £1,000, after accounting for disposals and acquisitions, then the company can claim the full amount of the residue as a writing down allowance. Where appropriate, it can claim a lesser amount.

26055
s 56A CAA 2001;
CA 23225

The **limit** is proportionately **reduced** where either:
– the accounting period is not 12 months; or
– the qualifying activity has not been carried on for at least 12 months.

MEMO POINTS   1. If there is more **than one activity** being carried on, the limit will apply to all such pools in isolation.
2. It is not possible to claim a **normal WDA** (i.e. at 18% or 8%) in addition to the small pools WDA.

EXAMPLE
1. E Ltd has a residue of £1,200 in the main pool, and claims £216 WDA. (1,200 @ 18%)
In the next accounting period, the written down value brought forward is £984. (1,200 – 216)
The small pools allowance would then be available.

2. F Ltd has a written down value brought forward of £1,900 in the main pool. The company acquires plant costing £55,000, and makes disposals valued at £6,000.
The capital allowances computation proceeds as follows:

	£
Written down value brought forward	1,900
Additions	55,000
Less: AIA	(50,000)
Disposal proceeds from sale	(6,000)
Residue unrelieved	900
Less: Small pool WDA	(900)
	Nil

4. Disposals

When an asset, in respect of which allowances have been claimed, is sold, the proceeds (as **restricted** to cost) are usually deducted from the pool. Any excess value is taxable under the chargeable gains rules (¶30000+).

26085
s 62 CAA 2001

MEMO POINTS   1. Where **no allowances** have been claimed, no disposal value is required to be brought into the capital allowances computation unless the asset has been acquired from a connected person, and anyone in the chain has recognised a disposal value.

s 64 CAA 2001

2. If the asset was acquired **from a connected person** (¶25190) (including a series of transactions involving connected persons), the disposal value is limited to the cost of the asset to anyone in the chain.
3. Where an asset is **acquired and disposed of** in the same accounting period, allowances are still available. This is also the case for enhancement expenditure which is incurred before a sale.
4. Where the asset is **computer software** (or a right to use or deal with computer software) and there are a series of disposal values, the total of these values cannot exceed the qualifying expenditure.

EXAMPLE   A Ltd and B Ltd are connected farming companies. A Ltd buys a tractor for £50,000 for use in the farming business. A couple of years later, A Ltd sells the tractor to B Ltd for £10,000. As B Ltd can claim capital allowances, the disposal value is £10,000.
B Ltd decides to upgrade to a better tractor in the same accounting period, and sells the one bought from A Ltd for £14,000. B Ltd shows an addition of £10,000 in the main pool, and a disposal value of £14,000.

So overall the tractor moves through each computation as follows:

	£	£
A Ltd		
Addition	50,000	
Disposal	(10,000)	
Loss on sale		40,000
B Ltd	10,000	
Addition	(14,000)	
Disposal		
		(4,000)
Overall loss on disposal (original cost £50,000 less proceeds of £14,000)		36,000

Disposal events

26090
ss 60, 61, 72
CAA 2001;
CA 23240

An adjustment will be required when any of the following occur:
- ceasing to own the asset;
- permanent loss or destruction of the asset;
- a right to use computer software is granted to another party for a capital sum;
- the asset starts to be used for a purpose other than for the qualifying activity;
- the qualifying activity is permanently discontinued;
- the asset begins to be leased under a long funding lease; or
- the abandonment of an asset used for mineral exploration and access.

Where **more than one event occurs**, an adjustment is only brought into account on the first event e.g. if an asset starts to be used for a purpose other than the qualifying activity, and then the activity is discontinued, the disposal would only be recognised on the change of use.

Balancing adjustments

26095

Unless an asset is in a single pool or short life asset pool, **balancing allowances** are only given on cessation of the trade even if no assets remain in the trader's ownership.

Balancing charges will arise where the disposal value exceeds the expenditure in any pool.

Disposal value

26100
ss 61 – 64
CAA 2001

The value taken into account depends on the event which occurs:

Disposal event	Detail	Disposal value
Sale of the asset	At market value	Net proceeds of sale[1] plus: – any insurance money received as a result of an event affecting the sale price; and – any other capital compensation received
	At less than market value but not nil	Market value unless the buyer: – is entitled to claim capital allowances on the asset; or – is assessable under the employment income rules in respect of the asset
	For nil proceeds i.e. a gift	The disposal value will be taken as nil where the asset is gifted to either: **a.** an employee who is assessable under the employment income rules in respect of the asset. In this case no trading deduction should have been claimed by the employer; or **b.** the asset is gifted to a/an: – charitable trust; – charitable company; – eligible body[2]; – designated educational establishment[3]; or – community amateur sports club (¶86270+)

Disposal event	Detail	Disposal value
Loss of asset	Destruction or demolition	Net amount received for the remains of the asset plus: – any insurance money received; and – any other capital compensation
	Permanent loss other than by destruction etc	Any insurance money received for the loss and any other capital compensation
Computer software – right to use granted to another party	Some non-monetary consideration	Market value of the right when it is granted
	No consideration or it is made at less than market value	Market value unless the buyer: – is entitled to claim capital allowances on the asset; or – is assessable under the employment income rules in respect of the asset
	Any other case	Net consideration received plus: – any insurance money received as result of an event affecting the consideration; and – other compensation received
Permanent discontinuance of the qualifying activity		Disposal value for the event (¶61305)
Commencement of a long funding lease	Finance lease	An amount equal to the lessors' net investment in the lease (as recognised under GAAP)
	Operating lease	Market value of the asset at the start of the lease
Abandonment of an asset used for mineral exploration and access		Any insurance money received for the abandonment and any other capital compensation
Any other event		Market value

Note:
1. The **net proceeds of sale** are what the seller actually receives, so where some of the agreed sale price is irrecoverable, it should be ignored.
2. An **eligible body** is one of the following:
– the National Heritage Memorial Fund;
– the Historic Buildings and Monuments Commission for England;
– the National Endowment for Science, Technology and the Arts;
– the British Museum; or
– the Natural History Museum.
3. This refers to **establishments** which are designated under regulations as made by the Secretary of State, or in the case of Wales and Northern Ireland, the Welsh Ministers and Department of Education respectively.

Specific rules for the special rate pool

Anti-avoidance provisions apply where:

26105
s 104E CAA 2001

a. a **scheme to secure a tax advantage** involves an asset being sold for less than its notional written down value (i.e. cost less the maximum allowances that could have been claimed in respect of the asset). In this case, the seller's disposal proceeds will be deemed to be the notional written down value, although the purchaser will only be able to claim allowances based on the acquisition value; and

b. connected parties (¶25190) transfer an asset in order to obtain allowances which were not available prior to 1 April 2008. The asset will not be treated as a qualifying asset and no allowances will be due. However, there are special rules for intra-group transfers.

> MEMO POINTS For **groups** where an asset was in the transferor's main pool before the transfer, but would enter the transferee's special rate pool, a joint election can be made by both companies (within the normal time limits (¶25160)) to quantify the notional written down value of the asset. This figure is used as both the disposal and acquisition cost, with the cost entering the transferee's main pool. If the buyer sells the asset, the proceeds are not capped at the transfer value but at the original acquisition price.

F. Special situations

Summary

26135

Topic	¶¶
Non-qualifying use	¶26165+
Partial depreciation subsidy	¶26210
Fixtures	¶26230+
Hire purchase contracts	¶26335+
Ships	¶26385+

---

1. Non-qualifying use

26165
A company may buy an asset partly to use in a qualifying activity and partly for other purposes.

Exception

26170
CA 27100

Where a company provides an asset for a **director's or an employee's private use**, and this is assessed as employment income, HMRC usually treat this as incurred wholly and exclusively for the purposes of the qualifying activity.

In respect of **machinery** HMRC will always accept the capital allowance claim e.g. cars, aircraft, yachts, washing machines and dishwashers, unless the asset is seemingly provided as a result of personal choice of the director e.g. enabling a director to drive a Bentley which does not fulfil an obvious purpose in a farm business. *G H Chambers (Northiam Farms) Ltd v Watmough* [1956]

For **plant** HMRC state that the company is only entitled to capital allowances if the asset has a function in the qualifying activity e.g. this would exclude paintings and furniture provided for the director's home.

Computation

26175
ss 205 – 207
CAA 2001;
CA 27005

Assets which are only partly used for a qualifying activity should be put in a single asset **pool**.

Where the asset is eligible for an **FYA or AIA**, the allowance should be reduced on a just and reasonable basis. However, the amount added to the pool assumes a full allowance has been given with no reduction. Hence WDA will be given on a smaller balance.

Similarly, the **WDA** is reduced for the non-qualifying use of the asset, but the full WDA is deducted from the pool balance. The rate of WDA depends on whether the asset would ordinarily be placed in the special rate pool or the main rate pool.

On **disposal**, the balancing adjustment should be reduced on a just and reasonable basis to reflect the non-qualifying use of the asset over its ownership period.

Any **VAT adjustments** arising as a result of the capital goods scheme are reduced in the same way as the allowance.

> EXAMPLE   C Ltd acquires an asset costing £10,000, which is only used for the UK trade 60% of the time in Year 1 and 70% in Year 2. It is disposed of in Year 3 for £3,000. The average qualifying use over the asset's ownership period is 65%. $\dfrac{(60\% + 70\%)}{2}$

	Single asset pool £	Non-qualifying use reduction £	Allowances given £
Year 1			
Addition	10,000		
WDA @ 20% as reduced for 60% use	(2,000)	800	1,200
Year 2			
WDV b/fwd	8,000		
WDA @ 20% as reduced for 70% use	(1,600)	480	1,120
Year 3			
WDV b/fwd	6,400		
Disposal	(3,000)		
Balancing allowance	(3,400)	1,190	2,210
	Nil		

Reduction in qualifying use

On a **change of circumstances** where:
- the qualifying use of an asset significantly falls; and
- the market value of the asset exceeds the brought forward balance in the single asset pool by more than £1 million,

a disposal is deemed to occur at market value, and the asset is transferred to another single asset pool.

26180
s 208 CAA 2001;
CA 27300

> EXAMPLE D Ltd buys an asset for £50 million in Year 1, and uses it for a qualifying activity 80% of the time. Assume an FYA at 50%.
> In Year 2, the qualifying use changes to only 30%. The market value of the asset is £30 million at the end of this year, which exceeds the written down value by more than £1 million.
>
> | | Single asset pool 1 | Single asset pool 2 | Non-qualifying use reduction | Allowances given |
> |---|---|---|---|---|
> | **Year 1** | £m | £m | £m | £m |
> | Addition | 50 | | | |
> | FYA @ 50% | (25) | | 5 | 20 |
> | **Year 2** | | | | |
> | WDV b/fwd | 25 | | | |
> | Disposal | (30) | | | |
> | Balancing charge[1] | 5 | | (1) | (4) |
> | **Year 3** | | | | |
> | WDV b/fwd | Nil | 30 | | |
>
> Note:
> 1. The balancing charge is restricted by 20% to reflect the qualifying use made of the asset during Year 1.

2. Partial depreciation subsidy

Where a payment is received to cover the depreciation of an asset used in a qualifying activity, allowances are **restricted** on a just and reasonable basis e.g. if a subsidy is intended to cover 50% of the depreciation, then allowances should be restricted by 50%.

In order for the restriction to operate, the asset must be placed in a single asset pool (¶25920).

26210
ss 209–212
CAA 2001

> MEMO POINTS A partial depreciation subsidy is **defined** as a payment which is:
> - payable directly or indirectly in respect of qualifying expenditure for a qualifying activity;
> - intended to take account of part of the depreciation of the asset resulting from its use for the qualifying activity; and
> - not taken into account as taxable income or profits.

3. Fixtures

26230
CA 26000

Fixtures may have become so integral to the building that they no longer qualify for capital allowances as plant. Even where qualifying as plant, the party who can claim allowances may not be the owner.

> MEMO POINTS 1. The special rules for fixtures do not apply to assets leased under a **long funding lease** (¶82215+) (including a chain of leases, where any of the leases involved are long funding ones).
> 2. For the interaction between the fixtures rules and **hire purchase** contracts see ¶26345.

Definition

26250
s 173 CAA 2001

A fixture is an asset that is installed in, or otherwise fixed in or to, a building or land so as to become part of that building or land in law.

A **chattel** is an asset, which is tangible and moveable. A chattel **can become** a fixture if it is subsequently fixed to a building or land e.g. a radiator.

Chattel or fixture?

26255
CA 26025

Over time, case law has focused on the following issues when deciding whether an item is a fixture:

Issue	Detail
Object and purpose of annexation	If attachment is: – permanent and is intended to provide a lasting improvement to the property, indicates item is a fixture; or – temporary, and only for the asset to be used and enjoyed, indicates item is a chattel
Method and degree of annexation	Of less importance Some degree of physical affixation is required If the asset is unable to be removed without serious damage to the property, indicates item is a fixture

Ownership

26260
CA 26025

The **usual rules** require a company to own an asset in order to claim allowances, so that only a freeholder would be able to claim in respect of fixtures.

However, **special rules** apply so that allowances can be claimed by the company who incurs expenditure on the provision of a fixture (either by paying for its installation or as a result of taking on a lease) so long as another party is not also making a claim.

> MEMO POINTS 1. If a company **accounts for a disposal** in respect of the fixture, the asset is not treated as owned any longer.

s 537 CAA 2001

> 2. Where a party makes a **contribution** towards the cost of a fixture and pays it to the person who is treated as the owner of the asset, that party can claim allowances on its share of the cost.

Interest in the property

26265
ss 173–176
CAA 2001;
CA 26150

On incurring expenditure on a fixture which is to be used for the purposes of a qualifying activity, capital allowances can be claimed so long as the company has an interest in the relevant property when the plant or machinery becomes a fixture. For this purpose the **relevant property** is the building or land of which the fixture becomes part.

Where **more than one party owns an interest** in the property and incurs costs relating to a fixture, only the party with the lowest interest can claim allowances. However, the party unable to claim allowances could make a contribution to the cost (¶26260). If both parties have the same interest, they can both claim allowances on their share of the expenditure.

> MEMO POINTS 1. An interest in a property is **defined** as:
> **a.** the freehold interest;
> **b.** an agreement to acquire the freehold interest;
> **c.** the Scottish equivalent of either of the above;

d. a lease;
e. an easement or servitude;
f. an agreement to acquire an easement or servitude; or
g. a licence to occupy land.
This list is **ordered** so that the greatest interest is shown first.
2. A **lease** is:
– a leasehold interest;
– an agreement to acquire a leasehold interest; or
– the Scottish equivalent of either of the above.
3. A **licence to occupy land** is not an interest in land unless it is an exclusive licence i.e. it allows the licensee to control the land.
4. **Mortgaged property** is still treated as owned by the company rather than by the party providing the mortgage.

EXAMPLE

1. E plc owns the freehold of an office block which is leased to F Ltd.
If F Ltd installs air conditioning which keeps the office at a good temperature for its employees and is fixed to the building, this is for the purpose of its qualifying activity.
As F Ltd has a leasehold interest in the property when incurring the expenditure, the company can claim capital allowances.

2. If E plc and F Ltd shared the cost of the air conditioning, only F Ltd could claim allowances on its share of the cost.
However, if E plc makes a contribution to F Ltd's cost instead, it could claim allowances on its share.

Leased equipment which is a fixture

Under an equipment lease, the equipment **lessor** will not have an interest in the relevant property but will own the equipment which becomes the fixture.

However, where the equipment lessor and equipment lessee are unconnected (¶25190) and make a joint election (within the usual time limits (¶25160)), the equipment lessor is **treated as owning** the fixture at the time when the expenditure is incurred if any of the following situations apply, and certain conditions are met:
a. the equipment lessee is carrying on a qualifying activity;
b. the fixture is not part of a building and the equipment lessor has the right to sever it; or
c. the equipment lease is part of the affordable warmth programme (and the equipment lessor incurred the expenditure before 1 January 2008).

26270
ss 174, 177
CAA 2001

MEMO POINTS   An **equipment lease** is an agreement where a person incurs capital expenditure on the provision of a fixture and leases it, directly or indirectly, to another person. The lessor will have no interest in the property to which the fixture is attached.

Situation	Conditions	Reference
Lessee is carrying on a qualifying activity	– the fixture is not for use in a dwelling house (¶25285); – the lease is entered into for the purposes of a qualifying activity that the lessee carries on or is going to carry on; and – if the lessee had incurred the expenditure on the fixture, the expenditure would have qualified for allowances	s 178 CAA 2001
Fixture is not part of a building and the equipment lessor has the right to sever it e.g. portaloos, bus shelters, and information signs	– the fixture is not for use in a dwelling house (¶25285); – the fixture is fixed to land that is neither a building nor part of a building; – the lessee has an interest in the land; – the lessor is entitled to sever the fixture at the end of the lease, and as a result will own it; – the nature of the asset and the way in which it is fixed mean that it can be used again for the same purposes once it has been severed; and – under GAAP, the lease would be accounted for as an operating lease in the lessor's accounts (¶82085)	s 179 CAA 2001

Situation	Conditions	Reference
Lease is part of the affordable warmth programme	– the lease is of a boiler, heat exchanger, radiator or heating control that is installed in a building as part of a space or water heating system; and – the equipment lease is approved as entered into as part of the affordable warmth programme[1]	s 180 CAA 2001

Note:
1. **Approval** is given by the Secretary of State or the appropriate authorities in Wales, Scotland and Northern Ireland.

EXAMPLE G Ltd's office block has a lift. This lift is leased from H plc (an unconnected party) who is the equipment lessor and has no interest in the property. G Ltd is the equipment lessee.
Assuming G Ltd has a qualifying activity which is carried on at the property, G Ltd and H plc can make a joint election to enable H plc to claim capital allowances.

Acquiring property with fixture already attached

26275
s 181 CAA 2001;
CA 26250

Normally, the purchaser of a property which includes a fixture would become the owner of the fixture, **unless** the same person, or another person, is claiming (or has claimed) capital allowances because of another interest held in the property (e.g. a superior or inferior interest).

s 562 CAA 2001;
CA 12100

The **total sum** paid for the purchase needs to be apportioned in order to ascertain the expenditure on which allowances are due. Where no prior claim to capital allowances has been made by the vendor, the apportionment is made on a just and reasonable basis, and the result for the vendor and the purchaser must be the same, as HMRC will challenge any discrepancy. In most cases, apportionment based on negotiation between the parties for the property's purchase would be taken as made at arm's length.

There are stringent new rules for **post-March 2012 acquisitions** where capital allowances have already been claimed (¶26290).

s 182 CAA 2001

MEMO POINTS 1. Where the property includes a **fixture previously let under an equipment lease**, and the purchaser of the property pays a capital sum to discharge the obligations of the equipment lessee, the fixture is treated as belonging to the purchaser. However, if another person has an interest in the property and is claiming allowances on the fixture, the purchaser cannot claim allowances.

s 183 CAA 2001

2. When a **property** with fixtures is **leased** and the **lessor** is:
a. entitled to claim allowances, the lessor and lessee can make a joint election to transfer ownership of the fixture to the lessee (i.e. effect a disposal for the part of the premium which relates to the fixture), and therefore allow the lessee to claim capital allowances. The lessor and lessee must not be connected (¶25190), and the election must be made in writing within 2 years of the date that the lease commences; or

s 184 CAA 2011

b. is not entitled to claim allowances, then the lessee is treated as owning the fixture so long as:
– the fixture has not previously been used for the purposes of a trade by the lessor or any person connected to the lessor (¶25190); or
– the lessee or some other person is not claiming allowances because of some other interest in the property.

s 186A CAA 2001

3. Since 1 April 2012, where fixtures are acquired with a building which qualifies for **business premises renovation allowance** (BPRA) (¶26515+), the purchaser can claim plant and machinery capital allowances on any fixtures expenditure not already relieved by BPRA.

EXAMPLE A property is constructed by A plc, a property developer, who installs central heating. A plc grants a 50-year lease to B Ltd for a premium, and part of the premium is apportioned to the fixture and B Ltd claims allowances accordingly.
If A plc later grants a 999-year lease of the same property to C plc, C plc cannot claim allowances on the central heating as B Ltd has a prior interest.

26280
ss 198 – 200
CAA 2001;
CA 26800

The parties involved can make an irrevocable **joint election** to fix the apportionment (although this has no effect for capital gains purposes) where either:
– a sale of the qualifying interest occurs at or above market value; or
– a premium is paid by an incoming lessee.

The **amount apportioned** to a fixture may not exceed any of the following:
- the amount that the seller was able to claim allowances on in respect of the fixture; or
- the sale price of the interest in land, or where relevant, the premium.

No election can be made in cases of avoidance (¶26305).

s 197 CAA 2001

As fixtures may fall within the **special rate pool or the main pool**, HMRC will not accept one apportionment which is supposed to cover all fixtures in a particular property. While an asset by asset apportionment would be completely impractical, the apportionment should take into account high value fixtures and ensure reasonable total values enter each pool.

| MEMO POINTS | 1. An election must be made by notice **in writing** to HMRC, and contain the following **information**:
- the amount apportioned to the fixture by the election;
- the name of each party making the election;
- information sufficient to identify the fixture and the relevant land;
- particulars of the interest in the property acquired; and
- the tax district references of each of the parties making the election.

s 201 CAA 2001

2. The **time limit** for making the election is 2 years after the date of the acquisition of the interest in the property, although where a referral to a tribunal is necessary (¶26290), this is extended to when the tribunal makes a determination.

3. A copy of the election must be included with each party's **tax return** for the first accounting period affected by it.

4. Where **circumstances change**, and the maximum figure which could be apportioned to the fixture is reduced, the election is automatically changed to the lower amount.

Prior claim to allowances

Where a party has treated the fixture as **revenue expenditure**, no allowances would have been claimed.

26285
s 185 CAA 2001;
CA 26400

Otherwise, unless the asset forming the fixture has been sold as a chattel (¶26255) and the vendor and purchaser are unconnected, the **total allowances** given in a chain of transactions **should not exceed** their original cost. This restriction operates so that the acquisition expenditure of the new owner cannot exceed the disposal value recognised by the vendor or any past owner (ignoring owners who claimed allowances as a result of a contribution (¶25185) but including those who treated the fixture as part of an industrial building or claimed research and development allowances).

Post-March 2012 acquisitions   For acquisitions of fixtures on or after 1 April 2012 from a business, **new restrictions** have been imposed so that a purchaser will only be able to claim capital allowances where the pooling requirement is satisfied i.e. previous business expenditure on qualifying fixtures has been notified to HMRC via a tax return by the seller in an accounting period beginning on or before the day of transfer, or the seller claimed a first year allowance on the expenditure (or any part of it) and either:

26290
ss 187A, 187B
CAA 2001

a. within 2 years of the transfer one of the following has happened:
- the parties to the transfer make a joint election (¶26280) to apportion value between a building and the fixtures;
- where such an agreement proves impossible, by referring the matter to the First-tier Tribunal for an independent determination; or
- where the immediate vendor was not able to claim any capital allowances (e.g. a charity), the purchaser obtains statements from a prior owner of the fixtures, which confirm the disposal value that has been used for tax purposes, and that the criteria immediately above can no longer be met (due to the 2-year time limit already having expired); or exceptionally
b. the vendor provides a written statement supporting the disposal value which has been brought into account for tax purposes e.g. if the vendor had previously permanently ceased its business activity, a deemed disposal of the fixtures at market value would have occurred. If the vendor then sells the property and associated fixtures some years later, a written statement would be required to enable the new purchaser to claim allowances.

| MEMO POINTS | 1. The onus is on the **purchaser** to demonstrate whether **b.** or **c.** above is satisfied. HMRC may request copies of supporting evidence.

2. For the purposes of ascertaining the vendor's **disposal value** (¶26300), these rules have no effect.

3. For a **non-business**:
– **vendor**, the pooling requirement in **a**. has no effect until April 2014; and
– **purchaser**, who wishes to pass on a possible entitlement to allowances to a future purchaser, the rules in **b**. (or more unusually **c**.) above must still be satisfied. This would most commonly mean that the non-business should make a joint election with the past owner, even though this would have no actual beneficial effect for the non-business.

Disposal events

26295
s 188 CAA 2001

As the fixtures rules mean that very often the party claiming the allowances may not necessarily be the true owner, when the claimant ceases to have a **qualifying interest** in the property, a deemed disposal of the fixture occurs, and a disposal value is brought into the capital allowances computation.

ss 190 – 195
CAA 2001

A disposal will also occur when:
a. the fixture is **permanently severed** from the property;
b. the **property lessor** enables the lessee to claim allowances (¶26275); or
c. in relation to **equipment leases** either:
– the rights of an equipment lessor (¶26270) are assigned. In this case the assignee is treated like an equipment lessor, and the expenditure incurred for capital allowances purposes is the consideration given for the assignment; or
– the financial obligations of an equipment lessee under the equipment lease are discharged, whether on the payment of a capital sum or otherwise. In this case, the equipment lessee is treated as owning the fixture once the payment is made.

s 189 CAA 2001

[MEMO POINTS] Whilst the **interest** in the property is obvious in most cases, where the qualifying interest:
– is an **agreement** to acquire an interest in land that is subsequently transferred or granted, the interest that is transferred or granted becomes the qualifying interest;
– ceases to exist because it is **merged** with another interest, the interest with which it is merged becomes the qualifying interest e.g., if the qualifying interest is a lease and the leaseholder acquires the freehold, the freehold interest becomes the qualifying interest;
– is a lease and a **new lease** of the relevant land is granted when it terminates, the new lease becomes the qualifying interest;
– is a lease and the **lessee remains in possession** of the relevant land after the lease terminates (with the lessor's consent without a new lease being granted), the qualifying interest continues; or
– is a **licence**, and on its termination a new licence to occupy the relevant land is granted to the licensee, the new licence becomes the qualifying interest.

26300
s 196 CAA 2001

Valuation Except in cases of avoidance (¶26305), the following disposal values apply:

Disposal event	Detail	Disposal value
Sale of the qualifying interest	At or above market value	Part of the sale price apportioned to fixtures, on which the buyer can claim allowances (or would be able to if eligible)
	For less than market value	Market value unless: – the buyer's expenditure on the acquisition of the fixture qualifies for allowances, and – the buyer is not a dual resident investing company (¶91480+) that is connected with the seller (¶25190), in which case the disposal value is that part of the sale price apportioned to fixtures on which the buyer can claim allowances
Transfer of the qualifying interest other than by way of sale		Market value
Expiry of the qualifying interest		Nil unless the person receives a capital sum by way of compensation so that the disposal value would be the value of that sum

Disposal event	Detail	Disposal value
Premium paid by incoming lessee		Part of the premium apportioned to fixtures on which the lessee can claim allowances (or would be able to if eligible)
Severance of fixture		Market value of the fixture when it is severed
Equipment lease ends	Assignment of rights by equipment lessor	Consideration given by the assignee for the assignment
	Discharge of equipment lessee's obligations	Capital sum paid
Permanent discontinuance of the qualifying activity	Followed by the sale of the qualifying interest	The part of the sale price apportioned to fixtures, on which the buyer can claim allowances (or would be able to if eligible)
	Followed by the demolition or destruction of the fixture	Net amount received for the remains of the fixture plus: – any insurance money received; and – any other capital compensation
	Followed by permanent loss other than by destruction etc	Any insurance money received in respect of the loss and any other capital compensation
Beginning to use the fixture wholly or partly for purposes other than those of the qualifying activity		Market value when the use begins i.e. that part of the price paid for the qualifying interest, which, if the qualifying interest had been sold in the open market immediately before the event, would have been treated as expenditure by the buyer on the provision of the fixture

Avoidance Where the disposal is part of a **scheme to secure a tax advantage**, which involves an asset being sold for less than its notional written down value (cost less the maximum allowances that could have been claimed in respect of the asset i.e. possibly an FYA, then WDA at either 18% or 8%), the seller's disposal proceeds will be deemed to be the notional written down value. The purchaser will only be able to claim allowances based on the actual acquisition value.

26305
s 197 CAA 2001

4. Hire purchase contracts

Who can claim allowances

The lessee of a hire purchase contract can claim capital allowances where:
– the hire purchase contract is accounted for under GAAP as a finance lease by the lessee (¶82080) (or would be so if accounts were prepared); and
– the assets are used for a qualifying activity (¶25270+).

26335
s 67 CAA 2001

If the above **conditions are not met** neither the lessor nor the lessee can claim capital allowances until the lessee is treated as the owner of the asset (e.g. when the contract terms are fulfilled, such as an option to buy the asset at the contract's end).

> ⸻ MEMO POINTS ⸻ 1. If the **lessor has claimed capital allowances** before the contract commences, it must bring a disposal value into account (¶26085+) when the contract starts, irrespective of whether the lessee is able to claim allowances.
> 2. If the **lessee stops being entitled to the benefit of the contract** without ever becoming the real owner of the asset, a disposal occurs, and the lessee is treated as ceasing to own the asset.

Timing

Capital **expenditure** that is **incurred before the asset is brought into use** for the purposes of the qualifying activity is deemed to be incurred as soon as there is an unconditional obligation to pay for the goods.

26340
s 67 CAA 2001

All **other** capital **expenditure** is deemed to be incurred when the asset is brought into use (i.e. allowances can be claimed on future payments as soon as the asset is used).

For assets acquired via hire purchase for the purposes of a future finance lease see ¶82535.

> [EXAMPLE]   F Ltd has an accounting period end date of 30 September. On 1 September, it entered into a hire purchase contract to acquire a printing press. The cash price was £100,000 but, under the terms of the hire purchase agreement, F Ltd had to pay a total price of £125,000 (a deposit of £20,000 to be paid on 1 September, with the balance of £105,000 to be paid in 25 monthly instalments, representing monthly payments of £1,000 hire charge and £3,200 capital). The printing equipment was delivered on 1 October, and brought into use by 31 October. The deposit of £20,000 will qualify for capital allowances for the accounting period in which it is paid.
> The balance of the cash price will qualify for capital allowances in the next accounting period.
> The finance charges (totalling £25,000) will be allowed as a deduction against profits in the accounting period when they are incurred. (125,000 – 100,000)

Fixtures

26345
s 69 CAA 2001

There are special rules which apply to fixtures (¶26230+), in particular the **identity of the claimant**, who may not be the true owner of the asset, or the lessee of the hire purchase contract. When a fixture is acquired via a hire purchase contract the fixtures rules apply.

If an asset that is being **bought under a hire purchase contract becomes a fixture**, and the fixtures rules deem some other person to be the owner of the asset, the lessee of the hire purchase contract is treated as ceasing to own the asset, so that a disposal event occurs.

Disposals

26350
s 68 CAA 2001;
CA 23330

When a lessee ceases to be entitled to the benefit of the contract **after bringing the asset into use**, a disposal must be brought into the capital allowances computation.

The disposal **value** is the sum of:
– capital amounts received as consideration, compensation, damages or insurance for the lessee's rights under the contract or the asset; and
– expenditure treated as incurred when the asset was brought into use (i.e. including any future contractual payments yet to be made, but on which allowances have been claimed).

If the asset **has not been brought into use**, the disposal value is any capital sums received as consideration, compensation, damages or insurance in respect of the lessee's rights under the contract or the asset.

> [EXAMPLE]
> **1.** G Ltd buys a combine harvester for £70,000 on hire purchase, paying a deposit of £30,000 and then four annual instalments of £10,000.
> The plant is brought into use immediately. G Ltd is treated as incurring expenditure of £70,000 for allowances purposes.
> After making the first instalment payment, the contract is assigned to E Ltd for £35,000. G Ltd was still due to pay £30,000 under the contract. G Ltd must bring in a disposal value of £65,000. (35,000 + (3 × 10,000).
>
> **2.** If G Ltd had not brought the combine harvester into use before assigning the contract, the disposal value would have been £35,000.

26355
s 229 CAA 2001;
CA 28700

Where the anti-avoidance rule of ¶25460 applies on the **assigning of the benefit** of a contract, usually in the context of a connected party transaction, this could produce an unfair result, as the buyer's qualifying expenditure is restricted to the vendor's disposal value.

In this case the vendor's disposal value (deemed to arise in the accounting period of assignment) is the sum of the following:
– the capital amounts received for consideration, compensation, damages or insurance for the rights under the contract or the asset; and
– any capital expenditure that has not yet been incurred under the contract.

> [EXAMPLE]   H Ltd is a trucking company, and enters into a hire purchase contract to buy a truck for £50,000. A deposit of £10,000 is paid, but then the directors decide that the truck is not suitable,

and so the contract is assigned to another group company, A Ltd which is a connected party, for £10,000.

H Ltd's disposal value is £10,000, and A Ltd will incur a total cost of £50,000 (being the £10,000 payable to H Ltd plus the amount still due under the contract).

If the normal rules about assignment of a hire purchase contract applied (¶25460), A Ltd's qualifying expenditure would be restricted to £10,000, even though A Ltd will incur capital expenditure of £50,000 on the truck.

So the revised rules above mean that the £40,000 still to be incurred under the contract is added to H Ltd's qualifying expenditure and disposal value.

So the limit on A Ltd's qualifying expenditure is also £50,000.

5. Ships

As the sums involved are so large, there are a number of modifications to the usual rules to facilitate flexibility in claiming allowances, and minimise the impact of balancing charges for ships which are used solely for the purposes of a trade.

26385

Scope

A ship is not specifically **defined** but is given its normal everyday meaning based on the Maritime Shipping Acts. HMRC state that any vessel that is capable of being manoeuvred under direct or indirect power is a ship.

26390
CA 25100

The following are **excluded**:
– oilrigs and platforms;
– accommodation barges; and
– light and weather ships.

There are further restrictions imposed where balancing charges are to be rolled over (¶26415).

Pooling

The rate of allowance and calculation method are the same as for other plant, but the expenditure is **automatically allocated** to a single pool (one for each ship) **unless**:
– an election is made to include it within the main pool, in which case the ship cannot be subsequently treated separately;
– the qualifying activity (¶25270+) is the leasing of assets other than in the course of a trade; or
– the ship is provided for leasing, although it can be put into a single pool where, for 10 years from the date it is brought into use, the ship is only used for a qualifying purpose (¶82610) and not leased overseas (other than for protected leasing (¶82615)).

26395
ss 127, 128
CAA 2001

MEMO POINTS The **pooling election** may relate to the total expenditure on the ship, or any proportion thereof, and may be made before any allowances have been given. Alternatively, where allowances have already been claimed, an election may be made to transfer the balance of any ship expenditure (or proportion thereof) into the main pool. The election must be in writing and made within the usual time limits (¶25160).

s 129 CAA 2001;
CA 25150

EXAMPLE A Ltd has the following balances:
– main pool balance brought forward of £5,000;
– disposal proceeds for general plant of £20,000; and
– expenditure in a single ship pool of £30,000.
Ordinarily, a balancing charge of £15,000 would result. (5,000 – 20,000)
However, A Ltd can elect to transfer £15,000 from the single ship pool to the main pool to avoid the balancing charge.

Deferral of allowances

To allow flexibility, **elections** can be made to defer allowances due (both WDA (which requires the ship to be shown in a single ship pool) and FYA, where applicable). The deferred allowances are kept in a separate pool (one for each ship), and may be claimed at any

26400
ss 130, 131
CAA 2001

time whilst the trade is carried on. Allowances for future accounting periods are calculated as if the usual allowance claim had been made i.e. the WDV is reduced.

The claim must be made within the usual **time limits** (¶25160), applying from the end of the accounting period in which the allowances are to be utilised, and **specify** the amount to be postponed.

When they are so claimed they are treated as allowances of the period of the claim, not as brought forward losses. Deferred allowances are not affected by the sale of the ship to which they relate.

> EXAMPLE B Ltd has a calendar year accounting period, and acquires a ship for its trade on 4 July which costs £1 million.
> The WDA available is £180,000. (1,000,000 @ 18%)
> B Ltd postpones £100,000 of the allowance.
> The balance on the single ship pool at the end of the accounting period is £820,000. (1,000,000 – 180,000)
> The postponed allowance can be claimed in any accounting period so long as the ship trade continues, and will be in addition to the WDA available in the later accounting period.

Disposals

26405
s 132 CAA 2001

Unless a pooling election (¶26395) has been made, each ship will be treated as being in a separate pool of its own, so a **balancing adjustment** would normally arise on disposal. However, to avoid this, the expenditure in the single ship pool is transferred to the appropriate pool and the disposal value is brought to account in that pool.

If the disposal value exceeds the balance of expenditure in the main pool, a balancing charge will arise, although an election can be made to roll it over (¶26410).

> MEMO POINTS 1. If a ship is provided for **leasing**, and it then begins to be used other than for a qualifying purpose at some time during the designated period (¶82605), a disposal event is deemed to occur.

s 133 CAA 2001

> 2. A ship may cease to belong to a person **without** it **ever having been used**, in which case:
> – the single ship pool is discontinued and a disposal value is brought to account in the normal way; and
> – any allowances which have been claimed or postponed are withdrawn, and added back to the main pool in the accounting period of disposal.

Comment As deferred allowances may be claimed at any time (¶26400), they may be used to offset the balancing adjustment, if required.

> EXAMPLE C Ltd has a calendar year accounting period. At the beginning of Year 10, C Ltd had a WDV brought forward on the main pool of £22,000 and on a ship of £950,000. For Year 10, C Ltd elected to defer allowances of £100,000 in respect of the ship. The ship was sold for £820,000 during Year 11, and the company wishes to utilise the deferred allowances to offset any balancing charge.
>
> | | Main pool £ | Ship £ | Deferred £ | Allowances £ |
> |---|---|---|---|---|
> | **Year 10** | | | | |
> | WDV b/fwd | 22,000 | 950,000 | | |
> | WDA @ 18% | (3,960) | (171,000) | 100,000 | 74,960 |
> | | 18,040 | 779,000 | | |
> | **Year 11** | | | | |
> | Transfer to main pool | 779,000 | (779,000) | | |
> | Proceeds | (820,000) | | | |
> | | (22,960) | | | |
> | Deferred allowances | 22,960 | | (22,960) | Nil |
> | WDV c/fwd | Nil | Nil | 77,040 | |

Rollover on replacement

If there is a **balancing charge** following the disposal of a qualifying ship, the company can make a rollover claim where a replacement is acquired within 6 years of the disposal.

26410
ss 134, 135
CAA 2001

> `MEMO POINTS` This rule also applies to **75% groups** so that a disposal by one group member can be rolled over against a replacement acquired by another member where:
> – the replacement ship remains in the ownership of the company which acquired it, and
> – that company remains a member of the same group as the disposing company for the next 3 years, or until the total loss of, or irreparable damage to, the ship if sooner.

Qualifying ship Specifically **excluded** from these provisions are ships, other than passenger ships and cruise liners, which are of a kind used or chartered primarily for sport or recreation.

26415
ss 151 – 154
CAA 2001;
CA 25350

Both the old ship and the replacement must be:
a. ships of a sea-going kind with a **gross tonnage** of at least 100 tons, **unless** the disposal of the original ship is caused by its loss or destruction, or where the ship is damaged to such an extent that it is uneconomical to repair; and
b. registered in one of the following places:
– the UK (or one of its colonies);
– the Channel Islands or the Isle of Man; or
– the EU/EEA (¶82585).

The registration requirement must be met for the old ship immediately prior to disposal, and for the replacement ship for 3 years from the date of first use (unless the ship is disposed of in the meantime). Registration of the replacement ship should take place within 3 months of first use.

> `MEMO POINTS` 1. The following are **UK colonies**:
>
> | | | |
> |---|---|---|
> | Anguilla | Cayman Islands | Montserrat |
> | Bermuda | Falklands | St Helena |
> | British Virgin Islands | Gibraltar | Turks & Caicos |
>
> 2. **Hong Kong** ceased to be a colony on 30 June 1997, so ships registered there after this date do not qualify. Ships registered in Hong Kong on or before this date continue to be qualifying ships provided the other conditions are met.

Other conditions All of the following criteria must be met for a balancing charge to be rolled over:

26420
ss 130 – 137
CAA 2001

– the **old ship** is disposed of in the accounting period (i.e. cessation of belonging, permanent loss of possession, abandonment, or ceasing to exist), having been owned in that accounting period by the company and wholly **used for** a qualifying activity (¶25270+) (i.e. not leased overseas or where the special leasing rules apply);
– no subsidies (¶26210) were received towards its **partial depreciation**; and
– the company has not made a **loss** for the accounting period.

Limit on amount The maximum amount that can be rolled over is the **lowest of** the amount:

26425
s 138 CAA 2001;
CA 25450

– of the actual balancing charge that would otherwise accrue on the main pool;
– of the balancing charge relating solely to the ship;
– of expenditure that is (or is expected to be) incurred on the replacement ship; and
– that would reduce the company's profits for the period, in which the rollover is claimed, to nil.

Where the **ship is in its own pool**, the balancing charge relating solely to the ship is easy to ascertain. Where the ship has **already entered the main pool**, the company should assume that all allowances available (both first year, if any, and writing down) have been claimed in respect of the ship i.e. effectively treat the ship as if it had stayed in its single ship pool. The disposal proceeds should be set against this notional value to obtain the balancing charge in respect of the ship.

EXAMPLE D Ltd owns a qualifying ship which is in a single ship pool with a WDV of £400,000, and which is sold for £1,000,000 in Year 4. E Ltd intends to acquire a new ship within 6 years for £1.25m. The WDV for the main pool is £250,000. E Ltd's accounts for Year 4 show a loss of £50,000, and brought forward losses are £200,000.

	Main pool £	Ship £
WDV b/fwd	250,000	400,000
Disposal		(1,000,000)
		(600,000)
Transfer to main pool	(600,000)	600,000
Balancing charge	(350,000)	
Current year loss	50,000	
	300,000	

The amount of the balancing charge that may be deferred is the smallest of:
– the balancing charge on the main pool i.e. £350,000;
– the amount taken into account in respect of the ship i.e. £600,000;
– the intended cost of the replacement ship i.e. £1.25m; and
– the amount which would reduce E Ltd's profits to nil i.e. £300,000. (The brought forward losses are ignored.)
So the balancing charge which may be deferred is £300,000. So the pools now look like this:

	Main pool £	Ship £
WDV b/fwd	250,000	400,000
Deferred balancing charge	300,000	
	550,000	
Disposal		(1,000,000)
		(600,000)
Transfer to main pool	(600,000)	600,000
Balancing charge (350,000 – 300,000)	(50,000)	
Current year loss	50,000	
	Nil	

26430
ss 140–146
CAA 2001

Replacement ship acquisition The rolled over balancing **charge is set against** the costs of the first ship which is expected to be used wholly for the purposes of the trade for a minimum period of 3 years, and which is entered into a separate ship pool.

The company must give **notice** to HMRC when rolling over the charge. In the case of groups, both companies must give notice.

MEMO POINTS 1. Where **more than one ship is acquired** within the 6 years, the balancing charge is rolled over against the earliest purchase.

CA 25500

2. If **more than one balancing charge has been deferred**, they must be rolled over in the order in which they arose i.e. a balancing charge arising in an earlier accounting period must be attributed to new shipping before a balancing charge arising in a later accounting period.

ss 146–150
CAA 2001

3. The **new ship** must not:
– have been previously owned by the company (or a connected person (¶25190)) in the 6 years prior to its acquisition;
– be used for overseas leasing;
– be put into the main pool; or
– be acquired as a transaction (or part of a series of transactions) whose main object is to defer a balancing charge.
4. The **trade** is treated as being the same, for both the old ship, and the new ship, when there are changes in ownership which simply continue the trade (¶60545+) (e.g. the addition of a new partner or a hive down).
5. For **groups** the member acquiring the new ship must:
– bring it into use for the purposes of its qualifying activity,
– continue to own it for 3 years after it is brought into use, and
– stay a member of the same group as the disposing company for 3 years after the ship is brought into use.

The 3-year period is reduced where the ship is lost or irreparably damaged in the meantime. If a company, which acquired a new ship, stops being a member of the same group as the disposing company, the rolled over balancing charge should be reinstated in the disposing company's computation.

EXAMPLE Continuing the example at ¶26425 above, D Ltd acquires a new ship in the following accounting period for £1.25m.

	Ship 2 £	Allowances £
Purchase	1,250,000	
Less: Deferred balancing charge	(300,000)	
	950,000	
WDA @ 18%	(171,000)	171,000
WDV c/fwd	779,000	

Claim Claims to roll over the balancing charge must be made in writing within the normal **time limits** (¶25160) based on the accounting period in which the old ship was sold.

26435
s 135 CAA 2001

Given the time limit for making claims, it is possible that a claim may need to be submitted before a replacement ship has been acquired. If a claim is made but a **suitable replacement is not purchased** within the 6-year period, the balancing charge will be reinstated for the accounting period in which it arose and interest will be charged on any unpaid tax. In this case, the company must notify HMRC of the change in circumstances within 3 months after the end of the relevant accounting period.

s 145 CAA 2001

SECTION 4

Buildings

In recent years, allowances for buildings have been phased out, so that from 1 April 2011, only the following still apply:
- business premises renovation allowances; and
- flat conversions.

26485

As a consequence it is important to claim the maximum plant and machinery allowances, which makes the distinction between building and plant even more vital (¶25365+).

A. Business premises renovation

Business premises renovation allowance (BPRA) is available for qualifying expenditure incurred until at least April 2017. The available 100% allowance is intended to stimulate redevelopment of vacant and derelict sites in certain disadvantaged areas.

26515
CA 45000

1. Scope

BPRA is available to a company which incurs qualifying expenditure whilst having a relevant interest in the qualifying building.

26545
s 360A CAA 2001

However, since 11 April 2012, an **exception** applies which **excludes** any company which is in financial difficulty, or is subject to an outstanding recovery order i.e. where a company

SI 2007/107 reg 4

falls within the Community Guidelines on State Aid for Rescuing and Restructuring firms in difficulty.

Qualifying expenditure

26550
s 360B CAA 2001;
SI 2007/107 reg 5

Qualifying expenditure is the costs incurred by the company when undertaking works which bring a qualifying building back into commercial use. Since 11 April 2012 the **maximum** qualifying cost for each building project is €20 million (taking into account any cost incurred by any person within the previous 3 years on the same project).

For this purpose, the following are **works**:
– conversion;
– renovation; or
– repairs.

s 360L CAA 2001

However, where the **cost is subsidised** by either:
– a notified State Aid (i.e. approved by the European Commission) other than BPRA; or
– a grant which is not a notified State Aid but which is declared by Treasury order to be relevant for the purposes of withholding initial allowance or WDA,
no BPRA is available, unless the subsidy is repaid (¶25185).

Qualifying building

26555
s 360C CAA 2001

A qualifying building is a commercial building or structure (or part) which is **situated** in a disadvantaged area. From 1 January 2014 this must be so **at the time** when the expenditure is incurred.

Expenditure on acquiring **land**, extending a building, or developing land next to a building does not qualify e.g. adding another storey to a qualifying building.

26560
SI 2007/107

Disadvantaged areas   Otherwise known as assisted areas, these are **designated by** Treasury regulations (see flmemo.co.uk/ctm26560).

If a qualifying building is **situated partly** in a disadvantaged area i.e. on the boundary, a just and reasonable apportionment of the qualifying expenditure should be made (e.g. based on floor area).

26565
s 360C CAA 2001

Use   Prior to the renovation work, the building must not have been used:
– for any trading or other business activity, or as offices, for at least 1 year immediately preceding the date when those works began; or
– most recently as a dwelling (¶25285).

If **part of a building** has been unused for more than a year, and is converted to qualifying business premises, the cost will qualify for BPRA.

> EXAMPLE   F Ltd owns an office block. It leases out all of the floors except for the run-down retail premises on the ground floor.
> After the ground floor has been derelict for over a year, F Ltd leases it to G Ltd who converts into a café.
> G Ltd's expenditure will qualify for BPRA.

26570
SI 2007/945

After the works are complete, the building must be available for business or commercial use, **excluding**:
– farming;
– fisheries;
– aquaculture e.g. fish farming;
– the manufacture of substitute milk products;
– synthetic fibres;
– shipbuilding; and
– steel or coal industries.

Where premises are **temporarily unavailable for use** as a commercial building e.g. broken heating or gas leak, they will still qualify for BPRA (and no adjustment need be made to the allowances given) so long as they qualified immediately before the event which has caused the break in use.

Relevant interest

The relevant interest is **defined** as the interest to which the company incurring the qualifying expenditure was entitled at the time when it was incurred.

26575
ss 360E, 360F
CAA 2001

If the company **acquires an interest** in the building **as a result of** the renovation, it is treated as having had that interest when the expenditure was incurred e.g. where the company owns an agreement for a lease which is only actually granted once the expenditure has been incurred.

> MEMO POINTS 1. If the company has **more than one interest** in the building, the relevant interest is the reversionary interest.
> 2. Where the company **creates another interest** which is subordinate to the relevant interest (e.g. where the company owns the freehold and grants a lease), the relevant interest is not affected.
> 3. Where the company has a relevant interest which is a leasehold interest, and then the company **acquires the reversionary interest as well** (e.g. the freehold) so that the two interests merge, the reversionary interest becomes the relevant interest.

> EXAMPLE
> 1. A Ltd owns the freehold of a qualifying building which is then leased to B Ltd for 45 years. A Ltd then leases the building from B Ltd for 8 years.
> A Ltd has two interests in the building, but the relevant interest is the freehold interest.
>
> 2. If A Ltd doesn't lease the building back from B Ltd, but converts a portion of the building for retail use, the relevant interest is still the freehold interest even where the expenditure is incurred after the creation of the lease.
>
> 3. If B Ltd (an existing lessee) decides to acquire the freehold from A Ltd, its relevant interest in the building becomes the freehold.

2. How allowances are given

An initial allowance of 100% of the qualifying expenditure is made for the accounting period in which it is incurred, by making a claim on the CTSA return.

26605
s 360G CAA 2001

Where the full IA is not claimed writing down allowances are available on the balance of expenditure which remains.

A balancing adjustment will occur when certain balancing events occur within 7 years of the date of first use of the building (subsequent to its renovation). Where no such events occur the benefit of the allowances is retained.

> MEMO POINTS 1. Where an **additional VAT liability** (¶25135) is incurred in respect of the building, and an initial allowance has already been claimed, the VAT also qualifies for IA. Where the building has already come into use, or been made available for letting, the additional IA is written off when the VAT liability is incurred.

ss 360U, 360W
CAA 2001

> 2. Since 1 April 2012 where **fixtures** (¶26230+) are acquired, the purchaser can claim plant and machinery capital allowances on any fixtures expenditure not already relieved by BPRA.

s 186A CAA 2001

Giving effect to allowances

Any allowances or balancing charges arising from the BPRA rules are **usually** treated the same as any capital allowances i.e. as part of a trade or property business.

26610
ss 360Z, 360Z1
CAA 2001

Exceptionally, where the company has **no trade, and no property business**, the adjustments fall to be treated as if the company had a virtual property business.

Withdrawal of initial allowance

26615
s 360H CAA 2001

The initial allowance is withdrawn if either of the following occurs:
– the building is **not available** for commercial **use** (either by the company which carried out the works or it is not available for letting); or
– the company **sells the relevant interest** before the building is brought into use.

Withdrawal is usually effected by HMRC raising an assessment.

s 360L CAA 2001

If a **subsidy is received** after an initial allowance (or WDA) has been claimed, the allowance is withdrawn to that extent, unless the subsidy is repaid. Any adjustments needing to be made to any BPRA claim may be made within 3 years of the end of the accounting period in which the subsidy is paid (or repayment is made).

> EXAMPLE   C Ltd incurs qualifying expenditure of £1.4 million converting a building into a department store, and claims a full IA.
> At the audit, it is discovered that a government grant (notified State Aid) was available for a portion of the cost. C Ltd makes an application and receives £500,000. So £500,000 of the IA is withdrawn.

Writing down allowances

26620
ss 360I – 360K,
360R CAA 2001

The company can claim writing down allowances where all of the following **conditions** are met at the end of the accounting period:
– the company still holds the relevant interest in the building;
– no long lease (i.e. in excess of 50 years) has been granted out of the relevant interest for a premium;
– a reduced claim, or no claim, for IA was made; and
– there is still some expenditure remaining which has not yet been written off.

The applicable **rate** of WDA is of 25% on a straight line basis, although this would be limited where the residue of unrelieved expenditure was less than 25% of the original cost.

It is possible to claim a WDA in the same accounting period as the initial allowance.

s 360V CAA 2001

MEMO POINTS   Where an **additional VAT liability** (¶25135) is treated as qualifying expenditure, this is added to the residue at the time that the VAT arises.

> EXAMPLE   D Ltd spends £100,000 on converting a disused warehouse into offices in Year 1, which are immediately available for letting.
> The company chooses to make the following claims:
>
> | Year | | Expenditure £ | Allowances claimed £ |
> |---|---|---|---|
> | 1 | Costs incurred | 100,000 | |
> | | IA claimed | (20,000) | 20,000 |
> | 2 | Residue b/fwd | 80,000 | |
> | | WDA: 100,000 @ 25% | (25,000) | 25,000 |
> | 3 | Residue b/fwd | 55,000 | |
> | | WDA: 100,000 @ 25% | (25,000) | 25,000 |
> | 4 | Residue b/fwd | 30,000 | |
> | | WDA: 100,000 @ 25% | (25,000) | 25,000 |
> | 5 | Residue b/fwd | 5,000 | |
> | | WDA: 100,000 @ 25% (restricted to residue) | (5,000) | 5,000 |
> | | | Nil | |

3. Balancing adjustments

A balancing adjustment (i.e. allowance or charge) will be made in the accounting period in which a balancing event occurs, so long as that **event happens within** 7 years of the first use of the building.

26650
s 360M CAA 2001

Where **more than one** balancing event occurs, a balancing adjustment is only made on the first one.

> EXAMPLE E Ltd buys a warehouse and converts it into offices, claiming a full IA.
> The company sells the office building 8 years later.
> As this is outside the 7-year time limit, no balancing adjustment is required.

Balancing events

A balancing event is any of the following:
- the sale of the building;
- the grant of a long lease out of the relevant interest for a premium;
- the ending of a lease that is the relevant interest, without the lessee acquiring the reversionary interest i.e. a lease surrender;
- the demolition or destruction of the qualifying building; or
- the building ceasing to be used for a commercial purpose.

26655
s 360N CAA 2001

> MEMO POINTS 1. Where a **lease terminates**, the following rules apply:
> **a.** where the lessee remains in possession of the building with the lessor's consent, without a new lease being granted, the lease that has terminated is treated as continuing for as long as the lessee remains in possession;
> **b.** if there was an option in the terminated lease for the lessee to be granted a new lease and the lessee exercises that option, the new lease is treated as a continuation of the old lease;
> **c.** if the lessor pays a sum to the lessee when the lease terminates, this is treated as a lease surrender by the lessee; and
> **d.** if another lease is granted to a different lessee, and that lessee pays a sum to the original lessee, this is treated as an assignment of the original lease (i.e. the two leases are treated as the same lease).
> 2. The making of an **additional VAT rebate** (¶25135) to the company holding the relevant interest is also a balancing event.

s 360Z3 CAA 2001;
CA 45950

s 360X CAA 2001

Deemed proceeds

The following table shows the **value** to be brought into the BPRA computation.

26660
ss 360O, 360S,
360X, 360Z2
CAA 2001

> MEMO POINTS If **proceeds are only partly attributable** to assets qualifying for BPRA, a just apportionment is made.

Disposal event	Disposal value
Sale of the building	Net sale proceeds
Grant of a long lease	Capital sum involved, or if greater, the amount that would have been paid had the transaction been undertaken on arm's length terms
Ending of lease without lessee acquiring reversionary interest	Where the lessee and the person owning the superior interest are connected (¶25190), the market value of the relevant interest in the qualifying building at the time of the event
Demolition or destruction of building[1]	Net amount received, plus any insurance or compensation monies
Property ceases to be used for commercial purpose	The market value of the relevant interest at the time of the event
Additional VAT rebate	Amount of the rebate
Note: 1. If any **demolition costs** are incurred (and these exceed monies received for the remaining property), they are added to the residue of qualifying expenditure immediately before demolition.	

Anti-avoidance

26662
ss 568, 569
CAA 2001

Anti-avoidance provisions apply in connection with sales where either:
– the control test is met, or the sale has been artificially arranged in order to obtain a tax advantage; or
– as part of a tax avoidance scheme, the proceeds are less than they would be on the open market.

> ⌐MEMO POINTS⌐ 1. In general, when an asset is sold, the net **sale proceeds** will be the disposal proceeds. However, a market value figure will be substituted where either:
> **a.** the **control test** is met. That is where:
> – the buyer has control over the seller (or vice versa);
> – a third party has control over both the buyer and the seller; or
> – the buyer and seller are connected;
> **b.** the sale has been **artificially arranged** in order to obtain a tax advantage by all or any of the parties concerned.
> For **other types of disposal**, such as gift, demolition, destruction or the permanent cessation of the use of the building, the disposal value will be the total of any capital compensation, insurance or salvage money received. Any receipts chargeable as income are excluded from the disposal value.
> 2. If, as a result of a **tax avoidance scheme** (i.e. a scheme or arrangement where the taxpayer's main purpose included the obtaining of a tax advantage), proceeds on the sale of a building are less than they would be on the open market, a balancing allowance will be denied to the vendor. (However, the residue after sale for both the purchaser and the vendor is still computed as if the balancing allowances had been given in full.)

Computation

26665
ss 360P, 360S
CAA 2001

The deemed proceeds from ¶26660 need to be compared with the residue of qualifying expenditure immediately before the balancing event.

For this purpose, the **residue** is calculated as follows:
– initial allowances are written off at the time when the qualifying business premises are first used or suitable for letting (which might be quite some time after the initial allowance is claimed (¶26605)); and
– writing down allowances are written off at the end of each accounting period.

> ⌐EXAMPLE⌐ F Ltd incurs expenditure of £100,000 qualifying for BPRA in the accounting period ended 31 December 2012.
> The premises are not available for letting until 1 December 2013.
> The initial allowance is claimed in the accounting period ended 31 December 2012, but is not written off until 1 December 2013.

26670

If:
– there are **no proceeds**, there will be a balancing allowance equal to the residue of the expenditure;
– the residue of **expenditure is greater** than the deemed proceeds, a balancing allowance of the difference will arise;
– there is **no residue of expenditure**, there will be a balancing charge equal to the deemed proceeds; or
– the **proceeds exceed the residue** of expenditure, a balancing charge of the difference will arise.

A **balancing charge** cannot exceed the total allowances already given before the balancing event i.e. the sum of the initial allowance and WDA.

ss 360X, 360Y
CAA 2001

Where a **VAT rebate** is received, it is written off the residue at the time when it accrues. No balancing allowance can result. Any balancing charge would be the difference between the VAT rebate and the residue.

> ⌐EXAMPLE⌐ G Ltd incurs qualifying expenditure of £150,000 and claims 100% initial allowance so the residue is nil.
> A couple of years later, the company sells the building for £180,000.

The balancing charge is restricted to £150,000, being the allowances made, even though the proceeds are greater. The profit will be charged as a capital gain (¶30000+).

B. Flat conversions

Flat conversion allowance (otherwise known as flats over the shop or FCA) was intended to attract investors to buy and develop spaces above commercial premises into dwellings, and is **only available** until 31 March 2013. Note that the conversion of a basement would also be eligible for the allowance where the building is a qualifying building.   **26700**

There is a limit on the subsequent rental value of the flat, and the lets must be short-term.

1. Scope

A company which incurred qualifying expenditure in respect of a qualifying flat, and which has the relevant interest in the flat, can claim FCA.   **26730**

Qualifying expenditure

Qualifying expenditure is the capital cost incurred when the company undertakes any of the following **works**:   **26735**
s 393B CAA 2001
- converting part of a qualifying building into a qualifying flat;
- renovating a flat in a qualifying building to create a qualifying flat;
- making repairs incidental to the conversion or renovation of a qualifying flat (so long as these are not revenue expenses); or
- providing access to a qualifying flat e.g. creation of stairwells or extensions to the building to contain this access.

Common examples of qualifying expenditure are the costs of: CA 43150
- dividing a single property to create a number of separate flats; or
- installing a new kitchen or bathroom.

Exclusions   The following expenditure is excluded: **26740**
ss 393B, 393C
CAA 2001
- the acquisition of land, or rights in or over land;
- an extension to the building (unless it is required to give access to a qualifying flat);
- works to an extension that was completed after 31 December 2000;
- the development of land adjoining or adjacent to the building. This includes conversions forming part of a larger scheme of development; and
- the provision of furnishings or other chattels.

Associated costs   Examples of associated costs that **may qualify** are: **26745**
CA 43150
- architect's and surveyor's fees;
- inserting or removing walls, windows, or doors;
- installing and upgrading plumbing, gas, electricity or central heating;
- reroofing incidental to the conversion/renovation; and
- providing external fire escapes where regulations require.

> EXAMPLE   A Ltd owns a clothing shop which has two upper floors, one used for storage, and the other unused.
> The company converts the two upper floors into flats for letting, incurring the following costs:
> - installing bathrooms;
> - central heating;

– outside staircase to provide separate entrances for the flats and also comply with fire safety regulations; and
– furniture.
Only the cost of the furniture does not qualify for FCA.

Qualifying building

26750
s 393C CAA 2001

A qualifying building has up to four **storeys** above the ground floor and meets the following **criteria**:
– constructed before 1 January 1980 (any subsequent extension must have been finished by 31 December 2000);
– all or most of the ground floor is authorised for business use; and
– it appears that when the building was constructed, the storeys above the ground floor (or basement) were for use primarily as one or more dwellings.

The **part of the building** on which the expenditure is incurred must either have been unused, or used only for storage, for at least 1 year before the conversion work begins.

CA 43200

⬚MEMO POINTS⬚ 1. The **ground floor** is the floor that contains the main entrance to the shop.
2. **Authorised for business use** means approved for use for specific business activities in the ratings legislation, such as retail shops, premises for the provision of financial and professional services, pubs, restaurants, cafés, doctors' and dentists' surgeries, other offices and premises for research and development activities and industrial processes (those which can be carried out in residential areas).
The specific rules depend on whether the property is located in:
– England or Wales, when it must be authorised for use within class A1, A2, A3, B1 or D1(a) as set out in the Schedule to the Town and Country Planning (Use Classes) Order 1987;
– Scotland, when it must be authorised for use within class 1, 2, 3 or 4, as set out in the Schedule to the Town and Country Planning (Use Classes)(Scotland) Order 1997 or specified in Article 3(5)(j) of that Order; or
– Northern Ireland, when it must be authorised for use within class 1, 2, 3, 4 or 15(a) as set out in the Schedule to the Town and Country Planning (Use Classes)(Northern Ireland) Order 1989 or specified in Article 3(5)(b), (c) or (h) of that Order.
3. An **attic** counts as a storey if it can be lived in e.g. it has windows in the roof and proper stair access. An attic or loft that is not suitable for living in does not count as a storey, even if it can be used for storage.
4. Provided that the greater part of the storeys above the ground floor were **for use primarily as dwellings** (¶25285), the building will qualify. HMRC give the example of a four-storey building which would qualify if it was built with a showroom or office on the first floor, provided that it appears that the original purpose of the second and third floors was residential.
5. Where **part** of the upper floors **have been used** (other than for storage) in the last year, the expenditure must be apportioned.

Qualifying flat

26755
ss 393D, 393E
CAA 2001;
CA 43250

A qualifying flat is **defined** as a dwelling that is a separate set of premises suitable for letting which is:
– in a qualifying building, and divided horizontally from another part of it;
– held for short-term letting;
– accessible without using the business premises;
– has no more than 4 rooms, ignoring kitchens and bathrooms, and closets, cloakrooms and hallways that are not more than 5m^2 in area; and
– not a high value flat.

Temporary unavailability for letting, such as redecoration between tenancies, does not jeopardise the flat's qualifying status.

⬚MEMO POINTS⬚ 1. The flat can be on **more than one floor**.
2. A **dwelling** is a building or part of a building occupied or intended to be occupied as a separate residence (¶25285).
3. A flat is **suitable for letting** from the time that the renovation has been completed. There is no need for the flat to be actually let. A flat could be held for letting if it is being actively marketed.

4. **Short-term letting** means that the lease to the eventual occupying tenant has a term of less than 5 years.

High value flats   The notional rent must not exceed the limits shown in the following table. This must be **measured at the time** when the renovation expenditure is first incurred by the company. It is irrelevant whether the achievable rent subsequently exceeds the limits (i.e. at some time after the renovation is completed).

26760
s 393E CAA 2001

   MEMO POINTS   For this purpose, the **notional rent** is the rent for which the flat could be reasonably let, assuming:
– the conversion or renovation has been completed;
– the flat is let furnished;
– the lease does not require a premium or other payment to be made to the landlord;
– the tenant is not connected (¶25190) with the company; and
– the flat is let on an assured short hold tenancy (or in Scotland, a short assured tenancy).

Number of rooms[1]	Flats in Greater London	Flats elsewhere
Up to 2	£350 per week	£150 per week
3	£425 per week	£225 per week
4	£480 per week	£300 per week
Note: 1. Ignoring kitchens and bathrooms and closets, cloakrooms and hallways that are not more than 5m² in area.		

Anti-avoidance   The renovation of the flat cannot be **part of a scheme** involving the creation or renovation of one or more high value flats.

26765
s 393D CAA 2001

The flat must not be **let to** a connected person (¶25190).

Relevant interest

The relevant interest is **defined** as the interest to which the company incurring the qualifying expenditure was entitled at the time when it was incurred.

26770
ss 393E, 393F
CAA 2001

If the company **acquires an interest** in the building **as a result of** the renovation, it is treated as having had that interest when the expenditure was incurred e.g. where the company owns an agreement for a lease which is only actually granted once the expenditure has been incurred.

   MEMO POINTS   1. If the company has **more than one interest** in the building, the relevant interest is the reversionary interest.
2. Where the company **creates another interest** which is subordinate to the relevant interest (e.g. where the company owns the freehold and grants a lease), the relevant interest is not affected.
3. Where the company has a relevant interest which is a leasehold interest, and then the company **acquires the reversionary interest as well** (e.g. the freehold) so that the two interests merge, the reversionary interest becomes the relevant interest.

2. How allowances are given

An initial allowance of 100% of the qualifying expenditure is made for the accounting period in which it is incurred, by making a claim on the CTSA return. This may pre-date the actual letting of the flat.

26800

A balancing adjustment will occur when certain balancing events occur within 7 years of the date when the flat was first suitable for letting as a dwelling. Where no such events occur, the benefit of the allowances is retained.

Giving effect to allowances

Any allowances or balancing charges arising from the FCA rules are **usually** treated the same as any capital allowances relating to a property business.

26805
s 393T CAA 2001

Exceptionally, where the company has **no property business**, the adjustments fall to be treated as if the company had a virtual property business.

Withdrawal of initial allowance

26810
s 393H CAA 2001

The initial allowance is withdrawn if either of the following occurs:
– the flat no longer qualifies when it is first suitable for letting as a dwelling; or
– the company sells the relevant interest before the flat is first suitable for letting as a dwelling.
Withdrawal is usually **effected** by HMRC raising an assessment.

Writing down allowances

26815
ss 393J – 393L
CAA 2001

The company can claim writing down allowances where all of the following **conditions** are met at the end of the accounting period:
– the company still holds the relevant interest in the flat;
– no long lease has been granted out of the relevant interest for a premium;
– a reduced claim or no claim for IA was made; and
– there is still some expenditure remaining which has not yet been written off.

The applicable **rate** of WDA is of 25% on a straight line basis, although this would be limited where the residue of unrelieved expenditure was less than 25% of the original cost.

Sch 38 para 41
FA 2012

As flat conversion allowances have been **abolished** from 1 April 2013, no writing down allowances will be available after 31 March 2013. Where an accounting period straddles this date, an apportionment of the usual WDA will be required using the following formula:

$$\frac{\text{Number of days in accounting period before 1 April 2013}}{\text{Number of days in accounting period}}$$

---

3. Balancing adjustments

26820
s 393M CAA 2001

A balancing adjustment (i.e. allowance or charge) will be made in the accounting period in which a balancing event occurs, so long as that **event happens within 7 years** of the date when the flat was first suitable for letting as a dwelling.

Where **more than one** balancing event occurs, a balancing adjustment is only made on the first one.

> EXAMPLE   C Ltd buys a restaurant, and converts the upper floors into flats, claiming a full IA.
> The company sells the building 8 years later.
> As this is outside the 7-year time limit, no balancing adjustment is required.

Balancing events

26825
s 393N CAA 2001

A balancing event is any of the following:
– the sale of the relevant interest;
– the grant of a long lease out of the relevant interest for a premium;
– the ending of a lease that is the relevant interest without the lessee acquiring the reversionary interest i.e. lease surrender;
– the demolition or destruction of the qualifying building; or
– the flat ceases to be a qualifying flat.

s 393V CAA 2001

MEMO POINTS   Where a **lease terminates**, the following rules apply:
a. where the lessee remains in possession of the building with the lessor's consent, without a new lease being granted, the lease that has terminated is treated as continuing for as long as the lessee remains in possession;
b. if there was an option in the terminated lease for the lessee to be granted a new lease, and the lessee exercises that option, the new lease is treated as a continuation of the old lease;
c. if the lessor pays a sum to the lessee when the lease terminates, this is treated as a lease surrender by the lessee; and

d. if another lease is granted to a different lessee, and that lessee pays a sum to the original lessee, this is treated as an assignment of the original lease (i.e. the two leases are treated as the same lease).

Deemed proceeds

The following table shows the **value** to be brought into the FCA computation.

26830
ss 393O, 393S,
393U CAA 2001

Disposal event	Disposal value
Sale of the relevant interest	Net sale proceeds
Grant of a long lease	Capital sum involved, or if greater, the amount that would have been paid had the transaction been undertaken on arm's length terms
Ending of lease without lessee acquiring reversionary interest	Where the lessee and the person owning the superior interest are connected (¶25190), the market value of the relevant interest in the flat at the time of the event
Demolition or destruction of flat[1]	Net amount received, plus any insurance or compensation monies
Flat ceases to be a qualifying flat	The market value of the relevant interest at the time of the event
Note: 1. If any **demolition costs** are incurred (and these exceed monies received for the remaining property), they are added to the residue of qualifying expenditure immediately before demolition.	

MEMO POINTS   If **proceeds are only partly attributable** to assets qualifying for FCA, a just apportionment is made.

Computation

The deemed proceeds from ¶26830 need to be compared with the residue of qualifying expenditure immediately before the balancing event.

26835
ss 393Q, 393R
CAA 2001

For this purpose, the **residue** is calculated as follows:
– initial allowances are written off at the time when the flat is first suitable for letting as a dwelling (which might be quite some time after the initial allowance is claimed (¶26800)); and
– writing down allowances are written off at the end of the accounting period.

If:
– there are **no proceeds**, there will be a balancing allowance equal to the residue of the expenditure;
– the residue of **expenditure is greater** than the deemed proceeds, a balancing allowance of the difference will arise;
– there is **no residue of expenditure**, there will be a balancing charge equal to the deemed proceeds; or
– the **proceeds exceed the residue** of expenditure, a balancing charge of the difference will arise.

26840
s 393P CAA 2001

A **balancing charge** cannot exceed the total allowances already given before the balancing event i.e. the sum of the initial allowances and WDA.

EXAMPLE   E Ltd incurs qualifying expenditure of £150,000 and claims 100% initial allowance so the residue is nil.
A couple of years later, the company sells the flat for £180,000.
The balancing charge is restricted to £150,000, being the allowances made, even though the proceeds are greater.

SECTION 5

Land

26890 The allowances which are focused on land are:
- land remediation relief;
- dredging allowances; and
- mineral extraction allowances.

A. Land remediation

26920 Land remediation **relief** (LRR) **applies to** both capital and revenue **expenditure** incurred by a company in bringing back land into productive use which has been blighted by either:
- contamination; or
- long-term dereliction.

The company may claim a deduction of 150% of the qualifying expenditure incurred when making the land usable, and loss-making companies can receive a payment of land remediation tax credit.

The key principle is that an unconnected third party must have caused the contamination or dereliction.

This commentary applies to expenditure incurred since 1 April 2009.

> ⌐MEMO POINTS⌐ A company that is a **partner** of a partnership is within the scope of this relief.

1. Scope

26950 Companies that have acquired contaminated or derelict land, or a major interest in it, and incur qualifying expenditure in making it usable, will be eligible for LRR. If no remediation work is carried out, there is no LRR.

s 1178A CTA 2009

> ⌐MEMO POINTS⌐ 1. **Land** includes buildings on the land.
> 2. The definition of a **major interest** in land covers the following:
> - owning the land outright;
> - being granted a lease of at least 7 years; or
> - being assigned a lease with at least 7 years remaining.

Exclusions

26955
s 1178 CTA 2009

Land remediation relief is not available in the following **situations** (although the expenditure may still qualify for a normal revenue deduction or capital allowances):

Situation	Detail	Reference
Arrangements have been put in place which either create or enhance a claim	This is anti-avoidance legislation to prevent bogus claims or claims being artificially increased Arrangements mean any scheme, agreement or understanding, whether or not legally enforceable Amount of relief is restricted to the amount that would have been available had the company not entered into those arrangements	s 1169 CTA 2009
Cleaning up nuclear sites	Any site which has a nuclear site licence	s 1145B CTA 2009
Foundations for new building	Where land has been disturbed in order to remove the contaminant etc, subsequent buildings may require stronger foundations, but this cost does not qualify	CIRD 61535

Situation	Detail	Reference
Dealing with ground gases arising from natural processes	With the exception of radon, gases present as a result of natural processes, or as a result of the decay of living organisms or their waste products, do not qualify for relief e.g. treating methane, carbon dioxide and hydrogen sulphide present as a result of peat bogs, river or lake sediments	CIRD 61540
Where the company, or a party connected to the company[1] was one of the polluters or allowed the site to become derelict	Any party which is responsible in any way (by action or inaction) for causing the contamination or dereliction, or additional contamination, cannot access the relief, including those who fail to take action to contain the spread of pollution e.g. by failing to take action to stop a leak[2] It is irrelevant whether the action which caused the contamination was acceptable practice at the time e.g. using asbestos in a building However, where a company acquires a site, and subsequently: – existing contamination is spread by movement in the groundwater; – a change in the law, or of recommended accepted levels of contamination, means that the site is deemed to be contaminated; or – previously unsuspected contamination is identified on the site, then the company is not automatically treated as the polluter Not knowing that contamination was present when the site was acquired does not make the company responsible for that contamination when it is later discovered	s 1150 CTA 2009, CIRD 60130
The polluter (or connected party) retains an interest in the land	Where the polluter: – disposes of the legal title to the land, but retains a beneficial interest in it; or – grants a long lease of the site but retains a reversionary interest; or – sells its entire interest in the property, but the sale contract gives the polluter an option to buy it back, or the consideration represents the future value of a subsequent sale of the cleaned-up land	s 1150 CTA 2009
Contamination caused by a tenant	If contamination was already present when the landlord acquired the property from an unconnected person, relief is still available, as long as the polluter does not receive any further income from the land i.e. a slice of the action payment	ss 1150, 1178A CTA 2009

Note:
1. The **connected party** was connected (¶31375) at any of the following times, either when:
– the contamination took place;
– the major interest in the land was acquired; or
– the land remediation work was undertaken by the company.
2. Putting ventilation into an **underground car park** does not qualify for LRR as the polluter is paying for the work, and the contamination is ongoing i.e. the land was not acquired in a contaminated state, and it is the use of the building which is causing the contamination.

Contaminated state

Land or buildings are in a contaminated state if there is contamination present when the land is acquired (except for Japanese Knotweed), usually **as a result of** industrial activity, such that:
– it is causing relevant harm; or
– there is a serious possibility that it could cause relevant harm, or
– it is causing, or there is a serious possibility that it could cause, significant pollution in the groundwater, streams, rivers or coastal waters.

26960
s 1145 CTA 2009

SI 2009/2037

There is a **specific inclusion** of the following contaminants which **do not arise from industrial activity**, and for which no source of contamination need be identified:
– naturally occurring arsenic and arsenical compounds;
– radon, where the level of radon exceeds the Health Protection Agency Action Level, which is 400 becquerels per cubic metre for workplaces and 200 becquerels per cubic metre for domestic properties; and
– Japanese Knotweed (¶26975), which is the only contaminant that need not be present when the land is acquired.

Most of the time planning requirements will make it clear whether the land is contaminated for the purposes of LRR.

MEMO POINTS 1. For this purpose **contaminant excludes**:
– the presence of air and water (although a pollutant may exist in the air or water table, when LRR would potentially be available); and
– living organisms (with the exception of those specified above) or decaying matter from living organisms.

CIRD 61260, 61265

2. **Evidence** of the contaminated land is required, and HMRC will accept the following documents, which are usually included in a preliminary risk assessment or desk study submitted to the local planning authority, provided that the risk assessment has been carried out in accordance with the appropriate guidance:
– National Grid Reference, maps and other details to identify the specific area covered;
– historic maps: it is important to note that the contamination could have been carried into the site from adjoining areas;
– historic photographs;
– previous planning history;
– historical information such as contemporary business directories;
– local history publications or corporate histories; and
– evidence as to the underlying geology.
Where the soil guideline value is exceeded (being a criteria used by the Environment Agency), HMRC will accept that the land is contaminated.

CIRD 61335

3. The **underlying geology** should show whether it is possible that the contamination could have occurred naturally, and if not, it is a fair conclusion that man has caused the contamination. Further, Department of the Environment **Industry Profiles** provide developers, local authorities, and anyone else interested in land contamination, with information on the processes, materials and wastes associated with individual industries, and HMRC will accept these as evidence that contamination has occurred due to a previous industrial use of the site.
For details see flmemo.co.uk/ctm26960.

26965

s 1145(2) CTA 2009;
CIRD 61250

Industrial activities These include:
– mining and quarrying, including extraction of fuels, minerals and oils;
– manufacturing, including fuel processing and production, manufacture of chemicals and man-made fibres, the metal goods, engineering and vehicles industries, and other manufacturing industries;
– supply of electricity, gas and water, the production and distribution of electricity, gas and water; and
– the construction industry.

Contamination may be present as a result of the use of the products of an industrial activity even where the land is **used for other purposes** e.g. asbestos is present as a result of industrial activity (the construction industry), even where the building is used as a shop.

26970

s 1145(4) CTA 2009

Relevant harm is defined as causing any of the following:
– death of living organisms, or significant injury or damage to living organisms;
– significant pollution of controlled waters;
– a significant adverse impact on the ecosystem; or
– structural or other significant damage to buildings or other structures, or interference with buildings or other structures, that significantly compromises their use.

26975

CIRD 61440, 61445

Japanese Knotweed Only infestations which were not **planted** by the company nor allowed to spread by the company are eligible for relief. There is no requirement that the infestation is present when the site is acquired.

The treatment **must not involve** its removal to a landfill site.

HMRC allow relief in cases where the company takes remedial action **as soon as** practically possible after discovering the infestation, and this could include taking appropriate specialist advice which may require any treatment to be delayed until the next growing season.

> EXAMPLE   A Ltd purchased a plot of land that had previously been used for flats, and at the time of acquisition, there was no Japanese Knotweed on the site. However, a couple of years later, it was discovered that Japanese Knotweed had subsequently spread on to the site as a result of fly-tipping. Unfortunately, A Ltd fails to take any action, and it is only when the site is about to be sold a couple of years later that A Ltd removes the infestation which is now covering most of the site. A Ltd is unable to claim LRR as the Japanese Knotweed spread due to the company's failure to take action within a reasonable time.

Long-term dereliction

Land is in a derelict state where both of the following **conditions** are met:
– the land is not in a productive state e.g. it cannot be put to economic use (such as a car park) or social use (for housing or as a site of special scientific interest); and
– it can only be changed into productive use by removing buildings or other structures.

26980
s 1145A CTA 2009

Long term **means** being in a derelict state since 1 April 1998.

> MEMO POINTS   1. **Temporary use** will not jeopardise the derelict status of the land where it is very limited i.e. less than 7 days a year, and the income generated is not substantial.
> 2. HMRC will accept the following as **evidence** that the land was derelict at the time of its acquisition, being appropriate classification:
> – on the National Land Use Database (NLUD), for England; or
> – by the Scottish Vacant and Derelict Land Survey.
> Further, evidence of the land's status at acquisition and since 1998 would include:
> – a survey;
> – insurance cover;
> – empty property business rates;
> – estate agent's literature; or
> – local newspaper articles.

CIRD 62001

CIRD 62030

> EXAMPLE
> 1. The site of a former warehouse has been used as a car park during the last couple of years. B Ltd purchases the site to turn it into offices, but first must remove the foundations and services relating to the former warehouse.
> LRR is not available as the site was in productive use as a car park. If the site had been an overflow car park for a couple of days a year then it would not have been in productive use.
>
> 2. A site next to a river has been vacant for a long time, and C Ltd acquires it for redevelopment. Before work can commence, the flood defences have to be improved.
> The land is not derelict for the purposes of LRR as it can be brought back into productive use without the removal of buildings or other structures.

Interaction between contaminated and derelict land

Whether a site qualifies as derelict or contaminated are separate issues. However, in practice, sites that are derelict are often contaminated as well. For the purposes of LRR, the two issues are dealt with separately.

26985
CIRD 61225

> EXAMPLE   D Ltd acquires the site of a former warehouse that has been derelict since 1996. For redevelopment to take place, the concrete bases for the machinery have to be removed, and contamination has to be contained.
> D Ltd can claim LRR for both the removal of the bases and the containment of the contamination.

---

2. Remediation works

Qualifying remediation activities include the doing of any works or operations **undertaken directly by or on behalf** of the company in order to:

27015
ss 1146, 1146A
CTA 2009

a. prevent, minimise, remedy or mitigate the effects of any harm or pollution of territorial waters;
b. restore the land or waters to their former state; or
c. in the case of derelict land, undertake removal of the following specified items from the land:
– post-tensioned concrete heavyweight construction where stressing is to be carried out on site after casting an in-situ component, or where a series of pre-cast concrete units are to be cast together to form the required member;
– building foundations and machinery bases;
– reinforced concrete pilecaps (concrete structures which combine weight-bearing piles into groups);
– reinforced concrete basements (which requires expensive stability works); and
– redundant services that are located below ground, including all piping, wiring, cabling, equipment, infrastructure or similar relating to gas and water supply, drainage, sewerage, electricity supply and telecommunications.

CIRD 61595

| MEMO POINTS | 1. Qualifying activities include any **preparatory activities** provided:
– they are for the purposes of assessing the condition of the land or waters concerned; and
– the work in respect of the land or waters itself qualifies for the relief.
2. **Abortive expenditure** qualifies for relief, where a company is appraised of all the available options, and decides on a remediation strategy that subsequently proved unsuccessful.

Methods

27020
CIRD 61501

The following methods are often used when cleaning up land which has been contaminated. Note that this list is not exhaustive, and HMRC are aware that new methods are always being developed:

Method	Detail	Reference
Cover systems	Mitigates the effects of the contamination by placing a layer of material over the contaminated ground in order either to: – provide a barrier between the contamination and the areas of use; or – prevent the infiltration of rain and drainage water into the ground to protect controlled waters	CIRD 61505
In-ground barriers and cut-off walls	Isolates the contamination by putting a physical barrier around it Barriers may be built of sheet piles, geomembranes or a cement-based slurry, depending on the requirements of the site	CIRD 61510
Dig and dump	Not allowed for Japanese Knotweed Excavation of contaminated material and its removal to landfill	CIRD 61515
Biological treatment	Involves stimulating the naturally occurring microbial communities or the introduction of other microbes to break down the contaminants Can take place in situ or contaminated material can be excavated and treated either at the site or at an off-site treatment centre	CIRD 61520
Cement based stabilisation/solidification	Cement-based material is used to chemically stabilise and seal off the contaminants May be necessary to use a higher (i.e. more expensive) grade of cement or concrete depending on the contaminant to comply with BS 8500	CIRD 61525

3. Qualifying expenditure

27025
s 1144 CTA 2009;
CIRD 63101

LRR gives an enhanced deduction on qualifying expenditure, which can include revenue costs and capital costs (subject to the necessary election being made (¶27100)).

The expenditure must:
- be incurred on land which is in a contaminated or a derelict state, and only incurred because of that state (this includes additional costs incurred i.e. where the cost of work is increased due to the contamination); and
- be relevant contaminated land remediation or relevant derelict land remediation.

MEMO POINTS **Common additional costs** include:
- greater expense of removing asbestos;
- higher grade fencing around a site; and
- alternative landfill sites which are more expensive.

EXAMPLE

1. E Ltd buys a brownfield site which is contaminated. The company installs a membrane to prevent the contaminants migrating to the surface. E Ltd also imports topsoil and subsoil for the gardens of the residential properties it is building.
The cost of the membrane qualifies for LRR as it is only installed due to the presence of the contaminant.
The topsoil and subsoil would have been used in any event, and so do not qualify for LRR.

2. F Ltd also buys a brownfield site which is contaminated, in order to construct a leisure centre. The company imports topsoil to create a 1200mm capping layer over the contamination, double the depth that F Ltd normally uses to create amenity areas.
Only the extra depth of topsoil qualifies for LRR.

Excluded costs

The following costs cannot qualify for LRR:
- preliminaries;
- any expenditure which is met by a third party, or covered by a subsidy, grant or compensation;
- landfill tax, although any payment to a landfill site operator will qualify; and
- work carried out under a statutory obligation imposed by legislation listed in a Treasury Order e.g. where the local authority requires a company to clean up land.

27030
s 1144 CTA 2009

Note that where a company **engages a contractor** to carry out the remediation work, it is the company who can claim LRR, and not the contractor.

MEMO POINTS 1. **Preliminaries** are costs that are not related to a particular part of the project e.g. site services, security, temporary works, or safety measures. They would be incurred in any event. However, LRR will be available for any increase in costs due to the poor state of the land.
2. If the **grant or subsidy** etc only covers part of the expenditure, the balance qualifies for relief provided it meets all the other conditions (¶27025). Where a payment is not designated against any particular expenditure, it should be allocated on a just and reasonable basis.
3. The types of work arising under a **statutory obligation** include the following:

CIRD 63270

s 1177 CTA 2009;
CIRD 63130

CIRD 63120

Area of statutory obligation	Arising from
Expenditure required on land or buildings adversely affecting the amenity of the neighbourhood	s 215 Town and Country Planning Act 1990
	s 179 Town and Country Planning (Scotland) Act 1997
	art 39 Planning (Northern Ireland) Order 1991
Expenditure incurred on work required for defective premises, dangerous buildings, ruinous and dilapidated buildings and neglected sites	ss 77, 79 Building Act 1984
	art 66 Pollution Control and Local Government (Northern Ireland) Order 1978
	s 28 Building (Scotland) Act 2003
Expenditure on work required for the abatement or prohibition of a nuisance	ss 79 – 82 Environmental Protection Act 1990
	art 65 Pollution Control and Local Government (Northern Ireland) Order 1978
Expenditure incurred on a listed building under a repairs notice	s 43 Planning (Listed Buildings and Conservation Areas) (Scotland) Act 1997
	s 48 Planning (Listed Buildings and Conservation Areas) Act 1990
	art 109 Planning (Northern Ireland) Order 1991

Summary

27035

Type of cost	¶¶
Preparatory activities	¶27040
Staffing	¶27045
Materials	¶27050
Subcontractors	¶27055+
Verification	¶27065

Preparatory activities

27040
ss 1146, 1146A
CTA 2009

Provided the company goes on to carry out the remediation, the costs of the following preparatory activities will qualify for LRR:
– ascertaining the level of contamination in the site itself, any land adjoining it, and any controlled waters affected by that land (i.e. where significant pollution is being caused, or there is a serious possibility of pollution being caused, because the land is in a contaminated state); and
– establishing the nature and condition of structures on a derelict site.

s 1179 CTA 2009

CIRD 63215

MEMO POINTS   1. **Controlled waters** are broadly the territorial waters within the 3 nautical mile limit, coastal waters extending inland, inland waters and ground water.
2. The cost of an **initial desk study** does not qualify for relief as it would have been carried out anyway, although where contamination is a possibility, the costs of further work to establish the level of contamination together with the cost of the risk assessment is qualifying preparatory work.

CIRD 63220

EXAMPLE
1. G Ltd purchases a site for redevelopment, carrying out a desk study to identify potential hazards. This is followed by carrying out further work, including tests, to establish the levels of contamination, and remediation work is then completed to mitigate it.
G Ltd can claim the cost of the further work for LRR.
However, the cost of the desk study is excluded.

2. H Ltd acquires a brownfield site, and initial tests indicate that there is heavy metal contamination which poses a health hazard. However, before carrying out remediation work, H Ltd becomes aware of a new test, and those results show that there is only a low risk of the contamination becoming a danger and so no remedial work is needed.
As no remediation work is undertaken no LRR is available.

Staffing costs

27045
ss 1170, 1171
CTA 2009

Staffing costs **exclude**:
– benefits in kind;
– payments to an employee benefit trust;
– employment costs of secretarial, administrative and support staff; and
– payments under a share incentive scheme.

The following costs, which relate to directors or employees directly and **totally engaged** in the relevant land remediation, will qualify for LRR:
– all earnings consisting of money, paid because of the employment of the director or employee;
– secondary Class 1 NIC paid by the company;
– contributions paid by the company to any pension fund operated for the benefit of directors or employees of the company; and
– expenses (other than benefits in kind) paid to directors or employees to cover expenses that they have paid because of their employment.

Where an individual is directly and actively **engaged** in relevant land remediation for **only part of the total working time** in an accounting period, the following rules apply:

Proportion of working time engaged on land remediation	Employment costs which qualify for LRR
< 20%	None
20% to 80%	Appropriate proportion
> 80%	All

Materials

Materials must be used **directly** in the remediation work e.g. chemicals used to treat Japanese Knotweed.

Hiring of plant or equipment is excluded, although hiring plant with an operator would qualify as paying a subcontractor.

27050
s 1172 CTA 2009;
CIRD 69020

Subcontractors

Relief for payments to **unconnected** subcontractors, including professional advisers who inform the company how to remediate the land, is not subject to any special rules.

27055

If the company and the subcontractor are **connected** persons (¶31375) then any payments must meet the following **conditions** to qualify for LRR:
– the company must physically pay the subcontractor;
– the subcontractor must recognise the whole payment in its profit and loss account, in accordance with GAAP, for an accounting period that ends not more than 12 months after the accounting period in which the contracting company recognises a deduction; and
– all of the subcontractor's relevant expenditure must similarly be brought into account.

27060
s 1175 CTA 2009;
CIRD 63245

The qualifying expenditure is **limited** to the subcontractor's relevant revenue costs of carrying out the land remediation activities, including payments to third parties to carry out that work, which can only include:
– unsubsidised expenditure;
– employee costs; and
– materials.
Note that the subcontractor's capital costs are excluded.

> EXAMPLE A Ltd engages the services of a group company, B Ltd, to construct a residential estate on a site infested with Japanese Knotweed. B Ltd engages an unconnected firm, C Ltd, to remove it. A Ltd can claim LRR in respect of the payment made by B Ltd to C Ltd in respect of staffing or material costs. This is because B Ltd incurred these costs when it arranged for C Ltd to carry out the work on behalf of A Ltd.

Verification work

As a condition of **granting planning permission**, a verification report may be required, to show what work has been carried out and provide evidence that the site has been decontaminated to an acceptable standard.

27065
CIRD 63265

The cost of preparing the verification report is qualifying land remediation expenditure.

---

4. How relief is given

LRR is available for both capital and revenue expenditure, and is given as a 150% deduction against trading profits, or profits from a UK property business. In certain cases a tax credit will be available.

27095
s 1147 CTA 2009

Capital expenditure

To treat qualifying capital expenditure as a deduction in computing taxable profits, the company must make an **election** within 2 years of the end of the accounting period in which the expenditure is incurred.

27100
s 1147 CTA 2009

Note that any capital expenditure which is covered by the election cannot qualify for capital allowances or as a deduction for the purposes of chargeable gains.

Any **pre-trading expenditure** is incurred on the first day of trading or business activity.

Enhanced deduction

27105   The original qualifying expenditure plus an additional 50% is allowed as a deduction.

> EXAMPLE   D Ltd acquires contaminated land, and incurs £100,000 when cleaning it up.
> D Ltd can claim a deduction of £150,000.

Tax credit

27110
ss 1151, 1154
CTA 2009

A company that has a qualifying land remediation **loss** for an accounting period can make a claim to surrender all or part of that loss in return for a payment of 16% of the amount surrendered (known as the land remediation tax credit).

s 1155 CTA 2009;
CIRD 68055

However, a tax credit will **not be paid until** the company has paid any PAYE or Class 1 NIC amounts owing for any payment period (i.e. each month ending on the 5th) ending in that accounting period. Further, if HMRC commence an enquiry into the relevant CTSA return, no payment need be made until the enquiry is concluded, although HMRC may make a provisional payment.

The tax credit itself may be **set against** any corporation tax liability of the company (in which case no payment would be made by HMRC).

ss 1152, 1153
CTA 2009

MEMO POINTS   1. A **qualifying land remediation loss** is the lower of:
a. 150% of the qualifying remediation expenditure; and
b. the unrelieved trading or property loss for the accounting period, calculated in the normal manner but:
– ignoring any losses brought forward or carried back;
– assuming the maximum loss has been set against other income of the accounting period (¶36080); and
– taking into account any actual claims to carry back the loss against profits of earlier accounting periods (¶36100+), or to surrender the loss as group/consortium relief (¶66000+).

s 1156 CTA 2009
s 1157 CTA 2009

2. The tax credit paid to a company is not the company's **income** for any tax purpose.
3. Any qualifying land remediation expenditure, related to the qualifying land remediation loss surrendered, is not an allowable deduction in computing **chargeable gains**.

> EXAMPLE   E Ltd incurs qualifying land remediation expenditure of £50,000 in an accounting period (and claims a further 50% of this expenditure as land remediation relief). After taking other expenses into account, the company has an overall trading loss for the accounting period of £70,000. It makes a claim to surrender the full amount of the land remediation loss in exchange for a payment of land remediation tax credit. No other loss relief or group relief claims for the period were made.
> E Ltd's qualifying land remediation loss is £70,000, being the lower of:
> – 150% of the qualifying land remediation expenditure i.e. £75,000 (50,000 × 1.5); and
> – the company's unrelieved trading loss for the accounting period i.e. £70,000.
> The tax credit payable is £11,200 and no losses can be carried forward to later periods. (70,000 × 16%)

27115
s 1158 CTA 2009

Where a land remediation credit is claimed, the company is deemed to have surrendered the loss such that it is not **available for carry forward** against future profits.

For this purpose, the **amount of the loss surrendered** is usually the whole of the qualifying land remediation loss unless the tax credit is less than the maximum amount that could be claimed. In the latter case, a corresponding proportion (found by grossing up the tax credit by 100/16) of the qualifying land remediation loss for that accounting period is deducted from the loss to be carried forward.

> EXAMPLE   F Ltd is a stand-alone company with a trading loss of £200,000, of which £75,000 is a qualifying land remediation loss. It has no other income or gains in the accounting period. The company claims a payable tax credit of £8,000 and makes no other loss claims.
> The £8,000 tax credit equates to a qualifying land remediation loss of £50,000. (8,000 × 100/16)
> The loss available to carry forward is therefore £150,000. (200,000 – 50,000)

Administration The tax credit must be quantified and **claimed** on the company's CTSA return, and the usual time limit applies (¶25160), although HMRC may allow a late claim. Claims can only be changed or withdrawn by submitting an amended return.

27120
Sch 18 paras 83H
– 83K FA 1998;
CIRD 68030

Interest is payable on the tax credit, and runs from the filing date of the return on which the claim is made to the tax credit payment date.

If a change in circumstances means that a **claim** for a tax credit **has become excessive**, then the company must notify HMRC, and, if possible, submit an amended return. Otherwise, HMRC will open an enquiry or raise a discovery assessment, and the company could be liable to penalties.

Penalties also apply where the company fraudulently or negligently makes a claim, and that claim is incorrect. The maximum penalty payable is the difference between the amount actually claimed and the amount to which the company is entitled in the accounting period.

B. Dredging

Capital expenditure on dredging may qualify for writing down allowances. There is no initial allowance. A balancing allowance may only arise on the cessation of the trade.

27150

1. Scope

Dredging allowances write off capital expenditure incurred on dredging by a company which is carrying on a qualifying trade. The allowances are treated as an expense of the trade.

27180
s 489 CAA 2001

Definition

Dredging must be done **in the interests of** navigation (i.e. improving the waterway or channel for the passage of ships), which **includes**:
– removal of anything forming part of, or projecting from, the sea bed or the floor of any inland water. It does not matter how the removal is done, or whether the item removed is wholly or partly above water; and
– the widening of an inland waterway.

27185
s 484 CAA 2001

Dredging **excludes** normal maintenance work on an existing channel.

Qualifying expenditure

Qualifying expenditure is capital expenditure (less any amount of subsidy or contribution (¶25185)) where either:
– the company is **carrying on** a trade consisting of the maintenance or improvement of the navigation of a harbour, estuary or waterway; or
– the dredging is **for the benefit of** vessels coming to, leaving, or using a dock or other premises occupied by that company for the purposes of its qualifying trade.

27190
s 485 CAA 2001;
CA 80500

> EXAMPLE G Ltd constructs sofabeds for the wholesale market. The company occupies a dock that receives imported raw materials, and ships out the finished products.
> If G Ltd incurs capital expenditure on deepening the dock this would be eligible for dredging allowances.

A third party which makes a **capital contribution** towards a company's dredging expenditure is treated as incurring capital expenditure on dredging and, therefore, the third party can claim dredging allowances.

27195
ss 533, 543
CAA 2001

Qualifying trade

27200
ss 274, 484(2)
CAA 2001

A qualifying trade is a trade or undertaking which falls within either of the categories below:
– consists of the maintenance or improvement of the navigation of a harbour, estuary or waterway; or
– a trade as shown in the table below.

s 486 CAA 2001

> MEMO POINTS 1. Where only **part of a trade satisfies the required conditions**, the expenditure should be apportioned, and the qualifying part of the trade should be treated separately.
> 2. Capital expenditure incurred on dredging before the:
> – **qualifying trade begins**, is deemed to be incurred on the day that the trade commences; and
> – **dock etc is occupied**, is deemed to be incurred on the first day on which both the trade is carried on and occupation occurs.

Activity	Detail	Qualifying trade	Undertakings carried on by way of trade
Manufacturing	Any trade consisting of manufacturing goods or materials	✓	
Processing	Any trade consisting of subjecting goods or materials to a process (this includes repair or maintenance of goods or materials) Excludes: – site preparation (as land is not goods or materials); – testing and inspection of cars for MOTs; – taking photographs; and – accelerating the normal process of growth e.g. plants in greenhouses or chickens in broiler houses	✓	
Storage	Any trade consisting of storing goods or materials: – which are to be used in the manufacture of other goods or materials; – which are to be subjected, in the course of the trade, to any process; – which have manufactured, produced or subjected to a process in the course of a trade and have not yet been delivered to the purchaser; or – on their arrival in any part of the UK from a place outside the UK	✓	
Agricultural	Any trade consisting of: – ploughing or cultivation of land occupied by another; – carrying out any other agricultural operation on land occupied by another, or – threshing another's crops	✓	
Utilities	Including the following: – the generation, transformation, conversion, transmission or distribution of electrical energy; – the supply of water or hydraulic power; or – the provision of sewerage services		✓
Infrastructure	Either: – the design, building, financing or operation of highways; or – a transport, tunnel, bridge, inland navigation or a dock undertaking (including a marina)		✓
Working foreign plantations	Any trade consisting of working land outside the UK used for: – growing and harvesting crops; – husbandry; or – forestry	✓	
Fishing	Any trade consisting of catching or taking fish/shellfish	✓	
Mineral extraction	Any trade consisting of working a source of mineral deposits	✓	

> EXAMPLE A Ltd owns and operates ships, some of which carry freight, whilst the others are used for pleasure cruises. A Ltd occupies a dock.
> If A Ltd incurs capital expenditure on dredging the dock, it must be apportioned between the two different parts of the trade.
> Dredging allowances are only given on the part that is allocated to the freight trade.

2. How allowances are given

Qualifying expenditure is usually written off at a rate of 4% on a straight line basis during the writing down period. Total allowances cannot exceed the amount of the qualifying expenditure.

27230

Writing down period

The writing down period is the 25-year period that **begins** with the accounting period in which the qualifying expenditure was incurred.

27235
s 487 CAA 2001

No allowances are available for an **accounting period** if it **falls outside** the writing down period, even if there is still expenditure which is not written off.

Writing down allowance

Writing down allowances are available provided that qualifying expenditure has been incurred, and all of the following **conditions** are satisfied:
– during that accounting period the company is carrying on the qualifying trade (for the purposes of which the qualifying expenditure was incurred);
– the accounting period is at least partly within the writing down period; and
– no balancing allowance is due for that accounting period.

27240
s 487 CAA 2001

The **rate** of WDA is 4% straight line, assuming a 12-month accounting period.

> MEMO POINTS 1. A **partial claim** can be made (i.e. not the full 4%), although this will mean that not all of the expenditure will be written off during the writing down period.
> 2. The rate is proportionately reduced for a **short accounting period**.
> 3. Where the **accounting period is only partly** within the writing down period, that part is treated as a separate chargeable period for the purposes of the WDA.

3. Cessation of trade

If the trade is permanently discontinued or sold, a balancing allowance will arise, so long as the cumulative allowances do not exceed the qualifying expenditure. There are no balancing charges.

27270
s 488 CAA 2001

Exception

For this purpose, a **deemed cessation** (where the company is no longer within the charge to UK corporation tax in respect of the trade) is not treated as a permanent discontinuance.

27275
s 41 CTA 2009

Sale of the trade

The sale of the trade (i.e. where there is a change of ownership) will result in a balancing allowance **unless**:
– the trade is treated as continuing under a company reconstruction (¶79290+), or on the transfer of a UK business to one or more companies resident in another EU member state;
– the sale is to a connected person; or
– the sole or main benefit of the sale is to obtain a tax advantage.

27280
s 488 CAA 2001

> MEMO POINTS 1. A **connected person sale** is a sale where:
> – the seller is a body of persons and the buyer controls the seller;
> – the buyer is a body of persons and the seller controls the buyer;

– the seller and the buyer are both bodies of persons and another person controls both of them; or
– the buyer and seller are connected persons (¶25190).
2. A sale undertaken to obtain a **tax advantage** would include:
– the obtaining of an allowance or deduction (or a greater one); or
– the avoidance or reduction of a charge.

Balancing allowance

27285　A balancing allowance is available for the accounting period in which the trade is discontinued, and gives relief for any expenditure not yet written off.

It is **computed** by using:

$$E - A$$

where:
– E is the qualifying expenditure; and
– A is all the allowances made up to, and including, the accounting period before the one in which the trade is permanently discontinued. It is irrelevant to whom the allowances were made.

| EXAMPLE | C Ltd incurred capital expenditure on dredging of £25,000 in Year 6. At the end of Year 9, the company sells its trade to E Ltd, an unconnected company. C Ltd's dredging computation shows the following: |

		£	£
Year 6	Addition	25,000	
	WDA	(1,000)	1,000
Year 7	WDV b/fwd	24,000	
	WDA	(1,000)	1,000
Year 8	WDV b/fwd	23,000	
	WDA	(1,000)	1,000
Year 9	WDV b/fwd	22,000	
	Balancing allowance	(22,000)	22,000
		Nil	

C. Mineral extraction

27315
s 394 CAA 2001

Mineral extraction allowances potentially apply to any company which is carrying on a trade of mineral extraction, wherever that trade is located.

1. Scope

27345
s 394 CAA 2001

Allowances are available in respect of qualifying expenditure incurred by a company for the purposes of a mineral extraction trade.

Exclusions

27350　As the company must be carrying on a mineral extraction trade, **lessors** of land containing minerals will not qualify.

Further, the following **costs** are excluded:
a. land on which the mineral deposits are located, or land which gives access to adjacent mineral deposits (even where its value is consequently inflated);
b. works constructed wholly or mainly for the processing of the raw products, unless the process is designed to prepare the raw products for use as such;
c. plant and machinery other than in ¶27365 below; and
d. buildings and structures, either for occupation by workers, or for use as an office (although an office which takes up no more than 10% of the whole will be treated as qualifying).

s 399 CAA 2001

Trade of mineral extraction

A trade of mineral extraction is **defined** as a trade that consists of, or includes the working of, a source of mineral deposits.

27355
s 394 CAA 2001

Mineral deposits include:
– any natural deposits capable of being lifted or extracted from the earth; and
– geothermal energy, whether in the form of aquifers, hot dry rocks or otherwise.

So the following **activities** would qualify:
– sand and gravel extraction;
– hard rock mining;
– oil industry; and
– geothermal energy.

Exploration without extraction is a non-trading, or pre-trading, activity. However, where expenditure is incurred during the exploration phase, and the company subsequently undertakes some form of mineral extraction, relief is available (¶27360).

s 400 CAA 2001;
CA 50130

Qualifying expenditure

The following types of expenditure qualify for relief:

27360
s 395 CAA 2001

Type of cost	Detail	Rate of WDA	Reference
Mineral exploration and access [1]	This is defined as the costs incurred when searching for, or discovering and testing, the mineral deposits of any source, or winning access to any such deposits Costs incurred in gaining access to a deep mine via a shaft until the target mineral is reached Includes expenditure on unsuccessful planning applications (and related appeals) where permission was sought for mineral extraction or access to be undertaken For the treatment of plant acquired, see ¶27365	25%	ss 396, 401 CAA 2001, CA 50230
Acquisition of mineral assets [1]	Mineral asset means: – any mineral deposits; – land comprising mineral deposits; or – any interests in or rights over such deposits or land This category also includes the costs of: – obtaining an option over mineral deposits; – successful planning applications; – production licences; – restoration of the site subsequent to the extraction activities ceasing (¶27370)	10%	ss 397, 398 CAA 2001, CA 50220

Type of cost	Detail	Rate of WDA	Reference
Construction of works	In connection with the working of a source of mineral deposits, as long as they are likely to be of little or no value to the company immediately before the source ceases to be worked Works can include railway lines, roads and jetties at the site of the mineral extraction Where the mineral deposits are located outside the UK, works include the cost of accommodation buildings, utility buildings and welfare works for employees engaged in the extraction trade	25%	ss 414, 415 CAA 2001, CA 50230

Note:
1. Where an item of expenditure could fall under either of these categories, it should be treated as an acquisition of a mineral asset, thereby attracting a lower rate of allowance.

s 404 CAA 2001

MEMO POINTS   1. Where the costs relate to the **acquisition of land and associated mineral deposits**, the element which represents the undeveloped market value of the land is excluded from the qualifying expenditure. This is to ensure that allowances are given on the value of the mineral deposits contained in the land rather than the land itself.
2. For **second-hand assets** see ¶27450+.

27365
ss 402, 426
CAA 2001

Pre-trading expenditure   Where **plant and machinery costs** are incurred during the mineral **exploration and access** phase, and the assets are disposed of before the trade commences, those costs are treated as being incurred on the first day on which the trade of mineral extraction is carried on. A balancing allowance of the costs less any associated income received (i.e. sale, insurance, salvage or compensation monies) will arise (¶27420).

Other types of costs incurred during the exploration and access phase are relieved under the normal rules (¶27360).

MEMO POINTS   1. **Disposed of** includes sold, destroyed or abandoned.
2. If the mineral **exploration and access activity ceases** before the first day of trading (i.e. when extraction actually begins), only expenditure incurred within 6 years prior to the date of trading is eligible for relief.

27370
ss 416, 418, 430
CAA 2001

Restoration costs   Where the **company is continuing its trade**, but capital restoration costs are incurred after the cessation of extraction activity at a particular mineral deposit, these will normally qualify for writing down allowances. A further balancing allowance will normally be due in respect of any unrelieved qualifying expenditure once the restoration of the site is complete.

Where the **company completely ceases its trade** of mineral extraction, restoration costs (net of any receipts received) are qualifying expenditure provided that they:
– are incurred within the 3 years following the last day that the trade was carried on;
– have not yet been relieved; and
– would have been qualifying expenditure had the trade continued.

Qualifying expenditure is treated as incurred on the last day of trading, and is relieved in full as a balancing allowance.

2. How allowances are given

27400

Allowances are given on each individual item of expenditure, which often results in balancing adjustments.

CA 50410

HMRC state that they will not object if assets are grouped together for computational convenience, provided that:
– individual sources are dealt with separately; and
– the costs of acquiring mineral assets are distinguished from other expenditure.

ss 416A – 416E
CAA 2001

MEMO POINTS   Certain **oil companies** (with a ringfenced trade) may qualify for a 100% FYA on their qualifying expenditure, which excludes the costs of acquiring a mineral asset.

Giving effect to allowances

Any allowances or balancing charges arising from the MEA rules are treated as expenses and income respectively of the trade.

27405
s 432 CAA 2001

Writing down allowances

Allowances are **claimed on** the balance of unrelieved qualifying expenditure remaining after any proceeds arising from part disposals have been accounted for. Where the proceeds exceed the balance, a balancing charge will arise, and no further WDA will be due.

27410
s 418 CAA 2001

The **rate** of WDA is 25%, unless the expenditure is on the acquisition of a mineral asset, when it is 10%.

Disposals

Proceeds from a disposal are **recognised** where an asset ceases to be permanently used for the purposes of the trade. The receipt is brought into account for the accounting period related to the disposal or cessation of use.

27415
ss 420 – 424
CAA 2001

The **value** of the disposal mirrors the rules for plant and machinery allowances (¶26100), and cannot exceed the original cost incurred. Where assets qualifying for mineral extraction allowances are disposed of together with other non-qualifying assets, a just and reasonable apportionment of the proceeds should be undertaken.

For a **part disposal**, the company may choose whether to claim a balancing allowance, or deduct the disposal receipt from the balance of qualifying expenditure (so long as the disposal is not made to a mineral trader).

CA 50470

MEMO POINTS 1. **Permanent cessation of use** includes:
– a sale;
– abandonment or dismantling;
– destruction;
– using the asset for development which is outside the terms of a development order, or where the development was not started before the asset was acquired;
– a company ceasing to be resident in the UK through a permanent establishment; and
– compliance with restoration criteria as set out in planning permission documents etc.
2. Any **capital sum** reasonably attributable to qualifying expenditure is brought into account as a disposal receipt.
3. Where **proceeds exceed historic cost**, a chargeable gain may arise (¶30000+).
4. If any **demolition costs** are incurred (and these exceed monies received for the remaining property), these are added to the residue of qualifying expenditure immediately before demolition.

s 430 CAA 2001

s 425 CAA 2001

s 433 CAA 2001

Balancing allowances

The following table summarises the occasions when a balancing allowance will arise:

27420

Situation	Detail	Reference
Pre-trading expenditure	Where plant and machinery costs are incurred during the mineral exploration and access phase (¶27365), a balancing allowance of the costs less any associated income received (i.e. sale, insurance, salvage or compensation monies) will arise Where pre-trading expenditure is incurred and exploration etc ceases before the first day of trading, a balancing allowance will arise	s 426 CAA 2001
Giving up exploration, search or inquiry	Qualifying expenditure was incurred on mineral exploration and access, which is then aborted before the mineral deposits were ever worked	s 427 CAA 2001
Disposal of an asset	Where proceeds less than historic cost	s 430 CAA 2001
Buildings for benefit of employees overseas (¶27360) ceasing to be used	Where the mineral deposits are located outside the UK, a balancing allowance will be available for buildings which are no longer used for the mineral extraction trade	s 429 CAA 2001

Situation	Detail	Reference
Company permanently ceases to work a particular mineral deposit, without ceasing to trade	Balancing allowance will arise in respect of unrelieved qualifying expenditure on: – mineral exploration and access relating solely to those deposits; or – the acquisition of a mineral asset consisting of those deposits or any part of them. Where two or more mineral assets derive from a single asset, this applies only when all the relevant mineral deposits cease to be worked Further balancing allowance may arise on the completion of restoration (¶27370)	s 428 CAA 2001
Discontinuance of trade	Where mineral extraction trade completely ceases	s 431 CAA 2001

3. Second-hand assets

27450   The allowances available to the buyer of a second-hand asset will be restricted where the vendor, or any previous owner, incurred the expense of the asset for the purposes of a mineral extraction trade.

Restriction

27455
ss 407, 411
CAA 2001

CA 50630

Broadly, the buyer's qualifying expenditure is restricted to the vendor's residue i.e. the vendor's qualifying expenditure less net allowances given to him.

Where the buyer's asset is **derived from one or more assets** of the vendor, the buyer's qualifying expenditure is determined by reference to just and reasonable apportionments of both:
– the vendor's qualifying expenditure; and
– any balancing allowances given to or balancing charges made on the vendor.

Vendor's situation	Qualifying expenditure for buyer
No allowances claimed	Lesser of: – buyer's expenditure; and – vendor's qualifying expenditure
Balancing charge	
Balancing allowance	Lesser of: – buyer's expenditure; and – vendor's residue i.e. the vendor's qualifying expenditure less the total of all allowances claimed in respect of that expenditure (as reduced by any balancing charges)
Allowances claimed	

Amounts qualifying for allowances

27460
ss 407, 409, 411
CAA 2001

The buyer's expenditure should be **allocated** on a just and reasonable basis between:
– mineral exploration and access; and
– other mineral assets.

The method of allocation depends on whether the **vendor** was:
a. carrying on a mineral extraction trade, when the lower of the following is to be allocated to exploration and access (attracting WDA at 25%), with the remainder attracting WDA at 10%:
– the proportion of the buyer's expenditure corresponding to the vendor's expenditure on mineral exploration and access; and
– the vendor's expenditure on mineral exploration and access which can be attributed to the asset acquired by the buyer; or
b. not carrying on a mineral extraction trade, when the amount allocated to exploration and access is the same value as incurred by the vendor (as represented by the asset acquired).

CHAPTER 2

Acquiring and holding intangible fixed assets

28000   Whilst it is more usual for a company to acquire intellectual property rather than create it itself, all intellectual property tends to have a finite life, beyond which its value becomes negligible.

There is a strong link between research and development activity (which requires extensive funds but can yield significant tax relief), and the eventual creation of valuable intellectual property (the value of which would be uncertain at the outset of the project).

For details of the various tax incentives for research and development activity see ¶78000+.

Comment   Intellectual property is often acquired via shares in a company, which gives the vendor relief in the form of the substantial shareholdings regime (¶32090+). However, purchasers are more likely to prefer acquiring intellectual property directly, as tax relief is available under the intangibles regime.

SECTION 1

Scope

Accounting classification

28050
FRS 10;
FRSSE;
IAS 38

For accounting purposes, intangible assets are **defined** as identifiable assets that do not have a physical substance, but where the company has access to future economic benefits generated by the asset, either through custody or legal protection of the asset.

Intangible assets can either be purchased separately, as part of a business acquisition, or developed internally by the business.

Under GAAP only intangible assets capable of separate **recognition** can be capitalised (usually at cost). The cost of developing intangible assets internally is usually not capitalised, but charged as an expense to the profit and loss account as it is incurred. The exceptions are intangible assets that are clearly identifiable and have a readily ascertainable market value.

s 396 CA 2006   Intangible fixed assets fall into the following **categories**, each requiring classification in order to determine the appropriate accounting treatment and disclosures:
– development costs;
– concessions, patents, licences, trade marks and similar rights and assets; and
– goodwill.

28055   **Goodwill**   This may be purchased or generated internally, and only purchased goodwill is recognised on the balance sheet, being the difference between the cost of an acquired entity and the aggregate fair values attributed to the individual identifiable assets and liabilities acquired. Usually, positive goodwill arises i.e. when the acquisition cost exceeds the fair value.

Goodwill is **distinguished from other assets** because of the following characteristics:
– valuations of goodwill are subjective;
– goodwill cannot be sold as an asset separately from the rest of the business; and
– there is no reliable correlation between goodwill and the costs incurred in creating it.

Goodwill is generated through a number of factors, such as the expertise of the workforce, product reputation, or location. The factors that generate goodwill also make it difficult to value objectively.

> MEMO POINTS   **Negative goodwill** occurs when the acquisition cost is less than the fair value of the identifiable assets because either:
> – the seller requires a quick sale and has sold at a "bargain" price;
> – the purchase price has been reduced to take account of future expected costs such as reorganisation costs; or
> – the seller decides to divest of a business that no longer fits with the strategic direction of the company.
> Negative goodwill can also arise where an acquired business is expected to generate losses in the immediate future.

28060   **Amortisation**   As with other fixed assets, the cost less the asset's expected residual value should be amortised over its expected useful economic life.

There is a rebuttable presumption that the **useful economic life** of goodwill and intangibles will not exceed 20 years. Where certain conditions are met, a longer economic life may be used.

Impairment   There is a requirement for annual impairment **reviews** for intangible assets and goodwill amortised over a period of 20 years or more, or with indefinite useful economic lives. Further, a special first-year impairment review should be undertaken for goodwill and intangible assets relating to new business acquisitions.

28065
FRS 11

Where an impairment **loss** is recognised, for instance through a deterioration in the quality of service provided, the remaining useful economic life and residual value should also be reviewed, and, where appropriate, revised. The new carrying amount should be amortised over the revised estimate of the asset's useful economic life. The reduction in the carrying amount should be charged to the profit and loss account.

Tax classification

For tax purposes, intangible fixed assets are assets **used** on a continuing basis for the company's activities (whether capitalised in the accounts or not), including intellectual property located in the UK and overseas such as:
- patents;
- trademarks;
- know-how;
- copyright or design rights;
- database rights;
- licences (e.g. mobile phone licences);
- brands;
- domain names;
- customer lists;
- plant breeders' rights;
- registered designs;
- royalties;
- agricultural quota;
- payment entitlements under the single payment scheme for farmers;
- franchises; and
- telecommunication rights.

28070
ss 712 – 714
CTA 2009

Note that the asset may have commercial, industrial, or some other economic value.

Goodwill   **HMRC** have recently issued **guidance** on the apportionment of goodwill for transactions involving the sale of a business run from trade-related premises, such as public houses, cinemas, restaurants, care homes, petrol stations or hotels. When a business operated from a trade-related property is sold as a going concern, the sale price usually includes an element of goodwill.

28075

The **value** of this goodwill (along with the other assets acquired) will depend on the facts of the case. In general, companies are now being advised to take an accounting-based approach when calculating goodwill, as opposed to simply interpreting previous legal rulings, which involves taking the following **steps**:
a. estimate the market value of all the tangible assets together as an operational entity;
b. identify the sum attributable to goodwill and any other intangible assets included in the sale by deducting the existing use value of the property, licences and chattels from the sale price (or market value) of the business as a going concern;
c. identify the sum attributable to the chattels by estimating their value to an incoming purchaser;
d. identify the sum attributable to the property by deducting the value of the chattels; and then
e. stand back and consider whether the answer produced is reasonable in the particular circumstances of the case.

Further information can be found in the HMRC practice note at flmemo.co.uk/ctm28075.

Comment   HMRC are currently debating these issues with the CIOT and other interested parties but, so far, a consensus has failed to emerge.

Which set of rules?

28080   The **current tax regime** was introduced on 1 April 2002, and broadly **applies** to assets:
– created by the company on or after this date; and
– acquired on or after this date from an unrelated party (as assessed at the asset's acquisition).

The intention behind this regime is to mirror very closely the entries in accounts prepared under GAAP, although there are exceptions.

For assets which **existed before 1 April 2002**, or have been acquired from a related party who held them on that date, the old rules, which are dictated by the kind of asset concerned, continue to apply.

For this purpose, an asset which is **internally generated** by a business which was in existence before 1 April 2002 will be subject to the old rules.

MEMO POINTS   For details of the new **patent box** regime, available from 1 April 2013, see ¶29235+.

28085
s 835 CTA 2009

Related parties   The following table shows all instances where a company and another party are related. Note that the related party relationship continues regardless of any administration, liquidation or other insolvency proceedings or equivalent arrangements that may affect any party.

Identity of parties	Related if	Detail
Both companies	One controls the other	Control is the power of a person to secure that the affairs of a company are carried out in accordance with his wishes
	One has a major interest in the other	Major interest means that a person and another person together have control, and each person controls at least 40% of the relevant rights and powers
	Members of the same 75% group	See ¶65090+
Both under control of same person	Unless other party is a public body[1]	Control is the power of a person to secure that the affairs of a company are carried out in accordance with his wishes
Company is close	Other party is a participator or an associate of a participator	A company is basically close where it is controlled either by five or fewer shareholders or by any number of its directors. See ¶78050 for full details A participator is any person having an interest in the capital or income of the company, specifically including a person who: – possesses or is entitled to acquire issued share capital or voting rights in the company; – is a loan creditor of the company; – possesses or is entitled to acquire a right to receive or participate in distributions of the company, or in any amounts payable by the company (in cash or kind) to loan creditors by way of premium or redemption; or – is entitled to secure that income or assets (whether present or future) of the company will be applied directly or indirectly for their benefit For associates see ¶75390+

Note:
1. A **public body** is any of the following:
– the Crown;
– a Minister of the Crown or a government department (and Northern Ireland equivalents);
– the Ministers of the Scottish Parliament;
– the National Assembly of Wales;
– a foreign sovereign power; or
– an international organisation i.e. where members are at least two sovereign powers, or the governments of two or more sovereign powers.

SECTION 2

Intangible assets regime

A. Scope

To come within the intangible assets regime, the asset must not be specifically excluded (¶28165) and must:

a. satisfy the asset conditions; and

b. generally be created or acquired from an unrelated party after 31 March 2002.

For the details of how the regime affects assets acquired from **related parties** see ¶28820+.

For details of how the controlled foreign company rules treat intellectual property held overseas see ¶90780+.

28135

---

1. Exclusions

The following table shows all assets which are excluded from the intangible asset regime. Note that options or other rights to acquire or dispose of an excluded asset are themselves excluded.

In general, assets in existence prior to 1 April 2002 (¶28240+), and remaining within the same economic family, are also excluded.

For royalties and other situations which are subject to special tax rules see ¶28260+.

28165
ss 800 – 802
CTA 2009

Excluded assets	Reference
Rights over tangible assets i.e. either: – enjoyed by virtue of an estate, interest or right over land; or – rights in relation to tangible movable property	s 805 CTA 2009
Intangible assets that were previously accounted for as tangible and in respect of which capital allowances have been claimed e.g. website where IAS is then adopted	s 804 CTA 2009
Oil licences	s 809 CTA 2009
Financial assets i.e. those accounted for under the loan relationship, derivatives, or insurance contracts rules See ¶28210 for options, futures and contracts for differences	s 806 CTA 2009
Any of the following: – shares or other rights in the profits or in the winding up of a company (or in its governance); – rights under a trust; and – the interest of a partner in a partnership, although the exclusion does not apply to the extent that the accounting treatment is to look through the trust or partnership to the underlying intangible asset	s 807 CTA 2009
Assets held for non-commercial or non-business purpose	s 803 CTA 2009
Assets held for purposes outside the charge to corporation tax i.e. a non-resident company holds intangible assets that are used for purposes outside any UK permanent establishment	s 803 CTA 2009
Assets representing production expenditure on films	s 808 CTA 2009

Assets subject to special tax rules

28170 The following table summarises assets and items which are not within the intangibles regime as a result of being taxed under other rules:

Asset	Detail	Items within intangibles regime	Reference
Computer software that is treated as part of the cost of related hardware	Software development costs that are directly attributable to bringing a computer system or other computer-operated machinery into working condition for its intended use within the business	Royalties	s 813 CTA 2009
Represents capital expenditure by a company on computer software in respect of which an irrevocable election has been made	Election can be made to preserve capital allowances, which must: – specify the expenditure to which it relates; and – be submitted in writing to HMRC within 2 years of the end of the accounting period in which the expenditure was incurred	– royalties – receipts not recognised under the capital allowances rules, including any on asset's realisation	s 71 CAA 2001, s 815 CTA 2009
Represents expenditure on research and development	See ¶78000+ for tax relief	– royalties; – receipts recognised as they accrue; – debits on reversal of any of those receipts; and – realisation of the asset (ignoring any R&D expenditure when deducting cost)	s 814 CTA 2009
Held for the purposes of a mutual trade[1] or business	Assets remain subject to chargeable gains rules	Royalties	s 810 CTA 2009
Held for life insurance business		– royalties; and – computer software	s 902 CTA 2009
Representing the production or acquisition or the master version of a sound recording or film	Film criteria are as follows, either: – production costs of the master version of a film where the principal photography began before 1 January 2007; or – acquisition costs of the master version of a film before 1 October 2007 whose principal photography began before 1 January 2007	Royalties	ss 811, 812 CTA 2009

Note:
1. Where a company either:
– starts to use an asset for a mutual trade, a deemed disposal will occur (and there is no deferral mechanism (¶28780+)); or
– ceases to use an asset for a mutual trade, the provisions of ¶28790 apply.

2. Asset conditions

The asset conditions require an asset to be either: **28200**
– goodwill, as the term is used for accounting purposes; or
– an intangible fixed asset.

Comment The **distinction** between goodwill and other intangibles is not important for tax purposes e.g. whether the value of a business resides in its goodwill or customer lists.

Goodwill

Goodwill is defined under GAAP (¶28055), and for the purposes of the intangibles regime,   **28205**
goodwill **includes** internally generated goodwill (¶28300), but **excludes** goodwill which is   s 715 CTA 2009
accounted for by a holding company of a group when preparing consolidated accounts.

Other intangibles

Other intangibles **include** intellectual property and internally generated intangible assets.   **28210**
There is no requirement for an asset to appear on a company's balance sheet. However,   ss 712, 713
assets acquired as dealing or trading stock, and prepaid expenses, are not intangible fixed   CTA 2009
assets.

Fungible assets (i.e. those which can be dealt in without identifying the particular assets   s 858 CTA 2009
involved) of the same kind, held by the same company in the same industry, are treated as
one single asset (e.g. milk quota in the farming industry), so that each acquisition of milk
quota is treated as further expenditure on the same asset, and any disposal is treated as a
part disposal.

Options and other rights (e.g. futures) to acquire or dispose of an intangible are treated as
a fixed asset, even though they may not be of the required duration.

> ⌐MEMO POINTS⌐ 1. Where the **subject matter** of an option or other right is partly an intangible fixed
> asset and **partly another asset**, the rules for intangibles and derivatives contracts (¶16775) will
> apply to each asset respectively, and a just and reasonable apportionment will be required.
> 2. A **contract for differences**, where the subject matter is an intangible asset, is taxed under the
> derivative rules.
> 3. For the rules relating to **fungible assets held before 1 April 2002** see ¶28270.
> 4. **Finance leases** of intangible assets (including hire purchase and conditional sale contracts)   SI 2002/1967
> are specifically treated as intangible assets in the hands of the lessor.

3. When created or acquired

The intangibles regime **applies to** intellectual property: **28240**
– acquired after 31 March 2002 from an unrelated party (as tested at the time of acquisition),   s 882 CTA 2009
irrespective of the date of creation by the other party;
– created by the company after 31 March 2002; and
– acquired after 31 March 2002 from a related party (¶28085) in certain circumstances.

For this purpose the **date** of acquisition is when the expenditure is incurred for accountancy   s 883 CTA 2009
purposes, unless:
– the asset would qualify for capital allowances, when it is the date when an unconditional
obligation to pay arises; or
– the expenditure does not qualify for any form of tax relief against income under the law
as it was before 1 April 2002, and under the capital gains rules the asset would have been
disposed of and acquired prior to 1 April 2002.

For creation see ¶28300.

There are **exceptions** relating to:
– transfers at no gain/no loss for capital gains purposes;
– royalties; and
– reinvestment relief (¶28565).

ss 897, 905
CTA 2009

> MEMO POINTS 1. Except for internally generated goodwill, **expenditure** incurred on an item of intellectual property **both before and after** 1 April 2002 is treated as two separate assets, and the amounts incurred post-31 March 2002 fall within the intangibles regime. The expenditure should be apportioned on a just and reasonable basis e.g. based on time.
> 2. Dates are irrelevant in respect of the following assets, which were already treated as revenue items for accounting periods prior to 1 April 2002:
> – **telecommunications** rights and licences; and
> – syndicate capacity at **Lloyd's**.

a. Exceptions

Royalties

28260
s 714 CTA 2009

For this purpose, a royalty is **defined** as income in respect of the enjoyment or exercise of rights that constitute an intangible fixed asset.

Royalties come within the intangibles regime regardless of the **date** that the intellectual property was created or acquired, subject to certain transitional rules.

> MEMO POINTS The following **transitional rules** apply (to ensure no double taxation):
> – where the royalty was taxed before 1 April 2002, it will not be taxed again i.e. it is irrelevant when it is recognised in the accounts; and
> – if not already taxed before 1 April 2002, but also recognised for accounting purposes before 1 April 2002, the payment is deemed to be received for tax purposes on 1 April 2002.

No gain/no loss transfers

28265
s 892 CTA 2009

Most no gain/no loss transfers involve related parties. However, in certain situations (e.g. a transfer of trade), the parties may not be related, and so a special override is required **to avoid** the transferee **gaining an advantage** by being able to amortise an asset value which was not taxed on the transferor (as it was transferred at a tax neutral value under the capital gains code).

In such a case, the asset remains outside the intangibles regime, and so the capital gains rules continue to apply.

Fungible assets

28270
ss 890, 891
CTA 2009

Where **additions** to fungible assets are made both **pre- and post-1 April 2002**, the two amounts of expenditure are treated completely separately when considering the tests at ¶28240.

When some of the fungible assets are **sold**, the disposal must be matched first with the assets outside the intangibles regime.

CIRD 11780

There is an anti-avoidance rule where **additions** are made which **replace pre-April 2002** assets, so that additions are to be identified as far as possible with assets realised within 30 days before or 30 days after the acquisition. For this purpose assets realised earlier are to be identified before assets realised later, and assets acquired earlier before assets acquired later.

b. Detail

Acquisitions from related parties

28290
s 882 CTA 2009

To be within the intangibles regime, the asset must either have been:
a. already subject to the intangibles regime in the hands of the transferor (i.e. a taxable credit arose on the asset's disposal (ignoring reliefs and tax neutral transfers));

b. acquired from a person who in turn acquired the asset after 31 March 2002 from a sufficiently unrelated transferor; or

c. created (by any party) on or after 1 April 2002.

HMRC will rebuff any argument that goodwill is created through **synergies** achieved on merging a business acquired with an existing business. HMRC's view is that goodwill:

– includes internally generated goodwill;

– is neither created by the purchaser on acquisition nor created when recognised in the purchaser's accounts; and

– recognised by the purchaser is the same asset as that disposed of by the vendor.

HMRC Brief 25/11

> ☐ MEMO POINTS ☐ Condition **b.**, where Company A acquires the asset from an independent party (C) via a related party (B), means that all of the following criteria must be met:
> – B acquired the asset after 31 March 2002 from C;
> – C is not a related party of Company A at the time of the asset's acquisition by Company A; and
> – where either B or C (or both) is a company, one must not be a related party of the other at the time B acquired the asset from C.
> If the disposal by B is at no gain/no loss see ¶28265.

CIRD 11640

> ☐ EXAMPLE ☐ In 2003, A Ltd purchased the goodwill of another group company, B Ltd (which had been in business before 1 April 2002 but had never recognised any goodwill in its accounts), and claimed a deduction for amortisation, treating the goodwill as a post-April 2002 intangible fixed asset. A Ltd's contention was that the goodwill was only created when it capitalised the goodwill on its own balance sheet after the acquisition.
> HMRC rejected the claim on the grounds that the goodwill had been created by B Ltd before 1 April 2002.
> It was held that B Ltd had sold goodwill to A Ltd in 2003, which was an asset which had already been brought into existence before it was transferred. The fact that A Ltd had applied the correct accounting treatment did not mean that the goodwill either came into existence, or was a different asset to that held by B Ltd, after the acquisition. *Greenbank Holidays Ltd v HMRC [2011]*

Anti-avoidance Special rules apply for credits and debits, accruing on or after 5 December 2005, to prevent certain assets falling within the intangibles regime as a result of transfers between related parties involving assets:

a. whose **value is derived** in whole or in part from a pre-April 2002 asset held by the transferor or a related party. In this case, either the whole asset, or the relevant part (which is treated separately for the purposes of these rules), is itself treated as a pre-April 2002 asset; or

b. acquired directly or indirectly (whatever the timing) **as a result of** a disposal of a pre-April 2002 asset held by a related party. A classic example would be a disposal of a pre-April 2002 asset to a third party, and the acquisition by the company of a different asset from the same third party.

28295
ss 893 – 895
CTA 2009

Internally generated assets

In respect of internally generated assets, **other than** those previously eligible for capital allowances, the following rules apply:

– **expenditure** after 31 March 2002 does not create a new asset, and does not fall within the intangibles regime if the intellectual property was created before 1 April 2002 (i.e. held by the company or by a related party before 1 April 2002). It is a question of fact whether expenditure incurred after 31 March 2002 is on the creation of a new asset or the enhancement of a pre-April 2002 asset; and

– internally generated **goodwill** is treated as created before 1 April 2002 if the business in question had been begun by the company, or by a related party, before that date.

Internally generated intellectual property, that already **qualifies for capital allowances** (e.g. computer software), can either enter the regime or continue to be within the capital allowances rules (¶25110+).

28300

s 885 CTA 2009

s 884 CTA 2009

B. Amounts

28330 All of the profits and losses relating to intangible assets are subject to corporation tax as income and expenses respectively, no matter whether the company treats them as revenue or as capital in its accounts.

The taxable amounts usually reflect the figures in the accounts, and expenditure is known as debits whilst income is known as credits.

Accounting practice

28335
s 716 CTA 2009

There is heavy reliance on the company accounts, as the debits and credits that are included in a corporation tax computation essentially mirror those that are computed for accounts purposes, **providing** an acceptable method has been adopted i.e. UK or International GAAP. Note that this also explains the emphasis on period of account, rather than accounting period.

Most taxable items will **appear in** the company's profit and loss account, but where appropriate, items in the statement of total recognised gains and losses (or statement of changes in equity where IAS apply) should also be taken into account.

> ⌐MEMO POINTS⌐ 1. Since 1 January 2005 listed companies are required to use **international accounting standards** (IAS) for the preparation of consolidated accounts (other companies can choose to adopt IAS).

s 717 CTA 2009

> 2. Where the accounts **do not comply with GAAP**, the company will still be taxed on the amounts which would have been shown had GAAP-compliant accounts been compiled. For example, amounts may be incorrectly debited or credited in an earlier period when they should be included in the accounts for a later period. The later intangibles computations should be prepared on the basis that correct accounting was used for the earlier period. This is the case even if, viewed in isolation, the accounts for the later period might be said to be in accordance with GAAP.

s 718 CTA 2009;
CIRD 30080

> 3. In determining whether GAAP has been properly and consistently applied, HMRC may look at any **consolidated accounts** drawn up in respect of the group of which the taxpayer company is a member, especially with regard to any view taken of the useful life or economic value of an asset. However, consolidated accounts will not be used in this way where they are prepared under foreign law and the accounting treatment substantially diverges from that under GAAP.

Anti-avoidance

28340
s 864 CTA 2009

Where there are arrangements, which have as their object tax avoidance, debits and credits are to be taxed as if no arrangements existed.

> ⌐MEMO POINTS⌐ 1. For this purpose arrangements **include** any scheme, agreement or understanding, whether or not legally enforceable.
> 2. **Tax avoidance** occurs where the company avoids having to bring into account a credit, or is able to reduce the amount of the credit brought into account.

---

1. Debits

28370 The accounting entries leading to deductible debits are either:
– expenditure relating to the intangible asset; or
– the reversal of previous accounting gains.

Expenditure

28375
s 727 CTA 2009

Qualifying expenditure is incurred for any of the following **purposes**, and it is irrelevant whether the amount would normally be a capital or revenue item, or whether the expenditure is abortive:
– acquiring, creating or establishing title to an intangible asset;
– maintaining, preserving, enhancing or defending title to an intangible asset; or
– by way of royalties for the use of an intangible asset.

The **accounting entries** which would result in a debit are as follows:
- revenue items taken to the profit and loss account as they accrue;
- accounting losses (e.g. amortisation debits) in respect of capitalised expenditure on an intangible asset; and
- amounts deducted from the proceeds on the realisation of an intangible asset (¶28485+).

  MEMO POINTS   1. Expenditure on **tangible assets** which is treated as capital expenditure (¶25060), even where incurred for one of the purposes above, is not within the intangibles regime.
2. Where expenditure is incurred only **partly for a qualifying purpose**, a just and reasonable apportionment of the amount should be made.

Revenue items

Expenditure on an intangible asset gives rise to a deductible debit for the period of account in which it is written off to the company's profit and loss account, so long as it does not represent previously capitalised costs. Where transactions are **not undertaken at arm's length** a transfer pricing adjustment is required (¶70000+).

28380
s 728 CTA 2009

The following table summarises those costs where there are restrictions on the deductibility.

Expenditure relates to	Detail	Reference
Entertaining and gifts	Complete disallowance of this type of cost (¶14585)	s 865 CTA 2009
Crime	Complete disallowance where company makes a payment which either: - constitutes a criminal offence; or - is induced by blackmail or extortion	
Hire of cars	For leases entered into: - before 1 April 2009, restriction applies where car cost more than £12,000; or - on or after 1 April 2009, restriction applies where car has CO_2 emissions exceeding 130g/km [1]	
Employer financed retirement benefit schemes	Broadly, payments made to an unapproved pension scheme (¶14890)	
Delayed payment of pension contributions	Deductible debit is allowed when payment is actually made (regardless of entries in accounts (¶14910))	s 868 CTA 2009
Delayed payment of remuneration	If remuneration remains unpaid more than 9 months after the accounting period end, it is disallowed in that accounting period A deduction is then allowed in the accounting period of payment (¶14615)	ss 866, 867 CTA 2009
Delayed payment of royalties to related parties	Where a royalty is payable by a company to, or for the benefit of, a related party (¶28085) and it is: - not paid within 12 months of the end of the period of account in which it is charged against profits; and - not at some time fully brought into account for tax purposes by the recipient, a deductible debit will only arise when the royalty is actually paid	s 851 CTA 2009
Bad debts	Allowable bad debts are either those which: - give rise to an impairment loss (¶16435+); or - have been released as part of a statutory insolvency agreement	s 869 CTA 2009
Note: 1. For expenditure prior to 1 April 2013 the limit was 160g/km.		

Capitalised expenditure

28385   The tax deductions relating to the capitalised cost of an intangible asset are normally based on the sums written off in the accounts i.e. through amortisation or impairment. However, a company can **irrevocably elect** to write off an asset for tax purposes at a fixed rate of 4% per annum.

28390
s 729 CTA 2009

Accounts basis   In general, the amortisation charge in the profit and loss account is an allowable debit, assuming the accounts have been prepared under GAAP.

However, where the **cost** of the asset for the purposes of accounting and tax **is not the same** (e.g. due to reinvestment relief), the amortisation charge will need to be adjusted using the following **formula**:

$$\text{Amortisation charge} \times \frac{\text{Tax cost}}{\text{Accounting cost}}$$

where:
– amortisation charge is the amount charged to the profit and loss account as amortisation (or impairment);
– tax cost is expenditure on the asset that is recognised for tax purposes (or tax written down value for subsequent periods); and
– accounting cost is expenditure on the asset capitalised for accounting purposes.

s 744 CTA 2009   <u>MEMO POINTS</u>   1. Following the **part realisation** of an asset, the tax written down value is reduced to an appropriate proportion as shown by the following formula:

$$\text{Tax written down value} \times \frac{\text{Accounting value of part retained}}{\text{Accounting value prior to disposal}}$$

s 857 CTA 2009   2. Where the **accounting cost is nil** (e.g. where an asset is transferred at market value but the recipient only shows a nil value in the accounts), the amortisation charge and cost are deemed to be the amounts that would have arisen had market value been used.

EXAMPLE
1. A Ltd acquires an asset at a capitalised cost of £1,000, which is amortised over 10 years on a straight line basis.
For tax purposes, the acquisition cost is reduced to £800 following a reinvestment relief claim.

In Year 1 the deductible debit would be £80. $(100 \times \frac{800}{1,000})$

Year 1	Accounts £	Tax regime £
Cost	1,000	800
Amortisation/Debit	(100)	(80)
Net book value c/fwd/Tax written down value c/fwd	900	720

During Year 2 A Ltd incurs enhancement expenditure of £300.

Year 2	Accounts £	Tax regime £
Net book value b/fwd/Tax written down value b/fwd	900	720
Enhancement expenditure	300	300
	1,200	1,020
Amortisation/Debit $(120 \times \frac{1,020}{1,200})$	(120)	(102)
Net book value c/fwd/Tax written down value c/fwd	1,080	918

2. An asset with an accounting value (and TWDV) of £1,000 is partially realised for £750, and the accounting value of the part of the asset retained is £375.

The TWDV of £1,000 is adjusted to £375. $(1,000 \times \frac{375}{1,000})$

3. An asset with an accounting value of £1,000 is partially realised for £750, and the accounting value of the part of the asset retained is £375. The TWDV of the asset prior to the disposal was £800.

The TWDV after the part disposal is £300. $(800 \times \frac{375}{1,000})$

Fixed rate election Excluding lessors, a company may irrevocably elect for an annual fixed rate **deduction equal to** a 4% straight line writing down allowance of the tax cost of the asset (or the remaining tax written down value of the asset, if less).

28395
ss 730, 731
CTA 2009

For **accounting periods of less than 12 months** the deduction is proportionately reduced.

> MEMO POINTS 1. After a **part disposal** the tax cost of the asset is proportionately reduced.
> 2. The **time limit** for the election is 2 years after the end of the accounting period in which the asset was acquired or created.
> 3. This fixed 4% deduction is not available for **finance leased** assets that are treated as intangible assets (¶28210).

> EXAMPLE B Ltd buys an asset for £100,000 and elects for fixed rate treatment.
> In Year 5, the company makes a part disposal of the asset for £60,000, setting £50,000 of the acquisition cost against this disposal, which results in a profit of £10,000. The net book value remaining is £50,000. (100,000 − 50,000)
> The tax written down value brought forward is £84,000. (100,000 − (4,000 × 4))
> The amount of the remaining tax written down value attributable to the disposal is £42,000.
> $(84,000 \times \dfrac{50,000}{100,000})$
> The taxable profit on sale is £18,000. (60,000 − 42,000)
> The fixed rate deductions now relate to the remaining book value expenditure of £50,000 and are therefore reduced to £2,000 p.a. (50,000 @ 4%)
> These deductions will be set against the tax written down value until the amount has expired.

Reversal of previous accounting gain

The rules below **do not apply** to the writing off of revaluation surpluses (i.e. where an asset has previously been revalued and the uplift is then written off (¶28445+)).

28400
s 732 CTA 2009;
CIRD 12560

Where an accounting gain has been recognised in a previous period of account (resulting in a taxable credit (¶28430+)), which is subsequently reversed, a deductible debit will arise.

The amount of the debit will depend on whether the **taxable credit** was:
– the **same as the accounting gain**, when the deductible debit will be the same as the accounting loss; or
– **different from the accounting gain**, when the deductible debit is computed using the following formula:

$$\text{Accounting loss} \times \frac{\text{Previous credit}}{\text{Accounting gain}}$$

where:
– accounting loss is the amount recognised for accounting purposes;
– accounting gain is the item that is in whole or part reversed; and
– previous credit is the credit previously brought into account for tax purposes.

> EXAMPLE C Ltd recognised an earlier accounting gain of £100 but the taxable credit was only £80. In the next accounting period £50 of that gain is reversed in the accounts.
> The allowable debit is £40. (80/100 × 50)

2. Credits

The credits which might arise in the intangible assets regime are as follows:

28430

Situation	¶¶
Royalties on assets held by companies prior to 1 April 2002	¶28260
Receipts taken to the profit and loss account as they accrue	¶28435
Negative goodwill taken to the profit and loss account	¶28440
Revaluations	¶28445

Situation	¶¶
Reversal of a previous accounting debit	¶28455
Catch-up adjustments arising on a change of accounting policy	¶28730+
Profit on disposal of an asset	¶28485+

Receipts taken to the profit and loss account

28435
s 721 CTA 2009

All receipts arising from the exploitation of intangible assets are taxed as they are recognised in the accounts prepared under GAAP, **excluding**:
– proceeds arising from the disposal of an asset (¶28485+); and
– grants made in Northern Ireland out of UK public funds.

When transactions are not undertaken on arm's length terms, a **transfer pricing** adjustment to increase the taxable credit may be required (¶70000+).

Negative goodwill

28440
s 724 CTA 2009

Exceptionally, when a business is acquired, the **aggregate fair value** of the assets may **exceed** the total price paid for the business i.e. the business is acquired at a bargain price. The excess is known as negative goodwill, which is written off as a credit to the profit and loss account.

For tax purposes, negative goodwill is not an asset, but it is necessary to treat the amount written off as taxable credits to the extent that it can be attributed to intangible fixed assets i.e. the shortfall between the price paid for those assets and their market value (where ascertainable).

Comment In most cases negative goodwill would not be attributable to intangible fixed assets.

Revaluation

28445
s 723 CTA 2009

Under GAAP intangible assets should not be revalued, either to increase the carrying value above original cost or to reverse prior period losses arising from impairment or amortisation.
However, there are exceptions for:
– intangible assets with **readily ascertainable market values**, which may be revalued by reference to those market values; and
– an **impairment loss**, which was recognised as a result of an external event and, as a result of other external events that were not foreseen in the original impairment calculations, has now reversed.
Other than when a fixed rate election (¶28395) has been made (when the revaluation is not taxable), the **resulting uplift** in the value of the asset gives rise to a taxable credit that is the lesser of:
– the uplift, as adjusted for any difference between the accounting value and the tax written down value of the asset; and
– the total debits deducted for sums written off the asset, less any revaluation credits recognised for past periods.

After the revaluation, the **tax written down value** is increased by the amount of the taxable credit.

MEMO POINTS   1. The **uplift as adjusted** is calculated using the following formula:

$$\text{Revaluation gain} \times \frac{\text{Tax written down value}}{\text{Net book value}}$$

where:
– revaluation gain is the increase in value recognised in the accounts;
– tax written down value is the TWDV before the asset is revalued; and
– net book value is the NBV before the asset is revalued.
2. If one intangible asset is revalued then all other capitalised intangible assets in the **same class** should be revalued.

3. After an intangible asset has been revalued, **further revaluations** should then be carried out regularly to ensure that the carrying value does not differ greatly from the market value at the balance sheet date.

4. Where an **internally generated asset** is capitalised in the accounts at a valuation, no taxable credits or deductible debits arise (either as a revaluation or amortisation). However, where:
– the company incurs costs relating to either the creation or enhancement of an internally generated asset and these are capitalised, taxable debits would be available for the writing off of this expenditure; and
– expenditure is initially charged against profits but the entry is subsequently reversed on the capitalisation of the expenditure, this would be the reversal of an accounting loss (¶28455).

EXAMPLE D Ltd owns an intangible asset that has a readily ascertainable market value, which was purchased for £10,000 and amortised at £1,000 p.a. At the end of Year 4 it had a carrying value of £6,000. It is then revalued to £11,000 in the accounts, and an accounting gain of £5,000 is recognised.
The asset's tax cost on acquisition was £8,000. The annual deductible debits have been £800. (8,000/10,000 × 1,000)
So the total deductions have been £3,200, resulting in a tax written down value at the end of Year 4 of £4,800. (8,000 − (4 × 800))
The taxable credit on the revaluation is £3,200, being the lesser of:
– the proportion of the revaluation gain i.e. 4,000; (4,800/6,000 × 5,000) and
– the total deductions of £3,200.

CIRD 13060

Subsequent deductions   For accounting purposes the **amortisation charge** will be based on the revalued amount and the remaining useful economic life of the asset.

28450
CIRD 12790

For tax purposes, the deductible debit should be calculated by reference to the revised tax written down value, using the following formula:

$$\text{Amortisation charge} \times \frac{\text{Tax written down value}}{\text{Net book value}}$$

where:
– amortisation charge is the charge in the profit and loss account;
– tax written down value is the amount after the revaluation has taken place; and
– net book value is the accounts value.

EXAMPLE E Ltd owns an intangible asset that cost £1,000. When the net book value was £700 in the accounts (all of the amortisation being allowed for tax purposes), the asset was revalued to £1,200 and then amortised over a further 10 years at £120 p.a.
The taxable credit on revaluation is restricted to the tax deductions previously given of £300. This means that £200 of the uplift is not taxed.
The revised tax written down value of the asset is £1,000.
The deductible debit is £100, calculated by taking an appropriate proportion of the amortisation charge. (120 × 1,000/1,200)
This calculation is performed for each accounting period. So for the next year:
– the net book value will be £1,080; (1,200 − 120)
– the tax written down value will be £900; (1,000 − 100) and
– the deductible debit will be £100. (120 × 900/1,080)

Reversal of previous accounting loss

The rules below do not apply to the reversal of amortisation or impairment losses by way of revaluation gains (¶28445).

28455
s 725 CTA 2009

Very rarely a company may recognise an accounting gain which reverses some or all of a previous accounting loss.

Where the previous loss resulted in a deductible debit the gain must be recognised as a taxable credit.

The amount of the credit will depend on whether the **deductible debt** was:
– the **same as the accounting loss**, when the taxable credit will be the same as the accounting gain; or

– **different from the accounting loss**, when the taxable credit is computed using the following formula:

$$\text{Accounting gain} \times \frac{\text{Previous debit}}{\text{Accounting loss}}$$

where:
– accounting gain is the amount recognised for accounting purposes;
– accounting loss is the item that is in whole or part reversed; and
– previous debit is the debit previously brought into account for tax purposes.

> EXAMPLE F Ltd recognised an earlier accounting loss of £100 but the deductible debit was only £80.
> In the next accounting period £50 of that loss is reversed in the accounts.
> The taxable credit is £40. (80/100 × 50)

3. Disposals

28485
s 734 CTA 2009

A disposal (referred to in the legislation as a realisation) is **defined** as any transaction whereby:
– the asset ceases to be recognised on the company balance sheet; or
– there is a reduction in the accounting value of the asset (i.e. a part sale (¶28510)), excluding adjustments resulting from amortisation or impairment.

A taxable credit/deductible debit will arise based on the difference between the proceeds received for the asset and its tax written down value. A taxable credit may be deferred by using reinvestment relief (¶28540+).

> MEMO POINTS 1. An asset **ceases to be recognised** for accounting purposes where a transaction transfers to others all significant rights, or other access to benefits, relating to that asset.
> 2. A transaction will cause a **reduction in the value** of an asset for accounting purposes where it leads to a significant change in the company's right to benefits deriving from that asset.
> 3. For **deemed disposals** when:
> – a company becomes non-UK resident; or
> – a foreign company starts to use an asset outside the UK,
> see ¶28775+.

Proceeds

28490
s 739 CTA 2009

The proceeds of realisation are, subject to tax adjustments, the amount recognised for accounting purposes as those proceeds, net of the incidental costs.

s 856 CTA 2009

Where intangible assets are disposed of together **with tangible assets**, a just and reasonable apportionment of the proceeds must be made.

> MEMO POINTS 1. A common situation which involves a **tax adjustment** is a transfer between related parties, where market value must be substituted for the actual proceeds.
> 2. Allowable **incidental costs** follow the usual rules (¶28380). The most likely disallowable cost would be entertaining potential buyers of the asset.

s 740 CTA 2009

> 3. Where a **transaction is aborted**, and the end result would have been a disposal, any incidental expenditure incurred is a deductible debit for that period (subject to the usual restrictions).

Tax written down value

28495

The tax written down value is computed differently depending on whether a fixed rate election has been made.

> MEMO POINTS 1. Where the asset **has not been amortised** the taxable credit or deductible debit is the difference between the net realisation proceeds and the tax cost of the asset, as reduced by any net proceeds of any earlier part disposal.
> 2. If the **asset has not appeared on the company's balance sheet** (either because it is internally generated, or already completely written off) the taxable credit will be the net disposal proceeds.

Fixed rate election made The tax written down value is found by using the following **formula**:

$$\text{Tax cost} - \text{Debits}$$

where:
- tax cost is the cost of the asset recognised for tax purposes; and
- debits are the total debits previously brought into account under the fixed rate basis (¶28395).

28500
s 743 CTA 2009

No election The tax written down value is found by using the following **formula**:

$$\text{Tax cost} - \text{Debits} + \text{Credits}$$

where:
- tax cost is the cost of the asset recognised for tax purposes;
- debits are the total debits brought into account by way of amortisation (¶28390); and
- credits are the total credits brought into account by way of revaluation or as a result of a change in accounting policy.

28505
s 742 CTA 2009

Part disposals

Where only part of an intangible asset is disposed of, a proportion of the tax written down value is deducted as determined by the following **formula**:

$$\text{Tax written down value} \times \frac{\text{Reduction in net book value due to disposal}}{\text{Net book value before disposal}}$$

Where the tax written down value is the same as the net book value, the taxable credit/deductible debit will be the same as the profit or loss on disposal for accounting purposes.

The remaining tax written down value is then the benchmark with regard to any **future transaction** involving the asset, to which enhancement expenditure is added, and in respect of which debits and credits are calculated.

28510
ss 737, 744
CTA 2009;
CIRD 13260

> EXAMPLE
> 1. G Ltd holds an asset with a net book value of £1,000, and makes a part disposal, for proceeds of £750. The net book value of the part retained is £375. The profit on disposal is £125. (750 – (1,000 – 375))
> The asset's tax cost is the same as the accounting cost so that the taxable credit is also £125.
>
> 2. H Ltd holds an asset with a net book value of £1,000 and makes a part disposal, receiving proceeds of £750. The net book value of the part retained is £375, which means there is a reduction of £625 as a result of the disposal. The profit on disposal is £125. (750 – 625)
> In this case the tax cost is only £800, so that the net book value and the tax written down value are not the same.
> The proportion of the tax written down value to be set against the proceeds is £500. (800 × 625/1,000)
> So the taxable credit is £250. (750 – 500)

4. Reinvestment relief

Taxable credits on the disposal of a chargeable intangible asset can be deferred by claiming reinvestment relief. Broadly, the relief deducts an amount from the proceeds arising on disposal of the old asset, and also deducts the same amount from the company's expenditure on the replacement intangible asset(s), thereby reducing the subsequent deductible debits (both in respect of amortisation and eventual sale).

A company can make a provisional claim when it intends to acquire replacement assets (¶28570).

Comment Reinvestment relief allows gains from disposals of any class of intellectual property (including goodwill) to be rolled over against reinvestment in any type of intellectual property. The purpose to which the intellectual property is put (i.e. trade or investment) is irrelevant.

28540

Scope

28545   **Intangibles which are outside the regime** (e.g. goodwill arising before 1 April 2002) are nevertheless included in the reinvestment provisions when disposed of, as capital gains rollover no longer applies. This includes assets of a type which would not have qualified for capital gains rollover relief.

Part disposals to related parties (¶28085) are excluded from the relief.

Conditions

28550   The following conditions need to be satisfied to make a claim:

Asset	Conditions to be satisfied	Reference
Old asset[1]	Asset must have been a qualifying intangible asset of the company throughout the company's period of ownership[2] i.e. its disposal would give rise to a taxable credit within the intangible assets regime	s 755 CTA 2009
	Sale proceeds must exceed its tax cost	
Replacement asset(s)[1]	Expenditure must be incurred in the period from 1 year before to 3 years after the disposal of the old asset	s 756 CTA 2009
	Expenditure must be capitalised in the company accounts (an asset that is unexpectedly sold after acquisition and is not therefore capitalised in the accounts may nonetheless still qualify)	
	Asset must be a qualifying intangible asset in the company's hands immediately after acquisition	

Note:
1. Where an asset is disposed of and **subsequently reacquired** it is treated as two different assets.
2. If the old asset was **not a qualifying intangible asset** throughout the company's period of ownership, it may still qualify providing:
– it was a qualifying intangible asset when it was sold; and
– for a substantial part of the company's period of ownership, it was a qualifying intangible asset (in which case a just and reasonable apportionment is made).

Full disposal of old asset

28555
s 758 CTA 2009

Reinvestment relief reduces the disposal proceeds of the old asset and the acquisition cost of the new asset by the amount of the claim.

The relief is the **amount** by which the lower of the:
– disposal proceeds of the old asset; and
– acquisition cost of the replacement asset,

exceeds the cost of the old asset.

> EXAMPLE   A Ltd buys an asset for £75 and sells it for £125, when its tax and net book value is £40.
> The sale triggers a taxable credit of £85. (125 – 40)
> If a replacement asset was purchased for £150, the amount eligible for relief would be £50. (125 – 75)
> Proceeds are therefore reduced by £50, and the taxable credit would become £35. (125 – 50 – 40)
> If a replacement asset was purchased for £100, the amount eligible for relief would be £25. (100 – 75)
> Proceeds are therefore reduced by £25, and the taxable credit would become £60. (125 – 25 – 40)

Part disposal of old asset

28560
s 759 CTA 2009

On a part disposal only a proportion of the old asset's cost needs to be taken into account, by using the following **formula**:

$$\text{Full cost} \times \frac{\text{Reduction in net book value}}{\text{Net book value before disposal}}$$

When the **remainder** of the old asset is **sold** (either all at once or as subsequent part disposals) the remaining cost is the original acquisition cost as reduced by amounts taken into account in previous part disposals.

EXAMPLE B Ltd buys an asset for £100, and receives proceeds of £90 on a part disposal at a time when its net book value immediately prior to the disposal was £50, and immediately afterwards £40. The net book value is therefore reduced by £10.

The proportion of the cost which is taken into account is £20. (100 × 10/50)

If a replacement asset was purchased for £110 the amount eligible for relief would be £70. (90 – 20)

If a replacement asset was purchased for £60 the amount eligible for relief would be £40. (60 – 20)

B Ltd then makes another part disposal of the same asset for proceeds of £60, when its net book value immediately prior to the disposal was £30, and immediately afterwards was £15. The net book value is therefore reduced by £15.

The original cost remaining after taking into account the first part disposal (whether or not reinvestment relief was actually claimed on the first disposal), is £80. (100 – 20)

The proportion of this cost which is to be taken into account for the second disposal is £40. (80 × 15/30)

If a replacement asset was purchased for £80 the amount eligible for relief would be £20. (60 – 40)

If a replacement asset was purchased for £50 the amount eligible for relief would be £10. (50 – 40)

If the remainder of the asset is then sold the cost to be set against the proceeds is £40. (100 – 20 – 40)

CIRD 20235

Pre-1 April 2002 assets

Although intangible assets that existed before 1 April 2002 are subject to chargeable gains (¶30000+) on disposal, only reinvestment relief is available, and not capital gains rollover relief.

28565
s 898 CTA 2009

The net proceeds received (i.e. proceeds less incidental cost of disposal) are compared to indexed cost.

EXAMPLE C Ltd sells goodwill which it acquired in 2000. The disposal proceeds are £400,000, and the acquisition cost was £60,000. Incidental costs of disposal are £50,000. Assume indexation allowance (¶30530+) is 20%. C Ltd is considering two investments in a new intangible asset, one costing £360,000 and the other costing £300,000.

The gain arising on the sale of the goodwill is:

	£
Proceeds	400,000
Less: Expenses	(50,000)
Net proceeds	350,000
Less: Cost	(60,000)
	290,000
Indexation allowance (60,000 × 20%)	(12,000)
Chargeable gain	278,000

Note that the indexed cost is £72,000. (60,000 + 12,000)

The £360,000 asset costs more than the net proceeds for the old asset of £350,000. Reinvestment relief of £278,000 can be claimed.

The cheaper £300,000 asset costs less than the net proceeds of the old asset, so only the excess of the new asset's cost over the old asset's indexed cost can be claimed, i.e. £228,000. (300,000 – 72,000)

Making a claim

A claim must **specify**:
- the old assets which have been disposed of;
- the expenditure on replacement assets; and
- the amount of relief.

28570
s 757 CTA 2009

The usual **time limits** apply (¶46425).

Relief can be provisionally claimed where the company makes a **provisional declaration** on its CTSA return in the accounting period of disposal which states that it:
- has realised an intangible fixed asset;
- proposes to reinvest the proceeds in a new intangible asset; and
- is entitled to relief of a specified amount.

s 761 CTA 2009

The declaration automatically lapses 4 years after the end of the accounting period of the disposal, although it will be superseded in the meantime where it is either withdrawn or an actual claim is made (i.e. the replacement asset is acquired).

C. Computation

28600

Once the amounts involved have been established the treatment of credits and debits (i.e. income and expenditure) arising on intangible assets depends upon whether the assets are held for trading (including a property business) or non-trading purposes.

s 750 CTA 2009

> ⌐MEMO POINTS⌐ 1. Where an intangible asset is held for **more than one purpose** a just and reasonable apportionment of the taxable amounts should be made.
> 2. Where the **period of account exceeds 12 months** the taxable amounts will need to be apportioned to each accounting period (¶3060).

1. Trading or property business

28630

ss 747 – 749
CTA 2009

Credits and debits arising on assets held for the purposes of the trade are taxed as trading income (or as property income if the trade is a property business).

> ⌐MEMO POINTS⌐ 1. For this purpose a **property** business would **include** furnished lettings and overseas property.
> 2. Trade includes mines, transport undertakings and other profits **derived from the exploitation of land** (¶14125+).

2. Non-trading purpose

28650

Intangible assets may be held by a company for non-trading purposes, but which still constitute a business or commercial activity. The most common example is an investment business.

Overview

28655

ss 751, 752
CTA 2009

Non-trading items are pooled. If the **net position** is a:
a. gain, it is assessable as miscellaneous income; or
b. loss, this is either:
– set off against profits of any kind of the current period;
– surrendered as group relief; or
– automatically carried forward against non-trading profits of later periods.

Set off against profits

28660

s 753 CTA 2009

The company must make a **claim** to set the non-trading debits against its total profits within 2 years of the end of the accounting period in which the profits arose.

Group relief

28665

A group or consortium claim for non-trading losses from intangibles falls within the general rules for group relief (¶66000+), and requires a 75% holding in each group company (whether direct or indirect).

ss 99, 105
CTA 2010

The non-trading losses on intangible fixed assets are pooled with other non-trading type losses (i.e. qualifying charitable donations, property business losses and management expenses). The **amount available for surrender** is the amount by which the pooled losses exceed the gross profits, and the losses on intangibles are deemed to be surrendered last (i.e. after the other types of non-trading type losses).

For this purpose a company's **gross profits** are the profits for the accounting period before they are reduced by any losses and other allowances of the same or any other accounting period (¶66150).

EXAMPLE D Ltd has trading losses brought forward of £10,000. In the current accounting period, it makes a trading profit of £8,000. The non-trading loss on intangible assets is £3,000.
The tax computation is as follows:

	£
Trading profits	8,000
Less: Trading losses brought forward	(10,000)
Losses carried forward	(2,000)

Ignoring the trading losses the non-trading loss could be set against the trading profits, and hence there are no excess non-trading losses to surrender.

Carried forward

Unused non-trading losses from intangibles are automatically carried forward and can be set against the company's profits of later accounting periods. They may not be surrendered by way of group relief in later accounting periods.

28670

D. Special situations

Summary

28700

Topic	¶¶
Intra-group transfers	¶69180+
Leaving a group	¶69220+
Change of accounting policy	¶28730+
Transfer pricing	¶70000+
Migration	¶28775+
Related party transactions	¶28820+

---

1. Change of accounting policy

On a change of accounting policy (including where a company adopts IAS for the first time) which results in a difference between the closing accounts value in one period, and the opening value in the next, a debit or credit will arise in the later period, although only to the extent that the difference is not recognised under another rule within the intangibles regime.

28730
s 872 CTA 2009

The **exceptions** are:
– assets which are subject to a fixed rate election (¶28395), where no difference is recognised, unless a single asset is subsequently recognised as multiple assets (known as disaggregation (¶28740+));
– where the difference is recognised as a gain on revaluation (¶28445); or
– where the difference is recognised as either the reversal of an accounting loss (¶28455) or reversal of an accounting gain (¶28400).

s 878 CTA 2009

Amount

28735
ss 872, 873
CTA 2009

The amount of the credit or debit is calculated using the following **formula**:

$$\text{Accounting difference} \times \frac{\text{Tax written down value at end of earlier period}}{\text{Net book value at end of earlier period}}$$

If the **result is a credit** this will be capped to the net amount of previous debits on the asset less previous credits on the asset.

The tax written down value for the **later period** will be the TWDV of the earlier period plus the credit or minus the debit (whichever applies).

Disaggregation

28740
s 874 CTA 2009;
CIRD 12310

Sometimes a change of accounting policy, such as when adopting IAS, will result in a single asset at the end of the earlier period being recognised as multiple assets in the later period.

The **tax written down value** of the original asset is pro-rated among the resulting assets, based on their net book values. Any credit or debit resulting from the change of policy must be added to, or deducted from, the tax written down value to find the tax cost going forward.

> EXAMPLE   E Ltd decides to adopt IAS at the beginning of Year 5. The original intangible asset has a tax written down value at the end of Year 4 of £120.
> Under IAS, the asset must be disaggregated into three assets (X, Y and Z), with net book values of £100, £200 and £300 respectively.
> The tax written down value for each asset is as follows:
> – asset X, £20; (120 × 100/600)
> – asset Y, £40; (120 × 200/600)
> – asset Z, £60. (120 × 300/600)

28745
s 876 CTA 2009;
CIRD 12320

Fixed rate election   If the **original asset** was subject to a fixed rate election (¶28395) the resulting assets are also subject to this election. The tax written down value of the original asset is pro-rated among the resulting assets based on their net book values.

A company may make a fixed rate election in respect of a **resulting asset** so long as the time limit for making the election in respect of the original asset has not expired. For this purpose it is necessary to identify the cost of the notional original asset which relates to the resulting asset, and amortise it accordingly as if a fixed rate election had already taken effect.

> EXAMPLE
> **1.** F Ltd acquires an intangible asset in Year 4 for £10,000, which is amortised at 10% p.a. A fixed rate election is made in respect of it. The tax debit is £400, which reduces the TWDV at the end of Year 4 to £9,600. The net book value is £9,000. (10,000 – 1,000)
> In Year 5 F Ltd adopts IAS, which results in two assets, X and Y, with net book values of £6,000 and £3,000 respectively.
> The TWDV for each asset is as follows:
> – asset X, £6,400; (9,600 × 6,000/9,000) and
> – asset Y, £3,200. (9,600 × 3,000/9,000)
> So in Year 5 the total deductible debit relating to amortisation is £384. ((6,400 @ 4%) + (3,200 @ 4%)).
>
> **2.** G Ltd acquires an asset for £12,000 in Year 6 which is amortised at 10% p.a. In Year 7 G Ltd adopts IAS, which results in four assets W, X, Y and Z, with tax written down values of £1,800, £2,100, £3,300 and £3,600 respectively (a total of £10,800). If a fixed rate election is made in respect of Z alone a change will be needed to the amortisation that has been claimed in respect of it.
> Z's TWDV is one third of the total, which means that the notional original asset would have cost £4,000. $(12,000 \times \frac{3,600}{10,800})$
> So the amortisation charge for Year 6 at 4% must be corrected to £160. (4,000 @ 4%)
> The cost of £4,000 is used for all subsequent periods for asset Z.

2. Migration

Special rules apply when a company either leaves the UK or becomes UK-resident. **28775**

Leaving the UK

The following situations give rise to a **deemed disposal** and reacquisition at market value: **28780**
– a company becomes non-UK resident; or
– a foreign company, which has a permanent UK establishment, starts to use an asset outside the UK, although there is an option to defer any taxable credit which arises.

s 859 CTA 2009

Deferral of taxable credit

Where a company ceases to be UK-resident, the resultant charge can be postponed where the following **conditions** are met:
– the asset is held for the purpose of a non-UK trade carried on through a permanent establishment;
– the company remains a 75% subsidiary of its UK-resident parent company;
– the deemed disposal proceeds of the asset exceed the original cost of the asset recognised for tax purposes; and
– the company and its parent jointly elect for this rule to apply.

28785
ss 860 – 862
CTA 2009;
CIRD 47050

The **amount deferred** is the excess of the market value of the asset over its tax cost (not its tax written down value).

The deferred **gain is brought back into charge** (in the UK parent company as a non-trading credit) if any of the following occur:
– the non-resident company ceases to be a 75% subsidiary of the UK parent company;
– the parent company leaves the UK; or
– the non-UK company disposes of the intangible fixed asset within 6 years of its becoming non-resident.

Where only a **part disposal** is made by the non-UK company, only a proportion of the deferred amount will become chargeable.

MEMO POINTS 1. **Tax cost** is the accounting cost as adjusted for tax purposes (before any debits or credits).
2. **Tax written down value** is the tax cost less debits and plus credits i.e. the running total for tax purposes.

> EXAMPLE A Ltd leaves the UK and elects for the resulting taxable credit of £1,200 to be deferred. A couple of years later A Ltd makes a part disposal for £1,500, and the value of the asset retained is £1,000.
>
> The proportion of the credit which becomes taxable is £400. $1,200 \times (\frac{1,500 - 1,000}{1,500})$

MEMO POINTS For exit charges falling due **on or after 11 December 2012** where the company leaves the UK and becomes resident in another EEA state it may be able to enter an exit charge payment plan. For full details see ¶91447+. Sch 3ZB TMA 1970

Coming within the UK tax net

An asset will become a qualifying intangible asset when: **28790**
– a company, holding an intangible asset, becomes resident in the UK; or
– a non-resident company begins to use an intangible asset for the purposes of a trade in the UK through a permanent establishment (¶92140+).

s 863 CTA 2009

The company will be treated as acquiring the asset at its net book **value** at the time of change (as determined under UK GAAP), although if the asset was originally created/acquired before 1 April 2002, it will not be within the scope of the intangible asset regime.

MEMO POINTS The same rules apply to foreign companies coming within the **controlled foreign companies** rules (¶90555+).

3. Related party transactions

28820   Transactions involving related parties are subject to special rules as follows (for groups of companies see ¶69115+):

Situation	Consequence	¶¶
Pre-April 2002 assets purchased from related parties	Excluded – subject to capital gains rules	¶28240
Transfer between related parties (other than between group members)	Market value	¶28825+
Part disposal to related party	No reinvestment relief	¶28840
Royalties are delayed in being paid to a related party	Deductible debit not available until royalty is paid	¶28845

Transfers between

28825
ss 845–849
CTA 2009

Transfers of intangible assets between related parties (i.e. where the asset falls to be taxed under the intangibles regime for at least one of the parties) are deemed to occur at market value (for all tax purposes) **unless**:
a. the transfer is a tax neutral transfer (e.g. intra-group transfer (¶69180+));
b. the transfer pricing regulations apply (¶70000+), in which case the asset is deemed to be transferred at the price determined under the transfer pricing regulations;
c. the asset is transferred to a company by a related party on or after 16 March 2005, and gift holdover relief (see *Tax Memo*) was claimed on the transfer. In this case the transfer will be deemed to take place at market value less the amount of the heldover gain; or
d. the asset is transferred on or after 16 March 2005, and the amount at which the asset is transferred is taken into account as a distribution or earnings (¶28835).

28830
s 845 CTA 2009

Market value   The market value of an asset is **defined** as the price that the asset might reasonably be expected to fetch on a sale in the open market (¶30410+).

28835
s 847 CTA 2009

Distribution or earnings   For this purpose the related party would not normally be a company.

Where an intangible asset is transferred:
– from a company to a related party at under-value; or
– to a company from a related party at over-value,

the application of the market value rule is modified in a way that does not prevent a **taxable distribution or employment income** from arising. However, computations and debits or credits arising under the intangibles regime are unaffected i.e. market value still applies.

> EXAMPLE   A controlling shareholder transfers an intangible asset to a company for £10,000 (when it is worth £1,000).
> For the purposes of income tax the transfer will be deemed to take place at £1,000, and the consideration received in excess of its market value will be taxed as a distribution on the shareholder.
> However, for the purposes of the intangibles regime, the company will account for the intangible asset at market value.

Part disposals

28840
s 850 CTA 2009

Reinvestment relief (¶28540+) is unavailable where the company makes a part disposal of an asset to a related party.

This is very broadly defined to include the case where the related party, in connection with the part disposal, acquires any interest in the asset, or in another asset which derives at least some of its value from the partly disposed asset.

Delayed payment of royalties

Where royalties are **paid more than** 12 months after the end of the accounting period in which they are deducted in the profit and loss account, and the **recipient** does not include a taxable credit for the royalty, a deduction will only arise when payment is made.

28845
s 851 CTA 2009

SECTION 3

Assets outside the intangibles regime

Intellectual property acquired or internally generated before 1 April 2002 (¶28080+) will continue to be taxed under the old rules, which means that:
– capital allowances at 25% on a reducing balance basis will continue for patents, industrial know-how and computer software;
– expenditure on internally generated intellectual property may be disallowed as capital;
– profits on the sale of intellectual property will be taxed as capital gains, with indexation relief; and
– capital gains rollover relief is very limited (¶30985).

28895

Summary

The following table summarises the assets which have special rules. Other assets are subject to the capital gains rules, with the following caveats:
– only proceeds not taxable as income are liable; and
– most assets will probably fall to be treated as wasting assets (¶31605+), if they have a useful life of 50 years or less.

28900

Type of asset	¶¶
Patent rights acquired before 1 April 2002	¶28930+
Industrial know-how acquired before 1 April 2002	¶29105+
Capital expenditure on R&D	¶78610+
Computer software	¶25405

A. Patent rights acquired before 1 April 2002

An invention which is new, but not obvious, and is capable of industrial application, may be granted patent protection for a maximum of 20 years.

28930
Patents Act 1977;
CA 75010

A patent consists of rights conferred by letters patent to the exclusive use and benefits of the particular invention. Patent **rights are defined** as the right to do, or authorise the doing of, anything which would be, but for that right, the infringement of a patent.

Potential users of the invention must pay to acquire rights to use the patent, or be granted a **licence** to use it, which allows the inventor both to control the invention and also secure an income stream from it.

s 466 CAA 2001

The new patent box regime, which commenced on 1 April 2013, is potentially available to all companies (¶29235+).

1. Scope

Commencement

28960
The commencement of a **UK patent** is the date from which the patent rights become effective i.e. when the Patent Office accepts the complete specification of the patent.

Foreign patent rights commence as determined by the patent law of the territory in respect of which they are granted.

Patent yet to be granted

28965
s 465 CAA 2001
Where a company incurs expenditure on a right **to acquire** patent rights in an invention, for which a patent has not yet been granted, it is treated as incurring expenditure on the purchase of patent rights. If the patent rights are later acquired, the expenditure on the right to acquire them is treated as expenditure on buying them.

The party who receives a payment for a right to acquire patent rights is treated as receiving the proceeds of a **sale** of patent rights, irrespective of whether the patent is actually granted.

Income

28970
s 483 CAA 2001
Income from patents is the **sum** of the following:
a. royalties or other sums paid in respect of the user of a patent;
b. any balancing charge; and
c. the sale of future patent rights.

2. Capital allowances

Qualifying expenditure

29000
ss 467 – 469
CAA 2001
Expenditure must **exclude** any licence paid for in royalties, as royalties are deducted as revenue expenditure.

Two types of capital expenditure are eligible for allowances:
a. qualifying **trade** expenditure on the purchase of patent rights for the purposes of the trade carried on by the purchaser; and
b. qualifying **non-trade** expenditure on the purchase of patent rights where any of the income receivable in respect of the rights would be chargeable to tax (i.e. the expenditure must either be incurred for existing patent rights, or in order to acquire patent rights in the future for inventions where no patent has been granted yet).

Pre-trading expenditure on buying patent rights is treated as incurred on the first day of trading, provided that the company owns the rights on that date.

29005
s 481 CAA 2001
Restriction Qualifying expenditure is restricted if the company acquires patent rights and either:
– the company is **connected** with the seller; or
– the sale is a **sole or main benefit** transaction i.e. where the sole or main benefit, which might be expected to accrue to the parties, is the obtaining of a patents allowance.

The expenditure qualifying for capital allowances is restricted to the amounts below (in order):
a. the seller's disposal value, if there is one;
b. where there is no disposal value, the capital sum payable to the seller; or
c. where neither of the above apply, the smallest of:
– the open market value of the patent rights;
– any capital expenditure incurred by the seller; and
– any capital expenditure incurred by anyone connected with the seller (¶25190).

Writing down allowances

29010
ss 470 – 475
CAA 2001
Writing down allowances (WDA) are **first given** in the accounting period in which the qualifying expenditure is incurred.

To **calculate** the allowances the expenditure is separately pooled between each trade (if there is more than one) and non-trade expenditure.

The **rate** of WDA is 25% of the pool balance at the end of the period in question, calculated in accordance with the general rules (¶25890+), unless a balancing adjustment is required.

> MEMO POINTS   1. Where the **trade is carried on for only part** of the accounting period the WDA is proportionately reduced.
> 2. A **partial claim** may be made.
> 3. Any qualifying expenditure incurred **in previous accounting periods** on patent rights that the company still owns, but which was not added to the pool already, can be added in a later accounting period.
> 4. Where the trade (and associated patent right) is transferred without a **significant change in ownership**, allowances continue to be available to the successor on the same basis as the transferor. For this purpose there is no significant change of ownership where there is a company reconstruction without change of ownership (¶79290+), or a transfer between companies which are under common control (¶79600+).

> EXAMPLE   B Ltd acquired patent rights before 1 April 2002. The balance of the pool is £10,000 and disposal values of £4,000 occur in the current accounting period.
> B Ltd can claim a WDA of any amount up to £1,500. ((10,000 – 4,000) @ 25%)

Balancing adjustments

The following balancing adjustments may occur:

29015
s 471 CAA 2001

Situation	Adjustment	Result
Accounting period when trade permanently ceases	Deduct disposal value from the balance of the pool	If: – positive – balancing allowance; or – negative – balancing charge
Last of the patent rights in the non-trade pool come to an end	Deduct disposal value from the balance of the pool	If: – positive – balancing allowance; or – negative – balancing charge
Pool balance is less than disposal value		Balancing charge

For this purpose the **disposal value** of patent rights is the net proceeds of sale, although this is restricted to cost unless the patent rights were acquired in a connected person transaction.

ss 476, 477
CAA 2001

Any excess over cost is taxed as miscellaneous income (¶29050+). The granting of an exclusive licence is treated as a sale of the whole of the patent rights relating to a specific invention.

s 466 CAA 2001

For **connected party** (¶25190) **transactions** (including a series of connected party transactions) the disposal value is limited to the greatest amount of capital expenditure incurred by any of the parties involved in those transactions.

> EXAMPLE   C Ltd spent £10,000 in January 2002 when acquiring patent rights, and claims capital allowances. The company grants Licence 1 for £6,000 and Licence 2 for £6,000.
> In respect of the first licence C Ltd recognises a disposal value of £6,000.
> However, the proceeds for Licence 2 exceed the remaining cost of £4,000. (10,000 – 6,000)
> So £2,000 is assessable as miscellaneous income.

Giving effect to allowances

Allowances on:
- **trade** expenditure are treated as trade expenses in the usual manner; and
- **non-trade** patent expenditure are set against the company's non-trade patent income for the same accounting period, with any excess being carried forward without time limit against such income for subsequent accounting periods.

29020
ss 478 – 480
CAA 2001

Balancing charges are treated as either trading receipts or, where no trade exists, miscellaneous income.

3. Profits

29050 Under these provisions there are two sets of rules, depending on whether the receipt is capital or income in nature.

In either case the profits from a sale of patent rights are the proceeds less the acquisition cost and any incidental expenses of the sale.

Capital receipt

29055 The sale of future patent rights for a capital sum is charged to tax as patent income.

ss 912 – 920
CTA 2009

Subject to an election to the contrary, receipts are automatically **spread** over a period of 6 years beginning on the first day of the chargeable period in which payment is received.

> ⌑ MEMO POINTS ⌑   1. An **election** can be made to disapply the spreading provisions and treat the full amount as taxable in the year of receipt if appropriate. This may be beneficial where, for example, there are expenses incurred on patents in the year of receipt which can be set against the patent receipt, or where spreading the payment would result in a company being liable to tax at the marginal rate (¶40110+).
> This election must be made within 2 years of the end of the accounting period in which payment is actually received.
>
> s 911 ITA 2007
>
> 2. If a **non-UK resident company** sells a UK patent right for a capital sum, it is taxed under the miscellaneous income provisions and the payer must deduct tax at the basic rate (¶41050), unless the recipient is covered by a double tax treaty, when the appropriate rate of deduction should be made.

> EXAMPLE   D Ltd prepares its accounts regularly for the 12 months to 31 December, and receives capital proceeds of £18,000 on the disposal of patent rights in the year ended 31 December 2013. For each accounting period between 1 January 2013 and 31 December 2018, £3,000 will be assessable. (18,000/6)

29060 Where a **chargeable period is less than 12 months**, the amount assessable is reduced proportionately on a daily basis, with the assessable amount for the final period being proportionately reduced for the remainder of the 6 years.

> EXAMPLE   Taking the facts from the example in ¶29055 above, if D Ltd prepared accounts for the 6 months to 30 June 2015 before resuming regular 12-month accounts, the receipt would be spread as follows:

Period ended	Length		Assessable amount £
31 December 2013	12 months		3,000
31 December 2014	12 months		3,000
30 June 2015	1 Jan to 30 June, 181 days	181/365 × 3,000	1,488
30 June 2016	12 months		3,000
30 June 2017	12 months		3,000
30 June 2018	12 months		3,000
30 June 2019	1 July to 31 Dec, 184 days	184/365 × 3,000	1,512

Income receipt

29065 The receipt of a royalty (or other such payment) for the prior use of a patented invention is either:

s 527 ICTA 1988

– treated as an income receipt, taxable in the year of receipt; or
– spread backwards over a number of years (if an appropriate claim is made).

29070 **Spreading** A spreading claim may only be made where income tax is deductible on the payments received, and the payments are **receivable for a period in excess of 2 years**, in which case they may be spread over a period of between 2 and 6 years, depending on the number of complete years for which they are receivable. Fractions of a year are ignored.

s 527 ICTA 1988

Where **receipts are due for a period in excess of 6 years**, they are spread over the maximum 6-year period. For example, receipts under a 3-year agreement can be spread over 3 years, whereas receipts under a 9-year agreement can only be spread over 6 years.

A claim to spread income receipts must be made within 4 years of the end of the accounting period in which a payment is received. Any other relief or allowance that becomes due as a result of the claim can also be given.

Sch 18 para 55
FA 1998

When spreading income receipts, the income is deemed to be received in equal annual instalments on the same **date** in each year as the actual receipt, with the final instalment being the date of the actual receipt.

29075

For example, a payment of £20,000 under a 4-year agreement which was received on 1 July 2013 would be deemed to be received in £5,000 instalments on 1 July 2010, 2011, 2012 and 2013. The length of each individual accounting period is therefore irrelevant when spreading income receipts.

EXAMPLE E Ltd receives income in respect of a patent it owns under a 3-year agreement as follows:

Period ended	31 Dec 2009	31 Dec 2010	31 Dec 2011	31 Dec 2012	31 Dec 2013
Other profits	50,000	55,000	60,000	70,000	72,000
Patent income	-	-	30,000	36,000	12,000
PCTCT	50,000	55,000	90,000	106,000	84,000

If a claim is made for the patent income to be spread, PCTCT will be as follows:

Period ended	31 Dec 2009	31 Dec 2010	31 Dec 2011	31 Dec 2012	31 Dec 2013
Other profits	50,000	55,000	60,000	70,000	72,000
Patent income 1	10,000	10,000	10,000	-	-
Patent income 2	-	12,000	12,000	12,000	-
Patent income 3	-	-	4,000	4,000	4,000
PCTCT	60,000	77,000	86,000	86,000	76,000

B. Industrial know-how acquired before 1 April 2002

Know-how is **defined** as industrial information or techniques which are likely to assist in:
- the manufacture or processing of goods or materials;
- the working of a source of mineral deposits (¶27355); or
- the carrying out of any agricultural, forestry or fishing operations.

For this purpose know-how is treated as property.

29105
s 452 CAA 2001

s 453 CAA 2001

1. Scope

Exclusions

HMRC state that commercial know-how i.e. information relating to the **selling of goods or materials** once they have been manufactured, such as the following, is excluded from allowances:
- market research;
- customer lists; and
- sales techniques.

This also means that know-how transferred by a **franchise** agreement is also excluded.

Know-how acquired in a **control** transaction does not qualify for capital allowances i.e. where the seller controls (¶25190) the buyer, or the buyer controls the seller, or some other person controls both the buyer and the seller.

Expenditure is not qualifying expenditure if it is **already deductible** for tax purposes.

29135
CA 70030

s 455 CAA 2001

Qualifying expenditure

29140
ss 454, 455
CAA 2001

Capital expenditure, incurred by a company on the acquisition of know-how before 1 April 2002, will qualify for capital allowances where the know-how is acquired either:

a. on its own for use in a trade which the company is either carrying on already, or which will be commenced after the acquisition; or

b. together with the trade or part trade in which it is used, and either:
- the parties to the transaction make an election to avoid goodwill treatment; or
- the trade or part trade was carried on wholly outside the UK before the acquisition.

A **holding company** may acquire industrial know-how for use in trades carried on by its subsidiary companies, and so long as the conditions are met, the holding company will qualify, as the know-how is also used in its trade of providing management services to its subsidiaries.

---

2. Capital allowances

29170
ss 456, 460
CAA 2001

Qualifying expenditure is pooled (with a separate pool for each trade carried on by the company), and a writing down allowance is available for each accounting period.

A balancing adjustment will occur when know-how is disposed of, or where the trade permanently ceases.

Writing down allowances

29175
ss 457, 458, 461
CAA 2001

Writing down allowances (WDA) are **first given** in the accounting period in which the qualifying expenditure is incurred.

The **rate** of WDA is 25% of the pool balance at the end of the accounting period in question, calculated in accordance with the general rules (¶25890+), unless the company ceases to trade in the accounting period.

> ‾MEMO POINTS‾ 1. Where the **trade is carried on for only part** of the accounting period the WDA is proportionately reduced.
> 2. A **partial claim** may be made.
> 3. Any qualifying expenditure incurred **in previous accounting periods** on know-how that the company still owns, but which was not added to the pool already, can be added in a later accounting period.
> 4. Where the trade (and associated know-how) is transferred without a **significant change in ownership**, allowances continue to be available to the successor on the same basis as the transferor. For this purpose there is no significant change of ownership where there is a company reconstruction without change of ownership (¶79290+), or a transfer between companies which are under common control (¶79600+).

> ‾EXAMPLE‾ F Ltd acquired know-how before 1 April 2002. The balance of the pool is £10,000 and disposal values of £4,000 occur in the current accounting period.
> F Ltd can claim a WDA of any amount up to £1,500. ((10,000 – 4,000) @ 25%)
> If F Ltd claims £1,500 the balance on the pool at the start of the next accounting period is £4,500. (10,000 – 4,000 – 1,500)

Balancing adjustments

29180
s 462 CAA 2001

A balancing allowance can only occur when the trade is permanently ceased, assuming that the disposal value is less than the pool balance.

Where disposal values for know-how exceed the pool balance at any time a balancing charge will arise.

For this purpose the **disposal value** of know-how is the net proceeds of a capital sale, and this amount is not restricted to cost.

No disposal value is brought into account if the sale is treated as a sale of goodwill.

MEMO POINTS 1. Proceeds will arise on a **capital sale** where either: CA72200
– know-how is disposed of as one element of a comprehensive arrangement under which a trader effectively gives up an established business in a particular territory; *Evans Medical Supplies Ltd v Moriarty* [1957] or
– the receipt is wholly or partly attributable to a covenant against competition, and that covenant is ancillary to the grant of a licence under a patent which is a fixed capital asset of the grantor. *Murray v Imperial Chemical Industries Ltd* [1967]
2. A **sale of goodwill** occurs when know-how is disposed of along with a trade or a part of a s178 CTA 2009 trade, unless either:
– the parties jointly elect (within 2 years of the disposal) that the transaction should not be treated as a sale and purchase of goodwill. Such an election cannot be made where the sale is a control sale. Where the election is made the buyer is treated as acquiring know-how (which will fall within the intangibles regime where the buyer is a company); or
– the trade was carried out wholly outside the UK before the acquisition of the know-how.
In the absence of an election, the vendor does not include any disposal value in the capital allowances computation, although the receipt may be liable to tax as a chargeable gain. The buyer is treated as acquiring goodwill.
3. A **control sale** is one where either party controls the other, or both are under the control of another person, including a partnership.
4. A **receipt** from a disposal of know-how which is brought into account as any of the following CA72500 will be taxable as miscellaneous income:
– disposal value;
– trading receipt; or
– payment for goodwill.
HMRC state that a likely scenario would involve know-how built up by the trading members of a group prior to 1 April 2002 which is then exploited by a non-trading holding company.

EXAMPLE G Ltd has a pool of qualifying expenditure for the current accounting period of £35,000. If:
– the disposal values total £40,000, there is a balancing charge of £5,000; (40,000 – 35,000)
– there is a disposal value of £3,000, the resulting WDA is £8,000; ((35,000 – 3,000) @ 25%) and
– the trade is discontinued in the accounting period and there are disposal values of £3,000, there is a balancing allowance of £32,000. (35,000 – 3,000)

Giving effect to allowances

Allowances are treated as trade expenses in the usual manner. **29185**
s 463 CAA 2001

Balancing charges are treated as trading receipts.

SECTION 4

Patent box

In order to improve the UK's attractiveness as a place to do business the government introdu- **29235**
s 357A CTA 2010 ced an elective patent box regime for income arising on or after 1 April 2013. Profits that are in the box are taxed at a lower rate, which is achieved by applying a reduction to the profits, then taxing the balance in the normal way.

Comment 1. This incentive may not be that **useful** for many companies, as it is restricted to UK and EU patents only (thereby excluding US patents). Further, several companies avoid applying for patents in order to maintain a level of secrecy from competitors. Certain other countries, including Luxembourg, Belgium, and Spain, have introduced an Innovation Box, which applies not only to a much wider range of intellectual property, but also results in a much lower tax rate. So, internationally, the patent box will not be that influential when companies are deciding where to locate their intellectual property, and the main benefit will be to UK companies who already hold domestic patents.
2. Those companies who wish to **obtain the most advantage** from the UK patent box regime should consider the following:
– identifying all possible patented items which the company or group owns, and whether to apply for further UK patents where this is commercially viable; and

– working through the various possible patent box calculations, especially in respect of the simplified claim (¶29400+) procedure, to ensure the company is benefiting from the maximum tax break.

A. Scope

29265
ss 357B, 357G,
357GA CTA 2010

A company must hold interests in qualifying patents (or an exclusive licence in respect of qualifying patents) from which it derives qualifying income. Additionally, companies who previously held such interests may also qualify where income is received in the current accounting period which is derived from patents (e.g. compensation for infringement).

An **election** into the regime is made on a company by company basis, so that certain companies in a group can elect without any consequences falling on other group members. The election must be notified to HMRC, and will be effective from the beginning of the specified accounting period until it is revoked.

A company is free to **opt out** of the box at any time, by giving notice of revocation to HMRC, although in order to prevent exploitation, a company will not then be able to opt back into it for 5 years.

> MEMO POINTS   1. **Notice** of the election must specify the first accounting period to which it is to apply. The time limit for submission to HMRC is 12 months after the usual filing due date of the return for that accounting period (¶46110). In practice, HMRC will accept a corporation tax computation including a box deduction as evidence of an election, so long as it is submitted by the usual due date. The same rules apply for the **revocation** of an election.
> 2. If a company has **more than one trade** the election will apply to all the company's trades. In this case the patent box deduction is calculated separately for each trade, and any resulting loss (¶29395) must be set against the profits of the other trades.

s 357BA CTA 2010
> 3. An **exclusive licence** is one granted by the proprietor, being someone who holds either the qualifying IP right or an exclusive licence over that right, which gives the licensee exclusive rights over at least some of the IP rights extending throughout an entire national territory. On intra-group transfers of rights under an exclusive licence, the transferee company is treated as holding the licence for the purposes of these rules.

s 357CE CTA 2010
> 4. Licences which include **both exclusive and non-exclusive** elements are treated as two separate licences, and only income relating to the exclusive part is qualifying income.

Qualifying patents

29275
s 357BB CTA 2010

Qualifying patents and rights are **restricted to** the following:
– those granted by the UK Intellectual Property Office (IPO) or under the European Patent Convention, irrespective of whether local overseas patent registrations also apply i.e. the worldwide income of these patents will qualify;
– Supplementary Protection Certificates (SPC), which extend the protection afforded by qualifying patents in respect of pharmaceutical and agrochemical products;
– plant variety rights;
– medicinal and veterinary products which are granted marketing authorisations and marketing or data protection; and
– plant protection products with data protection benefits.

Further, patent rights granted by the following **EU member states**, which are equivalent to those granted in the UK, are also included:

Austria	Bulgaria	Czech Republic	Denmark	Estonia
Finland	Germany	Hungary	Poland	Portugal
Romania	Slovak Republic	Sweden		

A patent will **cease to qualify** for the box once the patent or associated SPC has expired.

SI 2012/420
> MEMO POINTS   1. Where an EU state has **multiple processes** that lead to a right similar to a UK patent, only rights granted under the most rigorous test in that jurisdiction will qualify.
> 2. **Utility patents**, and any similar "**second tier**" rights, are excluded.

Development

Either the company itself or a group company must have performed sufficient **activity** to develop the invention or its application.

29280
s 357BC CTA 2010

Comment   The intention behind this rule is to restrict the box to companies and groups which have been properly involved in the innovation lying behind the patent.

For this purpose HMRC state that the following are **excluded**:

29285

– simply applying for a patent in respect of acquired rights;
– acquiring rights to and marketing a fully developed patent or invention, or product incorporating the invention;
– commercialisation of a product or process that is otherwise fully developed; or
– activities which are limited to other commercial and legal matters, such as the negotiation of a licence, or the challenging or defending of a patent.

MEMO POINTS   Development is **defined** as either:
– creating, or significantly contributing to the creation of, the patented invention; or
– performing a significant amount of activity to develop the patented invention, or any product or process which incorporates it,
and satisfying one of the four conditions shown in the table below:

s 357GD CTA 2010

Situation	Conditions to be met
A company has carried out the qualifying development activity itself	Since that time the company has not ceased to be, or become, a controlled member of a group [1]
	A change of ownership occurs which means that the company has ceased to be [2], or becomes [3], a controlled member of a group. The company must continue to perform development activity of the same description for at least 12 months after the change of ownership
A company has not carried out the qualifying development activity itself but is a member of a group [1]	Another company in the group has carried out the qualifying development activity. The claimant company need not have been a member of the group at the time that the activity was performed
A group [1] acquires company which has carried out qualifying development activity	The acquired company must continue with the same qualifying development activity for at least 12 months after acquisition. The qualifying IP can be transferred to another company in the group, as can the trade (to either the same company or yet another group company)

Note:
1. A group is **defined** as a company ("Company A"), and every company with which Company A is associated, which means one of the following tests is met:
– the financial results of Company A and the other company are fully consolidated into a single set of financial statements;
– Company A and the other company are connected (¶16580); or
– Company A has a major interest in the other company or vice versa (¶16610).
2. A company **ceases to be a controlled member of a group** if every other member of that group that controlled it, or held a major interest in it, ceases to do so and, as a result, the company ceases to be associated with any of those companies. So the company can leave the group on its own, or as a member of a subgroup.
3. A company **becomes a controlled member of a group** if another company ("Company X") becomes the holder of a major interest in it or begins to control it and, immediately before that time, the company was not associated with Company X or any company associated with Company X.

Ownership

Beneficial ownership determines the eligibility of patents rather than legal ownership.

29290
ss 357GB, 357GC
CTA 2010

This means that the box rules include:

a. partnerships, so that certain (but not necessarily all) partners can elect to be taxed as if the partnership itself had elected into the regime, and the profit allocated to the partner will then be reduced through the patent box calculation to ensure the actual profits are charged at 10%. The partnership meets the development condition (¶29280) if it has itself carried out qualifying development in relation to the right, or if a relevant corporate partner (entitled to at least a 40% share of the partnership's profits or losses) has done so; and

b. cost-sharing arrangements, which may be established as a separate legal entity (to which the patent box rules will apply as usual) or as a contractual arrangement. In the latter case, where only one of the parties to the arrangement holds a qualifying IP right or exclusive licence, all of the parties to the arrangements will be treated as owning it, so long as they are:
– required to contribute to the development of the item to which the right relates (or any product incorporating it); and
– entitled to a proportionate share of the income from exploiting the right.

Comment   When **companies are acquired or sold** it will be necessary to ensure that the development and ownership criteria are both met if the benefit of the patent box is to continue.

29295
s 357BE CTA 2010

Groups   Patents can be transferred intra-group whilst still remaining in the box. For the definition of group see ¶29285.

Any company claiming the box reduction must be actively involved in the ongoing **decision-making** which is required for the exploitation of the patent. For example, deciding on:
– whether to maintain protection in particular jurisdictions;
– whether to grant licences;
– whether to research alternative applications for the innovation or licensing others to do so;
– which products, incorporating the invention, will go to market; and
– what features those products will have, and how and where they will be sold.

HMRC state that the company is not required to take all decisions relating to the patent's management (particularly where certain issues must be considered by the holding company's board). Further, there may be minimal management activity in some accounting periods, as dictated by commercial necessity.

Relevant IP income

29300
ss 357CA – 357CF
CTA 2010

Relevant IP income **excludes** financial income and income derived from oil extraction, but **includes** worldwide income derived from any of the categories shown in the table below.

Type of income	Details
Income from the sale of qualifying items i.e. the invention covered by the qualifying patent (¶29275)	Includes items: – incorporating the patented invention (or designed to incorporate it) if sold together as a single unit and at a single price[1]; or – which form spare parts
All royalties or licence fees received for use of qualifying patent protected inventions, including notional royalties[2]	Receipts must derive from an agreement that grants at least one of the following rights[3] in respect of either: – any qualifying patent e.g. an exclusive licence in respect of a UK patent; – a qualifying item or process e.g. where a company licenses worldwide patent rights to another company, any non-UK or EPO licence income which is derived from the same item or process as covered by the UK patent will be included; – non-patented items, if the purpose of granting those rights is the same as for the rights over the qualifying patent; or – fees or royalties received in respect of a qualifying process i.e. a process in respect of which a company holds a qualifying patent

Type of income	Details
Income from the sale or other disposal of a qualifying patent right or exclusive licence	For patent rights acquired: – on or after 1 April 2002, the income will be the difference between the disposal proceeds and the tax written down value (¶28485); or – before 1 April 2002, spreading may apply, so that the relevant income will be the amount calculated under those rules (¶29070+) Excludes all sales and other disposals of non-qualifying patents, even if they relate to inventions that the company also protects by qualifying patents
Infringement income	Includes income received: – from an alleged infringement; and – after expiry or sale of the relevant patent right, provided that the infringement took place when the right was a qualifying patent right, and the company had elected into the patent box Where income relates to a period prior to 1 April 2013, an appropriate portion of the income should be included
Insurance, compensation or other damages	Such receipts must either be: – in respect of qualifying items (see above); or – an amount in respect of lost income which, if it had been received, would have represented qualifying income For example, if a UK company agrees an out of court settlement of £10 million in respect of an alleged infringement of both its UK and US patents, the compensation relating to the UK patent comes within this category

Note:
1. For this purpose **packaging/containers** and their contents are separate items, unless the packaging etc performs an additional function which is essential to allow the contents to be used as intended e.g. a medical inhaler which includes a sleeve and canister, which are both needed to deliver the active ingredient. HMRC state that where the packaging is not patented but the contents are, there will generally be no real difference in practice to distinguish income from packaging separately, due to the apportionment rules (see note 3 below).
2. **Notional royalties** relate to patents used in processes that create non-patented products or to provide services e.g. a patented tool is used in the manufacturing process of non-patented items which are sold by the company. Using transfer pricing principles (¶70155+), the qualifying income is an amount equal to the royalty that would be paid to an independent owner of the qualifying patent rights for the company's exclusive use of those rights.
3. Where a single licence grants a **bundle of rights**, some of which are non-qualifying, the income must be apportioned on a just and reasonable basis, unless the non-qualifying part is trivial (which HMRC take to mean less than 5%), when the entire income will qualify. This rule also applies to non-patented containers and packaging.

MEMO POINTS 1. **Financial income** includes: s 357CB CTA 2010
– trading loan relationships credits;
– any amounts that GAAP treats as arising from a financial asset e.g. dividends or the sale of shares;
– any return that is economically equivalent to interest (¶16610); and
– credits in respect of a company's derivative contracts.
2. Where the accounts **do not comply with GAAP** qualifying income will still be computed by using the amounts which would have been shown had GAAP compliant accounts been prepared.

Timing

The usual **date** from which income will fall within the regime will be the date of grant of approval to the patent, and not the date of the patent application.

29305
s 357CQ CTA 2010

However, a company can elect to recognise income received during a **retrospective period** of up to 6 years from the date of grant, so that income arising since the date of the patent application will also benefit from the box rate. The actual benefit will be delayed until the accounting period when the patent is granted. Such an election also extends to the situation where a company received income whilst the patent was pending, but disposed of its rights before the patent was actually granted.

The **additional amount** is the difference between the actual box profits (¶29395+) of each accounting period in the retrospective period (disregarding any amounts set off by a loss), and what they would have been had the patent in question been granted.

MEMO POINTS 1. No formal **election** procedure is set down, so an appropriate note in the tax computation will be sufficient.

2. For this purpose the company will be deemed to be a **qualifying company** (¶29265) for an accounting period even though the patent has not yet been granted.

3. Where a **loss** (¶29395) results from the patent box calculation for a particular accounting period, and the company has elected to include this accounting period within its retrospective period, it must still be set off against box profits arising from other accounting periods i.e. only the net figure is available as the additional amount.

Commencement

29310
Sch 2 paras 7, 8
FA 2012

The box is being **phased in** over 5 years, as follows:

Financial year beginning	% of full benefit available
1 April 2013	60
1 April 2014	70
1 April 2015	80
1 April 2016	90
1 April 2017	100

Where a company's accounting period **straddles 1 April 2013** the box will only apply to income arising on or after this date. Apportionment should be done on a just and reasonable basis.

For **subsequent accounting periods**, patent profits must be apportioned between the two applicable financial years.

Where a company has a **set off amount** (¶29395) (i.e. the calculation results in a box loss) which is carried forward during the transitional period, the amount brought forward is reduced incrementally by 10% p.a.

EXAMPLE A Ltd has box profits of £100,000 for the year ended 31 December 2014. This is dealt with as follows:

FY	% of box available	Days in period	Calculation	Adjusted box profits
FY 2013	60%	90	90/365 x 100,000 x 60%	14,795
FY 2014	70%	275	275/365 x 100,000 x 70%	52,740
				67,535

B. Calculation

29340

To achieve an effective tax rate of 10% the box requires the profit relating to patents to be isolated, and then for the resulting trading deduction to be computed.

Comment This procedure avoids complications if the company claims trading losses or other reliefs.

1. Quantifying the box profit

29370
s 357C CTA 2010

To calculate the profits which are attributable to qualifying patents, the following **three-step process** is required:

a. determine how much (adjusted) taxable trading profit is attributable to relevant IP income i.e. that which relates to patents and products containing patented inventions;

b. deduct a routine profit from the trading profits relating to IP in order to calculate the residual IP profit. The routine profit is basically 10% of almost all trading expenses; and
c. of the residual IP profit, isolate how much actually relates to patents.

Apportionment

Unless mandatory streaming is required or advantageous, the apportionment calculation compares the relevant IP income (¶29300) with the total gross income of the trade, and applies that same proportion to profits of the trade, in order to establish the trading profit attributable to qualifying IP income. Note that only relevant IP income which is included within the company's total gross trading income is necessary to the calculation.

29375
ss 357CB, 357CG
CTA 2010

For this purpose the company's **total gross trading income** and PCTCT will need to be adjusted to **exclude**:
- interest payable;
- financial income (¶29300); and
- any amounts which are equivalent to interest, including credits on derivative contracts.

Further adjustments will be required in respect of research and development (R&D).

> ⌐MEMO POINTS⌐ 1. **Mandatory streaming** applies when any of the following conditions are satisfied: s 357DC CTA 2010
> **a.** the total gross income of the trade includes a substantial amount of credits brought into account for computing the profits of the trade, but these are not fully recognised as revenue in accordance with GAAP e.g. transfer pricing adjustments;
> **b.** the total gross income of the trade includes a substantial amount of licensing income that is not relevant IP income; or
> **c.** conduit arrangements, where a company is relicensing rights it already holds.
> For the purposes of **a.**, **b.**, and **c.** above, **substantial** means the lower of £2 million or 20% of the total gross income of the trade for the accounting period, subject to a de minimis threshold of £50,000, below which mandatory streaming does not apply.
> 2. Where the normal **apportionment calculation gives an unfair result**, there is a streaming   s 357D CTA 2010
> alternative, which means that the company elects to allocate income and expenses between IP and non-relevant activities on a just and reasonable basis, consistently year on year. Briefly, all amounts brought in as taxable credits (excluding finance income) of the trade in the accounting period are divided into two streams of income, by identifying how much is relevant IP income and how much is not. Similarly, all deductions (ignoring loan relationship debits etc but including the R&D adjustment (¶29380)) are allocated to the stream to which they relate. The deductions relating to IP income are then subject to the 10% mark up (¶29390). The small claims treatment is available as usual as an alternative to deducting a marketing assets return figure (if calculating the latter (¶29410), the full amount of the actual marketing royalty is used).

> ⌐EXAMPLE⌐ B Ltd manufactures and sells a range of established products which are not protected by qualifying IP, giving a turnover of £900,000 with net profits of £50,000. The company also owns qualifying IP which it has licensed out to another business for a fee of £100,000. So B Ltd's total trading profits are £150,000. (50,000 + 100,000)
> B Ltd's total trading income is £1 million. (900,000 + 100,000)
> Using the usual apportionment method would give profits attributable to IP income of only £15,000. (100,000/1 million x 150,000)
> Streaming would enable the company to have profits attributable to IP income of £100,000.

Research and development costs Any research and development (R&D) **enhanced deduction** (¶78330+ and ¶78435+) (but not the actual R&D costs themselves) must be excluded from PCTCT.

29380
s 357CH CTA 2010

Within the **first 4 years** after electing into the patent box, a special calculation is required in order to include an average amount of R&D expenditure, so that the full development cost of the patent is taken into account. First, the average R&D spend in the 4 years prior to entry to the box must be computed. This figure is then compared to the actual R&D spend in each accounting period in the 4 years after entry to the box, and where there is a shortfall (i.e. the actual amount is less than 75% of the average), this is added back to the profits.

> ⌐MEMO POINTS⌐ 1. Where an **accounting period is less than 12 months** the average amount of R&D spend is proportionately reduced.

2. If the company has **traded for less than 4 years** before electing into the box, the average amount of R&D spend is calculated since the first day of trading.

3. For this purpose R&D expenditure is **defined** as that recognised in the company's statutory accounts under UK GAAP, and brought into account in calculating the profits of the trade.

EXAMPLE   C Ltd has an average R&D spend of £1,000 in the 4 years before entering the box. The results of the first 4 years after entering the box are as follows:

	Year 1 £	Year 2 £	Year 3 £	Year 4 £
R&D spend	1,500	800	350	200
PCTCT	700	4,000	3,500	4,600

The R&D adjustments are as follows:

	Year 1 £	Year 2 £	Year 3 £	Year 4 £
Actual R&D spend	1,500	800	350	200
Average R&D in 4 years prior to box	(1,000)	(1,000)	(1,000)	(1,000)
Excess/(shortfall)	500	(200)	(650)	(800)
Shortfall (only recognise if more than 25% of average R&D i.e. £250)	n/a	less than £250	400[1]	550[1]
Difference brought forward	-	500	500	100
Difference carried forward	500	500	100	Nil
Shortfall to take account in PCTCT	n/a	n/a	n/a	450

So only Year 4 is affected by the shortfall adjustment, which proceeds as follows:

		Year 4 £
Original R&D spend		200
Shortfall		450
Revised R&D spend		650
Original PCTCT		4,600
Revised PCTCT	(4,600 – 450)	4,150

Note:
1. The actual shortfall is reduced by £250 each time i.e. 25% of the average R&D.

29385   **Calculation**   The adjusted PCTCT is allocated to qualifying IP income by using the following **formula**:

$$\text{Adjusted PCTCT} \times \frac{\text{Relevant IP income}}{\text{Total gross income}}$$

MEMO POINTS   The same formula applies in the case of a **loss-making** company, and the result will obviously be a negative figure.

EXAMPLE   D Ltd has trading turnover of £1 million, of which £700,000 is from the sale of qualifying patented products. Its initial tax computation is as follows:

		£	£
Trading turnover			1,000,000
R&D	Does not qualify for R&D tax credits	100,000	
Other expenses		675,000	
			(775,000)
PCTCT			225,000

The qualifying income of £700,000 represents 70% of the trading turnover. (700,000/1,000,000)
So 70% of the PCTCT is deemed to relate to the qualifying income i.e. £157,500. (225,000 x 70%)

Qualifying residual profit

29390
ss 357CI – 357CK
CTA 2010

To compute the residual profit which relates to IP (otherwise known as qualifying residual profit) the **routine profit** (i.e. the profit which is not eligible for the box) must be stripped out.

In order to calculate the routine profit a 10% mark up is applied to **routine deductions**. For this purpose these deductions comprise various elements as shown in the following table.

Trading deduction	Excluded	Included
Capital allowances	Allowances in respect of patents and R&D	All other allowances
Research and development	Cost in accounts plus any additional deduction computed under the R&D rules (¶78295+)	
Premises expenses		Rent, rates, repair and maintenance, water, fuel and power costs etc
Personnel costs	Costs relating to employees who are engaged in relevant R&D	Any expenditure incurred in respect of directors or employees, including: – Class 1 and Class 1A NIC; – share scheme deductions; – pension contributions; and – amounts paid in respect of externally provided workers (¶78250)
Plant and machinery costs		Any deductible costs associated with plant and machinery owned or leased by the company e.g. costs of leasing, constructing, modifying, maintaining, servicing, operating etc
Professional services		Legal services, financial services including accounting, audit and valuation functions, and costs associated with the administration and management of the company
Miscellaneous services	All finance costs	Computer software costs, consultancy and professional costs, telecommunications, postal, computing, transport and waste disposal services

MEMO POINTS   Routine deductions **incurred by another group company** on behalf of the patent box company are also included e.g. premises costs, which should be apportioned between the companies on a reasonable basis, so that the patent box company includes its appropriate share of the total expense.

Box profit

Unless the result of ¶29390 above is a loss (subject to any adjustment in respect of a retrospective period (¶29305)), the box profit (i.e. the profits **directly attributable to** patents) must be isolated from profits derived from brands and marketing assets.

29395

There are two available **methods** for calculating the box profits, either:
– the small claims treatment, which is simpler, but only available where certain conditions are met; or
– the default method, available to all companies.

MEMO POINTS   1. Where a **loss** arises from the calculation so far (either because the IP is not producing profits yet, or the IP profit is less than a routine return on expenses), it is ringfenced and carried forward for the purposes of the box calculation only, unless the company is a member of a group, or it has more than one trade, when the loss must be set against any box profits arising in the other trade.

ss 357E – 357EF
CTA 2010

2. A **group** company must set off any box loss against another group company's box profit, where the accounting period of the loss-making company ends at the same time or within an accounting period of another group member. The loss-making company can compensate the other company for the resulting restriction in its box profit, and the amount paid will be ignored for tax purposes.

3. **Box losses carried forward** must be set against the first available box profit, either in the company itself, or in a group company. If the company ceases to trade the losses are extinguished

unless the company has another ongoing trade, or is a member of a group. On a transfer of trade the loss goes to the transferee.

29400
ss 357CL, 357CM
CTA 2010

Small claims treatment The small claims treatment is available where the qualifying residual profits (¶29390) of all trades in aggregate do not exceed £3 million. This limit is apportioned where there are associated companies (¶40185) that have also made patent box elections and to account for periods shorter than a year.

Where the qualifying residual profits **do not exceed £1 million** (ignoring any negative qualifying residual profits which may arise where a company has numerous trades) the small claims treatment is automatically available.

If the profits **exceed £1 million**, but are still under the £3 million limit, provided the company has not used the default method (¶29410) for any accounting period beginning in the previous 4 years then the small claims treatment will be available.

29405 Where either of the conditions in ¶29400 is met, a company can elect to adopt the following approach, so if it has only **one trade**, the box profits will be the lower of:
– 75% of the qualifying residual profit (¶29390); and
– £1 million (as adjusted for associated companies (¶40185) which have also made a patent box election, and accounting periods of less than 1 year).

> ⌐MEMO POINTS⌐ 1. There is no formal **election procedure**, so a company includes the election for small claims treatment by way of a note to the computation in its corporation tax return.
> 2. Where a company has **more than one trade** the qualifying residual profit of each of the trades is aggregated to determine whether the small claims limit has been exceeded. Any negative amounts of qualifying residual profit in a trade are ignored. Where the total does not exceed £1,333,333, the box profits are 75% of the qualifying residual profit in each trade. Otherwise, the box profits will be £1,000,000 (for the company as a whole), as adjusted for associated companies (¶40185) which have also made a patent box election, and accounting periods of less than 1 year.

29410
s 357CN – 357CP
CTA 2010

Default method If a company does not elect for small claims treatment it must deduct a marketing assets return figure in order to calculate its box profits. Note that where a loss would result from this the company should make a small claims election.

For this purpose the **marketing assets return figure**, in respect of the trade for the accounting period, is calculated as:

$$\text{Notional marketing royalty} - \text{Actual marketing royalty}$$

where:
– the notional marketing royalty is the appropriate percentage of the relevant patent income that a company would pay to a third party for the exclusive right to exploit the relevant marketing assets; and
– actual marketing royalty is the amounts that are deductible in the accounting period for payments actually made to acquire or exploit the relevant marketing assets e.g. a royalty paid to use a marketing asset, or an amortisation charge in relation to an acquired marketing asset.

Where either:
– the **actual royalty exceeds the notional royalty**; or
– the **difference between the two is less than** 10% of qualifying residual profits (¶29390) for the accounting period,

the marketing assets return figure will be nil.

HMRC state that this will be helpful to companies where it is evident that **marketing activities are minimal** and make no significant contribution to the generation of profit, or where an arm's length royalty is actually paid. In these cases there is no need to carry out a detailed calculation.

Although the marketing assets return figure should be **recomputed** at the beginning of each accounting period, HMRC state this is only necessary where there have been significant changes in the relevant contributions of marketing assets.

MEMO POINTS 1. **Marketing assets** are those that are exploited in generating the relevant IP income, and comprise any of the following:
– anything in respect of which proceedings for passing off could be brought i.e. the company's goodwill or reputation has been damaged by the misrepresentations of another party e.g. use of the company's trademark without permission;
– equivalent rights recognised under the law of another country;
– signs or indications of geographical origin of goods or services; and
– information about actual or potential customers which is used for marketing purposes.
2. The **notional marketing royalty** assumes that an agreement can be made for the company to exploit the assets to the exclusion of all others, even if the assets cannot, in fact, be separately transferred or assigned. The royalty should be the full amount that the company would be willing to pay to be able to use the marketing assets in an arm's length situation, and the usual transfer pricing methodologies may be used (¶70155+).
3. To calculate the **actual marketing royalty** the total marketing amounts paid are split between relevant IP income (¶29300) and other income on the same pro-rata basis as other expenses (¶29390).

2. Tax liability

The 10% tax rate is **given effect** by means of a deduction in computing taxable profits.

29440
s 357A CTA 2010

The resulting reduced profits are then taxed at the usual rate of corporation tax (i.e. either the small profits rate or mainstream rate).

Where **no box profit arises** because the result of the calculation is a loss (¶29395) the company will be taxed on its actual profits, or will be able to relieve its losses, as if it had made no patent box election for that accounting period.

Deduction

The tax deduction is calculated using the following **formula**:

29445

$$\text{Total box profit} \times \frac{(\text{Main corporation tax rate} - \text{Box rate})}{\text{Main corporation tax rate}}$$

EXAMPLE E Ltd has trading profits of £1,000, all of which qualify for the patent box. The required calculation is as follows:

		£
Profits subject to patent box		1,000
Patent box deduction	$1,000 \times \dfrac{(23\% - 10\%)}{23\%}$	(565)
Taxable profits		435
Tax charge	$435 \times 23\%$	100

The result of £100 is 10% of the qualifying profits.

3. Anti-avoidance

The rules include three anti-avoidance provisions, which **prevent** the following:

29475
ss 357F – 357FB
CTA 2010

a. exclusive rights being conferred which are commercially irrelevant, just to generate income which will qualify for the box in the licensee's hands. However, where a choice is made between two validly commercial options, one of which will qualify for the box, this anti-avoidance rule will not apply;

b. qualifying items being incorporated into a product with the motive of generating qualifying income. Again, HMRC state that this rule is not intended to affect any reasonable commercial choice, including applying for patents which will qualify for the box instead of relying on secrecy; and

c. schemes whose main purpose is to secure a relevant tax advantage from the box.

s 167A TIOPA 2010 Additionally, the exemption from the **transfer pricing** rules for small and medium sized enterprises (¶70050+) will be disapplied where HMRC issue a transfer pricing notice in respect of a transaction which involves shifting profits into a company so that it can take advantage of the patent box regime.

Schemes

29480
s 357FB CTA 2010

A **relevant tax advantage** arises where either:

a. box profits are increased as a result of the scheme; or

b. the scheme is one of those shown in the table below.

However, HMRC state that the following **do not constitute a scheme** for this purpose:

– making a patent box election, or delaying it until the company starts to make box profits;

– opting out of the patent box once box profits become box losses (though no further box election will be possible within 5 years);

– creating IP holding companies to crystallise income from qualifying IP in the form of royalties;

– separating trades with profitable qualifying IP income streams and those with non profit-able income streams into different companies, to allow decisions about whether or not to elect in to the regime to be made more easily; and

– bringing qualifying IP into the UK.

Further, where **group restructuring** is undertaken to maximise the patent box benefits, this will not constitute tax avoidance where the transactions are reasonable and commercially appropriate, and they would not have been treated as a scheme if set up from scratch.

Scheme	Details
Schemes designed to circumvent the patent box rules	This applies to any arrangement which avoids any of the rules so as to inflate the tax advantage
Mismatch schemes	Designed to create a mismatch between the expense of acquiring or developing a qualifying IP right (or an exclusive licence over a qualifying IP right) and the income arising from that right or licence e.g. an expense is incurred whilst the company (or a company with which it is grouped) is outside the regime, but the income arises once the company has elected into the regime
Inflating relevant IP income	HMRC give the example of a single agreement which is made for the sale of both qualifying and non-qualifying items, so that the sale proceeds are allocated unreasonably towards the qualifying items

CHAPTER 3

Disposals

30000 The basic rules for calculating chargeable gains are common to all persons (i.e. companies, individuals, trusts etc), although there have been additional refinements in respect of non-corporates in recent years.

s 8 TCGA 1992　Companies are liable to corporation tax on any chargeable gains (less allowable losses) arising in the particular accounting period, which are included in the profits chargeable to corporation tax (PCTCT) as another source of income, and disclosed on the CTSA return. Note that although gains and income are merged together for the purposes of assessing the corporation tax charge, they must retain their individual identity due to the separate loss relief rules which apply to revenue and capital losses (¶35005).

The assets affected by the chargeable gains rules are disposals of investments i.e. land and property, and shares. For disposals of most intangible assets see ¶28135+. Disposals of securities (rather than shares) are taxed under the loan relationship rules (¶16050+).

> ⎍MEMO POINTS⎍　For details of what chargeable gains arise on a company that is being wound up see ¶61000+, including the new **disincorporation** relief.

SECTION 1

General principles

Overview

30050 There are **two key principles** when computing chargeable gains:
− a capital gain is the amount by which the disposal value of a chargeable asset in the hands of a chargeable person exceeds its acquisition value (and the cost of any permanent improvements); and
− a capital loss arises when the proceeds are less than the acquisition cost etc (and there are specific rules for the set-off of these losses (¶37000+)).

Other important factors include:
− ascertaining whether a disposal has actually occurred;
− the timing of the transaction, in respect of the dates of both acquisition and disposal;
− the residence of the company;
− the location of the asset;
− whether capital allowances have been claimed in respect of the asset; and
− indexation allowance.

1. What is a disposal?

The term disposal is not **defined** by statute but is taken to mean more than just a transfer for consideration in respect of an asset.

30080
s 1 TCGA 1992

CG 12704

However, no disposal will take place in the following **excluded situations**:

Exclusions	¶¶
A reorganisation of share capital i.e. where either: – persons are allotted shares in a company in proportion to their existing shareholdings; or – the respective rights attaching to various classes of shares in the company are altered	¶32235+
Conversion of securities	¶32285
Company reconstructions e.g. involving an exchange of shares, or acquiring a business by issuing shares	¶79290+
Transfer of legal ownership between a nominee and beneficial owner	

Natural disposals

The most **common form** of disposal is a change in the ownership of an asset, as a result of sale, exchange or gift.

30085

Other forms of disposal include:
a. the grant and exercise of an option;
b. capital sums received:
– as compensation for damage or destruction;
– in return for surrendering rights or refraining from exercising rights; or
– as consideration for the use or exploitation of an asset;
c. the entire loss, destruction, dissipation or extinction of an asset, irrespective of whether a capital sum is received as compensation or insurance.

A disposal can arise where part of the asset is retained (¶31130+), or where an interest or right in or over an asset is created.

Note that where no chargeable gain could accrue in respect of a transaction, there will be no allowable loss.

Deemed disposals

Tax may also be charged if the legislation **specifically provides** for a transaction to be treated as if it were a disposal, as in the following cases:

30090
CG 12703

Situation	¶¶
Value shifting	¶32410+
Company migration	¶91435+
Non-resident company carrying on a business through a UK permanent establishment	¶92105+
A company leaving a group and taking with it assets transferred to it by other group members in the previous 6 years	¶67425+
Appropriations to and from trading stock	¶11710
A claim by the owner of an asset that it is of negligible value	¶31720+

Identifying the asset disposed of

As with disposal, asset is not **defined** in statute and so must be given its natural meaning.

30095
CG 12760

HMRC state that an asset is whatever is covered by a specific item of expenditure on an acquisition, whether made by purchase or otherwise.

With regard to **land** a part disposal may be treated as a separate asset (¶31790+).

There are also special rules with regard to the grant of an **option** (¶31445+).

Enhancement expenditure may alter the character of the asset, but does not create a new asset.

2. Time of disposal

30125
s 28 TCGA 1992

The date of disposal is **generally** taken to be the date when contracts are made (i.e. when the purchaser legally acquires the asset), although there are numerous **exceptions**:

Transaction	Date of disposal	Reference
Receipt of a capital sum (e.g. insurance money)	When the capital sum is received	s 22 TCGA 1992
Conditional contracts	When the condition is fulfilled	s 28 TCGA 1992
Hire purchase	When use or enjoyment of asset is received	s 27 TCGA 1992
Value of asset becomes negligible	When company claims, unless an earlier time is specified	s 24 TCGA 1992
Compulsory land purchase orders	When compensation is agreed (or otherwise determined i.e. by arbitration)	s 246 TCGA 1992
Entire loss or destruction of an asset	When the loss or destruction takes place	s 24 TCGA 1992
Gifts	When the donor has done everything possible to transfer the asset	

3. Chargeable persons

30145
s 2 TCGA 1992

A chargeable person is essentially any company which is not exempt but trading in the UK.

Exempt bodies

30150
ss 256, 271
TCGA 1992

The following bodies are exempt from tax on chargeable gains:
– **charities** (¶86000+) provided they use gains for charitable purposes;
– **local authorities**;
– **co-operative housing associations**, where the gains relate to a property occupied by a tenant;
– authorised **unit trusts** and open-ended investment companies;
– registered **friendly societies**;
– approved **superannuation** funds; and
– **scientific research associations** (¶22085).

MEMO POINTS   Chargeable gains realised by a company in a **fiduciary or representative capacity** are excluded from the charge to corporation tax, as capital gains tax applies instead. For details of capital gains tax see *Tax Memo*.

Residence issues

30155
ss 2, 10B, 276
TCGA 1992

All **UK-resident** companies are subject to corporation tax on all gains arising, regardless of where the assets are located.

Non-UK-resident companies trading:
– **in the UK** through a permanent establishment (¶92140+) are only taxable on gains accruing on assets situated in the UK and used for the purposes of the trade; or
– **outside the UK** through a foreign permanent establishment are not taxable in the UK, regardless of where the assets are situated.

MEMO POINTS   **UK means** Great Britain and Northern Ireland including the surrounding territorial sea, and excludes the Irish Republic, the Isle of Man and the Channel Islands.

Ownership

For tax purposes, it is **beneficial** ownership which is important, rather than legal ownership. This is particularly relevant for transactions involving land.

30160

---

4. Chargeable assets

A chargeable asset is **defined** as any form of property (wherever situated) including:
- options, debts and other similar property;
- any currency other than sterling; and
- any property created by the person disposing of it (excluding intangible assets created by a company after 31 March 2002); and
- intellectual property acquired or created by the company itself before 1 April 2002.

The asset must be capital in nature (¶13000+).

30190
s 21 TCGA 1992

MEMO POINTS   1. **Sterling** is not an asset for capital gains purposes because it is the unit by reference to which chargeable gains are measured.

2. There is an exemption for **foreign currency** held for an individual's personal use abroad.

Exclusions

Subject to meeting certain criteria, the following assets do not give rise to a chargeable gain (for investments see ¶30200):

30195

Type of asset	Detail	Reference
Intangible assets (¶28135+)	Used on a continuing basis for the company's activities including intellectual property located in the UK and overseas Only applies to assets: – created by the company on or after 1 April 2002; or – acquired on or after this date from an unrelated party (as tested on the asset's acquisition)	s 882 CTA 2009
Car	Only applies to normal passenger vehicles (including classic cars) The following are therefore chargeable assets: – private number plates; – racing cars; – taxis; – vans; – commercial vehicles; and – motorcycles	s 263 TCGA 1992
Woodlands	Where managed by occupier on commercial basis	s 250 TCGA 1992
Chattels	Either: – worth less than £6,000; or – with a predictable life of 50 years or less (unless used for the purposes of a trade, profession or vocation and qualified for capital allowances (¶31655))	ss 45, 262 TCGA 1992
Assets to which the structured finance arrangements apply (¶21915+)	The disposal of the asset by the borrower and/or any subsequent reacquisition	s 263E TCGA 1992

Type of asset	Detail	Reference
Life assurance policies	Where the disposal is made by the original beneficiary, unless purchased The rights of the insurer under a policy of insurance are not considered to be an asset However, the rights of the insured are a chargeable asset where the insured asset is chargeable	s 210 TCGA 1992
Non-life policies of insurance	This exemption does not apply where the insured assets are chargeable assets	s 204 TCGA 1992
Non-marketable government securities	This includes the following securities issued under the National Loans Act 1939 and 1968 (and the corresponding Northern Ireland Acts): – savings certificates and securities; – development bonds; – defence bonds; and – premium bonds	s 121 TCGA 1992
Pension rights	Where the disposal is made by the original beneficiary The fund in question need not be an approved scheme, but it must be established for persons employed in a trade, profession or vocation	s 237 TCGA 1992
Annuity rights	Where they are granted in the ordinary course of a business (unless they are deferred annuities)	s 237 TCGA 1992
Heritage property	Only if certain conditions are met, which broadly means that: – the general public have access to the asset; – the assets are properly maintained; and – they are retained in the UK Common examples include certain works of art, manuscripts, scientific collections, historic buildings, and outstanding scenic land	s 258 TCGA 1992

30200 **Investments** The following investments are exempt:
– EIS shares (¶80055+);
– shares in a VCT (¶80355+);
– gilt edged securities;
– qualifying corporate bonds (broadly, any asset that represents a loan relationship of the company (¶16080+) other than a convertible security or an asset linked to the value of a non-trading asset).

30205 **Receipts** The following receipts are exempt:

ss 51, 268B
TCGA 1992
– compensation from foreign governments in respect of confiscated, expropriated or destroyed assets;

s 148(2) FA 1996
– compensation for mis-sold pensions;
– compensation for professional or personal injury;
– gambling winnings; and

SP 4/97
– mortgage cash backs.

---

5. Location of assets

30235

s 275 TCGA 1992
The location of an asset is determined by statute.

As a general rule an asset will be located where it is physically situated.

  MEMO POINTS 1. The specific rules for **intangibles** will only be of relevance for pre-April 2002 assets, as the intangibles regime otherwise applies (¶28135+).

s 275C TCGA 1992
2. Assets may be **co-owned** i.e. either jointly or in common, and in equal or unequal parts. The location of each owner's interest is the same as the location of the asset were it to be wholly owned.

Asset	Location
Rights or interests over immovable property (e.g. land)	Same country as the immovable property
Rights or interests over chattels	Same country as where the chattel is located
Government issued shares and debentures	Country where issuing authority is located
Other registered shares and debentures	Shares or debentures of any company incorporated in the UK are located in the UK Otherwise country where register is kept
Ships and aircraft	Situated in the country where owner is resident
Options/futures where the underlying subject matter is located (or treated as located) in the UK	Located in the UK
Business goodwill (only relevant where pre-1 April 2002 asset)	Situated in the country where the trade is carried on
Patents, trademarks, designs and corresponding rights (only relevant where pre-1 April 2002 asset)	Country where they are registered Rights or licences to use patents etc are located in the UK if they are exercisable in the UK
Copyright, design rights, franchises and corresponding rights (only relevant where pre-1 April 2002 asset)	Located in UK if they, or any rights derived from them, are exercisable in the UK
Other intangible assets (only relevant where pre-1 April 2002 asset)	Located in the UK if created in the UK

SECTION 2

Computation

The basic computation which must be carried out for each disposal is as follows:

30285

	£	£
Disposal proceeds (¶30320+)		x
Less: Incidental costs of disposal (¶30500)		(x)
		x
Less: Acquisition cost (¶30485)	x	
Incidental costs of acquisition (¶30500)	x	
Enhancement expenditure (¶30490)	x	
Unindexed gain		x
Less: Indexation allowance (¶30530+)		(x)
Indexed gain		x

The following **reliefs** are available to reduce the amount of gains chargeable to tax, and in some cases to extinguish the gain altogether.

30290

Relief	Overview	¶¶
Rollover	Defers the point at which a gain, on an asset used in the trade, becomes chargeable by rolling it over into the base cost of a replacement asset The effect is to reduce the allowable expenditure on the replacement asset	¶30940+
Substantial shareholding exemption	Exemption in respect of the disposal by a company of a substantial shareholding (broadly a holding in excess of 10%)	¶32090+

Relief	Overview	¶¶
Intra-group asset transfers	Assets transferred at no gain/no loss	¶67050+
Losses on unquoted shares of trading companies	Investment company can set capital loss arising against income	¶37230+
Corporate venturing scheme (CVS)	Defer gains on eligible CVS shares by rolling over into new acquisition of CVS shares	¶80545+
Reconstructions	New shares stand in the shoes of the original shares, taking on their date of acquisition and allowable cost	¶79290+

A. Disposal proceeds

30320 Disposal proceeds will usually be the actual consideration received, unless certain circumstances arise which mean that the open market value of an asset should be used instead. In either case, the disposal proceeds may be reduced by incidental costs of disposal.

1. Actual consideration

Definition

30350 Consideration is not defined for capital gains purposes, but where the disposal takes place at **arm's length** between unconnected persons, the consideration is the amount of money or money's worth that changes hands.

CG 14500 Consideration can include:
a. money;
b. the value of any asset received in exchange; and
c. the capitalised value of any of the following:
– the right to receive income or payments in the nature of income;
– relief from liability e.g. the waiver of rent or a loan;
– the benefit of free or low-interest loans; and
– the benefit of rights to obtain goods or services free, or at a discount.

Exclusions

30355 Consideration excludes:
s 37 TCGA 1992 – amounts treated as **income** for corporation tax purposes in respect of the company making the disposal;
– **receipts** which are included in such income (whether resulting in a profit or a loss); and
– **VAT** charged on the disposal.

If the consideration is in a **foreign currency**, it must be converted to sterling at the exchange rate applying at the date of disposal (¶17215).

s 9C TCGA 1992; SI 2013/1815 [MEMO POINTS] For disposals **on or after 1 September 2013** calculations need to be carried out in a company's functional or designated currency (¶17205) where the disposal is of a ship, aircraft, shares or interest in shares.

Recipient of proceeds

30360 Payment does not have to be made to the vendor for it to be deemed to be consideration.

Where a payment is made **to a third party** at the request of the vendor, as opposed to the sum being received by him, this is deemed to be part of the consideration. *Crusader v HMRC* [2007]

Similarly, where the purchaser of a company made a separate payment, on the basis that the target company would then use it to make a contribution into its pension plan, it was held that the payment should be taken into account as part of the consideration. *HMRC v Collins* [2008]

Future payments

Deferred consideration can either be ascertainable at the date of disposal (i.e. the amount is known but is not yet payable), or unascertainable (both the amount and possibly the date of payment are unknown). **30365**

Ascertainable consideration In this case the amount is known, can be calculated or is ascertainable by taking account of **events which have happened by** the date of disposal e.g. the agreement for the disposal includes a sum equal to half of the taxable profits of the business for the year ended on the date of disposal, payable 9 months after the date of the contract, when no discount will be available to take account of the risk of non-payment. If the amount concerned is subsequently deemed to be irrecoverable, a claim may be submitted for an adjustment to be made. **30370**

Where ascertainable consideration is payable in **instalments**, there is a single disposal and the full amount of consideration must be brought into the computation at the date of disposal, assuming that the sums received are indeed capital (¶13050+) as determined by the contract of disposal.

If the instalment **period** is more than 18 months, and instalments fall after the company's usual due date of payment of tax (¶48050+), the company may request for the related tax to be paid in instalments. *s 280 TCGA 1992*

> ⬜ MEMO POINTS 1. Where the company opts to **pay tax in instalments**, the number and frequency of the instalments must be agreed with HMRC, usually comprising instalments of tax equal to 50% of each instalment of consideration due under the contract until the total tax liability has been discharged. However, the instalment period cannot be longer than 8 years, and cannot extend beyond the date on which the final instalment of the consideration is received. *CG 14912*
> 2. Where an instalment arrangement is agreed, **interest** will be charged on any instalment paid after the agreed date, and will run from the date the instalment was due to the date of payment.
> 3. Where instalments are received in relation to a **land disposal** see ¶19490+.

> ⬜ EXAMPLE
> 1. The agreement for the sale of a business provides for a consideration of £300,000, of which £200,000 is payable on completion and £100,000 is payable if the profits of the year, following the date of disposal, exceed £130,000.
> Both elements are quantifiable at the date of disposal, although the £100,000 is contingent.
>
> 2. The agreement for the sale of a piece of land provides for a consideration of £80,000, of which £50,000 is payable on completion and £30,000 is payable if planning permission is granted within a set time limit.
> Again this is all ascertainable consideration.

Unascertainable consideration Where consideration is unquantifiable at the date of disposal and contingent (relying on events which occur after the date of disposal), this is treated as the acquisition of a new asset (i.e. the right to future consideration which is therefore received and cannot become irrecoverable). *Marren v Ingles* [1980] **30375**
s 48 TCGA 1992;
CG 14881

The proceeds for the disposal of the asset must therefore include an amount for the market value of the **right to future consideration** (which requires some method or basis of valuation). This amount is also allowable expenditure for the new asset. There is a separate chargeable occasion when each instalment of future payment is received.

> ⬜ EXAMPLE 1. The agreement for the sale of shares in a company provides for an initial payment of £60,000, plus two further payments equal to the excess of the company's profits over £200,000 in each of the 2 years following the date of the contract. *CG 14888*
> The profits cannot be ascertained at the disposal date.

CG 14970

2. The agreement for the sale of an asset provides for an immediate payment of £250,000, plus a further payment of half the profit made by the purchaser on a subsequent sale of the asset, subject to a maximum of £500,000 on the total to be paid.

Similarly, the profit cannot be ascertained at the disposal date.

3. A Ltd sells its business premises in return for cash plus a right to unascertainable future consideration. It acquires replacement premises and claims rollover relief (¶30940+).

However, rollover relief will not be available to the company on the later disposal of the right, as the right itself is not a qualifying asset for rollover relief purposes.

4. B Ltd acquired a parcel of land in Year 4 for £20,000. The land was sold in Year 10 for £50,000 plus a right to 2% of any profit made on selling smaller parcels of the land. At the date of sale, this was estimated to be a further £15,000.

The position on the disposal of the land is as follows:

	£	£
Proceeds	50,000	
Expected future consideration	15,000	
		65,000
Less: Allowable expenditure (ignoring indexation)		
Original cost		(20,000)
Chargeable gain		45,000

B Ltd receives further consideration of £22,000 in Year 17, once the land is sold.

	£
Proceeds	22,000
Less: Allowable expenditure	
Value at acquisition	(15,000)
Chargeable gain	7,000

If the further consideration had been only £10,000, the calculation would be as follows:

	£
Proceeds	10,000
Less: Allowable expenditure	
Value at acquisition	(15,000)
Allowable loss	(5,000)

Liabilities transferred

30380
ss 48, 49
TCGA 1992

The **assumption of a liability by the vendor**, in connection with the disposal of an asset, will reduce the disposal consideration by the value of the liability assumed.

However, this provision does not apply to liabilities which are **contingent** on a future event relating to:
– the default by an assignee in relation to his obligations under a lease;
– a covenant for quiet enjoyment, or any other obligation assumed as vendor of land, or of any estate or interest in land; or
– a warranty or representation made on a disposal, by way of sale or lease of any property other than land.

If the liability **later becomes enforceable**, an adjustment may be made to the computation.

s 26(3) TCGA 1992 If a mortgage or other similar security is **taken over by the purchaser**, it will be included in the disposal consideration for the asset, along with the other consideration received.

EXAMPLE C Ltd acquires land from D Ltd for £10,000, and agrees to assume the outstanding obligations under D Ltd's mortgage which, at the date of disposal, amount to £50,000. D Ltd's disposal proceeds will be:

	£
Cost	10,000
Liabilities assumed	50,000
Disposal proceeds	60,000

2. Open market value

Market value is **defined** as the price that an asset might reasonably be expected to fetch if it was sold on the open market by a willing vendor to a willing purchaser.

30410

When used

The open market value of an asset will be used as disposal proceeds in the following **circumstances**:

30415
ss 17, 18
TCGA 1992

a. the transaction was not made on arm's length terms i.e. one of the parties to the transaction did not intend to get the best deal for themselves, such as a gift, a transfer between connected persons (¶31370+) or a transfer into a settlement. The subjective intention test has to be applied to each individual transaction, even where the overall effect of a larger plan is not to confer gratuitous benefit. A transaction between connected persons can never be at arm's length, even if the consideration is freely negotiated;

b. the consideration cannot be valued (such as on an exchange of assets);

c. the disposal was made in connection with a loss of employment, reduction of emoluments, or in recognition of past or future services;

d. a claim is made for assets of negligible value (¶31720+);

e. assets are appropriated to or from trading stock; or

f. UK permanent establishment (¶92140+) assets are taken out of the charge to UK corporation tax by a non-resident company.

MEMO POINTS HMRC give the following **factors** which would indicate that a transaction was **not made on arm's length terms**:

CG 14545

– the presence or absence of real negotiations between the parties about the terms of the transaction;

– how the terms of the transaction compare with those in similar commercial transactions;

– whether the parties have separate legal or other professional representation;

– whether the parties have received independent advice;

– the character of any comparable prior dealings between the parties;

– whether the transaction between the parties may be linked with any other transaction between the same parties; and

– the relationship between the parties outside the particular transaction.

EXAMPLE
1. E Ltd wants to sell its business premises quickly. F Ltd is aware of this, so makes a low offer which is accepted.
E Ltd accepts the price F Ltd has offered. Although this is not the best possible price which could have been achieved if the property had been marketed for longer, it is the best deal available given the circumstances, and is a transaction undertaken on arm's length terms.

2. If G Ltd is selling a painting for £500 when the art dealer acquiring it knows it is worth £5,000, this is still a bargain at arm's length.

How to ascertain market value

The valuation should be made on the **basis** of the information which was available, or could have been made available, at the valuation date.

30420
s 272 TCGA 1992

Where two taxpayers are affected by the same valuation, HMRC will look at their case together.

MEMO POINTS 1. If an asset or collection of assets can be broken up and **sold in lots**, HMRC state that they should be valued on the assumption that they will be lotted in such a way as to maximise the proceeds of sale, unless this gives a lower result than keeping the asset whole. Any flooding effect in the market, by having assets of the same type available for sale at the same time, should be ignored.

CG 16340

2. A **special purchaser** i.e. a party with a specific reason to acquire an asset, may be prepared to pay an abnormally high price. Whilst this price is not deemed to be market value, the very existence of the special purchaser may drive up the market value.

CG 16352

30425   **Securities**   The following special provisions apply for the valuation of securities.

Type of security	Market value	Reference
Listed shares and securities	Lower of: – one quarter up on the lower of the two quoted prices; and – the average of the highest and lowest markings at which bargains were recorded for a given date	s 272(3) TCGA 1992
Unit trusts	Lower of two prices quoted i.e. the buying price	s 272(5) TCGA 1992
Unquoted shares	Open market value on the assumption that the purchaser has all of the information that a prudent buyer reasonably requires for a purchase at arm's length	s 273 TCGA 1992

EXAMPLE   Shares in H plc are quoted at 1091p to 1101p. The highest and lowest marked bargains were 1090p and 1101p.
The value will be the lower of:

– 1093.5; $(1091 + \dfrac{1101 - 1091}{4})$ and

– 1095.5. $(\dfrac{1090 + 1101}{2})$

Post-transaction valuation check

30430
CG 16600

There is a mechanism by which HMRC will check company-provided valuations, of any type of asset, for free after the relevant transaction has occurred, including:
– deemed disposals when an asset's value has become negligible (¶31720+); and
– simple apportionments e.g. where a number of assets have been disposed of in a single transaction, but excluding complex areas such as business/non-business use of an asset.

CG 16612

This allows companies to make entries on their CTSA returns with the knowledge that HMRC will not query the valuation used. HMRC consider themselves bound by any prior agreement to a valuation, unless there are any material issues that were not brought to their attention and which affect the basis on which agreement has been reached.

MEMO POINTS   1. HMRC will not give any **pre-transaction** valuations.
2. HMRC will not provide a **valuation for an asset on request** i.e. the company must put forward a valuation which can be checked, although HMRC may suggest an alternative valuation.
3. **Joint owners** of an asset can approach HMRC together when valuing an asset.

CG 16615

4. HMRC state that the **costs** reasonably incurred by a company in determining the valuation or apportionment, which is the subject of the check, are allowable deductions. Any costs incurred in actually making the submission, or in furthering subsequent negotiations, are not deductible in computing the gain or loss on the relevant disposal.

30435   **Timing**   A **request** for a post-transaction valuation check (PTVC) can be made at any time after the transaction has taken place, but before the affected CTSA return is filed.

CG 16611

HMRC state that an **agreement** to a valuation **will take** at least 56 days from making the request, and that in many cases it may take substantially longer. Note that failure to reach agreement on a PTVC is not an acceptable reason for failing to submit a CTSA return within the usual time limit.

30440
CG 16603

How to make a request   Form CG34 should be used to provide information about the disposal, and about the context in which the valuation is required. The **form** and accompanying notes are available at flmemo.co.uk/ctm30440.
In addition to the CG34, the following **information** should also be submitted:
– a copy of the capital gains computation for the accounting period, showing how each valuation has been used and an estimate of the tax liability resulting from the disposal;
– details of any reliefs due or to be claimed in respect of the disposal; and
– a copy of any professional valuer's report obtained, or an explanation of how the valuation has been arrived at.

For **unquoted shares**, and pre-1 April 2002 **goodwill**, the last 3 years' company accounts (up to the valuation date) should be provided.

If **incomplete information** is provided HMRC will not accept the request for the check, unless it is clear that full information is not available.

HMRC's scope of work As HMRC's only responsibility at this stage is to check the valuation, any **computations** may not be reviewed in detail, so the company cannot assume that the computations themselves are agreed as a result of the check.

30445

B. Allowable expenditure

Allowable expenditure is broadly the total cost incurred by the vendor on the acquisition and disposal of the asset, and is comprised of:
- the cost of acquiring the asset;
- enhancement expenditure;
- expenditure incurred wholly and exclusively in connection with the title to the asset; and
- incidental costs.

30475
s 38 TCGA 1992

> MEMO POINTS Where **tax has been suffered overseas** on a disposal, tax credit relief is available, so that the foreign tax is deducted from the part of the corporation tax chargeable in the UK which relates to that gain. Alternatively, the company can choose to have the foreign tax treated as a deduction in the computation of the gain. In this latter case, no indexation is available on the deduction. For further details of double tax relief see ¶90480+.

ss 277, 278
TCGA 1992

Exclusions

The following expenditure is not allowable:
- expenditure which is otherwise deductible in calculating corporation tax;
- contingent liabilities;
- discounts for the postponement of receipt of consideration;
- interest, which is dealt with under the loan relationship provisions (¶16050+);
- insurance premiums paid to cover the risk of damage, loss or depreciation of the asset; and
- expenditure reimbursed out of public funds (such as local authority housing grants).

30480
s 39 TCGA 1992

s 38(3) TCGA 1992
s 205 TCGA 1992
s 50 TCGA 1992

Acquisition

The acquisition cost of the asset is simply the actual or deemed consideration paid by the vendor (or on his behalf) on the initial acquisition of the asset.

Where the asset was **acquired with other assets** in a composite acquisition (e.g. a single contract of purchase at an inclusive price embracing more than one asset), the acquisition price should be apportioned on the basis of market value at the date of acquisition.

30485

s 52 TCGA 1992

Enhancement

Enhancement expenditure (incurred by the owner of the asset or on his behalf) will be included in allowable expenditure if it is:
- incurred wholly and exclusively for the **purposes** of enhancing the asset (not merely connected with the asset); and
- reflected in the **state or nature** of the asset at the date of disposal, so this excludes costs which were futile or have wasted away by the time of disposal.

30490

> MEMO POINTS 1. Where the enhancement expenditure was incurred **before 31 March 1982**, no deduction will be available if the gain is calculated using the market value on 31 March 1982 (¶30785+).
> 2. Expenditure incurred on **initial repairs to a property** (including decoration), in order to put it into a fit state for letting, will be allowed as enhancement expenditure, providing it was not given as a deduction for a property trade.
> 3. **Demolition** costs of a building will be allowed where the demolition enhances the value of the land.

CG 15201

CG 15200

EXAMPLE A Ltd acquired a disused barn in Year 1 for £62,000. A couple of years later, it was converted into a warehouse at a cost of £18,000. The conversion was made without planning permission, and the council stipulated that the building had to be returned to its original state. Shortly thereafter, the building was sold.

The enhancement expenditure is not reflected in the property at the date of sale, and therefore does not form part of the allowable cost.

Title to an asset

30495
s 38(1) TCGA 1992

Expenditure incurred wholly and exclusively for the purposes of **establishing** title to an asset, or defending or **preserving** the title to an asset or rights over it, will usually constitute allowable expenditure.

However, the expenditure must be **incurred by** the owner of the asset and not on his behalf (in contrast to enhancement and acquisition expenditure).

Incidental costs

30500
s 38(2) TCGA 1992

The following are allowable incidental costs (where incurred wholly and exclusively for the sale or purchase (as appropriate)):
– fees, commission or remuneration paid for the **professional services** of any surveyor, valuer, auctioneer, accountant, agent or legal adviser;
– costs of transfer or **conveyance** (including stamp duty and stamp duty land tax);
– **advertising** to find a seller/buyer; and
– costs reasonably incurred in making any **valuation** or apportionment required for the purposes of computing the gain or loss, including expenses incurred in ascertaining market value where this is required by the legislation. Any fees for negotiating with Valuation Division or agreeing a value with a District Valuer are not allowable.

CG 14207

MEMO POINTS 1. For larger businesses (¶46225) **rounding** (to the nearest £1,000) is only allowed for incidental costs of acquisition and disposal.
2. Incidental costs of disposal incurred by a shareholder on a **company takeover reconstruction** (¶79290+) are treated as additional consideration paid for the new shares.

C. Indexation allowance

30530
s 53 TCGA 1992

Indexation allowance aims to take account of inflation between the dates of acquisition and disposal, and is effectively used to increase the original cost of an asset.

The two elements to an indexation allowance calculation are identification of:
– expenditure qualifying for indexation allowance; and
– dates of acquisition and disposal.

1. Qualifying expenditure

30560
s 38 TCGA 1992

Indexation allowance is available for expenditure **incurred wholly and exclusively**:
– on the acquisition of an asset (including any incidental associated costs);
– for the purpose of enhancing the value of an asset (if reflected in the nature of the asset when it is sold); and
– in establishing or defending title or right to an asset.

Incidental costs of disposal are not indexed.

MEMO POINTS 1. For assets acquired **before 31 March 1982** see ¶30785+.
2. For assets acquired **before 1 April 1965** see ¶30675+.
3. Where the **cost** of the asset is **restricted** or adjusted e.g. wasting assets, the qualifying expenditure will similarly be adjusted.

2. Timing

In order to calculate indexation allowance it is necessary to determine the dates of expenditure for each asset. For shares see ¶32190+.

30580

Transaction	Deemed date for indexation purposes
Acquisition	Date the asset itself is acquired or provided
Enhancement	Date expenditure becomes due and payable Where asset is enhanced between the date of acquisition and the date of disposal, the indexation allowance on the original cost and the enhancement expenditure will be calculated separately, based on the dates on which each item of expenditure was incurred Where the enhancement took place before 31 March 1982 and market value has been used (¶30785+) for the calculation of the gain, any enhancement expenditure is ignored
Disposal	See ¶30125

3. Calculation

Indexation allowance is calculated by applying the indexation factor to the qualifying expenditure.

30600

Indexation factor

The indexation factor is based on the retail price index (RPI) (¶95160) and is calculated using the following **formula**:

30605

$$\frac{RD - RI}{RI}$$

where:
- RD is the RPI for the month of disposal; and
- RI is the RPI for the month in which the expenditure was incurred (or, if later, March 1982).

If **RD does not exceed RI** the indexation factor will be nil.

The indexation factor is generally **expressed** as a decimal rounded to three decimal places (unless the disposal relates to certain shares (¶32205)), although HMRC will accept unrounded calculations for all computations where these are used consistently by the company.

> [EXAMPLE] A Ltd buys an asset in October 1987 for £18,000 and sells it for £50,000 in March 2013. The RPIs for October 1987 and March 2013 are 102.90 and 248.70 respectively.
>
> The indexation factor is therefore 1.417. $\left(\frac{248.70 - 102.90}{102.90}\right)$
>
> The indexed gain is:
>
> | | £ |
> |---|---|
> | Disposal proceeds | 50,000 |
> | Less: Cost | (18,000) |
> | Gain before indexation | 32,000 |
> | Indexation: Oct 87 to Mar 13 | |
> | 18,000 × 1.417 | (25,506) |
> | Indexed gain | 6,494 |

Losses

Indexation allowance can never be used to **create or increase** a loss and is therefore restricted to the amount of the unindexed gain.

30610

> EXAMPLE B Ltd buys an asset in August 1983 at a cost of £13,000. It sells the asset for £25,000 in March 2013.
> The RPIs for August 1983 and March 2013 are 85.68 and 248.70 respectively.
>
> The indexation factor is therefore 1.903. $\left(\dfrac{248.7 - 85.68}{85.68}\right)$
>
> | | £ |
> |---|---|
> | Disposal proceeds | 25,000 |
> | Cost | (13,000) |
> | Unindexed gain | 12,000 |
> | Indexation: Aug 83 to Mar 13 | |
> | 13,000 × 1.903 = 24,739 | |
> | Restricted to unindexed gain | (12,000) |
> | Indexed gain | Nil |

4. Special situations

Part disposals

30640 In general on the disposal of part of an asset, indexation allowance is calculated for the proportion of the qualifying expenditure relating to the part disposed of.

However, in the following circumstances a claim may be made to simply **adjust the base cost** of the asset. This means that indexation will be calculated in full on the original cost, and then a notional indexation will be calculated on the adjustment (i.e. from the date of the part disposal to the date of the disposal of the remainder). The **notional indexation** is deducted from the original indexation.

Circumstance	Reference	¶¶
Compensation or insurance policy payouts for lost or destroyed assets	s 23 TCGA 1992	¶31240+
Small part disposals of land	s 242 TCGA 1992	¶31800+
Small part disposals of land as a result of a compulsory purchase order	s 243 TCGA 1992	¶31955+
Small cash receipts in respect of shares	s 122 TCGA 1992	¶32250

> EXAMPLE C Ltd owns land which it acquired in August 1995 for £75,000. In June 1997, it sold part of the land for £16,000. This was the only land transaction made in the accounting period. The value of the entire holding immediately prior to the disposal was £100,000.
> As the transaction qualifies as a small part disposal, the allowable expenditure of the remaining land will be reduced as follows:
>
> | | £ |
> |---|---|
> | Allowable expenditure | 75,000 |
> | Less: Proceeds from small part disposal | (16,000) |
> | Adjusted expenditure | 59,000 |
>
> If the remaining land was disposed of in June 2013 for £100,000, the resulting gain would be calculated as follows:
>
> | | £ | £ |
> |---|---|---|
> | Disposal proceeds | | 100,000 |
> | Adjusted expenditure | 59,000 | |
> | Indexation: Aug 95 to Jun 13 | | |
> | $\dfrac{249.70 - 149.90}{149.90} = 0.666 \times 75,000$ | 49,950 | |
> | Notional indexation: Jun 97 to Jun 13 | | |
> | $\dfrac{249.70 - 157.50}{157.50} = 0.585 \times 16,000$ | (9,360) | |
> | | | (99,590) |
> | Gain | | 410 |

Options

Where the asset being disposed of was acquired by way of an option (¶31415+), indexation allowance is **calculated separately on** the cost of:
- the option (deemed to occur when the option was granted); and
- acquiring the asset (deemed to occur on the exercise of the option).

30645
s 145 TCGA 1992

D. Assets held on 6 April 1965

As capital gains tax did not exist before 6 April 1965, gains arising on assets held on this date are deemed to accrue equally over the period of ownership, and only the part of the gain which arises after 6 April 1965 is chargeable.

30675
Sch 2 para 16
TCGA 1992

1. General principles

Exclusions

The rules in the following paragraphs only apply if a global rebasing election (¶30835) is not in force.

For quoted shares see ¶32220+.

30705

> MEMO POINTS Special rules apply where **UK land**, which was held at 6 April 1965, **has development value**, and it is disposed of either:
> - at a price exceeding the value of the land if the valuation had been made on the basis that development would be unlawful; or
> - where any material development has been carried out by the vendor after 17 December 1973.
> Where this provision applies the computation of the chargeable gain or allowable loss is made by reference to the original cost or the market value at 6 April 1965.
> The computation which results in the smaller gain or loss will prevail.
> Where one computation results in a gain and the other a loss, the disposal is treated as giving rise to neither a gain nor a loss. The chargeable gain/allowable loss will then be compared to the 31 March 1982 value in accordance with the rebasing provisions (¶30785+).

Sch 2 paras 9 - 15
TCGA 1992

Apportionment

The apportionment is calculated using the following **formula**:

$$\frac{\text{Period after 6 April 1965}}{\text{Period of ownership}} \times \text{Indexed gain}$$

For the purposes of the above formula, assets **acquired before 6 April 1945** are deemed to have been acquired on 6 April 1945.

30710
Sch 2 para 16
TCGA 1992

Indexation allowance

Indexation allowance will always be calculated using the **higher of** the:
- original cost; or
- value on 31 March 1982 (¶30785+).

The resulting gain is then used to determine whether rebasing should apply. Special rules apply where a loss arises (¶30755).

30715

> EXAMPLE A Ltd acquired an asset on 1 October 1953 for £25,000 and sold it on 1 October 2011 for £250,000. The value at 31 March 1982 was £75,000. The indexation factor is 1.996.

The indexed gain is calculated as follows;

	Original cost	March 1982 value
	£	£
Disposal proceeds	250,000	250,000
Less: Cost/31 March 1982 value	(25,000)	(75,000)
Indexation allowance on higher of cost and March 1982 value 1.996 × 75,000	(149,700)	(149,700)
Indexed gain	75,300	25,300

The total period of ownership is 58 years. The period from 6 April 1965 to October 2011 is 46.5 years.
The time-apportioned gain is therefore £60,370. (75,300 × 46.5/58)
The gain of £25,300 resulting from using the 31 March 1982 value is less than the time-apportioned gain, and will therefore be the chargeable gain.

Enhancement expenditure

30720   Where enhancement expenditure was **incurred before** 6 April 1965, the chargeable gain will be apportioned between the original cost and the enhancement expenditure, and each part is then separately time apportioned based on the dates on which the expenditure was incurred.

Sch 2 para 16(5)
TCGA 1992

MEMO POINTS   Where the **initial expenditure is disproportionately small** compared with the value of the asset immediately before the enhancement expenditure is incurred, apportionment of the gain may be made on the basis of fact if this gives a more realistic result. In this case, the actual gain attributable to the enhancement expenditure will be used, and the balance will be deemed to apply to the initial expenditure.

EXAMPLE   B Ltd acquired an asset on 1 April 1953 for £50,000. On 1 April 1963, it spent £45,000 enhancing the asset. The asset was sold on 1 April 2012 for £350,000. The value at 31 March 1982 was £100,000. The indexation factor is 2.053.
The period:
– of ownership from 1 April 1953 to 1 April 2012 is 59 years;
– since the enhancement works were done (from 1 April 1963 to 1 April 2012) is 49 years; and
– from 6 April 1965 to 1 April 2012 is 47 years.

	Original cost	March 1982 value
	£	£
Disposal proceeds	350,000	350,000
Less: Cost/March 1982 value	(50,000)	(100,000)
Enhancement expenditure	(45,000)	
Indexation allowance on higher of cost and March 1982 value 2.053 × 100,000	(205,300)	(205,300)
Indexed gain	49,700	44,700

	£
Allocated to:	
Original cost (50,000/95,000 × 49,700)	26,158
Enhancement expenditure (45,000/95,000 × 49,700)	23,542
	49,700
Time-apportioned gain:	
Original cost 26,158 × 47 years / 59 years	20,838
Enhancement expenditure 23,542 × 47 years / 49 years	22,581
	43,419

The time-apportioned gain is compared to the gain using the 31 March 1982 value (£44,700), and the lower one taken.

2. Market value election

A company may elect for the gain to be calculated using the market value at 6 April 1965. The election, which is irrevocable, must be **submitted** within 2 years of the end of the accounting period in which the disposal takes place.

30750
Sch 2 para 17
TCGA 1992

Indexation allowance in this case will be calculated using the higher of the values on:
- 6 April 1965; and
- 31 March 1982.

EXAMPLE C Ltd acquired an asset on 6 April 1952 for £20,000. The asset was sold on 6 April 2012 for £240,000. The value on 6 April 1965 was £70,000 and on 31 March 1982 it was £80,000. The indexation factor is 2.053.

	Original cost	6 April 1965 value
	£	£
Disposal proceeds	240,000	240,000
Less: Cost/April 1965 value	(20,000)	(70,000)
Indexation allowance on higher of April 65 and March 1982 (2.053 × 80,000)	(164,240)	(164,240)
	55,760	5,760
Time-apportioned gain: $55{,}760 \times \dfrac{47 \text{ years}}{60 \text{ years}}$	43,679	

C Ltd should make an election to use the 6 April 1965 value for this asset as this gives rise to a smaller gain than under time apportionment. The resulting gain of £5,760 is then compared to the gain under the rebasing rules (¶30785).

Losses

As the election to use the 6 April 1965 value is voluntary, a **company is not obliged** to apply the 6 April 1965 value when that gives rise to a smaller loss than when using the original cost.

30755
Sch 2 para 17(2)
TCGA 1992

The following table summarises the position with respect to losses. The final column indicates whether the company should then go on to apply the March 1982 rebasing provisions (¶30785+).

Gain/loss under time apportionment	Gain/loss using 6 April 1965 value	Treatment	Rebasing?
Loss	Gain	No election	Rebasing applies
Loss	Smaller loss	No election	Rebasing applies
Loss	Larger loss	Loss restricted[1]	Rebasing applies
Gain	Loss	No gain/no loss	No rebasing

Note:
1. Where **the 6 April 1965 value gives rise to a larger loss** than under time apportionment, the allowable loss is restricted to the actual loss incurred before time apportionment was applied.

EXAMPLE D Ltd acquired an asset on 6 April 1958 for £30,000. The asset was sold on 6 April 2012 for £11,000. The value on 6 April 1965 was £35,000 and on 31 March 1982 it was £40,000.

	Original cost	6 April 1965 value
	£	£
Disposal proceeds	11,000	11,000
Less: Cost/April 1965 value	(30,000)	(35,000)
	(19,000)	(24,000)
Time-apportioned loss: Original cost $19{,}000 \times \dfrac{47 \text{ years}}{54 \text{ years}}$	(16,537)	

The 6 April 1965 value gives rise to a larger loss so an election should be made. The loss will, however, be restricted to the actual loss before time apportionment i.e. £19,000. This amount will then be compared to the result of the rebasing exercise as follows:

	£
Disposal proceeds	11,000
Less: 31 March 1982 value	(40,000)
	(29,000)

The restricted loss of £19,000 arising from the 6 April 1965 election will be used, as it gives rise to a smaller loss than the 31 March 1982 value.

E. Assets held on 31 March 1982

30785
s 35 TCGA 1992

Rebasing is the term used to describe the treatment of assets held on 31 March 1982.

Essentially it means that when calculating a gain or loss on a disposal of an asset which was held on 31 March 1982, it is possible to use the value of the asset on 31 March 1982 as the allowable expenditure (i.e. the value is rebased).

Rebasing may either be carried out on the disposal of each single relevant asset (¶30815), or an irrevocable election may be made for all assets held on 31 March 1982 to be revalued at that date, and this is known as a global rebasing election (¶30835).

1. Single asset treatment

30815

On the disposal of an asset that was held on 31 March 1982, **two computations** are prepared as follows:

a. one based on the original cost of the asset; and

b. the other on the assumption that the asset was sold and immediately reacquired on 31 March 1982, at the market value at that date.

s 55 TCGA 1992 **Indexation allowance** is calculated on the higher of the original cost and March 1982 value.

The computation that results in the smaller gain or loss will prevail. Where one computation results in a gain, and the other in a loss, the disposal is treated as giving rise to neither a gain nor a loss.

EXAMPLE

1. A Ltd acquired an asset on 1 December 1978 for £100,000 and sold it on 1 May 2013 for £800,000. The March 1982 value was £150,000.
The indexation factor is 2.131.

	Cost	March 1982
	£	£
Disposal proceeds	800,000	800,000
Less: Cost/March 1982 value	(100,000)	(150,000)
Indexation allowance (150,000 × 2.131)	(319,650)	(319,650)
Indexed gain	380,350	330,350

In this case, the value on March 1982 will apply because it gives rise to the smaller gain.

2. Assume the facts are as in 1. above, but A Ltd sold the asset for £425,000.

	Cost	March 1982
	£	£
Disposal proceeds	425,000	425,000
Less: Cost/March 1982 value	(100,000)	(150,000)
Indexation allowance (150,000 × 2.131)[1]	(319,650)	(275,000)
Indexed gain	5,350	Nil

Note:
1. Restricted for the March 1982 disposal as indexation cannot create or augment a loss.
In this case the disposal will be treated as giving rise to neither a gain nor a loss.

3. Assume the facts are as in 1. above, but A Ltd sold the asset for £75,000.

	Cost	March 1982
	£	£
Disposal proceeds	75,000	75,000
Less: Cost/March 1982 value	(100,000)	(150,000)
Allowable loss	(25,000)	(75,000)

In this case the original cost will apply because it gives rise to a smaller loss.

---

2. Global rebasing election

A company may elect for the gains on all disposals of assets (other than machinery and plant qualifying for capital allowances (¶25240+)) held on 31 March 1982, and disposed of after 5 April 1988, to be calculated only by reference to the 31 March 1982 value.

30835
s 35(5) TCGA 1992

The election, which is irrevocable, must be made in writing within 2 years of the end of the accounting period in which the first disposal of an asset held on 31 March 1982 occurs.

Once the **election** has been made, all gains will be calculated using the 31 March 1982 value even if the original cost is higher. Similarly, indexation allowance will always be based on the 31 March 1982 value.

MEMO POINTS 1. An election made by a **company in one capacity** does not cover disposals made by it in another capacity e.g. an election made by the company itself would not bind any partnership of which the company was a member.

s 35(7) TCGA 1992

2. An election could have a **retrospective effect**, because an election covers not only disposals made after the election has been made but all disposals on or after 6 April 1988. Where necessary, adjustments will therefore need to be made to prior CTSA returns.

CG 16765

---

3. Special situations

Rolled over gains

If a gain on the disposal of an asset was rolled over (¶30940+) into another asset **before** 31 March 1982, the gain will effectively be eliminated because the 31 March 1982 value will be the full value rather than the original cost reduced by the rolled over gain.

30855
Sch 4 para 2
TCGA 1992

Alternatively, a claim can be made for the **rolled over gain to be reduced** by half if:
– the rolled over gain was made before 31 March 1982;
– the asset into which the gain was rolled was acquired between 1 April 1982 and 5 April 1988; and
– that asset was disposed of on or after 6 April 1988.

A claim for this relief must be submitted no later than 2 years after the end of the relevant accounting period.

Shares transferred from group company

Where a company disposes of shares that:
– were transferred to it from a group company after 31 March 1982; and
– formed part of a larger holding when held by the group company at 31 March 1982,
the **valuation of the smaller holding** can be based on a proportion of the value of the larger holding. Depending on the level of the original holding, this may increase the value of each share.

30860
Sch 3 para 1A
TCGA 1992

SECTION 3

Specific types of disposal

Summary

30910

Topic	¶¶
Assets used in a trade	¶30940+
Part disposals	¶31130+
Compensation	¶31165+
No gain/no loss disposals	¶31280+
Gifts	¶31320+
Connected persons	¶31370+
Options	¶31415+
Hire purchase	¶31520+
Close non-resident companies	¶76040+
Disposal of assets leased under a long funding lease	¶82455
Appropriations between fixed assets and trading stock by company	¶11710
Appropriations between fixed assets and trading stock involving a group	¶67130+
Liquidation	¶61295+
Change of residence	¶91435+

A. Assets used in a trade

30940　Where a gain arises on the disposal of an asset which has been used for the purposes of a trade, it may be possible to **defer** the point at which **the gain** becomes chargeable by rolling over the gain into the base cost of a replacement asset.

The effect is to reduce the allowable expenditure on the replacement asset, thus increasing the gain which arises on its disposal.

To qualify for **full relief** the proceeds of the original asset (net of the costs of disposal) must be fully reinvested in a replacement asset (again, net of the costs of acquisition).

Where only **partial reinvestment** occurs (¶31035) the relief is restricted.

There is no requirement for the disposal to be by way of sale, nor is there a requirement for any disposal proceeds to be in the form of cash. This means that, for example, gifts of assets, or disposals in exchange for shares, may also qualify for relief.

> MEMO POINTS　1. A similar relief, known as **holdover relief**, is available where the replacement asset is a depreciating asset (¶31040+).
> 2. For details of rollover relief and **groups** of companies see ¶67315+.

1. Scope

30970　To be **eligible** for this relief:
– both the original and replacement assets must be qualifying assets; and
– the replacement asset must be acquired within a set period.

If the replacement asset itself is disposed of in the future, it too can be the subject of a rollover claim into another new asset.

Original asset

The original asset must be used throughout the period of ownership for the **purposes of** one of the following qualifying **activities**:

a. a trade (including furnished holiday lettings (¶19410+) and the management of woodlands on a commercial basis) carried on by the taxpayer, or the taxpayer's personal company (for example a building owned by a shareholder and used by the company for the purposes of its trade);

b. an office or employment;

c. a not-for-profit:

– unincorporated association;

– body chargeable to corporation tax; or

– professional or trade organisation;

d. the partition of farmland; or

e. discharging the responsibilities of a public authority.

30975
ss 152, 157
TCGA 1992

s 158 TCGA 1992

> MEMO POINTS   1. A **personal company** is one in which the taxpayer exercises not less than 5% of the voting rights. The company must be a personal company at the time that the old asset is disposed of and also when the new asset is acquired. The same personal company must use both the old and new asset.
> 2. Any **non-trade use** in the period before 31 March 1982 is ignored. In limited circumstances, a restricted relief may be available for assets which are used only partly for trade purposes (¶31050+).
> 3. A **non-UK-resident** company trading in the UK through a permanent establishment (¶92140+) will be able to claim rollover relief if the old asset and the new asset are both within the charge to UK tax.

s 157 TCGA 1992

s 159 TCGA 1992

The asset must also fall within one of the following qualifying **classes**:

30980
s 155 TCGA 1992;
CG 61020

Class	Asset	Detail
1A	Land and buildings	The land and any building are treated as separate assets for rollover purposes, and separate claims can be made in respect of each, requiring an apportionment of proceeds and costs Buildings include: – part of a building; and – permanent or semi-permanent structures in the nature of a building Buildings used in a trade of dealing or developing land are excluded if the profits on sale are treated as trading profits Rollover relief may be available on the grant of an option over land, if the underlying asset itself would have qualified for this relief Land and buildings which are let by the owner and where the tenant has the exclusive right to occupation (e.g. a house let to a director) are excluded from relief unless the company is letting: – tied premises; – furnished premises and caravan sites which amount to a trade; or – furnished holiday accommodation
1B	Fixed plant and machinery	Fixed is taken to mean normally in one place, and not easily moved HMRC will accept items such as washing machines and dryers in a launderette It is not necessary for the plant or machinery to be attached to a building Lifts and escalators that have become part of the building are not plant and machinery

Class	Asset	Detail
2	Ships, aircraft and hovercraft	Ships and aircraft take their ordinary everyday meaning HMRC accept that aircraft includes aeroplanes, helicopters, airships and hot air balloons HMRC also accept that ship includes vessels such as fishing boats, motorised cruisers and yachts i.e. any vessel used in navigation other than one which is propelled by oars
3	Satellites, space stations and spacecraft, including launch vehicles	
7A	Payment to farmers under the EU single payment scheme	The single payment scheme is a subsidy scheme introduced by the EU under which farmers receive a single payment linked to various environmental conditions Initially this payment was to be related to a farmer's historical subsidy record, but it is now an entirely flat rate payment Further details can be found at flmemo.co.uk/ctm30980
8A	Syndicate rights of an underwriting member of Lloyds	

30985
ss 156ZA, 156ZB TCGA 1992

Intellectual property As a result of the introduction of the intangibles regime on 1 April 2002 (¶28135+), the rules outlined below apply to the following **types of asset** held by a company (which were previously eligible for rollover relief):
– goodwill;
– milk quotas and potato quotas;
– ewe and suckler cow premium quotas; and
– fish quotas.

Situation	Tax treatment
New asset is intellectual property acquired from an unrelated party on or after 1 April 2002	Gain arising from any disposal of an asset in ¶30980 above cannot be rolled over into new asset New asset falls completely within the intangibles regime (¶28135+)
Company disposed of intellectual property prior to 1 April 2002	Rollover relief is available against any capital gain from that disposal into the acquisition of assets, other than goodwill or quota, after 1 April 2002
Company disposed of intellectual property on or after 1 April 2002 but before 1 April 2003	Rollover relief is available against any gain arising from that disposal into the pre-1 April 2002 acquisition of any of the qualifying assets, subject to the normal rules including the reinvestment time limit of 12 months before the date of disposal Company may split the claim to relief between intangible asset reinvestment relief (¶28540+) and rollover relief

Replacement assets

30990
s 152 TCGA 1992

Subject to certain concessions, the replacement asset must:
a. be **acquired** (or contracted for under an unconditional contract i.e. obtaining beneficial ownership) during a qualifying period which:
– starts 1 year before the disposal of the original asset; and
– finishes 3 years after the disposal of the original asset;
b. be used for one of the qualifying **activities** (¶30975) immediately after acquisition; and
c. fall within one of the qualifying **classes** (¶30980). There is no requirement for the original and replacement asset to fall within the same class. Similarly, there is no requirement for

the assets to be used for the purposes of the same trade, provided the gap between the trades is no more than 3 years.

HMRC state that rollover relief will not be available where the assets are acquired with a view to **resale** at a profit. However, relief will not be denied merely because it is expected the asset will one day be sold at a profit, and the intended use by the company is for a qualifying activity in the intervening period. If the intention on acquisition is to dispose of the asset, and its trade use is merely a temporary convenience, relief will be denied.

CG 60390

> MEMO POINTS 1. HMRC have powers to **extend the time limit** in which a replacement asset can be acquired in certain circumstances. This is only likely to be done where the intention to acquire a replacement asset existed and can be evidenced, but circumstances beyond the company's control prevented an acquisition taking place before the time limit expired. However, no decision on a possible extension of the time limit can be made until the old asset has been disposed of, the new asset has been acquired, and all other conditions of the relief are satisfied.
> 2. Assets **in the course of construction** are deemed to be acquired when the construction works are finished.
> 3. Rollover relief will be available on **deemed gains** arising, for example, on the gift of an asset, appropriation to trading stock etc.
> 4. Where an asset is deemed to be **sold and reacquired** for chargeable gains purposes, this is not a qualifying acquisition for rollover relief purposes.
> 5. Where reinvestment is made in **more than one asset**, a just and reasonable apportionment is made. HMRC will accept the company's allocation of the disposal proceeds against the cost of the new assets. However, amounts must be identified in respect of each asset.

CG 60640

CG 60770

Concessions By concession, rollover relief is also available in the following situations, including where assets are exchanged or partitioned.

30995

Situation	Reference
Disposal proceeds from the old asset are used to enhance the value of other assets, provided these assets are used in a trade (or will be so used once the enhancement is completed)	ESC D22
Disposal proceeds from the old asset are used to acquire a further interest in an existing asset already used in the trade e.g. extending an existing lease. However, relief will be denied if a tenant acquires the freehold interest in land, immediately selling part of it off, for example, to finance the original purchase. Any capital gain on the sale cannot be rolled over into the original purchase as HMRC take the view that the acquisition was not expenditure on a new asset	ESC D25
The asset is not brought into immediate use because work of a capital nature is to be carried out on it (provided that it is brought into use once this work is completed)	ESC D24
The asset is sold and then reacquired for purely commercial reasons	ESC D16

2. Calculation

The rollover calculation depends on whether the asset is:
– non-depreciating i.e. has a maximum life of more than 60 years; or
– depreciating i.e. a wasting asset, or likely to become a wasting asset within the next 10 years.

31025

Non-depreciating assets

To be eligible for full relief an amount which equals the **proceeds** derived from the disposal (net of the costs of disposal) of the original asset must be fully **reinvested** in the replacement asset (including incidental costs of acquisition). Note that there is no need to track the funds from one asset to the other.

31030

CG 60350

The relief is determined by calculating the gain on the original asset and reducing the allowable expenditure on the replacement asset by the same amount.

Indexation allowance is available for both assets. For the old asset it will be calculated in accordance with the normal rules (¶30530+). On the subsequent disposal of the new asset, indexation allowance will be based on the cost of the new asset after deducting the rolled over gain, and will run from the date of the new asset's acquisition.

> EXAMPLE In March 2005, D Ltd buys a warehouse for £50,000 which is used exclusively for trade purposes until March 2010 when it is sold for £98,000 (net of expenses of sale). The indexation factor is 0.159, and the resulting chargeable gain on the disposal is £40,050. Also in March 2010, the company acquires a larger warehouse at a cost of £120,000 (including expenses of purchase) and moves the trade to the warehouse
> If a claim to rollover relief is made, the following computation occurs:
>
> | | £ |
> | --- | --- |
> | Net disposal proceeds | 98,000 |
> | Less: Cost (including expenses of purchase) | (50,000) |
> | Rollover relief | (40,050) |
> | Unindexed gain | 7,950 |
> | Indexation: 0.159 × 50,000 | (7,950) |
> | Chargeable gain | Nil |
>
> Due to the rollover relief claim, the cost of the new warehouse is also reduced by £40,050 to £79,950. (120,000 - 40,050)
> In March 2013, D Ltd sells the second warehouse for £130,000 (incurring £2,000 expenses of sale) and does not reinvest the proceeds. The indexation factor is 0.127, and the chargeable gain on disposal of the second warehouse is:
>
> | | £ | £ |
> | --- | --- | --- |
> | Net disposal proceeds | | 128,000 |
> | Less: Cost (including expenses of purchase) | 120,000 | |
> | Rollover relief | (40,050) | |
> | | | (79,950) |
> | Unindexed gain | | 48,050 |
> | Indexation: 79,950 × 0.127 | | (10,154) |
> | Chargeable gain | | 37,896 |
>
> **Note:**
> As a result of indexation allowance, the chargeable gain on the second disposal can be less than the amount of gain rolled over even where the sale price of the replacement asset exceeds its actual cost.

31035
s 153 TCGA 1992

Where the **proceeds** from the sale of the original asset are only **partially reinvested**, the amount not reinvested becomes chargeable, and the balance is then rolled over.

If the proceeds which are not reinvested exceed the amount of the gain, no rollover relief is available.

> EXAMPLE E Ltd bought a factory for trade use on 1 December 1999 for £200,000 which was sold on 1 June 2007 for £425,000, realising a gain after indexation of £214,400. On 31 March 2010, the company acquired a freehold office building, again for trade use, at a cost of £400,000.
> So the proceeds which are not reinvested are £25,000, and these become chargeable. (425,000 - 400,000)
> The remaining part of the gain can be rolled over as follows:
>
> | | £ |
> | --- | --- |
> | Expenditure on office building | 400,000 |
> | Less: Rolled over gain (214,400 - 25,000) | (189,400) |
> | Qualifying expenditure | 210,600 |

Depreciating assets

If a replacement asset is a depreciating asset (broadly, one with a **useful life** of 60 years or less), the gain is simply held over and **becomes chargeable** on the earliest of the following:
- 10 years from the acquisition of the replacement asset;
- the disposal of the replacement asset; or
- the cessation of trading use of the replacement asset.

The amount of the gain which can be held over is calculated in exactly the same way as for non-depreciating assets.

31040
s 154 TCGA 1992

However, if a qualifying **non-depreciating asset is purchased subsequently**, but before the gain becomes chargeable, a further claim may be made to roll over the original gain into the new asset. The qualifying expenditure on the new asset will be reduced by the heldover gain in the usual way. If only part of the heldover gain can be set against the cost of the new non-depreciating asset, the heldover gain can be split so that:
- part is deducted from the new non-depreciating asset; and
- the remainder is held over until the one of the situations in ¶31040 occurs.

31045

> [EXAMPLE] F Ltd sold fixed plant in Year 1 for £600,000, realising a gain after indexation of £170,000.
> In Year 2, a 25-year lease on a building, used for trade purposes, was acquired at a cost of £650,000. As this lease is a wasting asset, a claim for holdover relief was made.
> In Year 9, F Ltd purchased the freehold of a building, also used for trade purposes, at a cost of £900,000. As the leasehold building was still owned and used for trade purposes, and less than 10 years had elapsed since its acquisition, F Ltd could claim to roll over the original gain of £170,000 against the qualifying expenditure on the freehold building, reducing the qualifying expenditure to £730,000. (900,000 - 170,000)

Partial trade use

Assets which are only partially used for trade purposes may be eligible for relief where:
- the original asset has been used for periods of exclusive trade use and periods of exclusive non-trade use; or
- either the original or replacement asset (or both) are subject to mixed use, and the mixed use asset is a building or structure.

31050

Exclusive non-trade use Where the original asset has been subject to periods of exclusive non-trade use, the amount of the gain eligible for rollover relief is restricted. This is achieved by treating the asset as two separate assets, one a qualifying trade asset, and one not eligible for relief. The proportion of the gain attributable to the trade asset is determined by the period of qualifying use compared to the total period of ownership. Periods before 31 March 1982 are ignored.

31055
s 152(7) TCGA 1992

> [EXAMPLE] G Ltd sold a factory on 31 March 2013 for £500,000, realising a chargeable gain of £75,000. The factory had been acquired 20 years ago, and in that period had been let for a period of 5 years.
> On 31 July 2013, the company acquired another factory at a cost of £600,000.
> The chargeable gain is apportioned between trade and non-trade assets, based on a period of ownership of 20 years, of which 15 were exclusively trade use.
>
> | | Total | Trade (15/20) | Non-trade (5/20) |
> |---|---|---|---|
> | | £ | £ | £ |
> | Total gain | 75,000 | 56,250 | 18,750 |
> | Less: Rolled over gain | (56,250) | (56,250) | - |
> | Chargeable gain | 18,750 | Nil | 18,750 |

The qualifying expenditure on the office building would be reduced as follows:

	£
Expenditure on new factory	600,000
Less: Rolled over gain	(56,250)
Qualifying expenditure	543,750

31060
s 152(6) TCGA 1992

Mixed use   Where a building or structure is **used simultaneously** for trade and non-trade use, it is again treated as two separate assets for calculating rollover relief. Similarly, if the replacement asset is a building or structure which is used only partly for trade purposes, it is treated as two assets and the gain on the original asset can only be rolled over into the expenditure apportioned to trade use.

Disposals of assets with heldover gains

31065

In some cases a company may receive, and then dispose of, an asset where a gain has been subject to gift relief or rollover relief.

The heldover or rolled over gain will be reduced by half where:
– the **original asset** was disposed of before 31 March 1982; and
– the **replacement asset** was acquired between 1 April 1982 and 5 April 1988, and disposed of on or after 6 April 1988.

For this relief to apply, a claim must be made no later than 2 years after the end of the accounting period in which the final disposal occurred.

> MEMO POINTS   If **holdover** relief was originally claimed, but before the charge was triggered, the claim was **withdrawn** and the gain rolled over into a replacement asset, then the 50% reduction is only available if it would have been available on the original asset into which the gain was held over.

---

3. Claiming relief

31095

Rollover and holdover relief must be claimed in writing within 4 years of the end of the accounting period to which it relates.

The **time limit** starts on the later of the end of the accounting period in which:
– the disposal takes place; or
– the new assets are acquired.

CG 60605

> MEMO POINTS   1. The claim should **specify** the following:
> – identity of original asset(s);
> – date of disposal;
> – disposal proceeds;
> – identity of replacement asset(s);
> – acquisition expenditure;
> – date of acquisition; and
> – amount of disposal proceeds reinvested.
> 2. Where **more than one asset** is disposed of or acquired, the claim must also specify how the proceeds have been allocated to the replacement assets.
> 3. Although **limited liability partnerships** (LLPs) are treated as partnerships, an LLP is treated as a corporate entity from the date of commencement of a liquidation, and any gains originally rolled over into a qualifying asset within the LLP will be brought into charge.

31100
s 153A TCGA 1992

A claim cannot be made until a replacement asset is actually acquired. However, it is possible to make a **provisional declaration** of intention to claim relief before a replacement asset is acquired. This declaration must be made on the CTSA return for the accounting period in which the disposal occurs, and the tax liability for the year can be calculated on the basis that the gain is to be rolled over. However, if a suitable replacement asset is not purchased within the time limit, the claim is invalid and HMRC will raise an assessment for the tax which will be payable with interest, calculated as though no claim had ever been made.

B. Part disposals

A part disposal arises where:
- part of an asset is retained following disposal; or
- an interest or right is granted over an asset.

<u>MEMO POINTS</u> 1. For the rules relating to small parcels of **land** see ¶31800+.
2. For **options** see ¶31415+.

31130
s 21 TCGA 1992

Calculation

The chargeable gain or allowable loss arising on a part disposal is calculated in accordance with the normal rules, but the **allowable expenditure** (and 31 March 1982 value) must be apportioned between the part disposed of and the part retained.

31135
s 42 TCGA 1992

Other than when a sublease is granted out of a short lease (¶31885+), expenditure which relates:
- directly to **one of the parts** will be allocated to that part; and
- to the **asset as a whole** will be apportioned between the two parts on the basis of the following formula:

$$\frac{A}{A+B}$$

where:
- A is the disposal proceeds of the part disposed of; and
- B is the market value of the part retained.

However, where the part sold is a **definite fraction** of the whole, HMRC will allow that fraction to be applied to the allowable expenditure.

CG 12733

On a **subsequent disposal** of all or part of the remaining asset, the allowable expenditure will be reduced by the part allocated to the earlier disposal.

<u>MEMO POINTS</u> Where an **asset has been eligible for capital allowances**, the formula above is applied first, and then the capital allowances are taken into account only to the extent that they relate to the part being disposed of. If a previous part disposal resulted in a loss which was restricted by capital allowances (¶31690), then only the balance of the capital allowances should be used to restrict any further loss.

s 41 TCGA 1992;
CG 12738

[EXAMPLE] A Ltd bought a set of four paintings in January 2006 for £40,000. Two of them were sold in an arm's length transaction in March 2013 for £48,000, and the other two were kept, for which a value of £10,000 was agreed. The indexation factor is 0.286.
The chargeable gain on the part disposal will be calculated as follows:

	£
Disposal proceeds	48,000
Less: Allowable expenditure	
$\frac{48,000}{48,000 + 10,000} \times 40,000$	(33,103)
Indexation (33,103 × 0.286)	(9,467)
Indexed gain	5,430

In an unconnected transaction, A Ltd sells the two remaining paintings in June 2013 for £25,000. The indexation factor is 0.291.
The chargeable gain on the disposal will be calculated as follows:

	£
Disposal proceeds	25,000
Less: Allowable expenditure (40,000 - 33,103)	(6,897)
Indexation allowance (6,897 × 0.291)	(2,007)
Indexed gain	16,096

C. Compensation

31165
ss 22, 24
TCGA 1992

Where a capital sum is derived from an asset (i.e. money or money's worth is received which is not taxed as income, irrespective of whether the payer receives an asset in return), this is a deemed disposal (¶30125). *Marren v Ingles* [1980]

The treatment of compensation receipts differs, depending upon whether the asset concerned is either:
– lost or destroyed; or
– damaged.

In both situations, relief may be available where:
– the capital sum is used to replace or restore the asset; or
– the amount of the capital sum received is small.

CG 12940

⌐MEMO POINTS⌐   1. "**Derived from an asset**" requires the asset itself to be identified, which may not be the immediate source of the capital sum e.g. where a building is damaged and the insurance rights are assigned, the asset concerned would be the building and not the insurance rights. As long as the person receiving the compensation has had beneficial ownership of the asset, and receives a capital sum in respect of that ownership, the compensation will be treated as derived from the asset e.g. where compensation is received after the damaged asset is sold.

CG 12980

2. "**Money's worth**" means anything which, although not money, can be recognised as equivalent to, or can be converted into, money. The receipt must therefore be assessed as to whether:
– it can be turned into money; or
– its value can be expressed in monetary terms.
Whilst there does not have to be an actual conversion into money, there must be the potential for an actual conversion.

CG 12952

3. There is also a deemed disposal where a capital sum is received as compensation in return for either:
– forfeiting or surrendering **rights**; or
– refraining from exercising rights,
provided that those rights constitute an asset (¶30190).

CG 12955

4. Similarly, a capital sum received as compensation or consideration for the **use or exploitation** of assets is also a deemed disposal. HMRC give the example of lump sum payments made to landowners for the granting of easements or wayleaves (¶19175), for perpetuity or a specific number of years, to lay cables, pipelines etc.

ESC D33

5. The **right to take court action** for compensation or damages is itself an asset (i.e. where there is no statutory or contractual right) and the settlement of such an action is a disposal of that right. *Zim v Proctor* [1985] Associated legal fees are an allowable cost, even where the court action is unsuccessful. However, consideration received in respect of an action taken for personal or professional injury remains exempt. Under a statutory concession, the disposal of the right can be treated as the disposal of the underlying asset (where one exists e.g. the disposal of that asset may be exempt or another relief, such as rollover relief, might apply), or otherwise exempt where there is no underlying asset.

1. Lost or destroyed assets

31195

Where a capital sum, such as compensation or a payment under an insurance policy, is received for an asset which has been lost or destroyed, the capital sum received will be treated as disposal proceeds. If **compensation is not received** for the asset, the disposal proceeds will be equal to any salvage money received. The resulting loss will be allowable for offset against chargeable gains.

Land and buildings may be treated as separate assets for these purposes. This means that if a building is completely destroyed (and therefore the subject of a deemed disposal), the related land is treated as if it were sold and immediately reacquired at market value.

Replacement asset acquired

If, within a year from receipt, the **whole of the capital sum** is used to acquire an asset to replace the one which was lost or destroyed, the company may elect that a chargeable gain will not arise.

31200
s 23(4) TCGA 1992;
CG 15745

The term replacement asset is not **defined** by the legislation, but HMRC interpret the term as meaning an asset which is of a similar type and function to the original asset. On submission of the appropriate claim, the **disposal proceeds** of the original asset are deemed to be such that neither a gain nor loss arises.

The **allowable cost** of the replacement asset is then reduced to take account of the difference between:
- the capital sum received, plus any residual or scrap value of the original asset; and
- the deemed disposal proceeds of the original asset.

If the **capital sum** received on the loss or destruction of an asset is only **partly used** to acquire a replacement asset, then relief is still available.

31205
s 23(5) TCGA 1992

On submission of a claim, the amount of:
- the gain is restricted to the excess of the capital sum that was not used to acquire the replacement asset; over
- the allowable cost of the new asset, as reduced by the difference between the original gain and the restricted gain.

EXAMPLE B Ltd bought a painting in December 2000 for £10,000, which was stolen in July 2010. B Ltd received insurance money of £18,000 in June 2011. In December 2011, B Ltd bought a similar painting for £15,000. Assuming a claim for relief was made:
- the chargeable gain will be restricted to the amount not used to acquire the replacement asset i.e. £3,000; and
- the allowable cost of the replacement asset will be:

	£	£
Actual cost		15,000
Less: Chargeable gain on original asset (see 2. below)	4,340	
Capital sum not used to acquire replacement asset	(3,000)	
		(1,340)
Allowable cost		13,660

2. Using the same facts as for 1. above, but no claim was made. Indexation runs from December 2000 to June 2011, so the indexation factor is 0.366.

	£
Disposal proceeds	18,000
Less: Allowable expenditure	(10,000)
Indexation allowance (10,000 × 0.366)	(3,660)
Indexed gain	4,340

---

2. Damaged assets

General rule

In general, where a capital sum is received as a result of damage to an asset, it is treated as a part disposal, **provided** the asset is still in existence and has not been disposed of by the company i.e. it is not compensation in respect of any right of action or statutory right which came into existence as a result of the damage.

31235

The chargeable gain is calculated in accordance with the normal part disposal rules (¶31130+), using the following **formula** to calculate the allowable expenditure:

$$\frac{A}{A+B}$$

where:
– A is the capital sum received; and
– B is the market value of the asset at the date of receipt of the capital sum.

If expenditure has been incurred on **restoration** of the damaged asset **before the receipt** of the capital sum, it will be treated as enhancement expenditure (¶30490) and will be apportioned using the part disposal formula described above.

ⒺⓍⒶⓂⓅⓁⒺ　C Ltd purchased a sculpture in June 1997 for £38,000. The sculpture was vandalised in August 2002 and, in December 2002, the company incurred restoration costs of £5,000. C Ltd received compensation in January 2013 of £8,000, when the sculpture was valued at £65,000. The chargeable gain on receipt of the compensation would be:

	£	£
Disposal proceeds		8,000
Less: Allowable expenditure		
$\dfrac{8,000}{8,000 + 65,000} \times 38,000$	4,164	
Indexation: Jun 97 to Jan 13		
$\dfrac{245.80 - 157.50}{157.50} = 0.561 \times 4,164$	2,336	
		(6,497)
Restoration expenditure		
$\dfrac{8,000}{8,000 + 65,000} \times 5,000$	548	
Indexation: Dec 02 to Jan 13		
$\dfrac{245.80 - 178.50}{178.50} = 0.377 \times 548$	207	
		(755)
Indexed gain		748

Modifications

31240
s 23 TCGA 1992

The general rule is modified according to whether:
a. all of the capital sum is used to restore the asset, when, provided the appropriate claim is made, a part disposal will not be deemed to take place and instead the capital sum which would have been treated as disposal proceeds will be deducted from the allowable cost of the asset;
b. part of the capital sum is used to restore the asset (¶31245); or
c. the capital sum exceeds the allowable cost of the asset (¶31250).

RI 157

⎣ MEMO POINTS ⎦　1. **Small** is not defined by the legislation but for these purposes it is generally understood to mean:
– 5% or less of the value of the asset; or
– £3,000 or less (whether or not this is within the 5% limit).
2. Where the asset concerned is a **wasting asset** (¶31605+), relief will only be available where the whole amount of the capital sum is used in the restoration.

31245
s 23(3) TCGA 1992

Part is used to restore asset　Where only part of the capital sum is applied in restoring the asset, and the **unused part** is:
– not reasonably required for restoration; and
– small when compared to the value of the asset,
the company can claim to treat the unused part as the consideration for a part disposal.

In this case the part disposal **formula is applied to** both cost (or 31 March 1982 value) and restoration expenses, but is amended as follows:

$$\frac{A}{A + B}$$

where:
– A is the unused part of the capital sum; and
– B is the restored value of the asset.

The part of the capital sum which is used in restoration is deducted from the allowable cost as described in ¶31240.

Where the asset concerned is a wasting asset, the allowable cost is restricted in accordance with the wasting asset rules (¶31605+).

EXAMPLE D Ltd bought a painting in March 1985 for £30,000. In October 1995, it was damaged and D Ltd spent £6,250 on restoration in January 1996. The company received insurance money of £16,750 in March 1996 when the restored value of the painting was £48,000. D Ltd sold the painting in March 2013 for £70,000.
The chargeable gains are calculated as follows:

	£	£
Part disposal on receipt of capital sum (March 1996)		
Disposal proceeds (16,750 - 6,250)		10,500
Less: Allowable expenditure		
$\frac{10,500}{10,500 + 48,000} \times 30,000$	5,385	
Indexation: Mar 85 to Mar 96		
$\frac{151.50 - 92.80}{92.80} = 0.633 \times 5,385$	3,409	
		(8,794)
Restoration expenditure		
$\frac{10,500}{10,500 + 48,000} \times 6,250$	1,122	
Indexation: Jan 96 to Mar 96		
$\frac{151.50 - 150.20}{150.20} = 0.009 \times 1,122$	10	
		(1,132)
Chargeable gain		574
Gain on subsequent disposal (March 2013)		
Disposal proceeds		70,000
Less: Allowable expenditure		
Balance of cost (30,000 - 5,385)	24,615	
Indexation: Mar 85 to Mar 13		
$\frac{248.70 - 92.80}{92.80} = 1.680 \times 24,615$	41,353	
Balance of restoration expenditure (6,250 - 1,122)	5,128	
Indexation: Jan 96 to Mar 13		
$\frac{248.70 - 150.20}{150.20} = 0.656 \times 5,128$	3,364	
	74,460	
Less: Capital sum used in restoration	(6,250)	
		(68,210)
Gain		1,790

Capital sum exceeds allowable cost If the capital sum received exceeds the allowable cost of the asset, then relief will only be available if the **entire capital sum** is used in restoration (¶31240).

31250
s 23(2) TCGA 1992

Except for wasting assets (¶31605+), where **part of the capital sum** is used and the unused part qualifies as small (or where the capital sum itself qualifies as small (¶31240)), the company may claim to treat the whole of the capital sum as disposal proceeds, and the entire allowable cost will be set against it. The allowable cost available for use against subsequent disposals will therefore be reduced to nil.

EXAMPLE E Ltd bought a painting in June 1990 for £1,000. In May 1996, the painting was damaged and E Ltd spent £22,500 on restoration in August 1996. An insurance payout of £25,000 was received in December 1996. E Ltd sold the painting in March 2013 for £100,000.

The chargeable gains are calculated as follows:

	£	£
Gain on receipt of capital sum:		
Disposal proceeds		25,000
Less: Allowable expenditure:		
Original cost	1,000	
Indexation: Jun 90 to Dec 96		
$\dfrac{154.40 - 126.70}{126.70} = 0.219 \times 1,000$	219	
		(1,219)
Restoration expenditure	22,500	
Indexation: Aug 96 to Dec 96		
$\dfrac{154.40 - 153.10}{153.10} = 0.008 \times 22,500$	180	
		(22,680)
Indexed gain		1,101
Gain on subsequent disposal:		
Disposal proceeds		100,000
Less: Allowable cost		-
Gain		100,000

D. No gain/no loss disposals

31280
s 55 TCGA 1992

No gain/no loss disposals arise because of the **relationship between the parties** involved in the transaction. This means that although neither a chargeable gain nor allowable loss is generated in connection with the current disposal, later disposals of the same asset may be chargeable to tax.

The acquisition cost for the new owner of the asset will therefore be equal to the allowable expenditure on the asset in the hands of the original owner.

> MEMO POINTS   1. **Indexation** will be available to the date of the no gain/no loss disposal.
> 2. A company which acquires an asset after 31 March 1982 in a no gain/no loss transaction will be treated, for **rebasing purposes**, as if it held the asset on 31 March 1982 providing:
> – the asset was originally acquired before 31 March 1982; and
> – all of the disposals of the asset between 31 March 1982 and the date of disposal were also no gain/no loss transactions.

Scope

31285

In the following **situations**, a disposal is deemed to be a no gain/no loss disposal:
– transfers within a 75% CG group of companies (¶65415+);
– certain transfers as part of a company scheme of reconstruction (¶79290+);
– certain transfers of UK trades (¶61200+);
– certain gifts (¶31320+); and
– transfers to a harbour authority.

Comment   A no gain/no loss transfer must not be confused with a disposal giving rise to neither a gain nor a loss (for example, the deemed disposal on March 1982 rebasing). In a disposal giving rise to neither a gain nor a loss, the vendor's allowable expenditure is deemed to be that which results in neither a gain nor a loss. The transferee is therefore not affected, and his acquisition cost is the actual consideration.

Calculation

31290

The acquisition cost for the new owner of the asset is equal to the allowable expenditure on the asset in the hands of the original owner.

EXAMPLE Asset A was acquired by F Ltd in May 1995 at a cost of £10,000. A no gain/no loss disposal took place in June 2010 to G Ltd. On a subsequent disposal, the allowable expenditure will be F Ltd's original acquisition cost plus indexation to the date of the no gain/no loss disposal.

	£
F Ltd's acquisition cost	10,000
Indexation: May 95 to Jun 10	
$\frac{224.10 - 149.60}{149.60} = 0.498 \times 10,000$	4,980
G Ltd's allowable expenditure on a subsequent disposal	14,980

E. Gifts

The general rule is that where assets are disposed by way of a gift (i.e. for little or no consideration), the disposal, and the connected acquisition, are deemed to take place at market value (¶30410+). Once the market value has been established, the disposal is treated like any other.

31320

However, there are special rules for certain types of gift.

Type of gift	Treatment	Reference
To charities (¶86000+)	Treated as transaction at no gain/no loss (¶31280)	s 257 TCGA 1992
To CASCs (¶86270+)		
To employee trusts		s 239 TCGA 1992
To housing associations		s 259 TCGA 1992

Charity recipients

A donor may claim both corporation tax relief and the relief from capital gains on the same donation to a charity (¶22085+).

31325
s 257 TCGA 1992

If the disposal:

CG 66621

– is a gift, or for a consideration **less than the allowable cost**, both the disposal and the acquisition are treated as taking place for an amount which gives neither a gain nor a loss to the donor; or

– consideration **exceeds the allowable cost**, only the actual consideration is taken into account.

MEMO POINTS 1. If this exemption has applied to the previous disposal of an asset, and the **charity is liable to capital gains tax**, the charity is treated as having acquired the asset at the same time as the donor acquired it and having owned the asset throughout, e.g. if the donor owned the asset on 31 March 1982, the charity will be treated as owning it on that date.

CG 66622

2. A disposal, to a charity, of **qualifying corporate bonds** which were received by the donor on a takeover, and in relation to which there is a deferred gain (¶32280), will not crystallise that deferred gain on either the donor or the charity.
3. For gifts of **land and buildings** to a charity, the whole ownership of the property must be transferred to the charity, and the charity needs to provide the donor with a certificate containing:
– a description of the qualifying interest in the land;
– the date of disposal; and
– a statement that the charity has acquired the interest in the land.

EXAMPLE
1. A Ltd gifts shares which cost £150,000 to a charity at a time when they have a market value of £250,000.
A Ltd is treated as having disposed of the shares for a consideration of £150,000, and the charity as acquiring them for £150,000.

2. Instead, if A Ltd sells the shares for a consideration of £75,000 at a time when they have a market value of £250,000, the company is treated as having disposed of the shares for a consideration of £150,000 and the charity as acquiring them for £150,000.

3. If, instead, A Ltd sells the shares for a consideration of £200,000 at a time when they have a market value of £250,000, the company is treated as having sold them for a consideration of £200,000, thereby realising a gain before indexation of £50,000. The charity acquires the shares for £200,000.

4. If A Ltd gifts the shares at a time when they have a market value of £100,000, the company is treated as having disposed of the shares for a consideration of £150,000 and the charity as acquiring them for £150,000. A Ltd does not make an allowable loss on this transaction.

5. Finally, if A Ltd sells the shares for a consideration of £40,000 at a time when they have a market value of £80,000, the company is treated as having disposed of the shares for a consideration of £150,000 and the charity as acquiring them for £150,000. Again, A Ltd does not make an allowable loss on this transaction.

31330

CG 66630

Corporation tax relief claimed   If the donor is eligible for corporation tax relief on the disposal (¶22055), the **charity's acquisition cost** is reduced by the amount of the relief. There is no requirement that the relief is actually given.

> EXAMPLE   B Ltd owns shares in a quoted company which were acquired at a cost of £22,000. B Ltd sells the shares to a charity for £40,000 when they are worth £60,000, incurring £100 dealing costs. B Ltd can claim a qualifying charitable donation deduction of £20,100. (60,000 + 100 - 40,000)
> B Ltd is taxed on a gain (before indexation) of £17,900. (40,000 - 22,000 - 100)
> The charity's acquisition cost of £40,000 is reduced to £19,900. (40,000 - 20,100)

Employee trusts

31335
s 239 TCGA 1992;
CG 36000

Where a close company transfers assets to an employee trust, a relief automatically applies (i.e. no claim is required), which means that no gain and no loss results.

The transfer must not be a transfer of value for inheritance tax purposes i.e. it must be a disposition of **property** to be held on trust, and **applied for** the benefit of most of the employees of the company.

The following persons must be **excluded from benefiting** from the trust:
a. a participator in the company unless he:
– is not beneficially entitled to 5% or more of any class of its shares; and
– would not be entitled, on a winding up of the company, to 5% or more of its assets; and
– does not have rights entitling him to acquire 5% or more of any class of shares;
b. a participator in another company which has made a qualifying transfer to that trust; or
c. a **person** connected with such a participator.

> MEMO POINTS   1. A **close company** (¶75000+) is broadly a company controlled by five or fewer participators, or any number of directors. Non-resident companies which would be close (if UK-resident) can also qualify for this relief.
> 2. A **participator** is defined as any person having an interest in the capital or income of the company, specifically including a person who:
> – possesses (or is entitled to acquire) issued share capital or voting rights in the company;
> – is a loan creditor (¶75365) of the company;
> – possesses (or is entitled to acquire) a right to receive or participate in distributions of the company, or in any amounts payable by the company (in cash or kind) to loan creditors by way of premium or redemption; or
> – is entitled to secure that income or assets (whether present or future) of the company will be applied directly or indirectly for their benefit.

31340
CA 36070

Computation   If the assets are transferred as a **gift or for a value below cost**:
– the asset is treated as passing at such a price that there is no gain and no loss, including indexation;

– except for indexation purposes, the employee trust is treated as having acquired the asset at the same date and cost as the company (including on 31 March 1982 where the company held the asset at this date).

If the **consideration paid exceeds the allowable cost** to the company, the chargeable gain or allowable loss is computed by reference to the actual consideration given.

| EXAMPLE | C Ltd acquired an asset in June 2005 for £10,000. In June 2013, this asset was sold to an employee benefit trust for £11,000, when the asset was valued at £25,000. The indexation factor is 0.299. |

	£
Proceeds	11,000
Cost	(10,000)
Indexation: 10,000 x 0.299 = 2,990 but limited to 1,000	(1,000)
Chargeable gain	Nil

F. Connected persons

There are special rules when an asset is transferred between connected parties.   **31370**

Scope

The following table summarises all the **situations** where one party is connected with another.   **31375**

ss 286, 288 TCGA 1992; ss 1122, 1124 CTA 2010

Identity of the party/parties	Situations where connected
Two companies C Ltd and D Ltd	– the same person (Mr G) has control[1] of both companies; – Mr G has control of C Ltd, and individuals connected with Mr G have control of D Ltd; – Mr G has control of C Ltd, and Mr G has control of D Ltd when taking into account the interests of individuals connected with him (see below); or – C Ltd and D Ltd are each controlled by a group of two or more persons, and the groups either consist of the same persons or could be regarded as consisting of the same persons if, in one or more cases, a member of either group were to be replaced by a person with whom that member is connected
A company and a person	The person has control[1] of the company either on his own account, or taking into account the interests of persons connected with him When a company is in liquidation, it is the liquidator who has control of its assets
Two or more persons acting together[2] to control any body corporate (including a company)	Connected with one another, and also any person acting on the directions of any of them, to secure or exercise control[1] of the company
Two individuals A and B	– A is B's spouse or civil partner[3]; – A is B's relative[4]; – A is the spouse or civil partner of a relative of B; – A is a relative of B's spouse or civil partner; – A is the spouse or civil partner of a relative of B's spouse or civil partner
Members of a partnership[5]	Are connected with: – any other partner in the partnership; – the spouse or civil partner[3] of any other partner; or – a relative[4] of any other partner

Identity of the party/parties	Situations where connected
Trustee of a settlement	Is connected with: – any settlor of the settlement and anyone connected with him; – a company connected with the settlement; and – trustees of any subfunds of the settlement, or where the settlement is itself a subfund of a principal settlement, the trustees of any other subfunds of the same principal settlement For the strict **definitions** of settlement, settlor, subfund and principal settlement, see *Tax Memo*

Note:
1. A person **controls** a company if that person can use the following to ensure that the company conducts its affairs in accordance with their wishes:
– shareholding;
– voting power; or
– powers given to the person by the Articles of Association.
Each of these criteria may apply to the company itself, or to another company which is able to exercise control of the original company.
2. **Acting together** does require both parties to act in some way to control the company e.g. refraining from voting in a particular way.
3. **Spouses/civil partners** will remain connected despite the issue of a decree nisi until such time as a decree absolute is issued.
4. A **relative** is a brother, sister, ancestor or lineal descendant.
5. If the only connection is by **reason of partnership**, bona fide commercial transactions for acquisitions or disposals of partnership assets will not be treated as being carried out by connected persons.

EXAMPLE

1. Mr D owns 100% of Z Ltd. Z Ltd is therefore connected with Mr D as he has control of the company.

2. Mr D owns 40% of Z Ltd and his three children, F, G and H, each own 20%.
Mr D is connected with his children, and the company is therefore controlled by Mr D and persons connected with him. The company is therefore connected with Mr D and with each of his children.

3. Mr D owns 100% of the shares in Z Ltd and Y Ltd.
As the same person controls both companies, Z Ltd and Y Ltd are connected.

4. Mr D owns 100% of the shares in Z Ltd, and his son, F owns 100% of the shares in Y Ltd.
As Mr D and F are connected, the companies are also connected with each other.

5. Mr D owns 100% of the shares in Z Ltd, and 40% of Y Ltd. The remaining shares in Y Ltd are owned by his three children.
As Mr D is connected with his children, he, together with persons connected with him, controls both companies, and therefore Z Ltd and Y Ltd are connected.

6. Four friends, Mr A, Mr B, Mr C and Mr D, each own 25% of the shares in Z Ltd and Y Ltd.
Both companies are controlled by the same group of persons, and therefore Z Ltd and Y Ltd are connected.

7. Four friends, Mr A, Mr B, Mr C and Mr D each own 25% of the shares in Z Ltd.
Mrs A, B's sister, C's son and D's father each own 25% of Y Ltd. Substituting a connected person for each of the shareholders in Y Ltd produces the same group as the holders of Z Ltd. Z Ltd and Y Ltd are therefore connected.

Disposal value

31380
s 18 TCGA 1992

In general, consideration for a transaction between connected persons is deemed to be the open market value. This amount will be used to calculate the chargeable gain arising on the transfer, and will represent the base cost for the subsequent sale of the asset.

Where a disposal to a connected person gives rise to an **allowable loss**, that loss may only be offset against chargeable gains arising in the same or later accounting periods on disposals to the same connected person (¶37080).

Anti-avoidance

31385
ss 19, 20
TCGA 1992

Where a company makes a **series of linked disposals** (excluding intra-group transfers) to one or more connected persons, the deemed proceeds on each of the disposals may be adjusted if the total consideration for the assets disposed of is less than it would be if the assets were sold in a single transaction. The most common example of this is a series of disposals of shares in an unquoted company, where the single shareholding constituted a majority holding, and would command a higher price as a single sale, compared to a series of smaller minority shareholdings.

This provision applies where a company disposes of assets by separate transactions to connected persons and:

– those transactions occur **within a period** of 6 years ending on the date of the last transaction; and

– the original market **value of an individual transaction** is less than a reasonable proportion of the total value of all of the assets disposed of in the series of transactions taken together.

The **value attributable to each disposal** in the series will be deemed to be the relevant proportion of the total market value of all of the assets concerned.

> ⌐ MEMO POINTS ⌐ 1. The **total market value** of all of the assets disposed of, in the series of transactions, is found by establishing what the market value of the assets would have been if all of the assets had been disposed of together at the time of the transaction concerned (ignoring any assets acquired after the date of the transaction in question).
> 2. The **total number of assets** taken into account is limited to the maximum number, held by the vendor, at any time during the period immediately before the first transaction until immediately before the last transaction.
> 3. In respect of **groups** see ¶67280.

> ⌐ EXAMPLE ⌐ E Ltd owns 800 shares in an unquoted company, and makes the following gifts to a connected party.
>
> | | |
> |---|---|
> | June 2010 | 200 shares |
> | June 2013 | 400 shares |
>
> The aggregate market values of 600 shares at the relevant dates are:
>
> | | £ |
> |---|---|
> | June 2010 | 48,000 |
> | June 2013 | 60,000 |
>
> The appropriate portion of the aggregate market value at each date is arrived at as follows:
>
> | | | £ |
> |---|---|---|
> | June 2010 | $\frac{200}{600} \times 48,000$ | 16,000 |
> | June 2013 | $\frac{400}{600} \times 60,000$ | 40,000 |

G. Options

An option, and the asset over which it is granted, are two separate assets for chargeable gains purposes.

31415

The party granting the option is known as the grantor, and the party exercising the option is known as the grantee.

> ⌐ MEMO POINTS ⌐ 1. An option is **defined** as a right, binding in law, to accept or reject a present offer within a specified time in the future, and usually requires consideration to change hands.
> 2. A **put option** is an option binding the grantor to buy.
> 3. A **call option** is an option binding the grantor to sell, or to grant a lease.
> 4. If the option is **not exercised**, it lapses, and the owner of the asset is free to exploit the asset or make a disposal.

1. Grant of an option

Although the granting of an option creates an interest in the asset, the grant is treated as a disposal of an asset, i.e. the option itself. It is not a part disposal of the underlying asset. The only allowable expenditure is the costs directly associated with the grant.

31445
s 144 TCGA 1992

MEMO POINTS 1. **Except for** the following, an option with a **life of 50 years** or less is a wasting asset (¶31605+):
– quoted options to subscribe for shares in a company;
– traded options;
– financial options; and
– any option where the person is intending to use the assets so acquired for the purposes of a trade.
2. For the interaction between the **substantial shareholding exemption** and options, see ¶32145.

EXAMPLE A Ltd owns a painting, valued at £25,000, which it had acquired in May 1998 for £5,000. Several years later, A Ltd grants an option to B Ltd to acquire the painting for £50,000 in the next 5 years. B Ltd pays £6,000 for the option, and A Ltd incurs professional fees of £1,200 in connection with the grant.
A Ltd has disposed of the option, for £6,000. The allowable expenditure is £1,200 and a gain of £4,800 therefore results. (6,000 - 1,200)

31450

Where an option is sold **without being exercised**, the gain or loss is computed in the normal manner. If the option is a wasting asset (¶31445), the allowable expenditure on the option will be reduced in accordance with the wasting asset rules (¶31605+).

s 22 TCGA 1992

The **abandonment** of an option is not a disposal, unless the grantee of the option receives a capital sum for the abandonment, in which case an allowable loss will arise.

2. Exercise of an option

31480

Both the grantor and grantee are affected by the exercise of the option.

Grantor

31485
s 145 TCGA 1992

When a call option is exercised, the **grant** of the option **and the disposal** of the underlying asset are treated as a single transaction taking place on the date on which the option is exercised.

Any tax charged on the grant of the option will be set against any tax due on its exercise.

MEMO POINTS 1. **Indexation** will run to the date of exercise of the option.
2. Where the option **binds the grantor to buy an asset** (a put option), the consideration paid for the option is deducted from the allowable cost of the asset.
3. Where the option binds a **grantor both to buy and to sell**, the consideration is divided equally so there are two options for tax purposes.
4. An exercise of an option to acquire an asset on **non-arm's length terms** is treated as if it were a sale of the underlying asset at market value. The exercise price and any consideration given for the option will be ignored. An exercise price will be on non-arm's length terms when it is an option to:
– buy assets and the exercise price is more than the market value of the underlying assets; or
– sell assets and the exercise price is less than the market value of the underlying assets.

EXAMPLE
1. Continuing the example at ¶31445, B Ltd exercises the option in January 2013, when the painting is valued at £75,000.
A Ltd has therefore made a disposal of the painting and the chargeable gain is calculated as follows:

	£	£
Proceeds (6,000 + 50,000)		56,000
Costs of disposal		(1,200)
Less: Allowable expenditure		
Original cost	5,000	
Indexation: May 85 to Jan 13		
$\dfrac{245.80 - 95.21}{95.21} = 1.582 \times 5,000$	7,910	
		(12,910)
Chargeable gain		41,890

Note:
The chargeable gain originally arising on the grant is reduced to nil, and any tax charged is repaid or set off against the tax due on exercise. B Ltd's acquisition cost is £56,000. On a subsequent disposal of the painting, indexation will run as follows:
– on £6,000 from the date of grant of the option to acquire the painting; and
– on £50,000 from the date of exercise.

2. On 1 March 2006, C Ltd granted an option (for £7,000) to D Ltd, under which D Ltd could sell shares in X Ltd to C Ltd for £120,000.
Assuming there are no associated costs arising on the grant of the option, a chargeable gain will arise to C Ltd of £7,000.
In March 2013, D Ltd exercised the option and sold the shares to C Ltd. The chargeable gain arising on grant is reduced to nil. Any tax charged is repaid, and the allowable expenditure of the shares for C Ltd will be £113,000. (120,000 - 7,000)
On a subsequent disposal, the capital gains arising to C Ltd will be computed in the usual manner.

Grantee

Where a call option is exercised by the person to whom it is granted, there are no tax consequences for the grantee. On a **subsequent sale** of the asset acquired by the exercise of the option, the allowable expenditure is increased by the amount (if any) paid for the exercise of the option.

31490

Indexation (where applicable) will be applied separately to the cost of the option and the cost of the asset itself.

MEMO POINTS 1. Where **shares** forming part of a section 104 pool (¶32200+) are acquired as a result of an option, the cost of the option is added to the pool.
2. An exercise of an option to acquire an asset **on non-arm's length terms** is treated as if it were a sale of the underlying asset at market value.
3. Where the option **binds the grantor to buy** (a put option), the cost of the option is treated as an incidental cost of the grantee on a subsequent disposal of the asset.

EXAMPLE On 1 January 2005, E Ltd granted an option to F Ltd for £15,000 under which F Ltd could acquire an asset for £200,000. F Ltd exercised the option on 1 April 2008, and subsequently sold the asset on 1 March 2013 for £300,000.
The chargeable gain arising on sale will be computed as follows:

	£	£
Disposal proceeds		300,000
Less: Allowable expenditure		
Cost on exercise	200,000	
Indexation: April 08 to Mar 13		
$\frac{248.70 - 214.00}{214.00} = 0.162 \times 200,000$	32,400	
Amount paid for option	15,000	
Indexation: Jan 05 to Mar 13		
$\frac{248.70 - 188.90}{188.90} = 0.317 \times 15,000$	4,755	
		(252,155)
Chargeable gain		47,845

H. Hire purchase

In respect of a hire purchase agreement, the vendor is regarded as having disposed of the asset at the beginning of the contract, even though legal ownership does not pass until the end of the hire period.

31520
s 27 TCGA 1992

MEMO POINTS 1. A hire purchase agreement will contain the following **terms**:
– the hire period i.e. the period during which the eventual purchaser of the asset can use it;
– the deposit i.e. the initial sum paid at the beginning of the hire period;

– the hire charge i.e. the regular amounts paid during the hire period; and
– the date of the transfer of ownership i.e. when the purchaser takes ownership and the hire period ceases.
2. For capital allowances see ¶26335+.

Deferred consideration

31525
s 48 TCGA 1992

Unless the vendor is **treating the hire charges as revenue receipts**, the payments will be deferred consideration. However, as the future payments are certain and can be quantified at the beginning of the hire period, the total consideration is brought into the computation as disposal proceeds. Subject to certain conditions, the related tax may be paid by instalments (¶30370).

The date of disposal for the purposes of **indexation** is the beginning of the hire contract.

> ⌐ MEMO POINTS ⌐ Where the vendor **repossesses the asset**, usually due to the purchaser defaulting, the actual amounts received will be taxable. In this case, the original computation will need to be revisited.

SECTION 4

Specific types of asset

Summary

31575

Type of asset	¶¶
Wasting assets	¶31605+
Chattels	¶31645+
Assets eligible for capital allowances	¶31685+
Negligible value assets	¶31720+
Land and interests in land	¶31760+
Shares and securities	¶32020+

A. Wasting assets

Scope

31605
s 44 TCGA 1992

An asset is **defined** as a wasting asset if its predicted useful life is 50 years or less, always **excluding** freehold land.

Plant and machinery is always treated as a wasting asset (although see ¶31655).

> ⌐ MEMO POINTS ⌐ 1. For **chattels** see ¶31645+.
> 2. For **land and leases** see ¶31840+.

31610
s 146 TCGA 1992;
CG 76745

Exclusions The wasting assets rules do not apply to
– freehold land;
– a quoted option to subscribe for shares in a company;
– a traded option;
– a financial option; and
– an option over assets which is exercisable by a person to use the assets for the purposes of a trade.

Valuation The value of a wasting asset is **deemed to diminish** on a straight line basis over the course of its life (i.e. very similar to the accounting concept of depreciation for tangible fixed assets). Therefore, the allowable expenditure is restricted proportionately, depending on how much time has lapsed between the asset's acquisition and disposal.

31615
s 46(1) TCGA 1992

If an asset has any estimated **scrap value** (as assessed at the time when the asset was acquired by the company making the disposal), the restriction will be made to the cost after deducting the scrap value, and the scrap value will then be added back to reach the qualifying expenditure. Where additional expenditure is made which increases the scrap value, this new value is used on the basis that the expenditure was incurred when the asset was originally acquired, not when it was actually incurred.

CG 76700

EXAMPLE

1. A Ltd purchased a wasting asset in March 2006 for £12,000. The wasting asset had a life of 12 years from the date of purchase. In March 2013, A Ltd sells the asset for £18,000.

	£	£
Disposal proceeds		18,000
Less: Allowable expenditure		
Restricted cost:		
Life at acquisition: 12 years		
Life at disposal: 5 years		
5 /12 × 12,000	5,000	
Indexation: Mar 06 to Mar 13		
$\frac{248.70 - 195.00}{195.00} = 0.275 \times 5,000$	1,375	
		(6,375)
Chargeable gain		11,625

2. B Ltd acquires an asset for £11,000 in Year 1 with an estimated useful life of 10 years and a scrap value of £1,000. It is sold in Year 8 for £20,000.

	£	£	£
Disposal proceeds			20,000
Less: Allowable expenditure:			
Cost		11,000	
Less: Scrap value		(1,000)	
		10,000	
Restricted:			
Life at acquisition: 10 years			
Life at disposal: 2 years			
2 / 10 × 10,000		2,000	
Add: Scrap value		1,000	
			(3,000)
Gain before indexation			17,000

B. Chattels

The reliefs available for chattels (i.e. tangible moveable property such as plant and paintings) are different depending on whether or not the asset is a wasting asset (i.e. has a predicted useful life of 50 years or less).

31645

MEMO POINTS 1. To be **tangible** the asset has to be a physical asset e.g. a piece of machinery.
2. A **moveable** asset is one which can be moved easily and without damaging its surroundings.

CG 76550

Non-wasting chattels

31650
s 262 TCGA 1992

The following rules apply to non-wasting chattels.

Consideration on disposal	Detail	Tax treatment
£6,000 or less	Resulting in a gain	Exempt
	Resulting in a loss	Substitute £6,000 for proceeds and if this produces: – a lower loss, this is the allowable loss; or – a gain, the result is deemed to be neither a gain nor a loss
Less than £6,000		Amount of gain is lower of: – computed gain; and – 5/3 of excess of the consideration over £6,000

CG 76631

MEMO POINTS   1. For **joint owners** of a chattel the £6,000 limit is applied to each owner's share of the consideration.

2. In the case of a **part disposal** (¶31130+), it is necessary to consider the disposal proceeds and the market value of the part remaining, to establish whether the exemption will be available.

3. If assets which form part of a **set of articles** are sold on different occasions to the same person, or a connected person, the sales will be treated as a single transaction. Whether assets form part of a set of articles is a question of fact. Broadly, HMRC will treat assets as part of a set if they are essentially similar in nature, and their value together is greater than the value of the parts. It is irrelevant whether individual items are sold in different accounting periods.

EXAMPLE

1. A Ltd sells a Regency chest of drawers for £6,600, realising a gain after indexation of £1,500. As the consideration exceeds £6,000, the gain is chargeable, although it is restricted to a maximum of £1,000. (5/3 × (6,600 - 6,000))

2. B Ltd sold an asset costing £6,500 for £5,800, realising a loss on disposal of £900. The loss will be restricted as follows:

	Actual loss £	Restricted loss £
Disposal proceeds	5,800	6,000
Less:		
Costs of disposal	(200)	(200)
Acquisition cost	(6,500)	(6,500)
Net loss	(900)	(700)

In this case the allowable loss is restricted to £700.

3. C Ltd sold one third of an asset for £2,000, realising a gain of £1,200. The market value of the remaining part of the asset is £5,000.

As the aggregate of the disposal proceeds and the part retained exceeds £6,000, C Ltd's chargeable gain (before indexation) will be computed as follows (using the part disposal formula from ¶31135):

$$\frac{2,000}{2,000 + 5,000} \times (5 / 3 \times (7,000 - 6,000)) = £476$$

Wasting chattels

31655
s 45 TCGA 1992

Where a chattel is a wasting asset (i.e. an asset with a predicted useful life of 50 years or less), any chargeable gain on disposal will be exempt **unless** the asset has been used for business purposes and could have been subject to a claim for capital allowances (¶31685+).

If an asset was used **partly for a trade**, any consideration and allowable expenditure is apportioned appropriately between the trade and non-trade elements.

MEMO POINTS   1. When assessing the predictable life of **plant and machinery**, it should be based on the following assumptions:
– the predictable life will end when the item of plant or machinery is unfit for further use;
– it is put out of use at that date;
– it will be utilised normally and not overused; and
– it will be exploited throughout its life in this way.
2. If **capital allowances were withdrawn** on an asset before sale (because, for example, the asset was never actually used as intended), then the taxpayer is treated as if the allowances had never been made.
3. Where a chattel **is not exempt as a wasting asset**, the £6,000 chattel exemption may apply instead (¶31650).
4. For wasting assets which are **not chattels** see ¶31605+.

C. Assets eligible for capital allowances

Where the asset is a chattel, and the **disposal proceeds** are less than £6,000, any gain will be exempt (¶31650).

31685
s 47 TCGA 1992

Otherwise, where a disposal of an asset on which capital allowances could be claimed results in:
– a capital **gain**, any allowances already given are clawed back by way of a balancing charge (¶26095), but there is no change to the capital gains computation; or
– a capital **loss**, special rules apply to restrict the amount of the allowable loss by any capital allowances given. In practice, this means that the allowable loss is restricted to any incidental costs of acquisition or disposal.

Comment   **Plant and machinery** is always treated as a wasting asset (¶31605+). No rebasing election can be made for this type of asset.

MEMO POINTS   1. For this purpose the **definition** of capital allowance **includes**:
– any normal capital allowance (¶25120);
– relief given in respect of expenditure on sea walls; and
– any deduction in computing profits or gains in relation to cemeteries.
2. A **renewals allowance**, granted on the acquisition of a new asset, should be regarded as an allowance for expenditure incurred on the old asset.

s 52(5) TCGA 1992

Asset disposed of at a loss

If an asset is disposed of at a loss, the **allowable expenditure** for chargeable gains purposes will be restricted to prevent double relief being given for the same costs (i.e. in the form of both capital allowances and also a capital loss). This could restrict a loss to nil, but would never create a gain.

31690
s 41 TCGA 1992

As the allowable cost is reduced, this also affects the **indexation allowance**.

EXAMPLE
1. A Ltd owns an item of machinery which it acquired in Year 4 for £12,000. The machinery is sold in Year 9 for £15,000 and the company incurred incidental costs of sale amounting to £1,500.
As the proceeds exceed the cost of the asset, all capital allowances will be withdrawn by way of a balancing charge. Ignoring indexation, the position on the disposal of the asset is as follows:

	£	£
Proceeds	15,000	
Less: Incidental costs of sale	(1,500)	
		13,500
Less: Allowable expenditure		
Original cost		(12,000)
Chargeable gain		1,500

2. Taking the facts from 1. above, but the machine is sold for £10,000.

On the disposal of the machine, part of the capital allowances on the asset will be withdrawn by way of a balancing charge; however, a total of £2,000 allowances, previously given, will still remain. The position on the disposal of the asset is therefore as follows:

	£	£
Proceeds	10,000	
Less: Incidental costs of sale	(1,500)	
		8,500
Less: Allowable expenditure		
Original cost	12,000	
Less: Capital allowances given and retained	(2,000)	
		(10,000)
Allowable loss		(1,500)

D. Negligible value assets

31720 Where an asset has become worthless, it may be impossible to find a purchaser, so that the resulting loss cannot be realised. However, when a negligible value claim is made, the asset is treated as having been sold and immediately reacquired at market value, thereby crystallising a capital loss.

Conditions

31725

s 24(2) TCGA 1992

A claim can be made once an asset's value has become negligible.

There is no statutory **definition** of negligible, although small is defined as 5%, and negligible is therefore taken to be considerably less than 5%.

> ▭ MEMO POINTS ▭　1. When considering **buildings**, HMRC will accept a negligible value claim based solely on the value of the building becoming negligible, and not the land on which it stands. However, as a building and the land are strictly a single asset, the land will be deemed to be sold separately and reacquired on the same date, which may give rise to a chargeable gain.
> 2. HMRC maintain a list of **quoted shares** (at flmemo.co.uk/ctm31725) which are accepted as being of negligible value. A claim is automatically accepted for any shares on this list. Claims may be made for other shares, but the owner will need to prove that the value has become negligible.

Time limits

31730 A negligible value **claim** may be made at any time whilst the value remains negligible. In this situation the asset is deemed to be sold and immediately reacquired on the date on which the claim is made.

Alternatively, a claim may be made **specifying a date** on which the asset was of negligible value. The claim must be made within 2 years of the end of the accounting period in which the specified date falls, and the asset must be of negligible value both on the date that the claim is made and also on the specified date.

E. Land and interests in land

31760 There are special rules in relation to land in respect of the following:
- part disposals;
- leases;
- buildings qualifying for capital allowances (i.e. BPRA or flat conversion allowance);

– compulsory purchase; and
– land exchanges.

> [MEMO POINTS] 1. Where a company holds land **as stock** (i.e. a land bank), any sale will be treated
> as trading income.
> 2. Land **includes** dwellings and other buildings or structures situated on it (whether owned   s 288 TCGA 1992
> or leased), and any right or interest over land. Land covered by water is also included in the
> definition.
> 3. Any **interest in land** is situated in the same place as the land itself.   s 275 TCGA 1992
> 4. The **time of acquisition/disposal** of land is deemed to be the date of the contract, irrespective   s 28 TCGA 1992
> of whether the conveyance takes place at a later date.
> 5. For **sale and leaseback** transactions, or **sale and repurchase** transactions see ¶19220.

1. Part disposals

Except for small disposals of land (¶31800+), the computation of a gain arising from a part **31790**
disposal of land follows the usual rules (¶31130+).

Valuation

However, as the valuation of land is a potentially contentious issue, there are **two methods** **31795**
which can be followed:

SP D1

Method	Detail
General method	Requires the engagement of a professional to make a valuation, which therefore incurs cost HMRC can require this method where alternative method is deemed unsatisfactory
Alternative method	Must be fair, reasonable and realistic Usually attribute a reasonable value to the part disposed of at the date it was acquired

> [EXAMPLE] A Ltd acquires 80 acres of land for £80,000 in Year 3. In Year 9, the directors decide to
> sell 30 acres at a price of £60,000.
> **General method**
> Assuming the value of the remaining land in Year 9 is £90,000, the chargeable gain will be calcul-
> ated as follows:
>
> | | £ |
> |---|---|
> | Disposal proceeds | 60,000 |
> | Cost $\frac{60,000}{60,000 + 90,000} \times 80,000$ | (32,000) |
> | Gain before indexation | 28,000 |
>
> The cost for the remaining 50 acres is deemed to be £48,000. (80,000 - 32,000)
> **Alternative method**
>
> | | £ |
> |---|---|
> | Disposal proceeds | 60,000 |
> | Cost (say, 30/80 × 80,000) | (30,000) |
> | Gain before indexation | 30,000 |
>
> The cost for the remaining 50 acres is deemed to be £50,000. (80,000 - 30,000)
> Although the gain is higher under the alternative method than the general method, there would be
> significant valuation fees to be incurred in order to apply the general method.

Small part disposals

A small part disposal of land will not trigger a gain where the company **elects** to deduct the **31800**
proceeds from a future sale of the remaining land (¶31810).   s 242 TCGA 1992

31805
s 244 TCGA 1992

Exclusions   The small part disposal rules do not apply if:
– the **allowable expenditure** of the original asset is nil; or
– the **consideration received** for the part disposal exceeds the original allowable expenditure of the land.
In such a case, the company may elect to calculate the gain or loss on the part disposal by deducting the total original allowable expenditure from the proceeds of the part disposal. The allowable expenditure (and 31 March 1982 value, if applicable) for the remaining land will therefore be reduced to nil, and only expenditure incurred since the part disposal will be available on any subsequent disposals. This election must be submitted to HMRC within 2 years after the end of the accounting period in which the disposal took place.

> [EXAMPLE]   B Ltd owns land which was acquired in June 2007 for £9,000. In December 2012, when the value of the entire holding had increased to £100,000, part of the land is sold for £17,000. This was the only land transaction made by the company during the current accounting period. Assuming that B Ltd submits an election, the chargeable gain on the part disposal will be calculated as follows:
>
> | | £ |
> |---|---:|
> | Disposal proceeds | 17,000 |
> | Less: Allowable expenditure of entire holding | (9,000) |
> | Gain before indexation | 8,000 |
>
> The cost available for use on the subsequent disposal of the remaining land is reduced to nil.

31810

Subject to the above exclusions, the following **conditions** must be satisfied:

Area	Condition	Detail
Proceeds	Must not exceed £20,000, as applied to all part disposals of land in the same accounting period	Exclude following from the £20,000 threshold: – land which is the subject of compulsory acquisition (¶31945+); – no gain/no loss transfers between group companies (¶67080+); and – an estate or interest in land which is a wasting asset such as a short lease (¶31605+)
	Must not exceed 20% of the value of the entire holding prior to the part disposal	Where transaction not made for full consideration, market value is used
Claim	Must be submitted to HMRC within 2 years after the end of the accounting period in which the disposal took place	

2. Leases

31840

As short leases (i.e. with 50 years or less to run) are wasting assets, the rules for calculating chargeable gains must take their diminishing value into account i.e. the longer into the term the lease is, the less it is worth.

To ascertain the correct treatment, it is therefore vital to identify whether or not a lease is a short lease.

Scope

31845
Sch 8 paras 8, 10
TCGA 1992

The **definition** of a lease includes underleases, subleases and any tenancy or licence and any agreements for such.

For chargeable gains purposes only, the **duration** of a lease is determined by the terms of the contract, subject to anti-avoidance rules which deem a lease to expire on:
– the first date on which the landlord has the right to terminate the lease; or
– the date beyond which the terms of the lease render it unlikely that the lease will continue (e.g. because of a substantial increase in rents).

Summary

Subject	Meaning	¶¶
Assignment of a long lease	Sale of an existing long lease	¶31855
Assignment of a short lease	Sale of an existing short lease	¶31860+
Grant of a lease out of a long lease or freehold	Creating a new lease out of a long lease or freehold [1]	¶31880
Grant of a sublease out of a short lease	Creating a new lease out of a short lease [1]	¶31885+

Note:
1. The **grant** of a lease **to follow on from a previous lease** will be deemed to be the grant of a new lease unless all of the following conditions are satisfied:
– the lease (whether or not it is between connected or unconnected persons) is made on terms which would have been made between unconnected persons who are bargaining at arm's length;
– the grant of the follow-on lease is not part of a larger scheme;
– the lessee did not receive a capital sum in respect of the transaction; and
– the property and terms of the lease (other than duration and rent) remain the same as the old lease.

31850

ESC D39

Assignment of a long lease

There are no special rules for the assignment of a long lease for capital gains purposes. Any chargeable gain or allowable loss is therefore calculated in accordance with the normal rules.

31855

Assignment of a short lease

As short leases are wasting assets, the original expenditure which is **allowed as a deduction** in the capital gains calculation reduces each year. However, this is not on a straight line basis but is based on a series of percentages shown below.

31860

Short lease depreciation factors					
Years	Percentage	Years	Percentage	Years	Percentage
50 (or more)	100	33	90.280	16	64.116
49	99.657	32	89.354	15	61.617
48	99.289	31	88.371	14	58.971
47	98.902	30	87.330	13	56.167
46	98.490	29	86.226	12	53.191
45	98.059	28	85.053	11	50.038
44	97.595	27	83.816	10	46.695
43	97.107	26	82.496	9	43.154
42	96.593	25	81.100	8	39.399
41	96.041	24	79.622	7	35.414
40	95.457	23	78.055	6	31.195
39	94.842	22	76.399	5	26.722
38	94.189	21	74.635	4	21.983
37	93.497	20	72.770	3	16.959
36	92.761	19	70.791	2	11.629
35	91.981	18	68.697	1	5.983
34	91.156	17	66.470	0	0

Note that the provisions outlined here **exclude** land:
– used throughout the period of ownership for the purposes of a trade, profession or vocation; and

– where capital allowances have (or could have) been claimed in respect of the cost (¶31685+).

Where the land disposed of has **partly qualified** for capital allowances or business use, the allowable expenditure relating to the land should be apportioned accordingly.

There are also special rules where a lease is subject to an onerous sublease (¶31875).

31865
Sch 8 para 1
TCGA 1992

Allowable cost   The following **formula** is used to calculated the allowable cost, based on the percentages from the table in ¶31860:

$$\text{Allowable expenditure for original lease} \times \frac{\text{\% for years left to run at assignment}}{\text{\% for years left to run from original acquisition}}$$

Indexation is then applied as normal to the result.

> ⌐MEMO POINTS⌐   1. If the lease was acquired **before 31 March 1982**, the formula is amended to calculate the proportion of the 31 March 1982 value available:
>
> $$31 \text{ March } 1982 \text{ value of original lease} \times \frac{\text{\% for years left to run at assignment}}{\text{\% for years left to run from 31 March 1982}}$$
>
> 2. Where the **duration** of the lease is **not a complete number of years**, the relevant percentage is obtained by taking the whole year, and adding one twelfth of the difference between the whole year and the next highest year for each extra month.
>
> 3. If a lease was **originally a long lease** but was assigned at a time when there were 50 years or less to run, then the percentage for the number of years left to run on the lease at the original acquisition will always be 100 (i.e. 50 years or more).

s 43 TCGA 1992;
ESC D42

> 4. If the leaseholder company acquires a **superior interest** in land (either a superior lease or the freehold reversion), the two leases are merged, and on a subsequent assignment the following rules apply:
>
> – allowable expenditure will be the cost of the first lease (wasted if it is less than 50 years), together with the cost of the superior interest (again, wasted if it is a lease of less than 50 years); and
>
> – indexation is given on the first lease and the superior interest from their respective dates of acquisition.

⌐EXAMPLE⌐

1. C Ltd acquired a 30-year lease on 30 June 2008 for £150,000. The lease was assigned on 30 June 2013 for £200,000.
The cost available for deduction from the disposal proceeds will be calculated as follows:

$$150,000 \times \frac{\text{\% for 25 years}}{\text{\% for 30 years}} = 150,000 \times \frac{81.100}{87.330} = £139,299$$

2. D Ltd acquired a 40-year lease on 31 January 2008 for £120,000. The lease was assigned on 31 March 2013 for £150,000.

	£
Disposal proceeds	150,000
Cost[1]	(115,458)
Gain before indexation	34,542

Note:
1. The period from acquisition of the lease to assignment is 5 years 2 months. This is deducted from the years left to run at the date of acquisition to reach the years left to run at assignment:

$$120,000 \times \frac{\text{\% for 34 years 10 months}}{\text{\% for 40 years}} = 120,000 \times \frac{91.844^*}{95.457} = 115,458$$

* % for	34 years		91.156
	35 years	91.981	
	34 years	(91.156)	
		0.825	
	10/12 × 0.825		0.688
			91.844

Enhancement Where the property, which is the subject of a short lease, is enhanced   **31870**
before it is assigned (and this is reflected in the lease's value), the deductible enhancement
expenditure is also restricted.

For these purposes the **formula** is amended as follows:

$$\text{Enhancement expenditure} \times \frac{\text{\% for years left to run at assignment}}{\text{\% for years left to run from enhancement}}$$

The formula should be applied separately for each item of enhancement expenditure.

Onerous sublease A lease is not a wasting asset if, at the date of assignment, it is subject   **31875**
to an onerous sublease.

An onerous sublease is **defined** as one where:
– the rent payable under the sublease is less than the full annual rental value of the property;
and
– the value of the reversionary interest exceeds the allowable expenditure of the acquisition
of the asset.

On the **original assignment** of such a lease, there is no wasting asset restriction applied to
the cost.

However, once the **sublease term ends**, the lease will revert back to a wasting asset, and on
a **subsequent assignment** the formula is amended as follows:

$$\text{Allowable expenditure} \times \frac{\text{\% for years left to run at assignment}}{\text{\% for years left to run from date sublease expired}}$$

Grant of a lease out of a long lease or freehold

The grant of a lease out of a long lease or freehold is deemed to be a part disposal. The   **31880**
allowable expenditure for the entire holding must be apportioned on the following basis: Sch 8 para 2
TCGA 1992

$$\frac{A}{A + B}$$

where:
– A is the value of the part disposed of (i.e. the premium received on the grant of the lease);
and
– B is the value of the remainder (i.e. the market value of the remainder of the property
together with the value of the right to receive rent under the lease).

> MEMO POINTS 1. If the grant of the lease is **not at arm's length** (between connected parties, for
> example) the premium is valued at market value at the time of the grant.
> 2. Where the **sublease is for 50 years or less**, an adjustment is required to take account of the
> fact that some of the premium will be taxable as income (¶19215). The amount of the premium
> included in the above calculation will be reduced by the amount treated as property income.
> However, the value of the part disposed of, included in the denominator of the part disposal
> fraction, will be the whole of the premium received.
> 3. If a leaseholder charges a **premium for the grant of a further sublease** out of a lease, corpor-   Sch 8 para 6
> ation tax relief is available (¶19405). Any capital loss will be restricted by the amount of tax relief   TCGA 1992
> already received (but not so as to turn a loss into a gain).

EXAMPLE
1. In June 2006, E Ltd acquired a property under a 99-year lease for £60,000. In March 2013, the
company granted a 60-year sublease for a premium of £90,000. The value of the remainder was
agreed to be £40,000.

	£
Disposal proceeds	90,000
Cost ($60,000 \times \dfrac{90,000}{90,000 + 40,000}$)	(41,538)
Gain before indexation	48,462

2. Carrying on from the previous example, if the sublease granted by E Ltd had been 40 years in length, the following would apply:

	£
Premium received	90,000

Premium taxed as income from property:

$$90,000 \times \left(\frac{50 - 39}{50}\right) \qquad\qquad \underline{(19,800)}$$

Balance for chargeable gains purposes	<u>70,200</u>

	£
Disposal proceeds	70,200
Cost $\left(60,000 \times \dfrac{70,200}{90,000 + 40,000}\right)$	<u>(32,400)</u>
Gain	<u>37,800</u>

3. F Ltd grants a 25-year lease on a property to G Ltd for rent of £12,000 p.a. and a premium of £12,000. After a couple of years, G Ltd sublets the property to H Ltd on a 10-year lease at a premium of £5,000.

For income purposes:
F Ltd is taxable on the premium as follows:

$$12,000 \times \frac{(50 - 24)}{50} = £6,240$$

G Ltd is taxable on the premium from H Ltd as follows:

		£
Premium $5,000 \times \dfrac{(50 - 9)}{50}$		4,100
Less:		
$\dfrac{\text{Years of sublease}}{\text{Years of head lease}} \times$ Taxable element of head lease premium	10 / 25 × 6,240	<u>(2,496)</u>
Liable to corporation tax as income		<u>1,604</u>

For chargeable gains purposes:
G Ltd is taxed on the grant of the sublease to H Ltd as follows:

	£
Premium received	5,000
Less:	
$\dfrac{\text{Years of sublease}}{\text{Years of head lease}} \times$ Premium paid to F Ltd	
$\dfrac{10 \text{ years}}{25 \text{ years}} \times 12,000 = 46.695[1] \, / \, 81.100[1] \times 12,000$	<u>(6,909)</u>
	(1,909)
Less	
Relief already given for corporation tax (restricted)	<u>1,909</u>
Allowable loss	<u>Nil</u>

Note:
1. The value of a short lease is determined by the short lease table of percentages (¶31860)

Grant of a sublease out of a short lease

31885   The grant of a sublease out of a short lease is also a part disposal. However, because the original lease is a wasting asset, the required **formula** is as follows:

$$O \times \frac{G - S}{A}$$

where:
– O is the allowable expenditure for the original lease;
– G is the % for the years left to run on the original lease at the grant of the sublease;

– S is the % for the years left to run on the original lease at the expiry of the sublease; and
– A is the % for the years left at the date of the acquisition of the original lease.

An adjustment must also be made to take account of the fact that some of the premium will be subject to corporation tax as income (¶19215).

MEMO POINTS If the **lease was acquired before 31 March 1982**, the formula is amended to calculate the proportion of the 31 March 1982 value available, so that in the formula above:
– O is the 31 March 1982 value of original lease; and
– A is the % for the years left on the original lease at 31 March 1982.

EXAMPLE On 1 April 2002, E Ltd acquired a 40-year lease from F Ltd for £60,000. On 1 April 2012, E Ltd granted a 20-year sublease for £80,000.

	£
Premium taxed as income from property:	
On grant of sublease	
$80,000 \times \dfrac{(50 - 19)}{50}$	49,600
Less: Proportion of amount taxed on F Ltd	
$60,000 \times \dfrac{(50 - 39)}{50} \times 20/40$	(6,600)
Property income	43,000

Chargeable gains	£
Disposal proceeds	80,000
Less: Cost[1]	(25,541)
	54,459
Less: Income already assessed	(43,000)
Gain before indexation	11,459

Note:
1. $60,000 \times \dfrac{\% \text{ for 30 years } - \% \text{ for 10 years}}{\% \text{ for 40 years}} = 60,000 \times \dfrac{87.330 - 46.695}{95.457} = £25,541$

Sublease at higher rent If the sublease is granted at a higher annual rent compared to the rent payable on the original lease, the premium will often be reduced as a result. Hence, the allowable expenditure, as calculated above, must be reduced as follows:

31890

$$\text{Allowable expenditure as restricted} \times \frac{\text{Actual premium paid}}{\text{Notional premium}}$$

The **notional premium** is the amount that would have been payable if the rent on the sublease was the same as on the original lease.

EXAMPLE Following on from the example in ¶31885 above, if the rent on the headlease was £2,000 p.a. and the rent on the sublease was £3,000 p.a., then it becomes necessary to calculate what the premium on the sublease would have been if the rent had been £2,000. If it is assumed that the premium would have been £90,000, the calculation would become:

	£
Disposal proceeds	80,000
Less: Cost $(25,541 \times \dfrac{80,000}{90,000})$	(22,703)
	57,297
Less: Property income	(43,000)
Gain before indexation	14,297

Enhancement Where the property, which is the subject of a short lease, is enhanced before the grant of a sublease (and this is reflected in the value of the short lease), the **deductible** enhancement expenditure is also restricted.

31895

For these purposes the formula becomes:

$$\text{Enhancement expenditure} \times \frac{G-S}{E}$$

where:
- G is the % for the years left to run on the original lease at the grant of the sublease;
- S is the % for the years left to run on the original lease on the expiry of the sublease; and
- E is the % for the years left to run on the original lease at the date of the enhancement expenditure.

The formula should be applied separately for each item of enhancement expenditure.

3. Buildings qualifying for capital allowances

31925
s 41 TCGA 1992

A building is treated as being part of the land and, where there is an **overall loss** arising on the sale of the land and building taken together, the losses will be restricted to take account of capital allowances previously given (¶26485+).

One computation must be prepared for both the land and building, and the allowable expenditure included for the building is reduced by the amount of capital allowances received. The effect of the computation is shown at ¶31685.

4. Compulsory purchase

31945

Where land is compulsorily purchased, the following may be relevant:
- rollover relief; and
- part disposal, including a relief for small part disposals.

Rollover relief

31950
s 247 TCGA 1992

This may be available where land is **acquired by** authorities exercising compulsory powers. The relief applies where:
- the owner of the land did not take any steps to dispose of the land whether by advertising or by otherwise making his willingness to sell known to the authority; and
- the consideration for the disposal was applied in acquiring new land (the replacement land).

However, relief will not be available if the **replacement land is a dwelling house** which qualifies for principal private residence relief. Similarly, rollover relief which has been given will be withdrawn if the new land becomes eligible for principal private residence relief within 6 years from the date of acquisition.

Rollover relief may be given on a **provisional basis** on:
- an exchange of contracts for the replacement land; or
- a declaration being made by the company that it intends to acquire replacement land.

> ☐ *MEMO POINTS*   1. **Principal private residence relief** broadly applies where an individual disposes of a dwelling house which has been his only or main residence during his period of ownership. For further details see *Tax Memo*.
> 2. If proceeds are **reinvested into a depreciating asset** the gain will be held over (¶31040+).
> 3. Any gain arising on the disposal of a qualifying asset may be rolled (or held) over into the acquisition of a qualifying replacement asset by **another group member** (¶67315+), subject to a joint election being made. There is no requirement for both companies to be members of the group at the same time. The disposing company must be a member of the group at the time of disposal, and the acquiring company must be a member at the time at which the replacement asset is acquired.
> 4. The rollover relief provisions are extended to cover gains made by a landlord following the exercise by a:

– **tenant** of a statutory right to acquire the freehold reversion of a property or extend the lease; or
– **crofting community body** of a statutory right to acquire croft land.

Part disposals

Where only part of the holding of land is acquired in a compulsory purchase then a part disposal under the normal rules will arise (¶31130+), **unless** the company elects for the small part disposal rules to apply.

31955
ss 243, 245
TCGA 1992

If the consideration for that part disposal **includes compensation for severance of land** (or any other injurious effect on the remaining land), a part disposal of the remaining land will also arise. For this rule to apply, both parcels of the land must have been held in the same capacity.

Small part disposal The following are **excluded** from this relief, as another special election (¶31805+) is available:
– the allowable expenditure of the original asset is nil; or
– the consideration received for the part disposal exceeds the original allowable expenditure of the land.

31960
s 244 TCGA 1992

Otherwise, on a small part disposal as a result of a compulsory purchase, the company may elect that a disposal will not arise, and instead the **consideration** will be deducted from the allowable expenditure on the subsequent disposal of the remaining land.

> ⌐MEMO POINTS⌐ 1. Small is not **defined** by the legislation, but for these purposes it is generally understood to mean:
> – 5% or less of the value of the asset; or
> – £3,000 or less (whether or not this is within the 5% limit).
> 2. **Indexation allowance** on a subsequent disposal by the company will need to be adjusted (¶30640).
> 3. The **claim** must be submitted within 2 years after the end of the accounting period in which the disposal took place.

RI 157

5. Exchanges of land

Land can be owned jointly in two ways: as joint tenants, or as tenants in common.

31990

Where jointly owned land is **partitioned** between the joint owners, a disposal will be deemed to arise, so that each owner will be deemed to have acquired a new interest in the part of the land allotted to him, and to have disposed of the part of the land which is released to the other owner.

Rollover relief can, however, be claimed provided that, as **a result** of the exchange, each owner becomes the sole owner of part of the land that was previously owned jointly.

ss 248A - 248D
TCGA 1992

> ⌐MEMO POINTS⌐ 1. A **joint tenancy** requires the tenants to have equal interests in the land which were acquired at the same time. A joint tenant is not the absolute owner of a fractional share in the land, and so where the interest ceases, it is the other joint tenants who are deemed to own the land. On the disposal of land subject to a joint tenancy, each tenant is entitled to an equal share of the net sale proceeds, irrespective of the amount paid at acquisition.
> 2. The interests held by **tenants in common** can be any proportion e.g. 75% and 25%. On the disposal of the land, the net sale proceeds are apportioned in the same way.

F. Shares and securities

Shares and securities are subject to a number of special rules due to the very nature of these assets. For companies only, certain disposals of shares are exempt from tax.

32020

1. Scope

32050
s 104(3) TCGA 1992

For the purposes of this section, the word share will be used to include securities other than:
– qualifying corporate bonds (QCBs) (as determined at the time of disposal); and
– relevant securities,
unless the distinction is vital.

s 132 TCGA 1992

Security includes any loan stock or similar security whether of the UK government or of any other government, or of any public or local authority in the UK or elsewhere, or of any company, and whether secured or unsecured.

s 108 TCGA 1992

[MEMO POINTS]   A **relevant security** is:
a. a security within the accrued income scheme i.e. any security except for:
– shares in a company;
– national savings certificates;
– war savings certificates;
– certificates of deposit;
– zero coupon redeemable securities; and
– deeply discounted securities;
b. a qualifying corporate bond; or
c. a security which at any time is, or has been, an interest in a non-reporting offshore fund (¶21800+).
Disposals are taken in the order in which they occur, and matched against:
– acquisitions on the same day;
– securities acquired within the previous 12 months on a FIFO basis; and
– other acquisitions on a LIFO basis,
unless securities are disposed of for transfer or delivery on a particular date, when they must be identified with acquisitions of securities for transfer or delivery on or before that date.

Qualifying corporate bonds

32055
s 117 TCGA 1992

A QCB means any asset representing a loan relationship of a company (¶16050+).

QCBs are subject to the loan relationship rules, and hence their **disposal** does not create a chargeable gain or allowable loss. However, where a gain arising from a share disposal is deferred on the receipt of a QCB, the disposal of the QCB will cause that gain to fall into charge (¶32280).

Share

32060

A share is a definite portion of a company's share capital, and gives the shareholder **rights** to:
– receive dividends;
– vote at general meetings; and
– receive a distribution of assets if the company is wound up.

Some larger companies may issue different **classes** of share, which will have different entitlements in respect of the rights. These might include preference shares, non-voting ordinary shares, and redeemable shares.

CG 50207

Shares are issued for a subscription price, which is usually fully paid. However, it is possible for a share to be **partly paid**, and the remaining amount will be payable subsequently (e.g. if a £1 share is issued for 75p, the company can ask for the extra 25p in the future). Partly paid shares are treated the same as fully paid shares provided that the balance of the subscription price is payable within 6 months of the issue of the shares.

There is a very important distinction between a subscription for shares and a purchase of shares, namely the recipient of the consideration. A **subscription** involves the issue of new shares by the company, and so the consideration is paid to the company. A **purchase** involves the acquisition of shares which have already been issued, and so it is the current owner of the shares who receives the consideration. Certain reliefs (¶37230+, ¶41350+, ¶80000+) only apply to issued shares.

2. Exemption

In order to keep the UK corporation tax regime competitive with other countries, an exemption was introduced in respect of the disposal by a company of substantial shareholdings. This means that no chargeable gain or allowable loss arises. As the exemption is automatic, no **claim** is required.

32090

Exclusions

The following disposals do not fall within the substantial shareholding exemption (SSE):
– no gain/no loss disposals (¶31280+);
– where the gain would not have been a chargeable gain because of some other provision, although the reorganisation provisions are superseded by the operation of the SSE; or
– where one of the anti-avoidance rules (¶32155) applies.

32095
Sch 7AC
TCGA 1992

Substantial shareholding

A substantial shareholding is **defined** as a holding of not less than 10% of the ordinary share capital of a company (of any residence), which carries an **entitlement** to not less than 10% of both:
– the profits available for distribution to its equity holders; and
– the assets on a winding up available to its equity holders.

32100
Sch 7AC para 8
TCGA 1992

> MEMO POINTS   1. **Ordinary share capital** is all a company's issued share capital, however named, excluding share capital which only has a right to fixed rate dividends and no other right to share in the company's profits.
>
> 2. **Equity holders** include any person who:
> – holds ordinary shares in the company;
> – is a loan creditor (other than in relation to a normal commercial loan); or
> – has provided new consideration for shares in the company, and used assets belonging to the company on which the company has claimed capital allowances. Where this condition is satisfied, that person alone is treated as an equity holder in relation to the shares referred to in the condition.
>
> 3. In looking at the level of shareholding, other 51% **group** company (¶69055) **holdings** can be aggregated.
>
> 4. On **liquidation**, although the company no longer has beneficial ownership of its assets, it is still deemed to own the shares for the purposes of the SSE.

s 1119 CTA 2010

ss 158, 159
CTA 2010

Sch 7AC para 9
TCGA 1992

Sch 7AC para 16
TCGA 1992

> EXAMPLE   A Ltd owns 100% of the shares in B Ltd. If A Ltd holds 6% of C Ltd, and B Ltd owns 7% of C Ltd, then the following consequences occur:
> – A Ltd and B Ltd are both treated as holding 13% of C Ltd's ordinary share capital; and
> – both companies are treated as being entitled to the rights to distributable profits and assets etc attributable to a 13% shareholder.

The exemption applies not only to shares, but also:
a. interests in shares i.e. an interest as co-owner of the shares, whether owned jointly or in common, equally or unequally; and
b. assets related to shares i.e. either:
– an option to acquire or dispose of shares, or an interest in shares; or
– a security that could be converted into, or exchanged for, shares in that company by the exercise of rights granted to the holder of the security (and where those rights have more than a negligible chance of being exercised).

32105
Sch 7AC paras 29,
30 TCGA 1992

Conditions

The following three conditions must be **met** either at the **time** of disposal or within the last 2 years (assuming the disposal had taken place up to 2 years earlier (the "2 year look back" exemption)):

32110
CG 53113

Criteria	Condition	Detail	Reference
Size of interest and length of ownership	Investing company must have held a substantial shareholding (¶32100) in the target company for a continuous 12-month period[1] beginning not more than 2 years prior to the disposal[2]	This means that it is possible for a company to have less than 10% holding for up to a year, and still make an exempt disposal Periods of ownership relating to no gain/no loss transfers, or where the shares currently owned have derived from a reorganisation, are added to the ownership period of the shares in their current form i.e. the total period during which the gain to be exempted has arisen is taken into account However, where shares are deemed to be disposed of and reacquired, the period of ownership runs from the date of reacquisition, including where a degrouping charge arises (¶67425+) Where shares are transferred either in a repurchase transaction or for stock lending, only the original owner of the shares can use SSE	Sch 7AC paras 7 - 11, 14, 15 TCGA 1992
Investing company and target company	Must be carrying on trading activities[3] throughout the 12-month period[1] (and immediately after the date of disposal)[2], and the company's activities do not, to a substantial extent (¶32125), include non-trading activities The target company must be either: – a stand-alone trading company; – the holding company of a trading group; or – the holding company of a trading subgroup (i.e. it would be a holding company were it not itself a 51% subsidiary) - in this case intra-group transactions outside the subgroup do count as a trading activity	Trade means anything that is a trade, profession or vocation, provided it is conducted on a commercial basis and with a view to the realisation of profits, including: – intending or preparing to start to trade[4]; – intending to acquire a trading company (including the case where one business has been sold and the company is actively looking for another acquisition)[4]; or – a furnished holiday letting business (¶19410+) Where the company is a member of a 51% group, the group must be carrying on trading activities (ignoring intra-group transactions)	Sch 7AC paras 18 - 28 TCGA 1992

Note:

1. **Parts of days** are not taken into account, so where shares were acquired at midday on 1 January, the exemption would still apply if they were disposed of at 9am on the following 31 December. Provided that the shares were owned at some point on the 365th day after their acquisition, the exemption will apply.

2. Where the investing company cannot satisfy these conditions but **another group member** can, then the disposal will be treated as made by that other group member, and so SSE will apply (¶69065). Note also the 2 year look back (¶32150), which may assist holding companies which are selling off their only subsidiary.

3. **Activities** include engaging in trading operations, making and holding investments, planning, holding meetings etc. A company may have trading activities both when it is trading and before it commences to trade. Investment may be so closely aligned with the trading purpose as to not constitute a separate activity e.g. a travel agent who is required to keep a fixed level of cash on deposit by ABTA.

4. Companies are allowed whatever **time** is reasonable, having regard to the particular circumstances, to prepare to carry on a new trade or to acquire a trade or trading company. HMRC state that what is reasonably practicable in the circumstances will depend on the facts in each case (e.g. delays in an acquisition caused by factors outside the control of the investing company would not jeopardise the relief).

EXAMPLE

1. D Ltd has two wholly owned subsidiaries, E Ltd and F Ltd. D Ltd holds 20% of X Ltd for 6 months, when X Ltd is then taken over by Y Ltd, and D Ltd receives a 12% holding in Y Ltd as a result. The Y Ltd shares stand in the shoes of the previous X Ltd shares (i.e. no disposal occurs,

and the Y Ltd shares are deemed to have been owned for 6 months). After a further 3 months, D Ltd transfers its Y shareholding to E Ltd at no gain/no loss. E Ltd then transfers these shares to F Ltd after 2 months, again at no gain/no loss. After a further 5 months, F Ltd sells the shares in Y Ltd.

For the purposes of SSE, F Ltd is deemed to have owned the shares from the date on which D Ltd acquired them (i.e. a total of 16 months). The disposal is therefore exempt.

2. H Ltd, a trading company, is owned 55% by A Ltd and 45% by B Ltd. The owners of B Ltd wish to dispose of the shares but still qualify for SSE.

Unless B Ltd has its own trade, it will not qualify, as it is not a holding company because its does not own more than 50% of H Ltd.

Joint venture companies

A company is a joint venture where 75% of its ordinary share capital is owned by five or fewer persons. For this purpose all shares held by the members of a 51% group (¶65505+) are treated as if held by a single person.

32115
Sch 7AC paras 23, 24 TCGA 1992

When determining whether the **investing company** can satisfy the trading requirement, and the joint venture company is **not in its group**:

a. the investment activity of holding of shares in the joint venture company is disregarded; and

b. a proportion of the activities of the joint venture company, and any 51% subsidiaries (¶65505+) it has, are attributed to the investing company (or where relevant, to all the companies in a group or subgroup), based on the shareholding of each of the owners. Where the joint venture company itself is a holding company, any intra-group activities with its subsidiaries are ignored.

Where the investing company and joint venture company are **in the same group**:
– all the group's holdings of shares in the joint venture company are disregarded as an intra-group activity; and
– all the activities of the joint venture company are taken into account, rather than only a proportion of the activities.

Other owned entities

Where a group has an interest in a company which falls outside the definition of a joint venture company, the treatment of the company for SSE purposes will be a question of fact. For example, if the **effective management of the joint enterprise** is closely integrated with that of the group, and it conducts a trade which is similar to, or complements, that of the wider group, then that would suggest that the group's involvement in the enterprise does not represent a separate non-trading activity.

32120
HMRC Brief 29/11

Similarly, where a group has an interest in an entity which **does not have issued share capital**, the trading or non-trading characteristic of the entity should be decided on first principles.

Non-trading activities

Most companies and groups tend to have certain activities which are not trading. Provided that these are not **substantial** (i.e. not more than 20% according to HMRC), the SSE will still be available.

32125
Sch 7AC paras 20 - 22 TCGA 1992; CG 53116

HMRC give the following **indicators** which should be assessed when deciding whether a non-trading activity is substantial:

Comment   HMRC state that these indicators should not be regarded as individual definitive tests to which a 20% "limit" applies. Where the indicators give contradictory results, the company should weigh up the relevance of each, in the context of the individual case, and judge the matter "in the round".

Indicator	Detail	Reference
Turnover received from non-trading activities	Compare the turnover derived from each of the company's or group's activities	CG 53316a
Value of non-trading assets compared to total assets	Where an asset is no longer used for the trade, this could lead to non-trading use, although **surplus trading premises** in the following situations do not create a non-trading activity: – letting part of the trading premises; – letting properties which are no longer required for the purpose of the trade in question, where the company's objective is to sell those properties; – subletting property where it would be impractical or uneconomic, in terms of the trade, to assign or surrender the lease; and – the acquisition of property (whether vacant or already let) where it can be shown that the intention is that it will be brought into use for trading activities The company may include the value of **intangible assets** which are off balance sheet **Share investments** may be required as a result of trading conditions e.g. shares received in lieu of payment of a trade debt, or a necessary shareholding in a trade organisation **Historic cost** could be replaced by current market value depending on the facts of the case	CG 53316b, 53317, 53319
Expenditure incurred, or time spent by officers and employees, on non-trading activities	Review expenses incurred by the company Also look at use of staff resources, both on basis of cost and time	CG 53316c
Company's history	Whilst there may be moments when certain receipts or expenses etc may point to a company having a substantial non-trading activity, this may not be the case where information is looked at on a longer time scale	CG 53316d

Confirming status of companies

32130
CG 53120

Companies can **apply** to HMRC for an opinion about whether they themselves qualify as an investing company using the other non-statutory clearance guidance procedure (¶54050+). HMRC should not be approached about the status of another company.

MEMO POINTS   1. HMRC will accept applications from any company, or its advisers, as long as they can demonstrate uncertainty, and will give an opinion both **before and after transactions**. For clearance to be given pre-transaction, the company will need to demonstrate that the transaction is being genuinely contemplated.
2. The company must provide full **details** about itself, including commercial background, and full particulars of the transaction (¶54065).
3. It will not be possible for HMRC to confirm a company's status for **future periods**, as the status of a company, group or subgroup is a question of fact and this may alter as the balance of their activities changes. In particular, vendors should obtain warranties from the buyer that the target company will maintain its trading status for the requisite period.
4. Where an opinion has been expressed on the company's trading status pre-transaction, and HMRC then **dispute the status**, this can only be resolved through enquiry into a return.

Operation of the exemption

32135

The exemption applies to disposals of:
– shares;
– interests in shares; and
– assets relating to shares,
provided that various anti-avoidance rules do not prohibit its operation.

Shares and interests in shares   Provided that the company (or group) has a substantial shareholding and meets the other requirements, any disposal of any shares will be exempt. It is not necessary for the exemption to apply to the same shares as are taken into account when assessing whether the company owns a substantial shareholding.

32140
Sch 7AC para 1
TCGA 1992;
CG 53155

Assets relating to shares   A disposal of options etc (¶32105) will be exempt where:
– immediately before the disposal of the assets relating to shares, the investing company held shares in the target company which, if sold, would qualify as an exempt disposal of a substantial shareholding; or
– a 51% group company (¶69050+) held such shares.

32145
Sch 7AC para 2
TCGA 1992

2 year look back   This applies where the conditions for the exemption are not met at the time of a disposal, but they were met at some time during the previous 2 years. This means that when the investing company is in liquidation, disposals can potentially still be exempt.

32150
Sch 7AC para 3
TCGA 1992

The 2 year look back exemption is not available if the **investing company** was not a trading company after the disposal, unless it was being, or about to be, wound up.

If the **target company** was not trading immediately after the date of disposal, the 2 year look back exemption is only available if, at some time during the 2-year period, the target company was controlled by:
– the investing company (plus any connected persons); or
– a group company of the investing company.

Anti-avoidance   This rule prevents exploitation of the exemption where arrangements are put in place whose **sole or main benefit** is to obtain an exemption on a disposal where an untaxed gain arises in Company A on a disposal of shares, (or an interest in shares or an asset related to shares), in another Company, B, and **before the gain accrued** either:
– Company A acquired control of Company B, or the same person or persons acquired control of both companies; or
– there was a significant change of trading activities affecting Company B at a time when it was controlled by Company A, or when both companies were controlled by the same person or persons.

32155
Sch 7AC para 5
TCGA 1992;
SP 5/02

> ⌐MEMO POINTS⌐   1. An **untaxed gain** represents profits which have not been taxed anywhere in the world for a period ending on or before the disposal which would result in the exempt gain. "Profits" means income or gains, including unrealised income or gains. HMRC give the following examples which do not represent untaxed gains:
> – a dividend received by a holding company which is paid out of taxed profits of a subsidiary;
> – profits derived from an exempt gain which arose from the disposal of a substantial shareholding; and
> – no tax was payable because of a specific relief (e.g. loss relief).
> 2. There is a **significant change** of trading activities if:
> – there is a major change in the nature or conduct of a trade (¶60260) carried on by Company B (or a 51% subsidiary of Company B);
> – there is a major change in the scale of the activities of a trade carried on by Company B (or a 51% subsidiary of Company B); or
> – Company B (or a 51% subsidiary of Company B) begins to carry on a trade.

Interaction with other reliefs

The substantial shareholding exemption is ignored for the purposes of determining whether an asset is a chargeable asset for the purposes of any other reliefs etc.

32160
Sch 7AC paras 4, 32
- 38 TCGA 1992;
CG 53170

In particular:
– on an **appropriation to trading stock** there is normally a deemed disposal and reacquisition of the assets concerned at market value (¶11710). An appropriation of assets that would qualify as exempt under these provisions is still an exempt disposal, and the acquisition cost of the assets concerned on an appropriation will be market value;
– a **negligible value claim** (¶31720+) cannot be backdated for claims made where the substantial shareholding exemption applies; and

– **heldover gains** (e.g. gift relief etc) do not fall within this exemption. On a disposal of exempt assets, any gains held over will be chargeable to capital gains.

> EXAMPLE   D Ltd has owned shares in E Ltd for many years and a disposal of those shares would qualify for exemption. E Ltd is taken over by F Ltd such that D Ltd receives shares in F Ltd in exchange for its shares in E Ltd.
> The following consequences occur:
> – the exemption overrules the usual "stand in the shoes" provisions;
> – a disposal is deemed to occur, but it is exempt; and
> – D Ltd acquires the shares in F Ltd at their market value.
> Note that for the purposes of any further SSE in respect of the F Ltd shares, the period of ownership before the takeover is ignored, because there was a deemed disposal of E Ltd shares.

---

3. Chargeable disposals

32190   Disposals of shares which do not fall within the substantial shareholding exemption will be chargeable disposals.

As shares are fungible assets (i.e. one share is exactly like another, and separate identification of each asset is impossible), it is necessary for special identification rules to apply in order to match disposals with acquisitions, so that a gain or loss can be calculated. This is particularly pertinent where several acquisitions and disposals have occurred.

Identification rules

32195   Except for those subject to certain tax reliefs, shares are split into three main groups, depending on whether they were **acquired**:
– on or after 1 April 1982 (the section 104 pool (¶32200+));
– on or after 6 April 1965 but before 1 April 1982 (the 1982 pool (¶32215)); and
– before 6 April 1965 (known as 1965 shares (¶32220+)), although a pooling election can be made which then includes theses shares in the 1982 pool.

s 107 TCGA 1992   On a disposal, shares are **matched** in the following **order**:
a. shares acquired on the same day as the disposal;
b. shares acquired in the 9 days prior to the date of disposal (in which case no indexation applies, even where the acquisition and disposal occur in different months);
c. shares forming part of the section 104 pool;
d. shares from the 1982 pool;
e. 1965 shares on a last in first out (LIFO) basis; and
f. shares acquired after the disposal, on a first in first out (FIFO) basis.

> MEMO POINTS   The following shares which are the **subject of tax relief** have their own identification rules:
> – EIS or VCT shares;
> – shares subject to corporate venturing scheme relief (¶80825+); and
> – shares subject to community investment tax relief (¶41350+).

Section 104 pool

32200   All shares acquired after 31 March 1982 are put in this pool and treated as a single asset.

As the section 104 pool is treated as coming into existence at 6 April 1985, all shares acquired before that date are indexed before they are added to the pool.

On the occurrence of any of the following **operative events**, indexation is added to the pool:
– addition of shares after 6 April 1985;
– disposals;
– scrip issues in lieu of dividends; and
– rights issues.

To calculate the **indexation**, the total value of the indexed pool of expenditure to date is multiplied by the following indexation formula: **32205** s 110 TCGA 1992

$$\frac{RE - RL}{RL}$$

where:
– RE is the RPI for the month in which the operative event occurs; and
– RL is the RPI for the month of the previous operative event (or, if this is the first operative event, the month in which the pool commenced).

For this purpose only there is no requirement to **round** the indexation to 3 decimal places.

When a **disposal** occurs the acquisition cost is determined by taking a proportion of the indexed pool of expenditure, based on the number of shares disposed of compared to the total number of shares in the pool. If the indexed cost exceeds the disposal proceeds, the indexation will be restricted (as indexation cannot create or augment a loss). **32210**

EXAMPLE G Ltd made the following acquisitions and disposals of ordinary shares in H Ltd, an unquoted company:

Date	Holding	Acquisition cost £
October 1984	1,500	15,000
March 1990	1,500	20,000
May 1992 (disposal)	(600)	
September 1995	2,800	44,000

On 19 June 2006, G Ltd sold 4,000 shares for £90,000. The resulting chargeable gain/allowable loss will be calculated as follows:

Section 104 pool:

	Holding	Cost £	Indexed cost £
Indexed pool at 6 April 1985[1]	1,500	15,000	15,675
Indexation to Mar 90 $\frac{121.40 - 94.78}{94.78} \times 15,675$			4,402
			20,077
Addition Mar 1990	1,500	20,000	20,000
	3,000	35,000	40,077
Indexation to May 92 $\frac{139.30 - 121.40}{121.40} \times 40,077$			5,909
			45,986
Disposal May 1992	(600)		
600/3,000 × 35,000		(7,000)	
600/3,000 × 45,986			(9,197)
	2,400	28,000	36,789
Indexation to Sep 1995 $\frac{150.60 - 139.30}{139.30} \times 36,789$			2,984
			39,773
Addition Sep 1995	2,800	44,000	44,000
	5,200	72,000	83,773
Indexation to Jun 06 $\frac{198.50 - 150.60}{150.60} \times 83,773$			26,645
			110,418
Disposal June 2006	(4,000)		
4,000/5,200 × 72,000		(55,385)	
4,000/5,200 × 110,418			(84,937)
Balance of pool c/fwd at June 2006	1,200	16,615	25,481

	£
Chargeable gain June 2006:	
Disposal proceeds	90,000
Indexed cost	(84,937)
Gain	5,063

On 22 March 2013, the company sold a further 1,000 shares for £30,000. The resulting chargeable gain/allowable loss will be calculated as follows:

Section 104 pool:

	Holding	Cost	Indexed cost
		£	£
Balance of pool b/fwd	1,200	16,615	25,481
Indexation to Mar 13			
$\frac{248.70 - 198.50}{198.50} \times 25,481$			6,444
			31,925
Disposal Mar 13	(1,000)		
1,000/1,200 × 16,615		(13,846)	
1,000/1,200 × 31,925			(26,604)
	200	2,769	5,321

	£
Chargeable gain Mar 13:	
Disposal proceeds	30,000
Indexed cost	(26,604)
Gain	3,596

Note:
1. Pool at 6 April 1985

	£
Cost	15,000
Add: Indexation Oct 84 to Apr 85:	
$\frac{94.78 - 90.67}{90.67} = 0.045 \times 15,000$	675
Value of pool at 6 April 1985	15,675

1982 pool

32215   Shares of the same class, acquired after 5 April 1965 and before 1 April 1982, are placed in the 1982 pool (also known as the frozen 1982 pool). The pool is not indexed but the number of shares at 1 April 1982, the original cost and the March 1982 value should be recorded.

On disposal, the cost and March 1982 value are apportioned between the number of shares in the pool.

EXAMPLE A Ltd made the following acquisitions of ordinary shares in B Ltd, an unquoted company:

Date	Holding	Acquisition cost
		£
October 1976	1,500	10,000
June 1978	2,800	28,000
August 1980	2,200	26,000
Total	6,500	64,000

At March 1982, the value of each share was £15, which made the value of the shareholding £97,500.
A Ltd sold 3,000 of the shares on 24 March 2013 for £150,000. The resulting chargeable gain/allowable loss is calculated as follows:

1982 pool:

	Holding	Cost	March 1982 value
		£	£
Value of pool b/fwd	6,500	64,000	97,500
Disposal	(3,000)		
3,000/6,500 × 64,000		(29,538)	
3,000/6,500 × 97,500			(45,000)
Value of pool c/fwd	3,500	34,462	52,500

Chargeable gain Mar 2013:

	Cost	March 1982 value
	£	£
Disposal proceeds	150,000	150,000
Less: Cost/March 1982 value	(29,538)	(45,000)
Less: Indexation Mar 82 to Mar 13		
$\frac{248.70 - 79.44}{79.44} = 2.131 \times 45,000$	(95,895)	(95,895)
Gain	24,567	9,105
The smaller gain will be taken	9,105	

Shares acquired before 6 April 1965

There is a different treatment depending on whether the shares are quoted or unquoted. **32220**

Quoted shares There are **two possible treatments** of quoted shares: **32225**
a. elect for all shares held at 6 April 1965 to be valued at market value, in which case the shares are included in the 1982 pool; or
b. provided no global rebasing election has been made (¶30835), carry out three calculations based on:
– actual cost;
– market value at 6 April 1965; and
– market value at 31 March 1982, when the shares are identified on a LIFO basis, and indexation is based on the higher of cost or March 1982 value.

Sch 2 para 4
TCGA 1992

Sch 2 para 2
TCGA 1992

The following table applies in respect of **b.** above:

Actual cost	6 April 1965	31 March 1982	Overall result
Gain	Gain	Gain	Smallest gain
Loss	Loss	Loss	Smallest loss
Gain	Loss	Loss	No gain/no loss
Gain	Gain	Loss	No gain/no loss
Gain	Loss	Gain	No gain/no loss
Loss	Loss	Gain	No gain/no loss
Loss	Gain	Loss	No gain/no loss
Loss	Gain	Gain	No gain/no loss

MEMO POINTS The irrevocable **election** must be submitted within 2 years of the end of the accounting period in which the first disposal of pre-April 1965 shares is made, and can be made in respect of:
– quoted shares;
– fixed interest securities; or
– preference shares.

EXAMPLE C Ltd made the following acquisitions of ordinary shares in D plc, a quoted company:

Date	Holding	Acquisition cost £
1 April 1955	5,000	25,000
1 April 1960	8,000	56,000

The market value at 6 April 1965 was £10 per share and at 31 March 1982 it was £13 per share. On 24 March 2013, A Ltd sold 10,000 shares for £420,000. All of the shares acquired on 1 April 1960 and 2,000 of the shares acquired on 1 April 1955 will be treated as disposed of. The resulting chargeable gain/allowable loss is calculated as follows:

1 April 1960 holding (8,000 shares):	Cost £	April 1965 £	March 1982 £
Disposal proceeds (8,000/10,000 × 420,000)	336,000	336,000	336,000
Less: Cost/April 1965/March 1982 value	(56,000)	(80,000)	(104,000)
Less: Indexation Mar 82 to Mar 12 $\frac{248.70 - 79.44}{79.44} = 2.131^1 \times 104,000$	(221,622)	(221,622)	(221,622)
	58,378	34,378	10,378
Gain (the smaller gain will be taken)			10,378

1 April 1955 holding (2,000 shares):	Cost £	April 1965 £	March 1982 £
Disposal proceeds (2,000/10,000 × 420,000)	84,000	84,000	84,000
Less: Cost (2,000/5,000 × 25,000)	(10,000)		
(April 1965/March 1982 value)		(20,000)	(26,000)
Less: Indexation Mar 82 to Mar 13 $\frac{248.70 - 79.44}{79.44} = 2.131^1 \times 26,000$	(55,406)	(55,406)	(55,406)
	18,594	8,594	2,594
Gain (the smaller gain will be taken)			2,594

The total gain on the disposal of the shares is therefore £12,970. (10,376 + 2,594)
Note:
1. Indexation is applied to the higher of cost or March 1982 value.

32230 **Unquoted shares** Provided no rebasing election for March 1982 value (¶30835) has been submitted, unquoted shares acquired before 6 April 1965 are treated as being disposed of on a last in first out (LIFO) basis rather than being pooled. The calculation of the chargeable gain or allowable loss for each separate acquisition is subject to time apportionment in order to ensure that only the post–1965 proportion of the gain is brought into charge.

The apportionment is calculated using the following **formula**:

$$\frac{\text{Period after 6 April 1965}}{\text{Period of ownership}} \times \text{Indexed gain}$$

An **election** may be made for the original cost of unquoted shares acquired before 6 April 1965 to be replaced with the market value at that date (¶30750+).

EXAMPLE E Ltd made the following acquisitions of ordinary shares in F Ltd, an unquoted company:

Date	Holding	Acquisition cost £
1 April 1951	6,000	54,000
1 April 1953	4,000	40,000

The market value at 31 March 1982 was £15 per share.

On 1 October 2012, E Ltd sold 7,000 shares for £329,000. All of the shares acquired on 1 April 1953 and 3,000 of the shares acquired on 1 April 1951 will be treated as disposed of. The resulting chargeable gain/allowable loss is calculated as follows:

1 April 1953 holding (4,000 shares):	Cost	March 1982
	£	£
Disposal proceeds (4,000/7,000 × 329,000)	188,000	188,000
Less: Cost/March 82 value	(40,000)	(60,000)
Less: Indexation Mar 82 to Oct 12		
$\frac{245.6 - 79.44}{79.44} = 2.092 \times 60,000$	(125,520)	(125,520)
Gain before time apportionment	22,480	2,480
Time apportionment:		
47.5 / 59.5 × 22,480	17,946	
Gain (the smaller gain will be taken)	2,480	

1 April 1951 holding (3,000 shares):	Cost	March 1982
	£	£
Disposal proceeds (3,000/7,000 × 329,000)	141,000	141,000
Less: Cost	(27,000)	(45,000)
Less: Indexation Mar 82 to Oct 12		
$\frac{245.60 - 79.44}{79.44} = 2.092 \times 45,000$	(94,140)	(94,140)
Gain before time apportionment	19,860	1,860
Time apportionment:		
47.5 / 61.5 × 19,860	15,200	
Gain (the smaller gain will be taken)	1,860	

The total gain on the disposal of the shares is therefore £4,340. (2,480 + 1,860)

Reorganisations

A company may receive new shares by way of a bonus issue, rights issue or scrip issue. In each case the shares may be issued in the same **class** as those held, or in a different class.

32235

MEMO POINTS   1. A **bonus or scrip issue** arises when a company capitalises reserves and distributes additional shares to existing shareholders in proportion to their existing shareholding, or where existing shares are split to reduce the nominal value. For companies, scrip issues are treated the same as bonus issues. Certain bonus issues are treated as distributions (¶18240+).
2. A **rights issue** is a method by which companies raise additional capital through the issue of additional shares to existing shareholders. The shares are issued in proportion to the holdings, for a consideration which is usually below their market value. Similar in nature are **warrants to subscribe**, which are a separate right allowing someone to subscribe for shares at a given price.
3. For schemes of reconstruction and mergers, see ¶79000+.

Topic	¶¶
Bonus issue of same class	¶32240
Bonus issue of different class	¶32245
Rights issue of same class	¶32250
Rights issue of different class	¶32255
Sale of rights nil paid	¶32260

Bonus issue of the same class   Where shares of the same class are issued without any **payment** from the shareholder, the bonus shares are deemed to have been acquired on the same date as the original holding.

32240
s 127 TCGA 1992

Where the original holding is in:

a. the **section 104 pool**, the effect of a bonus issue is to increase the number of shares in the pool. The acquisition is not an operative event (¶32200) for the purposes of indexing; or

b. the **1982 pool**, it is important to ensure that the March 1982 value is correctly calculated. The share value at March 1982 may be based on either:

– the actual shares in issue on 31 March 1982; or

– the shares as adjusted for the bonus issue.

The value must therefore be applied to the correct number of shares.

Where the bonus issue relates to shares **acquired before 6 April 1965**, again, the 6 April 1965 values must be correctly calculated, following the same principles as for the 1982 pool above.

EXAMPLE

1. G Ltd acquired 1,000 ordinary shares in H Ltd in June 1979 at a cost of £1,000. On 31 March 1982, their market value was £1,400. H Ltd made a 1 for 4 bonus issue of ordinary shares in June 1985.

The bonus issue means that G Ltd holds a total of 1,250 shares. $(1,000 + \frac{1,000}{4})$

The March 1982 value of £1,400 now therefore corresponds to 1,250 shares, which makes the value per share £1.12.

2. A Ltd made the following acquisitions of ordinary shares in B Ltd, an unquoted company.

Date	Holding	Acquisition cost £
January 1982	2,000	10,000
June 1995	3,000	25,000
October 1998	7,000	70,000

In September 1999, B Ltd made a 1 for 2 bonus issue of ordinary shares. The March 1982 value of the shares was £6 per share (£4 as adjusted for the bonus issue). In October 2012, A Ltd sold 16,000 shares for £200,000.

The disposal is matched to the acquisitions as follows:

	1982 pool		Section 104 pool	
	Holding	£	Holding	£
Original	2,000	10,000	10,000	95,000
Bonus 1: 2	1,000	-	5,000	-
	3,000	10,000	15,000	95,000
Disposal	(1,000)	(3,333)	(15,000)	(95,000)
	2,000	6,667	Nil	Nil

Section 104 pool (15,000 shares):

	Holding	Cost £	Indexed cost £
Jun 1995 purchase	3,000	25,000	25,000
Indexation to Oct 98			
$\frac{164.50 - 149.80}{149.80} \times 25,000$			2,453
			27,453
Oct 1998 purchase	7,000	70,000	70,000
	10,000	95,000	97,453
Sept 1999 bonus issue[1]	5,000		
	15,000		
Indexation to Oct 12			
$\frac{245.60 - 164.50}{164.50} \times 97,453$			48,045
			145,498
Disposal Oct 12	(15,000)	(95,000)	(145,498)
	Nil	Nil	Nil

Chargeable gain October 2012

Proceeds ($\frac{15,000}{16,000} \times 200,000$)	187,500
Indexed cost	(145,498)
Gain	42,002

1982 pool (1,000 shares):

	Cost £	March 1982 £
Disposal proceeds ($\frac{1,000}{16,000} \times 200,000$)	12,500	12,500
Less: Cost ($\frac{1,000}{3,000} \times 10,000$)	(3,333)	
March 1982 value (1,000 × 4)		(4,000)
Less: Indexation Mar 82 to Oct 12		
$\frac{245.60 - 79.44}{79.44} = 2.092 \times 4,000$	(8,368)	(8,368)
	799	132

Gain (smaller gain taken)	132

The total gain on the disposal will therefore be £42,134. (42,002 + 132)

Note:
1. As a bonus issue is not an operative event no indexation allowance is added at this point.

Bonus issue of a different class Where the shares received under a bonus issue are of a different class to the original holding, the original acquisition cost must be apportioned between the two classes. Once the apportionment is made, the bonus shares are deemed to have been acquired on the same date as the original holding.

32245
ss 128 - 130
TCGA 1992

The **method of apportionment** will depend on whether the new shares are quoted or unquoted as follows:

Type of shares	Method of apportionment
Quoted (i.e. quoted on a recognised stock exchange (¶95320) within 3 months of the issue)	Original acquisition cost is apportioned on the basis of the market values of the different classes of shares on the date when the revised quotations, reflecting the bonus issue, are published
Unquoted	The original and bonus shares are treated as comprising one single holding, despite being different classes of share On each subsequent disposal of shares (of whichever class), the cost will be apportioned based on the market values at the date of disposal, using the following formula: $\dfrac{\text{No of shares sold}}{\text{No of shares of that class held}} \times \dfrac{\text{MV of class holding}}{\text{MV of all class holdings}} \times \text{Cost b/fwd}^{1}$

Note:
1. Or indexed cost as appropriate.

EXAMPLE

1. C Ltd purchased 20,000 ordinary shares in D plc for £20,000 in Year 1. In Year 5, there was a 1 for 5 bonus issue of convertible preference shares of £1 nominal value per share. On the first day after the issue, the ordinary shares had a market value of 150p and the preference shares had a value of 120p, giving a value to C Ltd of £30,000 for the ordinary shares and £4,800 for the preference shares.

The acquisition cost of the shares is apportioned between the shareholdings as follows:

		Cost £
Ordinary shares	$\dfrac{30,000}{30,000 + 4,800} \times 20,000$	17,241
Preference shares	Balance	2,759
		20,000

2. In Year 1, E Ltd acquired 1,200 ordinary shares in F Ltd at a cost of £10,000.

In Year 2, F Ltd made a bonus issue of one £1 preference share for every four £1 ordinary shares held, and E Ltd received 300 £1 preference shares.

In Year 7, E Ltd sells 300 ordinary £1 shares at a time when the market value of the ordinary shares is £3 per share, and the preference shares is £2.60 per share.

The total value of the holding of:
– ordinary shares is £3,600 (3 × 1,200); and
– preference shares is £780. (2.60 × 300)

The total value overall is therefore £4,380.

The apportioned cost of the ordinary shares will be calculated as:

$$\frac{300}{1,200} \times \frac{3,600}{4,380} \times 10,000 = £2,055$$

32250　**Rights issue of shares of the same class**　Where the shareholder **does not take up** any new shares, the rights issue is disregarded for capital gains purposes. Consequently, where the market value at 6 April 1965 or 31 March 1982 is quoted at an adjusted figure which assumes that shareholders have taken up all rights issues, that quotation does not apply to the shareholder. Note the rights may still be sold on the shareholder's behalf, which will result in cash received.

Where a rights issue of the same class of shares as the original holding **is taken up**, the shares are deemed to have been acquired on the same date as the original holding for **matching** purposes. For **indexation** purposes the actual date of acquisition is used.

Where the original holding is in:
– the **section 104 pool**, a rights issue is an operative event (¶32200), and will increase the cost as well as the number of shares in the pool. Indexation allowance must be added to the pool, before adding the cost of the rights issue;
– the **1982 pool**, the cost of the rights issue shares is included in the pool value. On a subsequent disposal from the 1982 pool, the shares must be separated into two parts for the purposes of calculating indexation allowance. Indexation allowance on the rights issue shares will only be available from the date of the issue. Indexation allowance on the original shares in the pool will run from March 1982.

The share value at March 1982 may be based on either:
– the actual shares in issue on 31 March 1982; or
– the shares as adjusted for the rights issue.

s 122 TCGA 1992　　MEMO POINTS　**Fractional entitlements** may arise from a rights issue e.g. if a shareholder holds 13 shares, and there is a 1 for 3 rights issue, the shareholder would be entitled to 4.25 shares. Most of the time, these fractional entitlements are sold to other shareholders, so that a capital receipt is received, which is likely to be small, and hence will be deducted from the allowable cost of the entire holding.

EXAMPLE　G Ltd acquired 5,000 shares in H Ltd in July 1980. The market value of the shares on 31 March 1982 was £1.50 each. In July 2013, H Ltd made a 1 for 5 rights issue of shares of the same class. G Ltd took up the rights issue, paying £1.00 per share.

	Number of shares		£
At 31 March 1982	5,000	@ £1·50	7,500
Rights issue	1,000	@ £1·00	1,000
	6,000		8,500

The market value on 31 March 1982 (as adjusted) is therefore £1.42 per share. (8,500/6,000)

2. A Ltd acquired 1,000 ordinary shares in B Ltd in June 1979 at a cost of £1,000. On 31 March 1982, their market value was £1,400. B Ltd made a 1 for 4 rights issue of ordinary shares in June 2013, and the subscription price was £1.20 per share.

The rights issue means that A Ltd holds a total of 1,250 shares. $(1,000 + \frac{1,000}{4})$

The price that A Ltd pays to acquire the shares under the rights issue is £300. (250 × 1.20)
The March 1982 value is therefore £1,700. (1,400 + 300)
Apportioning this over the 1,250 shares gives a March 1982 value per share of £1.36.

Rights issue of shares of a different class Where the new shares received in a rights issue are of a different class to the original shares, the calculation rules are the same as for bonus issues of a different class (¶32245). The acquisition cost of the rights issue shares must be added to the original cost before apportioning the total between the classes.

32255
s 130 TCGA 1992

Sale of rights nil paid This arises where the shareholder sells the rights before the new securities are actually allotted. The proceeds for this disposal are a capital distribution, and will be treated as a part disposal (¶31130+) of the holding, unless the consideration is small.

32260
s 129 TCGA 1992

The amount of the acquisition cost attributable to the **part disposed** of is calculated using the following formula:

$$\frac{\text{Amount of capital distribution}}{\text{Amount of capital distribution} + \text{Market value of remaining holding}} \times \text{Acquisition cost}$$

However, where the **consideration is small** (i.e. 5% or less of the value of the shareholding, or up to £3,000 in value), and is:
− **more than the allowable expenditure** on the shares, the company can elect to offset the total acquisition cost of the shares against the cash received. The acquisition cost of the remaining shares will therefore be nil; or
− **equal to or less than the allowable expenditure**, the company can elect for the cash received to be simply deducted from the original cost (or March 1982 value, where appropriate). Indexation allowance will need to be adjusted for shares in the 1982 pool.

EXAMPLE C Ltd acquired 1,000 shares in D Ltd for £1,000. Some years later, when C Ltd's shareholding was worth £30,000, there is a 1:5 rights issue, but C Ltd sells the rights nil paid for £500.
As the consideration for the sale is less than 5% of the market value of the existing shareholding, C Ltd can elect to deduct £500 from the original cost, which will only come into effect once there is a subsequent disposal.
If the consideration for the sale had been £1,100 (i.e. still small but more than the original cost), an election can be made to deduct £1,000, and only the balance of £100 is chargeable.

Earn-outs

When a company is sold, **part of the consideration** is often deferred so that it can be based on the future results of the company (i.e. on events which will occur after the disposal date), and will usually be in the form of paper in the acquiring company i.e. shares or loan stock. This includes cases where consideration is potentially payable, but due to the poor performance of the company, no consideration is actually paid.

32265
s 138A TCGA 1992

At the point of disposal, the vendor's right to receive future consideration is **unascertainable**, and is known as an earn-out, which is treated as a separate asset for capital gains purposes. However, its value must be included in the sale proceeds, along with any cash received for the disposal of the original shares.

MEMO POINTS 1. Any element of deferred but **ascertainable** consideration must be excluded, and treated in accordance with the normal rules (¶30370).
2. Where the vendor has the **choice to take the consideration in cash** rather than paper, all of the consideration is chargeable as normal at the date of disposal.
3. Where the earn-out element is payable partly in shares and **partly in cash**, the elements must be treated separately.

s 138 TCGA 1992

4. Technically, the earn-out itself is treated as a security, so that the paper for paper rules (¶32270) can apply.

5. Where the purchasing company in an earn-out is itself **taken over** during the earn-out period, the initial earn-out may be replaced by a new one. In this case, the same rules can apply, as one security is being swapped for another.

6. There is a **clearance** procedure available (¶79365) so that all parties involved can obtain certainty as to how the transaction should be taxed.

CG 58026

> EXAMPLE
> **1.** E Ltd sells the shares of X Ltd to F plc for £1,000,000 payable in cash, and £100,000 to be paid in F Ltd's shares in 1 year's time.
> Although the number of shares to be received will depend on their future value, the value of the consideration can be determined at the point of disposal, so that there is no unascertainable consideration.
>
> **2.** If E Ltd instead agrees to receive 100,000 shares in F plc in 1 year's time, this is again not unascertainable consideration.

32270

s 135 TCGA 1992

Shares   Where the future consideration is unascertainable and in the form of shares in the acquiring company, the disposal will be treated as a paper for paper exchange and no gain will crystallise i.e. the new shares are deemed to "stand in the shoes" of the old shares, with the same acquisition cost and date of acquisition.

An irrevocable **election** can be made to disapply this rule (thereby crystallising a gain). This election must be made within 2 years of the end of the accounting period in which the earn-out right is conferred.

> EXAMPLE   In Year 2, G Ltd acquires all the shares in X Ltd for £100,000. In Year 10, G Ltd sells the shares in X Ltd to H Ltd for the following consideration:
> – cash of £800,000;
> – 40,000 shares in H Ltd at current market value of £1.50 each (total £60,000); and
> – a right to a single payment of deferred consideration, which is dependent on the future profits of X Ltd, and payable in shares of H Ltd, deemed to be valued at £120,000 at the date of the sale. In Year 11, 50,000 shares in H Ltd are issued to G Ltd, when a share is worth £2.50.
> The indexation factor from:
> – Year 2 to Year 10 is 20%; and
> – Year 10 to Year 11 is 2%.
>
> **Year 10**
>
> | | | £ |
> |---|---|---:|
> | Cash received | | 800,000 |
> | Less: Apportioned cost | $100,000 \times \dfrac{800,000}{800,000 + 60,000 + 120,000}$ | (81,633) |
> | Unindexed gain | | 718,367 |
> | Less: Indexation | $81,633 \times 0.200$ | (16,327) |
> | Chargeable gain | | 702,040 |
>
> The shares and earn-out do not crystallise a gain in Year 10.
>
> **Year 11**
> Earn-out received
>
> | | | Cost | Indexed cost |
> |---|---|---:|---:|
> | | | £ | £ |
> | Received in Year 10 | $100,000 \times \dfrac{120,000}{800,000 + 60,000 + 120,000}$ | 12,245 | 12,245 |
> | Indexation to Year 10 | $12,245 \times 0.200$ | | 2,449 |
> | | | | 14,694 |
> | Indexation to Year 11 | $14,694 \times 0.020$ | | 294 |
> | Carried forward to share pool | | 12,245 | 14,988 |

Share pool - shares in H Ltd

		Holding	Cost	Indexed cost
			£	£
Received in Year 10	$100,000 \times \dfrac{60,000}{800,000 + 60,000 + 120,000}$	40,000	6,122	6,122
Indexation to Year 10	$6,122 \times 0.200$			1,224
				7,346
Indexation to Year 11	$7,346 \times 0.020$			147
			6,122	7,493
Shares issued in Year 11		50,000	12,245	14,988
Allowable cost c/fwd		90,000	18,367	22,481

A chargeable gain will arise when the shares in H Ltd are disposed of.

Non-QCBs   Loan stock to be received as future consideration is treated the same as shares (¶32270).

32275

QCBs   Where the consideration is in the form of QCBs (¶32055), a gain crystallises, but is then held over until they are disposed of. The proceeds for this gain are equal to the market value of the QCBs on their acquisition.

32280

s 116 TCGA 1992

EXAMPLE   In Year 2, A Ltd acquires all the shares in Y Ltd for £100,000. In Year 10, A Ltd sells the shares in Y Ltd to B Ltd for the following consideration:
– cash of £800,000;
– 40,000 shares in B Ltd at current market value of £1.50 each (total £60,000); and
– a right to a single payment of deferred consideration which is dependent on the future profits of Y Ltd, and payable in QCBs of B Ltd, deemed to be valued at £120,000 at the date of the sale.
In Year 11, QCBs are issued to A Ltd, valued at £125,000.
The indexation factor from:
– Year 2 to Year 10 is 20%; and
– Year 10 to Year 11 is 2%.

Year 10

		£
Cash received		800,000
Less: Apportioned cost	$100,000 \times \dfrac{800,000}{800,000 + 60,000 + 120,000}$	(81,633)
Unindexed gain		718,367
Less: Indexation	$81,633 \times 0.200$	(16,327)
Chargeable gain		702,040

The shares and earn-out do not crystallise a gain in Year 10.

Year 11
Earn-out received

		Cost	Indexed cost
		£	£
Received in Year 10	$100,000 \times \dfrac{120,000}{800,000 + 60,000 + 120,000}$	12,245	12,245
Indexation to Year 10	$12,245 \times 0.200$		2,449
			14,694
Indexation to Year 11	$14,694 \times 0.020$		294
		12,245	14,988

Heldover gain

	£
Proceeds	125,000
Less: Indexed cost	(14,988)
Gain - will not crystallise until QCBs are disposed of	110,012

Share pool - shares in B Ltd		Holding	Cost	Indexed cost
			£	£
Received in Year 10	$100,000 \times \dfrac{60,000}{800,000 + 60,000 + 120,000}$	40,000	6,122	6,122
Indexation to Year 10	$6,122 \times 0.200$			1,224
				7,346
Indexation to Year 11	$7,346 \times 0.020$			147
Allowable cost c/fwd			6,122	7,493

A chargeable gain will arise when the shares in B Ltd are disposed of.

Conversions

32285
ss 132, 133
TCGA 1992

Where a holding of securities is converted into shares, the new holding is deemed to have been acquired at the same time as the original holding for the same acquisition cost i.e. the shares stand in the shoes of the securities.

> MEMO POINTS 1. The conversion of securities **includes**:
> – a conversion of securities into shares of the same company;
> – a conversion of a non-QCB into a QCB;
> – a conversion of a QCB into a non-QCB; and
> – where the company holder of the securities chooses, conversion instead of redemption.
> 2. If the holder receives a **premium on the conversion** of the holding, the premium may give rise to a gain, which is subject to the same rules as for rights nil paid (¶32260).

> EXAMPLE C Ltd acquired £6,000 8% convertible loan stock in D plc in March 1999 for a cost of £5,500. In March 2008, C Ltd chose to convert the loan stock into shares. C Ltd received 1 share for each £1 of loan stock, and therefore received 6,000 shares. In March 2013, C Ltd sells the shareholding for £20,000.
>
> | | £ |
> |---|---|
> | Proceeds | 20,000 |
> | Less: Cost | (5,500) |
> | Gain before indexation | 14,500 |

SECTION 5

Anti-avoidance

32335

As chargeable gains rely on a disposal actually occurring, there are various ways in which a charge to tax could be avoided by transferring value out of assets without crystallising a disposal. There are therefore special rules to combat this type of avoidance.

Summary

32340

Rule	¶¶
Depreciatory transactions	¶67625+
Dividend stripping	¶32370+
Value shifting	¶32410+
Manipulation of capital losses	¶37120+

A. Dividend stripping

Dividend stripping means reducing the value of shares in a company by payment of a dividend prior to disposal. The rules here are very similar to the depreciatory transaction rules (¶67625+), even though there is no requirement for a group of companies to be involved.

32370
s 177(1) TCGA 1992

> MEMO POINTS Broadly, a **depreciatory transaction** can be defined as a transfer of assets between group members which materially reduces the value of shares or securities in a company, and there is subsequently a sale of those shares or securities.

Scope

These provisions apply where:
- company A holds shares in another company, B;
- the **holding amounts** to at least 10% of all of the shares in that class;
- company A is not a share-dealing company; and
- a distribution is made to company A which materially reduces the value of the holding.

32375
s 177(6), (7)
TCGA 1992;
CG 46540

However, dividends paid out of **post-acquisition profits** are not subject to the dividend stripping provisions, as these profits are not reflected in the acquisition price of the share. Where a company has both pre and post-acquisition reserves, any distribution is matched with post-acquisition profits as far as possible. Note that it is profits accrued which are important here, not profits realised. If the cost of the acquisition reflects an accrued capital profit which is then stripped out by a dividend when the profit is realised, the dividend stripping rules will still apply.

> MEMO POINTS 1. For the purposes of these rules, all **holdings** owned in a particular company are treated as one holding, unless they are of shares in a different class, or which carry different entitlements or obligations.
> 2. In deciding whether a company owns **10%** or **more of a class of shares**, shares held by connected persons (¶31375) must be taken into account.
> 3. There is no statutory definition of **material reduction** although HMRC take the view that any reduction is material unless it is negligible.

> EXAMPLE In Year 1, A Ltd buys 100% of B Ltd for £7 million. B Ltd's assets include a property with a book value of £500,000 which is actually worth £2.5 million (an accrued capital profit of £2 million). In Year 5, B Ltd sells the property for £3.5 million and realises a commercial profit of £3 million, which is then paid out as a dividend to A Ltd. A Ltd sells B Ltd for £4 million and claims a capital loss.
> B Ltd paid the dividend out of a profit realised after A Ltd bought it, but £2 million related to a profit which had accrued at the time of the acquisition. So only £1 million of the dividend is treated as relating to post-acquisition profits. (3 million - 2 million)

Consequences

The distribution is treated as a depreciatory transaction in relation to a **subsequent disposal of those shares** and, for these purposes, the companies are deemed to be members of the same CG group (¶65415+).

32380

The **allowable loss** is reduced to such extent as is just and reasonable i.e. the value of the shares on their sale should be increased to ignore the effect of the depreciatory transaction. Note that although a loss can be reduced to nil, the rules cannot create a gain.

> EXAMPLE C Ltd acquires 12% of the ordinary share capital of D Ltd, and the following week D Ltd pays a distribution equal to the full amount of its distributable reserves. Shortly thereafter, C Ltd sells the shares for significantly less than the acquisition cost.
> This will be caught by the dividend stripping provisions and therefore treated as a depreciatory transaction. The capital loss will be restricted by the amount of the dividend.

B. Value shifting

32410   Value shifting means taking value out of an asset prior to sale, so that a tax-free benefit can be enjoyed i.e. as a consequence of the arrangements, a capital gain is reduced or a capital loss is increased. Tax avoidance must be one of the main purposes of the scheme or arrangements.

For disposals occurring on or after 19 July 2011, the previous complex rules have been replaced by a simpler anti-avoidance rule which applies to disposals of shares or securities. For details relating to groups of companies see ¶67695+.

---

1. Rules applying until 18 July 2011

Exclusions

32440
s 32 TCGA 1992

These provisions do not apply to:
a. ordinary payments for group relief;
b. transfers between members of the same 75% CG group of companies, (unless the asset is transferred for consideration lower than both the cost and the market value of the asset); and:
c. bona fide commercial transactions which are not undertaken with the aim of avoiding tax.

Scope

32445   The provisions apply in the following distinct **situations**:
a. there is a movement of value out of an asset, without an actual disposal needing to occur; or
b. as part of an arrangement, value passes out of an asset, and as a consequence, a tax-free benefit arises. In this case, a subsequent disposal of the asset must occur.

For the detailed rules applying to **groups** see ¶67715+.

Movement of value

32450
s 29 TCGA 1992

Where value shifts out of an asset, without an actual disposal, a deemed disposal is nevertheless treated as occurring at market value (irrespective of the value of any actual consideration received for the arrangement), although the usual reliefs (such as rollover relief) are still available.

This rule can apply in the following **situations**:
a. a person exercises control over a company such that value passes out of one shareholding into another i.e. a shareholding is diluted;
b. the owner of land (or any other property) sells it and becomes the lessee, and there are subsequently arrangements which are favourable to the lessor; or
c. rights or restrictions over any asset are reduced or removed by the person entitled to enforce them.
The adjustment applies equally to the person benefiting from the value shift.

> EXAMPLE   E Ltd owns F Ltd's entire issued share capital of 10,000 £1 shares which were acquired by subscription at par. Several years later, G Ltd (which is connected with E Ltd but not part of the same 75% CG group) acquired 12,000 £1 shares in F Ltd by subscription at par, when the company was worth £525,000. The market value of the new shares was £310,200.
> E Ltd's interest has reduced to 45%, which has a value of £214,800, and E Ltd is deemed to make a disposal as follows:

	£
Deemed proceeds on disposal	310,200
Less: Allowable cost	
$\dfrac{310,200}{310,200 + 214,800} \times 10,000$	(5,909)
Chargeable gain (before indexation)	304,291

The allowable cost of G Ltd's shares will be adjusted to reflect the market value at acquisition i.e. £310,200.

Tax-free benefit

The value shifting provisions will also apply where, as part of a scheme or arrangement, the value of an asset is materially reduced (¶32375) and a tax-free benefit arises.

32455
s 30 TCGA 1992

This most often occurs in the context of groups (¶67715+).

MEMO POINTS 1. Where the transaction is motivated by tax avoidance, the **person receiving the tax-free benefit** does not have to be the person making the disposal, or a person connected with him: any person receiving a tax-free benefit will cause the rules to apply.
2. A **benefit** includes money and money's worth, the increase in value of an asset, and being relieved of a liability.
3. The benefit is **tax-free** unless it is required to be brought into account for the purposes of computing income, profits or gains for the purposes of income tax, capital gains tax or corporation tax.

2. Rules applying from 19 July 2011

Scope

The following new targeted anti-avoidance rule **applies to** disposals of **shares or securities** on or after 19 July 2011 when:
– arrangements have been made whereby the value of those shares or securities, or any relevant asset, is materially reduced;
– the main purpose (or one of the main purposes) of the arrangements is to obtain a tax advantage; and
– the arrangements do not consist solely of the making of an exempt distribution i.e. the value shifting rules will not apply where a normal dividend is paid out before the sale.

32485
s 31 TCGA 1992

MEMO POINTS 1. **Arrangements** include any agreement, understanding, scheme, transaction or series of transactions (whether or not legally enforceable).
2. An asset is a **relevant asset** if, at the time of the disposal, it is owned by a company which is a member of the same group as the disposing company. It is irrelevant whether the tax advantage is obtained for the disposing company or any other person.
3. **Exempt distribution** means a distribution which is within the rules for:
– small companies (i.e. with less than 50 employees and where either the turnover or gross balance sheet total do not exceed €10 million) (¶18385); or
– other companies, in which case the distribution must fall within a particular class of exemption (¶18390).
4. For **HMRC guidance** on these new rules see ¶67775.

Consequences

Any allowable loss or chargeable gain accruing on the disposal is to be calculated as if the consideration for the disposal were increased by such amount as is just and reasonable i.e. ignoring the effect of the arrangements. This also applies where the disposal pre-dates the acquisition.

32490

The **adjustment** can reduce the amount of a loss, increase a gain, or even turn a loss into a gain.

PART 5

Losses

Losses
Summary

The numbers cross-refer to paragraphs.

Types and interaction

SECTION 1

Types of losses

Any transaction that could create a profit could also potentially create a loss. The legislation allows a company to make use of losses arising by setting off the losses against certain profits. Depending on the source of the loss, the way in which the loss can be used will be different.

35000

Possible sources

The following table illustrates the likely losses that may arise and the relevant paragraphs of *Corporation Tax Memo* that detail the provisions. Also highlighted is whether a particular loss could be the subject of a group relief claim (¶66050+).

35005

Source of loss	¶¶	Available for group relief?
Trading losses (UK and overseas)	¶36000+	✓[1]
UK property business	¶36235+	✓
Overseas property business	¶36275	
Non-trading loan relationship deficit	¶16360+	✓
Disposal of capital asset	¶37000+	
Disposal of certain shares by investment company	¶37230+	
Surplus capital allowances re special leasing	¶82565	✓
Derivatives	¶16970	
Non-trading losses on intangible fixed assets	¶28655	✓
Foreign exchange transaction	¶17245+	
Excess management expenses	¶17770	✓
Losses on miscellaneous transactions	¶21085	
Note: 1. Only **UK trading losses** can be surrendered.		

Order of set-off

35055   As the rules differ for each loss and how they can be utilised, there is an order of set-off that must be adhered to. The interaction of these rules may mean that the company has to consider a number of options before making various claims.

	£	£	£
Trading profits		x	
Less: Trade losses brought forward		(x)	
			x
Loan relationship non-trade credits (net after deducting current period non-trade debits)[1]	x		
Less: Loan relationship deficits of subsequent period brought back	(x)		
		x	
Overseas property business	x		
Less: Overseas property business losses b/fwd	(x)		
		x	
Profits from miscellaneous transactions	x		
Less: Losses arising from miscellaneous transactions b/fwd	(x)		
		x	
UK property business profits		x	
Chargeable gains	x		
Less: Capital losses b/fwd	(x)		
		x	
Non-trading income		x	
Less: Loan relationship deficits b/fwd[2]		(x)	
			x
			x
Less:			
Non-trading loan relationship deficits of current period			(x)
UK property business loss			(x)
Trading losses of current period			(x)
Trading losses of subsequent periods			(x)
Surplus capital allowances re special leasing			(x)
Qualifying charitable donations			(x)
Group relief			(x)
Profit chargeable to corporation tax			x

Note:
1. Net of deficits brought forward for which no specific claim has been made (¶16365+).
2. Deficits set against non-trading income of the subsequent period.

Choosing loss claims

35060   The prescribed order of claims means that, even in the simplest of cases, a company may have a choice to make as to the best way to utilise its losses.

EXAMPLE A Ltd has the following results over a 3 year period:			
	Year 1	Year 2	Year 3
	£	£	£
Trading profit/(loss)	(10,000)	6,000	8,000
Qualifying charitable donations	2,000	2,000	2,000
Chargeable gain	8,000		

For **Year 1** a choice can be made either to offset the trading loss against the gain, so wasting relief for the charitable donation, or to carry forward the losses to be set against future trading profits. A Ltd decides not to waste the donation and its profits chargeable will be £6,000. As it has not claimed the loss against the current year's profits, it cannot claim to carry the loss back to an earlier year.

In the following years, there are no choices available, and the profits chargeable to tax will be:

Year 2	**£**
Trading profit	6,000
Less: Trading losses brought forward	(6,000)
Profits chargeable	Nil
Losses to carry forward	4,000
Year 3	
Trading profit	8,000
Less: Trading losses brought forward	(4,000)
Trading profits left in charge	4,000
Less: Qualifying charitable donations	(2,000)
Profits chargeable	2,000

In **Year 2** the offset of losses is mandatory, and as such, no relief will be given for the qualifying donation.

SECTION 3

Claiming relief

Time limits

In order to be able to **carry back the loss** or **use it in the loss-making period** against other profits, the company must make a claim no later than 2 years after the end of the loss-making period.

35110
s 37(7) CTA 2010;
SP 5/01

Carrying forward losses happens automatically, and no claim is required.

> EXAMPLE B Ltd makes a trading loss in the year ended 30 September 2013. It has until 30 September 2015 to make an claim either to carry the loss back or use it against other profits of the year. If no claim is made, the loss will be carried forward for use against future profits of the same trade.

HMRC have power to accept **late claims**, although this will generally only apply if the claim could not have been made on time due to factors outside the company's control. This **interpretation** is applied strictly, and the conditions will usually only be satisfied when a number of factors combine. HMRC offer as an example the situation in which all of the following occur:

CTM04590

– an officer of the company was absent for good reason such as illness;
– the absence arose at a time preventing the claim being made at the appropriate time;
– a good reason exists as to why the claim was not made before the absence; and
– no other person could make the claim on behalf of the company within the usual time limit.

The claim should be made on the tax return. If claiming the loss against current year profits or gains, it will also be shown on the corporation tax computation (¶46220).

Proving the loss

Whilst it will usually be the case that accounts have been prepared and a corporation tax computation drawn up, there may be occasions when neither of these tasks has been completed. This typically happens when a company fails.

35115
CTM04570

HMRC guidance states that the lack of such documents does not make it impossible to claim relief. Where it is clear that the **trading losses significantly outweigh the claim** for relief, the relief will not be denied. In looking at this, regard is to be had to the Statement of Affairs prepared by the company's liquidators, management accounts or any other documentation that would assist in quantifying the position.

However, if the whole of the loss shown in unaudited or management accounts is claimed, HMRC may resist the claim.

SECTION 1

Trading losses

A. Calculation of the loss

A trading loss is calculated under the same rules as trading profits generally. However, only **losses made in a UK trade** are eligible for the reliefs detailed below, as there are no similar provisions for losses on foreign trades. Likewise, if the company was **not within the charge to corporation tax** when the loss arose, it will not be eligible for relief in later periods once the company comes within the charge. **36000**

Capital allowances are given as a deduction from trading income, so the allowances claimed become part of the loss available.

> MEMO POINTS 1. Where a company makes payments that are eligible for **charitable donations relief** (¶22055+), those are accounted for separately and do not form part of the trading loss.
> 2. Losses from **trades carried on overseas** can only be carried forward and used against future profits of the same trade.

1. Restrictions on losses available for relief

Relief for trading losses is **potentially restricted** in the circumstances shown in the following table: **36005**

Circumstances	¶¶
The trade is not carried on in a commercial way with a view to realising "gain"	¶36010
A Government investment in the company is written off	¶36015
The loss arises from a trade carried on by a limited partnership	¶36020
There is a change in ownership of the company	¶60245

Trading commercially

36010
s 44 CTA 2010;
CTM04600

Losses that arise from a trade that is not carried in a commercial way with a view to realising "gain" cannot be relieved against other profits. In this case "gain" is simply defined to mean an **accounting profit**, and so includes deductions such as depreciation (as opposed to capital allowances).

For relief to be restricted, it is not sufficient for HMRC to show that a number of years have shown accounting losses. If the trade is carried on in such a manner as to give a **reasonable expectation** of making a profit, this will be sufficient to allow relief. However, the **onus of proof** is on the company to show that the trade was carried on in such a manner. If the way in which a trade is carried on **changes during the period** from a non-commercial basis to a fully commercial one, it is the situation at the end of the period that is important. Provided the trade is run on a commercial basis at that time, there will be no restriction on the loss for the entire period.

HMRC say that this provision is not intended to catch anything other than extreme situations, in which expenditure greatly exceeds any possible income that the trade could generate over any period.

MEMO POINTS 1. For companies operating in **farming or market gardening** there is a further restriction (¶84455).
2. These provisions do not affect trades that are carried on in the exercise of functions conferred under statute (including an Act of the Scottish Parliament).

Reduction for Government investment write-offs

36015
s 92 CTA 2010

If a Government investment in a company (either by way of **shares or loan**) is written off, any losses available to the company are reduced by an amount equal to the amount written off. The **reduction** of the losses is made at the end of the last accounting period prior to the write-off.

If the amount written off is greater than the losses currently available, the excess must be carried forward and deducted from future trading losses until the whole of the write-off has been accounted for.

> EXAMPLE The Government makes a loan of £500,000 to A Ltd to allow it to pursue a project. The loan was advanced in March 2009, which fell in A Ltd's year ending 31 December 2009. In the year ended 31 December 2013, A Ltd incurred losses of £100,000. The loan is written off in March 2014.
> The write-off is deducted from the loss arising in the year ended 31 December 2013, thus eliminating it completely. The balance of £400,000 is carried forward and will be deducted from any future losses made by A Ltd.

Company as a limited partner

36020
s 56 CTA 2010

A company may join a partnership as a limited partner. This means that:
– the company is not entitled to take part in the **management** of the partnership; and
– its **exposure to risk is capped** at the amount it has contributed to the partnership (so if the partnership's losses extend beyond that, someone else is liable for the excess).

In this case, there is a **restriction** on the relief that can be claimed by the company for losses arising from the partnership trade either:

- against other profits or gains in the loss-making period or earlier periods; or
- by way of group relief (¶66000+).

The restriction covers all losses arising from that trade on a **cumulative basis**, so the total loss relieved cannot exceed the amount of the cap.

The **cap** is the amount of capital the company has contributed to the partnership, measured at the end of the loss-making period (or, if earlier, at the date it leaves the partnership).

Capital contributed is defined as that which the company has provided to the partnership and:
- has not withdrawn;
- is not entitled to withdraw whilst it is a limited partner; and
- is not entitled to have someone else repay to it.

This includes any profit share to which the company is entitled, and which it has not withdrawn. If this has already been added to the company's capital account, it will not be counted twice.

> EXAMPLE B Ltd is a limited partner in a partnership carrying on a trade. It made an initial contribution to the partnership of £20,000. In Year 1, B Ltd's share of the loss arising was £15,000. It used this against other profits of the same year and the previous year. In Year 2, its share of the loss was £8,000. However, it will only be able to utilise £5,000 of the loss against other profits, bringing its total losses used in that way to £20,000.
> The remaining loss of £3,000 can be carried forward against future profits only. Any loss arising after that will only be available for carry forward, unless a further contribution is made to the partnership.

B. Use of losses arising

There are several ways in which a company can use a trading loss arising in an accounting period, as shown in the following table:

36050

Method of relief	Conditions	¶¶
Set against other profits and gains of the same period	The trade must be carried on wholly within the UK	¶36080
Carried back and set against profits and gains arising in the previous 12 months		¶36100+
Carried forward and set against future profits of the same trade	Includes overseas trades	¶36150+
Surrendered to other companies in the same group or consortium	The trade must be carried on wholly within the UK	¶66000+
Carried back and set against profits and gains arising in the previous 36 months	Only applies to a loss incurred in the 12 months ending with the cessation of the trade	¶61080

1. Using in the current period

The company can make a claim to set the loss against other **profits and gains** arising in the same accounting period.

36080
s 37(3)(a) CTA 2010

This is an all-or-nothing election, as the company cannot choose against which sources or to what extent the losses will be relieved. If, for example, there are foreign profits with a foreign tax credit available (¶90480), the company cannot single out this source and exclude it from the loss claim.

EXAMPLE 1. C Ltd suffers a trading loss of £30,000 in an accounting period. In the same period, it also has property business profits of £30,000 and a non-trading loan relationship profit of £10,000. C Ltd makes a claim to offset the losses arising.

	£
UK property business profits	30,000
Profits from non-trading loan relationships	10,000
	40,000
Current year loss claim	(30,000)
Profits chargeable to corporation tax	10,000

2. D Ltd made a trading loss of £100,000 in an accounting period. In the same period, it realised chargeable gains of £30,000 and profits from an overseas operation of £40,000, with a foreign tax credit of £10,000. The company has a choice to make. It can either:
– claim relief for the trading loss and pay no corporation tax, but forego any credit for the foreign tax suffered; or
– pay tax on the chargeable gain, whilst using the foreign tax credit against the corporation tax due on the overseas profit.
It is not possible for D Ltd to offset only £30,000 of the loss and extinguish the gain.

A claim must be made within the normal time limit (¶35110).

2. Carrying back to earlier periods

36100
s 37(3)(b) CTA 2010;
CTM04510

A loss can be carried back and relieved against profits and gains of an earlier period, provided that:
– the company has made a claim against profits and gains (if any) of the current period; and
– there are **surplus losses** still unrelieved.

The carry-back is limited to profits arising in the 12 months immediately prior to the loss-making period. The **same trade** must have been carried on during the period in which the loss is offset, although not necessarily for the entire period: it is sufficient for it to have been carried on at some point during that time.

MEMO POINTS For **losses arising in accounting periods** ending after 23 November 2008 and before 24 November 2010, a limited extension of this loss carry back was available to enable the loss to be carried back 3 years.

Prior accounting period of 12 months

36105

The simplest situation is that in which the company has a chargeable accounting period of 12 months ending immediately before the start of the loss-making period.

EXAMPLE E Ltd makes a trading loss of £100,000 in the year ended 31 December 2013. In the same year it makes chargeable gains of £30,000. In the year ended 31 December 2012 it had trading profits of £85,000. The effect of a loss-relief claim would be as follows:

	£	Loss memorandum
Year ended 31 December 2013		
Trading loss		100,000
Chargeable gains	30,000	
Less: Current year trading losses	(30,000)	(30,000)
Profits chargeable to corporation tax	Nil	
Trading losses unrelieved		70,000
Year ended 31 December 2012		
Trading profits	85,000	
Less: Loss carried back from year ended 31 December 2013	(70,000)	(70,000)
Profits chargeable to corporation tax	15,000	
Trading loss unrelieved		Nil

Prior accounting period not 12 months

If the previous accounting period is not 12 months in length, the losses can be relieved against profits which arise within the 12 months ending immediately before the start of the loss-making period. Where necessary, an apportionment of the profits must be made.

36110

The loss will be relieved against the later period first.

> [EXAMPLE] F Ltd has the following trading results during the periods detailed.
>
> | | |
> |---|---|
> | Year ended 31 March 2012 | Profit £100,000 |
> | 9 months ended 31 December 2012 | Profit £75,000 |
> | Year ended 31 December 2013 | Loss £150,000 |
>
> F Ltd has no other profits or gains during these periods.
> The effect of making a claim to carry back the loss is as follows:
>
> | | £ | Loss memorandum |
> |---|---|---|
> | **9 months ended 31 December 2012** | | |
> | Trading profit | 75,000 | 150,000 |
> | Less: Losses carried back | (75,000) | (75,000) |
> | Profits chargeable to corporation tax | Nil | |
> | Trading loss unrelieved | | 75,000 |
> | **Year ended 31 March 2012** | | |
> | Period within the 12 months ending on 31 December 2012: | | |
> | 1 January 2012 – 31 March 2012 | | |
> | Trading profit for year | 100,000 | |
> | Available for loss offset (3/12 × 100,000) | (25,000) | (25,000) |
> | Profits chargeable to corporation tax | 75,000 | |
> | Trading loss unrelieved | | 50,000 |
>
> The remaining loss will be carried forward (¶36150).

Where it is possible to **offset losses from two periods** against the same profits, the loss from the earlier period is relieved first.

36115

> [EXAMPLE] E Ltd makes up accounts for 6 month periods to 30 June and 31 December. Its results are as follows.
>
> | | |
> |---|---|
> | 6 months ended 30 June 2012 | Profit £50,000 |
> | 6 months ended 31 December 2012 | Profit £30,000 |
> | 6 months ended 30 June 2013 | Loss £45,000 |
> | 6 months ended 31 December 2013 | Loss £20,000 |
>
> The loss from the period ended 30 June 2013 will be utilised first.
>
> | | £ |
> |---|---|
> | **Loss from 6 months ended 30 June 2013** | |
> | Against profits of 6 months ended 31 December 2012 | 30,000 |
> | Against profits of 6 months ended 30 June 2012 | 15,000 |
>
> The losses from the later period (the 6 months to 31 December 2013) could be carried back to cover both the 6 months ended 30 June 2013 and the 6 months to 31 December 2012. However, there are no profits remaining in these periods for relief.. The loss will therefore be carried forward to later periods (¶36150).

Interaction with losses brought forward

If the company makes a claim to carry back a loss to a period for which there are also losses brought forward (¶36150), the losses brought forward take precedence.

36120

> [EXAMPLE] H Ltd has the following trading results during the periods detailed.
>
> | | |
> |---|---|
> | Year ended 31 March 2011 | Loss £30,000 |
> | Year ended 31 March 2012 | Profit £75,000 |

The company has unused losses arising in the year ended 31 March 2013 of £60,000.
The losses will be utilised as follows:

	£
Year ended 31 March 2012	
Profit	75,000
Less: Losses brought forward from 2011	(30,000)
	45,000
Less: Losses carried back from 2013	(45,000)
Profits chargeable to corporation tax	Nil
Loss memorandum	
Year ended 31 March 2011	
Loss for the year	30,000
Used against the profits from year ended 31 March 2012	(30,000)
Losses remaining	Nil
Year ended 31 March 2013	
Loss for the year	60,000
Used against the profits from year ended 31 March 2012	(45,000)
Losses remaining	15,000

3. Carry forward of unrelieved losses

Carry forward

36150
s 45 CTA 2010

Where a loss is **not fully utilised** in any other manner, and arises in a period during which the company is within the charge to corporation tax, it will be carried forward **automatically** for use in later periods. The loss will then be set against the first profits arising from **the same trade**, without exception. The set-off is automatic and no claim needs to be made.

> EXAMPLE In Year 1 A Ltd makes a loss in a trade of £30,000. It makes no claim for relief, and the loss is carried forward. In Year 2 the same trade shows a profit of £50,000. The loss carried forward is automatically set off against the profit, leaving £20,000 chargeable to corporation tax (50,000 – 30,000).

s 46 CTA 2010

> MEMO POINTS 1. For this purpose other items of income such as **interest and dividends** can be relieved as profits of the trade if they would be considered as such profits but for specific provisions relating to them. This is only likely to apply to financial institutions. *Nuclear Electric Ltd v Bradley* [1996]
> 2. Where a company **admits a partner** to its trade, it will still be able to utilise any brought-forward losses against its share of profits.
> 3. Where the **company merges a trade** with an existing trade which carries a loss, the loss can only be set against profits from the original element of the trade. The allocation of profit of the merged trade between its constituent parts is based on the particular facts and circumstances of the situation.

36155

Same trade It is necessary to **identify** when a trade is the same, and when it has changed so that brought-forward losses can no longer be relieved. Whether or not the same trade is being carried on is a question of fact, to be decided on the circumstances of each particular case. As such, it is the tribunal (¶54335) who will decide, should there be a dispute.

BIM70535

HMRC guidance acknowledges there is a presumption that a company carries on only one trade unless:
– one activity is so different in nature from the other that it can be seen as quite separate; and
– the activities are separately organised and managed right up to board level.

> EXAMPLE
> 1. A company that manufactured gas appliances and gas chemical plant started to manufacture electric food mixers. This new activity was carried on under a new name and a separate bank

account was run for it. A separate works manager and suitably trained staff were employed in a separate part of the company's premises. Whilst the company accounts were produced with the existing and new activities aggregated, a separate account was attached for the new activity. This had its share of the management charges incurred by the company, along with its own material, labour, etc costs. Although the board was the same for both parts of the company, they rarely met, leaving the works director for the company and the secretary to make the decisions.

It was held that, although the factors in the case were finely balanced, the activity was not a new trade but an extension of the existing one. *Cannon Industries Ltd v Edwards* [1965]

2. An individual acted as a contractor for "processing" films, employing only clerical staff whilst subcontracting the technical work to a third party. At a later stage he entered into partnership with the individual processing the films. It was held that the introduction of a substantial amount of machinery, and the fact that the trade involved "making things" meant that its trade had changed significantly. *Humphries (George) & Co v Cook* [1934]

3. Moving from dealing in computer hardware and software to the provision of IT consultancy services has been considered to be a change in trade. *Kawthar Consulting Ltd v HMRC* [2005]

4. The owners of a fish and chip shop purchased another shop in another location and commenced operating it. Buying for the shops was centralised and only one set of accounts was prepared. It was held that this was an extension to an existing trade as the new shop had lost its existing identity and had been subsumed into their own. *Maidment v Kibby* [1993]

5. A company which had operated a brewery closed its own brewing operation, but continued to bottle and sell beer brewed for it.

The court considered that the company had ceased operating as a brewer and had started a new trade. *Gordon & Blair Ltd v IRC* [1962]

SECTION 2

Losses arising from a property business

The options for relieving a loss arising from a property business (¶19000+) differ from those available for trading losses, and depend on whether the property is located in the UK or overseas. However, the quantification of the loss is still based on the same principles as for property income generally. **36205**

The restrictions which apply to trading losses on a **change of ownership** also apply to losses from a property business, wherever it is situated (¶60290). If the company has an investment business, details of the restriction can be found at ¶60325.

A. UK property business

Relief will **only be available** where the trade was carried on: **36235**
− on a commercial basis such that it could reasonably be expected to make a profit; or s 64 CTA 2010
− in the exercise of a statutory function.

As such, where a nominal rent is charged to a **connected party**, any loss arising will not be available to be used as outlined here.

Set-off of losses

Unlike trading losses, the relief of a loss from a UK property business is **automatic**. **36240**
Firstly, any loss arising is offset against other profits or gains in the same period. If this is s 62 CTA 2010
against foreign profits, it may result in a foreign tax credit (¶90480) being lost.

Where the **property business continues in a future period**, any unrelieved loss is carried forward to the next period, and treated as if it arose in that period. This means that as the loss is brought forward, it is relieved against any other profits or gains at the first available opportunity. This process of carry forward and offset will continue until either:
– the loss is completely relieved; or
– the company ceases to carry on the UK property business.

EXAMPLE In the year ended 31 December 2012, A Ltd makes a loss in its UK property business of £30,000, whilst making a trading profit of £5,000. In the year ended 31 December 2013, it has a trading profit of £10,000 and a profit from the UK property business of £7,500. The loss is utilised as follows:

Year ended 31 December 2012
Trading profit	5,000
Less: UK property business loss	(5,000)
Profit chargeable to corporation tax	Nil

Year ended 31 December 2013
Trading profit	10,000
UK property business profit	7,500
	17,500
Less: UK property business losses brought forward	(17,500)
Profit chargeable to corporation tax	Nil

Loss memorandum	**£**
UK property business loss arising in year ended 31 December 2012	30,000
Utilised Trading profits year ended 31 December 2012	(5,000)
against:	
Trading profits year ended 31 December 2013	(10,000)
UK property business profits year ended 31 December 2013	(7,500)
Loss to carry forward	7,500

The loss will be available to utilise in future, provided that the UK property business continues.

Cessation of property business

36245
s 63 CTA 2010

If the company ceases its UK property business in a period, any **losses still not used** by the end of that period will be lost. However, this does not apply to **companies with investment business**. Where the property business ceases but the company continues to be classified as a company with investment business, the remaining losses at the end of the period in which the business ceased will be carried forward and treated as if they were management expenses of the following period (¶17620).

B. Overseas property business

36275
ss 66 – 67
CTA 2010

Where a loss arises from the carrying on of an overseas property business, and provided that the same conditions are met as for a UK property business (¶36235), the loss will be available for carry forward for relief only against future profits arising from the same property business.

EXAMPLE B Ltd has the following results:

Year ended 31 March 2012
Trading profit	20,000
Overseas property business loss	(10,000)

Year ended 31 March 2013
Trading profit	25,000
Overseas property business profit	5,000

This will give the following taxable profits:

Year ended 31 March 2012

Trading profit	20,000
Profits chargeable to corporation tax	20,000

Year ended 31 March 2013

Trading profit		25,000
Overseas property business profit	5,000	
Less: Loss brought forward	(5,000)	
		-
Profits chargeable to corporation tax		25,000

The balance of the loss will be available in future years to offset only against profits arising from the overseas property business.

C. Furnished holiday lettings

For accounting periods beginning on or after 1 April 2011, a loss arising from a commercial business of furnished holiday letting (¶19410) can only be relieved by carrying it forward against future profits arising from the same letting business. This works in a way analogous to that for an overseas property business (¶36275).

36305
ss 65, 67A
CTA 2010

MEMO POINTS 1. **Previously**, there was much more flexibility, in that losses from furnished holiday lettings were treated as trading losses (¶36050).

Capital losses

SECTION 1

All companies

37000
ss 8, 16 TCGA 1992
s 43 TMA 1970

The **computation** of a capital gain or loss is covered at ¶30285+.

In order **for the loss to be allowed**, it must be quantified and claimed within 4 years of the end of the accounting period in which it arises.

A. Disallowed and restricted losses

37030   The use of a loss to reduce other gains may be prohibited or restricted in the following circumstances:

Circumstance	Loss relief	¶¶
Company's gains are not subject to corporation tax	Disallowed	¶37060
Loss arises on a transaction with a connected person	Only against gains from transactions with the same person	¶37080
Loss created artificially to obtain a tax advantage	Disallowed	¶37100

Circumstance	Loss relief	¶¶
Income gain artificially converted to capital	Not allowed against that gain	¶37125
Artificial creation of a trading deduction in connection with a gain	Not allowed against that gain	¶37130
Artificial transactions among group companies	Restricted	¶67595+
Losses accruing to a company before it joins a group	Ring-fenced	¶67835+
Write-off of Government investment in the company	Available losses reduced by amount written off	¶36015

1. Not subject to UK tax

If a loss arises in a situation **where a gain would not have been subject to UK corporation tax** (for instance, if the company is not UK-resident when the loss arises), but it later has a gain chargeable in the UK, the loss will not be available for relief.

37060
s 8(2) TCGA 1992

2. Transactions with connected persons

Where a loss arises on a transaction with a connected party (¶31375), that **loss can only be used** against gains arising in transactions with that person whilst the parties in question remain connected. If they later lose their connection, any loss remaining will be lost.

37080
s 18 TCGA 1992

3. Creating losses artificially

A loss will not be available if a transaction is entered into and one of its main purposes is to **secure a tax advantage** (¶21450). The advantage does not have to be secured for the person to whom the loss accrues. For instance, in a group situation, a subsidiary transferring a loss-making asset could reduce the value of the parent. This would then result in further losses arising from the original transaction. Nor does the advantage have to result in an immediate impact on the tax position of the company. If the **loss cannot be utilised** at the time it arises, this will not stop the rules applying.

37100
s 16A TCGA 1992

Where the rules apply, such losses will be disallowed. HMRC have stated that a number of **factors will be taken into account** in looking at whether the tax advantage was one of the main reasons for the transaction. These include:
– if there are a number of steps, are the steps dependent on one another or can the chain of events be stopped at any point;
– the overall commercial objective that the parties involved sought to achieve (including members of the groups involved if applicable);
– if the objective appears reasonable in the circumstances and is genuinely being sought; and
– if the objective is achieved in a straightforward manner, or were complex, additional or added steps involved that resulted in the tax advantage accruing.

CG40240+

4. Specific anti-avoidance

As the general anti-avoidance rules only cover the position where a capital loss is created by way of a transaction designed to create a loss artificially, there are rules to prevent two specific circumstances where either:
– genuine losses could be used to shelter artificial gains; or
– a trading deduction is artificially created to cover gains.
These rules will only apply where a **notice is issued** by HMRC (¶37135).

37120

> MEMO POINTS   HMRC operate a non-statutory **clearance** system (¶54050) for transactions where the company concerned may be caught under the rules, either on an actual or proposed transaction.

Converting income to capital

37125
s 184G TCGA 1992

Where a genuine loss arises on the sale of an asset, or there are losses brought forward, a company may seek to convert an income source into capital in order to utilise the losses.

HMRC may issue a notice where they believe that all of the following may have occurred:
– due to an arrangement that has been entered into, the company has a **receipt connected to the disposal of an asset**;
– a gain accrues to the company on the **disposal against which losses could be offset**;
– without the arrangement, at least part of the **receipt would have been treated as income** and not capital, either of the company itself or of another company in its capital gains group (¶65415+); and
– one of the **main purposes** of the arrangement is to secure a tax advantage by deducting the losses from the gain.

In this case, **where a notice is issued** (¶37135), the company will not be able to set the losses against that particular gain.

Deduction of revenue expenditure

37130
s 184H TCGA 1992

HMRC may issue a notice where they believe that all of the following may have occurred:
– the company makes a **capital gain** in connection with an arrangement and **losses accrue** or are **already available for offset**;
– the company, or one connected with it (¶31375), incurs **expenditure that is allowed against income** but not gains in connection with the arrangement;
– one of the **main purposes** of the arrangement is to both secure a deduction against income for the expenditure, and to deduct the losses from the gain now being made; and
– the arrangements are not excluded arrangements.

In this case, **where a notice is issued** the company will not be able to set the losses against that particular gain.

> MEMO POINTS   An arrangement is **excluded** if:
> – it relates to land or an interest in land;
> – the transaction falls within the limitations for deductions on sale and leasebacks (¶82440);
> – payments are being made to a company that is not connected; or
> – the arrangements are made at arm's length.

Notices

37135
s 184I TCGA 1992

For either of these **restrictions to apply**, HMRC must issue a notice to the company specifying:
– the arrangement to which the notice relates;
– the accounting period in which the gain arises; and
– the effect of the notice.

Where a company receives such a notice, the procedure and rules differ slightly depending on the point in the company's compliance cycle at which the notice is sent. It is for the **company to decide** whether it must make an amendment to its return in order to comply with the notice. If it fails to make an amendment, but should have done so, it will be liable for a penalty for submitting an inaccurate return (¶52480).

37140

No return yet made for period   Where the company has not made a return for the period to which the notice relates, it is entitled to **make a return** within the next 90 days ignoring the notice, and then amend it within that 90 day period.

37145

Return submitted for the period   Where the company has made a return for the period, HMRC can only issue a notice if a **notice of enquiry** (¶50415) has been delivered to the company. The company then has 90 days to amend its return to comply with the notice. No **closure notice** (¶50550) can be issued until either the company amends its return, or the 90 day period expires.

Period previously subject to enquiry If HMRC have previously concluded enquiries into the return, two **conditions** must be met before they can issue a notice:

37150

– when the closure notice was issued, HMRC could not reasonably have been expected to know that circumstances existed in which a notice could be issued **based on the information** provided to them before that time; and

– a **request for information was made** during the enquiry that, if it had been complied with, would have resulted in a reasonable expectation that HMRC would issue a notice.

Where a notice is issued in these circumstances, HMRC cannot make any **discovery assessment** (¶50600) until either the company amends its return, or the 90 day period expires.

B. Order of set-off

Firstly, any losses arising on a disposal are used to reduce any gains in the period that remain chargeable (for instance, after any rollover relief (¶30940) is given).

37180

Any surplus is then carried forward to offset against the first available gain in future years, until such time when all of the losses have been utilised.

> EXAMPLE A Ltd makes two disposals of fixed assets during the year to 30 June 2012: one for a gain of £5,000, the other for a loss of £15,000. It also makes trading profits of £15,000. In the following year, it makes a trading profit of £17,000 and a capital gain of £3,000. This will result in the following position:
>
> | Year ended 30 June 2012 | £ | £ |
> |---|---|---|
> | Trading profits | | 15,000 |
> | Capital gains | 5,000 | |
> | Less: Capital losses | (5,000) | |
> | Net gains | | - |
> | Profits chargeable to corporation tax | | 15,000 |
>
> Capital loss to carry forward is £10,000 (15,000 – 5,000)
>
> | Year ended 30 June 2013 | | |
> |---|---|---|
> | Trading profits | | 17,000 |
> | Capital gains | 3,000 | |
> | Less: Capital losses brought forward | (3,000) | |
> | Net gains | | - |
> | Profits chargeable to corporation tax | | 17,000 |
>
> Capital loss remaining to carry forward is £7,000 (10,000 – 3,000)

Although the set off is automatic, the company must report the loss on its self-assessment return in order to secure its use in future years.

SECTION 2

Investment companies

A. Basic position

Where an investment company (¶6080) satisfies certain conditions, it can claim relief against its other profits if:

37230
s 68 CTA 2010

– it makes an allowable **capital loss**;

– on a disposal of **unquoted shares** in a **qualifying trading company**;

– for which it **subscribed** (as opposed to purchased from another party).

MEMO POINTS 1. The relief is not available to a company with investment business (¶6115) that is not an investment company,

2. In order to qualify, the **disposal** must be:
- made at arm's length (¶30415);
- deemed to occur by virtue of a negligible value claim (¶31720);
- by virtue of the receipt of a capital distribution on the dissolution or winding up of the company (¶61265); or
- due to the loss, dissipation or extinction of the asset (¶30085).

If the shares become part of a different holding as a result of a reconstruction or amalgamation (¶30080), that is not a disposal for these purposes.

Investing company

37235
ss 69, 90 CTA 2010

The company making the disposal must:
- have been an investment company throughout a **qualifying period**, normally 6 years in length, ending on (and including) the date of disposal;
- not be the **holding company** of a trading group; and
- not be **associated** (¶40185) with, or part of the same group as, the company of whose shares it disposes, at any time between the initial subscription and the date of disposal.

MEMO POINTS The **qualifying period** may be shortened, provided that prior to the commencement of that shorter period, the company was never either an excluded company (¶37240) or a trading company (this could apply, for instance, where a company was dormant or has been incorporated for less than 6 years).

37240
s 90 CTA 2010

Excluded company A company is an excluded company if it:
- **wholly or mainly deals** in land, commodities, futures, shares or securities, or other financial instruments;
- is a **holding company** of any group other than a trading group;
- is a **building society** or registered industrial or provident society; or
- carries out a trade **other than on a commercial basis** where there is a reasonable expectation of profit.

Qualifying trading company

37245
ss 78 – 85
CTA 2010

For **shares issued on or after 6 April 1998**, the following conditions must be satisfied by the investee company:

Requirement	When	For how long?
The company must carry on a trade on a commercial basis with an expectation of profit and the trade carried on cannot wholly or substantially consist of excluded activities[1]	At date of disposal or, if not, then within the last 3 years before the disposal, provided that the company has not been an excluded company (¶37240), a trading company, or an investment company since then	For 6 years ending on the date of disposal; or for a shorter period ending on the same date, provided that the company was never an excluded company, a trading company, or an investment company before the beginning of that shorter period
The company must not control any other companies other than its own 51% subsidiaries (¶65505); where the subsidiary is a property management company, the level of ownership required is raised to 90%		
The company cannot be a 51% subsidiary of, or controlled by, any other company, nor can there be arrangements in place to bring such a situation about		

Requirement	When	For how long?
Gross assets must be no more than £7 million before the issue of the shares on which relief is sought, and no more than £8 million after[2]	Immediately before and after making the subscription	
The company must be unquoted, with no arrangements in place to become quoted	At the date of the issue of the shares	For shares issued prior to 7 March 2001, the company had to be unquoted from the time of issue until 7 March 2001
The company must be carrying on business wholly or mainly in the UK	At incorporation or, if later, 12 months before the shares were issued	For the entire period up to the date of disposal

Note:
1. **Excluded activities** are defined as:
– dealing in land, commodities, futures, shares, securities or other financial instruments;
– dealing in goods other than in the course of an ordinary trade of wholesale or retail distribution;
– banking, insurance, money-lending, debt-factoring, hire-purchase financing or other financial activities;
– leasing;
– receiving royalties or licence fees;
– providing legal or accountancy services;
– property development;
– farming or market gardening;
– holding, managing or occupying woodlands, any other forestry activities or timber production;
– shipbuilding, producing coal or steel;
– operating or managing hotels or similar establishments or managing property used in such a way;
– operating or managing nursing homes or residential care homes or managing property used in such a way.
2. **Gross assets** are measured on a group basis, where applicable (i.e. the parent company plus its 51% subsidiaries) ignoring investments in subsidiaries and intra-group liabilities.

MEMO POINTS   When considering a **group**, all of its trades should be treated as if they are carried out by one company, and then the above rule applied. In doing so, the following activities are to be ignored: s79(5) CTA 2010
– intra-group shares or loans;
– the holding and managing of property used by another group company for the purposes of its trade (provided that this itself is not excluded); and
– the holding and managing of property used by another group company for the purposes of research and development (¶78000+), provided that it is intended that a trade will arise from it and a group company will carry this out, or it benefits an existing trade of a group company.

For **shares issued before 6 April 1998**, only the conditions below are relevant to the company invested in: **37250**

Requirement	When	For how long?
Must be a trading company[1]	At date of disposal or, if not, then within the last 3 years before the date of disposal, provided that it has not been an excluded[2] or investment company since then	For 6 years ending on the date of disposal, or for a shorter period ending on the date of disposal, provided that it has never been an excluded company or investment company before the beginning of that shorter period
Not listed on a recognised stock exchange (¶95320)	At incorporation or, if later, 12 months before the shares were issued	Throughout the period until the date of disposal
UK resident		From incorporation until date of disposal

Note:
1. A **trading company** is one carrying on one or more trades, or the holding company of a trading group. It cannot be an excluded company. A **trading group** is one where the business of the members, when taken together, consists wholly or mainly of trades, but the trades of excluded companies or non-UK-resident companies cannot be counted as trades for this purpose.
2. An **excluded company** is one that wholly or mainly deals in shares, securities, land, or commodity futures, or is not operated on a commercial basis with a view to making profit. The holding company of a non-trading group, a building society or registered industrial and provident society are also excluded companies.

B. Calculating and applying the relief

1. Amount of relief

Entire shareholding qualifies

37280
s 75 CTA 2010

As a general principle, the normal share identification rules (¶32195) are used for disposals of shares that attract relief. In a very straightforward case, the company will have only shares that qualify for relief. In this case, the amount of relief due will be the cost of the subscription.

> EXAMPLE A Ltd subscribes for 1,000 shares in B Ltd in June 2003 for £100,000. These shares all qualify for the relief. A Ltd disposes of the shares for £40,000 in an arm's length transaction. A Ltd can claim relief for the full capital loss of £60,000 (40,000 – 100,000).

Where only a **part of the shareholding** is disposed of, the normal method of calculating the loss (¶32195) will apply, and this will be the amount of relief available.

> MEMO POINTS Where the shareholding involved shares that qualified for relief under the **corporate venturing scheme** (¶80545) and which have been held throughout, the identification rules applying to that scheme will apply first.

Mixed shareholding

37285

It may be the case that the company making the disposal has acquired a **number of tranches** of shares over the years, some of which qualify and some which do not. When all of such a shareholding is disposed of, the loss available for relief against income is restricted to the cost of the qualifying shares.

> EXAMPLE C Ltd subscribed for 100 shares for £3,000 in D Ltd in June 1998. It then purchased a further 200 shares in May 2002 for £12,000. In May 2013, it made a negligible value claim for its entire shareholding. Both parcels of shares fall into the section 104 holding (¶32200), and the loss would be calculated as follows:
>
> | | £ |
> |---|---|
> | Proceeds | Nil |
> | Less: Cost | (15,000) |
> | Loss | (15,000) |
>
> **Note:**
> As there is a loss arising, there is no need to calcuate indexation allowance.
>
> This loss is then allocated across the acquisitions. The amount attributed to the 100 subscriber shares will be:
>
> $$\frac{100}{300} \times 15,000 = £5,000.$$
>
> However, this is more than would have been available if the qualifying holding had not formed part of the pool. If it had been separately identified, the loss arising would have been £3,000 (the original subscribed cost). The relief available is restricted to this lower figure. The remaining loss of £12,000 is still available as an ordinary capital loss.

37290 **Part disposal** Where there is a mixed shareholding and only a part of it is disposed of, the calculation is further complicated by the problem of **identifying the shares** that have been disposed of.

> EXAMPLE In December 1994 E Ltd subscribed for 2,000 shares in F Ltd for £5,000, then in August 1995, a further 1,000 shares were purchased for £15,000. In January 2013, 1,600 of the shares are disposed of in an arm's length transaction for £4,000. Both acquisitions would fall into the section 104 holding (¶32200), which would be:

	Holding	Cost £	Indexed cost £
December 1994 subscription	2,000	5,000	5,000
Indexation, at a rate of 0.027, to August 1995			135
	2,000	5,000	5,135
Addition August 1995	1,000	15,000	15,000
	3,000	20,000	20,135
Indexation at a rate of 0.640 to January 2013			12,886
	3,000	20,000	33,021
January 2013 part disposal	(1,600)	(10,667)	(17,611)
	1,400	9,333	15,410

The computation of the loss in the usual manner gives the following:

	£
Proceeds	4,000
Less: Cost[1]	(10,667)
Loss	(6,667)

Note:
1. No indexation applies, as indexation cannot increase a loss.
Identification of the shares for the purpose of quantifying the relief is based on last in first out (LIFO). In this case the 1,600 shares are matched firstly against the acquisition of 1,000 shares in August 1995 and then 600 shares from the original, qualifying subscription. As such the maximum loss attributable to the qualifying shares is:

$$\frac{600}{1,600} \times £6,667 = £2,500$$

Finally, this figure is compared against the purchase cost of the shares that have been identified as disposed of. In this case, 600 shares at £2.50 per share is £1,500. As this is the lower figure, it is this amount that is eligible for relief. The remainder of the loss will still be available for relief as a capital loss.

Bonus shares

If any bonus shares are issued during ownership, these will be treated as being acquired on the same date as the original shares to which they relate.

37295
s 73 CTA 2010

Reorganisations

If shares that would qualify for relief are **exchanged** for shares in another company (Newco), the new shares will **continue to qualify**, provided that:
– all the issued shares of Newco are subscriber shares;
– the consideration is payable wholly in Newco shares, in proportion to the original holdings, with new shares carrying the same rights as those they replace;
– the Newco shares were issued on or after 6 April 1998; and
– the general capital gains rules on reconstructions (¶30080) apply, such that there is deemed to be no disposal of the old shares.

37300
ss 87, 88 CTA 2010

MEMO POINTS Where the **new shares were issued before 6 April 2007**, either the acquiring company or the target company had to apply for clearance from HMRC to ensure that the transaction was for genuine commercial reasons, and did not form part of a scheme or arrangement to avoid corporation tax on chargeable gains. If this was not secured, the replacement shares could not take the place of the original ones.

2. Applying the relief

The loss arising is set against the total profits of the accounting period in which the loss arose. The loss is **used before** applying a deduction for management expenses (¶17620) or

37330
ss 71-72 CTA 2010

charitable donations (¶22055), **but after** any claim for relief under the corporate venturing scheme (¶80545).

If the **loss cannot be wholly relieved** in that period, the excess can be carried back and relieved against profits arising in the previous 12 months. If only part of a previous accounting period falls into those 12 months, an apportionment must be made (¶36110). The company must have been an investment company throughout the accounting period(s) concerned.

After applying both these reliefs, or if no claim is made, **any remaining loss** is carried forward, but only as a capital loss under the normal rules (¶37000+).

A **claim** must be made within 2 years of the end of the accounting period in which the loss arose.

PART 6

Calculation of the tax charge

Calculation of the tax charge
Summary

The numbers cross-refer to paragraphs.

Computation

| SECTION 1 |

Outline

Once the amount of chargeable income or allowable loss for each source has been calculated for the accounting period, it is necessary to calculate the total profits chargeable to corporation tax (PCTCT) before calculating the amount of corporation tax that is due. **40000**

In the tax computation, all taxable profits are aggregated, including any chargeable gains made, and any allowable deductions are taken from the total profit. Any amounts paid or received under deduction of tax are included in the computation gross. Any non-taxable items – for example, dividends that may receive exemption – are left out of the computation. Where a loss has been incurred from a particular source, the profit should be shown as "0" rather than as a negative. However, this line would typically be removed from the computation altogether. The extent to which any available losses may be utilised will depend on the nature of each loss (¶35000+). **40005**

Once PCTCT has been calculated, the corporation tax liability can be determined. Income tax suffered at source (¶41050) and any double tax relief (¶90480+) will reduce this figure to give the net corporation tax payable. The tax computation, including the calculation of the tax liability, will form the main supporting document for the company tax return (¶46050).

[MEMO POINTS] Since April 2013, new rules apply a different rate of tax to assets held in a "patent box". Further details of these can be found at ¶29235.

Basic format

40010   The basic format of the computation is as follows:

	£
Trading income	x
Income from UK land and property	x
Profits from loan relationships	x
Profits from overseas sources	x
Income from other sources	x
Income received under deduction of tax	x
Chargeable gains	x
	x
Less: Expenses of management	(x)
Losses claimed	(x)
Qualifying charitable donation payments	(x)
Profit chargeable to corporation tax	x
Corporation tax thereon @ x %	x.xx
Less: Community investment tax relief	(x.xx)
Less: Double tax relief	(x.xx)
Less: ACT	(x.xx)
Less: Income tax suffered at source	(x.xx)
Net corporation tax payable	x.xx

[MEMO POINTS] 1. In a tax computation, **numbers are generally** rounded to the nearest pound, except for the tax figures below the PCTCT line – for example, income tax suffered at source – which are always given in pence (i.e. two decimal places). See ¶46225 for when a computation can be produced using figures **rounded** to thousands.
2. The amount of tax due on loans to participators is also added to the tax due for the year (¶75750+).

Currency

40015
ss 5 – 9B CTA 2010   Where a company prepares its accounts in a foreign currency it will be **required to convert** the details of income and gains into sterling. Exactly how will differ slightly depending on how the company carries out its accounting process during the year. For full details see ¶17170.

Rates of tax

40020   The rates of corporation tax are set for "financial years" (FYs), which run from 1 April to 31 March and are designated by the year in which they start. So, FY2013 started on 1 April 2013 and ends on 31 March 2014.

The main rate of corporation tax is currently set at 23% for FY2013 (and will be 21% for FY2014). This applies for all companies which have taxable profits (plus any included franked investment income (¶40115)) over £1,500,000. It also applies to **close investment holding companies** (¶75945+), regardless of the level of profit.

For small companies – that is, companies with taxable profits (plus any included franked investment income) of **£300,000 or less** – there is a small profits rate of taxation, currently set at 20% (FY2013).

To account for those with profits between these two figures there is a marginal relief calculation (¶40110+) to smooth the transition from one rate to the other.

These limits are subject to division based on the number of **companies associated** (¶40185) with the company.

[MEMO POINTS] The main rate for companies with ring fence profits from **oil extraction and rights** in the UK and on the UK continental shelf is 30%. The small profits rate is 19%.

SECTION 2

Companies with no associates

A. Tax at one rate

Accounting period coinciding with financial year

Where the company's **accounting period coincides with the FY** (i.e. runs from 1 April   **40070**
through to 31 March), and PCTCT is either equal to or greater than £1,500,000, or less than
or equal to £300,000, corporation tax is calculated simply by multiplying the PCTCT by the
appropriate rate of tax.

> EXAMPLE A Ltd has PCTCT of £59,000 for the year to 31 March 2014 and the company received
> no dividend income. This falls within the small profits rate band and the corporation tax due is
> therefore £11,800 (£59,000 × 20%).

Accounting period straddling two financial years

Where the accounting period straddles two FYs and there is **no change in the rate of tax**,   **40075**
there is no requirement to apportion the profit between the FYs and the calculation can
proceed as if the period ended on 31 March.

However, where the accounting period straddles two FYs and there is a **change in the rate
of tax**, it is necessary to apportion the profit and apply the rates for each FY separately. The
apportionment should reflect the number of days falling into each FY.

> EXAMPLE B Ltd has PCTCT of £1,575,000 for the year to 31 December and is therefore subject to
> tax at the main rate. Assuming a main rate of 23% for the first FY and 21% for the subsequent FY,
> corporation tax is due as follows:
>
> | | | £ |
> |---|---|---|
> | First FY: | | |
> | 90/365 × £1,575,000 = | £388,356 @ 23% | 89,321.88 |
> | Subsequent FY: | | |
> | 275/365 × £1,575,000 = | £1,186,644 @ 21% | 249,195.24 |
> | Total corporation tax due | | 338,517.12 |

Accounting period of less than 12 months

Where the accounting period is less than 12 months, the profit thresholds must be correspon-   **40080**
dingly reduced to determine the rate of tax payable. In addition, any apportionment between
FYs should reflect the overall length of the accounting period.

> EXAMPLE C Ltd has PCTCT of £190,000 for the 9 months to 30 September. Tax will be due at the
> small profits rate, as profits do not exceed £224,384 (273/365 × £300,000). Assuming a rate of
> 21% for the first FY and 20% for the second FY, corporation tax is due as follows:
>
> | | | £ |
> |---|---|---|
> | First FY: | | |
> | 90/273 × £190,000 = | £62,637 @ 21% | 13,153.77 |
> | Subsequent FY: | | |
> | 183/273 × £190,000 = | £127,363 @ 20% | 25,472.60 |
> | Total corporation tax due | | 38,626.37 |

B. Marginal relief

40110
s 19 CTA 2010

Where a company's profits **exceed** £300,000 it will automatically be taxed at the higher corporation tax rate. However, where the profits are **below** £1,500,000 it will be entitled to marginal relief. This relief is intended to smooth the transition from one rate of tax to the other.

After having calculated the tax due at the full rate, the following fraction is applied:

$$(U - A) \times \frac{N}{A} \times F$$

where:
- N is PCTCT;
- F is the prescribed fraction (3/400 for FY2013);
- U is the upper limit of the margin (£1,500,000); and
- A is the augmented profits for the period (¶40115).

This gives the amount of relief that the company is entitled to claim.

EXAMPLE D Ltd has profits of £720,000 and receives no dividends during the year.		
		£
Tax at main rate	£720,000 @ 23%	165,600
Less: Marginal relief	$(£1{,}500{,}000 - £720{,}000) \times \dfrac{720{,}000}{720{,}000} \times \dfrac{3}{400}$	(5,850)
Total corporation tax due		159,750

Company with dividend income

40115
s 1126 CTA 2010

Where a company receives franked investment income during a period, this is added to the usual PCTCT to work out the augmented profits. **Franked investment income**, as it is termed, consists of dividends received by the company, along with the tax credit it would be entitled to (being 1/9th of the payment received). **Excluded** from this sum, for these purposes, are dividends received by the company from anyone that is its 51% subsidiary (¶65505), or a fellow 51% subsidiary in a group. This also extends to quasi-subsidiaries, being companies that are owned by a consortium that the receiving company is a member of, and where it is not (and no arrangements exist to make it) a 75% subsidiary of another company.

EXAMPLE E Ltd has profits of £330,000 and receives a dividend from another company, not a subsidiary, of £90,000.		
		£
Tax at main rate	£330,000 @ 23%	75,900.00
Less: Marginal relief	$(£1{,}500{,}000 - £430{,}000) \times \dfrac{330{,}000}{430{,}000} \times \dfrac{3}{400}$	(6,158.72)
Total corporation tax due		69,741.28

The dividend received is grossed up for the tax credit to make a total of £100,000 (£90,000 × 10/9).

40120

There is no longer any need for the company to claim either the small profits rate or marginal relief where they apply. These are now both automatic.

Accounting period straddling two financial years

40125

Where the company's accounting period straddles two FYs, it is necessary to calculate the marginal relief separately for each FY if there has been a change in the fraction and/or the thresholds.

EXAMPLE F Ltd has PCTCT of £360,000 for the year to 31 December. Assuming (for illustrative purposes) a main rate of 28% and a small profits rate of 21% for FY1, and rates of 26% and 20%, respectively, for FY2, the tax due would be as follows:

		£	£	£
First FY:				
Apportioned profit	90/365 × £360,000	88,767		
Upper limit of margin	90/365 × £1,500,000	369,863		
Tax at 28%	£88,767 @ 28%		24,854.76	
Less: Marginal relief	(£369,863 – £88,767)[1] × 7/400		(4,919.18)	
				19,935.58
Second FY:				
Apportioned profit	275/365 × £360,000	271,233		
Upper limit of margin	275/365 × £1,500,000	1,130,137		
Tax at 26%	£271,233 @ 26%		70,520.58	
Less: Marginal relief	(£1,130,137 – £271,233) × 3/200		(12,883.56)	
				57,637.02
Total corporation tax due				77,572.60

Note:
1. Where there is no franked investment income involved, the computation can be simplified to remove the fraction of PCTCT divided by the augmented profits, as these are the same.

Accounting period of less than 12 months

Where the accounting period is less than 12 months, the profit thresholds must be correspondingly reduced when calculating the marginal relief due. In addition, any apportionment between FYs should reflect the overall length of the accounting period.   **40130**

EXAMPLE G Ltd has PCTCT of £325,000 for the 8 months to 30 November. With a main rate of 23% for the FY and a fraction of 3/400, corporation tax is due as follows:

		£	£
Profit		325,000	
Upper limit of margin	244/365 × £1,500,000	1,002,740	
			£
Tax at 23%	£325,000 @ 23%		74,750.00
Less: Marginal relief	(£1,002,740 – £325,000) × 3/400		(5,083.05)
Total corporation tax due			69,666.95

SECTION 2

Companies with associates

A. General rule

As the lower rate of tax applies to companies with smaller profits in a year, a mechanism was required in order to stop the fragmentation of larger companies into smaller profit units to take advantage of the lower rate. This is the purpose behind the associated company rules. These received a major revision for accounting periods ending on or after 1 April 2011 in terms of the attribution of rights of connected persons (¶40255).   **40180**
s 24(3) CTA 2010

The rules ensure that the bands for **determining the rate of tax** are divided equally between all the associated companies involved. Therefore, if a company is associated with three other companies, the bands are divided by four (three plus the company itself) to determine the rate applicable.

Associated

40185   A company is associated with another company if **one controls the other**, or **both are controlled** by a third party.

It is usually fairly obvious if two companies are under the control of the same (singular) person. However, the position can become complicated when determining whether a **group of persons** controls two companies. HMRC treat a group of persons as controlling two companies if the same irreducible group of persons controls each company.

An irreducible group is any number of persons who together have control but who, if any one of those persons were removed, would no longer have control.

> [EXAMPLE]   Mr B, Mr C and Mr D each own 33% of A Ltd. Mr E holds the remaining 1%. In determining control, there are 3 irreducible groups:
> – Mr B and Mr C;
> – Mr B and Mr D; and
> – Mr C and Mr D.

Companies are then only under common control if the same irreducible group controls both companies.

> [EXAMPLE]   Mr F and Mr G own B Ltd and C Ltd as follows:
>
> | | Mr F | Mr G |
> | ------ | ---- | ---- |
> | B Ltd | 50% | 50% |
> | C Ltd | 60% | 40% |
>
> In this case Mr F and Mr G can control both B Ltd and C Ltd. However, Mr F is able to control C Ltd on his own account. As such the companies are not associated, because they are not controlled by the same irreducible group of individuals.

Exclusions

40190
ss 25(3), 26
CTA 2010;
CTM03590

A company can be ignored, when considering the definition of associated, where it has **not carried on a trade or business** during the period or, if it was only associated for part of the period, it has not carried on a trade or business during that part of the period. It is possible that a company is carrying on a business even where no income is received, for instance where it holds assets or pays expenses. Simply holding funds on deposit and receiving interest has been held not to be carrying on a business. *Jowett v O'Neill & Brennan Construction Ltd* [1998] Similarly, a company continuing to let property previously used in a now ceased trade has been held not to be carrying on a business. *HMRC v Salaried Persons Postal Loans Ltd* [2006]

However, a company managing and letting property, making and holding investments, and making loans to a company (and receiving interest on them) has been held to be in business. *Land Management Ltd v Fox* [2002] It would seem clear that the distinction in this last scenario is that an active position was involved, as opposed to the passive situation of leaving funds on deposit.

40195   Similarly excluded are **holding companies**, provided that all they do is hold shares in their 51% subsidiary companies (¶65505). This will only apply where the company:
– has no assets other than those shares in its 51% subsidiaries;
– is not entitled to any deductions for qualifying charitable donations (¶22085) or management expenses (¶17620); and
– has no other income or gains, other than dividends from the shares, which are fully distributed to its shareholders.

Where the company fails one of these tests, it can still argue that it is not carrying on a business and, as such, still not be considered to be an associate for the purposes of marginal relief. However, it is highly likely that a company claiming deductions will be considered to be in business.

B. Ascertaining control

The definition of control is the same as that used for the close company rules (¶75275+). However, there are several exceptions as to the rights that can be attributed to someone when looking at what that person controls.

40225
s 27 CTA 2010

1. Rights of associates

There **must be** substantial commercial interdependence between two companies **before** the rights of any associates (¶75390+) are attributed to an individual in specifying the companies over which that individual exercises control.

40255

> EXAMPLE Mr and Mrs A run two companies. Mr A's company is involved in importing goods, whereas Mrs A's company is an employment agency providing temp workers for legal firms. Prior to the change in rules in 2011 these two companies would have been associated, as Mr A would have been attributed the rights of his wife and so control both companies. This had the same effect in reverse for Mrs A.
> However, provided that the companies are not substantially commercially interdependent, the rights of Mrs A will not be attributed to Mr A (and vice versa), so that the companies will not be associated.

MEMO POINTS A company was able to **elect to defer** the application of these rules from the first period ending on or after 1 April 2011 to the period following.

s 55 FA 2011

Substantial commercial interdependence

Legislation gives guidance as to what "substantial commercial interdependence" means. In ascertaining the level of dependency, account should be taken of the degree of:
– **financial** interdependency – two companies will be financially interdependent if one gives support to the other (either directly or indirectly), or each has a financial interest in the affairs of another company;
– **economic** interdependency – this will apply where the companies are seeking the same economic objectives, the activities of one benefit the other, or the companies have common customers; and
– **organisational** interdependency – in this case two companies will be interdependent if they have common premises, employees, management or equipment.

40260
SI 2011/1784

2. Fixed rate preference shares

In looking at the issue of control, fixed rate preference shares are **ignored** where the company holding them is not a close company (¶75000+) and it:
– takes no part in the management or conduct of the company which issued the shares; and
– subscribed for shares in the ordinary course of its business, which includes the provision of finance.

40290
s 28 CTA 2010

> MEMO POINTS Fixed rate preference shares are shares issued wholly for new consideration, which cannot be converted into or exchanged for other shares, and which do not carry any rights to dividends other than those at a fixed rate and/or amount which, allowing for any sum repaid on redemption, only represents a reasonable commercial return.

3. Loan creditors

40310
s 29 CTA 2010

A company will not be under the control of another if the **only connection** between them is that one is a creditor of the other and either:
– the creditor company is not close; or
– the creditor, in acting as such, is simply carrying out its normal business.

4. Trustees

40330
s 30 CTA 2010

Provided that there is **no other connection** between the companies, where the same person acting as trustee controls two companies they will not be associated.

C. Applying marginal relief

Accounting period of 12 months

40360

Where the accounting period is 12 months long, the limits for marginal relief are simply divided by the number of associates plus one.

> EXAMPLE A Ltd has PCTCT of £520,000 for the year to 31 March 2014. It has two associated companies. The thresholds must be divided by three (i.e. 2 + 1) to determine the rate, as follows:
>
> | | PCTCT (£) | Threshold ÷ 3 (£) |
> |---|---|---|
> | Small profits rate: 20% | 0 – 300,000 | 0 – 100,000 |
> | Main rate: 23% | Over 1,500,000 | Over 500,000 |
>
> A Ltd's profits are therefore taxable at the main rate.

Accounting period of less than 12 months

40365

Where a company's accounting period is less than 12 months, the thresholds for determining the rate of tax are reduced correspondingly.

> EXAMPLE B Ltd has PCTCT of £105,000 for the 9 months to 31 March 2014. It has one associated company. The thresholds must be divided by two (i.e. 1 + 1) and reduced for the short accounting period, as follows:
>
> | | PCTCT (£) | Threshold ÷ 2 (£) | Threshold × 274/365 (£) |
> |---|---|---|---|
> | Small profits rate: 20% | 0 – 300,000 | 0 – 150,000 | 0 – 112,603 |
> | Main rate: 23% | Over 1,500,000 | Over 750,000 | Over 563,014 |
>
> B Ltd's profits are therefore taxable at the small profits rate.

Variable number of associated companies

40370

In general, where the number of associated companies varies throughout the accounting period, the **total number** of associated companies at any time during the accounting period is used.

> EXAMPLE C Ltd prepares its accounts to 31 December each year. It had three associated companies (D, E and F) at 1 January. On 1 June E Ltd ceased to be an associate and on 1 July C Ltd became associated with G Ltd.
> When determining the rate of tax, the thresholds should be divided by five (C, D, E, F and G) for the whole of the period. The fact that E and G were not associated at the same time is irrelevant.

MEMO POINTS Prior to the tax law rewrite, there was provision to cater for the situation where the associates either side of the end of a financial year were different and the profit thresholds also changed at that time. As the limits have not changed since 1994, this legislation was repealed but if a change in the thresholds should occur it is possible that a similar provision would be reintroduced.

CHAPTER 2

Adjustments to tax liability

41000 Whilst for most companies the basic calculation of corporation tax will suffice, there are several circumstances in which the liability will need to be adjusted to account for other factors. Principally, these involve income tax that the company has suffered, although there are also legacy rules relating to advance corporation tax for those companies that still have a surplus. Finally, there may be adjustments required where the company is involved in the rules relating to community investment tax relief.

SECTION 1

Income tax

A. Deduction of tax

41050
ss 952, 968
ITA 2007

Although companies are not generally subject to income tax, some forms of income that they receive may be received net of tax. It is not a simple case of allowing credit for any tax withheld, as the company is also **under an obligation** to deduct income tax from certain payments it makes. These two are offset when the company completes any necessary quarterly return (¶47115+), and where the net position at the end of an accounting period is that income tax has been suffered, this can be set against the corporation tax liability. If the income tax suffered exceeds the corporation tax due, a refund may be obtained.

B. Compulsory deduction

There are four common types of payment which must **generally** be made net of income tax:
– **annual payments**, which are characterised by a legal obligation to pay and by being treated as income in the hands of the recipient (if a payment forms part of the recipient's trading receipts it is not an annual payment; the word "annual" in this respect does not imply a payment once per year, but denotes a quality of recurrence; however, the obligation must cover a period of more than 1 year to be considered an annual payment – an example of an annual payment like this would be an annuity);
– **annual interest**, being interest paid by a company for a loan capable of lasting more than 1 year – loans from banks carrying on business in the UK (and from persons whose business consists wholly or mainly of dealing, as principal, in financial instruments) are **excluded** from this definition;
– **patent royalties**; and
– a **sale of a UK patent right** by a non-UK resident.

> MEMO POINTS   Where a **royalty** relates to copyright, income tax must be deducted if the recipient usually lives outside the UK.

41080
ss 901, 903
ITA 2007

However, the **general rule is modified** to allow such payments to be made gross if they are made by a company to one of the following recipients:
– a UK-resident company or permanent establishment (PE);
– a partnership in which all the partners are either UK-resident companies/PEs or approved bodies;
– an approved body; or
– a manager of an ISA.

The onus is on the payer to satisfy itself that the recipient falls within one of the above categories. An initial **penalty** of up to $3,000 (and a continuing penalty of $600 per day thereafter) can be imposed if HMRC are persuaded that the payer could not reasonably have believed that the payments could be made gross.

> MEMO POINTS   An **approved body** is:
> – a local authority;
> – a health service body;
> – a public office, crown department or charity;
> – a scientific research organisation;
> – the UK Atomic Energy Authority;
> – the National Radiological Protection Board;
> – an exempt approved superannuation scheme;
> – a parliamentary pension fund;
> – certain exempt colonial pension funds;
> – an exempt retirement annuity trust scheme; and
> – a registered pension scheme.

41085
ss 930, 933–937
ITA 2007

The **rate of tax** which must be deducted depends on the nature of the payment. Prior to 6 April 2008 the general rule was that income tax at the basic rate (22%) should be deducted. However, where the payment was annual interest, the lower rate of income tax applies (20%). From that date both rates are now the same and as such the distinction for these purposes is irrelevant, the deduction always being made at 20%.

41090

s 975 ITA 2007

MEMO POINTS   1. A **tax deduction certificate** listing the following information must be provided to the recipient of a payment made under deduction of tax, if requested:
– the gross amount of the payment;
– the rate and the amount of income tax deducted;
– the net payment actually made; and
– the date the payment was made.
2. Any tax deducted from payments must be **paid to HMRC** unless offset by tax suffered at source. For payment requirements see ¶47120.

C. Receipt of income taxed at source

Available relief

41120   Where a company has received income from which income tax has been deducted at source, relief for the tax suffered **may be obtained** in the following order:
– offset against payments made in the same quarter;
– carried forward to the next quarter within the same accounting period and offset;
– deduction from mainstream corporation tax liability;
– repayment from HMRC.

Offset against payments made

41125
ss 952, 953
ITA 2007
Companies need to account for income tax on form CT61 on a quarterly basis (¶47115). In any one quarter, receipts can be set against payments made by the company under deduction of tax. Only the net amount of tax needs to be paid to HMRC, with any **unrelieved amounts** being carried forward until the next quarter.

EXAMPLE   A Ltd pays annual interest of £10,000 (gross) during the period ended 30 June and receives income, under deduction of tax, of £12,000 (net). The income tax position is as follows:

		£
Tax deducted from annual interest	£10,000 @ 20%	2,000.00
Tax suffered	£12,000 × 20/80	(3,000.00)
Net income tax suffered		(1,000.00)

To the extent that **income tax suffered is less than income tax deducted** by the company, the company must pay the difference to HMRC.

EXAMPLE   B Ltd makes annual payments of £1,000 (gross) during the period ended 30 June and receives income under deduction of tax of £600 (net). The income tax position is as follows:

		£
Tax deducted from annual payments	£1,000 @ 20%	200.00
Tax suffered	£600 × 20/80	(150.00)
Net income tax payable to HMRC		50.00

Deduction from mainstream corporation tax liability

41130
s 967 CTA 2010
If any amounts have not been relieved via form CT61 at the end of the accounting period, the **balance** may be deducted from the corporation tax payable.

EXAMPLE   C Ltd has one associated company and has trading profits of £50,000. It received income under deduction of tax of £30,000 (net) for the period ended 31 March. The tax position is as follows:

	£	£
Trading profit	50,000	
Income received under deduction of tax (gross)		
£30,000 × 100/80	37,500	
Profit chargeable to corporation tax		87,500
Tax thereon @ 20%		17,500.00
Income tax suffered at source £37,500 @ 20%		(7,500.00)
Net corporation tax payable		10,000.00

Repayment from HMRC

If any **income tax remains unrelieved** (i.e. it exceeds the corporation tax liability), a repayment may be obtained from HMRC. Evidence will need to be submitted in support of any repayment, in the form of tax deduction certificates.   **41135**

EXAMPLE During the period ended 31 March D Ltd (which has three associated companies) incurred a trading loss of £5,000 and received annual payments of £15,000 (net). The tax position is as follows:

	£	£
Income received under deduction of tax (gross)		
£15,000 × 100/80	18,750	
Trading loss set against general income	(5,000)	
Profit chargeable to corporation tax		13,750
Tax thereon @ 20%		2,750
Income tax suffered at source 18,750 @ 20%		(3,750)
Net income tax repayable		(1,000)

Repayments of income tax in this way should be claimed by completing the appropriate section of the corporation tax return. HMRC are not required to make a repayment until the corporation tax liability has been finally agreed.   **41140**

A **provisional repayment** may be made where it is clear that a repayment will be due – for example, where evidence of substantial losses is available. If a provisional repayment is made which subsequently proves to be excessive, it must be repaid to HMRC and interest will be charged.

SECTION 2

ACT

A. Background

Historically, companies making qualifying distributions had to deduct tax from the dividend at source. This was known as advance corporation tax (ACT) and the net dividend was known as a franked payment. Any such payments received by a company were known as franked investment income (FII (¶40115)).   **41190**

If, during an accounting period, a company's franked payments had exceeded its FII, ACT would have to be paid to HMRC as, essentially, an advance on the company's mainstream corporation tax liability, as it could (up to a certain limit) either be:
– offset against the final tax liability; or
– surrendered to a subsidiary for offset against its corporation tax liability.
The restriction on the amount of offset meant that many companies had surplus ACT, which could be used in a number of ways, including being carried forward for offset against future corporation tax liabilities.

> ⌐MEMO POINTS⌐ **Surplus ACT** carried forward could not be surrendered to a subsidiary. However, the amount of current year ACT which could be surrendered to a subsidiary was not limited to the amount the subsidiary could use. In addition, an election for surrender had a time limit of 6 years from the end of the accounting period in which the ACT arose, so an election could be made subsequently if it became apparent that the subsidiary could utilise that ACT.

41195   When ACT was abolished in 1999, a number of companies still had surplus ACT which they had not been able to use. This surplus ACT can still be carried forward and set against future tax liabilities of the company holding a surplus at 5 April 1999.

However, the system of shadow ACT (¶41225+) limits the amount of surplus ACT which can be used, in a way similar to the old ACT rules.

> ⌐MEMO POINTS⌐ 1. If a company feels that it is unlikely to be able to recover its surplus ACT, it may **opt out of the shadow ACT scheme**. Where a company is a member of a 51% group of companies (¶65505), such an election may only be made by the parent company for the whole group. Individual members of the group cannot be excluded.
> 2. For modifications to these rules when applied to members of a 51% **group of companies** see ¶69665+.

B. Shadow ACT

Calculation

41225
SI 1999/358

The shadow ACT regime is simply a method used to calculate how much of the surplus ACT brought forward from dividends paid before 6 April 1999 can be utilised. It is calculated **as follows**:
a. calculate the shadow ACT (distributions paid × 25% (¶41230));
b. calculate the maximum ACT capacity (taxable profits × 20%); and
c. deduct **a.** from **b.** to give the ACT available for offset against the company's tax liability (¶41235).

Shadow ACT capacity

41230   When calculating shadow ACT, the 25% is applied to all distributions (whether qualifying or not) made by a company during an accounting period, with the exception of:
– intra-group dividends; and
– manufactured dividends.

The **calculation is modified** where a company has also received franked investment income during the accounting period, as follows:

$$\frac{FD}{\frac{(FI)}{\underset{\overline{FD}}{Net}}} \times 25\% = \text{shadow ACT}$$

Where:
FD is franked distributions, calculated as distributions made × 125%; and
FI is franked income, calculated as:
– franked investment income × 9/8; plus
– any surplus FII brought forward from earlier periods.

EXAMPLE A Ltd makes a distribution of £100,000 on 1 September and receives a distribution of £25,000. A Ltd has surplus FII brought forward of £22,000. Shadow ACT is calculated as follows:

		£
Franked distributions	£100,000 × 125%	125,000
Franked income	£25,000 × 9/8	(28,125)
	Surplus FII b/fwd	(22,000)
Net distributions		74,875
Shadow ACT	£74,875 × 25%	18,718.75

MEMO POINTS 1. ACT is always stated to 2 decimal places.
2. If the franked **income** for a period **exceeds** the franked **distributions**, this is surplus franked investment income and must be carried forward and included in the computation for the subsequent period.

ACT available for offset

The **maximum surplus ACT** which can be offset in an accounting period is calculated as follows:

41235

$$A - B$$

where:
- A is the company's ACT capacity – that is, 20% of the company's PCTCT (¶40000+); and
- B is the shadow ACT attributed to that period.

Assuming that a company has capacity to offset surplus ACT, the corporation tax liability for the period is reduced. The figure after deduction of ACT is known as the mainstream corporation tax payable. No reduction is made for shadow ACT. If the **capacity is less** than the full amount of surplus ACT, the balance is carried forward to the subsequent period.

MEMO POINTS If a company is liable to tax on an apportionment of profits from a **controlled foreign company** (¶90555+), the apportionment is included in PCTCT for these purposes.

EXAMPLE B Ltd has surplus ACT of £125,000. During its accounting period ended 31 March, it made a distribution of £50,000 and received franked investment income of £13,000. Assuming profits of £350,000 and a corporation tax liability (before ACT) of £105,000, the ACT position is as follows:

		£
Profit chargeable to corporation tax		350,000
Maximum ACT capacity	£350,000 × 20%	70,000
Distributions	£50,000 × 125%	62,500
Franked income	£13,000 × 9/8	(14,625)
Net distributions		47,875
Shadow ACT	£47,875 × 25%	11,968.75
Maximum ACT capacity		70,000.00
Less: Shadow ACT		(11,968.75)
Surplus ACT offset against corporation tax liability		58,031.25
Corporation tax liability		105,000.00
Less: Surplus ACT		(58,031.25)
Mainstream corporation tax payable		46,968.75
Surplus ACT c/fwd	£125,000 – £58,031.25	66,968.75

Interaction with income tax and double tax relief

41240   Surplus ACT is deducted from the company's corporation tax liability in **priority** to any income tax suffered (¶41050). **Double tax relief**, however, is allocated against any tax due on overseas profits in priority to surplus ACT.

These rules are generally to the company's advantage. If a company cannot fully recover income tax by deduction from the corporation tax liability, it can claim a refund from HMRC (¶41135), whereas unrelieved ACT is simply carried forward. The order of offset therefore restricts the amount of relief which may be lost.

C. Surplus shadow ACT

41270   It is possible that a company will have surplus shadow ACT for an accounting period. This is where the shadow ACT exceeds the maximum which can be utilised against the current year corporation tax liability.

Surplus shadow ACT is carried back and **treated as** shadow ACT of the previous 6 years, set against later years first.

However, shadow ACT carried back **displaces surplus ACT** offset during a certain period:
a. for companies with regular 12-month accounting periods, the period is the accounting period immediately prior to the one in which the surplus shadow ACT arises; and
b. for companies with irregular accounting periods, the period is determined as follows:
– the period begins 24 months before the end of the accounting period in which the surplus shadow ACT arises; and
– the period ends the day before the start of the accounting period in which the surplus shadow ACT arises.
A simple way to calculate the period is to deduct the length of the accounting period giving rise to surplus shadow ACT (in months) from 24. The number remaining is the number of months for which the surplus is carried back. Surplus shadow ACT carried back is used in the latest period first. Where an accounting period falls partly within the period, the surplus shadow ACT is apportioned on a time basis.

Any **displaced surplus ACT** continues to be carried forward, unless the company has opted out of the shadow ACT regime, in which case it is lost.

EXAMPLE   C Ltd prepares its accounts to 31 December regularly until 2012, when a set of accounts is prepared for the 8 months to 31 August 2013. Surplus shadow ACT of £27,500 arose in the period to 31 August 2013. Surplus ACT had been used as follows:
Year ended 31 December 2011 £16,000
Year ended 31 December 2012 £15,000
Balancing remaining unused £18,000.
The surplus shadow ACT will be carried back as follows:

Maximum period for carry back (in months)	24
Months in period in which surplus arose	(8)
Remaining period for carry back	16

i.e. the 12-month period ended 31 December 2012 and the 4 months to 31 December 2011.

		£
Surplus ACT position:		
Balance of surplus ACT		18,000
Year ended 31 December 2012		
Surplus ACT displaced		15,000
4 months to 31 December 2011		
Surplus ACT displaced	4/12 × 16,000	5,333
Total surplus ACT remaining at 31 August 2013		38,333

D. Opting out of the shadow ACT regime

Once a company has **fully utilised its surplus ACT**, it is no longer within the shadow ACT regulations.   **41300**

If, whilst **surplus ACT remains unused**, the company decides that it no longer wants to attempt to utilise the surplus ACT, it can notify HMRC that it wishes to opt out of the regime. In this case, its final accounting period for these purposes is the period in which the notification is made. No surplus ACT can be utilised after the end of the final accounting period. However, the company may still be affected by the shadow ACT regulations. Shadow ACT continues to be calculated for any accounting period beginning in the 12 months immediately following the accounting period in which the notification is given, and the normal rules for the carry back of surplus shadow ACT apply. If these rules result in the displacement of surplus ACT, that surplus ACT is no longer recoverable.

SECTION 3

Community investment tax relief

Community investment tax relief (CITR) is **designed to promote** investment in disadvantaged areas and communities by providing a measure of tax relief on such investments. The scheme is run jointly by HMRC and the Department for Business, Innovation and Skills (BIS). The investment mechanism is provided by Community Development Finance Institutions (CDFI), which either invest directly into projects or invest in other CDFIs. An investor can only obtain tax relief by investing in an accredited CDFI. CDFI accreditation is managed by BIS, while claims for tax relief are assessed by HMRC.   **41350**

Tax relief is given in the form of a reduction in the corporation tax liability, normally at a maximum of 5% of the amount invested, for the first five years of the investment. The relief for any accounting period is also limited by the amount of corporation tax due, so a tax liability cannot be turned into a refund, although surplus relief may be carried forward in certain circumstances. Total tax relief available is therefore normally 25% of the amount invested. The investor must have a tax relief certificate issued by the CDFI in order to make a claim for relief.   s 220 CTA 2010

Where an **investment is made** by a company **on or after 1 April 2013**, further rules allow for the possibility of carrying forward unused relief, and also set a maximum level of relief which can be granted over a 3-year period.

A. Types of qualifying investment

The taxpayer can invest in the CDFI by making a **loan** to it, or by **subscribing for shares** or securities in it. Where the investor is a **bank**, the provision of an overdraft does not count as making a loan for these purposes. A bank deposit would be regarded as a loan by the investor, so if the bank is an accredited CDFI the deposit could qualify for CITR if the terms are set correctly.   **41380**
ss 221, 225
CTA 2010;
CITM4020

Loans

A loan should be made in full but **drawdown** over a period no longer than 18 months is permitted. The loan is **deemed to be made** on the date of the first drawdown. In order to   **41385**
s 226 CTA 2010

qualify for relief the loan **should not** be convertible or exchangeable into a form which is redeemable within the 5-year investment period. **Repayments required** under the loan agreement should not exceed the amounts shown in the table below:

Year	Amount of permitted cumulative repayment
1	Nil
2	Nil
3	Up to 25% of the loan capital outstanding at the end of Year 2
4	Up to 50% of the loan capital outstanding at the end of Year 2
5	Up to 75% of the loan capital outstanding at the end of Year 2

s 226 CTA 2010

MEMO POINTS   1. Any repayments which result from **normal commercial terms being breached** will not count for this requirement, provided that the relevant loan term is no more likely to be breached than a reasonable term in a non-CITR loan.
2. Where a CDFI is in the form of a **partnership**, a partner's capital account will not qualify for relief.

Shares and securities

41390
ss 227, 228
CTA 2010

Shares and securities **must be** fully paid up in cash from the date of investment, meaning that there must be no undertaking to pay further cash in connection with the acquisition. They **must not be** convertible into, or exchangeable into, a form which is redeemable within the 5-year investment period.

s 230 CTA 2010

MEMO POINTS   The investment will **not qualify** if the investor arranges to protect itself against the investment risk in some way. The exception to this is if the risk protection would be expected commercially if the investment was made by a banking business.

B. Investor conditions

41420
ss 231 – 235
CTA 2010

In order to qualify for relief, an investor:
– must be the **sole beneficial owner**;
– **must not control** the CDFI (this also includes anyone connected with the investor, or where a situation exists that may allow the investor, or someone connected with them, to gain control);
– must **not be a CDFI** (to prevent a double layer of tax relief); and
– must not intend to **avoid tax** in relation to the investment.

C. Relief

41450
ss 220 – 223
CTA 2010

Where the **investment was made before 1 April 2013**, relief is limited to no more than 5% of the amount invested, or the amount of corporation tax due, whichever is lower. It is **given in the accounting period** in which the date of the investment falls, and the accounting periods in which the following four anniversaries of that date fall. Investors may not therefore get as much relief as they were expecting where a shorter than normal accounting period results in a lower tax liability before relief. As relief cannot be carried forward or back, any potential restriction needs to be taken into account before changing an accounting period end.

Where the **investment was made on or after 1 April 2013**, the above rules largely still apply, although relief which is unused in an accounting period will now be able to be carried forward and used in subsequent periods (to the extent that those accounting periods contain the four anniversaries of the date of the investment). In addition, in order to comply with rules regarding the granting of State Aid, a maximum relief of 200,000 euros can be granted over a 3-year period. This maximum amount will be further reduced by any de minimis aid which the investor receives from the EU.

Relief must be **claimed** after the end of the accounting period and within the usual time limits (¶46425).

EXAMPLE

1. A Ltd invested £150,000 in a CDFI on 1 July 2011. Its year end is 31 December. The CITR available for each year from 31 December 2011 to 31 December 2015 is £7,500 p.a.

2. The same facts as in 1. but the company changes its year end in 2013 to 30 June. The relief will now be spread as follows:

Period	Amount of relief (£)
Year ended 31 December 2011	7,500
Year ended 31 December 2012	7,500
Period ended 30 June 2013	Nil
Years ended 30 June 2014 to 2016	7,500 p.a.

Amount invested

Tax relief is given as a percentage of the invested amount. For **shares and securities** the invested amount is the amount subscribed and held continuously. Any deemed disposal and re-acquisition under the capital gains legislation will break continuous ownership for these purposes.

41455
ss 222, 267
CTA 2010

MEMO POINTS   1. If any **bonus** shares are subsequently issued, they are treated as forming part of the original issue still held.
2. **Rights** issues are acquired for all capital gains and CITR purposes at the time of the rights issue, for the consideration then given.

s 241 CTA 2010

s 151BB
TCGA 1992

The invested amount for a **loan** is more complex, as set out below:

41460

Accounting period	Invested amount
In which investment date falls	Average capital balance for Year 1 of 5-year period
In which anniversary of investment date falls	Average capital balance for Year 2 of 5-year period
In which the second, third and fourth anniversaries of the investment date fall	Lower of average capital balance for the: – 12 months beginning with the anniversary of the investment date in that period; and – 6 months beginning 18 months after the investment date.
Note: The average capital balance is the mean of the daily outstanding balances for that period.	

Permitted returns of value

An investor can receive certain returns that will **not affect the investor's relief**. These are:
– reasonable payment for goods, services or facilities provided by the investor;
– payment of interest at reasonable commercial rates;
– payment of a company dividend, or other distribution, that does not exceed a normal return on shares or securities in that company;
– payment for the acquisition of an asset at or below its market value;
– rental payments for the use of property, provided that they do not exceed a commercial rate; and
– payment to satisfy an ordinary trade debt.

41465

Investors are also allowed certain **returns on their investments**, within set limits. These are as shown below:

	Permitted return	
Period	Loans	Shares
Years 1 and 2[1]	No repayment allowed	No return allowed
Year 3	Up to 25% of the average capital balance for the period of 6 months beginning 18 months after the investment date	Up to 25% of the invested capital
Year 4	Up to 50% of the average capital balance for the period of 6 months beginning 18 months after the investment date	Up to 50% of the invested capital
Year 5	Up to 75% of the average capital balance for the period of 6 months beginning 18 months after the investment date	Up to 75% of the invested capital

Note:
1. No payments can be made in the year prior to the investment.

41470 Where there has been a return on investment within the permitted levels, the relief previously given will be unaffected but the relief for future periods will be reduced.

> EXAMPLE B Ltd made a qualifying investment of £100,000. In Year 4 it received a return of value of £50,000, which is within the permitted maximum.
> In Years 1 to 3 it will be entitled to claim relief of £5,000 p.a. (£100,000 x 5%). In Years 4 and 5 this will drop to £2,500 p.a. (£50,000 x 5%).

D. Withdrawal of relief

41500 Relief will be withdrawn for earlier years where either there is a disposal of the investment or there has been a return in excess of the permitted amounts (¶41465).

Disposal

41505
ss 243, 244
CTA 2010

Disposal in this situation is the same as that for the taxation of chargeable gains (¶30080). **Unless** the disposal falls into one of the following categories, all relief previously given will be withdrawn:
– distribution of a loan during a winding up of the CDFI:
– the entire loss, destruction, dissipation or extinction of the investment;
– a claim under the negligible value rules (¶31720); or
– disposal of the investment after the CDFI ceases to be accredited.

Where any of these occur, the relief withdrawn for earlier periods is restricted to 5% of the amount received (or if full relief was not given a proportion of it will be withdrawn). This will also be the case where **shares** are disposed of in an arm's-length transaction. Where the relief withdrawn relates to an **investment made on or after 1 April 2013**, then the rules relating to the carry forward of unused relief will also need to be considered if the disposal is of shares.

Excessive returns of value

41510
ss 236, 237
CTA 2010

If returns of value exceed the permitted limits (¶41465), CITR will be lost in full for any period for which it has been claimed.

> MEMO POINTS 1. In looking at the average balance certain **non-standard repayments** are ignored, such as discretionary repayments by the CDFI, where these do not arise from the terms of the loan or as a result of the CDFI breaching an obligation under the loan agreement.

2. Amounts that are **insignificant** are ignored in looking at this test. HMRC guidance states that amounts of more than £1,000 are unlikely to be considered insignificant. If more than one amount has been received, the aggregate is used to consider whether the total payments are insignificant or not.

Procedure

Where an event occurs that results in relief for earlier years being withdrawn, the company must **inform** HMRC no later than 12 months after the end of the period in which the event occurred.

41515

Relief is **withdrawn** by way of an assessment that can be raised up to 6 years after the end of the period for which relief was claimed.

PART 7

Compliance

Compliance
Summary

The numbers cross-refer to paragraphs.

Records

What has to be kept?

Statutory obligation

The records that a company is required to keep are those that enable it to deliver a complete and correct tax return. The records that **have to be kept** include records of:
– all receipts and expenses in the course of the company's activities, trading or otherwise, including details of what they relate to; and
– where a trade involves dealing in goods, all sales and purchases made in the course of that trade.

45000
Sch 18 para 21
FA 1998

Although HMRC have the power to specify, by way of regulation, what **specific information** must be kept, or not kept, no such regulations have yet been made.

HMRC guidance

The **type of records** that a business keeps will depend on the size and complexity of its affairs. As such there is no detailed requirement in the legislation. HMRC guidance splits the records to be kept into two separate categories: accounting records and business records.

45005
CH 10200

Accounting records include those required by Companies House (¶45125); if these regulations are complied with, that will be sufficient to satisfy HMRC also.

Business accounting records are more detailed in nature and can be described as those required to prepare the accounting records needed to satisfy Companies House. HMRC give **examples** of such records that it may be useful to keep:
– annual accounts, including profit and loss statement and balance sheet;
– bank statements and paying-in slips;

- a cash book and any other accounts books that are kept;
- purchases and sales books or ledgers;
- invoices and any record of daily takings such as till rolls;
- order records and delivery notes;
- a petty cash book; and
- other relevant business correspondence.

CH 217000

These records must be kept up to date and be easily accessible in the event of an enquiry by HMRC. However, HMRC have no objection to the records being held overseas, provided that they are produced upon request.

> MEMO POINTS   Certain legislation requires further records to be kept where the rules apply – for example, the transfer pricing legislation. These are detailed in the relevant parts of *Corporation Tax Memo*.

Failure to keep proper records

45010
Sch 18 para 23
FA 1998;
EM 04650

Failing to keep proper records could attract a **penalty** of up to £3,000. However, HMRC have said that they do not expect to charge a penalty in every case of poor record-keeping. They are more likely to calculate any penalty levied for understatement of tax based on the fact that records were not kept or preserved.

However, in more serious cases where, for example, there is evidence of deliberate destruction of records to obstruct an enquiry or a history of poor record-keeping, it is likely a penalty will be levied. HMRC guidance suggests that on the first occasion that it becomes apparent such action has been taken, but this cannot be proven, a warning letter will be issued. Further failures will most likely attract a penalty.

> MEMO POINTS   The situation regarding lost or destroyed records is covered at ¶45210.

SECTION 2

Format of records

45060
Sch 18 para 22
FA 1998

Historically, HMRC insisted on records being kept in their original form. However, they have updated their record-keeping requirements to keep pace with developments in information technology and storage media. Records can now be **preserved** in any form and by any means. Alternatively the **information** in them can be stored in any form or by any means. This means records do not need to be kept in their original form and can be stored in an electronic format rather than in the original paper version. The only current **exceptions** to this rule are:
- dividend vouchers;
- statements showing the tax withheld from discretionary trust payments;
- statements showing income tax withheld at source;
- records for tax withheld relating to subcontractors; and
- details of foreign taxes, including those not paid because of developmental reliefs allowed for in the double taxation arrangements.

> MEMO POINTS   HMRC have the **power** to make conditions or specify exclusions from these requirements.

45065
CH 13100

HMRC guidance suggests the following as examples of **how the information can be stored**:
- photography, so that an exact record of the document is kept but typically in a smaller format, such as microfiche;
- computerised invoicing system that can accurately reproduce invoices on demand; and
- electronic invoicing systems where two or more computers exchange invoicing details electronically without any paper having been generated.

> MEMO POINTS   **Both sides** of a document must be captured where there is information on the reverse. However, if this contains standard terms and conditions, it is only necessary to keep one copy of this, making a new copy when any changes are made.

Computer records

Records that are kept on computer may be kept either on the computer itself or on some external device, such as an external hard drive, magnetic tape or DVD. It is also possible for data to be held remotely or accessed online.

45070
CH 13400

It will still be necessary to retain the **paper documentation**, unless an exact replica can be reproduced by the system. In essence this requirement will only be satisfied by keeping accurate and clear scans of entire documents.

Companies have to ensure that the **information remains accessible** and can be legibly reproduced upon request. This may be an issue where software is changed or updated, or an annual licence is allowed to lapse. This may also be an issue where the software does not work on an upgraded operating system. Where any of these happen, arrangements must be in place to reproduce the information.

Taxpayers have to give reasonable assistance to **HMRC** where computer **access** is required in order for HMRC to inspect any document or information.

45075
s 114 FA 2008

SECTION 3

Companies House requirements

Companies are required by law to keep certain records. HMRC have said that where companies comply with these rules, they are highly likely to satisfy HMRC's own conditions regarding accounting records. The records **required by law** must show and explain the company's transactions and set out its financial position at any time, at that time. They must enable the directors to prepare accounts that comply with the Companies Act and International Accounting Standards, if applicable.

45125

Information

Accounting records must, in particular, contain entries showing all money received and expended by the company and a record of the assets and liabilities. Also, where the company's business involves dealing in goods, the records must contain:
– a statement of stock held by the company at the end of each financial year;
– all statements of stocktaking from which any statement of stock is taken or prepared; and
– a statement of all goods sold and purchased, other than by ordinary retail trade; this should list the goods, the buyers and sellers.

45130
s 386 CA 2006

Location

The company's records **must be kept at** the registered office or such other place as the directors think suitable. The records must always be open for inspection by the company's officers. Records can be kept outside the UK but only if accounts and returns prepared from those records are sent to the UK. The accounts and returns sent to the UK must show the financial position of the company at intervals of not more than 6 months and allow the company's directors to prepare accounts that comply with the Companies Act.

45135
s 388 CA 2006

Interpretation

The ICAEW has published a technical release providing guidance for directors on accounting records under the Companies Act 2006. This guidance says that the **accounting records should be** "an orderly, classified collection of information capable of timely retrieval" and that "an unorganised collection of vouchers and documents will not suffice". The accounting records should be kept up to date but need not be completed instantaneously, provided

45140
ICAEW TECH 01/11

that completion is within a reasonable period of time. What is "reasonable" will vary from business to business.

SECTION 4

Retention periods

Standard periods

45190

Sch 18 para 21
FA 1998

Whilst the type of records required by HMRC and Companies House overlap, HMRC specify a more stringent retention period. Companies Act 2006 mandates a 3-year period from the date when the records are made for **private companies**, or 6 years for **public limited companies**. HMRC's requirements start with a basic 6-year retention period.

For **taxation**, the retention period ends on the later of:
– 6 years from the end of the accounting period;
– when any HMRC enquiry is closed; and
– when the period during which HMRC can raise an enquiry ends (¶50445).

45195

In some cases a document may be **relevant to more than one accounting period**. This may be something as simple as a document relating to an insurance premium where the period of cover spans two accounting periods, or something more complex such as a loan agreement where deductions are made over a number of years. Where this is the case, the document must be retained until 6 years after the last accounting period to which it relates.

The same will be the case where **capital assets** are purchased. In such a case the documentation will be required to be held until 6 years after the asset is no longer held by the company, be this by sale, destruction or otherwise.

Shorter retention period

45200

CH 216000

HMRC have the power to set a shorter period for retention but have not currently done so. However, they will consider a **request** to shorten the period if approached by a taxpayer. HMRC will consider requests sympathetically, taking into account the taxpayer's compliance history, as well as the cost and effort involved if the taxpayer has to keep the records for the full period. Agreement should be reached in writing.

Late notice to file received

45205

Sch 18 para 21
FA 1998

If the company does not receive a notice to deliver a return until **after the sixth anniversary** of the end of the accounting period then, if it still has any of the records at that point, it must retain them until the end of any HMRC enquiry or until the enquiry window has passed.

Loss of records

45210

Where a company's records are lost, destroyed or stolen and they cannot be replaced, the company should inform HMRC as soon as possible. The company should then endeavour to recreate the records as accurately as is possible from whatever material is still available. How successful this will be will ultimately depend on the size and complexity of the company, along with what information can be gathered from other parties – for example, copy bank statements, or hire purchase documentation. This information should then be used to complete any necessary returns, highlighting to HMRC any figures that are provisional or estimated (¶46190).

There is no guidance covering the situation where records are lost or destroyed **and all returns are already complete**. However, it would be best practice to advise HMRC of this, so as to pre-empt any suspicion of deliberate destruction of records should an enquiry subsequently be initiated.

Reporting

The self-assessment regime was introduced in 1999 and squarely puts the **onus** on individual companies to ensure their corporation tax liability is properly calculated, reported and the liability paid on time, without the issue of an assessment by HMRC. The senior accounting officer duties also force large companies to verify that they have appropriate accounting processes in place. With the onus on companies in this way, HMRC are developing a more risk-assessed basis for their review of companies. The disclosure of tax avoidance schemes rules give HMRC an early opportunity to identify tax planning schemes by requiring users and promoters to disclose them before making a return. HMRC may, as a result, introduce legislation with immediate (or even restrospective) effect. Specific reporting obligations arising in these areas are discussed below.

46000

MEMO POINTS For information on when and how a company must notify its chargeability to corporation tax see ¶60050+.

SECTION 1

Corporation tax returns

46050   The self-assessment system for corporation tax requires companies to **file a complete annual return** within a specific deadline, in a specific format, containing relevant claims and elections. All returns made after 31 March 2011 for periods ending on or after 1 April 2010 must be made in an approved electronic format and filed online.

> MEMO POINTS   Companies that are either dormant (¶7000+) or treated as dormant (¶7205) are not required to complete returns annually.

A. Exemptions from electronic filing

46080
SI 2009/3218;
SI 2010/2942

The only businesses exempted from electronic filing are those where:
– **religious** observance prevents or is incompatible with the use of electronic methods; or
– the company involved is considered to be **insolvent**.

Exemption must be **confirmed** with HMRC.

B. Filing period and deadline

46110   A corporation tax return must be filed within 12 months of the end of the period of account (¶3040). The period of account for most companies will be the 12 months ending with the statutory accounting reference date, so the corporate tax return filing deadline will be 12 months after that. If later, the filing deadline will be 3 months after the **notice to file a return** is received. Such a notice is **deemed to be received** 4 days after it is issued by HMRC by post.

Sch 18 para 5
FA 1998

If the period on the **notice to file a return does not match** the accounting period, the following rules determine the return or returns required.

a. If an accounting period **ends during the notice period**, a return is required for that accounting period. If more than one accounting period ends within the notice period, returns are required for both.

> EXAMPLE   A Ltd prepares accounts for the 12 months to 31 December 2013. The specified period in the notice to file is 1 January 2013 to 31 December 2013. The return period is therefore 1 January 2013 to 31 December 2013. If the company ceased to trade on 30 June 2013 but continued to receive investment income, two returns would be required: 1 January 2013 to 30 June 2013 and 1 July 2013 to 31 December 2013.

b. If the company is **outside the scope** of corporation tax (for example, it is dormant) throughout the notice period, a nil return is required for the notice period, although in many cases HMRC will agree not to issue a notice in these circumstances.

c. If an accounting period **begins during the notice period** (for example, where a company starts to trade), a return is required for the period from the start of the notice period until the start of the accounting period.

> EXAMPLE   B Ltd was incorporated on 1 January 2013 but did not acquire a source of income until 8 July 2013. It prepares its first accounts to 30 June 2014. The notice to file specifies a period of

1 January 2013 to 31 December 2013. A return is required for the period 1 January 2013 to 7 July 2013.

d. If **none of the above** applies no return is required. In this case it is best practice to notify HMRC that a return will not be filed. Otherwise a penalty will automatically be charged and will need to be appealed.

EXAMPLE C Ltd was incorporated on 1 March 2012 but did not commence trading until 1 May 2012. Accounts are prepared for the year to 30 April 2013. The notice to file specifies a period of 1 June 2012 to 29 February 2013. No return will be required.

MEMO POINTS Where a company **does not receive a notice to file** it must advise HMRC of its chargeability for the period within 12 months of the end of the accounting period. On a practical level this is typically carried out by filing a return, although this is not necessary to satisfy the requirement. For the penalty for failing to notify chargeability see ¶52110.

Sch 18 para 2
FA 1998

Period of account longer than 12 months

Where the period of account is longer than 12 months, so that it is split into two accounting periods (¶3060) for tax purposes, the filing deadline is still based on the end of the period of account. For periods of account **longer than 18 months**, the filing deadline is 30 months after the start of the period for which accounts are prepared, or 3 months after the notice to file a return is received, if this is later. Note that the Companies Act 2006 does not permit accounting reference periods of longer than 18 months.

46115
Sch 18 para 14
FA 1998

C. Composition of return

In order for a company to satisfy its filing requirements for a self-assessment return it **must file** a corporate tax return (form CT600 and any supplementary pages required) in XML format, a computation for the period (in iXBRL format) and statutory accounts as prepared for the members (also in iXBRL format). If **any of these items are not present** the return will be considered incomplete.

46145

MEMO POINTS Where a small or medium-sized company prepares **abbreviated accounts** these will not be sufficient for filing with HMRC.

1. Return

Outline of main return

An electronic CT600 must be submitted in XML format. XML stands for eXtensible Mark-up Language. This can be **produced** by using the free HMRC template or commercial software. The CT600 **contains** a number of standard pages, together with supplementary pages that are submitted only if required.

46175

The short version is for most **straightforward companies and clubs** and is only 4 pages long. The full version of 8 pages is for **all other companies** and in particular must be used by companies:
- subject to the **controlled foreign companies** regime;
- claiming or surrendering **group** or consortium relief;
- subject to the **large companies** payment on account rules;
- with non-trading gains or losses from **intangible** assets;
- which are members of **group** payment arrangements;
- with **overseas** profits or losses; and
- with a number of other types of income or loss (¶46185).

46180 The full version of the form contains the following sections:

Page	Details
1	Summary of company information
2 – 3	Summary of turnover and profits from various sources, including deductions and reliefs
4 – 5	Detailed tax calculation, including reliefs in the forms of tax, and payment reconciliation
6	Information regarding capital allowances, and research and development expenditure
7	Losses, deficits and excess amounts
7 – 8	Repayments of tax
8	Declaration that the return is correct and complete

Supplementary pages

46185 The supplementary pages available are listed below with an indication of whether they can be used with a short return. Where they cannot but the pages are required, a long return must be completed.

Form	Description	Can be used with short return?	¶¶
600A	Loans to participators by close companies	✓	¶75575
600B	Controlled foreign companies (and bank levy)		¶90555
600C	Group and consortium relief		¶66050
600D	Overseas life assurance business		-
600E	Charity and community amateur sports clubs	✓	¶86000
600F	Tonnage tax		-
600G	Corporate venturing scheme		¶80545
600H	Cross-border royalties		¶90345
600I	Supplementary charge in respect of ring fence trades		-
600J	Disclosure of tax avoidance schemes	✓	¶46485

Complete and accurate return

46190 Each return must contain a **signed declaration** that, to the best of the knowledge of the person making the return, it is complete and correct. A complete and correct return is one that contains accurate figures and all other information that the company is required to include.

If the company has **not been able to establish a final figure** to be included in the return, it may include a best estimate, provided that it can show that it took all reasonable steps to reach the correct figure. A return submitted like this will not be regarded as incomplete. However, HMRC should be advised as soon as possible after the company becomes aware that an estimate is no longer the best one, or an accurate figure becomes available.

---

2. Corporate tax computation

46220 The computation acts as a **bridge** between the figures shown in the accounts and the figures shown in the return itself. For instance, the return only requires the turnover and taxable profit from a trade to be shown but this does not show how the profit from trade is made up. The accounts will show the various expenses but not all of these may be allowable and as such the profit shown in the accounts will not necessarily (and in most cases will not) match the taxable profit. The computation shows how the profit per the accounts is adjusted to reach the taxable profit shown on the return. This **must now be lodged** electronically in iXBRL format.

Rounding of figures

Companies with **turnover in excess of £5,000,000** may submit tax computations showing the figures rounded to thousands of pounds, where the business profit or loss figure has been prepared on that basis. The **limit applies** to turnover for the current year, or the previous year's turnover if the current year's is below the threshold. However, rounded figures **cannot be used** when calculating the actual tax payable.

46225
CTM 93220

The company will **need to provide a certificate** explaining the basis on which the rounding has been calculated, and stating that it has been prepared free of bias, is consistent and gives a fair result. The certificate must also say which software program (if any) has been used to produce the rounded figures. In **subsequent years** the certificate need only say that there has been no change in approach, should that be the case.

> <u>MEMO POINTS</u> 1. Where the company is part of a **group** it is the company's turnover only and not the group turnover that is considered.
> 2. For this purpose the turnover includes any investment and property receipts.
> 3. Rounding is **not available** for calculating:
> – amounts surrendered or claimed under the group relief provisions;
> – losses carried forward or back;
> – capital gains (apart from incidental costs of purchase or disposal);
> – tax credit relief; or
> – capital allowances.

iXBRL format

iXBRL stands for Inline eXtensible Business Reporting Language and is a refinement of eXtensible Business Reporting Language (XBRL). XBRL is an international standard for **identifying financial data electronically** using agreed labels (known as tags). This allows tagged data to be analysed electronically, so that, for example, the accounts of businesses from different territories can be compared without reference to the translated definitions of the accounts narratives. iXBRL has been developed by HMRC to allow both narrative text and data to be tagged so that it can be both analysed by computer for risk-assessment (without re-keying), and read by people for clarification and oversight. The tags, once applied, will normally be hidden from a human reader.

46230

iXBRL is divided into **dictionaries of tags**, known as taxonomies. The two currently in use in the UK are UK GAAP and UK IFRS. Each contains more than 5,000 separate tags. There is a third taxonomy called Corporation Tax, or "CT", Computational Taxonomy; this deals with the extra data found in the corporation tax computation. **HMRC have produced another, minimum, tagging list** based on these taxonomies. Companies and advisers were able to use this reduced list for tagging up to April 2013 in order to limit the effort involved and to gain familiarity with the tagging process.

The amount of effort involved in tagging will also depend on the strategy adopted to produce the iXBRL computation. The **basic options** available are:
– use accounts preparation/computation software that will automatically tag to at least HMRC's minimum tagging list;
– use HMRC's free template on their website for small and simple companies;
– use conversion software that allows data and text in other applications to be tagged in iXBRL; or
– outsource the work to a tagging service.

The **choice of which strategy** to adopt will depend on factors such as existing accounts preparation processes, complexity, and availability and cost of software.

> <u>MEMO POINTS</u> 1. HMRC publish a **list of software** that meets the required technical standard on their website.
> 2. HMRC have confirmed that no new iXBRL tagging requirements will be introduced until the second half of 2014. This is mainly due to the revision of a number of accounting standards and

the possible introduction of the EU directive on micro-sized entities. Any company that wishes to file accounts under the new standards can fulfil its obligations by using the current IFRS taxonomy (for those adopting the FRS changes early) or the UK GAAP taxonomy (for those taking account of changes arising from the micro-sized entities regulations).

Transitional arrangements

46235   HMRC have published guidance recognising that the move to iXBRL is a substantial change for companies and their advisers. Their **initial approach** is to offer help, guidance and education rather than impose penalties for incorrect or missing tags. Accounts and computations will **pass the government gateway** for online submission if a small number of key items have been tagged. HMRC have said that it is highly unlikely that a return will be **rejected for poor tagging** once it has passed through the gateway, unless it is clear that no reasonable attempt to tag it has been made. A **reasonable attempt** includes one where automatic tagging has been applied but there is no manual tagging of free-form items, or one where the return has been manually tagged and is complete and accurate as far as is reasonably possible.

As there is no existing **penalty** for tagging errors, there can only be penalties imposed if there has been a loss of tax or a late submission. HMRC have said that it seems hard to envisage a loss of tax simply through a tagging error if the documents in their human-readable format are complete and correct. Neither will errors automatically cause an enquiry to be opened, unless the tagging has caused, for example, risk-assessed ratios to be skewed and HMRC initiate contact. A **late submission** will incur the standard penalty (¶52255), unless there is a reasonable excuse.

3. Statutory accounts

46265   The accounts that accompany the corporation tax computation are also required to be in iXBRL format. Unlike the computation, there is an **exemption** for unincorporated charities, clubs and associations (and authorised investment funds), which may submit their accounts in PDF format instead.

A further transitional arrangement exists for **small incorporated charities** with income below $6,500,000 per annum. They may continue to submit accounts in PDF format until such time as HMRC make available a free template for them.

Special cases

46270   In certain circumstances the accounts that require to be lodged will **differ** from those normally required. The following table outlines these cases, giving details of what is required to be filed and in what format.

Type of company	Type of accounts	Format
Group holding company	Group consolidated accounts and individual company accounts for the holding company	Individual company accounts in iXBRL plus consolidated accounts in PDF format, unless same information for parent company is shown in iXBRL consolidated accounts
Non-resident company trading in the UK as a permanent establishment/branch/agency	Profit and loss account for both UK business and the company as a whole; balance sheet for the company; balance sheet for the UK business only if one is prepared	Profit and loss account and balance sheet for UK business must be in iXBRL; company figures can be submitted as a PDF
Overseas company resident in UK	Accounts which it must submit to the UK Registrar of Companies	iXBRL where there is a taxonomy for the accounting standards used for the accounts, otherwise PDF

D. Amendments to a submitted return

By the company

The company can amend its return where it becomes aware that an item on the return is wrong, or that the return has been made for the wrong period. The **time limit** for company-made amendments is 12 months from the filing date. The return can be amended in any format.

46300
Sch 18 para 15
FA 1998

By HMRC

HMRC can amend the return for any **obvious error or omission**, regardless of whether this is arithmetical, or an error of principle. They may also correct a return where information they have reflects a different position. They can make these amendments **within** 9 months of when the return was filed. Where the **company makes an amendment** to a return the deadline for HMRC is extended to 9 months from the date of the amendment.

46305
Sch 18 para 16
FA 1998

In order to amend a return HMRC must issue a **notice of correction** to the company advising it of the changes proposed. The **company may reject** the notice by amending the return or, if it is too late to amend its return, it must give notice of rejection of HMRC's notice within 3 months of the latter's issue. HMRC can **only enforce** such a notice by opening an enquiry.

E. Finality

As returns are self-assessed and then not subject to any scrutiny, bar checking for obvious errors and omissions, in order to give companies some closure a company can **consider its return final** 12 months after the latest date the return could be filed on time, since after that date the company cannot amend it, unless HMRC have opened an enquiry (¶50415) within that time. This is always subject to HMRC's power of discovery (¶50600).

46335

If a company tax **return is delivered late**, the enquiry window is extended to any time up to, and including, the 31 January, 30 April, 31 July or 31 October next following the first anniversary of the day on which the return was delivered.

Sch 18 para 24
FA 1998

F. Failing to make a return

HMRC assessment

If a company does not make a return by the filing date, HMRC have the power to make a **determination** of the taxable profit and the tax due. Essentially this acts as if the company had made a self-assessment and can be enforced in the same way. HMRC can **issue a determination up to** 3 years from the date it could have first been issued, being the due date for filing a return. If HMRC are **not able to ascertain when the filing date** would be (for instance, where they are unaware of the period end) they may issue a determination from the later of 18 months after the end of the period set out in the notice to file, or 3 months after the notice to file was served.

46365
Sch 18 para 36
FA 1998

> MEMO POINTS   The company will also be liable to a penalty (¶52255).

Company's actions after determination

46370
Sch 18 para 36
FA 1998

If the company can show that it has **no accounting period** ending in or at the end of the period shown in the notice to file, or that it has filed the return, the determination has no effect.

Sch 18 para 40
FA 1998

The only way a company can **displace** a determination for a period is to submit a valid tax return. This must be done no more than 3 years after the determination could first be issued, or 12 months after it was actually issued, whichever is the later.

SECTION 2

Claims and elections

How to make a claim

46420
Sch 18 paras 57 – 59
FA 1998

Once a notice to file has been issued for a period any claim that is capable of being made in a return, either when it is submitted or by way of amendment, must be made in the return. It is possible to make an amendment by letter but this will then result in the return being amended while an amendment is still possible (¶46335).

The following claims **must** be made in the return:
– group relief;
– capital allowances;
– research and development tax credits;
– land remediation tax credits; and
– vaccine research relief credits.

Sch 1A TMA 1970

In a case where either **no notice to file** has been issued, or the **time limit for amending** the return has expired but the time limit to make a claim itself has not, a claim can be made in writing and should include a declaration that the claim is correct to the best of the company's information and belief. Any claim must be **quantified** and cannot be framed as a formula.

Sch 18 para 56
FA 1998

[MEMO POINTS] 1. A company is entitled to **correct an error** in a claim, provided that it is still within the original time limit for making the claim.
2. Where a claim is made **outside the amendment** window no changes are made to the return but the claim will be given effect to by way of discharge or repayment of tax.

Time limit

46425
Sch 18 para 55
FA 1998

The **standard time** limit for a claim is 4 years from the end of the accounting year to which it relates, **unless** legislation for a particular claim specifies otherwise.

Extended time limits can apply to allow claims out of time where there has been:
– an amendment of a return (through a closure notice) following an HMRC enquiry which has increased the amount of tax payable;
– the issue of a discovery assessment (¶50600); or
– an assessment to recover excessive group relief (¶66050).

Sch 18 para 62
FA 1998

In these cases a claim may be made within 12 months after the end of the accounting period in which the amendment or assessment was made. The **claim has to reduce** the liability arising from the amendment or assessment, or any other tax liability for either the period to which the amendment or assessment relates, or any later period ending not more than 12 months after the period in which the amendment or assessment is made.

If the increased liability arises from an assessment to recover tax lost because of **careless or deliberate conduct**, any allowances or reliefs that would normally have been allowed to the company can be claimed, even if out of time. However, these can only be allowed against the assessment itself and so should be made prior to it being raised.

──────── MEMO POINTS ──────── 1. Claims that can only be **made on the original or amended** CT600 (¶46145) carry an effective 2-year time limit, rather than 4. However, the extended time limit may apply.
2. The **claim under the extended time limit** can only reduce the amount of additional tax created by the amendment or the assessment. Where the additional tax arises in more than one period, the effective restriction is apportioned across the relevant periods. *Sch 18 para 64 FA 1998*
3. If making the claim has the effect of **increasing another taxpayer's tax liability**, consent in writing needs to be obtained from that person. *Sch 18 para 63 FA 1998*

Late claims for group relief, capital allowances and losses

In exceptional cases HMRC will consider out-of-time claims if matters **outside the company's control** prevented the claim being made inside the time limit. The company has to write to HMRC setting out, at a minimum, why the claim is late, how late it is, what would happen if the claim were refused and any unusual aspects to the case. This has to be done as soon as the company realises it needs to make the claim and can do so, otherwise it may be refused. It is these elements that HMRC will consider in deciding whether refusing the claim would be unreasonable. **46430** *SP 5/01; CTM 97060*

HMRC give two **examples** in their guidance of cases that may warrant allowing late claims to be made:
– where, when the time limit expires, the company or its advisers are **unaware of profits** against which the company could claim relief; or
– where the amount of a profit or loss depends on **discussions with HMRC** which are not complete when the time limit expires and the delay in agreeing figures is not substantially the fault of the company or its advisers.

In either of these cases HMRC will only admit claims (or adjustments to claims) to the extent of the profit or loss in question.

Reasons beyond the company's control would also include a claim where all of the follow- **46435** ing features were present:
– an officer of the company was ill or otherwise absent for a good reason;
– the absence or illness arose at a critical time and prevented the making of a claim within the normal time limit;
– there was a good reason why the claim was not made before the time of the absence or illness; and
– there was no other person who could have made the claim on the company's behalf within the normal time limit.

However, the following are **not considered to be reasons** beyond the company's control:
– oversight or negligence on the part of the company or its agent;
– failure to calculate the necessary figure, without good reason;
– a wish to avoid commitment pending clarification of the effects of making the claim; or
– illness or absence of an agent or adviser to the company.

SECTION 3

Disclosure of tax avoidance schemes

In order to make review of certain tax planning schemes more timely and efficient for HMRC, **46485** disclosure rules cover scheme promoters and users. Schemes have to be **identified and described to HMRC** in advance of the submission of tax returns. A system of identifying numbers is then used to track the extent and impact of the various schemes in use. This allows HMRC both to target which schemes they will look at and also to co-ordinate their reviews across more than one taxpayer.

──────── MEMO POINTS ──────── HMRC have stated that **everyday advice and arrangements** should not be caught by these rules. In particular, advice on how the tax system operates should not create an obligation to disclose.

A. Notifiable schemes

46515
s 306 FA 2004

A scheme is only required to be disclosed where it is intended to provide, as one of its main purposes, a tax advantage and one of a number of prescribed characteristics, known as **hallmarks**, is evident in the implementation of the scheme.

A number of the hallmarks only apply if the scheme involves a promoter. Some of the hallmarks may also apply where there is no promoter but the company involved is large (being defined as one that is not small or medium-sized (¶95140)). The application can be summarised as below:

Hallmark	Applicable to schemes:		¶¶
	With a promoter	Designed in-house	
Confidentiality	✓	✓	¶46555
Premium fees	✓	✓	¶46590
Leasing arrangements	✓	✓	¶46610
Standardised tax products	✓		¶46645
Loss schemes	✓		¶46680

MEMO POINTS   **A notifiable proposal** is simply a proposal for arrangements that would then be considered notifiable and the same rules apply. Where proposals are notified there is no need to then disclose the entering into of the arrangements themselves.

Definition of scheme promoter

46520
s 307 FA 2004

A scheme promoter is one who, in the course of a business involving taxation services, or that of a bank or securities house:

a. designs the scheme, **unless** the person does not:
– take responsibility for any part of the scheme, i.e. is a specialist legal adviser;
– provide any tax advice; or
– have enough information to comply with the rules and might not reasonably be expected to know that disclosure is required;

b. makes available information about the scheme, including an explanation of the tax advantage, to someone with a view to either that party, or another, entering into the arrangement, at a point in time when the design of the scheme is sufficiently complete that it would be reasonable to believe someone wishing to secure that particular advantage would enter into it (or similar transactions) – this is termed making a **firm approach**;

c. makes the scheme **available for implementation**; or

d. organises or manages the scheme, **provided that** this person is connected with someone who designed or marketed the scheme.

46525
SI 2004/1865
regs 2 – 6

Exclusions from definition   The following are not promoters:
– a company in the same **51% group** (¶65505+) as the company to which it provides services relating to the scheme;
– an **employee** of either a promoter or user;
– someone providing tax advice **but not the design** of the scheme;
– someone designing the scheme but who **does not provide** the tax advice;
– someone who only **designs part of the scheme** and could not be expected to have enough information to know whether the scheme is notifiable or not, or enough information to comply with a promoter's duties (¶46730+); and
– someone who need not provide the required information about the scheme because of **legal professional privilege**.

B. Hallmarks

1. Confidentiality

Schemes involving a promoter

This hallmark applies where it might **reasonably be expected** that a promoter would want to keep confidential from any other promoter the way in which an element of a scheme secures, or might secure, a tax advantage. It is important to note that it is not necessary for the entire scheme to be considered confidential – simply an element of it.

This is an **objective test**, in the sense that it considers what a typical promoter would do. If the elements are well known to other advisers the scheme will not be caught by this hallmark, even if any particular scheme is kept confidential. If a **confidentiality agreement** is put in place between the promoter and the user before full details are revealed, and the adviser would not normally use such an agreement, HMRC will take this as indicative that the confidentiality hallmark will apply.

This hallmark will also apply if the promoter wants to keep the elements that secure the tax advantage **confidential from HMRC**, because the promoter intends to use that element or a similar one in future schemes. This is a **subjective test**, as it depends on the **intention** of the actual promoter.

46555
SI 2006/1543 reg 6

Schemes not involving a promoter

Where there is no UK promoter (or the promoter is covered by legal professional privilege) the confidentiality hallmark will apply if the **user would intend**, if the legislation did not apply, to keep the way an element of a scheme gives rise to the tax advantage confidential from HMRC for any of the following reasons:
– to facilitate repeated or continued use of the same element (or substantially the same element) in the future;
– to reduce the risk of HMRC using that information to open an enquiry into any return or account; or
– to reduce the risk of HMRC using that information to withhold payment of all or part of an amount claimed separately from a return relating to trade and employment losses.

46560
SI 2006/1543 reg 7

2. Premium fee

A premium fee is one that can be charged because of any element giving rise to a tax advantage, where the fee is significantly attributable to, or contingent (as a matter of law) on obtaining, that tax advantage. This is another **objective test**, in that the fee need only be reasonably expected to be charged to a person experienced in receiving this type of service; it does not need to be actually charged.

46590
SI 2006/1543 reg 8

3. Leasing arrangements

This hallmark is present where the arrangements include a long lease of **plant or machinery** that is of high value and at least one of the following applies:
– **one** of the **parties** to the lease(s) is **not**, or would not be, **within the charge** to corporation tax while the other could claim capital allowances;
– money or a money debt is used to **protect the lessor** from the risk of sustaining a loss if payments due under the lease are not made in accordance with its terms; or

46610
SI 2006/1543
regs 13, 15–17

– the arrangements are designed to consist of a **sale and finance leaseback** arrangement or a **lease and finance leaseback**.

> ☐ MEMO POINTS 1. For these purposes a lease is considered **long** if its term is more than 2 years. This will also include the situation where there exists an option for the **lessee to extend** the term to more than 2 years, or where there are **other arrangements** entered into at the same time that contemplate a lease for a term longer than 2 years. If the plant is also **leased to another connected party** and the aggregate of the lease periods exceeds 2 years, the lease will be long.
> 2. A lease is of **high value** where the lower of the cost or market value to the lessor of:
> – a single asset under the lease is at least £10,000,000; or
> – the aggregate of all the assets being leased under the arrangement is at least £25,000,000.

Sale and finance leaseback

46615 The finance leaseback condition **does not apply** where the leased **assets are new** – that is, not second-hand when they are acquired or created by the seller – and the sale prior to the leaseback is not more than 4 months after acquisition or creation. Neither does the condition apply if the asset is a **fixture leased together with land**, unless the plant or machinery is used for storage or production. However, this exemption for leased fixtures will not apply if the cost of the fixture is more than 50% of the aggregate value of the assets subject to the lease and the rent payable under the lease is dependent on the availability of capital allowances on any plant or machinery in the lease.

> ☐ MEMO POINTS In **valuing** the land and plant for these purposes it is the market value of the lessor's interest in the land and the open-market value of the plant (if it were not subject to a lease) which are considered.

---

4. Standardised tax products

46645
SI 2006/1543
reg 10

This hallmark covers schemes which a promoter intends to **market to more than one taxpayer**, with little or no variation, using standardised documentation. In these cases the documentation will be in a form determined by the promoter and will detail the various transactions that a client will enter into, which will be substantially the same from client to client.

Exemptions

46650
SI 2006/1543
reg 11

Exemptions are available from the need to disclose where the arrangements involve:
– only plant or machinery leases;
– the use of an enterprise investment scheme or venture capital trust;
– relief under the corporate venturing scheme or community investment tax relief;
– ISA accounts, approved share incentive plans, share option schemes, CSOP schemes, or grants of enterprise management incentives;
– registered pension schemes and certain overseas pension schemes; or
– schemes for periodical payments of personal injury damages.

If a scheme was **first made available for implementation** before 1 August 2006 it will also be exempt from disclosure.

---

5. Loss schemes

46680
SI 2006/1543
reg 12

Where a scheme is directed at generating **trading losses for individuals** which can then be set against income tax and capital gains tax liabilities, it will be covered by this hallmark. The promoter must expect more than one individual to implement the same (or substantially the same) arrangements and an informed observer should reasonably be able to conclude that the main benefit of those arrangements for the individuals participating in them is the losses arising, which will be used to reduce their income tax or capital gains tax liabilities.

> ☐ MEMO POINTS HMRC guidance makes clear that this hallmark is not meant to capture **genuine start-up losses**, even though they may be predictable.

6. Other schemes

HMRC can apply to the tribunal for an order that a scheme which **does not bear one of the hallmarks** should be disclosed. An order will **only be made** where the tribunal is satisfied that HMRC have reasonable grounds for suspecting that the scheme may be notifiable, having taken all reasonable steps to establish whether it is. This may include asking a possible promoter whether a scheme is notifiable and if the promoter considers it is not, why not (a pre-disclosure enquiry (¶46840)), or requiring the promoter to provide documents and/or information in support of the view that the scheme is not notifiable. **Justification** that a scheme is not notifiable must be made by reference to the hallmarks and cannot simply consist of referring to a professional opinion stating that it is not.

46700
s 306A FA 2004

> MEMO POINTS **Reasonable grounds for suspicion** can include whether the relevant arrangements fall within one of the hallmarks and attempts now or in the past to avoid providing information to HMRC when requested.

C. Obligations

1. Disclosure of schemes

Who is responsible?

Where a scheme is subject to disclosure it will typically be the promoter of the scheme, where one exists, who is required to disclose. However, where the **promoter** is either **not resident in the UK**, or is not subject to the rules due to the operation of **legal professional privilege**, this obligation will fall on the scheme user. It is also the scheme user's responsibility where the arrangement has been devised **in-house**. A scheme user is simply someone who implements the scheme in order to secure the tax advantage.

46730
ss 308, 309
FA 2004

Multiple promoters In some cases there may be more than one person termed as a promoter. For instance, someone may design the scheme, another may market it and a third party may then implement it. In such a case disclosure **by one person** will discharge the others' obligations, provided that the party not making the disclosure holds the information that would have been required to have been disclosed and either the:
– disclosing party has identified the identity and address of the non-disclosing party; or
– non-disclosing party holds the scheme reference number.

46735
s 408(4) – (4C)
FA 2004

Timing of disclosure

A scheme must be disclosed to HMRC within a short interval after a trigger point. The intervals and their various trigger points are:

46740

	Deadline[1]	Trigger point
Promoter of a **hallmarked** scheme	5 days	From the earliest of the date on which the promoter: – first makes a firm approach (¶46520) to another person in relation to a notifiable proposal; – makes the notifiable proposal available for implementation by any other person; or – first becomes aware of any transaction forming part of notifiable arrangements implementing the notifiable proposal

	Deadline [1]	Trigger point
Where a **tribunal** has given an **order** that a scheme should be disclosed despite not showing one of the main hallmarks (¶46700)	10 days	From the date the order is made
Users with **overseas promoters**		From the day on which the user enters into the first transaction forming part of the notifiable arrangements
Users where the promoter is protected by **legal professional privilege**	5 days	
All other users	30 days	From the day on which the user enters into the first transaction forming part of the notifiable arrangements

Note:
1. **Non-working days** are ignored for calculating the deadline.

Making the disclosure

46745
SI 2012/1836 reg 4

The **information that is required** to be disclosed is:
- the promoter's name and address;
- the provisions under which disclosure is required;
- a summary of the scheme and its name, if it has one;
- an explanation of how the tax advantage arises; and
- details of the legal provisions that apply.

If a **scheme user** is disclosing because there is an overseas promoter, the user's name and address and those of the promoter must be included. If a user has an obligation to disclose for any other reason, it should provide its name and address. Information does not have to be provided if disclosure has already been made about a scheme that is substantially the same.

Upon examining a disclosure HMRC will then issue a **scheme reference number**.

s 308A FA 2004   〔 MEMO POINTS 〕   Disclosure can be made on standard forms available from the HMRC website. The **essential test** as to whether enough information has been provided is whether HMRC can understand how the scheme is meant to operate. If HMRC do not think enough information has been provided, they can request more by obtaining a tribunal order (¶46850).

---

2. Disclosure of scheme users

46775
s 313ZA FA 2004

Promoters have a duty to provide lists of clients to HMRC. The obligation applies where a promoter has passed on, or would have been required to pass on if one had been issued, a scheme reference number issued by HMRC. All clients to whom numbers must be passed on or after 1 January 2011 must be listed, even if disclosure of the scheme was made before that date.

Lists are required for each **calendar quarter** and must be submitted within 30 days after the end of the quarter. However, **nil returns** are not required.

Client details which must be reported now include the user's National Insurance number or unique tax reference number. Users must, therefore, supply their **National Insurance number** or **unique tax reference number** to the promoter within 10 days of the date on which the user receives the scheme reference number or enters into a transaction forming part of the arrangement (whichever is later).

---

3. Scheme reference numbers

46795

After a scheme has been disclosed, **HMRC may issue** a scheme reference number to the party making the notification. Issue of a number does not mean that HMRC have cleared the scheme, or that they believe that it does not confer a tax advantage. Instead the number simply allows HMRC to co-ordinate and prioritise enquiries into returns.

Promoter

A promoter who receives a scheme reference number must pass it on to anyone to whom the promoter provides services in connection with the scheme. The person to whom services are provided by the promoter need not necessarily be the user implementing the scheme. **Notification of the number must** be on form AAG 6 (available from HMRC's website) and be provided within 30 days of the later of when the promoter becomes aware of any transaction forming part of the scheme or when the promoter receives the scheme reference number from HMRC.

46800
s 312 FA 2004

> MEMO POINTS **Form AAG 6** also requires the name and address of the promoter, brief details of the scheme and the date the reference number was passed on.

SI 2012/1836
reg 6

Client

A client who is in effect an **intermediary** between the promoter and the end user must pass the reference number on to any other party who might reasonably be expected to be a party to, and who might reasonably be expected to gain a tax advantage from, the scheme. This should be done on form AAG 6 within 30 days of the later of when the user receives the number from the promoter or when the user becomes aware of any transaction forming part of the scheme. This requirement **only applies** when there is sufficient commercial connection between the parties to give a reasonable expectation that the other party will benefit from a tax advantage.

46805
s 312A FA 2004

Scheme user

The scheme user must put the reference number on its **tax return** for the first period in which it enters into a transaction forming part of the scheme, and on the return for each subsequent period for which the tax advantage is obtained. If the return is not submitted, or the reference number is not included, the number should be provided separately by the filing date on form AAG 4.

46810
SI 2012/1836
reg 11

As noted above, users must also supply their details to the promoter (see ¶46775).

---

4. HMRC powers

Pre-disclosure enquiries

A pre-disclosure enquiry is used by HMRC to gain information from a promoter, or introducer (¶46845), about a scheme that they believe **may be notifiable**. The request for information will ask whether, in the promoter's opinion, the scheme is notifiable and if not, why the promoter considers that it does not require disclosure. The promoter has to **respond within** 10 days of the day after the notice is issued (or such longer period as HMRC may allow).

46840
ss 313A, 313B
FA 2004

The **promoter's argument** must be framed in terms of how the scheme does not fall within one of the hallmarks and not simply refer to a legal opinion. Sufficient information should be supplied by the promoter to evidence his assertions. If **sufficient information is not provided** HMRC can apply to the tribunal for an order to require the promoter to furnish specific information or documents to support the argument. Such information then has to be **provided within** 14 days (or such longer period as HMRC allow).

Requests to introducers

An **introducer** is someone who makes information available to another about a scheme with a view to having the latter, or another party, enter into it. This means that another party must have designed the scheme and provided the introducer with the information.

46845
s 313C FA 2004

HMRC have the power to force an introducer to disclose the identity of anyone who has given the introducer any such information in relation to arrangements specified in their request. Such a notice must be **complied with within** 10 days or such longer period as the notice states. This is intended to ensure that a promoter cannot avoid his obligations by remaining anonymous.

Forcing complete disclosure

46850
ss 308A, 314A
FA 2004

Where HMRC **believe that a scheme is notifiable** but has not been disclosed, they can apply to a tribunal for a disclosure order to be issued. The application must contain a description of the arrangements and the identity of the promoter. The tribunal will only grant an order where it believes that the arrangements are notifiable.

Where a scheme has been disclosed but HMRC believe that **not all the required information** has been provided, they can apply to the tribunal for an order to secure further information or documentation pertaining to the scheme. Such an order will only be issued where the tribunal believes that it forms part of the required information, or will support or explain it, and must be **complied with** no more than 10 days after its issue (or such longer period as HMRC may allow).

D. Penalties

46880

The penalty regime has three broad categories:
– disclosure penalties;
– penalties relating to a user failing to disclose the scheme reference number; and
– information penalties, being any other failure not already covered.

In order for penalties to be imposed for **failure to disclose**, or under the **information penalty** category, HMRC must apply to the tribunal. The tribunal will decide on the initial penalty and then HMRC have the ability to levy further penalties for continuing failures.

Disclosure penalties

46885

The failure to disclose penalties depend on whether a disclosure order (¶46700) has been made or not. Where **no disclosure order** has been made, a failure to make a disclosure by the due date, or making one not in the correct form, may result in the tribunal imposing a penalty of up to £600 a day. The period this runs from will be from the day after the disclosure should be made until the earlier of the filing of the disclosure or the decision of the tribunal. If the tribunal **considers** that this daily penalty would be **insufficient** to deter a further default arising it can determine a single penalty of up to £1,000,000.

Where the **failure continues** after the tribunal decision HMRC can levy a penalty of up to £600 for each day the failure continues.

Where a **disclosure order** has been made in relation to the scheme the maximum penalty that both the tribunal and HMRC can levy is £5,000 per day.

Failure to show scheme registration number

46890

A scheme user which fails to comply with an obligation to report a scheme reference number and related information (on a return or separately) is liable to a penalty of £100 per scheme for a **first failure**. Where there is a **second** failure inside 36 months the penalty is £500 per scheme; if there is a **third** failure, £1,000 per scheme. Any **further failures** in the period will also be penalised at £1,000 per scheme. It should be noted that the failures do not have to be in relation to the same scheme.

Information failures

These penalties are designed to cover the situations where:
- a promoter has not responded to a **pre-disclosure enquiry** (¶46700);
- an **introducer** does not provide, when required to, the identity of the person who supplied him with information about a scheme;
- a promoter or client **does not pass on the scheme registration number** as required; or
- a promoter **fails to provide details of a client** to whom he was obliged to pass on the scheme reference number.

This will cover failures to comply with any of the above, as well as not providing the information in the correct format.

In these cases a tribunal can levy an **initial** penalty for each failure of up to £5,000. HMRC may then impose a **further penalty** of up to £600 (£5,000 where a **disclosure order** has been made) **per day** should the failure continue after the tribunal imposes the initial penalty.

46895

SECTION 4

Senior accounting officers

A. Scope

Not all companies will be subject to the senior accounting officer (SAO) requirements. The following are **exempt**:
- companies with **turnover less** than £200 million and **assets less** than £2 billion (unless part of a group exceeding those limits);
- UK companies **incorporated under legislation other** than the Companies Act (for example, the Building Societies Act 2006);
- UK branches of companies **incorporated overseas**; and
- companies in **administration** or considered **insolvent**.

Overseas branches of UK companies are included but HMRC do not expect exhaustive checking of overseas accounting and filing where there has been suitable delegation. **Dormant companies** are within the legislation but can be identified as such on the certificate. Companies which are **not resident in the UK** are only covered to the extent of trading or other taxable activity in the UK.

46945
SAOG

Testing the size of the company

The test is **applied to** the accounts for the company's accounting year (as defined for the purposes of the Companies Acts) preceding the one for which certification (¶46990) is required.

If the company is a **51% subsidiary**, the same limits apply to the group totals, making the company part of the regime even if it appears too small. Group turnover and asset totals are simply computed by aggregating the amounts in the individual accounts, so HMRC acknowledge that there may be some double-counting of intra-group items.

46950

Sch 46 para 15
FA 2009

B. Responsibilities

46980
Sch 46 para 1
FA 2009

The legislation **imposes** on the SAO **personally** the obligation to establish, maintain and monitor suitable accounting arrangements that allow tax liabilities to be calculated correctly in all material respects, including record-keeping. As part of the ongoing compliance process the SAO must then **certify** annually that the company has appropriate accounting arrangements in place for designated taxes.

Sch 46 para 14
FA 2009

MEMO POINTS   1. The **taxes covered** are:
- corporation tax (including any amount assessable or chargeable as if it were corporation tax);
- VAT;
- PAYE (excluding National Insurance contributions and student loan repayments);
- insurance premium tax;
- stamp duty land tax;
- stamp duty reserve tax;
- petroleum revenue tax;
- customs duties; and
- excise duties (including air passenger duty).

HMRC Brief 19/13

2. The SAO of the representative member of a VAT group is considered by HMRC to be responsible for the accounting arrangements of the VAT group as a whole.

Suitable accounting arrangements

46985

HMRC's guidance says that **appropriate tax accounting arrangements** are the framework of responsibilities, policies, appropriate people and procedures in place for managing tax compliance risk, as well as the systems and processes which put this framework into practice. As such it is the entire process that allows the tax liabilities to be calculated. So this would cover all processes, from data input to producing the final numbers for returns.

HMRC suggest that appropriate arrangements might cover the following broad elements:
- a **process** for gathering and recording data in a systematic way;
- an **understanding** of the key tax compliance risks in the business;
- **designing and implementing** control activities to mitigate these risks – for example, separation of responsibilities and ensuring that people who undertake delegated activities have the right levels of skill and competency; and
- **mechanisms for communicating** roles and responsibilities, monitoring activities to ensure that controls are operating effectively – the level of monitoring required will vary according to the level of risk present.

Certification

46990
Sch 46 para 2
FA 2009

The SAO **must certify annually** that the company has had the appropriate tax accounting arrangements in place throughout the year. If the company **does not have such arrangements** in place, an explanation is required as to why they were not considered appropriate. As corporate tax returns are self-assessed, and many of the elements in the return will be based on the accounting treatment rather than any special taxation rules, self-certification **puts the onus** on senior management to ensure that accounting is fit for the purpose of accurately calculating the company's various liabilities.

The certificate can cover **more than one** company if the SAO acts for more than one company (¶47020).

The certificate **must be submitted before** the deadline for filing the accounts with Companies House. This deadline is 9 months for a private company and 6 months for a public company. As such, the certificate has to be submitted before the deadline for filing the corporation tax return.

C. Who is the senior accounting officer?

The SAO is the person who, in the **company's reasonable opinion**, has **overall responsibility** for the company's financial accounting arrangements. There can be **only one** SAO for each company at any time but there may be more than one in any year, as jobholders and responsibilities change.

HMRC **must be notified** of the identity of the designated SAO for each year before the filing deadline for the Companies House accounts.

As it is possible for one individual to **act for more than one company**, the notice should list every company for which that SAO acts, the financial year to which it relates and the name and contact details of the SAO.

47020
Sch 46 para 16
FA 2009

D. Penalties

Failure by the SAO

Where there is a **failure to establish**, maintain or monitor suitable accounting arrangements (¶46985) during an accounting period, or the **required certificate** is not provided within the time limit (or it contains a careless or deliberate **inaccuracy** (¶52575)), the penalty is £5,000 **levied on** the SAO personally, not the company. Each penalty can only be levied once per year per company.

47050
Sch 46 paras 4, 5
FA 2009

An SAO who acts for **more than one company** can only be liable for one of each penalty in respect of all the companies for which he so acts. This is the case even where the companies' **year ends are not the same**.

Sch 46 para 9
FA 2009

> EXAMPLE A Ltd and B Ltd are in a group and have the same SAO. A Ltd's year end is 31 March 2013 and B Ltd's is 31 December 2012. If the SAO of B Ltd is subject to a penalty for the year to 31 December 2012, he cannot be penalised for a failure in the year to 31 March 2013 in A Ltd, as a group company has been assessed for a penalty in a period that ends during A Ltd's financial year.

More than one SAO in a period Where the SAO changes during the period, only one SAO will be liable for a penalty. Where the failure is in respect of:
– the **main obligation**, it is the SAO at the period end; and
– not supplying a **certificate** on time, it is the SAO in place at the deadline date for submitting it. However, if a previous SAO has submitted a certificate for a period this will remove the necessity for his successor to provide one for the same period.

47055
Sch 46 para 6
FA 2009

> MEMO POINTS Someone who has been **replaced** as the SAO can still be liable to a penalty for providing a carelessly or deliberately inaccurate certificate.

Failure by the company

The **only obligation** placed on the company is to notify HMRC of who the SAO is for a period (¶47020). Where the company fails to do this the penalty is £5,000, **levied** on the company.

47060
Sch 46 para 7
FA 2009

Issue of penalties

HMRC must raise penalties within 6 months of the failure or inaccuracy coming to their attention, or no more than 6 years after the filing deadline for the accounts for that financial year. If the company or officer has a **reasonable excuse**, no penalty will be raised. HMRC

47065
Sch 46 para 9
FA 2009

guidance says that a reasonable excuse will depend on the circumstances of each case but it is likely to be an exceptional, unforeseeable event beyond a person's control. The following are **specifically not** considered to be a reasonable excuse:

Sch 46 para 8
FA 2009

– an insufficiency of funds, unless attributable to events outside the person's control;

– relying on anybody else, unless the first person took reasonable care to avoid the failure; or

– where there was a reasonable excuse that has now ceased and within a reasonable time no steps have been taken to remedy the failure.

The guidance also specifically refers to the situation where a **new SAO** takes over responsibility during a period. HMRC would not expect the new SAO to go back and check his predecessor's work, if the arrangements appeared to be in order. If, having provided a certificate, the arrangements then **prove to be inappropriate** and the new officer could not reasonably have known this, he will not be regarded as careless or having deliberately provided an inaccurate certificate.

MEMO POINTS   An **appeal** against a penalty can be made within 30 days of the penalty notification being given. It must be in writing to HMRC and state the grounds for appeal.

SECTION 5

Quarterly accounting and sundry returns

A. Income tax

Return periods

47115

s 949 ITA 2007

If a company **withholds** income tax from any payments it makes (¶41050), it must make a return of the tax withheld on form CT61. Such returns are required on a calendar quarterly basis. Where the company's year end **does not coincide** with a calendar quarter there will be an additional return required.

> EXAMPLE   A Ltd has a year end of 31 May. It withholds income tax from payments it makes. It must make a return for each of the following periods:
> – 1 June (the start of its accounting period) to 30 June;
> – 1 July to 30 September;
> – 1 October to 31 December;
> – 1 January to 31 March; and
> – 1 April to 31 May (the end of its accounting period).

Due date

47120

The return must be **submitted** within 14 days of the return period ending and the **tax must be paid** over by the same date. The payments to HMRC can be reduced by any income tax withheld by income received by the company and this should be included on the return. If there is a balance of income tax suffered in the year, net of the income tax payable, at the company's year end, this can be set against the company's tax liability. (See ¶41120 for full details of this.)

47125

A return does not need to be made if there are **no payments** in the return period, even if income is received net of income tax. The receipt should then be included in any later return in that accounting period if a payment is subsequently made. A payment later matched or exceeded by a receipt in the accounting period will generate a repayment of income tax to the company.

B. Distributions

Qualifying distributions

A company is not required to make any return to HMRC regarding the payment of qualifying distributions (¶18330). However, the company **does need to provide** each recipient of a qualifying distribution with a statement or voucher showing the:
– recipient's name;
– net amount of the distribution;
– tax credit attaching to it;
– period to which it relates; and
– date of payment.

47155
s 1106 CTA 2010

Non-qualifying distributions

There is **no formal return required** when non-qualifying distributions (¶18440) are made. Instead the company **must provide HMRC** with the:
– details of the transaction;
– name(s) and address(es) of the recipient(s); and
– value of the distribution received by each recipient.

The information must be **provided within** 14 days of the accounting period end. If the distribution is made on a date **not within an accounting period**, the information must be provided within 14 days of the distribution.

47160
s 1101 CTA 2010

Stock dividends

Stock dividends (¶18095) **must be reported** to HMRC. The **information** to be provided includes the:
– date of issue of the shares;
– date on which the company was first required to issue the shares, if this differs from the date of issue;
– terms of issue; and
– cash equivalent.

The **return periods** are the same as those used for income tax (¶47115). Each return **must be submitted** within 30 days of the end of the return period.

47165
s 1052 CTA 2010

C. Penalties

Penalties may be charged if the returns for **income tax withheld**, **non-qualifying distributions** or **stock dividends** are not made on time. The penalty is £300, with a further £60 per day that the failure continues. A penalty cannot be imposed after the position has been rectified.

47195

CHAPTER 3

Payment and repayment

48000 The corporation tax self-assessment regime encompasses payments as well as returns, so that companies are expected to calculate and pay their liabilities by the due date without receiving an assessment from HMRC. Another feature is the instalment regime for large companies, under which self-assessed payments are spread over a period that begins during the accounting period. HMRC will charge interest on late payments and pay it on repayments. Excessive repayments and repayment interest can be reclaimed by HMRC. If a company has no tax payment to make it should inform HMRC: see flmemo.co.uk/ctm48000.

SECTION 1

Due date

A. General rule

48050
s 59D TMA 1970;
CTM 01800

With the **exception of large companies** (¶48125), the due date for corporation tax payment is 9 months and 1 day after the end of the accounting period. Where the end of the accounting period is the **last day of a calendar month**, the due date is day 1 of the 10th month after the accounting period end. Where the end of the period is not the last day of a calendar month, the due date is the same day in the month, 9 months later, plus 1 day. However, if there is no such equivalent day, the due date reverts to day 1 of the 10th month.

> EXAMPLE The following shows the due date for a number of accounting period end dates.
>
> | Accounting period ended | Due date |
> |---|---|
> | 31 December 2012 | 1 October 2013 |
> | 29 January 2013 | 30 October 2013 |
> | 30 May 2013 | 1 March 2014 |

Where there is **more than one accounting period** in a period of account, each will have its own due date. This differs from the way that filing deadlines are calculated where there is more than one accounting period (¶46110). | **48055**

> EXAMPLE The 18-month period of account ended 31 March 2013 will be split into the two chargeable accounting periods ended 30 September 2012 and 31 March 2013.
> The due dates for these periods will be 1 July 2013 and 1 January 2014, respectively.

Postponement of tax

Where there is an **appeal against an amendment** of a self-assessment or an **assessment**, a postponement of the tax charged can be requested. The application for postponement must be made in writing to HMRC within 30 days of the date of issue of the amendment or assessment, setting out the amount to be postponed and the grounds for believing that the amount charged is excessive. If **HMRC do not agree** with the request, an appeal to the tribunal can be made within 30 days of HMRC's decision. | **48060**
s 55 TMA 1970

Applications for postponement can be made outside the 30 days, if there has been a **change in circumstances** such that the tax charged has become excessive. In HMRC's view this must be more than a mere change of mind about whether to apply for postponement, or how much tax to postpone. Examples of a sufficient change of circumstances are further accounts preparation work, or additional group relief becoming due.

Any agreement reached on the amount of tax to be postponed must be made or confirmed in writing. If an application to postpone any amount is not agreed or determined, the tax becomes due and payable as if it were the subject of an amendment or assessment issued on the date that the written agreement or determination was made of the amount which can be postponed. | **48065**

When the **appeal** against the amendment or assessment is **finally determined**, any tax previously postponed becomes due and payable as if it were subject to a notice issued on the date when HMRC advise the company of the total amount due as a result of the determination. Any overpaid tax is repaid.

B. Large company instalments

If a company is "large", as defined below, its corporation tax liability becomes due in instalments, based on its own estimate of its total corporation tax liability for the accounting period. The instalments begin before the period has ended, continuing thereafter. Depending on the accuracy of the company's estimate, there may be a need for a final balancing payment. Any **underestimates** will incur interest at a special rate. Any overestimates will earn interest on overpaid tax on each instalment, again at a special rate. | **48095**
s 59E TMA 1970

> MEMO POINTS The **tax due in instalments includes** tax on loans to participators (¶75575) and any sums due under the controlled foreign company provisions (¶90555).

1. Definition of large company

A company will be considered to be "large" if its taxable profits (including franked investment income (¶40115) other than from 51% group companies) exceed the upper limit for marginal relief in force at the end of its accounting period, currently £1,500,000. | **48125**
SI 1998/3175
regs 2, 3

If there are **associated companies** (¶40185), the upper limit must be divided amongst all the associated companies in existence at any point during the period. If the accounting period is less than 12 months, the limit must also be proportionately reduced.

Exceptions

48130   A company is not "large" if the:
– tax does not exceed £10,000; or
– profits do not exceed £10 million and the company was not large in the preceding 12 months for other reasons.

Both amounts are proportionately reduced for **periods of less than 12 months**. The £10 million limit is also reduced for the number of **associated companies** at the end of the immediately preceding period, or, if there was no such period, at the beginning of the period. A company cannot make use of the second exception in two consecutive periods.

EXAMPLE

1. A Ltd has profits for its first 12-month accounting period of £7 million. As these are less than £10 million, and A Ltd was not within the instalment regime in the previous period, it is not liable to pay tax by instalments.

2. B Ltd has profits for the following 12-month accounting periods:

Year ended 31 December	Profits (£)
2011	125,000
2012	6,000,000
2013	8,500,000

B Ltd is not within the instalment regime for the period ended 31 December 2011, as the profits are below the upper limit for marginal relief. Nor is it within the instalment regime for the period ended 31 December 2012, as the profits are below £10 million and it was not within the regime for the previous period. However, B Ltd is within the instalment regime for the period ended 31 December 2013, as although its profits are below £10 million, it was only outside the regime in the previous period because of the £10 million limit. That exemption cannot be used in two consecutive periods, so B Ltd must be within the instalments regime for the year ended 31 December 2013.

---

2. Calculating payment dates

12-month accounting period

48160   Instalments are spread over a period that starts before the end of the accounting period and
SI 1998/3175 reg 5   finishes after it. A 12-month accounting period will have four instalments as follows:

Instalment	Payable	Month
1	6 months and 13 days from the start of the accounting period	7
2	3 months after instalment 1	10
3	3 months after instalment 2	13
Final	3 months and 14 days after the end of the accounting period	16

EXAMPLE C Ltd's 12-month accounting period ended 31 December 2013 will have the following instalment dates:

Instalment	Payable	Payment Date
1	6 months and 13 days from the start of the accounting period	14 July 2013
2	3 months after instalment 1	14 October 2013
3	3 months after instalment 2	14 January 2014
Final	3 months and 14 days after the end of the accounting period	14 April 2014

Short accounting periods

48165   Where a company has an accounting period of **less than 12 months**, the steps to calculate the dates of the required payments are:

– **final instalment**: due 3 months and 14 days after the end of the accounting period;
– **first instalment**: 6 months and 13 days from the start of the accounting period; and
– **subsequent instalments**: 3 months after the preceding one, provided that this is before the final instalment is due.

EXAMPLE D Ltd has an 8-month accounting period ended 30 June 2013. Instalments will be due as follows:

Instalment	Payable	Payment date
1	6 months and 13 days from the start of the accounting period	14 May 2013
2	3 months after instalment 1	14 August 2013
Final	3 months and 14 days after the end of the accounting period	14 October 2013

If the **final instalment** proves to be **earlier than the first instalment**, the final instalment is the only one required.

EXAMPLE E Ltd has a 14-month period of account ending 28 February 2013. The instalment due dates for the short 2-month accounting period ended 28 February 2012 initially appear to be:

Instalment	Payable	Payment date
1	6 months and 13 days from the start of the accounting period	14 July 2013
Final	3 months and 14 days after the end of the accounting period	14 June 2013

However, as the final instalment is due earlier than the first instalment, only one instalment is required on 14 June 2013.

---

3. Amount of instalments

Calculation

Instalments are based on the current **estimate** of the **total corporation tax liability** for the period using the formula:

48195

$$3 \times \frac{\text{CTI}}{\text{n}}$$

where:
– CTI is the best estimate of the corporation tax liability for the accounting period; and
– n is the number of complete months in the accounting period.

More than one instalment If there is more than one instalment, the **first instalment** will be as given by the formula. **Subsequent instalments** will be the smaller of the balance of CTI due at that time and the amount given by the formula. The final instalment should bring the total of all payments up to CTI.

48200

In order to do this, it is essential that the best estimate of CTI is **reviewed** in time for each instalment in order to minimise the amount of any interest on overdue tax. If the **estimate of CTI increases**, an additional payment will need to be made in order to keep the cumulative position up to date (this need not wait until the next instalment date). If the **estimate decreases**, future instalments will be reduced. If there is a **cumulative overpayment**, the company can claim repayment of the excess, or offset it against the next instalment.

SI 1998/3175 reg 6

EXAMPLE
1. F Ltd has a 12-month accounting period ended 31 December 2013. It initially estimates its corporation tax liability for the year at £840,000. However, by the second instalment it expects that this will increase to £880,000. At the fourth instalment, the liability is self-assessed as £890,000. Instalment one will be calculated using the normal formula to give an instalment figure of £210,000. (3 × £840,000/12)

Instalment two is calculated on the revised estimate of £880,000. The calculation would give a result of £220,000. Once the second instalment has been made the company should have paid a total of £440,000 and should therefore make a top-up payment of £10,000.

Instalment three is based on the same calculation as instalment two.

The final instalment should be a balancing payment to ensure that the correct amount of tax has been paid for the year. In this case a final instalment of £230,000 is required. (£890,000 – £660,000)

2. G Ltd has a 10-month accounting period ended 31 October 2013. It initially estimates its corporation tax liability at £890,000. By the third instalment, it has revised this estimate downwards to £840,000. The final calculation of the corporation tax due is £860,000.

The due dates and calculations are as follows:

Instalment	Due date	Calculation £	£
1	14 July 2013	3 × 890,000/10	267,000
2	14 October 2013	3 × 890,000/10	267,000
3	14 January 2014	Lower of 3 × 840,000/10 and 756,000 – 534,000	222,000
Final	14 February 2014	860,000 – total instalments to date of 756,000	104,000

If G Ltd identifies the reduction in its corporation tax liability soon after 14 October 2013, it could reclaim a repayment rather than reduce its next instalment in January 2014 by the cumulative overpayment.

48205 **Single instalment** Where the calculation shows that **only the final instalment** has to be made, the entire corporation tax liability will be due on that date.

Periods involving part-months

48210 If the accounting period has an **incomplete month** in it, "n" is increased to reflect the extra days based on a complete month having 30 days. The fraction is always rounded to 2 decimal places.

> EXAMPLE H Ltd has an accounting period from 16 July 2013 to 31 December 2013. This period of 5 months and 16 days will result in n being 5.53. (5 + 16/30)

HMRC guidance on instalments

48215 HMRC **expect** that companies will follow normal commercial practices and governance in estimating quarterly payments. A company's approach can be tailored to its **size and complexity** and need not involve preparing a full corporation tax computation. Management information such as forecasts and budgets are relevant. Companies are **not expected** to have hindsight but should consider known plans. **One-off transactions** that do not turn out as expected – for example, the availability of rollover relief on a capital gain – should not cause a problem and would be an acceptable reason for underestimation of payments. It would be sensible for companies to **keep a record** of both their overall approach to estimating quarterly payments and where they have taken a view on items such as the outcome of an enquiry into an earlier year's return.

HMRC powers

48220
SI 1998/3175
regs 10, 11

Alongside HMRC's usual powers of enquiry (¶50415), they also have powers that **allow them to seek information** about the quarterly instalment calculations after the filing date for the tax return. They can require information so that they may check that:

– the payments were consistent with the quality and quantity of information available to the company about its total liability for the period when the payment(s) were due;

– any non-payment was reasonable; and

– any claim for repayment was properly made.

HMRC can also ask to see the **books and records** for the same reasons. Copies may be produced but they should be photographic or other facsimiles. HMRC may still require the originals. However, **no enquiry** can be carried out into the payments until the return has been filed.

HMRC regard interest on underestimated instalments as the principal incentive for compliant behaviour. Their guidance says that **enquiries will only be appropriate** if inspectors believe that the company has deliberately or recklessly failed to make payments in line with the company's own information, or fraudulently or negligently made a repayment claim. Where a **penalty is due**, it will not be more than twice the interest due on understated instalments. HMRC say that penalties will be sought only in the most serious cases involving flagrant abuse.

48225
s 59E TMA 1970;
SI 1998/3175
reg 13;
EM 08310

SECTION 2

Making payment

Methods

Since 1 April 2011 **all payments** of corporation tax, interest on overdue corporation tax and filing penalties have to be made electronically. HMRC **accept** the following as electronic methods (even though at first sight not all may appear electronic):
- payment by direct debit;
- credit or debit card from a UK card issuer via Internet (BillPay service);
- Internet or telephone banking;
- Bank Giros using an HMRC payslip;
- payment at a Post Office counter using an HMRC payslip; and
- BACS/CHAPS transfers.

Payments **sent by post** to HMRC are not electronic.

48275
SI 2003/282 reg 3

> ⌐MEMO POINTS⌐ 1. Payments made by **credit card via the Internet** incur a transaction fee of 1.4% of the amount to be paid.
> 2. Payments made by **credit card over the telephone** incur a transaction fee of 1.5% of the amount to be paid.
> 3. Payment can be made using **sterling or foreign currency** from a foreign bank account. If there is any shortfall because of the conversion rate used, extra payment must be made.
> 4. HMRC's bank now accepts payments using the **Faster Payments Service**. This will, in the correct circumstances (companies should always check with their own bank to ensure that the right circumstances are in place), allow payments to be made and received on the same day. Full details can be found by following this link: flmemo.co.uk/ctm48275

SI 2012/689 reg 2

SI 2011/711 reg 2

Group payment arrangements

Groups of companies can **apply** for a group payment arrangement so that one company in the group can make payments on behalf of the other group members in the arrangement. This is **available for instalment payments** as well as **annual payments**. Payments can be allocated across group members after liabilities are settled. For more information see ¶69815.

48280

Income tax accounted for quarterly

Companies that **withhold income tax from payments** must account for that tax to HMRC on a quarterly basis (¶47115). The returns must be filed within 14 days after the end of the quarter, with a further return due for the period to the year end if that is not a quarter end. The income tax **must be paid** to HMRC at the same time as the return is filed. No assessment is raised by HMRC.

The **amount due** is reduced by any amount of income tax that the company suffers on its own receipts in the reporting period. If there is an **excess of tax suffered** this is carried forward to offset against tax that the company withholds in the following period.

48285
ss 951 – 953
ITA 2007

If there is still a surplus by the end of the company's accounting period this is set off against the company's corporation tax liability (¶41130).

Help in making and managing payments

48290
s 59G TMA 1970

HMRC have recognised that economic constraints may make it difficult for companies to make timely payments of corporation tax. They have **introduced** the Business Payments Support Service and have also **proposed** the introduction of managed payment plans. Both are designed to help companies spread payments over a period of time.

The Business Payments Support Service is available to taxpayers who **identify in advance of payments becoming due** that they may have difficulty in paying the amount of tax they owe on time. If HMRC are satisfied that the business has genuine difficulty, but will be able to make the payments in due course and then return to a normal payment pattern, they may grant additional time to pay. This will be after asking questions about the business and, for example, why the difficulty has arisen and what steps have been taken to raise funds. In some more complex cases they may require documentary evidence. **Interest** on overdue tax will still apply, even where time to pay has been granted.

> ⌐MEMO POINTS¬   Managed payment plans were included in Finance Act 2009 but their implementation was deferred. Originally they were **expected to be available** from April 2011 but in June 2010 the Government announced they would be delayed. No new implementation date has been proposed. Managed payment plans will **not be available** to companies liable to make instalment payments, nor to those in group payment arrangements.
> The **intention** is that companies make payments regularly so that they are spread equally before and after the normal due date. The payments are to be treated as paid on the normal due date.

SECTION 3

Repayments and interest

A. Repayments

48340
s 59D TMA 1970

A company may find that it has overpaid tax, perhaps because the tax was paid on an estimated basis to eliminate an interest exposure before the corporation tax computation was finalised for submission. If there has been an overpayment, the excess is repaid to the company.

The **amounts that can be repaid** are:
- corporation tax paid and not yet repaid;
- a corporation tax refund surrendered to the company by another group company;
- an excess of income tax suffered on income; and
- construction industry scheme deductions treated as corporation tax.

A repayment can be claimed even where the **liability has not been finally established**. The company has to make a claim to HMRC, stating the amount of the refund required and why it thinks that the amount it has paid will exceed its probable final tax liability. A **claim** cannot be made before the material date, being the later of the date when the tax was paid and the normal due date (9 months and 1 day after the end of the accounting period). If the return has not been submitted when the refund claim is made, the amount to be repaid must ignore deductions under the construction industry scheme.

s 59DA TMA 1970

> ⌐MEMO POINTS¬   A company **awaiting the outcome of an appeal** against an amendment to a return, or against an assessment, can apply to the tribunal (¶54335) for determination of the amount to be repaid.

Overpaid instalments

A company which has overpaid instalment payments (because its estimate of profits has reduced) can also make a claim under the specific regulation rather than setting the overpayment off against the next instalment. The company must explain why it now believes its earlier estimates were excessive. It may also apply to the tribunal to determine the amount to be repaid if there is an outstanding appeal.

48345
SI 1998/3175 reg 6

B. Interest on repayments

HMRC will pay interest on overpayments of tax. Interest will be paid regardless of whether the corporation tax was paid in instalments or not. **Repayments of instalments** earn interest at a different rate for the period up to 9 months and 1 day after the period end. The standard rate applies after that date. The **interest is taxable income** for the company under the loan relationship rules (¶16050+) and is paid without deduction of income tax. The rate of interest on repayments is lower than the rate payable on underpaid tax, so the need to avoid underpaying should be balanced against the rate earned on repayments. Special rules apply where the repayment results from losses or loan relationship deficits carried back.

48375

Interest rate setting

The interest rate on overpayments is set by reference to the official bank rate decided by the Monetary Policy Committee of the Bank of England. The actual rate payable for tax **repaid more than 9 months and 1 day after the period end** is the bank rate less 1% (subject to a minimum of 0.5%); it is set monthly. This rate applies to any period between 9 months and 1 day after the period end and the date the tax is repaid. HMRC refer to this as repayment interest.

48380
SI 1989/1297

Where the repayment is of **instalments** paid by a large company, or corporation **tax paid early** by a company that is not a large company, the actual rate is the bank rate less 0.25%, set twice monthly. HMRC refer to this rate as credit interest. This rate applies to any period between the date on which the first instalment is due, or would be due if the company were large, and 9 months and 1 day after the period end.

> MEMO POINTS The actual rates and the periods over which they apply are published by HMRC and can be found at ¶95260. The harmonisation of interest rules that has applied to most other taxes since Finance Act 2009 does not yet apply to corporation tax. While the primary legislation is in place a start date is yet to be announced.

Calculation of interest

Non-instalment payments Interest is **due** from the material date, which is the later of:
– the date the tax was paid; and
– 9 months and 1 day after the period end,
until the order to repay the tax is issued by HMRC.

48385
s 826 ICTA 1988

The material date for a **repayment of income tax suffered** is the day after the end of the accounting period in which the income was received. Where there has been **more than one payment** of corporation tax, a later payment is treated as being repaid in priority to an earlier one.

> EXAMPLE E Ltd has a 12-month accounting period which ended on 30 September 2008. Its liability for the year was calculated to be £75,000. It made the following payments:
>
> | | |
> |---|---|
> | 1 July 2009 | £80,000 |
> | 31 July 2009 | £10,000 |
>
> The overpayment of £15,000 was repaid to the company on 17 November 2009. The repayment interest rate was 0% from 27 January 2009 to 28 September 2009, and then 0.5%.

The interest due to the company will be calculated as follows:

From payment made on	Amount of repayment	Interest calculation
31 July 2009	£10,000	0% from 31 July 2009 to 28 September 2009 0.5% from 29 September 2009 to 17 November 2009
1 July 2009	£5,000	0% from 1 July 2009 to 28 September 2009 0.5% from 29 September 2009 to 17 November 2009

48390

SI 1998/3175 reg 8;
CTM 92290

Instalment payments   Interest runs from **no earlier** than the day that the first instalment is due for large companies within the instalment regime (or when an excess arises) until the tax is repaid. For those companies that pay their tax early, interest also runs from the date that the first instalment would be due if the company was within the instalments regime or when the tax was paid, if later. The credit interest rate only applies up to the date 9 months and 1 day after the period end. **Credit interest is not normally** calculated by HMRC until after the normal due date has passed.

EXAMPLE   B Ltd is a large company subject to the instalment regime. It has a 12-month accounting period ending on 31 December 2009. It paid instalments as follows:

Payment date	Estimated liability £	Payments made £	Correct payments £	Overpayments £
14 July 2009	6,750,000	1,687,500	1,400,000	287,500
14 October 2009	6,300,000	1,575,000	1,400,000	175,000
14 January 2010	5,600,000	1,400,000	1,400,000	-
14 April 2010	5,600,000	1,400,000	1,400,000	-

In November 2009, the company made a repayment claim for excessive instalments. This was accepted and £462,500 was repaid to the company on 5 January 2010. Credit interest is due as follows:
- £287,500 interest at 0.25% from 14 July to 20 September 2009 (rate change);
- £287,500 interest at 0.50% from 21 Sept until 5 January 2010; and
- £175,000 interest at 0.50% from 14 October until 5 January 2010.

48395

SI 1998/3175 reg 8

If a large company does not make a claim for repayment but instead **reduces future instalments**, the credit interest period will run until the overpayment is extinguished.

EXAMPLE   C Ltd is a large company subject to the instalment regime. It has a 12-month accounting period ending on 31 December. It paid instalments as follows:

Payment date	Estimated liability £	Payments made £	Correct payments £	Overpayments £
14 July	2,000,000	500,000	500,000	-
14 October	2,500,000	750,000[1]	500,000	250,000
14 January	2,500,000	625,000	500,000	375,000
14 April	2,000,000	125,000	500,000	-

Note:
1. This sum is made up of the second instalment of £625,000 and the shortfall from the first instalment of £125,000.
The company will be due credit interest on £250,000 from 14 October to 13 January, and on £375,000 from 14 January to 14 April, when the overpayment is utilised against the final instalment.

Repayments following loss carry back

48400

s 826 ICTA 1988

If a **trade loss** is carried back to an earlier accounting period, this may result in overpaid tax for the earlier period. Repayment interest will be calculated from the normal payable date of the earlier period but only if the **earlier period is wholly within the 12 months preceding** the loss-making period.

EXAMPLE D Ltd has a 12-month accounting period ending on 31 March 2012 and pays the full liability of £150,000 on 1 January 2013. In the period ending 31 March 2013 it makes a loss, which it carries back to the previous year, generating a repayment of £45,000. Repayment interest will run from 1 January 2013 until the tax is repaid.

If the earlier period is **not within the preceding 12 months**, the repayment interest will only run from the normal payable date for the period in which the loss is made.

EXAMPLE D Ltd makes a further loss in the period ending 31 March 2014 and ceases to trade on that date. The loss is carried back to the year ended 31 March 2012 and generates a further repayment of £30,000. Repayment interest will only start running from 1 January 2015, as the earlier period is not within the 12 months preceding 31 March 2014.

MEMO POINTS Where a **non-trading loan relationship deficit** (¶16350) is carried back to an earlier period and a repayment of tax results, repayment interest will only run from the normal due date of the later period.

Repayments of tax paid on loans to participators

Tax paid on a loan to a participator (¶75575) in a close company becomes repayable after the loan has been repaid, released or written off. Unless this happens within 9 months of the period end in which the loan was originally made (in which case the tax need not be paid in the first place), the tax **repayment cannot become due** until 9 months after the end of the period in which the loan repayment, release or write-off took place. Repayment interest will not start running until that date (or the date the tax was paid, if later).

48405
s 826(4) ICTA 1988

EXAMPLE E Ltd paid £8,000 tax on a loan to a participator 9 months after the year ended 31 May 2012. The loan was repaid 2 months later, on 30 April 2013. The tax became repayable on 28 February 2014 and was repaid on 24 May 2014.
Repayment interest is due on £8,000 for the period 28 February 2014 to 24 May 2014.

Clawback of overpaid repayments and interest

If a repayment has been made that is later found to be excessive, HMRC can **raise an assessment** to recover the excess, just as if it were tax due. If repayment interest was paid to the company, this can be recovered in the same way. Repayments **include tax set off** against other liabilities. The assessment is treated as being for the accounting period for which the original refund or set-off was made. **Interest can be charged** on the amount due under the assessment from the date the refund was originally made to the company until it is repaid to HMRC.

48410
Sch 18 para 52
FA 1998;
ss 1110, 1111
CTA 2010

An extended time limit applies if the assessment would be **outside the normal 4-year time limit**. The extended time limit is up to the end of the accounting period following the one in which the refund was made to the company. The limit is extended to 3 months after HMRC complete an enquiry into a relevant tax return, if this would be later. The longer time limits of 6 years and 20 years still apply where there has been careless or deliberate behaviour resulting in a loss of tax.

Sch 18 para 53
FA 1998

SECTION 4

Overpayment relief

The company can make a claim **where it believes** that it has paid too much tax, or that an assessment or determination is excessive.

The claim must be made in writing within 4 years of the accounting period. It **must include**:
– a statement that the company is making a claim under the overpayment relief provisions;
– details of the period to which it relates;

48460
Sch 1A TMA 1970;
Sch 18 para 51
FA 1998;
SACM 12150

– the grounds on which the assessment or payment is believed to be excessive;
– whether there has been an appeal about the matter;
– proof that the tax has been paid if it is a claim for repayment; and
– a declaration signed on the company's behalf that the details in the claim are correct to the best of the company's knowledge and belief.

Denial of relief

48465
Sch 18 para 51A
FA 1998

The relief will not be available where:
– the tax is excessive because of a mistake in a claim, notice or election;
– the tax is excessive because of an error in a capital allowances claim;
– other relief is available;
– the company should have been aware and able to correct the matter in normal time limits;
– the matter has already been the subject of an appeal or put to a court or tribunal;
– the grounds could have been included in an appeal to a court or tribunal but it is now too late;
– the tax is the subject of enforcement proceedings; or
– there was a mistake in calculating the liability but it was prepared in line with generally prevailing practice at that time.

With effect from 17 January 2014 it will no longer be a bar to relief that the return in question was prepared based on the generally prevailing practice at the time of submission, provided that tax was charged contrary to EU law. From the same date the time limit for claims will run from the period to which the return containing the mistake relates.

HMRC guidance

48470
SACM 12065

HMRC have offered some guidance on cases where the taxpayer should have been aware and claimed some other relief within the relevant time limit. These should be considered on a case-by-case basis. The ability and circumstances of the taxpayer need to be taken into account in determining whether the taxpayer took reasonable care to pay the right amount of tax, and whether it had any reason to think it had paid the wrong amount. There is **no requirement** to take advice on everything, nor to avoid all possible mistakes. However, HMRC do expect that if there is uncertainty, advice is both taken and heeded.

48475
SACM 12105

Generally prevailing practice   HMRC believe that the **onus** is on them to demonstrate the generally prevailing practice in any appeal hearing on overpayment relief. The practice need not be something that is universally followed. If a tribunal or court has decided that a practice is wrong, it should be treated as such even if there is an appeal on the decision.

Double assessment claim

48480
Sch 18 para 50
FA 1998

A company can claim relief where it thinks it has been assessed to tax twice on the **same profits for the same accounting period**. The claim has to be made in writing. HMRC will amend the assessment or repay tax if they agree with the claim. If HMRC refuse, an appeal can be brought (¶54125+).

SECTION 5

HMRC set-off

48530
s 130 FA 2008;
DMBM 700010

HMRC can set off amounts owed to it against amounts due to the company. This only applies in **England, Wales and Northern Ireland** but HMRC say this aligns with the common law position in **Scotland**. This covers a wide range of amounts owed and therefore a debt relating to one tax can be set against a repayment due in respect of a different tax. If there is already a statutory right of set-off that will take priority.

Repayments for **post-insolvency periods** cannot be set off against amounts owed for pre-insolvency periods.

s 131 FA 2008

There is **no requirement to inform** the company in advance that set-off is being applied. However, HMRC must notify in writing that set-off has been made. For set-off to take place the amounts must have been properly established, be quantifiable and payable. There is no formal **appeal** process but HMRC say they will consider any concerns raised by a taxpayer after the set-off.

48535

PART 8

Enforcement

Enforcement
Summary

The numbers cross-refer to paragraphs.

CHAPTER 1

Powers

The Government's continuing efforts to harmonise the administration of taxes have resulted in significant changes to HMRC's powers. The power to look at documents and inspect premises gives HMRC the authority to conduct compliance checks even before a return is submitted. This means information on tax planning could be gathered at an early stage. Inadequacies in record-keeping could be identified before a return is made and improved through a mechanism such as the business record checks that HMRC are now implementing.

50000

SECTION 1

Information and documents

A. Power to request from company

50050
Sch 36 para 1
FA 2008

HMRC have the power to request, **at any time** (but see ¶50295 for requests after a self-assessment return has been filed), any information or documents (hereinafter referred to as information) that are reasonably required to check a company's tax position. They do this by issuing an information notice to the company.

CH 23260

Documents that are requested should be ones that are already in existence and as such HMRC cannot require someone to prepare a document that does not exist. However, in many cases this may be done by the company as a simple method of providing information that has been requested.

CH 23240

The dictionary definition of **information** covers knowledge and facts only. HMRC do not regard it as including opinion or speculation.

s 114 FA 2008

‾MEMO POINTS‾   Documents **include** those in electronic format.

Tax position

50055
Sch 36 para 64
FA 2008

The definition of tax position is drawn widely so that it **covers** any tax liability, past, present or future. It also covers penalties, any other amounts payable in connection with any tax, and any claims and elections. The inclusion of **future liabilities** is the most problematic of these categories, since there may be some uncertainty as to exactly when a company develops a tax position in relation to a transaction not yet undertaken.

This ability to request information about a future liability could also be used by HMRC to identify what they perceive as loopholes in tax legislation and close them earlier than might otherwise be the case.

Reasonably required

50060
CH 21620

There is no definition of what can be regarded as reasonably required. HMRC guidance states that reasonably required is **limited to** information which might affect the tax position. In some cases this cannot be known until the information is actually obtained but HMRC officers should be **prepared to show** why the information could help decide what the correct position is, how it might be corrected (if wrong) and how to ensure that the correct amount of tax is paid. At all times the balance needs to be managed between the burden of obtaining the information and how important it is in checking the tax position.

Tribunal approval for notice

50065

HMRC **may seek** the approval of the tribunal for the information notice. If the tribunal has approved the notice, the company cannot appeal (¶50145) against it once it is issued. There are several conditions for approval.

For the tribunal to issue a notice:
– the application needs the agreement of an authorised HMRC officer;
– the tribunal must be satisfied that the notice is justified in the particular circumstances;
– the recipient of the notice must have been told that the information is required and must have been given a reasonable opportunity to make representations to HMRC; and
– a summary of any representations made must have been presented to the tribunal.

The last two conditions can be **waived** where the tribunal believes that to comply with them would prejudice the collection of tax.

B. Power to request from third party

HMRC can issue an information notice about a **named taxpayer** to a third party. The information must be reasonably required (¶50060) to check the named taxpayer company's tax position. The **notice must** name the company **unless** the tribunal has approved the request and agreed that the company does not need to be identified, because this might seriously prejudice the collection of tax.

50095
Sch 36 para 2
FA 2008

HMRC suggest that a third-party notice is **most likely to be used** where information or a document is not in the company's power to provide, or facts need to be checked independently.

CH 23620

Conditions to issue notice

For HMRC to be able to issue a notice to a third party, either the **company** to which it relates has to agree to it or the **tribunal** must approve its issue. HMRC also have the ability to seek tribunal approval, even if the company agrees to the issuing of the notice.

50100
Sch 36 para 3
FA 2008

For the tribunal to issue a notice:
– the application needs the agreement of an authorised HMRC officer;
– the tribunal must be satisfied that the notice is justified in the particular circumstances;
– the recipient of the notice must have been told that the information is required and must have been given a reasonable opportunity to make representations to HMRC;
– a summary of any representations made must have been presented to the tribunal; and
– the company to whom the notice relates must have been given a summary of why HMRC require the information requested.

The last three conditions can be **waived** where the tribunal believes that to comply with them would prejudice the collection of tax.

> MEMO POINTS   A third-party notice **must be copied** to the company, unless HMRC believe that doing so would prejudice the collection of tax and the tribunal agrees that reasonable grounds exist for this belief.

Sch 36 para 4
FA 2008

Group situations

Where a third-party notice is issued to someone for the purpose of checking the tax position of **both** a **parent undertaking** and **one of its subsidiaries**, the information contained in the notice differs. It need only name the parent company, and state that it is for the purpose of checking its and its subsidiaries' tax position, but does not have to name the subsidiaries involved. Further, a copy of the notice only has to be given to the parent undertaking. If the **tribunal is approached** to approve the issue of a notice, HMRC need only give reasons why the notice is required with regard to the parent undertaking.

50105
Sch 36 para 35 (2),
(3) FA 2008

If a notice is **issued to the parent undertaking** in relation to **more than one of its subsidiaries** the rules are changed so that:
– no approval, from the tribunal or any of the subsidiaries, is required to issue the notice;
– there is no need to name the subsidiaries, provided that the notice states that it is in relation to more than one subsidiary;
– there is no requirement to issue a copy of the notice to any subsidiary; and
– the parent undertaking has full rights of appeal (¶50145) against the notice, rather than the restricted rights usually attaching to third-party notices.

Where **tribunal approval is sought** in these circumstances there is no requirement to:
– name the subsidiaries, provided that the notice states that it is for the purpose of checking the tax position of more than one subsidiary;
– issue a copy of the notice to the subsidiaries; or
– issue a summary of reasons why the information is required to the affected subsidiaries.

`MEMO POINTS`   Broadly speaking a **parent undertaking** is one that can control, either by way of voting rights, the ability to appoint a majority of the board, or having a dominant influence over, another company. For a full definition see *Company Law Memo*.

Identity of company unknown

50110
Sch 36 para 5
FA 2008;
CH 227100

HMRC can also issue requests where they do not know the identity of a company, or the individual identities of a group of taxpayers. This requires the **approval** of the tribunal. There must be reasonable grounds for believing that there has been a failure to comply with UK tax provisions, and the information must not be readily available from another source. HMRC operational guidance quotes **examples** of when the need for unnamed taxpayer notices might arise, ranging from serious tax evasion to offshore bank accounts.

Involved third parties

50115
Sch 36 para 34A
FA 2008

Within the definition of third party there is a further category of "involved" third parties. These parties **differ depending on the tax in question**. The only involved third party for corporation tax purposes is a Lloyd's managing agent as regards the activities of any syndicate it manages. The rules for third-party notices in these cases are amended so that:
– no prior approval is required to issue a notice to an involved third party;
– a copy does not need to be given to the company; and
– there is no appeal mechanism if the information is part of the involved third party's statutory records.

Other third-party powers

50120
s 222 FA 2013

HMRC have power to issue demands for information about third parties in order to comply with the UK's obligations under an agreement with the **US** to improve international tax compliance and implement FATCA (the Foreign Account Tax Compliance Act). Details of the compliance regime will be included in regulations.

50125
s 228 FA 2013

HMRC also can now demand information from **merchant acquirers** (businesses which process credit card transactions) and **aggregators** (businesses which act as intermediaries by aggregating a number of retailers under a single merchant account) about business transactions.

HMRC can require merchant acquirers and aggregators to provide information about credit, debit and charge card sales made by retailers, and each retailer's name, address, VAT number if available and bank account details. HMRC say they will not seek to identify the details of individual credit or debit card holders, just the total sales made by particular retailers in each month. HMRC will use this information to cross-check against business income declared on, inter alia, corporation tax returns.

Whilst the new power has only been available since 17 July 2013, demands for information may relate to periods ending in the 4 years up to the date of the notice.

C. Appeals

General right

50145
Sch 36 paras 29
– 31 FA 2008

A general right of appeal against the issue of an information notice exists to allow companies to counter a request that they do not believe to be reasonable. This **right does not apply** where the documents requested are statutory records, or if the tribunal approved the notice in advance (¶50065 and ¶50100).

In the case of notices **issued to third parties** the only ground for appeal is that a notice would be unduly onerous to comply with. Involved third parties (¶50115) do not have their rights of appeal restricted in this way.

Any appeal **must be made within** 30 days of the issue of the information notice in question.

MEMO POINTS 1. Where a company wishes to challenge a notice that was **approved by a tribunal** it must do so by way of judicial review.
2. **Statutory records** are those required to be kept under the Taxes Acts or under any other enactment where the document relates to tax matters. If such documentation is not related to a business and not required to be kept under any other legislation relating to tax, it only forms part of the statutory records once the chargeable period it relates to has ended.

Tribunal decision

The tribunal can confirm, vary or set aside the information notice. Its decision must then be complied with in the period it specifies, or if it does not specify, the period reasonably specified by HMRC. There is **no right of appeal** from the tribunal's decision, so any further challenge by the company must be through judicial review.

50150
Sch 36 para 32
FA 2008

Professional advisers

A number of protections are afforded to auditors, tax advisers and legal advisers, although the protection for auditors and tax advisers is more limited than that for legal advisers. Where the protection applies, a third party cannot be required to provide certain types of information.

50155
Sch 36 paras 23 -
26 FA 2008

Third-party adviser	Outside the scope of an information notice	Limitations
Auditor	Anything: – created in the role of auditor and held by the auditor; and – held for the purposes of the appointment as auditor	Information or a document relating to any information or document prepared by the adviser as tax accountant for the client to provide to HMRC
Tax adviser	Any: – information related to communications about tax advice to a client or another of its tax advisers; and – documents which are the tax adviser's property consisting of tax advice to a client or another of its tax advisers	Where a notice relates to unknown parties (¶50110) the exemption does not extend to the names and addresses of those parties, or anyone who has acted for them
Legal adviser	Any document or information which is subject to legal professional privilege	

The definition of **auditor is extended** in HMRC guidance so that it is not just an auditor appointed under the relevant Companies Acts requirements but also one appointed for a non-statutory purpose – for instance, to comply with the requirements of a professional body – provided that the adviser acts to the Companies Acts standards and separates auditing paperwork from accounts preparation paperwork.

CH 22280

Where the information relates to the third party's role as **tax accountant**, HMRC can ask how an item has been calculated, but not why it has been calculated one way rather than another. Where only part of a document is relevant, only that part need be revealed or provided.

CH 22340

Legal professional privilege A major exclusion that benefits legal advisers is that any information subject to legal professional privilege need not be provided. As this is likely to be an area where **disputes** could arise about which documents are covered by this exemption, the legislation allows for these to be **resolved by the tribunal**.

50160
Sch 36 para 23
FA 2008

Legal professional privilege was not originally a statutory term; it has developed over centuries as a common law concept in order to keep legal advice confidential. The prevailing view has been that this only extends to advice provided by solicitors or barristers, or foreign legal professionals. Tax advisers have therefore been at a commercial disadvantage, as their advice has not been protected in the same way, even if it covers the same matters. The

Supreme Court has confirmed, however, that legal professional privilege cannot be extended to accountants without statutory intervention. *R (oao Prudential plc and another) v Special Commissioner of Income Tax and another* [2013]

SI 2009/1916

If the **company**, on receipt of an information notice, **believes that any of the information** requested is covered by legal professional privilege, it must respond with a list of those items no more than 20 working days after the original delivery date. HMRC must then reply within a further 20 working days stating which information they believe is not covered by legal professional privilege. The company can then appeal to the tribunal for resolution of the dispute within a further 20 working days. The tribunal will decide which, if any, parts of a document must be disclosed, whilst ensuring that no inadvertent disclosure of the items takes place.

D. Complying with a notice

1. Provision of information

50190
Sch 36 para 7
FA 2008

Information requested has to be supplied:
- **within** a specified, reasonable period;
- in such **form** and manner as HMRC reasonably request; and
- at an agreed **place**.

Reasonable period

50195
CH 23420

HMRC accept that the **length of time** regarded as reasonable will vary depending on the circumstances. HMRC consider that 30 days will be an appropriate length of time to produce most information. They will also consider a request for an extension to the time to supply any information where there is sufficient reason for the deadline to be adjusted.

The guidance also envisages a situation where a notice may be **issued at a visit** to business premises to examine previously requested documents. These may indicate that further documents not previously specified should be examined. A notice could be issued for immediate compliance. However, the company could refuse to comply on the basis that it will appeal the notice (¶50145).

Place of delivery

50200

The regulations do not force someone complying with a notice to send the information to HMRC. Instead there is only a **requirement** to make the information available for examination. The company can suggest a time and place for this to happen. Where this is reasonable and practical HMRC should accept the company's suggestion. It will not be considered reasonable if the information is made available at an unsocial time of day or at an unreasonable location. For instance, the provision of information at around midnight at a private dwelling is not considered reasonable. *Johnson v IRC* [1996]

If the **company's suggestion** is **not** considered to be reasonable or practical, HMRC should advise the company as to why not, and suggest an alternative. Where agreement cannot be reached ultimately HMRC will decide on how the information will be provided.

2. Documents to be provided

Basic rule

50230
Sch 36 para 18
FA 2008;
CH 22120

As a basic principle HMRC can **only request documentation** that is in the physical control of the company from which it is requested, or which it is within that company's power to acquire, by legal channels or by influence over the holder of the relevant document. Beyond this the documents that have to be provided are those requested in the notice, unless any specific exemption applies.

It is generally acceptable for copies of documents to be provided, although HMRC can specifically request originals, or subsequently request them. HMRC can make copies, take extracts or remove the documents, as required.

A company cannot, nor arrange to, conceal, destroy or otherwise dispose of a document if HMRC have informed it that the document is, or is likely to be, the subject of an information notice. The document can be destroyed or disposed of only if at least 6 months have passed since the company was last informed of the need to retain the document. If an information notice **has been served**, concealment, destruction or disposal may amount to a criminal offence (¶50735).

Sch 36 paras 43, 53 FA 2008

Exclusions

The following documentation cannot be required to be provided:
– information relating to an **impending tax appeal**;
– **journalistic** material;
– **personal** information; and
– information relating to someone who **died** more than 4 years previously.

50235
Sch 36 paras 19, 22 FA 2008

Generally documents that are **more than 6 years old** in their entirety cannot be requested. However, where HMRC believe it is necessary to examine such a document, they can apply for it with the agreement of an authorised officer. HMRC suggest that a document this old is only likely to be requested where it sheds light on a later period, or where a deliberate error in a return is suspected.

Sch 36 para 20 FA 2008; CH 22140

E. Failure to comply

In order to encourage compliance with information notices, either those issued to the company itself or to third parties, a simple system of **penalties** applies.

50265

Where the party that has received the notice fails to comply within the time specified it will be liable to an initial penalty of £300. Where the failure continues, a further daily penalty of up to £60 can be imposed.

If the initial penalty has been levied and failure continues HMRC **can apply to the Upper Tribunal** to impose a tax-related penalty where they believe that the amount of additional tax at stake is significant. Where there is **no right of appeal against a notice** the application must be made within 12 months of the date of the initial penalty. Where a **right of appeal does exist** it must be made within 12 months of the later of the date on which the right of appeal against the notice expires or the appeal is decided. It is then for the Upper Tribunal to decide the penalty, based on the amount of tax considered to be at stake.

MEMO POINTS The initial, daily and tax-related penalties can **all be levied** in respect of a single failure.

F. Once return submitted

If a self-assessment corporation tax return has been submitted, HMRC **may not issue** a notice relating to information for that period.

50295
Sch 36 para 21 FA 2008

Notwithstanding this exclusion HMRC **can still issue** a notice and the company will have to comply if:

– an enquiry notice has been issued for that return, or a claim, or election, and the enquiry is still open;
– HMRC have reason to suspect that an assessment has not been raised which should have been, or that an assessment undercharges tax, or that too much tax relief has been given;
– the information is also required to check another tax; or
– the information is also required to check the operation of rules where the company is withholding tax on behalf of another, for instance under PAYE.

The **result of these limitations** is that in order to obtain information where a return has been submitted, HMRC are forced to open an enquiry (¶50415+).

SECTION 2

Power to inspect

General right of inspection

50345
Sch 36 paras 10,
10A FA 2008

As well as asking to see documents or be provided with information to check a company's tax position, HMRC can **enter business premises** in order to inspect the premises, and any business assets or business documents on the premises. This right is restricted so that no entry can be made into any part of premises used solely as a **dwelling**.

HMRC can also enter the premises of an **involved third party** (¶50115).

Sch 36 para 12A
FA 2008

Entry and inspection are also permitted to **value** the premises or other property. This can include those premises used solely as a dwelling. The inspection must be reasonably required in order to check someone's tax position.

> MEMO POINTS   1. In this context a **business** includes charitable activities, the letting of property and the activities of a public authority.
> 2. **Premises** includes any building, land or means of transport. This means any vehicle used for a business purpose can be inspected.
> 3. **Assets** which may be inspected include computers and associated equipment used to produce business documents; assistance with access must be provided if necessary, within a reasonable period.
> 4. Any **documents** can be copied, have an extract made of them, or be removed. Assets can also be marked to show that they have been inspected.

Restrictions

50350
CH 25120 – 25140

Entry **does not allow** for forced or clandestine entry, nor does it permit searching. Inspection does not include touching and opening items. The simple distinction is that inspection allows sight of what is in view but not looking for something that cannot be seen.

> EXAMPLE
> 1. Where an HMRC official is shown into a room in which the books, records and invoices that have been requested have been placed on a table for inspection, the official is allowed to open the files and boxes of records that have been collected. He is allowed to walk around and look at the pictures on the wall. He is not allowed to open the filing cabinet in the corner just to see what is in it.
>
> 2. An HMRC official is shown into a room in which the accounting records requested have been placed on a table for inspection. He is told the invoices are in the filing cabinet in the corner. He may open the filing cabinet to inspect any invoices that he may want to.

Documents inspected after entry on to business premises are **subject to the same limitations** as those subject to an information notice (¶50050+), so that the exclusions for auditors, tax advisers and privileged legal communications all apply (¶50155).

CH 25650, 25700

The power of entry is **not absolute**, so that entry may be refused by the occupier or the person whose tax position is being checked. HMRC do not have the right to override this, even when notice has been given and/or tribunal approval has been obtained. In these circumstances HMRC guidance suggests that the officer should try to arrange an alternative time and date. If the tribunal has approved the inspection, the officer has the power to levy a penalty for deliberate obstruction if entry is refused (¶50365).

Notification of inspection

The inspection **should be carried** out at an agreed time, or at a reasonable time, which is either:
- after 7 days' notice has been given (this does not have to be in writing); or
- at any time, if the inspection is carried out by, or with the approval of, an authorised officer of HMRC.

50355
Sch 36 para 12
FA 2008

If the inspection is by, or with the approval of, an authorised officer and **no notice has been given**, a written notice must be supplied to the occupier of the premises at the time of the inspection; if the occupier is not on site at the time, the notice must be supplied to the person who appears to be in charge. Failing these it should be left on the premises. The notice must state the consequences of obstructing the inspection. If the inspection has been approved by the tribunal, the notice must say so.

> MEMO POINTS If the property is to be entered for **valuation** purposes only, either the inspection must:
> - be at an agreed time for which notice has been given; or
> - have been approved by the tribunal and at least 7 days' notice of the inspection must have been given to anyone specified by the tribunal.

Sch 36 para 12B
FA 2008

Approval by tribunal

Tribunal approval for an inspection is **only given** where the application has been made by or with the approval of an authorised officer of HMRC and the tribunal believes that the inspection is justified. If the request relates to a valuation, the company and the premises occupier must have been allowed a reasonable opportunity to make representations. There is **no appeal** from such tribunal approval, so any challenge has to be by way of judicial review.

50360
Sch 36 para 13
FA 2008

Penalty

In terms of the inspection of business premises the only penalty that could arise is for **deliberately obstructing** an HMRC officer during a visit, when the visit has been approved by the tribunal. There is an initial penalty of £300, plus a penalty of up to £60 per day where the obstruction continues.

50365

If the initial penalty has been levied and failure continues, HMRC **can apply to the Upper Tribunal** to impose a tax-related penalty where they believe that the amount of additional tax at stake is significant. The application must be made within 12 months of the date of the initial penalty. It is then for the Upper Tribunal to decide the penalty, based on the amount of tax considered to be at stake.

> MEMO POINTS The initial, daily and tax-related penalties can **all be levied in** respect of a single failure.

SECTION 3

Enquiries

If HMRC want to make an examination of the detail of a return, they must initiate a formal enquiry. HMRC **do not need** to provide a reason why they have raised an enquiry: it could be random; or it could be that they believe there is an inaccuracy in the return. The opening

50415
Sch 18 para 24
FA 1998;
EM 1503

enquiry letter is likely to be neutral in tone and HMRC will seek information to help them determine whether they think an inaccuracy exists.

Although a limited number of random enquiries are still carried out each year, most cases are now identified by way of risk-assessment.

A. Time limit

50445
Sch 18 para 24
FA 1998

In order to start the enquiry HMRC must issue a formal enquiry notice. The notice must be issued within the enquiry window. The enquiry window is based on when the return is filed, as follows:

Self-assessment return	Enquiry window deadline
Filed on time – single company or small group	12 months after the actual date of filing
Filed on time – member of medium or large group	12 months after the due filing date[1]
Filed late	Up to and including the 31 January, 30 April, 31 July or 31 October next following the anniversary of when the return was filed
Company amends its return	Up to and including the 31 January, 30 April, 31 July or 31 October next following the anniversary of when the return was amended
Note: 1. HMRC have stated that, where possible, for companies in medium and large groups, they will open all enquiries within 12 months of the date the last group company files its return.	

s 383 CA 2006

MEMO POINTS 1. A **small group** is one that meets two of the following conditions:
– assets less than £3.26 million;
– turnover less than £6.5 million; or
– 50 or fewer employees.
2. For details of when returns are due to be lodged see ¶46110.

B. Scope of enquiry

50475
Sch 18 para 25
FA 1998

An enquiry **can cover** anything contained in the return (including any claim or election), or anything that affects the tax payable for another period of that company, or the tax payable of another company for any period. Where an enquiry is raised as a result of an amendment made by the company and the enquiry is raised outside the normal enquiry window, the enquiry can only relate to the matters covered by the amendment.

The enquiry **can also extend** to whether to issue a notice relating to:
– avoidance involving capital losses;
– arrangements designed to increase foreign tax credit relief;
– transfer pricing in a medium-sized enterprise; or
– avoidance involving tax arbitrage.

Return for incorrect period

50480

An enquiry can still be made, even if the return appears to be for the wrong period. A **wrong period is one** where the accounting period on the return is not in fact an accounting period of the company, or where the return claims that there is no accounting period ending in the period set out in the notice to file, but where there is in fact such a period. The filing deadline, on which the enquiry window is based, will be that for the period set out in the return.

C. During the enquiry

HMRC actions

During the course of an enquiry HMRC can amend the tax return if they need to do so immediately to avoid a loss of tax. **Otherwise** any amendments are not normally made until the conclusion of the enquiry. The company cannot ask HMRC to review this, nor can an appeal be made to the tribunal at the time. However, the company is able to appeal the amendment by giving notice in writing to HMRC, within 30 days of being notified of it.

50510

If the enquiry is limited to only looking at an **amendment** made by the company itself, the amendment made by HMRC can only relate to the understated liability arising from the company's amendment.

> MEMO POINTS HMRC may issue an **information notice** during the enquiry (¶50050) in order to secure more information.

Company actions

The company can also amend its return during the course of the enquiry but this will **only take effect** when the enquiry closes if the amendment affects the tax payable by:
- the company for that or another period; or
- another company for any period.

50515
Sch 18 paras 31, 33
FA 1998

The amendment will either be mentioned as part of the amendments in the closure notice or, if it is not, it is deemed to have been made on closure. This deferral does not prevent a claim for an **early repayment** if the company's circumstances change so that the company believes it has overpaid tax.

The **company can apply** to the tribunal to get an **enquiry closed** where it believes that HMRC are unnecessarily prolonging it. The tribunal will instruct HMRC to close the enquiry by a date it specifies, unless it is satisfied that HMRC have reasonable grounds for not yet closing the enquiry. This provision is often used by companies to force HMRC to highlight their concerns, where these have not already been disclosed.

Referral to tribunal

At any point during the enquiry the company and HMRC can **jointly** refer any issue to the tribunal (either may withdraw the referral). Referral is likely to be for complex and important questions that will affect the outcome of the enquiry. The enquiry cannot be closed until after the referral is finally determined. The tribunal determination is binding on the parties and has to be taken into account by HMRC in reaching their conclusions on the enquiry.

50520
Sch 18 paras 31A
– D FA 1998

D. Closing the enquiry

The enquiry closes when HMRC issue a closure notice showing their conclusions. HMRC will make any amendments they decide are required in the closure notice (including an amendment to make it the return for the correct period if this is needed), or else state that no changes are needed. They can also issue **additional notices** to give effect to any changes required to other company returns as a result of their findings.

50550

The company can then appeal in writing within 30 days if it does not agree with any of the amendments.

> MEMO POINTS If HMRC have decided that a return has been made for the **wrong period**, the closure notice will state what the right period should have been (both beginning and end dates). If there is more than one accounting period which ends in or at the end of the period shown on

the notice to file a return, the conclusions in the closure notice refer to the first of the accounting periods. The company will then be required to submit a return for the missing period(s) by the later of the original filing deadline and 30 days after it is finally determined what the correct periods should have been.

SECTION 4

Discovery assessments

Basic rule

50600
Sch 18 para 46
FA 1998

During an enquiry information may come to light that HMRC were not aware of previously. This may be as simple as discovering that the company has not been disallowing entertaining expenses in its computations, or it may be more complicated – for instance, that the company has not been making full disclosure of its income. In order to combat this situation HMRC are able to raise assessments that would otherwise be out of time. These are known as discovery assessments.

These **can only be made** where HMRC could not have reasonably been expected to be aware that there had been a loss of tax, on the basis of the information available to them at the time the enquiry window closed, or any open enquiry was completed (this requirement does not apply if the behaviour which resulted in the loss of tax was careless or deliberate). A discovery assessment can only be **raised within** 4 years of the end of the accounting period concerned.

Any **appeal** against the assessment must be made in writing within 30 days.

Careless or deliberate behaviour

50605

If the behaviour which has resulted in a loss of tax is careless the **time limit is extended** to 6 years. If the behaviour is deliberate, the time limit is 20 years.

> [MEMO POINTS]   The **definitions** of careless and deliberate can be found at ¶52580+.

Information available

50610

Information is made available if it is in:
– the relevant **return** and accompanying documents (this further **includes** the returns of the previous two periods);
– a relevant **claim** and accompanying documents; or
– any **accounts**, documents or information produced for HMRC during an enquiry.

If the existence and relevance of the information could be **inferred** by HMRC from anything in the list above, or they have specifically been told about it by the company (or someone acting on its behalf), that will also be considered to have been made available.

> [EXAMPLE]   A number of taxpayers entered into transactions that were subject to the **disclosure of tax avoidance schemes** (DOTAS) rules (see ¶46485+). All of the necessary paperwork was completed and the returns indicated the scheme reference number. HMRC challenged a similar scheme; the final decision of the Court of Appeal, given on 25 June 2009, was that the particular scheme was ineffective. HMRC later issued discovery assessments to the taxpayers in this case. The Upper Tribunal, confirming the decision made by the First-tier Tribunal, held that the fact that the returns had highlighted all of the issues involved, including the scheme reference number, along with the decision in the original case, meant that HMRC had full possession of the facts involved and had **not** later discovered anything that entitled them to issue assessments. *HMRC v Charlton and others* [2012]

Protection from discovery

50615

This leaves companies in a situation where, having made a self-assessment which they have certified as correct and complete, they will not finally know, even at the end of the enquiry window, whether HMRC regard them as having provided enough information to avoid a discovery assessment.

HMRC have therefore **issued guidance** on how to provide enough information in certain circumstances. If a company follows the guidance and no enquiry is opened, the statement says that the return can be regarded as finally closed.

EM 3200

It should be noted that a decided case has stated there is no requirement that the existence of information and the relevance of it should be communicated to HMRC within the same written communication. Also, the relevance should be ascribed to a particular period, suggesting that for ongoing matters the information is provided year on year. *HMRC v Lansdowne Partners Ltd* [2010]

> MEMO POINTS I IMRC do not believe that making available information about one company in a **group** will count as making available the same information about another company in the same group.

EM 8135

HMRC guidance The information provided must be enough for HMRC to realise that there might be insufficient tax self-assessed but does not need to be enough for them to calculate the amount. **Providing too much information** is inadvisable, since HMRC say they cannot be expected to pick out the relevant points from a lot of detail unless their attention is drawn to it. The common situations used in the guidance are:

50620
SP 1/06

a. where a **valuation** is used in the return (the return or accompanying documents should state who made the valuation, whether the valuer was independent of the company and suitably qualified, and that it was carried out on an appropriate basis);

b. where an **unusual item** appears, judgement has been used and a different view has been taken from HMRC (the guidance cites repairs as an example – where suitable analysis of what has been treated as capital and what as revenue is included, along with the basis of the split between the two, HMRC say that no discovery will be made unless the statement is obviously untrue or unreasonable enough to be negligent); and

c. where an **adjustment** has not been applied (the guidance acknowledges that taxpayers may take a different view of the law than HMRC do – provided that clear and sufficient disclosure is made, allowing HMRC to realise there might be an understated liability and open an enquiry, they say that finality will be achieved if the taxpayer's stance is not wholly unreasonable).

Generally prevailing practice Another form of protection from discovery, in a case where HMRC believe that a mistake was made in a return, is afforded if the **return was prepared** in accordance with practice generally prevailing at that time. There is no legislative definition of generally prevailing practice but HMRC manuals refer to a change in HMRC practice and thus imply that it is HMRC's practice which counts. However, case law suggests that the practice should be "accepted by HMRC and taxpayers' advisers alike". *HMRC v Household Estate Agents Ltd* [2007] If a company believes that the treatment it has adopted is generally prevailing practice it should ensure that it records the basis for that decision, since it may later **need to defend that view** if a discovery assessment is made.

50625
Sch 18 para 45
FA 1998;
CTM 95090, 95560

SECTION 5

Power to obtain contact details of debtors

Another power recently granted to HMRC entitles them to obtain from a third party the contact details of people who owe money to them. HMRC must reasonably require the details in order to pursue the debt, and they must have reasonable grounds for believing that the third party has the contact details.

50675
Sch 49 FA 2009

Third parties

50680   The third party must be a company, a local authority or a local authority association, or HMRC must have reasonable grounds for believing that the contact details were obtained in the course of carrying on a business (which includes professions and property businesses, wherever situated). There is an **exemption** if the third party obtained the details while providing charitable services free of charge or, if not a charity, obtained the details in the course of providing services on behalf of a charity free of charge. Advice received from a debt advisory charity about tax debts should, therefore, remain confidential.

Procedure

50685   The details must be **requested** by issuing a notice in writing to the third party. This must request the details at a time and in a manner which is reasonable. The third party can **appeal** within 30 days against any part of the notice if it would be unduly onerous to comply with it. The **penalty** for failing to comply is £300.

SECTION 6

Criminal investigation powers

50735   HMRC have various powers in order to investigate serious crime under the Police and Criminal Evidence Act 1984 and the Serious Crime Act 2007. Prosecutions are handled by the Revenue and Customs Prosecution Office, which is now part of the Crown Prosecution Service.

The **key powers** available that now apply to all criminal investigations, not just those that relate to customs and excise matters, are the power to:
– obtain a warrant to enter premises and search;
– search people found on the premises;
– make arrests; and
– obtain a judicial order for the production of a document, most notably in cases of serious tax fraud.

These powers can **only be carried out by** an appropriately authorised officer of HMRC.

HMRC's policy is that criminal investigations will **only be undertaken** where they need to send a strong deterrent message, or criminal sanction is appropriate. Normally they would expect to deal with a case under their civil investigation of fraud procedures. However, HMRC reserve the right to pursue cases on a criminal basis if that seems more appropriate.

CHAPTER 2

Interest levied

51000

The principal systems in place to ensure timely payment of tax by companies, be it **corporation or income tax**, are those of interest and penalties. The rules relating to penalties for late-paid tax are covered at ¶52415+.

A. Mainstream corporation tax

51030

Corporation tax for companies, other than large ones as defined, is normally due 9 months and 1 day after the end of the accounting period. For further information on how to identify the exact due date see ¶48050.

51035
s 59E TMA 1970

If a company is **large**, its corporation tax liability becomes due in instalments, based on its own estimate of its total corporation tax liability for the accounting period. Any **underestimates** will incur interest at a special rate. Any overestimates will earn interest on overpaid tax on each instalment, again at a special rate. The tax due in instalments includes tax on loans to participators and any sums due under the controlled foreign company provisions.

> MEMO POINTS   For the calculation of instalment due dates and amounts see ¶48095+. For the calculation of interest on overpaid instalments see ¶48345.

Late payments of mainstream tax

Interest runs from the date that the tax is due and payable until it is actually paid.

51040
s 87A TMA 1970

> EXAMPLE   A Ltd has a 12-month accounting period which ended on 30 September 2012. The due date was 1 July 2013. On 30 September 2013 it filed a corporation tax return showing a liability of £45,000. On 30 November 2013 it paid £30,000 of the tax due and the balance of £15,000 was paid on 31 December 2013. The interest rate in force was 3%. The interest due from the company was calculated as:
> – payment of £30,000: interest from 2 July 2013 to 30 November 2013 at 3%; and
> – payment of £15,000: interest from 2 July 2013 to 31 December 2013 at 3%.

Overdue or underpaid instalments

For companies within the instalment regime interest is due from no earlier than the day that the first instalment is due until the instalment is paid. The **debit interest rate**, as it is termed

51045
CTM 92660

by HMRC to distinguish it from the main rate of interest levied on underpayments, only applies for periods up to the date 9 months and 1 day after the period end, as thereafter the normal interest rate applies. Debit interest is not calculated by HMRC until after the normal due date has passed and the company has provided a self-assessment return, or HMRC make a determination in the absence of a return.

> EXAMPLE B Ltd is a large company subject to the instalment regime. It has a 12-month accounting period ending on 31 October 2012. It paid instalments as follows:
>
> | Payment date | Estimated liability £ | Payments made £ | Correct instalment £ | Cumulative underpayment £ |
> |---|---|---|---|---|
> | 14 May 2012 | 5,000,000 | 1,250,000 | 1,400,000 | 150,000 |
> | 14 August 2012 | 5,200,000 | 1,300,000 | 1,400,000 | 250,000 |
> | | Top up first instalment | 50,000 | | 200,000 |
> | 15 November 2012 | 5,300,000 | 1,325,000 | 1,400,000 | 275,000 |
> | | Top up first two instalments | 50,000 | | 225,000 |
> | 15 February 2013 | 5,400,000 | 1,350,000 | 1,400,000 | 275,000 |
> | | Top up first three instalments | 75,000 | | 200,000 |
> | 2 August 2013 | 5,600,000 | 200,000 | - | - |
>
> This results in the following amount of interest being levied on the company:
>
> | Due from | Due to | Days | Amount £ | Interest rate | Interest due £ |
> |---|---|---|---|---|---|
> | 15 May 2012 | 14 August 2012 | 91 | 150,000 | 1.5% | 2,048 |
> | 15 August 2012 | 15 November 2012 | 92 | 200,000 | 1.5% | 2,760 |
> | 15 November 2012 | 15 February 2013 | 92 | 225,000 | 1.5% | 3,105 |
> | 15 February 2013 | 2 August 2013 | 168 | 200,000 | 1.5% | 5,040 |
> | | | | | | 12,953 |
>
> If the outstanding tax had not been paid by 9 months and 1 day after the period end the underpayment would have been subjected to the normal interest rules from that date forward (¶51040).

> MEMO POINTS If an interest rate change occurs during the period the interest is to be calculated for, the interest at the old rate is calculated to the date of change and then the new rate applied from that date.

B. Other situations

Carry back of losses

51075
s 87A TMA 1970;
CTM 92240

In some cases tax for a period may not have been paid, as the company was aware that the following period's accounts would show a loss that it would be able to carry back (¶36100). Where a **trade loss** is carried back to an earlier accounting period, **wholly within the preceding 12 months**, late payment interest will run on the net amount unpaid for the earlier period after the loss has been set off.

> EXAMPLE C Ltd has a tax liability for the year ended 31 March 2012 of £21,000, based on profits of £100,000. As the due date for payment approaches the company's management accounts are showing a substantial loss in the following year. The decision is taken not to pay the tax and, once the accounts for the year to 31 March 2013 have been completed, a claim will be made to carry back the trading loss.
> 1. If the final loss is more than £100,000 no interest will be due on the original unpaid amount.
> 2. If the final loss is only £40,000, tax of £12,600 will still remain due and this amount will carry interest from the original due date (1 January 2013).

If the earlier period is **wholly or partly outside** the 12 months preceding the **trade loss** period, or the carry back is of a **non-trading loan relationship deficit** (¶16350), interest will be charged on overdue tax for that earlier period, if there would otherwise have been unpaid tax. Late payment interest will be calculated from the normal payable date of the earlier period until 9 months and 1 day after the end of the accounting period for which the loss arose.

> EXAMPLE D Ltd has a tax liability of £10,500 for its year ending on 31 March 2012. This amount remains unpaid and after the preparation of the following year's accounts and computation, a claim is made to carry back a non-trading loan relationship deficit to extinguish the tax liability that arose. Interest will be charged on £10,500 from 1 January 2013 (the original due date for payment of the tax) until 1 January 2014 (the date on which any tax for the loss-making period would have been due).

Tax on loan to a participator

51080
s 109 TMA 1970;
CTM 61610

Tax paid on a loan to a participator in a close company (¶75575) becomes due 9 months and 1 day after the period end, unless the loan is repaid, released or written off within that 9-month (and 1 day) period. Late payment interest starts running from the date that the tax is due until it is paid.

If the loan is **repaid, released or written off** before the tax is paid, interest will stop running from the date of repayment, release or write-off, despite the fact that the repayment itself would not be due until the due date of payment for the period in which the loan is repaid, etc.

> EXAMPLE E Ltd makes a loan to Mr Z in the year ended 31 December 2012. This is repaid on 15 November 2013. As this is outside the 9-month (and 1 day) time limit, the tax becomes due on 1 October 2013. The company never pays the tax due. As the loan repayment occurs during the year ended 31 December 2013, the loan repayment (if the company had paid the tax) would not be due until 1 October 2014. However, the interest only runs until the actual date of the loan repayment – that is, 15 November 2013.

Clawback of overpaid repayments and interest

51085
Sch 18 para 52
FA 1998;
ss 1110, 1111
CTA 2010;
CTM 92180

If a repayment has been made that is later found to be excessive, HMRC can raise an assessment to recover the excess and any associated repayment interest. The **assessment is treated** as being for the accounting period for which the original refund was made. Interest can be charged on the amount due under the assessment from the date that the refund was originally made to the company until the amount is repaid to HMRC.

Penalties

52000 Following consultation on "Modernising Powers, Deterrents and Safeguards", commencing in 2005, HMRC have been moving towards harmonisation of the penalties system across all taxes. Introduction has been phased, both for the rules themselves and the taxes they cover. First were the penalties for inaccuracies, introduced in 2007 but not applicable to corporation tax until 1 April 2009. In 2008 the penalties for failing to notify chargeability to tax and the information powers were introduced. Penalties for late payment of tax and late filing of returns were legislated for in 2009 but do not yet apply to corporation tax. Pre-existing penalties remain in force until the new penalties have effect.

The structure for most of the new penalties is the same, using standard penalty rates with discounts, all of which are designed to encourage compliant behaviour and reward co-operation once a failure is identified. Generally, the penalty will depend on the amount of potential lost revenue (¶52150) caused by the failure.

> MEMO POINTS   Penalties relating to the disclosure of tax avoidance scheme rules are dealt with at ¶46485+.

<hr>

SECTION 1

Failure to notify chargeability to tax

A company must notify HMRC within 3 months of the beginning of its **first accounting period**   **52050**
– that is, the first time it falls within the corporation tax net (¶60055). There is a separate obligation to **notify chargeability for each accounting period** (¶46110).

> MEMO POINTS   A number of the provisions relating to the new penalty regime for errors in documents also apply to these failures. See ¶52480+ for full details.

A. Notification of coming within the tax charge

Penalties were chargeable for failures to notify first coming within the charge to tax at £300   **52080**
for the initial failure and then at £60 per day for continuing failures. These penalties were **abolished** from 1 April 2010, although the obligation to notify overall chargeability remains. As such a new penalty may be put in place to encourage compliant behaviour.

B. Notification of chargeability for a specific period

Prior to 1 April 2010 the penalty for failure to notify for a particular period was up to 100%   **52110**
of the corporation tax unpaid 12 months after the end of the accounting period, before taking account of any relief arising from repayment of a loan to a close company participator.

Since 1 April 2010 this is still set at the same maximum but the calculation has been formalised so that it is now on a similar basis to the calculation of penalties for inaccuracies (¶52480+).

1. Amount of penalty

The penalty is based on the behaviour that leads to the failure and the potential lost revenue   **52140**
(PLR). This may then be discounted.

Behaviour

There are two elements to determining the percentage of the PLR which constitutes the   **52145**
penalty.

Firstly it has to be determined whether a **disclosure** was made and whether this was prompted or not. For further details on this see ¶52555.

Secondly the type of **behaviour** leading to the failure has to be categorised as:
– deliberate, where a company, knowing it needs to make a notification and is able to, chooses not to do so;

– deliberate and concealed, making the deliberate choice not to notify and taking steps to cover up that omission; and
– all other failures.

Behaviour	Maximum percentage of PLR	Minimum percentage of PLR for prompted disclosures	Minimum percentage of PLR for unprompted disclosures
Deliberate but not concealed	70%	35%	20%
Deliberate and concealed	100%	50%	30%
Other	30%	10%/20%[1]	0%/10%[1]

Note:
1. The lower rate is applicable where the failure comes to HMRC's attention within 12 months of the original deadline for notification.

CH 72240   ☐ *MEMO POINTS* ☐   The **onus of proof** is on HMRC to show that a particular failure was a result of deliberate behaviour, or that there was an attempt at concealment.

Potential lost revenue

52150
Sch 41 paras 7, 11
FA 2008
The potential lost revenue (PLR) is the amount of corporation tax due for an accounting period which is still outstanding 12 months after the end of the period. The unpaid tax is **calculated without** setting off any tax refund arising from a repayment of a loan made to a close company participator. Nor is any set-off allowed for an overpayment by another person, unless it is allowed by statute.

> *EXAMPLE*   A Ltd starts to trade in the UK through a permanent establishment on 1 February 2011. It fails to notify HMRC until 4 March 2014, when it makes a payment of £10,000 on account for the year ended 31 January 2012. Its return for that year, submitted on 7 March 2014, shows a corporation tax liability of £25,000. As it did not notify chargeability until after 31 January 2013 and all the tax was unpaid at 31 January 2013, the PLR is £25,000.

---

2. Discounts

52180   The legislation gives a range that a penalty can fall within based on the circumstances. For instance, a deliberate but unconcealed error that is notified to HMRC will result in a penalty of between 20% and 70% of the PLR where the disclosure is unprompted. In order to **arrive at the relevant percentage** within that band HMRC consider a number of factors. A full discussion of these can be found at ¶52760.

HMRC are also able to give discounts based on **special circumstances**. More details on this can be found at ¶52770.

Sch 41 para 15
FA 2008
The penalty can also be reduced if **another penalty is calculated** using the same tax liability.

---

3. Process and appeals

Assessing the penalty

52200
Sch 41 para 16
FA 2008
HMRC must issue an assessment for the penalty, which procedurally operates like an assessment for tax, **within** 12 months of the end of the appeal period for any assessment of the unpaid tax. If there is **no assessment of the unpaid tax**, the penalty assessment must be made within 12 months of the date on which the amount of tax unpaid (because of the failure to notify) is identified. HMRC can stay the penalty (i.e. choose not to issue it, or postpone it) or agree a compromise over payment of it. Otherwise the penalty has to be **paid** within 30 days of the issue of the penalty assessment.

Appealing

The company can appeal against the fact of the penalty itself, or its amount, and need not have paid the penalty to do so. The appeal can result in a review by HMRC or an appeal to the tribunal, just as if the penalty assessment were an assessment to tax (¶54125).

52205
Sch 41 paras 17, 18
FA 2008

Where a company has made an error that is not deliberate it may have a **reasonable excuse**. HMRC state that a reasonable excuse is normally an exceptional and unforeseeable event that is beyond the company's control. The key appears to be the inability to control events leading to the failure. So, whilst an insufficiency of funds is not considered a reasonable excuse, the failure of a major supplier resulting in that insufficiency of funds may be considered one. Other examples of reasonable excuse include disruptions in the postal service, or prolonged industrial action.

EXAMPLE A company appealed against late filing penalties levied against it for the years ended 31 March 2009 and 2010. The company had appointed a third party to act as company secretary and tax agent. All correspondence from HMRC was sent to the agent and the company never received any copies. The company signed its annual accounts for the year ended 31 March 2009 and at the same time approved the accompanying tax computations. It assumed that these were lodged on time and made payment of the tax it knew was due. In August 2010 it provided its agent with the records for the following year, as it was aware of the schedule for tax payments and returns. The company, having heard nothing, tried repeatedly to contact the agent via email and telephone. On 26 July 2011 the company discussed the matter with its solicitor and in August 2011 a new agent was appointed. At this point the failures were identified and corrected by lodging the necessary returns on 4 October and 5 December 2011.

The company argued that it had done everything in its power to comply and commented that no correspondence had been received by it (or its agent) once the earlier year's payment had been received by HMRC but a return had not. HMRC responded that they were under no obligation to inform the company that it had paid tax without making a return and noted that the company had made no attempt to contact HMRC to discuss the issues it was facing. The Tribunal held that the company did not have a reasonable excuse, although the Tribunal had considerable sympathy for it. *TJS Consulting Ltd* (TC02336) [2012]

SECTION 2

Failure to file a return on time

The alignment of penalties across taxes covers penalties for not filing a return on time, including a corporation tax return. The alignment of these penalties, like others, has been staggered and although the enabling legislation has been enacted, a **Treasury Order is awaited** giving the implementation date for corporation tax returns. The following sections therefore describe the current penalties for late filing, followed by details of the new rules.

52255

There also exists a general penalty provision for other returns that are either required by the legislation on the occurrence of a certain event, such as the company making a purchase of its own shares, or upon request from HMRC, such as returns of commission payments made.

A. Self-assessment returns

1. Current rules

Standard penalty

The existing penalties are:
- £100 for a return that is **no more than 3 months late**; and
- £200 for **all other returns**.

52285

Sch 18 para 17
FA 1998
The fines are increased if there is a **history of late filing** so that the initial 3 months' fine becomes £500 and the increased fine becomes £1,000. These apply where there have been three successive late filings, and apply from the third onwards.

Tax-geared penalty

52290
There is a tax-geared penalty if the return is **more than 18 months late**, which increases if it is more than 2 years late. The amounts are:
– 10% of the tax still unpaid at 18 months after the filing date for returns lodged between 18 months and 2 years late; and
– 20% of the tax still unpaid at 18 months after the filing date for returns lodged more than 2 years late.

Sch 18 para 18
FA 1998
The tax unpaid is calculated before any set-off for repayments of tax arising from repayments of loans to close company participators.

Extension of deadline

52295
Sch 18 para 19
FA 1998
There is **no penalty** if the return is filed by the last day on which the accounts can be filed with the Registrar of Companies. If a company has obtained a **filing extension** with the Registrar, it will effectively obtain a filing extension with HMRC to the same date.

---

2. New rules

Basic penalty

52325
Sch 55 paras 1, 3
FA 2009
When the new rules come into force there will be an initial penalty of £100 if the return is late.

There will be further penalties if the return is **more than 3 months late**, with increments where it is later than 6 months, and then later than 12 months. The rules refer to a penalty date, which is the day after the filing deadline.

How late?	Penalty
Between 3 and 6 months	£100 flat rate, plus £10 for each day (up to a maximum of 90) after the 3 months have elapsed
Between 6 and 12 months	The cumulative penalties so far, plus the greater of 5% of the tax shown on the return or £300
More than 12 months	The cumulative penalties so far plus: – where the **company co-operates** with HMRC so that they can assess the tax liability, the extra penalty will be 5% of the tax shown as due on the return or £300, whichever is greater; – if the **company deliberately withholds information** (by failing to make the return), the extra penalty will be 70% of the tax shown as due on the return or £300, whichever is greater; or – if the company **deliberately withholds information** (by failing to make the return) and **conceals** that fact, the extra penalty will be 100% of the tax shown as due on the return or £300, whichever is greater.

The penalties charged for returns filed more than 12 months late can be **discounted** but this element of the penalty cannot be reduced below £300.

> MEMO POINTS   The penalties for returns more than 12 months late are modelled on the penalty regime for errors in documents. For full details of the terms used and the possible discounts available see ¶52555.

Penalty cap

Whatever the eventual penalty charged, the **element calculated by reference to the tax liability** cannot exceed 100% of the tax due. Where other types of penalty (except for those relating to late payment of tax) are calculated by reference to the same tax liability, the payment for late filing will be reduced by the amount of that penalty.

52330
Sch 55 para 17
FA 2009;
CH 158100

B. Special returns

There are several other returns, documentation or information which are either requested by HMRC or required under legislation. A general penalty provision applies to failure to meet such requests and requirements.

52360
s 98 TMA 1970

An **initial penalty** of £300 can be levied, followed by a **daily** penalty of up to £60 for a continuing failure. Where the company has failed to comply with a **request from HMRC** within the time limit specified, the penalty must be levied prior to the request being complied with. This would mean that a return could be supplied late but not attract a penalty if HMRC have not already charged one.

If the company has failed to **provide something required** under the legislation, as opposed to something that is requested, the initial penalty can be assessed at any time after the deadline has passed. However, the daily penalty cannot be imposed once the failure has been remedied.

SECTION 3

Failure to pay on time

The **current rules** in relation to late paid tax only charge interest on late payments (¶51000+). However, there are **no penalties** to encourage payment. This has meant that in a number of cases companies have chosen to delay payment where the cost of borrowing was higher than the rate charged on late payments.

52410

From an as yet unannounced date there will be a new regime that introduces a penalty, along with provisions for appeal, to encourage companies to pay on time. It is these rules that are outlined below.

New rules

Level of penalty

The new structure will mean an increasing penalty reflecting the lateness of the tax, along-side the continuing interest regime. The penalties will also apply to late payments of tax due under the **large company instalment payment** regulations (¶48095).

52415
Sch 56 para 4
FA 2009

The penalty will be charged on any tax unpaid at key points after the **penalty date**. The penalty date is the day after the filing date (¶46110), not the payment date. This is graduated as follows:
- 5% immediately on any amount unpaid;
- a further 5% **3 months** after the penalty date on any amount still unpaid; and
- a further 5% **9 months** after the penalty date on any amount still unpaid.

Sch 56 para 1
FA 2009

    `MEMO POINTS` 1. The **tax due** is the amount shown as due on the corporation tax return.
2. **No penalty** will arise where, before the date the penalty arises, an agreement has been reached with HMRC regarding payment and the company adheres to it.

52420
Sch 56 para 9
FA 2009

Reduction A reduction in the penalty may be available if HMRC believe that special circumstances apply. This does not include an inability to pay, or the fact that another company has made an overpayment that balances the position. The penalty can be stayed or agreed with a compromise.

Issue of penalty notice

52425
Sch 56 para 11
FA 2009

HMRC must issue an **assessment for the penalty** by the later of:
– 2 years after the filing date for the corporation tax return; and
– 12 months after the end of the appeal period for the tax assessment relating to the return
or, if there was no assessment, 12 months after the liability was quantified.

The resulting assessment must be **paid** within 30 days.

    `MEMO POINTS` If it later becomes apparent that an earlier penalty was insufficient this can be increased.

Appealing a penalty

52430
Sch 56 paras 13
– 15 FA 2009

A penalty charged under these provisions can be appealed against, **either** about the fact that it has been levied or as to amount. It can result in a review by HMRC or an appeal to the tribunal just as if it were an assessment to tax (¶54125+); the penalty **does not** need to be paid before the appeal can be heard. If the appeal concerns the **size of the penalty**, the tribunal can determine what it considers the right amount should be.

SECTION 4

Errors in documents

52480

The first tranche of legislation to modernise and harmonise the penalty regime was enacted in Finance Act 2007 and deals with errors in documents (including, of course, returns). It set the pattern for the future structure of penalties by varying the level of the penalty depending on whether disclosures are prompted or not. It also gives discounts recognising the help the taxpayer gives HMRC in quantifying the error – that is, the quality of the disclosure. The penalty is based on the amount of potential lost revenue (PLR) and there are additional specific rules dealing with group relief and losses.

SI 2008/568

The rules **apply to** returns due on or after 1 April 2009 for periods beginning on or after 1 April 2008.

A. Conditions

52510

A penalty will arise if there is a **careless or deliberate** error in a document, which gives rise to an understatement of tax, a false (or increased) loss or a false (or increased) repayment of tax in any of the following:
– the corporation tax return;
– the accounts supporting the return;
– any return, statement or declaration used to make a claim for an allowance, deduction or relief; or

– any document which HMRC rely upon to determine the liability to tax, payments by the company (including penalties), a repayment or a credit.

Document

As the legislation applies in relation to a document which is given to HMRC, the **definition** of document is critical. A document is defined much more widely than its normal meaning and includes any method of communicating information to HMRC. This can include post, fax, email, telephone call or information supplied verbally during a meeting.

52515
Sch 27 para 28
FA 2007;
CH 81060

HMRC determination

If HMRC issue a determination (¶46365) in the absence of a self-assessment, a penalty may arise if this is an **under-assessment** and the company fails to draw HMRC's attention to this within 30 days, knowing that it is an under-estimate of the tax due. HMRC will take into account whether it would be reasonable for the company to have known about the under-assessment and what steps it would have been reasonable to expect it to take to tell HMRC.

52520

Third parties

A third party can be liable to a penalty if it deliberately withholds information, or provides false information, with the **intention** of causing someone to submit a document that is inaccurate. The person who submits the document can also be liable, although the overall penalty for the company and the third party cannot exceed 100% of the PLR.

52525
Sch 24 paras 1A, 24
FA 2007

B. Level of penalty

1. Basis of calculation

The penalty is based on the amount of potential lost revenue (PLR). The percentage of the PLR will depend on the type of behaviour that led to the penalty and whether HMRC believe the disclosure was prompted or unprompted. An **unprompted disclosure** is one where the company had no reason to believe that HMRC had discovered, or were about to discover, the inaccuracy. Anything else is considered a **prompted disclosure**.

52555
Sch 24 para 9
FA 2007

CH 82442

> EXAMPLE
>
> 1. A Ltd has just received notice that it is to be the subject of a corporation tax enquiry. Shortly afterwards it makes a disclosure relating to its corporation tax position. This would be considered to be prompted, as HMRC would take the prospect of the enquiry discovering the error as being a prompt to disclose.
>
> 2. B Ltd has received correspondence to say it is to have its PAYE records checked. At this time the company makes a disclosure regarding its transfer pricing adjustments. This will not be deemed to be prompted, as it does not relate to compliance as an employer.

2. Standard of error

Errors that give rise to a penalty are broken down into:
– those involving carelessness;
– deliberate errors that are not concealed; and
– deliberate errors that are concealed.

52575

The **onus of proof** as to which standard of error is considered to have occurred falls on HMRC. The level of proof required rises as the level of error does.

Sch 24 para 3
FA 2007

⌐ *MEMO POINTS* ⌐ 1. Errors that are **not considered** careless or deliberate are not liable to any penalty. 2. An error (which is neither careless nor deliberate) discovered after a document has been submitted to HMRC **becomes careless** if the company delays informing HMRC once it becomes aware of the error.

Careless

52580
CH 81140

A careless error is one where there was a lack of reasonable care, which HMRC have likened to the general law concept of **negligence**. What constitutes reasonable care will be **dependent on the particular circumstances** of the company and the error itself. A larger company would be expected to have more sophisticated systems and take more care than a small one.

HMRC **accept** that a company has taken **reasonable care** where:
– arrangements or systems exist that, if followed, could reasonably be expected to produce an accurate basis for the calculation of tax due;
– despite these systems inaccuracies arise in processing or coding items in these systems; and
– the effect of the inaccuracies is not significant in relation to the overall liability for the period.

HMRC also state that a company taking reasonable care would find out the correct tax treatment or take advice on any **unfamiliar transactions** it has entered into. Any remaining uncertainty could be managed by drawing attention to the matter in a return or document.

52585
CH 81130

Not careless   HMRC give the following examples of when a penalty would not be due:
– where the company takes a **differing viewpoint on a transaction** from HMRC, provided that the company's position is reasonably arguable;
– where a document is prepared based on **advice received** from HMRC, or a professional adviser, which later proved to be incorrect, provided that all relevant facts and circumstances were disclosed at the time the advice was sought; or
– small arithmetical or transpositional errors that would not be picked up by a reasonable quality check.

Deliberate

52590

Where a company knowingly, and intentionally, provides an inaccurate document this will attract the level of penalty attributable to deliberate failures. If there are then arrangements to conceal the deliberate error the error will fall into the **deliberate and concealed** category. In essence, the difference between the two categories is the positive act of doing something to conceal an error. For instance, knowingly not recording all of the sales of the company is clearly deliberate. However, it is not considered concealed until an attempt is made to cover the shortfall by, for example, destroying sales invoices.

CH 81160

Other acts that could be used to conceal an error could be submitting false invoices, backdating a contract, or creating false minutes of meetings.

3. Rate of penalty

52620
Sch 24 paras 4, 4B,
4C, 10 FA 2007

The scale of penalty based on the type of disclosure is:

Nature of failure	Maximum percentage of PLR	Minimum percentage of PLR for prompted disclosure	Minimum percentage of PLR for unprompted disclosure
Careless	30%	15%	0%
Deliberate, not concealed	70%	35%	20%
Deliberate and concealed	100%	50%	30%
Third-party failure	100%	-	-
Under-assessment not notified	30%	-	-

4. Potential lost revenue

Potential lost revenue (PLR) refers to the additional tax payable once the error (including an under-assessment) is corrected. The **basic definition** accommodates repayments and is expanded to cover the situation where there is more than one error in a document, as well as where losses are reduced or extinguished. Repayments are treated as additional tax due where a repayment was made which should not have been, and where a repayment would have been made but for the error being identified and corrected. Additional group relief claims are ignored, provided that the error **does not create or increase an aggregate group loss** (¶52705).

52640
Sch 24 para 5
FA 2007

EXAMPLE C Ltd, D Ltd and E Ltd form a group of companies. Their returned results, including original group relief claims, are:

	£	
C Ltd profit	50,000	less group relief £50,000
D Ltd loss	(75,000)	
E Ltd profit	60,000	less group relief £25,000
Aggregate profit	35,000	

C Ltd's return is found to contain an inaccuracy, deemed as careless, which results in the profit rising to £85,000. D Ltd then withdraws its surrender to E Ltd and re-allocates the loss to C Ltd, thus resulting in a profit after relief of £10,000. As the error did not create, or increase, a loss for the group overall, the changes in group relief are ignored in the calculation of PLR.
Assuming a small profits rate of 20% the PLR would be calculated as follows:

C Ltd	Correct position £	Original position £	Additional amount £
Trading income	85,000	50,000	35,000
Less: Group relief	(75,000)	(50,000)	-[1]
Profits chargeable to tax	10,000	-	35,000
Tax at small profits rate	2,000	-	7,000
D Ltd			
Trading income	60,000	60,000	-
Less: Group relief	-	(25,000)	-[1]
Profits chargeable to tax	60,000	35,000	-
Tax at small profits rate	12,000	7,000	-

Note:
1. The changes in the group relief claims are ignored for the purpose of the calculation.
The total PLR is £7,000 (£7,000 + £0).

MEMO POINTS Repayments due in relation to tax paid on a **loan to a participator** are always ignored.

a. Multiple errors

If the order of correction of errors would have an **impact on the size** of the PLR, the errors need to be adjusted in a specific order. Overstatements in the same period can be allowed for, but only those that belong to the company itself; overpayments made by another person will not count. The order of correction is based on culpability, so that careless errors are corrected first, followed by deliberate but not concealed and then deliberate and concealed errors.

52660
Sch 24 para 6
FA 2007

Overstatements are set against understatements in the same way: against non-careless errors first, then against careless, then deliberate and unconcealed, followed by deliberate and concealed.

EXAMPLE F Ltd is found to have made two errors in a return: a careless error resulting in additional profit of £10,000 and a deliberate error of £30,000. Its reported profits for the year were £280,000. It has no associated companies.

F Ltd's original tax liability, assuming a small profits rate of 20%, would have been £56,000. In order to find the PLR that applies in respect of each inaccuracy these must be corrected in order.

Correction for careless error of £10,000

Revised taxable profits	290,000
Tax at small profits rate of 20%	58,000
Less: Original liability	(56,000)
PLR in respect of careless error	2,000

Correction for deliberate error of £30,000

Taxable profits	320,000
Tax at main rate of 24%	76,800
Less: Marginal relief	(11,800)
Total tax due	65,000
Tax calculated as due after first correction	58,000
PLR in respect of deliberate error	7,000

MEMO POINTS   Where there are **several errors of one type** – for example, careless errors – but they cannot be grouped together, as they are not to be subjected to the same level of penalty, the adjustments must be applied so as to preserve the highest penalty liability.

b. Losses

52680
Sch 24 para 7
FA 2007

Where a loss is amended due to an error being discovered, it may be the case that **no further tax arises** at that time. This will be the case where the loss is not reduced sufficiently to bring any profit into tax. However, the loss that is carried forward may affect the tax due in future periods (where it can be used). In these cases the PLR relating to the unused loss that would be available to carry forward is calculated by taking 10% of the remaining loss.

Loss likely to remain unrelieved

52685
CH 82370, 82371

The unused portion is ignored completely if there is no reasonable prospect of the loss being used. There is no reference in the legislation as to how this prospect can be measured. HMRC regard the likelihood of there being no reasonable prospect for the use of losses as slim (other than where it is not possible legally or factually to use the losses). Within a **group of companies** they will consider the potential for reorganising the group's activities to make effective use of surplus losses when viewing the likelihood of the losses being used.

c. Group relief

52705

The normal rule that group relief must be ignored when calculating the PLR is amended where the error has **created or increased an aggregate group loss**. In other words, where the total of losses is not fully used as group relief, the group relief surrenders and the way the losses are used must be considered in calculating the PLR. HMRC provide the following example:

EXAMPLE   A Ltd, B Ltd, C Ltd and D Ltd are a group of companies with the following results:

	£	
A Ltd profit	110,000	Less group relief of 110,000 from C Ltd
B Ltd profit	160,000	Less group relief of 160,000 (90,000 from C Ltd and 70,000 from D Ltd)
C Ltd loss	(200,000)	
D Ltd loss	(85,000)	
Aggregate loss	(15,000)	

A Ltd's return is found to contain an inaccuracy of £40,000, increasing its correct profit to £150,000. In light of this C Ltd amends its loss surrenders so that £150,000 of its loss is allocated to A Ltd and £50,000 to B Ltd. D Ltd then amends its surrender to allocate all of its loss of £85,000 to B Ltd.

Under the normal rules for calculating the PLR, A Ltd's PLR would simply be £40,000 x 20% = £8,000. However, as this error created the aggregate loss of the group the rules for calculating the PLR in the case of losses apply.

The calculation of the PLR for the penalty is as follows:

	£	£
A Ltd: correct profit	150,000	
Less: Group relief claim	(150,000)	
Profits chargeable to tax	Nil	
Tax due		Nil
Less: Original tax liability		Nil
		Nil
B Ltd: profit	160,000	
Less: Group relief	(135,000)	
Profits chargeable to tax	25,000	
Tax due		5,000
Less: Original tax liability		Nil
		5,000
Unused loss rule		
Unused loss originally shown at appropriate percentage (£15,000 x 10%)		1,500
Total PLR		6,500

Note:
The unused loss rule applies as D Ltd had not utilised the remaining loss and the loss itself was attributable to the error.

Group relief will also be accounted for where the **error occurs in the group relief claim**.   **52710**

[EXAMPLE] E Ltd, a member of a group, group relieves all of its profit for a year. A careless error is later discovered, meaning that the group relief claims have to be reduced accordingly. The PLR will be calculated as the increase in tax due to the reduction in loss claims.

d. Delayed tax

A separate provision deals with any inaccuracy that causes tax to be **declared later** than it should be (other than the use of losses). The PLR is set at 5% of the delayed tax for each year of delay, pro-rated for periods of less than a year. Essentially this rate recognises the time delay in the tax reaching HMRC. This will be **in addition to** any **actual lost tax** as a result of the error. For it to be considered a delay, the error has to automatically reverse in a later period, without any extra action by the company to correct it.

52730
Sch 24 para 8
FA 2007

[EXAMPLE] F Ltd provides a return showing employee remuneration of £350,000 for a year when it was subject to the main rate of corporation tax of 28%. This included a bonus of £100,000 that was not paid until more than 9 months after the company's year end. As such the amount should have been disallowed for tax, then allowed against profits in the following period, when it was actually paid (¶14615). The main rate of tax applicable in the second year had dropped to 26%. The PLR will be calculated as:

Tax at 28% for Year 1	28,000
Less: Tax at 26% for Year 2	(26,000)
	2,000
Plus timing addition: £26,000 x 5%	1,300
Total PLR	3,300

The timing addition only applies to the amount of tax that is declared later than it should have been.

HMRC Brief 15/11 HMRC's policy until April 2011 was that if the **error was discovered prior** to the return for the second year having been filed, normal penalties would be levied. However, HMRC now accept that if the error would automatically have reversed in the second year, the delay rules will be applied.

C. Discounts that reduce the maximum penalty

52760
Sch 24 para 9
FA 2007

Discounts to penalties have always been available in the past through the notions of abatement and mitigation. These have now been formalised and are based on what has been termed the **quality of disclosure**.

The extent to which a penalty is reduced towards the minimum available is dependent on three main factors:
a. telling HMRC about the inaccuracy (this involves admitting the error (or under-assessment), explaining how it arose and disclosing it in full; the earlier an error is admitted the larger the potential discount);
b. the amount of **assistance** given to HMRC to quantify the inaccuracy, including helping with calculations and volunteering information (such help should be more effective than merely giving the appearance of assistance); and
c. allowing HMRC access to records to ensure that the inaccuracy is fully recorded (access should be given freely, without the need for HMRC to issue information notices).

CH 82430

A reduction will be given for each of these factors, the size of the reduction depending on the quality of each. The maximum reduction is 30% for telling, 40% for helping and 30% for giving access. Every set of circumstances will differ and so will the reductions.

> MEMO POINTS   1. If any element of the disclosure is **not needed** (for example, because HMRC can obtain information from another source) the full reduction for that element of the disclosure will nonetheless be provided.
> 2. A single action by the company may count for or against more than one element, depending on the circumstances.

Calculating the actual penalty rate

52765

There are several steps involved in calculating the final percentage to be applied to the PLR to ascertain the penalty.

Step 1: ascertain if disclosure was prompted or not and what category of failure has occurred.

Step 2: calculate the maximum reduction of the percentage applicable for that category.

Step 3: the percentage reduction for the quality of disclosure is identified.

Step 4: apply the percentage reduction to the maximum possible reduction.

Step 5: this reduction is then applied to the maximum penalty percentage, and the result of this is applied to the PLR.

> EXAMPLE   G Ltd has made an unprompted disclosure of a deliberate, but unconcealed, error in its last return. When looking at the penalty level, HMRC decided that the percentage reduction available for the quality of disclosure was 60%. The PLR was £100,000.
> Step 1: the maximum penalty for this sort of error is 70%.
> Step 2: the minimum is 20%, so the maximum reduction is 50%.
> Step 3: the percentage reduction for the quality of disclosure was 60%.
> Step 4: the percentage reduction available in this case will be 30% (50% × 60%).
> Step 5: the final penalty level is 40% (70% maximum less 30% reduction).
> On applying this to the PLR the penalty will be £40,000.

Further HMRC abatement of penalty

52770
CH 82490

HMRC can reduce a penalty for **special circumstances**, if they think it right to do so. Special circumstances do not include an inability to pay, or the fact that someone else has made an overpayment which offsets the loss of revenue. The actions HMRC can take include staying the penalty (that is, not issuing it or postponing it), or agreeing a compromise over proceedings for a penalty. The penalty can also be reduced if another penalty is calculated using the same tax liability.

D. Administration

1. Process

The harmonised assessment and appeal process for the penalty for inaccuracies and under-assessments is similar to the process for the other types of penalty. An assessment will be raised for the penalty and it must be paid within 30 days of issue. The assessment is procedurally the same as an assessment for tax.

52800

Issue of penalty

A penalty raised on the company or a third party has to be raised within 12 months of the end of the appeal period for the decision that corrected the inaccuracy or, if there was **no assessment** for the tax, within 12 months of the correction of the error.

52805
Sch 24 para 13
FA 2007

A penalty relating to an **under-assessment** by HMRC has to be raised within 12 months of the end of the appeal period relating to the assessment that corrected the under-assessment or, if there was no assessment, within 12 months of the correction of the under-assessment.

Suspension

A penalty levied under these provisions for a **careless inaccuracy** can now be suspended for a period of up to 2 years. This suspension mechanism does not feature in the penalty system for any of the other kinds of penalty, such as those for late notification or a late return. It does not apply to **deliberate errors**, or those for which a **third party** is liable to a penalty.

52810
Sch 24 para 14
FA 2007

A suspension will come with **conditions** which, if met, will mean that the penalty will be cancelled at the end of the period of suspension. If another penalty is raised during this period, the suspended penalty will become due immediately. HMRC will only offer a suspension if they believe that adhering to the conditions will help to avoid careless inaccuracies in future.

MEMO POINTS   The **conditions** set by HMRC must:
– be directly related to the company;
– be capable of being shown as having been met;
– be able to be achieved by the company;
– not be unreasonable; and
– have a known time limit.

CH 83153

EXAMPLE
1. In this VAT case the First-tier Tribunal upheld the taxpayer's appeal against HMRC's refusal to suspend penalties for careless inaccuracies. HMRC refused suspension because previous penalties had been suspended and similar errors had again been made; also the taxpayer had not contacted HMRC to seek assistance. However, the Tribunal held that:
– **simple repetition** of inaccuracies of the same sort should not of itself be a reason for refusing suspension if the inaccuracies are careless and relate to an area which the taxpayer finds confusing (this highlighted the need for education and so pointed towards suspension rather than penalisation);
– the fact that previous penalties have been suspended is not a relevant consideration in deciding whether to refuse suspension in relation to later VAT periods;
– whilst the taxpayer had made repeated errors of a single type, it had not failed to undertake a specific action included as a condition of a previous suspension;

– the conditions of previous suspension had been little more detailed than instructions to apply the rules correctly in future (but not instructions how to apply the rules correctly); and

– the requirement to seek assistance from HMRC should have been a condition of a previous suspension but was not (and therefore was not a valid reason for refusing suspension on this occasion).

Shelfside (Holdings) Ltd (TC01978) [2012]

2. The appellant in this income tax case failed to declare a redundancy payment on his tax return. HMRC refused to suspend the penalty, on the ground that it was not realistic to set a condition that the appellant should declare redundancy payments on his tax return in future. The First-tier Tribunal said this was "far too narrow a view and discloses a highly material error of law". HMRC had stated that the condition must be "specific to the careless inaccuracy" but the Tribunal said: "That is not a statutory requirement; nor is it implicit in the statutory regime set out in Schedule 24". The Tribunal ordered suspension of the penalty on condition that the appellant use a qualified accountant to prepare his tax returns during the period of suspension. *Boughey* (TC02082) [2012]

3. The First-tier Tribunal has since ruled that HMRC's **policy** not to suspend penalties in the case of "one-off" errors is **flawed**. A refusal to suspend issued simply because of the policy was unlawful. The Tribunal therefore considered whether the penalty should be suspended in the circumstances of this case (as, in its view, HMRC ought to have done). On the facts the Tribunal held that suspension was appropriate here: the appellant had offered to have a professional review of his reporting processes and have his tax returns submitted by a professional also. *Testa* (TC02549) [2013]

2. Appeals

52840

Sch 24 paras 15, 16
FA 2007

In relation to these penalties the following can be appealed:

– the fact a penalty was **levied** at all;

– the **amount** of the penalty (in this case the tribunal can adjust the penalty as it sees fit);

– a **failure** to be offered a suspension; or

– the **conditions** attaching to a suspension.

An appeal on the **suspension** or lack of it will only result in a changed decision if the tribunal thinks that the HMRC decision is flawed. What is regarded as flawed will be viewed in the light of the principles used in judicial review.

The appeal can result in a review by HMRC or an appeal to the tribunal, just as if it were an assessment to tax (¶54125+). The penalty **does not need** to be paid before the appeal is determined.

E. Involvement of others

52870

If other persons are involved in delivering returns and documents or providing information, they may be sufficiently involved to be liable to a penalty. The key categories are employees, officers of the company and agents.

Employees

52875

CH 75140

HMRC do not regard employees (provided that they are **not officers**) as agents of a company. They would not be liable for any part of a penalty.

Officers of the company

52880

Sch 24 para 19
FA 2007

If there has been a deliberate inaccuracy **attributable** to a manager, company secretary or director of the company, HMRC can assess the officer directly for part or all of a penalty, although the combined penalty charged to the company and the officer cannot exceed the total penalty. The officer has 30 days to pay the penalty and may appeal against its imposition.

HMRC would not usually **pursue** an officer personally for a penalty unless:
- there is evidence of personal gain by the officer;
- the company is insolvent; or
- there are grounds to believe the company will become insolvent.

> EXAMPLE Mr A is owed money by his company, H Ltd. This goes back to a significantly earlier period, when the company was trading. However, H Ltd has been unable to pay the debt. Mr A transfers his own sole trade into H Ltd and trades through the company for a period to enable the company to be able to repay his loan. He then winds up the company, without ever notifying HMRC of the fact the company traded or returning details of its profits. Mr A has benefited personally from the failure and the company no longer exists to pursue for any penalty. HMRC will pursue Mr A in such circumstances.

> MEMO POINTS 1. Merely **signing a document** would not automatically mean that a deliberate inaccuracy is attributable to an officer.
> 2. **Senior accounting officers** of large companies also have specific reporting duties (see ¶46945).

Agents

The involvement of an agent in submitting returns and providing information **would not normally** absolve the company of responsibility as principal. A penalty could be raised on the company even where the agent sends in a return with an error, or later discovers an error and does not take reasonable steps to tell HMRC about it. However, the company will **not be liable** to the penalty because of the agent's actions, or lack of them, if it can show that it took reasonable care to avoid a careless inaccuracy, or a failure to inform HMRC of an under-assessment. HMRC expect a company to be able to **provide evidence** that it took reasonable care. This includes taking responsibility by checking that the agent has done what the agent was supposed to do, following advice from a competent professional adviser and providing all relevant information.

52885
Sch 24 para 18
FA 2007;
CH 84540

SECTION 5

Failures in relation to information powers

HMRC have a range of powers to obtain information from a company (and also third parties) about its tax affairs. For details of these see ¶50050+. The following penalties apply where there is a failure to comply correctly with an information notice or an inspection.

52935

A. Penalty rates

---

1. Inaccuracies in information provided

If an inaccurate document or incorrect information is provided to HMRC in the course of complying with a notice there will be a penalty, not exceeding £3,000, if the inaccuracy is:
- careless or deliberate; or
- discovered later and the person who supplied the information or document does not take reasonable steps to tell HMRC.

No penalty will be charged if HMRC are told about the inaccuracy at the time they are given the information or document. The maximum penalty will only be charged in very serious cases of deliberate inaccuracy.

52965
Sch 36 para 40A
FA 2008

CH 26280, 26780

2. Failure to provide information

Initial penalty

52985   A fixed penalty of £300 applies to a failure to comply with an information notice or the **deliberate obstruction** of an HMRC officer carrying out an inspection that has been approved by the tribunal. Failure to comply **includes** the concealment, destruction or other disposal of a document, or arranging the same. If some, but not all, of the documents or information are supplied, HMRC should only consider a penalty if the missing items are significant.

Daily penalty

52990   If the failure or obstruction **continues** after a fixed penalty has been imposed, a daily penalty not exceeding £60 per day can be charged. If the penalty is because a document has been destroyed, a daily penalty will not be suitable and a tax-related penalty may be charged instead.

Tax-related penalty

52995   If the failure or obstruction continues after a penalty has been raised, HMRC can ask for a further penalty by **applying** to the Upper Tribunal. They can only do this if they believe that the amount of tax paid, or likely to be paid, is significantly less than ought to be paid because of the failure or obstruction. The Upper Tribunal can impose any penalty but it must have regard to the amount of unpaid tax.

Criminal offences

53000
Sch 36 paras 53, 54
FA 2008

There are two criminal offences related to **concealment or destruction of documents** where tribunal approval has been sought, or given, for the issue of an information notice. If the accused is found guilty, the punishment is a fine or imprisonment for up to 2 years, or both. The use of this sanction will only be considered in very serious cases.

The recipient of an information notice (approved by the tribunal) who has concealed or destroyed a document will have committed an offence, unless either:
– the document has already been produced and HMRC have not said they needed it to be kept; or
– more than 6 months have elapsed since a copy was provided and HMRC did not say within those 6 months that they wished to see the original.

An offence will also be committed if the act of concealment, destruction, or arrangement for either **takes place after the person has been informed** that HMRC intend to issue an information notice with the tribunal's approval. This is clearly designed to prevent early destruction. However, this offence **does not apply** if more than 6 months have passed since the taxpayer was informed of HMRC's intention to apply for a notice, or if an information notice has in fact been issued before the document was concealed or destroyed (since the former offence will be applicable in such a case).

B. Administration

1. Process

53030   All assessments for penalties are **due to be paid** within 30 days of the later of the issue of a notice, or the determination, or withdrawal, of an appeal. As such there is no requirement to pay a penalty before an appeal.

Incorrect documents

A penalty for supplying an erroneous document (¶52480) must be issued within 12 months of the date when the error became known to HMRC but in any case within 6 years of when the company became liable to the penalty.

53035
Sch 36 para 46
FA 2008

Failure to deliver documents

Assessments for the **initial or daily penalties** must be issued within 12 months of the latest of:
- when the company became liable to the penalty;
- the end of the period within which an appeal could be made; or
- the date on which an appeal is determined or withdrawn.

HMRC must apply to the Upper Tribunal for a **tax-related penalty**. This has to be done within 12 months of the date when an initial or daily penalty must be issued.

53040
Sch 36 para 46
FA 2008

---

2. Appeals

The company may appeal, in writing to HMRC, against either the penalty itself or its amount, within 30 days of the date of the penalty notice. HMRC can then review the penalty or settle by agreement. If an appeal is made the tribunal can cancel, confirm or amend the penalty.

A **tax-related penalty** cannot be appealed.

53070

> MEMO POINTS   One **common ground of appeal** will be that of having a reasonable excuse (¶52205).

SECTION 6

Tax defaulters

Since 1 April 2010 HMRC have had the power to "name and shame" publicly those they regard as the worst tax defaulters.

53120
s 94 FA 2009;
SI 2010/574

Conditions

If the **potential lost revenue** from a penalty situation, following a compliance check of some sort, **exceeds** £25,000, HMRC may publish the name and address of the taxpayer concerned where there has been a deliberate:
- inaccuracy in a document;
- supply of false information or withholding of information by a third party; or
- failure to notify chargeability to corporation tax.

However, the details will **not be published** if the full discounts for the quality of disclosure have been given, or there was unprompted disclosure.

53125
CH 190050

What can be published?

The full list of the information that can be published is:
- the company's **name** (including any trading name or previous name);
- the company's **address**;
- the **nature of any business** carried on by the company;
- the **amount** of the penalty or penalties and the potential lost revenue in relation to them;
- the **periods** or times to which the inaccuracy, failure or action giving rise to the penalty (or any of the penalties) relates; and
- any such further information as is considered appropriate in order to make clear the company's **identity**.

53130

The current list of "deliberate tax defaulters" can be found at: flmemo.co.uk/ctm53130.

Procedure

53135 The **company must be informed** of the proposed publication of the details and given a chance to make representations. No publication may be made before the penalty (or the last if there is more than one) is made final, or more than 12 months after that, and the publication may not last for more than a year.

Even if part or all of a company penalty has been sought from an **officer** (¶52880), it will still be the company's details that are published and not those of the officer.

There is no **right of appeal** against the decision to publish. However, a judicial review may be sought.

CHAPTER 4

Clearances, reviews, appeals and the GAAR

HMRC have been reviewing and harmonising elements of the administration system for UK taxation in recent years. The results of this have included a new **non-statutory clearance mechanism** for use where uncertainty exists about the interpretation of legislation, particularly new legislation, and there is insufficient guidance already available. The **appeal mechanism** beyond HMRC has also been reformed. The previous appeal to the Special or General Commissioners has now been replaced by appeal to the First-tier Tribunal and any **subsequent appeal** is to the Upper Tribunal (formerly to the High Court). Prior to the appeal stage, however, the taxpayer can now request an **internal independent review** by HMRC, which may resolve the case satisfactorily without the costs and formality of an appeal hearing.

54000

SECTION 1

Non-statutory clearances

54050   Following the 2006 Budget, and a review of how HMRC could work best with large businesses, the previous non-statutory clearance mechanism provided for businesses through a code of practice was replaced by a new, also non-statutory, system of clearances. This system, which is **not designed to replace** statutory clearances where they exist, is available to remove material uncertainty for companies which have undertaken, or are contemplating entering into, major transactions.

> [MEMO POINTS] Statutory clearances continue to exist for:
> – company reconstructions (¶79365);
> – purchase of own shares (¶18720);
> – CFC exemptions (¶90920); and
> – transactions in securities (¶21535).

When is clearance available?

54055
NBCG 1310

Clearance can be sought where there is **material uncertainty** relating to the application of new legislation, during the **period covered** by the four most recent Finance Acts. Uncertainty relating to older legislation is also included, but only where it affects a **transaction of commercial significance** to a company. The significance is determined by the scale of the business and the impact of the transaction upon it.

Exclusions

54060   HMRC will not provide clearance where the request relates to:
– **draft** legislation;
– **tax planning** advice;
– an application that is **essentially the same** as a previous one (unless there has been a change in the facts);
– a situation where the motive is to gain a **tax advantage**;
– a situation where **published guidance** on the issue already exists (HMRC will expect a company to have reviewed published guidance before deciding that the company's situation is not covered);
– a situation where there is already an open **enquiry** into the transaction, or into the relevant self-assessment tax return, or where the deadline for opening an enquiry has passed;
– a question which does not concern the **interpretation or application** of tax law (e.g. an asset valuation or transfer pricing);
– whether a project qualifies for **research and development** tax incentives (in this case a company should approach its Customer Relationship Manager, if it has one, or the R&D Specialist Unit); or
– the **tax consequences** of executing a trust deed or settlement.

Timing and content of application

54065
NBCG 2340

Applications can be made **before or after** a transaction has taken place, although a transaction must be genuinely contemplated before HMRC will make a pre-transaction clearance.

NBCG 3000 – 3500

A company should **supply** the full facts and context of a transaction, as well as explaining the legislative uncertainty, when applying for a clearance. In order to help companies to provide all the necessary elements, HMRC have provided a checklist for them to complete and submit with their applications. Details that HMRC would expect are the:
– nature of the transaction;
– date that it was or is to be entered into;
– parties involved;
– contractual information;

– contingencies, if any, together with an explanation of them;
– commercial context of the transaction and the reasons for it; and
– applicant's view of the tax consequences of the transaction, together with a clear statement of the points on which clarification is required.

> MEMO POINTS Clearance applications should be sent either to the company's Customer Relationship Manager (for large businesses) or the HMRC Non-Statutory Clearances Team, 5th Floor Alexander House, 21 Victoria Avenue, Southend-on-Sea SS99 1AA. There are separate addresses for Business Investment Relief and IHT Business Property Relief applications. Details and general guidance on making an application may be found by following this link: flmemo.co.uk/ctm54065.

Timing and content of clearance

A substantive response to an application will **normally be given within** 28 days and will be in one of four forms: **54070**
– acceptance of the company's interpretation of the legislation;
– a request for further information;
– rejection of the company's interpretation of the legislation; or
– rejection of the application for one or more of the reasons in ¶54060.

> MEMO POINTS 1. HMRC's **rejection** of, or **disagreement** with, an application does not prevent a company from going ahead with a transaction, or filing a self-assessment return based on its interpretation of the relevant legislation.
> 2. HMRC guidance says that a clearance application should be used to form part of the risk-assessment profile of the business but that the information in it should only be revisited if it is relevant to other significant risk factors.   NBCG 7500

Binding on HMRC

HMRC are only bound by a response where the company has set out all the facts and drawn attention to all the issues. The clearance applies only to that applicant and to that set of facts. HMRC will **not be bound** where the transaction entered into is materially different from the one that was contemplated, or where the clearance turns out to be based on incorrect or incomplete information.   **54075**
NBCG 7600, 7700

Changes in interpretation of the law, or new or revised laws enacted, can also affect the extent to which a clearance can be regarded as binding, as follows:
– where **interpretation** of the law **changes**, and a return has not yet been submitted or can still be amended, HMRC will expect the revised interpretation to apply;
– if there is a **change in statute** that takes place before the transaction is entered into and is prospective in effect, HMRC would not expect to be bound by the clearance previously given; and
– if a **change is retrospective**, HMRC would not expect to be bound, although they point out in their guidance that retrospective changes will be very infrequent.

Where **HMRC make a mistake** in the clearance they give, the company is still entitled to rely on it, provided that it was clear, unequivocal, explicit, the company relied on the advice, and it would suffer loss if the correct view were applied. The company also needs to have fully disclosed all relevant facts. Once HMRC notify the company that the advice they gave is incorrect, the company need only start accounting for tax on the correct basis from the date of notification.   NBCG 7800

SECTION 2

Reviews and appeals

The UK direct tax system allows a company to **disagree formally** with HMRC where it has been assessed to tax which it considers is not due, had a relief disallowed which had been sought, or not received a credit which was believed to be available. The formal process   **54125** commences with an appeal to an officer of HMRC within a specified time limit. Where resolution cannot be reached with the officer, there is both a statutory right to a review by an independent officer and/or further appeal through the legal channels of the Tax Chamber of the Tribunals Service.

A. Appeals to HMRC

54155
ARTG 2040

In general, where HMRC have assessed, amended, made a determination or a decision, or issued a notice, there will be a right of appeal. So an appeal could be about any of the following:
– whether a particular provision or relief applies;
– the amount of income or profits HMRC believe to be chargeable to tax;
– the amount of tax HMRC believe to be due;
– a penalty that is wrongly charged or is considered by the company to be too high (¶52000+);
– certain types of notice requiring the company or a third party to provide information to HMRC (¶50050+); or
– a claim refused by HMRC.

Time limit to appeal

54160

The right to appeal relating to **assessments**, **amendments**, **discovery assessments** and **determinations** is set out in legislation and usually allows for a 30-day period in which to appeal to HMRC. The provisions are:

Circumstance	Appeal period	Statutory reference	Further details
Assessment	30 days from issue of notice	Sch 18 para 48 FA 1998	¶46365
Amendment of self-assessment	30 days after amendment notified to company	Sch 18 para 30 FA 1998	¶46305
Discovery determination	30 days from issue of notice	Sch 18 para 49 FA 1998	¶50600+
Amendment of a return following an enquiry	30 days after amendment notified to company	Sch 18 para 34 FA 1998	¶50550
Refusal to allow a postponement of tax due	30 days	s 35 TMA 1970	¶54760

s 49 TMA 1970

HMRC may accept a **late appeal** if a written request is made and they are satisfied that there was a reasonable excuse for the delay. They also need to be satisfied that the request was made without unreasonable delay once the excuse finished. If HMRC **do not agree** their decision can be appealed to the tribunal.

HMRC actions

54165

If a formal appeal is launched under any of these provisions, **an officer of HMRC will consider** the grounds for appeal and the information supplied. Further discussions may take place with the company and/or its adviser. At the end of this process HMRC will issue their decision. If the **company does not wish to accept** this decision it can:
– request an internal review by an independent officer of HMRC (or accept a review offer from HMRC);
– appeal to the First-tier Tribunal; or
– if the case is complex, make an appeal directly to the Upper Tribunal, with the agreement of HMRC.

MEMO POINTS   A company can **withdraw** an appeal at any time by notifying HMRC orally or in writing. The matter is then treated as agreed in line with HMRC's view.

s 54 TMA 1970

B. Reviews

All taxpayers have been entitled to a **formal review within HMRC** of any case in dispute since 1 April 2009. The issue must be reviewed by someone independent of the case within HMRC. This is a useful way of progressing disputes where the taxpayer does not wish to incur the costs or formality of an appeal to the tribunal. If the company is not happy with the result of the review it cannot ask for another; the only further remedy is to appeal to the tribunal.

54195

1. Procedure

Request

A review is requested by writing to the HMRC case handler and this can be done at any time, provided that it is **before an appeal to the tribunal**. Making the request for a review prevents an appeal to the tribunal while the review is in progress.

54225

HMRC response

HMRC will then write to the company directly and send a copy to the tax agent, if there is one. The letter will **set out the timetable** for the review and explain HMRC's view and decision at that point. This letter must be **sent out within** 30 days of the request, unless HMRC seek and achieve agreement for a delayed response.

54230
s 49B TMA 1970;
ARTG 4290

The review must be **completed** within 45 days of the HMRC letter that acknowledged the request. HMRC can **seek an extended timetable** if this is necessary. If the company is happy with the outcome of the review, the case is then treated as settled on that basis. If the company is **dissatisfied**, it must appeal to the tribunal within 30 days of the date of the review conclusion letter.

s 49G TMA 1970;
ARTG 4030, 4690

If a **review decision is not issued** within 45 days, or by the end of any extended review period, the case is treated as finalised (unless the company agrees to a further extension) on the basis set out in the review acknowledgement letter (in other words, on the basis that HMRC have not changed their original view). The company then has 30 days, from the date of the letter informing it that the case is treated as finalised, in which to appeal to the tribunal. If the **company does not appeal**, the matter is treated as settled by agreement and the company can only take the matter further by applying to the tribunal to have its appeal heard out of time (¶54375).

54235
ss 49E, 49F
TMA 1970;
ARTG 4850

Alternatively HMRC **may offer a review**. The company has 30 days to accept this offer once made. If it does not accept the offer and does not appeal to the tribunal, the case is treated as settled by agreement in writing.

54240

2. Reviewer's obligations

The reviewer is required to **form his own independent view** of the facts and the decision made. The nature and extent of the review will depend on the complexity of the case and the work already carried out by HMRC. A case that has already been widely considered may need less work than one that initially appeared straightforward but which raises hidden uncertainties.

54270
ARTG 4620

The reviewer **should not** normally contact the original case handler during the review in order to preserve independence, but if it does become necessary the company must be offered the opportunity to make representations in the same way.

The reviewer will **consider** whether the appropriate **technical and legal** input has already been obtained. If it has not, he will organise it and, if appropriate, agree an extended time-table with the company. HMRC describe the reviewer as acting as a "ringmaster" in this respect.

54275

ARTG 4080

HMRC guidance states that in making a decision on the review, the reviewer should consider the **chances of the decision being upheld** by a tribunal. The following should be factored in when doing so:
- whether the facts have been established and whether there is any disagreement about them;
- the technical and legal merits of the case;
- the materiality and proportionality of the tax compared to the costs of pursuing it;
- the likelihood of success for HMRC; and
- the wider implications of the case, including those relating to law and policy.

Company's actions during review

54280

ARTG 4630

The company **may provide further information** during the review. If this is regarded as substantial, it will be referred back to the original case handler for consideration. Only if the new information is limited in scope, and can be handled most efficiently by the reviewer, will the latter deal with it directly. HMRC may seek an extension of the time limit so that they can deal with the extra information, particularly where specialist input is required (such as from the Valuation Office).

New arguments might also be proffered by the company. If these are substantially different from those submitted before, they will be passed to the case handler. If they are based on existing information, the reviewer may include them in the review without involving the case handler. A case handler who is satisfied by the new arguments can settle the case directly, in which case no review conclusion letter will be issued.

Further negotiation

54285

ARTG 4620

A review **does not automatically** rule out the possibility of further negotiation. The reviewer may refer the case back for further negotiation where previous negotiations seem inadequate, or where the company asked for a review because the case handler was unwilling to reach a reasonable negotiated position. In these cases the reviewer will set out the parameters for negotiation. If settlement by negotiation is expected to be relatively simple to achieve the reviewer may carry it out directly.

SECTION 3

Tribunals

54335

The system for hearing appeals on direct tax was reformed from 1 April 2009. Direct tax appeals are now heard in the Tax Chamber of the First-tier Tribunal. There are five other chambers, including the Social Entitlement Chamber (where tax credit appeals are heard) and the Lands Chamber of the Upper Tribunal (where land valuation disputes are resolved). All the tribunals fall under Her Majesty's Courts and Tribunal Service, which is an agency of the Ministry of Justice.

SI 2009/273
rules 2, 3

As well as an overriding objective of fairness and justice, there are a number of **obligations on the tribunals**, including the need to avoid unnecessary formality, seek flexibility and deal with the case proportionally to its complexity, and the costs and resources of the parties involved. Any special expertise must be used effectively and delays avoided.

There is an **obligation on the parties** to help achieve the overriding objective and to co-operate generally. The tribunal should encourage the parties to use alternative dispute resolution (ADR) methods if that would settle the matter more quickly, at less cost, than pursuing the dispute through the tribunal system. For more information about ADR see flmemo.co.uk/ctm54335.

Constitution of tribunals

Appeals to the **First-tier Tribunal** are heard by a panel with a mixture of legally qualified judges and non-legally qualified, but expert, members. The number and mixture depend on the requirements of the case. Appeals from the First-tier Tribunal are to the Upper Tribunal (Tax and Chancery Chamber) and **permission to appeal** must be granted by the First-tier Tribunal or, if refused at that level, sought directly from the Upper Tribunal.

54340

> MEMO POINTS   An appeal may go **directly to the Upper Tribunal**, bypassing the First-tier Tribunal, if the case is complex and the Presidents of the Tax Chamber and the Tax and Chancery Chamber agree.   SI 2009/273 rule 28

A. Commencing an appeal

Timing of appeal

An **initial appeal** on a point of dispute is always to HMRC (¶54155). Whether and when an appeal is then made to the Tribunal depends on HMRC's reaction to the initial appeal. If they offer a review, any appeal to the Tribunal must be made before that offer, or after either the offer or an accepted review's conclusions have been rejected by the company. If HMRC offer a review and then fail to issue a decision after that offer is accepted, the company may appeal after the 45-day time limit expires. If the company requests a review, it can then appeal at any time (subject to the deadlines described below).

54370
ss 49D, 49G
TMA 1970

An appeal to the tribunal must be made **within 30 days** of the:
– date that an offer of review is declined; or
– date of the review conclusion letter (or letter advising there were no findings).

> MEMO POINTS   **HMRC cannot take an appeal** relating to corporation tax directly to the tribunal; instead they must offer a review first.   ARTG 8210

Power to allow late appeals

The tribunal has power to admit a late appeal, provided that a request is made as part of the appeal notice, together with an explanation as to why it is being made out of time. HMRC will decide whether to **oppose the request** for a late appeal, taking into account:
– the length of time since the time limit expired;
– whether there is a reasonable excuse for it being late; and
– what the tribunal is likely to think, given its objective of being fair and just and its wide discretion.

54375
SI 2009/273 rule 20;
ARTG 8240

If **permission** for a late appeal is **refused** by the First-tier Tribunal, a request for judicial review of that decision by the Upper Tribunal can be made.

ARTG 12010

Making an appeal application

Appeals to the tribunal **must be in writing**, either by letter or on a standard form that can be downloaded from the Tribunals Service website or ordered by phone. The **following information** should be included:
– the name and address of the company;
– the name and address of the company's representative;

54380
SI 2009/273;
ARTG 2410

- an address where documents for the company may be sent or delivered;
- details of the decision appealed against;
- the grounds of appeal; and
- the result the company is seeking.

The company **must include** a copy of the decision, assessment or review conclusion against which it is appealing.

> [MEMO POINTS] The address for delivery of the appeal is:
> Tribunals Service
> Tax
> 2nd Floor
> 54 Hagley Road
> Birmingham
> B16 8PE

B. Before the hearing

1. Procedural issues

54410   Once the **appeal has been received**, the Tribunals Service will inform HRMC of the appeal and tell the company what will happen next. The Tribunals Service will not proceed with the appeal if HMRC believe that an appeal to them has not been made first. HMRC may choose to treat the appeal to the tribunal as an appeal to them.

Representative

54415
ARTG 8530

The **company may appoint** a representative to act for it and attend the hearing, provided that the name and address of the representative is sent to HMRC and the tribunal prior to the hearing. Documents should be supplied to the representative but **need not** then also be provided to the company.

> [MEMO POINTS]   A person may also attend the hearing to provide support **without being** a nominated representative.

Case categorisation

54420   When the Tribunals Service receives the appeal, it will allocate it to one of four categories:
- **default paper**, where the cases are the most straightforward and do not usually require a hearing (this includes an appeal against a penalty for late filing of a corporation tax return);
- **basic**, where cases usually involve a hearing and the exchange of some documents prior to it (this includes appeals against information notices, penalties not involving deliberate behaviour, applications for permission to make a late appeal, applications to postpone tax and applications to close an HMRC enquiry);
- **standard**, requiring more detailed case management (this becomes a catch-all category for those not allocated elsewhere); or
- **complex**, where hearings are expected to be lengthy and involve a complex matter of principle or large sums of tax.

> [MEMO POINTS]   A **complex case** may be sent straight to the Upper Tribunal, in which case, as with all complex cases, an order as to which party must bear the costs may be made, unless the company opts out of that procedure.

Similar cases

54425
SI 2009/273 rule 18

Where there are **common or related issues of law or fact** on undecided cases, the tribunal may decide that one of the cases should be designated as the lead case. Consequently, the other cases are suspended (or "stayed") until the lead case is decided. The decision in the lead case will be **binding** on any of the other parties who did not object within 28 days of the designation decision being notified to them. If the **lead case is dropped**, the tribunal will determine if another should become the new lead case.

2. Statements of case

Statements of case are **prepared by** the person that responds to an appeal, known as the respondent. Generally this will be HMRC after an appeal by a company that disagrees with HMRC's original decision.   **54455**

For **default paper** cases a statement of case must be produced within 42 days of the respondent being given notice of the appeal. For **standard and complex** cases this time limit is extended to 60 days.

The statement **must include** the reasons for the decision that is being appealed against and the legal basis for it. The statement may also include a request for the appeal to be heard at a hearing. It must be copied to the tribunal, the company making the appeal ("the appellant") and anybody else involved.

> MEMO POINTS   A statement of case is required in all cases **except** those categorised as **basic**.

C. Consideration of the appeal

Default paper cases

After receiving the statement of case the **appellant** has a further 30 days in which to make its own response and provide any further information (which should be copied to HMRC). The appellant may also ask for a **hearing**. Thereafter the tribunal will decide the matter without a hearing and notify its decision (which may be to allow a hearing).   **54485**
SI 2009/273 rule 25

Basic cases

No statement of case is required for a basic case. Instead an **informal hearing** will be held at which the decision will be made. Any **witness** evidence will not need to be given under oath or affirmation. If HMRC intend to **raise fresh arguments** they must notify the appellant so that it may deal with them at the hearing.   **54490**
SI 2009/273 rule 26

Standard and complex cases

If either party **intends to produce or rely on documents** in the hearing, a list of those documents must be provided within 42 days of receipt of the statement of case. The documents will be those that are in that party's possession, or to which that party has access. The other party must be allowed to inspect or take copies, unless the documents are privileged.   **54495**
SI 2009/273 rule 27

Obtaining further information

HMRC **may issue** information notices to obtain copies of documents under the normal powers afforded to them (¶50050+). This includes the right to inspect premises and remove documents. However, they are not permitted to see documents that are protected by **legal professional privilege** (¶50160). Where there is a dispute over whether any particular document is covered by the protection, the tribunal can decide on its status. There is no right of appeal once the tribunal has determined which, if any, part of the document should be disclosed. HMRC and the company can agree over the documents at any time prior to the hearing.   **54500**

> MEMO POINTS   If documents are **potentially privileged** and identified as such during an inspection, they must be sealed in a container so that they cannot be seen and delivered to the tribunal intact.   SI 2009/1916 reg 6

Withdrawal from an appeal

54505
SI 2009/273 rule 17

A **company** may withdraw its appeal, or part of its case, at any time up to and including the appeal proceedings themselves. The tribunal will ensure that other parties are informed that the appeal has been withdrawn. The company can then apply to **reinstate** its appeal, provided that this is within 28 days of its withdrawal notice, or the hearing (if the withdrawal was oral).

ARTG 8420

HMRC may decide **not to defend** the case at the tribunal. If they then agree the issues with the company, a formal agreement will be concluded and HMRC will inform the tribunal. If **HMRC withdraw** and do not enter into an agreement, they will invite the company to withdraw its appeal.

D. Conduct of hearings

1. Notice and location

54535
SI 2009/273
rules 29, 31;
ARTG 8490

The tribunal must give 14 days' notice of hearings, although a **shorter period is permitted** if the parties agree, or if there are exceptional or urgent circumstances. Complex hearings are usually held in London, Manchester, or Edinburgh; others are held at venues around the country. A hearing is **not required** if both parties decide one is not necessary and the tribunal believes it can decide the issues without one.

2. Public nature

54555
SI 2009/273 rule 32

While hearings are normally held in public the **tribunal may consent** to a wholly or partly private hearing if:
– it is in the interests of public order or national security;
– it is necessary to protect a person's right to private and family life;
– it is necessary to maintain the confidentiality of sensitive information;
– it is necessary to avoid serious harm to the public interest; or
– a public hearing would prejudice the interests of justice.

Where all or part of the hearing is **held in private**, the tribunal has to ensure that the report of its decision does not inadvertently lead to disclosure of the matters that were discussed privately, so defeating the object of holding the hearing in private.

Tribunal powers

54560
SI 2009/273 rule 14

The tribunal has the **power to withhold** the publishing of certain documents or information if to do so would lead to a member of the public being identified and the tribunal thinks it would not be right for that to happen.

SI 2009/273 rule 32

Further, the tribunal can prevent anyone attending a hearing if:
– it believes the person is, or will be, disruptive;
– the presence of the person will hamper the giving of evidence or submissions;
– the person's attendance would defeat the object of the hearing being in private; or
– that person is under the age of 18.

3. Procedure during hearing

54590

The **usual order** for the hearing is that the appellant will present its case and evidence first, bringing out all relevant facts. It would be expected to explain:
– what is in agreement;

- what is in dispute;
- what evidence is being put forward; and
- the basic points being made.

The respondent would then follow. Each party is allowed to ask questions of the other. The tribunal panel members may also ask questions.

Evidence

The company can put forward **witnesses** to give evidence on its behalf; each witness may be required to take an oath or make an affirmation before doing so. If a witness **does not agree to attend**, the tribunal can issue a summons requiring him to do so. The tribunal can specify whether it requires evidence on specific points, what sort of evidence, and how many witnesses it will allow. It can also say whether it wants expert testimony, and whether this should be from a single witness or not. Witness evidence **can be given** orally or via a written statement (which would of course not allow for cross-examination).

54595

The tribunal can **refuse to accept** evidence where:
- it was not provided within the time required;
- it was not provided in the manner required; or
- it would be unfair to allow it.

SI 2009/273 rule 15

> ⌐MEMO POINTS⌐ 1. The Tribunals Service guidance suggests that a **written statement** might be used where the evidence is not likely to be disputed by the other party.
> 2. If a **summons** is issued for a **witness to attend**, it must allow for payment of that person's expenses for attending and say who is to pay them (provided that the witness is not a party to the appeal).

Failing to appear or comply

If a party to the appeal fails to attend the hearing, the tribunal **may proceed** if it thinks that proper notice was given, and that it would be in the interests of justice to continue.

54600

If the **appellant does not comply** with any part of the rules, or does not comply with any direction given by the tribunal, the tribunal can:
- ignore the failing;
- issue instructions on how it can be remedied;
- restrict participation in the case;
- strike out the case; or
- refer the matter to the Upper Tribunal if it relates to **witnesses** refusing to appear, give evidence, swear an oath, or make documents available.

The tribunal can strike out all or part of a case if it **warns the appellant in a direction** that failure to comply will, or could, lead to that result. The tribunal may also strike out the case if it believes that the **lack of co-operation** by the appellant is such that it cannot proceed fairly or justly. Similarly, it can strike out the case if it believes that the appellant has **no reasonable hope of winning** the case. The appellant can object to the striking out and may apply for reinstatement within 28 days after the notice of striking out is given.

54605
SI 2009/273 rule 8

HMRC (the respondent) can be treated in a similar way, except that they can only be barred from the proceedings, rather than their case being struck out. HMRC can then apply for the bar to be lifted. If **HMRC are barred** the tribunal can then ignore any submissions by HMRC and summarily decide against them.

No jurisdiction

The tribunal must strike out the case if it does not have jurisdiction to hear it and **does not transfer the case** to a tribunal that does. If, for example, an appeal was sent to the tribunal while a review was being carried out by an independent HMRC officer, the tribunal would not have jurisdiction.

54610

E. Conclusion of appeal

Timing of decision

54640   The tribunal **may give a decision orally** at the conclusion of a hearing, but must in any event provide a **written decision** within 28 days. It would be usual for a decision on a basic category case to be notified at the hearing, whereas decisions relating to standard and complex cases will usually be provided later in writing. A default paper case will only have a written decision, sent out after the papers have been considered.

Contents of written notice

54645
SI 2009/273 rule 35   The written notice has to include the tribunal's decision and, unless agreed by both parties that it is unnecessary, also include a summary of the facts and reasons for the decision, or full written findings of the facts and the tribunal's reasoning. It must also state how and when any appeal against the decision can be made.

If the tribunal does not give full details of its findings and reasons, a party can apply for these within 28 days of the decision notice. The tribunal must then send the full decision within 28 days of the request. A party must apply for the full written findings before it can make any further appeal.

F. Awarding costs

Basic principle

54675   The normal principle for dealing with the costs of a hearing before the **First-tier Tribunal** is that each party is responsible for its **own costs**. This principle can be overridden where the tribunal believes that a party or its representative has **acted unreasonably** in bringing, conducting or defending the proceedings, in which case that party may be asked to pay some or all of the costs of the other party.

Complex cases

54680   If the case is categorised as complex, the payment of costs will be subject to an order by the tribunal, unless a taxpayer has elected to opt out of this part of the rules. It must do this within 28 days of receiving notice that it will be a complex case. If the taxpayer does not elect to opt out, it could be asked to pay some or all of HMRC's costs.

Application for costs

54685   An application for an order as to who should pay costs can be made **at any time** during proceedings, and should be made no later than 28 days after the final decision in the case. The tribunal cannot make an order for costs without letting the paying party make representations.

G. Further appeals

54715   If a party does not agree with a decision of the First-tier Tribunal it can apply for **permission to appeal** to the Upper Tribunal within 56 days of the latest of the date it received:
– full written reasons;

– amended reasons or a corrected decision; or
– notice that a request to set the decision aside has been refused.

The **request must identify** the decision to which it relates, point out what are regarded as the error(s) in the decision and state the result that the applicant is seeking. A **late request** for permission can be made, provided that it is accompanied by the reason why it is late.

SI 2009/273 rule 39

Basis of appeal

An appeal to the Upper Tribunal **can only be made** on a point of law. Examples of how an error in law might arise are where the tribunal:
– did not apply the correct law or wrongly interpreted the law;
– made a procedural error;
– had no evidence, or not enough evidence, to support its decision; or
– did not give adequate reasons for its decision in the written statement of its reasons.

54720

Tribunal's actions

When the tribunal receives a request for permission to appeal it **must first decide** whether it should review the case. It **can only review** the case if it believes it has made an error on a point of law. If it does not review it, or reviews it and takes no further action after review, it can then agree to or refuse the request for an appeal. If the tribunal **does not grant permission** to appeal for any part of the case, it must advise the applicant on how it can seek permission directly from the Upper Tribunal.

54725

SI 2009/273 rule 40

> MEMO POINTS If the tribunal **decides** to make any **changes** to its original decision, it must give the parties the chance to make representations.

The First-tier Tribunal can **correct** any part of a decision if there has been a clerical or other accidental error. It can also **set aside** and **remake** any part of a decision if it would be in the interests of justice to do so. In order for it to do this, a party must apply within 28 days of receiving notice of the decision and one of the following must have happened:
– a document relating to the proceedings was not sent, or was not received, at an appropriate time;
– there was some other procedural irregularity; or
– a party, or a representative, was not present at a hearing.

54730

SI 2009/273
rules 37, 38

H. Tax payments in dispute

Delaying payment until decision

The company can arrange to **postpone payment** of tax which is in dispute and the subject of an appeal. Application for postponement must be in writing and submitted within 30 days of the assessment or decision. The amount and grounds for postponement must be included with the application. If **HMRC do not agree** with the postponement application, the company can apply to the tribunal to agree the postponement instead.

54760

s 55(3) TMA 1970;
ARTG 2510

Payment becoming due

Once an **appeal is settled**, or the First-tier Tribunal reaches its decision, any further tax due must be paid in accordance with the settlement or decision, even if there may be a further appeal to the Upper Tribunal or beyond. Further tax must be paid within 30 days of when the notice requiring payment is sent to the company. If there is a **further appeal** HMRC may agree to withhold requests for payment informally pending the outcome of the appeal, if making the payment would force the company into bankruptcy or liquidation. Overpayments will be repaid to the company.

54765

ARTG 8930

SECTION 4

Appeals to the UK courts

54815   Appeals beyond the First-tier Tribunal are normally taken next to the Upper Tribunal and then to the relevant court of appeal (some appeals may skip a stage – known as leapfrogging). The Upper Tribunal rules are substantially the same as those for the First-tier Tribunal, with some minor differences. Details of the procedures involved in taking an appeal to these higher levels is beyond the scope of this work and practitioners and companies will therefore need to take **specialist advice**.

> MEMO POINTS   Appeals in **Scotland** are taken to the Court of Session and those in **Northern Ireland** to the Court of Appeal.

54820   The **Upper Tribunal** sits as a Superior Court of Record, meaning that its decisions have precedence over those of the First-tier Tribunal. It **can only hear appeals** on points of law, rather than matters of fact. Its hearings are presided over by legally qualified judges.

Costs in the Upper Tribunal

54825
SI 2008/2968
rule 10

The Upper Tribunal may make an **order for costs** on a case which is heard on appeal from the First-tier Tribunal. This may involve one party paying all or some of the costs of another party.

Appeal to the courts of appeal

54830
SI 2008/2968
rule 44

If a party does not agree with a decision of the Upper Tribunal it can **seek permission** from the Upper Tribunal to appeal on a point of law to the Court of Appeal, Court of Session, or the Court of Appeal in Northern Ireland. It must do so within 1 month of the latest of the date it received:
– full written reasons;
– amended reasons or a corrected decision; or
– notice that a request to set the decision aside has been refused.

The **application must identify** the decision to which it relates, point out what are regarded as the error(s) in the decision and state the result that the applicant is seeking. A late request for permission can be made, provided that it is accompanied by the reason why it is late.

Review

54835
SI 2008/2698
rule 45

The **Upper Tribunal** may review its decision before deciding whether to grant leave to appeal. It can only do so if it **overlooked** legislation or case law which would have had a material effect on its decision or, since it made its decision, a **superior court has made a decision** binding on the Upper Tribunal which would have had a material effect if it had been made before the Upper Tribunal's decision. If the Upper Tribunal **does not grant leave to appeal**, it will advise the party seeking leave on how to apply directly to the appellate court for permission.

Appeal to the Supreme Court

54840   An appeal to the Supreme Court lies from a court of appeal. **Permission** is needed from the appeal court, although it is **not normally needed** from the Court of Session. If permission is **not granted**, permission can be sought directly from the Supreme Court. The Supreme Court hears appeals on points of law of general public importance.

Judicial review

54845
ARTG 12010

Judicial review as a concept deals with the **review by the courts** of powers and decisions of public bodies. It will often be applied for when there is no other right of appeal available.

For example, judicial review may be sought of a decision by the First-tier Tribunal because there is no right of appeal from it, as there is no point of law involved. Judicial review may also be sought for decisions made by HMRC – for example, where the company believes that HMRC are not exercising their powers properly, have misdirected the company so that it has suffered disadvantage, have assumed powers to which they are not entitled, or have acted unfairly.

Judicial review is **exercised** by the High Court but it may transfer some of its responsibilities to the Upper Tribunal. A judicial review decision may:
– quash the original decision;
– make a specific order;
– award damages; or
– issue an injunction.

SECTION 5

The GAAR (general anti-abuse rule)

Commencement and taxes covered

Following a substantial consultation exercise, the UK now has an overarching form of statutory revenue-protection mechanism called the GAAR (general anti-abuse rule).

The GAAR applies in respect of arrangements entered into on or after 17 July 2013 to taxes including:
– corporation tax; and
– any amount chargeable as if it were corporation tax, or treated as if it were corporation tax, such as a CFC charge, the bank levy, the oil supplementary charge and tonnage tax.

55000
ss 206–215 and
Sch 43 FA 2013

When does the GAAR apply?

If tax arrangements are found to be abusive, HMRC will be able to counteract the tax advantage.

55005

Arrangements include any agreement, understanding, scheme, transaction or series of transactions (whether or not legally enforceable).

Arrangements are **tax arrangements** if it would be reasonable to conclude that the obtaining of a tax advantage was the main purpose, or one of the main purposes, of the arrangements.

Tax arrangements are **abusive** if they are arrangements which cannot reasonably be regarded as a reasonable course of action in relation to the relevant tax provisions, having regard to all the circumstances (the "double reasonableness" test).

All the circumstances includes:
– whether the result of the arrangements is consistent with the purposes of the relevant tax provisions;
– whether the means of achieving that result involves any contrived or abnormal steps; and
– whether the arrangements are intended to exploit any shortcomings in the relevant tax provisions.

The purpose of the **double reasonableness** test ("arrangements which cannot reasonably be regarded as a reasonable course of action") is to provide two levels of safeguard to the taxpayer. The first level asks whether the arrangements are, objectively, a reasonable course of action in relation to the relevant tax provisions. If the decision is that the arrangements are a reasonable course of action, the GAAR cannot be activated. If the decision is that the arrangements are not a reasonable course of action, the question must then be asked whether it would nonetheless be a reasonable view to decide that the arrangements are a reasonable course of action in relation to the relevant tax provisions. Only if it would not be reasonable to hold that view can the GAAR be activated.

In making decisions about reasonableness it is permissible to take into account any relevant material concerning the purpose of the legislation. This would include, for example, explanatory notes issued when the legislation was first published and comments by Ministers in Committee. It might also be relevant to consider whether the legislation manifestly fails to achieve its stated objective.

Published guidance on the GAAR states: "these safeguards (and particularly the 'double reasonableness' test) would prevent the GAAR operating in relation to arrangements entered into for the purpose of avoiding an inappropriate tax charge that would otherwise have been triggered by a more straightforward transaction. Tax charges of this sort (sometimes referred to as 'bear traps') can be encountered from time to time. For example where a taxpayer has to take what appear to be contrived steps in order to ensure that they are not taxed on more than the economic gain, such an arrangement would not generally be regarded as abusive."

A **tax advantage** includes (but is not limited to):
– relief or increased relief from tax;
– repayment or increased repayment of tax;
– avoidance or a reduction of a charge to tax or an assessment to tax;
– avoidance of a possible assessment to tax;
– a deferral of a payment of tax or an advancement of a repayment of tax; and
– avoidance of an obligation to deduct or account for tax.

Counteraction may only take the form of making just and reasonable adjustments but these should not lead to double taxation.

Advisory Panel

55010   A GAAR Advisory Panel has been formed, with two main objectives:
– to produce guidance, which HMRC, tribunals and the courts will take into account in deciding whether arrangements fall foul of the GAAR; and
– to supply (via a sub-Panel of, usually, three persons) an opinion in individual cases as to whether or not the actions taken were reasonable in all the circumstances.

Procedure

55015   The procedure under which application of the GAAR proceeds is as follows:
1. A specialist HMRC officer issues a notice to the taxpayer, advising of HMRC's intention to apply the GAAR and explaining why.
2. The taxpayer then has 45 days to make representations.
3. If the taxpayer makes representations, these are forwarded to the GAAR Advisory Panel along with HMRC's reference of the matter (should HMRC wish to proceed having considered the taxpayer's representations) and HMRC's comments on the taxpayer's representations.
4. The taxpayer must be informed that HMRC has decided to proceed, despite having considered the representations.
5. The taxpayer then has 21 days to make further representations to the Panel.
6. The Panel will produce a unanimous **opinion**, or separate opinions if unanimity is not achieved.
7. HMRC will then consider again whether to counteract the tax advantage achieved by the taxpayer.
8. HMRC do not have to follow the opinion(s) of the Panel.
9. The taxpayer may appeal should HMRC decide to go ahead with counteraction.
10. On appeal the tribunal or court must take into account both the Panel's **guidance** on the GAAR generally and the Panel's opinion(s) on the particular case.

Monitoring

55020   HMRC have announced that they will monitor and evaluate the GAAR through:
– recording how many abusive schemes are disclosed under the DOTAS rules (¶46485);
– noting attempts to circumvent the measure, whether disclosed or not;

– identifying potential GAAR cases as well as those which are authorised for counteraction under the GAAR, with a separate record of cases successfully litigated or settled by agreement using a GAAR challenge; and

– keeping in regular communication with taxpayers and practitioners affected by the measure.

Consideration will also be given to evaluating how effective the GAAR has been at **discouraging**, as well as preventing, abusive avoidance schemes.

PART 9

Starting and ceasing a business

Starting and ceasing a business
Summary

The numbers cross-refer to paragraphs.

CHAPTER 1

Starting a business

Whilst the only way to start a company is to incorporate by incorporating it, there are several **60000** in which it may commence activities. If a new trade is commenced, there may be little preparatory work prior to the company being set up, or considerable expense may have been incurred in such areas as market research or product development. Alternatively, the company may be incorporated in order to purchase another trade, or to receive the transfer of an existing unincorporated business.

In all cases, the company will face a number of issues after its incorporation. There are also factors that must be borne in mind when taking over another trade or company.

SECTION 1

Notification of trading

Initial action following incorporation

HMRC will usually send a letter to a **newly formed company** within 6 weeks of them being **60050** advised by Companies House that the company has been formed. The purpose of the letter is to advise the company of its unique taxpayer reference number (UTR) and provide a reminder of the company's tax obligations. The letter is sent from the tax office that is assigned to deal with the company's affairs, to the registered office of the company. This location may not be the one from which it is trading, and is often the address of the company's accountant or legal adviser.

The form CT41G, which was formerly used to register a company for corporation tax, is now seldom used and is no longer routinely sent out by HMRC. Instead, most companies are expected to register for tax online, either as part of the registration process at Companies House (known as the Joint Registration service), or separately via HMRC's website. The appropriate addresses are shown in the following table:

Situation	Website
Register for corporation tax (companies)	flmemo.co.uk/ctm60050a
Register for corporation tax (clubs and associations)	flmemo.co.uk/ctm60050b
Companies House joint registration facility	flmemo.co.uk/ctm60050c

At present there is no **time limit** for registering, if the company has not yet commenced any activity. HMRC guidance states that registration should be performed as soon as possible.

> ⎣_MEMO POINTS_⎦ At intervals, the company may receive a form 204, entitled **Corporation Tax Review**, which is used by HMRC to check whether a company is still dormant. If this is not the case, form 204 Active Company should be completed, or registration performed online as above.

Commencement of activities

60055
s 55 FA 2004

A company (**not an unincorporated association**) is obliged to notify HMRC when it comes within the charge to corporation tax. This will happen when an accounting period commences, and it is either:
– the **company's first accounting period**; or
– an accounting period which **does not start immediately after the previous one ends**, for instance, after a period of dormancy.

The **notice must be given** to HMRC within 3 months of the start of the accounting period.

Where this information has been **previously provided** to HMRC in relation to another tax area (usually VAT), the company must still notify HMRC as above.

> ⎣_MEMO POINTS_⎦ 1. Since 1 April 2010 there has been no **penalty** for failure to notify a commencement of activities.
> 2. The requirement to register should not be confused with the provisions relating to **notification of chargeablility** (¶46110).
> 3. Whilst it is commonly believed that only the commencement of a trade gives rise to the requirement to notify, any activity that results in the **commencement of an accounting period** falling within these provisions will trigger the requirement (for example, acquiring a source of income). See ¶3045 for full details. HMRC describe this as the company "becoming active".

SECTION 2

Expenditure prior to trading

60105   Expenditure may be incurred before the company is incorporated by someone else acting in relation to its affairs, or after incorporation but prior to any trade commencing.

Pre-incorporation expenditure

60110   Expenses may be **incurred in connection** with an activity that the company will commence or take over on its incorporation. For instance, it may be that someone has carried out market research on the potential sales level of a new service they intend to offer. If the company had incurred this expense after it had been incorporated, it would have been able to obtain tax relief for it (¶60115), but no statutory provision exists to enable a company to secure relief for expenditure incurred by another person. (Contrast this with the position for VAT: see *VAT Memo* for full details).

However, it should be possible for an individual who incurs expenditure in this situation to claim a **reimbursement** of the costs from the company once it is incorporated. This allows the company to treat the expenditure as if it had incurred it directly.

> MEMO POINTS 1. The **income tax position** of the individual can be more complex, as the reimbursed expenses cannot be incurred wholly and exclusively for the purpose of an employment which did not exist at the time. However, it would appear that HMRC accept that expenses reimbursed in such situations will not be taxable.
> 2. The expenditure may instead already be **attributable to a trade** because it was incurred by another person in relation to a trade that will be transferred to the company. Such expenditure is dealt with under the normal trading rules.

Pre-trading expenditure

Once the company is incorporated, it may incur expenditure as it prepares to trade. In some cases such expenditure will be accounted for under normal accounting principles at a later date. For instance, the **purchase of stock** will only be allowed as a deduction once there is a change in the stock level, or a **prepayment** of an expense may also cover a trading period.

60115
s 61 CTA 2009

However, where the costs are **not attributable to a trading period**, but would be allowable for tax purposes if they had been incurred once the company was trading, a deduction is allowed provided the expenses were incurred within 7 years before commencement of the trade. The deduction is given in the first trading period.

This rule does not apply to finance costs, for which see ¶60120.

> EXAMPLE A Ltd incurs the following expenses:
>
> | Date | Amount (£) | Purpose |
> |---|---|---|
> | 15 November 2010 | 25,000 | Market research |
> | 1 April 2012 | 60,000 | Rent until 31 March 2015 |
> | 22 March 2013 | 18,000 | Initial stock |
>
> The company begins to trade on 1 April 2013, drawing up accounts to 31 March. The expenditure on market research will qualify for a deduction, because it would have been allowable if the company had been trading, and was incurred within the 7 year period prior to trading commencing. As the payment of rent relates to a 3 year period, only one of which is prior to trading, only £20,000 will be allowed under these rules. A further £20,000 will be available under standard accounting principles for the year ended 31 March 2014, and the final £20,000 in the year ended 31 March 2015.
> The cost of stock will follow standard accounting principles and effectively be matched to items sold.
> The total amount of pre-trading expenditure that will be treated as having been incurred on 1 April 2013 will be £45,000 (25,000 + 20,000).

Interest and related costs If the company incurs interest charges or other finance expenses before it commences its trade, they will be treated as a **non-trade debit** for loan relationship purposes (¶16350+). Likewise, any money on deposit will be attracting interest, which under the loan relationship rules will be a **non-trade credit**.

60120
s 330 CTA 2009

If these debits and credits result in a **non-trading deficit**, the company is entitled to claim relief for it against any other income arising in that period. If (as is likely) the company has insufficient income, it can only carry the debit forward. Normally such a debit cannot be relieved against trading profits (¶16360). However, if the company **commences a trade within 7 years** of the end of the period in which such a debit occurs, it can treat the debit as a trade debit in the first trading period, provided that:
– it makes an election for this treatment within 2 years of the end of the period in which the debit arises; and
– if the debit had arisen once the trade had commenced, it would have been a trade debit.

⌐MEMO POINTS¬ 1. For this election to be available the **debits must arise** in an accounting period. This in essence means that the company must have some source of income.
2. If the election is made but **no trade commences** within the 7 year period then they are lost.

60125
s 12 CAA 2001

Expenditure qualifying for capital allowances Expenditure incurred before the trade commences on items that would qualify for plant and machinery allowances (¶25240+) is **deemed** to have been incurred on the first day of trading. However, this does not change the actual date of purchase for the purposes of any first year allowances that may be available.

SECTION 3

Impact on accounting periods

60175
ss 9 - 10 CTA 2009

As **most of the administrative requirements** are tied to accounting periods, and a number of the **reliefs** can only be used when attributed to accounting periods (¶60115), it is vital that accounting periods are identified correctly.

Typically, the **first accounting period** will **commence** when the company acquires a source of income, such as by opening an interest-bearing bank account, making a capital disposal or commencing a trade.

It is likely that the **period will then end** on the first of the following:
– the expiration of 12 months from the start of the period;
– the company's accounting date;
– the company starts to make up accounts, having previously not done so; or
– the company begins or ceases to trade.

⌐EXAMPLE¬ A Ltd deposits capital in an interest-bearing account on 5 January 2012. It continues its preparations to trade until 6 July 2013 when it acquires an existing business. To keep track of its expenses, it drew up accounts to 31 December 2012, and intends preparing accounts based on calendar years. Its accounting periods for corporation tax purposes will be as follows:

5 January 2012 - 31 December 2012	Commencement of accounting period to passing of accounting reference date
1 January 2013 - 5 July 2013	From end of last accounting period to commencement of a trade
6 July 2013 - 31 December 2013	Commencement of trade until accounting reference date
1 January 2014 - 31 December 2014	Following the company's accounting period

As the accounting periods do not match the periods that the accounts cover, an apportionment of profits must be made (¶3060+).

Determining the start of trading

60180

In most cases it will be clear when the trade commences. However, it may be difficult to distinguish in some cases between trading and preparing to trade. Whilst every case has to be judged based on its own circumstances, some **general guidance** can be taken from case law.

Firstly, trading has an **active nature** in that goods or services should be being provided to somebody. Anything leading up to this is likely to be considered preparatory. *Ransom v Higgs* [1974] Generally speaking, a **trade cannot commence until** the company is in a position to provide the goods or services it intends to, and actually does supply them, or offers to supply them, by way of trade. The preparatory phase may be lengthy, depending on the nature of the trade. A small retail outlet will commence trading on the day it opens to the public, having only had a relatively short preparation phase. *J & R O'Kane & Co v CIR* [1922] However, a company researching a new medical treatment will have a much longer preparatory phase before it commences trading.

There is **no requirement** for the trade to be commenced on a **large scale**; it will be sufficient to have started the sale of the goods or services. However, the sale of stock produced by a trial run of a process may not necessarily result in a trade having commenced. It is possible that such an action could be seen as a continuation of testing a product, rather than commencing to trade by selling it.

Where a company intends to provide **services** rather than goods, the relevant date, without any evidence to the contrary, will generally be considered to be the date on which its first contract of engagement is entered into. *Napier v Griffiths* [1990]

Manufacturing The **general principle** for manufacturing businesses is that trade only commences once the company takes in raw materials and makes its product. The following actions have all been held to be preparatory activities:
– visiting similar businesses in other parts of the country;
– having a factory built;
– outfitting the factory with the necessary plant and machinery;
– entering into agreements to purchase products for the business;
– entering into agreements for the sale of the finished products; and
– engaging a foreman of works. *Birmingham & District Cattle By-products Ltd v CIR* [1919]

60185
BIM70510

High-technology businesses Many technology businesses will raise funds based on a concept rather than a finished product, and at that stage will not know how they will exploit the intellectual property that will arise. They may license the use of it to another business, utilise it themselves, or a combination of both. Until the company has **decided how it will exploit** the intellectual property, it is unlikely to meet the criteria for trading.

60190
BIM70515

Investment company The main source of income for an investment company is the **receipt of dividends**, which will be excluded from tax. Without specific provisions, such a company might not be considered to have come within the charge to corporation tax. The company is therefore deemed to come within the charge when it commences business. This is interpreted to mean the date on which it first acquires shares in another, non-dormant, company.

60195
s 9(2) CTA 2009;
CTM01420

SECTION 4

Taking over a trade

A. Companies without investment business

1. Trading losses brought forward

Where a **company changes ownership** (¶60250), the use of trading losses brought forward will be restricted where either:
– in the period from 3 years before to 3 years after the change of ownership, there has been a **major change** in the nature or conduct of a trade (¶60260); or
– the scale of a company's activities has become **small or negligible**, and following a change of ownership there is a considerable **revival** of the trade.

Where these provisions apply, the accounting period in which the change of ownership occurs is **split into two notional periods** at the date of the change. Profits and losses are apportioned between the two notional periods on a just and reasonable basis. In practice, time apportionment will apply unless another method is considered more appropriate.

Trading **losses arising before the change** of ownership cannot be carried forward against profits after that date. Similarly, trading **losses arising after the change** of ownership cannot be carried back to a period before that date.

60245
ss 673 - 675
CTA 2010

MEMO POINTS   1. When computing a **balancing charge** (¶26085) that is triggered after a change in ownership, any capital allowances made before the change that could not be relieved against profits before the change are ignored.

2. A similar restriction applies in relation to brought forward surplus ACT (¶41190).

3. Where the **change in ownership occurs on or after 20 March 2013**, similar restrictions apply to **shell companies**. A shell (or dormant) company is one which does not carry on a trade or a UK property business, and is not a company with investment business. The **restrictions apply to** the carry forward of loan relationship deficits and losses on intangible fixed assets from periods prior to the date of change.

Change in ownership

60250
s 719 CTA 2010

A change in ownership of a company **occurs if** either:
– a single person acquires a holding of more than half the ordinary share capital;
– two or more persons each acquire a holding of at least 5% and jointly more than half of the ordinary share capital; or
– two or more persons each increase their holdings such that they each hold at least 5% and jointly more than half of the ordinary share capital.

> EXAMPLE A Ltd is owned by B Ltd (80 %) and C Ltd (20 %). B Ltd then sells 3% to C Ltd and 49% to a new shareholder, D Ltd. Neither C Ltd nor D Ltd have acquired more than 50% of the ordinary share capital. Although they have acquired more than 50% between them, the rules do not aggregate the acquisitions as C Ltd did not acquire at least 5%. However, the rules do allow the aggregation of C Ltd's total shareholding, as it is more than 5%. Consequently A Ltd has changed ownership.

s 720 CTA 2010

When considering changes in shareholdings, it is possible to look at any two points in time, provided they are not more than 3 years apart, and consider the resulting position over that period.

> EXAMPLE In the example above, suppose that C Ltd increased its shareholding on 1 April 2012, with D Ltd making its acquisition on 1 October 2013. The rules will still apply as the net change over the period will still be the same.

s 721 CTA 2010;
CTM06340

MEMO POINTS   1. HMRC may consider that the ordinary share capital test is not appropriate where persons have **extraordinary rights**. In this situation, an alternative basis for quantifying ownership may be proposed.

2. When considering a person's holding, shares held and acquisitions by **connected persons** (¶31375) are also taken into account.

3. Where an individual acquires shares through an unsolicited **bequest or gift**, such an acquisition may be ignored.

60255
s 724 CTA 2010

There is **no change in ownership** of a company where it remains a 75% subsidiary (¶65090) of one company, regardless of changes to intermediate direct shareholdings. This is to allow the situation where a company is a member of a group and its direct ownership is passed between members of the group whilst still being a subsidiary of the ultimate group holding company.

> EXAMPLE A group of companies is structured as follows:

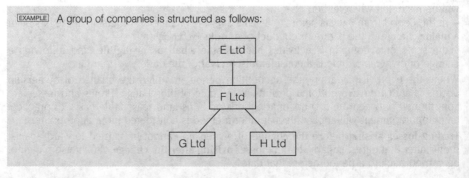

All companies are owned 100% by the company above them.
F Ltd sells its entire shareholding in H Ltd to E Ltd. Under the normal rules it is clear that a change in ownership has occurred. However, H Ltd was a 75% subsidiary of E Ltd before the transaction and remains so afterwards. As such the rules are disapplied.

Major change in nature or conduct of a trade

The **legislation** contains a **list of factors** which may be relevant when considering whether a major change has occurred. This includes the following:
– the type of property dealt in;
– the services or facilities provided; and
– the customers, outlets and markets.

60260
s 673 CTA 2010;
SP 10/91;
CTM06370

To clarify the position, HMRC have published guidance on what they consider to be a major change, and provide a number of examples to illustrate their view. In general, changes resulting from technological advances, efficiency measures or product rationalisation will not be considered a major change, although each case will be considered on its own facts.

The following **would not constitute a major change**:
– moving production from a number of outdated factories to a single modern production plant;
– replacing a product component with a different material without changing the overall nature of the product;
– changing the brand of product which is dealt with but not the actual product type; or
– withdrawing an unprofitable product line and increasing production of another existing and similar product.

The following **would constitute a major change**:
– ceasing to deal in one product and beginning to deal in a product with a totally different use;
– changing from being a service company to a production company; or
– changing from investments in stocks and shares to investment in property.

Anti-avoidance provisions

Two targeted anti-avoidance rules ("TAARs") apply to changes of ownership (as defined in¶60500) which take place **on or after 20 March 2013**. The first TAAR relates to the **transfer of deductible amounts** where the following items may be restricted:
– expenses of a trade or a property business;
– expenses of a management company's investment business; and
– non-trade debits relating to loan relationships or to intangible fixed assets.

60265
Sch 14 FA 2013

The **restriction applies** where, at the date of the change, it is highly likely that the expense will form part of a group relief claim, and one of the main purposes of the change in ownership is to allow the claim to be made. Where the restriction applies, the **expense can still be utilised** against profits of the same trade, but cannot be the subject of a group relief claim. These rules essentially seek to prevent manipulation of expenses during periods where a change of ownership occurs. It is often possible to defer a significant expense until after the date of the change of ownership so that it can be used by the purchaser, with the benefit of this advantage being reflected in the purchase price.

The second TAAR relates to situations where **profit is transferred** to the company which changes ownership, where one of the main benefits is to use the deduction arising from an expense against the profit which has been transferred. This provision will only apply where the use of the expense is, again, thought to be highly likely at the time of the change of ownership. It should be noted that no restriction will be made on the use of deductible amounts against profits which would have arisen without the existence of the profit transfer arrangements.

2. Losses from a property business

60290
ss 704, 705
CTA 2010

Where a **company changes ownership** (¶60250) the use of losses from a property business, **either UK or overseas**, brought forward will be restricted where either:
– in a period of 3 years before or after the change of ownership there has been a **major change** in the nature or conduct of a trade or the property business; or
– the scale of a company's activities has become **small or negligible** and subsequently, following a change of ownership, there is a considerable revival of the trade.

These provisions essentially mirror those applicable for companies with trading losses (¶60245). The provisions covered by the deduction transfer and profit transfer **TAARs** (¶60265) also apply to expenses of a property business.

60295

For these purposes a **major change** is deemed to occur where there is a:
– significant difference in the type of property dealt in, or the services or facilities provided; or
– significant change in the customers, outlets or markets of the business.

EXAMPLE A company moving from renting industrial units to providing domestic accommodation for rent will not only be a major change in the type of property but also in the customer base.

B. Companies with investment business

Management expenses

60325

Unrelieved management expenses **brought forward** may be restricted either:
– because of a change in the nature of the trade (¶60355);
– when there is an intra-group disposal of an asset (¶60400); or
– where specific anti-avoidance provisions apply (¶60265).

1. Change in nature of the business

Scope

60355
ss 677, 682
CTA 2010

Where a company with investment business changes ownership, the use of losses will be restricted if:
– in the period from 3 years before to 3 years after the change of ownership (¶60250) there is a **major change** (¶60260) in the nature or conduct of the business;
– after the change of ownership there is a **significant increase in the capital** (¶60360) of the company; or
– the scale of a company's activities have become **small or negligible** and subsequently, following a change of ownership, there is a considerable revival of the business.

Significant increase in capital

60360
ss 688 - 690
CTA 2010

In order to decide if there has been a significant increase in the capital of the company two figures have to be compared.

Amount A is defined as the lower of:
– the capital immediately before the change in ownership; and
– the highest 60 day minimum amount in the 12 months ending with the change of ownership.

Amount B is defined as the highest 60 day minimum amount in the 3 year period following the change of ownership.

A **60 day minimum** amount is the amount of capital that a company has maintained for a period of at least 60 days.

If Amount B is either:
- at least twice amount A; or
- over £1 million more than amount A

a significant increase in capital is deemed to have occurred.

> MEMO POINTS 1. **Capital** is defined as the total of the paid up share capital and share premiums, together with any outstanding redeemable loan capital and any outstanding debts (including interest on them). It must be expressed in sterling at the exchange rate applying when the capital was introduced or incurred.
> 2. The **debts** can be for money borrowed, capital assets acquired, any right to receive income or where the value of the consideration for the debt was less than the debt itself.

s 691 CTA 2010;
CTM08750

s 453 CTA 2010

> EXAMPLE C Ltd is acquired by D Ltd on 21 December 2013 and there are excess management charges at that date. C Ltd's capital history is:
>
> | Date | No of days | Capital (£) |
> |---|---|---|
> | 21 December 2012 | 72 | 100,000 |
> | 3 March 2013 | 240 | 150,000 |
> | 29 October 2013 | 54 | 175,000 |
> | 21 December 2013 | Change of ownership | |
> | 1 July 2014 | > 60 | 325,000 |
>
> Amount A: The capital immediately before the change in ownership was £175,000. This was also the highest level of capital in the preceding year. However, it was not maintained for a period of at least 60 days. The next highest level of capital was £150,000 and this was maintained for at least 60 days. So the highest 60 day minimum amount is £150,000. This is also amount A as it is lower than the level of capital at the date of change.
> Amount B will be £325,000 and as this is more than twice amount A there has been a significant increase in capital of the company.

Restrictions

Where these provisions apply, the accounting period in which the change in ownership occurs is **split into two notional periods** at the date of the change. **Management expenses** are apportioned between the two notional periods on a just and reasonable basis. In practice, time apportionment will apply unless another method is considered more appropriate.

60365
ss 678, 685
CTA 2010

Excess management expenses **brought forward** will be added to the earlier of the two periods. The expenses that are then allocated to the earlier period cannot be used in the later period, and vice versa.

> MEMO POINTS **Other deductions** or reliefs which are similarly restricted include:
> - losses of a property business;
> - excess capital allowances (as they are part of management expenses carried forward);
> - non-trading losses on intangible fixed assets;
> - qualifying charitable donations (¶22055); and
> - surplus ACT (¶41190).

ss 681-684
CTA 2010

Non-trade loan deficits A non-trade deficit **arising in the period of change** will be time apportioned, but specific rules affect certain types of debit.

60370
ss 679, 680, 685
CTA 2010

Any **deficit brought forward** will always be apportioned to the first of the two notional accounting periods.

Certain debits accounted for under the **amortised base cost** method are only brought into account in one period rather than being spread over a number of periods (¶16050+). Where such a debit falls to be accounted for in the period of change and it is either:
- treated as such, as it is interest paid late, where it is not allowed to be deducted until paid; or
- a deeply discounted security of a connected or close company subject to the postponement until redemption rules;

then all of the related debit will **fall into the first** notional period and will not form part of the overall deficit that is time apportioned. If the debit is accounted for under the amortised base cost method but does not fall into one of these categories, then the total debit is apportioned based on the length of the accrual period.

---

2. Transfers of assets intra-group

60400
s 699 CTA 2010

Management expenses brought forward across a change in ownership may be restricted from relief against chargeable gains made within the 3 years after the change in ownership. This restriction only applies where the expenses carried forward at the change of ownership have not already been disallowed (¶60245).

A new owner must therefore ensure that excess expenses are not restricted as a result of crystallising a gain on an asset transferred intra-group, even if they have not already been compromised by changes in activities or capital.

Scope

60405
s 692 CTA 2010

The restriction applies to the use of brought forward management expenses against a gain arising on the disposal of an asset which was **acquired after the date of change** from a group company by way of either:
– a **no gain/no loss transaction** (for tangible assets, ¶67080); or
– a **tax neutral transfer** (for intangible assets, ¶69180).

This includes the situation where the asset sold **derives its value** from the asset transferred (for example, the asset transferred was a leasehold, but the lessee also acquires the reversion and then sells the freehold).

Computation

60410
s 693 CTA 2010

Management expenses **brought forward** at the date of change of ownership cannot be set against the lower of:
– the total gains for the period in which the gain arises; and
– the gain on the asset transferred intra-group.

> EXAMPLE E Ltd was acquired by F Ltd, on 31 December 2012. E Ltd's accounting period end is 31 December. Excess expenses at 1 January 2013 were £28,000. On 4 September 2013 an asset was transferred intra-group to E Ltd. On 15 November 2013 the asset was sold at a gain of £15,000. Other capital gains in 2013 totalled £17,000.
>
> | | £ |
> |--|--------|
> | Gains on asset transferred intra-group | 15,000 |
> | Other gains | 17,000 |
> | Total gains for 2013 | 32,000 |
>
> None of the excess expenses at 1 January 2013 can be set against the gain of £15,000. They can be used against the other gains of £17,000.
> If the company had instead realised capital losses of £2,000 (not including the gain on the intra-group asset), the position would have been as follows:
>
> | | £ |
> |--|---------|
> | Gains on asset transferred intra-group | 15,000 |
> | Other gains/(losses) | (2,000) |
> | Total gains for 2013 | 13,000 |
>
> In this case none of the expenses brought forward could be used against the total gains of £13,000.

ss 697-701
CTA 2010

> MEMO POINTS **Other deductions** or reliefs which are similarly restricted include:
> – losses of a property business;
> excess capital allowances (as they are part of management expenses carried forward);
> – non-trading losses on intangible fixed assets;
> – deficits under the loan relationships regime;
> – qualifying charitable donations (¶22055); and
> – surplus ACT (¶41190).

Where the **date of change in ownership does not coincide with the end of an accounting period**, notional accounting periods are created, either side of the date of change.   **60415**

If the **gain** arises in the accounting period when the change of ownership occurs, it is allocated between the notional periods on the basis that **if the total gains** (including those realised on intangible assets (¶28485)):   s 702 CTA 2010

– are **greater than the gain** on the asset transferred intra-group, then the gain on that asset is allocated to the notional period after the date of change, and the excess is allocated to the notional period before the date of change; or

– are **less than the gain** on the asset transferred intra-group, the total amount is allocated to the later notional period (unless there are capital losses involved, this amount will equal the gain on the asset that was transferred intra-group).

Management expenses of the accounting period are allocated between the two notional periods on the basis of GAAP, unless this is unjust or unreasonable. Excess management expenses brought forward into the actual accounting period are allocated to the first of the notional periods, not time apportioned between them.

EXAMPLE Continuing the example at ¶60410, the same facts apply to E Ltd's acquisition except that it took place on 15 February 2013. This produces the following notional accounting periods:
– 1 January 2013 to 15 February 2013; and
– 16 February 2013 to 31 December 2013.
The excess expenses at 1 January 2013 of £28,000 are allocated to the period ended 15 February 2013.

	£
Gains on asset transferred intra-group (sold 15 November 2013)	15,000
Other gains	17,000
Total gains for 2013	32,000

As total gains are greater than the gain on the asset transferred intra-group, the gain of £15,000 is allocated to the period ended 31 December 2013 and gains of £17,000 are allocated to the period ended 15 February 2013.
Tax computation for the period ended 15 February 2013:

	£	£
Income (say)		4,000
Gains		17,000
		21,000
Management expenses:		
Expenses of the period	2,000	
Expenses brought forward	28,000	
Total	30,000	
Relieved in current period	(21,000)	
Expenses carried forward at the date of change that cannot be set against intra-group gains	9,000	

The remaining expenses of £9,000 can still be carried forward but their use will still be restricted in a similar way for future periods.
Instead, if there had been other capital losses of £2,000, the total gains of £13,000 would have been allocated to the notional period ended 31 December 2013 (the later period, because the intra-group asset gain exceeds total gains). The management expenses carried forward at 15 February 2013 would have been £30,000, but none of this amount could be set against the gains.

C. Capital allowances

Special rules apply to certain situations that arise where one company succeeds to the trade of another, as shown in the following table: **60445**

Situation	¶¶
Transfer of trade to a company under the same ownership	¶79600+
Manipulation of the succession rules to secure balancing allowances	¶60475
Purchase of capital allowances	¶60495+
Change in the person carrying on a trade where no sale has been made	¶60545+

1. Manipulation of allowances

60475
ss 954 - 957
CTA 2010

Where a company ceases to trade and another company begins the same trade (either as its only trade or as part of an existing trade), the succession to trade rules for capital allowances (¶79715) will apply where:
– under the normal rules the predecessor company would have been **entitled** to balancing allowances; and
– the **reason** the predecessor ceased to carry on the trade was to secure allowances to which it would not have been entitled otherwise.

> EXAMPLE A Ltd, a profitable trading company, and B Ltd, a loss making trading company, are under common ownership (¶79640). C Ltd, an unconnected third party, is interested in purchasing the trade of B Ltd. As B Ltd has been making losses, it has disclaimed all of its capital allowances for a number of years, and the written down value of the assets is significantly higher than their market value. If B Ltd transferred the trade directly to C Ltd, it would receive significant balancing allowances which it could not use. The decision is made to allow A Ltd to take over the trade, and then sell it on. If it were not for the rules above, A Ltd would obtain the balancing allowances that arise on the disposal. Instead, C Ltd will effectively succeed to the position of A Ltd, acquiring the assets at their written down value for the purposes of future allowances.

> MEMO POINTS This does not apply where the successor is a **dual resident investing company**.

2. Buying capital allowances

Scope

60495
s 212B CAA 2001;
Sch 26 FA 2013

A company is barred from acquiring capital allowances by purchasing another company and then using group relief (¶66050) to shelter the profits of other companies in the group.

The basic rules are outlined below, but where the change in ownership takes place **on or after 20 March 2013**, then the provisions are **extended to cover not merely trades**, but essentially any activity where capital allowance buying could occur.

If a company carrying on a trade/activity (by itself or in partnership):
– is subject to a **qualifying change** (¶60500); and
– the company (or partnership) has **excess capital allowances** (¶60510) in relation to that trade/activity; and
– one of the **main purposes** of the change arrangements is to gain a tax advantage by securing additional allowances;
then the use of some or all of those excess allowances will be restricted (¶60515).

Where the change in ownership takes place **on or after 20 March 2013**, the "main purpose" condition does not need to be satisfied if:
– the excess of allowances amounts to **at least £50 million**; or
– the excess is between £2 million and £50 million, and the benefit is "not insignificant" (not defined, but HMRC are likely to take the view that this will be 5% or more).

> MEMO POINTS In looking at the gaining of a tax advantage the rules will also apply where a claim is to be made in relation to postponed allowances for ships (¶26385+).

Qualifying change

In order for there to have been a qualifying change in relation to the company (C) on a given day, one of the following must apply:

a. There is a **change in the principal company** (or companies) of C, or C is not owned by a company at the start of the day but is so owned at the end of the day. This will apply where C joins a group, irrespective of whether it was part of a group beforehand.

b. Any company that is involved in a **consortium** where the consortium, if it was treated as a single company, would be considered the principal company, **increases its ownership** in C. This will also apply where the consortium holds another company, which in turn is the principal company of C. The rules will only apply to the company (or companies) that have increased their share in C.

c. C **ceases to carry on all or part of its trade/activity**, and a partnership begins to carry it out in circumstances where the provisions relating to the transfer of a trade without a change in ownership would apply (¶79600+). For instance, D Ltd may transfer its trade to a partnership of E Ltd and F Ltd, where E Ltd is a wholly owned subsidiary of D Ltd.

d. C carries on a trade/activity in partnership and its **share in the partnership decreases**. The rules will not apply to C but to the partner whose share has increased.

60500
ss 212C - 212I
CAA 2001

Principal company

The definition of principal company is extensive, in order to ensure that the legislation covers the situations intended. The definition relies on the definition of qualifying 75% subsidiary (¶65090+), referred to here simply as "subsidiary".

Simple case: A company, P, is considered a principal company of another, C, where:
– C is a subsidiary of P; and
– P is not a subsidiary of another company.

Chain of companies: P is the principal company of C where:
– C is a subsidiary of a third company, T;
– T is a subsidiary of P; and
– P is not a subsidiary of another company.

This chain is extended if there are more companies in the chain so that there will only be one principal company for a chain of companies.

Consortium: P is the principal company of C where:
– C is owned by a consortium of which P is a member; or
– C is a subsidiary of another company owned by a consortium of which P is a member,
provided P is not a subsidiary of another company.

If P was a subsidiary of another company, A, then A would be the principal company of C. If A is a subsidiary then the chain is extended to find the first company that is not a subsidiary.

60505
s 212E CAA 2001

> ⬛ *MEMO POINTS* For full details of what makes a company a **qualifying 75% subsidiary** see ¶65090+. These are amended so that **companies without share capital** can fall into them. In this case the parent company needs to control the subsidiary, along with being entitled to 75% of any profits available for distribution and 75% of the assets on winding up

Excess allowances

There is a relevant excess of allowances in relation to a trade where the tax written down value at the date of the change exceeds the balance sheet value of the same assets.

The **tax written down value** is calculated by adding together the expenditure that is available for carry forward for plant and machinery in any single asset pool, class pool and the main pool, and any postponed allowances in relation to ships (¶26385+).

The **balance sheet value** is the net asset value of the same assets (or net investment for assets subject to finance leases) shown in the accounts drawn up under GAAP for the start of the day of change, but adjusted for the disposal of any plant and machinery on that day. In the case of **fixtures** it is possible that these will be reflected in the accounts in land as

60510
s 212J CAA 2001

opposed to plant and machinery. Where this is the case a just and reasonable apportionment of the value shown in the accounts should be made.

Implications

60515
s 212P CAA 2001

Where the change of ownership occurs **on or after 20 March 2013**, the provisions do not merely apply to trades (¶60495), but the term "trade" is retained below for ease of reference.

Where there is an excess of allowances (taken across all the allowance pools), the existing **accounting period** ends on the day of change and a new one starts on the following day. It is then necessary to:
– **identify** which pool or pools have an excess; and
– then **reduce** the residue of expenditure in those pools by the excess as it stood immediately before the date of change.

In ascertaining the balance sheet value for each pool a just and reasonable apportionment will be necessary.

If **one pool has an excess greater than the total excess**, this implies that another pool has a written down value less than the balance sheet value attributed to it. Where this is the case the restriction applied is limited to the total amount of the excess across all pools.

A sum equal to the **restriction** which is applied for each pool then goes into a new pool of the same type, and attracts allowances at the same rates. The **use of these allowances** is restricted as follows:
a. The allowances can only be set against profits of the original trade. This means that a new trade transferred into the company (or partnership) will not be able to use the allowances generated from the excess pools.
b. Losses created or increased by the allowances can only be set against profits of that period, deriving from trades carried on by the company (or if the trade is carried on by a partnership then a trade carried on by one of the partners) at the date of change, and are restricted to the amount of loss that could have been relieved if there had been no change.
c. Losses created or increased by the allowances cannot be surrendered as group relief, unless they could have been surrendered if no change had occurred, and are restricted to the amount that could have been surrendered if there had been no change.

EXAMPLE   D Ltd falls within the above rules. It has overall excess allowances of £190,000, calculated as follows:

	Main pool	Single asset pool	Special rate pool
Tax written down value	100,000	200,000	200,000
Balance sheet value	80,000	210,000	20,000
Excess of TWDV over BSV	20,000	-	180,000
Excess of BSV over TWDV	-	10,000	-

As there is an excess of balance sheet value of £10,000 in the single asset pool, this can be allocated against the potential restriction in the other pools. D Ltd decides to allocate it against the main pool to maximise claims in the next few years.
The opening balances of the new period will be:

	Main pool	New main pool	Single asset pool	Special rate pool	New special rate pool
Tax written down value	90,000	10,000	200,000	20,000	180,000

MEMO POINTS   Adjustments for **disposals** of plant and machinery will require a just and reasonable apportionment in allocating them to affected pools.

---

3. Changes in person carrying on the trade

60545
s 265 CAA 2001

Special provisions apply where:
– a company **succeeds** to a trade that was carried on by another person; and
– the succession causes the **old trade** to be treated as **discontinued**.

In this situation, provided the assets are **transferred without being sold**, the assets of the trade are deemed to be transferred at the date of succession at their market value, and acquired by the new business at that price. The successor can claim writing down allowances in respect of the asset, but is not entitled to any first year allowance or annual investment allowance (¶25940).

> EXAMPLE E Ltd transfers its trade and assets to F Ltd without any charge being made. F Ltd will be deemed to have acquired the assets at their market value at the date of transfer and will claim WDA based on that value.

These rules are modified where the transfer is of plant and machinery and the **predecessor and successor are connected** (¶25190). In this situation, a joint election may be made to transfer the assets at tax WDV, which means that no allowances are due to the predecessor for the final period of trade. Such an election must be made within 2 years of the date of the succession.

60550
ss 266 - 268
CAA 2001

> MEMO POINTS 1. These provisions **do not apply if** the predecessor and successor are companies:
> – in **common ownership**, in which case the rules at ¶79600+ apply; or
> – which are carrying on a **business of leasing** plant and machinery. In this situation, no election is permitted and the capital allowances on disposal will be calculated using the consideration actually received.
> 2. There is no requirement for the transfer to have happened without the assets being purchased. Any transfer value will be ignored if an election is made.

D. Unpaid tax

Where HMRC consider that a company has had a **change of ownership** (¶60250) and:
– an assessment for corporation tax relating to a **period ending on or after** the change remains unpaid 6 months after it was assessed; and
– looking at the situation as a whole, there is a **reasonable expectation** that at least part of the transaction was undertaken on the basis that at least some element of a tax liability would go unpaid,
HMRC can recover the unpaid tax from a **linked person**.

60580
ss 710 - 718
CTA 2010

> MEMO POINTS The **assessment may also relate** to a company that either controlled, or was controlled by (¶75275), the company changing ownership at the time of assessment, or at some point prior to the change in ownership.

Reasonable expectation

In ascertaining whether there was a reasonable expectation that a potential tax liability would go unpaid, it is **necessary to look** not only at the transactions involved in the change of ownership, but also at the circumstances surrounding the change.

60585

> MEMO POINTS A **potential tax liability** is one that could reasonably be foreseen at the time of the change in ownership as likely to arise.

Linked persons

HMRC can assess anyone who, in the 3 years prior to the date of change, had **control** of the transferred company (either directly or via another company). This period is shortened to the date of the last change of ownership, if this occurred inside the previous 3 years.

60590
ss 706 - 709
CTA 2010

The definition is **further extended** to any other company that the same person controlled in the 3 years prior to the change of ownership.

Ceasing a business

61000   It is important to distinguish between a company which ceases to trade (or ceases one of its trades) and a company which ceases to exist. There will generally be a period between these two dates during which the company tidies up its affairs and ensures that it has complied with all its statutory requirements, before any remaining assets are distributed to its shareholders.

SECTION 1

Cessation of trade

A. When does a trade cease?

61050   The date of cessation is relevant to the timing of certain elections, as well as identifying the end of an **accounting period** (¶3050). It is therefore important to identify that date correctly. There are no statutory rules, and each situation must be judged on its facts and circumstances. However, case law does give some indication of what constitutes a cessation.

BIM70565

Cessation means the permanent discontinuance of the trade. A trade ceases when its activities are brought to an end, even if it is initially intended that the trade should recommence at a later date. *Marriot v Lane* [1996] The intention of the company will be relevant only where the trade appears to cease, has a period of inactivity, and then is recommenced.

Simply deciding to wind down a trade, or making a decision to sell it, will not bring about its cessation if the trade actually continues beyond that date. *J & R O'Kane & Co v CIR* [1922]

If the trade is deemed to have ceased, the ongoing collection of outstanding trade debts will not change that position. (Note that in this respect tax law differs from bankruptcy law.) *Tryka v Newall* [1963]

EXAMPLE

1. A company closed its brick manufacturing works. Some 5 months later, after being taken over, it recommenced the same trade but at a different premises using different staff. It was decided that because of the shortness of the intervening period, this was the continuation of the previous trade, and not a cessation of trade followed by the commencement of a new one. *Robroyston Brickworks Ltd v CIR* [1976]

2. A company ceased its brewing operations but continued to sell beer that another company brewed to its request. In this case it was decided that the original brewing trade had ceased and a new trade of beer selling had commenced. *Gordon & Blair Ltd v IRC* [1962]

MEMO POINTS   1. A company that ceases to trade does not become a company with investment business simply by virtue of having surplus cash. In order to be a company with investment business it must have investments which it manages as a distinguishable activity. Where this is not the case the company will not have expenses of management to offset against its income.
2. The **ending of investment activity** does not bring an accounting period to an end for a company with investment business.

B. Losses on cessation of trade

A company which suffers a loss in its final 12 months of trading can carry back certain losses for 36 months, rather than the normal 12 months (¶36100+). These losses are known as **terminal losses**.

61080
s 39 CTA 2010

MEMO POINTS   The terminal loss rules **do not apply** if:
– when the trade ceases, some other person who is not within the charge to corporation tax begins to undertake any of the activities previously carried on; or
– the cessation of trade is part of a scheme to obtain terminal loss relief.

s 41 CTA 2010

Quantifying the loss

The terminal loss is **calculated** as:
– the full amount of any trading loss arising in the final period of trade, provided that it commenced less than 12 months before the cessation; and
– a time-apportioned amount of any trading loss arising in an accounting period commencing earlier than 12 months before the cessation, but ending later than 12 months before the cessation.

61085

If either of these two **amounts is a profit**, it is excluded from the calculation of the terminal loss.

EXAMPLE

1. A Ltd ceased trading on 30 June 2013 having made up accounts to 31 December previously. In the period to 30 June 2013 it had a trade loss of £10,000. In the year ended 31 December 2012 it had a loss of £12,000. The terminal loss is calculated as follows:

Loss from final period completely within final 12 months	£10,000
6 months of loss from penultimate period (6/12 x 12,000)	£6,000
Total terminal loss	£16,000

2. B Ltd ceased trading on 30 April 2013, having made up accounts to 31 December previously. In the period to 30 April 2013 it had a trade loss of £8,000. In the year ended 31 December 2012 it made a profit of £22,000. The terminal loss is calculated as follows:

Loss from final period completely within final 12 months	£8,000
Penultimate period result is a profit, so is ignored	-
Total terminal loss	£8,000

Using the loss

61090   Firstly, the loss arising in the final period itself must **extinguish** the profits from that period. This is the standard rule for any loss carry-back claim (¶36100+).

> EXAMPLE   C Ltd has a final 12 month trading loss of £24,000 and a capital gain of £10,000. Only so much of the loss as cannot be set off against the gain can be carried back under the terminal loss provisions.

The remaining losses can be carried back up to 36 months before the commencement of the loss-making period, **provided** that the same trade was carried on in at least part of that period. Relief is given:
– for earlier loss-making periods before later ones; and
– against later profit-making periods before earlier ones.

If there has been a change of accounting period during that time, it is likely that only part of one accounting period will fall into the 36 month period. In this case the loss can be offset against a time-apportioned amount of the profit.

> EXAMPLE   D Ltd has the following results:
>
> | | |
> |---|---:|
> | Year ended 30 June 2010 | £14,000 |
> | Year ended 30 June 2011 | £12,000 |
> | 6 months ended 31 December 2011 | £6,000 |
> | Year ended 31 December 2012 | £10,000 |
> | Year ended 31 December 2013 | (£50,000) |
>
> The terminal loss is £50,000. It can be carried back against profits arising in the 36 months preceding the period of the loss: that is, the period from 1 January 2010 to 31 December 2012. This includes the whole of the profits from:
> – the year ended 31 December 2012;
> – the 6 months ended 31 December 2011; and
> – the year ended 30 June 2011.
> Only half of the year ended 30 June 2010 falls into the carry-back period, so only half of the profits for that period can be relieved. The total terminal loss used will be £35,000 (10,000 + 6,000 + 12,000 + 7,000) and £15,000 will remain unused.

61095   Where the **final accounting period** of a company is **not 12 months long**, it is possible that part of the arising terminal loss may be carried back to a period more than 4 years prior to the cessation of trade.

> EXAMPLE   E Ltd ceased to trade on 31 March 2013. Recent results were as follows:
>
> | | |
> |---|---|
> | 4 months ended 31 March 2013 | Loss £18,000 |
> | Year ended 30 November 2012 | Loss £24,000 |
> | Year ended 30 November 2011 | Nil |
> | Year ended 30 November 2010 | Profit £12,000 |
> | Year ended 30 November 2009 | Profit £11,000 |
> | Year ended 30 November 2008 | Profit £3,000 |
>
> The terminal loss available is calculated as follows:
>
> | | |
> |---|---:|
> | Loss of the final 4 month period | £18,000 |
> | 8 months of the loss for the year ended 30 November 2012 | £16,000 |
> | Total terminal loss available | £34,000 |

Losses are relieved so that earlier period losses are used first, so the £16,000 arising from the portion of the year ended 30 November 2012 must be used before the £18,000 from the final period.

Losses from year ended 30 November 2012: the terminal loss element can be carried back to any period falling within the 36 months immediately preceding that accounting period (1 December 2008 to 30 November 2011). The loss will be set off against later period profits first, meaning the terminal loss claim would shelter the following profits:

Year ended 30 November 2010	£ 12,000
Year ended 30 November 2009	£ 4,000

The remainder of the loss for the period that did not form part of the terminal loss will be unused, as there no profits arising in the year ended 30 November 2011.

Losses from 4 months ended 31 March 2013: this can be carried back to cover profits arising since 1 December 2009. However, the profits for this period have already been extinguished by the losses from the earlier period. As such this element of the loss will also be unused.

Time to claim

Terminal loss relief must be claimed within the normal **time limit** (¶46425). HMRC have the power to extend this time limit in exceptional circumstances.

61100

C. Post cessation receipts and expenses

Receipts

The collection of outstanding debts is not an issue in determining profits, because the sales will have been recognised in the profit and loss account and taxed accordingly. However, there will be occasions when sums are received after the trade has ceased which were not previously accounted for. These are taxable if they constitute **post cessation receipts**. Whilst this can include general items, such as trade commissions received after the trade has ceased, certain specific circumstances are also included.

61130

   MEMO POINTS   This discussion specifically refers to trades, but there are similar provisions relating to the cessation of a UK property business.

ss 280 – 286
CTA 2009

Debts If a deduction for a bad debt provision or write-off has previously been claimed in respect of a debt, any sum received after cessation in settlement of that debt will be taxable as a post cessation receipt.

61135
ss 192, 193
CTA 2009

If the company is released from the liability to pay a debt after its trade has ceased, the amount released is taxable as a post cessation receipt, unless the release was part of a statutory insolvency arrangement.

Transfer of right to receive a sum A company may transfer the right to a post cessation receipt to another person which does not itself trade. Any value which the company receives for the transfer is a taxable post cessation receipt. If the transfer was not on an arm's length basis, market value is used instead.

61140
s 194 CTA 2009

When the **transferee** then **receives** the sums due, they are not taxable in his hands.

   MEMO POINTS   1. Where the payment is for **trading stock**, the payment will not be treated as a post cessation receipt, to the extent that the stock value was brought into account in the final set of accounts.

s 195 CTA 2009

2. If someone **succeeds to the trade** and receives sums that were due to the transferor, but not already accounted for in the transferor's accounts, the successor will be taxed on them as trading receipts. They do not constitute post cessation receipts of the transferor.

s 95 CTA 2009

Expenses

61145
s 196 CTA 2009

A company with taxable post cessation receipts **may deduct** any expense, loss or capital allowance that would have been available if the trade had not ceased, and which:
– does not arise, either directly or indirectly, as a result of the cessation itself; and
– has not already been relieved.

A deduction is given against the first available post cessation receipts arising after the expense itself.

Election

61150
s 198 CTA 2009

Where a company has a post cessation receipt in an accounting period beginning no later than **6 years after** after the trade ceased, it can elect to carry the receipt back and treat it as if it had been received on the final day of trading. This election must be made within 2 years of the end of the accounting period in which the receipt arises.

The additional tax is **calculated** by working out the tax that would have been due on the increased profit, and deducting the tax originally due. This additional tax is then due at the usual time for the accounting period in which the receipt arose.

SECTION 2

Transfer of trade

61200

Rather than selling its assets and/or trade as separate items, a company may transfer the trade as a whole. From the point of view of a company taking over such a trade, the rules are covered at ¶60245+. However, the following issues impact the transferor company more than the transferee.

With effect from 1 April 2013, a company is also, in certain circumstances, able to disincorporate and dispose of the land, buildings and goodwill used in its trade to its shareholders, at a value which results in no gain or loss to the company (ignoring the use of indexation).

> ‹MEMO POINTS› Reference should also be made to the reconstruction section (¶79050+) for the rules applying where a **UK trade** is transferred from one **UK company to another**.
> 2. For specific rules on the treatment of **capital allowances** on the transfer of a trade, see ¶60545.

Transfer of UK trade between EU resident companies

61205
s 140A TCGA 1992

Where a UK trade (or part of a UK trade) is transferred between two companies that are resident in **different EU member states**, a joint election can be made to transfer the assets by way of a no gain/no loss disposal (¶31280), provided that:
a. the transfer is made wholly in exchange for shares or debentures in the transferee company;
b. the avoidance of tax was not the main purpose, or one of the main purposes, of the transaction; and
c. immediately after the transfer, if the transferee is resident in:
– **the UK**, none of the assets concerned fall outside the UK tax charge by virtue of a double tax agreement; or
– **another EU member state**, any gain that would arise on an immediate disposal of the assets by it would form part of its profits for UK tax.

> ‹MEMO POINTS› Where these provisions apply, there will be no balancing allowances or charges for **capital allowances** purposes.

Transfer of non-UK trade to EU resident company

61210
s 140C TCGA 1992

Where a **UK resident company** transfers a trade (or part of a trade) carried on through an EU permanent establishment to another EU resident company, EU regulations prohibit the

member state where the trade is carried on from charging capital gains tax. However, in the UK the transfer will be treated as a chargeable event and taxed accordingly, but credit will be given in the form of double tax relief (¶90480), for the deemed local member state tax that would have been charged had the EU regulations not prohibited it. A **claim** can only be made for double tax relief by the UK resident company if:
– all the assets of the trade are transferred (cash is excepted); and
– the transaction was carried out for bona fide commercial reasons, i.e. the avoidance of tax was not the main purpose, or one of the main purposes, of the transaction.

A claim can be made to **defer the tax on the transfer** where the overall gains exceed the losses, provided the following conditions are met:
– all the assets of the trade are transferred (or all except cash);
– the consideration for the transfer is wholly in the form of shares (or loan stock) issued by the transferee company (if the consideration is only partly in the form of shares or stock, the amount of corporation tax that can be deferred is proportionately reduced); and
– as a result of the share issue, the UK company holds at least 25% of the ordinary issued share capital of the overseas company.

61215
s 140 TCGA 1992

The **deferred gain** is brought back into charge on a disposal, either:
– by the UK company, of any of the shares in the overseas company (pro-rated if only part are so disposed of); or
– by the overseas company, of any of the assets transferred within 6 years of the transfer (pro-rated if only part are so disposed of).

> ⌐MEMO POINTS⌐ A claim under this provision **cannot be made** if a claim has been made for relief on the transfer of a trade to an EU company (¶61210).

Disincorporation relief

This relief applies between **1 April 2013 and 31 March 2018**, and allows a company to disincorporate and dispose of the land, buildings and goodwill used in its trade to some or all of the shareholders in the company. The value of the disposal is that which (ignoring indexation) results in neither a gain nor a loss to the company.

61220
ss 58 – 61 FA 2013

The relief is available where:
– the business is transferred as a going concern together with all the assets of the business (although this can exclude cash);
– the total market value of the assets to which the relief can apply does not exceed £100,000; and
– all the shareholders are individuals and have held the shares throughout the period of 12 months ending on the date of disincorporation.

An **election**, which is irrevocable, must be made jointly by the company and the shareholders within 2 years of the date of disincorporation.

> ⌐MEMO POINTS⌐ 1. A similar relief applies to goodwill which is taxed under the **intangibles regime**.
> 2. An **individual** includes an individual acting as a partner in a partnership (but not as a member of a limited liability partnership).

SECTION 3

Dissolving the company

There are two ways to close down a company so that it no longer exists:
– a formal liquidation process (¶61295+); or
– by striking the company off the Register of Companies (¶61350+).

61265

A. Liquidation

61295   A company may be liquidated either by virtue of an order of court or by a voluntary resolution of the company. Either of these actions may also be referred to as the company being "**wound up**".

A voluntary liquidation may be either:
– a members' voluntary liquidation, in which a statement is made by the company that it can meet all of its debts within 12 months; or
– a creditors' voluntary liquidation.

In any of these cases, a liquidator will be appointed who will seek to realise as much value as possible from the assets of the company, in order to pay its debts and secure a return for the company's shareholders.

> ⬚MEMO POINTS⬚   1. For full details of the **procedures** involved see *Company Law Memo*.
> 2. This should not be confused with **administration**, where the aim is to rescue a company and allow it to continue trading after the administrator has completed his appointment. In cases where the administrator does not succeed in his task, the company will then enter one of the forms of liquidation.
> 3. Where a **UK resident liquidator** is appointed to deal with the affairs of a company resident abroad, it will be brought within the charge to UK corporation tax by virtue of its central control and management (¶2040) being exercised in the UK.

Accounting periods

61300
s 12 CTA 2009

An accounting period **ends** immediately before a company starts being wound up, and a new period commences as winding up begins. Winding up is **deemed to start** when:
– the company passes a resolution to commence winding up;
– a petition for winding up is presented (provided that the company has not already passed such a resolution) and the petition results in an order being made; or
– a similar sort of action is undertaken where the company does not enter a formal liquidation procedure.

Subsequent accounting periods will end on the earliest of:
– 12 months from the commencement of the period;
– the completion of the winding up; and
– the date on which the liquidator has stated the winding up will be completed, even if the winding up is not complete on that date.

> ⬚MEMO POINTS⬚   A liquidator is entitled to set a date to complete the winding up, in order to simplify a number of administrative matters.

What is chargeable?

61305
s 633 CTA 2010

The **normal rules** for computing the profit of a company still apply. In addition, the costs of the liquidator, provided that they are incurred wholly and exclusively for the purposes of the trade, will also be allowed against any income received.

Any assessments that arise from profits or gains are still made on the company, not the liquidator.

In the **final accounting period** (that is, the accounting period that ends with the completion of the winding up), interest received from HMRC in relation to overpaid tax will not be taxed if the amount does not exceed £2,000.

Rates of tax

61310
ss 628, 629
CTA 2010

During the period of winding up, the normal rules for the calculation of the tax charge still apply, with the exception of profits that arise in the final financial year (¶40020) of the company. In this case, the applicable rate of corporation tax is the rate for the previous financial year, unless the rate for the final year has been:

– **fixed**, in that it has been enacted in statute; or
– **proposed**, in that a Budget statement has indicated what it will be.

In either case it is the fixed or, failing that, the proposed rate which should then be used.

Distribution of assets

During the course of a winding up the liquidator will distribute surplus assets (usually cash) to the shareholders. Ordinarily such payments would be distributions and taxed in the share-holders' hands as dividends (see *Tax Memo* for full details). However, where distributions are made in the **course of a winding up**, they are specifically exempt from distribution status. As such, they will be taxed in the hands of the recipients as capital receipts under the relevant capital gains provisions.

61315
s 1030 CTA 2010

Any **transfer in kind** will result in a chargeable gain on the company as if the asset had been sold, with deemed consideration being the market value at the time of the disposal (¶30410+).

Group issues

When a winding up starts, the **assets** of the company become **beneficially owned** by the liquidator. This in itself does not trigger a chargeable gain, because he is seen as a bare trustee, but it does affect a company's group relationships if it owns shares in other companies.

61320
CTM36125

> [EXAMPLE] A Ltd is owned by X Ltd (60 %), Y Ltd (30 %) and a number of individuals (10 %), and as such is a consortium company (¶65350+). X Ltd goes into liquidation, meaning that it is no longer beneficially entitled to the shares in A Ltd. As such, the consortium ceases to exist.

Appointment of the liquidator will not result in the company leaving a group for **capital gains purposes**, so no degrouping charge (¶67425+) arises, and the provisions relating to transfers of assets within a group (¶67050+) will still be relevant.

> [MEMO POINTS] The most likely issues arising from the loss in beneficial ownership will relate to:
> – group relationships for **group relief purposes**; and
> – the rules on **successions to trade** (¶79600+) will no longer apply. Consequently, if the intention is to hive down a trade, this should be done before any insolvency proceedings commence.

B. Striking off

In many cases the company will **not want** to incur the expense of a **formal liquidation**. Instead, the company will either wait until the Registrar of Companies strikes it from the Register, or apply for this to be done sooner. An application should only be made after all the assets of a company have been distributed, because any assets held by the company at the time it is struck off are deemed to be *bona vacantia*, and pass to the Crown.

61350
ss 1000 – 1003,
1012 CA 2006

Distributions prior to striking off

Unless a distribution is made during a formal winding up process, it will be **treated** as an income distribution in the hands of the recipients. For corporate recipients this is unlikely to give rise to any difficulty, as it is likely that the distribution will be exempt (¶18380+). However, for recipients within the charge to income tax this may give rise to an increased tax charge compared to a formal liquidation.

61355
ss 1030A – 1030B
CA 2006

To counter this problem, once the striking off procedure has been started (either by the Registrar or by the company), any distributions will be treated as capital receipts for the shareholders provided that:

– at the time of the distribution, the company has secured (or intends to secure) payment of all amounts owing to it, and has satisfied (or intends to satisfy) all its debts; and
– the total of all such distributions does not exceed £25,000.

This provision applies equally to overseas companies.

The capital treatment will be revoked if within 2 years of the distribution being made:
– the striking-off does not in fact take place; or
– the company fails to secure (so far as is practicable) payment of all sums owing to it, or to satisfy all its debts.

It appears that all distributions will be treated as income if the total of distributions exceeds £25,000.

> ⌐MEMO POINTS⌐ The former extra-statutory concession C16, which offered a similar but unlimited treatment, was replaced by the above provisions with effect from 1 March 2012. HMRC have said that capital treatment will apply without limit as long as a company complied with the requirements of ESC C16, and the distribution was in fact made before 1 March 2012. For details of ESC C16, see previous editions of *Corporation Tax Memo*.

Share capital

61360   Technically the share capital of a company can only be returned to the shareholders under specific circumstances, none of which includes the striking off of the company. As such, if the funds are passed to shareholders, the company retains a right to have it repaid. Upon striking off, this right would pass to the Crown under the *bona vacantia* rule.

However, the Treasury Solicitor has stated that provided the amounts that could be recovered **do not exceed £4,000**, no action will be taken to obtain recovery.

PART 10

Groups
and consortia

Groups and consortia
Summary

The numbers cross-refer to paragraphs.

Forming a group or consortium

A group consists of a parent company and its subsidiaries. The extent of the relationship between two companies which is required to form a group depends on which particular group provisions are being considered. Group status requires a more significant relationship between the companies than being connected or associated.

65000

Note that the taxable entity is still the individual company irrespective of the fact that it is a member of a group. Being a member of a group for tax purposes merely enables various reliefs to be accessed. These reliefs are of course subject to various anti-avoidance rules to stop their exploitation.

MEMO POINTS   1. **Group relief** enables a company which has incurred losses (the surrendering company) to surrender those losses to a group company with taxable profits (the claimant company). The losses are set against the claimant company's profits in order to reduce its profits chargeable to corporation tax.
2. A company which is a **consortium** company, or a member of a consortium, may also surrender losses to another company in the consortium, provided of course that the latter has taxable profits. Although this is also called group relief, there are **differences** in the corporate structure of a consortium, and different **restrictions** on the amounts which can be surrendered under the rules for consortia.
3. The **chargeable gains** rules for groups enable group companies to transfer assets between themselves without tax consequences, although there are also provisions which prevent groups of companies using these rules to dispose of assets outside the group in a tax-free manner.

Additionally, there are specific provisions about the capital losses which can be surrendered when a company joins or leaves a group.

4. For the specific requirements to form a group for **VAT, stamp duty** or **stamp duty land tax purposes** see *Tax Memo.*

Summary

65005   In addition to the main types of group detailed below, a 51% group is sometimes relevant (¶65505).

Condition	Loss relief group	Consortium	Capital gains group
Subsidiary relationship	Parent owns 75% (directly or indirectly)	At least two companies own at least 75%	Uppermost parent owns at least 50% of any group company
		Any sub-subsidiary must be directly 90% owned	Any subsidiary is 75% owned by its immediate parent
Ownership tests	Shares, profits and assets	Shares, profits and assets	More than 50% subsidiary – shares, profits and assets
			75% subsidiary – shares only
Shares held as trading stock included when testing ownership	n	n	y
Company can be member of more than one group	y	y	n
Anti-avoidance tests			
Rights of equity holders in the accounting period	✓	✓	✓
Rights of equity holders ignoring limited share rights	✓	✓	✓
Rights of equity holders ignoring future rights	✓	✓	✓
Rights of equity holders ignoring arrangements for future rights	✓	✓	x
Rights of equity holders ignoring options for share rights	✓	✓	x
Arrangements test	✓	✓	x

SECTION 1

Formation to qualify for group relief

65055   One of the **main purposes**, for which companies under common ownership may wish to form a group, is to surrender losses from certain companies in the group to companies with taxable profits. This will reduce the corporation tax liability of the group as a whole.

There are three main **tests** to determine whether companies form a group for this purpose, as shown in the following table:

Test	¶¶
Share capital	¶65090
Profits available for distribution to equity holders	¶65145
Assets available for distribution to equity holders on a winding up	¶65205

Comment These tests will be straightforward to apply for many groups, particularly those where subsidiaries only have one class of share capital and any loans are normal commercial loans (¶65165).

It is possible for the same company to be a member of more than one group or consortium but not more than one capital gains group (¶65415).

Exclusions

The following are excluded for group relief purposes: **65060**
- unincorporated associations; and
- companies limited by guarantee.

A. Share capital requirement

The main requirement is that one company must be a 75% subsidiary of another company,   **65090**
or both companies must be 75% subsidiaries of another company.   s 152 CTA 2010

A 75% subsidiary is **defined** as one in which the parent company beneficially owns at least   s 1154 CTA 2010
75% of the subsidiary's ordinary share capital.

Shares which are held as a **trading asset** are excluded when applying this test.   s 151(3) CTA 2010

Ordinary share capital

Ordinary share capital is **defined as** all of a company's issued share capital (including shares   **65095**
with no voting rights), **excluding** shares with a right to a fixed dividend and no other right   s 1119 CTA 2010
to share in the company's profits.

The rights attached to shares can usually be found in the Articles of Association.

Beneficial ownership

Beneficial ownership is equated with equitable ownership, as opposed to legal ownership.   **65100**
So the legal owner of shares may also be the equitable or beneficial owner of those shares;   CTM 06030, 36125
but the legal owner may likewise only be a nominee or trustee for the true, or beneficial, owner – the owner in equity.

Where a company cannot enjoy the benefit of the shares it legally owns, it does not have beneficial ownership, as shown in the following table:

Situation	Severs group relationship?
An unconditional contract for sale is made	y
A conditional contract for sale is made	n
Parent company enters liquidation or resolution passed to wind up the company	y
Parent company going into administration	n
Options granted over shares which may or may not be taken up	n

Body corporate

65105
s 1121 CTA 2010

For the group relief provisions to be available, a subsidiary must be a body corporate.

Body corporate is **defined** as any body which has legal status conferred upon it by law. This includes not only companies registered under the various Companies Acts (whether limited by share or by guarantee) but also building societies registered under the Building Societies Acts, and societies registered under the Industrial and Provident Societies Acts.

Residence

65110

Any company, whatever its country of residence, can be a member of a group.

It is therefore possible for a **non-resident** company to be a member of a group and to trace ownership of a UK-resident company through a non-resident company. *ICI v Colmer* [1999] For further details see ¶66365.

Calculation of the holding

65115
ss 1156, 1157
CTA 2010

For the majority of the grouping provisions, ownership of the shares may be **direct or indirect** (that is, through one or more other bodies corporate). For example, if company A owns 100% of company B, which in turn owns 100% of company C, company A directly owns company B and indirectly owns company C.

Where the holdings are **less than 100%** the ownership is determined by multiplying the fraction of ownership throughout the series.

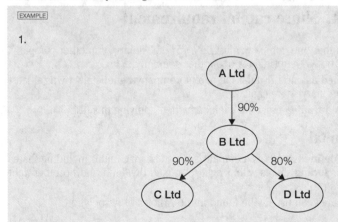

EXAMPLE

1.

A Ltd is in a group with B Ltd, in which it directly owns more than 75%.
It is also in a group with C Ltd, in which it indirectly owns 81%. (90% × 90%)
However, A Ltd's indirect interest in D Ltd of 72% (90% × 80%) is less than 75% and therefore not sufficient for D Ltd to belong to the group.

2. In the above example, if A Ltd also owned 4% of D Ltd directly, its overall ownership of D Ltd would be 76% and D Ltd would, therefore, belong to the group. (4% + (90% × 80%))

MEMO POINTS   For consortium relief 90% subsidiaries (¶65355) must always be directly owned.

B. Distributable profits

65145

The amount of profits available for distribution to equity holders is another key test as to the availability of group relief. Again, the requirement is that at least 75% should be due to the parent.

Definition

This test looks at the profits before distributions to equity holders (i.e. the profits as shown in the financial statements), but after deducting relevant preference dividends and commercial loan interest. Note that the amount of profits actually distributed is irrelevant. Repayments of share capital to shareholders which do not represent distributions are ignored.

65150
s 165(2) CTA 2010

If there are **no profits** available for distribution, a notional figure of £100 is used instead.

MEMO POINTS 1. For **non-resident** companies, the profits are computed assuming that the company is UK-resident. However, where the result of either of the following is less, that amount is used instead, being the profits of:
– the non-resident company as a whole; or
– the UK permanent establishment by itself.
2. **Prior year adjustments** are ignored.

ss 180, 181
CTA 2010

EXAMPLE E Ltd's accounts for the accounting period ended 31 December show profits of £5,000 as follows:

	£
Sales	50,000
Costs of sale	(30,000)
Gross profit	20,000
Loan interest to shareholder	(5,000)
Other expenses	(10,000)
Profits	5,000
Dividends	
On 5% fixed rate preference shares	2,000
On ordinary shares	2,000

The loan interest is in respect of a loan made by the principal shareholder, which has the right to be converted into ordinary shares at a later date. So it is not a commercial loan (¶65165) and the interest must be added back.
The dividends on the fixed rate preference shares must be deducted.
The profits available for distribution to equity holders are therefore calculated as follows:

	£
Profits	5,000
Add: Loan interest	5,000
Less: Dividend on fixed rate shares	(2,000)
Total	8,000

Equity holders

An equity holder is **defined** as any person who either:
a. holds ordinary shares in the company;
b. is a loan creditor (other than in relation to a normal commercial loan (¶65165)); or
c. has provided new consideration for any type of shares or securities in the company and used assets belonging to the company, on which the company has claimed capital allowances.

65155
ss 158, 159
CTA 2010

Ordinary shares For this purpose ordinary shares are defined by exclusion so that **all shares except** restricted preference shares are considered to be ordinary.

65160
s 160 CTA 2010

Restricted preference shares are those which:
– are issued for consideration which is, or includes, new consideration;
– do not carry rights of conversion into shares or securities (apart from into shares or securities in the company's parent company whose ordinary shares are listed on a recognised stock exchange (¶95320));
– do not carry a right to the acquisition of shares or securities;
– do not carry a right to dividends or carry a restricted right to dividends; and
– on repayment, do not carry rights to an amount exceeding the new consideration for which they were issued, except to the extent that such a right is reasonably comparable with those generally carried by fixed dividend shares listed on a recognised stock exchange.

> ☐ MEMO POINTS ☐   The rules relating to restricted preference shares were introduced for accounting periods commencing on or after 1 January 2008. Companies were able to make an irrevocable election for the rules not to apply to **shares issued before 18 December 2008**. The election must have been made on the CTSA return for the first accounting period beginning on or after 1 January 2008.

65165
s 162 CTA 2010

Loan creditor   All loan creditors, except in respect of a normal commercial loan, are equity holders.

For this purpose a **normal commercial loan** is one which:
a. is not convertible into shares or securities; and
b. does not charge interest at a rate which:
– depends on the company's results;
– depends on the value of the company's assets; or
– exceeds a normal commercial return on the loan.

For loans **commencing on or after 21 March 2012** this definition has been amended so that it is possible for shares to have a right to conversion, provided that the right relates to stock of an unconnected company and the stock is listed on a recognised stock exchange (¶95320).

s 163 CTA 2010;
CTM 81020

It is, however, acceptable for the **interest rate to reduce** as the company's results improve and vice versa, to reflect the fluctuating investment risk.

Where a loan is made solely **in order to acquire land** for investment purposes (i.e. not for resale), the terms of the loan can be linked to the value of the land and the loan can be secured on the land e.g. as with a mortgage.

65170

Provision of new consideration   Where a person is an equity holder by virtue of providing new consideration etc, that **person** alone is treated as an equity holder in relation to the shares referred to in the condition.

Similarly, where the new consideration is in the form of a commercial loan provided **by a bank**, the bank will only be an equity holder to the extent of the cost of the company's assets which are used by the bank.

Measuring the entitlement

65175
CTM 81045

The amount to which the parent company is beneficially entitled **depends on the rights attaching to** all of the following:
– ordinary shares in the subsidiary held by the parent;
– loans made by the parent to the subsidiary which are not normal commercial loans; and
– shares and loans in respect of which the parent is treated as an equity holder.

CTM 81095

> ☐ MEMO POINTS ☐   If there are unexercised **options** in respect of any shares which could vary the entitlements of any equity holders at any time during the accounting period, it is assumed that all outstanding option rights are exercised (even if this is not actually possible at the time this test is undertaken), so that the parent's entitlement is the lowest possible percentage.

C. Assets available on a winding up

65205

For a group relationship to exist the parent must be **entitled** to 75% of the subsidiary's assets available for distribution to equity holders on a notional winding up.

Scope

65210
s 166 CTA 2010

The assets referred to in this test **comprise** the net assets as shown in the subsidiary's accounts **excluding** liabilities to equity holders (in their capacity as equity holders (¶65155)). Note that amounts repayable to fixed rate preference shareholders are not liabilities to equity holders, unless the shareholder is himself an equity holder in another capacity, ignoring any interest of persons connected to him.

If an equity holder would be entitled to an amount of assets on a **notional winding up**, other than by way of distribution, that amount shall be treated as being available as a distribution of assets.

If there are **no assets** available on a notional winding up, a notional figure of £100 is used instead.

> ⌐MEMO POINTS⌐ 1. Where an equity holder has provided new consideration in return for shares or securities in a company and the **company has made a loan or acquired shares in the equity holder** (or in a person connected with him (¶31370)) using that consideration, both the assets available, and the assets to which that equity holder are entitled, are reduced by the amount of new consideration applied in this way.
>
> 2. For **non-resident** companies, the assets are calculated assuming that the company is UK-resident. However, where the result of either of the following is less, that amount is used instead, being the assets relating to:
> – the non-resident company as a whole; or
> – the UK permanent establishment by itself.

(margin: ss 180, 181 CTA 2010)

⌐EXAMPLE⌐ F Ltd's balance sheet is as follows:

	£
Land and buildings	100,000
Equipment	50,000
Stock	25,000
Total	175,000
Loan from shareholder	(40,000)
Net assets	135,000
Capital and reserves	
5% fixed rate preference shares	10,000
Ordinary shares	50,000
Retained profits	75,000
Total	135,000

The loan of £40,000 is not a normal commercial loan, so it is a liability to an equity holder.
The fixed rate preference shares are owned by a shareholder's husband but are not a liability to an equity holder, as he himself has no other interest in F Ltd.
The assets available for distribution to equity holders are £165,000. (£175,000 – £10,000)

Measuring the entitlement

The amount to which the parent company is beneficially entitled **depends on the rights attaching to** all of the following:
– ordinary shares in the subsidiary held by the parent;
– loans made by the parent to the subsidiary which are not normal commercial loans;
– shares and loans in respect of which the parent is treated as an equity holder (i.e. ignoring any fixed rate preference shares); and
– option rights in respect of shares or securities.

65215
CTM 81050

> ⌐MEMO POINTS⌐ If there are unexercised **options** in respect of any shares which could vary the entitlements of any equity holders during the accounting period, it is assumed that all outstanding option rights are exercised (even if this is not actually possible at the time this test is undertaken), so that the parent's entitlement is the lowest possible percentage.

(margin: CTM 81095)

D. Anti-avoidance tests

To **counteract abuse** two additional anti-avoidance provisions seek to prevent manipulation of the grouping tests.

65245

---

1. Economic ownership

65275
ss 170–174
CTA 2010

In addition to the requirements that the parent company must hold, in the accounting period in question, 75% of the rights to both distributable profits and assets available on a winding up, the **75% test must be met**:
– even if any shares with rights limited to a specified amount are ignored;
– by reference to any future accounting period, if the rights of the equity holders for that period are different from their rights in the current accounting period;
– if any arrangements in place in the relevant accounting period to change an equity holder's rights to profits or assets were given effect in any future accounting period; and
– if any option, the effect of which would change an equity holder's rights to profits or assets, were exercised in the relevant accounting period.

ss 179–182
CTA 2010

Further, the economic ownership tests are **extended** where an equity holder's entitlement to profits or assets of a non-resident company is, or could be, different from the equity holder's rights to profits or assets of the UK permanent establishment of the non-resident company.

In this **situation** the lower of the two percentages is used to determine the equity holder's rights in the profits and assets tests described above.

---

2. Arrangements

65295
s 154 CTA 2010

Even if the conditions for group relief are otherwise satisfied, relief will still be **denied** if, during the period in which the loss is incurred (or the one after it), arrangements are in place as a result of which:
– the company will become a member of another group;
– the company is under the control of persons who do not control the other companies in the group; or
– a company outside the group could begin to carry on the group company's trade as its successor.

CTM 80165

For this purpose arrangements need not be in writing and may be informal.

Where group relief is denied as a result of any arrangements, relief is only denied for the part of the **accounting period** in which the arrangements are actually in place. *Shepherd v Law Land plc* [1990]

s 155A CTA 2010

> MEMO POINTS   There are exceptions to these rules for **joint venture companies** where the arrangements involve either:
> – an agreement providing for the transfer of stock in the joint venture company to one or more of the existing members of the company due to a specific contingency; or
> – a provision in a constitutional document of the joint venture company that provides for the suspension of a member's voting rights due to a specified contingency.
> The **specified contingencies** are:
> – the voluntary departure of a member;
> – the commencement of liquidation, administration or similar, in any territory;
> – a serious deterioration in the financial condition of a member;
> – a change of control of a member;
> – a default by a member in performing its obligations under any agreement involving the joint venture;
> – an external change in the commercial circumstances affecting the joint venture company so that its financial viability is threatened;
> – an unresolved disagreement between any members; and
> – any contingency similar to those listed above that is provided for but not intended to happen at the time the arrangements are made.

> EXAMPLE   A loss-making company attaches one of its subsidiaries to the ABC group for a temporary period during which the ABC group claims group relief in respect of the subsidiary's capital allowances on a major investment project.
> However, as agreed between the parties beforehand, the subsidiary subsequently leaves the ABC group to return to its original group.
> This constitutes an arrangement where group relief would be denied.

Control

Control is acquired where a person has the right to secure that the company's affairs are conducted in accordance with his wishes. It may be **acquired through**:
– holding a majority of the company's shares;
– holding a majority of the company's voting rights;
– any powers given by the company's Articles of Association or other documents.

65300
s 1124 CTA 2010

In particular, an ability to determine the composition of the board of directors would be indicative of control.

CTM 80170

SECTION 2

Consortia

A consortium exists where at least 75% of the ordinary share capital of a company (known as the consortium company) is owned by at least two companies, both or all of which own at least 5% of the consortium company. The number of members is therefore between 2 and 20.

65350
s 153(1) CTA 2010

Qualifying for group relief

The **requirements** for a consortium company to be able to claim or surrender losses are that the company is either:
– a trading company (i.e. one whose business consists wholly or mainly in carrying on a trade or trades) owned by the consortium which is not a 75% subsidiary of any other company;
– a holding company (i.e. one whose business consists wholly or mainly in holding shares or securities in its 90% trading subsidiaries); or
– a trading company which is a 90% subsidiary of a holding company owned by a consortium which is not a 75% subsidiary of any other company.

65355
ss 132, 133
CTA 2010

It is also possible for a consortium company to claim and surrender losses to or from a company which is not a member of the consortium but which is a **member of a group** to which one of the consortium members (known as the link company) belongs (¶66665).

> ⌐MEMO POINTS⌐ 1. In determining whether a company is a 75% or a 90% **subsidiary** for the purposes of these requirements, the following tests apply:
> – ordinary share capital (¶65090),
> – rights to profits available for distribution to equity holders (¶65145); and
> – rights to assets available for distribution on a winding up (¶65205).
> 2. When deciding whether a company is a **90% subsidiary**, indirect shareholdings are ignored.
> 3. At the **time when the claim is made**, neither the surrendering nor claimant company need be a member of the consortium.

⌐EXAMPLE⌐

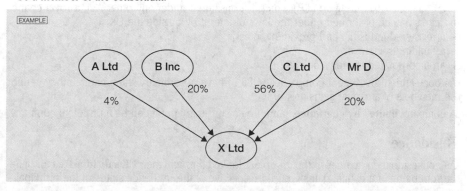

> As more than 75% of X Ltd is owned by companies, it is a consortium company.
> However, consortium relief can only be claimed by C Ltd because:
> – A Ltd only owns 4%;
> – B Inc is non-resident; and
> – Mr D is an individual.

Residence

65360
ss 133, 134A
CTA 2010

The residence of the companies is irrelevant in determining whether a consortium exists, including any link company. For further details see ¶66665.

Anti-avoidance tests

65365
s 155 CTA 2010

Consortia must also satisfy anti-avoidance tests similar to those applied to groups of companies.

The **arrangements** test prevents a company from belonging to a consortium when there are arrangements in place, as a result of which:
– the company could become a 75% subsidiary of a third company;
– the company becomes, or could become, controlled by a person or persons who together currently own less than 50% of the ordinary share capital of the company; or
– one or more persons acquire 75% of the votes or voting control over the company.

The **economic ownership tests** (¶65275) also apply to consortia.

SECTION 3

Capital gains groups

65415
s 170(3) TCGA 1992

A capital gains group requires any subsidiary to be:
– a 75% subsidiary of its immediate parent company; and
– an effective 51% subsidiary of the principal company (the uppermost company in the group).

A company can only be a member of one capital gains group at any time (¶65440), in contrast to group relief.

Company

65420
s 170(9) TCGA 1992

The **definition** of a company is more restricted than for group relief, so that any capital gains group company must be one of the following:
– a company within the Companies Act 1986;
– a company (excluding an LLP) which is constituted under any other Act, a royal charter or letters patent, or formed under the laws of a territory outside the UK;
– a registered industrial and provident society;
– a building society; or
– an incorporated friendly society.

As open-ended investment companies (OEICs) have no ordinary share capital, they cannot be members of a capital gains group.

A company **limited by guarantee** cannot be a subsidiary but it can be a principal company.

Residence

65425

As non-resident companies in the group are looked through, their **UK subsidiaries** can benefit from being in a capital gains group, irrespective of the residence status of the principal.

Where the non-resident company has a **UK permanent establishment**, this could also transfer assets at no gain/no loss to other members of the group.

> ___MEMO POINTS___   To include a non-resident company in a group requires a shareholding to be determined.   CG/APP 11
> HMRC state that the following factors may need to be taken into account when deciding if a foreign entity has **issued share capital** (factors will be given different weight and some may be completely irrelevant):
> – the foreign company must be a distinct legal entity, separate from its members and able to hold assets;
> – whether the member's interest is like shares (i.e. a portion of the fixed capital of the corporate body) or like debt (i.e. money owed by the body corporate to the members);
> – whether any subscription for the member's interest is payable;
> – whether the subscription payable for the shares remains the member's property, or whether it becomes the property of the company;
> – what proprietary rights (such as rights to participate in control by voting, rights to receive a dividend out of the company's profits and rights to share in a distribution out of the company's assets in the event of a winding up) attach to the member's interest and what responsibilities (such as a responsibility to pay up on the share if called) attach to the member;
> – whether the member's interest can be legally evidenced in accordance with local laws e.g. by being registered in a company-held document, or with a public authority, or by a certificate or similar document;
> – whether the member's interest is denominated in a stated fixed value;
> – whether the member's interest forms a fixed and certain amount of capital, or a part of that, to which creditors can look as security;
> – whether the non-UK law concerned requires amounts subscribed to be allocated to capital of the company which is fixed capital, and the extent to which subscriptions are so allocated; and
> – whether the member's interest is capable of transfer and, if so, whether such a transfer would be similar to a transfer of a portion of the capital of the company, with attendant proprietary rights, rather than similar to a transfer of money or a loan account.
> **Sources of information** would include the company's balance sheet, Articles of Association, Memorandum and the overseas territory's company law.

> ⌐EXAMPLE⌐
> **1.** A Ltd owns 75% of B Inc, which owns 100% of C Ltd.
> If B Inc has a UK permanent establishment, A Ltd or C Ltd can transfer an asset to it at no gain/no loss, provided that the asset is used for the purposes of the UK trade of B Inc.
>
> **2.** D Inc has two 100% UK subsidiaries, E Ltd and F plc.
> E Ltd and F plc can transfer assets at no gain/no loss as they are both in D Inc's capital gains group.

75% subsidiary

The requirements for a 75% subsidiary to exist are **much simpler** than for group relief in that:
– only the ordinary share capital test applies (¶65090); and
– a subsidiary need only be a 75% subsidiary of its immediate parent and not of the principal company in the group.

65430
s 1154 CTA 2010

Effective 51% subsidiary

A company is an effective 51% subsidiary where the **principal company**:
– is entitled to more than 50% of the profits available for distribution to equity holders; and
– would be entitled to more than 50% of the assets available for distribution on a winding up.

The profits available for distribution and assets available on a winding up are determined using the same principles as for group relief (¶65145+), **except**:
– no account is taken of outstanding **options**; and
– a **bank** is not an equity holder through making a normal business loan to the company.

65435
s 170(7) TCGA 1992

Principal company

65440
ss 170(4), (5)
TCGA 1992

A **75% subsidiary** is prohibited from being a principal company unless it cannot be in the same capital gains group as its parent because it is not an effective 51% subsidiary of the parent's principal company.

CG 45195

This rule must be applied to make a higher-tier company the principal company of the separate group in preference to a lower-tier company.

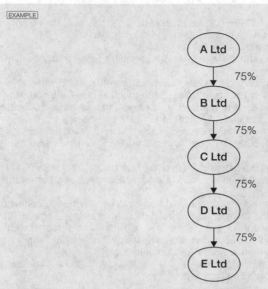

EXAMPLE

A Ltd is the principal company, whose effective interest in C Ltd is 56.25%. (75% × 75%)
However, D Ltd is not in A Ltd's group because it is only 42% effectively owned. (75% × 75% × 75%)
So D Ltd can be a principal company, and D Ltd and E Ltd form a separate group.
Note that C Ltd and D Ltd cannot form a group, because C Ltd is a member of the A Ltd group.
If E Ltd had its own subsidiaries, D Ltd would still be the principal company, as it is higher up the chain of ownership than E Ltd.

Anti-avoidance

65445

Only the **economic ownership** test (¶65275) applies, although no account is taken of options or arrangements to alter share rights.

How to decide which group

65450
s 170(6) TCGA 1992

Where a company could potentially be a member of more than one group, the following **tests** must be applied in this order (usually test **a**. is sufficient):

a. leave out of account any interest which the principal company in one group has in the distributable profits and assets (¶65145+) of the other principal company – if the result is that the company is an effective 51% subsidiary of only one principal company, the company is a member of that group;

b. look at only the entitlement to distributable profits, so that the principal company with the greatest entitlement has the subsidiary in its group;

c. look at only the entitlement to assets on a winding up, so that the principal company with the greatest entitlement has the subsidiary in its group; and

s 1154 CTA 2010

d. look at only the ownership of the subsidiary's ordinary share capital, taking into account direct and indirect holdings, so that the principal company with the greatest percentage has the subsidiary in its group.

EXAMPLE A Ltd owns the share capital of a group of companies as follows:

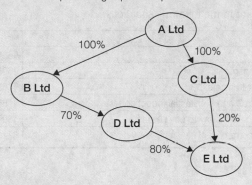

The same percentages as above apply in respect of assets and distributable profits, except that B
Ltd only has a 45% share of the assets and profits of D Ltd.
E Ltd could be a member of A Ltd's group or D Ltd's group.
A Ltd owns 56% of E Ltd through B Ltd and D Ltd. (100% × 70% × 80%)
A Ltd also owns a further 20% through its interest in C Ltd, so that A Ltd's total interest in E Ltd
is 76%. (56% + 20%)
B Ltd is only entitled to 45% of D Ltd's profits and assets, so that A Ltd's effective interest in E
Ltd through B Ltd and D Ltd is only 36%. (100% × 45% × 80%)
As C Ltd is also entitled to 20% of E Ltd's profits, etc, E Ltd is an effective 51% subsidiary of A
Ltd at 56%. (36% + 20%)
D Ltd is not a 75% subsidiary of B Ltd, so D Ltd could be a principal company of the DE group.
To determine which group E Ltd should be a member of, the interest of A Ltd in the assets and
profits of D Ltd must be excluded. This means that A Ltd only has an interest of 20% through C
Ltd and that fails the 51% effective control requirement.
So E Ltd is a member of D Ltd's group.

Changes to the group

A group remains the same group while the same company remains the principal company
of the group.

65455
s 170(10)
TCGA 1992

Where the **principal company joins another group** – for example, due to a takeover – the
first group and the other group are regarded as the same group, although subsidiaries may
fall out of the new group insofar as each is no longer an effective 51% subsidiary (¶67480).

The commencement of the **winding up** of a company does not break group relationships
for capital gains purposes, so a liquidator can transfer assets between existing group
companies at no gain/no loss.

s 170(11)
TCGA 1992

MEMO POINTS Where the principal company becomes a **European Company** (also known as an
SE (¶93000)), or a subsidiary of a SE, again the two groups will be treated as the same group.
The same caveat applies as to whether subsidiaries still remain effective 51% subsidiaries in the
new group.

s 170(10A)
TCGA 1992

SECTION 4

51% groups

In determining whether a 51% group is in existence, the factor to consider is ownership of
share capital (¶65095).

65505
s 1154(2) CTA 2009

Despite its name, a 51% group exists where a company owns more than 50% of the share
capital of another company (a 51% subsidiary).

Application

65510   A 51% group is relevant to the following situations:

Situation	¶¶
Shadow ACT	¶69665
Group payment arrangements	¶69815
Close company asset transfers	¶75895
Purchase of own shares and substantial reduction test	¶18655
Failure by non-resident company to pay UK tax	¶69925, ¶91240
Non-trading holding company	¶7145

CHAPTER 2

Loss relief

Group relief is available to companies in a group, or a consortium (when the relief is also **66000** known as consortium relief). However, once the requisite relationship has been established s 130 CTA 2010 (¶65055), there are further rules governing what losses may be surrendered, the order in which they are surrendered, and how claims for surrender must be made.

SECTION 1

75% group relief

66050 A qualifying loss can be transferred between any of the following group companies:
- from a parent to a subsidiary;
- from a subsidiary to a parent; and
- between two subsidiaries of the same parent.

A claim to group relief is not valid unless, at the time of the claim, the surrendering company has submitted its CTSA return and formally forgone the loss involved.

A. Surrenderable losses

66080
s 99 CTA 2010

The types of loss which can be surrendered from one group company to another are shown in the table below.

> MEMO POINTS **Capital losses** are not covered by the group relief rules. For details on ways in which capital losses can be used to relieve capital gains in a group situation see ¶67000+.

Type of loss	Can be surrendered even if company has other profits which could use losses	¶¶
Trading losses	y	¶66085
Excess capital allowances	y	¶66090
Non-trading deficits from loan relationships	y	¶66095
Excess qualifying charitable donations	n[1]	¶22215
UK property business losses	n[1]	¶66100
Management expenses	n[1]	¶66105
Non-trading debits on intangible fixed assets	n[1]	¶66110

Note:
1. These losses must be aggregated and can only be surrendered to the extent that the total amount exceeds the surrendering company's gross profit in the same accounting period (¶66150).

Trading losses

66085
s 100 CTA 2010

A company can surrender any trading losses **excluding**:
- losses from a trade which is not carried out on a commercial basis with a view to a profit (¶36005);
- disallowed farming and market gardening losses (¶84455); and
- overseas trading losses.

> MEMO POINTS 1. For the position where the surrendering company is **resident in another EEA state** see ¶66365+.
> 2. For the position where the surrendering company is a **consortium company** see ¶66475+.

Capital allowances

66090
s 101 CTA 2010

Capital allowances are normally taken into account in computing a company's trading profit or loss and therefore do not need to be specifically relieved (as they are included in the overall trading result).

s 260 CAA 2001

However, current period excess allowances arising on plant and machinery used for **special leasing** (¶82565) by a lessee can either be deducted from income from the qualifying activity of special leasing, or surrendered to the extent that they exceed the income from that activity. For this purpose the income is taken to be the amount before any losses of any other period and before capital allowances.

MEMO POINTS   1. Excess capital allowances **brought forward** cannot be surrendered.
2. Even after surrender, the capital allowances must still be taken into account in the surrendering **company's capital allowances computation** for the purposes of the balancing allowance and balancing charge rules (¶26085) i.e. the surrendered amount will still reduce the tax written down value.
3. Where the lessee is not undertaking a qualifying activity and the **lessor** is therefore claiming capital allowances, no group relief surrender is available.

s 184 CTA 2010;
ss 99, 259
CAA 2001

EXAMPLE   A Ltd is a 75% subsidiary of B Ltd for the whole of the current accounting period. The two companies have the following results:

	A Ltd £	B Ltd £
Trading result	6,000	(2,000)
Losses brought forward	(3,000)	
Income from special leasing	1,000	
Capital allowances in respect of special leasing	(1,600)	
Non-trading loan relationship credit/(deficit)	(1,200)	600

B Ltd claims relief in respect of its trading loss against its other profits.
A Ltd claims relief in respect of its excess capital allowances and then claims the maximum amount of group relief from B Ltd.
The corporation tax computations are as follows:

	A Ltd £	B Ltd £
Trading profits	6,000	-
Losses brought forward	(3,000)	-
Net trading profits	3,000	-
Miscellaneous income (£1,000 – £1,000)	-	-
Loan relationship credit	-	600
Trading loss	-	(600)
Excess capital allowances in respect of special leasing (£1,600 – £1,000)	(600)	-
Non-trading loan relationship deficit	(1,200)	-
PCTCT before group relief claim	1,200	-
Group relief claimed	(1,200)	-
PCTCT	Nil	Nil
Loss memo		
Trading losses		2,000
Set off against other profits		(600)
Group surrender		(1,200)
Trading losses to carry forward		200

Even if A Ltd decided not to set the excess capital allowances off in this accounting period, the group relief would still be restricted to £1,200.
If A Ltd's trading profits had been £8,000 instead of £6,000, B Ltd could have surrendered all of its £2,000 loss to A Ltd without having to set off the loan relationship credit first.

Non-trading deficits from loan relationships

Depending on the **purpose of the loan** upon which the interest has arisen, interest may either be surrendered as a non-trading deficit from a loan relationship or as a trading loss.
For details of what constitutes a non-trading deficit from a loan relationship see ¶16350.
For an example of group relief in this context see ¶16375.

66095
s 459 CTA 2009

UK property business losses

A UK property business loss is one incurred in a UK property business carried on by a company (¶19105) with a view to making a profit, **excluding** a property business loss brought forward from an earlier accounting period.

66100
s 102 CTA 2010

Management expenses

Management expenses are incurred when a company is pursuing an investment business (¶17620).

66105
s 103 CTA 2010

It is not possible to surrender losses of this type **brought forward** from an earlier accounting period.

Note that there is no requirement for the **claimant company** to carry on an investment business.

EXAMPLE E Ltd is a 75% subsidiary of D Ltd for the whole of the current accounting period. The two companies have the following results:

	D Ltd £	E Ltd £
Trading profits		2,000
Management expenses	(10,000)	
Management expenses brought forward	(1,000)	
UK property income	1,600	
Qualifying charitable donations		(400)
Non-trading loan relationship credit	6,000	1,000

E Ltd claims group relief from D Ltd, which is limited to the smaller of:
– D Ltd's excess of management expenses over the total profits for the accounting period, which is £2,400 (£10,000 – £1,600 – £6,000); and
– E Ltd's total profits as reduced by the charitable donation, which are £2,600. (£2,000 + £1,000 – £400)
So the group relief is limited to £2,400.
The tax computations for both companies are as follows:

	D Ltd £	E Ltd £
Trading profits		2,000
UK property income	1,600	
Loan relationship credits	6,000	1,000
	7,600	3,000
Less: Management expenses	(7,600)	
Qualifying charitable donations		(400)
Group relief claimed	-	(2,400)
PCTCT	Nil	200

Loss memo	
Current year management expenses	10,000
Management expenses brought forward	1,000
	11,000
Set off against other profits	(7,600)
Group surrender	(2,400)
Management expenses to carry forward (i.e. those brought forward)	1,000

Non-trading debits from intangible fixed assets

66110
s 104 CTA 2010

Brought forward debits from earlier accounting periods cannot be surrendered.
For full details of the intangibles regime see ¶28135.

B. Order of claims

1. Prioritising different types of loss

66140
Surrenderable losses can be split into two categories, depending on how flexible the loss claim can be.

Irrespective of surrendering company's profits

66145
s 99(3) CTA 2010

The following losses can be surrendered in any **amount**, even if the surrendering company has other profits against which the losses could be used:
– trading losses;

– excess capital allowances; and
– non-trading deficits from loan relationships.

There is no statutory **order** in which losses of these types must be used, so it is open to a group to specify its preferred order.

Other losses

The following losses must be aggregated and can only be surrendered to the extent that the total **amount** exceeds the surrendering company's gross profit in the same accounting period.

66150
s 105 CTA 2010

Also they must be used in the following **order**:
a. excess qualifying charitable donations;
b. losses from a UK property business;
c. management expenses; and
d. non-trading debits on intangible fixed assets.

For accounting periods ending on or after 20 March 2013 a company's profits for this purpose include apportioned profits under the CFC rules. However, when examining the amount of profit for periods straddling 20 March 2013 no account should be taken of apportioned profits arising prior to that date.

CTM 80142

The **gross profits** are the profits for the accounting period before they are reduced by any of the following losses and allowances of the same or any other accounting period:
– trading losses;
– excess capital allowances;
– non-trading deficits on loan relationships;
– excess qualifying charitable donations;
– UK property losses;
– management expenses; and
– non-trading debits on intangible fixed assets.

However, capital losses from an earlier period are not ignored i.e. they should be set against chargeable gains before calculating the gross profits. *MEPC Holdings Ltd v Taylor* [2003]

EXAMPLE F Ltd is a 75% subsidiary of G Ltd for the whole of the current accounting period. The two companies have the following results:

	F Ltd £	G Ltd £
Trading profits	2,000	3,000
Trading losses brought forward		(3,000)
Chargeable gains		2,400
Capital losses brought forward		(2,400)
Qualifying charitable donations	(600)	(12,000)
Non-trading loan relationship credit	1,500	7,000

F Ltd claims group relief from G Ltd, which is limited to the smaller of:
– G Ltd's excess of charitable donations over the total profits for the accounting period, which are £2,000 (see below); and
– F Ltd's total profits as reduced by the charitable donation, which are £2,900. (£2,000 + £1,500 – £600)
G Ltd's **total profits** must be calculated without taking into account the trading loss brought forward, but still allowing for the capital losses brought forward, as follows:

	£	G Ltd £
Qualifying charitable donations		12,000
Loan relationship credit	7,000	
Trading profit	3,000	
Chargeable gains	2,400	
Less: Capital losses brought forward	(2,400)	
	Nil	
		(10,000)
Excess charitable donations		2,000

The **computations** for both companies are then as follows:

	F Ltd £	G Ltd £
Trading profits	2,000	3,000
Less: Trading losses brought forward		(3,000)
		Nil
Chargeable gains (£2,400 – £2,400)	-	-
Loan relationship credits	1,500	7,000
	3,500	7,000
Less: Qualifying charitable donations	(600)	(7,000)
Group relief claimed	(2,000)	-
PCTCT	900	Nil

Loss memo

Current year qualifying charitable donations	12,000
Less: Set against other profits	(7,000)
Group relieved	(2,000)
Wasted (see ¶22215)	3,000

---

2. Losses arising from different accounting periods

66180
s 137 CTA 2010

The **order** in which a company may claim relief for losses is as follows:
a. reliefs from the same and earlier accounting periods (which are always deemed to be taken, irrespective of whether the claimant company actually claims relief);
b. group relief; and then
c. reliefs from later accounting periods.

So a loss carried back from a subsequent accounting period does not displace a group relief claim.

EXAMPLE H Ltd, which is a member of a 75% group, has the following results for two consecutive accounting periods:

	Year 4 £	Year 5 £
Current period trading profit/(loss)	4,000	(2,000)
Trading loss brought forward	(1,000)	
UK property income	1,500	1,500
Qualifying charitable donations	(500)	(500)

The tax computations will be as follows, before any claim for group relief is made:

	Year 4 £	Year 5 £
Current period trading profit	4,000	-
Trading loss brought forward	(1,000)	-
	3,000	-
UK property income	1,500	1,500
Trading loss	-	(1,500)
Qualifying charitable donations	(500)	-
PCTCT	4,000	Nil
Unrelieved trading loss (£2,000 – £1,500)		(500)

In Year 4 H Ltd could accept a group relief surrender of up to £4,000. The trading loss brought forward and charitable donation must be relieved first.

In Year 5 H Ltd cannot accept any group relief. If the unrelieved trading loss of £500 is carried back to Year 4, this would be superseded by any group relief claim. H Ltd itself may surrender any amount of trading loss, which would then enable the qualifying charitable donation to be relieved, otherwise it will be wasted.

C. Calculation of group relief

It is only possible for companies to surrender losses which arise in an overlapping accounting period i.e. one which is common to both the surrendering company and the claimant company, and during which both surrendering and claimant companies form a group. The surrendered loss must be utilised by the claimant company in that accounting period, as it cannot be carried back, carried forward or resurrendered.

66210
s 142 CTA 2010

For example, losses which arise before a company joins, or after it leaves, a group, and losses arising when a non-UK-resident company is not carrying on a trade in the UK through a permanent establishment, must be excluded when calculating the amount which can be surrendered.

Same accounting periods

The **maximum amount** which can be surrendered by the surrendering company is the lower of:
- the surrendering company's available loss; and
- the claimant company's total income.

66215
CTM 80210

> EXAMPLE
> 1. A Ltd and B Ltd are in the same 75% group.
> If A Ltd has losses of £100 and B Ltd has profits of £50, A Ltd can only surrender losses of £50 and will have remaining losses of £50, which it will need to relieve elsewhere, or carry forward.
>
> 2. If A Ltd has profits of £100 and B Ltd has losses of £50, B Ltd can surrender losses of £50 to A Ltd.

Different accounting periods

Where two companies have differing accounting periods, it is necessary to calculate:
- the loss of the surrendering company; and
- the profit of the claimant company,
in the **overlapping** period.

66220

The amounts are **calculated** on a time apportionment basis, except where this would produce an unjust or unreasonable result, in which case it is open to the companies to use an alternative method of apportionment. HMRC suggest that the following scenarios may lead to an unjust result:
- a one-off event, such as a significant acquisition or disposal of an asset;
- disposals are large but sporadic (this might be relevant to, for example, shipping companies and property developers); or
- the company's business is both substantial and seasonal.

s 141(3) CTA 2010;
CTM 80260

An alternative method may use management accounts as its basis.

The **maximum** amount which can be surrendered is the lower of the unused part of:
- the surrendering company's loss; and
- the claimant company's profit,
for the overlapping period.

66225

In each case the **unused part** refers to the amount of the loss or profit which remains after deducting any previous surrenders or claims for group relief, as the case may be (remembering that there may well be other group members with different accounting periods involved).

s 141(1) CTA 2010

If claims are submitted **at the same time**, the companies can decide the order in which losses should be relieved. If the companies choose not to specify the order, HMRC may do so.

> EXAMPLE
> 1. A Ltd and its wholly owned subsidiary, B Ltd, have calendar year accounting periods. A Ltd has a loss for the period. On 1 July C Ltd, which has a year end of 31 March, joined A Ltd's group. The accounting period common to both the surrendering and the claimant companies runs from 1 April to 31 December but as C Ltd only joined the group on 1 July, the overlapping accounting period runs from 1 July to 31 December.

2. The DEFGH group has the following results:

Company	Accounting period	Profit/(loss) £
D	12 months to 31 Dec 2012	80,000
E	12 months to 31 Dec 2012	(110,000)
F	6 months to 30 June 2012	8,000
G	12 months to 30 Sept 2012	(120,000)
H	12 months to 31 Mar 2013	150,000

The following claims and surrenders are made in the following order:

1. F Ltd claims group relief from G Ltd:

	Start	End		£
F Ltd	1 Jan 2012	30 June 2012		
G Ltd	1 Oct 2011	30 Sept 2012		
Overlapping period	1 Jan 2012	30 June 2012	6 months	

		£
Eligible loss: 6/12 x £120,000		(60,000)
Eligible profit: 6/6 x £8,000		8,000
Maximum group relief surrender	Lower of £60,000 and £8,000	8,000

2. D Ltd claims group relief from G Ltd:

	Start	End		£
D Ltd	1 Jan 2012	31 Dec 2012		
G Ltd	1 Oct 2011	30 Sept 2012		
Overlapping period	1 Jan 2012	30 Sept 2012	9 months	

		£
Eligible profit: 9/12 x £80,000		60,000
Eligible loss: 9/12 x £120,000		(90,000)
Less: Already claimed by F Ltd[1]		8,000
		(82,000)
Maximum group relief surrender	Lower of £60,000 and £82,000	60,000

3. D Ltd claims group relief from E Ltd:

	Start	End		£
D Ltd	1 Jan 2012	31 Dec 2012		
E Ltd	1 Jan 2012	31 Dec 2012		
Overlapping period	1 Jan 2012	31 Dec 2012	12 months	

		£
Eligible loss: 12/12 x £110,000		(110,000)
Eligible profit: 12/12 x £80,000		80,000
Less: Already claimed from G Ltd[2]		(60,000)
		20,000
Maximum group relief surrender	Lower of £110,000 and £20,000	20,000

4. H Ltd claims group relief from G Ltd

	Start	End		£
H Ltd	1 Apr 2012	31 Mar 2013		
G Ltd	1 Oct 2011	30 Sept 2012		
Overlapping period	1 Apr 2012	30 Sept 2012	6 months	

		£
Eligible profit: 6/12 x £150,000		75,000
Eligible loss: 6/12 x £120,000		(60,000)
Less: Already claimed by F Ltd[3]		4,000
Already claimed by D Ltd[4]		40,000
		(16,000)
Maximum group relief surrender	Lower of £75,000 and £16,000	16,000

5. H Ltd claims group relief from E Ltd

	Start	End		£
H Ltd	1 April 2012	31 Mar 2013		
E Ltd	1 Jan 2012	31 Dec 2012		
Overlapping period	1 April 2012	31 Dec 2012	9 months	

Eligible profit: 9/12 x £150,000	112,500
Less: Already claimed from G Ltd[5]	(16,000)
	96,500
Eligible loss: 9/12 x £110,000	(82,500)
Less: Already surrendered to D Ltd[6]	15,000
	(67,500)
Maximum group relief surrender Lower of £67,500 and £96,500	67,500

Note:
1. The period common to D Ltd's claim and F Ltd's claim is the 6 months from 1 Jan 2012 to 30 June 2012. So all of F Ltd's claim is deemed to relate to the 9-month period of D Ltd's claim.
2. The period common to G Ltd's surrender and E Ltd's surrender is the 9 months from 1 Jan 2012 to 30 Sept 2012. So all of G Ltd's surrender is deemed to relate to the 12-month period of E Ltd's surrender.
3. The period common to H Ltd's claim and F Ltd's claim is the 3 months from 1 Apr 2012 to 30 June 2012. So 3/6 of F Ltd's claim is deemed to relate to the 6-month period of H Ltd's claim i.e. £4,000. (£8,000 x 3/6)
4. The period common to H Ltd's claim and D Ltd's claim is the 6 months from 1 Apr 2012 to 30 Sept 2012. So 6/9 of D Ltd's claim is deemed to relate to the 6-month period of H Ltd's claim i.e. £40,000. (£60,000 x 6/9)
5. The period common to G Ltd's surrender and E Ltd's surrender is the 6 months from 1 Apr 2012 to 30 Sept 2012. So all of G Ltd's surrender is deemed to relate to the 9-month period of E Ltd's surrender i.e. £16,000.
6. The period common to H Ltd's claim and D Ltd's claim is the 9 months from 1 Apr 2012 to 31 Dec 2012. So 9/12 of D Ltd's claim is deemed to relate to the 9-month period of H Ltd's claim i.e. £15,000. (£20,000 x 9/12)

D. Tax planning

The **objective** of group relief is to reduce the taxable profits of the group as a whole.   **66255**

A well run group will therefore plan carefully how, where and when losses are used within the group, to maximise the reduction in its overall liability to corporation tax, taking into account the following **principles**:
– some group members should not be in a taxpaying position when other group members have unrelieved losses available;
– losses should be relieved as soon as possible;
– losses should be used to reduce tax which would be paid at the highest rate;
– no double tax relief in relation to overseas income should be wasted, so sufficient taxable profits should be left in charge where relevant; and
– losses should not be carried forward in a company which is unlikely to be able to utilise them in the future.

Tax rates

In most group situations there is a choice as to how a loss should be relieved, so decisions   **66260**
should be made in accordance with an overall group planning strategy. As the use of losses is very flexible (i.e. a surrender can be made to any group company), it is usually the tax rate applying in the current and future accounting periods which is the determining factor (assuming of course that up-front cash flow is not more of a concern).

Companies paying the **highest rate of tax** are always those with profits attracting the marginal rate of tax. This is the tax rate which applies when a company's profits exceed the lower profit limit (¶40110) but are not large enough to attract the full rate of corporation tax. The exact amounts involved will be different for each group, as these limits depend on the number of associated companies for each group member (¶40180).

EXAMPLE   A Ltd has two wholly owned subsidiaries, B Ltd and C Ltd. The companies have the following results for the year to 31 March 2013:

Company		£
A Ltd	Trading loss	(130,000)
	Loan relationship credit	40,000
B Ltd	Trading profit	580,000
C Ltd	Trading profit	160,000

The profits limits for the ABC group are as follows:
– lower limit, £100,000; (300,000/3); and
– upper limit, £500,000. (1,500,000/3)
This means that the companies are paying tax at the following rates (without taking the loss into account at this stage):
– A Ltd, 20%;
– B Ltd, 24%; and
– C Ltd, 25% (¶95020).
So the losses should be used to reduce C Ltd's profits to £100,000 (at which point its tax rate is 20%), before giving the remainder to B Ltd.
This gives the following results:

	A Ltd £	B Ltd £	C Ltd £	Total £
Trading profits	-	580,000	160,000	740,000
Loan relationship credit	40,000	-	-	40,000
Group relief	-	(70,000)	(60,000)	(130,000)
PCTCT	40,000	510,000	100,000	650,000
Rate of tax	20%	24%	20%	

Tax value of losses to the group is therefore £31,800. ((£60,000 x 25%) + (£70,000 x 24%))

E. Overseas issues

Summary

66290

Topic	¶¶
UK permanent establishment of a non-resident company	¶66325
Overseas permanent establishment of a UK-resident company	¶66335
Non-resident company trading in the EEA	¶66365
Dual resident companies	¶66425

The European Commission has referred the UK to the CJEU in relation to the UK's alleged failure to correctly implement the decision in the *Marks & Spencer plc* case in 2005. Although the legislation was amended after that decision the Commission considers that it still contains provisions contrary to the principles of freedom of establishment and non-discrimination.

---

1. Permanent establishments

66320 There are specific rules **restricting** group relief for:
– UK permanent establishments of non-UK-resident companies; and
– overseas permanent establishments of UK-resident companies.

Located in the UK

Group relief can only be claimed in respect of a **loss** of a UK permanent establishment where the loss:

1. relates to an activity which, if profitable, would have been within the charge to UK corporation tax and not exempted under a double tax treaty (¶90055) (assuming any eligible claims are made); and

2. is not available for relief against any non-UK income for the purposes of calculating foreign tax.

HMRC take the view that test 2. is an all-or-nothing test, so that if any part of a loss is relievable against non-UK profits, none of the remaining part may be group-relieved. However, the CJEU ruled in 2009 that HMRC's interpretation is contrary to EU law. *Philips Electronics UK Ltd v HMRC* [2009] As a consequence, with effect from 1 April 2013, where the surrendering company is established in the EEA, group relief is unavailable only **to the extent** that losses are available for relief against non-UK income.

For more about losses arising from a permanent establishment located elsewhere in the EEA see ¶66365.

> MEMO POINTS   1. **Not available for relief** means that where:
> – the overseas territory exempts the loss altogether, it has not been made available for relief against non-UK income, unless the territory allows consolidation of the loss with other overseas profits;
> – the overseas relief depends on whether it can be relieved in the UK, the loss is treated as being relieved overseas in priority, so that no group surrender is available;
> – relief is given overseas but is then subsequently recouped, this still prohibits any UK group surrender; and
> – the loss is unrelieved in the current accounting period but is carried forward, it is still available for relief overseas, unless a future set-off is deemed impossible – for example, because the company is in liquidation and there is no capacity overseas to set it off.
> 2. **Non-UK income** means any amount which is taken into account in computing profits, income or gains on which foreign tax is charged, and is not included in any UK tax computation for any accounting period.
> 3. **Foreign tax** means any tax chargeable under the laws of an overseas territory which is charged on income and/or chargeable gains, and is analogous to either UK corporation tax or income tax. The overseas territory tax law may derive from states or provinces, local authorities, or municipalities etc.

66325
s 107 CTA 2010,
CTM 80310, 80320,
80325, 80330,
80335

Where the non-resident company is claiming group relief, the **profits** which can be offset by group relief are only those which are:
– otherwise subject to UK corporation tax; and
– not exempted by the terms of a double tax treaty.

66330

Located overseas

A UK-resident company is **prohibited** from claiming group relief in respect of a loss of an overseas permanent establishment where the loss:
– is attributable to a permanent establishment outside the UK through which the company carries on a trade (¶90140); and
– all or part of the loss can be relieved against non-UK income for the purposes of calculating foreign tax (¶66325).

66335
s 106 CTA 2010

Comment   As a result of the **tie breaker clause** often found in double tax treaties, the territory of residence has priority in relieving the loss, so that the deemed residence of the permanent establishment will often be crucial in deciding whether group relief can be surrendered.

2. Non-resident companies

A non-resident company, which is resident or carrying on a trade in an **EEA member state** (¶82585) (other than through a UK permanent establishment (¶66325)), may surrender losses to a UK-resident company where the non-resident company is either:
– a 75% subsidiary of the UK-resident claimant company; or
– a fellow 75% subsidiary of a UK-resident company.

66365
s 136 CTA 2010

s 113 CTA 2010

The companies also need to meet the following **four conditions**:
- the equivalence condition;
- the EEA tax loss condition;
- the qualifying loss condition; and
- the precedence condition.

> [MEMO POINTS]   **Consortium** companies are outside the scope of these rules, unless the particular company is also a link company (¶66665).

Equivalence

66370
s 114 CTA 2010

The amount surrendered must be a **loss of a type** which would qualify for group relief, had it arisen in the UK (¶66080).

CTM 81515

For example, a capital loss will not satisfy the equivalence condition. Interest payable may be equivalent to a trading loss or non-trading loan relationship deficit, depending on the facts.

EEA tax loss

66375
ss 115, 116
CTA 2010

The loss must be calculated in accordance with the rules of the EEA state where it has arisen and if the **surrendering company is resident**:
- in the EEA, the loss must not relate to a UK permanent establishment of the company; or
- elsewhere and carries on a trade through a permanent establishment in the EEA, the amount does not relate to an activity which is exempt from tax (¶66325) in the EEA state under a double tax agreement.

Qualifying loss

66380
ss 117 – 120
CTA 2010;
CTM 81525

As stated above, HMRC take the view that test 2. in ¶66325 is an all-or-nothing test, so that if any part of a loss is relievable against non-UK profits, none of the remaining part may be group-relieved. However, the CJEU ruled in 2009 that HMRC's interpretation is contrary to EU law. *Philips Electronics UK Ltd v HMRC* [2009] As a consequence, with effect from 1 April 2013, where the surrendering company is established in the EEA, group relief is unavailable only **to the extent** that losses are available for relief against non-UK income.

The Supreme Court has recently ruled on the timing of when the tests relating to the availability of other reliefs should be applied. HMRC contended that the test should be applied at the end of the period in which the losses arose, whereas the taxpayer contended, and the Court agreed, that all relevant circumstances should be taken into account at the time the claim is made. Although in many cases this will make no difference, in this case the overseas activities had been brought to a close after the end of the accounting period involved, so there was no possibility of the losses being utilised against their own future trading profits. *HMRC v Marks & Spencer plc* [2013]

This was considered previously to be a very **restrictive test**, as the loss could apparently not be available for any other type of relief in any shape or form, and this must be assessed immediately after the end of the accounting period. Forgetting or failing to take steps to access overseas loss relief did not mean that UK group relief becomes available.

Since all of the following points apply, the test is still fairly described as "restrictive":
- neither the surrendering company nor any other **person** must be entitled to relief for the loss (whether by way of credit, the elimination or reduction of a tax liability, or otherwise);
- in any **territory** where the surrendering company is resident (assuming that any steps required to claim any relief are taken);
- in either the current **accounting period**, or any future or previous accounting period (as judged the end of the current accounting period). So the carry forward of a loss makes it available for relief overseas, even if actual events mean that it becomes time-barred and is never actually set off.

Most commentators believe that this rule (as it currently stands) means that only subsidiaries which have stopped trading, or are otherwise prohibited from carrying forward losses in their home territory, will satisfy this condition.

Comment   As stated at the beginning of this chapter, the UK is to be subject to infraction proceedings over the compatibility of these restrictions with EU law. It is certainly possible that further changes will be made in due course.

Precedence

The precedence condition applies where there is an **intermediate company** between the UK parent and the 75% EEA subsidiary, irrespective of the level of ownership of the intermediate company.

66385
s 121 CTA 2010

Where relief is possible in the territory where the intermediate company is resident (as determined under the laws of that territory), no UK group relief will be available.

Where there is **more than one UK parent company** in the group, the precedence condition only applies in relation to intermediate companies between the surrendering company and the nearest such UK-resident company in the ownership chain.

> EXAMPLE D plc is a UK parent company with a 75% subsidiary, X SA. The group is very large and there are several intermediate companies in the ownership chain, including E Ltd, F Ltd and G Ltd.
> The UK company nearest to X SA in the chain is G Ltd.
> Only H SA, resident in France, is an intermediate company between X SA and G Ltd.
> So, in this example, the precedence condition prevents a claim for relief where loss relief is available in France.

Recalculating the foreign loss

The ability for a group to surrender losses of a non-UK-resident company **only applies** where the foreign loss, having been recomputed under UK tax principles, remains a loss. This rule applies separately to all types of loss originating in the EEA state (¶66080).

66390
ss 122 – 126
CTA 2010;
CTM 81560

This will require the surrendering company's **accounting figures** to be drawn up under UK GAAP or IAS.

Then the **assumptions** as set out in the following table apply, in addition to the normal trading income principles (¶14200).

Topic	Assumptions
Residence	The company: – is resident in the UK throughout the loss period[1]; and – became UK-resident from the beginning of that period
Place of trading	Any trade carried on in the loss period[1] wholly or partly in the EEA territory concerned is carried on wholly or partly in the UK
Interest in land	Any interest in land in the EEA territory relates to land in the UK
Accounting period	An accounting period begins at the start of the loss period[1] and ends on the earlier of: – 12 months from the beginning of the loss period; and – the end of the loss period Where the loss period is longer than 12 months, a further accounting period then begins
Capital allowances	Plant and machinery was not brought into use for the purposes of the activity until the beginning of the loss period[1] The value to be used in the capital allowances computation is the lower of cost and market value (¶25130)
Intangible assets	The asset is treated as being acquired by the company at the start of the loss period[1] for its net book value (¶28790)
Loans and derivatives	All the usual UK rules apply In particular, the transition to IAS or FRS 26 must be taken into account (¶16200)
Note: 1. **Loss period** is defined by the rules of the relevant EEA territory for which the EEA tax loss is computed.	

> ☐ *MEMO POINTS*   1. Not all cases require a **full recomputation**, as it might be possible to start with the foreign tax profits and make adjustments to reflect any differences with UK tax practice.
> 2. Where recomputation actually **increases the loss** (e.g. due to timing differences in the recognition of revenue and expenses), only the original foreign loss is available for group relief.

Anti-avoidance

66395
s 127 CTA 2010

Anti-avoidance provisions apply to **deny group relief** where:
a. arrangements exist which either:
– turn an existing loss into a loss which will qualify for relief; or
– give rise to a new loss that qualifies for relief; and
b. obtaining that relief was one of the main purposes of those arrangements.

Arrangements include any agreement, understanding, scheme, transaction or series of transactions, whether or not legally enforceable.

---

3. Dual resident investing companies

66425
s 109 CTA 2010

A dual resident investing company (¶91480) cannot surrender losses under group relief. This is to prevent a company which is resident for tax purposes in more than one jurisdiction from claiming relief twice for the same loss.

SECTION 2

Relief for consortia

66475

There are some differences between the rules for claiming group relief and consortium relief, the main one being the restriction on the amount of loss which can be group relieved.

All of the consortium members must consent to a claim for consortium relief for it to be valid.

Further, the provisions enabling **non-UK-resident companies** which are resident or carrying on a trade in the EEA to surrender losses to a UK-resident group member do not apply to consortia, except in the case of link companies (¶66665).

A. General principles

Residence

66505

Consortium relief is **only available where** both the surrendering and the claimant companies are either UK-resident companies or non-resident companies carrying on a trade through a UK permanent establishment.

For an exception which now applies to link companies (i.e. consortium members which are also members of a group) see ¶66665.

Transfer of losses

66510

It is **impossible** for losses to be transferred between consortium members.

However, it is **possible** to transfer losses between a consortium member and:
– a consortium company (¶65350) which is a trading company or a holding company; and
– a trading company that is a 90% subsidiary of a consortium company that is itself a holding company.

Member's interest in the consortium company

The consortium member's interest in the consortium company is usually the percentage of the consortium company's ordinary share capital held.

66515
ss 143, 144
CTA 2010

Where there is **more than one class of share** in issue, it is the lowest of:
– the percentage of the consortium member's ownership of the consortium company's ordinary share capital;
– the percentage of the consortium company's profits available for distribution to which the consortium member is entitled;
– the percentage of the consortium company's assets available to equity holders on a winding up to which the consortium member is entitled; and
– the proportion of voting power in the consortium company which is directly held by the consortium member.

If the member's interest **varies during an accounting period**, the average is taken, based on time apportionment.

Where the surrendering or claimant company is a subsidiary of the consortium company, it is still the interests of the members in the consortium company which are looked at.

MEMO POINTS   Although this is calculated for each company, it is highly likely (because of the "lowest" test) that the aggregate **percentages will not total 100%**. Any shortfall is not eligible for relief.

CTM 80540

B. Cap on relief

The amount of relief available depends upon whether the claimant company is the consortium member or consortium company. Both situations require the member's interest in the consortium company to be determined.

66545

1. Claimant company is consortium member

The **surrenderable losses** are calculated by deeming the consortium company to use any trading loss against its own profits arising from the current accounting period first.

66575
ss 143, 144, 147
CTA 2010

The overlapping **accounting period** must be identified (¶66220).

The **maximum** amount of relief which can then be claimed is the lower of:
– the proportion of the surrenderable loss equal to the claimant company's interest in the consortium company; and
– the claimant company's available profit.

EXAMPLE
1. ABC is a consortium which owns X Ltd. X Ltd has made losses of £100,000 in the current accounting period. A Ltd, B Ltd and C Ltd have made profits of £50,000, £20,000 and £70,000, respectively.

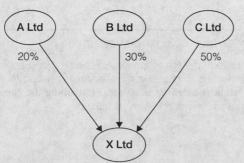

The maximum consortium relief which can be claimed by each member is as follows:

Member	Lower of	Maximum amount £
A Ltd	20% of £100,000 and available profit of £50,000	20,000
B Ltd	30% of £100,000 and available profit of £20,000	20,000
C Ltd	50% of £100,000 and available profit of £70,000	50,000

2. D Ltd is a consortium company owned 55% by E Ltd and 45% by F Ltd.
D Ltd has a calendar year end and makes a trading loss of £100,000 in the current accounting period to 31 Dec 2012.
E Ltd prepares its accounts to 30 Sept 2012 and has a profit of £60,000.
The overlapping period (¶66220) is 9 months:

	Start	End		£
D Ltd	1 Jan 2012	31 Dec 2012		
G Ltd	1 Oct 2012	30 Sept 2012		
Overlapping period	1 Jan 2012	30 Sept 2012	9 months	
Eligible loss: 9/12 x £100,000				(75,000)
E Ltd can claim 55% of this	£75,000 @ 55%			(41,250)
Eligible profit: 9/12 x £60,000				45,000
Maximum consortium relief	Lower of £41,250 and £45,000			41,250

---

2. Claimant company is consortium company

66595
s 144 CTA 2010

Where the claimant company is the consortium company, the **maximum** amount which can be surrendered is the lower of:
– the consortium member's loss; and
– the proportion of the claimant company's profit which is equal to the surrendering company's interest in the consortium company.

In effect the maximum amount of profit that can be sheltered will be the amount of profit the consortium member would be entitled to from the consortium company.

The same rules in respect of overlapping accounting periods apply as in ¶66220.

EXAMPLE Taking the example in ¶66575 above but assuming X Ltd has made a profit of £100,000, whereas the consortium members have each made losses, the maximum consortium relief which can be surrendered to X Ltd is £90,000, calculated as follows:

Member	Lower of	Maximum amount £
A Ltd	20% of £100,000 and available loss of £50,000	20,000
B Ltd	30% of £100,000 and available loss of £20,000	20,000
C Ltd	50% of £100,000 and available loss of £70,000	50,000
		90,000

---

3. Anti-avoidance

66615
ss 146A, 146B
CTA 2010

Where arrangements are put in place at any time during the overlapping accounting period, the main purpose of which is to obtain a tax advantage relating to group relief, and their effect is to **prevent certain consortium members controlling the consortium company**, the relievable loss (or profit as the case may be) is halved.

In detail, the following conditions must be met:

Situation	Conditions	Consequence
Surrendering company is owned by a consortium	Claimant company is either: – a consortium member; or – a member of a consortium member's group (where the consortium member is a link company (¶66665))	Loss surrendered to claimant is half of what it would otherwise be
	Arrangements are in place which enable a person to prevent the claimant company (or the link company where relevant) from controlling the surrendering company	
	The purpose of the arrangements is to enable the claimant company to obtain a tax advantage	
Claimant company is owned by a consortium	Surrendering company is either: – a consortium member; or – a member of a consortium member's group (where the consortium member is a link company (¶66665))	Amount of claimant company's profits, against which the surrendered loss can be offset, are half of what they would otherwise be
	Arrangements are in place which enable a person to prevent the surrendering company (or the link company where relevant) from controlling the claimant company	
	The purpose of the arrangements is to enable the claimant company to obtain a tax advantage	

C. Interaction of consortium relief and group relief

The interaction of both reliefs depends on the identity of the group member i.e. whether it is the consortium company or a consortium member. **66645**

Consortium company is a group member

Where a consortium company is also a member of a group (known as a group/consortium company), a loss may be relieved partly by group relief and partly by consortium relief. In this case, the group relief rules will take **precedence** over the consortium relief provisions, so that any potential group relief claim (whether actually made or not) reduces the consortium relief available. **66650**

The **group/consortium company** must be one of the following:
– a 90% subsidiary of a consortium company whose main activity is the holding of shares in 90% trading subsidiaries;
– a holding company itself; or
– a trading company which has its own 90% subsidiaries.

When the group/consortium company makes a **loss**, the amount available for consortium relief is calculated as follows: **66655**
a. reduce loss by any profits of the same accounting period;
b. assume that the maximum group relief claim is made, taking into account actual loss surrenders in respect of other loss-making members of the group (so that where these losses are surrendered to other group members, they cannot be surrendered to the group/consortium company); and
c. the remaining amount is the loss available for consortium relief.

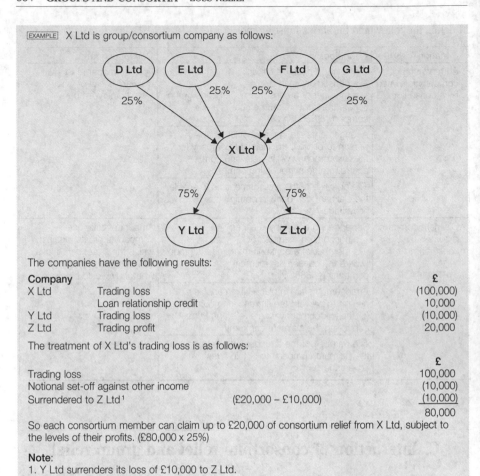

EXAMPLE X Ltd is group/consortium company as follows:

The companies have the following results:

Company		£
X Ltd	Trading loss	(100,000)
	Loan relationship credit	10,000
Y Ltd	Trading loss	(10,000)
Z Ltd	Trading profit	20,000

The treatment of X Ltd's trading loss is as follows:

		£
Trading loss		100,000
Notional set-off against other income		(10,000)
Surrendered to Z Ltd[1]	(£20,000 – £10,000)	(10,000)
		80,000

So each consortium member can claim up to £20,000 of consortium relief from X Ltd, subject to the levels of their profits. (£80,000 x 25%)

Note:
1. Y Ltd surrenders its loss of £10,000 to Z Ltd.

66660 When a **consortium member makes a loss**, the maximum amount which can be surrendered to the group/consortium company is calculated as follows:
a. identify any potential group relief claims the group/consortium company could make in respect of losses surrenderable from other members of its group; and
b. determine the consortium member's ownership percentage (¶66515) and apply this to the balance of the group/consortium company's profits.

EXAMPLE The same group as in ¶66655 above now has the following results:

Company		£
X Ltd	Trading profit	100,000
Y Ltd	Trading loss	(12,000)
Z Ltd	Trading profit	8,000

If Y Ltd surrenders its loss of £12,000 to X Ltd, the maximum consortium relief which can be surrendered to X Ltd is £88,000. (£100,000 – £12,000)
This makes the maximum surrender by each consortium member £22,000, subject to the level of their losses. (£88,000 x 25%)
If Y Ltd surrenders £8,000 to Z Ltd, this leaves £4,000 to be surrendered to X Ltd.
So the maximum consortium relief surrender is then £96,000. (£100,000 – £4,000)

Consortium member is a group company

66665 If the consortium member is also a member of a group (known as a **link company**), there are no priority rules.

Consortium relief can flow through the link company, so that a company in the link company's group can make a consortium claim in respect of the losses of the consortium company. The maximum amount of consortium relief is still restricted by the consortium member's interest in the consortium company (assuming that it has sufficient profits).

Similarly, a group member can surrender its losses via **group relief** through the link company to the consortium company.

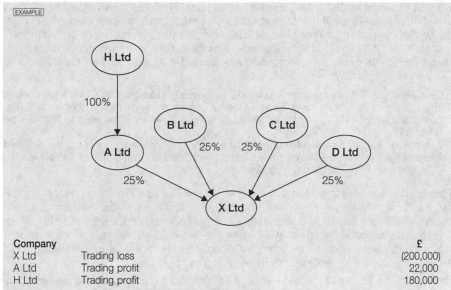

| EXAMPLE |

Company		£
X Ltd	Trading loss	(200,000)
A Ltd	Trading profit	22,000
H Ltd	Trading profit	180,000

The consortium relief available to A Ltd is £50,000. (£200,000 x 25%)
This can be shared between A Ltd and H Ltd in several different ways.
If there are only two companies in the group, it would be efficient to give H Ltd £30,000 of the losses to reduce its PCTCT to £150,000 and therefore enable it to access the small profits tax rate. The remaining £20,000 could be used by A Ltd.

| MEMO POINTS | 1. A **link company** must be either:
– UK-resident;
– carrying on a trade in the UK through a permanent establishment; or
– resident in the EEA and be in the same group as the claimant or surrendering company without needing to look through a non-EEA company.
2. If a group **relationship has not existed throughout the entire accounting period**, only the period when the group member was in a group relationship with the link company can be part of an overlapping period (¶66220).

ss 132–134
CTA 2010

Administration

Group relief claims historically involved paperwork from both surrendering and claimant companies, which made any subsequent amendments unwieldy and time-consuming.

66715

Happily, a simplified procedure is now available (¶66730).

Normal method

The **surrendering company** or, where the claim is in respect of a consortium, each consortium member, must give **consent** to a claim no later than the date on which the claim is submitted, including the following details:

66720
Sch 18 paras 70, 71
FA 1998

- the name of the surrendering company;
- the name of the company to which relief is being surrendered;
- the amount of relief being surrendered;
- the accounting period of the surrendering company to which the surrender relates; and
- the tax district references of the surrendering company and the company to which relief is being surrendered.

Sch 18 para 75
FA 1998

Where the **amount available for surrender subsequently reduces**, the company has 30 days to withdraw some or all of the consents and replace them with ones which do not exceed the new amount (note that the claimant company does need to agree with the withdrawal in this case). Otherwise, HMRC will direct which claims are to be withdrawn or reduced (against which there is a right of appeal). Any affected claimant company must amend its CTSA return accordingly.

Sch 18 para 72
FA 1998

[MEMO POINTS] 1. If the surrendering company has **already submitted its CTSA return** before giving consent, that return must be amended. If losses have been carried forward to future accounting periods and utilised, any affected subsequent period CTSA returns must also be amended.

Sch 18 para 71
FA 1998

2. A consent cannot be **amended** but can be withdrawn (with the agreement of the claimant company) and substituted with a fresh consent. The claimant company must amend its own CTSA return to reflect the changed consent.

66725
Sch 18 para 67
FA 1998

The **claimant company** must formally claim group relief on its CTSA return, quantifying the claim and also identifying the surrendering company. Any non-resident company, by reference to which the claimant and surrendering companies are related, must also be identified. A copy of the surrendering company's consent (or the original in the case of a non-resident surrendering company) must be submitted along with the CTSA return. Where the claim exceeds the amount surrendered, it will be ineffective.

Sch 18 paras 73, 74
FA 1998

Once submitted, claims cannot be **amended** but they can be withdrawn and replaced by a fresh claim, within the following time limits (although HMRC have discretion to accept a late claim or late withdrawal should the circumstances warrant it):
- 12 months following the filing due date for the CTSA return;
- 30 days after the completion of an enquiry into the return;
- 30 days after an amendment made by HMRC following an enquiry; or
- 30 days after the settlement of an appeal against such an amendment.

Sch 18 para 69
FA 1998

SP 5/01

[MEMO POINTS] 1. Where **more than one claim** is received by HMRC on the same day and the total exceeds the amount surrendered, HMRC can determine which claims must be withdrawn.
2. HMRC may accept a **late claim** where it was not possible to quantify either a loss or profit within the usual time limits, perhaps due to a degrouping charge (¶67425).

Simplified procedure

66730
SI 1999/2975

A group or consortium may apply to HMRC to adopt a simplified procedure for claiming group relief which avoids the need for formal claims in CTSA returns and notices of consent. An **application** must identify an authorised company within the group, which will act on behalf of the other group members.

The procedure allows the **authorised company** to:
- make and withdraw group relief claims and surrenders; and
- show the effects of the various claims, etc, on each company's CTSA returns,
by submitting a single statement to HMRC.

It is not necessary to include **all group members** in this procedure; indeed, HMRC may exclude companies which have not complied with all of their tax obligations. The authorised company can subsequently exclude a group member by giving appropriate notice at any time.

The application, unless formally accepted or rejected by HMRC, has **automatic effect** 3 months after being made.

The procedure may be **terminated** at the option of the authorised company or HMRC.

`MEMO POINTS`   1. The application must detail the following **information**:
- tax offices and references of all the companies in the group/consortium;
- signed statements that each company agrees to be bound by the agreement; and
- a copy of a specimen group relief schedule.

2. It is not necessary for group companies to have the same **accounting period end**.

3. The simplified procedure is separate from any **group payment arrangement** which may be in place (¶69815).

Excessive group relief claims

Where a company has claimed excessive group relief, HMRC may make an assessment to recover that amount. The assessment must be made within the normal time limits (¶46425).

Where, following an assessment, a company **does not pay the tax** due within 6 months of the latest date for submitting a claim for group relief, HMRC may, within 2 years, make an assessment to recover the tax from any other company in the group.

Where such an assessment has been made, the company which discharges the tax liability **may recover** the amount paid from the company against which the assessment was made.

66735
Sch 18 para 76
FA 1998

Sch 18 para 75A
FA 1998

Payments for group relief

Where a claimant company makes a payment to a surrendering company in return for the surrender of group relief, that payment (up to an **amount** equal to the loss surrendered, not the amount of relief in terms of tax) is not taken into account in calculating the profits or losses of either the claimant company or the surrendering company. The payment must be made under an agreement between the claimant and surrendering company.

The amount is also specifically **excluded** from being treated as a distribution.

Comment   Payment would be made to ensure minority shareholders were not disadvantaged (as a 75%-owned subsidiary can surrender its entire loss to its parent).

66740
s 183 CTA 2010;
CTM 80145

CHAPTER 3

Chargeable gains

The chargeable gains provisions seek to treat a group as a single entity so that the transfer **67000** of assets between group members is basically ignored for tax purposes.

As this opportunity carries the potential for abuse, there are many anti-avoidance rules which restrict the set-off of capital losses against gains, and also nullify the advantage of a no gain/no loss transfer in certain situations.

SECTION 1

Asset transfers

In addition to a no gain/no loss asset transfer between group members, it is possible to roll **67050** over a gain arising in one company against an asset acquisition by another group company.

Further, there are particular rules for the transfer of an asset which is treated as trading stock by one group member but as a capital asset by another.

A. Capital assets

Unless the following special provisions existed, when a group company (the transferor) **67080** transferred an asset to another group company (known as the transferee), a tax charge ss 17, 18 would arise on the disposal as a result of the market value rule which applies to transactions TCGA 1992 between connected persons (¶31380).

Instead, most intra-group transfers are undertaken at no gain/no loss i.e. the deemed s 171(1) TCGA 1992 proceeds for the disposal is the allowable expenditure plus indexation. Therefore the rules enable companies within a chargeable gains group to transfer assets freely around the group, without incurring a tax liability on each occasion. All that happens is the indexation allowance increases the longer that the asset is held by the group.

> MEMO POINTS 1. Where the relevant conditions are met, no gain/no loss treatment is mandatory, so no **election** is required. This does, however, mean that it is not possible to realise a gain in order to utilise capital losses brought forward.
> 2. **Plant and machinery**, which attract capital allowances, are transferred at the actual transfer price. For successions see ¶60445.
> 3. For **intangible fixed assets** see ¶69115.
> 4. For **loan relationships and derivatives** see ¶69375 and ¶69550, respectively.
> 5. Where a no gain/no loss transfer follows a **change of ownership of an investment company**, there are restrictions on the set-off of:
> – surplus ACT (¶41190); and
> – management expenses and charitable donations (¶60325).

Exceptions

The no gain/no loss rules do not apply to the following, so that all transfers occur at market **67085** **value**: s 171(2), (3), (6) TCGA 1992

Situation	Detail
Consortia	Transfers of assets between members of a consortium and consortium company
Deemed disposals	Where the group company paying the consideration does not itself acquire an asset e.g. capital sums derived from assets such as compensation (¶31165), the issue or redemption of shares, or purchase of own shares

Situation	Detail
Disposal of a debt on its repayment	Only applies to the disposal of the debt itself at the time it is wholly or partly repaid
Disposals to an investment trust	As disposals by an investment trust are exempt
Disposals to a venture capital trust (VCT)	As disposals by a VCT are exempt
Disposals to a qualifying friendly society	As disposals by a qualifying friendly society are exempt
Disposals to a dual resident investing company	To prevent avoidance (¶91480)
Disposals to a real estate investment trust (REIT) which is the head of a capital gains group	REITs have their own tax regime (¶19635)
Disposals resulting from the exercise of an option which was granted when the companies were not grouped (see example below)	Exercise occurs after 5 March 2007 For options generally see ¶31415
A disposal of shares in a company in consideration for a capital distribution from the company	Where a fractional entitlement is sold (¶32250)
A disposal of shares by way of a share-for-share exchange	See ¶79290

EXAMPLE A Ltd granted an option to B Ltd that enabled B Ltd to acquire an asset from A Ltd for £50,000.
After the grant A Ltd joined B Ltd's group. Some time later B Ltd exercised the option.
The no gain/no loss provisions will not apply on the transfer of the asset to B Ltd. Instead, A Ltd has disposed of the asset for £50,000.

Residence

67090
s 171(1A)
TCGA 1992

Although a company resident **anywhere in the world** can be a member of a group for chargeable gains purposes, an intra-group transfer only takes place on a no/gain no loss basis if the assets remain within the charge to UK corporation tax.

This means that both of the following **criteria** must be satisfied:
– the transferor is UK-resident, or the asset is a chargeable asset immediately before the transfer; and
– the transferee is UK-resident, or the asset is a chargeable asset immediately after the transfer.

MEMO POINTS For this purpose a **chargeable asset** is an asset that would be liable to UK corporation tax rules on its disposal, which usually means that it used for a UK trade carried on by a UK permanent establishment (¶92140).

Part disposals

67095
s 42(5) TCGA 1992;
CG 45350

In order to calculate the allowable cost for a part disposal (¶31130), market values have to be used initially.

EXAMPLE C Ltd acquires an asset for £100,000 and then makes a part disposal to fellow group member, D Ltd. The market value of the part disposed of is £60,000. The market value of the part retained by C Ltd is £140,000. The indexation factor is 0.20.

	£
Market value proceeds	60,000
Less: Allowable cost	
$100,000 \times \dfrac{60,000}{60,000 + 140,000}$	(30,000)
Unindexed gain	30,000
Indexation: $0.20 \times £30,000$	(6,000)
Gain before no gain/no loss rule	24,000

The no gain/no loss rule means that the deemed proceeds are £36,000, so that D Ltd takes over the proportion of C Ltd's indexed cost attributable to the part of the asset acquired by D Ltd. (£30,000 + £6,000)

After the transfer

While the **asset remains within the group** as a capital asset, no tax consequences occur. **67100**

However, should any of the following occur, a tax charge will result:
- the asset is appropriated to **trading stock** (¶67160);
- the **asset** is disposed of outside the group (¶67260);
- the asset is **no longer within the scope of UK** corporation tax (¶91440); or
- the **company** owning the asset leaves the group (¶67425).

B. Trading stock

Specific rules apply to the transfer of an asset where the asset is held by the transferor as trading stock, and by the transferee as a capital item, or vice versa. **67130**
s 173(3) TCGA 1992

The rules, which are set out below, **only apply** where the trade in which the asset is used is carried on by a UK-resident company or through a UK permanent establishment.

If this is **not the case**, the transferor will be making a disposal at market value.

1. Appropriations to trading stock

Where an asset owned by one group company as a **capital asset** is transferred to another group company for use as trading stock, this is treated as: **67160**
s 173(1) TCGA 1992
a. an intra-group transfer of a capital asset; which is then
b. transferred into trading stock by the transferee company.

So the intra-group transfer takes place at no gain/no loss.

The transfer into trading stock takes place at market value, so that the transferee company will realise a chargeable **gain**, although an election can be made to convert this gain into a trading profit (¶11710).

Where the transfer results in a **loss**, the election has the effect of turning a capital loss into a trading loss (¶36000), which is then available for current year set-off, carry back or group relief. However, where HMRC suspect there is a scheme to acquire a tax advantage, they will attack the arrangements. *Coates v Arndale Properties Ltd* [1984]; *Reed v Nova Securities Ltd* [1985]

EXAMPLE A chargeable asset which cost £30,000 on 1 March 2000 is transferred from E Ltd to F Ltd on 1 March 2013, when its value is £60,000. The indexation factor is 0.477.
E Ltd uses the asset as a capital asset but F Ltd appropriates it to trading stock and sells it for £70,000.
The asset is transferred between E Ltd and F Ltd at no gain/no loss.

	£
Cost	30,000
Indexation: Mar 00 to Mar 13 £30,000 × 0.477	14,310
	44,310

F Ltd is then treated as disposing of the asset into trading stock for £60,000, so that a chargeable gain of £16,690 arises. (£60,000 – £43,310)
The subsequent sale of the asset results in a trading profit of £10,000.
However, if F Ltd makes an election, the trading profit becomes £26,690. (£16,690 + £10,000)

2. Appropriations from trading stock

67180
s 173(2) TCGA 1992

Where trading stock owned by one group company is transferred to another group company to hold as a capital asset, this is treated as:

a. a transfer into a capital asset by the transferor; which is then

b. transferred to the transferee.

The transfer into a capital asset takes place at market **value**, so that the transferor company will have a trading profit/loss.

The intra-group transfer takes place at no gain/no loss, so that the transferee's base cost is the market value as at the date of the transfer.

> EXAMPLE Trading stock with a book value of £10,000 is transferred between G Ltd and H Ltd, which are both members of the same group. The market value of the stock is £15,000. H Ltd intends to hold the stock on its capital account.
> G Ltd is treated as selling the stock at market value into its capital account, giving a trading profit of £5,000. (£15,000 – £10,000)
> H Ltd acquires the asset with a base cost of £15,000.

SECTION 2

Transfers outside the group

67230

Transfers outside the group may involve:
- the disposal of the asset itself;
- the potential to claim rollover relief; or
- the company, which currently owns the asset, actually leaving the group.

A. Disposal of the asset

67260

Where a group company disposes of an asset outside the group, the usual rules apply.

The **cost** for the purposes of the disposal calculation will be the original cost to the group plus indexation (i.e. the cost to the initial member of the group which acquired the asset from outside the group).

This applies equally to a **disposal of shares** in another group company, although the substantial shareholding exemption (¶32090) may apply to exempt the gain (or disallow any loss).

> MEMO POINTS 1. **Indexation** cannot create a loss, except in relation to transfers which pre-date 30 November 1993. So any indexation creating or increasing a loss relating to transfers since 30 November 1993 must be disallowed when the asset is disposed of outside the group.
> 2. Any resulting **capital loss** can be set against the company's or group's gains (¶67285) in the same accounting period, or carried forward indefinitely (subject to the pre-entry loss rules where the company is acquired by another group (¶67865)). There is no mechanism to carry back a capital loss or to set it against other income (with limited exceptions for investment companies (¶37230) and corporate venturing scheme relief (¶80845)).

s 53 TCGA 1992

> EXAMPLE
> 1. The ABC group consists of A Ltd, B Ltd and C Ltd. On 1 June 1991 (when the RPI was 134.10), A Ltd acquired an asset which cost £200,000. The asset was then transferred around the group as follows:
> – to B Ltd on 1 June 1992 (when the RPI was 139.30);
> – to C Ltd on 1 June 2000 (when the RPI was 171.10); and
> – sold outside the group on 1 April 2013 for £205,000, when the RPI was 249.50.

Transfer on 1 June 1992:

		£
Cost to A Ltd		200,000

Indexation: Jun 91 to Jun 92

$$\frac{139.30 - 134.10}{134.10} = 0.039 \times £200,000 \qquad \underline{7,800}$$

| | | 207,800 |

Transfer on 1 June 2000:

		£
Cost to B Ltd		207,800

Indexation: Jun 92 to Jun 00

$$\frac{171.10 - 139.30}{139.30} = 0.228 \times £207,800 \qquad \underline{47,378}$$

| | | 255,178 |

Disposal on 1 April 2013

	£	£
Disposal proceeds		205,000
Allowable cost to C Ltd	255,178	

Indexation: Jun 00 to April 13

$$\frac{249.50 - 171.10}{171.10} = 0.458 \times £255,178 \qquad \underline{116,872}$$

		(372,050)
Indexed loss		(167,050)
Add back: Indexation disallowed (£47,378 + £116,872)		164,250
Allowable loss		(2,800)

The indexation (£7,800) involved in the group transfer in June 1992 is allowed as this occurred before 30 November 1993.

If the proceeds had been £215,000, the resulting loss of £157,050 is less than the indexation disallowed. In this case, neither a gain nor a loss would result.

March 1982 assets

Where the asset was held by any group member on 31 March 1982 and any intervening disposals have been at no gain/no loss, the disposing company will be eligible for indexation allowance from that date to the date of disposal. However, no double **indexation** allowance can be given i.e. in respect of the March 1982 value and also in respect of the base cost inherited from another group member. **67265**

Rebasing election A company may elect for the gains on all disposals of assets (other than machinery and plant qualifying for capital allowances (¶25240)) held on 31 March 1982, and disposed of after 5 April 1988, to be calculated only by reference to the 31 March 1982 value (¶30785). **67270**
Sch 3 para 8
TCGA 1992

For groups a **global election** can be made so that any disposal of assets held by the group on 31 March 1982 will be computed by reference to the March 1982 value. The following rules apply:

– only the principal company of the group can make the election;
– the election binds the whole group; and
– disposals by subsidiary companies and incoming companies are taken into account in determining the first relevant disposal (¶30835). However, disposals by an outgoing company are ignored. Where accounting periods are not aligned, the time limit for the election is 2 years from the end of the accounting period of the company making the first relevant disposal (in which that disposal is made). HMRC have discretion to accept late elections. CG 46374

MEMO POINTS 1. Where an incoming company **joins a group** which has already made an election, the joining company has the right to makes its own election. CG 46369

CG 46368

2. Where a company **leaves the group** (i.e. an outgoing company), it is not covered by an election which is made subsequent to its date of leaving. However, any company which leaves the group after the election is made will continue to be covered by it.

3. For the **valuation of shareholdings** transferred between group members see ¶30860.

67275
Sch 3 para 2
TCGA 1992

There are specific anti-avoidance rules relating to the use of a March 1982 election by groups.

For intra-group transfers of an asset, any **election made by** the transferee will be ignored. The asset will be covered by the election or non-election of the vendor.

Where there is a **series** of such transfers, the asset will be covered by the election or non-election made by:
– the last person by whom the asset was acquired after 5 April 1988, otherwise than from an intra-group transfer; or
– if there is no such person, the person who held the asset on 5 April 1988.

Linked transactions

67280
ss 19, 20
TCGA 1992;
CG 14701

Where a company makes a series of linked disposals to **one or more connected persons** (other than intra-group), the deemed proceeds on each of the disposals may be adjusted if the total consideration for the assets disposed of is less than it would have been if the assets had been sold in a single transaction.

However, to avoid exploitation of these provisions (either by the **fragmentation** of an asset to different group members which are then the subject of simultaneous disposals to a connected party, or the **reassembling** of a single asset from different group members before disposal to a connected party), the non-group disposal (to a person who is connected both with that company and with one of the other companies earlier in the chain) at the end of a series of intra-group transfers is treated as made by the original transferor company in the group. So the disposal to the connected party can be linked to other disposals made by that company.

Any resulting **increase in corporation tax** will be chargeable on the vendor (i.e. the company which is actually making the disposal to the connected party).

MEMO POINTS   1. For **valuation** purposes, assets disposed of in a later transaction which had not been acquired at the time when the connected party transaction occurred must be taken into account (unlike the general rule for non-group companies).
2. The **total number of assets** taken into account is usually limited to the maximum number held by the vendor at any time during the period immediately before the first transaction until immediately before the last transaction. However, in a group situation, any disposal by way of an intra-group transfer before the first transaction in the series of linked transactions is assumed to have been made after that transaction.

Reallocating gains and losses

67285
ss 171A, 171B
TCGA 1992

It is possible to elect for a chargeable gain or loss arising in one group company to be treated as having arisen in another (**excluding** degrouping charges prior to 18 July 2011 (¶67490)), **provided that**:
– both were members of the same group at the time that the gain or loss arose; and
– any transfer between them would have been at no gain/no loss (if the second company is actually non-resident, it is assumed that it is UK-resident for the purpose of this rule).

Note that as there is no longer any deemed transfer of the asset, the chargeable gain or loss is always **computed** in relation to the first group company's circumstances (e.g. in respect of exemptions and reliefs).

The scope of the election includes deemed as well as actual **disposals**, for example:
– negligible value claims (¶31720);
– capital distributions; and
– capital sums derived from an asset, such as compensation.

A joint **election** (which is revocable) must be made, in writing, within 2 years of the end of the accounting period in which the chargeable gain or loss accrued. It will be invalid where it attempts to transfer an amount which exceeds the actual gain or loss.

Comment The reallocation rules allow a group to review gains and losses retrospectively and allocate them in the most tax-effective way, having regard to the use of losses and also each individual company's marginal rate of tax (¶66260).

> MEMO POINTS 1. An election can be made for just **part** of a gain or loss; this **may be expressed as an amount**, a fraction or a percentage. An election need not identify particular gains and losses if it clearly states that all of the first company's gains and losses accruing in the accounting period are to be transferred.
> 2. **Multiple elections** are possible. A later election will have no effect where it tries to transfer more than the total available gain or loss.
> 3. Any **payment** that passes between the two companies, in connection with an election, is not taken into account in computing the profits or losses of either company for corporation tax purposes.
> 4. It is possible to show the election on the **schedule** used for the group simplified arrangements relating to group loss relief (¶66730).

B. Assets used in a trade

Rollover relief, which enables a company to roll over the chargeable gain arising on the disposal of certain business assets into the base cost of a new asset acquired within a certain period (¶30940), is also available to groups of companies.

67315

1. Group treated as a single entity

Rollover relief can be claimed where the disposal of the original asset and acquisition of the replacement asset are made by two different companies in the same group.

A **claim** must be made by both companies.

67345
s 175(1) TCGA 1992

Scope

For this purpose all of the **trades** carried on by group members are treated as a single trade. Additionally, a **non-trading group member** which acquires or disposes of assets used by other group members for the purposes of their trade will qualify for the relief.

67350
s 175(2B)
TCGA 1992

Exclusions

The following situations are excluded:

67355

Situation	Detail	Reference
Gain arises before company joins the group	Gain cannot be rolled over against group acquisitions Group gains cannot be rolled over against assets acquired before company joined the group	s 175 TCGA 1992
Gain arises after company leaves the group	No group rollover relief for gain	SP D19
Appropriations to trading stock	As proceeds from the deemed disposal cannot be used to acquire another asset, no rollover available No rollover where a chargeable asset is transferred at no gain/no loss and then appropriated into stock by another group member (¶67160)	s 173 TCGA 1992

Conditions

67360
s 175(2A), (2AA)
TCGA 1992

Relief can only be claimed where the following criteria are met:
a. the **company making the disposal** is a group member at the time of the disposal;
b. the **company acquiring the replacement asset** is a group member at the time of the acquisition and is not a dual resident investing company;
c. the gain arising on the disposal of both the original asset and the replacement asset would be a **chargeable gain** (i.e. not exempt under a double tax treaty) – the replacement asset cannot be acquired as a result of a no gain/no loss transfer (although where the asset's acquisition from outside the group falls within the relevant time limits (¶30990), this would just change the identity of the claimant); and
d. any gain arising on the disposal would be **within the charge to UK corporation tax** i.e. the trade is carried on by either:
– a UK-resident company; or
– a UK permanent establishment of a non-resident company.

CG 45949

[MEMO POINTS]   1. HMRC have confirmed that there is no need for the company disposing of the old asset and the company acquiring the new asset to be **members of the group at the same time**.
2. Neither company needs to be a member of the group **at the time that the actual claim** is made.

CG 45950

3. On a **takeover** of the principal company of a group, a gain realised by an original group member can be rolled over against an asset acquired by any member of the new group.
4. Any **payment** that passes between the two companies, in connection with a rollover relief claim, is not taken into account in computing the profits or losses of either company for corporation tax purposes.

> [EXAMPLE]
> 1. A Ltd has two wholly owned subsidiaries, B Ltd and C Ltd. B Ltd sells a factory for £500,000, realising a gain of £200,000. C Ltd acquires another factory 4 months later for £450,000.
> The amount not reinvested by the group of £50,000 is chargeable and not rolled over. (£500,000 – £450,000)
> The remaining amount of the gain of £150,000 is rolled over. (£200,000 – £50,000)
> So C Ltd's base cost for the replacement factory is £300,000. (£450,000 – £150,000)
>
> 2. D Ltd, which is a member of the DEF group, acquired an asset from outside the group in Year 6. In the same year E Ltd sold another asset, realising a gain. In Year 7 D Ltd transferred the asset at no gain/no loss to F Ltd.
> E Ltd's gain can be rolled over against the cost of the original acquisition of the asset by D Ltd, even though it has subsequently been transferred intra-group.
>
> 3. G Ltd, which is a member of D Ltd's group, disposes of an asset in Year 10. In Year 11 D Ltd is acquired by A Ltd, which has a subsidiary, B Ltd. In Year 11 B Ltd acquires a replacement asset.
> G Ltd's gain can be rolled over against the replacement asset acquired by B Ltd.

Depreciating assets

67365
s 175(3)
TCGA 1992;
CG 45945

If the replacement asset is a depreciating asset (broadly, one with a **useful life** of 60 years or less), the gain is simply held over instead of being rolled over (¶31040) and crystallises on the occurrence of certain events.

However, the gain held over will **not crystallise** when either of the following occurs:
– an intra-group transfer of the depreciating asset; or
– the cessation of trade of the company which owns the depreciating asset, provided that the owner remains in the group and the asset continues to be used only for the purposes of a UK trade carried on by a member of the group.

The gain held over **crystallises** on the earliest of:
– a disposal outside the group;
– cessation of use by any and every group member for the purposes of the single group trade (including the case where the owner leaves the group); or
– the expiry of 10 years after the acquisition of the depreciating asset.

The gain is **chargeable on** the company which happens to own the asset at the time.

Comment   The fact that the charge may not arise for 10 years will allow the group to arrange where the charge should arise in future.

2. Rollover of degrouping charge

Prior to 19 July 2011 it was possible for a group to claim rollover relief in respect of a degrouping charge. The **replacement asset** had to be acquired within 1 year before, and 3 years after, the date that the degrouping charge was deemed to accrue.

Where the degrouping charge had been **reallocated** to another group member (¶67490), the claim needed to be made by the company to which the degrouping charge had been transferred.

From 19 July 2011 (or 1 April 2011 where an election (¶67425) is made), there is no longer any facility to roll over a degrouping charge except in relation to intangible fixed assets and loan relationships.

67395

C. Company leaves the group

The aim of the degrouping charge is to ensure that the increase in value of an asset during its period of ownership by a group is crystallised, even if the asset leaves the group otherwise than by disposal of the company.

The rules, which apply when a company leaves a group within 6 years after receiving an asset transferred to it at no gain/no loss, were simplified in 2011. However, the new regime **does not extend** to **intangible fixed assets** or **loan relationships**. In particular, groups must correctly identify whether goodwill falls within the intangibles regime or is to be treated as a capital asset (¶30190). Further, the degrouping charge relating to stamp duty land tax is unchanged (see *Tax Memo* for details).

Because the old rules continue to apply in limited circumstances, they are laid out here, with the 2011 changes noted in context and explained individually afterwards.

Although the key date for the changes was nominally 19 July 2011, the principal company of a group could make an **election** to apply the new rules to all group companies which left the group on or after 1 April 2011. This election (which did not have to be made in any particular form or on a CTSA return) had to be made in writing by 31 March 2012, as had any revocation of it. Because the election may have been made after a company had left the group, the departing company must also have agreed to the election (and the same was true of any revocation).

67425

CG 45421

1. Old rules

These rules apply in respect of intangible fixed assets and loan relationships (and to all other assets subject to the amendments noted from ¶67525 under the heading "Current rules").

67455

Scope

A degrouping charge will arise if a company leaves the group while **holding an asset** (not as trading stock):

67460
s 179 TCGA 1992

– acquired intra-group in the 6 years prior to its departure date; or
– against which a gain has been rolled over, where the original asset was transferred at no gain/no loss within the 6 years prior to its departure date.

This rule **also operates** where:
– an associated company of the departing company holds the asset and leaves the group with the departing company i.e. it is not possible to avoid the degrouping charge merely by transferring the asset to another group member which also leaves the group (for this purpose a company is associated with another when both are in a 75% group relationship (¶65415)); or
– an asset derives its value from another asset transferred at no gain/no loss e.g. a lease is acquired at no gain/no loss and the transferee subsequently acquires the freehold reversion then leaves the group.

The charge **accrues to** the departing company, unless there is an election to reallocate it to another group member (¶67490) or roll it over (¶67395).

The charge itself may be a gain or a loss.

Comment   As the departing company is liable for the charge under these rules (but see ¶67495), it is imperative that adequate due diligence work is undertaken by the purchaser of the company, and appropriate warranties and indemnities are obtained.

> [EXAMPLE]   In Year 1 A Ltd transfers Asset 1 to B Ltd, a fellow group company. B Ltd disposes of the asset to a third party in Year 3 for £100,000, realising a gain of £20,000. B Ltd acquires Asset 2 by fully reinvesting the proceeds and claims rollover relief so that on a future disposal of Asset 2, its base cost will be reduced by £20,000.
> In Year 4 B Ltd is sold by A Ltd, whilst still owning Asset 2.
> The conditions for a degrouping charge in respect of Asset 1 are satisfied, because the gain on that asset has been rolled over into an asset that is still owned by a company that leaves the group.

67465   There is no requirement that both companies are members of the group **at the time of the no gain/no loss transfer**.

This means that a degrouping charge could be triggered even where an unconnected company:
– acquires an asset at arm's length;
– subsequently joins the vendor's group; and
– within 6 years of the asset transfer, leaves that group while still holding the asset.

Comment   This unfair result has been rectified since 19 July 2011 (¶67530), other than in relation to intangible fixed assets and loan relationships.

Exclusions

67470
s 179 TCGA 1992;
CG 45410

A degrouping charge does **not arise** in the following situations:

Situation	Detail
Company ungrouped	A company ceases to be in a group because its only subsidiary leaves the group
	A company ceases to be in a group because another company (which HMRC consider must be its only subsidiary) ceases to exist i.e. on its actual dissolution This also applies where all of a company's subsidiaries cease to exist simultaneously
Transfer of trade overseas	A trade carried on in the UK is transferred to a non-resident company (¶61205)
	A UK-resident company transfers a trade carried on through a permanent establishment in another member state of the EU (¶93195)
Mergers	A merger of a UK-resident company with a company resident in another member state of the EU, including a Societas Europaea (¶93000+)
	A demerger (¶79050+)
Became an investment trust or venture capital trust	A degrouping charge has already arisen after receiving an asset via an intra-group transfer
Two companies leave the group together	See ¶67475

67475
s 179(2), (2A), (2AA)
TCGA 1992

Two associated companies leaving together   No degrouping charge arises where the transferor and transferee company **form a subgroup** and leave the original group together. This exception only applies where the companies also formed a subgroup at the time when the asset was originally transferred.

However, if the **transferee company subsequently leaves** the second group within 6 years of the original intra-group transfer, and the second group is connected with the original group, a degrouping charge will be imposed at that time.

Similarly, where the subgroup leaves the original group on or after 23 March 2011, a degrouping charge will arise where the **original group and subgroup cease to be connected**, without a company actually leaving the subgroup.

MEMO POINTS 1. For this purpose **connected** means that the parent companies of both the original group and subgroup are under common control (¶75275) at any time on or after the subgroup leaves the original group.
2. See ¶67530 for the amended current rules.

EXAMPLE
1. A Ltd owns 100% of B Ltd, which in turn owns 100% of C Ltd. A Ltd is therefore the principal member of the group with B Ltd and C Ltd as subsidiaries.
B Ltd transfers an asset to C Ltd on 1 January 2009. In January 2012 A Ltd sells its entire shareholding in B Ltd.
Although C Ltd is no longer in the same chargeable gains group as A Ltd, the gain in respect of the asset transferred from B Ltd does not crystallise, as the subgroup consisting of B Ltd and C Ltd is sold and the transfer was between members of that subgroup.
If C Ltd had been sold separately, a degrouping charge would have arisen.

2. The XBCDE group is as follows:

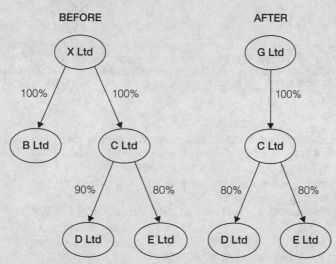

BEFORE / AFTER

If X Ltd sells C Ltd in 2008, the CDE subgroup is formed. Any assets transferred between C Ltd, D Ltd and E Ltd do not create a degrouping charge. Any assets transferred from B Ltd or X Ltd within the last 6 years will create a degrouping charge.
After the sale C Ltd is controlled by G Ltd, which is owned by the same individuals who control X Ltd. If C Ltd subsequently sells D Ltd in 2011, any assets transferred to D Ltd since 2005 from either C Ltd or E Ltd will result in a degrouping charge. If C Ltd transferred an asset to D Ltd in 2007, because X Ltd and G Ltd are under common control, the degrouping charge still applies even though D Ltd is leaving the G Ltd group and the intra-group transfer occurred when D Ltd was a member of X Ltd's group. The degrouping charge is calculated by deeming a disposal to occur in 2007 but is chargeable in 2011.

Parent company joins another group Where two groups join together, some companies in the target group **may not be effective 51% subsidiaries** of the new principal company (¶65435).

67480
s 179(5), (6)
TCGA 1992

No degrouping charge applies in this situation, **provided that** the company is a 75% subsidiary and also an effective 51% subsidiary of at least one member of the new group. Where this **condition is broken** within 6 years of the transfer of the asset and the same company, or another group member, holds the asset (or has rolled over a gain on its disposal into a replacement asset), a degrouping charge will arise.

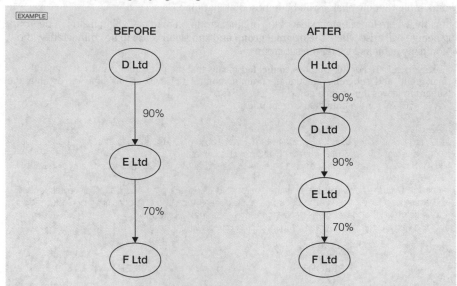

EXAMPLE

In 2010 D Ltd transfers an asset to F Ltd at no gain/no loss. When H Ltd takes over D Ltd in 2012, F Ltd is no longer an effective 51% subsidiary of the principal company (i.e. H Ltd). However, no degrouping charge arises because it is still a 75% subsidiary and an effective 51% subsidiary of D Ltd. If F Ltd is subsequently sold by E Ltd before 2016, a degrouping charge will apply.

Calculation

67485 The degrouping charge is calculated by **deeming the asset** to have been disposed of and reacquired for its market **value** at the time that the intra-group transfer took place. The base cost of the asset going forward is therefore the market value.

The charge is treated as **arising** on the later of:
– the date of the intra-group transfer; and
– the start of the accounting period in which the company leaves the group.

So the amount of the charge will be based on circumstances existing when the asset was transferred intra-group (i.e. indexation will be up to the date of the transfer) but will be chargeable to tax in the accounting period when the company leaves the group.

> *MEMO POINTS* Prior to 19 July 2011 (or 1 April 2011 where an appropriate election was made (¶67425)), **rollover relief** was available for a degrouping charge (¶67395) but that is now only the case in relation to intangible fixed assets and loan relationships.

EXAMPLE A Ltd acquired an office block on 1 April 2002 for £250,000. On 1 April 2006, when it was valued at £350,000, the block was transferred to B Ltd, a fellow group member. On 1 April 2011 A Ltd sold its shares in B Ltd. B Ltd has a calendar year end.
A degrouping charge will apply to B Ltd as follows:

	£	£
Market value at 1 April 2006		350,000
Less: Cost	250,000	
Indexation: Apr 02 to Apr 06		
$\dfrac{196.50 - 175.70}{175.70} = 0.118 \times 250,000$	29,500	
		(279,500)
Indexed gain		70,500

B Ltd will have a base cost of £350,000 for the office block, dating from 1 April 2006.
The degrouping charge of £70,500 will arise on 1 January 2011.

Reallocation

A group can **elect** that a degrouping charge arising in one group company is deemed to arise in another.

67490

The election must be made within 2 years of the end of the accounting period during which the departing company left the group.

Any payment for the transfer is ignored for tax purposes, provided that it is not excessive.

See ¶67545 for the current rules for all assets except intangibles and loan relationships.

Unpaid degrouping charge

Where a degrouping charge remains unpaid 6 months after the due date for payment, HMRC may **recover** the amount **from**:

67495
s 190 TCGA 1992

– the principal member of the group (at the date when the gain accrued); or
– any other company which had an interest in the asset and was a group member at any time up to 12 months before the gain accrued.

---

2. Current rules

The degrouping rules were changed significantly for companies leaving a group on or after 19 July 2011 (or from 1 April 2011 where an appropriate election is made (¶67425)). The stated intention is to improve the interaction of the substantial shareholding exemption with the degrouping charge.

67525

The commentary below identifies those aspects which have been amended.

When does the charge arise?

From 19 July 2011 the companies involved in the **no gain/no loss transfer** of the asset must be members of the group at the time of the transfer of the asset.

67530

The **associated company exception** (¶67475) is now redrafted to make it simpler, so that no degrouping charge will arise where either:

s 179(2ZA), (2ZB)
TCGA 1992

– the transferor and transferee companies are both subsidiaries of another company at the time of the transfer and remain so until immediately after they leave the group; or
– one is the subsidiary of the other and remains so until immediately after they leave the group.

Where does the charge arise?

The usual rules apply (¶67460+), **except** where the departing company leaves the group as a result of an actual **disposal of shares**, in which case the degrouping charge is deemed to accrue in the hands of the vendor (as opposed to the departing company).

67535
s 179(3A) – (3E)
TCGA 1992

Where there is a **share-for-share exchange** of old shares for new (¶79290), the degrouping charge is treated as an adjustment to the allowable cost for the acquisition of the new shares (i.e. a gain reduces the cost, a loss increases it). If the degrouping charge exceeds the allowable cost, the excess will be chargeable when the new shares are disposed of.

> ⬚ MEMO POINTS 1. A company may leave a group **other than by way of a share disposal**, for example through an issue of new shares, or a change in the rights in existing shares. In such a case the rules of ¶67460+ apply where there is no movement of value out of the existing shares.
> 2. Where a company leaves a group as a result of a **share disposal by more than one company**, the adjustment is shared equally, or in the proportions specified by the disposing companies in an election.

s 179(3F), (3G)
TCGA 1992

Treatment of the charge

The degrouping charge attaches to the departing company's shares so that there is no separate charge as such, and where it is a:

67540
s 179(3A)
TCGA 1992

– **gain**, it is treated as an increase to the **consideration** for the sale of the departing company's shares; or

– **loss**, it decreases that consideration.

This means that where the conditions for the **substantial shareholding** exemption (SSE) are met (¶32090), the degrouping charge will also be exempt. This is good news where the charge is a gain, but also means that any resulting loss is not available for relief (i.e. where the base cost exceeds current market value). Therefore, in order to access a loss, a group would need to plan to prevent the SSE from applying.

Rollover relief is not available for degrouping charges, mainly because of the availability of the SSE in most cases.

Comment   A vendor will need to be certain that SSE will shield a degrouping gain before undertaking a company sale. The vendor should seek a non-statutory clearance in this case (¶32130).

> | MEMO POINTS | 1. On a **share-for-share exchange** the degrouping charge is held over until the new shares are disposed of, unless the SSE applies to the exchange (¶32090).
>
> 2. The degrouping charge does not jeopardise the tax treatment of **reconstructions** (¶79290).

s 179ZA
TCGA 1992

> 3. In order to prevent any double taxation, where the SSE does not apply, a company is able to make a claim for the just and reasonable **reduction** of the amount by which a degrouping charge adjusts a chargeable gain e.g. where the consideration for an intra-group transfer is at book value, even though the market value of the asset at the time of the transfer is higher. This should enable groups to dissolve dormant companies, from which a trade has been hived out (¶79600), without waiting for 6 years first.

Sch 7AC para 38
TCGA 1992

> 4. The **date of the deemed disposal** at market value may be modified by the SSE rules, so that where an asset disposal immediately before the departing company leaves the group would have been exempt as a result of the SSE, the deemed date of disposal and reacquisition is to be treated as taking place on the same day as the company left the group. This ensures that if it is possible for the exemption to apply, at either the date of the asset transfer or at the time the asset leaves the group, it will apply.

s 179(3A)
TCGA 1992

> 5. The consideration for a disposal is also amended in the following special cases:
>
> – the group company making the disposal is **not within the scope of UK corporation tax** in respect of the disposal of shares but, were it to be so, the disposal would be within the SSE; and
>
> – where a gain is attributed under the **close company** rules (¶76040).

> | EXAMPLE | A Ltd is the principal company of a CG group and transfers a 20% shareholding in X Ltd to a subsidiary, B Ltd, on 1 March 2007. On 1 March 2011 B Ltd leaves the A group, taking with it the X Ltd shares.
> Any disposal of the X Ltd shares by B Ltd would be exempt under SSE.
> The deemed date of B Ltd's disposal and reacquisition of the shares in X Ltd is 1 March 2011.
> The degrouping charge is therefore exempt.

Reallocation

67545   Under the current rules the reallocation rules of ¶67285 apply instead of those in ¶67490.

SECTION 3

Anti-avoidance rules

Summary

67595

Rule	¶¶
Depreciatory transactions	¶67625
Dividend stripping	¶67675
Value shifting	¶67695

1. Depreciatory transactions

Without specific rules, it would be possible for groups to use the rules for intra-group transfers to reduce the value of one group member by transferring its assets intra-group, and then selling the shares in that group member at a loss. The depreciatory transaction rules are designed to prevent this activity, and restrict any loss arising by an amount which is just and reasonable. They cannot create a gain.

67625

Scope

The rules **apply** to transactions after 31 March 1982, in which:
a. there is a disposal of shares or securities;
b. the value of those shares or securities has been materially reduced; and
c. the reduction arises as a result of a depreciatory transaction – that is, one:
– which involves a disposal of assets from one group member to another, other than at market value; or
– involving two or more companies in the same group, where the company which is sold, or any of its 75% subsidiaries, is a party.

67630
s 176(1) TCGA 1992

Note that for share **disposals occurring on or after 19 July 2011**, it is only depreciatory transactions which have happened within the 6 years prior to the date of the share disposal which need to be taken into account. Prior to that date no time limit applied.

> MEMO POINTS 1. **Shares or securities** include loan stock and other securities, both secured and unsecured.
> 2. HMRC consider a reduction to be **material** if it is more than negligible. Whether a transaction reduces the value of shares or securities depends solely on their value at the time that the transaction takes place and not on their acquisition value.
> 3. A **disposal of assets** includes any other method by which the goodwill of one group company is appropriated by another. A disposal also includes the deemed disposal which arises when a negligible value claim is made (¶31720).

CG 46550

s 176(8) TCGA 1992

EXAMPLE The ABCDEFG group is comprised as follows:

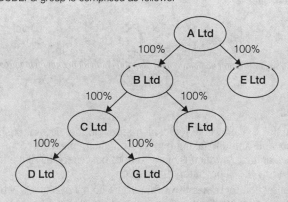

1. C Ltd disposes of an asset at less than market value to D Ltd.
This does not reduce the value of C's assets because the asset disposal is matched by the increase in value of D Ltd's shares.
The disposal from C Ltd is not a depreciatory transaction in relation to a disposal of C Ltd by B Ltd, or of B Ltd by A Ltd.

2. C Ltd disposes of an asset at less than market value to F Ltd.
This reduces the value of C Ltd's shares which are held by B Ltd. The disposal does not reduce the value of B Ltd's shares which are held by A Ltd, as C Ltd's reduction is matched by F Ltd's increase.
The disposal from C Ltd is a depreciatory transaction in relation to a disposal of C Ltd by B Ltd, but not in relation to a disposal of B Ltd by A Ltd.

3. D Ltd disposes of an asset to E Ltd at less than market value.
This reduces the value of:
– D Ltd's shares which are held by C Ltd;
– C Ltd's shares which are held by B Ltd; and
– B Ltd's shares which are held by A Ltd.
The disposal by D Ltd is a depreciatory transaction in relation to a disposal of D Ltd by C Ltd, of C Ltd by B Ltd, or of B Ltd by A Ltd.

Exclusions

67635
s 176(1) TCGA 1992

The rules do not apply to:
– a **payment which is brought into account** (or required to be brought into account) for the purposes of computing a chargeable gain or loss on the company which makes the share disposal – for example, a capital distribution (¶32250); and

CG 46580

– a **dividend** which is made out of post-acquisition profits (¶32375).

Types of depreciatory transactions

67640
s 176(3)
TCGA 1992;
CG 46564

In addition to an intra-group transfer of an asset, the following transactions **may be caught** by the depreciatory transaction rules:
– payment of a dividend (other than one out of post-acquisition profits);
– the cancellation of a loan;
– excessive payments for the use of services or assets;
– excessive payments for group relief; and
– the cancellation of shares where, immediately before their cancellation, the shares are the property of another group member.

> EXAMPLE
> **1.** A Ltd owns two subsidiaries, B Ltd and C Ltd. B Ltd surrenders group relief of £5 million to C Ltd and this reduces C Ltd's tax liability by £1.3 million. 2 years later, A Ltd sells C Ltd and sustains a loss. If C Ltd paid more than £1.3 million in respect of the group relief surrender, this would be a depreciatory transaction and a loss restriction should be made in respect of the excess. It should be noted that a payment up to £5 million could have been made without any implications at the time (¶66740).
>
> **2.** D Ltd owns two subsidiaries, E Ltd and F Ltd. E Ltd surrenders group relief of £5 million to F Ltd and this reduces F Ltd's tax liability by £1.3 million. F Ltd pays £1 million to E Ltd for the group relief surrendered. 2 years later, D Ltd sells E Ltd and sustains a loss.
> Here there is no depreciatory transaction, even though F Ltd did not pay the full amount of its tax advantage to E Ltd.

Consequences

67645
s 176(4), (5)
TCGA 1992

Where the rules apply, the allowable loss which arises on the disposal of shares is reduced by a just and reasonable amount, taking into account the depreciatory transaction. The **aim** of the reduction is that the loss which is allowed does not reflect the diminution in the value of the shares caused by the depreciatory transaction.

Where another transaction **increases the value** of the company's assets, while depreciating the value of the assets of any other member of the group, this can be taken into account.

s 176(6) TCGA 1992

To prevent **double taxation**, any chargeable gain which arises on a disposal within 6 years of the depreciatory transaction will also be reduced by a just and reasonable amount. However, the total reductions to chargeable gains cannot exceed the reduction in the allowable loss.

> EXAMPLE G Ltd buys H Ltd in 2009. In 2010 H Ltd sells an asset for £1 million (when it is worth £5 million) to another group member. A year later, H Ltd acquires an asset for £6 million (when it is worth £7 million) from another group member, so depreciating the value of the other company's assets.
> In 2013 G Ltd sells H Ltd at a loss.
> The loss should be adjusted by the net reduction in the value of H Ltd, which is £3 million. ((5 – 1) – (7 – 6))

2. Dividend stripping

The depreciatory transaction rules also **apply** to the practice of dividend stripping (that is, reducing the value of shares in a company by payment of a dividend prior its disposal). For details see ¶32370.

67675
s 177(1) TCGA 1992

3. Value shifting

The value shifting rules have a wider scope than the depreciatory transaction rules and are **intended** to prevent groups of companies from reducing their tax liabilities by artificially shifting value from one asset to another.

67695

The value shifting rules have **particular relevance to groups** in the following situations:
– on the disposal of shares in another company;
– on an intra-group distribution followed by the sale of a group company;
– where a company holding an asset leaves the group;
– on an intra-group transfer of an asset; or
– on the reorganisation of a group's share capital.

The original rules, which applied until 19 July 2011, have been replaced but only in respect of share disposals (¶67770+). Other types of disposal are still covered by the rules at ¶67715+.

The effect of the value shifting provisions is to increase the consideration for a disposal by a just and reasonable amount; they can restrict a loss, or create or increase a gain.

Comment Contrast these consequences to those of depreciatory transactions, which can only restrict a loss.
In practice, a loss situation would probably be covered by the depreciatory transaction rules (¶67625) or the manipulation of capital losses provisions (¶37120), in preference to value shifting.

a. Rules for disposals other than share disposals

Scope

The provisions apply in **situations** where:
a. there is a movement of value out of an asset (¶32450), without an actual disposal needing to occur; or
b. as part of an arrangement value passes out of an asset and, as a consequence, a tax-free benefit arises. In this case, a subsequent disposal of the asset must occur (¶32455).

67715

Exclusions

These provisions do not apply to:
a. ordinary payments for group relief;
b. transfers between members of the same 75% CG group of companies (unless the asset is transferred for consideration lower than both the cost and the market value of the asset); and:
c. bona fide commercial transactions which are not undertaken with the aim of avoiding tax.

67720

Movement of value

Where value shifts out of an asset, without an actual disposal, a deemed disposal is nevertheless treated as occurring at market value (irrespective of the value of any actual consideration received for the arrangement), although the usual reliefs (such as rollover relief) are still available.

67725
s 29 TCGA 1992

This rule can apply in the following **situations**:

a. a person exercises control over a company such that value passes out of one shareholding into another i.e. a shareholding is diluted;

b. the owner of land (or any other property) sells it and becomes the lessee, and there are subsequently arrangements which are favourable to the lessor; or

c. rights or restrictions over any asset are reduced or removed by the person entitled to enforce them.

The adjustment applies equally to the person benefiting from the value shift.

EXAMPLE E Ltd owns F Ltd's entire issued share capital of 10,000 £1 shares which were acquired by subscription at par. Several years later, G Ltd (which is connected with E Ltd but not part of the same 75% CG group) acquired 12,000 £1 shares in F Ltd by subscription at par, when the company was worth £525,000. The market value of the new shares was £310,200.

E Ltd's interest has reduced to 45%, which has a value of £214,800, and E Ltd is deemed to make a disposal as follows:

	£
Deemed proceeds on disposal	310,200
Less: Allowable cost	
$\dfrac{310,200}{310,200 + 214,800} \times 10,000$	(5,909)
Chargeable gain (before indexation)	304,291

The allowable cost of G Ltd's shares will be adjusted to reflect the market value at acquisition i.e. £310,200.

Tax-free benefit

67730
s 30 TCGA 1992

The value shifting provisions will also apply where, as part of a scheme or arrangement, the value of an asset is materially reduced (¶32375) and a tax-free benefit arises.

> MEMO POINTS 1. Where the transaction is motivated by tax avoidance, the **person receiving the tax-free benefit** does not have to be the person making the disposal, or a person connected with him: any person receiving a tax-free benefit will cause the rules to apply.
> 2. A **benefit** includes money and money's worth, the increase in value of an asset, and being relieved of a liability.
> 3. The benefit is **tax free** unless it is required to be brought into account for the purposes of computing income, profits or gains for the purposes of income tax, capital gains tax or corporation tax.

---

b. Rules for share disposals

67770
s 31 TCGA 1992

A targeted anti-avoidance rule **applies to** disposals of shares or securities on or after 19 July 2011 when:

– arrangements have been made whereby the value of those shares or securities, or any relevant asset, is materially reduced;

– the main purpose, or one of the main purposes, of the arrangements is to obtain a tax advantage; and

– the arrangements do not consist solely of the making of an exempt distribution i.e. the value shifting rules will not apply where a normal dividend is paid out before the sale.

> MEMO POINTS 1. **Arrangements** include any agreement, understanding, scheme, transaction or series of transactions (whether or not legally enforceable).
> 2. An asset is a **relevant asset** if, at the time of the disposal, it is owned by a company which is a member of the same group as the disposing company.

CG 48540

> 3. It is irrelevant whether the **tax advantage** is obtained for the disposing company or any other person, although usually it would be obtained for a member of the vendor's group. HMRC state that it will be relevant to compare whether, in the absence of the tax considerations:
> – the transaction giving rise to the advantage would have taken place at all;
> – if so, whether the tax advantage would have been of the same amount; and
> – whether the transaction would have been made under the same terms and conditions.

4. **Exempt distribution** means a distribution which is within the rules for:
– small companies (i.e. with less than 50 employees and either the turnover or gross balance sheet total do not exceed €10 million) (¶18385); or
– other companies, which requires the distribution to fall within a particular class of exemption (¶18390).

HMRC guidance

HMRC emphasise that the rule is **targeted against** deliberate tax avoidance and does not apply generally where surplus value is simply taken out of a target company before sale e.g. normal pre-sale transactions that reduce the value of a target company, where the disposal consideration for the shares is a true measure of the value passing from the vendor group.

67775
CG 48520

HMRC give the following list of **features** when the rule will apply, subject to the caveat that routine pre-sale transactions will not amount to avoidance:
– capital gains disposal consideration that does not represent the true economic worth of the assets disposed of;
– transactions designed to create a distributable reserve before disposal of the target company, although in some jurisdictions it may be possible to distribute share capital directly;
– the passing of value from a target company to its vendor group, typically by way of distribution; and
– funding the payments by way of loan to the target company, whether by a connected or unconnected lender.

So the rule will **principally apply** in a convoluted arrangement where the vendor group subscribes for additional share capital in a target company before a disposal, in order to increase its allowable cost but receives the value of the amount subscribed.

Practical illustration   HMRC give the following examples of the application of this rule:

67780
CG 48560

EXAMPLE

1. The target company has a large cash balance which it pays up to its group parent as a dividend prior to the sale. The purchaser pays an amount which it considers to be appropriate after the dividend has been paid.
HMRC state that this arrangement is the payment of an exempt dividend, so the value shifting rules do not apply.

2. The target company has issued share capital of 100,000 £1 ordinary shares. A purchaser has offered to buy the target company for £1 million.
The vendor group parent subscribes for a further £900,000 of share capital in the target company, so as to increase its base cost to £1 million.
The target company then reduces its share capital by re-denominating the £1 shares as 1p shares and credits the amount of reduction (£990,000) to distributable reserves. This amount is then paid out to the parent as a dividend. As the target company's base cost is £1 million, no gain will arise on its disposal.
HMRC state that the subscription for further shares, the reduction in share capital and the payment of the dividend comprise arrangements whereby a tax advantage is obtained. Therefore the sale consideration is adjusted to reflect the uplift in base cost.

3. The target company has distributable profit reserves but no cash. It borrows money from its parent (it could be from a third party) and uses this to pay a dividend. It is then sold to the purchaser and afterwards repays the loan.
HMRC state that these arrangements do not consist solely of the payment of an exempt dividend because the target company needs to borrow the funds to make the payment. The issue is whether the arrangements have a main purpose of obtaining a tax advantage.
The payment of existing distributable reserves before the sale of a company is normal commercial practice, so HMRC do not regard this as being tax-motivated.
However, where a transaction takes place before the disposal in order to create a reserve of untaxed profits, this has the purpose of obtaining a tax advantage.

Consequences

Any allowable loss or chargeable gain accruing on the disposal is to be calculated as if the **consideration** for the disposal were increased by such amount as is just and reasonable

67785

– that is, ignoring the effect of the arrangements. This also applies where the disposal pre-dates the acquisition.

s 31(2) TCGA 1992　The **adjustment** will take into account the overall tax consequences of the arrangements so, for example, where a tax charge is triggered by the arrangements, this will mitigate the increase to the consideration.

CG 48530　Where a scheme or arrangement reduces the value of an asset and the disposal in relation to which the value shifting provisions need to be applied is a **deemed disposal** for the purposes of the **degrouping charge**, the market value for that deemed disposal is increased by a just and reasonable amount. HMRC give the example of a group transferring an artifi-cially depreciated asset to a newly incorporated company, which leaves the group as a result of issuing shares to an unconnected, third-party purchaser.

Comment　Even where a group has elected for the new degrouping rules to apply from 1 April 2011, the new value shifting rules did not come into effect until 19 July 2011.

SECTION 4

Acquiring companies with losses and gains

67835　As the legislation allows groups flexibility when transferring assets, it would be very easy to acquire a company with accrued capital losses and use them to shelter any gains. An asset pregnant with gain could be transferred at no gain/no loss to the capital loss company and then sold, with the gain relieved by the losses accrued in that company. The pre-entry loss rules prevent this type of planning.

A. Pre-entry losses

67865　There are **two sets of rules** which prevent a company's losses from being set against group gains:
– the loss-buying rules; and
– general restrictions on pre-entry losses, which were significantly amended for set-offs occurring on or after 19 July 2011.

The loss-buying rules apply **in precedence** to the general restrictions.

1. Loss-buying rules

67895　These rules do not apply where there is a **genuine commercial transaction** which results in a capital loss.

They take precedence over the general pre-entry loss rules.

Where the loss-buying provisions do not apply, the rules in ¶67955+ may still do so, particu-larly in relation to bona fide mergers and acquisitions.

Scope

67900　Where a company changes ownership **as part of a scheme**, the main purpose of which is to
s 184A TCGA 1992　secure a tax advantage, and the company incurs a gain or a loss on a disposal of an asset which was owned before the change in ownership, the set-off of that gain or loss is restricted. The pre-entry loss can only be offset against gains on a pre-entry asset and vice versa.

The intention behind this rule is that a company's capital losses should only be available against its own capital gains, or those of companies that were under the same economic ownership when the loss arose and when the loss is utilised.

> MEMO POINTS   1. Scheme or **arrangement** includes any agreement, understanding, scheme, transaction or series of transactions, whether or not legally enforceable. HMRC state that in any case where one transaction would not have taken place without another transaction, or would have taken place on different terms without that other transaction, they will view this as an arrangement.
> 2. The **disposal could occur** either before or after the change in ownership, and the loss or gain may be realised in a different group company due to an intervening no gain/no loss transfer.
> 3. For pre-entry **gains** see ¶68105.

CG 47024

Purpose of the arrangements

The purpose of the arrangements is determined by the purpose of any of the **participants** in entering into the arrangements. The tax advantage may arise to any company.

67905
CG 47025, 47027

However, the mere existence of a tax advantage does not itself lead to the conclusion that the main purpose of the arrangements was to secure that advantage. There may have been **more than one way of securing a commercial objective**, and the company's choice may have been influenced by commercial factors rather than a beneficial tax position. HMRC state that where the tax advantage secured is significant, this will indicate that achieving a tax advantage was a main purpose, excluding the case where no additional, complex or costly steps have been included solely to secure that advantage.

To this end, all of the circumstances in which the arrangements were entered into need to be taken into account.

Further, the company will also need to consider whether, **in the absence of the tax advantage**:
- the transaction giving rise to the advantage would have taken place at all;
- if so, whether the tax advantage would have been of the same amount; and
- whether the transaction would have been made under the same terms and conditions.

CG 47028

> MEMO POINTS   1. A **tax advantage** includes all of the following situations:
> - a relief from corporation tax;
> - a repayment of corporation tax;
> - the avoidance or reduction of a charge to corporation tax or an assessment to corporation tax; and
> - the avoidance of a possible assessment to corporation tax.
> 2. HMRC give the following as examples of **factors** which need to be considered:
> - the overall commercial objective, excluding beneficial tax reasons;
> - whether this objective is one which the parties involved might ordinarily be expected to have, and which is genuinely being sought;
> - whether the objective is being fulfilled in a straightforward way; or
> - whether additional complex or costly steps have been introduced, which were only necessary due to the tax advantage being obtained.

s 184D TCGA 1992

CG 47026

Qualifying change of ownership

A qualifying change of ownership **occurs** where:
- a company joins a group;
- a company leaves a group; or
- a company becomes subject to different control.

67910
s 184C TCGA 1992

> MEMO POINTS   1. For this purpose a **group** is a chargeable gains group (¶65415).
> 2. A **change of control** occurs when:
> - a person has control who did not previously have control;
> - a person who previously had control alone has control with other persons; or
> - a person ceases to have control.
> **No change of control** arises:
> - on a company reconstruction, where a direct 75% subsidiary becomes an indirect 75% subsidiary; or
> - where a group acquires a new holding company but there is no change to the ultimate shareholders.

s 184C(5)
TCGA 1992

CG 47023   3. HMRC state that they would not normally consider the incorporation of a company, or the acquisition from a company formation agent of a **newly formed company**, as amounting to a change of control.

Pre-change asset

67915
ss 184A, 184E
TCGA 1992

An asset which is transferred intra-group **otherwise than at no gain/no loss**, after the qualifying change in ownership, is not a pre-change asset.

A pre-change asset is otherwise **defined** as one which is held by the company before a qualifying change in ownership occurs.

A pre-change asset **also includes**:
a. a new asset which derives its value from a pre-change asset, for example:
– assets have been divided or merged;
– assets have changed their nature; or
– rights or interests over assets have been created or extinguished; and
b. a replacement holding of shares of securities, following a company reorganisation or reduction of share capital.

CG 47033B   In certain situations the pre-change asset rules also apply where the following **deferral and rollover reliefs** have been claimed, so that the gain or loss is not recognised immediately on disposal. In such a case the gain or loss that would otherwise have arisen on the disposal of a pre-change asset is tracked through to a subsequent event where that gain or loss is wholly or partly recognised:
– a demerger of part or all of a company's business to another company in return for an issue of shares to the shareholder (¶79050);
– the transfer of a non-UK trade (carried on by a UK company) to a non-UK company in exchange for shares;
– transfers of a trade carried on in the UK to another company resident in a different EU member state (¶61205);
– transfers of assets to a Societas Europaea (¶93195);
– the rollover of a gain on an asset used in a trade (¶30940); and
– the postponement of a charge on a deemed disposal on the migration of a company (¶91440).

Shares and securities

67920
s 184F TCGA 1992

There are also specific rules for **pooled** assets, so that these are split into separate pools before and after the change in ownership.

Shares which are disposed of after the qualifying change in ownership are **matched** in the following order:
a. with shares acquired after the change;
b. with the pre-change shares; and then
c. in accordance with the normal matching rules (¶32195).

⌐MEMO POINTS¬ For this purpose **shares** include all securities, excluding relevant securities (¶32050).

Consequences

67925
s 184A TCGA 1992

A loss arising on the disposal of a pre-change asset on or after 21 March 2007 can only be set against gains arising on pre-change assets. This prevents a company from utilising the loss against a gain on the disposal of shares in a subsidiary, where the value of the shares has increased as a result of the value of assets acquired after the change in ownership.

The rules apply irrespective of whether the **qualifying loss arose** before or after the change in ownership.

⌐EXAMPLE¬ A stand-alone property owning company, A Ltd, has sustained capital losses. It owns two properties.
A Ltd issues ordinary shares to a third party, with a nominal value of 30% of A Ltd.

The remaining shareholders, owning 70% of A Ltd, sell their shares to B Ltd's group. As B Ltd does not own 75% of A Ltd, A Ltd does not join B Ltd's chargeable gains group. B Ltd intends to transfer all of its assets that have not yet risen in value, but which it expects to rise in value, to A Ltd in the expectation that any resulting chargeable gains could be covered by purchased losses. A Ltd has neither left nor joined a chargeable gains group but it has become subject to different control, so there has been a qualifying change of ownership. A Ltd has accrued losses on pre-change assets and the change of ownership has occurred in connection with arrangements, the main purpose of which is to secure a tax advantage for the B group.

The losses of A Ltd cannot be deducted from any gains arising to the company, except those accruing to A Ltd on a disposal of pre-change assets. If the properties owned by A Ltd at the time of the change of ownership are then sold, giving rise to a chargeable gain, this gain can be covered by the losses.

2. General restrictions on pre-entry losses

In addition to the loss-buying rules, there are also further restrictions on the offset of capital losses which apply where there is **no tax avoidance motive**, such as on a merger or takeover. Broadly, these rules prevent the use of a loss, which has accrued before a company joins a group, against chargeable gains arising after joining the group. So the pre-entry losses are ringfenced.

67955
Sch 7A TCGA 1992

However, for pre-entry losses which are to be set off on or after 19 July 2011, the rules have been significantly simplified.

a. Rules up to 18 July 2011

Scope

The **situations** which lead to a restriction on the set-off of losses (in relation to a pre-entry asset) are as follows:
– a company brings a realised loss (i.e. from a disposal which has already occurred) into a relevant group which is unrelieved;
– a company brings an asset into a relevant group and there is a loss on a subsequent disposal of the asset by any group company;
– a non-resident group member becomes resident in the UK and subsequently there is a loss on a disposal, by any group company, of an asset which the non-resident company owned at the time that it became resident; or
– a non-resident group member introduces an asset into a UK permanent establishment other than immediately upon acquisition of the asset and subsequently there is a loss on a disposal of that asset by any group company.

67975

However, where a **subgroup** of two or more companies (which were previously members of another 75% CG group) join a new group at the same time, there is no restriction on the offset of losses against assets held by that subgroup at the date of joining.

Sch 7A para 11
TCGA 1992

> MEMO POINTS 1. A pre-entry asset which is **disposed of outside the group** and then reacquired, ceases to be a pre-entry asset.
> 2. Where a pre-entry loss arises on an **appropriation of an asset to trading stock**, it is not possible to make an election for that loss to be taken into account in computing the trading profit. This prevents the conversion of a capital loss into a trading deduction, thereby avoiding the capital loss rules.
> 3. Where **qualifying corporate bonds** are issued on a reorganisation, so that a pre-entry asset is exchanged for a QCB, these will be subject to the pre-entry loss rules (¶67990).
> 4. Where an **asset derives its value** from a pre-entry asset (for example, a lessee acquires the freehold reversion), the second asset is also subject to the pre-entry loss restrictions.

Sch 7A para 10
TCGA 1992

Relevant group

The relevant group is the group into which the company brings the pre-entry loss or the asset on which the loss subsequently arose.

67980
CG 47910–47929

Most of the time it will be obvious which group is affected by the pre-entry loss rules.

However, a company may:

- move into and out of different groups, carrying forward a realised capital loss; or
- bring into different groups at different times an asset which is later disposed of at a loss.

Where there is **more than one group** which would be a relevant group in relation to that company, it is necessary to establish the particular group or groups where the loss set-off restrictions might apply. Similarly, to **stop companies trying to manipulate the rules**, there must be some provision for different groups being created which are under common control.

This means that there are five categories of relevant group:

Category	Relevant group	Detail
1 Company brings a realised loss into a group	Group which is joined by company	The company was not a member of a group at the time of making a loss Where the company has joined more than one company since making the loss, the relevant group is the latest one to be joined
2 Company has not brought a realised loss into any group	Group of which company was a member of at time of disposal	Category **1** cannot apply because company was a member of a group at the time of the asset disposal, or has not joined a new group Where company is not a member of a group at time of disposal, the relevant group is the most recent group of which the company was a member
3 There is a group into which a company has brought a realised loss, but the company was a member of another group in the same accounting period	Both groups are relevant groups	Pre-entry rules apply in relation to both groups (it is possible to have more than two groups if the company has changed groups more than once in the same accounting period, especially if the loss was realised in the second group and the company then joins a third group) For example, if A Ltd has a calendar-year accounting period and joins Group B on 1 February while holding an asset, which is disposed of on 30 June, then A Ltd leaves Group B and joins Group C, the following occurs: – Group C is the category **1** group which A Ltd joins with a realised loss; and – A Ltd was also a member of Group B in the same accounting period
4 Any group where either: – the company realising the loss is the principal company, or controls the principal company; or – the principal company is any company within any of the groups in categories **1** to **3**, or under control of such a company	All affected groups are relevant groups	This is intended to counter artificial avoidance devices, which exploit the 75% beneficial ownership requirement (which can be sidestepped by the subsidiary issuing deferred shares or similar) For example, within the D Group there is E Ltd, which holds an asset with an unrealised gain E Ltd leaves the D Group and joins the F Group, which is controlled by the D Group Another company, X Ltd, which has a realised loss, leaves the Y Group and joins the F Group The F Group then disposes of E Ltd and X Ltd to the D Group E Ltd transfers the asset at no gain/no loss to X Ltd, which sells it and tries to set its loss against the resulting gain However, the D Group is a relevant group, because it is the most recent group into which X Ltd has brought its loss F Group is also a relevant group, because it has been controlled by D Group

Category	Relevant group	Detail
5 If there is a relevant group under categories **1**, **2**, or **3**, any other group which includes, or has included, either: – the principal company of the first group; or – a company which has had that principal company under its control	All affected groups are relevant companies	This would apply where a company is not an effective 51% subsidiary of the principal company of a group For example, G Ltd, which holds Asset Y (which has an unrealised loss), leaves the H group and joins the A group with principal company A Ltd Within the A Group there is B Ltd, which holds Asset Z, which has an unrealised gain A Ltd artificially degroups G Ltd and B Ltd into a separate capital gains group, Group C, which has C Ltd as its principal company C Ltd is controlled by A Ltd Within the C Group both assets are disposed of The pre-entry loss rules apply to both A Group (which is a category **2** group) and C Group, which is controlled by A Group

Unrealised losses

When an asset owned at the relevant date is subsequently disposed of and this results in a capital loss, the proportion of the loss which relates to the period before the relevant date is treated as an unrealised loss. **67985**

For this purpose the **relevant date** is usually the date of joining the group, except where the joining company was non-UK-resident or the asset was outside the scope of UK corporation tax, in which case it is the earlier of:
– the time when the company becomes UK-resident; and
– when the asset comes within the scope of UK corporation tax.

In calculating this proportion there is a **choice** between:
– time-apportioning the loss actually realised on disposal subsequent to the relevant date; and
– electing for a market value treatment at the relevant date.

Time apportionment is calculated by applying the following formula to each item of expenditure: **67990**

$$A \times \frac{B}{C} \times \frac{D}{E}$$

where:
– A is the total capital loss;
– B is the allowable item of expenditure;
– C is the total allowable expenditure;
– D is the period from the date of the asset's acquisition (or 1 April 1982, if later) to the relevant date; and
– E is the period from the date of the asset's acquisition (or 1 April 1982, if later) to the date of disposal.

MEMO POINTS 1. Where the **expenditure is not just incurred at acquisition**, the date that the particular item of expenditure is incurred is substituted for the date of acquisition for D and E above.
2. Where an **asset was transferred** (on a no gain/no loss basis) **to the company before it joined** the relevant group, its period of ownership for the purposes of computing the pre-entry loss will run from the date that the original transferor company had acquired the asset. (If there have been several no gain/no loss transfers, it is necessary to look back to the date of the first acquisition that was not by way of an intra-group transfer.)
3. Where a pre-entry **asset**, standing at a loss, is **transferred intra-group after the company has joined** the relevant group, the pre-entry loss is still calculated by reference to the period of ownership of the company joining the group.
4. On a **share reorganisation** any allowable expenditure incurred for the new holding of shares (e.g. on a rights issue) is treated as if it had been incurred when the original shares were acquired, for the purposes of the time apportionment rules only.

5. When **qualifying corporate bonds** are issued on a share exchange, the pre-entry loss is calculated up to the time that the QCBs are issued but deferred until they are disposed of. So for the time apportionment rules, the date of the exchange is substituted for the date of disposal in E above.

> [EXAMPLE] A Ltd joins the BCD group on 1 January 2011. A Ltd has an accounting period which ends on 30 September. At 1 October 2010 A Ltd had capital losses brought forward of £50,000. A Ltd makes the following disposals:
> – on 15 November 2010 Asset X, which gives rise to a capital loss of £10,000; and
> – on 31 March 2011 Asset Y, which gives rise to a capital loss of £15,000. It was acquired on 1 March 2000.
> The realised pre-entry losses are £60,000. (£50,000 + £10,000)
>
> | | | Number of months |
> |---|---|---|
> | Pre-entry period of ownership | 1 Mar 2000 to 1 Jan 2011 | 130 |
> | Total period of ownership | 1 Mar 2000 to 31 Mar 2011 | 133 |
>
> The unrealised pre-entry loss is therefore £14,662. (£15,000 × 130/133)

67995   **Market value election**   Where an election for the market value method is made, the pre-entry proportion is treated as being the **lower of**:
– the loss which would have accrued if the company had disposed of the asset for its market value at the relevant date; and
– the allowable loss which actually accrued on the disposal of the asset.

The election **must be made** within 2 years of the end of the accounting period in which the loss is actually realised, although HMRC do have discretion to accept a late election.

> [EXAMPLE] Taking the facts of the example in ¶67990, above, Asset Y was purchased for £70,000 on 1 March 2000 and sold for £55,000. Its market value on 1 January 2011 was £58,000.
> If an election is made, the pre-entry loss is the lower of:
> – the loss using the market value of £58,000 i.e. £12,000 (£58,000 – £70,000); and
> – the actual loss of £15,000.
> As the intention should be to reduce the pre-entry loss as much as possible, the election is beneficial and should be made.
> So A Ltd's total pre-entry losses are £72,000. (£12,000 + £50,000 + £10,000)
> The balance of £3,000 can be offset without restriction. (£15,000 – £12,000)

Shares

68000
CG 47644

To determine the total capital loss, the usual pooling rules (¶32195) apply to shares, with the following modifications.

If an asset **pool has at any time contained a pre-entry asset**, the pool is treated as including a part referable to those assets until they have all been disposed of.

A disposal is **matched first** with any shares acquired after the company joined the group.

Where the number of **shares disposed of exceeds the post-joining acquisitions**, a pre-entry asset has also been disposed of.

For **time apportionment** the resulting pre-entry loss must be computed broadly on a first in, first out basis, using the following identification rules (which apply in this **order**):
a. an asset with an earlier acquisition date is disposed of before an asset with a later acquisition date (if there is more than one acquisition date for the asset, the earliest such date is used, although options are ignored);
b. assets brought into the group at an earlier time are disposed of before assets brought into the group at a later time;
c. for a realised loss (i.e. the asset was disposed of before the company joined its current group), the above rules apply with reference to the group of which the company was a member at the time of the disposal, or of which it had most recently been a member; and
d. a company is treated as disposing of assets in the order in which it acquired them.

CG 47742   It is possible to make a **market value election** which assumes that all of the shares were disposed of at the relevant time (i.e. a notional disposal when the pre-entry assets are brought into the group); the loss is then apportioned based on the number of shares.

The **notional disposal** is a disposal of the assets which immediately before the relevant time:
– formed part of a pool which consisted of or included assets falling to be treated for time apportionment purposes as pre-entry assets disposed of on the real disposal; and
– were comprised in a pooled asset held immediately after that time by a member of the relevant group.

EXAMPLE

1. A Ltd's share pool contains 500 shares acquired before it joined B Ltd's group and 400 shares acquired afterwards.
A Ltd subsequently disposes of 700 shares out of the pool.
The more recently acquired shares are treated as disposed of first.
This leaves 300 shares which relate to the pre-entry acquisition.
For the purposes of time apportionment these 300 shares are treated as a notionally separate asset which has never been pooled.
The remaining share pool now contains 200 pre-entry shares.

2. C Ltd joins the D group on 1 March 2008 holding 100 shares in X Ltd. In 2011 C Ltd sells 30 shares in X Ltd and realises a loss with a pre-entry proportion. C Ltd elects to compute the pre-entry loss by reference to market value at the relevant time.
For the purposes of the market value calculation the 100 shares are treated as disposed of on 1 March 2008 for their market value at that date.
Then 30/100 of this loss is taken to be the pre-entry loss.

3. On 1 January 2000 E Ltd joins the F group whilst owning 10 of the 100 issued shares in Y Ltd, which E Ltd acquired in 1997.
On 1 January 2005 G Ltd also joins the F group holding 60 shares in Y Ltd, which G Ltd acquired in 1998.
In 2006 G Ltd transfers its 60 shares in Y Ltd to E Ltd at no gain/no loss.
In 2010 E Ltd sells 30 shares in Y Ltd and realises a loss with a pre-entry proportion.
The time apportionment rules identify the 30 shares disposed of in 2010 with the 10 shares acquired by E Ltd in 1997 and with 20 of the 60 shares acquired by G Ltd in 1998 (using a first in, first out basis).
If E Ltd makes an election for the pre-entry loss to be computed by reference to the market value of the shares at the relevant time, the following steps should be taken:
– compute the loss on a market value disposal of the 10 shares brought into the group by E Ltd on 1 January 2000;
– compute the market value pre-entry loss on the other 20 shares brought into the group by G Ltd on 1 January 2005, taking 20/60 of the loss on a notional disposal of all 60 shares originally held by G Ltd; and
– add the loss on these 20 shares to the loss on the market value disposal of the 10 shares.
The resulting total is the pre-entry loss on the disposal of the 30 shares.

More then one relevant group

The capital loss rules apply separately to each relevant group (¶67980) when determining whether there is a pre-entry loss, and also for the purpose of quantifying it. **68005**

Where the loss was **realised before the company joined** a particular group, it is the whole loss which is the pre-entry loss.

If there is a loss on an asset which is a **pre-entry asset in relation to more than one** of the relevant groups, the pre-entry proportion of the loss is the largest calculated in relation to any of those groups.

EXAMPLE   A Ltd acquired Asset X on 1 March 2000. Exactly 3 years later A Ltd joined the B Group. On 1 January 2005 a member of the B Group transferred Asset Y to A Ltd at no gain/no loss. On 1 March 2007 A Ltd left the B group and joined the D group. On 1 March 2011 A Ltd sold both assets, realising a loss of £150,000 in relation to Asset X and a gain of £70,000 in relation to Asset Y. The B group and the D group are both relevant groups.
For the B Group the periods of ownership in respect of Asset X are as follows:

		Number of months
Pre-entry period of ownership	1 Mar 2000 to 1 Mar 2003	36
Total period of ownership	1 Mar 2000 to 1 Mar 2011	132

The unrealised pre-entry loss is therefore £40,909. (£150,000 × 36/132)

For the D Group the periods of ownership are as follows:

		Number of months
Pre-entry period of ownership	1 Mar 2000 to 1 Mar 2007	84
Total period of ownership	1 Mar 2000 to 1 Mar 2011	132

The unrealised pre-entry loss is therefore £95,455. (£150,000 × 84/132)
The largest pre-entry loss is taken.
So the loss which can be deducted from the chargeable gain is £54,545. (£150,000 − £95,455)

Relieving a pre-entry loss

68010 A pre-entry loss can only be set off against a gain arising from either:

a. a disposal made before the company joined the group (i.e. a gain arising in the same accounting period as the loss but before the date of joining);

b. a disposal of an asset acquired after joining the group if the asset was:
– acquired from outside the group; and
– used for the purposes of a trade carried on by the company both at the time of joining the group and when the disposal occurred; or

c. gains realised after joining the group in respect of assets brought into the group at the same time as the loss.

MEMO POINTS For **non-resident companies** the relevant date (¶67985) should be substituted for the date of joining in **a.**, **b.** and **c.**, above.

b. Rules from 19 July 2011

68030
Sch 7A FA 2011;
CG 47400+

The following rules for the deduction of a pre-entry capital loss apply when a company deducts a loss from a gain on or after 19 July 2011. This is subject to the loss-buying rules of ¶67895, above.

Latent losses that are not realised until after the company joins the group (i.e. a loss-making asset is not disposed of until the company is a member of the group) are no longer restricted in their use.

Therefore restrictions only apply to the set-off of losses that have been realised before a company joins a group.

Transitional rules

68035
Sch 11 para 12
FA 2011

The new rules apply to the set-off of accrued losses in **accounting periods** that end on or after 19 July 2011, irrespective of:
– whether the loss accrued before 19 July 2011; and
– the date that the company joined the group.

Where a company had **previously joined a group** with an asset standing at a loss, and then a loss on the asset accrued before 19 July 2011, that remains a restricted loss for the purposes of these rules.

Scope

68040 Where a company with unused accrued capital losses (i.e. a loss company) becomes a member of a group of companies, relief for those losses is restricted so that they can only be deducted from certain types of gains (¶68055).

MEMO POINTS 1. Where a **reorganisation** takes place prior to a company joining a group and **qualifying corporate bonds** are issued, any loss which is crystallised on the disposal of the QCBs will be a pre-entry loss (¶68060).

Sch 7A para 1(6)
TCGA 1992

2. On a **company takeover**, where the principal company of one group becomes a member of another group and the following exception does not apply, the members of the first group are treated as joining a new group for the purposes of these rules and therefore any accrued losses

will be restricted. The **exception** is the insertion of a new principal company at the top of the group and all of the following conditions apply, where the principal company:
– has the same shareholders as the former one;
– was not previously a member of a group; and
– has only assets which consist entirely, or almost entirely, of the issued share capital of the former principal company, immediately after the change.

3. Where a pre-entry loss arises on an **appropriation of an asset to trading stock**, it is not possible to make an election for that loss to be taken into account in computing the trading profit in respect of the asset. This prevents the conversion of a capital loss into a trading deduction, thereby avoiding the capital loss rules.

Sch 7A para 10 TCGA 1992

> EXAMPLE A Ltd appropriates an asset with an unrealised capital loss of £300,000 to trading stock, of which £200,000 is a pre-entry loss.
> A Ltd can only make an election (¶11710) in respect of the remaining £100,000 so that the pre-entry loss stays in the capital loss regime.

Changing group on reconstruction A company may leave one group and join another on a disposal of shares or securities which is a no gain/no loss disposal, usually as a result of a reconstruction e.g. where the loss company itself is transferred, or its parent company etc is transferred. This will not lead to a restriction of losses that accrued before the change.

68045
Sch 7A para 12 TCGA 1992

> EXAMPLE B Ltd is the principal company of a group, which is a chain of two 100%-owned subsidiaries, C Ltd and D Ltd (owned by C Ltd).
> In a scheme of reconstruction B Ltd transfers its shares in C Ltd at no gain/no loss to X Ltd.
> Accordingly, C Ltd and D Ltd leave the B group and join the X group.
> Any losses that had accrued to either C Ltd or D Ltd before they joined the X group will not be restricted.

Identifying the pre-entry loss

Where both **restricted and unrestricted** losses are available it may be necessary to identify which losses are deducted from the total chargeable gains of the accounting period and to determine which type of losses are carried forward.

68050
Sch 7A para 6 TCGA 1992

The **order** of set-off is as follows:
a. any restricted losses accruing in the period, to the extent that they are deductible;
b. any restricted losses brought forward to the accounting period, to the extent that they are deductible; and
c. any unrestricted losses.

> MEMO POINTS Where a company has **joined more than one group** there may be several restrictions involved. In this case the company may specify the deduction of any particular restricted loss from any particular gain in an election, which must be made 2 years from the end of the accounting period in which the gain accrued. If no election is made, the following priority rules apply:
> – earlier accrued losses are set off before later accrued losses; and
> – losses are set off against earlier gains in priority to later gains.

Setting off a pre-entry loss

The detailed provisions depend on whether a single company or multiple companies have joined a group.

68055

Single company Restricted losses may be set against **gains** that:
a. accrued before the company with restricted losses became a member of the group;
b. accrue after joining the group, on disposals of assets that were owned by the company with restricted losses when it joined; and
c. accrue on disposals of assets acquired from outside the group and are used for the purposes of the same trade or business that was carried on by the loss company at the time it became a member of the group. Another group company can acquire the loss company's business and use the asset for that business. However, the asset must be used only for the

68060
Sch 7A para 7 TCGA 1992

purposes of that trade or business from the time of its acquisition to its disposal. Where there is a major change in the nature of the trade, the losses cannot be deducted.

A company may be affected by a loss restriction even if it is **no longer a member of any group** e.g. where it joins and then leaves a group without becoming a member of any other group.

<table>
<tr><td>Sch 7A para 8
TCGA 1992</td><td>MEMO POINTS 1. Restricted losses may not be set against the gains arising on **assets used in a trade** where either of the following applies:
– within the 3-year period before or after the company with restricted losses becomes a member of the group, there is a major change in the nature or conduct of the trade or business that was carried on by the company when it joined the group; or
– when the company with restricted losses joined the group, the scale of its trading or business activity had become small or negligible and there followed a considerable revival.
2. For this purpose a **major change in the nature or conduct of a trade** or business includes:
– a major change in the type of property dealt in, or the services or facilities provided;
– a major change in customers, markets or outlets; or
– in the case of an investment business, a major change in the nature of the investments held.
A major change may result from a gradual process beginning outside the 3-year period. For further details see ¶60260.</td></tr>
<tr><td>Sch 7A para 7(6)
TCGA 1992</td><td>3. A restricted loss can be set off against a gain arising on the disposal of **qualifying corporate bonds** (QCBs), if the QCBs were acquired subsequent to the date of joining the group, as a result of a reorganisation where assets held at the time of joining are exchanged for the QCBs. HMRC will accept any reasonable method of apportionment which means that only gains relating to the pre-entry assets are set off by the restricted loss.</td></tr>
</table>

68070
Sch 7A para 7
TCGA 1992

More than one company Where two or more companies leave one group and **join another group at the same time**, an accrued loss brought into the new group by one of the companies can be deducted from a gain accruing to that company on the disposal of an asset held by another of those companies immediately before it joined the new group.

Similarly, an accrued loss brought into the new group by one of the companies can be set against a gain accruing to that company on the disposal of an asset that was acquired by another of those companies (from a third party) for use in the trade or business of the company with losses.

> EXAMPLE In 2011 A Ltd realises a capital loss. A Ltd has a subsidiary, B Ltd, which owns Asset X.
> In 2012 A Ltd is acquired by C Ltd.
> In 2013 B Ltd sells Asset X and a gain results. A Ltd and B Ltd elect to reallocate the gain to A Ltd (¶67285).
> The rules treat A Ltd as holding Asset X immediately before it joined the C Group. Therefore A Ltd can deduct the restricted loss from the gain.

Pooled assets

68075
Sch 7A para 7(5)
TCGA 1992

Where pooled assets are disposed of after a company joins a group, any **resulting gain** must be apportioned in order to ascertain the amount against which a pre-entry loss can be offset. The offset is restricted to the extent of the proportion of the gain attributable to assets held at the time that the company joined the group.

HMRC will accept any reasonable **method of apportionment**.

B. Pre-entry gains

68105
s 184B TCGA 1992

There are similar provisions to the loss-buying rules (¶67895) for pre-entry gains, which apply where a tax advantage arises on or after 5 December 2005, even if the loss, which is to be set against the gain, arose before this date.

Scope

The pre-entry gains rules apply where all of the following are satisfied and the tax advantage involves the deduction of a loss from a pre-change asset gain when calculating the PCTCT of any company:

68110
ss 184B – 184F
TCGA 1992

Condition	Detail	¶¶
Qualifying change in ownership	A qualifying change of ownership occurs where: – a company joins a group; – a company leaves a group; or – a company becomes subject to different control	¶67910
The change of ownership arises in connection with arrangements, the main or one of the main purposes of which is to secure a tax advantage	Arrangement includes any agreement, understanding, scheme, transaction or series of transactions, whether or not legally enforceable The tax advantage may arise to any company	¶67905
A chargeable gain accrues (whether before or after the change in ownership) to the company on the disposal of a pre-change asset	An asset which is transferred intra-group otherwise than at no gain/no loss after the qualifying change in ownership is not a pre-change asset A pre-change asset is otherwise defined as one which is held by the company before a qualifying change in ownership occurs	¶67915

Implications

Any gains arising on assets owned by a company at the time of its change of ownership will only be capable of being offset by capital losses deriving from the assets it held before the change.

68115

MEMO POINTS Between **5 December 2005 and 21 March 2007** a loss on an asset disposed of by the company which changed ownership could be set off, provided that the asset giving rise to the gain was either:
– disposed of before the change of ownership; or
– owned by the company before the change of ownership and disposed of subsequently.

EXAMPLE The ABC group owns all of the share capital of X Ltd that holds pre-April 2002 intellectual property (¶28240).
If X Ltd is sold the gain on the shares would be covered by the substantial shareholding exemption. Y Ltd wants to buy the intellectual property, so that it will qualify for the amortisation under the intangibles regime (being acquired after April 2002).
The ABC group sells X Ltd to F Ltd, which has substantial capital losses available. The share sale is exempt.
F Ltd then arranges for the sale of intellectual property out of X Ltd to Y Ltd. F Ltd hopes to use its capital loss to set off the resulting gain.
F Ltd only became involved in the scheme because it has surplus capital losses. There has been a qualifying change of ownership of X Ltd and X Ltd has disposed of a pre-change asset – that is, the intellectual property. So the gain arising on the sale of intellectual property cannot be set off by F Ltd's loss.

CHAPTER 4

Special situations

69000   In addition to the rules on group loss relief and the capital gains regime for groups of companies, there are several other topic areas where there are specific rules for groups.

SECTION 1

Substantial shareholding exemption

69050   An exemption applies to the disposal by a company of a substantial shareholding (¶32090), known as the SSE. This means that no chargeable gain or allowable loss arises. As the exemption is automatic, no claim is required.

There are particular rules which apply when a group is using the SSE. For this purpose group means a 75% CG group (¶65415), **except** that subsidiaries need only be 51% owned.

For the interaction of the SSE and degrouping charge when a company leaves a group see ¶67540.

Comment These provisions allow a group to transfer shares to a newly incorporated company and then dispose of the shares in the new company, without losing the benefit of SSE.

Size of the shareholding

A substantial shareholding is **defined** as a holding of not less than 10% of the ordinary share capital of a company, which carries an **entitlement** to not less than 10% of both the:
– profits available for distribution to its equity holders; and
– assets on a winding up available to its equity holders.

69055
Sch 7AC para 9
TCGA 1992

In determining whether a company has a substantial shareholding in a target company, any shares or interests in shares **held by other 51% group members** (¶65505) in the target company are aggregated. For this purpose, companies may be located anywhere in the world (assuming they have the equivalent to ordinary share capital – note that some Limited Liability Companies in the USA have no share capital, so they cannot be part of such a group).

The investing company is deemed to have the same entitlement to any rights enjoyed, by virtue of the shares, as the group member to which the shares actually belong.

Period of ownership

The investing company must have held a substantial shareholding (¶32100) in the target company for a continuous 12-month period, beginning not more than 2 years prior to the disposal.

69060
Sch 7AC para 10
TCGA 1992

Where shares held by the company were **previously transferred** to it at **no gain/no loss**, the transferor's period of ownership is included.

Qualifying activity

The **investing company** must be carrying on trading activities throughout the continuous 12-month period (and immediately after the date of disposal); and its activities cannot, to a substantial extent (¶32125), include non-trading activities.

69065
Sch 7AC para 18(4)
TCGA 1992

In determining whether this condition has been met, the activities of a **fellow group company** can be taken into account.

For **joint ventures** see ¶32115+.

SECTION 2

Intangible fixed assets

There are particular rules in respect of intangible fixed assets which affect groups.

69115

> MEMO POINTS 1. For details of the **intangibles regime** generally see ¶28135.
> 2. For the **group relief** of non-trading debits on intangible assets see ¶66080.

---

1. Definition of group

A group, for the purposes of these rules, means a principal company and its 75% subsidiaries. A subsidiary must also be an effective 51% subsidiary of the principal company.

69145
ss 765, 766, 771,
772 CTA 2009

A company can only be a member of one group at any one time.

> MEMO POINTS 1. An **effective 51% subsidiary** is one in which the principal company holds the rights to more than 50% of:
> – profits available to equity holders on a distribution; and
> – assets available to equity holders on a winding up.
> For further details see ¶65435.

Determining the relevant group

69150
s 768 CTA 2009

A 75% **subsidiary is prohibited from being a principal company**, unless it cannot be in the same capital gains group as its parent because it is not an effective 51% subsidiary of the parent's principal company.

For details of how to ascertain which group a particular subsidiary is in see ¶65450.

---

2. Intra-group transfers

69180
ss 775, 776
CTA 2009

Even though group members are related parties, the transfer of intangible fixed assets from one group company to another is tax-neutral (which effectively is the same as taking place on a no gain/no loss basis for capital gains purposes), provided that the assets are within the scope of the intangibles regime (¶28135).

CIRD 40250

> ⌐MEMO POINTS¬ 1. If a group member **subsequently leaves the group**, while still holding the intangible asset, there may be a degrouping charge (¶69220).
> 2. Note that there must actually be an asset **transfer** for these rules to apply. So the grant of a licence to exploit a patent, for example, is not a transfer.
> 3. Assets **not within the scope of the intangibles regime**, primarily due to the date of acquisition, will probably qualify for a no gain/no loss transfer under the capital gains code (¶67080).
> 4. **Non-resident companies** may be members of a group but the asset will not be within the scope of the intangibles regime unless it is held for the purposes of a trade carried on in the UK through a UK permanent establishment (¶92140) by the non-resident group member. Where a tax-neutral transfer is not available, the transfer pricing rules (¶70000) should be considered.

Exclusions

69185
s 775(4)(a), (b)
CTA 2009

The tax-neutral treatment of an intra-group transfer of intangible fixed assets does not apply where:
– the transferor or the transferee is a friendly society; or
– the transferee is a dual resident investing company (¶91480).

Consequences

69190

The **transfer is treated** as though it involves neither a disposal nor an acquisition.

Additionally, the **transferee** is treated as the owner of the asset throughout, inheriting the transferor's tax history, including the tax cost (which is basically the cost recognised for accounting purposes less any reinvestment relief (¶28540)) and all debits and credits already accounted for. So the transferee stands in the shoes of the transferor.

---

3. Leaving a group

69220
s 780 CTA 2009;
CIRD 40510

A degrouping charge **will arise** when a company leaves a group while still holding an intangible fixed asset which had been transferred to it (from another group member) within the previous 6 years.

Comment The aim of the degrouping charge is to ensure that the increase in value of an asset during its period of ownership is crystallised even if the asset leaves the group within a company.

Scope

69225
s 788(3) CTA 2009

This rule also operates where:
– an **associated company** of the departing company holds the asset and leaves the group with the departing company, so it is not possible to avoid the degrouping charge merely by transferring the asset to another group member which also leaves the group (for this purpose, a company is associated with another when both are in a 75% group relationship); or
s 788(2) CTA 2009
– an asset **derives** its value from another asset which was transferred.

The charge **accrues to** the departing company, unless there is an election to reallocate it to another group member (¶69260) or roll it over (¶69255).

The charge itself may be a debit or a credit.

Comment Unlike the capital gains rules for tangible fixed assets, no degrouping charge will arise when an asset leaves the group against which a credit has been rolled over.

Exclusions

A degrouping charge does **not arise** in the following situations:

69230
ss 782 – 789
CTA 2009

Situation	Detail
Company ungrouped	As a result of an exempt distribution (¶79120) Where there is a chargeable payment (¶79160) within 5 years, the degrouping charge will be reinstated Any necessary adjustments can be made within 3 years of the date of the chargeable payment
	A company ceases to be in a group because another company (which HMRC consider must be its only subsidiary) ceases to exist – that is, on its actual dissolution This also applies where all of a company's subsidiaries cease to exist simultaneously
Mergers (¶79825)	A commercial merger of a UK-resident company with a company resident in another member state of the EU, including a Societas Europaea
	A demerger taking place (¶79050)
Two companies leave the group together	See ¶69235+

Two associated companies leaving together No degrouping charge arises where the transferor and transferee company **form a subgroup** and leave the original group together. This exception only applies where the companies also formed a subgroup at the time when the asset was originally transferred. Where a company has left a group on or after 19 July 2011 (or 1 April 2011, where an appropriate election (¶67425) has been made), no degrouping charge arises where the transferor and transferee are part of the same subgroup at all times from when the asset is transferred until immediately after they leave the original group.

69235
s 783 CTA 2009

However, if the **transferee company subsequently leaves** the second group within 6 years of the original intra-group transfer and there is a relevant connection between the first group and the second group, a degrouping charge will be imposed at that time. For this purpose, the asset is deemed to have been transferred when both companies were members of the second group, so creating a degrouping adjustment at the time that the company leaves the second group.

MEMO POINTS 1. Being **part of the same subgroup** means that either:
– both companies are 75% subsidiaries and 51% effective subsidiaries of another company; or
– one is such a subsidiary of the other.
2. A **relevant connection** exists where, when the transferee leaves the second group, the parent company of the second group is under the control of:
– the principal company of the first group;
– any person who controlled the first group, or has done so since the transferee ceased to be a member;
– any persons who controlled the parent company of the parent company of the first group, where that company has ceased to exist; or
– any person who controls any person above which is a company.

s 784 CTA 2009

Parent company joins another group Where two groups join together, some companies in the target group **may not be effective 51% subsidiaries** of the new principal company (¶65435).

69240
s 785 CTA 2009

No degrouping charge applies in this situation, provided that the company is a 75% subsidiary and also an effective 51% subsidiary of at least one member of the new group. Where this condition is broken within 6 years of the transfer of the asset and the same company, or another group member, holds the asset, a degrouping charge will arise.

Calculation

69245 The degrouping charge is calculated by **deeming the asset** to have been disposed of and reacquired for its market value **immediately after** the intra-group transfer took place.

The **tax written down value** going forward is therefore market value.

The charge is treated as **arising** immediately before the company left the group.

So the amount of the charge will be based on circumstances existing when the asset was transferred intra-group but will be chargeable to tax in the accounting period when the company leaves the group.

s 781 CTA 2009 The **charge to tax** depends on whether the use made of the intangible asset by the transferee is a:
– trading purpose or property business (¶28630); or
– non-trading purpose (¶28650).

If the transferee has ceased to trade, the asset will be treated as a non-trading item.

69250 In the **accounting period of departure** the degrouping charge must be aggregated with the adjustments required to the credits and debits occurring in the intervening accounting periods – that is, between the date of the intra-group transfer and the accounting period in which the company leaves the group (as the tax written down value on the intra-group transfer is now deemed to be market value).

> EXAMPLE
> 1. Asset X has a 10-year life and is acquired by A Ltd for £10,000 in Year 4. Asset X is amortised at a rate of £1,000 per year. By the end of Year 6 the total amortisation is £3,000. (3 x £1,000)
> At the beginning of Year 7 Asset X is transferred to B Ltd, a group company, for its book value of £7,000. Its market value at this date is £9,000. In Years 7 and 8 B Ltd amortises the asset at £1,000 per year.
> B Ltd leaves A Ltd's group at the end of Year 8.
> B Ltd is deemed to have sold and reacquired the asset for £9,000 at the time of the asset transfer, leading to a credit of £2,000. (£9,000 – £7,000)
> B Ltd's amortisation deduction for Year 7 is adjusted to reflect an acquisition cost of £9,000 rather than £7,000, so the revised amortisation charge is £1,286. ($\frac{9,000}{7,000} \times £1,000$)
>
> The increase in amortisation is therefore £286. (£1,286 – £1,000)
> This is netted off against the degrouping charge and the amount of £1,714 is brought into account in Year 8. (£2,000 – £286)
> The amortisation debit for Year 8 is £1,286.
> The tax written down value when B leaves the group is therefore £6,428.
> These adjustments are summarised below:
>
> | **Year 7** | £ |
> |---|---|
> | Tax written down value b/fwd | 7,000 |
> | Degrouping credit | 2,000 |
> | | 9,000 |
> | Amortisation | (1,286) |
>
> | **Year 8** | |
> |---|---|
> | Tax written down value b/fwd | 7,714 |
> | Amortisation | (1,286) |
> | Tax written down value c/fwd | 6,428 |
>
> 2. At the beginning of Year 1 C Ltd transfers its business as a going concern to D Ltd for its book value. As the market value of the business exceeds the book value by £20,000, this is the amount of internally generated goodwill. D Ltd leaves C Ltd's group at the end of Year 3.
> D Ltd is deemed to have sold and reacquired the asset for £20,000. This gives rise to a taxable credit of £20,000 (as C Ltd had no acquisition cost).
> Amortisation charges will depend on the estimated useful life of the goodwill. If this is assumed to be 10 years, amortisation of £2,000 per year will apply in Years 1 and 2.
> This is netted off against the degrouping charge and the amount of £16,000 is brought into account in Year 3. (£20,000 – £2,000 – £2,000)

> An amortisation debit of £2,000 is also given in Year 3, so that the TWDV of the asset when D Ltd leaves the group is £14,000. (£16,000 − £2,000)

Rollover

Where a degrouping charge arises, it is possible to roll it over into replacement expenditure (¶69295).

69255
s 791 CTA 2009

Reallocation

No reallocation is possible if the degrouping charge gives rise to a deductible **debit**.

69260
ss 792, 793
CTA 2009

Any **further adjustments** which result from the degrouping charge, such as changes to amortisation between the date of the asset transfer and the date of departure from the group, stay with the departing company and cannot be reallocated.

It is possible to reallocate a degrouping charge which is a **credit** where the companies are:
– in the same group immediately before the transferee left the group; and
– both within the charge to UK corporation tax i.e. resident in the UK or trading through a UK permanent establishment (¶92140).

A joint **election** must be made within 2 years of the end of the accounting period in which the transferee leaves the group.

The degrouping charge is treated as a non-trading credit of the recipient.

  ┌─────────────┐
  │ MEMO POINTS │ 1. Any **payment between the companies for the transfer** is ignored for tax
  └─────────────┘
purposes, provided that it does not exceed the amount reallocated and is made under a formal agreement.
2. In the event of the degrouping charge arising as a result of the **transferee leaving a second group** (¶69235), the company to which the charge is reallocated must be in that group immediately before the transferee leaves.

s 799 CTA 2009

Unpaid degrouping charge

Where a degrouping charge remains unpaid 6 months after the due date for payment, HMRC may **recover** the amount due **from**:
– the principal member of the group (at the date when the gain accrued); or
– any other company which had owned the asset and was a group member at any time up to 12 months before the company left the group.

69265
ss 795, 797
CTA 2009

HMRC will serve a notice **demanding payment** within 3 years from the date when the amount of the degrouping charge is determined. A 30-day payment period is given by the notice and the tax due is treated as a liability of that person. There is a right of appeal against the notice.

The person paying the liability has a legal right to recover the amount from the defaulting company.

  ┌─────────────┐
  │ MEMO POINTS │ 1. The **notice** must state the amount of:
  └─────────────┘
– the tax referable to the degrouping charge; and
– corporation tax which remains unpaid for the relevant accounting period (and the date when it became payable).
The **amount due** is the lesser of:
– the unpaid corporation tax assessed on the company for the accounting period in which the gain accrued; and
– the tax referable to the amount of degrouping charge.
2. **Interest** will be due on the amount shown on the notice if payment is not made within the 30-day period. The amount is treated as overdue corporation tax for this purpose.
3. If the company is **non-UK-resident**, recovery can also be made from a controlling director i.e. any person who is, or was within the period of 12 months up to the departure date, a controlling director of:
– that company, or
– another company which, within that 12-month period, had control of that company.
4. **Controlling director** is defined as a director who controls (¶75275) the company.

CIRD 40740

s 87A TMA 1970

4. Reinvestment relief

69295
s 777(1) CTA 2009

Taxable credits on the disposal of a chargeable intangible asset can be **deferred** by claiming reinvestment relief, which deducts an amount from the proceeds arising on the disposal of the old asset and also deducts the same amount from the company's expenditure on the replacement intangible asset(s). This reduces the subsequent deductible debits (both in respect of amortisation and eventual sale).

In relation to groups, reinvestment relief is **extended** where a disposal is made by one group member and expenditure on the replacement asset(s) is incurred by another.

Summary

69300

The following points apply in respect of groups:

Relief	¶¶
Normal reinvestment relief on intangible assets sold by one group member and acquired by another	¶69305
Reinvestment via an acquisition of a controlling interest in a company already holding chargeable intangible assets	¶69310
Can be used in connection with degrouping charges	¶69325
Reinvestment relief is also available where an election is made to reallocate the taxable credit on degrouping to another group member	¶69325
Capital gain on pre-April 2002 asset can also be reinvested where another group member reinvests in an intangible asset	¶28565

Normal reinvestment relief

69305
s 777(2) CTA 2009;
CIRD 20410

The relief is available where all of the **criteria** in the following table are met. The disposing company and reinvesting company do not need to be members of the group at the same time.

Area	Condition
Disposing company	Must be a member of the group at the time of realisation
Acquiring company	Must be a member of the group when incurring expenditure to acquire replacement asset
	Not a dual resident investing company (¶91480)
Replacement asset	Must be within the intangibles regime immediately after acquisition
	Must not be acquired by virtue of a tax-neutral transfer (¶69180) from another group member
Election	Must be made jointly by both companies

> EXAMPLE   The A Group comprises A Ltd, B Ltd and C Ltd. B Ltd sells an intangible asset and then leaves the group. A year later D Ltd joins the group and acquires a patent.
> Reinvestment relief can apply, even though B Ltd and D Ltd are not in the group at the same time.

Acquisition of company holding intangible fixed assets

69310
s 778 CTA 2009

Where expenditure is incurred on the acquisition of shares in a company which owns intangible assets, either directly or indirectly, this cost can be taken into account for the purposes of reinvestment relief.

The following **conditions** must all be satisfied:

a. a company acquires shares in the target company (which was not previously a member of the acquirer's group);

b. as a result of the acquisition the target company becomes a member of the same group as the acquirer (note that the exact percentage shareholding is irrelevant to the amount of relief obtained); and

c. immediately before the transaction either:
– the target company holds the intangible assets; or
– another company holds the assets and becomes a member of the acquirer's group (for example, a subsidiary of the target) as a result of the transaction.

The cost of the shares will be deemed to relate directly to the acquisition of the intangible assets, so that the shares themselves are looked through.

As the replacement **assets are held indirectly** through a corporate vehicle, the normal rules are amended as follows:
– the condition that the assets must be chargeable intangible assets immediately after their acquisition is satisfied if they are such assets in the hands of the target company or its subsidiary;
– the tax written down value of those assets is reduced by the amount of reinvestment relief;
– the target company may allocate the reduction among its chargeable intangible assets as it sees fit;
– where more than one company held the assets by reference to which relief is sought, the allocation of the proceeds of realisation to the various assets is as agreed by the companies concerned; and
– a joint claim has to be made by the acquiring company and the company which holds the intangible assets.

69315
s 779 CTA 2009

As with the usual reinvestment relief, **gains** on pre-April 2002 assets can also be rolled over in this way.

A **taxable credit or gain** can be held over, provided that it arises somewhere in the acquirer's group.

The amount of the **deemed expenditure** is the lesser of:
– the cost of acquiring the shares in the target company; and
– the tax written down value of the intangible assets held by the target or its subsidiary.

69320

CIRD 20440

EXAMPLE HMRC give the following examples:

Tax value of old asset £	Original cost of old asset £	Proceeds of old asset £	Cost of shares £	TWDV of new assets £	Relief £	Explanation
80	100	150	200	90	Nil	Tax value of new assets is less than original cost of old asset
80	100	150	200	180	50	Tax value of new assets and cost of shares exceed sale proceeds Profit over original cost rolled over (£150 – £100)
80	100	150	200	140	40	Tax value of new assets is less than sale proceeds of old asset So profit to be rolled over restricted to the excess of the tax value over the cost of the old asset (£140 – £100)
80	100	150	140	200	40	Cost of shares is less than both the sale proceeds and tax value of new assets (which exceeds the proceeds) Relief restricted as if the cost of the shares is equal to the tax value of the new assets (£140 – £100)
80	100	150	130	140	30	Cost of shares is less than sale proceeds and tax value of new assets does not exceed the sale proceeds Relief is restricted as if the cost of shares is the tax value of the new assets (£130 – £100)

Degrouping charges

69325
s 791 CTA 2009;
CIRD 20460

Where a degrouping charge (¶69220) is rolled over, the reinvestment rollover relief rules are modified so that the **reinvestment period** begins 12 months before, and ends 3 years after, the transferee ceased to be a member of the group.

s 799 CTA 2009

> MEMO POINTS   1. Any **payment made between the companies** for the rollover relief is ignored for tax purposes, provided that it does not exceed the reduction in the acquisition cost or tax written down value of the asset(s), against which the degrouping charge is rolled over. The payment must be made under an agreement between the two companies.
> 2. It is possible to roll over a **reallocated degrouping charge** (¶69260).

SECTION 3

Loan relationships

Summary

69375

Topic	¶¶
Intra-group transfers	¶69405
Leaving the group	¶69445
Group mismatch schemes	¶69490

A. Intra-group transfers

69405
s 335 CTA 2009

Where a company transfers a loan relationship to another company in the same group, and both are within the charge to corporation tax in respect of the transaction (i.e. not located overseas, nor charities), special rules apply.

> MEMO POINTS   1. For this purpose a group is **defined** as a 75% CG group (¶65415). Broadly, this requires each subsidiary to be 75% owned by its immediate parent and the holding company to have at least a 50% interest in each group member.
> 2. **Repos and stock lending** come within these rules.

New party to the relationship

69410
s 340 CTA 2009

Other than when fair value accounting is used or avoidance is intended (¶69415), where one company directly or indirectly replaces another as a party to the loan relationship, any **credits or debits arising from the transfer** (e.g. a profit or loss on disposal) are ignored. The transferor is deemed to have disposed of the loan relationship for its notional carrying value and the transferee is treated as having acquired it for the same notional carrying value.

Any **other credits and debits** (e.g. interest) continue to be treated normally, according to each party's period of ownership.

s 336 CTA 2009

> MEMO POINTS   1. One group company **replaces another as a party** to a loan relationship where:
> − a loan relationship is transferred between two companies that are members of the same group; or
> − a series of transactions has the effect of a transfer between two such companies i.e. the company transferring the debt, and the company ultimately receiving it, have been members of the same group at any time in the course of a series of transactions.

s 338 CTA 2009

> 2. A transfer includes the case where a company becomes party to **equivalent rights and obligations** i.e. the capital, interest and dividends are the same, and there are the same remedies

available in the event of default. A debtor company may wish to transfer the debt to another group member with the agreement of the lender, which can happen by novation (¶16260).

3. **Notional carrying value** means the value of the loan relationship immediately before it is transferred i.e. assuming a period of account ended at the date of transfer and a balance sheet was drawn up for the transferor.

> EXAMPLE A Ltd and B Ltd are both members of a group. On 1 January A Ltd lends £20,000 to X Ltd, a third party, with interest of £500 due every quarter and repayment due in 5 years' time.
> On 1 July A Ltd sells the loan to B Ltd for £21,000, making a profit of £1,000. This profit is ignored for tax purposes and B Ltd is deemed to have acquired the debt for £20,000.
> A Ltd is taxed on interest of £1,000 (relating to the period from 1 January to 30 June) and B Ltd is taxed on the remainder of the interest as it accrues.
> On the date of repayment X Ltd only pays £15,000 and B Ltd writes off the remaining loan. As the loan entered B Ltd's accounts at £20,000, the resulting loss is £5,000. (£20,000 – £15,000)

Exclusions

In the unusual case where **fair value accounting** is required (¶16195), the loan relationship is disposed of at its fair value. The transferee should recognise the same value as the transferor but exclude any discount that the transferor is required to bring into account.

69415
s 341 CTA 2009

Where an intra-group transfer of a loan relationship on or after 16 May 2008 is likely to be followed by a disposal to a third party and the main, or one of the main, purposes of that disposal is to **secure a tax advantage** for the transferor, or a connected person, the special rules set out above do not apply (so that any profits are taxable).

s 347 CTA 2009

B. Leaving the group

Except in the case of demergers and the formation of a Societas Europaea (¶69460), a degrouping charge applies where there has been an intra-group transfer of the loan relationship and the transferee company ceases to be a member of the group **within** 6 years of the date of transfer. This means that there is a **deemed disposal** and reacquisition of the loan relationship at its fair value immediately before the transferee leaves the group. However, only a resulting credit is taxable, so if the fair value gives a loss, this is not crystallised for tax purposes.

69445
ss 344, 345
CTA 2009;
CFM 34110

Comment   Unlike a degrouping charge for chargeable gains purposes, there is no exemption from a degrouping charge where associated companies leave the group together (¶67475) and no way to reallocate the charge to another group company (¶67285).

> MEMO POINTS 1. When the intra-group transfer was effected through a **series of transactions**, the 6-year period starts on the date that the last of the series of transactions took place.
> 2. Where a **derivative contract** has been used to hedge a loan relationship, a deemed disposal will occur where the following criteria are met:
> – the transferred loan relationship must be a creditor loan relationship;
> – the effect of a deemed disposal at fair value would be a debit; and
> – when the transferee company leaves the group, a credit is brought into account under the derivative rules (¶69615).
> All this means is that the debit arising on the loan relationship will balance the credit arising on the derivative contract when the company leaves the group.

69450

Exclusions

A **demerger** will not give rise to a chargeable distribution when it is effected for genuine commercial reasons. In order to facilitate corporate restructuring, no degrouping charge applies either. However, where a company undertakes transfers for the purposes of tax avoidance within the next 5 years, a degrouping charge will then apply.

69455
s 346 CTA 2009

Where the **principal company itself becomes the 75% subsidiary** of another company, this does not result in any company leaving the group.

Societas Europaea

69460
s 421 CTA 2009

A special type of company, known as a Societas Europaea (SE), can be formed to **enable groups to operate throughout the EU** using a single corporate entity. They are subject to the tax law of the state of residence. Further details can be found at ¶93000.

Where such an entity is formed by way of a merger of two or more companies and the SE (i.e. the transferee) is **subject to tax** as a UK resident or as a UK permanent establishment of a non-resident, the following provisions apply, provided that the merger is carried out for bona fide commercial reasons and the SE is not a transparent entity:

a. when using the **amortised cost basis**, the transfer of an asset or liability representing a loan relationship is disregarded (i.e. the transferor and transferee are treated as the same company), except for calculating:
– the exchange gains and losses to be brought into account; and
– any debits or credits that do not relate to the merger (e.g. interest); and

b. when using the **fair value basis** of accounting, the transfer is treated by both companies as being at fair value i.e. the amount to be brought into account by the transferor is the fair value of the asset or liability at the date on which the transferee becomes a party to the loan relationship. The transferee is treated as acquiring the asset or liability for the same amount.

s 427 CTA 2009

‒‒‒ MEMO POINTS ‒‒‒ 1. A **clearance procedure** exists to ensure that HMRC agree the purpose of the merger is commercial (¶79365).

s 429 CTA 2009

2. A **transparent entity** is an entity which:
– has no ordinary share capital;
– is resident in a member state other than the UK; and
– is listed as a company in the Annex to the Mergers Directive.

C. Group mismatch schemes

69490

Group mismatch schemes use intra-group loans or derivatives to give rise to tax deductions that are not matched by corresponding taxable receipts (either in amounts or as a result of timing differences). One example would be an intra-group loan that has no impact on the group's consolidated accounts but which is taxed asymmetrically, so as to reduce the overall amount of corporation tax paid by the group.

For scheme losses or profits relating to a time on or after 19 July 2011, any tax advantage will be eliminated by excluding the relevant debits and credits from taxation.

s 938N CTA 2010

These rules **take priority** over certain other anti-avoidance rules as follows:
– unallowable purpose;
– transfer pricing;
– arbitrage; and
– worldwide debt cap rules.

Scope

69495
s 938L CTA 2010

The **geographical** scope of the rules is limited to schemes involving UK-to-UK transactions only.

Companies which are party to schemes with either of the following **features**, on or after 19 July 2011, will be subject to this anti-avoidance provision:

s 938B CTA 2010

a. when viewed at the outset, the scheme is practically certain to give rise to a reduction of at least £2 million in the amount of corporation tax due (note that a tax avoidance motive is therefore not necessary); or

b. group members enter into the scheme for the main purpose of securing the chance to obtain a relevant tax advantage (of any amount) and the scheme is more likely to produce a relevant tax advantage than a relevant tax disadvantage (where a disadvantage is possible, the expected value of the scheme is still positive).

The requirement in **b**. means that normal commercial hedging arrangements do not fall within these rules.

If the **length** of the scheme (that is, the scheme period) is uncertain, either condition should be treated as satisfied if it would be so were a reasonable assumption made as to the duration of the scheme at its outset.

> ▭ MEMO POINTS   1. A **scheme** involves members of the same group and includes any scheme, arran- gements or understanding of any kind whatever, whether or not legally enforceable, involving a single transaction or multiple transactions.
> 2. **Group** is widely defined, with two companies (A and B) being part of a group if any of the following conditions are met at any time during the scheme period:
> **a.** treated as connected for loan relationships purposes (¶16580);
> **b.** their financial results are included in the same set of consolidated accounts (or would be but for an accounting exemption);
> **c.** one company has a major interest in the other (¶16610);
> **d.** the financial results of A are included in consolidated accounts along with a third company and that third company has a major interest in B; or
> **e.** A is connected with a third company and that third company has a major interest in B.
> 3. A **relevant tax**:
> – **advantage** is defined as an economic profit made by the group over the period of the scheme which is not negligible and which only arises as a result of asymmetries in the way different members of the group bring, or do not bring, amounts into account as debits or credits; and
> – **disadvantage** is defined as an economic loss made by the group over the period of the scheme which is not negligible and which only arises as a result of asymmetries in the way different members of the group bring, or do not bring, amounts into account as debits or credits.
> 4. An **economic profit or loss** must take the provisions of the Corporation Taxes Acts into account and also the time value of money. It should be looked at from the view of the group as a whole.

(margin references: s 938H CTA 2010; s 938E CTA 2010; s 938D CTA 2010; s 938F CTA 2010)

Consequences

Scheme losses or profits relating to a time before 19 July 2011 are outside the scope of these rules.

69500
Sch 5 para 6
FA 2011;
s 938C CTA 2010

Where the rules do apply, scheme profits or losses are not brought into account.

For this purpose **scheme profits or losses**:
– arise from a transaction, or series of transactions, forming part of the scheme;
– are an amount (or comprise part of an amount) that is brought into account for the purposes of the loan relationship or derivative rules; and either
– affect the amount of any relevant tax advantage secured by the scheme; or
– arise from a transaction, or series of transactions, that might (if events had turned out differently) have affected the amount of any relevant tax advantage secured by the scheme.

SECTION 4

Derivatives

Summary

69550

Topic	¶¶
Intra-group transfers	¶69580
Leaving the group	¶69615
Group mismatch schemes	¶69490

A. Intra-group transfers

69580
s 626 CTA 2009;
CFM 53010

Where a company transfers a derivative to another company in the same group and both are within the charge to corporation tax in respect of the transaction (i.e. not located overseas, nor charities), special rules apply.

> MEMO POINTS   For this purpose a group is **defined** as a 75% CG group (¶65415).

New party to the derivative

69585
ss 625, 627
CTA 2009

Except when fair value accounting or hedging applies, where one company directly or indirectly replaces (for example, through novation) another as a party to the derivative, any **credits or debits arising from the transfer** (e.g. a profit or loss on disposal) are ignored. The transferor is deemed to have disposed of the derivative for its notional carrying value and the transferee is treated as having acquired it for the same notional carrying value.

> MEMO POINTS   1. One group company **replaces another as a party** to a derivative where:
> – a derivative is transferred between two companies that are members of the same group, or
> – a series of transactions has the effect of a transfer between two such companies i.e. the company transferring the derivative and the company ultimately receiving it have been members of the same group at any time in the course of a series of transactions.

CFM 53030

> 2. Under **novation** the transferee enters into a new but equivalent contract with the counterparty. So the existing parties to the contract (i.e. the transferor company and the counterparty) terminate their contract.
> 3. **Notional carrying value** means the value of the derivative immediately before it is transferred i.e. assuming a period of account ends at the date of transfer and a balance sheet is drawn up for the transferor.

s 628 CTA 2009

> 4. Where **fair value accounting** is required, the derivative is disposed of at its fair value. The transferee should recognise the same value as the transferor.
> 5. For **hedging** see ¶17075.

B. Leaving the group

69615
s 631 CTA 2009;
CFM 53110

Except in the case of demergers and the formation of a Societas Europaea, a degrouping charge applies where there has been an intra-group transfer of the derivative and the transferee company ceases to be a member of the group **within** 6 years of the date of transfer (see ¶69445+ for the rules, which are the same as for loan relationships). This means that there is a **deemed disposal** and reacquisition of the derivative at its fair value immediately before the transferee leaves the group.

However, only a resulting credit is taxable, so if the fair value gives a loss, this cannot be crystallised for tax purposes, unless the derivative is used to hedge a loan relationship (¶69450).

s 632 CTA 2009

> MEMO POINTS   1. A **demerger** will not give rise to a chargeable distribution when it is effected for genuine commercial reasons. In order to facilitate corporate restructuring, no degrouping charge applies either. However, where a company undertakes transfers for the purposes of tax avoidance within the next 5 years, a degrouping charge will then apply.
> 2. For **Societas Europaea** see ¶69460 above.
> 3. Where the **principal company itself becomes the 75% subsidiary** of another company, this does not result in any company leaving the group.
> 4. When the intra-group transfer was effected through a **series of transactions**, the 6-year period starts on the date that the last of the series of transactions took place.

Shadow ACT

There are several special provisions for groups in relation to shadow ACT. The main rules applying to all companies are discussed at ¶41190.

69665

A. Intra-group distributions

Subject to an appropriate election being made, an intra-group distribution does not give rise to shadow ACT and does not constitute franked investment income (FII) in the hands of the recipient. Hence intra-group dividends are excluded from the shadow ACT regime.

69695
SI 1999/358 reg 6

MEMO POINTS   A group is **defined** as a company and all of its UK-resident 51% subsidiaries. The parent must own more than 50% of the ordinary share capital and have more than 50% of the rights to both distributable profits and assets on a winding up (¶65505).

Election

An irrevocable election (on the CTSA return) can be made by the subsidiary to treat the distribution as giving rise to shadow ACT, which therefore creates FII for the **recipient**. This would be advantageous where the recipient needed to reduce its shadow ACT (and therefore enable it to recover surplus real ACT).

69700
SI 1999/358 reg 11

The election can only be made if the **paying company** has itself received sufficient FII (in the current accounting period or as a surplus brought forward), either from:
– a non-group company; or
– a group company in relation to which another election has already been made.

The **amount** covered by the election will be limited to this FII, although the election may specify a lower amount.

MEMO POINTS   1. The **time limit** for the election is 2 years after the end of the accounting period in which the distribution is paid.
2. When a company **leaves the group**, the election will only have effect for distributions paid before the date of leaving.
3. Similarly, when a company **joins the group**, any election will only have effect for distributions paid after the date of joining.

B. Surplus shadow ACT

Within a company's own tax computation, shadow ACT **must first be used** in the current accounting period, then carried back for 6 years in that company (possibly displacing surplus real ACT).

69730
SI 1999/358 reg 13

In a group context, any remaining surplus shadow ACT must be compulsorily allocated to other group members after utilisation of their own shadow ACT. For this purpose the company where the shadow ACT originates is known as the transferring company.

No other group member may utilise surplus real ACT until all the surplus shadow ACT for that accounting period has been allocated.

Allocation

69735 It is the parent company's choice as to how to make this allocation, although should the parent fail to do so, HMRC will make a determination.

The **maximum amount** of shadow ACT must be used and in the following order:

a. current accounting period (where another group company has the same accounting period);

b. any accounting period of a fellow group company which straddles the accounting period of the transferring company (taking earlier periods before later ones); and

c. any accounting period beginning up to 2 years before the end of the transferring company's accounting period.

Any remaining shadow ACT which has **not been allocated** stays with the transferring company and is carried forward.

However, where a **subsidiary is sold** to an unconnected third party, any current period shadow ACT that cannot be carried back in that company is treated as belonging to the old parent company.

EXAMPLE A Ltd owns 70% of B Ltd. Both companies have a year end of 31 March. For the year ended 31 March 2013 A Ltd has no surplus real ACT brought forward, but B Ltd has surplus real ACT of £100,000. The companies have the following results:

		A Ltd £	B Ltd £
PCTCT		300,000	600,000
Dividends paid		400,000	400,000
Dividends received (from unrelated company)		-	140,000

The ACT computation is as follows:

		A Ltd £	B Ltd £
Maximum ACT capacity	PCTCT x 20%	60,000	120,000
Shadow ACT	400,000 x 25%	(100,000)	-
		(40,000)	-
Deemed surrender		40,000	(40,000)
Real ACT capacity		Nil	80,000
Real ACT brought forward			(100,000)
Real ACT carried forward			(20,000)

Note:
B Ltd's shadow ACT is nil, as the non-group dividend paid of £120,000 is less than the dividends received.

SECTION 6

Administration

Summary

69785

Topic	¶¶
Group payment arrangements	¶69815
Tax refund surrenders	¶69870
Recovery procedures re non-residents	¶69925

A. Group payment arrangements

Group payment arrangements may be used to simplify the administration involved in the payment of corporation tax by **instalments**. Broadly, one company (known as the nominated company, which must be UK-resident) becomes **responsible** for making payment of one amount to HMRC on each instalment date on behalf of all the companies within the arrangement; this is then allocated amongst the participating members (some of which may be non-resident, or subsidiaries of non-resident companies).

69815
s 59F TMA 1970

Note that the nominated company does not take on the liability of each participating company; the arrangement is purely a payment mechanism.

Comment   As there is often uncertainty over group relief claims and surrenders, it is sometimes more efficient for one company to have an overview of the entire group and make payments based on group forecasts. Such an arrangement can also mitigate any interest charges.

Eligibility

At least one company in a 51% group (¶65505) must be liable to pay corporation tax by instalments (¶48095). However, not **all group members** need be included in the arrangement; it is possible to have several arrangements for multiple subgroups (although any company can only be covered by one arrangement).

69820

The following **conditions** must also be satisfied, which require the participating companies to:
– have the same accounting period end as the nominated company;
– have up-to-date tax affairs (all returns submitted and tax liabilities settled for the last but one accounting period); and
– sign a written contract with HMRC agreeing to the arrangement, which must be submitted to HMRC at least 2 months before the first payment is due.

> ⎡ MEMO POINTS ⎤   1. **New companies** and **companies which join** the group must align their accounting reference date with that of the nominated company. They cannot be included in the arrangement for accounting periods beginning before the start of the nominated company's period of account.
> 2. Where a **company ceases to trade**, it can remain in the arrangement, provided that it still prepares accounts for the same period as the nominated company
> 3. The text of the **contract** is stipulated by HMRC.

CTM 97430

Application

A group wishing to enter a group payment arrangement must contact the group payment team in the usual accounts office to which it pays its corporation tax (¶95380).

69825
CTM 97410

Effect

A group payment arrangement may cover:
– the payment of corporation tax (including any tax relating to close company loans (¶75750) and tax on profits of controlled foreign companies (¶91045));
– liabilities for interest; and
– any penalties due.

69830
s 59F(6) TMA 1970

The nominated company must make payments on the instalment dates, calculated by reference to the participating companies' most recent estimates of **profits**. The nominated company must also make top-up payments and claim repayments where necessary.

Payment must be made by means of an electronic transfer.

Until the closing date HMRC are prohibited from **collecting liabilities** directly from the participating companies, as it is the nominated company which is the conduit for all payments.

After the closing date the nominated company must allocate the payments between the participating companies as it sees fit. HMRC can then pursue the individual companies for any shortfall.

> MEMO POINTS   1. The **closing date** is usually the date by which all participating companies have submitted their returns (although this cannot be earlier than the statutory filing date). Where a determination is required, the date when all companies have either submitted returns or received a determination is the closing date.
> 2. Where **returns are filed late**, this has two effects:
> – the closing date becomes the date when determinations have been made; and
> – any shortfall in the payments made will be allocated by HMRC so as to maximise any tax-geared penalty.
> 3. The group payment arrangement is separate from any **group relief simplified procedure** (¶66730) which may be in place, although the nominated company can also be the authorised company for that purpose.

Duration

69835   Once the arrangements are entered into, they **automatically apply** to future periods. It is therefore vital that the nominated company informs HMRC (before the first instalment due date for each period) about any companies that wish to join or leave the arrangement.

Companies which **leave** the group, or do not have an aligned accounting period, must be removed from the arrangement.

Termination

69840   The arrangement may be terminated by:
– the **nominated company**, provided that HMRC are notified before the first instalment due date; or
– **HMRC**, where any of the terms in ¶69820 is breached.
A group payment arrangement may also be terminated if any of the participating companies is liable to tax under anti-avoidance legislation on a change of ownership (¶60580).

B. Surrender of tax refund between group members

69870
s 963 CTA 2010

A company which is a member of a group for group relief purposes (¶65055) may also elect to surrender a tax refund received from HMRC to another group member, in order to mitigate interest charges.

For this purpose a refund is **either** a repayment of:
– corporation tax paid by the surrendering company for a period; or
– income tax deducted from a payment received by that company in the period.

Conditions

69875   In order to surrender a refund from one group member to another, both companies must be in the same group throughout the accounting period and **until** the surrender is made.

The companies must also have the same **accounting period end**.

Both companies must provide a signed written **notice** of the surrender to HMRC, specifying the amount involved. If the actual **amount of the refund is less**, HMRC will require the amounts to be corrected within 30 days, otherwise the notice to surrender is void.

CTM 92460

> MEMO POINTS   1. HMRC state that although the notice can be in any **format**, it must show:
> – the name and tax reference of the surrendering company;
> – the name and tax reference of the recipient company; and
> – the type and amount of each refund surrendered.
> 2. The surrendering company **claims its refund** on form CT600E.

3. The **recipient company** can show an intended surrender on its CT600 return; a copy of the joint notice should be submitted along with the return.

Effect

No instalments   Where a tax refund is surrendered in this way, the **surrendering company** is treated as though it has received a repayment of tax on the later of the date on which the tax was paid and the date on which the tax was payable.

69880
s 964 CTA 2010

The company **receiving the surrender** is treated as though it originally paid corporation tax equal to the amount surrendered, including any interest which was originally paid by the surrendering company.

> [EXAMPLE]   A Ltd is the parent company of two wholly owned subsidiaries, B Ltd and C Ltd. None of the companies is liable to make instalment payments.
> For the year ended 30 September 2012 B Ltd has a corporation tax liability of £50,000. The amount actually paid on 1 June 2013 is only £30,000, as B Ltd expects to make a group relief claim. A Ltd has a trading loss and C Ltd paid its total corporation tax liability on time.
> When viewed as a whole, the group decides that A Ltd should surrender its group relief to C Ltd instead of B Ltd, which means C Ltd has overpaid its corporation tax liability by £25,000 but B Ltd has underpaid its by £20,000. An interest rate of 3% applies to underpayments and a rate of 0.5% applies to overpayments.
>
> a. If C Ltd surrenders £20,000 of its repayment to B Ltd, there is no interest charge on the underpayment, as B Ltd is treated as paying an extra £20,000 of corporation tax on 1 June 2013. C Ltd receives the remaining £5,000 of overpayment and interest supplement runs from 1 June 2013.
>
> b. However, if no surrender takes place and B Ltd pays the remaining £20,000 on 31 May 2014 (and C Ltd receives its refund on this date), the following interest payments are due:
> – B Ltd must pay interest of £600 (£20,000 x 3%); and
> – C Ltd will receive interest of £125. (£25,000 x 0.5%)
> So a tax refund surrender saves the group a net interest charge of £475. (£600 – £125)

If the repayment arises because the surrendering company has made a **claim to carry back losses or a loan relationship deficit**, the receiving company will have the same interest entitlement as the surrendering company (¶48390).

69885
s 965 CTA 2010

If **part** of the repayment is to be **set against a liability** of the receiving company and part repaid, then, for the purposes of calculating the repayment interest, any element which does not bear repayment interest is to be set against any liability in preference.

Instalments   If the surrendering company has paid corporation tax by instalments, the same rules as in ¶69880 apply, except that the **refund date** is treated as being the later of:
– the date that the tax was paid; and
– the due date for the first instalment for that accounting period.

69890
s 964 CTA 2010

The surrendering company can surrender part of each instalment payment to the recipient company, provided that this is identified to HMRC.

Payment for surrender

Any payment made for the surrender of a tax refund between group members is ignored for corporation tax purposes, up to an **amount** equal to the surrendered refund.

69895
s 966 CTA 2010

C. Recovery of tax payable by non-resident group member

Where a non-UK-resident member of a group fails to pay corporation tax within 6 months of an assessment being made, HMRC may serve notice to **recover** the unpaid tax **from** any company which, in the **period** starting 12 months before the accounting period in which the tax liability arose and ending when the tax first became due:

69925
ss 974 – 980
CTA 2010

– was a 51% subsidiary of the non-resident company,
– owned 51% of the shares in the non-resident company;
– along with the non-resident company, was a 51% subsidiary of a third party; or
– was a member of the same group as a company which was also a member of a consortium owning the non-resident company.

Where HMRC recover tax under this provision the **company which pays the tax** is entitled to recover the amount paid from the non-resident company.

> MEMO POINTS   1. HMRC may serve a **notice** demanding payment within 3 years from the date when the amount of the tax is finally determined. The notice must specify a 30-day payment period, and state:
> – the amount of unpaid tax;
> – its original due date; and
> – the amount to be paid by the company which receives the notice.
> 2. Where the company from which the tax is recovered is a member of a **consortium**, or a member of the same group as a consortium member, the tax recoverable is limited to the member's share (or in the case of a member of the same group as a consortium member, the group's share) in the consortium.
> 3. For a similar recovery mechanism in respect of **migrating companies** see ¶91240.

CHAPTER 5

Transfer pricing

SECTION 1

Scope

Where parties are **related** and **carry out transactions between themselves**, there is the **70000** opportunity to manipulate the price of the goods or services in order to minimise the overall tax position. Whilst this is most apparent in international group situations, where profit could effectively be moved to a territory with a lower rate of taxation, it could also be used in a UK group situation to move profits from a company paying tax at the mainstream rate to a company paying at the small profits rate.

In order to **counteract** such manipulation, there are rules that regulate the allowable level of deductions for tax purposes. These are collectively known as the transfer pricing regulations. The regulations ensure that, for tax purposes, the costs charged are similar to those that would be charged if there were an arm's length relationship. Sufficient documentation must be kept to substantiate this.

A. Exemptions from the rules

1. Dormant companies

70030

ss 165–167 TIOPA 2010

A dormant company will be exempt from the application of the transfer pricing regulations. A **company is regarded as dormant** (¶7000+) in an accounting period if no transactions have been recorded for that period. However, a company **cannot be regarded as dormant** for this purpose if it owns assets that should have been earning revenue in the period. In this case, even where **no transaction was recorded**, a transaction will be deemed to have occurred. So for a company to be considered dormant, any assets that are used by group companies should be transferred out.

> EXAMPLE A Ltd owns an office that B SA, a group company resident overseas, uses without charge. A Ltd will not be considered dormant, as an arm's length transaction in the same circumstances would not have resulted in the use of the asset without charge.

2. Small and medium-sized enterprises

70050

Generally speaking, an SME will be exempt from the regulations. However, there are exceptions to this (¶70055 and ¶70060).

For the purposes of transfer pricing, SMEs are defined by the European Commission as:

Condition	Small enterprise	Medium enterprise
Maximum number of employees	Less than 50	Less than 250
And then either:		
Maximum turnover	€10m	€50m
Or		
Maximum gross balance sheet assets	€10m	€43m

> MEMO POINTS 1. The transfer pricing rules apply to a **REIT** (¶19635+), whether or not the REIT is an SME.
> 2. These thresholds are applied on an annualised basis to the worldwide consolidated group, and will include any **linked enterprises** (broadly any enterprises that the SME controls (¶75275)).

Small enterprises

70055

The **exemption will not apply** if:
– an **election** is made by the company for the exemption not to apply for that period. Such an election, once made, is irrevocable; or
– the other party to the transaction is resident and liable to tax in a **non-qualifying territory**.

> MEMO POINTS 1. A party to the transaction will be **resident in a non-qualifying territory** if it is liable to tax in the territory by reason of domicile, residence or place of management. This, therefore, does not include a person who is liable to tax in the territory simply by virtue of income from sources in that territory.

2. A territory may be considered **qualifying** if it is specifically included in a regulation or there is a suitable non-discrimination clause in a tax treaty with that territory.

3. For accounting periods beginning **on or after 1 April 2013** a **further restriction** to the exemption is imposed. Where a transaction (or series of transactions) is taken into account in calculating profits for the patent box regime (¶28775+), HMRC may issue a notice to the company that the transfer pricing rules must be implemented. The only basis of appeal against such a notice is that the transaction was not taken into account in calculating patent box profits.

s 167A TIOPA 2010

Medium-sized enterprises

As well as being subject to the same rules as a small enterprise (¶70055), a medium-sized company may fall within the rules where HMRC consider that a transfer pricing misstatement will give rise to a significant loss of tax in an accounting period, and they issue a transfer pricing notice to that effect. This is only used in exceptional circumstances, and the transfer pricing notice can only be issued after an enquiry notice has been issued to the company.

70060
s 168 TIOPA 2010

Where a company receives a transfer pricing notice it can **appeal** (within 30 days) against the notice, but only on the **grounds** that it is not a medium-sized enterprise for the purposes of the transfer pricing regulations. Following receipt of the notice, the enterprise has 90 days to amend its return. The 90 day limit is extended where an appeal has been made. HMRC will not be able to issue a closure notice to the enquiry until the 90 day period has elapsed or the return has been amended.

B. When do the rules apply?

The UK transfer pricing rules apply where:
– a **provision exists** between two or more parties which does not follow the arm's length standard;
– one of the parties is either **involved** in the management, control or capital of the other, **directly or indirectly**, or a **third party** is involved in both; and
– the provision creates a **potential UK tax advantage** for at least one of the parties.

70090
ss 147, 148 TIOPA
2010

Involved

One company is directly involved in the management, control or capital of a company or partnership if it controls it. The ability to **control** how a company's business is conducted can be **gained** through a shareholding, voting rights, or power given by the Articles of the company or by some other document that regulates the affairs of the company.

70095

Another definition of control for the purposes of the transfer pricing legislation relates to a major participation in the management, control or capital of another person where the controlling party is one of a number of major participants in a **joint venture**. A company is a major participant in the venture for this purpose where:
– it and another person together control the joint venture entity; and
– each of the participants has interests, rights and powers amounting to at least 40% of the holdings, rights or powers relating to control of the joint venture.

MEMO POINTS   In the case of a **partnership**, control involves the right to more than half the income or assets.

Extended definition for financing arrangements

The meaning of control, in the context of financing arrangements, can extend to a situation where the rights and powers of persons who have **acted together** in relation to financing arrangements are combined to determine if there is control. For this purpose, the term **financing arrangement is defined** widely to include arrangements made for providing or guaranteeing in respect of any debt, capital or other form of finance. This could cover not only loans but also share capital, other financial instruments or guarantees.

70100
ss 161, 162 TIOPA
2010

The acting together rules were introduced mainly to include situations in which a private equity fund may thinly capitalise (¶70490) acquisitions, but they are applicable more widely than this. There does not need to have been any **direct agreement** between the parties to act together for these provisions to apply, though any shareholders' agreement or loan agreement may be examined as part of an enquiry.

Also, it is not necessary for both or all parties to hold equity shareholdings for them to be considered to be acting together – a **shareholder and a lender** could be regarded as acting together in some circumstances. Whilst shareholder debt may create a situation where lending may be on non-arm's length terms, there may also be situations where non-shareholder debt will be scrutinised.

EXAMPLE
1. A management buyout is partly financed by loans from the vendor of the business. As this lending takes place as part of a deal in which shares in the business are also being sold by the lender, HMRC may wish to look at the link between the sale of the shares and the granting of the loan, examining the terms of the transaction to determine if there are implications for the arm's length nature of the transactions.
2. A borrower (B Ltd) is in a distressed situation and undergoes financial restructuring. As a result of this restructuring, the previously unrelated lender acquires an equity shareholding in B Ltd. HMRC will now consider whether the terms of the refinancing are influenced by the lender's equity stake in the business, and will examine the terms to see if they are at arm's length.

Timing of involvement

70105 The period in which the involvement condition is required to be satisfied for the rules to apply depends on the nature of the transaction.

Where the transaction is a **financing arrangement**, an involvement on the day of the imposition of the provision, or in the 6 months following, will result in the regulations applying.

In **all other cases**, the involvement condition is only checked at the time of the transaction.

SECTION 2

General pricing methods

70155
INTM421020

There are a number of ways to ascertain the arm's length value of a transaction for the purposes of the transfer pricing legislation. Before deciding on a suitable transfer pricing method, the company should make a **comparison of the conditions imposed** between the related enterprises with those that would prevail between independent enterprises. This comparison should take account of wider conditions and involves consideration of all the various factors that **could affect the cost** such as:
- the nature of the goods or services provided;
- the functional analysis;
- contractual terms;
- economic conditions; and
- business strategy.

The **process of choosing** a method should be sufficiently transparent and well documented to enable HMRC to assess the reliability of the comparables used. The OECD considers that the transactional based methods (comparison with similar transactions, resale price and one based on cost) are the strongest, but the guidelines advise that the appropriate transfer pricing method should be used as determined by the factual and functional analysis of the parties and transactions involved. Correctly identifying the functions performed by each of the related parties is essential in determining the appropriate transfer pricing method.

By using one of these methods, the price charged can then be compared to the accounts and then, if need be, adjusted for tax purposes (¶70655+).

> ⌐ *MEMO POINTS* ⌐   The decision in *DSG Retail v HMRC* [2009] suggests that HMRC will not blindly adhere to any "hierarchy" of transfer pricing methods. The company had used the comparable uncontrolled price method, but the comparables were challenged by HMRC and a profit split approach was put forward as an alternative which was accepted.

A. Comparison with similar suppliers

The **comparable uncontrolled price** (CUP) method compares the price charged for the goods or services with the **prices charged by independent enterprises** engaging in similar uncontrolled transactions in comparable circumstances. Any **differences** between the price charged by the related parties and the range of prices charged by comparable independent enterprises may indicate that the price is not at arm's length and needs to be adjusted.

70185
INTM421030

A transaction of an independent enterprise is **comparable to the transaction** in question if the differences between the enterprises or the transactions are not sufficient to materially affect the open market price. Where these differences would affect the price, the transactions can still be regarded as comparable if reasonable adjustments can be computed to take into account the effect of the differences.

> ⌐ *MEMO POINTS* ⌐   The CUP method is considered to be particularly reliable where the independent enterprise is **selling the same product** as that transferred between the related enterprises.

B. Resale price

The resale price method takes, as a **starting point**, the price at which a product acquired from a related enterprise is sold to an independent enterprise. This resale price is reduced by a suitable gross profit margin to arrive at an arm's length price for the transaction between the related enterprises. The **gross profit margin** should be sufficient to cover the selling and other operating expenses and achieve a suitable net profit. The appropriate gross margin may be determined by reference to sales to third parties. If **no such internal comparison exists**, the resale price margin achieved by independent enterprises engaging in similar activities may be used as a reference. Such comparison may be adjusted where differences in the enterprises or transactions being compared materially affect the resale price margin, and the effect on the margin can be quantified.

70215
INTM421050

This method will be **most suitable** where the related enterprise selling on the goods to third parties is not itself processing or adding value to those goods, and not contributing to the creation of intangible property (such as trademarks) relating to the products. The resale price method is therefore considered suitable for marketing and distribution operations.

> ⌐ *MEMO POINTS* ⌐   When looking at comparable transactions to establish an appropriate gross margin under the resale price method, adjustments may need to be made for **differences in accounting practices** between different jurisdictions. An example is research and development expenses which could be included in cost of sales or operating expenses. Gross margins would not be comparable without ensuring that the treatment of such expenses is consistent in the controlled and uncontrolled transactions being compared.

C. Cost plus

The **cost plus method** takes as its basis the costs incurred by the supplier of the goods or services. A **suitable mark up** is than added to these costs, based on the appropriate level of

70245
INTM421060

profit that would be expected from the transaction. In determining the mark up, consideration should be given to the functions of the parties and the market conditions. The cost plus mark up could be established by considering the mark up charged from **performing similar services for third party** customers, or if there are none, reference could be made to the mark up charged by independent enterprises for similar transactions in similar circumstances. The cost plus method is considered **suitable for** the transfer of semi-finished goods, or for the supply of services between related enterprises.

D. Work by more than one company

Group activities highly integrated

70275
INTM421070

The **profit split method** can be the most suitable transfer pricing method to use where the operations of a group are highly integrated, for example in the case of a banking group or where two or more related parties are contributing unique, valuable, intangible assets. Any transfer pricing method aims to arrive at an approximation to what independent parties might determine at arm's length, and in these situations those independent parties might decide to share the profits in proportion to their relative contributions.

Another factor pointing to the suitability of a profit split method is that there may be insufficient reliable information on comparable transactions.

The **first step in applying** the profit split method is to determine the profit from the controlled transactions which is to be split, and to determine which related enterprises are involved in the transactions.

The following step is to divide those profits between the participating related parties in an economically sound manner, which approximates to what would have been done by independent enterprises involved in similar transactions in similar circumstances.

Two possible approaches to profit split mentioned by the OECD are contribution analysis and residual analysis, though these are not necessarily mutually exclusive.

Under a **contribution analysis**, the profit would be split according to the relative value of the functions performed by each of the related parties, as determined by the functional analysis. The ratio in which profits are split can be supported by other external information showing how independent enterprises engaging in similar transactions in similar circumstances would have split the profits.

A **residual analysis** would first attribute to each of the related parties an appropriate arm's length return for the activities in which it has participated, determined by reference to the return received by enterprises engaged in similar activities in similar circumstances. This would account for the routine functions performed by each of the parties, and any residual profit would then be allocated among the parties based on factors such as their unique contributions (e.g. intangible assets) used in performing the transactions.

One party contributing more

70280
INTM421080

Where only **one party** to a transaction is making a **unique contribution**, and the **other party** is performing relatively **routine functions**, a profit split would not be appropriate and a one-sided method such as the transactional net margin method (TNMM) or a traditional method should be considered. The TNMM is one-sided because it is only necessary to examine the functions of one of the related parties to the transactions, as compared, for example, to the profit split method where it is necessary to examine the functions of all the related parties amongst which the combined profit is to be split.

The **TNMM compares the net profit margin** from a transaction with a suitable base such as costs, assets or sales. The net margin from the transaction with a related party is compared to the net margin achieved from similar transactions with third parties or, where these do not exist, with the net margin achieved by independent enterprises engaging in similar transactions in similar circumstances. A functional analysis needs to be performed for the related enterprise and the independent enterprises whose transactions are being compared.

MEMO POINTS The company must ensure that there is **consistency** in the way that net margins are measured for the related enterprise and the independent enterprises. Differences in the way that operating or other expenses are treated could result in differences in margins, and appropriate adjustments may be needed to achieve reasonable comparability.

SECTION 3
Specific situations

A. Intangibles

As **problems** can arise with respect to **identification and valuation** of intangible assets (¶28070), accurate transfer pricing on the assignment or licensing of intangibles becomes more difficult.

70330
INTM440110

The OECD guidelines state that the term intangible property **includes**:
– rights to use industrial assets such as patents, trademarks, trade names, designs or models;
– literary and artistic property rights; and
– intangible property such as know-how and trade secrets.
Intangibles may be relatively easy to identify where, for example, there is patent or copyright protection, but for intellectual property that is not formally registered this is more difficult.

Licensed assets

Where intellectual property is licensed, **consideration for its use** may be included in the price of goods transferred or a separate royalty may be charged. In the case of a **separate royalty**, an arm's length rate must be found by an appropriate transfer pricing method. The OECD transfer pricing guidelines suggest that the comparable uncontrolled price method (¶70185) is the most appropriate, giving consideration to factors such as the:
– expected benefit to be gained from the asset;
– extent of the geographical area of its intended use;
– licensee's distribution network; and
– possibility of sublicensing.

70335
INTM440120

The effect of such factors on the value of the intangible may be considered by looking at the supernormal profit that can be earned on transactions as a result of the intangible.

B. Intercompany services

HMRC's guidance on transfer pricing for services is **not intended** to be prescriptive, and it is emphasised that businesses may use appropriate approaches to arrive at an arm's length price, drawing on the provisions of the OECD transfer pricing guidelines.

70365
INTM440060

The cost plus method (¶70245) is generally considered suitable in the case of intercompany services. HMRC **lay down certain issues** that the company should be looking at when considering whether to use a cost plus method for services. The criteria are:

– that there is **actually a service being provided**, and this service would be taken up by the recipient from an independent supplier at arm's length;
– the service **could be provided by a third party** at relatively low commercial risk, and would typically be charged out at a relatively modest margin (up to 10%);
– the service is of a **routine and administrative nature** and ancillary to the core business of the recipient;
– the service provider does **not provide** the service to **independent parties** (as in this case a comparable uncontrolled price method should be considered);
– the transaction does not involve the provision of **finance** or financial instruments;
– the transaction does not involve the creation, enhancement or transfer of **intellectual property**; and
– the service does not relate to the long-term **insurance** fund of an insurance company.

HMRC's guidance emphasises that the costs of the services before application of the mark up, for the purpose of applying the cost plus method, should be based on the total costs involved, including the appropriate proportion of overhead costs.

---

1. Services to multiple companies

70395
INTM440090

Where a service is bought in by one company and then provided to multiple group companies, HMRC's guidance suggests that a direct charging method based on the **cost relating to each recipient** should be applied where possible. However, an **indirect charging method** is permitted for routine services where the level, intensity, type and quality of service delivered to different recipients is similar, and there is a good correlation between the volume of service provided and the benefit to the recipient.

> ⌐MEMO POINTS⌐   HMRC emphasise the need for **consistency** in the treatment of intragroup service fees across the group year on year, unless there are specific reasons for differences in treatment. The basis for computing the arm's length charge should be consistent regardless of which group company is providing the service, and where there is a difference this should be justified on the basis of what independent service providers would have charged in similar circumstances.

Indirect charge method

70400

The OECD guidelines concede that, in view of the difficulties of directly computing and charging certain intercompany services, it will often be a practical necessity for groups to adopt an indirect charge method. This **involves** identification of the costs of providing the services, which make up the cost pool to be allocated among the parties receiving the services. An **appropriate allocation key**, or set of allocation keys, is then used to allocate the costs of the services between the various recipients of the services, applying a mark up to the costs as appropriate. The allocation key used should make sense, taking into account the type of service and the circumstances of its provision, and the cost base should be computed on sound accounting principles, with safeguards against manipulation. The allocation of charges among group companies should relate to the benefit received by each company that uses the services.

> ⌐MEMO POINTS⌐   The OECD **guidance on the allocation key** gives an example of the costs of payroll services, where the number of employees in each company would provide an improved basis of allocation than turnover, whilst the costs of computer back ups may be better allocated based on the levels of expenditure on computer equipment.

---

2. Intercompany service agreements

70430

Written agreements are not always required in an intra-group context, and where they exist with a significant amount of detail, they may provide the same type of information that would otherwise need to be given to the tax authorities in support of the transfer pricing for service fees. Such written intercompany service agreements may be **useful for other reasons**, such as helping the companies within the group to correctly implement the group's agreed transfer pricing policy. Although the tax authorities will always want to look beyond the legal contracts to the substance of the transactions, contracts between legal entities must be taken into account. Even within a company where the headquarters and a branch have made a service contract, this is a good starting point for the tax authorities to establish the basis for transfer pricing. Further evidence for the transactions would, however, be required in this case.

> ☐ MEMO POINTS ☐ An intercompany service contract is also a **guide for staff** within the group on the transfer pricing policy, and helps to ensure that the agreed transfer pricing policy is implemented correctly.

C. Cost contribution arrangements

HMRC's guidance states that cost contribution arrangements (CCA) can be extremely varied and, as such, it does not cover them in great detail. However, it does refer to the OECD guidelines which suggests that HMRC will look at cost contribution arrangements in the light of the guidelines.

70460
INTM421090

The OECD Guidelines describe a CCA as "a framework agreed among business enterprises to share the costs and risks of developing, producing or obtaining assets, services, or rights and to determine the nature and extent of the interests of each participant in those assets, services, or rights". CCAs are **mostly associated with** the development of intangible assets, but may also be used for intercompany services.

Under a cost contribution arrangement, related companies can make contributions at cost, **without the need** to compute the arm's length price. The contributions a company makes to the arrangement must be proportional to the expected benefits from the arrangement. This means that the group must produce documentation to support the relative contributions of the group companies compared to the expected benefits from the intangibles developed or services received.

A CCA needs to be **evidenced** by a detailed agreement that specifies precisely which transactions are included. These transactions can be charged at cost, whilst transactions that are not part of the CCA must be considered for arm's length pricing. Some analysis of proportional contributions and expected benefits will be required periodically.

> ☐ MEMO POINTS ☐ A CCA can save compliance costs for group companies by removing the necessity to compute an arm's length service fee, but there **must be evidence** that the contributions made are proportional to the expected benefits received. There would still be a need to distinguish between those transactions that were part of the CCA, and those that were not, as these would require a separate computation of an arm's length charge. This would include an arm's length charge by the **company administering** the CCA.

D. Financing

1. Interest

The transfer pricing rules also apply to financing situations. Most tax systems, including that of the UK, generally allow a tax deduction for interest paid on debt (¶16095+), whereas there is no tax deduction for dividends paid to holders of share capital. A group of companies may, therefore, gain a tax advantage from **making loans to subsidiaries** so as to benefit from the tax deductions obtained on the interest payments. This may result in a company having a debt to equity ratio that is significantly higher than would be expected if a commercial, third party lender had been used. This is known as being **thinly capitalised**.

70490
ss 152 – 154 TIOPA
2010;
INTM571000+

The question to be determined is the amount that could have been borrowed from a third party borrower, and on what terms. Also relevant is the question of whether the **third party would have been willing** to lend on these terms. HMRC will apply the arm's length principle based on the facts, rather than relying on any fixed formula such as a particular debt/equity ratio or level of interest cover.

HMRC will wish to take into account the amount of the loan and the interest rate charged, and any other relevant term of the loan agreement, to determine if the loan has been made at arm's length. They will also look at the **credit rating** of the borrower, to determine if a similar amount would have been loaned at a similar interest rate by an independent third party in similar circumstances. When the borrowing company also has third party debt, this may be evidence of the arm's length terms that it can obtain.

The **borrower must be able to demonstrate** that it can repay the loan, over the repayment period, on commercial terms. This can be demonstrated by means of factors such as the interest cover (the extent to which profits cover interest, expressed as a ratio). Another important factor is the security given for the loan.

Where HMRC consider that the level of borrowing **could not have been obtained** from an independent third party on the same terms, the excess debt is disallowed, leading to a higher corporation tax charge (and possibly interest and penalties). This gives rise to the possibility of double taxation within the group of companies, as the lending company may still be taxed in its own jurisdiction on the full amount of interest received.

2. Guarantees

70510
s 153 TIOPA 2010;

As the transfer pricing legislation refers to "provisions" rather than "transactions" they can apply to a **loan from an unrelated third party** lender where the borrower receives a guarantee from a related party, because a "provision" has been made between the related parties. A guarantee is defined very widely, and can cover informal guarantees.

HMRC guidance clarifies that the **creditworthiness** of the borrower must be considered as if it were a separate company, not part of a group. Therefore, cross-guarantees within a group of companies would be disregarded when considering the transfer pricing rules in relation to the creditworthiness of a particular company.

As the expenses relating to debt finance should not exceed those that would be incurred if the borrower was a single independent company, guarantee fees may be subject to a transfer pricing adjustment or disallowed altogether. On occasion the profits of the company giving the guarantee may be increased to allow for a guarantee fee that should have been paid by a related party.

> ⸺MEMO POINTS⸺ A guarantee **normally provides a benefit** in the form of a lower interest rate or a longer borrowing capacity. The transfer price would therefore be based on the interest actually paid compared to the interest that would have been payable without the guarantee. This amount would be split on a reasonable basis between the related parties.

3. Worldwide debt cap

70530
ss 260 – 353B
TIOPA 2010

The worldwide debt cap rules apply from 1 January 2010 to large, worldwide groups that have at least one member company within the UK corporation tax net (either a company or a branch). The **rules apply independently** of the transfer pricing provisions, and are intended to ensure that interest deductions in the UK are not greater than the group's external financing costs, looking at the worldwide position of the group. As such, the circumstances they will **most likely apply to** are:
– where a UK group arranges for most of its external debt to be borrowed by UK members of the group, and the amount of that debt is less than the amount borrowed by UK group members from overseas subsidiaries (upstream loans); and
– where a non-UK group arranges its borrowing so that the UK part of the group borrows more net debt (usually intra-group debt) than the external debt of the group.

MEMO POINTS   1. **Financial services companies** do not come under these rules.
2. A **large group** is one that contains any company that is larger than medium under the EU definition (¶70050).

Gateway test

In order to simplify the application of the rules, a **group will only fall within them** where the UK net debt of the group exceeds 75% of the worldwide group's gross debt, and this is **tested** in each period to ascertain if the rules apply.

70535
ss 262 – 265 TIOPA
2010

The **UK net debt** of a company is the average of the opening and closing balances shown for:
– all borrowings, liabilities under finance leases, alternative finance arrangements and any amounts designated by HMRC; less
– all cash, cash equivalents, loans, assets arising from finance leases, any alternative finance arrangements, any long term relationships that have the characteristics of a loan, including an interest-like return, and any further amounts designated by HMRC.

Where the net debt calculation shows a **surplus of assets**, the result is ignored for these purposes. This will mean that in the situation of an intercompany debt, only the debt side of the relationship will be taken into account. Further, where the **net debt is less than £3 million**, the company is treated as having no net debt.

The **worldwide gross debt** is the average of the liabilities shown in the consolidated balance sheet of the ultimate parent company at the end of both the current and previous periods.

MEMO POINTS   1. There is a facility for the **percentage threshold** and the **disregarded net debt figure** to be changed by Treasury Order although this may not have retrospective effect.
2. Where an **equity interest** is accounted for as a financial asset, it is excluded from the calculation of net debt.
3. Companies that have been **dormant** throughout the period are not taken into account for this calculation.

EXAMPLE   A Ltd and B Ltd are members of a worldwide group containing a number of large companies. The gross debt for the group is shown in the accounts for the year ended 31 March 2012 and 2013 as £62 million and £66 million respectively, giving an average of £64 million. The net debt figures shown in the accounts for the UK companies are as follows:

	Year ended 31 March 2012	Year ended 31 March 2013
A Ltd	£2 million	£3 million
B Ltd	£40 million	£52 million

A Ltd will be treated as if it has no net debt as the average is below £3 million. The average for B Ltd is £46 million. The total UK net debt therefore is calculated at £46 million. This is below 75% of the worldwide gross debt (£48 million) and, as such, the rules will not apply to the UK based companies.

Restricting the expense

The legislation works by **disallowing** the excess of the tested expense amount over the available amount in the tax computation for the period. Where there is **more than one UK company** involved, the group can allocate the disallowance as it sees fit.

70540
s 274 TIOPA 2010

The **available amount** is simply the amount disclosed in the financial statements of the group as finance costs.

To determine the **tested expense amount**, it is necessary to calculate the net financing deduction of each UK company or branch. This is defined as the excess of the financing deductions over the financing income. The relevant **financing deductions** are:
– the total of the loan relationship debits in the period, with the exception of impairment losses, exchange losses and costs related to these;
– debts brought into account with regard to finance leases; and
– financing costs on debt factoring or other costs relating to it.

Relevant **financing income** is:
– the total of loan relationship credits during the period, with the exception of exchange gains, reversals of impairment losses or costs related to these;

- amounts brought into account in respect of a finance lease;
- sums received as part of a debt factoring arrangement; and
- amounts receivable from another company in respect of the provision of a guarantee of the borrowing of that other company.

Where there is **no excess**, or the **excess is less than £500,000**, the company will be treated as having no net financing deduction.

> ☐ *MEMO POINTS*   1. The **de minimis** figure of £500,000 can be amended by Treasury Order but this cannot have retrospective effect.
> 2. Where an amount is disallowed under these provisions, another company in the group that is subject to UK corporation tax can exempt an equivalent amount of financing income in that period.

Reporting

70545
ss 277 – 281 TIOPA
2010

Where there is a restriction required in a UK company's tax computation by reason of these provisions, a **return** has to be made to HMRC within 12 months of the end of the period of account. This can be superseded, at any time within 3 years of the end of the period, by submitting a further return highlighting the differences from the prior return. If there is **more than one UK company** involved, all of the companies involved must act jointly in making the return.

The return must contain **details** of:
- the tested amount, the available amount and the total disallowed amount; and
- the companies that the provisions apply to and the amounts to be disallowed in respect of each. This must also include what type of cost is being disallowed (¶70540) and the accounting period affected.

s 276 TIOPA 2010

> ☐ *MEMO POINTS*   Where there is **more than one company** involved, it is possible to appoint a representative company by way of a joint notice. This company alone then deals with the administration imposed under these provisions.

E. Share incentive schemes

70575
INTM440210+

HMRC guidance emphasises that in the case of share incentive plans provided by a group company (normally the parent company) to its **employees and to employees of other group companies**, there are two elements that must be compensated at arm's length:
- the **provision to the employees** of the shares or share options. The payment for this element will normally be taken to the reserves of the **provider of the scheme** and will not need to feature in the tax computation. For the **payer**, this amount is not in itself tax deductible but the payer will be able to obtain the statutory deduction for providing employees with shares, subject to satisfying certain qualifying conditions (¶15120+); and
- an element relating to **administrative services** of operating the share incentive plan. This payment will be taxable on the recipient (the provider of the scheme) and tax deductible for the payer (¶15095+).

Where a transfer pricing adjustment imputes a further payment or receipt, this is treated in the same way as the original payment for taxation purposes.

F. Business restructuring

70605

In a restructuring it is necessary to examine the question of whether the **contractual terms** provide for an arm's length allocation of risk, and whether the parties have **conformed to the contractual terms** in practice. It is then necessary to consider if the risks are economically significant and their transfer pricing consequences. Tax authorities will want to determine if the allocation of risk is one that would have been agreed between independent parties in similar circumstances.

Also important is the extent to which the restructured companies should receive arm's length **compensation** for the functions, assets and risks transferred in the course of the restructuring, or an indemnification for the termination or renegotiation of the previous arrangements existing within the group. This involves understanding how the changes made have affected the functional analysis between the parties, the business reasons for, and anticipated benefits from, the restructuring, and the options that would have been available to independent parties.

The OECD has drafted discussion documents covering:
- the allocation of risk between the parties;
- compensation for the restructuring;
- application of the arm's length principle to the post-restructuring arrangements; and
- circumstances in which the transaction or structure adopted by the company may be disregarded by the tax authority.

SECTION 4

Adjustments and payments

A. All parties subject to UK tax

---

1. Compensating adjustments

General reduction available

Where profits of one enterprise (the advantaged person) have been increased by a transfer pricing adjustment, a compensating adjustment may be available to correspondingly decrease the taxable profits of the **other party to the transaction**. The compensating adjustment is only available if that other party (the disadvantaged person) is within the charge to income tax or corporation tax on profits arising from the relevant activities.

70655
s 174 TIOPA 2010;
INTM412130

The **disadvantaged person** must make the claim to a reduction in its taxable profits within 2 years of the date on which:
- the advantaged party files a return including an adjustment reflecting the arm's length position; or
- a relevant notice of determination is issued to the advantaged person i.e. a closure notice in relation to an enquiry, a notice of assessment or notice of a discovery assessment.

Specific adjustments

Specific rules apply to certain situations, including:
- transactions involving **trading stock**. Where a transfer pricing adjustment arises on a transfer of trading stock at a non-arm's length price, the transferee can obtain a compensating adjustment in the same period that the original transfer pricing adjustment was made, rather than waiting until the period when the stock is sold on;
- where the advantaged person is a **controlled foreign company** (¶90555+), the disadvantaged person (if a UK company) can claim a compensating adjustment provided that the profits of the CFC, as adjusted, are wholly apportioned to UK shareholders;

70660
INTM440030

– where interest is disallowed because a UK company is **thinly capitalised**, a compensating adjustment is available to a UK lender or to another group company;

– a UK borrower that has **interest payments disallowed** under the transfer pricing provisions is not required to deduct withholding tax from those payments;

– where a transfer pricing adjustment is made as a result of a **guarantee** on a security, for the purpose of a compensating adjustment, the sponsor can be treated as if it had paid the disallowed interest; the compensating adjustment is limited to the extent that a third party lender would take account of the guarantee when determining the debt capacity of the borrower; and

– a compensating adjustment cannot be made in relation to a provision relating to a security where the **guarantor participates** (directly or indirectly) in the management, control or capital of the business.

A compensating adjustment is **not available** in a situation where the "acting together" rules apply (¶70100).

2. Balancing payments

70690
ss 195, 196 TIOPA 2010;
INTM412140

Even where a compensating adjustment is made, there is still an imbalance because **one party has paid tax on income it did not receive**, whilst the other party has claimed a tax deduction for payments that it did not actually make. The related parties may choose to rectify this position by making a balancing payment between them. This may be important where, for example, the **distributable profits** of one party have been reduced below the desired level or where a **minority shareholder** objects to the situation that has arisen.

Where a compensating adjustment is available, a balancing payment can be made provided that the **main reason** for making it is that there has been a transfer pricing adjustment. The net tax position will not be altered by the balancing payment, which can be of any amount up to the amount of the transfer pricing adjustment. The payment is not deductible for the paying company and is not taxable income for the recipient.

INTM486010

‎⌐MEMO POINTS⌐   HMRC guidance indicates that transfer pricing adjustments or compensating adjust-ments have no direct **VAT consequences**, but where the original transaction was not at arm's length there might be reason to consider whether it was a transaction made at less than market value. This might lead to a direction to use the open market value for VAT purposes. Making a balancing payment also does not in itself have any VAT consequences. However, where agree-ment to make a balancing payment is conditional on the making of a further supply, this could be considered as non-monetary consideration for that supply and a liability to VAT could arise.

B. Involving parties not subject to UK tax

Double tax conventions

70720
INTM423000+

Where intercompany costs are **challenged by one of the tax authorities** involved, it may be possible to obtain relief from double taxation through the mutual agreement procedure (MAP) in the relevant double tax treaty. In this respect, the UK has a wide network of double tax treaties which are generally based on the OECD Model Tax Convention and most of which provide for a mutual agreement procedure similar to that outlined in Article 25 of the OECD Model. Under the previous version of Article 25, which was followed in most of the UK's tax treaties, the competent authorities in the two tax administrations **agree that they will endeavour** to reach agreement, but are not actually committed to reach agreement. This means that a company could go to the time and expense of invoking the mutual agree-ment procedure under a tax treaty, only to find that the competent authorities fail to reach agreement and the double taxation remains.

The latest version of the OECD Model Tax Convention provides for an **arbitration procedure** if the competent authorities do not reach agreement within 2 years. In this case, the unresolved issues can be submitted to arbitration at the request of the company. The mutual agreement that implements the arbitration decision is **binding on both contracting states unless a person** "directly affected by the case" does not accept the agreement. The UK has already begun to introduce the arbitration provision into its double tax treaties.

European Union

Another possibility for relief from double taxation is the EU Arbitration Convention, as strengthened by the Code of Conduct drawn up by the EU Joint Transfer Pricing Forum and adopted by the European Commission. The **EU Arbitration Convention**, officially known as the "Convention on the elimination of double taxation in connection with the adjustment of profits of associated enterprises", provides for a mutual agreement procedure (similar to that provided for in the OECD Model Tax Convention) **where a company considers that double taxation** has not been eliminated as provided for in the Convention, and the competent authorities of the member states concerned must then endeavour to resolve the case by mutual agreement. However, if there is **no resolution of the issues within 2 years** after the first notification of the case by the company to the competent authority, the case goes to an advisory commission for arbitration. The advisory commission must deliver an opinion within 6 months, after which the competent authorities are given a further 6 months to reach an agreement, which may deviate from the opinion of the arbitration commission. However, if the competent authorities are unable to reach an opinion within those further 6 months, they are obliged to adopt the opinion of the arbitration commission.

70725

SECTION 5

Advance agreements

As the transfer pricing regulations are complex and HMRC may dispute the use of a pricing method, there exists the facility to **agree with HMRC**, in advance, the method used to avoid adjustments or enquiries at a later date.

70775
INTM422020

A. Financing

HMRC has set out the **procedure for applications** for an advance thin capitalisation agreement (ATCA), and has provided a suggested model format for an agreement. **Situations** where an application for an ATCA could be made include:
– certain funding arrangements that do not require withholding tax treaty clearance, for example arrangements involving quoted Eurobonds;
– financing arrangements that are caught by the "acting together" rules (¶70100); or
– financing arrangements previously dealt with under the tax treaty clearance procedure.

Any UK business entering financial arrangements where the transfer pricing rules can be involved can apply for an ATCA. The company must outline the transactions in respect of which the proposed ATCA would apply, including background on the relevant business and transactions. The application may be made in electronic form. The typical period covered by an ATCA is 3 to 5 years, and "roll-back" to preceding periods may be possible in certain circumstances (¶70835).

If HMRC consider that the issues involved **would not materially affect** the profits or losses for the period concerned, they may reject the application. Where HMRC **cannot reach any agreement**, they will issue a statement setting out the reasons why.

70805
SP 1/12;
INTM573000+

The provisions of the **model ATCA** suggested by HMRC include the following:
- a description of the financial transactions covered;
- the term of the agreement (e.g. 3 to 5 years);
- monitoring of the financial conditions;
- a statement of the consequences of not meeting the financial conditions;
- circumstances where the agreement may be revoked; and
- the calculation of any interest disallowance.

> MEMO POINTS   **Use of the model agreement** is not obligatory and the suggested format may not be suitable for some transactions.

B. Other provisions

70835
ss 218 – 230 TIOPA
2010;
INTM422000+

An **application** can be made to HMRC for a unilateral or bilateral advance pricing agreement (APA), which could provide certainty that the tax administrations involved would not challenge the transfer pricing for the transactions covered by the agreement. This is on the basis that the information initially provided to them was accurate, and that any change in the circumstances in which the transactions are made is communicated to them.

An APA is a written agreement between a company and HMRC to determine a method for resolving transfer pricing issues in advance of making a tax return. The application can be **made by a UK resident company or partnership** engaging in transactions to which the transfer pricing legislation applies, or by a **foreign resident** with a branch or permanent establishment in the UK. HMRC may turn down a request for an APA where they consider that the transactions concerned are not of sufficient complexity to necessitate the negotiation of an APA, and would therefore not be a reasonable use of their resources.

The **scope** of an APA is flexible, covering specific transactions or all transfer pricing issues of a business. The **term** for which the APA runs is likely to be a minimum of 3 years and a maximum of 5 years. An APA may apply retrospectively to a period ending before the agreement is concluded, and the company and HMRC may agree to a "roll-back" of the agreement to resolve transfer pricing issues open from previous years.

> MEMO POINTS   A **multilateral APA** is essentially a series of bilateral APAs, and may be appropriate where there is one activity such as **global trading** and several group companies or branches are taking part in it in various jurisdictions.

Application process

70840

The process of application for an APA has **four stages** – expression of interest; formal submission of the application; evaluation and finalising the agreement.

The **expression of interest** should clarify:
- the transfer pricing issues to be covered;
- the parties involved;
- the proposed transfer pricing method and why it ensures conformity to the arm's length principle;
- the nature of any current transfer pricing enquiries underway or APAs already in force; and
- confirmation of whether a unilateral or bilateral APA is being sought.

The **formal submission** of the application for clarification should include:
- the applicant's understanding of the application of the transfer pricing legislation and of any double tax treaty relating to the transactions;
- the areas where clarification is required, due to the complexity of the legislation; and
- a proposal of how the effects of the transfer pricing legislation can be clarified.

The application should **identify** the critical assumptions made when proposing the transfer pricing method, and that method must be able to accommodate changes in economic and commercial conditions during the course of the agreement. A significant change to the critical assumptions at any stage would be a reason for reviewing the agreement and making appropriate changes.

At the **evaluation stage**, HMRC will review the application and seek further information and clarification of the background and the relevant transactions. They will be looking for a co-operative process and open exchange of information. In the case of a **bilateral APA**, the company will be expected to make information available to both tax administrations involved, and HMRC will discuss issues arising with the treaty partner. HMRC may consider meetings with both the company and the other tax authority to discuss and clarify issues.

Where **agreement** is reached, this is binding on both parties, and the relevant transfer pricing issues will be dealt with according to the agreement provided that its terms are observed. These **terms will include** a commitment by the business to determine its transfer pricing according to the terms of the agreement, and the identification of the critical assumptions which, if they change, will trigger a review of the agreement. Where **no agreement** can be achieved, HMRC will issue a statement explaining why they were unable to reach agreement.

The APA will set out the **nature and frequency of reports** required to be submitted by the company to HMRC in the course of the agreement. The APA would normally require a report on at least an annual basis confirming that the agreed method was used in the year, the financial results of the method and reconciliation to the accounts and tax computations. The report would include details of adjustments made as a result of any mismatch between the prices of the relevant transactions and those arrived at by the agreed transfer pricing method. The report would also normally confirm that the critical assumptions have been sound during the course of the APA and continue to be so.

> MEMO POINTS Where the company submits a tax return that reflects **pricing that does not conform** to the APA, this constitutes an incorrect return and could render the company liable to penalties (¶52480+).

SECTION 6

Documentation

UK requirements

Whilst some countries prescribe lists of required transfer pricing documentation, transfer pricing documentation requirements in the UK are part of the general provisions for a correct tax return under the self-assessment regime. Where **insufficient documentation** is kept to evidence a group's transfer pricing evaluation, the general tax penalty regime for an incorrect tax return will apply (¶52480+).

70890
INTM483030

HMRC divide the documentation requirements into **four classes of evidence** that may be required:
- primary accounting records;
- tax adjustment records;
- records of transactions with associated businesses; and
- evidence to demonstrate an arm's length result.

Whilst the **primary accounting records** should be created at the time that the information enters the accounting system, the tax adjustment records and the records of transactions with associated businesses could be created later than the primary accounting records but before a tax return is submitted for the period concerned.

The **evidence for an arm's length result** would need to be made available to HMRC in response to a reasonable request in relation to a tax return that has already been made. This means that, although the enterprise would need to be in possession of evidence on which it based its transfer pricing at the time the tax return was made (to ensure that the return was correct), this evidence need not necessarily be in a suitable format to submit to HMRC at that time. The enterprise could do further work to provide adequate evidence to HMRC after a reasonable request is made for this. Therefore, although there would be sufficient evidence for the transfer pricing at the time the tax return was made, this could be clarified and backed up by further evidence obtained at a later date.

⬛ MEMO POINTS In addition to the guidance on documentation given in the International Manual, HMRC, under the risk-based approach to transfer pricing enquiries, are giving the company the chance to engage in **pre-filing meetings** at which high-risk and complex transactions would be identified. These meetings would give companies a chance to clarify any questions they may have about the extent of documentation that might be required on these matters, and to gain an indication of the issues and transactions considered by HMRC to be relatively low-risk from a transfer pricing perspective. This would enable the company to prepare targeted documentation, in discussion with HMRC, and thereby reduce compliance costs.

EU documentation requirements

70895   The Code of Conduct on EU transfer pricing documentation sets out **guidelines** on the transfer pricing documentation for enterprises operating in the EU. These guidelines are not compulsory, and would not prevent HMRC requesting further information if required. The Code of Conduct provides for companies doing business in a number of countries in the EU to keep a "masterfile" on their EU business and "country specific documentation" for each EU member state in which they are operating. The aim is for enough information to be contained in the file to enable each EU tax administration to select cases for audit on the basis of a risk assessment, and to ask relevant and precise questions where they decide to investigate further.

SECTION 7

Enquiries

70945   HMRC have adopted a risk-based approach to corporation tax enquiries for large companies,
INTM481010+   which **analyses the tax risk** of large companies in respect of their inherent risk and their behavioural risk. The **inherent risk** would relate to the complexity of the business in terms of the:
– number of companies in the group;
– number and type of cross-border transactions; and
– activity in respect of mergers and acquisitions.

The **behavioural risk** would relate to the behaviour of the group as regards controlling its risk, taking into account:
– corporate governance factors;
– the adequacy of the internal systems and processes; and
– the tax strategy of the group e.g. the issue of whether the group engages in "aggressive" tax planning.

HMRC have set out **specific guidelines** as to how this risk management approach is to be applied to transfer pricing enquiries, and HMRC policy is that transfer pricing enquiries should be **completed** within 18 months where the company provided the necessary information in good time, with a longer period for particularly complex or high-risk enquiries which would not, however, exceed 36 months.

The governance process for transfer pricing and the "stage gates" through which transfer pricing enquiries must now pass are set out in HMRC guidance.

Comment The **effect of the risk-based approach** for companies cooperating with HMRC should be a reduction in transfer pricing compliance costs, because the enquiry would be focused on the high risk issues, and unnecessary compliance work with regard to other issues would be reduced to a minimum.

PART 11

Particular situations

Particular situations
Summary

The numbers cross-refer to paragraphs.

Close companies

Most UK companies are close for tax purposes, which broadly means that an extended definition of distribution applies, loans to shareholders are subject to special rules, and investment companies are subject to the full rate of corporation tax. **75000**

The aim of the rules is to is maintain a level playing field between companies where a few key people have control (and could potentially manipulate the company to their own advantage so as to avoid income tax) and those where shareholders have virtually no say in the extraction of the company's profits and assets.

Scope

The rules are drawn very widely, and encompass many companies. It is irrelevant whether **75050** the company is quoted, unquoted, unlimited or limited. A company is basically close where it is **controlled** either by five or fewer shareholders or by its directors, regardless of how many there are. See ¶75240 for the full definition.

A. Exclusions

Summary

75080
ss 439, 446, 447
CTA 2010;
CTM60105, 60280

The following table details those companies which cannot be close and are therefore unaffected by the special rules:

Company which cannot be close	Details
Not resident in the UK	Close company rules do not apply to a non-resident company trading in the UK through a permanent establishment (¶92140) For details of how to determine a company's residency see ¶2030
Certain companies controlled[1] by open companies (i.e. not close)	¶75110+
Quoted companies in which the public controls[1] 35% or more of the voting power	¶75145+
A company controlled[1] by an overseas government or local authority	¶75190
A company controlled[1] by or on behalf of the Crown	¶75210
A society registered under the Industrial and Provident Societies Acts	Either the Industrial and Provident Societies Act 1965 or the Industrial and Provident Societies Act (Northern Ireland) 1969
A building society	Within the meaning of the Building Societies Act 1986

Note:
1. Control is determined by applying various tests (¶75310+).

---

1. Controlled by open companies

75110
s 444 CTA 2010;
CTM60290

A company is **not to be treated** as close where either:
a. both of the following apply:
– it is controlled (under any test (¶75310+)) by an open company, or by two or more open companies; and
– it cannot be treated as a close company under any of the tests except by including an open company in the group of five or fewer participators (¶75355+); or
b. the company can only be shown to be close under the assets on a winding up test (¶75485+), but the company would not be close if certain loan creditors were excluded from being participators (¶75115).

s 444(4) CTA 2010

 MEMO POINTS 1. If a **non-resident company** is involved in the group, then it should be deemed to be close for these purposes, if it would be so were it to be resident in the UK.

s 445 CTA 2010

2. **Shares held by trustees** are deemed to be in the beneficial ownership of an open company where:
a. the shares are held in trust for a registered pension scheme; and
b. the fund or scheme is established for the benefit of employees of an unrelated open company, and not for persons who are employees or directors (including those who have left employment and all dependants) of either:
– the company being considered;
– any company associated with it;
– a company controlled by directors and/or associates of directors of the company being tested; or
– a close company.
A joint fund for the benefit of employees of two or more companies is deemed to be in the beneficial ownership of an open company if the majority of the beneficiaries are employees or dependants of an unrelated open company.

> EXAMPLE A Ltd's ordinary share capital is issued as follows:
>
> | Ordinary shares | Shareholding |
> |---|---|
> | B Ltd - open company | 290 |
> | C Ltd - open company | 220 |
> | D Ltd - close company | 260 |
> | Mr E | 50 |
> | Mr F | 30 |
> | Mr G | 30 |
> | Other shareholders (each holding less than 10 shares) | 120 |
> | | 1,000 |
>
> B Ltd and C Ltd control A Ltd as they own more than 50% of the shares. There is no combination of participators which would make A Ltd a close company, as an open company must always be included in the group in order for control to exist.
> A Ltd is therefore not a close company.
> If Mr F holds redeemable loan stock such that he has the majority of the assets on a winding up, then A Ltd is a close company even though the share capital is controlled by B Ltd and C Ltd.

Open company loan creditors

If the **only reason** that a company would be close is because of the right to assets test (¶75320 and ¶75485), then it is important to check whether there are any participators which are loan creditors and open companies. If the company can only satisfy the control tests by including an open company loan creditor then it will not be close.

75115
s 444 CTA 2010;
CTM60300

If the open company loan creditor **also holds shares** in the company, it will remain a participator in respect of that holding.

> EXAMPLE A national bank is entitled to the majority of assets on the winding up of H Ltd. The company's shares are held by individuals, five of whom have control.
> Although the bank would control the company under the assets test, H Ltd is a close company because of the individual shareholders who are the participators.

2. Quoted companies

A company in which 35% or more of the **voting power is held by the public** is usually not a close company. The conditions which must all be satisfied are shown in the following table:

75145
ss 446, 447, 449
CTA 2010;
CTM60310

Condition	Detail
The principal members do not hold more than 85% of the voting power	The principal members are the top five participators (¶75355+), each having an interest of at least 5%
Public beneficially hold at least 35% of the voting power	General public excludes: – directors and their associates (¶75395+); – companies controlled by the directors and their associates; – associated companies[1] of the quoted company; – funds (e.g. pensions) where the capital or income is applied wholly or mainly for the benefit of employees or directors of the company, its associated companies, or other companies which are controlled by the directors and their associates; – the principal members (other than open companies or pension funds who are principal members); and – nominees of any of the above The shares: – have been allotted or acquired unconditionally; and – have been the subject of dealings on a recognised stock exchange (¶95320) and been quoted in the official list of a recognised stock exchange within the preceding 12 months

Note:
1. Two **companies are associated** if, within the last 12 months, one of the two has control of the other or both are under the control of the same person or persons.

Voting power

75150   Voting power is not defined, but is usually easy to **identify** by looking at the various classes of issued share capital, their respective voting rights, and who holds the shares.

When a person holds **more than one class of share**, it is simply a case of adding up the votes to which he is entitled.

> EXAMPLE   X plc has issued:
> – 100,000 ordinary shares, each having one vote per share;
> – 20,000 A shares, each having 10 votes per share; and
> – 10,000 B shares, each having 30 votes per share.
> The total of the issued votes is 600,000. (100,000 + 200,000 + 300,000)
> Mr C and Mr D are two shareholders, and their voting power is calculated as follows:
>
> | Shareholder | Ordinary shares | A shares | B Shares | | Total votes |
> |---|---|---|---|---|---|
> | Mr C | 10,000 | 1,000 | 600 | (10,000 + 10,000 + 18,000) | 38,000 |
> | Mr D | 5,000 | 5,000 | 200 | (5,000 + 50,000 + 6,000) | 61,000 |

75155
s 447 CTA 2010

Held by the public   The voting rights held by the public exclude any rights attached to **preference shares** entitled to some sort of fixed dividend. However, when calculating the percentage held by the public, the total number of votes must include preference rights unless these are conditional and that condition would not be met at the time of the test (e.g. a vote only comes into being when the dividend is paid late, and dividends have always been paid on time).

75160   **Held by principal members**   Voting rights held by the principal members **include** those attached to all preference shares i.e. those with a fixed dividend.

Voting rights held by the following are to be **attributed** to a member:
– his nominee (¶75370);
– his associates (¶75395+); and
– a company which the member controls (or controls together with his associates).

Where more than one participator is eligible for the **fifth participator position** (because of equal shareholdings), they may all be treated as principal members (so in this case there would be more than five).

> EXAMPLE
> 1. The shares of A plc (which is quoted) are held as follows:
>
> | Shareholder | % of shares held |
> |---|---|
> | Mr A | 11% |
> | Mr B | 7% |
> | Mr C | 8% |
> | Mr D | 8% |
> | Mr E | 6% |
> | Mr F | 6% |
> | Other shareholders - unassociated individuals with holdings of less than 5% each | 54% |
> | | 100% |
>
> Mr A, Mr B, Mr C, Mr D and Mr E each hold more than 5% and are principal members of the company. Mr F is also a principal member, as he has an equal shareholding with Mr E. So there are six principal members in all.
>
> 2. The shares in B plc (a quoted company) are held as follows:
>
> | Shareholder | % of shares held |
> |---|---|
> | Mr A | 11% |
> | Mr B | 7% |
> | Mr C | 15% |
> | Mr D | 8% |
> | E plc (open company) | 25% |
> | Mr F (not connected to any other shareholder) | 9% |
> | Mr G | 17% |
> | Unassociated individuals | 8% |
> | | 100% |

The public own 42% of the company, taking the holdings of E plc, Mr F and the unassociated individuals into account. (25 + 9 + 8)
The principal members do not hold more than 85% of the voting power, taking into account the holdings of E plc, Mr G, Mr C, Mr A and Mr F. (25 + 17 + 15 + 11 + 9)
B plc is therefore not a close company.

3. Controlled by overseas government or local authority

A company will **not be close** where it is controlled by either:
- an overseas government;
- the Crown Agents for Overseas Governments and Administrations; or
- local authorities or local authority associations exempt from UK tax.

This is HMRC practice.

A company will also not be close if the only persons who can be taken to have control of that company are any of the above **together with** at least one open company (whether UK resident or not).

75190
CTM60280

4. Controlled by the Crown

The Crown for this purpose **includes** any Minister, government department or other person acting on behalf of the Crown.

If, under any control test (¶75310+), **someone other than the Crown** controls the company, then the company is still close.

75210
s 443 CTA 2010

B. Definition

A close company must be resident in the UK and is either:
a. under the **control** of:
- five or fewer participators; or
- any number of participators who are directors; or
b. bound to distribute the majority of the company's assets to five or fewer participators, or the participators who are directors, on a **winding up**.

The **time** when these criteria should be considered depends on which event is relevant, so for:
- loans to participators, the tests are considered when the loan is made; and
- distributions, the date of the dividend or when the benefits are made available is pertinent.

For investment companies see ¶75945+.

75240
s 439 CTA 2010

EXAMPLE The issued share capital of A Ltd is held as follows:

	Shareholding	Total shares issued
Ordinary shares		
Mr A	5	
Mr B	10	
Other shareholders (each holding less than 5 shares)	85	
Preference shares		100
Mr A	1,000	1,000
		1,100

Mr A owns more than 50% of the issued share capital so the company is close.

Summary of how to determine a close company

75245

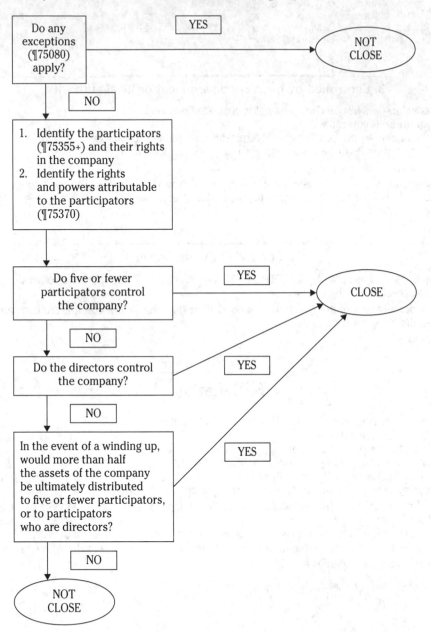

C. Control

75275
CTM60220

Control **means** that a person has the ability or potential (i.e. through future acquisitions) to control a company, either directly or indirectly. This is looking at the participator or general meeting level, not at administrative or board level.

As a person is deemed to possess the rights of his associates, his nominees and any companies he himself controls, the web can get quite large when deciding who has control of a particular company.

It is usually straightforward to see who controls a company, as long as a complete list of shareholders is available, and those shareholders do not include trustees or other companies.

> MEMO POINTS 1. **Indirect** control arises when the influence of a person's associates (¶75395+) are amalgamated with that of the person himself, so that together they control the company.
> 2. **Participator** is defined at ¶75360.

Comment 1. When considering any of the control tests, it is essential to have available an up-to-date copy of the company's **Memorandum and Articles of Association** and copies of relevant trust deeds etc.
2. It may be very difficult for a company with **bearer shares** to know whether it is a close company. HMRC have powers which can oblige possible shareholders to give relevant information on this issue.
3. Control is also relevant when considering **associated companies** for the purposes of tax rates (¶40185).

75280

---

1. What is controlled?

Control can be **tested** by looking at who owns the majority (i.e. more than 50%) of either the:
– issued share capital;
– voting power;
– income distribution, assuming that the whole of the income of the company is to be distributed amongst the participators; and
– rights to a company's assets (usually in the event of winding up).

75310
ss 450, 451
CTA 2010

In determining whether any person has control, the rights and powers of certain other persons may be attributed to them.

Each test must be considered in relation to participators who are not directors first. If the company is not close under any of those tests, it is then necessary to consider whether the directors (¶75445+) control the company. Failing that, the notional winding up test (¶75485+) is relevant.

> EXAMPLE
> 1. A Ltd has issued the following types of share:
> A shares which have full voting rights, held by 20 unassociated individuals. Nominal value £20.
> B shares (having no voting rights), held by four individuals. Nominal value £200.
> As the B shares have greater nominal value, A Ltd is close because they are held by four participators, who are deemed to control the company.
>
> 2. B Ltd has issued £1,000 of ordinary share capital with one vote per share, and 120 A shares, each having 10 votes per share. The ordinary share capital is held by 50 unassociated individuals. The A shares are held by Mr C and Mr D.
>
> | Shareholder | | Number of votes |
> |---|---|---|
> | Mr C | 10 × 60 | 600 |
> | Mr D | 10 × 60 | 600 |
> | | | 1,200 |
> | Other shareholders | | 1,000 |
> | | | 2,200 |
>
> As Mr C and Mr D have the right to more than 50% of the votes, B Ltd is a close company.
>
> 3. A joint venture company was owned 50% by an Italian company and 50% by a UK corporate group. The company had a 100% UK subsidiary, from which it received dividends. It was important to establish who controlled the joint venture company in order to correctly tax these dividends.

> It was held that the two parties acted together to exercise control of the company, in accordance with the detailed shareholders' agreement. Their control at the general meeting level allowed them to direct the company in its policy and business activity. *Steele v EVC International NV* [1996]
>
> 4. E Ltd was controlled by the trustees of Mr E's will trust which gave a life interest to Mrs E. It was argued that E Ltd was associated with F Ltd (which was controlled by the trustees of a discretionary trust set up by Mr E), because both sets of trustees were associates of Mrs E.
> The House of Lords held that the companies were associated. *R v CIR (ex parte Newfields Developments Ltd)* [2001]

Distributed income

75315
s 450(3)(c)
CTA 2010

This test looks at who has the right to distributed income, based on the issued share capital, and for this purpose the rights of any **loan creditor** are disregarded. The nominal value of the share capital is relevant rather than the number of shares. *Canada Safeway v IRC* [1973]

This will mainly be of relevance where **shares with no voting rights** carry the right to a high dividend.

Right to assets

75320
s 450(3)(d)
CTA 2010

This test is normally **only needed** where loan creditors are participators (excluding open companies (¶75115)), or there are special rights to the assets on a winding up or on the redemption of share capital.

A person has control of a company where he has a right to receive the majority of the assets which are available for distribution among participators (including loan creditors) in any **circumstances**, such as on:
– redemption of redeemable share capital;
– repayment of loans to the company; and
– a winding up of the company.

The test only applies to the assets that would come to a participator in that **capacity**. Where a bank has loaned money to a company in the ordinary course of its business, it would not therefore count as a participator.

Comment   Note that this test is distinct from the separate consideration of winding up which has its own rules (¶75485+).

Multiple control

75325

It is possible for more than one person or one group of persons to have control, because different groups may **satisfy different control tests** e.g. voting power, rights to dividends, or rights to assets.

> EXAMPLE
> 1. Mr A owns 60% of the voting power in A Ltd. Mr B and Mr C together own 70% of the share capital, and Mr D, Mr E and Mr F are entitled to 60% of the assets on a winding up.
> All three combinations of people can be taken to have control of the company at the same time.
>
> 2. Mrs F, Mrs G and Mrs H (who are unrelated) each own a third of B Ltd's shares.
> The company is controlled by either:
> – Mrs F and Mrs G;
> – Mrs G and Mrs H; or
> – Mrs F and Mrs H.
> However, the company is not controlled by Mrs F, Mrs G and Mrs H, as only two individuals are necessary to exert control.
>
> 3. Mr X, Mr Y and Mr Z together control A Ltd via voting rights. They also control B Ltd because of their rights to assets on a winding up.
> A Ltd and B Ltd are associated, even though different tests for control are satisfied in each company. The group of people who control each company is Mr X, Mr Y and Mr Z, and not the individuals or pairings e.g. Mr X and Mr Y.

2. Who exerts control?

a. Participators

The identity and rights of the company's participators are crucial when deciding whether a company is close. As the rights of a participator's associates are attributed to him when assessing who controls the company, it is important to understand the various personal and business relationships between the shareholders and loan creditors.

75355

Definition

A participator is any person having an interest in the capital or income of the company, **specifically including** a person who:
– possesses or is entitled to acquire issued share capital or voting rights in the company;
– is a loan creditor (¶75365) of the company;
– possesses or is entitled to acquire a right to receive, or participate in, distributions of the company, or in any amounts payable by the company (in cash or kind) to loan creditors by way of premium or redemption; or
– is entitled to secure that income or assets (whether present or future) of the company will be applied directly, or indirectly, for his benefit.

75360
s 454 CTA 2010

> MEMO POINTS 1. **Entitled to acquire** means that a person has a current or future contractual right, or a right arising under a trust deed, to either:
> – require a shareholder to transfer shares to him;
> – secure the issue of new share capital to him;
> – secure that if the company makes a distribution, he has a share in the distribution; or
> – secure that if a loan is redeemed by the company at a premium, he has a share in the premium.
> A common example would be a share option.
> 2. **Entitled to secure** means that a person is a participator if, by means of a current or future contractual right or some other arrangement, he can secure that income or assets of the company will be applied directly or indirectly for his benefit.

EXAMPLE A Ltd has £6,000 of authorised share capital, of which £4,000 is issued as follows:

Shareholder	Number of shares held
Mr A - director	300
Mr B - director	300
Mr C - director	300
Mr D - director	300
Mr E	400
Mr F	400
Other shareholders - unassociated individuals with holdings of less than 100 shares	2,000
	4,000

The four directors enter into service agreements stating that they will remain in post for 5 years, and in the 4th year, they will have the right to purchase 400 shares each at par. Taking this into account, each director is entitled to acquire rights in 700 shares.
The total share capital which should be considered is £5,600. (4,000 + (4 × 400))
This means that overall, the top five participators (the directors plus either Mr E or Mr F) control 3,200 shares, out of a total of 5,600, which means A Ltd is close from the beginning of the directors' service period.

Loan creditors

Loan creditor **excludes** normal trade creditors of the company.

The term means a creditor in respect of any:
a. redeemable **loan capital** (e.g. debentures) issued by the company; or
b. debt incurred by the company, being a debt for:
– money borrowed or capital assets acquired by the company;

75365
s 453 CTA 2010

– any right to receive income created in favour of the company (e.g. a person contracts to make annual payments to the company, in return for a capital sum due at some later date); or

– consideration which was substantially less than the amount of the debt (including any premium).

s 453(3) CTA 2010   ⎍MEMO POINTS⎍   1. A person who has a **beneficial interest in a debt or loan capital**, in respect of which some other person is the loan creditor, is to be treated as a loan creditor to the extent of that interest.

CTM60130   2. The supplier of goods under a **hire purchase** agreement is not normally regarded as a loan creditor because the goods remain in his ownership until the amount due is paid by the company. The payments are therefore akin to rent, and the amount due is not a debt for this purpose.

s 453(4) CTA 2010   3. A **bank**, which has made a **loan** to the company in the ordinary course of its business, would not normally be treated as a loan creditor. *United Dominions Trust Ltd v Kirkwood* [1966]

Rights of other persons

75370
s 451 CTA 2010

The rights and powers held by the following are **attributed to** a participator:
– his nominee i.e. another person who acts on the participator's behalf or at his direction;
– his associates (including the rights held by nominees of associates); and
– any companies of which he has control (either alone, or including the rights held by his associates and nominees of his associates).

---

b. Associates

75390

The associates of a participator are summarised in the table at ¶75395. Note that the rights of associates of associates are not attributed to the participator e.g. the spouse of a brother.

Summary

75395
s 448 CTA 2010

Associate	Details	Scope
A person in the participator's family excluding an uncle, aunt, nephew or niece, and spouses of relatives e.g. brother-in-law	Spouse	Includes separated spouses Excludes divorced persons
	Parent or remoter forebear	Only if blood relationship unless adopted (when associated)
	Child or remoter issue	
	Brother or sister	
	Business partner	¶75405
The trustees of any settlement where the participator (or any of his family) is the settlor	¶75410	Excludes will trusts (i.e. personal representatives are not associates) *Willingale v Islington Green Investment Co* [1972]
The trustees of a settlement or personal representatives of an estate, where the participator is interested in any company shares which are subject to a trust or held within an estate	The participator would be interested in the shares where he was a trust beneficiary or legatee of an estate	Where the participator is a company, any other company interested in those shares is also an associate

Family

75400

With several family members involved in a company, there are usually **several combinations** which yield control, but if the company would be close under any combination then that is the one which counts. There can be no double counting of rights, so that once rights have been attributed, they are not available to attribute again in the same combination.

EXAMPLE

1. Mr A, Mrs A and Miss B (Mrs A's sister) own shares in a company.
The following shareholdings could be amalgamated:
– Mr A and Mrs A, if Mr A is the participator;
– Miss B and Mrs A, if Miss B is the participator; or
– all three, if Mrs A is the participator.
However, if Mr A is treated as a participator, the shareholdings of Mrs A are attributable to him and are therefore not available to attribute to Miss B because they have already been used up.

2. The issued share capital of C Ltd is held as shown below:

Shareholder	Number of shares held
Mr A - director	150
Mr B - director	200
Mr C - director	40
Mr D - director	40
Mr E	30
F Ltd (controlled by Mr E's son)	100
Other shareholders - unassociated individuals with holdings of less than 30 shares	440
	1,000

Mr E's son is his associate, but the shares held by F Ltd cannot be attributed to Mr E, as F Ltd is an associate of Mr E's associate.
As neither of the control tests involving participators or directors are met, C Ltd is not a close company.

3. As above, except that Mr E's son holds a single share in C Ltd, and the other shareholders have 439 shares.
This time, the shares held by Mr E, his son, and F Ltd are all attributable to Mr E's son - a total of 131 shares.
This makes C Ltd a close company as the following five participators have control:

	Number of shares held
Mr A	150
Mr B	200
Mr E's son	131
Mr C	40
Mr D	40
	561

Business partner

As business partners are associates, this can lead to some companies becoming close whilst being owned by many **individuals who are unknown to each other** but are classed as business partners. This is particularly relevant in the case of investment businesses, which means that the company would be treated as a CIHC (¶75945+).

75405

Participator is settlor

The participator (or a family member) may have entered into the settlement directly or indirectly. **Funds** must have been provided for the purpose of the settlement, or reciprocal arrangements made for another person to make or enter into the settlement.

75410
CTM60150

The **rights or powers possessed by the trustee(s)** may be attributed to the participator, excluding any rights or powers held by them:
– in a personal capacity; or
– as trustees for other settlements, where the participator and his family are not the settlor.

The **rights and powers of the settlor and his family** are not attributed back to the trustees i.e. the settlor and his family are not associates of the trustees.

MEMO POINTS 1. **Settlement** includes any disposition, trust, covenant, agreement or arrangement (whether for the family's benefit or not) but excludes an estate still in the course of administration.

2. **Settlor** means any person by whom the settlement was made. If the settlor is a member of the participator's family, he may be living or dead.

EXAMPLE F Ltd has 100 issued ordinary shares, held by the following:

Shareholder	Number of shares held
Mr F (the settlor)	6
Trustees of F settlement	45
Other shareholders (each holding less than 5 shares)	49
	100

The other shareholders are not associated with Mr F or the settlement.
F Ltd is a close company because Mr F and the settlement are associated, so together they own more than 50% of the shares.

Interests in shares subject to any settlement or estate

75415
CTM60160

In this case, anyone could be the settlor. It is necessary to determine whether the participator is **interested in** such shares. The following table gives common examples:

Shares held by	Persons interested	Reference
Trustees	- the trustees; - the beneficiaries; and - the remainderman (if any)	
Trustees under a will for persons in succession	- the trustees; - the life tenant; and - the remainderman	*CIR v Park Investments Ltd* [1964] *CIR v Tring Investments Ltd* [1939] *Alexander Drew and Sons Ltd v CIR* [1932]
Estate	- the administrators during the period of administration; and - the potential beneficiaries of estate assets	*Willingale v Islington Green Investment Co* [1972]

MEMO POINTS For the definition of **settlement** see ¶75410 above.

75420

The **rights or powers possessed by the trustee(s)** may be attributed to the participator, excluding any rights or powers held by them in any other capacity.

The rights and powers of the participator and his family are not attributed back to the trustees i.e. the settlor and his family are not associates of the trustees.

s 448 CTA 2010

A **company participator** is associated with other beneficiaries which are also companies. However, individual beneficiaries are not associated with each other.

Groups

75425
s 459(4) CTA 2010

When a company (i.e. a subsidiary) is controlled by another company (i.e. a parent), the **participators of the parent company** are treated as being participators of the subsidiary when considering loans made to participators and distributions (¶75545).

EXAMPLE G Ltd is owned 60% by Mr A. G Ltd owns 100% of H Ltd.
If H Ltd loans money to Mr A, this is treated as a loan to a participator in H Ltd, because Mr A is a participator in G Ltd i.e. Mr A is deemed to be a participator of H Ltd.

c. Directors

75445

The control tests for directors are the same as for participators generally (¶75360). However, for this purpose, non-directors are excluded from the group who could control the company, and there is no limit on the number of directors who might exercise control.

Definition

The term director **covers persons** who occupy the position of director within a company, whatever their job title (i.e. attends board meetings as of right, and has a vote).

Further, any **person in accordance with whose directions** or instructions the directors are accustomed to act is also a director for this purpose i.e. a shadow director. However, this excludes someone merely giving professional advice, and for someone to be treated as a shadow director there must be a constant expectation that the person will make policy which the directors will follow.

75450
s 452 CTA 2010

Manager

A manager of the company will be deemed to be a director where he **controls at least** 20% of the ordinary share capital of the company. Control may be on his own account, or via amalgamation with his associates (in which case, the manager himself may not own or control any of the share capital).

Indirect control, arising where the manager controls 20% of the company through his ownership of another company, also deems him to be a director.

75455
s 452(2) CTA 2010

> MEMO POINTS 1. **Ordinary share capital** means all the issued share capital, by whatever name called, of the company other than share capital carrying a right to a dividend only at a fixed rate.
> 2. For the definition of **associates** see ¶75395.

> EXAMPLE A Ltd is owned by the following persons:
>
> | Shareholder | | Number of shares held |
> |---|---|---|
> | Mr A | Director | 7 |
> | Mr B | Director | 10 |
> | Mr C | Director | 10 |
> | Mr D | Director | 11 |
> | Mr E | Manager | - |
> | Mrs E | | 21 |
> | Others (less than 4 each) | | 41 |
> | | | 100 |
>
> The company is close because the directors control 59% of the shares. Mr E is deemed to be a director because he is a manager and more than 20% of the shares are attributed to him through his wife's shareholding.

D. Notional winding up

A company is close if five or fewer participators, or participators who are directors, together possess such rights as would, in the event of the winding up of the company, entitle them to receive the greater part of the company's assets then available for distribution among the participators. This includes participators and directors who are entitled to acquire (¶75360) such rights. **Loan creditors** can be included or excluded as participators i.e. if the test is satisfied on either basis, the company is close.

75485
ss 439(3), 440
CTA 2010;
CTM60320

> EXAMPLE The share capital of £36,000 of D Ltd is owned equally by twelve unassociated individual shareholders. There are two loan creditors as follows:
>
> | | £ |
> |---|---|
> | Mr A - director and shareholder | 33,000 |
> | Mr B - unconnected to D Ltd | 13,000 |
>
> In a winding up, the value of the net assets distributable among members, including loan creditors, would be £130,000, distributed as follows:

	£
Mr A - as loan creditor	33,000
Mr B	13,000
Shareholders (£7,000 each)	84,000
	130,000

D Ltd is controlled by four participators due to the inclusion of loan creditors, so it is a close company.

		£
Mr A	(33,000 + 7,000)	40,000
Mr B		13,000
Another shareholder #1		7,000
Another shareholder #2		7,000
Distribution to four participators		67,000

Corporate participators

75490
s 440 CTA 2010

If a participator is a company (**except** a company which possesses rights in a purely fiduciary or representative capacity), it is **assumed** that the corporate participator is itself wound up and that the assets it would receive from the winding up are distributed to its own participators in proportion to their respective entitlement. This process is known as "look through", and is repeated (where the company participator itself has corporate participators) until all of the assets of the possibly close company are distributed to individuals (or companies holding the rights in a fiduciary capacity only). It is irrelevant whether the participator company is open or close.

For the purposes of this provision, a person is treated as a participator in the possibly close company if he is a participator in any company itself entitled to receive assets, directly or indirectly, in the winding up.

> EXAMPLE The 100 ordinary shares in A Ltd are owned as follows:
>
> | | Shares |
> |---|---|
> | Mr A | 9 |
> | Mr B | 6 |
> | Mr C | 8 |
> | Mr D | 8 |
> | E Ltd | 9 |
> | F Ltd | 11 |
> | Other shareholders | 49 |
> | | 100 |
>
> The 100 shares in each of E Ltd and F Ltd are held as follows:
>
> | | E Ltd | F Ltd |
> |---|---|---|
> | Mr A | 40 | |
> | Mr B | | 70 |
> | Mr G | 60 | |
> | Mr H | | 30 |
>
> As E Ltd owns 9% of A Ltd, Mr A would be entitled to 4% of A Ltd on the winding up of E Ltd (9 x 40%) and Mr G would be entitled to 5% of A Ltd. (9 x 60%) So Mr A's total holding in A Ltd is 13% when including the shares he holds on his own account. (4 + 9)
> As Mr B controls F Ltd which owns 11% of A Ltd, Mr B is deemed to control the entire 11% plus the holding on his own account, so he controls 17%. (11 + 6)
> On looking through the company participators, the control of the assets on the winding up of A Ltd would therefore be as follows:
>
> | | | % controlled |
> |---|---|---|
> | Mr A | 9 + 4 | 13 |
> | Mr B | 6 + 11 | 17 |
> | Mr C | | 8 |
> | Mr D | | 8 |
> | Mr G | | 5 |
> | | | 51 |
>
> A Ltd is therefore a close company.

Consequences

Various consequences arise as a result of being a close company, which mainly focus on preventing the tax-free extraction of funds from the company.   **75540**

Comment   Due to the numerous consequences of being a close company, any corporate acquisition should be covered by the appropriate **indemnities and warranties**. This is especially vital where the purchaser believes his acquisition to be an open company, but it subsequently transpires that the company is indeed close.

Summary

75545

Consequence	Detail	¶¶
Loans to participators	Tax charge on company while loan remains outstanding unless repaid within 9 months of accounting period end	¶75575+
Benefits treated as distributions	Valued in line with the employment income rules, but assessed as dividend income	¶75875+
Investment holding company	No small profits tax rate	¶75945+
Transfer of assets at undervalue	Reduces base cost of shares for shareholders who are not employees or participators	¶75995+
Disposal of asset by non-resident company	Gain attributed to participators with at least a 10% interest in the company	¶76040+

A. Loans to participators

There are special rules to discourage participators from taking money out of a company in the form of a loan, and therefore avoiding a tax liability which would otherwise apply to dividends or earnings.   **75575**

Any loan or advance made by a close company to a participator (or one of his associates (¶75395)), except where the loan is excluded, will lead to a tax charge on the company.   s 455 CTA 2010

Comment   The opposite money flow i.e. the **individual lending funds to a close company**, offers the chance of tax relief on the cost of borrowing for this purpose. See *Tax Memo* for further details.

1. Excluded loans

In the following circumstances, a tax charge on a close company loan does not arise: **75605**
– where the loan arises in an accounting period and is repaid within 9 months of that   s 456 CTA 2010
accounting period end (¶75790);
– loans to employees and directors which satisfy strict criteria; and
– certain loans by money lending companies.

Comment   The first exception means that it is possible to make a **short-term loan** for a maximum period of 21 months, without a tax charge occurring. However, there will be income tax consequences for the recipient of an interest-free loan.

a. Loans to employees

75625
s 456 CTA 2010;
CTM61540

Where a close company makes a loan or advance, for any purpose, to a director or employee of the close company or of any associated company (¶75145), that loan or advance will not be liable to a tax charge where all of the following **criteria** are satisfied:
– the total amount outstanding from the borrower does not exceed £15,000;
– the borrower works full time for the close company or any of its associated companies (i.e. at least 75% of the normal working hours of the company); and
– the borrower does not have a material interest in the close company or any of its associated companies.

Loan amount

75630
CTM61550

If **separate accounts** are maintained in the participator's name, any loan will be subject to tax i.e. accounts with a credit balance cannot be netted off against outstanding loans.

However, it is possible to discharge the loan by making a book entry (¶75800) from the account in credit.

If a **genuine joint account** is maintained with the company e.g. between spouses, then netting off of one spouse's balance against the other's is permitted. Otherwise, loans **to spouses** are not taken into account when determining the amount of borrowing.

Where both husband and wife are directors or employees, they will each be entitled to a separate limit of £15,000.

Material interest

75635
s 457 CTA 2010

Material interest is tested by looking at the ability to control share capital and any entitlement to the company's assets on its winding up.

If a borrower **subsequently acquires** a material interest after the loan is taken out, the loan is then subject to tax on the amount outstanding at the time that the material interest is acquired.

75640
CTM61560

Share capital   A person has a material interest in a company if he is able to control more than 5% of the ordinary share capital. Control may be either through his shareholding alone, or by taking into account the holdings of his associates (¶75395), and may be indirect i.e. by looking through holdings in other companies.

For this purpose, **ordinary share capital** means all the issued share capital other than share capital carrying a right to a dividend only at a fixed rate.

75645
CTM61560

Winding up   A person has a material interest in a company if he is entitled to more than 5% of the distributable assets on its winding up. Again, this must be assessed by taking into account the rights of his associates (¶75395).

b. Money lending companies

75665
s 456(1) CTA 2010

There are **two tests** to be satisfied for the loan (of any amount) to escape a tax charge:
a. the company's business includes the lending of money; and
b. the loan was made in the ordinary course of that business.

Lending of money

75670
CTM61520

A company must have a trade of lending money which would imply a recurrence of lending to a variety of borrowers. A **single loan** made by a company to a participator, even on commercial terms, is not adequate evidence of the existence of a commercially constituted business of lending money.

Typical traits of a money lender include:
– advertising the money lending business to the public;

- publishing the rates of interest (which are at a commercial rate);
- receiving applications for loans from the public;
- having a system to enforce debt collection;
- using official documentation which clearly sets out the terms of repayment of the loan in a legally enforceable form;
- having a reasonable number of loans (HMRC expect at least 200) to ensure that profits on the good loans can cover the inevitable loan write offs; and
- matching of borrowing and lending e.g. a trader would not generally borrow short term funds, repayable on demand, and lend them on a long term basis.

> [EXAMPLE] A close company made a loan of £30,000 to its chairman. Although it was claimed that the company was making loans in the ordinary course of its business, only 8 loans were made over 14 years to the same person, who was the associate of a participator.
> It was held that this situation could not amount to a business of lending money. *Brennan v The Deanby Investment Company Ltd* [2001]

Ordinary course of business

Where the loan to a participator does not mirror the **size, terms or conditions** of the loan offered to the public, then it will be chargeable to tax.

75675
CTM61520

---

2. Scope

Meaning of loan

For this purpose, a loan includes the case where:
- a person incurs a **debt** to the close company, **excluding** a debt arising as a result of the supply of goods and services in the ordinary course of the close company's business and the period of credit is no more generous than that extended to the company's customers (not exceeding 6 months); and
- a **debt** due from the person to a third party is **assigned** to the close company in return for consideration. Note that it is the creditor who must assign the debt.

75705
s 455 CTA 2010;
CTM61535

Comment Where HMRC ascertain that a company has **understated its profits**, they will often conclude that the company has made a loan of this sum to the directors or participators. *Powerlaunch Ltd v HMRC* [2012]

> [EXAMPLE] A Ltd, a third party, loans £6,000 to Mr X who is a participator in B Ltd. A Ltd assigns the debt to B Ltd for £2,000.
> Mr X now has to pay his debt to B Ltd, but is still obligated to A Ltd. However, due to the assignment, this still falls to be treated as a close company loan to a participator.

> [MEMO POINTS] **From 20 March 2013** the meaning of loan has been **extended** to include any extractions of value from the company, unless such amounts are fully taxed on the individual as income. This is intended to counter arrangements involving corporate partners and the manipulation of capital accounts and drawings.

Indirect loans In the following circumstances, a loan will still be chargeable to tax even though it is not made directly to an individual participator in the company (or an associate of a participator):
- the loan **facilitates** the making of a payment, the meeting of a liability or the transferring of property to such a person; and
- this is part of an **arrangement**.

75710
s 459 CTA 2010;
CTM61670

However, as an **exception**, if the recipient's taxable income includes at least the full amount of the payment, transfer, or release etc, then no tax arises on the company. This would occur, for example, where the payment is treated as a distribution, or a settlor of a trust is deemed to have received a capital payment.

> [EXAMPLE]
> 1. A Ltd is a close company and loans money to B Ltd, an associated company. B Ltd loans money to Mr A who is a participator in A Ltd.
> A Ltd is liable to tax on the loan as if it had been made to direct to Mr A.
>
> 2. C Ltd makes a loan to Mr D who is a participator in D Ltd. As part of the same arrangements, D Ltd then makes a loan to Mr C, a participator in C Ltd.
> Both companies are treated as if they had loaned money direct to their respective participators.

75715
s 460 CTA 2010;
CTM61690

Third party provides the loan Where a loan is provided to a participator (or his associate) by a third party, but the loan is effectively **financed by** the close company, the company will become liable to tax. Such arrangements normally involve the close company having (or acquiring) **control of the lender** which may itself not be close e.g. a non-resident or quoted subsidiary loans money to participators in the parent company.

If there is no **connection** between either the loan and acquisition of control, or the loan and the funds provided by the close company, then a tax charge cannot apply.

> [MEMO POINTS] 1. A close company **provides funds** where it either:
> – makes any payment to;
> – transfers any property to; or
> – releases or satisfies (in whole or in part) a liability of;
> the lender.
> 2. If the lender **loaned money before coming under the control** of the close company, the loan is deemed to have been made immediately after the close company acquired the lender.

CTM61720

> 3. Where **two or more close companies** control the lender, each is deemed to have loaned an appropriate proportion of the money based on their respective ownership interests in the lender.

Recipients

75720
s 455(6) CTA 2010;
CTM61510

Particular situations where a tax charge will arise include the following where a loan is made **to**:
– a **company** which is acting in a fiduciary or representative capacity;
– a **partnership** (including limited partnerships and limited liability partnerships) and one of the partners is a participator in the company; or
– a **trustee** or trustees, and any shares or obligations of the company are subject to the trust.

> [MEMO POINTS] 1. A **Scottish partnership** has a separate legal identity from the persons carrying on the partnership, so a loan to such a partnership will not give rise to a tax charge. However, where a partner has a deficit in their capital account, HMRC may argue that the loan by the company has facilitated the overdrawn capital account, in itself effectively a loan (¶75710).

CTM61515

> 2. If a **company is a member of a partnership**, and makes a loan to the partnership, this should not be viewed by HMRC as a loan to the other partners.

CTM61525

> 3. A loan to an **employee share scheme or an employee benefit trust** (¶15035) may be liable to tax where either:
> – the trust itself holds shares in the company at the time of the loan, or if the individual trustees were all participators in the company; or
> – the trustees make payments to existing shareholders for their shares.

---

3. Tax charge

75750
s 455 CTA 2010

A loan will be charged to tax at 25%, and this is a liability of the company which is treated like corporation tax. The tax due must be disclosed on the CTSA return (¶46050) and paid on the normal due date(s) for corporation tax (¶48050). Interest will apply to any late payment.

> [MEMO POINTS] If the **recipient** of the loan is an employee or director, the loan may give rise to an income tax as a benefit in kind. See *Tax Memo* for further details.

Amount levied

75755
s 458 CTA 2010

The tax charge is levied on the **lower** of the balance outstanding at:
– the accounting period end; and
– 9 months and 1 day after the accounting period end.

> [EXAMPLE] On 14 March 2013, E Ltd lends a participator £60,000. This loan is repaid via annual instalments of £20,000, starting on 14 March 2014. E Ltd's accounting period ends on 30 June. The amount outstanding on 30 June 2013 is £60,000, but this is reduced to £40,000 by 1 April 2014. So the tax due is £10,000. (40,000 @ 25%)

Insolvent companies

Where a company has become insolvent and is unable to meet its creditors, the company should take steps to call in the loan, and so any tax charge would either be **waived** or repaid.

75760
CTM61530

However, if the **loan is irrecoverable** and the tax charge would reduce the funds available for arm's length creditors, HMRC will consider whether the tax charge should be waived.

4. Repayment of the loan

Where the whole or part of a loan is repaid, the tax charge already paid will be due back to the company.

75790
s 458 CTA 2010;
CTM61605

Where repayment is **made within** 9 months of the end of the accounting period in which the loan first arose, then the original tax charge is cancelled, so no tax is payable to HMRC. If the loan is repaid later than the 9 month deadline see ¶75815.

> [MEMO POINTS] 1. The loan may be **repaid by** someone other than the original borrower. *Collins v Addies* [1992]
> 2. If there are **multiple loans**, any parties involved can make a specific appropriation against a particular debt. If no such appropriation is made, HMRC will set the repayment against the earliest debt first.
> 3. A **novation** (¶16260) would be treated as the release of the original loan to be substituted by a new loan.

Disclosure

Full details of the loan repayment and the payer must be disclosed on the CTSA return on form CT600A.

75795

For loans which are **repaid within 9 months** of the accounting period end, there is no practical tax effect on the company, but the result of disclosing the information is that HMRC can ensure that the recipient is appropriately taxed.

Book entries

Properly recorded book entries can effect a repayment so long as they **represent** the commercial reality of a transaction. *Minsham Properties Ltd v Price* [1990]

75800
CTM61605

The effective **date of repayment** will be the date that the book entries are made.

Artificial entries to the loan account just before the year end, which are reversed in the next accounting period, would be viewed as careless errors and thus lead to a penalty (¶52510).

CTM61615

Cleared by earnings

When clearing a loan by the payment of earnings, those earnings will be **liable** to tax and also Class 1 NIC (the liability for which will fall on both the employee and company). The company will be able to deduct the bonus from its taxable profits.

75805
s 18 ITEPA 2003

It is important to be clear **when** those earnings become available.

Earnings **for employees other than directors** are treated as received on the earlier of when:
– the payment of earnings is made; or
– the employee becomes entitled to the payment.

For **directors**, the rules are extended so that earnings (whether arising from the directorship or a different role) are treated as received on the earliest of the following dates:

- when the payment of earnings is made;
- when the director becomes entitled to the payment;
- when sums on account of earnings are credited in the company accounts or records (regardless of whether the director has the right to draw the money);
- where the amount of earnings for a period has already been determined, the date on which the period of account ends; or
- where the period of account has already ended, the date when the amount of earnings for a period is determined.

s 18(3) ITEPA 2003

MEMO POINTS   For these purposes, a **director is defined** as:
- a member of the board of directors which manages the company;
- a single director who manages the company;
- a member of the company if the company is managed by its members; or
- any person in accordance with whose directions or instructions (other than in a professional capacity), the company directors are accustomed to act.

EXAMPLE

1. Mr G, who is not a director, is entitled to receive a bonus of £10,000 on 28 February 2013. Payment is actually made on the following 28 June, once the accounts for the year ended 28 February 2013 have been approved.
For income tax purposes, the bonus is received in 2012/13 when the entitlement arose.
If Mr G's entitlement only arose on 28 June, the bonus would be taxed in 2013/14.

2. Mr H is a director of H Ltd. The company year end is 31 October 2013. The amount of each director's bonus is decided at a board meeting in the following March.
The accounts are approved at the company's AGM 6 weeks later, in May, and the bonuses are paid after that, in July.
Mr H's bonus is assessed in 2013/14, because the bonus was determined in March and the period of account, to which it related, had already ended.

Cleared by dividends

75810
CTM 61605

A loan can be cleared by the **payment** of dividends (which is not a deductible cost to the company but does avoid NIC), although it is only when the dividend is actually paid that the loan is discharged i.e. the money is actually put at the person's disposal which would most likely be evidenced by a book entry in the accounts. So audit adjustments made after the year end would not be effective during the year.

This method of clearing the loan can be fraught with difficulties where **not all of the shareholders have an overdrawn loan account** i.e. dividends are payable on the entirety of a particular class of share.

The company should ensure that sufficient distributable **profits** exist in order to pay the dividend. See *Company Law Memo* for further details.

Repayment of tax

75815
s 458 CTA 2010

A **claim** must be made within 4 years of the end of the financial year in which the loan is repaid (or written off), and it is irrelevant whether the company is still close at the time of the loan repayment.

CTM61620

The **date** of the tax repayment is 9 months after the end of the accounting period in which the loan itself was repaid (or written off), leading to an undesirable delay in cash flow.

s 109 TMA 1970

Where tax on a loan is unpaid, the tax repayment does not reduce any **interest** charge already accrued. However, interest stops running on the date that the loan is repaid, released or written off (¶51080).

Comment   Given that there may be a significant period of time between the date of the initial tax payment and when the loan is repaid, the company should keep clear evidence of the tax payment, so that the claim for its repayment is irrefutable. HMRC cannot be relied upon to maintain sufficient records in this case.

EXAMPLE
1. Continuing the example at ¶75755, E Ltd is due a tax repayment of £5,000 on each of 1 April 2015 and 1 April 2016, in relation to the £20,000 instalments paid by the participator. Relief is due 9 months and 1 day after the end of each accounting period in which the instalments are paid.

2. B Ltd, a close company, makes a loan to a participator in the accounting period ended 30 June 2012. The tax charge is paid on 1 April 2013. The loan is repaid during the year ended 30 June 2014.
Relief for the loan repayment is not due until 1 April 2015.

Short-term repayments For repayments made **or on after 20 March 2013** new anti-avoidance rules have been introduced to counter short-term repayments and repayments where arrangements exist to replace the loan.

75817
s 464C CTA 2010

Where:
– repayments of at **least £5,000** (toward a loan of at least £5,000) are made;
– the repayment is **outside of the period** in which the original loan is made; and
– within 30 days of the repayment a **further loan** is taken;

then the repayments will be matched against the further advances, not the original loan. This is intended to stop the practice of making a repayment before the tax on it is due, only to re-advance the same sum shortly afterwards.

If the outstanding loan is **at least £15,000**, then if there are arrangements put in place to secure a further advance of at least £5,000 the rules will also apply, but without time limit.

MEMO POINTS 1. If the further advance is **repaid** within 30 days the advance can be disregarded in looking at the matching process.
2. Where repayments are made from **taxed income**, such as salary or dividends (including those effected by book entry only), these will not be further loans and will still count as repayments in the normal way.

5. Loan written off

Since 24 March 2010, there is no facility to claim a loan relationship debit (¶16540) in respect of the written off loan i.e. no deduction is available for the **company**.

75845
s 321A CTA 2009

However, the 25% tax charge will be repaid (¶75815).

The **borrower** will be taxable on the resulting deemed dividend income which arises in the tax year when the release or write off occurs. The taxable amount is the loan amount grossed up by 100/90, and there is a non-repayable 10% tax credit, which can be set off against the taxpayer's liability. HMRC accept that this procedure takes priority over taxing the release as employment income. However, Class 1 NIC may still be due where HMRC take the view that the write-off is earnings for NIC purposes.

s 463 CTA 2010;
s 415 ITTOIA 2005;
CTM61630

MEMO POINTS This is **intended** to make sure that a loan that is written off is treated in the same way as a distribution, rather than securing a tax advantage.

EXAMPLE F Ltd loaned Mr F £80,000 on 19 June 2012. F Ltd has a year end of 30 September. Mr F repays £62,000 on 2 May 2013, and the remainder of the loan is written off on 24 March 2014. F Ltd is liable to pay tax of £4,500 on 1 June 2013. ((80,000 - 62,000) @ 25%) This tax is repaid on 1 June 2015.
Mr F is taxable on income of £20,000 in 2013/14. (18,000 x 100/90) The associated tax credit is £2,000.

B. Benefits treated as distributions

75875
ss 1064 - 1069
CTA 2010

For a close company, the **meaning** of distribution is **extended to** certain benefits provided for participators, including:
– any expense incurred by the company in connection with the provision for any participator (or an associate of a participator) of living or other accommodation;
– entertainment;
– domestic or other services; and
– other benefits or facilities of whatever nature (including monetary gifts), to the extent that the expense is not made good to the company by the participator or the associate.

CTM60670

> ⌐MEMO POINTS⌐ **Pensions, rents, royalties and other payments** may be paid in excessive amounts where the recipient is a participator (or an associate). Any amount disallowed in computing the company's profits chargeable to corporation tax, purely because of the size of the payment, would be treated as a distribution in the hands of the recipient.

Exclusions

75880
s 1065 CTA 2010

No distribution arises when:
– the benefit is connected to employment;
– the recipient works for a charity or company carrying out educational work; or
– assets are transferred between certain members of a group.

75885
CTM60600

Any of the following incurred in relation to **employment** are not treated as a distribution for this purpose:
– benefits provided to an employee or director;
– benefits provided to the lower paid (i.e. earning less than £8,500 p.a.);
– living accommodation which is provided by reason of employment; and
– a pension payment or gratuity made to retired employees, their spouses or dependants.

The normal employment tax rules will apply in this case, which means the benefit may be treated as earnings.

> ⌐MEMO POINTS⌐ 1. When determining whether the threshold of £8,500 has been breached for a **lower paid employee**, the following items should be added together:
> – salary;
> – all benefits received;
> – any deemed income arising from the personal service company rules (also known as IR35 (¶77000+)); and
> – expenses incurred by the employee and reimbursed by the employer (other than when a dispensation is in force).
> Deductions may be made for pension contributions and payroll giving donations. For further details, see *Tax Memo*.

75890
CTM60600

Benefits provided to a participator (or his associate) can be ignored when the **recipient** is:
– a director or employee of a charity; or
– employed by a company which carries on business as a school or other educational establishment;
unless the benefits are excessive when compared to those provided to another individual holding the same position.

75895
s 1066 CTA 2010;
CTM60610

Transfers of assets between members of corporate 51% **groups** (¶65505) will not be treated as a distribution. For this purpose, the following are **excluded** from such a group:
– non-resident companies; and
– companies where the sale of the share capital of the other company would be treated as a trading receipt.

Chargeable amount

The benefit is **valued** using the general employment income rules. Full details are given in *Tax Memo*. In summary:

75900
s 1064 CTA 2010

Benefit	How valued	Reference
Accommodation	Annual value of property less rent paid by occupier Extra charge where property costs £75,000 or more	s 102 ITEPA 2003
Use of assets	20% of asset's market value	s 205 ITEPA 2003
Transfer of assets	Higher of market value when asset: – transferred; or – first made available less any amounts already taxed for use	s 206 ITEPA 2003
Company cars	List price multiplied by a percentage (maximum 35%) based on carbon dioxide emissions of car	s 114 ITEPA 2003
Company vans	£3,000	s 154 ITEPA 2003
Medical insurance	Cost incurred by company	s 204 ITEPA 2003

Income tax implications

The **recipient** will be taxable on the grossed up value of the benefit.

As the individual may be liable to income tax at higher rates, HMRC will ensure that the individual's own tax office is notified.

75905
CTM60530

> EXAMPLE Mr A is provided with a flat by A Ltd, which costs the company £10,000 p.a. in rent and service charges. Mr A does not work for the company. He pays £100 per month for the flat.
> The value of the deemed distribution is £8,800 p.a. (10,000 - 1,200).
> Mr A is treated as receiving dividend income of £9,778 (8,800 × 100/90), with an associated tax credit of £978.

Corporation tax implications

Any **expense incurred** by the company in providing these benefits is not deductible against profits.

75910

> EXAMPLE Continuing the example at ¶75905 above, £10,000 must be added back to A Ltd's PCTCT.

Companies acting in concert

If two or more close companies provide benefits to a person who is not a participator, this will still fall to be treated as a distribution where:
– the payment would be a distribution if it were made to a participator; and
– the companies are acting in concert or under arrangements made by any person.

75915
s 1067 CTA 2010

> EXAMPLE B Ltd (with a participator Mr X) and C Ltd (with a participator Mr Y) arrange for:
> – B Ltd to make a payment to Mr Y; and
> – C Ltd to make a payment to Mr X.
> B Ltd and C Ltd are both treated as having paid a distribution.

C. Close investment holding companies

Close investment holding companies (CIHC) cannot benefit from the small profits **rate of corporation tax**, and so are subject to the standard rate. This is irrespective of the level of profits or number of associated companies.

75945

Definition

75950
s 34 CTA 2010;
CTM60710

The legislation defines CIHCs by exclusion. In broad terms, a close company will be a CIHC **unless**, throughout the accounting period (¶3040), its whole or main purpose of existence is:
– trading;
– investing in land for (unconnected) letting; or
– acting as a holding or service company within a group which exists wholly or mainly to trade or invest in land for letting.

So the only companies **within the scope** of the definition are those:
– dealing purely with investments; or
– letting property to connected persons.

CTM60720

$\boxed{\textit{MEMO POINTS}}$ 1. A company may be currently undertaking an activity which would seem to imply it was a CIHC, when its actual **purpose** in existing is to trade etc (i.e. where it would not be a CIHC). Each case must be evaluated on the facts.
2. The purpose of a company's existence may be difficult to determine where there are **multiple sources of income** or other factors are inconclusive.

CTM60730

In this case, HMRC state that a common sense approach is needed, and regard should be had to the following:
– the relative levels, and sources, of income;
– the activities undertaken by the company;
– the content of board meeting minutes etc; and
– the type of assets held by the company and their respective uses.

Letting of land

75955
s 34(3) CTA 2010;
CTM60740

Unconnected letting means that the **tenant** cannot be:
a. connected with the company, or
b. the spouse or relative of an individual who is connected with the company. This also applies to relatives of the individual's spouse. So if the letting is to a relative of the individual's spouse, or the spouse of a relative of the individual, the company will be a CIHC.

s 1122 CTA 2010

$\boxed{\textit{MEMO POINTS}}$ 1. A **company is connected** with:
– any person who has control of that company;
– a person, if that person, acting alone or with persons connected with him, has control of it;
– another company if the same person controls both companies;
– another company if one is controlled by a person and the other is controlled by persons connected with that person;
– another company if one is controlled by a person who, together with persons connected with him, controls the other;
– another company if the same group of persons controls both; and
– another company, if each company is controlled by a separate group of persons but each group could be the same if the actual members were replaced by connected persons.
For a detailed discussion of these rules and numerous examples see ¶31375.
2. An **individual is connected** with:
– his spouse/civil partner;
– his relatives;
– a relative's spouse/civil partner (or the spouse/civil partner of a relative of his own spouse/civil partner);
– any person he is in partnership with;
– a partner's spouse/civil partner; and
– a partner's relatives.
3. A **relative** is a brother, sister, ancestor or lineal descendant.

Groups

75960

Broadly, a company that owns only trading subsidiaries or is part of a trading group will not be a CIHC (e.g. a company making loans to a fellow trading subsidiary).

Holding companies are not CIHCs where they exist wholly or mainly for the purpose of holding shares in, or making loans to, at least one trading or property investment subsidiary. This rule also includes an ultimate holding company where an intermediate holding company is interposed between it and the trading or property investment subsidiaries.

A **service company**, which exists to co-ordinate the administration of two or more trading or property investment companies, is not a CIHC.

A **caveat** applies where a company is involved in a trading/property investment group, but also acts as a holding company or service company to a non-trading company, because, depending on the level of activity, the non-CIHC status may be prejudiced by the latter.

Liquidation

Where a non-CIHC **commences** liquidation, it will not to be treated as a CIHC during the accounting period immediately following the start of the winding up. Thereafter, a company in liquidation is usually a CIHC unless it meets the normal criteria (¶75950).

75965
s 34(5) CTA 2010

If there is an unavoidable **gap** between the cessation of trade and the commencement of liquidation, strictly the company will be a CIHC from the liquidation date, although HMRC will consider whether this unduly disadvantages the company.

D. Transfer of assets at undervalue

If a close company transfers an asset to a shareholder for less than market value, there is a provision which restricts the advantage enjoyed by that shareholder.

75995
s 125 TCGA 1992

Shareholder receives asset

When a company transfers an asset to a recipient **other than another group member, participator or employee**, any discount in value is apportioned between the shareholders, and reduces the base cost of their shares (to nil in some cases).

76000

> ⌐MEMO POINTS⌐ If a **shareholder is itself a close company**, the value of its own shares may have been reduced as a result of the transfer. So the discount has to be apportioned between its own shareholders.

CG57126

⌐EXAMPLE⌐
1. Mr A bought a 10% shareholding in A Ltd, a close company, for £40,000. A couple of years later, the company sells an asset to another shareholder at a discount of £100,000.
As Mr A held a 10% shareholding, 10% of the discount is apportioned to his shares, so his base cost is reduced by £10,000 to £30,000. (100,000 @ 10%)

2. B Ltd bought a 10% shareholding in A Ltd above, also for £40,000. Mr B holds 50% of the shares in B Ltd, which he bought for £60,000.
In this case, the £10,000 undervalue relating to B Ltd's shareholding in A Ltd is then apportioned to B Ltd's own shares. So Mr B's base cost for his shares is reduced by £5,000 to £55,000. (10,000 @ 50%)

Transferee is a participator

Depending on the circumstances of the case, the discount will be taxed either as an income distribution (i.e. a dividend) or a capital distribution (i.e. any other type of distribution such as on the company's winding up).

76005
s 122 TCGA 1992

Transferee is an employee

The discount will be treated as a benefit in kind, and assessed as employment income. See *Tax Memo* for further details.

76010

E. UK participator in non-resident company

76040
s 13(1) TCGA 1992
There is a special rule which only affects UK investors in a non-resident company that would be close if it was UK resident.

Comment One of the ways of avoiding these rules is to ensure that the non-resident company is not close i.e. introduce more shareholders (with full voting rights etc), although HMRC will challenge artificial structures.

Having been issued with an infraction notice in 2011, these rules were changed for disposals on or after 6 April 2012.

Disposal of assets

76045
s 13(2) TCGA 1992
Where the non-resident company disposes of an asset (other than an asset used in its trade or as an intra-group transfer) and a **gain** arises, any participator resident in the UK at the time of the disposal is attributed, on a just and reasonable basis, with a proportion of that gain (usually based on the interest held in the company).

> MEMO POINTS 1. For this purpose, the **participator** could be a shareholder, loan creditor, or option holder.

s 13(9) TCGA 1992
2. Any **intermediate non-resident** companies are looked through in order to attribute the gain to the ultimate UK participator, unless the participators include non-resident trustees (when the gain is attributed to them).

3. The **just and reasonable** requirement is necessary because the different factors that determine which persons are participators in the non-resident company may each give a different proportion to the extent of the participator's interest. For example, entitlement to income may give one result, and entitlement to capital may result in a different proportion for each participator. The provisions aim to ensure that the apportionment is based on the real economic interest of the participator in the non-resident company, as a simple arithmetical apportionment based on a particular factor may not correspond to the real economic interest. The just and reasonable requirement would, for example, prevent an inappropriately large part of the gain being apportioned to a loan creditor, who did not have a real economic interest in the non-resident company.

4. The **gain is calculated** under the UK tax rules e.g. using indexation allowance.

s 13(8) TCGA 1992
5. Any **loss** realised on the disposal will only be attributed where it reduces gains realised in the same year of assessment which relate to that company.

Exclusions

76050
s 13(5) TCGA 1992
The following **assets** are excluded from these rules, and so no gain is attributed when:

a. the asset disposed of is used only for the purposes of:
– a trade carried on by the company wholly outside the UK; or
– the part of a trade carried on outside the UK, carried on by the company when the trade is partly within and partly outside the UK;
b. a gain on the disposal of money used for the purposes of a trade carried on by the company wholly outside the UK (e.g. foreign currency); or
c. for disposals on or after 6 April 2012, the gain arises on the disposal of an asset used only for the purposes of an economically significant activity which is carried on outside the UK through a business establishment outside the UK.

Further, the rules will not apply (for disposals on or after 6 April 2012) where it can be shown that neither the disposal of the asset nor the acquisition of it formed part of an arrangement to avoid capital gains or corporation tax.

s 14 TCGA 1992
An **intra-group transfer** of assets between two non-resident companies in a 75% CG group (¶65415) will be at no gain/no loss so no chargeable gain will arise, although where the transferee company leaves the group within 6 years of the transfer (¶67425), the gain which should have arisen, had the disposal not been at no gain/no loss, will be attributed. Note that transfers of assets between a non-resident company and a UK resident company will not benefit from this relief.

CG57380
Where a **double tax agreement** (¶90055) provides that gains of the type realised by the non-resident company are only taxable in that company's country of residence, the gain cannot be attributed back to the participators.

MEMO POINTS 1. An activity is considered to be **economically significant** if it:
– consists of the provision of goods or services on a commercial basis;
– requires the use of premises and staff (who are competent and have the required degree of authority); and
– involves the addition of economic value, by the company, to those to whom the goods or services are provided.
2. For disposals **prior to 6 April 2012**, the rules did not apply where the asset was disposed of by a permanent establishment that was liable to UK corporation tax.
3. For disposals **between 6 April 2012 and 5 April 2013** inclusive, it is possible to elect to disapply the changes to the rules. The time limit to do this is 4 years from the end of the accounting period in which the disposal occurred.
4. If the asset is **accommodation** (or any form of interest in accommodation), then for it to be considered to have been used for the purposes of a trade outside the UK it must have been furnished holiday accommodation which had been let commercially in the 12 months before the date of disposal, and in both the two 12–month periods prior to that. Where the company has had beneficial ownership of the property for more than 36 months it must have qualified in every 12–month period of its ownership, using the disposal date as the reference point.

UK tax consequences

Only if the **gain attributed** to the participator and his associates **exceeds** 25% of the total gain will there be any UK tax consequences. For disposals prior to 6 April 2012 this limit was 10%.

76055
s 13(4) TCGA 1992

The **amount** of the gain will be reduced by any overseas tax paid in respect of the gain by the non-resident company, unless the participator chooses to claim tax credit relief instead (¶90480).

A company participator will be liable to UK corporation tax on the attributed gain. The gain may be attributed to another group member, where appropriate (¶67285).

s 171A TCGA 1992

If any amount corresponding to the gain is then **distributed** to shareholders by the non-resident company within 3 years of the accounting period end in which the gain arose, the UK tax already paid can be set off against the tax arising on the distribution.

s 13(5A) TCGA 1992

If set off does not occur, the tax paid on the attributed gain will be available as allowable expenditure on any **disposal of the company's shares** by the participator.

s 13(7) TCGA 1992

In either case above, where the **company reimburses** the participator for the tax on the attributed gain, the set off mechanism is not available.

EXAMPLE
1. Mr A, Mr B, Mr C and Mrs D are all unconnected, and each own 25% of X Ltd, an overseas company. Mr A is liable to capital gains tax at 28%, having used his annual allowance already. He is also liable to income tax at 40%.
X Ltd disposes of a non-trading asset, realising a gain of £200,000. This amount is declared as a dividend 6 months later.
Each participator is attributed with a gain of £50,000. (200,000/4)
So Mr A pays capital gains tax of £14,000. (50,000 @ 28%)
The tax due on the dividend of £50,000 is computed as follows:

	£	£
Income	50,000	
Tax @ 40%		20,000
Less: Tax paid on attributed gain		(14,000)
Income tax liability		6,000

2. As above, except that Mr A disposes of his shares before the distribution is received. His shares cost £18,000, and he receives proceeds of £100,000.
The tax due on the disposal is computed as follows:

	£	£
Proceeds	100,000	
Less: Cost	(18,000)	
Less: Tax paid on attributed gain	(14,000)	
		68,000
Capital gains liability	68,000 @ 28%	19,040

CHAPTER 2

Trading through an intermediary

SECTION 1

Background

77000   In 1999 HMRC released Budget Press Release IR35, announcing action to counter what was perceived to be unacceptable tax avoidance involving the use of corporate structures. Although these rules have been subject to many changes they are still widely referred to as **IR35**.

These provisions are aimed at the situation in which an individual (the worker), who provides services to an organisation (the end user), **inserts an intermediary company** into the relationship.

The intermediary is usually referred to as a **personal service company** (¶77060+).

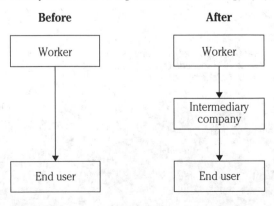

Before / After

Worker → End user

Worker → Intermediary company → End user

Without the intermediary, the worker provides services directly to the end user, either as a sole trader or as the end user's employee. When the intermediary is added, the worker becomes an employee of the intermediary, and the intermediary supplies the service to the end user.

Although this was initially a situation forced upon some freelance workers in order to safeguard the end user's position, it is widely used in certain industries as a method of tax avoidance.

The amounts of tax at stake can be substantial, with the **difference** attributable both to NIC, and to the comparative rates of income and corporation tax.

77005

To circumvent the IR35 rules, taxpayers started to form composite companies. A **composite company** entails a number of individuals owning shares in a company, each having a different class of share. Worker A has A class shares, worker B has B class shares, and so on. The company is run by an agency which takes an administration fee.

77010

Each worker then receives the income he has earned for the company, after allowing for corporation tax. The earnings are paid out in the most tax efficient manner (often including non-taxable expenses).

Although HMRC considered that the IR35 rules applied equally to composite companies, they had limited success in enforcing them. This led them to introduce specific rules to combat "**managed service companies**" (¶77140+), which took effect from April 2007. These rules apply both to composite companies, and to a company owned by a single individual where the administration and management is performed by a third party.

The IR35 provisions are **extended to office holders** with effect from 6 April 2013.

SECTION 2

Personal service companies

Applicable situations

Under the personal service company legislation, some or all of the income of the intermediary is deemed to be, and is taxed as, income of the worker.

77060
00 10, 61
ITEPA 2003

These rules come into operation if all of the following conditions apply:
– a worker performs (or is obliged to perform) **personal services** for a client (end user);
– the contract for those services is placed through an **intermediary**;
– the **relationship** between the worker and the client would be considered to be one of employment if the contract were directly between the two of them; and
– the intermediary satisfies certain conditions (¶77065).

The legislation **tests each contract** and not the overall situation. So where a company has contracts with a number of end users, some of its income may be subject to these rules whereas the balance is not.

Contracts to which the intermediary rules apply are termed **relevant engagements**.

> ⬜ *MEMO POINTS* 1. For a brief discussion on the factors affecting the employment status of the worker see ¶77205+.
> 2. The following commentary deals with the situation in which the intermediary is a company. There is analogous legislation dealing with the much less common situations in which the intermediary is a partnership or an individual.
> 3. For **NIC purposes**, the test is whether the worker would be regarded as employed in an employed earner's employment by the client. This means that the following could be deemed to be an employee for NIC purposes (but not necessarily for income tax purposes):

Tax Bulletin 74

- non-executive directors without a service contract;
- cleaners; and
- entertainers.

The intermediary

77065
s 51 ITEPA 2003

The rules only apply if the following conditions are satisfied:
a. the intermediary company is not an associated company of the client; and
b. the worker either:
- has a material interest in the intermediary; or
- is paid for his services directly by the client rather than through the intermediary.

The worker has a **material interest** in the intermediary if:
- he controls more than 5% of the ordinary share capital in the intermediary;
- he is entitled to receive more than 5% of any distributions by the intermediary; or
- the intermediary is a close company (¶75000+), and he is entitled to more than 5% of its assets in a winding-up.

A worker's shareholdings and other entitlements are taken to include those of his associates (¶75395+).

> MEMO POINTS   If the intermediary is a **partnership**, an individual may be caught by these provisions if any of the following apply:
s 52 ITEPA 2003
> - the individual is entitled to at least 60% of the partnership's profits; or
> - all or most of the partnership's profits relate to a single client; or
> - the profit sharing agreement allows the individual to receive an amount which reflects the client's payments in respect of his services.

Exclusions

77070

The rules do not apply if:
- the worker receives sufficient actual employment income from the intermediary (because of the way the income computation is performed (¶77075)); or
- the worker is a **non-resident entertainer or sportsman**; or
- the intermediary is a managed service company (¶77140+).

Implications for the worker

77075
s 54 ITEPA 2003

The worker is taxed on an annual amount which includes:
- the **gross income** of the intermediary from all relevant engagements (¶77060); and
- any other payments and benefits which the worker received in relation to those engagements, and which:
    - did not come from the intermediary;
    - are not taxable as his employment income; and
    - would be taxable on him if he were employed directly by the client.

This latter condition catches payments from the client to the worker which bypass the intermediary.

The following **expenses** are deductible from the taxable amount:
- a flat 5% of the gross income of the intermediary from the relevant engagements;
- expenses paid by the intermediary and which would be allowable if incurred by an employee;
- capital allowances arising from expenditure incurred by the intermediary, and which would be given if it were incurred by an employee;
- pension contributions paid by the intermediary to a registered scheme;
- any taxable employment income and benefits actually received by the worker from the intermediary (gross of employer's NIC); and
- other employer's Class 1 NIC and Class 1A NIC paid in respect of the worker, including NIC on the deemed earnings payment (¶77080).

The following pro-forma shows a typical calculation:

		£	£
1.	Gross income received by the intermediary on relevant engagements	X	
	Flat rate deduction of 5%:	(X)	
			X
2.	Add other payments or benefits received by the worker, in respect of the relevant engagements, but not received by the intermediary		X
			X
3.	Deduct the following:		
	Expenses incurred that would be deductible by an employee (See *Tax Memo* for full details)	X	
	Capital allowances deductible by an employee	X	
	Pension contributions paid by the intermediary to a registered scheme	X	
	Employer's NIC paid in respect of the worker	X	
	Amounts paid to the worker already assessed as employment income	X	
			(X)
			A
4.	Calculate employer's NIC: Employer's rate /(Employer's rate + 100) x A		(B)
	Deemed earnings payment		C

Where **no employment income** is actually paid in the year the NIC calculation at step 4 should reduce amount A by the earnings threshold.

The taxable amount is otherwise known as the **deemed earnings payment**. PAYE and NIC are due and payable as if this amount were paid on 5 April at the end of the tax year (even though it may never actually be paid at all).

77080
s 50 ITEPA 2003

If the individual stops working for the intermediary during the tax year, the deemed earnings payment will be assessed at the date of cessation.

Implications for the company

The deemed earnings payment and its related NIC are deductible from the **intermediary's taxable profits** as if they were incurred on 5 April. Trading losses may result from the increased employment costs.

77085
s 139 CTA 2009

From 6 April 2013, the company is almost certain to be subject to the **Real Time Information** provisions relating to the supply of payroll information to HMRC (see *Tax Memo* for further details), with the provisional calculation of the deemed payment being reported on or before 5 April. Any related tax and NIC which has not been paid (or provisionally paid) by 19 April (or 22 April where payment is made electronically) following the end of the tax year will potentially be liable to interest charges.

If the intermediary has a **year end of 31 March**, relief for the deemed earnings payment will be delayed by almost a year, so it is advisable for an intermediary to have a year end of 5 April.

EXAMPLE In 2012/13, A Ltd receives gross income of £100,000 from relevant engagements involving Mr B. Mr B also receives vouchers worth £500 as a Christmas present from A Ltd's clients. Mr B receives an annual salary of £40,000 (with employer's NIC thereon being £4,500) from A Ltd. Allowable travel expenses of £4,000 are incurred, and A Ltd pays a pension contribution of £5,000 to Mr B's pension scheme. A Ltd's year end is 31 March.

The deemed earnings payment is calculated as follows:

		£	£
1.	Gross income received by the intermediary on relevant engagements	100,000	
	Flat rate deduction of 5%:	(5,000)	
			95,000
2.	Amounts received by Mr B directly from clients		500
			95,500
3.	Less expenses:		
	Travel expenses	4,000	
	Pension contributions paid by the company	5,000	
	Employer's NIC paid in respect of Mr B	4,500	
	Amounts paid to Mr B and already assessed as employment income	40,000	
			(53,500)
			42,000
4.	Calculate employer's NIC: 13.8 /113.8 x 42,000		(5,093)
	Deemed earnings payment		36,907

Mr B will therefore be taxed as if he received extra salary of £36,907 on 5 April 2013. A Ltd only claims relief for the extra salary in the year ended on 31 March 2014. So if A Ltd receives £105,000 of income, incurs other costs of £20,000, and all other expenses are the same, the taxable result of A Ltd will be:

	£	£
Turnover		105,000
Less: Expenses		
Travel expenses	4,000	
Pension contributions paid	5,000	
Employer's NIC paid	4,500	
Salary paid	40,000	
Other costs	20,000	
		(73,500)
Taxable profits before adjusting for deemed earnings payment		31,500
Less: Deemed earnings payment	36,907	
Employer's NIC on deemed earnings	5,093	
		42,000
Trading loss		(10,500)

Relief for dividends paid

77090
s 58 ITEPA 2003

Where income of the intermediary has been taxed on the worker as a deemed payment, the payment of a dividend to him would result in the same profits being taxed twice. To ensure this does not happen, **relief is available** for dividends paid in the same year as the deemed payment arises, or in following years.

Relief will be given upon making a **claim**, provided that HMRC believe that it is necessary to ensure that double taxation does not arise. The effect is to reduce the amount of the taxable dividend by the amount of the deemed payment.

The deemed payment will be **offset** in order against dividends:
– in the same year in priority to other years;
– received by the worker before those received by another shareholder; and
– of earlier years before later years.

> MEMO POINTS   1. The **claim** must be made within 5 years of 31 January following the tax year in which the dividend is paid.
> 2. Where relief is given, the corresponding **tax credit** is reduced accordingly.

SECTION 3

Managed service companies

Scope

A managed service company (MSC) is **defined** as a company:
a. whose business consists wholly or mainly of providing (directly or indirectly) the services of an individual to other persons;
b. which pays the majority (if not all) of the consideration it receives for the individual's services to him (including his associates) in a way which saves tax and NIC, so that the remuneration exceeds that which would be received if the payment for the services were employment income of the individual; and
c. which is involved with an MSC provider (i.e. a person who is in the business of promoting or facilitating the use of companies to provide the services of individuals).

77140
s 61B ITEPA 2003

> MEMO POINTS   For this purpose, an MSC provider does not include someone who is merely providing normal accounting or legal services to small businesses in a professional capacity (that is, a person professionally qualified (or training for a professional qualification) and regulated by a regulatory body).
> To be an MSC provider, the person must have **considerable influence** over the running of the MSC, and the payment from the MSC must be linked to the individual's services. A provider would normally indemnify the individual against any personal tax liability arising as a result of using a MSC structure.

Consequences

All **income paid out** of an MSC is taxed as employment income and liable to PAYE and Class 1 NIC when received. The normal relief for employment expenses operates, treating the client as the employer (so, for example, travel to clients is not deductible because it is deemed to be commuting).

77145
s 61D ITEPA 2003

> MEMO POINTS   1. In addition, any **debt owed to HMRC** by an MSC (which normally has no assets) will be recoverable from certain persons, including:
> – the MSC's director, any other office holders and associates;
> – the MSC provider and associates; and
> – anyone else who encourages the use of MSCs or who is actively involved, but excluding a person who merely provides accountancy and legal services in a professional capacity and employment agencies who merely place individuals with clients.
> 2. Where a company pays out a dividend from a sum that is taxed as a deemed payment under these provisions, the recipient may be able to benefit from a reduction of the dividend amount (¶77090).

s 688A ITEPA 2003

The following pro-forma shows a **typical calculation** which must be performed every time that the worker receives a payment from the MSC.

77150

		£
1.	Amount received by the worker in respect of services provided through the MSC which are not paid as earnings	X
2.	Deduct expenses paid by MSC which would have been allowable as expenses of employment if incurred by the worker	(X)
	Only continue if A is positive	
3.	Calculate employer's NIC[1]	(B)
	Deemed earnings payment	C

Note:
1. The calculation of the employer's NIC must be done on a cumulative basis, applying the appropriate threshold at the date that the payment is made. For details of NIC see *Tax Memo*. For worked examples of the employer's NIC computation on an MSC payment see flmemo.co.uk/ctm77150

77155
s 141 CTA 2009

When calculating its **taxable profits**, the MSC can deduct the deemed employment income and employer's NIC in the accounting period when the payments to the individual are taxable.

SECTION 4

Deemed employment

77205

Central to both sets of rules is that in the absence of the intermediary, or chain of intermediaries, the worker would be an employee of the end user.

For tax purposes, the terms employed and self-employed are **not defined by statute**, and it is therefore necessary to consider a **series of factors** derived from case law. Note that because these tests have been developed in relation to simple employment relationships, they can be difficult to apply to more complex arrangements.

General employment issues

77210

The main conclusion that can be drawn from case law is that **no single factor** will give a definitive answer. The following table summarises some of the elements (in approximate order of importance) that commonly occur in decided cases. The list is not exhaustive, and other factors may be relevant, depending on the particular case.

It must also be understood that deciding the employment status of an individual "is not a mechanical exercise of running through items on a checklist", but requires a qualitative judgement of the overall position. *Hall v Lorimer* [1994]

	Factors indicating that a taxpayer is:	
	Employed	Self-employed
Mutuality of obligation	Individual required to accept work Other party required to provide work	Individual not obliged to accept work Other party not obliged to provide work
Control	Individual is supervised, and must obtain permission for absence etc	Individual has autonomy and can decide how work will be performed
Substitution/subcontracting	Individual is unable to subcontract his work to another without permission of other party	Individual can genuinely engage a substitute without permission of the other party
Integration	Central part of the other party's business	Peripheral to other party's business
Risk	Individual does not risk any of his own money in performing the work Other party responsible for professional liability insurance	Individual can profit from good work, but risks his own money in performing the work Individual responsible for professional liability insurance
Length of engagement	Usually long term	Usually short term
Equipment	Other party provides equipment	Individual provides own equipment
Location	Work is performed in premises provided or controlled by the other party	Individual decides where work will be performed
Hours of work	Hours of work are regular and defined by the other party	Individual determines when work will be performed
Payment	Paid regularly, usually on a weekly or monthly basis	Paid subject to the performance of the work

The **terms** of the **agreement** between the parties will never be the sole factor in determining
employment status, but it has been held that the agreement can be decisive if all of the
other factors are consistent with its terms. In an exceptional case, a taxpayer who worked
as a technician purely for his father's firm, and never raised any invoices, argued that he
was an employee but it was held that he was in fact self-employed because:
- he could control his hours of work and absences;
- he had already accepted assessments for being self-employed; and
- the terms of agreement indicated as such. *Barnett v Brabyn* [1996]

77215

In a case involving a lorry driver who owned his own vehicle, it was held that his contract was
an agreement to provide carriage services, rather than a contract of employment. The crucial
element was that the driver had to bear the risk of purchasing the lorry without the guarantee
of future work.*Ready Mixed Concrete (South East) Ltd v Minister of Pensions and National Insurance* [1968]

77220

In a more recent case concerning a construction company, it was held that the bricklayers
and scaffolders were self-employed, as they **provided their own tools and protective
clothing**, worked flexible hours (coming and leaving of their own accord, including sudden
absence to look after a sick child), and were not subject to much control by the contractor.
It was stated, however, that the substitution clause within each contract was a "fiction" (for
more on the right of substitution see ¶77235).

In contrast, it was held that the fork-lift truck drivers and one lorry driver were employed,
because they operated expensive plant made available by the contractor, who exercised
more control as a consequence. *Castle Construction (Chesterfield) Ltd v HMRC* [2008]

In business on own account

In order to be deemed as self-employed (and hence outside the scope of the IR35 rules) the
individual, or more appropriately the company, must be seen to have engaged in a contract
for services with the end user. This effectively means that the company must be seen to be
in business on its own account. This requires a **review of the whole situation** and not just
one single factor.

77225

In a case involving a market research interviewer (who was found to be employed), the
following criteria were examined:
- terms of the contract;
- extent of control by the organisation;
- level of financial risk faced;
- degree of integration into the organisation;
- ownership of the equipment used;
- responsibility for investment and management; and
- opportunity for profiting from sound management of tasks. *Market Investigations Ltd v Minister
of Social Security* [1969]

Actions of the parties

In a more recent case involving an individual working for a client through his company, the
following **factors** were indicative of a **non-employment relationship** with the company's
clients:
- there was no obligation on the individual to work a set number of hours, whether per day
or throughout the entire period of the engagement;
- similarly there was no obligation on the client to provide the individual with work during
the period of the engagement;
- the client could terminate the contract with minimal notice, and there was no obligation
on the client to engage the individual in the future;
- the individual could take time off without obtaining permission from the client's
management;
- the contract included a genuine substitution clause which would allow the individual to
suggest an alternative person to fulfil his role; and
- there was no provision of sick pay, holiday pay or social club membership.

77230

The **factors** indicating **employment** (which were of limited application because the individual worked in an area requiring security clearance) were:
- the limited financial risk faced by the individual;
- the main equipment used for the task was provided by the client; and
- the individual could not manage his tasks autonomously. *Ansell Computer Services Ltd v Richardson* [2004]

Right of substitution

77235   One of the most common arguments by which taxpayers seek to ensure they are not within the IR35 rules is to claim that they have the right to send a substitute to work in their place. This is due to the fact that an **unfettered right** to send a substitute has been held to be inconsistent with employment. *Express and Echo Publications v Tanton* [1999]

Whilst a contract may include the right to send a substitute, HMRC will always look to see whether the parties act in line with such a clause, in case it has been varied, or they consider it to be a sham. This can **cause a number of difficulties**, particularly if:
- the intermediary or worker has chosen not to exercise the right over the duration of the contract; or
- the worker has specialised skills, and the intermediary would be unable to provide a suitable replacement.

In such circumstances the actions of the parties have neither confirmed nor denied the reality of the contract terms.

ESM3350   [*MEMO POINTS*]   In any case, HMRC do not consider that an **unfettered right** to send a substitute is conclusive. The case of *Express and Echo Publications v Tanton* involved an obligation to provide a substitute, and HMRC argue that the case is unique.

77240   **Agencies and service companies**   Often an intermediary or worker will secure engagements **via an agency**, which then contracts with the end user. HMRC will not merely look at the contract between the intermediary and the agency, where an unfettered right of substitution may exist, but also the contract between the agency and the end user. This may have no right of substitution, or may allow the agency to send a substitute rather than the intermediary. In these cases it is more likely that HMRC will consider the right to be a sham and disregard it.

[EXAMPLE]   A software engineer's company contracted with an agency to provide his services almost exclusively to the Automobile Association (AA) for a period of 3 years. It was held that the engineer should be regarded as an employee of the AA because he was:
- integrated into the business, working mainly at the AA's premises or at home with an internet connection to the office server;
- working as part of a highly skilled team; and
- subject to control by the AA, as his work allocation was decreed by the team leader.
Whilst there was an effective substitution clause in the contract between the company and the agency, this was not the case in the contract between the agency and the AA. The **paperwork retrospectively put in place** to confirm that the AA would indeed accept a substitute, if the need arose, did not reflect the reality of the relationship. *Dragonfly Consulting Ltd v HMRC* [2008]

In another case, it was held that despite the existence of a **service company**, an individual remained employed by his original employer. The individual had been forced into using a service company which was engaged by an agency, but continued to provide the same services to his previous employer. Although there was a contract of employment between the individual and the service company, and there was an intervening agency agreement, this did not preclude the existence of an **implied and enforceable contract** of employment between the individual and the employer. In addition, the employer supplied a mobile phone and laptop to the individual, and paid his phone bills. Internally, the individual still had an employee number. *Cable & Wireless v Muscat* [2006]

In a third case, an **agent** was involved in finding work for the intermediary company. In the contract between these two parties, there was a **substitution clause** so that another individual could carry out the work instead of the taxpayer. However, there was no similar substitution clause in the contract between the intermediary company and the client, and this counted against the worker being self-employed. The taxpayer also **worked for a period** of 17 months for the client, with average weekly hours of 58 hours per week, which suggested that the client was obliged to find work for the taxpayer. It was held that this situation was caught by the IR35 rules. *Usetech Ltd v Young* [2004]

CHAPTER 3

Research and development

A number of reliefs beyond those normally given are available to encourage spending on research and development (R&D). As well as an enhanced relief for capital expenditure, there are further supplements available for qualifying revenue expenditure. A similar supplement exists for work involved in vaccine research.

78000

SECTION 1

Qualifying activities

In order to determine which activities qualify as R&D, it is necessary to look primarily at the **statutory definition** and then the Department of Business, Innovation and Skills guidelines, which have been given statutory force by way of regulation.

78050
SI 2004/712

> MEMO POINTS **HMRC** will generally use the BIS guidelines to operate the relief and only refer to the accounting standards, which the statutory definition relies on, to understand the accounting treatment of the expenditure.

CIRD 81300

1. Statutory definition

78080
s 1138 CTA 2010;
SSAP 13;
IAS 38

The statutory definition is that R&D is determined based on generally acceptable accounting principles.

In order to satisfy this definition, the work must show the presence of an **appreciable element of innovation**. As such a simple upgrade on a product or process will not be sufficient to qualify.

The accounting standards split the types of R&D into 3 broad categories:

Category	Description
Pure research	Experimental or theoretical work that is undertaken primarily to acquire new scientific or technical knowledge simply for the purposes of discovering something new, rather than research aimed at a particular aim
Applied research	Original or critical investigation designed to obtain new scientific or technical knowledge, or to develop existing knowledge moving toward a chosen commercial objective
Development	Using scientific or technical knowledge to either: – produce new or substantially improved materials, devices, products or services; or – install new processes or systems prior to the commencement of commercial production or application, or substantially improve those already produced or installed

2. BIS guidelines

78100

The accounting definition of R&D is restricted by the BIS guidelines. These guidelines state that any R&D **project must** seek to achieve an advance in overall knowledge or capability in science or technology. It is not sufficient that something is created using science or technology. Examples of R&D are given as projects that:
– extend overall knowledge or capability in a field of science or technology;
– create a process, material, device, product or service which incorporates or represents an increase in overall knowledge or capability in a field of science or technology;
– make an appreciable improvement to an existing process, material, device, product or service through scientific or technological changes; or
– use science or technology to duplicate the effect of an existing process, materials, device, product or service in a new or appreciably improved way.

MEMO POINTS   Even if the advance sought is **not achieved** the project may still qualify as R&D.

Advance in science or technology

78105

The advance must be an **overall advance**, as opposed to an advance made only by that company. However, if the details of an advance have not been made available, work to achieve a similar advance as another company may qualify. This could be the case where an advance is a trade secret, for instance.

The overall advance could be a new product, process, system, etc or an **appreciable improvement** to an existing one. Whether an appreciable improvement has been made is based on an objective test – would a competent professional working in that field consider that the improvement was genuine and non-trivial?

An advance may have tangible **consequences**, such as a new product or process, or intangible ones. It is likely that intangible consequences will arise from pure research where an improvement in knowledge is usually the end result.

MEMO POINTS 1. **Science** is defined as being the study of the nature and behaviour of the physical and material universe. As such, works in humanities, social sciences (including economics) and art will not be considered to be science.
2. **Technology** is the practical application of scientific principles.

Project and activities

Most companies will classify their R&D work into projects. However, there will be a number of activities that may lead to the overall advance that the project sought. These activities are conducted in a systematic, planned method in order to resolve any **scientific or technological uncertainty** that may exist. It is the costs of these activities that may or may not qualify as R&D within the overall project.

78110

Activities may lead to the resolution of an uncertainty either directly, where the work is targeted directly at resolving the uncertainty, or indirectly. The guidelines give examples of both of these and also what activities will not qualify as either.

Qualifying direct activities are:
– activities to create or adapt software, materials or equipment needed to resolve the uncertainty, **provided that** it is created or adapted solely for that purpose;
– scientific or technological planning activities; and
– scientific or technological design, testing and analysis undertaken to resolve the uncertainty.

78115

Qualifying indirect activities are:
– scientific and technical information services, provided that they are conducted to support the R&D work (such work may include preparing reports of the original R&D findings);
– indirect supporting activities, such as maintenance, security administration, etc insofar as they are undertaken for R&D;
– ancillary activities that are essential to the performance of the R&D (examples given are paying staff, leasing premises and equipment, and maintaining any equipment used for R&D purposes);
– training required to directly support a project;
– research by students and universities;
– research to devise new scientific or technological testing, survey or sampling methods, where this work would not qualify as R&D in its own right; and
– feasibility studies to ascertain the strategy for progress of the activity

78120

Non-qualifying activities are:
– commercial and financial steps taken with regard to the innovation, development and marketing of the product, process etc (such work may include market research);
– work to develop non-scientific or non-technological aspects of the advancement;
– production and distribution of goods; and
– general support services i.e. transportation, storage, maintenance, as opposed to those directly aimed at the R&D project.

78125

Scientific or technological uncertainty

Activities that replicate known results will not qualify as R&D. In order to qualify, an activity **must seek to answer** an uncertainty. This is the case where knowledge of whether something is possible or feasible is unknown and could not be deduced from existing knowledge by a competent professional. However, uncertainty can also arise where something has been established as being **feasible** but the development is then turning it into a cost-effective, reliable, reproducible process, material, device, product or service. For instance, the writing of data to DVDs was at one time technologically possible, but significant further R&D was required to turn this into a mass consumer product.

78130

While it may be known how a number of products work, **system uncertainty** may exist where it is not known how a combination of them will react or there is uncertainty as to the optimum way to combine the products. It is the complexity that leads to the uncertainty. However, this will not extend to the simple placing of components following established patterns or a routine method.

Fine tuning or small changes in the development process will not be considered to be R&D.

Commencement and cessation of work

78135   Qualifying activities are **deemed to begin** when work on the resolution commences, and this may include planning, provided that the planning relates to solving the uncertainty, as opposed to non-qualifying activities such as market research. **Planning** will also be included where a decision is made not to pursue the work.

Work will be **considered to be completed** when the uncertainty no longer exists. This is generally when the results are codified in a usable form, or where a prototype is developed and has been **tested** to show that it has the functioning capabilities of the final model. There may be further R&D carried out beyond the prototype stage, but this activity must itself satisfy all the necessary conditions to qualify.

Applying the principles

78140   The application of these guidelines can be complex with various stages of a project qualifying, while others do not. The following examples apply these guidelines to particular situations.

> EXAMPLE
> 1. A company wishes to manufacture a new blu-ray player, and carries out market research in order to ascertain which features a new player should have to make it appeal to the public. The result of this suggests that a number of improvements, considered to be non-trivial, should be investigated. A scheme is then devised to design several new parts to test and integrate with existing technology. This planning also devises a strategy to secure intellectual property rights to the intended developments and decisions on the design of the final product. The work culminates in the production and testing of a prototype. There are still some issues with this, because the components do not work together as expected, and further work is undertaken until a final prototype is built. Based on this, several copies are made and used at focus groups to garner further consumer feedback. This feedback suggests that the drive is too noisy and that the design of the case is unattractive. Further work is carried out to remedy these defects, including redesigning the drive mechanism.
> The activities above that **qualify** as R&D will be:
> – the planning of, and the actual work in relation to, the development of the new constituent parts;
> – production and testing of initial and successive prototypes; and
> – further development of the new drive mechanism.
> The following activities will **not qualify**:
> – initial market research;
> – planning and work involved in securing intellectual property rights and design;
> – production of consumer test models and testing works; and
> – redesign of casing.
>
> 2. A company develops a new water-breathable fabric intended to be used in outdoor clothing. A test fabric showing the required characteristics is produced in small amounts to allow consumer testing. Part of the feedback from this is that the new fabric feels coarse against the skin. Based on this the company examines new weaves and the physical structure of the fabric to overcome this. In this situation the redesign work, although apparently cosmetic or aesthetic in nature, will qualify because there still exists uncertainty as to whether the required result can be produced.

SECTION 2

Reliefs for revenue expenditure

A. Gateway conditions

Where a company incurs certain types of qualifying expenditure while undertaking relevant R&D it will be able to claim an additional deduction in its tax computation.

78190

1. Relevant R&D

In order to secure any of the reliefs the company must be undertaking R&D that is **relevant to** its trade. This could be an existing trade, an extension to an existing trade, or R&D being carried out with a view to commencing a new trade. This will include medical research carried out where there is a special relationship to the welfare of the workers involved in the trade. This may apply in the case of something such as an occupational disease. Where the work does not relate specifically to the workers of the trade but to the wider community, this will not apply. However, in such circumstances the work may qualify as R&D in the usual way.

78220
s 1042 CTA 2009;
CIRD 81400

Simply carrying out research is unlikely to constitute a trade in its own right. However, having contracts to do so with a reward available will be sufficient to constitute trading in these circumstances.

2. Qualifying expenditure

Only certain costs can **receive relief**. These are:
- staffing costs and externally provided workers;
- software or consumable items;
- subcontracted work; and
- clinical trial volunteers.

78240
ss 1050, 1064,
1069, 1075, 1097
CTA 2009

For **large companies** only, contributions to independent R&D can also receive relief (¶78455).

In some cases these costs may have been capitalised as part of an intangible asset under GAAP. Where this is the case, it will still be available for relief, provided that it would have been allowed as a deduction had it been expensed through the profit and loss account. However, there will be no further relief when these costs are passed to the profit and loss account by way of amortisation for instance.

s 53 FA 2004;
CIRD 81450

Staffing costs

Where staffing costs are incurred in relation to directors or employees **directly or actively engaged** in the qualifying R&D, the total cost will be available for relief. HMRC take the phrase directly or actively engaged to mean hands-on.

78245
ss 1123, 1124
CTA 2009;
CIRD 83000

EXAMPLE A Ltd is carrying out qualifying R&D. Much of Doctor X's time is spent carrying out the actual research, with the balance of her time being spent on qualifying indirect activities (¶78120). Her assistant also works full-time on the qualifying project. He ensures the laboratory is clean, researches related studies online, and ensures the necessary equipment is in good working order. His costs will also qualify, as he is actively involved in performing qualifying indirect activities.
Where a defect is found in the equipment a member of the maintenance team will carry out the repair work. The cost of carrying out this work will qualify, again, as an indirect activity. However,

the balance of the maintenance man's cost will not qualify, as it is not related to the repair of assets used specifically and solely for the research.

Time spent by the assistant filing reports of past experiments would qualify, but the time of a maintenance clerk completing job sheets for the repairs to the equipment will not.

Where Doctor X carries out interviews to recruit a further assistant, these costs will also be allowed. However, the cost of the HR manager will not be allowed.

Where a director or employee is only **partly engaged directly or actively** in the R&D project, the cost should be apportioned based on time spent on the project. So, if it is estimated that the director or employee spends 30 hours from a 40 hour week working on the project, 75% of the cost will qualify. However, the costs of support staff, such as those in providing services in the secretarial or administrative sphere, will not be attributable to the project.

The **costs that will qualify** include:
- sums paid as earnings to the director/employee;
- the reimbursement of expenses, provided that these are not considered to be benefits in kind;
- secondary Class 1 National Insurance contributions paid by the company on the above (or similar compulsory payments made elsewhere in the EEA or Switzerland); and
- contributions paid to a pension fund operated for the benefit of the director/employee.

> **MEMO POINTS** 1. **Redundancy payments** are not included within this definition.
> 2. The staffing costs are those of **staff employed** by the company only. So a recharge for staffing costs paid to a group company will not qualify under this heading. However, such a payment may qualify under the externally provided workers heading (¶78250).

Externally provided workers

78250
ss 1127–1132
CTA 2009;
CIRD 84000

Where a company makes a payment to an intermediary for the provision of staff, 65% of the payment made will qualify for relief. This may be an agency or another associated company. This does not cover subcontracting costs (for which see ¶78260) but only the **costs of labour** provided by an intermediary. An externally provided worker:
- is an individual and not a director or employee of the engaging company;
- personally carries out the work required by virtue of a contract between him and someone other than the engaging company; and
- is subject to the company's supervision in carrying out the work.

Where the company and the agency are **connected** (¶31375), and in line with GAAP all of the payments made to, and qualifying costs incurred by, the agency have been brought into account, the payment made by the company can qualify for relief in its entirety, subject to being **capped** at the costs incurred by the agency in providing the staff member. Where the parties are **not connected**, a joint election can be entered into to apply the connected parties provisions to all payments made under the contract. Such an election must be made within 2 years of the end of the accounting period during which the contract is first entered into and is irrevocable.

> **MEMO POINTS** For payments **prior to 1 April 2012** the contract had to be between the staff provider and the employee. In many situations this did not have the desired result and as such it is now only a requirement that the employee has a contract with a staff controller, being anyone in the chain other than the engaging company.
> However, this new definition will still not include payments made to **employment agencies** for finding staff that become employed by the company.

Software or consumable items

78255
ss 1125, 1126
CTA 2009

The cost of software, consumable or transformable items used directly in the R&D project will qualify for relief. For these purposes consumable and transformable items include water, fuel and power. For something to qualify as either consumable or transformed, it will be **incapable of being used again** in its original form. However, the cost of either used in support or administrative services will not qualify for relief.

> **MEMO POINTS** An apportionment is possible if a cost incurred **does not relate entirely** to qualifying R&D. For instance, the cost of power to heat and light an area of the property used for the R&D will be allowed.

Subcontracted work

Only certain payments to subcontractors qualify for relief depending on the status of both the contractor and subcontractor:

78260
ss 1133–1136
CTA 2009;
CIRD 84200

Category	Description
SME – no capping or subsidy involved	No further conditions
SME – relief capped or subsidy involved	Only where subcontractor carries out the work and is either: – a large company; – an individual or partnership containing only individuals; or – a qualifying body.
Large company	Work must be subcontracted to, and then performed by, either: – a large company; – an individual or partnership containing only individuals; or – a qualifying body.
Company acting as subcontractor, contracting work to another	

The work of the subcontractor does not have to qualify as R&D by itself, but it must form part of a larger project that, from the contracting company's perspective, is qualifying R&D.

Where the costs are available for relief, the **amount will be restricted** to 65% of the payment made in order to ensure that no profit element or general overheads of the subcontracting company become eligible for the company contracting the work.

Where the company and the subcontractor are **connected** (¶31375), and in line with GAAP, all of the payments made to, and qualifying costs incurred by, the subcontractor have been brought into account, the payment made by the contractor can qualify for relief in its entirety, subject to being capped at the costs incurred by the subcontractor. Where the parties are **not connected**, a joint election can be entered into to apply the connected parties provisions to all payments made under the contract. Such an election must be made within 2 years of the end of the accounting period in which the contract was entered into and is irrevocable.

> [MEMO POINTS] A **qualifying body** is a charity, scientific research organisation, an institution of higher education or a health service body. This list can be added to by way of Treasury Order.

s 1142 CTA 2009;
SI 2012/286

Payments to clinical trial volunteers

In many R&D projects, volunteers are recruited to test products in order to ascertain any likely side effects or similar. Any payment made to a person for participating in such a trial, where the **intended outcome of the trial is to** investigate the subject's reaction to a health care treatment or procedure, will qualify in full.

78265
s 1140 CTA 2009

B. Reliefs

There are a number of situations that attract enhanced relief under the R&D schemes. These can be generally classified as:
– SMEs performing their own work;
– large companies performing their own work; and
– any size company acting as subcontractor.

78295

Small or medium-sized enterprise

In order to be considered small or medium-sized (SME) for these purposes a company must fall within one of the following categories. In each case it must satisfy the headcount condition and then either the turnover or balance sheet condition to qualify. This is **wider than**

78300
s 1119 CTA 2009

the standard definition of small or medium-sized so that companies which generally would not be able to benefit from these enhanced reliefs can now do so.

Category	Larger SME	Medium	Small	Micro
Staff headcount	Less than 500	Less than 250	Less than 50	Less than 10
Turnover	Not exceeding €100 million	Not exceeding €50 million	Not exceeding €10 million	Not exceeding €2 million
Balance sheet total	Not exceeding €86 million	Not exceeding €43 million	Not exceeding €10 million	Not exceeding €2 million

The staff, income and assets of linked and partner enterprises must also be taken into account. In looking at the test, it is the **accounts** for the previous 12 months that should be examined.

CIRD 92000

A company that **breaches the limits** will not become a large company until it has breached the limits for 2 consecutive years. Similarly a company will not become small or medium-sized until its second year below the limit. Where this occurs, it will be deemed to be large from the commencement of the second period. However, this is not the case where a company is taken over or joins a group where the group is large, when it will automatically be considered large from the start of the period in which it is taken over.

> MEMO POINTS 1. **Linked enterprises** are those that can exert control, directly or indirectly, over the company.
> 2. **Partner enterprises** are enterprises that are not linked but hold at least 25% of the capital or voting rights in the company (aggregating any linked enterprises' holdings). In this case, only the relevant proportion of the partner enterprise's staff, turnover and assets are taken into account.

1. SMEs carrying out own work

a. Additional deduction

78330

Where an SME carries out its own research i.e. it is **not work that is subcontracted to it** by another party, it will be entitled to an additional deduction of 125% of the qualifying costs where it carries on a trade in the period concerned, provided that:
– it is a going concern when it claims the relief; and
– it is not in receipt of a notified State Aid with regard to any part of the project.

The relief available at this rate may be restricted by virtue of being partly subsidised (other than by notified State Aid (¶78400)) or via the capping provisions (¶78405).

> EXAMPLE B Ltd carries out qualifying R&D in a period incurring total qualifying costs of £800,000. As well as being entitled to the normal revenue deduction for this sum B Ltd will also be entitled to claim relief for a further £1,000,000.

> MEMO POINTS The **rate** at which relief has been given over the period the relief has been available has been changed regularly. For details of the rates prior to 1 April 2012 see ¶95100.

Going concern

78335
s 1046 CTA 2009

For an SME to be considered a going concern for these purposes, its **last published accounts** should have been prepared on the basis that the company is a going concern and, further, this should be without having regard to the possibility that the company may receive the enhanced tax relief or a repayable tax credit (¶78360). A company that is in **administration or liquidation** at the time the claim is made is not considered to be a going concern.

Pre-trading expenditure

78340

The normal rules for expenditure incurred before trading commences apply in the case of expenditure on R&D (¶60115). However, there are provisions to allow a company which incurred qualifying expenditure on R&D, provided that it is a going concern, to claim relief in the **accounting period** the expenses were actually incurred if they would have been so allowable if the trade had commenced. Upon making a claim, a trading loss equal to 225% of the expenditure will be incurred and the normal methods of obtaining relief for this will be possible (¶36000), with the exception that a loss can only be carried back if the company was entitled to relief in that earlier period. Such a **claim**, which can only apply to all of the expenditure in a period, must be made within 2 years of the end of the period to which it relates.

The loss so arising can also, and will most likely be, surrendered for a tax credit (¶78360).

> ☐ *MEMO POINTS* ☐ 1. It may be the case that there is **no accounting period**, because the company has no source of income. Where this is the case, HMRC will treat an accounting period as commencing when the comany's R&D activities commenced.
> 2. The **rate** at which relief has been given over the period the relief has been available has been changed regularly. For details of the rates prior to 1 April 2012 see ¶95100.

b. Tax credit

Where a company has expenditure that qualifies for the additional deduction of 125%, whether it is trading or has made an election under the pre-trading expenditure rules, and this results in the company incurring a **loss**, it can surrender the loss in return for an immediately payable tax credit.

78360
s 1054 CTA 2009

Amount that can be surrendered

Where a company makes a claim, the amount that can be surrendered will be the **lower of**:
- the loss incurred for the period; and
- 225% of the qualifying expenditure.

78365
s 1055 CTA 2009

This amount is **further reduced** by any amounts:
- that could have been offset against other profits of that or an earlier period;
- that have been carried back to an earlier period; and
- surrendered by way of group or consortium relief.

> ☐ *EXAMPLE* ☐ C Ltd incurs a loss of £300,000 and has no income in the same year. If the qualifying expenditure receiving the 125% uplift was £100,000, the loss that could be surrendered would be £225,000. (100,000 × 225%)
> If the expenditure had been £200,000 the loss that could be surrendered would be £300,000.

Where a surrender is made, the amount of the loss so surrendered cannot be used in any other way.

Amount and treatment of credit

The amount of credit given is 11% of the amount of the loss surrendered.

78370
s 1058 – 1061
CTA 2009

Where the company is in **arrears** with its PAYE and NIC liability for the accounting period concerned, the credit will not be paid out. Where there were **outstanding corporation tax** liabilities, the credits will be set against these, and any excess will then be paid to the company.

Any amount claimed will not be considered to be **income** of the company for any period.

c. Restrictions on relief

The additional 125% relief available is restricted to 30%, or removed entirely, where certain situations occur. If the circumstances mean that the additional deduction is limited to 30% the **new R&D expenditure credits** may be available (¶78490).

78390

Subsidised expenditure

78395
s 1068 CTA 2009

Notified State Aid   This is typically government funding, such as the Grant for Research and Development. However, not all government funding is notified State Aid. The matter should be clarified with the provider of the funding. Where any such aid is given for any **part of a project**, this will disqualify the project from receiving any additional relief. This is the case where only part of the project is covered, or where only part of the costs are funded, regardless of the type of costs that are funded. It is ineffective, once State Aid has been received, to **repay** this in an attempt to secure the enhanced SME relief.

78400

Other subsidies   Where the subsidy is not notified State Aid the expenditure that can qualify for the 125% additional deduction is reduced by the subsidy received. The **subsidised expenditure** will still qualify for an additional deduction, but only at the rate of 30%. If the subsidy is not allocated by the provider, it should be allocated across the project and categories of cost on a just and reasonable basis. It is most likely that this would be based on a proportion of total spending on the project.

> MEMO POINTS   The **going concern** condition applying to the higher rate of relief does not apply where the expenditure is subsidised.

Capped expenditure

78405
s 1113–1118
CTA 2009

Where the additional 125% relief is available, the amount of aid that can be obtained is capped at €7.5 million per project; that is the amount of relief it has received in excess of what a large company would have been able to claim. The total amount of relief aid is **calculated** as:

$$TC + R + (P \times CT) - (N \times CT)$$

where:
– TC is the total of any tax credit received, including any amounts claimed for but not yet received, provided that the claim has not been refused;
– R is the actual reduction in the tax liability (this can either be through an R&D claim by the company or by way of a loss being surrendered to it from a company making a similar claim);
– P is the potential amount of relief, where a claim has been made for relief but no account has been taken of it in ascertaining the tax liability of the company or any other company;
– CT is the main rate of corporation tax when this calculation is performed; and
– N is the notional relief that would have been available if the company had been able to claim under the large company scheme throughout the period in question.

Where the **maximum relief available has been reached**, the excess will qualify for relief at the lower rate of 30%.

> EXAMPLE   E Ltd has incurred the following expenditure and made the following claims over the life of a qualifying R&D project (this presumes a CT rate of 24%, a rate of relief of 125%, and payable credits at 11%).
>
> | Year | Expenditure | Claims |
> |---|---|---|
> | 1 | €8,000,000 | Tax credits of €1,980,000 |
> | 2 | €8,000,000 | Additional relief of €10,000,000 resulting in a reduction in tax of €2,400,000 |
> | 3 | €6,000,000 | Additional relief of €7,500,000 |
>
> The costs in Year 3 have been claimed but not yet allowed. The total additional expenditure available if the company had been able to claim as a large company would have been €6,600,000.
> ((8,000,000 + 8,000,000 + 6,000,000) × 30%)
> The total R&D aid received would be calculated as follows:
> (1,980,000 + 2,400,000 + (7,500,000 × 24%) – (6,600,000 × 24%) = €4,596,000.

> MEMO POINTS   1. In calculating the relief already given, it is necessary to aggregate any **reduction in tax liabilities another company** has received by virtue of a loss being surrendered by the qualifying company to it by way of group or consortium relief (¶66000+).

2. As the cap was only **introduced** on 1 August 2008, it is not necessary to aggregate any of the relief given prior to this date.

2. Large companies carrying out own work

a. Additional deduction

A company that is not an SME can qualify for an additional deduction of 30% of the amount of the qualifying costs it incurs when carrying out its own work, as **opposed to being engaged as a subcontractor** (see ¶78485 for when it acts as subcontractor). There is no requirement for a large company to be a going concern, the company only needs to trade during the period concerned in order to secure the deduction.

78435
s 1074 CTA 2009

For expenditure incurred on or after 1 April 2013 a new scheme of R&D expenditure credits has been introduced (¶78490).

b. Contributions to independent research

Where a large company makes a contribution to independent R&D, which is relevant R&D for its own trade, the expenditure incurred will count towards the threshold and be entitled to relief, provided that:
– the contribution is made to an individual, partnership consisting only of individuals, or a qualifying body; and
– the company is not connected to the individual or partnership when the payment is made.

78455
s 1079 CTA 2009;
CIRD 82200

Unlike payments to subcontractors, the payment will qualify in full where the conditions are satisfied.

> MEMO POINTS   For these purposes a **qualifying body** is one that is:
> – a charity;
> – an institute of higher education;
> – a scientific research organisation;
> – a health service body; or
> – any other body specified by Treasury Order.

3. Companies acting as subcontractors

Where any company acts as a subcontractor for another company it may qualify for relief at 30% where the work is subcontracted to it by:
– a large company; or
– any person (for example, a government agency, charity or overseas resident) where the profits from the trade are not subject to either income or corporation tax in the UK.

78485
ss 1063, 1077,
1078 CTA 2009

4. R&D expenditure credits

This new credit scheme was introduced for expenditure incurred on or after 1 April 2013, and is available for **all companies** where the current enhancement of 30% may apply. At present it is possible to elect as to whether to take advantage of the new scheme or the enhanced deduction. However, the enhanced deduction scheme will **not be available** for expenditure incurred on or after 1 April 2016.

78490
ss 104A – 104Y
CTA 2009

Amount and treatment of credit

The level of the credit is 10% of the qualifying expenditure incurred. The expenditure that qualifies under the scheme is the same as under the existing scheme (¶78240+). However, any credit claimed under the new scheme is shown in the accounts and will be taxed as

78495

income. There is a prescribed order that has to be applied in looking at the application of any available credit, with a number of limits being imposed during the full calculation.

Step 1: Firstly the credit is set off against the corporation tax liability for the period in which the expenditure was incurred

Step 2: Any excess is then restricted by reducing the amount of the credit by the amount of tax that would be charged on it at the main rate in that year. The amount of the reduction is available to offset against corporation tax liabilities in future years or it can be surrendered to other group companies.

Step 3: The remaining credit is then compared to the company's total PAYE and NIC liability for the accounting period. If the credit exceeds this then the credit is limited to this amount, any excess is then treated as a credit of the following period. However the credit carried forward into the following period is to be ignored in making the calculation at step 2 in future years.

Step 4: The credit as adjusted through the above steps is then used to settle any corporation tax for any accounting period.

Step 5: If the company is a member of a group it can surrender any remaining credit to another group member. If the accounting periods are not the same then an apportionment has to be made of both the credit of the surrendering company and the tax liability of the claimant company.

Step 6: If there is still any credit available it can be used to settle any liability with HMRC, including any negotiated settlement following an enquiry.

Step 7: Finally, if the company still has an entitlement to any credit for the period HMRC will pay the sum to it, if it is a going concern (without having regard to the available credit) and its PAYE and NIC for the period is fully paid.

5. Companies involved in vaccine research

78505
s 1086 CTA 2009

For these purposes, qualifying R&D is **defined** as R&D into vaccines (or medicines, where applicable) for the prevention of:
- tuberculosis or malaria (or their treatment);
- infection by human immunodeficiency virus; or
- the onset, or for the treatment, of acquired immune deficiency syndrome resulting from the infection by human immunodeficiency virus in clades A, C, D and E only.

a. Small and medium-sized enterprises

Relief available

78525

For expenditure incurred on or after 1 April 2012 SMEs are not entitled to receive any further relief under the vaccine research relief heading.

Prior to that date, where a company was trading, was classed as an SME, and was a going concern (¶78335), it could claim an **additional deduction** of 20% of the qualifying expenditure.

If the company was a larger SME (¶78300) and it obtained a **tax credit under the R&D scheme** (¶78360), it was entitled to claim 20% of the expenditure that did not qualify under the R&D scheme.

Pre-trading expenditure

78530

In the case of pre-trading expenditure, the company could elect to treat it as arising in the accounting period it was incurred and as such create a **loss** for the period. This loss could then be used in the normal ways (¶36000), with the exception that it could not be carried back unless the company was entitled to relief in that earlier period. In this case the amount of loss that could be claimed was 20% of the qualifying expenditure where this also qualified under the R&D scheme, and 120% of any sums that did not so qualify. A larger SME was only able to claim the additional uplift of 20% on costs that did not qualify under the R&D scheme.

This treatment had to be claimed by way of election made within 2 years of the end of the period in which the loss arose.

Tax credits

A company with a surrenderable loss could claim an R&D tax credit of 16% of the loss. The **amount** that could be claimed under this rule, together with any credits claimed under ¶78370, was **limited** to the company's PAYE and NIC liability for the period. The surrenderable loss in this case was calculated as the lower of the amount of the loss and:
– for an SME, 20% of the expenditure eligible for relief under the R&D scheme plus 140% of the expenditure that did not qualify; or
– for a larger SME (¶78300), 120% of the expenditure that did not qualify under the R&D scheme.

In the case of a company making an election under ¶78530, the surrenderable loss was also the deemed loss.

The surrenderable loss was then **further reduced** by any amounts:
– that could have been offset against other profits of that or an earlier period;
– that had been carried back to an earlier period; and
– surrendered by way of group or consortium relief.

Where a surrender was made, the amount of the loss so surrendered could be used in any other way.

78535

---

b. Large companies

Additional condition

In order for a large company (i.e. any company that does not qualify as an SME) to secure this relief, it must make a **declaration** that the existence of the relief has in some way incentivised it to carry out the research. This may be evidenced by showing an increased level of expenditure on the project, an enlargement of its scope or an increase in the speed at which the project is carried out.

78555
s 1088 CTA 2009

Relief available

For a large company, the relief is given by way of allowing a **deduction** of 140% of the qualifying expenditure.

78560
s 1091 CTA 2009

SECTION 3

Relief for capital expenditure

The enhanced revenue reliefs are complemented by an enhanced relief for capital expenditure incurred on qualifying R&D. The rules are modelled on those for capital allowances generally (¶25000+).

78610

A. Extended definition of R&D

78640
s 437 CAA 2001

The definition of R&D in this case is extended beyond that outlined by the Department of Business, Innovation and Skills (¶78100), to **include** oil and gas exploration and appraisal, meaning activities involving:
a. searching for petroleum or gas in an area; or
b. ascertaining:
– the extent or characteristics of any petroleum or gas bearing area; or
– the level of petroleum or gas reserves in an effort to decide on its commercial viability.

B. Eligible expenditure

78670
ss 438, 439
CAA 2001

Qualifying expenditure must be incurred:
a. either for **carrying out the research** itself or in **providing the facilities** in order to allow the research to be conducted. This will further include expenditure on **assets used by employees** conducting the research. However, purchasing land does not qualify, regardless of the purpose to which it is put. If a building is purchased, a just and reasonable apportionment is required to be made between the non-qualifying land and the qualifying building element;
b. on **R&D undertaken by that** company or on its behalf. Where the R&D is carried out by another party this must be as agent or by way of contractual agreement. The link should be clear, close and directly related to the R&D; and
c. on R&D that **relates to a trade** that is currently being carried on, or after the expenditure is incurred a trade connected to the R&D is commenced.

> EXAMPLE
> 1. A company buys a laboratory to conduct its research in. As the expenditure is on facilities to carry out research the costs will qualify for relief. However, the element relating to the purchase of the land will not qualify.
>
> 2. A company buys a car for an employee to use to travel between research sites. This expenditure will qualify as it is an asset used by an employee carrying out research.
>
> 3. A contract committed the company to fund the costs of exploration in return for ownership of oil found. This was not considered to be sufficiently close, as the contract was not for R&D but for the ownership of the fruits of the R&D. *Gaspet Ltd v Ellis* [1987]
>
> 4. An individual ran three separate trades: one as a publisher, one as an author and a third which he considered a research arm. In his tax return he claimed for an R&D allowance on capital expenditure incurred by the publishing trade. The research carried out by it related to the research that was ultimately included in new works produced by the author. As such, even though the publishing trade actually published the work, the research was not for its trade but for that of the author. Accordingly relief was denied. *Salt v Golding* [1996]

The R&D may also facilitate an extension of the trade or be medical research carried out in relation to a specific issue faced by its workers (¶78220).

Expenditure on acquiring rights arising from R&D will not qualify for relief.

> MEMO POINTS   It may be the case that a **company only performs R&D** work that qualifies, either as a member of a group or by contract for third parties. In this situation all of the assets will qualify for the enhanced allowance.

> EXAMPLE In order to use a patented invention in its research a company has to buy the patent rights. This will not qualify, as it is expenditure on rights arising from research. However, the rights may qualify for capital allowances as intellectual property (¶28000+).

Assets changing use

Where an **asset previously used** in another part of the company is then transferred into the R&D trade, it will not qualify for the R&D allowance, as this is not expenditure incurred. However, it may still be eligible for allowances under other categories, such as plant and machinery allowances.

78675

Conversely an asset that qualified for the R&D allowance will not be deemed to be disposed of, if it is **later used in another trade** of the company. This may happen where machinery that previously qualified for allowances is then used for production purposes. Any balancing charge will be recovered through the usual plant and machinery regime (¶26085).

Dwellings

While the general rule allows assets used by employees to qualify, this does not extend to the provision of a dwelling house. However, if the dwelling is **part of** a qualifying building, and accounts for not more than 25% of the total cost of the building, it will be deemed to form part of the building, and the cost of the entire building will then qualify for relief.

78680
s 438(3), (4)
CAA 2001

C. Amount and timing of allowance

For qualifying expenditure, the **rate** of allowance is 100% of the expenditure incurred in that period. The company does not have to claim the full amount of the allowance, but where it does not, there is no future writing down allowance available.

78710
s 441 CTA 2009

Where there is a **disposal of the asset in the same period** as the expenditure is incurred, the allowance will be the difference between the expenditure incurred and the proceeds of sale.

Where the expenditure is **incurred before the trade commenced**, the allowance will fall to be made in the first chargeable period for the company.

> MEMO POINTS   If a company does **not** wish to **claim** the **full amount** of the allowance, it could choose to claim allowances on the expenditure under another allowance where such an option is available. However, once any allowance has been claimed, the company cannot change the type of allowance that applies.

> EXAMPLE   A Ltd purchases new equipment that it is going to use in its qualifying research. This equipment can qualify for either plant and machinery allowances or R&D allowances. Typically it would choose the 100% allowance available under the R&D scheme. However, it may wish to not claim any allowances under this scheme so as to claim plant and machinery allowances in future.

Disposal

Where the company ceases to own the asset or, while it is still owned by the company, it is demolished or destroyed, there will be a balancing event. Where the disposal value exceeds the remaining expenditure, the excess is brought into charge as a **balancing charge**, in the period of disposal or demolition, up to the total amount of allowances claimed. If the event occurs after the trade has ceased, the charge will be made in the final period.

78715
ss 442 – 445
CTA 2009

The **disposal value** will differ depending on the circumstances of the disposal:
– for a **sale** at market value it is the net proceeds of sale,
– for **loss or destruction** of an asset it is the net amount received for any remains, plus any capital compensation or insurance proceeds received, less any demolition costs (if the demolition costs exceed the disposal value, the excess is taken for these purposes only to be qualifying expenditure with allowances being available, provided that the asset is still being used for a qualifying purpose); and
– for a **disposal at less than market value**, the market value of the asset at that time.

Impact of VAT adjustments

78720
ss 446 – 449
CAA 2001

Adjustments under the VAT capital goods scheme (¶25135) impact on the possible allowances available in two ways.

Firstly, where a **rebate** is received under the capital goods scheme, this will be treated as a part disposal of the asset. This will only apply where the asset is still in existence and is still owned by the company.

Secondly, if a **payment** is required under the capital goods scheme, the further payment will qualify for allowances in the period when the liability arises, provided that the asset is still owned and in existence at the time.

CHAPTER 4

Reconstructions and mergers

79000

Any transaction has a potential tax consequence and in many cases such consequences can present barriers to businesses reorganising themselves as they develop. This is most evident in the development of **group structures** as companies purchase businesses. They can be left with a structure dictated by the way a business is acquired rather than what is most commercially efficient for them. Without reliefs a company could easily find the tax charges outweigh any long-term benefit of reorganising a group, as well as passing on substantial tax charges to its shareholders. There are several reliefs available, which alleviate these issues where the transactions are carried out in one of the prescribed ways.

Types of demerger

What is a demerger?

79050 When a company or group of companies runs more than one business it may be desirable to separate out those businesses and run them under separate management. The **separation of the businesses**, or the division of the corporate group in order to achieve this separation, is known as a demerger.

In any demerger the company which holds the shares or assets to be demerged **transfers** those shares or assets by way of a distribution. A **distribution** means any dividend (including a capital dividend) paid by the company and any other distribution out of the company's assets in respect of its shares, other than any amount representing repayment of share capital or any amount of the distribution for which the company receives new consideration.

Main types of demerger

79055 There are three main types of demerger:
– **direct dividend** demerger (referred to throughout as a direct demerger);
– **indirect** or **three-cornered** demerger (referred to throughout as an indirect demerger); and
– **scheme of reconstruction** under section 110 Insolvency Act 1986.

Direct and indirect demergers benefit from tax relief under the same statutory provisions and together are known as **statutory demergers**. The term **reconstruction** is also frequently used to describe a demerger, although it is used more widely in tax legislation to describe any scheme of merger, division or other restructuring which involves the exchanging of shares by the shareholders of one company for shares in another company. A **scheme of reconstruction** which meets the conditions prescribed in the legislation obtains beneficial tax treatment (¶79290).

Reasons to demerge

79060 There are several reasons why a group of companies may wish to demerge. It may be **commercially desirable to separate businesses** within the same group which have different commercial strategies, or the shareholders may no longer wish to run the businesses together. The share price of a strongly performing business may be depressed by the weaker performance of other businesses within the group. A demerger may, therefore, unlock the value of certain businesses and increase the share price, which will improve the returns to shareholders.

A further benefit of a demerger may be that on a subsequent disposal of the demerged company, the **sellers would receive the sale proceeds directly** rather than through the selling company. They would, therefore, be liable to CGT on the capital gain made, rather than incurring a liability to income tax on the distribution of the sale proceeds. The extent of this benefit depends on the rates of income tax and CGT in force at the time of the disposal. Additionally, as a demerger cannot be implemented in order to facilitate an immediate onward sale, this benefit would be merely incidental.

Corporate law issues on demergers

79065 A demerger typically involves a number of transactions by the company or group concerned. For details of the relevant implications please refer to *Company Law Memo*. In summary, a demerger invariably involves a distribution (¶18050+) and the restrictions on a company's ability to make a distribution are therefore relevant.

In particular, a company may only make a distribution out of its distributable reserves. **Distributable reserves** are calculated as follows:

Realised profits	x
Less: Realised losses	x
Previous distributions	x
Amounts utilised in capitalisation	x
Distributable reserves	x

Where a company has **insufficient distributable reserves** to make a distribution, it may be possible for subsidiary companies to make distributions up to that company in order to boost its distributable reserves.

Consequences of demergers

Any demerger involves a number of steps which, without specific reliefs, would give rise to costly tax charges for the company or companies involved and the shareholders.   **79070**

In particular, the distribution of shares or assets which is made on a demerger would normally give rise to:
– shadow ACT (¶41225) for the **distributing company**, thereby reducing its capacity to utilise surplus ACT; and
– a charge to income tax for any **individual shareholders**.

Additionally, the disposal of shares or assets by the **company** making the distribution would normally give rise to a chargeable gain for that company; also **shareholders** receiving a capital distribution would be liable to CGT in respect of a deemed part disposal of their shareholdings.

Finally, if the demerger results in a **company leaving the group** while holding an asset acquired from another group company within the previous 6 years, a degrouping charge (¶67425) could arise.

However, as stated above, there are several reliefs designed to facilitate demergers and most transactions are therefore structured in order to satisfy the conditions of these reliefs.

A. Direct demerger

1. Structure

In a direct demerger the parent company of a group distributes the shares in its subsidiary directly to its members. The **result** of the demerger will be that the shareholders will hold shares in two separate companies and there will be no corporate group.   **79100**

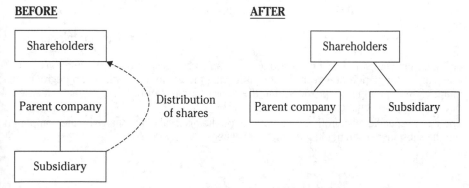

2. Distributions

Exempt distribution

79120
s 1076 CTA 2010

An exempt distribution is one which consists of the transfer by a company to all or any of its **members** of **shares in one or more 75% subsidiaries** (¶65055).

ss 1081, 1082
CTA 2010

In order to qualify as an exempt distribution the following must be satisfied:
a. all the companies involved must be **resident** in a member state;
b. all the companies involved must be **trading** companies or the **holding company of a trading group**;
c. the distribution must be made wholly or mainly for the purpose of **benefiting the trading activities** of the company or group (which activities will, after the distribution, be carried out by two or more companies or groups);
d. the distribution must **not be part of a scheme or arrangement**, the main purpose, or one of the main purposes, of which is:
– tax **avoidance**;
– the making of a **chargeable payment** (¶79160);
– the **acquisition by any person(s)** (other than members of the distributing company) of control of that company, or any other company involved in the demerger; or
– the **cessation or sale** of a trade after the distribution;
e. the **shares to be distributed** must:
– not be redeemable;
– constitute the whole or substantially the whole of the distributing company's shares in that company; and
– confer the whole or substantially the whole of the distributing company's voting rights in that company; and
f. after the distribution the distributing company must remain a trading company or the holding company of a trading group (unless the distributing company is itself a 75% subsidiary or the distribution is of two or more subsidiaries and the distributing company is dissolved without any assets available for distribution on a winding up).

79125
s 1085 CTA 2010

If the **distributing company is a subsidiary** of another company, the following conditions also apply:
a. the group must be a **trading group**; and
b. the distribution **must be followed by** one or more further exempt distributions which result in the shareholders of the parent company also becoming shareholders of:
– the company or companies to which a trade has been transferred;
– the subsidiary or subsidiaries whose shares have been demerged; or
– another company of which either of the above are 75% subsidiaries.

79130
s 192 TCGA 1992

Where a demerger qualifies as an exempt distribution the following happens:
a. the **shareholders** will not be treated as having received:
– a distribution of income (and as such will not be taxed on the value received); or
– a capital distribution (and as such no capital gains charge will be levied) – the shares received will be treated as if they were part of the original shareholding (see *Tax Memo* for full details);
b. the **distributing company** is not treated as having made a distribution for the purposes of calculating its shadow ACT (¶41225); and
c. where the **company leaving the group** holds an asset transferred to it by another group company in the period of 6 years prior to it leaving the group there will be no degrouping charge (¶67425+) imposed, provided that the transfer forms part of a merger that is carried out for bona fide commercial purposes.

There is no specific relief from the gain arising on the disposal of the shares by the company but the substantial shareholding exemption is likely to apply (¶69050).

3. Payments within 5 years

A payment made within 5 years of a demerger, in **connection with the shares** of any company involved, is termed a chargeable payment where it is made:
– **by any company concerned** in the distribution; and
– to a member of any company concerned in the distribution.

79160
s 1086 CTA 2010

A **repayment of share capital** or a **share buy-back** would, for example, constitute a chargeable payment.

A demerger will not qualify for relief under the statutory demerger provisions if it is **intended** that a chargeable payment is to be made.

Exemptions

The following payments are **excluded** from the chargeable payment rules:
– dividends and other distributions made in the normal course of an investment;
– distributions that are exempt under the general rules (¶18380+);
– payments between group companies; and
– payments made for bona fide commercial reasons not forming part of a scheme or arrangement for the avoidance of tax.

79165

Effect

If a chargeable payment is **made within 5 years** of the demerger taking place, a liability to income tax or to corporation tax (under the provisions which charge corporation tax on income) will arise on the recipient of the payment. The paying company will be required to **deduct** this income tax at the basic rate and account for it to HMRC.

A **return** must be made to HMRC within 30 days of a chargeable payment being made.

79170

B. Indirect demerger

1. Structure

On an indirect demerger the distributing company distributes **shares** in one or more subsidiaries, or one or more **trades**, to one or more **new companies**, in consideration of which the new companies issue shares to the original shareholders.

79200

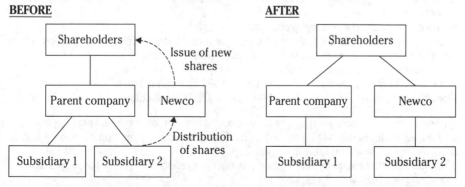

HMRC take the view that a **trade comprises** a parcel of assets which have been, or are capable of being, used to carry on a trade. However, a **trade does not include** dealing in shares, securities, land, trades or commodity futures.

s 1099 CTA 2010; SP 13/80

2. Distributions

Exempt distributions

79220
ss 1075, 1077
CTA 2010

An exempt distribution is one where the transfer by a company to one or more other companies **of a trade or shares** in one or more 75% subsidiaries (¶65055+) takes place, in consideration of which the **transferee companies issue shares** to all or any members of the transferor company (i.e. an indirect demerger).

ss 1081, 1083
CTA 2010;
SP 13/80

In order to qualify as an exempt distribution the following must be satisfied:

a. all the companies involved must be **resident** in a member state;

b. all the companies must be **trading** companies, or the holding company of a trading group;

c. the distribution must be made wholly or mainly for the purpose of **benefiting the trading activities** of the company or group (which activities will, after the distribution, be carried out by two or more companies or groups);

d. the distribution must **not be part of a scheme or arrangement**, the main purpose or one of the main purposes of which is:

– tax **avoidance**;

– the making of a **chargeable payment** (¶79260);

– the **acquisition by any person(s)** (other than members of the distributing company) of control of that company, or any other company involved in the demerger; or

– the **cessation or sale** of a trade after the distribution;

e. if the demerger involves the **transfer of shares**, the shares must:

– constitute the whole or substantially the whole of the distributing company's shareholding; and

– confer the whole or substantially the whole of its voting rights in the subsidiary;

f. after the distribution, the only or main activity of the transferee companies must be the holding of the shares acquired under the demerger or carrying on the trade transferred;

g. the **shares issued** by the transferee companies must:

– not be redeemable;

– constitute the whole or substantially the whole of the distributing company's shares in that company; and

– confer the whole or substantially the whole of the distributing company's voting rights in that company; and

h. the **distributing company** must remain a trading company, or the holding company of a trading group.

79225
s 1085 CTA 2010

If the **distributing company is a subsidiary** of another company, the following conditions also apply:

a. the group must be a **trading group**; and

b. the distribution **must be followed by** one or more further exempt distributions which result in the shareholders of the parent company also becoming shareholders of:

– the company or companies to which a trade has been transferred;

– the subsidiary or subsidiaries whose shares have been demerged; or

– another company of which either of the above are 75% subsidiaries.

79230

Where an indirect demerger qualifies as an exempt distribution the following happens:

a. the **shareholders** will not be treated as having received a distribution of income and as such will not be taxed on the value received;

b. the **distributing company** is not treated as having made a distribution for the purposes of calculating its shadow ACT (¶41225); and

s 192(3) TCGA 1992

c. where the **company leaving the group** holds an asset transferred to it by another group company in the period of 6 years prior to it leaving the group, there will be no degrouping charge (¶67425+) imposed, provided that the transfer forms part of a merger that is carried out for bona fide commercial purposes.

There is no specific relief from the **gain arising on the disposal of the shares** by the company but the substantial shareholding exemption is likely to apply (¶69050).

Nor is there any specific relief for the **capital gains tax** implications that arise. However, if the transaction meets the requirements both the company and the shareholders will qualify for relief under the scheme of reconstruction provisions (¶79290).

> MEMO POINTS Historically, indirect demergers were frequently **used in preference** to direct demergers where scheme of reconstruction relief was not available. To some degree this problem has been alleviated by the introduction of the substantial shareholding exemption which, if available, exempts the chargeable gain that arises on a direct demerger.

3. Payments within 5 years

The provisions relating to direct demergers also apply fully in relation to indirect demergers. See ¶79160 for full details.

79260
s 1086 CTA 2010

C. Schemes of reconstruction

1. Structure

The scheme of reconstruction provisions can apply in one of two cases. Firstly, where the effect of the transaction is that the business or substantially the **whole of the business** carried on by the company is **carried on by one or more successor** companies. Secondly, where the scheme is a **scheme of arrangement or a compromise** within the Companies Act and no part of the business of the original company is transferred.

79290

For the provisions to apply the:
– shares must be issued in one company to the shareholders in another company and to no-one else;
– shareholders of the original company must have an equal entitlement to shares in the new company (or, if there is more than one class of shares, shareholders of the same class must have an equal entitlement);
– reconstruction must be for bona fide commercial reasons;
– transferee company receives no consideration for the transfer (the assumption of its liabilities is ignored);
– transferee company must be either UK-resident at the time of acquisition or the assets must become chargeable assets immediately after the transfer; and
– transferor company must be either UK-resident at the time of transfer or the assets must be chargeable assets immediately prior to the transfer.

> MEMO POINTS A **controlling holding of shares** in a trading subsidiary is treated as being part of the parent company's business for the purposes of the scheme of reconstruction rules, thereby applying the relief to transfers of shares as well as transfers of assets. Apart from this situation, **whether a business exists** is a question of fact in each case. However, HMRC accept that the holding and managing (but not the mere holding) of a portfolio of investments can constitute a business.

Sch 5AA para 4(3)
TCGA 1992;
CG 52709

Examples of qualifying reconstructions

Demerger of trade   In this case a company is owned by its two shareholders equally. It is decided that the two trades it carries out, Trade A and Trade B, should be held in separate companies for commercial reasons.

79295
CG 52720+

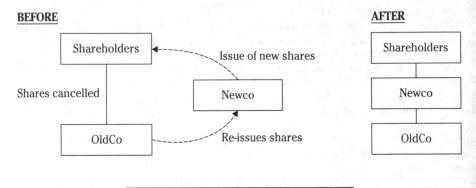

BEFORE   **AFTER**

In order to do this, shares in Newco are issued to the existing shareholders in the same proportions as their current holdings. Trade B is then transferred to Newco, which carries on that trade subsequently.

79300   **Companies Act arrangement**   A company, OldCo, wishes to insert a new holding company, NewCo, above itself in order to restructure its group. Under the Companies Act it receives permission to do so. The shares in OldCo are cancelled and reissued to NewCo. Meanwhile, NewCo issues replacement shares to the original shareholders in OldCo in the same proportions as before. There is no transfer of business, as OldCo is still carrying on the trade but as this is a scheme of arrangement under the Companies Acts it will still qualify for the relief.

BEFORE   **AFTER**

Shareholders ◄------- Issue of new shares   Shareholders

Shares cancelled   Newco   Newco

OldCo ------► Re-issues shares   OldCo

---

2. Reliefs applicable

Disposing company

79330
s 139 TCGA 1992

Where the provisions apply, the company disposing of the shares, or the assets in the case of a demerger of a trade, will not incur corporation tax on the chargeable gain that would arise ordinarily. The **transferee company** takes over the shares or assets at a price that results in no gain or loss arising (¶31280); the date of acquisition will be deemed to be the date the shares or assets were originally acquired.

Shareholders

79335
ss 126–131, 136
TCGA 1992

Where the provisions apply the shareholders will be treated as **not having made a disposal** of the shares but will be treated as having acquired the new shares at the date the original ones were acquired. This will defer the gain arising until a future disposal. For full details see *Tax Memo*.

D. Administration issues

1. Clearances

Reasons to seek clearance

As the transactions involved in a demerger or reconstruction would give rise to costly tax charges if the conditions for the various reliefs were not met, it is **common practice** to apply to HMRC for clearance that the relevant conditions will be met.

79365

Available clearances

Clearance can be sought in relation to the following matters:
- that a distribution will be an **exempt distribution** (statutory demergers);
- that a payment will **not be a chargeable payment** (statutory demergers);
- that on the **exchanging of shares** by shareholders in one company for shares in another company, anti-avoidance provisions will not prevent the new shares from being treated as the same asset as the original shares; and
- that on the **transfer of a business** from one company to another under a reconstruction, anti-avoidance provisions will not prevent the transfer from being considered to be a disposal at no gain/no loss (¶31280).

79370
ss 1091 – 1093
CTA 2010;
s 138 TCGA 1992

A **single letter** may be sent in respect of clearance under multiple provisions, as the application will be reviewed and clearance granted under all provisions by one person within the HMRC clearance team.

Procedure

An application for tax clearance **must be made** in writing to HMRC to the address given at ¶95380. Clearance can be **sought on behalf** of the transferor or recipient company (or companies) but not on behalf of the shareholders (who stand to receive the main benefit of the transaction).

79375
s 1093 CTA 2010

The clearance application **must contain certain information and confirmations** in relation to the transaction. In the case of a statutory demerger, the application must contain the following information as a minimum:
- the name, tax district and reference, country of residence, trading status, and involvement in the transactions of each of the companies included in the application;
- an explanation or diagram of any group structure;
- a statement of the purpose of the demerger, the trading activities to be divided, the trading benefits which will result and any other benefits which may arise;
- details of the number and class of any shares being transferred or issued;
- details of the assets and liabilities of trades being transferred and retained;
- details of any restructuring transactions undertaken, or to be undertaken, prior to the demerger;
- confirmation that the transactions do not form part of a scheme for tax avoidance;
- a statement of any circumstances in which any change of control of any of the companies involved, or any cessation or sale of a trade involved in the demerger might occur; and
- a copy of the latest audited accounts and details of any material changes since that date.

SP 13/80

In practice, an application relating to any other provision is likely to contain a similar degree of information to the above, since a clearance which is not given on the basis of full and accurate disclosure will be void in any event.

HMRC have 30 days in which to respond to an application for clearance, or to raise further enquiries. In the event of **further enquiries**, the applicant is granted 30 days in which to respond and the response will then allow HMRC a further 30 days. Theoretically, the clearance procedure could therefore take 60 days or more, although in practice this would be unusual and could cause commercial difficulties for the transaction.

2. Returns

79405 A return must be made to HMRC within 30 days of the making of:
– an **exempt distribution**;
– a **chargeable payment** within 5 years of an exempt distribution; and
– a **payment** which is made for **genuine commercial reasons** and which does not form part of a scheme or arrangement to avoid tax but which would otherwise be taxed as a chargeable payment.

HMRC require certain information about the transaction to be provided on the return, although this requirement is relaxed in relation to exempt distributions where advance clearance has already been obtained.

SECTION 2

Specific forms of demerger

A. Liquidation schemes

1. Reasons to use

79455 The conditions to obtain relief under the statutory demerger provisions (¶79100+) are strictly applied and mean that a statutory demerger is not a viable route for some companies. This may be because:
– the demerger is **intended to facilitate** a stock market flotation or a private sale;
– some or all of the **companies are not trading**;
– the company to be demerged does **not have sufficient distributable reserves**; or
– the **75% relationship between the companies** required for a statutory demerger does not exist.

In these circumstances it may be appropriate to consider the relatively complex (and therefore costly) structure of a liquidation scheme.

> MEMO POINTS Liquidation schemes are particularly useful for **property groups**, because dealing in land does not constitute trading for the purposes of the statutory demerger rules and in any event many property companies hold their assets as investments, which does not count as a trade for the statutory demerger rules but does count as a "business" for the scheme of reconstruction rules (¶79290).

2. Structure

79475 A liquidation scheme involves the **liquidation of the parent company** of a group, which distributes its assets (businesses or shares) to two or more new companies in the course of its winding up. In consideration for the transfers the **new companies issue shares** to the original shareholders. The parent company is then liquidated, leaving the shareholders holding shares in two or more new companies.

BEFORE

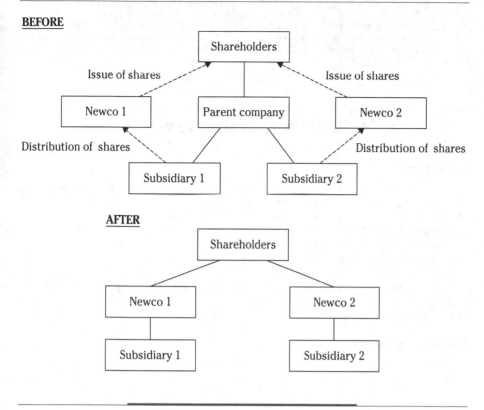

AFTER

---

3. Consequences

Shareholders

As the transaction will not be treated as a distribution there will be no income tax charge for the shareholders. If scheme of reconstruction relief applies, their base cost in their original shares will be allocated to the base cost of their new shares.

79495

Company

An allocation of assets made in respect of share capital on a winding up **is not treated** as a distribution. As such there is no shadow ACT (¶41225) for the company.

79500
s 1030 CTA 2010

Provided that the scheme qualifies as a scheme of reconstruction (¶79290), the transfers of any shares or assets by the company being reconstructed will be a no gain/no loss transaction (¶31280), so any **chargeable gain** will be held over.

Alternatively, if the **substantial shareholding exemption** (¶69050) applies, any chargeable gain will crystallise but be exempt from the charge to corporation tax. The substantial shareholding exemption is available even if the disposing company is to be wound up immediately after the disposal.

There is no exemption from the **degrouping charge** (¶67425) for a scheme of reconstruction. However, it may be possible to mitigate any degrouping charge by ensuring that the company which transferred the asset leaves the group with the transferee, although this will only be effective if the companies formed a group at the time the transfer was made. *Johnston Publishing (North) Limited v HMRC* [2008] Alternatively, the asset may be **hived out** of the company leaving the group, although care will need to be taken if the asset concerned is land, to avoid creating a charge to stamp duty land tax (see *Tax Memo* for full details).

> MEMO POINTS Confusingly, there is an exemption from a degrouping charge where a company leaves the group because **another member of its group ceases to exist**. This applies where a

subsidiary is liquidated, leaving a parent company holding assets acquired in the previous 6 years, but does not apply where a parent company is liquidated, because in the latter situation the subsidiaries leave the group as a result of the distributions or sales made during the course of winding up, not as a result of the parent ceasing to exist.

B. Schemes of arrangement

Definition

79530　A scheme of arrangement is a compromise or **arrangement between a company and its shareholders or creditors**, which is sanctioned by the court. In order to carry out a scheme of arrangement a company **must follow a statutory procedure** involving:
– an application to the court to convene a meeting of the shareholders or creditors;
– notice to the shareholders or creditors, summoning them to the meeting;
– the holding of a meeting at which the scheme is approved; and
– delivery of an order from the court to the Registrar of Companies, approving the scheme.
By following this procedure a company will be able to implement any kind of demerger, regardless of whether it can meet the conditions to qualify as a statutory demerger or a scheme of reconstruction.

Reasons for using

79535　A scheme of arrangement is a more costly and time-consuming procedure than a statutory demerger or scheme of reconstruction. It will be used where there are **practical difficulties** in implementing one of the simpler procedures; examples might include where the distributing company has insufficient distributable reserves to make a distribution.

Alternatively, a scheme of arrangement may be used where it is desirable to **insert a new holding company** on top of the distributing company in a statutory demerger, or the parent company in a liquidation scheme.

> ‾MEMO POINTS‾　1. Schemes of arrangement are often **combined** with a reduction in share capital (¶79545) to resolve issues with distributable reserves.
> 2. Although the insertion of a new holding company can **also be done** by way of a share-for-share exchange, a scheme of arrangement requires a lower majority of shareholder approval.

Structure

79540　There are **no specific tax reliefs** available to a transaction simply because it has been approved as a scheme of arrangement. Accordingly, such a scheme will normally be structured as an indirect demerger (¶79200), or a liquidation scheme (¶79455), in order to take advantage of the statutory demerger code and/or scheme of reconstruction relief.

Reduction of share capital

79545　A company limited by shares is permitted to reduce its share capital. The **effect** of a reduction in share capital is to create a reserve treated as realised profit, which in turn boosts distributable reserves. A reduction in share capital is, therefore, a useful procedure for a company wishing to demerge but which has **insufficient distributable reserves** to make a distribution.

A **public company** can only reduce its share capital with the approval of the court; for this reason a reduction in share capital is frequently combined with a court-approved scheme of arrangement.

Since 1 October 2008 a **private company limited by shares** can reduce its share capital either by approval of the court or by making a solvency statement. For full details of these see *Company Law Memo*.

Consequences

Provided that the value of the assets being transferred is not less than the nominal value of the shares which are cancelled in the reduction, a reduction of share capital does not involve the making of a **distribution**.

As there is no distribution, there are no income tax consequences for **shareholders**. If structured as an indirect demerger, scheme of reconstruction relief will apply to relieve any charge to CGT for the shareholders.

For the **company**, there will be no shadow ACT (¶41225) and if structured as an indirect demerger, the transaction will fall within the scheme of reconstruction relief and there will be no chargeable gain on the disposal of shares or assets.

For the position in relation to the degrouping charge see (¶79230).

79550

SECTION 3

Hive-downs

A. Structure

A hive-down occurs when the predecessor company transfers its trade (or part of its trade) to the successor company. Although the successor company is generally a newly incorporated company, there is no requirement for this. The **existence of another trade** in the successor company will not change the position. Typically this will be followed by a sale of the shares in the successor company to a third company.

79600
s 940A CTA 2010

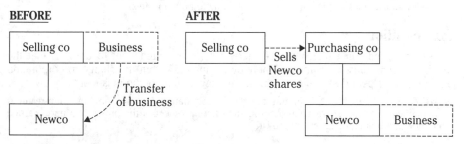

BEFORE | **AFTER**

Where a company (referred to in this section as the predecessor company) **transfers a trade to another company** (referred to in this section as the successor company), the default position is that the trade is treated as ceasing. However, where a trade is transferred **without a change in its ultimate ownership** and certain conditions are satisfied, this rule is disapplied for specific tax purposes.

79605
s 41 CTA 2010

Where a hive-down occurs, the following tax advantages arise:
– any **unused trading losses** arising from the trade are transferred to the successor company and can be used against future profits of the same trade; and
– the **capital allowances** position of any plant and machinery used in the trade is preserved and no balancing charge will arise in the predecessor company on the transfer of the assets.

These tax advantages would not exist on a transfer of the trade direct from its original owner to a third company; a hive-down may therefore be a tax-efficient way to dispose of a business in certain circumstances.

B. Conditions

79635
s 940C CTA 2010

Two conditions must be satisfied for a hive-down transaction to secure any reliefs: the ownership condition and the tax condition. Where the conditions are satisfied hive-down treatment is **mandatory**, so there is no requirement for it to be claimed on a return.

Ownership condition

79640
ss 941, 942
CTA 2010

Hive-down treatment will apply where a 75% interest in the trade is under **common ownership**:
- at some time within the 12 months prior to the transfer taking place; and
- at any time during the 2-year period from the date of transfer.

Ownership of the trade can be **determined** by any of the following:
a. the company carrying on the trade;
b. the ownership of the ordinary share capital of the company carrying on the trade; or
c. if the company carrying on the trade is a subsidiary of another company:
- the parent company of the company carrying on the trade;
- the ownership of the ordinary share capital of the parent company; or
- a person who has a majority of voting rights in a company which owns the ordinary share capital of the company carrying on the trade.

To establish common ownership of the trade both before and after the transfer of the trade, it must be possible to satisfy a combination of any of these tests.

ss 941(6);
942(8) CTA 2010

s 953 CTA 2010

[MEMO POINTS] 1. For the purposes of the tests **ownership** of share capital refers to beneficial ownership.
2. Hive-down treatment can apply where a transfer which does not meet the ownership condition is **followed by a further transfer** and the first and third companies are able to satisfy the common ownership test at some time in the 12 months prior to and during the 2 years from the first transfer. Where this unusual situation arises, hive-down treatment will apply to both transfers and the relevant liabilities restriction (¶79680) will apply to both transfers.

Tax condition

79645
s 943 CTA 2010

The second condition which must be met for hive-down treatment to apply is that the transferred **trade** must be carried on only by companies within the charge to corporation tax for the same period as that during which the ownership condition is met.

[MEMO POINTS] Companies within the charge to corporation tax may include **non-resident companies** which are chargeable to corporation tax in respect of the profits of a trade carried on through a branch or agency in the UK.

C. Consequences

1. Trading losses

79675
s 944 CTA 2010

When the conditions set out above are satisfied, any trading losses relating to the transferred trade will be available to the successor company for use against future profits from the **same trade**. Consequently, the predecessor company cannot then make a claim for terminal loss relief (¶61080) in respect of those same losses.

The losses arising on a hive-down will be **streamed in the successor** company according to the following principles:
- the successor company will only be entitled to losses arising from the trade or part trade transferred; and

– any losses transferred will only be available to be set against profits from the trade or part trade transferred.

In accordance with these principles, the following rules apply:
– where the predecessor company **ceases to carry on its entire trade** and the **successor company merges that trade with its own trade**, all of the losses can be used but against profits of the transferred trade only;
– where the predecessor company **ceases to carry on part of its trade** and that part becomes the **successor company's entire trade**, only the losses relating to the part trade can be used but against any profits subsequently arising;
– where the predecessor company **ceases to carry on part of its trade** and that part is **merged** with the successor company's existing trade, only the losses relating to the part trade can be used, and against future profits of that trade only.

The transferred trade is notionally treated as a separate trade in relation to utilisation of the losses transferred but for no other purpose. This means that if the successor company has generated any trading losses from its existing trade prior to the hive-down, those losses will be available to be carried forward and used against profits of the entire trade. Any losses arising from the existing trade after the hive-down will be available to be used against profits of the same trade.

The rules are not applicable where a whole trade is transferred and it is the only trade carried on by the successor company.

> ⌐MEMO POINTS⌐ Where **only part of a trade** is transferred, the loss that attaches must be allocated on a just and reasonable basis.

Restriction

Where a hive-down takes place and the assets attaching to the trade are transferred to the successor company but **some of its liabilities are retained by the predecessor company**, the relevant liabilities restriction prevents the successor company from carrying forward some or all of the losses relating to that trade. The intended effect of this rule is that losses equal to the amount of debt which the predecessor cannot pay as a result of the transfer are denied.

79680
s 945 CTA 2010

The amount of the restriction is calculated as follows:
– add up the liabilities not transferred (excluding share capital and reserves but including any intra-group debt left behind);
– deduct the value of any assets not transferred; and
– deduct the sale consideration given for the transfer.

If the result is a **positive number**, that amount is the amount of the restriction. An amount of the losses transferred up to and including this figure will be disallowed. Any losses disallowed in this way are not returned to the predecessor company but are effectively cancelled. If the amount is a **negative number** there is no restriction.

These rules do not apply to any **capital allowances** transferred under the hive-down.

> ⌐MEMO POINTS⌐ 1. Where **only part of a trade** is transferred, the assets and liabilities used for the purposes of this calculation are apportioned on a just and reasonable basis.
> 2. The legislation contains anti-avoidance provisions which are designed to **counteract attempts to eliminate liabilities** in order to avoid the relevant liabilities restriction. Where a liability which has been transferred from the successor company to the predecessor company is partially waived by the creditor, the liability is treated as covering only the actual amount repaid, rather than the full amount. Further, the conversion of any debt into share capital which takes place in the 12 months preceding the transfer is ignored in calculating the liabilities which are not transferred.

s 946 CTA 2010

Care should be taken following a hive-down to avoid a **major change in the nature or conduct of the trade** acquired under the transfer inside three years of the acquisition. Such a change could result in the losses transferred under the hive-down being disallowed. However, the transfer of part of a trade will not, of itself, normally be regarded a major change in the nature or conduct of a trade for the purposes of these provisions. For full details see ¶60245.

79685

2. Capital allowances

79715
s 948 CTA 2010

Where hive-down treatment applies the **successor company** will inherit the capital allowances position of the predecessor company in relation to the assets transferred. In other words, there will be no balancing charge at the time of the transfer and the successor company will be entitled to continue claiming the capital allowances which would have been available to the predecessor company.

s 949 CTA 2010

⬚ *MEMO POINTS* ⬚   The general rule does not apply to a **dual resident investing company**. A dual resident investing company is one which is UK-resident for tax purposes, is within the charge to tax in another territory and meets one of the following three conditions:
– it is not a trading company at any point during the accounting period in which the hive-down takes place;
– its trade during the accounting period in which the hive-down takes place consists of holding shares or investments, making loans or charitable payments, or obtaining funding for any of these activities; or
– it carries on one or more of the above activities to an extent which is unjustified by its trade, or which is not relevant to its trade.

SECTION 4

Dissolution

79765   Following a demerger or hive-down, it may be appropriate to dissolve one or more companies which have become surplus to requirements.

Liquidations

79770   If the company is extinguished through a formal liquidation, any **distributions made during the course of winding up** will not be treated as chargeable (¶79500) and will not give rise to any income tax charge for the recipients. Instead, the shareholders will be liable for CGT on receipt of the distribution.

Striking off

79775
ss 1000–1011
CA 2006

A company may be struck off the register of companies pursuant to a statutory procedure, provided that:
– it **does not intend to carry on any business** in the future;
– it will **collect any debts** owed to it; and
– it **intends** to seek dissolution.

Striking off may be requested by the directors of the company, or carried out by the Registrar of Companies with 3 months' notice.

The exemption for distributions made during the course of a liquidation is extended to distributions made during the course of striking off under this procedure. Full details of this exemption can be found at ¶61355+.

SECTION 5

Mergers

79825   A merger involves the joining together of the businesses of two previously separate companies. A true merger occurs when both companies dissolve and their assets and liabilities are transferred into a new company. This is **distinct from an acquisition**, which involves the purchase by one company or group of the shares in another company or group.

Mergers of this type are relatively uncommon in the UK, although company law does contain provision for the **dissolution of a company without its winding up**, and the **transfer of its assets to a new company** through a scheme of reconstruction, with the sanction of the court. Accordingly, if a merger of this type is implemented, scheme of reconstruction relief should apply to mitigate any charge to corporation tax on chargeable gains (for the company) or capital gains tax (for the shareholders).

s 900 CA 2006

Joint ventures

A joint venture is a **commercial agreement entered into by two or more separate entities**. A joint venture may be implemented by way of a simple contract, or it may take the form of a partnership or joint venture company. Only the last is considered in this book.

79830

The creation of a joint venture company is a common way to achieve a merger. Typically, two (or more) shareholders acquire shareholdings (which may or may not be equal) in the joint venture company. This can be achieved by the acquisition by one company of some of the shares in a company in another group. **More commonly**, each of the parties to the joint venture transfers the business assets to be used in the venture into a new subsidiary. One of the parties then incorporates the joint venture company and the shares in the subsidiaries are transferred to the new company by way of a share-for-share exchange. The business is then conducted by the joint venture company under the governance of a joint venture agreement made between the shareholders.

There is virtually no specific legislation which governs the creation or operation of a joint venture company. Accordingly, any transactions are taxed under the general principles of corporation tax. However, merger relief may facilitate the transfer of assets into the joint venture company on its creation.

Merger relief

A merger, or creation of a **joint venture company**, often involves the transfer of shares in a company which holds assets acquired from another group company within the previous 6 years. Under normal circumstances this would give rise to a degrouping charge (¶67425+).

79835
s 181 TCGA 1992

However, a specific exemption from the **degrouping charge** applies where:
– the merger is implemented for bona fide reasons and is not for the avoidance of tax;
– the merger does not take place with a view to the disposal of the business transferred;
– the activities transferred are sufficient to constitute a business (which extends the relief beyond mere trading companies);
– at least 25% of the consideration given for the business transfer is in the form of ordinary share capital, with the remainder comprising other share capital and/or debentures (but not cash); and
– the value of a party's interest in the joint venture is equal to the value of the business given up (effectively extending the provisions beyond 50: 50 joint ventures to other arrangements where the original 75% group relationship is broken).

An identical relief applies to the transfer of **intangible assets** in this situation.

s 789 CTA 2009

The relief applies **only** to any **initial transfers**, so all of the assets must be transferred together and it is essential for all the parties to contribute a business. HMRC offer an informal clearance procedure for the availability of the relief.

Cross-border mergers

A merger between a **UK-resident company** and a **company resident in another member state** of the European Union is governed by specific EU legislation. Such a transaction may still qualify for relief under the provisions which govern transactions between UK companies.

79840
ss 136, 139
TCGA 1992

In the event that these provisions do not apply, further provisions (¶61200) provide relief from corporation tax on chargeable gains (for the company) and capital gains tax (for the shareholders) on a cross-border transaction. These apply where a company transfers all of its assets and liabilities to another company and ceases to exist without entering liquidation.

CHAPTER 5

Attracting third party investment

80000   Given the recent improvements made to the following tax efficient investment schemes (in particular their attractiveness to smaller companies), it is likely that more companies will be seeking funding from these sources.

Scheme	¶¶
Enterprise investment scheme (EIS)	¶80055
Venture capital trust scheme (VCT)	¶80355
Corporate venturing scheme (CVS) (no longer available for fresh share issues)	¶80545
Seed enterprise investment scheme (SEIS)	¶81035

Overall funding level

The **amount which may be raised** by the company through risk capital schemes in the year ending on the date of issue of the shares must not exceed £5 million. For this purpose, risk capital schemes include the EIS, VCT and SEIS, and any other EU-approved risk capital schemes. This limit applies to:
– EIS and SEIS shares issued on or after 6 April 2012; and
– VCT investments made on or after 19 July 2012.

80005
ss 173A, 292A
IIA 2007

> MEMO POINTS   For earlier share issues and investments the limit was £2 million.

SECTION 1

Enterprise investment scheme

Unconnected individuals (of any country of residence) may invest in a company through the Enterprise Investment Scheme (EIS) for a minimum period of 3 years, and receive income tax relief.

80055

The scheme is intended to help small unquoted trading companies (¶80175) to raise finance by encouraging individuals to subscribe for shares in return for the following tax reliefs (which are fully detailed in *Tax Memo*):
– income tax relief at 30% is available on amounts subscribed for qualifying EIS shares;
– no chargeable gain arises on disposal of the shares;
– any loss arising (net of income tax relief received) can be set against income rather than capital gains; and
– amounts invested may be used to defer tax on other chargeable gains (for this relief only, there is no limit on the amount invested, no minimum period of ownership, and the investor can be connected to the company).

The requirements for EIS income tax relief are that:
– a **qualifying investor** (¶80090)
– must subscribe for **eligible shares** (¶80135)
– in a **qualifying company** (¶80170).
In addition, there must be no disqualifying arrangements in place.

> MEMO POINTS   1. A **claim for relief** cannot be made until the trade has been carried on for 4 months, and must be made within 4 years from the end of the tax year in which the shares were issued.
> 2. **Disqualifying arrangements** are any arrangements entered into with the purpose of obtaining tax relief for any person, if either or both of the following conditions apply:
> – all or most of the money raised is paid to or for the benefit of a party to the arrangements (or a person connected with such a party); or
> – in the absence of those arrangements, it would be reasonable to expect that the business would be carried on as part of another business by a person who is a party to the arrangements or a person connected with such a party.
> This requirement applies to shares issued on or after 6 April 2012, irrespective of when the disqualifying arrangements were entered into.

s 176 ITA 2007

s 179A ITA 2007

Periods A, B and C

The EIS is subject to many conditions, most of which must be fulfilled throughout one of the following periods:

80060
s 159 ITA 2007

Period	Starts	Ends
Period A	Date of incorporation of the company[1]	Immediately before the termination date[2] in relation to the shares
Period B	Date of issue of the shares	
Period C	12 months before the date of issue of the shares	

> **Note:**
> 1. If the company was incorporated more than two years before the date of issue of the shares, Period A starts two years before the latter date.
> 2. The **termination date** is the later of:
> – the third anniversary of the issue of the shares; and
> – the third anniversary of the commencement of the trade.

A. Qualifying investors

80090
ss 157, 163 - 165,
ITA 2007

The requirements for a qualifying investor are shown in the following table. The investor must:

Requirement	Qualifying period [1]	¶¶
Be an individual	(None)	
Have subscribed for the shares for genuine commercial reasons, and not as part of a tax avoidance scheme [2]	(None)	
Not be connected with the issuing company	Period A	¶80095
Not received a linked loan [3]	Period A	

> **Note:**
> 1. The condition must be satisfied throughout the period indicated.
> 2. In particular, relief is not available where the investment is made as part of a **reciprocal arrangement** in order to meet the conditions of the scheme. For example, EIS relief will not be available for an individual who is connected with company B but subscribes for shares in a company with which he is not connected (company A) on the condition that another person, who is connected with company A, will subscribe for shares in company B.
> 3. A linked loan (which includes the giving of any credit, or any debt assignment) is a loan made to the investor or his associate (¶80095) which would not have been made, or would not have been made on the same terms, if the investor had not subscribed or proposed to subscribe for the shares in question.

Connected persons

80095
ss 166 - 170
ITA 2007

A person is connected with the issuing company where the situations shown in the following table apply (either involving the potential investor or his associate). Where a person subsequently becomes connected (for example, a 15% investment is made, followed by a further 20% stake a couple of years later), the income tax relief will be withdrawn.

> `MEMO POINTS`   1. For the purposes of EIS relief, a person is **associated** with:
> – his relatives or partners (a relative is as detailed in ¶75955, with the exclusion of brothers and sisters);
> – the trustees of a settlement of which the investor or his relative was the settlor; and
> – the trustees or personal representatives of any trust or estate holding shares in which the investor has an interest.
> 2. It is important that the shares are subscribed for before the individual **becomes a director**.

Situation	Details
Employee, director or partner of the company	Directorships may be ignored where the director is either: **a.** unpaid i.e. the only payments received comprise: – payment or reimbursement of expenses allowable for employment income purposes; – normal commercial payments in respect of interest on loans, rent for property, supplies of goods and dividends; or – reasonable remuneration provided to the director (directly or indirectly) for services in the course of a trade or profession; or **b.** a business angel (¶80100) – a person unconnected with the company, who is prepared to provide finance and expertise to the company A company secretary who receives no payment, has no benefits in kind or employment contract and carries out only company secretarial duties is not an employee for EIS purposes

Situation	Details
Has control of the company	A person has control of the issuing company where, by virtue of his (or his associates') shareholding or voting rights, or under the Articles of Association or other regulatory document, he can secure that the company's affairs are conducted in accordance with his wishes[2]
Has a substantial interest in the company	A person has a substantial interest[2, 3] in a company if he (together with his associates) has possession of, or is entitled to acquire, over 30% of the company's or any 51% subsidiary's[1]: – issued ordinary share capital (nominal value); – voting rights; – net assets on a winding up (directly or indirectly)

Note:
1. In this context, a **subsidiary company** means a company which at any time in the period beginning on the incorporation of the company (or, if later, 2 years before the share issue) and ending on the termination date (¶80060) is a 51% subsidiary (¶65505).
2. The **right to acquire** shares in the future e.g. under options or where convertible debt is held, must be taken into account.
3. For shares issued before 6 April 2012, a person's holding of loan capital in the company was also taken into account. The 30% limit then applied to the total of a person's issued share capital and loans made to the company, rather than being applied to each category separately *HMRC v Taylor and another* [2011].

Business angels

A subscription by a business angel will qualify for relief if, **at the time of the subscription** for the EIS shares, the business angel was never:
a. connected with the issuing company; or
b. involved in the trade of the issuing company (either on his own, in partnership or as a director or employee).

80100
s 169 ITA 2007

A business angel will continue to qualify for relief even if he **subsequently** becomes a paid director of the company (or a subsidiary or partner of the company), provided any remuneration he receives is reasonable in relation to services performed.

Any **further subscription** after he becomes a paid director will qualify for EIS relief if the shares are issued before the termination date (¶80060) relating to the first EIS issue to him i.e. within 3 years, and provided he is not otherwise connected with the company e.g. by holding a 30% interest.

Limits on investment

Although there is no **upper limit** on the amount of the investment, the maximum amount which will attract tax relief in any tax year is £1 million.

80105

MEMO POINTS For shares issued before 6 April 2012 there was a minimum qualifying subscription of £500, and the maximum amount on which relief was given was £500,000.

B. Eligible shares

The shares must be newly-issued, fully paid-up ordinary shares acquired by subscription for cash (or related bonus shares).

80135
ss 172 - 178
ITA 2007

The purpose of the share issue must be to raise money for a **qualifying business activity** (¶80140). There is also a general requirement that shares must be issued for genuine commercial purposes and not as part of a tax avoidance scheme.

Shares are not eligible if, prior to the termination date (¶80060), they carry the following present or future **rights**:
– preferential rights to dividends;
– preferential rights to assets on a winding up; or
– rights to redemption.

For shares issued on or after 6 April 2012, a preferential right to dividends does not make the shares ineligible unless:
– the amount or timing of the dividend depends on a decision of the company or any other person; or
– the rights are cumulative.

> ⌐*MEMO POINTS*⌐   For the shares to be eligible, there must also be no **pre-arranged exits**, defined as any arrangements:
> – for disposal of the shares;
> – for the cessation of the trade or disposal of the company's assets; or
> – having as a main purpose the protection of the shareholder from the normal risks of investment.

Use of funds raised

80140
ss 173A, 175 - 179
ITA 2007

All of the money raised by the issue of shares must be used for the **purposes of** a qualifying business activity.

There is a specific **time limit** which applies, so that monies must be expended within 2 years from the later of:
– the date of the share issue; and
– the commencement of the trade.

> ⌐*MEMO POINTS*⌐   A **qualifying business activity** means any of the following:
> – carrying on a qualifying trade (¶80185);
> – preparing to carry on a qualifying trade which begins within two years of the date of issue of the shares;
> – research and development which is intended to leads to the carrying on of a qualifying trade, or to benefit one which is already being carried on.
> The qualifying trade or the R & D must be carried out for a **minimum period** of at least four months ending on or after the date of issue in order for the company to be a qualifying company.

C. Qualifying companies

80170
ss 180 - 199
ITA 2007

The company must satisfy two sets of conditions:
– one set at the date the shares are issued; and
– a further set throughout Period B (¶80060).

Conditions to be satisfied at the date of issue The company must:

Requirement	¶¶
Be unquoted[1] (and there must be no arrangements in place for it to cease being so)	
Not exceed a maximum permitted level of gross assets and number of employees	¶80175
Not be in financial difficulty[2]	

Note:
1. Shares on the Alternative Investment Market (AIM) and the PLUS Quoted and PLUS Traded Markets are not considered to be quoted for this purpose.
2. **Financial difficulty** is defined by the EC Guidelines on State Aid for Rescuing and Restructuring Firms in Difficulty: see flmemo.co.uk/ctm8471. However, HMRC will not regard a company as being in difficulty where, at the date of the subsequent share issue, it:
– is within the first 3 years of trading; and/or
– has been able to raise funds from its existing shareholders, or from the market, sufficient to meet its anticipated funding requirements at that time.

Conditions to be satisfied throughout Period B (¶80060) The company must:

Requirement	¶¶
Have a permanent establishment in the UK	¶80180
Exist wholly for the purposes of carrying on one or more qualifying trades, or be the parent company of a trading group	¶80185
Carry on a qualifying business activity	¶80140
Control no non-qualifying subsidiaries	¶80190
Have no property-managing subsidiary that is not a qualifying 90% subsidiary	¶80190
Be neither the 51% subsidiary of another company nor controlled by another company	¶80190

Maximum size The company must not exceed the following size limits:

80175
ss 186 - 186A
ITA 2007

Requirement[1]	
Maximum number of employees[2]	250
Maximum gross relevant assets[3] immediately before the investment is made	£15 million
Maximum gross relevant assets[3] immediately after the investment is made	£16 million

Note:
1. These limits apply to shares issued on or after 6 April 2012, but did not take effect until 19 July 2012.
2. Employee includes a director, but does not include an employee on maternity or paternity leave, or a student on vocational training. Employees working less than 35 hours a week (including lunch breaks and overtime) are ignored.
3. Relevant assets are the assets of the company (or group, where appropriate, ignoring intra-group holdings and obligations) calculated as the aggregate of the assets which would be shown on a balance sheet prepared to that date, without any deduction for liabilities.

Permanent establishment

80180
s 191A ITA 2007

A company has a permanent establishment in the UK if (and only if):

- it has a fixed place of business in the UK through which the business of the company is wholly or partly carried on; or

- an agent acting on behalf of the company has the authority to enter into contracts on behalf of the company and habitually exercises that authority in the UK.

The activities carried on at the fixed place of business or by the agent must, when considered in relation to the company's business as a whole, have more than a simply preparatory or auxiliary character (such as mere storage of goods).

> _MEMO POINTS_   1. A company does **not** have a permanent establishment in the UK simply because:
> – it carries on business in the UK through an independent agent or a broker; or
> – it controls a UK resident company or a company carrying on business in the UK (whether through a permanent establishment or not).

Carrying on a qualifying trade

A qualifying trade is the carrying on (or the preparing to carry on) of a trade, on a commercial basis with a view to making a profit.

80185
ss 181-183, 189,
192 -199 ITA 2007

When considering whether a company exists wholly for the purposes of a qualifying trade, **holding or managing property** for the purposes of the trade is ignored.

If the company (or group) carries on any of the following **excluded activities**, and they comprise more than 20% of the trade (e.g. in terms of turnover or capital employed), the trade does not qualify:

s 192 ITA 2007

Activity	Reference
Dealing in goods other than as part of an ordinary wholesale or retail distribution trade	s 193 ITA 2007, VCM 3030
Property dealing and development	s 196 ITA 2007, VCM 3020, 3080
Financial activities, including: – banking; – debt factoring; – money lending; – hire purchase financing; – dealing in commodities, futures, securities and shares; and – insurance	s 192 ITA 2007; VCM 3040
Leasing or hiring goods, including chartering ships (other than short term hiring or chartering)	s 194 ITA 2007, VCM 3050
Receiving royalties and licence fees, but excluding those attributable to film production, research and development and relevant intangible assets [1]	s 195 ITA 2007, VCM 3060
Farming and market gardening	VCM 3090
Holding, managing or occupying woodlands, any other forestry activities or timber production	VCM 3100
Operating or managing hotels, nursing homes and residential care homes	ss 197, 198 ITA 2007, VCM 3140, 3150
Providing legal or accountancy services	VCM 3070
Providing services for a trade carried on by another person (which consists substantially of non-qualifying activities) if the person has a controlling interest in both	s 199 ITA 2007, VCM 3170
Shipbuilding	s 196A ITA 2007
Producing coal	s 196B ITA 2007
Producing steel	s 196C ITA 2007

Note:
1. **Relevant intangible assets** are where the whole or greater part of the value of the asset was created by the share issuing company (or by a company that was a qualifying subsidiary of the issuing company at all times during which it created the asset). For intellectual property, creation means creation in circumstances such that the exploitation rights vest in the company.

VCM 13050, 13060

☐ *MEMO POINTS* 1. Where the share issue takes place **before the trade commences**, the company must be preparing to trade and intend to begin trading within 2 years of the date of issue. For this purpose, HMRC do not consider preliminary activities, such as raising capital or market research to establish whether a trade would be successful, to constitute preparing to trade.

2. **Research and development** qualifies whether it is carried out to benefit an existing trade or to develop a new one. However, preparing to carry out research and development will not qualify.

Groups

80190
s 181 ITA 2007

The EIS company may be a parent company of a trading group (and either trade itself or merely hold trading subsidiaries). For this purpose, the **activities** of the group are taken as a whole when deciding whether the trading criterion is met, and so the following are ignored:
– holding shares in a subsidiary, making loans to a subsidiary, and making loans to the parent company;
– holding and managing property used by any group company for the purpose of a trade or of research and development; and
– insignificant activities, where the particular company which carries them on exists for the purpose of carrying on a trade.

ss 183, 190
ITA 2007

Where the EIS company is a **holding company**, only a 90% subsidiary which fulfils the trading requirement can use the money raised by the EIS issue. For this purpose, the company carrying on the trade can also be a 100% subsidiary of a directly owned 90% subsidiary, or a 90% subsidiary of a directly owned 100% subsidiary. There is no requirement that the same company must carry on the trade throughout, so it is possible for a trade to move around a group.

Other subsidiaries must be 51% subsidiaries (¶65505), except for property managing subsidiaries (whose business consists wholly or mainly in the holding or managing of land or any property deriving its value from land) which must be 90% owned.

ss 187, 191
ITA 2007

Clearance

In order to provide comfort to potential investors, and therefore make the company more attractive, the company can seek **advance** clearance from HMRC that it is a qualifying company (by applying to the Small Company Enterprise Centre (¶95380).

80195
VCM 14030

Requests can be dealt with only if they come from a person authorised to represent the company, and not from a potential investor. It is not necessary for the request to identify the intending subscribers, and indeed the clearance will not apply to specific investors. Form EIS(AA) can be used to submit all the necessary information, but its use is not compulsory.

Sufficient **time** should be given to HMRC to consider the request before the company needs to issue the shares.

HMRC will be bound by any **assurance** given, provided the information supplied was correct and complete at the time it was given and has not been superseded by subsequent events. The assurance may be subject to caveats (for example, that the company's excluded activities do not become more pervasive).

VCM 14050

Where HMRC is **unable to give assurance**, a brief explanation of the reason will be given. In this case, the company should amend its plans if it still wants to attract EIS investors.

‎MEMO POINTS The following **information** must be submitted:
– a copy of the latest available accounts of the company, and of any subsidiary company;
– details of all trading or other activities to be carried on by the company and any subsidiary, and a note of which company or companies will use the money raised;
– the approximate sum that the company hopes to raise, and how it will be used;
– confirmation that the company expects to be able to complete the declaration on form EIS1 in due course;
– a copy of the latest draft of any prospectus or similar document to be issued to potential investors;
– an up to date copy of the Memorandum and Articles of Association of the company and of any subsidiary, and details of any changes to be made; and
– details of any subscription agreement or other side agreement to be entered into by the shareholders.

VCM 14040

D. Administration

When a company issues shares which qualify for EIS relief, there are certain statutory requirements which must be satisfied. Further, as investors may have obtained warranties etc from the company about its qualifying status, any instance where the company is at fault may require the payment of damages etc. In any event, the company may feel it has a duty not to jeopardise EIS relief for its investors.

80225

1. Initial requirements

The company must provide HMRC with sufficient **information** to establish that the qualifying conditions are satisfied, by completing form EIS 1 (available from HMRC's website) which requires details of:
– the capital structure of the company;
– the activities; and
– the subscribers.

80255
s 204 ITA 2007

The form must be **submitted**:
– no earlier than 4 months after the qualifying activity commences; and
– no later than 2 years from the end of the year of assessment in which the shares are issued (or, if later, 2 years and 4 months from the commencement of the qualifying activity).

After HMRC approval

80260

Where HMRC are satisfied that the conditions are met, **authority** will be given (via EIS 2) to the company to issue certificates of **eligibility** (EIS 3) to the investors.

Form EIS 3 can be issued to any eligible investor, regardless of whether relief is actually claimed.

HMRC will subsequently check the company's accounts etc to ensure that it continues to meet the requirements of the scheme.

Getting it wrong

80265
s 98 TMA 1970

If the company either:
– **fraudulently or negligently** completes form EIS 1, or issues form EIS 3; or
– issues form EIS 3 **without authority** from HMRC,
a penalty of up to £3,000 may be charged.

2. Ongoing requirements

80295
ss 240 - 244
ITA 2007

The company may feel it has a moral obligation not to do anything which would result in a withdrawal of EIS relief from investors. It is therefore important that the company continues to satisfy all the qualifying conditions and makes no returns of value.

However, the company must **notify** HMRC (¶80305) where it:
– becomes aware of any event resulting in a breach of the qualifying conditions; or
– makes a return of value, or issues replacement capital, which results in the withdrawal of relief.

Withdrawal of relief

80300
s 235 ITA 2007

Income tax relief for the investor may be withdrawn in certain circumstances as shown in the following table. For details of the income tax recovery mechanism, see *Tax Memo*.

Situation	Details	Reference
Breach of conditions by the investor, the company or the shares	Relief is withdrawn in full except for: – a takeover of the EIS company in a share-for-share exchange undertaken for bona fide commercial reasons, where the entire company is acquired for total share consideration (not involving any cash), and advance HMRC clearance is obtained (¶79365). This would often occur when a new holding company is inserted prior to the investors making an exit; or – a winding up, when company will not cease to be a qualifying company or 90% subsidiary company simply because the company, subsidiary or any other company is wound up, or is in receivership/administration, provided the winding up etc is for bona fide commercial reasons and does not form part of an arrangement to avoid a liability to tax	ss 177, s 247 ITA 2007

Situation	Details	Reference
A receipt of replacement capital	Relief will be withdrawn in full if, during Period A (¶80060), the EIS company (or one of its subsidiaries) either: **a.** acquires the entire issued share capital of another company, and the investor (or group of persons including the investor), at any time in the period, controlled the EIS company and the company whose shares were acquired; or **b.** acquires the trade, or most of the assets of a trade, and the investor (or a group of persons including the investor), at any time in the period, either: – owned more than a half share in that trade; or – controlled the EIS company and another company which carried on the trade	s 232 ITA 2007
Disposal of the shares	Relief will be withdrawn (the amount depending on the consideration received) if the investor disposes (or makes a deemed disposal[1]) of the shares during Period A (¶80060) The following are excluded from being a disposal: – a disposal on death; – transfers of shares between spouses - the receiving spouse stands in the shoes of the original investor; or – standard provisions in a company's Articles of Association requiring a shareholder to sell his shares if the majority of the shareholders accept an offer from a third party to purchase the company's entire issued share capital	ss 209, s 245 ITA 2007
Return of value	Relief will be withdrawn if the company, or a person connected with the company, makes a payment which is not insignificant (broadly, at least £1,000) to the investor, directly or indirectly, during Period C (¶80060), and which is not reimbursed by the investor (during that period) A return of value includes: – the repayment, redemption or repurchase of shares or securities; – payment for giving up rights to share capital or securities on its redemption; – repayment of a debt to the investor incurred before the subscription for EIS shares, if made in connection with any arrangement for their acquisition; – payment to investors for giving up rights to repayment of debt (except an ordinary trade debt); – company releases or waives any liability of the investor to the company; – company discharges the investor's liability to a third party; – company transfers an asset to the investor at less than market value; – company acquires an asset from the investor at more than market value; – company makes a loan to the investor which is not fully repaid before share issue; – company provides any benefit or facility to the investor; or – investor receives a payment/asset in the course of winding up the company The amount of relief withdrawn varies according to the circumstances.	ss 213 - 230 ITA 2007

Situation	Details	Reference
Payments to non-EIS investors	Relief is withdrawn from EIS investors where the company repays, redeems or repurchases any share capital belonging to non-EIS investors during Period C (¶80060), providing such a payment is not insignificant (broadly, at least £1,000) or the redemption within 12 months is to enable the company to comply with the Companies Acts provisions	ss 224 – 231 ITA 2007

Note:
1. For this purpose, a **deemed disposal** occurs on the grant of a:
– put option on the EIS shares, requiring the grantor of the option to purchase the EIS shares. (Any shares acquired by the investor after the granting of the put option are ignored and are not deemed to be disposed of); or
– call option on the EIS shares, requiring the investor to sell the shares.

Notification

80305
s 240 ITA 2007

Notification must be made in writing and, in all cases, the applicable **time limit** is 60 days from later of the date:
– of the event; and
– on which the company became aware of the relevant event.

s 98 TMA 1970

Where the company **fails** to notify HMRC, a penalty of up to £300 may be imposed, with a further penalty of up to £60 per day for continuing failure. If a company gives notice fraudulently or negligently, a penalty of up to £3,000 may be imposed.

SECTION 2

Venture capital trust scheme

80355

The Venture Capital Trust (VCT) scheme is designed to encourage individuals to invest indirectly in a range of small, higher risk, trading companies whose shares are unlisted. As a VCT will invest in a range of companies, the scheme allows investors to spread their risk.

VCT entity

80360

VCTs themselves are companies listed on an EU regulated market (such as the London Stock Exchange). They are approved by HMRC and run by fund managers. Investors can subscribe for, or buy, shares in a VCT, which uses the money to invest in a portfolio of trading companies. After a certain period of time, the VCT's investment is realised and the monies reinvested in another company.

A. Reliefs available to investors

80390
s 260 ITA 2007

The following tax reliefs are available to investors aged 18 or over, provided the shares in the VCT are acquired for bona fide commercial reasons and not as part of an arrangement to avoid tax. Fuller details can be found in *Tax Memo*.

Comment   Unlike EIS relief, the VCT scheme has no mechanism for setting off capital losses against income.

Tax relief	Requirements as to shares in VCT itself
Exemption from income tax on dividends from ordinary shares in VCTs	Must be ordinary shares Not limited to subscribed shares: purchased shares also qualify
Income tax relief at the rate of 30% of the amount subscribed for shares issued in the tax year	Must be newly subscribed ordinary shares which do not carry any preferential rights (to dividends or on a winding up), or rights of redemption at any time in the period of 5 years beginning with their date of issue Shares must be owned for at least 5 years No loan-linked investments within 2 years before the share issue or 5 years afterwards (meaning that the individual or his associate receives a loan which would not have been made but for the share subscription)
No chargeable gain arises on a disposal of the shares (known as disposal relief)	Must be ordinary shares Not limited to subscribed shares: purchased shares bought also qualify

Amounts on which relief is due

Where more than **£200,000 of VCT shares** are acquired in the same tax year, the following rules apply in order to identify which shares qualify for a particular relief: **80395**

Relief	Amount attracting relief
Dividend relief	Shares up to the permitted maximum of £200,000 in any tax year
Disposal relief	Shares acquired earlier in the tax year count first Ordinary shares of different classes or in different VCTs acquired on the same day are identified on a proportionate basis Irrelevant whether shares subscribed for or acquired - all treated the same
Income tax relief	First £200,000 worth of eligible shares which are issued in tax year

EXAMPLE On 1 May 2013, Mr A subscribed for (and was issued with) £80,000 of eligible shares in a VCT. On 1 June 2013, Mr A bought £100,000 of second-hand ordinary shares in a VCT. On the same date, he also subscribed for £140,000 of eligible shares in a VCT. So on 1 June, he received a total value of £240,000.

The shares on which the various tax reliefs are available are as follows.

Tax relief	1 May £	1 June bought £	1 June subscribed £	Total £
Dividend and disposal	80,000	$\frac{100,000}{240,000} \times 120,000 =$ 50,000	$\frac{140,000}{240,000} \times 120,000 =$ 70,000	200,000
Income tax relief	80,000		120,000	200,000

B. The VCT company

In order for its investors to be eligible for the reliefs, the VCT must be a quoted, non-close company, **approved by HMRC** as a VCT. **80425**

Conditions for approval fall into two classes:
– conditions which must be satisfied by the VCT itself; and
– conditions which must be satisfied by companies in which the VCT invests ("qualifying holdings").

80430
s 274 ITA 2007

Conditions upon the VCT HMRC will only grant approval if the VCT company meets **all** of the following conditions:
a. each class of the VCT's ordinary share capital is quoted on the official list of any EEA stock market;
b. its income derives wholly or mainly from shares or securities;
c. at least 85% of its income from shares and securities is distributed;
d. no more than 15% of its investments are in one single company (other than another VCT);
e. at least 70% of its investments are in the form of shares or securities which are qualifying holdings (¶80435);
f. at least 70% of the value of qualifying holdings is in the form of eligible shares; and
g. it has not made any investment which exceeds the permitted limits (¶80435).

Eligible shares are ordinary shares which throughout the five years following the date of issue carry none of the following present or future rights:
− preferential rights to dividends;
− preferential rights to assets on a winding up; or
− to redemption.

> ⌐MEMO POINTS⌐   1. In accounting periods ending before 6 April 2011, VCTs were required to be **quoted** on the UK Stock Exchange.
> 2. When determining the VCT's **income** (conditions **b** and **c**), the sums to be included in respect of loan relationships (¶16050+) are exclusive of interest and other amounts in respect of money borrowed by the VCT.
> 3. For the purposes of conditions **e.** and **f.**, **investments** include all money held by a company (or owed to it, where the company has account-holder's rights). A period of 6 months is however allowed for the reinvestment or distribution of monetary or non-monetary proceeds of investment disposals.
> 4. In accounting periods ending before 6 April 2011, the **minimum holding** of eligible shares was 30%. HMRC have indicated that the definition may be amended to include shares that may carry certain preferential rights to dividends, but no date has been set for this change.

80435
s 299A ITA 2007

Qualifying holdings For an investment by a VCT to be a qualifying holding:
− the disqualifying arrangements test (¶80055) must be satisfied in relation to shares issued on or after 6 April 2012; and
− the target company must meet all the same qualifying conditions as those for an **EIS company**: see ¶80170+.

The following **additional conditions** must also be satisfied:
a. At least 10% of the target company's shares are eligible shares (¶80430).
b. The securities held by the VCT are not related to a guaranteed loan.
c. For shares issued on or after 6 April 2012, if the target company carries on its qualifying trade in **partnership or a joint venture** with at least one other company, the maximum investment in the target company by the VCT is limited. The limit is £1 million, divided by the number of companies (including the target company) in the partnership or joint venture, and it applies for the period ending with the issue of the shares and beginning on the earlier of:
− 6 months before the issue of the shares; or
− the start of the tax year in which the shares were issued.

> ⌐MEMO POINTS⌐   1. Securities are related to a **guaranteed loan** if there are arrangements for the VCT to receive anything from a third party in the event of the failure by any person to comply with the terms of a loan to which the security relates, or the terms of the security itself.
> s 287 ITA 2007   2. If the shares were issued before 6 April 2012 the £1 million limit applied irrespective of the existence of a partnership or joint venture, but was available in full.

Unquoted company

80440
s 295 ITA 2007

Only an unquoted company (including one listed on AIM, PLUS Quoted and PLUS Traded Markets) can be a VCT investment, as determined at the time of the share issue (and there must be no arrangements in place for that unquoted status to change).

However, a subsequent listing of the shares on a recognised stock exchange (¶95320) will not affect the VCT relief already given, and such companies will be treated as qualifying VCT investments for the next 5 years.

Use of funds

All of the money raised by the issue of shares must be used for the **purposes of** a qualifying trade (not necessarily located in the UK), or research and development (¶80185).

80445
s 293 ITA 2007

The funds must be expended within 2 years from the later of:
- the date of the share issue; and
- the commencement of the trade.

> ⌐ *MEMO POINTS* ¬ 1. A **qualifying trade** is defined at ¶80185, along with the excluded activities which deny a company qualifying status where these constitute more than 20% of the company's trade.
> 2. Where **only some of the money** is expended (and this is more than insignificant) for the trading purpose, the VCT's holding in the company is divided into two: a qualifying holding and a non-qualifying holding, and the division is made in a just and reasonable way so as to maximise the qualifying holding.

ss 291, 300, 303 ITA 2007

s 293 ITA 2007; VCM 55150

Groups

The target company may be the parent company of a trading group (and either trade itself or merely hold trading subsidiaries).

80450
s 332 ITA 2007

For this purpose, the **activities** of the group are taken as a whole when deciding whether the trading criterion is met, and so the following are ignored:
- holding shares in a subsidiary, making loans to a subsidiary, and making loans to the parent company;
- holding and managing property used by any group company for the purpose of a trade or of research and development; and
- insignificant activities, where the particular company which carries them on exists for the purpose of carrying on a trade.

s 290 ITA 2007

Where the company is a **holding company**, only a 90% subsidiary which fulfils the trading requirement can use the money raised by the VCT issue. For this purpose, the company carrying on the trade can also be a 100% subsidiary of a directly owned 90% subsidiary, or a 90% subsidiary of a directly owned 100% subsidiary. There is no requirement that the same company must carry on the trade throughout, so it is possible for a trade to move around a group.

s 301 ITA 2007

Other subsidiaries must be 51% subsidiaries (¶65505), except for property managing subsidiaries (whose business consists wholly or mainly in the holding or managing of land or any property deriving its value from land) which must be 90% owned.

ss 298, 299, 302 ITA 2007

C. Administration

Clearance for the VCT

In order to provide comfort to a potential VCT, and therefore make it more attractive to investors, the company can seek advance **clearance** from HMRC that it will qualify, as a VCT by applying to the Small Company Enterprise Centre (¶95380).

80480
VCM 54250

It is also possible to seek provisional clearance before the VCT has been fully established (for example, before it has obtained a listing on an EEA stock market).

Assurance for the target company

A company which has been or hopes to be offered funding by a VCT may seek assurance from HMRC that:

80485
VCM 55360

- all or some of the shares to be issued will be eligible shares; and/or
- the shares it issues to the VCT will be regarded as a qualifying holding (¶80435).

Requests can be dealt with only if they come from a person authorised to represent the company, such as the company secretary or directors.

Sufficient **time** should be given to HMRC to consider the request before the company needs to issue the shares.

HMRC will be bound by any **assurance** given, provided the information supplied was correct and complete at the time it was given and has not been superseded by subsequent events. The assurance may be subject to caveats (for example, that the company's excluded activities do not become more substantial).

Where HMRC is **unable to give assurance**, a brief explanation of the reason will be given. In this case, the company will need to amend its plans if it still wants to attract VCT investors.

VCM 55370

[MEMO POINTS] The following **information** must be submitted:
- a copy of the latest available accounts of the company, and of any subsidiary company;
- details of all trading or other activities to be carried on by the company and any subsidiary, and a note of which company or companies will use the money raised;
- the approximate sum that the company hopes to raise, and how it will be used;
- an up to date copy of the Memorandum and Articles of Association of the company and of any subsidiary, and details of any changes to be made; and
- (where an investment by a particular VCT is in prospect) details of any subscription agreement or other side agreement to be entered into by the company and the VCT.

Withdrawal of relief

80490 VCT income tax relief may be withdrawn in the following circumstances:
- a breach of conditions; or
- the disposal of some or all of the shares by the investor.

Breach of conditions

80495 Relief will be withdrawn in full where:
- the VCT company or investor breaches the conditions; or
- the investor disposes of the shares within the period of 5 years from the date of acquisition.
The **amount of relief withdrawn** is calculated in the same way as for EIS shares (¶80300).

HMRC have the power not to withdraw approval from a VCT which breaches its approval conditions as a result of events outside its control.

ss 314, 321
ITA 2007

[MEMO POINTS] VCTs can retain approval:
- when they merge, provided the merger is for bona fide commercial reasons; and
- whilst being wound up, provided the winding up is for bona fide commercial reasons.

SECTION 3

Corporate venturing scheme

80545 The Corporate Venturing Scheme (CVS) was aimed at companies considering owning a minority shareholding in small independent trading companies (or groups). It is **no longer available** for **shares issued** on or after 1 April 2010.

Comment   As the CVS is still pertinent to those companies making delayed claims, and also where CVS shares are still held, full information about the scheme is given in this section.

For shares issued before 1 April 2010, the CVS gave the following tax reliefs to the investing company.

Tax relief	Brief detail	¶¶
Investment relief	Deduction against corporation tax liability based on 20% of the amount of the investment	¶80720
Deferral relief	Defers gains on CVS shares by rolling over into other CVS share acquisitions	¶80840
Loss relief	Can set losses against income rather than just capital gains	¶80845

A. Investing company

An investing company must satisfy a series of conditions throughout the 3 year **qualification period** commencing with the issue of the shares (or the start of the issuing company's trade, if later).

80575
Sch 15 para 3
FA 2000

Comment The latest possible end date for a qualification period is 31 March 2013, except for companies which started trading after the issue of the shares (¶80580), for which it is 31 March 2015.

The conditions are summarised in the following table

Condition	Detail	Reference
Must not own a material interest (including the interests of connected companies (¶31375) and associates (¶75390))	A material interest defined as owning, or being entitled to acquire, more than 30% of the ordinary share capital or voting rights in the issuing company (or a 51% subsidiary of the issuing company). Ordinary share capital means all shares issued by the company and any loan capital which carries the right of conversion into, or to acquisition of, shares, but excludes relevant preference shares[1]	Sch 15 paras 5, 7, 9 FA 2000
Must not control the issuing company (again the interests of connected companies (¶31375) and associates (¶75390) must be taken into account, along with those of directors[2])	A company has control of the issuing company where it exercises, is able to exercise, or is entitled to acquire, direct or indirect control over the affairs of the company For this purpose, control includes the possession of, or right to acquire, more than 50% of the issuing company's: – share capital (¶65095); – voting power; – distributable profits (¶65145); or – net assets on a winding up (¶65210) However, the following are excluded when determining control: – any rights as a loan creditor; and – any relevant preference shares[1]	Sch 15 paras 8,9 FA 2000, ss 450, 451 CTA 2010
Must be a trading company, or a member of a trading group, not involved in financial trades	See ¶80580	Sch 15 paras 10 -12 FA 2000
Must hold the shares in the issuing company as capital assets (and not as trading stock)	It is irrelevant whether shares qualify for the substantial shareholdings exemption i.e. it does not matter whether the shares are chargeable to corporation tax	Sch 15 para 13 FA 2000

Note:
1. **Relevant preference shares** are defined as shares which:
– are issued for wholly new consideration;
– do not carry voting rights;
– have no right of conversion into, or to the acquisition of, other shares; and
– are only entitled to preference dividends (i.e. dividends which are not dependent on the results of the company or the value of its assets, and which represent no more than a reasonable commercial return, including any redemption premium).
2. Any rights or powers held by any of its **directors** (or by any spouse, civil partner, parent or child of such a director), or by any director (or spouse, civil partner etc) of any company connected with it.

Non-financial trade

A qualifying investing company or group must, throughout the qualification period (¶80575), carry on a non-financial trade. If it was not trading when the shares were issued, a qualifying trade must commence within 2 years of that date.

80580
Sch 15 paras 10, 23
FA 2000

Sch 15 para 11
FA 2000
A non-financial trade is one carried out on a commercial basis with the view to the realisation of profits, and which does not consist wholly, or substantially, of carrying on financial activities.

VCM 91170
HMRC interpret substantially as generally meaning more than 20% of the trade (for example, in terms of turnover or capital employed), but a strict percentage is not applied.

For this purpose, **financial activities** include:
− banking or money-lending;
− debt factoring;
− finance leasing;
− hire purchase financing;
− insurance;
− dealing in shares, securities, currency, debts or other financial assets; and
− dealing in commodities, financial futures or options.

In determining whether a **stand-alone company** exists wholly for the purpose of carrying on a non-financial trade, the following are to be disregarded:
− purposes which have no significant effect on the extent of the company's activities, except in relation to incidental matters;
− the holding and managing of property used by the company for a non-financial trade; and
− the holding of any shares to which investment relief is attributable, unless the holding of such shares forms a substantial part of the company's business.

Groups

80585
Sch 15 para 12
FA 2000
Where the investing company is the **parent** of a group, that group must be a non-financial trading group. For this purpose, the following types of activity are ignored:
− the holding of shares in a subsidiary, and the making of loans to other group companies,
− the holding and managing of property used by any group company for the purposes of a non-financial trade,
− the holding by a group company of any shares to which investment relief is attributable, except where the holding of such shares amounts to a substantial part of the business of that company.

If the investing company is a **group member**, without being the parent, both the group and the company must exist wholly for the purpose of carrying on a non-financial trade. So in addition to the list above, incidental matters which have no significant effect on the company's activities are ignored.

B. Qualifying shares

80615
The shares must be newly issued ordinary shares **acquired by** subscription before 1 April 2010 and fully paid up in cash (unless bonus shares).

Throughout the qualification period (¶80575), the shares must not carry the following present or future **rights**:
− preferential rights to dividends;
− preferential rights to assets on a winding up; or
− rights to redemption.

The **purpose** of the share issue must be to raise money for a qualifying business activity.

Sch 15 paras 14,
37, 38 FA 2000
There are also general requirements that:
− shares must be subscribed for and issued for genuine commercial purposes, and not as part of a tax avoidance scheme; and
− there are no pre-arranged **exit arrangements** including arrangements for the sale of shares, discontinuance of the trade, the sale of the assets, or where the investor has insurance, indemnities or guarantees against the risk of making the investment.

Sch 15 para 6
FA 2000
Further, the investment cannot be made as part of a **reciprocal arrangement** (one in which a company subscribes for shares in an unconnected company on condition that another company invests in the issuing company).

Use of funds

All of the money raised by the issue of shares must be used for the **purposes of** a qualifying trade, or research and development from which it is intended that a trade, carried on or to be carried on within the same group, will benefit or will be derived.

80620
Sch 15 para 36
FA 2000

There is a specific **time limit** which applies, so that monies must be expended within 2 years from the later of:
- the date of the share issue; and
- the commencement of the trade.

C. Issuing company

Only unquoted companies (including those listed on AIM, PLUS Quoted and PLUS Traded Markets) can be CVS issuing companies, as determined at the time of the share issue (and there must be no arrangements in place for that unquoted status to change).

80650
Sch 15 para 16
FA 2000

However, a subsequent listing of the shares on a recognised stock exchange (¶95320) will not affect the CVS relief.

Criteria

In addition, the company must satisfy the following conditions **during** the 3 year **period** from the share issue (or date of commencement of trade, if later), although the employee numbers test only applies at the time of the share issue:

80655

Condition	Detail	Reference
It is independent, meaning that: – it is not a 51% subsidiary of another company (¶65505); – it is not controlled by another company; and – at least 20% of the ordinary shares are held by independent individuals Further there can be no arrangements where the company's independence could be compromised, and the qualifying trade cannot be carried on through a non-qualifying partnership or joint venture	Control is defined at ¶80095 For this purpose an independent individual excludes: – a director or employee of the investing company or of any company connected with it; and – a relative of such an individual (i.e. a spouse, civil partner, lineal ancestor or lineal descendant) A non-qualifying partnership or joint venture is one that carries on the qualifying trade where: – another member of the partnership or joint venture is a company; and – another person(s) owns more than 75% of the issued share capital of both the issuing company and at least one other party to the partnership/joint venture	Sch 15 paras 17 - 19 FA 2000
All subsidiaries are qualifying subsidiaries	Either 51% subsidiaries if trading, or 90% owned if activity relates to land or where CVS money used by subsidiary Control is defined at ¶75310 Subsidiaries affected by any of the following situations will still be controlled for this purpose, so long as the situation is brought about for genuinely commercial reasons: – a winding up or dissolution of the subsidiary or any other company; – the disposal of the shares in the subsidiary; or – anything done in consequence of the company, or any other company, being in administration or receivership	Sch 15 paras 20 - 21A FA 2000

Condition	Detail	Reference
Total number of full time employees (working at least 35 hours per week excluding lunch breaks and overtime), or their equivalent, is less than 50 at the time that the shares are issued	As measured in the company itself and any qualifying subsidiaries (the total for the entire group) must be less than 50 Employee includes a director, but excludes: – an employee on maternity or paternity leave; or – a student on vocational training Part-time employees are treated as an appropriate fraction of a full-time employee	Sch 15 para 22A FA 2000
Exists wholly for the purposes of carrying on one or more qualifying trades, or it is the parent company of a trading group	Throughout the qualification period (¶80575), a qualifying trade must be carried on This consists of any trade that is carried out: – wholly or mainly in the UK; and – on a commercial basis with a view to the realisation of profits. For further details, see ¶80185	Sch 15 paras 23 - 33 FA 2000
Must be a small company based on amount of relevant assets	Both of the following tests apply, so that immediately: – before the share issue, its relevant assets do not exceed £7 million; and – after the issue they do not exceed £8 million Relevant assets are the assets of the company (or group, where appropriate, ignoring intra-group holdings and obligations) calculated as the aggregate of the assets which would be shown on a balance sheet prepared to that date, without any deduction for liabilities	Sch 15 para 22 FA 2000, SP 2/06

Clearance

80660
Sch 15 para 89
FA 2000;

In order to provide comfort to potential investors, and therefore make the company more attractive, there was a procedure enabling the issuing company to seek **advance** clearance from HMRC that it was a qualifying company (by applying to the Small Company Enterprise Centre (¶95380).

D. Tax reliefs

80690   The CVS gives three possible tax reliefs to investing companies:
– investment relief (¶80720);
– deferral relief (¶80840); and
– loss relief (¶80845).

1. Investment relief

80720   An investing company is only eligible to claim relief where:
– it has received a compliance certificate (¶80910) from the issuing company; and
– the qualifying trade has been carried on for a minimum of 4 months by the issuing company or its qualifying 90% subsidiary.

VCM 91210

> *MEMO POINTS*   1. Investment relief is **claimed** on the CTSA tax return for the appropriate accounting period, on page CT600G.
> 2. The **time limit** is 6 years from the end of the accounting period in which the shares were issued.
> 3. The minimum trading period is waived if the company is **wound up, dissolved or put into administration** or receivership during the first 4 months, and the action is taken for commercial reasons and does not form part of an arrangement for the avoidance of tax.

a. Computation

The investing company is entitled to claim a corporation tax **deduction** of the lower of:
- tax at 20% on the amount invested; and
- the corporation tax payable for the accounting period in which the shares are issued.

The relief is given after any marginal relief but before any reduction in respect of community investment tax relief (¶41350) or double tax relief (¶90480).

80740
Sch 15 paras 39, 40
FA 2000

EXAMPLE A Ltd subscribed for 20,000 shares in B Ltd at a cost of £200,000. The shares were issued on 1 March 2010. A Ltd's corporation tax liability for the accounting period ended 30 September 2010 is £56,000.
CVS investment relief would be given as follows:

	£	£
Corporation tax due		56,000
Less: Lower of:		
Amount invested i.e. 200,000 x 20%; and	40,000	
Corporation tax liability for the period	56,000	
		(40,000)
Corporation tax payable		16,000

Attribution to shares

The reduction in the corporation tax liability is associated with the CVS shares issued in that period, so that a proportion of the investment relief is attributed to each underlying share.

Where more than one issue of shares qualifies for relief in a year, the relief is apportioned equally between each issue based on the cost incurred. This is of importance only where the subscriptions in an accounting period exceed the maximum for which relief is available.

If **bonus shares** (which are of the same class and have the same rights) are issued in respect of original CVS shares which are still held at the bonus issue date, the relief must be apportioned between the original shares and the bonus shares. For this purpose, the bonus shares are deemed to have the same issue date and ownership period as the original shares.

Shares resulting from a **rights issue** are treated as a separate holding, so they do not qualify for investment relief simply because the original holding so qualified.

An exchange of shares for **qualifying corporate bonds** is a disposal (¶80770) and will give rise to a chargeable gain or allowable loss.

80745
Sch 15 para 45
FA 2000

Sch 15 para 81
FA 2000

EXAMPLE
1. If A Ltd in ¶80740 only claims investment relief in respect of the B Ltd investment in the accounting period ended 30 September 2010, the corporation tax reduction of £40,000 is allocated to each share comprised in the issue.

The relief per share is therefore £2. ($\frac{40,000}{20,000}$)

2. However, if A Ltd made another CVS investment in C Ltd in the same accounting period, subscribing for 5,000 shares at a value of £100,000, the total investment relief due for the accounting period would be:

	£	£
Corporation tax due		56,000
Less: Lower of:		
Amount invested i.e. 300,000 @ 20%; and	60,000	
Corporation tax liability for the period	56,000	
		(56,000)
Corporation tax payable		Nil

The corporation tax relief is attributed proportionately to each issue:

		£
B Ltd	$\frac{200,000}{300,000} \times 56,000$	37,333

C Ltd $\dfrac{100,000}{300,000} \times 56,000$ 18,667

The relief is then attributed to the underlying shares as follows:

- B Ltd, £1.86665 per share; $(\dfrac{37,333}{20,000})$

- C Ltd, £3.7334 per shares. $(\dfrac{18,667}{5,000})$

3. If C Ltd made a bonus issue of one new share for every five original shares, A Ltd would acquire a further 1,000 shares. The relief attributable to the original shares of £18,667 is now allocated to the total shareholding of 6,000 shares, giving a relief per share of £3.1112. $(\dfrac{18,667}{6,000})$

---

b. Withdrawal of relief

80765
Sch 15 para 60
FA 2000

Investment relief for the investor may be withdrawn in the certain circumstances as shown in the following table. The withdrawal of the relief results in an amount becoming taxable as miscellaneous income (¶21050).

> MEMO POINTS   1. In general where relief is withdrawn, an **assessment** will be issued for the accounting period in which relief was obtained.

Sch 15 para 62
FA 2000

2. The **time limit** for such an assessment is 6 years after the end of the relevant accounting period i.e. the latest accounting period in which:
- the latest date for employing the funds raised by the issue falls (¶80620); or
- the event triggering the withdrawal of relief falls.

3. Any amounts assessed carry **interest** from the date of the event triggering the withdrawal.

Situation	Details	Reference
Breach of conditions by the investor, the company or the shares	Relief is withdrawn in full except for: – a takeover of the issuing company in a share-for-share exchange undertaken for bona fide commercial reasons, where the entire company is acquired for consideration wholly in shares (no cash is involved), and advance HMRC clearance is obtained (¶79365). This would often occur when a new holding company is inserted prior to the investors making an exit; or – a winding up, when company will not cease to be a qualifying company or 90% subsidiary company simply because the company, subsidiary or any other company is wound up, or is in receivership/administration, provided the winding up etc is for bona fide commercial reasons and does not form part of an arrangement to avoid a liability to tax	Sch 15 paras 60, 83 - 85 FA 2000
Disposal of the shares	Relief will be withdrawn (the amount depending on the consideration received (¶80770)) if the investor disposes of the shares in the qualification period (¶80575)	Sch 15 para 46 FA 2000
Return of value	Relief will be withdrawn (¶80775) if the issuing company, or a person connected with that company, makes a payment (which is not insignificant, meaning broadly at least £1,000) to the investor, directly or indirectly, in the period commencing 1 year before the issue of the shares and ending at the end of the qualification period (¶80575), which is not reimbursed by the investor (also during this period)	Sch 15 paras 47 - 55 FA 2000

Situation	Details	Reference
Payments to non-CVS investors	Relief is withdrawn (¶80790) from CVS investors where the issuing company either: – repays, redeems or repurchases any share capital belonging to non-CVS investors: or – makes a payment to any member in return for the cancellation or extinguishment of his interest in the share capital of the company or a subsidiary, during the period commencing 1 year before the issue of shares and ending at the end of the qualification period (¶80575), providing such a payment is not insignificant (it is at least £1,000) or the redemption within 12 months is to enable the company to comply with Companies Acts provisions	Sch 15 para 56 FA 2000
Options	Where an option (either put or call) is granted during the qualification period (¶80575) in respect of shares on which investment relief has been given, any relief attributable to those shares will be withdrawn The withdrawal of relief occurs when the option is granted It is irrelevant whether the option is exercised.	Sch 15 para 59 FA 2000

Share disposal

Relief will only be withdrawn if the investing company disposes of the shares within the qualification period (¶80575). Note that deferral relief and loss relief may be in point (¶80840+).

80770
Sch 15 para 46
FA 2000

Where investment **relief was not restricted** by the corporation tax liability, the amount of relief withdrawn is the lower of
– 20% of the disposal proceeds; and
– the relief originally given.

However, where the **corporation tax liability could not absorb the available relief**, the withdrawal is apportioned using the formula:

$$\frac{\text{CVS relief originally given}}{20\% \text{ of the amount subscribed for the shares}}$$

> EXAMPLE
>
> 1. D Ltd subscribed for 20,000 shares in E Ltd under the CVS scheme in Year 1 at a cost of £200,000. Investment relief of £40,000 was claimed. (200,000 × 20%)
> In Year 2, the shares were disposed to a third party for £210,000.
> The amount of investment relief withdrawn is £40,000, being the lower of:
> – the relief originally given of £40,000; and
> – 20% of the proceeds, meaning £42,000. (210,000 × 20%)
>
> 2. If D Ltd's relief in respect of the E Ltd shares had been restricted because the corporation tax liability for the accounting period was only £25,000, the relief withdrawn on the disposal of E Ltd shares would be £25,000, being the lower of:
> – the relief originally given of £25,000; and
> – the appropriate fraction of 20% of the proceeds, meaning £26,250. $(210,000 \times 20\% \times \frac{25,000}{40,000})$

Return of value

A return of value, broadly a payment made by the issuing company to the investing company (either directly, or involving connected persons (¶31375)) within the **restriction period** (beginning 1 year before the issue of the shares and ending at the end of the qualification period (¶80575)), will lead to a withdrawal of investment relief, **unless**:
a. it is **insignificant**, meaning a payment not exceeding £1,000, or a payment which is considered insignificant in relation to the amount subscribed for the shares (although all payments

80775
Sch 15 para 47
FA 2000

VCM 91330

will be treated as significant where there were arrangements in force, during the year prior to the share issue, for the investing company to receive any value from the issuing company before the end of the qualification period (¶80575)); or

Sch 15 para 54
FA 2000

b. the investing company wholly **restores the value** to the issuing company (either before or after the return of value itself, and via the same route) within a certain time by any of the following means:

– a cash payment, other than a qualifying payment ((¶80780) or a payment for shares or securities of the company (unless the receipt of value in question arose from the receipt of those shares or securities);

– a payment intended to reverse the release or waiver of a liability of the investing company or the discharge of the investing company's liability to a third party;

– a transfer of an asset at an overvalue to reverse the transfer of an asset to the investing company at less than market value; or

– a transfer of an asset at an undervalue to reverse the transfer of an asset at more than market value to the issuing company.

> MEMO POINTS   1. The restrictions on the **time** period within which the **restoration of value** must occur is:
> – not before the 12 months predating the share issue;
> – not after a period of unreasonable delay; or
> – not more than 60 days after the amount of relief to be withdrawn is determined, following the issue of an appeal against an assessment to withdraw relief.

VCM 91340

> 2. The **same route** means:
> – where the value comes from a person connected with the issuing company, it should be returned to that person; and
> – where it is received by a person connected with the investing company, it should be returned by that person.

> EXAMPLE   F Ltd made a qualifying CVS investment in G Ltd, and received a sum of £600 every 3 months, starting on 1 January 2010.
> Assuming £1,200 was not regarded as insignificant, F Ltd would be regarded as receiving value of £1,200 on 1 April 2010, a further £1,200 on 1 October 2010 etc.

80780

Sch 15 paras 49, 50
FA 2000;
VCM 91310, 91320

A return of value is **quantified** as follows:

Event	Value returned
Repayment, redemption or repurchase of shares or securities	Greater of amount received or market value of shares or securities
Payment for giving up rights to share capital or securities on its redemption	
Repayment of a debt to the investing company incurred before the subscription for CVS shares	Greater of amount of loan repaid or market value of debt
Payment to the investing company for giving up rights to repayment of any debt (except an ordinary trade debt)	Greater of amount received or market value of debt
Issuing company waives or releases any liability of the investing company to the company (meaning that a liability is not discharged within 12 months of the date on which it ought to have been discharged)	Amount of liability
Issuing company discharges the investing company's liability to a third party	
Issuing company makes a loan to the investing company which is not fully repaid before the share issue	Amount of loan outstanding, less any repayment made before issue of shares
Issuing company provides any benefit or facility to a director or employee (or their associates (¶75390)) of the investing company	Cost of providing benefit, reduced by any contribution from recipient (or his associate)
Issuing company transfers an asset to the investing company at less than market value	Excess of market value over consideration given
Issuing company acquires an asset from the investing company at more than market value	Excess of consideration given over market value

Event	Value returned
Issuing company makes any payment, **other than** any of the following qualifying payments, to the investing company: – payments for goods, services or facilities supplied by the investing company which are reasonable in relation to the market value of the supply; – interest payments which represent no more than a reasonable commercial return; – dividends or distributions which are no more than a normal return on investments in that company; – payments to acquire assets which do not exceed the market value of the assets; – payments of rent at commercial rates for the use of property; and – payments to discharge ordinary trade debts	Amount of the payment

The rules for withdrawing relief mirror those for a share disposal (¶80770).

80785
Sch 15 paras 47, 51, 52 FA 2000

Where the investing company has made **more than one subscription** for shares qualifying for investment relief, and they fall within the restriction period (¶80775), the value must be apportioned using the following formula:

$$\frac{\text{Amount subscribed for the particular issue}}{\text{Aggregate amount subscribed for the relevant issues}}$$

EXAMPLE

1. A Ltd subscribed for shares in B Ltd at a cost of £300,000 and obtained investment relief of £60,000 which was fully absorbed by the corporation tax liability. (300,000 × 20%)
A couple of years after the subscription, B Ltd purchased plant from A Ltd for £300,000 at a time when its market value was £200,000.
A Ltd has received a return of value of £100,000. (300,000 - 200,000)
The amount of investment relief withdrawn is therefore £20,000. (100,000 × 20%)

2. If A Ltd's investment relief had been restricted by a lower corporation tax liability to £45,000, the return of value on the disposal of B Ltd shares would be restricted to £75,000. (100,000 × $\frac{45,000}{60,000}$)

The amount of investment relief withdrawn is therefore £15,000. (75,000 × 20%)

3. C Ltd, which has a calendar year accounting period, subscribed for shares in D Ltd, a company which commenced trading on 1 July 2006. CVS investment relief was received as follows:

Issue	Date of issue	Number of shares	Cost	Relief	Comment
			£	£	
1	1 June 2007	50,000	50,000	9,000	Restricted by CT liability
2	1 December 2007	25,000	30,000	6,000	
3	1 June 2008	30,000	20,000	3,000	Restricted by CT liability

On 25 July 2010, C Ltd receives a return of value and the value returned is calculated at £6,000. Issue 1 is not a relevant issue in respect of this payment as the restriction period (¶80775) has ended.
Ignoring Issue 1, the subscription value (i.e. cost) for the CVS shares is £50,000.
The return of value is therefore attributed to Issues 2 and 3 as follows:

		£
Issue 2	$\frac{30,000}{50,000} \times 6,000$	3,600
Issue 3	$\frac{20,000}{50,000} \times 6,000$	2,400
		6,000

The amount of relief withdrawn is calculated as follows:
– Issue 2, £720; (3,600 @ 20%) and

– Issue 3, £360, as the relief was restricted by the original CT liability. (2,400 × $\frac{3,000}{4,000}$ × 20%)

Payments to other investors

80790
Sch 15 paras 56-
58 FA 2000

Where the issuing company (or its 51% subsidiary) makes a payment (¶80765) to any member during the restriction period (¶80775), and that member does not suffer a reduction of either investment relief or relief under the EIS as a result (including the crystallisation of a deferred gain), the CVS relief for the investing company will be reduced or withdrawn altogether **unless**:
– the payment itself, or the market value of the shares (before the payment), is insignificant (¶80775) compared to the market value of the remaining issued share capital after it is made; or
– the company is redeeming shares within 12 months of their issue, and these shares were issued in order to comply with the minimum share capital requirements of the Companies Acts.

80795

The rules for withdrawing relief mirror those for a share disposal (¶80770), except that:
– **if more than one company received CVS relief**, the relief withdrawn is apportioned between them in proportion to their shareholdings; and
– where the investing company made **more than one subscription** for shares in the issuing company and the payment to the member falls within the restriction period (¶80775), see ¶80785.

> [EXAMPLE]
> 1. E Ltd subscribed for shares in F Ltd at a cost of £150,000 and obtained investment relief of £30,000. (150,000 × 20%)
> A couple of years after the subscription, F Ltd redeemed shares for £80,000.
> If E Ltd was the only CVS investor, the relief withdrawn is £16,000, being the lower of:
> – the relief initially given of £30,000; and
> – 20% of the redemption value, being £16,000. (80,000 × 20%)
>
> 2. If there were other CVS investors in addition to E Ltd, the withdrawal would be apportioned based on the total CVS subscription value of, say, £1 million.
> So the redemption value applicable to E Ltd's shares is £12,000. $(80,000 \times \frac{150,000}{1,000,000})$
>
> This means that the relief withdrawn from E Ltd is £2,400, being the lower of:
> – the relief initially given of £30,000; and
> – 20% of the redemption value, being £2,400. (12,000 × 20%)
>
> 3. If E Ltd's relief had originally been restricted to £20,000, and the total CVS subscription was £1 million (including other CVS investing companies), the redemption value applicable to E Ltd's shares would be £8,000. $(12,000 \times \frac{20,000}{30,000})$
>
> This means that the relief withdrawn from E Ltd is £1,600, being the lower of:
> – the relief initially given of £20,000; and
> – 20% of the revised redemption value, being £1,600. (8,000 × 20%)

---

2. Disposals and chargeable gains

80825

Shares on which investment relief has been claimed are subject to the usual chargeable gains regime (¶32020), with minor modifications to the provisions relating to share identification and share reorganisations.

There are two types of reliefs available; deferral relief and loss relief.

Share identification

80830
Sch 15 para 93
FA 2000

The usual **pooling rules** do not apply to CVS shares, as the shares are deemed to be disposed of on a first in first out basis.

Where more than one batch of shares is **purchased on the same day**, shares to which no investment relief is attributable are deemed to be sold in priority to those with investment relief.

Reorganisations

A **rights issue** is treated as a separate acquisition: that is, the share reorganisation rules (¶32250) are disapplied where investment relief is attributable to the original holding or the new shares.

Where there is a **bonus issue** of shares (¶32240), any CVS relief attributable to the original holdings is also attributable to the bonus shares (the share reorganisation rules are not disapplied).

When shares are exchanged for **qualifying corporate bonds** (¶32055) on a company reorganisation, they are treated as disposing of the original shares, giving rise to a chargeable gain or allowable loss.

80835
Sch 15 paras 80 -
88 FA 2000

Deferral relief

It was possible to defer a gain on the disposal of CVS shares if:
– the shares qualified for investment relief;
– the shares were held continuously by the company since the date of issue;
– some or all of the gain (as distinct from the proceeds) was reinvested in replacement shares; and
– an appropriate claim was made.

The **replacement shares** were required to:
– themselves qualify for CVS relief (so the investment must be in shares issued to the company before 1 April 2010);
– not be in a prohibited company (meaning the company and its 51% group which were the subject of the original investment;
– be acquired in the 4 year period beginning 1 year before the disposal of the original shares.

If the replacement shares were acquired before the disposal of the original shares, the replacement shares must still be held and qualify for investment relief at the date of the disposal.

80840
Sch 15 paras 73, 74
FA 2000

Comment The latest possible disposal date on which a gain could have been made and deferred was therefore 31 March 2011. The **time limit** for a claim to deferral is 4 years from the end of the accounting period in which the replacement investment is made, so claims could still be available.

The **maximum gain** which could be deferred was the amount of the subscription for the replacement shares.

Sch 15 para 76
FA 2000

The original gain is **deferred** until the occurrence of a chargeable event (defined as the disposal of the replacement shares or the withdrawal of investment relief from those shares). The deferred gain must be included in the tax computation for the accounting period in which the event occurs. The deferred gain is apportioned equally between all the shares in the replacement holding.

Sch 15 para 79
FA 2000

> MEMO POINTS A **claim** can only be submitted once a form CVS3 is held by the investing company (¶80910), and must include the following details:
> - the amount paid on subscription for the shares;
> - the company in which the investment has been made;
> - the date the shares were issued;
> - the HMRC office which deals with the issuing company and that company's tax reference; and
> - the chargeable gains against which deferral relief is claimed.

VCM 93010

> EXAMPLE G Ltd realised the following gains in respect of CVS investments:
> – £30,000 in respect of H Ltd; and
> – £100,000 in respect of Y Ltd.
> G Ltd made a claim to defer the full amount of both gains, having acquired 80,000 shares in X Ltd at a cost of £200,000.
> If G Ltd sold 20,000 shares in X Ltd, the following gains would crystallise:
>
> – H Ltd: £7,500; ($\frac{20,000}{80,000} \times 30,000$) and
>
> – Y Ltd: £25,000. ($\frac{20,000}{80,000} \times 100,000$)

Loss relief

80845

Where the disposal of CVS shares gives rise to a loss, and the shareholding is not covered by the substantial shareholding exemption (¶32090), that loss can either be set against other chargeable gains (as normal (¶37180)), or, where a specific claim is made, set against income.

Sch 15 para 94
FA 2000

When calculating the **amount** of the loss for either relief, the allowable expenditure must be reduced to take account of any investment relief given and not withdrawn, although this cannot create a chargeable gain. In many cases, investment relief would be completely withdrawn so that no such adjustment would be required.

> MEMO POINTS The **substantial shareholding exemption** will normally apply to investments in trading companies, where the shareholding is 10% or more of the investee company's ordinary share capital and the investment is held for at least 12 months.

> EXAMPLE In June 2007, A Ltd subscribed £100,000 for 50,000 shares in a qualifying issuing company, B Ltd, which was less than 10% of the issued share capital of B Ltd. A Ltd claimed investment relief of £20,000 for its accounting period ending on 31 December 2007.
> In January 2010, A Ltd sold all 50,000 shares for £60,000. As the shares are disposed of within 3 years of their issue, investment relief of £12,000 is withdrawn. (60,000 × 20%)
> A Ltd retained investment relief of £8,000. (20,000 - 12,000)
> So the allowable cost of the shares was reduced to £92,000. (100,000 - 8,000)
>
> | | £ |
> |-------------------|----------|
> | Disposal proceeds | 60,000 |
> | Less: Cost | (92,000) |
> | Allowable loss | (32,000) |

80850

Sch 15 paras 67 -
72 FA 2000

Set against income This relief is only available where the shares have been held continuously by the company since their issue and investment relief has not been fully withdrawn.

The disposal must result from one of the following:
- by way of a bargain at arm's length for full consideration;
- by way of a distribution in the course of dissolving or winding up the issuing company;
- a deemed disposal following a negligible value claim (¶31720); or
- a disposal arising from the loss, destruction or extinction of the asset.

If the loss **exceeds the income** for the accounting period in which the loss arises, it may be carried back and set against income of the previous 12 months. There is no facility to carry forward a CVS revenue loss, so this relief should be carefully considered as it may be more beneficial to retain it as a capital loss.

VCM 92020

This loss relief is given **in priority to** all other deductions, including qualifying charitable donations and losses on unquoted shares for investment companies (¶37230). Where it is claimed, the same loss cannot also be treated as a capital loss or as a loss on unquoted shares.

> MEMO POINTS 1. Relief must be **claimed** within 2 years of the end of the accounting period in which the loss arises.
> 2. Where an accounting period falls partly within the **previous 12 months**, the loss can only be set against income attributable to the specified period (¶36110), and therefore profits of the accounting period must be apportioned on a time basis.
> 3. If a company claims loss relief in respect of **two or more disposals** in the same accounting period, relief for a loss arising from an earlier disposal is given before that arising from a later disposal.

Sch 15 para 71
FA 2000

> 4. If the disposal giving rise to the loss is part of a **scheme involving tax avoidance**, the value shifting provisions (¶32410) will apply. The disposal proceeds will be increased by the amount of the benefit (the loss), so that the loss is cancelled out.

E. Administration

When a company issued shares which qualify for investment relief, certain statutory requirements had to be satisfied. Further, as investors may have obtained warranties from the company about its qualifying status, any instance where the company is at fault may require the payment of damages.

For company investors in a CVS company, see ¶80985.

80880

---

1. Initial requirements

The issuing company was required to provide HMRC with sufficient **information** to establish that the qualifying conditions were satisfied, by submitting a compliance statement (on form CVS1):
– no earlier than 4 months after the qualifying activity commences; and
– no later than 2 years from the end of the accounting period in which the shares are issued (or, if later, 2 years and 4 months from the commencement of the qualifying activity).

When HMRC were satisfied that the conditions are met, they sent a blank form CVS3 (a compliance certificate) to the company, and authorised it to complete and issue the certificate to the investors.

80910
Sch 15 paras 41 -
43 FA 2000

Getting it wrong

If the company either:
– **fraudulently or negligently** provided or issued a compliance certificate; or
– issued a compliance certificate **without authority** from HMRC,
a penalty of up to £3,000 could be charged.

80915
Sch 15 para 44
FA 2000

---

2. Ongoing requirements

The issuing company is required to **notify** HMRC if it:
– becomes aware of any event resulting in a breach of the qualifying conditions; or
– makes a return of value or issues replacement capital which results in the withdrawal of relief.

See ¶80765 for details.

80945
Sch 15 para 65
FA 2000

Notification

Notification must be made in writing and, in all cases, the **time limit** for giving notification is 60 days from the date of the event, or, if later, 60 days from the date on which the company became aware of the relevant event.

Where the company **fails** to notify HMRC, a penalty of up to £300 may be imposed, with a further penalty of up to £60 per day for continuing failure. If a company gives notice fraudulently or negligently, a penalty of up to £3,000 may be imposed.

80950

s 98 TMA 1970

HMRC action

HMRC may issue a **notice** to any person or company requiring the production of information where they believe that a person or company:
– has not given any required notification; or
– has made or received a return of value.

The notice must specify the information required and the deadline for its production, which must be at least 60 days from the issue of the notice.

Failure to comply with a notice may result in a penalty of up to £300 being charged. Where a company or person provides fraudulent or negligent information in response to a notice, a penalty of up to £3,000 may be charged.

80955
Sch 15 para 66
FA 2000

s 98 TMA 1970

3. Investing company

80985
Sch 15 para 64
FA 2000

Once investment relief has been obtained, the investing company must **notify** HMRC (¶80950) if it:
– becomes aware of any event resulting in a breach of the qualifying conditions;
– receives a return of value or issued replacement capital which results in the withdrawal of relief; or
– is granted options.

SECTION 4

Seed Enterprise Investment Scheme (SEIS)

81035
ss 257A - 257HJ
ITA 2007

This new relief is available for shares issued between **6 April 2012 and 5 April 2017** inclusive. It is intended to help small new start-up companies.

The SEIS legislation is closely modelled on that for the EIS. Its main features are as follows:

Relief
Income tax relief at 50% on amounts of up to £100,000 a year subscribed for qualifying SEIS shares
No chargeable gain arises on disposal of the shares
Amounts invested may be used to defer tax on other chargeable gains arising in 2012/13 and 2013/14

Fuller details of the reliefs are given in *Tax Memo*.

---

1. Conditions for relief

81065

The requirements for SEIS income tax relief are that:
– a **qualifying investor** (¶81070)
– must subscribe for **eligible shares** (¶81075)
– in a **qualifying company** (¶81085).

In addition, there must be no **disqualifying arrangements** in place (¶80055).

A breach of any of the conditions may lead to relief being withdrawn.

For 2012/13 onwards, the maximum subscription by an individual in one tax year for which income tax relief may be given is £100,000.

For the meaning of Periods A and B in this section, see ¶80060.

Qualifying investor

81070
ss 257B - 257BF
ITA 2007

The requirements for a qualifying investor are shown in the following table. The investor must:

Requirement[1]	Qualifying period[2]	¶¶
Be an individual	(None)	
Have subscribed for the shares for genuine commercial reasons, and not as part of a tax avoidance scheme.	(None)	¶80090
Not be connected with the issuing company	Period A except as noted below	See below
Not received a **linked loan**	Period A	¶80090
Note: 1. In general the requirements are very similar to those for the EIS, and reference should be made to the indicated paragraphs. 2. The condition must be satisfied throughout the period indicated.		

An individual is **connected** with the company in the same circumstances as for an EIS company (¶80095), with the **exception** that the prohibition on being an employee is confined to Period B. For this purpose, the individual is not connected simply by reason of being a director (unlike the EIS).

> MEMO POINTS The investor can be **non-resident**.

Eligible shares

The conditions for eligibility are similar to those for the EIS. In particular:
- shares must be newly-issued, fully paid-up ordinary shares acquired by subscription for cash;
- the purpose of the share issue must be to raise money for a **qualifying business activity**;
- the shares must be issued for genuine commercial purposes and not as part of a tax avoidance scheme;
- shares may not be redeemable, or certain types of preference share; and
- there must be no pre-arranged exit arrangements

For full details see ¶80135.

The **principal difference** from the EIS is that the shares must be issued **within two years of the incorporation** of the company.

81075
ss 172 - 179
ITA 2007

Funds raised

The amount which may be raised by the company through the SEIS in the three years ending on the date of issue of the shares must not exceed **$150,000**. The company must not have previously raised any funds through the **EIS or VCT**.

All of the money (or all but an insignificant amount) raised by the issue of shares must be used for the purposes of the qualifying business activity for which it was raised, by the company (or its qualifying 90% subsidiary), by the end of **Period B**. The rules for determining whether this condition has been met are similar to those for the EIS (¶80140).

> MEMO POINTS If money is raised under the SEIS, at least 75% of it must be utilised as above before any investment in the company can qualify for the EIS or a VCT.

81080
ss 257CC, 257DK-
257DL ITA 2007

ss 173B, 292B
ITA 2007

Qualifying company

The company. must satisfy three sets of conditions:
- one set at the date the shares are issued;
- another set throughout Period A (¶80060); and
- a further set throughout Period B.

Conditions to be satisfied at the date of issue The company must:

81085
ss 257D - 257DN
ITA 2007

Requirement	¶¶
Be unquoted[1] (and there must be no arrangements in place for it to cease being so)	
Not exceed a maximum permitted level of gross assets[2] and number of employees[2]	
Not be in financial difficulty	¶80170
Not have previously raised funds under the EIS or VCT	
Have a qualifying trade that is less than 2 years old[3].	¶80185

Note:
1. Shares on the Alternative Investment Market (AIM) and the PLUS Quoted and PLUS Traded Markets are not considered to be quoted for this purpose.
2. The company may not have gross assets of more than £200,000 and must have fewer than 25 employees. For details of how assets are measured and who counts as an employee, see ¶80175.
3. This condition applies whether the trade was first begun by the company, or whether it was first begun by another person who then transferred it to the company.

Conditions to be satisfied throughout Period A (¶80060) The company must:

Requirement	¶¶
Be neither the 51% subsidiary of another company[1] nor controlled by another company.	¶80190
Not be a member of a partnership or LLP	
Note 1. In relation to shares issued on or after 6 April 2013, this requirement does not apply providing that the company was a subsidiary only during a period when it had: – issued only subscriber shares; and – not begun, or begun preparations for, its trade or business. This ensures that a company established by a corporate formation agent before being sold on to its new owners will not inadvertently be disqualified from the SEIS.	

Conditions to be satisfied throughout Period B (¶80060) The company must:

Requirement	¶¶
Have a permanent establishment in the UK.	¶80180
Exist wholly for the purposes of carrying on one or more qualifying trades, or be the parent company of a trading group	¶80185, ¶80190
Carry on a qualifying business activity	¶80140
Control no non-qualifying subsidiaries.	¶80190
Have no property-managing subsidiary that is not a qualifying 90% subsidiary	¶80190
Note The details of these conditions are similar to those for the EIS.	

2. Using the relief

81115
ss 257AB, 257E - 257EA ITA 2007

Provided all the conditions are met, the individual **may claim** relief either on the self-assessment tax return, or by submitting a claim accompanied by form SEIS1 which will be issued by the company. Relief is given as a tax reduction.

There is no maximum investment limit, but the maximum amount on which relief will be given in one tax year is £100,000.

Relief may be carried back by treating the shares as acquired in a previous year. However, a claim may not be carried back to any year before 2012/13.

> MEMO POINTS A **claim for relief** cannot be made until either:
> – the trade has been carried on for 4 months; or
> – at least 70% of the money raised has been spent for the qualifying business purpose.
> The claim must be made within **5 years from the filing date** for the tax year in which the shares were issued.

3. Withdrawal of relief

81135
ss 257F - 257FR ITA 2007

Income tax relief may be withdrawn in the following circumstances:
– A breach of conditions by the investor, the company or the shares
– A receipt of replacement capital
– A disposal of the shares
– A return of value to the investor
– The making of payments to non-SEIS investors

The details of these conditions, and the way in which the withdrawal operates, are similar to those for the EIS (¶80300).

4. Administration

The SEIS will be administered by the Small Companies Enterprise Centre (SCEC) of HMRC. The investor and the company both have a **duty to notify** HMRC within 60 days of any change in circumstances that means that the investor is no longer a qualifying individual or the company is no longer a qualifying company.

If the inspector believes that the individual or company has not given him the required information, he may issue a notice requesting the details.

MEMO POINTS   Information may also be requested in connection with:
- the winding up, dissolution, administration or receivership of the company or a subsidiary; or
- arrangements that are in place for a company to cease to be a qualifying 90% or 50% subsidiary.

81155
ss 257G - 257GI
ITA 2007

CHAPTER 6

The leasing industry

82000　Under a leasing agreement, the lessor hires an asset to the lessee, and in return receives a series of rental payments over a period of time. A leasing agreement can cover any asset and any period of time. Common examples include plant, cars and property.

SECTION 1

Presentation in the accounts

82050　All leases transfer some of the risks and rewards of ownership to the lessee, and the distinction between an operating lease and a finance lease is essentially one of degree, as discerned from the terms of the contract between the lessor and lessee. In the case of both finance and operating leases, the **legal ownership** of the asset is held by the lessor, and the lessee has a right to use the asset.

Lease accounting is a complex subject, and is covered by numerous accounting standards and sources of guidance.

MEMO POINTS 1. **Hire purchase contracts** are structured in a similar way to leasing arrangements. However, there is one fundamental difference: at the end of the contract there is a further payment by the hirer, sometimes optional and often for a notional amount, which the hirer pays to acquire ownership of the asset. For the tax consequences of these contracts see ¶26335+.

2. For **full details** of lease accounting see *Accountancy and Financial Reporting Memo*.

3. Where leasing **accounting standards** (either UK or International) are **newly issued** or changed on or after 1 January 2011, a company should continue to apply all tax rules as if the changes to leasing accounting standards had not taken place. This will of course mean that companies will incur extra cost in maintaining two sets of records – one for accounting purposes, and one for tax purposes.

s 53 FA 2011

---

1. Definitions

Finance lease

Commercially, a finance lease is a method of financing. The **economic substance** of the transaction comprises a loan of funds with the asset as security, so in reality the lessee has bought the asset with a secured loan from the lessor. The leasing agreement for the finance lease includes a return to the lessor for providing the funds, which is effectively interest on the loan made to purchase the asset.

82080
SSAP 21

Substantially all the **risks and rewards of ownership** are transferred to the lessee under a finance lease. This is tested at the lease's inception by looking at the net present value (NPV) of the minimum lease payments, and comparing that figure to the fair value of the leased asset (or an estimate). If the NPV is 90% or more of the fair value, there is a presumption that the lease is a finance lease.

MEMO POINTS 1. **Minimum lease payments** are classified as the minimum payments over the remaining part of the lease term (excluding charges for services and taxes to be paid by the lessor), plus:
– in the case of the lessee, any residual amounts guaranteed by him or by a party related to him, or;
– in the case of the lessor, any residual amounts guaranteed by the lessee or by an independent third party.
2. **Net present value** is the current value of money due to be received at a later date. It is calculated by discounting the minimum lease payments at the rate of interest implicit in the lease. For details of discounting see *Accountancy and Financial Reporting Memo*.
3. **Fair value** is the price at which an asset could be exchanged in an arm's length transaction less, where applicable, any grants receivable towards the purchase or use of the asset.

Comment A lease which fails the 90% test may still be a long funding lease for tax purposes (¶82215+).

Operating lease

An operating lease for accounting purposes is any lease that is not a finance lease.

82085

Both the **legal and the economic ownership** remain with the lessor, who retains the equity risk.

---

2. Accounting treatment

The accounting treatment of a finance lease differs from that of an operating lease, and reflects the economic and commercial reality of the transaction. Broadly, the treatment is dependent on which party holds substantially all the risks and rewards of ownership of the asset.

82115

Note that the commentary below outlines UK GAAP. For details of International GAAP see *Accountancy and Financial Reporting Memo*.

Finance lease

82120   The **lessor's accounts** do not show the asset on the balance sheet, but show the loan effectively made to the lessee (generally the cost of the leased asset).

The lease payment received by the lessor consists of a capital element (repayments of the loan), and a finance charge that passes through the profit and loss account.

82125   The finance **lessee** shows the asset on the balance sheet, with the capital element of the amount owed to the finance lessor also included as a loan on the balance sheet. The capital element of the leasing payments reduce the loan, whilst the interest element is charged to the profit and loss account. The finance lessee also includes a charge for depreciation of the asset in the profit and loss account.

The apportionment of the lessee's payment between capital and interest can be undertaken using any of the following methods:
- straight line;
- sum-of-the-digits; or
- actuarial method.

Operating lease

82130   Operating lease accounting is very simple in comparison.

The **lessor** shows the leased asset on the balance sheet, and the rental income in its profit and loss account, usually on a straight line basis (i.e. spread out evenly over the term of the lease).

The **lessee** shows only the rental charges in the profit and loss account, again on a straight line basis.

SECTION 2

Capital allowances

82180   When an asset is acquired for the purposes of leasing, capital allowances are available to the lessor except where the lease is classified as a long funding lease.

Comment   As the lessor and lessee must independently assess the lease, a long funding lease for a lessor may not be a long funding lease for the corresponding lessee, and vice versa. Further, lessors may elect for leases to be treated as long funding leases, and lessees may stay outside the regime by choice (¶82395)

No double claim to allowances

82185
s 70Q CAA 2001

Where each party could claim allowances, **priority** is always given to the lessor.

A. Long funding leases

82215
s 70G CAA 2001

Since 1 April 2006, longer leases (i.e. with a **term** exceeding 5 years (or in some cases 7 years)) of plant or machinery (¶25240+) that function effectively as financing transactions (equivalent to a secured loan and known as funding leases (¶82310+)), are treated for tax purposes in line with their commercial substance rather than their legal form. This definition includes finance leases, finance leasebacks (from 9 October 2007), and some operating leases.

On the whole, this means that:
– capital allowances are only available to the lessee;
– the lessee is entitled to relief for only part of the lease rentals; and
– the lessor is taxed only on that proportion of the rental income that represents the finance charge.

MEMO POINTS   All leases of **cushion gas** (¶25750) are treated as long funding leases.

s 28 FA 2010

1. Exclusions

The following are specifically excluded from the long funding lease rules:
– a short lease;
– hire purchase contracts (¶26335+);
– a lease of plant with land where the plant has a low percentage value;
– an excluded lease of background plant and machinery for a building;
– leases finalised before 21 July 2005 (provided that the lessor was also within the charge to tax on 17 May 2006);
– assets already leased out for at least 10 years prior to 1 April 2006, including subsequent capital expenditure incurred on updating or improvement, so long as a separate asset is not created; and
– assets that have previously been leased out by the current owner, where none of the previous leases were a funding lease, and the aggregate of the terms of the previous leases was more than 65% of the useful economic life of the asset when first leased out.

82245
ss 70G, 70J
CAA 2001

MEMO POINTS   1. For this purpose, a lease is **considered to be finalised** when:
– a written contract exists between the lessor and lessee;
– this contract is either unconditional or the conditions have already been met; and
– there are no terms outstanding that still require to be agreed.
2. A further exclusion applies to the lease of a qualifying ship to a **tonnage tax company**.
3. For **leaseback** contracts before 9 October 2007 see ¶82680+.

Short lease

Except in cases of avoidance (¶82265), a short lease is **generally** a lease of plant or machinery with a term of 5 years or less. However, the lessor may elect to treat a short lease as a long funding lease (¶82260).

82250
s 70I CAA 2001

The **decision** as to whether a lease is a short lease should be taken at its inception. Any change that might arise due to variations in interest rates should be ignored, although other predicted variations should be taken into account. It is possible for the lessor and lessee to take different views regarding the term of the lease.

MEMO POINTS   1. For this purpose, **term** is defined as:
– the period following inception that is not cancellable; plus
– any periods covered by one or more options that, at the inception of the lease, it is reasonably certain the lessee will exercise.

s 70YF(1), (2)
CAA 2001

2. The lease's **inception** is the earliest date when all of the following apply:
– there is a contract in writing for the lease between the lessor and lessee;
– the contract is unconditional or, if it is conditional, the conditions have been met; and
– no terms remain to be agreed.

s 70YI CAA 2001

3. A period is **not cancellable** if it can be cancelled only by:
– the occurrence of a remote contingency; or
– payment of a sum that is unlikely to be paid (as assessed at the beginning of the lease), so that continuation of the lease is reasonably certain.

s 70YF(4) CAA 2001

However, a finance lease of **between 5 and 7 years** will be treated as a short lease where all of the following **conditions** are met:
a. the residual value of the plant and machinery is not more that 5% of the market value of the asset at the start of the lease (as estimated at the lease's inception); and

82255
s 70I(3) – (8)
CAA 2001

b. the rents do not vary considerably i.e.:
– the rent in the first reference year must not be more than 10% less than the rentals of the second reference year; and
– the rentals payable in any reference year after the second, and in the final year, must not be more than the rentals due for the second reference year.

Broadly, this means that the first year's rental may be much higher than those payable in subsequent years, and that rentals may decrease by any amount over the term of the lease. This would exclude any lease containing a **balloon payment** i.e. a payment at or near the end of the lease that is much larger than the previous rental payments.

> ☐ *MEMO POINTS*　1. The **residual value** is the fair value of the asset which cannot reasonably be expected to be recovered by the lessor from the lease payments.
> 2. The **first reference year** is the period of 12 months beginning on the day after the lease term commences.
> 3. The **subsequent reference years** are 12 month periods beginning on the anniversary of the day after the lease commences, and ending before the last day of the lease term.
> 4. The **final year** is the period of 12 months ending on the last day of the lease's term.

> ☐ EXAMPLE　A lease commences on 1 June 2008 for a period of 78 months, ending on 30 November 2014. Payments are made as follows.
>
> | Date | £ |
> | --- | --- |
> | 1 June 2008 | 2,000 |
> | 1 June 2009 | 6,000 |
> | 1 June 2010 | 6,400 |
> | 1 June 2011 | 5,750 |
> | 1 June 2012 | 5,500 |
> | 1 June 2013 | 4,000 |
> | 1 June 2014 | 2,000 |
>
> Putting this into reference years (which ignores the first payment as it occurs on the day of inception, and includes the last payment twice):
>
> | Reference year | Dates | Rentals payable £ |
> | --- | --- | --- |
> | 1st | 2 June 2008 to 1 June 2009 | 6,000 |
> | 2nd | 2 June 2009 to 1 June 2010 | 6,400 |
> | 3rd | 2 June 2010 to 1 June 2011 | 5,750 |
> | 4th | 2 June 2011 to 1 June 2012 | 5,500 |
> | 5th | 2 June 2012 to 1 June 2013 | 4,000 |
> | 6th | 2 June 2013 to 1 June 2014 | 2,000 |
> | Final | 1 December 2013 to 30 November 2014 | 2,000 |
>
> The lease is a short lease because:
> – the rentals in the first reference year are only 6.25% less than the rentals for the second reference year (£6,000 is 93.75% of £6,400); and
> – none of the rentals payable in the 3rd to 6th reference years, and final year, is greater than the rentals due for the second reference year.

82260
SI 2007/304

In the case of leases for plant and machinery (excluding cars (¶25785)), the **lessor** can make an irrevocable election and **opt into** the long funding lease regime for all eligible leases.

For this purpose, an eligible lease must satisfy the following **conditions**:
– the lease runs for a term (¶82250) of at least 12 months, and is finalised on or after 1 April 2006;
– the asset's value does not exceed £10 million;
– the asset is not background plant and machinery (¶82275+);
– the value of the asset does not fall within the low percentage limits (¶82270); and
– at the commencement of the lease, the asset was either new, previously only leased on a long funding lease, or subject to a sale and leaseback election, before the lessor made a tax return for the accounting period in which the lease commenced.

> ☐ *MEMO POINTS*　1. Where the **original lessor's interest has been assigned**, an election can still be made so long as the assignment occurred within 4 months of the lease's inception, and the original lessor (and any subsequent owners) did not claim capital allowances.

2. Where a company has acquired equipment with short term finance, it might wish to substitute this with longer term funding. This can be achieved by a **sale and leaseback**, where a lessor buys the asset and leases it back to the lessee under a finance lease. Although anti-avoidance rules would normally apply, the lessor can make an election (¶82770) where the sale and lease-back occurs within 4 months of the first use of the plant or machinery, and as no capital allowances will have been claimed, the leaseback is an eligible lease.

s 227 CAA 2001

An **anti-avoidance rule** applies where a lease would otherwise be a short lease but at the time of its inception:

82265
s 70I(9) CAA 2001

– there are arrangements for the asset to be leased to others, including persons who are connected to the first lessee; and
– the total of the terms of the lease to the first lessee, and any person connected to that lessee, exceeds 5 years.

In this case, the lease does not fulfil the criteria for being a short lease.

Similarly, where there is a sale and **leaseback**, or a lease and leaseback, and the seller (or grantor of the head lease) has leased the plant or machinery to another person under a long funding lease, the leaseback is also a long funding lease for both parties to the leaseback (¶82440).

s 70Y CAA 2001

Plant has a low percentage value

Plant and machinery **leased with land** is not a long funding lease if the **value does not exceed** both:

82270
s 70U CAA 2001

– 10% of the value of any background plant and machinery (¶82275+); and
– 5% of the market value of the land (including buildings).

> MEMO POINTS 1. When determining the market value of the land, **mortgages** and other encumbrances are ignored.
> 2. **Anti-avoidance provisions** exist to treat a lease as a long funding lease where the following conditions apply:
> – the rentals paid under the lease by the lessee vary according to the value of capital allowances that are available to the lessor; and
> – the main purpose of the transaction is to ensure that the lessor obtains capital allowances.

BLM21600

s 70S CAA 2001

Background plant and machinery

Where the lease relates to land that **includes a building**, any plant and machinery that would reasonably be expected to be installed on the land, and is there primarily to **contribute to** the **functionality** of the building or the location, will not be a long funding lease.

82275
s 70R CAA 2001

The same anti-avoidance rule as in ¶82270 applies.

s 70S CAA 2001

The following table shows the **statutory guidance** as to which items comprise background plant or machinery:

82280
SI 2007/303 reg 2;
BLM21330

Item	Background plant or machinery?
Lighting installations including all fixed light fittings and emergency lighting systems	Always
Intruder alarm systems and other security equipment including surveillance equipment	Always
Telephone, audio-visual and data installations incidental to the occupation of the building	Always
Computer networking facilities incidental to the occupation of the building	Always
Sanitary appliances and other bathroom fittings including hand driers, counters, partitions, mirrors, shower and locker facilities	Always
Kitchen and catering facilities for producing, and storing, food and drink for the occupants of the building	Always
Fixed seating	Always

Item	Background plant or machinery?
Signs	Always
Public address systems	Always
Used for moving or displaying goods to be sold as part of the trade	x
Used for: – manufacturing goods or materials; or – subjecting goods to a process in the course of a trade	x
Used to store goods or materials: – on their arrival to the UK from a place outside the UK; – pending delivery or sale to a customer after having been manufactured or subjected to a process in the course of the trade; – to be used in the manufacture of other goods or materials; or – to be subjected to a process in the course of the trade	x
Heating, hot water and air conditioning installations (including ceilings with integral air conditioning)	Maybe[1]
Electrical installations that provide power to a building (e.g. high and low voltage switchgear, standby generators etc)	Maybe[1]
Protective installations (e.g. sprinklers, lightning protection etc)	Maybe[1]
Mechanisms for opening and closing doors, windows and vents	Maybe[1]
Escalators and passenger lifts	Maybe[1]
Window cleaning installations	Maybe[1]
Fittings (e.g. fitted cupboards, blinds, curtains etc)	Maybe[1]
Demountable partitions	Maybe[1]
Building management systems	Maybe[1]

Note:
1. These items only **are subject to the prohibitions** involving use as marked with x. HMRC state that these items are just examples, so the definitions should not be interpreted too narrowly.

2. Funding lease

82310 The lease must meet one or more of the following tests to be a funding lease:

Test	Applicable to:	
	Operating leases	Finance leases
Accounted for as a finance lease under GAAP	x	✓
Present value of the minimum lease payments amounts to at least 80% of the fair value of the leased plant and machinery	✓	✓
Lease term exceeds 65% of the remaining useful economic life of the leased plant and machinery	✓	✓

Accounts show finance lease

82315
s 70N CAA 2001

This test requires the lease to be accounted for as a finance lease under GAAP, either UK or IAS (¶82080).

In respect of the **lessor**, the accounts may be consolidated or stand-alone, and the lease may be shown in the accounts of a connected party (¶25190).

Present value of minimum lease payments

82320
s 70O CAA 2001

Under this test, the present value must be at least 80% of the asset's **fair value** (which is market value as reduced by any grants received for the asset's purchase).

The present value of the minimum lease payments is **calculated by** using the interest rate implicit in the lease, which is the interest rate that would apply in accordance with GAAP.

Where the asset's cost and residual value are known, the **interest rate implicit** in the lease is the rate which, when applied to the lease rentals, gives a present value of the cost.

> MEMO POINTS 1. For this purpose, minimum lease payments are **defined** as the minimum payments under the lease over the term of the lease excluding any charges for services or tax, but including:
> – any initial payment;
> – any residual amount guaranteed by the lessee; and
> – in the case of a lessee, any residual amount guaranteed by anyone connected with the lessee; or
> – in the case of the lessor, any residual amount guaranteed by a person unconnected with the lessor.
> 2. The **residual amount** is so much of the fair value of the asset as cannot reasonably be expected to be recovered by the lessor from the payments under the lease.

s 70YE CAA 2001

> EXAMPLE A Ltd leases plant to B Ltd which has a market value of £1.2 million. A Ltd received a grant of £200,000 towards the purchase. So the fair value is £1 million. (1,200,000 – 200,000)
> If the present value of the payments under the lease is £820,000, this means that the lease rentals are expected to recover £820,000 of the original cost (plus interest), so the residual amount is £180,000. (1,000,000 – 820,000)
> As the present value of the lease rentals is 82% of the fair value, this makes the lease a funding lease. (820,000/1,000,000)

Useful economic life

Where the lease term exceeds 65% of the remaining useful economic life of the asset, the lease is a funding lease.

82325
ss 70P, 70YI
CAA 2001

The remaining useful economic life is **defined as** the period running from:
– the commencement of the lease term of the lease; to
– the time when the asset is no longer used, or no longer likely to be used, by any party for any purpose as a fixed asset of a business.

The asset's **life** should be **estimated** by reference to the known facts at the commencement of the lease e.g. based on how it will be used, whether it will physically deteriorate, whether it will become obsolete etc. For further details of useful economic life see ¶25725+.

3. Tax consequences

Summary

82355

Party	Topic	¶¶
Lessor	Capital allowances generally	¶82375
	Incurs additional expenditure on asset	¶82400
	Transfers or assigns a long funding lease	¶82430
	Asset ceases to be used on a long funding lease but is retained by the lessor	¶82450
Lessee	Capital allowances generally	¶82395
	Disposals	¶82425+

a. Lessors

Long funding lessors are treated as if they had made a loan to the lessee for the purchase of the asset, and are taxed on an amount equivalent to the commercial profit in each period (effectively, from interest received on the loan).

82375
s 70A CAA 2001

Capital allowances are not available to the lessor.

b. Lessees

82395

ss 70H, 70Q
CAA 2001

Long funding lessees are treated, for tax purposes, similarly to a situation where the lessee has purchased an asset by taking out a loan.

Capital allowances are available to the lessee (who bears most of the economic risks of ownership) so long as:
- the **asset** is used for a qualifying activity (¶25270+);
- the **lease** is a long funding lease, or the lessor has elected for it to be treated as one (¶82260);
- no other person in a **chain of leasing** is, or would be, entitled to claim capital allowances (i.e. the lessor or a superior lessor); and
- the **first tax return affected by the lease** treats it as a long funding lease. Once the tax return becomes final, it is not possible to make an overpayment relief claim on the basis that the lease should, or should not, have been treated as a long funding lease.

Further tax relief for the lessee is only due on the **interest element** of the leasing payments, not on the capital element.

Amount of expenditure

82400

s 70B CAA 2001

The amount of capital expenditure on which the claim is based differs depending upon whether the lease is a long funding operating or finance lease.

Under a long funding **operating lease**, the eligible capital expenditure is the market value of the plant and machinery at the later of:
- the commencement of the lease; and
- the date that the asset is first brought into use for the qualifying activity.

s 70C CAA 2001

Under a long funding **finance lease**, the eligible capital expenditure is the total of:
- the present value of the minimum lease payments (¶82320); plus
- the amount (if any) of rentals paid before the lease commenced, but for which relief is not otherwise available.

s 70D CAA 2001

> ⌐MEMO POINTS¬   1. Anti-avoidance provisions counter **arrangements intended to artificially inflate the amount of expenditure**. If a lease is entered into with the intention of claiming capital allowances in excess of the market value of the asset, the amount of capital allowances that can be claimed are restricted to the market value of the asset.
> 2. If the **lessor incurs additional capital expenditure** on the leased asset with the result that the lease payments increase, the lessee can be treated as incurring additional expenditure for the purpose of capital allowances at the time when the additional expenditure is first recognised.

ss 70C(4A) – 70D
CAA 2001

> 3. As aggressive tax schemes were claiming capital allowances twice (once on the **guaranteed residual value** of the asset, and again on the amount of the guarantee which was physically paid), an anti-avoidance provision was put in place, from 9 March 2011, to ensure that tax relief is only available on the actual amount expended. A lessee cannot include a guaranteed amount in the computation of capital allowances for the period of the lease where it is reasonable to assume tax relief would otherwise be available in respect of a payment under that guarantee.

Which pool?

82405

Assets enter the main pool by default, unless the provisions in the capital allowances regime require them to be separately identified.

The assets requiring **separate identification** by a company are:
- short life assets (¶25835+);
- ships (¶26385+); and
- special rate pool items (¶25920).

c. Disposal events

Termination generally

82425

s 70E CAA 2001

The termination of a long funding lease is treated as a disposal event for capital allowance purposes, and the lessee must bring a disposal value into the capital allowances computation.

The disposal **value** depends on whether the lease was:

a. a long funding **operating lease**, when it is the amount by which the market value of the plant and machinery at the start of the lease (or date the plant and machinery is first brought into use, if later) exceeds the total of:
– the trading deductions allowed; and
– the payments made to the lessee when the lease terminates; or

b. a long funding **finance lease**, when it is the total of the amounts payable on termination plus the net present value (¶82080) of the balance of the minimum lease rentals (less any payments made to the lessor as a result of the termination). The balance of the minimum lease rentals is the difference between the minimum lease payment (¶82080) at the start of the lease and the amount that would have been the minimum lease payment, if the lease had been intended to expire on the date of termination.

For termination events happening **on or after** 21 March 2012 the disposal value is increased by any other payment relating to the lease. These include payments made, directly or indirectly, for the lessee's (or someone connected with the lessee's) benefit, that is connected to the lease and is not:
– an initial payment by the lessor under the lease (a reverse premium);
– a payment made to the lessor under any residual value guarantee agreement;
– a payment made under a superior lease to the lessor of that lease by the lessee of that lease; and
– a payment to the seller of the proceeds of sale of plant or machinery under a sale and leaseback agreement.

Where the transaction is **not at arm's length**, the value is based on what would have been reasonably expected to fall into this category.

A long funding lease is treated as coming to an end (¶82425), and a new lease will commence, if either:

82430
ss 70W, 70X
CAA 2001

a. the **lessor** transfers or **assigns** a long funding lease. In this case, the assignee can elect to opt into the long funding lease regime, provided:
– the relevant conditions are met;
– the assignment occurs within 4 months of the commencement of the original lease; and
– the original lessor has not claimed capital allowances on the assets; or

b. the **lessee transfers plant or machinery** (that is leased under a long funding lease) to another person, who continues to lease the asset.

As long as the **term and the amount receivable** under the new lease are equivalent to the old terms, then the new lease will continue to be treated as a long funding lease.

Extension of lease term

Where the term of a long funding operating lease is extended **as a result of** certain specified events, the lease is treated as coming to an end at the expiration of the original term. The commencement of the extended term is treated as the start of a new long funding lease, which runs for the remainder of the extended lease term.

82435
s 70YB CAA 2001

The **specified events** include:
– variations to the provisions of the lease;
– the granting or exercise of options; or
– where the effect is that the lessee will continue, or is reasonably certain to continue, to lease the plant or machinery for a further period.

> ⌐MEMO POINTS¬ Where the term of a **lease that is not a long funding lease** is extended, the new lease, which runs for the remainder of the extended term, may fulfil the relevant conditions for a long funding lease, in which case it will be treated as a long funding lease.

s 70YC CAA 2001

Sale and leasebacks

Where a long funding lease asset is subject to a sale and leaseback, or lease and leaseback, the **new lease** is treated as a long funding lease. This ensures that the head lessor cannot claim capital allowances.

82440
s 70Y CAA 2001

> ⌐*MEMO POINTS*¬   1. Most transactions involving finance leasebacks must be **disclosed** to HMRC (¶46610+).
> 2. For the anti-avoidance rules relating to leasebacks contracted **before 9 October 2007** see ¶82680+.

> ⌐EXAMPLE¬   An existing long funding lessor, D plc, sells plant and machinery to C Ltd and leases it back. The leaseback is treated as a long funding lease, thereby ensuring that the new head lessor cannot claim capital allowances, and the existing lease becomes a sublease.

Change in accounting treatment

82445
s 70YA CAA 2001

Where there is a change in the GAAP with respect to a long funding lease, for example a change from treatment as a finance lease to treatment as an operating lease, the **old lease** is treated as having come to an end and the lease is treated as a new lease.

Cessation of use

82450
ss 13A, 70YG
CAA 2001

When an asset ceases to be used on a long funding lease, but **is retained by the lessor** and continues to be used for a qualifying activity, the lessor can obtain capital allowances on the asset.

The **amount of allowances** available to the lessor is calculated by reference to the termination amount. This is the value of the plant and machinery at, or about, the time that the long funding lease ceases.

The lessor cannot claim **first year allowances or short life asset** treatment for such assets, except in the case of:
– cars with low carbon dioxide emissions (¶25550); or
– energy-saving or environmentally beneficial plant and machinery that was leased with a building as background plant and machinery (¶82275+).

Chargeable gains implications

82455
s 25A TCGA 1992

When a long funding lease of plant or machinery **commences**, it is treated as disposed of, and immediately reacquired, at the date of commencement for the following **values**, depending on whether the long funding lease is:
– an operating lease, for the market value of the plant and machinery at the commencement of the lease; or
– a finance lease, for the lessor's net investment (as would be first recognised in the accounts if they were prepared in accordance with GAAP).

On a **subsequent termination** of a long funding lease it is treated as disposed of, and immediately reacquired, at the date of termination for the value of the plant and machinery at, or about, the time when the lease terminates.

s 41A TCGA 1992

Where the above deemed disposal and reacquisition gives rise to a **capital loss**, the loss is restricted depending on whether the plant and machinery has been leased:
– only once, when the loss is limited by the amount the asset has fallen in value over the term of the lease; or
– more than once, when the loss is restricted by the amount that the asset has fallen in value in each period it was leased.

For this purpose, the **fall in value** is based on the market values at the start and end of the lease.

B. Other leases (not long funding leases)

82485

From 1 April 2006, the capital allowances treatment of assets that are not leased under long funding leases can be divided into those assets that are leased:
– in the course of a trade; and
– for some other purpose, known as special leasing.

In considering whether the leasing activity constitutes a trade, reference should be made to the general question of whether a trade exists and the factors that need to be considered (¶5000+).

For assets leased overseas where the lease was finalised before 1 April 2006 see ¶82585+.

---

1. Asset leased in course of a trade

The lessor's trade would constitute the lease of plant or machinery for commercial profit.

82515

Where the lease is finalised on or after 1 April 2006, the capital expenditure incurred on the provision of assets for leasing in the UK or overseas is included in the main pool (unless required to be separately identified (¶25920)), and the normal rules apply for WDAs (¶26035+).

First year allowances

Generally, no first year allowances are available for assets that have been purchased for leasing, **unless** the asset is:
– a car with low carbon dioxide emissions (¶25550); or
– energy-saving or environmentally beneficial plant and machinery purchased as background plant and machinery (¶82275+).

82520
s 46 CAA 2001

Anti-avoidance

In cases **other than normal commercial** leases, the amount of allowances available is restricted where arrangements are made from 9 December 2009, whereby the expected economic value of the asset to the lessor is less than the capital expenditure incurred on the acquisition of the asset.

82525
ss 228MA – 228MC
CAA 2001

In this case, the allowances are limited to the expected economic return.

> MEMO POINTS 1. For this purpose, **expected economic value** is defined as the sum of the following present values:
> – the lessor's anticipated taxable income from the lease; plus
> – the residual value of the asset (as reduced by any rental rebate).
> 2. **Present value** is computed by using the interest rate implicit in the lease (¶82320).

Acquisitions by other group companies

Capital allowances on **assets acquired outright** by a company for leasing on or after 1 April 2006 are restricted in the following situations:
a. the leasing company acquiring the plant and machinery is a member of the same 75% CG group (¶65415+), and does not have the same accounting date as the principal company of the group; and
b. the lease is either:
– a finance lease; or
– an operating lease with a term of between 4 and 5 years.

82530
s 220 CAA 2001

The **restriction** is computed by using the following formula:

$$\text{Capital expenditure} \times \frac{\text{Days from acquisition of asset to the end of chargeable period}}{\text{Days in the chargeable period}}$$

The balance of any **unrelieved expenditure** in the period of acquisition is added to the pool for the next accounting period.

> EXAMPLE E Ltd is a member of the EFG group and it prepares accounts to 31 December each year, although the other group companies prepare their accounts to 31 March. On 1 October 2012, it acquires an asset to lease under a finance lease to F Ltd, for £30,000. E Ltd has a brought forward balance of £80,000 in the main pool as at 1 January 2012. Assume that WDA is given at 20% in the year to 31 December 2012, and 18% in the year to 31 December 2013 (but see also ¶26050). The capital allowances computation will be as follows:

	Main pool £	Allowances £
Year ended 31 December 2012		
WDV b/fwd	80,000	
Addition (92/366 x 30,000)	7,541	
	87,541	
WDA @ 20%	(17,508)	17,508
Year ended 31 December 2013		
WDV b/fwd	70,033	
Addition (30,000 – 7,541)	22,459	
	92,492	
WDA @ 18%	(16,649)	16,649
WDV c/fwd	75,843	

Acquired via hire purchase

82535
s 229 CAA 2001

Where the asset is acquired via a hire purchase contract **for the purposes of** a finance lease, the restriction in ¶82530 applies to all payments made under the contract.

> EXAMPLE   A Ltd prepares accounts to 31 December each year. On 1 May 2012, it acquires an asset under a hire purchase contract which is to be leased under a finance lease.
> The initial payment under the contract is £20,000, and quarterly payments of £2,500 (including a finance charge of £500) are also due on 1 January, 1 April, 1 July and 1 October.
> A Ltd has a brought forward balance of £80,000 in the main pool as at 1 January 2012. Assume that WDA is given at 20% in the year to 31 December 2012, and 18% in the year to 31 December 2013 (but see also ¶26050). The capital allowances computation will be as follows:
>
> | | Main pool £ | Allowances £ |
> |---|---:|---:|
> | **Year ended 31 December 2012** | | |
> | WDV b/fwd | 80,000 | |
> | Initial payment (245/366 x 20,000) | 13,388 | |
> | Instalment on 1 July 2012 (184/366 x 2,000) | 1,005 | |
> | Instalment on 1 October 2012 (92/366 x 2,000) | 503 | |
> | | 94,896 | |
> | WDA @ 20% | (18,979) | 18,979 |
> | **Year ended 31 December 2013** | | |
> | WDV b/fwd | 75,917 | |
> | Balance of initial payment (20,000 – 13,388) | 6,612 | |
> | Balance of instalments (4,000 – 1,005 – 503) | 2,492 | |
> | Instalment on 1 January 2013 (no restriction) | 2,000 | |
> | Instalment on 1 April 2013 (275/365 x 2,000) | 1,507 | |
> | Instalment on 1 July 2013 (184/365 x 2,000) | 1,008 | |
> | Instalment on 1 October 2013 (92/365 x 2,000) | 504 | |
> | | 90,040 | |
> | WDA @ 18% | (16,207) | 16,207 |
> | WDV c/fwd | 73,833 | |

2. Assets leased other than in the course of a trade (special leasing)

82565
ss 19, 259, 260
CAA 2001;
CA29450

Each asset (**excluding** a dwelling house) acquired for leasing other than in the course of a qualifying activity (otherwise known as special leasing), is placed in an individual **pool** attracting allowances at the rate applying to the main plant and machinery pool (¶26035+), and each asset is treated as having a separate qualifying activity.

A person who has more than one item of plant or machinery, which is the subject of special leasing, has a separate qualifying activity in respect of each item.

Capital **allowances** given for assets leased other than in the course of a qualifying activity may be **relieved**:
– against income from leasing (and any allowances that remain unrelieved are carried forward to the next accounting period); or
– by deduction from profits generally in the immediately preceding accounting period, in which case, a claim must be made within 2 years of the end of the accounting period in which the loss arose.

Where the asset is **used** only **partly** for leasing, the allowances are restricted accordingly.

A **claim** for these allowances must be made within 4 years of the end of the accounting period.

Sch 18 para 55
FA 1998

3. Overseas leases finalised before 1 April 2006

Assets acquired for leasing overseas, when the lease was finalised (¶82245) before 1 April 2006, are subject to different rules depending on whether the lessee is located within the EEA.

82585
s 105 CAA 2001

> MEMO POINTS   1. Plant or machinery is used for overseas leasing if it is leased **to a person** who:
> – is not resident in the UK; and
> – does not use the plant or machinery exclusively for earning profits chargeable to UK tax (including profits from exploration or exploitation activities carried on in the UK or its territorial sea).
> This includes a chain of leases where at least one satisfies this criteria.
> 2. The **EEA** comprises the following countries:

Austria	Finland	Ireland	Netherlands	Spain
Belgium	France	Italy	Norway	Sweden
Bulgaria	Germany	Latvia	Poland	Switzerland
Cyprus	Gibraltar	Liechtenstein	Portugal	United Kingdom
Czech Republic	Greece	Lithuania	Romania	
Denmark	Hungary	Luxembourg	Slovak Republic	
Estonia	Iceland	Malta	Slovenia	

a. Lessee resident outside EEA

Where assets are leased overseas to a non-EEA resident and the lease was finalised (¶82245) before 1 April 2006, the availability of capital allowances depends on the following:

82605
ss 105, 106, 109,
110 CAA 2001

Situation	Capital allowances [2]	¶¶
Asset is not used for a qualifying purpose	None	¶82610
Protected lease i.e. short term lease or lease in respect of a ship, aircraft or transport container	Main rate	¶82615
Asset leased overseas within the designated period [1]	10% WDA	¶82620

Note:
1. The **designated period** is the period of 10 years beginning on the date that the asset is first brought into use by the company which incurred the expenditure. If the company ceases to own the asset within that 10 year period, the designated period ends on that date.
2. Where events mean that a lease which did qualify for allowances now **no longer fulfils the criteria**, allowances previously given will be clawed back (¶82625).

Prohibition of allowances

Capital allowances are not available where the assets are **not used** for a qualifying purpose, and one of the following applies:
– there is more than a year between consecutive payments due under the lease;
– the lease is for a period in excess of 13 years, or can be extended by agreement or renewed to be in excess of 13 years;
– payments in addition to the periodical payments are due under the lease;

82610
s 110 CAA 2001

– the payment terms under the lease agreement are not standard terms;
– the rates of payment under the lease change (excluding any changes attributable to variations in tax rates, capital allowance rates, bank interest rates or insurance premiums); or
– at any time, the lessor (or a connected person) could be entitled to receive a payment of an amount determined before the expiry of the lease, which is referable to the asset's value on or after the expiry of the lease, whether or not the payment is related to its disposal.

ss 122, 125
CAA 2001

MEMO POINTS   1. In this context, a **qualifying purpose** is:
a. where the lessee or the original buyer uses the asset for the purposes of a qualifying activity without leasing it;
b. the buyer uses the asset for short term leasing; or
c. the lessee uses the asset for short term leasing and is either:
– UK resident; or
– using the asset in the course of a qualifying activity carried on in the UK.
2. Where the asset is **disposed of to a connected person** (¶25190), the new owner is treated as the buyer.

s 121 CAA 2001

3. A **short term lease** is a lease to the same person with a term of:
– up to 30 consecutive days and up to 90 days in total in any 12 month period; or
– up to 365 consecutive days, and, during any 4 year period in the designated period (¶82605), the total period in which it is leased directly to a person carrying on a qualifying activity does not exceed 2 years.
For this purpose, connected persons (¶25190) are treated as the same person.

Protected lease

82615
s 105(5) CAA 2001

Assets subject to a protected lease are **treated** as normal assets for the purposes of capital allowances, so, for example, where the relevant criteria are met, FYA would be available. They are placed in the main **pool**, and in the absence of any other allowance, qualify for WDA at the main rate (¶26035+).

A protected lease is **defined** as one which relates to assets which are either:
a. used for short term leasing (¶82610); or

ss 123, 124
CAA 2001

b. a ship, aircraft or transport container that is used in the course of a qualifying activity for capital allowances purposes i.e.:
– all the factors discussed at ¶25270+;
– ships or aircraft that are let on a charter by a UK resident person who carries on a trade of operating ships or aircraft in the UK; and
– transport containers that are let in the course of a UK trade of operating ships or aircraft, and the container is at other times used by the lessor for the operation of ships or aircraft.

Where there is a **chain of leases** which contains at least one non-protected lease, allowances will be restricted to 10% WDA.

Other leases

82620
ss 107, 108
CAA 2001

Assets which do not fall within the prohibition of ¶82610, or the remit of protected leases, will be placed in the overseas leasing pool, unless required to be put in a separate asset pool by another rule of the capital allowances regime (¶25920). The applicable rate of WDA is 10%.

The **final chargeable period** for the overseas leasing pool will occur when it is impossible for there to be any more disposal receipts.

When an asset in the overseas leasing pool is **disposed of to a connected person** (¶25190) (other than in a reconstruction where the qualifying activity is treated as continuing), the disposal value is the lower of market value and original cost.

Clawback of allowances

82625
ss 111, 112, 114,
115 CAA 2001

A balancing charge is due in respect of such overseas leases in the following situations, where WDA at:
a. 10% has been given but, within the designated period (¶82605), an event occurs such that no allowances should have been given. A balancing charge is due equal to the aggregate of

allowances already claimed. The amount of unused expenditure is brought into the pool as a disposal value. The balancing charge is made in the period in which the event occurs; or
b. the normal rate is given, or even an FYA, but within the designated period, the asset is used for (non-protected) overseas leasing. In this case, the balancing charge is equivalent to the sum of the allowances given in the accounting periods up to and including that in which the asset is first used for leasing overseas, less the maximum allowances that could have been given if the 10% rate had been used instead. The balancing charge is made in the accounting period in which the asset is first used for leasing purposes. In the following accounting period, an amount equal to the balancing charge and the disposal value together is treated as an addition to the overseas leasing pool. The effect of this is to ensure that the written down value in the overseas leasing pool is the same as it would have been if the asset had been used for overseas leasing from the time at which it was first acquired.

> ☐ MEMO POINTS Except in the case where the qualifying activity is treated as continuing (e.g. a company reconstruction without a change of ownership), a clawback of allowances occurs when plant and machinery is **acquired from a connected person** (¶25190) and that person has claimed an FYA, WDA or a balancing allowance on the asset. The clawback is calculated on the basis of the allowances given to the owner and the connected party.

Provision of information to HMRC

Information must be provided to HMRC in the following circumstances, where:
– expenditure on plant and machinery has qualified for a normal WDA or for an FYA, which is then **subsequently used for overseas leasing** (excluding protected leasing (¶82615)) in the designated period (¶82605); or
– plant and machinery is **leased to joint lessees**, and at least one of those joint lessees falls into the relevant definition to constitute overseas leasing, the lessor must provide information to HMRC.

82630
ss 119, 120
CAA 2001

The **time limit** for providing the information is 3 months after the end of the accounting period in which the plant is first so used. This time limit can be **extended** to 30 days after the informant acquired knowledge that the plant was being so used, where that informant could not reasonably have been expected to know this earlier.

Where the expenditure on the plant and machinery has not yet qualified for a normal WDA or FYA, and the plant is used for **protected leasing**, the capital allowances claim must be accompanied by a certificate that describes the protected leasing.

s 118 CAA 2001

---

b. Lessee resident inside EEA

Some commentators suggested that the overseas leasing rules, as they applied to EEA residents before 1 April 2006, were contrary to EU law as possibly being a restriction on the freedom to provide services.

82650
HMRC Brief 40/07

In response, **HMRC** issued **specific guidance**, where the EEA country (¶82585):
– gives the lessee relief broadly equivalent to capital allowances, a WDA of 10% continues to be available (and the rules relating to situations where allowances are not given do not apply (¶82610)); or
– gives no relief to the lessee which is broadly equivalent to capital allowances, the lessor receives the normal applicable rate of WDA.

C. Pre 9 October 2007 leaseback contracts

In addition to the general anti-avoidance rule at ¶25460, pre 9 October 2007 sale and lease-back, or lease and leaseback, transactions are subject to specific anti-avoidance rules in order to stop the artificial acceleration of capital allowances, or the avoidance of tax on income.

82680

Leases relating to post 8 October 2007 sales (or the first lease in a lease and leaseback transaction) fall under the long funding lease rules (¶82215+).

Transactions involving sale and leasebacks must be disclosed to HMRC (¶46610+)

1. Sale and leasebacks

82710   The accounting treatment of a sale and leaseback transaction is to treat it as refinancing, so that the asset continues to be recognised on the vendor's balance sheet.

a. General anti-avoidance

82730
ss 214 – 218
CAA 2001

When an asset is transferred under a sale and leaseback as part of a relevant transaction, no first year allowances or annual investment allowance can be claimed.

For this purpose, a **relevant transaction** is either:
– a sale of plant or machinery;
– a hire purchase or similar contract; or
– an assignment of a hire purchase or similar contract.

However, **no relevant transaction** can occur where plant has been sold to the buyer in the normal course of the seller's business of manufacturing or supplying such plant, and it has never been used before the sale or the making of the contract.

Where the **main purpose** of the transaction is the obtaining of a writing down allowance, the capital expenditure deemed to be incurred by the new purchaser is either:
– the disposal value that the vendor is required to bring into account on the transaction (¶26085+); or
– if there is no such amount, the lower of the current market value of the plant or machinery or the amount originally incurred by the vendor.

> MEMO POINTS   For **expenditure incurred on or after 1 April 2012** the test is no longer if the transaction was entered into to secure an allowance, but if the transaction (or a scheme of which it forms part) was undertaken with the intention of securing a tax advantage. If the result of the transaction is that the purchaser increases the rate at which they obtain allowances or obtain them earlier, then the legislation will reduce the rate to what it should have been or postpone the allowance until such time as it would normally have been available.

b. Finance leasebacks

82750
s 221 CAA 2001;
CA28500

Excluding certain assets with a long build time, a sale and finance leaseback **occurs** where a person sells an asset used in a qualifying activity and leases it back under a finance lease (or a person connected with the seller leases it back), irrespective of whether there is a period of time between the sale and the leaseback. Provided that the asset is not used for any qualifying activity other than leasing **during the gap**, this is still a sale and finance leaseback. The use to which the asset is put after the leaseback is irrelevant.

> MEMO POINTS   Assets with a **long build time** are outside the scope of these rules where:
> – the asset is ordered by the lessor initially, or the purchase contract is novated to the lessor, before the asset is brought into use for the purposes of the trade;
> – neither the lessee, nor anyone connected with the lessee, will claim plant and machinery allowances on the asset; and
> – the purpose of the transaction is not to obtain allowances.

> EXAMPLE   A Ltd has a yacht that is used in a cruising trade. A Ltd sells the yacht to B Ltd, which leases it out to third parties for a few months and then leases it back to A Ltd under a finance lease.
> This is a sale and finance leaseback, as B Ltd used the yacht only for leasing during the period of time between the sale and the finance leaseback.

Summary

The following rules apply to plant and machinery acquired for leasing out under a finance lease **before** 9 October 2007.

82755

For leases **commencing subsequently**, the rules in ¶82215+ apply i.e. the leaseback transaction is treated as a long funding lease.

Area	Rule	¶¶
Qualifying expenditure	Time apportioned in the first year, so that using a finance lease does not accelerate the benefit of capital allowances	¶82535
Transfer value for capital allowances purposes (i.e. between the seller and the buyer)	Limited to the notional written down value, unless election made	¶82760
FYAs for buyer	No	
No risk that lessee will default	No allowances available to the buyer (i.e. the lessor)	¶82765

Transfer value

Unless the buyer is prohibited from claiming allowances because the company bears no risk of lessee default (¶82765), or an election is made (¶82770), the **seller's disposal value** is restricted to the lowest of:

82760
ss 222 – 224, 226
CAA 2001

– the true disposal value;
– market value;
– the notional written down value of the seller's capital expenditure (i.e. cost less the maximum allowances that could have been claimed in respect of the asset, including any FYA); or
– the notional written down value of the capital expenditure incurred by anyone connected with the seller.

The **buyer's qualifying expenditure** (and that of any future owner) is also limited to the seller's disposal value as calculated above, plus any installation costs incurred. If the seller does not have a disposal value, the buyer's qualifying expenditure is the lowest of:
– the market value;
– the notional written down value of the seller's capital expenditure, if there is any; or
– the notional written down value of any capital expenditure incurred by anyone connected with the seller.

No risk of lessee default

Subject to one exception, no capital allowances at all are available to the lessor where plant or machinery is sold and leased back under a finance lease and, as part of the leasing arrangements, the greater part of the risk that the lessee's obligations under the lease will not be met has been removed (other than by means of a guarantee from persons connected with the lessee).

82765
s 225 CAA 2001

The **exception** relates to guarantees provided by the following:
– a person connected with the lessee;
– jointly, by a person connected with the lessee and a bank where that person's credit rating is higher than that of the bank; or
– a bank, which is itself counter-guaranteed by a non-resident person connected with the lessee of equal or superior creditworthiness, where the lessee does not have an established credit rating in the UK (primarily because it has been trading in the UK for a short period); or
– a parent bank (where the lessor is part of a banking group) to meet the capital adequacy requirements related to the large exposures regime, provided that the guarantee is not part of any wider arrangements.

⎡*MEMO POINTS*⎤   1. For this purpose, HMRC interpret the **greater part of the default risk** as meaning reducing the risk of loss to the lessor by more than 50%.

2. **Typical examples** of when this rule applies are where the lessee's obligations are:
– secured by cash deposits or by the pledging of assets or income; or
– backed by a third party guarantee or letter of credit.

Asset sold within 4 months of first use

82770
ss 227, 228
CAA 2001

An irrevocable **election** can be made where the sale occurs no more than 4 months after the asset is first brought into use, and all of the following **conditions** are satisfied:
– the asset was not acquired from a connected person (¶25190) or a transaction that aimed to obtain allowances;
– no capital allowances have been claimed on the capital expenditure incurred on the asset;
– the seller incurred capital expenditure on the asset (i.e. it was neither a gift nor acquired as trading stock); and
– the asset was acquired by the seller when it was new.

If an election is made, the **qualifying expenditure** is considered to be the smallest of the following amounts:
– the actual expenditure by the buyer;
– the capital expenditure that the seller incurs on the asset; or
– the capital expenditure that any person connected with the seller incurs on the asset.

⎡*MEMO POINTS*⎤   The **time limit** for the election to be made is 2 years after the date of the sale and leaseback.

Lease rentals

82775
s 228B CAA 2001;
CA28920

There is a restriction on the lease rentals that can be **deducted by a lessee** in computing profits for tax purposes.

This **permitted maximum**, for any accounting period, is the total of:
– the finance charge as shown in the accounts (assuming GAAP has been followed); and
– the annual depreciation amount, which deems the value of the plant and machinery at the start of the leaseback to be equal to the transfer value in ¶82760. The depreciation rate already used in the accounts should suffice.

When the lease **terminates**, the following amount is added to the permitted maximum in the accounting period of termination:

$$\frac{\text{Original consideration} \times \text{Current book value}}{\text{Original book value}}$$

where:
– the original consideration is the consideration payable to the person who sold the plant and entered into the leaseback;
– the current book value is the net book value of the leased plant or machinery immediately before the termination; and
– the original book value is the net book value of the leased plant or machinery at the beginning of the leaseback.

s 228G CAA 2001

⎡*MEMO POINTS*⎤   Where the **lessee treats the leaseback as an operating lease**, even though the lessor treats it as a finance lease, the amounts above should be calculated by reference to a connected person's accounts. Where this is not possible, increase the lessee's profits for the accounting period in which the leaseback begins by the net consideration (i.e. the tax-free amount received by the vendor (¶82790+)).

⎡EXAMPLE⎤
1. In Year 10, E Ltd sells equipment to F SA, a bank resident in Spain, for its market value (and net book value) of £500,000, and finance leases it back over 10 years. E Ltd acquired the equipment in Year 1 for £1,000,000 and it is depreciated on a straight line basis over 20 years, giving an annual depreciation charge of £50,000.
The transfer value (¶82760) of the equipment is £55,000, which is E Ltd's disposal value.

The permitted maximum for an accounting period is the sum of the finance charge shown in E Ltd's accounts, plus the depreciation that would have been charged if the equipment had cost £55,000 and had been written off over the 10 year leaseback (i.e. an annual depreciation charge of £5,500).

The actual depreciation shown in the accounts of £50,000 should be added back.

2. If a premium of £600,000 was due on the leaseback (being the original consideration), payable over 10 years, then the annual payment would be £60,000. If E Ltd cancels the lease in Year 5, £300,000 is still owed to F SA.

If the current book value before termination is £250,000, the permitted maximum is increased by

£300,000. $\dfrac{(600,000 \times 250,000)}{500,000}$

Where a person leasing plant or machinery under a sale and finance leaseback **leases it out under a further operating lease**, and the following conditions are satisfied, the deduction available to the operating lease **lessee** is restricted to the permitted maximum (¶82775):
– the term of the lease begins on or after 18 May 2004;
– the lessee, or a person connected with the lessee, is the person who entered into the sale and finance leaseback; and
– the lessee accounts for the lease as an operating lease.

82780
s 228J CAA 2001;
CA28970

The operating lease **lessor** is taxable on the full amount of the lease rentals, irrespective of any payments due to the lessee under the operating lease, although the taxable income cannot exceed the permitted maximum.

Where only some of the plant or machinery is leased under the operating lease, a just and reasonable apportionment should be made.

> EXAMPLE Taking the facts from example 1 in ¶82775, E Ltd leases the equipment to G Ltd on an operating lease for an annual rent of £50,000. If E Ltd's permitted maximum for the lease rentals to F SA is £8,000 a year, the following consequences occur:
> – G Ltd can only deduct rent of £8,000 a year in computing its profits;
> – if E Ltd is due to give G Ltd a rebate of £3,000, E Ltd's rental income is £50,000 and not £47,000; but
> – E Ltd's rental income from G Ltd is restricted to £8,000, as this is the permitted maximum.

The **lessor's qualifying expenditure** is limited to the transfer value (¶82760), which may be less than the amount that the lessor actually paid.

82785

In respect of the **rental income received**, a permitted threshold applies, above which any amounts are left out of account e.g. if the threshold is £10,000, and the lessor receives rents of £13,000, the extra £3,000 should be ignored.

s 228D CAA 2001;
CA28940

To calculate the **permitted threshold**, the following formula is used:

$$\text{Gross earnings} + \frac{(\text{Transfer value} \times \text{Investment reduction})}{\text{Net investment}}$$

where:
– the gross earnings are the amount shown in the lessor's accounts as the gross earnings under the leaseback;
– transfer value is as given at ¶82760;
– investment reduction is the amount shown in the lessor's accounts in respect of the reduction of net investment in the leaseback for the accounting period; and
– net investment is the amount shown in the lessor's accounts as the lessor's net investment in the leaseback at the beginning of its term.

Termination of leaseback

As the rules aim to recover any tax-free sum that has been received by the **lessee** over the life of the leaseback, where the leaseback terminates early, a special mechanism comes into play to ensure that the balance is still taxable. Note this does not affect the treatment of any refund of rentals, which is still taxed in full.

82790
s 228C CAA 2001;
CA28930

In the accounting period of termination, the lessee's **profits** are **increased** by the following:

$$\frac{\text{Net consideration} \times \text{Current book value}}{\text{Original book value}}$$

where:
– the net consideration is the difference between the amount received by the seller for entering into the sale and finance leaseback, and the restricted disposal value (i.e. it is equivalent to the tax-free amount that the seller received);
– the current book value is measured immediately before the termination; and
– the original book value is measured at the commencement of the leaseback.

82795
s 228E CAA 2001;
CA28950

When a leaseback terminates, the **lessor** may sell the asset and refund the lessee in respect of some of the rentals.

The disposal value will be restricted to the original transfer value (¶82760), as will any refund of rentals.

> EXAMPLE   A Ltd sells an asset to B Ltd for £20,000 and leases it back over 10 years for £2,000 p.a. When A Ltd sells the asset, the disposal value is restricted to £1,000 under the rules in ¶82760.
> B Ltd's qualifying expenditure is therefore £1,000.
> A Ltd cancels the lease after 2 years, and B Ltd sells the asset for £18,500. However, B Ltd's disposal value is restricted to £1,000 (i.e. to the level of qualifying expenditure).
> A Ltd has to pay a termination charge of £16,000, but B Ltd gives A Ltd a refund of £18,000 which relates to the rentals. B Ltd can only deduct £1,000 of the £18,000 in computing taxable profits.

2. Lease and leasebacks

82825
s 228F CAA 2001;
CA28910

Broadly, there is a lease and finance leaseback where the owner of plant or machinery, company A, leases the plant or machinery to a finance provider, B, for a premium, and then leases it back from B. This also includes the case where a connected party of company A uses the asset.

The same rules apply as for sale and leasebacks with the following modifications (note that the lessee is company A, and the lessor is B):

Topic	Detail	Reference	¶¶
Lessee's deduction	Permitted maximum includes only the finance charge as depreciation is excluded	s 228B CAA 2001	¶82775
Lessee treats leaseback as an operating lease	Increase the lessee's profits by the premium received by the original owner	s 228G CAA 2001	¶82775
Taxation of lessee on termination of lease	Any refund of rentals is taxed in full even if there are amounts owing to the lessor	s 228C CAA 2001, CA28930	¶82790
Lessor's rental income	Normally applies to lease and leaseback transactions before 6 December 2006	s 228D CAA 2001, CA28940	¶82785

SECTION 3

Sale of lessor companies

82875

Where a company that is carrying on the business of leasing plant or machinery comes under new ownership, provisions apply to impose a tax charge on the original owner and give tax relief to the new owner.

> MEMO POINTS   Leasing business carried on by a company **in partnership** is outside the scope of this book.

1. Qualifying change of ownership

Generally, a change of ownership occurs when there is a change in the flow of group relief to or from the lessor company. The change may be partial or complete.

Such a change **would be effected by** either:
– the sale of all or some of the shares in the lessor company or its immediate (or higher) parent company;
– equity dilution i.e. where the lessor company issues shares to the purchasing group so that it gains a majority interest; or
– the granting of an option over shares entitling a third party to obtain control over the lessor company.

The test looks at the changes in the **relationship between** the lessor company and the top company in a structure (i.e. usually a parent in a group), so that where the 75% relationship is broken, there is a change in ownership. For example, a change from 100% to 75% would not constitute such a change for these purposes.

In most cases, it will be obvious that a lessor company has changed ownership.

> MEMO POINTS 1. The **definition of a 75% shareholding** mirrors the rules for group relief (¶65055).
> 2. A company is automatically deemed to have a change in ownership where it enters a **tonnage tax group** on or after:
> – 21 March 2012 if it enters the tonnage tax regime at the same time; or
> – 23 April 2012 where it does not.
> This was introduced to counter a number of avoidance schemes of which HMRC had become aware.

> EXAMPLE E Ltd owns 75% of D Ltd, a lessor company. F Ltd owns 100% of E Ltd.
> If F Ltd sells all of the shares in E Ltd to G Ltd, there is a break in the chain of ownership between D Ltd and F Ltd, who is the principal company. D Ltd is no longer a 75% subsidiary of F Ltd.

82905
BLM80305

Who is the principal company?

The identity of the principal company is **established by** looking upwards from the lessor company and seeing if it is a 75% subsidiary of another company.

Where there is a **chain of companies**, each 75% parent-subsidiary relationship above the lessor company should be identified. The chain is broken when there is no 75% relationship, and the uppermost company is then the principal company.

> EXAMPLE A Ltd is a lessor company and a 100% subsidiary of B Ltd. B Ltd is a 100% subsidiary of C Ltd. C Ltd is not a 75% subsidiary of another company.
> The test looks at one link of the chain at a time so:
> – A Ltd is a 75% subsidiary of B Ltd;
> – B Ltd is a 75% subsidiary of C Ltd; but
> – C Ltd is not a 75% subsidiary of another company.
> So C Ltd is the principal company of A Ltd. It is irrelevant whether A Ltd is a 75% subsidiary of C Ltd.

82910
s 393 CTA 2010;
BLM80310

Exception

Where the lessor company **remains in the same group** (i.e. in a chain of 75% subsidiaries with the same principal company) after an intra-group transaction, there is no relevant change of ownership.

82915
s 395 CTA 2010

Consortia

The usual test does not work for consortia, as no single company will own at least 75% of a consortium company.

So where a **consortium company is a lessor**, it will have more than one principal company, as each consortium member is treated as a principal company (unless the consortium member is itself a 75% subsidiary of another company, in which case that other company is the principal company).

82920
ss 394, 397
CTA 2010;
BLM80320

⸂ *MEMO POINTS* ⸃ 1. A company is treated as **owned by a consortium** (and known as a consortium company) when it is:
– not a 75% subsidiary of any company; and
– 75% or more of its ordinary share capital is beneficially owned by two or more companies (a consortium); and
– none of those other companies owns less than 5% of that capital.
2. Where a consortium owns a **holding company**, which owns 90% trading subsidiaries, all of the companies are treated as owned by the consortium.

82925
BLM80325

Changing proportion of shareholdings   Where a consortium changes the shareholdings in the lessor consortium company, so that the relevant fraction is less at the end of the day (compared with the beginning of the day), there is a change of ownership.

For this purpose, the **relevant fraction** is the smallest of the percentage of any of the following in the lessor company:
– ordinary share capital of company;
– beneficial entitlement to any profits available for distribution to equity holders; or
– beneficial entitlement to any assets available for distribution to its equity holders on a winding up.

⸂ *MEMO POINTS* ⸃ 1. Where the **lessor company is a 90% subsidiary of a holding company** owned by a consortium, the relevant fraction is calculated by looking at the shareholdings in the holding company.
2. When a **consortium member is a 75% subsidiary of another company**, the member's shareholding is looked through all the way up to the principal company, so that there is a relevant change in the relationship between the lessor company and its principal company whenever there is either:
– a change in the relevant fraction; or
– a company, which is part of the chain of ownership between the lessor company and the principal company, stops being a 75% subsidiary.

⸂EXAMPLE⸃
1. D Ltd is a lessor company, owned 74% by Y Ltd and 26% by Z Ltd.
If Y Ltd is a member of a profit-making group, 74% of the early tax losses of D Ltd can flow to the Y group.
When D Ltd moves into profit, Y Ltd sells shares in D Ltd to Z Ltd so that after the sale, D Ltd is owned 74% by Z Ltd and 26% by Y Ltd.
If Z Ltd is a member of a loss-making group, 74% of the taxable profits of D Ltd can be absorbed by group relief flowing from the Z group.
This fall in the shareholding of Y Ltd in D Ltd is a relevant change in the relationship.

2. E Ltd is a lessor company, owned by F Ltd and X Ltd. F Ltd is owned by G Ltd, and the principal company for this chain is H Ltd.
G Ltd sells all of its holding in F Ltd to X Ltd. So F Ltd is no longer a 75% subsidiary of G Ltd, and no longer a member of H Ltd's group.
There is a qualifying change of ownership in relation to E Ltd, because H Ltd is no longer a principal company.

---

2. Tax charge on original owner

82955

Often, in the first years of a relatively long lease, the capital allowances available to the lessor company are greater than the rental income received from the lessee, resulting in tax losses. These losses can be surrendered to other group members.

When the lease moves into its profitable phase, the lessor company could be sold to a loss-making group, and hence the profits would be sheltered via group relief from the new group. There are tax rules to stop this tax saving.

Overview

82960

The charge to the **original owner**, on a disposal of the lessor company, equates roughly to the amount of benefit received from those tax losses.

A corresponding deduction is available to the **leasing company** immediately after the change in ownership, but with restrictions on how this deduction can be offset.

Accounting period

Where a leasing business is carried on by a company, an accounting period ends on the **relevant day** (i.e. the date of the company's sale) where all of the following **conditions** apply:
- the company carries on the business of leasing plant and machinery;
- the company is within the charge to corporation tax; and
- there is a qualifying change of ownership (¶82905+) in relation to the company.

82965
s 383 CTA 2010

In the accounting period:
- **ending** on the relevant day, the company is regarded as receiving a taxable business receipt; and
- **beginning** the day after the relevant day, the company is treated as incurring a tax deductible business expense of the same amount.

> MEMO POINTS 1. For this purpose, a company carries on a **business of leasing plant or machinery** if **at least half** of:
> - the relevant plant or machinery value relates to qualifying leased plant or machinery; or
> - the company's (or one of its associate's) income over the 12 months ending on the relevant day derives from qualifying leased plant or machinery, as apportioned on a just and reasonable basis, where necessary.
>
> 2. Except in the case of long funding leases, the **relevant plant or machinery value** is the sum of:
> - the value of plant and machinery in the company's balance sheet as at the start of the relevant day; and
> - any such value which would be shown in the company's balance sheet drawn up at the end of the relevant day, and would also have been shown in the balance sheet of an associated company.
> Where the company leases the plant or machinery under a **long funding lease**, the ascribed value replaces the balance sheet value. **Ascribed value** is the higher of:
> - the market value of the asset unencumbered by the lease; and
> - the present value of the leased asset (which is calculated by reference to the value of the remaining payments under the lease and the residual value of the asset that will not be recovered through the lease, and using the interest rate implicit in the lease).
>
> 3. A company is an **associated company** of another company on any day if, at the start of that day:
> - one of the two has control of the other; or
> - both are under the control of the same person(s).
> For the meaning of control see ¶75275+. This also includes consortium members where the relevant company is a consortium company or a 75% subsidiary of a consortium company.
>
> 4. **Qualifying leased plant or machinery** must meet all of the following conditions:
> - it is, or at any time in the past 12 months has been, leased out by the relevant company or an associate, although where the associate is the lessor, the lessee cannot be the relevant company; and
> - it must have been subject to a plant or machinery lease (excluding a lease of background plant or machinery for a building (¶82275+)) at some time in the 12 months ending with the relevant day.

ss 387 – 391
CTA 2010

ss 388 – 390
CTA 2010

ss 437A – 437C
CTA 2010

s 408 CTA 2010

s 387(7) CTA 2010

Taxable receipt

The taxable receipt is computed using the following **formula**:

$$PM - TWDV$$

where:
a. PM is the net book value of the relevant plant and machinery (excluding any assets leased under long funding leases) shown:
- on the lessor's balance sheet, determined on the assumption that the balance sheet is drawn up in accordance with GAAP, including the ascribed value (¶82965) of plant or machinery transferred to the lessor company from connected parties at any time;

82970
s 399 CTA 2010;
BLM80510 +

– in the balance sheets of each associated company in respect of all plant or machinery transferred to the lessor company at the start of the relevant day; and

– as a fixture in land in the accounts (which may not be shown on the balance sheet as plant or machinery); and

b. TWDV is the tax written down value of that plant and machinery, this being the unrelieved qualifying expenditure on plant or machinery in any relevant pools carried forward under the normal capital allowances provisions, excluding any additions on the relevant day (other than assets acquired from an associated company).

s 385 CTA 2010

[MEMO POINTS]   1. As accounts are unlikely to be drawn up on the relevant day, the values above should be determined as if accounts had been drawn up under GAAP.

2. It is not possible to carry back a loss from a later period to extinguish this charge.

[EXAMPLE]   F Ltd is a lessor company which is a subsidiary of H Ltd. F Ltd owns a number of printing presses which are leased out under operating leases.
On 31 December 2012,
– all the shares in F Ltd are sold by H Ltd; and
– F Ltd acquires plant from group company G Ltd, and a lathe from an unconnected party.
PM should reflect the printing presses.
TWDV should reflect the printing presses and the plant from G Ltd (which is an associated company). The lathe is excluded as it is an addition on the relevant day, and acquired from an unconnected party.

82975

ss 405, 406
CTA 2010;
BLM80545

If the **economic control of the company has changed**, for example, from being a 75% subsidiary of a company to being owned by a consortium of which that company is a member, an adjustment may be made to reflect the fact that the original owner still has some economic control over the lessor company.

The **adjustment** restricts the taxable receipt to an appropriate percentage. Except in the case of the lessor company being owned by a consortium before the sale, the appropriate percentage is determined by subtracting the relevant fraction (i.e. the interest remaining in the lessor company at the end of the relevant day) from 100%.

Where the lessor company is **owned by a consortium**, the appropriate percentage is found by deducting the relevant fraction at the end of the day from that at the start of the day. Where a consortium member leaves a consortium altogether there will be no relevant fraction at the end of the day. In this case, the taxable receipt is limited to the relevant fraction at the start of the day.

[EXAMPLE]   A Ltd is a lessor company which is a 75% subsidiary of B Ltd (and so group relief is fully available).
After the sale A Ltd is owned by a consortium, of which B Ltd is a member, and B Ltd now owns 50% of A Ltd.
B Ltd has therefore not sold all of its interest in A Ltd.
The amount of the taxable receipt is restricted to the appropriate percentage, which is 50%.

Deductible expense

82980

s 384 CTA 2010

A deductible expense of the same **amount** as the taxable receipt is treated as an expense in the new accounting period.

s 386 CTA 2010

As any **loss** arising from the expense cannot be carried back, and its use as a loss being carried forward may be limited, the legislation treats an amount equal to the sum of:
– the amount of loss deriving from the expense; and
– an amount equivalent to the rate of interest on overpaid tax applied to that amount (adjusted proportionately where the accounting period does not equal 365 days),
as a notional expense of the following period.

Where the **loss is carried forward again** in a subsequent accounting period, the amount of loss deriving from the notional expense is subject to the same calculation and carried forward again, this being repeated if necessary up to the end of the 5 year period following the relevant day.

Farming activity encompasses food production (including cultivation, breeding, rearing and keeping animals), and maintaining the land in good agricultural and environmental condition.

84000

Increasingly, farmers have sought to diversify, both in their business structures and activities, in order to stabilise their often precarious financial situation.

SECTION 1

Scope

Any farming activity carried out in the UK is treated as a trade for corporation tax purposes. Where a company **runs more than one farm** in the UK, all such activity is treated as a single trade. This includes situations in which the company:

84050
ss 36, 1270
CTA 2009

– moves from one farm to another without a break;
– gives up a portion of land; or
– takes over additional land.

However, where a company runs certain of the farms **in partnership** with another entity (rather than entirely in its own name), each partnership is treated as a separate trade.

BIM55115

> MEMO POINTS Husbandry conducted on land **outside the UK** is not within the definition of farming but will probably constitute trading, applying the usual principles (¶5000+). Any losses sustained on such an activity are still subject to restriction (¶84455+).

Definition

84055   Farming is defined as the occupation of land wholly or mainly for the **purposes** of husbandry, excluding market gardening.

Occupation

84060
BIM55055

HMRC take the view that occupation **involves**:
– activity requiring acts by the occupier as user of the property;
– physical possession and actual presence;
– a degree of permanence; and
– the conveying of a benefit to the possessor.

HMRC consider that the definition should be given a common sense **interpretation**, to include activities normally recognisable as farming such as growing crops (including short rotation coppice) and the raising of farm livestock. *Lowe v J W Ashmore Ltd* [1970]

BIM55105

    MEMO POINTS   1. **Intensive production** of livestock, which are kept entirely separate from the land (e.g. indoors) being fed entirely on purchased feed, is not farming. *Lean & Dickson v Ball* [1925], *Jones v Nuttall* [1926], *Peter Reid v CIR* [1947]

BIM55120;
s 154 FA 1995

2. **Short rotation coppice** consists of densely planted, high-yielding varieties of either willow or poplar, commonly harvested every 3 years. The roots are not disturbed and send up shoots, which are cut down to ground level and used for fuel. HMRC regard the initial cultivation of the land (spraying, ploughing, fencing, and planting of the cuttings) as a capital cost, against which Woodland Grants received (¶84345) should be matched. All subsequent costs are revenue expenses. Direct costs (such as weeding, disease prevention, harvesting and the costs of the first cut) can be carried forward and matched against subsequent receipts from the sale of the crop. Indirect costs (such as rent, maintenance of farm buildings and general management costs) should be treated in the same way, although HMRC also accept a general deduction in the farming account as overheads.
3. For details of income arising from **land exploitation** such as rents, wayleaves, and easements, see ¶14125+.

SECTION 2

Accounting for livestock

84110
BIM55410

Farm animals may be either:
– capital assets of the farm (animals retained because of their produce, such as milk or wool, or because they are of a particular pedigree); or
– trading stock, when the animals themselves are purchased and sold.

The tax treatment of farm animals recognises this dichotomy, and instead of stock, farmers may elect to treat certain of their animals as capital assets under the herd basis (¶84190+).

BIM55440

    MEMO POINTS   1. A **share** in an animal should be treated as trading stock, unless it is a production animal of a class for which the farmer has made a herd basis election (¶84200).
2. **Working horses** may be treated either as trading stock or as a fixed capital asset (when the cost of a home-bred horse added to working horses may be estimated at 85% of its current market value). Once a method of accounting has been chosen, it must be applied consistently: it is not acceptable to treat the same working horse as stock in one period and as a capital asset in another.

---

1. Trading stock

84140   The **default treatment** is for farm animals to be accounted for as trading stock. The usual principles of stock valuation apply (lower of cost and net realisable value (¶11695+)), but HMRC have also given specific guidance in relation to livestock.

Strictly, livestock should be valued on an animal by animal basis, but it is acceptable for farmers to value animals of a similar type and quality together on a global or average basis classified according to age.

BIM55410

Production cost

The production costs of getting the stock into its **condition** and location at the balance sheet date include direct and indirect costs.

84145
BIM55410

Where **grants and subsidies** are intended to cover specific expenses, only the reduced cost should be included in the stock valuation.

Type of cost	Examples
Direct costs	Price paid or insemination costs plus additional maternal feed costs in excess of maintenance Costs of rearing to the valuation date or maturity if earlier including: – feed costs including forage; – vets' fees including drugs; – drenches and other medicines; – ringing, cutting and dehorning; and – supervisory employee or contract labour costs
Indirect costs	Depreciation and maintenance of farm buildings Rent and rates General employee (including director) or contract labour Machinery costs

Deemed cost Where the **actual cost cannot be determined**, deemed cost (a specific percentage of open market value) can be used for home-bred stock, or stock acquired some time before maturity and matured on the farm. Deemed cost is not appropriate for pedigree stock or thoroughbred horses.

84150
BIM55410;
55420

The following **percentages** apply:
– cattle, 60%; and
– sheep and pigs, 75%.

Open market value should be based on the assumption that there is a willing buyer and a willing seller free from restrictions (such as DEFRA movement restrictions). It is not acceptable to treat cull value as the open market value, because that does not recognise the value of the future income stream from produce and/or progeny.

84155

HMRC prefer deemed cost to be fixed **at maturity**, although they will accept deemed cost based on open market value at each balance sheet date if that method is used consistently, although it may increase taxable profits.

> MEMO POINTS Deemed cost of **immature and unweaned** animals can be based on the open market value of animals of a similar age and type, except where the mother is accounted for via the herd basis (¶84190+) and there is a very limited market in unweaned progeny. In the latter case, the costs of producing the progeny should be carried forward to be set against the eventual sale price.

Net realisable value

In general, net realisable value should be calculated as for other types of stock, using anticipated sale proceeds based on the animal's condition at the balance sheet date, less marketing and other costs.

84160
BIM55410

However, the following should also be **taken into account**:
– grants and subsidies intended to augment the sale prices of stocks; and
– for breeding and production animals, the ancillary stream of income from the sale of their progeny and produce.

Where there are **insufficient records** for every animal, HMRC also allow the following approaches:

Type of animal	Net realisable value
Not usually sold except for slaughter at end of useful life (e.g. laying hens, breeding sows)	Consistently writing off the cost, down to anticipated cull value, on a straight line or other appropriate basis over the animal's expected productive life
Other production animals	Open market value of animals of the same kind, quality and condition based on the assumption that there is a willing buyer and a willing seller of the particular animal as a production animal at the balance sheet date

2. Herd basis

84190
ss 109–110
CTA 2009

Where a herd of animals has an enduring benefit to a company (for example a production dairy herd), it may be possible to make a herd basis election for it to be treated as a single capital asset, with the following **implications**:
– any profit on the eventual disposal of the herd is not taxable; and
– the set up costs and additions to the herd are not a deductible expense.

The election must be made early in the life of the herd (although no election can be made for the first year of trade), and once made it is irrevocable.

BIM55640

> ⌐MEMO POINTS⌐ 1. Herd in this context is a generic term, **encompassing** the terms flock, gaggle and any other collective noun relating to animals.
> 2. Whilst most **claimants** will be actively engaged in farming, the herd basis can apply to any company which keeps a herd for the purposes of a trade (such as fish breeding).
> 3. The herd basis may be used by one or both of the parties to a **share farming** agreement, where:
> – neither party has an existing herd basis election and each qualifies to make an election (for example, because this is the first time either has kept a herd of the class in question);
> – both parties already have an election in respect of a herd of the same class (the elections will extend to the jointly owned herd); or
> – only one party has an existing election and the other does not (but nevertheless qualifies to make one).
> Where both parties are on the herd basis, each is treated as having a separate herd. It is useful to convert the shares into "animal units": for instance, a 60% undivided interest in a herd of 100 animals represents 60 animal units.

84195

Comment A herd basis election gives greatest **advantage** when the market value of the herd is much greater than its cost, and the value is expected to appreciate further. This could be particularly relevant for homebred animals or pedigree stock. On disposal of the production herd, a tax free profit will result. However, if the market were to suffer a downturn, there would be no relief for a resulting loss.

Scope

84200

A **production herd** is a collection of animals of the same species kept for produce, which includes the live young and other products such as wool, eggs and milk. Items that can only be obtained by fattening or slaughtering the animal are not produce for these purposes.

A herd can consist of any **number** of animals, including just one, or even a share in an animal. Temporary additions are excluded, although an animal which is sold soon after joining the herd for reasons which could not have been anticipated at the time of acquisition can still be part of the herd.

The following table shows those animals which are able to be included in a herd for this basis.

Type of animal collection	Included within herd?
Kept for exhibition or racing	x
Working dogs	x
Dairy herds	✓
Cattle held for resale	x
Ewe flocks	✓
Sheep held for resale	x
Pigs	✓
Poultry	✓
Thoroughbred horses kept for breeding	✓
Working horses	x
Bees	✓

In general, only **mature** animals can be part of the herd. The exception to this is animals such as acclimatised hill sheep, where immature animals which are bred and reared can only be kept with the herd, with the sole intention of replacing mature animals.

84205
s 110(4) CTA 2009;
BIM55575

Immature animals are accounted for as trading stock (¶84140+) until they are old enough to join the herd.

MEMO POINTS 1. **Female** animals are deemed to be mature when they produce their first offspring, or in the case of hens, when they first lay.
2. **Male** animals are treated as mature when they are first used for breeding.
3. Where mature animals are acquired **whilst in calf**, the herd value is the acquisition cost reduced by the value of the unborn calf, and the value of the unborn calf is a trading expense.

An election applies to all animals of the same **species** kept for the same produce (otherwise known as "a herd of the same class"), whether past, present or future, and wherever maintained. For example, an election in respect of egg-laying hens applies not only to the flock owned at the time that the election is made, but also to any previous or subsequent flocks of egg-laying hens.

84210
BIM55590

The only exception is where a herd is **fully disposed of** and an interval of at least 5 years elapses before a subsequent herd of the same class is acquired. In this case, the original election lapses and the farmer may decide whether to make a new election in respect of the new herd.

EXAMPLE If a company has both a Friesian dairy herd and a Jersey dairy herd, these are of the same class. Consequently, it cannot make the election solely in respect of the Jerseys; any election must relate to all the dairy cattle.
However, where a company keeps angora goats for their wool, and another herd of goats is kept for their milk which is made into cheese, these are different classes and a separate election can be made in respect of each herd.

Consequences

The tax treatment of expenditure on, or proceeds from, any specific animal will **depend upon** when, and why, it is acquired or sold as follows:

84215

Situation	Detail	Tax treatment	Reference	Example
Initial costs of herd		Costs not deductible If the animal has been transferred from trading stock, a trading receipt must be accounted for[1]	s 112 CTA 2009	¶84220
Additions to herd	Not replacing an animal which has left the herd	Costs not deductible If the animal has been transferred from trading stock, a trading receipt must be accounted for[1]	s 113 CTA 2009	¶84220

Situation	Detail	Tax treatment	Reference	Example
Replacement	Replacing animal which has left the herd[2]	Deductible cost is restricted to the amount which would have been incurred on an animal of the same quality (i.e. the cost of replacement is allowable but not the cost of improvement)	s 114 CTA 2009	¶84225
Animal leaves herd (not substantially reducing herd size)	Sold or died and replaced by another animal	Any proceeds are taxable	s 114 CTA 2009	¶84225
	Compulsorily slaughtered and replaced by animal of lower quality	Taxable proceeds are limited to the deductible cost of the replacement	s 115 CTA 2009	
	Sold and not replaced	Profit is taxable (i.e. proceeds less cost[3])	s 116 CTA 2009	¶84230
Substantial reduction in size of herd	20% or more of the herd is disposed of within a 12 month period	If, within 5 years of the date of sale, the herd is: – replaced[4], the proceeds for the original animals will be brought into the trading account in the year in which the replacement is acquired; or – not replaced[4], no taxable proceeds or profits arise and similarly no loss is allowed	ss 117 –120 CTA 2009	¶84235
	Less than 20% of the herd is disposed of[5]	Treated as sale without replacement, so profit is taxable	s 116 CTA 2009	¶84230

Note:
1. The **receipt** should be equivalent to the cost of breeding and rearing the animal. To simplify matters, HMRC will generally accept a percentage of the open market value (¶84150+) at the time of transfer. However, if a farmer believes this to be inappropriate, HMRC will usually accept an alternative basis of valuation, such as actual cost, as long as it is consistently applied.
2. To identify whether an animal has been **replaced**, it is customary to look at the overall size of the herd at the start and the end of the period of account. HMRC accept that an animal will be treated as a replacement if it is brought into the herd within 12 months of the related disposal, even though this may be in a different accounting period. (Where an animal disposed of in one accounting period is known to have been replaced in the following accounting period, the proceeds of the disposal can be held in suspense until the second period when both adjustments can be made.) Exceptionally, replacement treatment may also be applied to animals joining the herd after the 12 month period has elapsed if the company can demonstrate that there is a causal connection between the departure of the old animal and the introduction of the new e.g. where there are insufficient homebred animals to replace unexpected disposals (perhaps resulting from injury or illness).
3. The **cost** of animals is the purchase price plus any costs incurred by the farmer in maturing the animal. If a farmer does not have records enabling him to identify the cost of the actual animals disposed of, HMRC will accept either a first in first out basis (¶11695) or a percentage of the sale proceeds (¶84150).
4. Where the **new herd is a different size** to the old herd, three scenarios are possible, either the new herd is:
a. larger than the old herd so the extra animals are treated as additions;
b. slightly smaller than the old herd and the reduction is treated as animals leaving the herd; or
c. substantially smaller than the old herd, so that part of the original herd is not replaced.
5. Although **substantial** is defined as at least 20%, depending on the circumstances, a lesser percentage may be deemed to be substantial.

Examples

84220   ## Increasing the herd

EXAMPLE   Year 1: A Ltd acquires a dairy herd of 30 mature cattle at a cost of £400 per head and 15 calves at £300 per head. A valid herd basis election is made. The entries in the accounts in respect of the herd are as follows:

Trading account				Capital account			
	No		£		No		£
Calves	15	15 × 300	4,500	Cows	30	30 × 400	12,000
Allowable trading expense			4,500	C/fwd			12,000

Year 2: A Ltd receives proceeds of £60 as a result of the death of three of the cows. The company purchases replacements of same quality at a cost of £450 each and decides to also purchase an

additional seven cows at the same price. Eight of the calves have reached maturity and are transferred into the herd. A Ltd cannot identify the cost of the calves and decides to adopt the accepted percentage of market value. For this purpose, the open market value is taken to be £350.

Trading account				Capital account			
	No		£		No		£
				B/fwd	30	30 × 400	12,000
Deaths	(3)		(60)				
Replacements 3		3 × 450	1,350				
				Additions	7	7 × 450	3,150
Transfers from stock	(8)	8 × (350 × 60%)	(1,680)		8	8 × (350 × 60%)	1,680
Trading receipt			(390)	C/fwd	45		16,830

Replacements   84225

EXAMPLE B Ltd has a flock of 100 sheep valued at £2,000 (£20 each). During the year, 25 sheep (valued at £500) are sold for £800 and replaced with another 25 sheep costing £1,000.
These transactions are both trading transactions, giving an overall deduction of £200. (1,000 – 800)
B Ltd shows the sheep as a fixed asset, and so the profit on disposal of the 25 sheep is £300. (800 – 500)
The following adjustment is made to the trading profit:

	£	£
Profit on disposal		300
Adjustment in computation: Cost of disposed animals	500	
Cost of replacements	(1,000)	
		(500)
Net effect (as above)		(200)

The herd has not changed, only the individual sheep making up the herd. The net cost of £200 is akin to the cost of maintaining the condition of the herd.

Animals sold and not replaced   84230

EXAMPLE C Ltd started its herd in 1962 with an initial purchase of 60 cows costing £100 each. Over the years the herd was maintained by regularly replacing the stock with animals of the same quality. This year, ten of the cattle are to be sold without replacement, five of which were recently bought for £450 a head. The sale proceeds were £5,500.
The profit is calculated as follows:

		£
Proceeds		5,500
Cost of cattle recently purchased	5 × 450	(2,250)
Net decrease in herd	5 × 100	(500)
Profit		2,750

Reducing the herd   84235

EXAMPLE Continuing the example at ¶84220:
Year 3: A Ltd sells 5 cattle at a price of £600 per head. It also sells three calves at £500 per head and transfers the remaining four to the herd on reaching maturity, when the market value is £525 per head.

Trading account				Capital account			
	No		£		No		£
				B/fwd	30	30 × 400	12,000
					7	7 × 450	3,150
					8	8 × (350 × 60%)	1,680
					45		16,830
Sales – cattle	(5)	5 × (600 – 400)	(1,000)	Reduction	(5)	5 × 400	(2,000)
– calves	(3)	3 × 500	(1,500)				
Transfers from stock	(4)	4 × (525 × 60%)	(1,260)	Additions	4	4 × (525 × 60%)	1,260
Trading receipt			(3,760)		44	C/fwd	16,090

Year 4: A Ltd is forced to slaughter the entire herd due to disease. Compensation is received, but the company quits farming rather than acquire a replacement herd. There is no trading entry, and the capital account is reduced to nil.

Capital account	No		£
B/fwd	25	25 × 400	10,000
	7	7 × 450	3,150
	8	8 × (350 × 60%)	1,680
Additions	4	4 × (525 × 60%)	1,260
	44	C/fwd	16,090
Disposal	(44)		(16,090)
	Nil		Nil

Note:
1. An entry in the trading account would be required in respect of compensation for any calves slaughtered, but compensation for the herd is a capital receipt and therefore not taxable.
2. If, however, A Ltd did decide to acquire a replacement herd within 5 years, the trading account would include a trading receipt equivalent to the proceeds for the slaughtered cattle less their original cost, and a trading deduction for the cost of the replacement herd.

Administration

84240

s 122 CTA 2009;
BIM55585

An election must be made in writing and specify the class of production herd to which it relates. As there is no required **format** or any need for the election to be signed, HMRC will accept accounts and tax computations which have the herd basis as their method of calculation.

For companies, the **time limit** for submitting a herd basis election is 2 years after the end of the accounting period in which the herd is acquired.

s 124 CTA 2009

Where a farmer receives **compensation for the compulsory slaughter** of animals due to disease, the time limit is extended to 2 years after the end of the accounting period in which the compensation is received. As the election is deemed to come into force at the beginning of the period of receipt, an adjustment will be required to transfer those animals from stock to the production herd, although the accounts for earlier periods will not be affected.

84245

s 122 CTA 2009

Once an election is made, it **applies from** the date that the herd is acquired. Where the trade is transferred to a new owner, the new farmer will need to make a fresh election if he wants to continue the herd basis.

The company is required to maintain adequate **records** such that any movement in the herd can be readily identified. Indeed, it is recommended that a herd account be maintained and submitted to HMRC with the tax computation and accounts.

s 123 CTA 2009

If a company **previously made a herd election**, but disposed of that herd over 5 years ago, and then subsequently acquires a new herd, the period of account in which the acquisition occurs is treated afresh, and any previous election ceases to have effect. The company can therefore choose whether to make a herd election in respect of the new herd.

SECTION 3

Special situations

84295

A farming company may have various types of income or expenses to consider, in addition to restricted relief for recurrent losses.

Summary

84300

Topic	¶¶
Grants and subsidies	¶84330+
Single payment scheme	¶84375+
Compensation from DEFRA	¶84415+
Losses	¶84455+
Milk quota	¶84495+
Sugar beet tonnage	¶84530

1. Grants and subsidies

Whether a grant received is capital or revenue should be decided by the purpose for which the grant is paid. Most farming grants will be revenue in nature.

84330
BIM55160

Recognition

HMRC take the view that the application of UK GAAP is a valid basis for determining **timing issues** (provided of course that there is no specific tax law contradicting it (¶11050+)). Where there is more than one acceptable basis, a single one should be chosen and then used consistently.

84335

HMRC will not challenge the recognition of income unless either:
- a substantial deferment of tax is potentially involved; or
- some of the income is never brought into the computation of profit.

BIM55160

Accounting for grants tends to be governed by their intended **purpose** as follows:

84340

Purpose of grant	Accounting
Non-specific	Any amount of grant which is quantifiable with reasonable accuracy is a trading receipt for the period of account when the entitlement to the grant is established[1]
To set against costs	Reduces costs in accounts Only net costs to be carried forward in stock
Subsidising sale of crop	Treated as income when crop is sold, consumed or abandoned
Note: 1. HMRC's view is that **entitlement** does not arise until the company has fulfilled the material obligations required under the particular scheme (such as by keeping an animal to the end of a specified retention period). Grants payable by instalments should be accounted for based on the information available before the financial statements are completed and signed.	

Particular types of grants

HMRC give the following **guidance** in relation to the following grants:

84345
BIM55165

Name of grant	Nature	Tax treatment
Farm woodland premium scheme[1]	Annual payments of up to £300 per hectare to compensate for lost farming profits	Farming profits
Management agreements	Payments for managing the land in a particular way	Farming profits
Environmental stewardship scheme	Farmers enter into legally binding agreements lasting 5 or 10 years to deliver certain specific environmental benefits as defined in each bespoke agreement	Recognise the income as accruing on a monthly basis over the whole period of the agreement with expenses matched

Name of grant	Nature	Tax treatment
Oilseed support scheme	Subsidises sales	Recognised as income at the time of sale, taking into account adjusting events occurring after the balance sheet date (¶11555)
Note: 1. The Forestry Commission runs a Woodland Grant Scheme which provides non-taxable grants for the establishment and maintenance of woodlands. The exploitation of commercial woodlands is exempt from corporation tax.		

s 980 CTA 2009

2. Single payment scheme

84375

Tax Bulletin Special Edition June 2005

The single payment scheme (SP) was introduced in 2005 as a result of the reform of the EU's Common Agricultural Policy. It replaced many of the previous types of agricultural grant, and is now the main subsidy available to farmers.

In order to receive the SP, a farmer must have Payment Entitlement (PE) matched against eligible land and comply with a series of standards, covering areas such as environmental, public, animal and plant health, animal welfare, and good farming/environmental practice. Unlike previous subsidies, it is not linked to production.

A comprehensive explanation of the scheme can be found at flmemo.co.uk/ctm84375 This includes HMRC's views on the correct tax and accounting treatments.

Type of income

84380

BIM55130+

The tax treatment of the subsidy income depends on the circumstances of the **recipient** as follows, although see ¶84385 where PE is accounted for as an intangible asset:

Recipient	Taxable as	Reference
Commercial farming company using land for production	Revenue trade receipt	s 36(1) CTA 2009
Company occupying land but not producing i.e. keeping land in good agricultural and environmental condition	Revenue trade receipt	s 38 CTA 2009
Not occupying e.g. letting out land for grazing	Miscellaneous income (with letting income treated appropriately)[1]	s 979 CTA 2009
Note: 1. The EU regulations specify that when PE is leased, it must be accompanied by an equivalent area of qualifying agricultural land with both assets being let from the same date and for the same period. Where agreements do not specify the rental amounts appropriate to each, it will be necessary to apply an apportionment based on market values.		

BIM55134

Recognition

84385

BIM55140

To remain **eligible for SP**, farmers do not need to hold the land for the whole of the calendar year, although they remain responsible for ensuring that the eligibility conditions are met for the entire period.

There is therefore a **choice** between recognising the income on:
– 15 May, as this is the only day on which the farmer is required to hold the land; or
– 31 December, when it is certain that the criteria have been met for the entire calendar year.

HMRC will not challenge either treatment, so long as payments are accounted for on a consistent basis.

HMRC state that where **PE** is acquired for continuing use in the business, they would expect a company to account for it as an intangible fixed asset. This includes options to acquire or sell PEs. On the disposal of PEs, a reinvestment claim into another asset may be possible. The SP income in this case would be treated as a taxable credit. For further details of the intangible asset regime, see ¶28135+.

3. Compensation from DEFRA

DEFRA requires the **slaughter of animals** which are at risk of being infected with certain diseases, and will pay compensation. As the company would show an abnormal profit in the accounting period of slaughter, HMRC allow the income to be spread equally over the next 3 accounting periods, so long as the affected animals are not (and could not be) accounted for under the herd basis (¶84200).

84415
ss 127A – 127G
CTA 2009;
BIM55180

Where the herd basis applies, compensation receipts are brought into profit only when the corresponding replacement animals join the new herd. If the company could have made a herd election but has not done so, a retrospective election is permitted.

Scope

In practice, **spreading** applies to the following types of animals:
– immature animals (followers) in a production herd;
– mature animals which do not constitute the whole, or a substantial part, of a production herd;
– animals kept for sale or slaughter e.g. store cattle; and
– flying flocks or herds.

84420
BIM55185

> MEMO POINTS 1. If the farming trade should **cease**, spreading applies up to the date of cessation.
> 2. A **flying flock or herd** usually involves cattle or sheep where animals are continually purchased or sold so that they do not generally remain in the herd or flock for a normal productive life.

Spreading

The following **amounts** can be spread, depending on the situation of the slaughtered animal:

84425
BIM55185

Situation of animal	Amount to be spread
Born or bought in a year prior to the year of slaughter	The compensation, less the amount at which the animal was valued at the beginning of the accounting period in which the slaughter took place
Born in year of slaughter [1]	25% of the compensation
Bought in year of slaughter [1]	Purchase price
Note: 1. If sufficient records do not exist to ascertain which animals were born or purchased in the year of slaughter, a reasonable estimate will be acceptable.	

EXAMPLE A Ltd has cows with the following details which are slaughtered:

Type of cow	Number	Opening stock valuation (£)	Compensation received (£)	Profit (£)
Milking	80	48,000	72,000	24,000
Followers	40	12,000	24,000	12,000
Newborns	20	-	3,600	3,600

The milking cows are subject to a herd basis election.
The followers and newborns are eligible for spreading relief as follows:
Followers (compensation less initial valuation): £12,000 (24,000 – 12,000)
Newborns £900 (3,600 @ 25%)
So a total of £12,900 is taken out of the profits in the accounting period of slaughter and £4,300 is recognised in each of the following three accounting periods.

---

4. Losses

Farming is treated as a trade, and, as with all trades, relief for losses is only available where the trade is carried out with a view to realising a profit. However, the legislation for farming takes this one step further. If a farmer incurs a loss (before taking account of capital allowan-

84455
s 48 CTA 2010

ces, including balancing charges) in the accounting period and in each of the chargeable periods which falls wholly or partly in the 5 years prior to the accounting period, relief for the current period loss will not be available against general profits of that accounting period or the preceding period. The loss can, however, be carried forward against future profits of the same trade.

However, this **restriction will not apply** where the farm:

– is part of, and ancillary to, a larger trading undertaking (such as a butcher who makes a practice of fattening bullocks for his business, or a manufacturer who grows his own raw materials (¶84460);

– is a long term venture and certain conditions are met (¶84465); or

– was set up and commenced within the 5 years prior to the beginning of the accounting period (or treated as discontinued and a new trade set up e.g. a sole trader incorporates during the 5 year period).

BIM75650

┌ *MEMO POINTS* ┐ 1. Note that the **year of commencement** is ignored so that in effect it is only when a new company has made losses for 6 years that the relief may be restricted in the 7th year.

2. A farm may validly make an **isolated profit** against which losses can be relieved. HMRC will only challenge cases of avoidance such as:

– excluding expenses from the accounts;

– recognising sales or expenses in the wrong accounting period; or

– manipulating opening or closing stock valuations.

3. The restricted loss relief rule also applies to farming carried on **outside the UK**.

Ancillary to larger trade

84460
BIM75645

Although many farms have diversified, HMRC will carefully examine any claim to ensure that the **diversified activity** has actually become the major part of the business. HMRC apply the word ancillary strictly, and they take it to mean "subservient and annexed to", implying a close operating link with, and contribution to, the larger undertaking.

HMRC give the example of a working farm being converted into a tourist attraction where the farm animals are an integral part of the attraction. In such a case, tourist income is likely to exceed traditional farm receipts, and employees will be more involved in the tourism business than their traditional farming roles.

Long term ventures

84465
s 49 CTA 2010;
BIM75640

For long term ventures, losses will not be restricted if the following apply:

a. a competent person carrying on the entire farming activities in the current year would reasonably expect **future profits** (relief will be denied where the activities could never make a profit, however efficiently they were carried out); and

b. such a person, if running the farm in the previous years, could not **reasonably have expected** the activities to become profitable until after the current year.

HMRC state that the onus is on the farmer to produce hard evidence supporting the aspiration to future profits and the circumstances causing the previous losses.

┌ *MEMO POINTS* ┐ 1. HMRC state that good **evidence** would be documents provided to a bank manager as to the viability of the farming for a farmer who did not have other resources or assets to provide security for a loan. If the company has sought advice from consultants, then such a report may be requested by HMRC.

2. A **competent person** is obviously hypothetical, but HMRC state that his expectations of the farm's potential for profit in **a.** above would probably match or exceed those of the company, given the same set of circumstances in the previous 5 years. Note that the expectation of profit could be as a result of changes to the business which may well have been recommended to the company.

3. The test in **b.** above assumes that a competent farmer had carried out the **activities** from the start of the prior period of loss, but does not set constraints about **the way they are carried on** e.g. where results have been adversely affected by excessive borrowing due to the inexperience of the company, a competent farmer would not have taken on such debt.

5. Milk quota

A milk quota allows a farmer to produce a certain **quantity** of milk from the farm in any single year.

If production **exceeds** the quota then a tax deductible superlevy may be payable, depending on the total UK production figure.

Milk quota is treated as an intangible asset for corporation tax purposes. Any amortisation charge (¶28385+) is allowable against trading profits.

84495
BIM55335

BIM55340

Disposal

Milk quota is often sold or leased.

Milk quota is treated as a chargeable asset, separate and distinct from the land to which it relates. Disposal of milk quota is therefore a chargeable disposal, although reinvestment relief may be available (¶28540+).

Payments for quota **leasing** are allowable expenses, whilst receipts for quotas leased out are trading income.

84500
BIM55315

6. Sugar beet tonnage

There is a scheme agreed between farmers and British Sugar that allows sugar beet growers to relinquish all or part of their Contract Tonnage Entitlement. The **Contract Tonnage Entitlement** is a maximum tonnage of sugar beet which can be supplied and delivered to an identified processing plant

The amounts relating to the **sale or acquisition** of Contract Tonnage Entitlement are revenue and so are taxed as receipts and expenses of the trade. Where accounts prepared under UK GAAP show the payments on the balance sheet and an amortisation charge in the profit and loss, the amortisation charge is an allowable deduction.

84530
Tax Bulletin 55

85000　Unlike a company, a partnership is not a separate legal entity (except in Scotland), and partners are therefore liable for their own actions and those of their partners. Partnerships can involve many different types of entity, most commonly individuals. A corporate partnership requires at least one company partner. In all cases, the members of the partnership, not the partnership itself, are taxable on the profits made by the partnership (i.e. the partnership is transparent). The partnership's profits and gains must therefore be attributed between the partners, and a company partner will be liable to corporation tax on its allocation.

BIM 72005　 　☐ *MEMO POINTS* ☐　1. **When deciding whether a partnership exists**, HMRC will consider the following factors:
   – a partnership agreement;
   – all of the partners having the power to bind the firm in transactions and authorise payments;
   – the business being registered as a partnership for VAT;
   – the presence of partners' names on letter headings; and
   – the partners sharing losses as well as profits.
Sharing the fruits on joint endeavours, for instance taking your share of oil from an oilfield, is not considered to indicate a partnership exists as it is not profits that are being shared.
2. **Non-resident** partners (¶85530) are taxed on the profits of the UK trade in the same way as residents.
3. For **structured finance** arrangements see ¶21915+.

4. Corporate partners of partnerships can claim **research and development** tax credits (¶78000+), even though the partnership itself cannot.
5. For **derivatives** see ¶16860.
6. For full details of partnerships **in general**, and in particular, the administrative requirements, see *Tax Memo*.

SECTION 1

Scope

There are **three main types** of partnership vehicle which are seen in the corporate arena: **85050**
- general partnership;
- limited partnership; and
- limited liability partnership.

General partnership

This is the default formation in the absence of any special action to limit the liability of any partners.   **85055**
s 1 Partnership Act
1890

Partnership is the **relation which exists between** persons carrying on business in common with a view to profit. Whilst sharing the spoils of business, partners are jointly and severally **liable** for the debts and obligations of the firm, resulting from normal activity as well as from negligence, wrongful doing etc. This liability subsists during the company's membership of the partnership, and in some cases afterwards.

> MEMO POINTS   1. **New partners** are only liable for the debts incurred after they became partners, unless they have been held out to be partners previously, or there is an express agreement to take on extra liability.
> 2. **Leaving partners** will continue to be liable for debts incurred before the date of leaving, although the partnership and creditors may agree to release them.

Limited partnership

A limited partnership is the same as in ¶85055 above, except that **certain of the partners**   **85060**
have applied for limited liability (i.e. in relation to debts and obligations) on the basis that   Limited Partnership
they only contribute capital to the business and have no management role etc.   Act 1907

A limited partnership must have at least one **general partner** who has unlimited liability, although often this would be a company, so that the shareholders would have limited liability through the usual mechanism of the company having a separate legal identity.

A limited partner can only access restricted **losses** arising from the trade of the partnership (¶85245).

Limited liability partnership

Limited liability partnerships have been available since April 2001, and must consist of at   **85065**
least two registered members. This type of entity **differs** from other types of partnership because it is incorporated and, like other types of bodies corporate, it has a separate legal **identity** from its members. A member's liability is restricted to the amount of capital in the LLP. In contrast to limited partnerships, members can be involved in the management of the LLP.

LLPs must file annual accounts and returns with Companies House. Despite its corporate identity, an LLP is taxed in the same way as other partnerships, except for minor differences in the treatment of losses (¶85245). Further, on a winding up which is either unusually prolonged, or connected with tax avoidance, the LLP itself will be subject to corporation tax on its own account.

Accounting entries

85115
FRS 9

Most companies account for a partnership interest as a joint venture: broadly, a long-term interest in a jointly controlled entity. However, the partnership may instead be considered a joint arrangement which is not an entity in its own right (JANE), or even an arrangement that is a joint venture in form but not substance.

> MEMO POINTS 1. "**Joint arrangements**" is an umbrella term covering joint ventures, joint arrangements that are not entities and arrangements that are joint ventures in form but not substance. Joint arrangements are **governed by** a formal agreement and comprise two or more investors. In practice, it can be hard to differentiate a joint venture from other types of joint arrangement. In addition, the nature of the joint arrangement may change over time.
> 2. **Full details** of all accounting requirements can be found in *Accountancy and Financial Reporting Memo*.

Joint venture

85120
FRS 9 (4)

A joint venture is **defined** as an entity in which the reporting undertaking holds an interest:
– on a long-term basis; and
– is jointly controlled by the reporting entity and one or more other venturers under a contractual arrangement.

Where an investor does not share **control** of the entity, it is merely an investment and should be accounted for as such.

> MEMO POINTS 1. A **long term interest** is defined as an interest held other than exclusively for subsequent resale, and where the business is reasonably expected to be retained for more than a year from the date of its acquisition.
> 2. **Jointly controlled** means that no one particular party alone can assume overall control of that entity. Decisions on financial and operating policy, essential to the activities, economic performance and financial position of the venture, require the consent of each venturer, usually evidenced by the joint venture agreement.

85125
FRS 9 (20)

Individual company accounts The company's partnership interest will be shown as a fixed asset investment, **valued** either at cost (less any amounts written off) or fair value.

85130
FRS 9 (21)

Consolidated financial statements An appropriate **share** of the partnership's results and net asset base should be shown in the consolidated accounts, using the gross equity method. There are particular disclosure requirements.

Joint arrangement which is not an entity (JANE)

85135

A contractual arrangement under which the constituent parties engage in joint business activities, but where those activities do not constitute a separate **business** from that of its investors is a JANE e.g. an agreement covering joint distribution or marketing.

The company should include an appropriate proportion of the partnership's profits, cash flow and net assets in its own accounts.

Joint venture in form but not substance

85140

An entity may operate through a structure that has the appearance of a joint venture, in that the participants hold a long term interest in an entity and exercise joint management, but there is no common **business activity** between the venturers.

As an application of the substance over form principle, each venturer should account directly for its share of the assets, liabilities and cash flows arising within the entity, as **stated in the agreement** governing the venture.

Ascertaining taxable income

As it has no separate legal identity, a partnership is not liable to tax, although it is obliged to submit a separate tax return. Instead, each partner is liable to tax on its share of the partnership income as summarised in the following table:

85190

Type	Scope of partnership interest	Treatment of profit share	Restrictions on losses
Company partner	Shares in both profits and losses and has an active role in running the business	Profits and losses are subject to corporation tax	No
Partner of LLP	Commercial liability is limited to the capital contributed to the partnership		Yes

A. Trading profits

Two profit computations are often required, one using income tax principles and one using corporation tax principles, as some partners will be individuals and others will be companies.

85220
ss 1259, 1260
CTA 2009

The relevant computation forms the basis of the corporate partner's share of profits.

MEMO POINTS 1. **Changes of partner** are ignored by the company provided it remains a partner both before and after the change.
2. When a company **becomes or ceases to be a partner** it is deemed to commence or discontinue a trade. However, this alone does not cause an accounting period to end.
3. For **non-resident** partners see ¶85530.

Computation

In order to calculate the company partner's share, the following **three steps** should be taken:

85225
s 38A(3) CAA 2001;
CTM 36510

Step	Overview	Action
1	Compute profits of partnership	Calculate the profits of the partnership's trade, profession or business for its accounting period as though the partnership was a company (taking the residence status of the company partner) Interest paid to partners, and other prior allocations of profit, are deductible from the taxable profits In relation to capital allowances, any partnership with at least one corporate partner is not eligible for the annual investment allowance
2	Allocate profits to company partner	The partnership's profits are apportioned in accordance with the partnership's profit sharing arrangements (which are entirely separate from the capital ratios) The corporate partner's share of profit is subject to corporation tax as a separate trade carried on by the company If the accounting periods of the partnership and the company are different, the partnership profits are apportioned between the company's own accounting periods, usually on a time basis. However, where there is a more accurate way of identifying the profits which relate to each accounting period of the company, this should be used *Marshall Hus & Partners Ltd v Bolton* [1981] Qualifying charitable donations (¶22085+) made by the partnership are apportioned to the corporate partner by reference to the accounting period in which they are paid

Step	Overview	Action
3	Tax profits as a separate trade	Where a loss arises (¶85230+) the usual loss reliefs (¶35005) will apply, including group relief where applicable Companies' losses brought forward may not be relievable against profits from partnership, unless derived from the same trade Corporation tax arising is not a debt of the partnership, but a liability of the company only

---

EXAMPLE The ABC partnership comprises A Ltd, Mr B and Mr C. All partners share profits equally. The partnership makes a trading profit of £180,000 (as computed for corporation tax purposes) for the accounting period ending on 30 June.
A Ltd's share of the profit is £60,000. (180,000 x 1/3)

Losses

85230
ss 1259, 1263,
1264 CTA 2009

As salaries and interest on capital paid to partners are treated as a prior allocation of profit made before the main division between the partners, the company may derive a loss from the partnership in a variety of **circumstances**, as shown in the following table. The basic premise is that the allocation of the partnership's profit between the partners cannot create a loss and vice versa.

Partnership result	Company's share	Treatment
Profit	Loss	Company treated as making neither a loss nor profit, as its loss is reallocated to other partners
Profit	Profit but another partner makes a loss	Loss reallocated to other partners, including company
Loss	Loss but another partner makes a profit	Profit reallocated to other partners, including company
Loss	Profit	Company treated as making neither a loss nor profit, as its profit is reallocated to other partners

85235
s 1263 CTA 2009

Reallocation When the **partnership has made a profit**, but certain of the partners have made a loss, the following formula must be used to reallocate the loss:

$$FP \times \frac{PP}{PP + TCP}$$

where:
- FP is the amount of the partnership's profit;
- PP is the amount of that partner's profits; and
- TCP is the total of the comparable amounts attributed to other partners that are profits.

EXAMPLE Mr A, Mr B and C Ltd have been in partnership for many years and share profits in the ratio 50:30:20. During the current accounting period, the adjusted profits of the partnership are £25,000. Mr A and Mr B both receive salaries of £20,000.

	Total £	Mr A £	Mr B £	C Ltd £
Salary	40,000	20,000	20,000	-
Balance (50:30:20)	(15,000)	(7,500)	(4,500)	(3,000)
	25,000	12,500	15,500	(3,000)
Reallocation of C Ltd's loss				3,000
12,500/(12,500 + 15,500) x 25,000		11,161		
12,500/(12,500 + 15,500) x 25,000			13,839	
		11,161	13,839	-

Similarly, where the **partnership has made an overall loss**, but certain of the partners have made a profit, the following formula must be used:

$$FL \times \frac{PL}{PL + TCL}$$

where:
- FL is the amount of the partnership's loss;
- PL is the amount of that partner's loss; and
- TCL is the total of the comparable amounts attributed to other partners that are losses.

Limited partners Loss relief claims by limited or non-active partners of a **trading partnership** or LLP (but not of a professional or vocational partnership, or similar type of LLP) may be restricted. The **restrictions apply** only to claims for relief against non-partnership income or gains of the partner and group relief. There are no restrictions on the relief of losses against profits of the partnership's trade.

The **cap** on the loss relief is:
- the amount of the company's capital contribution; plus
- any allocated partnership profits not received in money (or money's worth); less
- any relief already given in earlier years.

The comparison of losses and capital contributed should be carried out at the end of the company's own accounting period. So where the partnership has a different accounting period, this will require a separate balance sheet to be drawn up at the company's accounting period end.

> ┌─────────┐
> │ MEMO POINTS │ 1. A limited partner is **defined** as a company carrying on a trade as:
> └─────────┘
> **a.** a limited partner in a limited partnership (¶85060); or
> **b.** a general partner in a partnership excluding any rights to managing the trade, where the liabilities for debts etc incurred for the purposes of the trade can be discharged by a third party. This also includes overseas partners where the criteria in **b.** are met under the overseas territory's domestic law.
> 2. **Capital contribution** means:
> – the net capital contributed by the company to the partnership at the end of the company's accounting period, excluding any amounts it can withdraw if it wishes; plus
> – any accounting profits (rather than taxable profits) to which the company is entitled, but has not received.
> Contributions are **excluded** if their main purpose was to enable the partner to have access to partnership losses, or if the contribution is:
> – financed by a loan which is either on less than arm's length terms or is to be repaid by another person (or by the partnership); or
> – to be reimbursed by another person (or by the partnership).
> Where the company guarantees a loan on behalf of the partnership, this is not capital contributed.
> 3. For **limited liability partnerships** with a trade, the same mechanism applies, so that loss relief is limited to the company's contribution to the LLP at the end of the loss-making period. For this purpose, the contribution (measured at any time) is the greater of the amount:
> **a.** subscribed i.e. the amount contributed less any that the company:
> – has previously, directly or indirectly, drawn out or received back;
> – so draws out or receives back in the next 5 years, or during any time when it is a member of the LLP; or
> – is entitled to require another person to reimburse to it; and
> **b.** payable by the partner in the event of the winding up of the LLP, including any amount so payable during the next 5 years.

> ┌─────────┐
> │ EXAMPLE │ The ABC limited partnership is formed on 1 May 2011. One of the partners, A Ltd, contributes £1,000 capital. One year later, a further £4,000 contribution is made.
> └─────────┘
> The partnership losses and how these are available to A Ltd are shown below:
>
> | Year end | Partnership's total loss | Allocated to A Ltd | Capital contributed by A Ltd | Loss relief available | Balance c/f |
> |---|---|---|---|---|---|
> | | £ | £ | £ | £ | £ |
> | 30 April 2012 | 18,000 | 6,000 | 1,000 | 1,000 | 5,000 |
> | 30 April 2013 | 16,000 | 7,000 | 4,000 | 4,000 | 8,000 |
> | | | 13,000 | 5,000 | 5,000 | |

> A Ltd will need to contribute further capital of £8,000 in order to utilise the balance of losses, or wait until the partnership starts to make a profit.

B. Non-trading income

85275
ss 1262, 1265
CTA 2009

As with trading income, the partnership's non-trading income is **allocated** to corporate partners **based on** the partnership agreement (usually the income sharing ratios). For these purposes, this income is akin to a second trade.

Where the company's **accounting period does not match** that of the partnership, the amount should be time apportioned.

When a company realises **capital from the untaxed profits** of a partnership, the disguised interest rules apply (¶16120).

C. Chargeable gains

85305

As with income, any tax on chargeable gains arising from partnership assets will be assessed and charged on the partners separately.

Corporate partners are **assessed** in the accounting period in which the gain arose. The gains and losses arising from partnership assets will be aggregated with the partner's other gains and losses for the same accounting period.

Sale of assets

85310
s 59 TCGA 1992;
SP D12;
CG 27350

If the partnership itself realises a capital gain or loss, arising from the sale of an asset, or part of the business, this will be allocated to each partner based on their own particular fractional share in that asset.

The chargeable gain arising to each partner is therefore **calculated** as the difference between the:
– disposal consideration, pro-rated according to the asset sharing ratio at the date of disposal; and
– allowable expenditure, pro-rated according to the asset sharing ratio at the date of acquisition.

The **asset sharing ratio** will generally be the same as the capital profit sharing ratio, but where no such ratio is specified, the profit sharing ratio will be used. The partners may specify a particular ratio with regard to a particular asset. In the absence of a written agreement or evidence of the above tests, HMRC take the view that the assets should be treated as if they were held equally.

> MEMO POINTS For **details of other partnership situations** such as changes in partners' shares, revaluation of assets, and asset distributions see *Tax Memo*.

> EXAMPLE A Ltd, B Ltd and Mr C carry on a business in partnership.
> The asset sharing ratios are 50:30:20 respectively.
> The partnership purchases a freehold property for £600,000 and sells it several years later for £900,000.
> The gains on disposal (ignoring expenses) for each partner is computed as follows:
>
> | | A Ltd £ | B Ltd £ | Mr C £ |
> |---|---|---|---|
> | Disposal proceeds 900,000 x 50%/30%/20% | 450,000 | 270,000 | 180,000 |
> | Less: Cost 600,000 x 50%/30%/20% | (300,000) | (180,000) | (120,000) |
> | Gain before indexation | 150,000 | 90,000 | 60,000 |

Mitigation A company partner can **defer** a capital gain by rolling it over into other trading assets (¶30940+), providing the new asset is acquired within the period beginning 1 year before the disposal, and ending 3 years after it.

85315
s 152 TCGA 1992

Alternatively, capital losses may **shelter** the gain, either in the company itself or, where the partner is a member of a group, via reallocation to another group company.

s 171A TCGA 1992

Sale of partnership

If the business of the corporate partnership is sold, this may be by route of the sale of the company itself i.e. a share sale.

85320

Where the **partnership and the corporate vendor are both trading**, the substantial shareholding exemption will apply where all relevant conditions are met (¶32090+).

Sch 7AC
TCGA 1992

However, **in other cases**, a capital gain will arise, which may be sheltered by capital losses. In a group situation the gain may be reallocated to other members of the group (¶67285+).

s 171A TCGA 1992

SECTION 4

Loan relationships

As income derived from debt is treated differently depending on whether the income is assessable on an individual or company, there are special rules when a company and a partnership, of which it is a member, are involved in a money debt (¶16100).

85370

A. External loans

Overview

When all of the following **criteria** are met, any debits or credits arising from the money debt must be excluded from the computation of the company partner's profits, and treated separately:
– a trade, profession or business is carried on by persons in partnership;
– any of those persons is a company; and
– a money debt is owed by or to the partnership.

85400
s 380 CTA 2009

The debits and credits are instead computed separately for each company partner, by:
a. calculating the gross debits and credits; and
b. then apportioning them between each partner.

Gross debits and credits

In order to calculate the gross debits and credits, the company is **deemed to stand** in the shoes of the partnership, so that each of the money debts owed by, or to, the partnership is treated as owed by, or to, the company partner.

85405
s 381 CTA 2009

Where the money debt is:
– a **transaction for the lending of money** (¶16110), the company partner is treated as if it is a party to a loan relationship and calculates the debits and credits accordingly; or
– **not a transaction for the lending of money** (¶16115), the company partner can be treated as being party to a deemed loan relationship i.e. interest and exchange differences are recognised.

> EXAMPLE The ABC partnership lends £150,000 to D Ltd, at an annual interest rate of 10%. The partnership comprises Mr A, B Ltd and C Ltd.
> B Ltd and C Ltd are each treated as being the creditor in a £150,000 loan relationship. The gross credit relating to each company is £15,000. (150,000 @ 10%)

CFM 36030

Apportionment

85410
s 381 CTA 2009;
CFM 36040

Allocation to each company partner is then made **on the basis** that gross credits and debits are apportioned according to the profit share agreement.

A loan involving a connected person (¶85455) has special rules.

> EXAMPLE Continuing the example at ¶85405 above, the partners share profits in the following proportions: 20:50:30.
> Therefore, B Ltd recognises a credit of £7,500. (15,000 x 50%)
> C Ltd recognises a credit of £4,500. (15,000 x 30%)

B. Loans between partners and the partnership

85440
CFM 36050

A loan made to the partnership from a company may in fact be more of a capital contribution than a true loan.

HMRC give the following list of **factors** which should be taken into account when deciding whether a loan relationship actually exists:
– whether the partnership can repay the loan without the departure of the lender, or the dissolution of the partnership;
– whether the debt is shown in the partnership accounts as a normal creditor or as partnership capital; and
– whether the terms of the loan agreement include normal commercial rates for interest and repayment conditions.

Loan to partnership

85445

When a company partner has made a loan to the partnership, two **entries** will appear **in its accounts**:
– a creditor entry to reflect the loan made; and
– a debit entry to reflect the partner's portion of the gross credits and debits (¶85405).

The partnership and partner may be connected parties (¶85455).

> EXAMPLE The ABC partnership has received a loan of £10,000 (with interest of 10% p.a.) from C Ltd, its corporate partner. C Ltd's profit share is 30%.
> To reflect the loan made, C Ltd will show a creditor entry in its accounts of £10,000.
> However, in its capacity as partner, it will also show a debit of £300, being its share of the interest payable. (10,000 x 10% x 30%)

Loan to company partner

85450

Where the company partner borrows from the partnership, two **entries** will appear **in its accounts**:
– a debtor entry to reflect the loan made; and
– a credit entry to reflect the partner's portion of the gross credits and debits (¶85405).

The partnership and partner may be connected parties (¶85455).

Connected parties

85455
ss 383, 472
CTA 2009;
CFM 36060

A company partner will **control a partnership** if it, alone or with another connected company partner, has rights to a share of more than one half of the assets or income of the partnership. The share is determined by the partnership's profit share agreement. However, for this purpose, the term partner **excludes** a general partner in a collective investment scheme (¶16610).

One company **partner** is **connected** with another if one has control of the other, or both are under the control of the same person, at any time during the accounting period.

EXAMPLE X Ltd owns 100% of the shares in both B Ltd and C Ltd, who are members of a partnership as shown below:

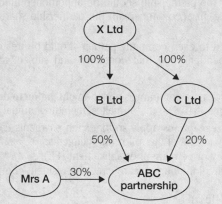

B Ltd and C Ltd are under the common control of X Ltd and are therefore connected. Together they are entitled to 70% of the partnership profits, so both B Ltd and C Ltd control the partnership.

Consequences   If the company partner and partnership are connected, the following rules apply:
– both parties must use the amortised cost basis (¶16580);
– there is no relief for impairment losses (¶16630+);
– relief for interest paid late is restricted (¶16605), and this includes situations where the company partner is a participator in the borrower (¶16610), or has a major interest (¶16610); and
– relief for relevant discounted securities is postponed (¶16685+).

85460

EXAMPLE If, in the example at ¶85455, both B Ltd and C Ltd lend £40,000 to the partnership, but £20,000 is written off in respect of both loans, the following treatment will apply:
– each company will recognise a creditor relationship in their own accounts, using the amortised cost basis;
– no impairment loss will be recognised (i.e. the £20,000 written off), so that the full amount of the loan will be shown; and
– the partnership will show a debtor relationship, and use the amortised cost basis to calculate the gross credits and debits.

SECTION 5

Particular situations

Summary

85510

Subject	¶¶
Annual interest	¶85515
Filing date	¶85525
Overseas issues	¶85530
Anti-avoidance	¶85540

Annual interest

85515 Any interest payable by the partnership should be apportioned amongst the partners, both individual and corporate, in accordance with the partnership sharing arrangements of the accounting period.

The amount apportioned to each company partner should be treated as it was a payment of interest made independently by that company, and subject to the loan relationship rules (¶85370+).

85520
ss 901, 903
ITA 2007

Subject to various exceptions, a company is under an **obligation to deduct** basic rate income tax from certain payments (¶41080+) that it makes, including annual interest.

However, the following **exceptions** apply so that such payments can be paid gross if they are made by a company to one of the following recipients:
– a UK-resident company or permanent establishment (PE);
– a partnership in which all the partners are either UK-resident companies/PEs or approved bodies;

ss 930 – 937
ITA 2007

– an approved body (¶41085); or
– a manager of a PEP or ISA.

For further details of the income deduction mechanism see ¶47115+.

Filing date of partnership return

85525
s 12AA(4), (5)
TMA 1970

A partnership consisting of:
– a **mix of individuals and companies** will have a return filing date which is the latest of the usual filing dates of any of the partners; and
– **companies only**, will have the same return filing date as its partners.

For further details of the partnership return and other administrative matters see *Tax Memo*.

> EXAMPLE The ABC partnership consists of two individuals and C Ltd.
> The partnership has an accounting period end of 30 June.
> The individuals would include the year ended 30 June 2012 in their 2012/13 self-assessment tax returns, when the last filing date is 31 January 2014.
> C Ltd has a year end of 31 December, so the year ended 30 June 2012 falls within C Ltd's accounting period ending 31 December 2012. The due date for C Ltd's CTSA return is 1 October 2013.
> So the latest filing date associated with any of the partners is 31 January 2014, and this is the due date for the partnership return.

Overseas issues

85530
CTM 36520

Non-resident partners If there is a non-resident corporate partner, a separate computation must be prepared for the non-resident, using the usual **principles** which apply to UK permanent establishments (¶92105+) i.e. only including those profits which are within the scope of UK corporation tax.

> EXAMPLE A UK partnership has two corporate members, A Ltd and B Inc (resident in the US), and profits are shared equally. The partnership's worldwide trading profits are £10,000, of which £7,500 is earned in the UK.
>
> | Step | | A Ltd £ | | B Ltd £ |
> |------|--|---------|--|---------|
> | 1 | Partnership profits assuming all partners are UK companies | 10,000 | Partnership profits assuming all partners are non-resident | 7,500 |
> | 2 | Allocate 50% to partner | 5,000 | Allocate 50% to partner | 3,750 |
> | 3 | Assessable to UK corporation tax | 5,000 | Assessable to UK corporation tax | 3,750 |

Non-resident partnership The same rules apply to the **computation of the profits** arising from a non-resident partnership as for UK partnerships.

85535
ss 1259, 1260
CTA 2009

Where a **double tax treaty exempts** the profits of a partnership, this has no effect on the UK-resident corporate partner, which still remains liable to UK corporation tax on its worldwide profits and gains. However, other double tax treaty provisions will apply.

Anti-avoidance

Where a company tries to **exploit partnership losses**, by entering into arrangements so that either:

85540
ss 959 – 961
CTA 2010

– another partner (including a connected person (¶31375)) receives a payment in respect of the company's partnership loss or profit; or
– the company itself receives a payment in respect of its loss,
special rules apply to restrict the treatment of partnership profits or losses.

Broadly, this means that any profits or losses derived from the partnership by the company are treated separately, so that the losses can only be set against partnership profits, and no other losses can be used to reduce the partnership profits allocated to the company.

CHAPTER 9

Charities and community amateur sports clubs

Charities

86000   The charities sector, or the third sector as it is often called, is a large part of the UK economy. There are estimated to be around 200,000 operating in the UK with income of over £56 billion. These charities differ hugely in size and structure, but the tax benefits available are of equal importance to them all. While there are a number of tax breaks given to charities, there are a large number of potential pitfalls that can result in the removal of the reliefs. This in turn can threaten a charity's viability.

While the exemptions have remained largely constant during recent times, there have been a number of changes in charity law and the administration in some jurisdictions in the past few years. This, along with changes in the way some charities are funded, has created a number of potential issues for all charities.

MEMO POINTS   There are also a number of **VAT reductions** that charities can also obtain. For full details of these see *VAT Memo*.

Structures

86005   There are a number of ways that a charity may be set up. Some of these are subjected to income tax rather than corporation tax, such as trusts. However, the **following** structures would potentially fall to be subject to corporation tax:
– an unincorporated association;

- a company limited by share or guarantee under the Companies Acts;
- a company registered under the Industrial and Provident Society Acts;
- statutory corporations; and
- a Charitable Incorporated Organisation (CIO).

> MEMO POINTS The **CIO** was introduced in March 2013 in England and Wales as an alternative structure intended to provide greater protection for trustees. At present there is no mechanism to convert from a charity to a CIO. In Scotland the **SCIO** was introduced in April 2011, and conversion is currently possible.

A. Eligibility for reliefs

There are four conditions set out in legislation that a body must pass in order to be eligible to claim any of the tax exemptions for charities.

86035
Sch 6 FA 2010

It must:
- be **established** for charitable purposes only;
- be **located** in the UK or an EU member state, or a country specified by statutory instrument;
- meet the **registration** condition; and
- meet the **management** condition.

> MEMO POINTS Iceland and Norway are the only two **countries specified** at present.

Charitable purposes

The following are **considered to be** charitable purposes:
- the advancement of education;
- the prevention or relief of poverty;
- the advancement of religion;
- the advancement of health or the saving of lives;
- the advancement of citizenship or community development;
- the advancement of the arts, culture, heritage or science;
- the advancement of amateur sport;
- the advancement of human rights, conflict resolution or reconciliation, or the promotion of religious or racial harmony or equality and diversity;
- the advancement of environmental protection or improvement;
- the relief of those in need by reason of youth, age, ill-health, disability, financial hardship or other disadvantage;
- the advancement of animal welfare;
- the promotion of the efficiency of the armed forces of the Crown, or the police, fire and rescue services or ambulance services; and
- any other purpose recognised as a charitable purpose under previous case law, the Recreational Charities Act 1958 or reasonably recognised as being within the spirit of charity law.

86040
s 2 Charities Act 2006

As the condition is that the body has to be established for charitable purposes only, its **constitution** must restrict it to using all of its income for its stated charitable purposes.

> MEMO POINTS 1. The Charities Act **definition** of charitable purpose is imported into the legislation but it should be noted that the Charities Act 2006 itself only applies to charities in England and Wales.
> 2. The following are also **included** within the legislation:
> - scientific research organisations;
> - the Trustees of the National Heritage Memorial Fund;
> - the Historic Buildings and Monuments Commission for England;
> - the National Endowment for Science, Technology and the Arts;
> - the Trustees of the British Museum; and
> - the Trustees of the National History Museum.
> In this case the relevant income is treated as if it is all applied for charitable purposes.

s 468, 490, 491
CTA 2010

Registration condition

86045
Sch 6 para 3
FA 2010

In order for a body to be eligible for the charities exemption it must be registered with the **appropriate regulator** for the jurisdiction in which it is established, if this is required by the relevant regulator. For bodies in England and Wales this will be the Charity Commission for England and Wales. In Scotland it will be the Office of the Scottish Charity Regulator. The position in Northern Ireland remains that charities must be registered with HMRC itself.

> MEMO POINTS   1. While the Charity Commission for **Northern Ireland** has been set up for some time it is not as yet accepting registrations due to issues with the relevant legislation.
> 2. In some jurisdictions bodies **may not be required to be registered** with the regulator. For example in England and Wales charities with income of less than £5,000 per annum will not be accepted for registration in order to simplify the administration of such charities. In such cases it is possible to register directly with HMRC.

Management condition

86050
Sch 6 paras 4, 5
FA 2010

Those who have general control and management of the charity must be considered to be fit and proper to hold that position. There is no statutory definition of fit and proper but HMRC guidance explains what it believes to be the relevant factors.

The **starting point** will be that anyone appointed is fit and proper unless HMRC holds information to the contrary. This means that so long as a body takes appropriate steps in selecting its management personnel it should assume it passes this test unless challenged by HMRC.

If it turns out that a member of the management team is **not considered to be fit and proper** HMRC has the discretion to say the body still passed the test where either:
– the manager in question had no ability to influence the charitable purposes of the charity or the application of its funds; or
– the circumstances are such that it is just and reasonable to treat the body as satisfying the condition.

> MEMO POINTS   Those that are **considered to have** general control and management will vary depending on the size of the body. For instance, in a large corporate body it will likely be the directors. However, in a smaller charity it will be the chairperson, treasurer, secretary and other members of the management committee.

86055   **Fit and proper**   While charity regulators are also interested in whether or not the management team consists of fit and proper persons, HMRC have different information available to them and as such they may decide that someone is not fit and proper for the purposes of securing the various reliefs.

Factors that may lead to HMRC deciding a manager is not fit and proper may include:
– a history of tax fraud;
– a history of other fraudulent behaviour, including misrepresentation or identity theft;
– involvement in attacks against, or abuse of, tax repayment systems; or
– being barred from acting as a charity trustee by a regulator or the Court, or being disqualified as a company director.

B. Reliefs, exemptions and restrictions

86085

Without specific exemptions charities would be subject to tax as any other business. However, there are a number of exemptions that may apply. These are **not blanket exemptions** and a charity should never assume simply because it is a charity that none of its income will be subjected to tax.

> MEMO POINTS   None of the exemptions are available for **subsidiaries** of charities unless they are charities in their own right. In this case the passing of profits via Gift Aid may be available (¶22120).

1. Reliefs and exemptions

Trading profits

Profits from a charitable trade carried on by a charitable company are not included in total profits of the company, **provided** that the profits are applied for the charitable purpose of the company only.

86115
s 478 CTA 2010

A **charitable trade** is one that is carried out:
- as part of the company's primary charitable purpose; or
- where the work relating to the trade is carried out mainly by beneficiaries of the charity.

s 479 CTA 2010

Where only **part of the trade** satisfies the above, i.e. the trade is not solely related to the company's primary purpose, it should be treated as two trades by making a just and reasonable apportionment of income and expenses.

> MEMO POINTS   This will also include **post-cessation receipts** if they would have been exempt had they been received prior to the cessation of trade.

Small trades   Profits of a trade carried on by a charity will also be exempt where:
- the **total income** from non-exempt trades and transactions that would be charged as miscellaneous profits does not exceed a given limit in an accounting period, or that at the start of the period it had a reasonable expectation it would be below the limit; and
- the **income is applied** to the charitable purposes of the company.

86120
s 480 CTA 2010

The **limit** for a 12-month accounting period is 25% of the total income for the period, with a minimum of £5,000 and a maximum of £50,000. Where the accounting period is less than 12 months in length the monetary limits will need to be pro-rated.

> MEMO POINTS   1. This also applies to **miscellaneous income** with the exception of:
> - gains from transactions in land (¶19490+); and
> - chargeable payments connected with exempt distributions (¶79160+, ¶79370+).
> 2. In looking at the **charity's expectation**, HMRC will examine a number of things including minutes of meetings at which the expectations were considered, copies of cash flow forecasts, business plans and earlier year's accounts.

s 481 CTA 2010

Small scale fundraising events   The profits from certain events can also be exempted from tax **provided**:
- the event is organised for charitable purposes;
- the primary purpose of the event is the raising of money;
- the event is promoted as being for the purpose of raising funds;
- the profits are applied to charitable purposes or are transferred to a charity; and
- there are no more than 15 events of the same kind in the same location during the year.

86125
s 483 CTA 2010

This is intended to cover **such events** as fairs, jumble sales, horticultural shows, discos and dinner dances. As the exemption covers events it is limited to irregular activities as opposed to something like running a shop or bar.

> MEMO POINTS   1. This exemption also extends to **voluntary organisations**.
> 2. The **15-event limit** does not apply to events that raise less than £1,000 per week, such as coffee mornings. However, it should be noted that such an activity may constitute a trade if it is sufficiently regular. If the £1,000 limit is breached in a week all of the potentially small scale activities in that week will not qualify for this exemption. The limit is intended to ensure that there is no distortion of competition with non-charitable organisations carrying out similar activities.

Lotteries

Charities may use a lottery to raise funds during the year. Where the proceeds are applied for charitable purposes the funds raised will be exempt from tax **provided** it is:
- considered an exempt lottery under the Gambling Act 2005; or
- promoted in accordance with a lottery operating licence under the same Act.

86130
s 484 CTA 2010

> MEMO POINTS   For lotteries in **Northern Ireland** the lottery must be promoted and conducted in accordance with the Betting, Gaming, Lotteries and Amusements (Northern Ireland) Order 1985.

Property income

86135
s 485 CTA 2010

Income from property, whether it falls to be treated as property income or as trading income (¶19170) will be exempt if the right, estate, income or land from which the income arises is vested in someone for charitable purposes, where it is applied for charitable purposes.

This is also extended to distributions from **REITs** (¶19635) provided the shares are held for charitable purposes.

Investment income

86140
ss 486 CTA 2010

Often a large proportion of a charity's income will be from investments it owns. Such income will be exempt from tax where it is applied for charitable purposes and it **represents**:
– non-trading profits from a loan relationship (¶16050+);
– a dividend or other distribution from a company (¶18000+); or
– a distribution from an unauthorised unit trust.

s 487 CTA 2010

MEMO POINTS This is **further extended** to public revenue dividends (being sums received that are paid out by the Government) where the income is only applied for the repair of a cathedral, college, church, chapel or any other building that is used solely for divine worship.

Estate income

86145
s 489 CTA 2010

Where a charity receives income from an estate that would be taxable it will be exempted where the income is applied for charitable purposes.

Capital gains

86150
s 256 TCGA 1992

It is not unusual for a charity to make a capital gain. Such a gain will be exempt from tax where the proceeds are applied for charitable purposes.

If a **calculation of a gain is required** due to the charity incurring non-charitable expenditure (¶86185+) care should be taken in establishing the asset's base cost. Where an asset has been gifted to the charity it is likely that the base cost will be set at the amount at which the donor was regarded as having incurred no gain or loss (¶31280).

---

2. Restrictions

86180

As the **intention** of the exemptions is to ensure that charities retain funds to be able to further their charitable purposes the tax free element will be restricted where the charity does not apply its exempt income accordingly.

Non-charitable expenditure

86185
s 496 CTA 2010

The restriction will **only apply** where:
– the charity incurs non-charitable expenditure in an accounting period; and
– it has income that is exempted in that period under any of the above headings.

Where the non-qualifying expenditure **exceeds** the exempt income, the amount that is charged to tax is limited to the expenditure.

The **definition** of non-charitable expenditure is wide to include a number of items that may not be immediately obvious. It is defined as:
– any expenditure that is not incurred for charitable purposes only, unless it is taken into account in calculating the profits or losses of any business carried out, or miscellaneous transaction entered into, by the charity;
– any loss incurred in a trade other than a charitable trade (or one that qualifies under the small trade, lottery or fundraising exemptions);
– any property business loss, where, if a profit had been made, it would not have qualified for exemption;

– any loss arising on a miscellaneous transaction entered into otherwise than in the course of carrying out its charitable purpose;
– amounts invested in an accounting period in an investment that is not an approved charitable investment; and
– amounts lent in an accounting period that do not represent an investment or an approved charitable loan.

MEMO POINTS   1. **Approved charitable investments** are: s511CTA2010
– investment in securities issued (or guaranteed) by the government of any EU member state;
– investment in securities issued (or guaranteed) by the government of any other territory (or part of one), an international entity acting as a public authority or whose role is recognised by an international treaty (and organisations like them), a building society, a mutual credit institution, an open-ended investment company, or company where they are listed;
– any investments in a common investment or deposit fund established under the various Charities Acts (or a similar fund where the fund is set up for the exclusive benefit of charities);
– any interest in land, other than that held as security for a debt;
– bills, certificates of tax deposits, savings certificates and tax reserve certificates issued by the UK government;
– Northern Irish Treasury Bills;
– units in a unit trust scheme;
– a deposit with a bank that receives a commercial rate of return and is not part of an arrangement involving a loan to another party by the bank;
– a deposit with the National Savings Bank, a building society or mutual credit institution;
– certificates of deposit; and
– any other investment that an HMRC officer considers, on application by the company, to be a suitable investment for the benefit of the charity.
2. **Approved charitable loans** are loans that are not considered to be investments and the loan: s511CTA2010
– is made to another charity for charitable purposes only;
– is made to a beneficiary in the course of carrying out the charity's purpose;
– is a deposit in a current account with a bank where there is no arrangement involving a loan to another party; and
– satisfies an HMRC officer, on application by the company, that it is made for the benefit of the charity and not for the avoidance of tax.
3. Where a non-qualifying investment is **realised or repaid**, either in whole or part, in the period in which it is made, no further restriction will be applied where this sum is then used to make a further non-qualifying loan. This is intended to avoid double counting the same sum.

Excess non-qualifying expenditure   A charity may postpone non-charitable expenditure from a period where it has substantial exempt income to another period, where there is little such income, in order to limit the amount of the expenditure that becomes taxable. In order to combat such a move **any excess** has to be carried back to the previous year, and then it is treated as arising in that year instead. This will then amend the tax position for that year. If this results in an excess in that year it is then carried back to the year prior to that one. This continues but **only as far back as** any periods that end within 6 years of the period in which the expenditure was actually incurred.   **86190**

EXAMPLE   A charity has exempted income as follows:

Year ended 30 April 2013	£5,000
Year ended 30 April 2012	£20,000
Year ended 30 April 2011	£25,000

The charity makes a non-qualifying investment during the year ended 30 April 2013 of £40,000. This will result in the following amounts being charged to tax:

Year ended 30 April 2013	£5,000
Year ended 30 April 2012	£20,000
Year ended 30 April 2011	£15,000

The non-qualifying expenditure extinguishes the exemption in full for the years ended 30 April 2013 and 2012. It will only eliminate part of the exemption in the year ended 30 April 2011. In order to effect this the two earlier years will have to be amended to recover the tax now due.

C. Administration

86220   In order to use any of the exemptions a **claim** has to be made by the charity. While there are provisions for this to be done as a stand-alone claim at any time up to the normal time limit (¶46425), the claim will almost certainly be made via the corporation tax return on the supplementary form CT600E. This will ensure that tax is not paid needlessly, rather than having to pay it and reclaim it on a stand-alone claim.

The details on any given return are subject to the usual powers of **enquiry** by HMRC (¶50415+) and the contents of a return may mean that HMRC may not issue a **notice to file** (¶46110) for a number of years. If HMRC do not require the charity to file a return they will advise by letter when the next review will be carried out.

However, if the **charity has non-qualifying expenditure** in a period, or is subject to tax on income arising, it is still obliged to notify HMRC of this.

SECTION 2

Community amateur sports clubs

Background

86270   Since April 2002, it has been possible for a community amateur sports club (CASC) to gain a number of exemptions from tax on its profits where it satisfies certain criteria, and where the club is **established** in an EU member state (or a territory that is approved for this purpose).

Conditions

86275
s 658 CTA 2010

The club must be:
– **registered** with HMRC; and
– under the **management and control** of people HMRC deem to be fit and proper (¶86055).

Further, it must, by virtue of its constitution, be:
– **open to all**, without discrimination, and at a price that does not exclude or pose a significant obstacle to participation;
– organised on an **amateur basis**; and
– in existence for a qualifying purpose as its main purpose (i.e. the provision of facilities for, and promotion of the participation in, one or more eligible sports).

> MEMO POINTS   A club is **run on an amateur basis** where:
> – any surplus funds have to be reinvested in the club with no provision for funds or assets to be distributed to the members or third parties (although donations to other CASCs or charities are within the rules);
> – it is only used to provide members and guests with the normal benefits of a members' sports club; and
> – upon dissolution any surplus funds which are available must be used for an approved purpose, being the purposes of the governing body of the sport involved, another CASC or a charity.

Available exemptions

86280
ss 662 – 665A
CTA 2010

Where the total **trading income** of a CASC, for a 12-month period (before allowing for deductions for expenses) does not exceed £30,000, and it applies the profits towards achieving its qualifying purpose, then the trading income will be exempt. There is a similar exemption for **property income** (where the maximum income is £20,000).

Finally, exemptions exist for **interest income**, **gift aid income** and **chargeable gains**, without limit, provided that the funds are applied for the purposes of the club. In order to secure any of these exemptions, a **claim** must be made within 4 years of the end of the accounting period.

> MEMO POINTS Where the **period is less than 12 months**, or where the club has been registered as a CASC for less than a 12-month period, the limits are proportionately reduced. Where it has been **registered for less than the full period**, only the amounts attributable to that period may be exempted; the remainder will be subject to tax in the usual way.

Withdrawal of exemptions

Any of the available exemptions can be withdrawn where the club incurs expenditure on anything other than a qualifying purpose during a period. Where this occurs, the exempt amount will be reduced by:

86285
s 666 CTA 2010

$$RIRG \times \frac{NQE}{IRCG}$$

where:
- RIRG is the exempt amount;
- NQE is the expenditure on purposes which do not qualify for relief; and
- IRCG is the total of the income and gains made in the year.

If the **expenditure exceeds the income and gains for the year**, the entire exemption is withdrawn in that year, with any surplus being carried back to earlier periods and applied using the above formula. This exercise can only continue until either the expenditure has been exhausted, or there are no more accounting periods ending within the period of 6 years from the end of the period in which the expenditure is incurred.

Change of use of assets

Where an asset, **previously used for a qualifying purpose**, is put to another purpose which does not qualify (without disposing of it), the club will be deemed to have disposed of it and immediately reacquired it at its market value at that date. Any gain arising on this will be subject to tax as normal (¶30050+) and not be able to benefit from the usual exemption for capital gains, as there will be no proceeds to apply for a qualifying purpose.

86290
s 669 CTA 2010

> MEMO POINTS This will also be the case where the club **ceases to qualify as a CASC**.

PART 12

Cross-border issues

Cross-border issues
Summary

The numbers cross-refer to paragraphs.

CHAPTER 1

Investing overseas

90000 Even small companies are now looking further afield in the pursuit of profits and new trading opportunities, which have been greatly facilitated by the worldwide web.

At the moment, UK resident companies with overseas income must ensure they comply with a UK tax system which is in a state of flux, particularly with regard to certain exemptions (including the transitional phase of the controlled foreign companies regime which potentially applies to interests of at least 25% in overseas investments).

Whereas overseas income has historically been taxable in the UK with a credit for foreign tax paid, the UK tax system is moving to a more territorial system of taxation based on exemption of foreign income.

Comment It is essential that any business obtains proper tax advice early on in relation to any plans for overseas expansion.

SECTION 1

Scope

Residency

90050 It is most important to ascertain the residence of the parties involved in any overseas transaction, and for this purpose, the relevant double tax treaty should be consulted (¶90055), which should ensure that companies are only **liable to tax** in one territory (i.e. treated as resident in one, and non-resident in the other). In cases where a company could be treated as resident in both territories, there is usually a tie-breaker clause which will determine its residence.

For UK residency issues see ¶2030+.

Double tax agreements

90055 The following table shows the countries with which the UK has concluded an agreement (and where applicable the statutory reference for the most recent treaty), excluding those dealing with only shipping or air transport. For up-to-date details of treaties currently in force, see HMRC's website at flmemo.co.uk/ctm90055.

Country	Reference (SI)	Country	Reference (SI)
Albania [4]		Latvia	1996/3167
Anguilla	2010/2677	Liechtenstein	2012/3077
Antigua & Barbuda	2011/1075	Lesotho	1997/2986
Argentina	1997/1777	Liberia	2011/2434
Armenia [4]		Libya	2010/243
Aruba	2011/2435	Lithuania	2001/3925
Australia	2003/3199	Luxembourg	1968/1100
Austria	1970/1947	Macedonia [2]	1981/1815
Azerbaijan	1995/762	Malawi	1956/619
Bangladesh	1980/708	Malaysia	1997/2987
Bahamas	2010/2684	Malta	1995/763
Bahrain	2012/3075	Mauritius	1981/1121 2011/2442
Barbados	2012/3076	Mexico	1994/3212
Belarus [1]	1986/224	Moldova	2008/1795
Belgium	1987/2053	Mongolia	1996/2598
Belize	2011/1685	Montenegro [2]	1981/1815

Country	Reference (SI)	Country	Reference (SI)
Bermuda	2008/1789	Montserrat	2011/1083
Bolivia	1995/2707	Morocco	1991/2881
Bosnia-Herzegovina[2]	1981/1815	Namibia	1967/2788
Botswana	2006/1925	Netherlands	2009/227
British Virgin Islands	2009/3013	Netherlands Antilles[5]	
Brunei	1950/1977	New Zealand	1984/365
Bulgaria	1987/2054	Nigeria	1987/2057
Burma (Myanmar)	1952/751	Norway[4]	2000/3247
Canada	1980/709	Oman	1998/2568
Cayman Islands	2010/2973	Pakistan	1987/2058
Chile	2003/3200	Panama[4]	
China[4]	1984/1826	Papua New Guinea	1991/2882
Croatia[2]	1981/1815	Philippines	1978/184
Cyprus	1975/425	Poland	1978/282
Czech Republic[3]	1991/2876	Portugal	1969/599
Denmark	1980/1960	Qatar	2010/241
Dominica[4]	2011/1686	Romania	1977/57
Egypt	1980/1091	Russia	1994/3213
Estonia	1994/3207	St Kitts & Nevis	2011/1077
Ethiopia	2011/2725	St Lucia	2011/1076
Falkland Islands	1997/2985	St Vincent	2011/1078
Faroes	2007/3469	San Marino	2011/1688
Fiji	1976/1342	Saudi Arabia	2008/1770
Finland	1970/153	Serbia[2]	1981/1815
France	2009/226	Sierra Leone	1947/2873
Gambia	1980/1963	Singapore[5]	1997/2988
Georgia	2004/3325	Slovak Republic[3]	1991/2876
Germany	2010/2975	Slovenia[2]	2008/1796
Ghana	1993/1800	Solomon Islands	1950/748
Gibraltar	2010/2680	South Africa	2002/3138 2011/2441
Greece	1954/142	Spain[4]	1976/1919
Grenada	2011/1687	Sri Lanka	1980/713
Guernsey	1952/1215	Sudan	1977/1719
Guyana	1992/3207	Swaziland	1969/380
Hong Kong	2010/2974	Sweden	1984/366
Hungary	2011/2726	Switzerland	1978/1408
Iceland	1991/2879	Taiwan	2002/3137
India	1993/1801	Tajikistan[1]	1986/224
Indonesia	1994/769	Thailand	1981/1546
Ireland	1976/2151	Trinidad & Tobago	1983/1903
Isle of Man	1955/1205	Tunisia	1984/133
Israel	1963/616	Turkey	1988/932
Italy	1990/2590	Turkmenistan[1]	1986/224
Ivory Coast	1987/169	Tuvalu	1950/750
Jamaica	1973/1329	Turks & Caicos Islands	2010/2679
Japan	2006/1924	Uganda	1993/1802

Country	Reference (SI)	Country	Reference (SI)
Jersey	1952/1216	Ukraine	1993/1803
Jordan	2001/3924	United States of America	2002/2848
Kazakhstan	1994/3211	Uzbekistan	1994/770
Kenya	1977/1299	Venezuela	1996/2599
Kiribati and Tuvalu	1950/750	Vietnam	1994/3216
Korea	1996/3168	Zambia	1972/1721
Kuwait	1999/2036	Zimbabwe	1982/1842

Note:
1. Formerly part of the USSR, and the convention with the USSR published in SI 1986/224 is deemed to apply.
2. Formerly part of Yugoslavia, and the convention with Yugoslavia, published in SI 1981/1815 is deemed to apply.
3. Formerly part of Czechoslovakia, and the convention with Czechoslovakia, published in SI 1991/2876 is deemed to apply.
4. A new double taxation treaty has been signed but has not yet come into force.
5. A new Protocol has recently been signed but has not yet entered into force.

UK-resident company

90060   UK-resident companies are **liable** to UK corporation tax on:
- all profits and income, whatever the source; and
- all gains, wherever the asset giving rise to the gain is located,

whether the income/proceeds are remitted to the UK or not. Where income cannot be remitted to the UK because of third party action see ¶90210.

For non-resident companies with UK income see ¶92000.

SECTION 2

Overseas branches

90110   Overseas branch profits are usually subject to tax in both territories i.e. where the branch is located and also in the UK.

Subject to an election for exemption (¶90160), foreign branch profits are subject to UK taxation with a credit for foreign tax. The credit cannot reduce the UK tax liability on that income below nil, so some foreign tax may not be relieved. There is also a mechanism for relief where the UK company is loss-making.

Trading income of a UK trade derived from overseas is treated as part of the UK trading profits.

Comment   Although the strictly technical term for a branch is **permanent establishment**, in most cases the terms are interchangeable. A company has a permanent establishment when it trades through a branch or other fixed place of business, or through an agent (excluding an independent agent). For further details see ¶92140.

---

1. Trading activity

90140   The **profit** from an overseas trade is **calculated** using the same rules as for UK trades (¶14000), the net foreign profits representing the gross foreign income less direct expenses, attributable to earning that income, and a reasonable proportion of the indirect expenses.

The terms of any relevant **double tax treaty** (¶90055) may contain rules for the attribution of profits to a permanent establishment and to the operation of the arm's length principle, which will govern the assessment of the overseas branch to tax in the territory where it is operating. For the attribution rules in the context of a UK branch (which mirrors the requirements of the OECD Model Tax Convention) see ¶92285.

MEMO POINTS 1. For the translation of **foreign currency** amounts into sterling for the purposes of the CTSA return see ¶17170.
2. For **overseas letting** see ¶90345.
3. For **loan relationships** see ¶90345.

2. Exemption

For accounting periods commencing on or after 19 July 2011, an irrevocable election is available to certain companies to exempt profits from overseas permanent establishments. This puts the taxation of foreign branch profits on a similar footing to the taxation of dividends received from foreign subsidiaries (¶90290).

90160
ss 18A, 18F
CTA 2009

MEMO POINTS Prior to **1 April 2013** the company also had to be UK-resident.

Exclusions

The following companies are excluded:
– companies whose main activity is **investment business**;
– **insurance** companies;
– companies where the branch is a **lessor** of plant in respect of which capital allowances have been claimed;
– **close companies** whose profits are derived from chargeable gains (¶76040); and
– those undertaking **international shipping and air transport**.

90165
ss 18P, 18Q
CTA 2009

A **transaction** between an overseas branch and a UK resident, which would have required the UK resident to withhold tax, for which no refund would apply under the applicable double tax treaty, is also excluded.

s 18D CTA 2009

Effect of election

When the election is made (which **applies** from the date specified and then for all future accounting periods), the foreign permanent establishments amount (including gains (¶90175)) is not subject to UK corporation tax. As the profits and gains are not taxable, no relief is given for any **net loss** that may arise. Likewise, no relief is available for foreign tax suffered on those profits.

90170

Note that it is possible to make an election before a company has any foreign permanent establishments.

MEMO POINTS 1. An election can be made in an **accounting period** so long as the company has carried on business in a territory outside the UK through a permanent establishment for at least part of it. It can only be **withdrawn** before the start of the first accounting period to which it relates.
2. **Transitional rules** apply in the case of overseas branches that have generated **more losses than profits** in the 6 years prior to the election being made, so that branch profits are only exempt when the losses have been used up (i.e. matched by subsequent profits in the overseas territory. For this purpose any sideways relief of foreign losses set off against UK profits is ignored). For cumulative branch losses in any one territory of at least £50 million the 6-year period is extended back indefinitely (although not beyond 6 years prior to the commencement of the regime, so that this rule will have greater effect for companies making elections in future years). However, it is possible to stream separately a particular territory whose foreign branches have losses carried forward from the previous 6 years, so that branches in profitable territories can be exempt from when the election is actually made.

s 18F CTA 2009

ss 18J – 18N
CTA 2009

Foreign permanent establishments amount

The foreign permanent establishments amount is the **aggregate** of the relevant profits less the relevant losses amount for each territory where the company carries on business through a permanent establishment.

90175
s 18A CTA 2009

The profits/losses will be determined as follows, so that where there is:
– a **double tax treaty** with the overseas territory which contains a non-discrimination article, the exempt income will be based on the UK measure of profits of the permanent establishment that are taxable by the other territory in accordance with the double tax treaty; or

– **no bilateral double tax treaty**, the principles of the OECD Model Tax Convention will be applied in determining the amount of overseas profits to be exempted.

s 18B CTA 2009

⌐*MEMO POINTS*¬ 1. **Chargeable gains** or allowable losses realised on assets held by the branch are included within the exempt amount, although an adjustment will be required where the gain is not totally attributable to the branch e.g. where the asset has not been held by the branch for the entirety of the company's ownership period.

s 18C CTA 2009

2. For **capital allowances** purposes, notional allowances or charges are required to be taken into account i.e. the branch is deemed to acquire the assets at tax written down value, and the notional allowances are calculated in each accounting period by applying the usual rules (¶25490).

3. The **OECD Model Tax Convention** contains provisions for resolving the commonly encountered problems of international juridical double taxation (i.e. two or more territories taxing the same income at the same time), which is perceived to be an obstacle to the development of economic co-operation between countries. For further details see flmemo.co.uk/ctm90175.

Anti-avoidance

90180
ss 18G, 18H
CTA 2009

Anti-avoidance provisions apply to stop the diversion of income to an exempt foreign branch, although the following situations are **outside the scope** of these rules:
– the territory in which the branch is located does not charge a lower level of tax i.e. less than 75% of the equivalent UK tax (¶90610);
– the company's branches which are located within the same territory together do not have profits of £200,000 or more; or
– the branch satisfies a motive test.

s 18I CTA 2009

A just and reasonable reduction of the amount of the exempted branch profits will apply where the foreign branch has entered into **one or more transactions** which have essentially achieved a reduction in UK tax, but the branch does not exist for the main reason of reducing UK tax.

⌐*MEMO POINTS*¬ 1. The **motive test** is assumed to be met in the company's first accounting period after making the election so long as the company:
– carried on business through the branch throughout the 12 months before making the election;
– has not entered into any transactions with UK residents with a main purpose of achieving a more than minimal reduction in UK tax (see ¶90875 for how to interpret this kind of rule);
– has not undertaken a major change in the nature or conduct of the business (¶60260) in the period running from 12 months prior to the election being made to the end of the first accounting period within the regime; and
– does not enjoy more than a 10% increase in the gross income of the branch, comparing the first period in the regime with the previous period.
In addition, no asset attributable to the branch must be previously owned, or part of its business carried on, by a CFC which has previously been subject to an apportionment (¶90555).

2. To ensure that these rules **reflect changes in the controlled foreign companies** regime (¶90555+) the anti-avoidance rules have been amended for accounting periods beginning on or after 1 April 2013. In essence, these provisions ensure that any profits that would pass through the CFC gateway test (¶91270+) will be considered to have been diverted and will not be included in the calculation of the profit of the overseas branch but of the UK company. The exemptions detailed at (¶91210) will also apply in order to reduce the diverted amount.

3. Income that cannot be remitted to the UK

90210
ss 1274 – 1278
CTA 2009

Relief may be available in certain specified circumstances for overseas income that cannot be remitted to the UK **due to the following reasons**:
– the remittance is prevented by the laws or the government of the overseas territory; or
– it is not possible to obtain foreign currency in that territory.

Relief is not available if the company has been able to convert the amounts into another currency outside that territory, or an Export Credit Guarantee Department (ECGD) payment has been made.

Otherwise, the assessable income for an accounting period is **reduced** by the amount that cannot be remitted to the UK. Where the income subsequently becomes remittable an amount becomes subject to tax (as measured at the date that the income ceases to be unremittable) in the accounting period in which the restriction is lifted. A claim for relief must be made within 2 years of the end of the accounting period in which the income arises.

> MEMO POINTS 1. Where the income becomes remittable, but the company has **permanently ceased to trade** etc in the meantime, it will be treated as a post-cessation receipt.
> 2. HMRC may allow **tax** on unremittable income or gains tax to **remain uncollected**, without payment of interest.

s 92 TMA 1970

SECTION 3

Overseas subsidiaries

Although overseas income is taxable whatever its territory of source, overseas dividends received are exempt if they satisfy certain conditions.

90260

Companies who control at least 25% of an overseas company must also consider the controlled foreign company rules at ¶90555.

A. Dividends received

The taxation of distributions received by UK companies fundamentally changed from 1 July 2009, so that virtually all distributions received by UK-resident companies (i.e. from both UK and non-UK companies) are exempt from UK corporation tax (¶18325). However, exempt dividends (excluding intra-group dividends) are still treated as franked investment income (¶18330).

90290

While this means that no UK corporation tax is payable in respect of the dividends, there will no longer be a credit for foreign tax suffered. As most foreign dividends will be received under deduction of withholding tax, UK companies should examine the terms of any relevant double tax treaty (¶90055) carefully to ensure that any reduced rate of foreign withholding tax available under the treaty is being applied.

Non-exempt dividends

Where a dividend does not fulfil the conditions for one of the exemptions the gross **amount** of the dividend is subject to UK corporation tax, and double **tax relief** is available for the foreign tax paid.

90295

Irrespective of the level of shareholding relief is available for withholding tax on all dividends paid to the UK.

Where the company **owns at least 10%** of the ordinary share capital of the paying company relief is also available for underlying tax, unless a tax deduction in respect of the dividend has been given in another territory (i.e. because that jurisdiction treats the payment as interest).

ss 57(3), 63 TIOPA 2010

> MEMO POINTS For the translation of **foreign currency** amounts into sterling for the purposes of the CTSA return see ¶17170.

Withholding tax

Withholding tax is the tax **deducted** at source by the payer of the dividend and, therefore, is directly suffered by the recipient.

90300
s 13 TIOPA 2010

INTM 162060

A claim to double tax relief will need to be **evidenced by** documents such as a foreign notice of assessment, evidence of foreign tax deducted etc.

The relief will be the lower of the foreign tax suffered and the mainstream rate of UK corporation tax (¶90480).

Underlying tax

90305
s 59 TIOPA 2010

The rate of underlying tax relating to a foreign dividend is **computed** by using the following formula:

$$\frac{\text{Actual tax paid} \times 100}{\text{Actual tax paid} + \text{Relevant profits}}$$

where:
– the actual tax paid is the tax paid in the territory by the overseas company paying the dividend in the accounting period to which the dividend relates. A company can specify the accounting period to which a dividend relates, but cannot specify the profits out of which the dividend was paid; and
– the relevant profits are the profits available for distribution as shown in the overseas company's accounts (usually for the last accounting period ending before the payment of the dividend), including capital profits that have been credited to capital reserves, but excluding provisions, bad debts or contingencies other than as required to be made under the foreign territory's law. In cases of avoidance, where the recipient is not a small company (¶18385), the profits relating to the avoidance activity are the relevant profits.

90310
s 58 TIOPA 2010

Mixer cap The mixer cap **applies only to** the underlying tax, and **restricts** the amount relieved where the underlying tax exceeds the mainstream tax rate in force when the dividend is received. The mixer cap is **computed** using the following formula:

$$(D + PA) \times M\%$$

where:
– D is the dividend received, including any withholding tax;
– PA is the amount of tax attributed to the dividend; and
– M% is the rate of corporation tax applying in the UK when the dividend is paid.

Although the mixer cap does not apply to withholding tax, where the **dividend has passed through an intermediate company** it should be noted that withholding tax then becomes underlying tax on the dividend paid to the UK company, and is therefore subject to the mixer cap.

EXAMPLE The ABCD group comprises a UK holding company, Company A, with an intermediate holding company in Belgium, Company B, which owns 100% of two subsidiaries located in Germany, Companies C and D.
Company C pays a dividend of 80 (with an underlying tax rate of 20%) and Company D pays a dividend of 70 (with an underlying tax rate of 30%). Company B then pays a dividend of 140 to Company A.
The mixer cap will apply as follows:

Dividend	Tax attributable	Mixer cap	Credit allowable to UK parent
C to B	20	$(80 + 20) \times 24\% = 24$	20
D to B	30	$(70 + 30) \times 24\% = 24$	24
			44

The total underlying tax available to Company A is therefore restricted to 44 and the excess underlying tax of 6 is lost. (30 – 24)

90315
s 71 TIOPA 2010

The mixer cap will generally not apply to **two companies resident in the same territory** if they are taxed in that territory on a consolidated basis. The companies will be treated as a single entity with aggregated profits, losses and tax.

A consolidated group of companies which is resident overseas has the following results:

	Company E	Company F	Total
Accounting profits before domestic tax	60,000	120,000	180,000
Foreign tax @ 30%	(18,000)	(36,000)	(54,000)
Local tax	(4,000)	(5,000)	(9,000)
Accounting profit after tax	38,000	79,000	117,000

Total tax paid is 63,000. (54,000 + 9,000)
If a full dividend was paid to its UK parent, the underlying tax would be calculated as follows:

	Company E	Company F	Total
Relevant profits	38,000	79,000	117,000
Tax paid $\frac{38,000}{117,000} \times 63,000, \frac{79,000}{117,000} \times 63,000$	20,462	42,538	63,000
Underlying tax rate $\frac{63,000 \times 100}{(117,000 + 63,000)}$			35%

As the underlying rate is more than 24%, the mixer cap will apply to restrict the amount of underlying tax relief in the UK.

B. Other income

For interest and royalties two different regimes exist depending on whether or not the transaction is wholly carried out inside the EU.

90345

MEMO POINTS 1. Income from **overseas property letting** is also taxable in the UK, subject to double taxation relief and the provisions of double tax treaties. Profits on overseas rental properties are computed for UK tax purposes using the same rules as for UK property (¶19105).
2. Profits or losses arising from overseas **loan relationships** are treated in the same way as UK source loan relationships (¶16050). However, tax may need to be withheld on payments of interest.
3. For **intangible assets** see ¶28775.

1. Both parties in the EU

The European Union Interest and Royalties Directive has as its objective the achievement of equal treatment of domestic and cross-border interest and royalty payments within the EU, and to eliminate double taxation and double non-taxation of cross-border payments.

90375
EC Directive
2003/49

Where the terms of the Directive are not met, interest and royalties will be subject to deduction of tax at source.

Exemption

Interest or patent royalty payments between EU companies are exempt from income tax if the following **conditions** are satisfied:
– the recipient and paying company are 25% associates;
– the paying company is either a UK company or a UK permanent establishment of an EU company; and
– the recipient company is an EU company (and not a UK or non-EU permanent establishment of an EU company).

90380
ss 757–767
ITTOIA 2005

Anti-avoidance provisions prevent the exemption from applying if financing arrangements appear to have been structured where the main benefit was to obtain a tax advantage.

s 765 ITTOIA 2005

MEMO POINTS 1. Payments of interest or royalties by a **permanent establishment** will only qualify for exemption if the payment is directly connected with the business of that permanent establishment.

2. Companies are **25% associates** if:
– one holds directly 25% or more of the share capital or voting rights of the other; or
– a third company holds directly 25% or more of the share capital or voting rights of the other companies.
3. An **indirect shareholding** is not covered by the exemption. For example, where the parent company holds 25% of a subsidiary through:
– another entity such as a partnership; or
– intermediate holding company.

Interest

90385
SI 2004/2622

If the payment is of interest, tax-free payments cannot be made before an exemption **notice** is issued by HMRC after an appropriate application has been made on Form EU Interest and Royalties.

There can be a delay of up to 3 months before the notice is issued, and the notice will last for between 1 and 3 years. Exemption will only apply to arm's length amounts (i.e. where there is no special relationship between the companies).

INTM 400060

◁ MEMO POINTS ▷ 1. The following **information** is required in the claim form:
– proof of tax residence;
– information as to the claimant's beneficial entitlement to the income, in respect of which the payment is made;
– details of the tax to which the claimant is subject;
– information establishing that the 25% associated relationship condition is met; and
– a copy of the loan agreement or other legal document providing legal justification for the payment.
2. The beneficial owner of the interest or royalties may appeal to the First-tier Tribunal against a **refusal to issue an exemption notice** or its cancellation within 30 days. The decision of the tribunal is final.

s 131 TIOPA 2010;
INTM 400030

3. A **special relationship** generally means a 51% direct or indirect controlling interest. For example, both companies are under common control of a worldwide group. HMRC state that a small shareholding or inter-dependent trading relationship might constitute a special relationship. The following factors must be taken into account:
– whether the loan would have been made at all in the absence of the special relationship;
– the amount which the loan would have been; and
– the rate of interest, and the other terms, which would have been agreed in its absence.

Royalties

90390
s 914 ITA 2007

If the payment is a royalty, tax-free **payments** can be made immediately providing the paying company believes the recipient will be entitled to exemption. There is no requirement to obtain advance **approval** from HMRC, but if the belief of the taxpayer turns out to be mistaken, HMRC can recover the tax that should have been deducted.

Information about such payments must be disclosed on the CTSA **return**, and the company will be liable to penalties for an incorrect return and for failing to deduct tax where it could not have reasonably believed that the exemption could apply.

No exemption

90395

Interest and royalties are usually **paid** net of income tax (¶41050) unless the exemption applies.

A **repayment** of tax can be claimed if any interest or royalty payments are made under deduction of tax that should have qualified for the exemption. A claim should be made on Form EU Interest and Royalties.

2. One party outside the EU

Interest

90425
s 930(2) ITA 2007

When a company pays interest overseas, income tax (at the basic rate) **must** be deducted from the payments.

An application can be made to HMRC to pay this interest **gross** or at a **reduced** rate in line with the terms of a relevant treaty (¶90055), but until clearance is given, income tax must be withheld.

Royalties

When a company pays a patent royalty overseas, and believes that the non-resident recipient is entitled to relief from UK tax on the royalty under the **terms of a double tax treaty**, the company may pay the royalty gross, or at a reduced rate of deduction, in line with the terms of the relevant treaty. No prior clearance is required from HMRC, but if the belief of the taxpayer turns out to be mistaken, HMRC can recover the tax that should have been deducted.

90430
ss 911 – 913
ITA 2007

SECTION 4

Relief for foreign tax

Foreign source income may be subject to tax in more than one territory. However, under the terms of most double tax agreements, only one territory will tax the income, as it will be exempt from tax in the other territory.

90480

In the **absence of such arrangements**, foreign income commonly suffers foreign tax, either by deduction at source or by assessment. Relief is given for the foreign tax against any UK tax liability under:
– the terms of a double tax agreement between the UK and the other territory, where such an agreement exists; or
– under the unilateral double tax provisions contained in UK tax legislation.

Relief is usually given in the form of a credit against the UK tax liability, although in the case of loss-making companies, the foreign tax can be treated as an expense.

Treaty relief

The UK has concluded a wide network of double taxation treaties which provide for relief for foreign tax paid (in addition to a growing number of EU-wide agreements). The terms of the relevant treaty (¶90055) should be consulted where foreign income has been received. However, UK domestic tax law applies where this is **more favourable** to the taxpayer. A double taxation treaty will also generally provide for maximum **withholding tax** rates in respect of dividends, interest and royalties, which may benefit a UK company if they are lower than the rates laid down in the domestic law of the territory from which the income is received.

90485

> ‾MEMO POINTS‾ 1. For double tax treaty purposes, only a 50% interest is required for a company to be a **subsidiary** i.e. this is lower than most subsidiary requirements which usually need more than 50%.
> 2. An **anti-avoidance** provision was to be introduced in 2012 to deny relief when a claim is made under the UK's double taxation treaties but arrangements have been entered into in order to avoid UK tax. As there were practical problems with the proposed legislation, it has been abandoned, although HMRC will continue to challenge specific arrangements that clearly seek to abuse provisions in a treaty.

Unilateral relief

Where there is no applicable double tax treaty, unilateral relief is available for the foreign tax paid. Note that the provisions of a double tax treaty always take precedence. *Bayfine UK v HMRC* [2010]

90490
s 25 TIOPA 2010

Tax suffered on branch income

90495
s 44 TIOPA 2010

In the absence of an exemption election (¶90160), where a company claims relief for foreign tax paid in respect of overseas income from a **trade or property business**, the double tax relief is the lower of:

– the overseas tax paid; and
– the UK tax liability on the net profit of the overseas business.

The foreign tax relief is only available in respect of the corporation tax payable on that overseas income, and is not available in respect of **other unrelated UK profits**.

> EXAMPLE A Ltd has UK trading income of £400,000, and overseas trading income of £40,000 on which foreign tax of £10,000 has been paid.
> Assuming A Ltd claims credit relief, its tax computation will be as follows (assuming a tax rate of 23%):
>
> | | £ |
> |---|---:|
> | UK trading income | 400,000 |
> | Overseas income | 40,000 |
> | PCTCT | 440,000 |
>
> The total UK corporation tax will be:
>
> | | £ |
> |---|---:|
> | UK corporation tax @ 23% | 101,200 |
> | Less: Foreign tax (relief would be limited to 40,000 @ 23%) | (9,200) |
> | Total UK tax due | 92,000 |

Tax suffered on dividends

90500
s 18 TIOPA 2010

Relief for both withholding and underlying tax (where applicable) is usually given as a credit against the UK corporation tax liability in the accounting period in which the dividend is received.

Where a credit is claimed, any double tax relief given is **restricted to** the UK mainstream corporation tax rate in force at the time that the relief is claimed.

> EXAMPLE B Ltd receives a dividend from its 100% foreign subsidiary C SA of £120, net of 60% underlying tax.
> If credit relief is claimed, B Ltd's tax computation would be as follows (assuming a tax rate of 23%):
>
> | | £ |
> |---|---:|
> | Net dividend | 120 |
> | Underlying tax | 72 |
> | Foreign profits | 192 |
> | UK tax @ 23% | 44 |
> | Less DTR (restricted) | (44) |
> | UK tax payable | Nil |

Loss-making companies

90505
s 112 TIOPA 2010

A UK company that is loss-making in a particular period may consider claiming overseas tax as an expense, as this will increase the loss which may **mitigate** the company's other taxable income, and avoids wasting a relief which cannot be set against a non-existent tax liability.

Where a business is carried on wholly overseas this trade is treated as entirely separate from any UK trade for the purposes of loss relief.

> EXAMPLE C Ltd has made a UK trading loss of £150,000. It receives overseas trading income of £40,000 on which foreign tax of £10,000 has been paid.

C Ltd will have the following tax computation, assuming it decides to expense the foreign tax:

	UK £	Overseas £
UK result/Overseas result	(150,000)	40,000
Less: Foreign tax	-	(10,000)
Loss/PCTCT	(150,000)	30,000

SECTION 5

Controlled foreign companies

The controlled foreign company (CFC) rules were introduced to discourage the practice of setting up subsidiaries in low tax jurisdictions with the aim of accumulating income that would never become taxable in the UK.

90555

The CFC legislation aims to bring the profits of a CFC into the scope of UK tax by means of apportionment in certain defined circumstances. UK companies must take account of their shareholdings in CFCs when preparing the CTSA tax return.

A wholesale reform of the CFC rules has taken effect for accounting periods beginning on or after 1 April 2013 (¶91180).

Summary

90560

Topic	¶¶
Scope	¶90590
Exclusions	¶90645
Apportionment of profits	¶90980
Taxation of apportioned profits	¶91045
Changes for accounting periods beginning on or after 1 April 2013	¶91180

A. Scope

A controlled foreign company is **defined** as a company that is:
- resident outside the UK;
- controlled by UK resident persons (individuals or companies); and
- subject to a lower level of taxation in its territory of residence than it would be subject to in the UK.

90590
s 747, Sch 24
ICTA 1988

These criteria must be **assessed** during each accounting period. In addition to the normal rules (¶3040+), an accounting period is deemed to:
- start when the company comes under the control of UK residents; and
- end when it ceases to be controlled by UK residents, or if the territory of residence changes.

s 751 ICTA 1988

Where resident

For the purposes of these rules a company is regarded as resident in the territory where it is liable to tax throughout the accounting period **by reason of** domicile, residence or place of

90595
s 749 ICTA 1988

management. It is not necessary for the company to have actually paid tax in the overseas territory, provided that it was potentially liable to tax there.

Where there are **two or more territories** where the company could be deemed to be resident, and no applicable election or designation has been made, the company will be regarded as resident in only one of the territories, which will be decided on the basis of the following tests (taken in order) where:

a. the effective management takes place; or (if that is not conclusive)

b. the greater amount of its assets (as determined by the market value) are situated immediately before the end of the accounting period; or (if that is not conclusive)

c. the territory specified in an election, or, if no election is made in time, the territory designated by HMRC (on a just and reasonable basis) as being the territory of residence in that period.

> ☐ *MEMO POINTS* 1. The irrevocable **election** as to the company's territory of residence may be made by one or more persons who together hold a "majority assessable interest" in a particular accounting period. The persons will have this majority assessable interest if, in the event of an apportionment of the chargeable profits of the company for that period, it is likely that more than 50% of those aggregate chargeable profits would be chargeable on those persons. When this election takes effect for a particular accounting period, the CFC will then continue to be regarded as resident in that territory for subsequent accounting periods, until such a time as the territory in which the CFC is resident, by reason of its domicile, residence or place of management, is different.
>
> 2. The **time limit** for making the election is 12 months after the accounting period end of the CFC to which the election relates. The signed election must specify the percentage of the chargeable profits and tax of the CFC that would be likely to accrue to the persons making the election if an apportionment were to be made.
>
> 3. Where HMRC makes a **designation** in respect of the territory of residence of the CFC for a period, this is irrevocable and is notified to every UK-resident company that HMRC considers would be chargeable under the CFC provisions assuming an apportionment of its profits were to be made in that period.
>
> 4. A UK-resident company that is deemed to be non-resident as a result of a **double taxation treaty**:
>
> **a.** from 1 April 2002, remains subject to the CFC legislation; or
>
> **b.** before 1 April 2002, remains outside the CFC rules. However, such a company will come within the scope of the CFC rules if at any time on or after 22 March 2006 a non-resident company:
>
> – with no subsidiaries acquires, directly or indirectly, a UK subsidiary; or
>
> – that already has subsidiaries acquires, directly or indirectly, a UK subsidiary and there is a qualifying change in activities (i.e. any major change in the nature, conduct or size (¶60260)) of the non-resident company (or of the group of which it is a part) at the time of the acquisition of the subsidiary or at a later time.

Control

90600
s 755D ICTA 1988

The control of a company is **defined** as being the power of a person to ensure that the affairs of the company are conducted according to that person's wishes, by one of the following means:

– holding shares in the company or having voting powers in that or any other company; or

– arising from powers conferred by the Articles of Association or other document of the company or any other company.

Control also includes persons who are entitled to:

– acquire the greater part of the company's profits, if they were to be distributed;

– receive the greater part of the proceeds, if the company's share capital were to be disposed of; and

– receive the greater part of the company's assets on a winding up.

90605
s 755D(2)
ICTA 1988

If **two or more persons**, considered together, have such power, they are considered to control the company. For this purpose each person is also deemed to hold the rights and powers:

– which he is entitled to acquire (or will in future be entitled to acquire);

– which (now or in the future) may be exercised by other persons on his behalf, under his direction, or for his benefit; and
– if UK resident, of any person connected with him who is also a UK resident.

A company will also be treated as controlled by UK persons if two people control the company, one of whom is UK resident, and the following tests are satisfied:
a. both persons have interests, rights and powers amounting to 40% of their combined holdings, rights and powers; and
b. the holdings of the non-UK resident person do not exceed 55%.

Lower level of taxation

An overseas company is considered to be subject to a lower level of taxation if the **local tax** paid in respect of its income profits **is less than** 75% of the corresponding UK tax liability that would have been incurred if the company had been UK resident. For this purpose the small profits tax rate is available. Note it is amounts that are important here, not simply rates.

90610
s 750 ICTA 1988

Additionally, where the local tax is determined under a **designer rate tax provision** in a particular accounting period, the overseas company is treated as having been subject to a lower rate of tax for that period in that territory. A designer rate tax provision is a provision that HMRC regard as allowing companies to exert significant control over the amount of tax paid, and include companies of a certain status in Guernsey, Jersey, Isle of Man and Gibraltar.

s 750A ICTA 1988;
SI 2000/3158

> MEMO POINTS   1. Local taxes paid in respect of **turnover or capital gains** are excluded.
> 2. In calculating the local tax and hypothetical UK tax **double tax relief** relating to the local tax is disregarded. However, there is relief for tax paid in third countries.
> 3. **Anti-avoidance** provisions exist to combat schemes which:
> **a.** divert income into the overseas company that is only taxable in the overseas territory (i.e. not taxable in the UK). This has the effect of increasing the amount of foreign tax payable on the profits as a proportion of the UK tax that would have been payable on those profits. The anti-avoidance provision discounts the diverted income; or
> **b.** enable tax paid by the overseas company to be repaid to an associated person. The anti-avoidance provision reduces the local tax by the amount repaid to any other person, whether directly or indirectly.

> EXAMPLE   A Inc is resident in territory A which charges tax at 18%. Its income profits for an accounting period are £100,000, which includes income of £15,000 from territory B on which tax of £1,500 has been suffered.
>
> | | | | £ |
> |---|---|---|---:|
> | Tax paid in territory A | 100,000 @ 18% | | 18,000 |
> | Less: Territory B tax | | | (1,500) |
> | Local taxes paid | | | 16,500 |
> | | | | |
> | UK tax position would be: | | | |
> | Corporation tax | 100,000 @ 20% | | 20,000 |
> | Double tax relief | Territory A | | - |
> | | Territory B | 1,500 | |
> | | | | (1,500) |
> | Corresponding UK tax | | | 18,500 |
> | 75% thereof: | | | 13,875 |
>
> As the local taxes exceed 75% of the corresponding UK tax, A Inc is not a CFC. (£16,500 compared to £13,875)

The following assumptions are made when calculating the **hypothetical UK chargeable profit** and tax liability for this purpose:
– the overseas company is UK-resident, not a close company, and foreign profits are therefore included in the UK taxable profit;
– all of the appropriate claims and elections, including those relating to capital allowances, have been made;
– group relief is not available;

90615

– unremittable foreign income is subject to relief; and
– losses brought forward may be utilised if incurred in the previous 6 years.

B. Exclusions

90645
s 748 ICTA 1988

No apportionment of profits is required where the **UK company** is entitled to less than 25% of the apportioned profit (¶90980) or the **overseas company** falls within any of the following exemptions:

Type of exemption	Relief where not all conditions are met?	¶¶
Resident in an excluded country	n	¶90680
Low profits	n	¶90720
Engaging in exempt activities	n	¶90740
Engaging in trading activities or the exploitation of intellectual property, either of which has little connection with the UK	y	¶90780
Becoming a foreign subsidiary as a result of a reorganisation or change of ownership (note that this exemption only lasts for 3 years)	y	¶90830
Commercial motive	n	¶90870

90650

Where it is considered by the company that an exemption may apply **advance clearance** is available from HMRC to substantiate the availability of the exemption (¶90920). **Reporting requirements** (¶91090) apply unless the CFC is resident in an excluded country.

1. Excluded countries

90680
SI 1998/3081

Where a controlled foreign company is resident in a territory that is included in a list of excluded countries, and satisfies certain requirements, no apportionment will be made. There are two lists, with **different criteria** for each list, which must be met throughout the particular accounting period.

Comment   The list is intended to apply an exemption to those companies that, based on their territory of residence and the type of income they are receiving, can be reasonably assumed not to be involved in the diversion of profits from the scope of UK tax.

List 1

90685

A company resident in any country shown below must pass both the income and gains requirement and the anti-avoidance provision.

The **income and gains** of the CFC which are derived from outside the country must not exceed the greater of:
– 10% of its (commercially quantified) income in that period; or
– £50,000 (pro-rated where the accounting period is less than a year).

Anti-avoidance provisions apply where the CFC invests in a non-corporate entity, whose income is not included in the commercially quantified income of the CFC, and the entity:
– is controlled (or capable of being controlled) by the CFC or by the group of which the CFC is a part; and
– receives more than half its income from other entities (corporate or non-corporate) that are connected (¶31375) or associated (¶75390) with the CFC or the group.

Where UK tax would have been payable on the income of that non-corporate entity, the income must be included as part of the commercially quantifiable income of the CFC for the purpose of the limits above.

Australia	Gambia	
Austria	Germany	Papua New Guinea
Bangladesh	Ghana	Poland
Bolivia	Honduras	Romania
Botswana	Iceland	Senegal
Brazil	India	Sierra Leone
Bulgaria	Indonesia	Slovak Republic
Canada	Ivory Coast	Solomon Islands
Colombia	Japan	South Africa
Czech Republic	Korea, Republic of	Swaziland
Denmark	Lesotho	Sweden
Dominican Republic	Malawi	Trinidad and Tobago
Falkland Islands	Mexico	Turkey
Fiji	New Zealand	Zambia
Finland	Nigeria	Zimbabwe
France	Norway	

List 2

A company resident in any country shown below must pass both the income and gains requirement and the anti-avoidance provision, and **additionally**: **90690**
- not be entitled to any tax exemptions, reductions or other benefits; and
- not fall within any of the circumstances specified in the table below.

Country	Prohibited circumstances
Argentina	Companies obtaining exemption from tax on income from transactions, activities or operations carried on in, or from goods located in, tax-free areas in accordance with Law 19640 of 16 May 1972
Belgium	Companies which are regarded as Foreign Sales Corporations in s 922(a) of the United States Internal Revenue Code 1954, and which accordingly qualify for reduced Belgian taxation
	Companies approved under Royal Decree No 187 of 30 December 1982 as Co-ordination Centres
Brunei	Companies qualifying as "pioneer companies" under the Investment Incentives Enactment 1975
Chile	Companies obtaining exemption from tax under Law 16,441 of 1 March 1966 on income from property located in the Department of Isla da Pascua or from activities developed in that Department
China	Companies deriving income in or from the Hong Kong Special Administrative Region, and submitting tax returns to the authorities of that Region
	From 20 December 1999, companies deriving income in or from the Macao Special Administrative Region and submitting tax returns to the authorities of that Region
Egypt	Companies which do not fall within the scope of Article 111, Book 2 of Law 157 of 1981 because they do not operate in Egypt
Faroe Islands	Companies deriving interest from Faroese financial institutions from which tax is deducted at source under Law 4 of 26 March 1953
Greece	Companies whose profits are exempt from tax under Article 6(2)(c) of Law 3843/1958 (profits from the operation of ships under the Greek flag)
	Companies having profits exempt from company income tax by virtue of Article 25 of Law 25/1975 or by virtue of Law 89/1967 (profits from shipping and associated activities)

Country	Prohibited circumstances
Hungary	Companies benefiting from the reduced rate of tax for extra-territorial companies under s 19(2) of Act LXXXI of 1996 on Corporate Tax and Dividend Tax
Italy	Companies benefiting from paragraphs 12 to 14 of Article 11 of Law 413 of 30 December 1991 (Trieste Free Zone Financial and Insurance Centre)
Kenya	Companies having income exempted from tax under paragraph 11 of Schedule 1 to the Income Tax Act 1973
Luxembourg	Companies obtaining any special tax benefit under the Law of 31 July 1929, the decree of 17 December 1938 or the Grand Ducal Regulation of 29 July 1977 (holding companies)
	Any reinsurance company established in Luxembourg requiring authorisation under Article 92 of the law of 6 December 1991
Malaysia	Companies exempt from tax in accordance with s 54A of the Income Tax Act 1967 (shipping)
	Companies subject to tax at 5% in accordance with ss 60A and 60B of the Income Tax Act 1967 (inward reinsurance and offshore insurance)
	Companies deriving dividends from a company (or companies) deriving income from either: – shipping; – inward insurance; and – offshore insurance
	Companies obtaining a tax benefit under the Offshore Companies Act (Island of Labuan) 1990
Malta	Companies entitled to exemption or relief from tax at the discretion of the Minister responsible for finance under s 12(2) of the Income Tax Act 1948
	Companies obtaining exemption from tax under s 86 of the Merchant Shipping Act 1973
	Companies obtaining exemption or relief from tax under s 30 of the Malta International Business Activities Act 1988 or s 30 of the Malta Financial Services Centre Act 1988
	Companies obtaining exemption or relief from tax under s 18 of the Malta Freeports Act 1989
Morocco	Companies receiving a tax benefit under Law 58-90 of 1992 (offshore financial centres)
Netherlands	Companies which are regarded as Foreign Sales Corporations under s 922(a) of the United States Internal Revenue Code 1954
	A company ("the first company") receiving interest, rents or royalties in an accounting period directly, or indirectly, from a Dutch company ("the second company") which is connected with the first company within the meaning of s 839 of the Taxes Act, in circumstances where: **a.** the second company does not satisfy the income and gains requirement in regulation 5 as respects its accounting period in which the interest, rents or royalties were paid: and **b.** the aggregate of the non-local source income of the first company in its accounting period in question, and the interest, rents and royalties received by it from the second company in that period, exceeds whichever is the greater of: – £50,000 (pro-rated for accounting periods of less than 12 months); and – an amount equal to 10% of its commercially quantified income arising in that period
Pakistan	Companies deriving royalties, commissions or fees which are exempt from tax under paragraph 139 in Part I of the second Schedule to the Income Tax Ordinance 1979

Country	Prohibited circumstances
Philippines	Companies authorised under Presidential Decree 1034 of 30 September 1976, or under Presidential Decree 1035 of 30 September 1976, to operate an offshore Banking Unit or a Foreign Currency Deposit Unit as defined in those Decrees
	Companies receiving interest on deposits with a Foreign Currency Deposit Unit, or other interest subject to the reduced rates of tax under s 27(D) of the National Internal Revenue Code 1997
Portugal	Companies obtaining tax benefits under Decree Law 502/85 of 30 December 1985, Articles 41 and 51(g) of the Tax Benefits statute (EBF) approved by Decree Law 215/90 of 31 August 1989 (free zone in Madeira), or Decree Law 501/85 of 28 December 1985 as implemented by Decree Law 63/87 of 5 February 1987 (free zone in the Azores)
Puerto Rico	Companies obtaining a tax benefit under s 2(o) of the Industrial Incentive Act 1978 (designated service industries)
	Companies obtaining a tax benefit under s 25 of the International Banking Centre Regulatory Act 1989 (International Banking Entities)
Singapore	Any company obtaining tax concessions under Ministry of Finance Regulations pursuant to and s 43A, ss 43C to 43K of the Income Tax Act
	Companies obtaining exemption from tax on the income of a shipping enterprise in accordance with s 13A of the Income Tax Act
	Companies obtaining relief from tax in accordance with ss 45 to 55 (international trade incentives), and ss 75 to 84 (warehouse and service incentives), of the Economic Expansion Incentives (Relief from Income Tax) Act
	Companies deriving dividends from a company (or companies) deriving income from one or more of the following activities: – obtaining tax concessions under Ministry of Finance Regulations; – shipping; – international trade incentives; – warehouse and service incentives
Spain	Companies which are registered in the official register of the Canary Islands Special Zone (Zona Especial Canaria) established under Law 19/1994 and which benefit from the special low tax rate applied to such companies
	Companies benefiting from the alternative taxation regime for co-ordination centres established by the provincial governments of the Basque Country, under laws pursuant to Norma Foral 3/1996 of 26 June 1996, Norma Foral 7/1996 of 4 July 1996, and Norma Foral 24/1996 of 5 July 1996
Sri Lanka	Companies obtaining relief or exemption from income tax under any of the following provisions of the Inland Revenue Act 1979: – s 8(c)(iv) (foreign currency banking units); – ss 10(d) and 15(b) (income derived from approved bank accounts); – s 10(e) (interest of newly resident companies); – s 15(cc) (services rendered outside Sri Lanka); or – s 15(p) (re-export of approved products)
Tanzania	Companies relieved or exempted from income tax under s 15(1) or (1A) of the Income Tax Act 1973
Thailand	Companies obtaining a tax benefit under Royal Decree 280 of 22 September 1992 (offshore banking units)
Tunisia	Companies obtaining exemption from, or reduction of, tax under Law 76-63 of 12 July 1976 (financial and banking institutions dealing with non-residents)
United States	Domestic International Sales Corporations as defined in s 992(a) of the Internal Revenue Code 1954

2. Low profits

90720

ss 748 (1)(d),
748(1)(da)
ICTA 1988

For accounting periods beginning on or after 1 January 2011, there are two alternative ways of exempting a CFC based on the level of either:

a. its chargeable profits (i.e. as adjusted for UK tax purposes (¶90615)), which must be less than £50,000 in a 12-month accounting period; or

b. except in cases of avoidance, its accounting profits as prepared under GAAP, which must be less than £200,000 in a 12-month accounting period. For this purpose the profits must be adjusted to exclude exempt dividends and capital gains, but include trust and partnership income on a just and reasonable basis. Transfer pricing adjustments are ignored unless exceeding £50,000.

> ⸀MEMO POINTS⸀ 1. For accounting **periods beginning before 1 January 2011**, only the chargeable profits de minimis applied.
>
> 2. The anti-avoidance rules mentioned in **b**. above attack any of the following arrangements:
> – the CFC is party to a scheme where the main purpose, or one of the main purposes, of any party to the scheme is to ensure that the new de minimis exemption applies to the CFC;
> – the scheme shifts profits to a CFC from another company, and that the main purpose, or one of the main purposes, of any party to the scheme is to ensure that the new de minimis exemption applies to one or more CFCs for one or more accounting periods; or
> – which require that in computing the CFC's chargeable profits, there must be no adjustment as a consequence of either connected party loan relationships (¶16725) or group mismatch schemes (¶69490).

> ⸀EXAMPLE⸀
>
> 1. C Ltd owns X Inc, and X Inc owns Y Inc.
> X Inc has profits of £250,000 and Y Inc has profits of £100,000.
> Y Inc's profit level would satisfy the accounting profits exemption so will not be a CFC.
>
> 2. If Y Inc recharges £75,000 of expenses to X Inc, this will reduce X Inc's profits to £175,000. Even though this is now below the £200,000 threshold, the anti-avoidance rule will mean that neither X Inc nor Y Inc will be able to fall within the accounting profits exemption.

3. Exempt activities

90740

s 748(1)(b),
Sch 25 para 5
ICTA 1988

Where a CFC is carrying on activities in its territory of residence, the nature of which can reasonably be assumed not to be acting as a vehicle for avoidance of UK taxation, then no apportionment of its profits is required.

For this purpose the main activity of the company must **exclude**:

a. investment business;

b. dealing in goods for delivery to or from the UK or connected persons; or

c. wholesale, distributive, financial or service business where at least 50% of its gross trading income is derived from:

– connected persons (¶31375);

– persons connected with persons who control the CFC through the 40% test (¶90605);

– persons holding a stake of at least 25% in the overseas company; or

– UK-resident individuals, companies or permanent establishments.

Trading companies

90745

A CFC satisfies the exempt activities test in an accounting period where it has a real business presence in its territory of residence throughout the accounting period. It must also be effectively managed there.

Sch 25 paras 6(b), 8
ICTA 1988

Effectively managed means that the staff in that territory must be in sufficient numbers to deal with the volume of business of the company in the overseas territory, as well as having adequate qualifications and experience to supervise, control and carry out most of its activities. Further, for non EU/EEA CFCs, any services provided by the overseas company for persons resident outside its territory (except through a permanent establishment, branch or agency liable to UK tax on its profits) must not be performed in the UK.

> *MEMO POINTS* 1. **Business presence** means premises which are to be occupied and used with a reasonable degree of permanence e.g. office, shop, factory, mine etc, building site or construction project (with a duration of at least 12 months).
> 2. The **staff** may be the company's own employees or other staff who are wholly or mainly engaged in doing the business of the company, and who are remunerated by a person connected to the CFC and resident in the same overseas territory.

Holding companies

For this purpose a holding company is defined as a company whose business consists of owning shares in:
– 90% owned local holding companies; or
– 51% owned trading companies.

90750

Currently, the exempt activities test only applies to a **local** holding company, where:
– 90% of its gross income in the accounting period is derived directly from companies that are controlled by it, and actually received in the territory of residence;
– those companies are resident in the same territory as the holding company throughout the accounting period, and are not holding companies themselves; and
– are engaged in exempt activities or are exempt trading companies.

Sch 26 para 6(3) ICTA 1988

The same rules regarding **effective management** apply as for trading CFCs (¶90745). However, the staff remunerated by a person connected to the CFC in the overseas territory are not required to be wholly or mainly engaged in the company's business, just merely engaged in some capacity.

For **non-local** holding companies and **superior** holding companies which fell within a previous exemption in the last accounting period ending before 1 July 2009, that exemption will continue until periods commencing after 1 July 2012. Where the accounting period straddles the change in rules, it is to be treated as two periods on a just and reasonable apportionment.

> *MEMO POINTS* 1. The **previous exemption** applying up until 1 July 2009 meant that a superior holding company was exempt if 90% of its income derived from companies under its control, which were resident in the same territory as the superior holding company, and which themselves were:
> – holding companies, local holding companies or engaged in an exempt activity; or
> – superior holding companies with such qualifying exempt income from their subsidiaries.
> 2. A **superior holding company** is a company, whose business consists wholly or mainly in the holding of shares in companies which are holding companies or local holding companies, or are themselves superior holding companies.

4. Minimal business connection with UK

The following two exemptions, which apply for accounting periods beginning on or after 1 January 2011, rely on a minimal connection with the UK, and are available **regardless of** the extent of intra-group transactions:
a. carrying on trading activities; and
b. exploiting intellectual property.

90780

A CFC that **cannot fully satisfy the conditions** of either test can apply to HMRC for a reduction of the full CFC charge to reflect the extent to which the conditions have been satisfied (¶90790, ¶90800).

s 751AB ICTA 1988

Trading companies

90785   The CFC must satisfy all of the following conditions **for full exemption**:

Conditions	Detail	Reference
Business establishment	The CFC must have a business establishment **in** its territory of residence (¶90745)	Sch 25 para 12C ICTA 1988
Business activities	The CFC's business **cannot include**, to a substantial extent, the following activities: – the holding or managing of shares or securities; – the holding of intellectual property; – dealing in securities, other than in the capacity of a broker; – the leasing of any description of property or rights; – the investment of funds which would otherwise be available for investment, directly or indirectly, by any person (or connected person (¶31375)) who has control of the CFC HMRC state that the meaning of **substantial** will be a matter of facts and circumstances, but it can be taken to be a maximum of 20% of the total business activity, measured by reference to factors such as trading activity, income, or assets	Sch 25 para 12D ICTA 1988
No significant UK connection	A CFC will be treated as having a **significant** UK connection only if either of the following conditions are met: **a.** more than 10% of its **gross income**[1] is UK connected (i.e. derived from persons who are liable to UK corporation tax) and all of the following do not apply: – the CFC has sufficient staff based outside the UK to manage the CFC's business; – its profits do not exceed 10% of its relevant operating expenses (which, for this purpose, exclude the cost of goods sold and the UK connected expenditure); and – its UK connected income for the period does not exceed 50% of its gross income; or **b. expenditure** in the UK exceeds 50% of its total expenditure, and the company is involved in a **scheme** which has a main purpose of achieving a reduction in UK tax	Sch 25 para 12E ICTA 1988
Finance income and intellectual property income	The **sum of both** finance income and intellectual property income **cannot exceed** 5% of the CFC's gross income[1] for the accounting period If this condition is failed, see ¶90790 **Finance income** is defined as amounts arising from a financial asset as defined by UK GAAP plus any amounts that would be recognised as income under the loan relationship disguised interest rules (¶16120) **Intellectual property income** is defined as royalties and receipts of a similar nature	Sch 25 para 12F ICTA 1988

Note:
1. **Gross income** excludes distributions which would be exempt under the UK rules and chargeable gains, but includes income accruing to a settlement, of which the CFC is a settlor or a beneficiary, and income accruing to a partnership of which the CFC is a partner.

90790
s 751AB(2)
ICTA 1988

A **reduction** to the CFC charge may apply where either:
– the level of UK-connected income exceeds 10% but does not exceed 50%; and/or
– the combined finance and intellectual property income of the CFC exceeds 5% of gross income, but the relevant intellectual property income of the CFC does not exceed 5% of gross income.

In either case so long as an application to reduce a CFC charge in the same accounting period has not been made in respect of either EEA CFCs (¶91005) or a reorganisation

(¶90840), the company can apply to HMRC to reduce the CFC charge to a specified amount (which can be nil). The related creditable tax (¶91085) will also be reduced on a just and reasonable basis.

The **specified amount** is:
– the sum of the excess finance and intellectual property income (i.e. amounts over 5% of the gross income of the CFC, ignoring negligible amounts); and
– where the UK connection test is failed, the part of the CFC's net chargeable profits that arise from UK transactions or which does not represent the net economic value arising from staff activity in the overseas territory.

There is a right of appeal where HMRC refuse an application.

Holding intellectual property

The CFC must satisfy all of the conditions **for full exemption**:

90795

Conditions	Detail	Reference
Business establishment	The CFC must have a business establishment in its territory of residence (¶90745)	Sch 25 para 12I ICTA 1988
Intellectual property business	The CFC's main business throughout the accounting period must be the exploitation of intellectual property which has no relevant UK connection (ignoring any IP with a UK connection if it forms an insignificant part of the main business) IP has a **UK connection** if either: – it has been held in the UK at any time during the accounting period or the previous 6 years; or – any activities to create, maintain or enhance the IP have been carried on by a person who is within the charge to UK income or corporation tax, and is related to the CFC For this purpose **insignificant** is intended to cover small elements of the overall business activity, and HMRC state that 5% of the main business – measured by reference factors such as trading activity, income or assets – can be regarded as the upper limit of insignificant	Sch 25 para 12J ICTA 1988
Other business activities	The CFC must either carry on: **a.** no activities other than its main business; or **b.** other activities which either: – do not constitute a substantial part of the whole business; or – meet the business activity conditions in either ¶90740 or ¶90785 For this purpose, **substantial** can be taken to mean a maximum of 20% of total business activity, measured by reference to factors such as trading activity, income or assets	Sch 25 para 12K ICTA 1988
No significant UK connection	A CFC will be treated as having a **significant** UK connection only if either of the following apply: **a.** a substantial proportion of the CFC's gross income (see below) derives from persons within the charge to UK income or corporation tax; or **b.** the CFC incurs expenditure (other than incidental or insignificant expenditure) on either: – R&D subcontractor payments (¶78260), or – the creation, development or maintenance of intellectual property, and that expenditure forms part of the income of a related person who is within the charge to UK tax A **related person** is broadly connected (¶31375) or associated (¶75390) with the company, or has a 25% assessable interest in the company	Sch 25 para 12L ICTA 1988

Conditions	Detail	Reference
Finance income	The total finance income cannot exceed 5% of the CFC's gross income for the accounting period. Finance income is defined as amounts arising from a financial asset, as defined by UK GAAP, plus any amounts that would be recognised as income under the loan relationship disguised interest rules (¶16120). **Gross income** excludes distributions which would be exempt under the UK rules and chargeable gains, but includes income accruing to a settlement of which the CFC is a settlor or a beneficiary, and income accruing to a partnership of which the CFC is a partner	Sch 25 para 12M ICTA 1988

90800

s 751AB(2)
ICTA 1988

A **reduction** to the CFC charge may apply where the finance income exceeds 5% of the gross income.

So long as an application to reduce a CFC charge in the same accounting period has not been made in respect of either EEA CFCs (¶91005) or a reorganisation (¶90840), the company can apply to HMRC to reduce the CFC charge to a specified amount (which can be nil). The related creditable tax (¶91085) will also be reduced on a just and reasonable basis.

The **specified amount** is the amount of finance income in excess of 5% of the CFC's gross income, but ignoring negligible amounts.

There is a right of appeal where HMRC refuse an application.

5. Becoming a foreign subsidiary

90830

Certain foreign subsidiaries, whose accounting periods end within a set exempt period, will not be taxed as CFCs.

Sch 25 para 15F
ICTA 1988

The **exempt period**:
– starts when the overseas company first becomes subject to the UK CFC rules e.g. by acquiring a UK company investor; and
– effectively ends 3 years later, unless the company enters into certain types of arrangement in the meantime (although a reduction in the resulting CFC charge will be available in this case).

90835

The CFC must satisfy all of the conditions in the table below **for full exemption**, or alternatively meet the following criteria:

Sch 25 para 15D
ICTA 1988

– exempt period begins after 23 March 2011;
– the company was not a CFC in the accounting period which includes 23 March 2011;
– the company was not UK controlled before the exempt period began; and
– on becoming a CFC, the company is controlled by the group's ultimate parent.

This means that a foreign subsidiary that is not under UK control on 23 March 2011 can qualify for the exemption if its ultimate parent later becomes UK-resident, regardless of whether it has been under UK control and a CFC at some earlier time.

Situation	Conditions	Reference
Prior to becoming a UK-controlled foreign subsidiary	The company has not previously been controlled by a UK-resident person or persons	Sch 25 para 15C(1) ICTA 1988
	No part of its business or its assets were previously carried on, or owned, by a company under such control and related to the CFC	

Situation	Conditions	Reference
Circumstances when becoming a foreign subsidiary – the company was either:	**a.** in existence before it became a CFC, but was not a member of a UK-controlled group	Sch 25 para 15C(2) ICTA 1988
	b. controlled by a UK-resident company during the exempt period, but the controlling company was not a UK-resident beforehand i.e. a holding company moved into the UK	Sch 25 para 15C(3) ICTA 1988
	c. part of the group already, but control of it passed from a non-UK resident parent to a UK-resident intermediate holding company, as part of a group reorganisation	Sch 25 para 15C(4) ICTA 1988
	d. a CFC when formed, and was set up as an acquisition vehicle in preparation for acquiring other companies which would also qualify for this exemption	Sch 25 para 15C(5) ICTA 1988
No disqualifying transaction occurs	For this purpose a disqualifying transaction includes the following (ignoring any transaction which is negligible in value): – a loan or advance to a related person within the charge to UK tax, or a change in terms of such a loan. Arrangements put into place before the start of the exempt period are also caught; – any transactions referable to investment or other non-exempt activities carried on by the CFC which are reflected in its profits and which achieve a reduction in UK tax (i.e. where the transaction did not exist, a UK tax charge would be higher or a tax relief would be reduced); or – an acquisition vehicle engaging in activities other than simply holding shares in its subsidiaries A relevant transaction occurs either: – when the company becomes a UK-controlled foreign subsidiary (including transactions in relation to agreements entered into before that time); or – on or after 9 December 2010, if it is part of an avoidance scheme designed to exploit this exemption	Sch 25 para 15E ICTA 1988

Reduction in tax charge

A reduction to the CFC charge may apply where the exempt period has been terminated early by any of the events in ¶90835, **excluding** terminations in relation to acquisition vehicles.

90840
s 751AC ICTA 1988

So long as an application to reduce a CFC charge in the same accounting period has not been made in respect of either EEA CFCs (¶91005) or a trading or intellectual property exploiting company (¶90790, ¶90800), the company can apply to HMRC to reduce the CFC charge to a specified amount (which can be nil). The related creditable tax (¶91085) will also be reduced on a just and reasonable basis.

The **specified amount** is the amount (if any) of the chargeable profits as it is just and reasonable to relate to both the transaction which terminated the exempt period, and any subsequent transactions.

There is a right of appeal where HMRC refuse an application for a reduction.

6. Motive test

The motive test aims to exclude from the CFC rules those companies that have not been set up with the objective of avoiding UK tax, but do not otherwise fit within the other exemptions.

90870
s 748(3) ICTA 1988

If the overseas company exists for reasons other than gaining a UK tax advantage, and was therefore not set up with the aim of diverting profits away from the UK, the motive test will apply where both of the following **conditions** are satisfied:

Condition	Detail	¶¶
Transaction leg	A transaction that was reflected in the overseas company's profits for the period has led to a reduction in UK tax and either: – the reduction is minimal; or – achieving the reduction was not the main purpose, or one of the main purposes, of the transaction	¶90875
Diversion of profits leg	Achieving a reduction in UK tax by diversion of profits from the UK was not the main reason, or one of the main reasons, for the company's existence in the accounting period	¶90885

Transaction leg

90875   The transaction leg of the motive test consists of two elements:

The **first element** looks at the results of the transaction i.e. whether:
– the transactions are reflected in the profit of the overseas company;
– those transactions have achieved a reduction in UK tax; and
– the reduction in UK tax was more than minimal.

Where there is a positive answer to all of these points the transaction has achieved a reduction in UK tax that is more than minimal, and it is then necessary to go on to the second element of the transaction leg.

Sch 25 para 17
ICTA 1988

‎MEMO POINTS   1. A transaction achieves a **reduction** in UK tax if, but for that transaction, any person (whether connected or associated with the CFC or not) would have either:
– been liable to UK tax;
– been liable to a greater amount of UK tax;
– not been entitled to a relief or would have been entitled to a lower amount of relief; or
– not been entitled to a repayment of tax or would have been entitled to a smaller entitlement. This therefore involves determining what the tax position would have been **if the transactions had not been carried out**. It is not, however, necessary to speculate on what alternative courses of action would have been taken, but merely to examine the situation if the transactions had not taken place.
2. For this purpose **UK tax** includes only income tax, corporation tax or capital gains tax. Transactions that only result in reductions in foreign tax are not relevant.

INTM 208060

3. Where the **tax consequences** resulting from the transactions are **remote** from the transactions themselves, these are not taken into account e.g. a CFC gives tax planning advice to an unconnected UK resident which reduces UK tax, but the only transaction reflected in its profits is the receipt of a fee for that service.

90880
INTM 208080

Second element   Even if the reduction in tax is more than minimal, unless it was the main purpose or one of the main purposes of the transaction to achieve the reduction, the motive element will be satisfied.

When deciding whether the reduction in UK tax was one of the **main purposes** of the transactions, consideration must be given to both the purpose of the overseas company itself, and the purpose of any person who had an interest in the controlled foreign company during the period concerned. The motives of other persons are not relevant.

If the **reduction** in UK tax was only **incidental** to the main purpose of the transactions, this would not be a main purpose

In the view of **HMRC** if the transactions achieve a reduction in UK tax it is normally reasonable to assume that the reduction was anticipated, and if the tax reduction is substantial it is likely to be one of the main purposes of the transaction, even if the scheme does not achieve its purpose. This is also the case where the transaction also has a commercial purpose i.e. it is possible for transactions to have a number of purposes, one of which is tax reduction.

Diversion of profits leg

90885

The diversion of profits leg deals with the reason for the CFC's existence.

A diversion of profits has occurred if it can be reasonably assumed that the following would have applied **had it not been for the existence of the CFC** or a company associated or connected with it:
– the whole or a substantial part of the income received by the CFC would have been received by a UK-resident person (or by a company that can reasonably be supposed to have been set up in those circumstances); and
– the UK resident would have been liable to UK tax, or more UK tax, or entitled to less relief or a lower repayment of UK tax.

It is then necessary to consider whether the reduction in tax was the **main reason** behind the CFC's existence. HMRC believe that where the existence of a controlled foreign company achieves more than a negligible saving of tax, it would normally be reasonable to infer that the tax saving was one of the reasons for bringing the company into existence. Extending this further, if the tax saving is substantial, it would be reasonable to infer that it was a main reason for the company's existence.

INTM 208160

A company's **activities may change over time**, so that the original motives for bringing a company into existence may no longer exist some years later. This test is taking a snapshot of the CFC in the particular accounting period, with the company's activity in previous periods only being of limited bearing.

Holding companies

90890
INTM 208240

Whilst, in the opinion of **HMRC**, many overseas holding companies are set up with the purpose of reducing foreign tax (rather than UK tax) this does not mean that the motive test is necessarily satisfied. Reduction of UK tax may also be one of the main objectives. HMRC's view is that one of the main reasons for setting up an overseas holding company, rather than a UK holding company, is because of the UK tax liability that would otherwise be incurred.

HMRC suggest that, in considering the application of the motive test to holding companies, the following two basic questions (applicable to all CFCs) are important:
– whether the business of the CFC would have been carried out in the UK; and
– whether one of the main reasons why the company was not set up in the UK is the fact that the UK tax liability would have been greater than the foreign tax liability. Again this is a question of fact.

As HMRC hold the view that the main reason for locating a holding company, or group finance company, outside the UK is that the tax liability on **interest received** is lower, they will only accept that such a company (whose main receipt is interest) could only pass the motive test when set up for regulatory reasons or acting as a regional holding company.

INTM 208350

7. Obtaining clearance

90920
INTM 214120

HMRC can give clearance as to whether a foreign subsidiary falls within any of the exemptions, which will give a company and its group certainty about how to complete the CTSA return.

Further, clearance can be requested in respect of the way any area of the controlled foreign company legislation applies in respect of a particular case.

Who can request clearance?

90925

All UK shareholders of a foreign subsidiary are entitled to request clearance. Where there is **more than one UK shareholder** a clearance application may be made by one on behalf of the others.

Clearance application

90930
INTM 214130

An application for clearance should always include the following **details**:

a. name of the controlled foreign company;

b. UK company's interest in the controlled foreign company's share and loan capital (as measured under ¶90995);

c. tax district and reference number of UK companies (where known);

d. territory of residence and details of branches, including those in the UK;

e. place and, for new companies the date, of incorporation; and

f. a copy of the most recent accounts (where these have been drawn up).

The exact information and supporting material will obviously depend on the particular circumstances. HMRC give further guidance in respect of certain exemptions as shown in ¶90935 below.

> MEMO POINTS   The clearance application should be **sent to**:
> CTIAA, Outward Investment Team Registry (Controlled Foreign Company Clearances),
> 3rd Floor,
> 100 Parliament Street,
> London
> SW1A 2BQ

90935
INTM 214130

Information in respect of certain exemptions

Type of exemption	HMRC guidance
Excluded countries	Following information is required: – proof of commercially quantified income showing which capital items are not included; – computation of non-local source income; – a statement that the CFC is resident in a List 1 country (¶90685), or not falling within any of the prohibited circumstances shown in List 2 (¶90690)
Exempt activities	**a.** actual or expected equity at beginning and end of accounting period; **b.** full description of business including all transactions with associates; **c.** where there is more than one business: which is considered the main business and why; **d.** details of investments held, and actual or projected income from these during the accounting period for which clearance is sought; **e.** details of projected tax payable for the accounting period for which clearance is sought and how computed; **f.** full details (including address) of business establishment, number of hours, days etc occupied on company business, whether shared with other businesses and rent etc paid; **g.** full details of staff employed, place of employment and duties and salaries of each; **h.** details of management companies employed and amounts paid; **i.** details of services provided by the company for persons resident outside the territory of residence and where performed; **j.** details of persons engaged wholly or mainly in the business of the company whose remuneration is paid by a person connected with, and resident in the same territory as, the controlled foreign company; and **k.** reasons why it is considered the company satisfies the "exempt activities" test For **holding companies** sufficient information will be needed to establish whether the various definitions of holding company (¶90750) are satisfied, and whether the company derives 90% of its income from acceptable sources and in the appropriate form

Type of exemption	HMRC guidance
Motive test	Applications will need to be supported by sufficient information to allow HMRC to judge whether a reduction in UK tax has been achieved and if so, whether a main purpose for a transaction or reason for the existence of the company was the achievement of that reduction In particular: a. actual or expected equity at beginning and end of accounting period; b. full description of business including all transactions with associates; c. where there is more than one business, which is considered the main business and why; d. details of investments held, and actual or projected income from these during the accounting period for which clearance is sought; e. details of projected tax payable for the accounting period for which clearance is sought and how computed; f. details of any direct or indirect transactions between the UK and the controlled foreign company (including interest on loans (direct or indirect), royalties, payments for services, purchase or sale of goods); g. the effect on UK tax (including the effect on losses or repayments) if those transactions had not taken place; h. the reasons for the transactions; i. the reasons, if any, why the business of the controlled foreign company could not be carried on by a UK resident; j. the tax effect if that business could have been carried on in the UK; and k. the reasons for the company's existence in the accounting period

Response from HMRC

HMRC aim to work to a 28-day turnaround target from receipt of the application, provided all relevant information is included.

90940

If the company has a **particular need** for a clearance decision to be given **by a specific date**, it must specify this in the application.

INTM 214120

Comment   Companies should allow as long as possible for the clearance procedure to reach its conclusion (certainly at least 2 months), as further information is often requested by HMRC before they reach a decision.

When **clearance cannot be given**, HMRC will state the reasons why. Where the company disagrees with HMRC's reasons it is entitled to submit a tax return in accordance with its own view of the position. If the return is subsequently amended by HMRC, the company can appeal in the normal way (¶54155).

90945

Any **clearance given** by HMRC will state the **terms** under which it is given, and the **period** for which it applies (which is normally indefinitely provided that the facts and circumstances do not change).

90950

HMRC will consider themselves **bound** by the clearance given provided that all the relevant facts of the situation have been stated accurately by the company.

INTM 214120

HMRC may review the continued application of the clearance to ensure that the facts remain the same. Where there is a **change in the facts and circumstances**, the company should notify this to HMRC, otherwise penalties could be levied, if a return is submitted on the basis of a clearance which could no longer apply given the change in circumstances.

C. Apportionment of profits

When the overseas company is within the definition of a CFC and the exemptions do not apply, an apportionment takes place among persons who have a relevant interest in the CFC

90980

s 752 ICTA 1988

at some time in the accounting period, arising by virtue of direct or indirect holdings of ordinary shares in the CFC.

However, an assessment to tax under the provisions is only made on UK companies.

Chargeable profits

90985   **Unless** falling within an exclusion the chargeable profits of the overseas company must be **computed for the following reasons**, so as to:
– establish whether the profits have been subject to a lower level of tax in the overseas territory (¶90610);
– ensure that the profits exceed the de minimis limits (¶90720); and
– establish the amount of profits that will be apportioned among shareholders in situations where this is necessary.

The chargeable profits are a notional sum, and no part of those profits can be identified as coming from a particular source. *Bricom Holdings v CIR* [1997]

90990   Although chargeable profits are computed for the purposes of the CFC legislation in the
Sch 24 ICTA 1988   same way as they would be for UK corporation tax purposes, the following **assumptions** need to be made in order to perform the computation:
– the overseas company is assumed to be **resident** in the UK (from the beginning of the first accounting period in respect of which an apportionment has been made), and is therefore within the charge to UK corporation tax;
– the term **profits** has the same meaning as it does for corporation tax, **excluding** chargeable gains, but including income of a trust of which the CFC is the settlor or a beneficiary;
– the company is not a close company;
– all relevant **claims and elections** have been made so as to obtain maximum relief, though the UK-resident company that has a majority interest in the CFC may cancel or modify such claims or elections by notifying HMRC;
– the CFC is not a member of a **group or consortium**; however, where there is in fact a surrender of losses by the CFC under the group relief provisions, its profits are to be increased to the extent of the group relief surrendered;
– where the CFC has incurred **trading losses** in an accounting period ending within 6 years of the beginning of the first accounting period for which an apportionment is required to be made under the CFC provisions, the UK company having a majority interest may claim to set those losses against the profit of the CFC, assuming that the usual carry forward loss rules apply (i.e. the effect of the claim is to deem the CFC to be UK resident for loss purposes, so that its profits and losses are computed accordingly for every accounting period since the period of the loss);
– in computing **writing down allowances and balancing adjustments** these are given as if machinery or plant which had been bought before the commencement is brought into the computation at market value at the beginning of the period.

> MEMO POINTS   1. For CFCs **resident in the EEA** see also ¶91005.
> 2. On giving appropriate notice to HMRC, UK parent companies are able to apply the **designated currency** rules (¶17210) when determining the chargeable profits of their overseas subsidiaries.
> 3. Where the CFC's chargeable profits include a payment received from another company (the paying company), and the corporation tax relief available to the paying company is restricted by the **worldwide debt cap rules** see ¶91015.

Method of apportionment

90995   Where the CFC provisions apply for the accounting period of a CFC, apportionment of its chargeable profits and creditable tax takes place **amongst** all the persons that have an interest in the CFC in the accounting period.

s 749B ICTA 1988   The following **persons have an interest** in the CFC, being those:
– who possess or who have the right to acquire share capital or voting rights in the CFC;
– possessing or entitled to acquire the right to receive distributions of the CFC, or any amounts payable by the CFC to loan creditors;

– having the right to secure that present or future income or assets of the CFC will be applied either directly or indirectly for their benefit; or
– who have control of the CFC, with or without other persons.

The **basic rule can be modified** by HMRC so that the apportionment is made on a just and reasonable basis. This would only be necessary where a UK company controlled the CFC by means other than a large shareholding (although the interests of a loan creditor are ignored for this purpose). In this case the company can apply for clearance (¶90920), detailing the following in the application:
s 752(4) ICTA 1988;
INTM 214130

– the various interest holdings in the controlled foreign company, and the basis on which they are held;
– the basis of why a particular apportionment method has been adopted.

> MEMO POINTS 1. Where a **company** has an interest in a CFC, any person that has an interest in that company is treated as having a corresponding interest in the CFC.
> 2. A **joint interest** (except one in a fiduciary or representative capacity) is treated as being in equal shares.

EXAMPLE
1. The ordinary share capital of X Inc, a CFC, is owned as follows:

Person	Residency	Shareholding
Mr A	UK resident	30%
B SA	French resident	30%
C Ltd	UK resident	10%
D Ltd	UK resident	30%

No other shares are in issue.
No apportionment is made to C Ltd as its interest is less than 25%.
An apportionment would be made to B SA, but it is outside the scope of UK corporation tax.
Only D Ltd is affected by the apportionment rules.

2. E Ltd owns 100% of the non-voting preference shares in F Inc (a CFC), and is therefore entitled to all the assets on winding up. However, E Ltd owns only 10% of the ordinary voting shares, whilst G Ltd, an unrelated company, owns 90%.
Based on the ordinary shares, E Ltd might avoid an apportionment as its interest is less than 25%. However, it is likely that HMRC would seek to apply a just and reasonable basis, and apportion a greater percentage to E Ltd.

Indirect holdings Where a person has only an indirect holding (i.e. the connection with the CFC is more remote, usually by having to look through another entity), the following rules apply:

91000
ss 752A, 752B
ICTA 1988

– a UK company holding a direct interest must be treated as the sole holder of the shares;
– if the direct holder is not UK-resident and the only indirect shareholder is UK-resident, the UK resident with the indirect holding is treated as the owner; and
– if the direct holder is not resident in the UK and there is more than one UK-resident indirect shareholder (i.e. there is a chain or group of companies), the lowest UK resident in the chain of ownership is deemed to be the holder.

Where income arises to the trustees of a settlement and the company is a settlor or beneficiary, the income is included in the apportionment of profit. If there is more than one beneficiary, a just and reasonable apportionment is made.

EXAMPLE X Inc is a CFC owned 60% by Y Inc (a non-resident company) which is itself owned by Z Ltd, a UK-resident company. Z Ltd also owns 10% of X Inc directly. The other 30% of X Inc is owned by another non-resident company, T Inc, which is 100% owned by W Ltd, a UK-resident company, W Ltd being in turn 100% owned by V Ltd, another UK-resident company.

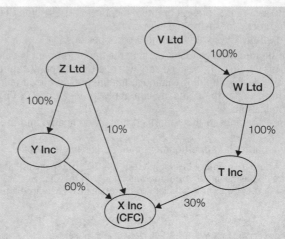

Under the CFC rules on indirect holdings, Z Ltd is deemed to hold 70% of X Inc (60% indirectly + 10% directly), while W Ltd is deemed to own the other 30% of X Inc (as it is the lowest UK resident company in the chain).

EEA territories

91005
s 751A ICTA 1988;
INTM 210540

As a consequence of the decision of the European Court of Justice in *Cadbury Schweppes v HMRC* [2006], a reduction in the amount of apportioned profits will be available where the **profits are generated by** genuine economic activity within an EEA state. Profits arising merely from holding assets in the overseas company would not be eligible for the EEA relief.

A UK resident may apply for the chargeable profits of the CFC to be reduced for a period if the following **conditions** are met:
– a CFC is liable to an apportionment in an accounting period;
– throughout that accounting period the CFC has had a business establishment in an EEA territory (this being a territory that is within the EEA at that time (¶82585));
– throughout that accounting period the CFC has had employees operating in the EEA territory;
– a UK company has a relevant interest in the CFC in the period; and
– no application for a reduction has been made in respect of other exemptions (¶90790 and ¶90800).

The **amount of the reduction** in apportioned profits is the amount that represents the net economic value to a group of companies, created by the work of staff in a business establishment in the EEA state. This is the real economic profit for the group created by those activities, after deducting the full economic costs of carrying on the work. In assessing the value of the work, attention must be paid to the actual content of the work and the level of competence of the staff carrying it out.

> MEMO POINTS 1. **Business establishment** means premises which are, or are intended to be, occupied and used with a reasonable degree of permanence for the purposes of the company's business.
> 2. An **application for the relief** to be deducted from the CFC's profits for a period must be made to HMRC's Outward Investment Team, together with appropriate detailed information about the CFC as specified by HMRC. Documentation must be submitted in support of the computation of the part of the CFC profits that represents net economic value. The level of documentation should be similar to that provided by a UK company in support of its transfer pricing position (¶70890).
> 3. The application should be **made by** the due date of the CTSA return of the UK company for the accounting period to which it relates.
> 4. Where the application is **refused**, the company may advise HMRC of its appeal within 30 days of the refusal of the application.

1. A UK company forms a CFC in another EEA state to deal with intra-group services, including accounting and payroll. The necessary equipment is installed and a management team is appointed. The management recruits staff locally. The group services company is rewarded for its work on a cost plus basis (¶70245).

An application for EEA relief is very likely to be granted, provided that the chargeable profits of the CFC are in line with the transfer pricing method chosen. The group services company is doing real business in the EEA location, and directly creating value for the group. The transfer pricing method used is appropriate to calculate the reward for intra-group services.

2. A UK company sets up a controlled foreign company in another EEA state, and transfers intellectual property to the CFC which receives the royalties. A small team of staff is appointed to administer the intellectual property and collect the royalty payments.

In this case the real economic value arises from the legal ownership of the intellectual property and not from the administrative work of the staff in the CFC. An application for EEA relief will not be accepted by HMRC unless it is limited to the arm's length return for the administrative work of the staff, rather than the royalty income from the intellectual property.

Worldwide debt cap

To prevent double taxation, where the chargeable profits of the CFC contain **an amount of income** in respect of a payment which has been reduced for tax purposes by the worldwide debt cap rules (¶70530), the UK company can apply to HMRC for a reduction in the apportioned profits. The related creditable tax (¶91085) will also be reduced on a just and reasonable basis.

91015
s 751AA ICTA 1988

D. Taxation of apportioned profits

Where at least 25% of the chargeable profits of a CFC are apportioned to a UK-resident company (or to persons connected or associated with it), the related tax charge is calculated by charging corporation tax at the appropriate rate, and deducting the relevant proportion of the CFC's creditable tax.

91045

The tax charge can then be reduced by various reliefs.

EXAMPLE The ordinary share capital of A Inc (a CFC) is owned by the following persons:

Person	Residency	Shareholding
B SA	French company	40%
C Ltd	UK company	30%
D Ltd	UK company	10%
Mr E	UK individual	20%

These are the only shares in issue.
If A Inc has profits of £575,000, including a chargeable gain of £75,000, the apportionment to C Ltd is:

		£
Profits		575,000
Less: Chargeable gain		(75,000)
		500,000
Apportionment	500,000 x 30%	150,000

1. General principles

Accounting period

The apportioned profit will be taxable in the hands of the UK company for its accounting period in which the CFC's accounting period (¶90590) ends.

91075

> EXAMPLE F Inc is a CFC wholly owned by G Ltd. F Inc prepares its accounts to 31 December, and G Ltd to 31 March. An apportionment of £100,000 is made for F Inc's accounting period ended 31 December 2012.
> This will be included on G Ltd's corporation tax return for the accounting period to 31 March 2013.

Tax rate

91080   The appropriate tax rate is **defined** as the mainstream corporation tax rate. The small profits rate never applies for this purpose.

Creditable tax

91085
s 751(6) ICTA 1988

The creditable tax is computed as the **aggregate** of any:
– income tax deducted at source from income received by the CFC;
– double tax relief available in the UK for foreign tax due against the chargeable profits, which would be available assuming the overseas company is liable to corporation tax on its chargeable profits, and given the other assumptions set out in the CFC rules in relation to the tax status and profits of the overseas company (¶90615); and
– corporation tax charged in the UK on income of the CFC that is taxable in the UK, less any tax repayments made.

> EXAMPLE H Inc, a CFC, is owned as follows:
>
> | | | |
> |---|---|---|
> | Mr H | UK resident | 30% |
> | A Ltd | UK resident | 70% |
>
> H Inc's results for the year to 31 March were as follows:
>
> | | £ |
> |---|---:|
> | Trading profits from overseas operations[1] | 425,000 |
> | Interest received from Swiss bank (Swiss tax paid £2,950) | 47,000 |
> | UK source taxed income (gross) | 15,000 |
> | UK rental income | 22,200 |
>
> **Note:**
> 1. The profits are as adjusted for tax purposes in the territory of residence. Entertaining and depreciation totalling £12,500 have been deducted. Capital allowances available under UK rules are £18,750. An adjusted loss of £2,950 would have been available in the previous 6 years, under UK rules.
>
> A Ltd's profits are calculated by:
> – adjusting H Inc's profits; and
> – including the apportioned profits in A Ltd's computation (which already show other profits for the period of £1m).
>
> **Adjustment of H Inc's profits**
>
> | | £ | £ |
> |---|---:|---:|
> | Overseas trading profit | | 425,000 |
> | Add: Disallowable items | 12,500 | |
> | Less: Capital allowances | (18,750) | |
> | | | (6,250) |
> | | | 418,750 |
> | Less: Losses brought forward | | (2,950) |
> | Foreign income | | 415,800 |
> | Loan relationship credit | | 47,000 |
> | UK property business | | 22,200 |
> | Taxed income | | 15,000 |
> | | | 500,000 |
> | | | |
> | Apportioned to A Ltd | 70% × 500,000 | £350,000 |

A Ltd's computation (presuming a tax rate of 23%)		£	£
Tax on UK profits:	1,000,000 @ 23%		230,000
Tax on apportioned CFC profit	350,000 @ 23%	80,500	
Less:			
Credit relief for Swiss tax		(2,950)	
UK income tax suffered	15,000 @ 20%	(3,000)	
Tax on H Inc's UK income	22,200 @ 23%	(5,106)	
			69,444
Gross corporation tax due			299,444

Reporting

The tax on the apportioned profit is charged as if it were corporation tax, and so the company must provide details of its apportionment computation in the **CTSA return** for the period in which the accounting period of the CFC ends. The supplementary page required is CT600B.

91090
s 754 ICTA 1988

No separate reporting is required where:
- the excluded countries exemption applies; or
- the relevant interest in the CFC is less than 25%.

INTM 214020

However, where an **exemption** would potentially apply, HMRC will allow a company to submit a CT600B and claim the exemption without checking that the overseas subsidiary is a CFC (i.e. particularly avoiding the need to check whether the CFC is liable to a lower tax charge) or whether the company's interest is at least 25%. In this case only the following information is required:
- name of the CFC;
- its territory of residence; and
- the exemption due.

Where the company is **liable to a CFC tax charge**, the following additional information is also required:
- the appropriate percentage of apportionable profits and creditable tax;
- the amount of chargeable profits apportioned to the company;
- tax on the chargeable profits;
- the creditable tax on the chargeable profits;
- reliefs in terms of tax;
- unrelieved surplus ACT; and
- the CFC tax due.

91095
INTM 214030

Whilst penalties would be levied for an **incorrect** return HMRC will take account of the following:
- the information which should have been available to the company;
- the understanding of the liability which might reasonably be expected; and
- the company's justification for taking an alternative interpretation of facts or legislation.

INTM 214080

Payment

The **due date** for the related payment is the same as for the normal corporation tax charge i.e. either 9 months and 1 day from the end of the accounting period (¶48050) or in quarterly instalments (¶48095). The normal rules for interest (¶51040) and penalties (¶52410) apply.

91100

Where the **CFC tax remains unpaid** by the due date, HMRC may initiate recovery proceedings against another UK resident company, where that company holds (or has held) all or part of the same interest in the CFC as the defaulting company. Payment must be made within a further 3 months.

s 754 ICTA 1988

2. Reliefs

91130   The following reliefs are available:
- offset of usual losses and allowances against the CFC charge;
- using surplus ACT to reduce the CFC charge;
- reducing the gain resulting from the disposal of the CFC shares; and
- a reduction in the tax on non-exempt dividends received from a CFC.

Offset

91135
Sch 26 para 1
ICTA 1988

A full or partial claim for relief can be made by offsetting **a proportion** (i.e. as computed using the mainstream rate of tax) of any of the following against the CFC tax charge:
- trading losses;
- property business losses;
- charitable donations;
- management expenses;
- excess capital allowances;
- group relief; or
- non-trading loan relationship deficits.

Comment   Where creditable tax is available against the apportioned profit the losses offset against the chargeable profits may be relieved at a rather lower rate.

> EXAMPLE   In the year to 31 March 2013, B Ltd made a trading loss of £100,000 and was charged to tax in respect of apportioned profits of £140,000.
> In the absence of a claim, B Ltd will be liable to pay tax of £33,600. (140,000 x 24%)
> However, B Ltd can make a claim to offset the trading losses against the apportioned profits. This relief will be expressed in terms of a tax reduction (i.e. the reduction in tax as a result of the claim will be £24,000). (100,000 @ 24%)
> So the CFC tax will actually be £9,600. (33,600 – 24,000)
> The trading losses will be deemed to have been fully utilised.

Surplus ACT

91140
SI 1999/358 reg 20

Where there is still surplus ACT from accounting periods beginning before 6 April 1999, this may be offset against the tax on the apportioned profits, subject to the provisions with respect to the shadow ACT rules (¶41225).

The ACT **available for offset** is restricted to the amount of shadow ACT that would be due if a dividend equal to the net chargeable profits were paid.

Gains on disposals of CFC shares

91145
Sch 26 para 3
ICTA 1988

When the shares in a CFC are disposed of, any chargeable gain arising may be **reduced** where tax has previously been paid on apportioned profits.

The **amount** of the reduction is calculated by using the following formula (all of the amounts refer to the particular accounting period):

$$\frac{\text{Average market value of shares disposed of}}{\text{Average market value of the entire holding}} \times \text{Total tax paid on the apportioned profits}$$

A **claim** for the reduction must be made within 3 months of the end of the accounting period in which the disposal of the CFC shares takes place.

> EXAMPLE   C Ltd holds 5,000 shares in D Inc (a CFC). In Year 1, C Ltd pays tax of £10,000 on apportioned profits. In Year 2, C Ltd sells 1,000 shares in D Inc, when each share is worth £30. C Ltd realises a chargeable gain of £12,000.
> This gain can be reduced by £2,400. ($\frac{30 \times 1,000}{30 \times 5,000} \times 10,000$)

Non-exempt dividends received

The rule below is **only of relevance** when the dividends from the CFCs are not exempt (¶18380).

91150
Sch 26 para 4
ICTA 1988

The **total assessments** under the CFC provisions (gross attributed tax) are treated as underlying tax, which can be offset against the corporation tax liability resulting from the receipt of the dividend.

This gross attributed tax does not increase the amount of dividend income received for tax purposes when computing the liability (i.e. the dividend from the CFC is not grossed up for this underlying tax).

> EXAMPLE   E Inc pays a non-exempt dividend to F Ltd of £104,000 (gross) out of profits of £520,000. F Ltd had paid tax at 26% on apportioned profits of £100,000.
>
> | | £ |
> |---|---:|
> | UK tax on apportioned profit
100,000 × 26% | 26,000 |
> | Effective rate of tax:
$\frac{26,000}{520,000} = 5\%$ | |
> | Underlying tax credit on dividend
104,000 × 5% | 5,200 |
>
> The credit of £5,200 can be set against the tax liability of F Ltd.

E. Changes to the rules

The new rules draw on a lot of the previous legislation and the mechanics of apportionment are still the same. However, the approach of the rules is somewhat different in an effort to simplify them and eliminate companies from the need to apply the rules by applying a gateway test as a first step. Only profits that pass the gateway test will be liable to the new rules. The changes to the scheme, outlined below, are effective for accounting periods beginning on or after 1 April 2013.

91180

1. Scope

The **definition** of a controlled foreign company under the new rules is wider than the previous definition, so that it is simply a company that is non-UK resident and is controlled by UK residents (but see below for an extension to include non-UK residents).

91190
s 371AA TIOPA
2010

A company will be considered to be under **control** of another where any of the following apply:

ss 371RA – 371RE
TIOPA 2010

a. Where a person (or persons) can ensure that the company's affairs are conducted in accordance with their wishes by virtue of voting power, holding of shares, the Articles of Association or another document.

b. Where it is reasonable to assume that a person (or persons) would receive more than 50% of the:
- proceeds, if the overseas company's shares were to be sold;
- distribution, if the overseas company were to distribute all of its funds; or
- assets, if the overseas company was wound up.

c. Where a person is considered to be the overseas company's parent undertaking according to accounting standards, provided, if the overseas company was deemed to be a CFC, the ensuing apportionment of profit under the CFC rules would give the parent undertaking a share of at least 50% of the profit.

Although an overseas company, under the normal rules, can only be a CFC where it is controlled by UK-residents, there is an **extension** where it is controlled by a UK-resident along with a non-UK resident. In this case the company will still be a CFC if:
– the UK-resident company holds at least 40% of whatever factor is used for ascertaining control; and
– the non-UK resident company holds at least 40%, but no more than 55%, of the same factor.

---

2. Entity level exemptions

91210   The first way that a company may be outside the new CFC regime is if it is considered to be exempt. The five ways a company may automatically be considered outside the rules are shown below.

Exemption	¶¶
Low profits	¶91215
Low profit margin	¶91220
Exempt period	¶91225
Excluded territories	¶91235
Tax	¶91240

MEMO POINTS   Care should be taken when **applying** the rules to ensure that the correct profits figure is being used as this changes between the accounting profit and the assumed taxable profits.

Low profits exemption

91215
s 371LB TIOPA 2010

This exemption will apply where the CFC has:
– accounting profits, or assumed taxable profits, of no more than £50,000; or
– accounting profits, or assumed taxable profits, of no more than £500,000 and the amount of non-trading income is no more than £50,000.

s 371LC TIOPA 2010

However, this exemption **cannot apply** where either:
– an **arrangement** is entered into at any time that secures the low profits exemption and this arrangement had, as at least one of its main purposes, the securing of the exemption for that period (or for that period and any other);
– the business of the CFC is the provision of UK **intermediary services**, being the personal provision of the services of a UK-resident individual without a contract directly between that person and the client, but under one between the client and the CFC; or
– where the exemption would otherwise be available after examining the **accounting profits** (rather than the assumed taxable profits) where a scheme is in place to exploit differences in accounting treatments, known as a group mismatch scheme (¶69375).

MEMO POINTS   1. These **limits** are for an accounting period of 12 months. Where the period is shorter the limits are reduced accordingly.
2. The **assumed taxable profits** are the profits that would be calculated by following UK legislation

Low profit margin exemption

91220
s 371MB TIOPA 2010

A CFC's profits will not be subject to apportionment where its accounting profits, before making any deductions for **interest payable**, for the period do not exceed 10% of its operating expenditure for the period excluding:
– the cost of goods purchased by the CFC unless those goods are used in the territory the CFC is resident in during that period; and
– any expenditure that gives rise to income of a person related to the CFC, either directly or indirectly.

However, this exemption **cannot apply** where an arrangement is entered into at any time that secures the low profit margin exemption and this arrangement had, as at least one of its main purposes, the securing of the exemption for that period (or for that period and any other).

s 371MC TIOPA
2010

Exempt period

There are a number of **conditions** to be met before a CFC can take advantage of this exemption:
– the accounting period must end during an exempt period for the CFC;
– the CFC does not cease trading prior to it having at least one chargeable period beginning after the end of the exempt period;
– the first accounting period beginning after the exempt period ends is not within the CFC charge; and
– at all times during the period from the first day of the exempt period to the end of the first period of the CFC beginning after the exempt period, a company would be chargeable if the profits were subject to apportionment and each company that would be chargeable but for this exemption would have been a chargeable company at the commencement of the exempt period.

91225
s 371JB TIOPA
2010

The exempt period, which lasts for 12 months, **begins** where:
– immediately before the relevant time the CFC is carrying on a business or, if the relevant time is when the CFC is formed to control another company with the expectation that it will start an exempt period on the date on which the CFC begins to control that company;
– one or more companies would be chargeable on an apportionment if the company would otherwise be deemed to be a CFC; and
– at no point during the preceding 12 months is there a company that would be chargeable to an apportionment.

Comment This exemption is essentially to allow groups to rearrange the affairs of a CFC while bringing the headquarters of group holding companies back to the UK.

> MEMO POINTS   1. A company can apply to HMRC to **extend** the exempt period. Such an application must be made before the expiration of the existing exempt period and must be made by a company that would be subject to tax on an apportionment.
> 2. Where the accounting period **does not end during** an exempt period any part of its profits arising during an exempt period will not pass the gateway test (¶91270).

s 371JD TIOPA
2010

s 371JE TIOPA
2010

The exempt period exemption will, however, be **denied** where either an arrangement is entered into to secure a tax advantage for that period (or that period plus any other period):
– where the arrangement is linked to the exempt period exemption, for that period (or that period plus any other) and it involves the CFC holding assets giving rise to non-trading financial profits or trading finance profits, or holding intellectual property that entitles the CFC to income; or
– where as a consequence of the arrangement the accounting period of the CFC is shortened to less than 12 months and at least one of the main purposes of this was to secure the exempt period exemption for that period (or that period plus any other).

91230

Excluded territories exemption

A CFC will be exempt for a period where:
– it is resident in one of the specified excluded territories;
– no intellectual property has been transferred to it from the UK in the previous 6 years;
– it is not involved in an arrangement to secure a tax advantage for any person; and
– certain types of income do not exceed a threshold level.

91235
s 371KB TIOPA
2010

Threshold test Four types of income of the CFC must be compared against its accounting profits in order to see if the threshold test is passed.

The following types of income must be aggregated:
– income that is not subjected to tax in the CFC's country of residence, or is subject to a reduced rate of tax (this may be by virtue of the type of income or as a tax holiday / incentive

scheme, as well as any credit type scheme for either the CFC or someone connected with it). This excludes any dividends or distributions received;
– any notional interest deducted from any income for tax purposes in the CFC's territory (or any territory in which it has a permanent establishment) but is not actually deducted in determining the CFCs assumed taxable profits for the period. This is limited to its non-local income (gross income received from someone outside the CFC's territory that arises during the period);
– income from a settlement of which the CFC is either settlor or beneficiary;
– the CFC's share of income from any partnership it is involved in; and
– any reduction in the CFC's profits as a result of a transfer pricing adjustment where there is no increase in the profits in another territory.

Where the sum of all of these does not exceed the greater of 10% of the CFC's accounting profits for the period and $50,000 the threshold test will be met.

> MEMO POINTS   1. Where any income falls into two headings it will only be counted once for the purposes of examining the threshold test.
> 2. The **specified territories** are:

Afghanistan	Fiji	Panama
Algeria	Finland	Papua New Guinea
Angola	France	Peru
Argentina	Gabon	Philippines
Armenia	Gambia	Poland
Aruba	Germany	Portugal
Australia	Ghana	Puerto Rico
Austria	Greece	Republic of Korea
Azerbaijan	Guyana	Russia
Bangladesh	Honduras	Saudi Arabia
Barbados	Iceland	Senegal
Belarus	India	Sierra Leone
Belgium	Indonesia	Slovakia
Belize	Iran	Slovenia
Benin	Israel	Solomon Islands
Bolivia	Italy	South Africa
Botswana	Ivory Coast	Spain
Brazil	Jamaica	Sri Lanka
Brunai	Japan	Swaziland
Burundi	Kenya	Sweden
Cameroon	Lesotho	Tanzania
Canada	Libya	Thailand
China	Luxembourg	Trinidad and Tobago
Colombia	Malawi	Tunisia
Croatia	Malaysia	Turkey
Cuba	Malta	Uganda
Czech Republic	Mexico	Ukraine
Democratic Republic of the Congo	Monaco	United States of America
Denmark	Morocco	Uruguay
Dominican Republic	Namibia	Venezuela
Ecuador	Netherlands	Vietnam
Egypt	New Zealand	Zambia
El Salvador	Nigeria	Zimbabwe
Falkland Islands	Norway	
Faroe Islands	Pakistan	

3. For companies in **Australia**, **Canada**, **France**, **Germany**, **Japan** or the **USA** there is a relaxation of the rules so that there is no intellectual property condition nor threshold test, provided the profits do not arise from a permanent establishment in another territory and all of the profits are subject to tax in that territory.

Tax exemption

This exemption **cannot apply** where the CFC:
- does not have a territory of residence; or
- is subject to a designer rate of tax, defined as a rate where the company has significant control over the amount of tax they pay and are specified as such in regulations.

For this exemption to **apply** the amount of tax paid in the CFC's territory of residence on local profits must be at least 75% of the amount of tax that would have been paid on the same profits in the UK. When looking at the local tax paid no account is taken of capital gains or losses, and the profit is calculated based on the local tax rules. The local tax amount may also be reduced where the CFC has net:
- income taken into account in calculating its local liability that would not be taxed in the UK; or
- expenditure disallowed that would have been allowed under UK rules.

In either case the amount of local tax is reduced to account for the difference in tax treatment so that the comparison of tax is based on a level of profit that is comparable.

> [MEMO POINTS] 1. Where the CFC has paid tax and a **repayment** of it, or a **credit** in respect of it, is made to someone other than the CFC under the local territory's rules, the local tax is reduced accordingly.
> 2. When carrying out the **calculation** of the equivalent UK tax:
> - any double tax relief available for the local tax is to be ignored; and
> - any amounts representing income tax deducted from payments received and any tax charged in respect of the CFC's profits must be deducted from the amount of tax calculated.
> 3. The **territory of residence** is determined by examining its liability to tax by virtue of its domicile, residence or place of management. This may result in a company being considered to be resident in more than one territory but for the CFC rules it can be resident in only one. If there are two territories the following are applied in order to break a tie:
> - if an election was made to prefer one territory in an earlier period;
> - the effective place of management if only in one territory;
> - where two or more territories have an effective place of management, one of these with more than 50% of the assets held based on the market value;
> - any other territory in which more than 50% of the assets are held;
> - by election; then
> - decision by HMRC on a just and reasonable basis.

91240
s 371NB TIOPA 2010

s 371NE TIOPA 2010

s 371TB TIOPA 2010

---

3. Gateway test

Where a company is not exempted from the charge it must ascertain what, if any, profits pass through the gateway. An initial gateway test is imposed to see if any profits pass the gateway test before considering the amount of profits that pass the gateway using more detailed rules.

91270
ss 371BB TIOPA2010

The **initial gateway test** comprises a test for each type of income category under the legislation:
- profits attributable to UK activities;
- non-trading finance profits;
- trading finance profits; and
- captive insurance business.

> [MEMO POINTS] The rules relating to captive insurance business are not covered in this book.

Profits attributable to UK activity

This gateway is **passed unless** one of four conditions are satisfied:
1. At no time during the period does the CFC hold assets or bear risks where:
- the main purpose of the arrangement is the reduction or elimination of any tax imposed in the UK and as a result of this arrangement the CFC expects its business to be more profitable at any point; and

91275
ss 371CA TIOPA2010

– there is an expectation that the arrangement will lead to a reduction or elimination of the liability of another party in another territory and its reasonable to suppose that the arrangement would not be in place if it wasn't for this expectation.

2. At no time during the period does the CFC have any UK-managed assets or bear any UK-managed risks. This means that the asset or risk is managed or controlled to a significant extent by the CFC in the UK, other than through a permanent establishment, or by a company connected with the CFC in circumstances that a third party would not be used.

3. At all times during the period the CFC has the capacity to ensure its business was commercially effective if its UK-managed assets or risks were no longer UK managed.

4. The CFC's profits consist only of non-trading finance profits or property business profits.

Non-trading finance profits

91280
ss 371CB TIOPA
2010

This gateway is **passed only** if the CFC has non-trading finance profits during the period excluding:

– any profits arising from the investment of funds held for the purposes of the CFC's trade where no trading profits of the CFC pass through the gateway (¶91275); and

– any profits arising from the investment of funds held by the CFC for any property business it carries on.

However, the exclusion of profits will **not apply** where the funds are held:

– only or mainly because of a restriction on the CFC paying dividends unless the restriction does not apply throughout the relevant 12-month period;

– with a view to paying dividends at a time after the relevant 12-month period;

– with a view to acquiring shares or making a capital contribution to a person;

– with a view to acquiring, developing or otherwise investing in land after the relevant 12-month period;

– only or mainly for contingencies; or

– only or mainly to reduce or eliminate the liability to any tax or duty of any person.

> MEMO POINTS   The **relevant 12-month period** is the 12 months following the end of the accounting period in question.

91285
s 371CC TIOPA
2010

Where a CFC **also has** trading profits, property business profits or exempt distribution income (where a substantial part of its business throughout the period is the holding of shares in its 51% subsidiaries) then the gateway test will not be passed if the non-trading finance profits are no more than 5% of the total of its trading and property business profits (before deductions for interest and locally imposed tax) and the exempt distribution income.

> MEMO POINTS   If a **51% subsidiary** is itself a CFC and has non-trading finance profits these have to be added in when looking at this test.

Trading finance profits

91290
s 371CE TIOPA
2010

Profits will **only pass** this gateway where at any time during the period the CFC has funds or assets that derive (directly or indirectly) from UK-connected capital contributions.

Trading finance profits can be treated as non-trading finance profits by a group treasury company provided it gives notice to HMRC. Such a notice must be given within 20 months of the end of the accounting period, although HMRC has the discretion to allow later notifications.

---

4. Trading profits safe harbour

91320
s 371DF TIOPA
2010

Before any apportionment is considered a company may be able to exempt all of its profits from the regime provided it meets a variety of criteria.

1. **Business** condition. At all times during the period the CFC has in its territory of residence premises with a reasonable degree of permanence that are, or intended to be, occupied or used, and that is the premises from which the CFC's activities are mainly carried on from.

2. **Income** conditions. No more than 20% of the CFC's trading income (excluding goods made in the CFC's territory of residence sold in the UK) is derived from UK-resident persons or UK permanent establishments of non-UK companies.

3. **Management expenditure** condition. No more than 20% of the total related management expenditure of the CFC is to be incurred in the UK. This includes staff costs for management, as well as the cost of individuals not employed by the company who perform a management function. This is extended to include the provision of such services through another company.

4. **Intellectual property** condition. This condition is automatically met unless the assumed total profits include income from the exploitation of intellectual property (IP) that has been transferred to the company from a related person (or derived from a related person's IP) in that period or any of the prior 6 years, and the value of that related person's IP has decreased as a result. This will also be the case where only **part** of IP being exploited was transferred provided this element is a significant part of what is being exploited and it has significantly raised the company's profits.

5. **Export of goods** condition. This is met if no more than 20% of the trading income of the CFC arises from goods exported from the UK (excluding exports to the CFC's territory of residence).

These provisions attempt to ensure that only the artificial diversion of profits falls under the new regime.

---

5. Quantification of income

Once a gateway test has been passed it is necessary to quantify the income that will be subject to apportionment among the participating companies (¶90980). Again, the way that the income is quantified will depend on the category of income.

91340

Profits from UK activities

There is an eight step calculation to follow in order to determine the amount of profit from UK activities that should be apportioned.

91345
ss 371DA – 371DL
TIOPA 2010

Step one: Identify the relevant assets and risks. These are the assets or risks giving rise to the CFC's profits for the period.

Step two: Exclude any assets or risks where the profits arising to the CFC are only negligibly higher than if they had not been held or borne.

Step three: Identify the significant people function or key entrepreneurial risk-taking function (SPF) carried out by the CFC that is relevant to the ownership of the assets and risks involved.

Step four: Determine to what extent the SPFs are carried out in the UK by the CFC or by a connected company. If there are no UK SPFs identified then no profits pass the gateway.

Step five: Assume the UK SPFs are carried out by a permanent establishment of the CFC in the UK and attribute the assets and risks already identified to it.

Step six: Exclude any assets or risks where the total of the gross amounts of income arising from the UK SPFs does not exceed 50% of the total income of the CFC.

Step seven: Recalculate the assumed profits after excluding the assets and risks that were attributed to the fictional permanent establishment at step five.

Step eight: Exclude any profits where the non-tax value of the arrangement i.e the economic value is more than 20% of the total value. It is highly unlikely this will be applicable as it would be difficult to ascertain the non-tax value of an arrangement like this once this stage of the calculation has been reached.

Non-trading finance profits

The same steps one to five (¶91345) as for profits from UK activities have to be undertaken, substituting non-trading finance profits for its total profits.

91350
s 371EA TIOPA
2010

The amounts that will be **included** within non-trading finance profits before applying the steps will be:
- profits arising from UK SPFs (¶91345);
- profits arising from UK funds or assets;
- arrangements, typically loans, with the UK; and
- UK finance leases.

Trading finance profits

91355
s 371EA TIOPA
2010

This heading covers profits that are **derived from** excess free capital. This is determined by considering what would be a reasonable level of free capital for a similar company that was not a 51% subsidiary of another company. The excess free capital is then considered to be the excess or, if less, the CFCs free assets deriving from UK connected contributions.

This sum is then adjusted to reflect what it is reasonable to assume arises from the use or investment of the free excess capital.

SECTION 6

Special situations

Summary

91405

Topic	¶¶
Leaving the UK	¶91435
Dual resident companies	¶91480
Non-resident close companies	¶76040
Transfer of UK trade	¶61205
Transfer of non-UK trade	¶61210

A. Leaving the UK

91435

On becoming non-resident, a company must notify HMRC and make arrangements to settle all UK tax liabilities, which will include corporation tax on the exit charge arising from the deemed disposal of all assets transferred out of the UK.

Comment Where a company migrates from the UK **to another EU member state**, and is subject to exit tax on chargeable assets, there is a danger of double taxation on these assets because of subsequent tax charges that may occur in the other member state at a later date when the asset is disposed of or another event triggers a charge to tax. Exit taxes on companies are not yet harmonised within the EU. However, in 2006, the European Commission issued a Communication entitled "Exit taxation and the need for coordination of Member States' tax policies". This was in response to a decision of the European Court of Justice in *Hughes de Lasteyrie du Saillant* which concerned exit taxation on individuals. The European Commission stated the opinion that the *Hughes de Lasteyrie du Saillant* case and the interpretation of freedom of establishment given by the ECJ have direct implications for the imposition of exit taxes on companies. So far, no actual changes have been implemented.

Company migration

A company migrates from the UK if it either:
- transfers its central management and control outside the UK; or
- becomes non-resident under the provisions of a relevant double tax treaty.

91440

An **accounting period** comes to an end at the date of migration, which means balancing adjustments must be calculated in relation to capital allowances.

s 10 CTA 2009

An **exit charge** applies if a company ceases to be resident in the UK, so that the company is deemed to have disposed of and immediately reacquired its chargeable assets at market value, although any assets relating to a trade that the company continues to carry on in the UK through a permanent establishment (¶92140) are excluded from the exit charge.

s 185 TCGA 1992

Where an exit charge accrues to a company that is a **75% subsidiary of a UK-resident company**, it is possible to make an election to **postpone** this gain. The gain will, however, become chargeable if:
- within 6 years of its departure, the company that left the UK disposes of the assets;
- the subsidiary ceases to be a 75% subsidiary of the principal company; or
- the principal company changes its residence.

> ⌐MEMO POINTS⌐ 1. For details of **chargeable assets** see ¶30190.
> 2. For details of **market value** see ¶30410.
> 3. An exit charge will also arise where a **permanent establishment** ceases to trade, unless there is a scheme of reconstruction (¶79290).
> 4. It is not possible to **roll over** the gain on a business asset (¶30940) into the acquisition of an asset which occurs after the cessation of residence, unless the new assets are purchased for use in a trade carried on in the UK via a permanent establishment.
> 5. For **European companies** who are transferring their registered office see ¶93245.

On becoming non-resident, a company must **notify HMRC** in advance, by providing the following information:
- the date of the intended migration;
- the estimated UK tax due in respect of accounting periods beginning before that date; and
- what arrangements will be made to settle that liability.

91445
s 109B TMA 1970

HMRC must approve the arrangements, which must be based on true information, otherwise the approval is void.

Where the company **does not comply** with these rules, it will be liable to a penalty. A penalty can also be levied on any person who is:
- a company which controls the migrating company;
- a director of that company or the migrating company; or
- a person who gives a direction or instruction to such a company or director to perform the act in question, otherwise than by way of advice given in a professional capacity.

Where the UK **tax due is not paid** within 6 months of migration, HMRC may serve a notice demanding payment from certain persons connected with the company, within 3 years from the date when the amount of the tax is finally determined. A 30-day payment period is given by the notice, and the tax due is then treated as a liability of that person.

> ⌐MEMO POINTS⌐ 1. For this purpose, **UK tax** includes:
> - PAYE;
> - income tax deducted from payments made by the company;
> - tax deducted from payments made to non-resident entertainers or sportsmen;
> - tax deducted from subcontractors in the construction industry; and
> - interest on overdue tax.
> 2. The **certain persons** to whom a notice demanding payment can be served are:
> - any member of the same 51% group (¶65505) as the migrating company (as the group was comprised for the 12 months prior to the migration); and
> - any person who was a controlling director (i.e. a director who has control) of the migrating company or of any company which controlled it.
> 3. **Control** is defined at ¶75275.

Exit payment plans

91447
s 59FA, Sch 3ZB
TMA 1970

For exit charges payable on or after 11 December 2012 new provisions were introduced for companies that leave the UK to become resident in another EEA state. In order to enter into such a plan in relation to an exit charge the company must carry on a business in the EEA state and not be considered to be resident somewhere outside of the EEA under any double taxation agreement.

Where the company satisfies these conditions it can apply to defer the tax due on:
– **capital gains** charges;
– charges levied under the **loan relationship** rules; and
– charges levied under the **intangibles** regime.

The company must **apply** to HMRC within 9 months and 1 day of the end of the migration period to enter such a plan. The application must contain:
– the date on which the company became non-resident;
– the EEA state it now resides in;
– the amount of corporation tax the company believes is due as a result of the migration and the amount it wishes to defer; and
– details of the method of deferment.

91448   **Deferment options**   Two methods of deferment are available – the standard method and the realisation method.

Standard method This is the simpler way to deal with the deferment, calculating the overall gains that arise at the time of migration, then paying the tax on these in 6 annual instalments. The first payment is due 9 months and 1 day after the end of the migration period.

Realisation method This option has a larger administrative burden but has the benefit of taxing gains as the assets are realised. In this option the gain on every asset is recorded separately. Every year the company is then required to complete a return showing what assets have been realised and paying the tax that arose at the time of migration on these assets. For **intangible assets**, **derivative contracts** and **loan relationships** the economic life of the asset must be calculated at the time of migration and the tax is then spread over the asset's lifetime (although this is subject to a 10 year maximum).

> MEMO POINTS   No matter which method of deferment is chosen the tax will carry **interest** from the date it would have been due normally until the time it is actually paid.

Asset migration

91450   Where a chargeable asset becomes located outside the UK, for example where a UK permanent establishment transfers an asset offshore, an exit charge (¶91440) will also arise.

B. Dual resident companies

91480
s 18 CTA 2009

Most companies are deemed to be resident in only one territory due to the terms of a double tax treaty.

However, certain companies fall to be treated as resident in both the UK and another territory, which would give ample opportunity for tax planning and double deductions were it not for special rules.

Comment   Although **territory** and country are usually interchangeable, territory additionally denotes a state or other political subdivision.

Scope

91485   A dual resident company is one that fulfils the requirements for residence in more than one territory at the same time. This is possible because different countries have different rules for

tax residence. Under UK tax law, a company is dual resident in any period in which it is resident in the UK under the UK tax rules for residence, and is also resident in another state or territory because:
– it derives its status as a company under the general law of that territory, for example it is incorporated there;
– the location of management or seat of business is in that other territory; or
– it is regarded as resident under the overseas law relating to taxation.

Legislation exists:
– to ensure that certain types of dual resident company are unable to offset **losses** under the group relief provisions; and
– to restrict the access of such companies to **other types of tax relief** that would normally be available to groups or associated companies.

Comment   While the legislation is potentially of wide scope, it was originally introduced to deal with certain dual resident companies that were being used to exploit the group relief provisions (both in the UK and in the overseas territory) by obtaining a double deduction. Companies used for this purpose were generally resident in both the UK and either the US or Australia. Residence in the US and Australia is based on the place of incorporation whereas in the UK it is generally based on where the central management and control is situated, and it was therefore possible for a company incorporated in the US or Australia, but managed in the UK, to obtain dual resident status.
Such companies would often have no taxable income but would make tax losses because they were making interest payments.

Investing company

The legislation only applies to dual resident investing companies i.e. all companies whose **business is not wholly or mainly** that of trading throughout the accounting period, or which are investment companies.

91490
s 109 CTA 2010

A company will also be a dual resident investing company if, although it carries on a trade, it carries on **finance type** activities as follows:
– a trade whose main function is to carry on one or all of certain financial activities (thereby potentially bringing a group finance company within the definition of a dual resident investing company);
– although the main function of the company is not carrying on financial activities, the company engages in those financial activities to an extent which is not justified by its trade, or for a purpose that is not appropriate to its trade;
– the acquisition and holding of investments, including interests in connected companies (¶31375) (whether or not resident in the UK);
– making qualifying charitable donations (¶22085);
– making payments in relation to loans which result in loan relationship debits (¶16295); or
– paying other deductible finance costs.

A dual resident company would therefore come under these provisions if, in addition to carrying on a trade, it was borrowing substantial amounts to invest in subsidiary companies or had issued bills of exchange or deeply discounted securities to the extent that the total interest payments (including the element of discount on the securities) exceeded its profit for a period.

> MEMO POINTS   A dual resident company whose **trade ceases or greatly diminishes** during a period will be treated as a dual resident investing company.

Consequences

The following table summarises the consequences of being a dual resident investing company:

91495

Relief	Restriction	Reference
Group relief	Company cannot surrender losses, excess management expenses, excess capital allowances etc to other group members	s 109 CTA 2010
Intra-group transfers of asset to dual resident company	Cannot be made on no gain/no loss basis Note that transfers from dual resident company to the group can be made at no gain/no loss	s 171(2)(d) TCGA 1992
Group rollover relief	Not available when company acquires replacement asset	s 175(2) TCGA 1992
Succession to trade	Trading losses cannot be carried forward	s 949 CTA 2010
	The sale or transfer of an asset between parties under common control cannot be treated as at written down value but will be treated as at market value	ss 266, 570 CAA 2001
	Where the parties are also connected persons, and the sale is of machinery or plant at less than market value, the disposal is at market value	s 61 CAA 2001

SECTION 7

Subsidiary or branch?

91545 A UK-resident company must decide whether to incorporate a separate company in the overseas territory (and make sure it is not controlled or managed in the UK otherwise it may be dual resident (¶91480)) or trade through a permanent establishment. Often, it would be better for a loss-making start-up to be taxed as a branch, before incorporating once the trade starts to take off, so that losses can be utilised in the UK and then advantage can be taken of lower overseas tax rates on subsequent profits.

> MEMO POINTS 1. Certain territories have **other types of entity** available, in addition to a subsidiary or permanent establishment, which can be useful options e.g. a representative office, which enables a company to have a local overseas presence to undertake preparatory activities without significant start-up costs, and may be entitled to lower overseas tax rates.
> 2. It is of paramount importance that the payroll taxes and social security liabilities of **staff working overseas** are correctly treated and that any shortfall in salary is anticipated, and where necessary, equalised to what the net pay would have been if the individual had stayed in the UK. For details see *Tax Memo*.
> 3. A UK resident may instead choose to **acquire an overseas interest** – either the shares of an existing company (whose profits would not be liable to UK tax unless attributed under the CFC rules (¶90555)) or assets with which to form a branch (profits liable to tax in both the UK and overseas territory with relief for double taxation). An intermediate holding company could also be formed, either in the overseas territory, or a third territory, depending on commercial and tax considerations.

Comparison

91550 The basic differences between a subsidiary and branch are summarised in the table below:

Topic	Subsidiary	Branch
Legal requirement	Certain territories require incorporation	May not be available as an option
Setting up and flexibility	Can be costly and time consuming Once subsidiary exists, it can only be offloaded by sale or winding up etc	Easier to set up and potentially less permanent

Topic	Subsidiary	Branch
Liability of parent company	UK parent protected as subsidiary is separate legal entity	No protection
Ascertaining chargeable profits	From accounts	Most be calculated by using attributed profits (¶90140)
Corporation tax	An overseas subsidiary company will not be liable to UK corporation tax Taxable on worldwide profits in territory of residence Beneficial where tax rates in overseas territory are lower than in the UK	Profits of an overseas branch are liable to UK corporation tax in the year that they arise, irrespective of whether they are remitted to the UK Double taxation will most likely occur (as also taxed in foreign territory), and relief available under double taxation agreement or under UK domestic rules Availability of election to exempt profits (¶90160)
Capital allowances	No UK capital allowances for expenditure incurred by an overseas subsidiary company	UK capital allowances will be available in respect of plant and machinery purchased by an overseas branch
Trading losses	No UK relief is available for trading losses incurred by an overseas subsidiary company, unless group relief is available (¶66365)	Relief will usually be available for trading losses if incurred by an overseas branch
Effect on UK company's tax charge	Treated as an associated company (¶40185), and so the UK corporation tax limits will be reduced accordingly, which may increase parent's tax charge May result in UK parent falling within payments on account regime (¶48095)	Branch not treated as an associate of UK company, but profits included in parent's PCTCT

CHAPTER 2

Inward investment

92000　Inbound investment now comes into the UK from all parts of the world, for example investments by sovereign wealth funds, and investments into the automobile industry from China and India.

For UK corporation tax purposes, an overseas company may operate in the UK through either a subsidiary or a branch (formally known as a permanent establishment (PE)).

A UK subsidiary will be treated like any other UK resident company, and the overseas parent will extract profits usually by a dividend, interest or intra-group charges. The method of funding of the subsidiary is a key issue to decide.

A UK permanent establishment will only be subject to UK corporation tax on the profits attributed to it.

> ⌐MEMO POINTS⌐　Where a company trades in the UK, other than through a permanent establishment, there is no charge to corporation tax, although an income tax charge could apply. For example, a non-resident company might make a **one-off sale** or carry out a door-to-door sales operation without a fixed base in the UK.

SECTION 1

UK subsidary

92050　A UK subsidiary must observe all of the UK tax and accounting compliance rules, in particular:
－ notifying HMRC of its existence (¶60050+);

– calculating the tax liability, with the small profits rate possibly available, although the associated companies rule must be taken into account (¶40180+);
– submitting CTSA returns (¶46050+);
– payment of corporation tax on time (¶48055+); and
– ensuring compliance with the accounting requirements of Companies House, and satisfying the need for an audit, where relevant (see *Accountancy and Financial Reporting Memo*).

Funding decision

The non-resident parent must decide how to fund its UK subsidiary i.e. via equity or debt.   **92055**

Whilst dividends are not deductible in the UK and **equity** is a longer term investment, no withholding tax applies.

Interest on **debt** is deductible in the UK, but may be subject to higher tax rates as a receipt in the parent's territory of residence. Foreign exchange gains on intercompany loans will be taxable (¶17135+).

The tax consequences of any funding structure must be looked at in the round e.g. if tax rates in the other territory are higher, it would not be beneficial to have interest deductions in the UK, unless it is more important to reduce UK tax which cannot be given relief in the other territory.

Other topics which must also be considered in relation to debt funding are:
– transfer pricing (¶70000+);
– thin capitalisation (¶70490+);
– worldwide debt cap (¶70530+);
– arbitrage (¶94000+);
– late paid interest (¶16605+); and
– unallowable purpose (¶16500+).

SECTION 2

UK branch

A **non-UK resident** company trading through a UK permanent establishment is subject to UK   **92105**
corporation tax on the profits of that permanent establishment (i.e. trading profits and   s 5II TOIA 2005
income from any property used by the UK permanent establishment). Capital gains on assets
used by the UK permanent establishment are also subject to UK corporation tax.

Other UK profits (not attributable to a permanent establishment) of a non-resident company are subject to income tax at the basic rate of 20%.

Comment   A non-resident company may prefer, instead, to form a subsidiary as the basis of its UK operations. For a comparison of a branch structure as against a subsidiary see ¶92570.

Trading in the UK?

There is a **distinction** between trading in the UK and trading with the UK. Trading by non-   **92110**
residents **with the UK** does not bring them within the charging provisions of corporation tax.

According to HMRC, some of the **differences between** trading in and trading with the UK   INTM263020
that have been established by case law are as follows:
– the mere purchase of goods does not amount to trading; *Sulley v Attorney General* [1860] and
– if contracts are regularly made in the UK by the overseas principal or by an agent, that is strong evidence of trading in the UK but is not decisive.

To determine if there is trading in the UK, it is necessary to identify the profit-making activities and where they are performed. *Smidth & Co v Greenwood* [1921]

> ⌐*MEMO POINTS*⌐ Any entity making taxable supplies in the UK is required to register for **VAT** if the value of those supplies exceeds the registration threshold. Irrespective of the requirement to register, VAT can be recovered through a special claim mechanism. For details see *VAT Memo*.

A. Permanent establishment

92140
s 1141 CTA 2010

For UK tax purposes, a permanent establishment is **defined** as either:
– a fixed place of business in the UK, through which the business is wholly or partly carried on; or
– an agent who is acting on behalf of the company, who has authority to conduct business on behalf of the company and habitually exercises that authority (unless the agent is of independent status acting in the ordinary course of his business).

Comment   The definition of a permanent establishment in UK domestic tax law is similar to the definition in the OECD Model Tax Convention. The Commentary to Article 5 (permanent establishment) of the OECD Model has not been imported into UK law, but the UK has agreed the content except for certain stated agreed reservations. The commentary can therefore be applied to the UK domestic law provisions on permanent establishments where the wording is the same. However, if in the course of periodic updates, the Commentary on the OECD Model changes significantly, the approval of the UK Parliament would be needed to apply the updated interpretation to the UK's domestic law.

1. Fixed place of business

92170
INTM264060

For a fixed place of business to exist, **HMRC** consider that there must be:
– a geographic place of business, such as business premises, although there may be situations in which equipment can represent a fixed place of business;
– the place of business must have a certain degree of permanence; and
– the business of the non-resident must be carried on through the fixed place of business.

The following are common **examples** of fixed places of business:
– a place of management;
– a branch;
– an office;
– a factory;
– a workshop;
– an installation or structure for exploring natural resources;
– a mine, oil or gas well, quarry, or other place of extraction of natural resources; or
– a building site or construction or installation project.

> ⌐*MEMO POINTS*⌐ There is no requirement as to how long a **building or construction project** must continue. Where there is a double tax treaty which follows the OECD Model, it will normally provide that a permanent establishment only exists where the project continues for at least 12 months. Some treaties, however, specify a shorter period such as 6 or 9 months. Where the non-resident company is involved in more than one construction site or project, each should be considered separately as a potential permanent establishment.

Exclusions

92175
s 1143 CTA 2010

If the activities, in relation to the business as a whole, are **preparatory or auxiliary** in character, there is no permanent establishment in the UK. For example:
– the use of facilities for the purpose of storage, display or delivery of goods or merchandise belonging to the company;
– the maintenance of a stock of goods or merchandise belonging to the company for the purpose of storage, display or delivery;
– the maintenance of a stock of goods or merchandise belonging to the company for the purposes of processing by another person; or
– purchasing goods or merchandise or collecting information for the company.

These activities are only excluded from the definition of a permanent establishment if they are **performed** only for the non-resident enterprise. If such activities are also performed for other enterprises (including other companies in the same group), the fixed place of business cannot be excluded from the definition of a permanent establishment.

> ⎡_MEMO POINTS_⎤ According to **HMRC**, factors that need to be taken into account in determining if a fixed place of business in the UK is performing preparatory or auxiliary activities include:
> **a.** whether the remoteness of the services performed in the UK from the realisation of profits by the enterprise make it difficult to allocate any of the company's profits to its activities in the UK. If the activities performed are essentially the same as those performed by the company generally, they cannot be preparatory or auxiliary, and a permanent establishment may exist; and
> **b.** where the activities of the fixed place of business in the UK form an essential and significant part of the whole enterprise or are the same as the general purpose of the enterprise, the activities cannot be preparatory or auxiliary e.g. managing the enterprise or supplying spare parts.

INTM266120

Geographic condition

The significance of the geographic condition is the requirement for a **distinct place** of business in the UK, used for carrying on the business. This might consist of business premises, facilities, equipment or a site, but it might also be merely a space that is used such as a place in a street, or market used by a street vendor.

92180
INTM266060

It would also be possible for a UK place of business of a non-resident company to exist at the business **premises of another company**, for example the offices of a client company or an affiliated company, where that company makes some office space available to the non-resident enterprise. In considering whether space has been put at the disposal of a non-resident enterprise it does not matter whether the space is shared or exclusively available to that enterprise.

A key deciding factor is whether the particular address is advertised to customers e.g. appearing on business cards or on the company's website.

> ⎡_MEMO POINTS_⎤ 1. Where a business is conducted through **automated machinery**, a permanent establishment may exist if personnel are required to set up, operate or maintain the machinery.
> 2. The UK takes the view that a **server** (either alone or together with **websites**) cannot in itself constitute a permanent establishment of an enterprise that is doing business in the nature of e-commerce through websites on that server. However, the view of other OECD countries is that a server could constitute a permanent establishment where the equipment is not moved and is located at a particular location for a sufficient period of time to be regarded as fixed.

INTM266100

> ⎡EXAMPLE⎤
> **1.** A travelling salesman regularly visits a large client company in the UK, and holds meetings with the purchasing director in his office. The company, for whom this salesman works, would not be considered to have a fixed place of business in the UK, as the premises of the client are not at the disposal of that company.
> However, a parent company that is given the use of an office in a UK subsidiary, so as to supervise the activities of that subsidiary company for a period of time, would be regarded as having that office space in the UK at its disposal, and it could, therefore, constitute a fixed place of business in the UK.
>
> **2.** B SA is a French manufacturer, who is attempting to break into the UK market. It has paid for a new website, hosted in the UK, which is aimed at UK customers. Customers are able to order and pay for their goods through the website.
> HMRC will not treat this arrangement as a permanent establishment, as the website does not constitute a fixed place of business.
> However, were B SA to engage personnel working from home in the UK to undertake advertising and marketing, it would be possible for a permanent establishment to exist, particularly if the personnel have the authority to agree contractual terms with the customers.

Degree of permanence

A UK permanent establishment can only exist if the fixed place of business has a certain degree of permanence, rather than being purely temporary. For this purpose, HMRC take the view that a place of business which **continues for less than** 6 months does not constitute a permanent establishment, subject to certain clarifications.

92185
INTM266070

For this purpose, a permanent establishment:
– **begins** to exist as soon as a company begins to carry on business through a fixed place of business in the UK, but this does not include the time when preparatory work is being carried out before commencement of the business; and
– **ends** when the fixed place of business is sold or the enterprise ceases to carry on business through it.

> *MEMO POINTS*   1. Where the business is of a **recurrent nature**, the period of time for which the business is carried on from a particular location needs to be considered in combination with the number of times that the location is used for business. Temporary interruptions in business activities do not, in themselves, cause a permanent establishment to cease to exist.
> 2. If a place of business is **initially intended** to be used only for a very short period of time but its **use extends** for a much longer period than anticipated, and can no longer be considered as temporary, it becomes a fixed place of business. It can, therefore, be regarded retrospectively as a permanent establishment.
> 3. A place of business that exists for a very short period of time could also be regarded as a permanent establishment if its existence is **cut short by an unexpected event**, such as the failure of an investment.
> 4. For **construction projects** see ¶92170.

Personnel condition

92190
INTM266080

If a fixed place of business is to constitute a permanent establishment, it must be manned by personnel carrying on the business. These **persons** could include either employees of the business, the entrepreneur or owner of the business, or other persons such as self-employed personnel who have received instructions from the business.

PAYE82000

> *MEMO POINTS*   Any **employees** engaged by the non-resident company, whether as part of a permanent establishment or not, must be treated correctly for the purpose of PAYE. In respect of those who are in the UK for:
> **a.** between 1 and 30 days a year, no requirements apply;
> **b.** between 31 and 60 days a year, confirmation must be provided to HMRC that no formal employment contract exists, and the period does not form part of a more substantial period in the UK, in which case no PAYE is applicable;
> **c.** between 61 and 90 days a year, the following information must be provided to HMRC:
> – employee's name;
> – last known UK and overseas addresses of employee;
> – nature of duties undertaken;
> – dates of commencing and ceasing employment; and
> – to which country a tax return covering worldwide income is submitted;
> **d.** between 91 and 183 days, the following should be supplied to HMRC:
> – all of the information in **c.** above;
> – a statement from the overseas tax authority which confirms that the employee is subject to tax in the overseas territory; and
> – details of the employee's links and visits to the UK in the last 5 years; and
> **e.** over 183 days, PAYE must be operated. For details see *Tax Memo*.

---

2. Agent

92220   If a non-resident does not have a fixed place of business in the UK, there may be an agency relationship which could create a permanent establishment for tax purposes.

Dependent agent

92225
s 1141(1)(b)
CTA 2010

A company could have a permanent establishment via a dependent agent under UK domestic tax law if the agent has, and habitually exercises, **authority** to do business on behalf of the company.

Comment   It should be noted that double tax treaties that follow the OECD Model have a narrower definition of an agency permanent establishment compared to UK tax law. Many treaties require the agent to enter into contracts, which is not as wide as the UK definition. The non-resident company doing business through an agent should therefore rely on the terms of the relevant double tax treaty (if any) if the treaty follows the provisions of the OECD Model.

Independent agent

Where an agent in the UK is an independent agent acting in the course of his ordinary business, the activities of the agent do not create a UK permanent establishment for the overseas principal.

92230
s 1142 CTA 2010

Which type of agent?

Whether the agent is independent is a question of the **business character of the relationship** between the agent and the overseas principal. If the relationship between them is of independent businesses dealing with each other at arm's length, the agent is regarded as an independent agent. For example, if the agent **acts for other** unrelated **businesses** on the same terms as he acts for the non-resident, and if the same activities were performed for other unrelated parties, this would indicate independence.

92235
INTM264080

The agent should be legally and economically independent of the non-resident company, with regard to the business conducted by the agent for the principal. HMRC suggest that the **factors** to be considered might include:
- whether the agent is given detailed instructions or is controlled comprehensively;
- the extent of the obligations of the agent to the principal;
- whether the agent bears the entrepreneurial risk for operations carried out for the principal;
- the extent to which the principal relies on the agent's particular skills and experience; and
- whether the agent refers to the principal for approval in the way that the business is conducted.

Particular kinds of agent

There are specific requirements in relation to:
- investment managers;
- brokers; and
- Lloyd's agents.

92240

Investment managers   Where profits are earned by a UK investment manager on behalf of a non-resident investor in respect of investment transactions, the **liability to tax** is limited to tax deducted at source.

92245
s 1146 CTA 2010

For the exemption to apply, the following **tests** must be satisfied:
- the UK investment manager is in the business of providing investment management services;
- the transactions are carried out in the course of the business;
- the investment manager is acting in an independent capacity;
- the "20% test" is met;
- the investment manager receives the customary remuneration for the services; and
- the investment manager does not act as the UK representative of the non-resident for any other transaction or income chargeable to UK tax in the same period.

SP 1/01

Where only the 20% test is not met the exemption may still apply but will be restricted.

> MEMO POINTS   1. An investment manager is **defined** as a person who provides investment management services.
> 2. The investment manager will be considered to be acting in an **independent capacity** if the relations with the non-resident are those of independent parties acting at arm's length i.e. if the non-resident is a widely held collective fund or is being marketed with the intention that it will become one, or is being wound up or dissolved.
> A fund is regarded as **widely held** if there is no majority interest in the fund held by five or fewer persons (including connected persons (¶31375)), or no one person holds more than 20% of the fund (with connected persons). Where one of these requirements is not met, other factors would require to be examined to establish if the fund can be regarded as widely held.

INTM269080

INTM269100

s 1147 CTA 2010

3. The **20% test** means that the investment manager, and persons connected with it, cannot have a beneficial entitlement to more than 20% of the chargeable profit of the non-resident arising from transactions carried out through the UK investment manager. If this 20% threshold is exceeded, the part of the non-resident's income to which the investment manager and connected persons are beneficially entitled is excluded from the limitation. The remainder of the non-resident's UK profits will remain eligible for the exemption provided that the other tests are met.

INTM269170

4. **Customary remuneration** is the amount which would be paid between independent entities acting at arm's length. HMRC will apply the principles outlined in the OECD transfer pricing guidelines (¶70365) to determine if the pricing structure is within the arm's length range. In applying the test, HMRC would look for any provision that uses a transaction or series of transactions to reduce the remuneration paid to the UK investment manager.

HMRC will look at remuneration received by the UK investment manager and amounts payable to any person for services provided to the non-resident, or in connection with the non-resident, or payments that relate to the performance of the non-resident. If such amounts cannot be shown to have been made at arm's length, HMRC would regard them as reducing the remuneration paid to the UK investment manager.

92250
s 1145 CTA 2010

Brokers If a transaction is carried out on behalf of a non-resident company in the course of its trade by a UK broker, the broker is regarded as an **independent** broker if the following conditions are met:
– at the time of the transaction the broker is carrying on the business of a broker;
– the transaction is carried out in the ordinary course of that business;
– the remuneration received for the provision of the services to the non-resident is not less than the customary remuneration (¶92245) for that class of business; and
– the broker does not otherwise fall to be treated as the permanent establishment of the non-UK resident company in relation to any other transaction in the same accounting period.

92255
s 1151 CTA 2010

Lloyd's agents If a transaction is carried out in the course of a trade on behalf of a non-resident by a person acting as a members' agent or managing agent at Lloyd's, the person is regarded as an agent of independent status acting in the ordinary course of the business if the following **conditions** are fulfilled:
– the non-resident company is a member of Lloyd's;
– the transaction is carried out in the course of the company's underwriting business; and
– the person acting on behalf of the company, in relation to the transaction, is a members' agent or managing agent of the syndicate in question.

> ▭ MEMO POINTS ▭ The trade of **underwriting** at Lloyd's is carried on at the Lloyd's building in London, so a non-resident corporate member has a UK permanent establishment which carries on its business of underwriting at Lloyd's, unless the non-resident company is represented by an independent agent.

B. Attribution of profits

92285
s 19 CTA 2009

Where a non-resident company has a **permanent establishment** in the UK, it is not necessarily a straightforward process to establish the profits attributable to the UK permanent establishment. UK tax law attributes profits to the permanent establishment based on the separate enterprise principle.

An analysis must be undertaken to determine the relevant functions of the permanent establishment and of the rest of the company, taking into account the location and nature of risk. The various types of transaction conducted by the permanent establishment can then be examined.

Comment Following a report on the attribution of profits to permanent establishments, the OECD has updated Article 7 (Business Profits) of the Model Tax Convention and the related commentary. Under this Article, profits are attributed to a permanent establishment following the same separate enterprise approach as required by UK domestic law. As UK double tax treaties are generally based on the provisions of the OECD Model Tax Convention, new tax treaties concluded by the UK are likely to follow this approach, and as older treaties are updated, by means of a replacement treaty or a protocol, they will tend to incorporate the new OECD article in many cases.

As a consequence, tax authorities around the world are more aware of permanent establishment issues, including dependent agent permanent establishments, and may be more alert in looking to attribute profits to such permanent establishments in line with the OECD approach.

Separate enterprise principle

The profits attributed to the permanent establishment are the profits it would have made had it been a separate, distinct enterprise engaging in similar business activities under similar conditions and dealing independently with the other (non-UK) parts of the company. Such **capital** is attributed to the permanent establishment as would be appropriate if it were a separate enterprise.

92290
s 21 CTA 2009

This means that the arm's length principle is applied to dealings between the permanent establishment and the other parts of the non-resident enterprise, and that transfer pricing methods (¶70155+) are applied to establish that transfers between the permanent establishment and the rest of the entity are at arm's length. Although the accounting records of the enterprise are important, the **dealings with other parts of the company** will need to be backed up by sufficient evidence to establish that they would have occurred between independent enterprises dealing at arm's length and that they are appropriately priced.

s 22 CTA 2009

The application of the arm's length principle has to make allowances for the fact that the permanent establishment and the rest of the non-resident enterprise are part of the same entity. As an entity cannot enter into contracts with itself, the significance of contractual terms will not be as great.

Expenses

Expenses are only allocated to the UK permanent establishment where the expenses were incurred for the purposes of the UK operations. It is irrelevant whether the expenses are **incurred**:
– directly by the UK permanent establishment; or
– elsewhere in the non-resident enterprise and reimbursed by the UK permanent establishment.

92295
s 29 CTA 2009

The expenses must be actually incurred as a **real cost** by the non-resident enterprise, and notional charges from the non-resident enterprise to its UK permanent establishment cannot be allowed for UK tax purposes.

s 30 CTA 2009

Where expenses are payable to third parties for the **whole non-resident company** including the UK permanent establishment, a reasonable apportionment can be made to find the attributable expenses.

> MEMO POINTS 1. Intra-entity payments for the use of **intangible property** are not allowable for UK tax purposes. However, where a payment is made by the non-resident for intellectual property used by the whole entity or a part of it that includes the UK permanent establishment, then a reasonable apportionment can be made to allocate some of the expense to the UK.

s 31 CTA 2009

> 2. Similarly, UK tax law does not allow any deduction for tax purposes for **interest or other financing costs** paid by a UK permanent establishment to the non-resident entity (except for the banking sector for which there are special rules). Part of an interest payment by the non-resident entity to a third party could, if appropriate, be allocated to a UK permanent establishment, although if the interest is deemed to arise in the UK as a consequence, UK withholding tax must be deducted.

s 32 CTA 2009

EXAMPLE A notional payment of rent by the UK permanent establishment to the non-resident company would not be allowable, but if the company as a whole paid rent to a third party for premises that are used in the UK operations, the part of this rent relating to the UK would be allowable for tax purposes.

Capital gains

92300
s 10B TCGA 1992

A capital gain will arise where the permanent establishment disposes of a **UK situs asset** and both of the following criteria are met:
– the disposal is made whilst the UK trade of the permanent establishment is continuing; and
– at or before the time of disposal, the asset has been used in or for the purposes of the trade, profession or vocation; or used, held or acquired for the purposes of the permanent establishment.

A disposal is also deemed to have been made if an asset is **transferred out of the UK**, or if it **ceases to be used** in the UK because the non-resident company's UK activities have ceased. The mergers provisions may apply (¶79825+).

Dependent agent involved

92305
INTM267040

Where a UK permanent establishment exists because of the activities of a dependent agent (¶92225), who is selling goods in the UK on behalf of the non-resident company, there may be **two elements** to the UK profits:
a. the profit of the dependent agent itself derived from its activities for the non-resident company, which might arise from a payment by the non-resident enterprise at arm's length for its services. This is chargeable to UK tax on the dependent agent as profits of a trade; and
b. the residual UK profit attributable to the non-resident company, which is a profit over and above the arm's length remuneration paid to the dependent agent. This is a profit chargeable to UK tax on the permanent establishment of the non-resident company.

To what extent taxable **profits** may arise in the UK (over and **above the arm's length reward** to the dependent agent entity in the UK) depends on the facts and circumstances of each case, how much risk is borne by the overseas principal, and the relationship of the parties including the location of functions, risks and assets.

> EXAMPLE A dependent agent enterprise enters into a sales agency agreement with C Inc whereby it does not take ownership of the goods that it sells. These remain the property of C Inc, in whose name they are sold by the agent.
> The dependent agent enterprise keeps a stock of goods in a warehouse to fulfil the orders that its sales activities have achieved, but the inventory risk is borne by C Inc. The arm's length fee paid by C Inc to the agent rewards the agent for its selling activities only.
> Where the inventory risk is being managed by qualified personnel of C Inc, who are operating from the premises of the dependent agent entity, the tax authorities may consider that an arm's length reward for these activities of managing the inventory risk should be attributed to the dependent agent permanent establishment, thereby constituting further taxable profits in the UK over and above the arm's length fee paid.
> There are therefore two elements to the taxable profit in the UK from these activities, being the arm's length:
> – fee paid by C Inc to the UK dependent agent entity, which is subject to UK tax as profit of the dependent agent entity in the UK; and
> – reward attributed to the inventory risk management function of C Inc, which may be subject to UK tax as profit of a UK permanent establishment.

C. Attribution of capital

92335
INTM267120

The attribution of capital is only relevant if an **interest deduction** is claimed in the UK tax computation. This is most likely to be the case in respect of non-resident companies in the banking sector.

As the separate enterprise principle looks at the profits that the permanent establishment would have made if it were an independent enterprise engaging in similar activities in similar circumstances, the rules provide for an amount of **equity and loan capital** to be attributed to it, akin to the capital that would be required by an independent enterprise in the same circumstances. The attribution of capital in this way effectively places a **limit** on the amount of the interest deduction that may be claimed by the UK permanent establishment.

Assets

The first step in capital attribution is to attribute assets to the permanent establishment. These are the **tangible** and **intangible** assets from which the permanent establishment derives its profits, and are not necessarily the same as those assets on its balance sheet.

92340

Capital requirement

Having established the assets of the permanent establishment, the next step is to perform the capital requirement calculation, so as to effectively construct a hypothetical balance sheet. The equity and loan capital are the balancing figure once the assets attributable to the UK permanent establishment have been established.

92345

> MEMO POINTS   1. **HMRC** do not accept that the permanent establishment should be assumed to have the most tax efficient mix of equity and loan capital, because this would not be the case with independent enterprises acting at arm's length.
> 2. Other **factors** which need to be considered in determining the amount of interest-bearing debt to attribute to the UK permanent establishment are:
> – the capital structure of the whole non-resident entity;
> – the capital structure of other entities of the same size that are trading in the UK;
> – the capital structure of other companies engaging in similar activities in the UK;
> – the capital structure of other companies trading in the UK that are comparable in size and structure to the UK permanent establishment; and
> – existing interest-free facilities of the UK permanent establishment – where part of the existing debt capital is on interest-free terms it can be considered to fulfil part of the equity capital requirement.
> 3. **Post-tax profits** of the permanent establishment can also be considered to be part of the equity capital, provided that they are retained in the UK rather than being remitted to the head office of the non-resident entity. On the other hand, where losses have been made, they would increase the requirement for equity capital.

INTM267130

The **activities** of the permanent establishment of a non-resident company may differ in many ways from the activities of a separate entity of the same size that is trading in the UK. Comparables may, therefore, be difficult to find when determining the capital to be attributed to the permanent establishment. For this reason it will often be most useful to look at how the non-resident enterprise as a whole funds itself. Consideration can then be given to the question of how far the funding of the permanent establishment itself would replicate the funding of the whole company.

92350

Unless the activities carried on by the permanent establishment are significantly more or less risky than those of the whole non-resident enterprise, it may be possible to take the capital ratios of the whole non-resident enterprise and apply the same ratios to the UK permanent establishment. Where the activities of the permanent establishment are clearly different to those of the whole non-resident enterprise, it may still be possible to take the capital ratios of the whole enterprise as a starting point, and then make adjustments to allow for the different activity and risk in the permanent establishment.

Notional funding costs

The notional funding costs of the permanent establishment are then computed.

92355

Nil funding costs would be attributed to the **equity** capital, whilst the notional interest and other costs of borrowing attributed to the **debt** capital should be based on the actual terms of loans taken out by the non-resident company and by its UK permanent establishment.

The attribution of the same **credit rating** to the permanent establishment as to the whole non-resident enterprise reflects the reality that the permanent establishment would be able to obtain funds at a lower cost than would an independent entity of similar size.

A tax adjustment is computed, being the difference between the funding costs claimed by the permanent establishment and the notional funding costs attributed to the permanent establishment by the capital attribution provisions.

D. Tax liability

92385 The UK has concluded a wide network of double taxation treaties with other countries (¶90055). The treaties are mostly based on the OECD Model Tax Convention, but the wording of the treaties differs as each is negotiated separately with the other contracting state. The treaties allocate taxing rights with respect to a number of different categories of income including business profits, dividends, interest and royalties.

Where both contracting states impose taxation on the same profits, the treaty will allow for the **elimination of double taxation** through a tax credit or a tax exemption for the profits in the other state. The treaty will normally also provide for dispute resolution procedures in the case that a dispute over the operation of the treaty cannot be resolved.

1. Business profits

92415 Generally, the business profits article of a UK double tax treaty states that the profits of an enterprise of one contracting state will only be taxable in the other contracting state if it carries on a business in that state through a permanent establishment.

The permanent establishment definition in the treaty may differ from the definition in UK domestic law, although in many cases differences will be small as the UK's domestic law is based on the OECD Model which is followed in many treaty negotiations. Where the **treaty is more favourable** to a taxpayer than the UK domestic law, the terms of the treaty will apply.

The rate of tax is usually the mainstream rate of corporation tax unless the double tax treaty contains a non-discrimination clause, when the small profits rate would then be available.

2. Other income

92435 Non-trading income can only be chargeable to corporation tax if the non-resident is trading through a permanent establishment. In this case, income such as interest, royalties or licence fees can be chargeable to corporation tax where the source of income is **connected** to the operations of the UK permanent establishment.

> MEMO POINTS 1. **Licence fees receivable** by the non-resident in respect of product lines developed by a permanent establishment in the UK would be subject to corporation tax as part of the profits of the permanent establishment.
> 2. If the trade of the permanent establishment generates **excess funds** that are put on deposit and earn interest, the interest will be subject to corporation tax as part of the profits of the permanent establishment in the UK.

No connection to permanent establishment

92440 If, however, there is no connection between the income earned by the non-resident in the UK and the permanent establishment of that non-resident in the UK, then that income would not be subject to corporation tax as part of the profits of the UK permanent establishment but would be **subject to** income tax on the non-resident entity (normally collected by deduction at source).

Where there is a relevant double tax treaty between the UK and the country of residence of the recipient of the income, the tax treaty withholding **tax rates** may apply if they are lower than the rate to be withheld under UK domestic law.

Type of income	Action
Rent	Where the following conditions are fulfilled, an overseas company can apply to HMRC for UK rental income to be paid without deduction of tax, using Form NRL2: – the company's UK affairs are up to date, or the company has not had any UK tax obligations to date; and – the company does not expect to be liable to UK tax in the current tax year. In other cases, where these conditions are not satisfied, UK tax is deducted at source from the rental income by the payer in the UK.
Royalty	UK royalty income received by a non-resident is subject to withholding tax at the basic rate of income tax unless the royalties come within the scope of the EU Interest and Royalties Directive (¶90375+). This may be reduced by the terms of a relevant tax treaty; however, the definition of royalties in the applicable treaty should be examined carefully as this could differ from the definition in UK law.
Interest	UK interest income received by a non-resident is subject to UK income tax which will be withheld at the basic rate of 20% unless the interest comes within the scope of the EU Interest and Royalties Directive (¶90375+). This may be reduced by the terms of a relevant double tax treaty.

3. Gains

A non-resident company that does not have a permanent establishment in the UK is outside the scope of corporation tax on capital gains arising in the UK.

92470
s 10B TCGA 1992

Otherwise, the provisions of any relevant **double tax treaty** will apply, which usually means that the capital gains will be taxable in the UK. The EU Mergers Directive may apply in the case of cross-border mergers, demergers, transfers of assets, or share exchanges (¶79840).

E. Administration

Interaction with Companies House

Non-resident companies with a branch or permanent establishment in the UK are required to register with Companies House. Registration is not required if there is no physical presence in the UK.

92500
SI 2009/1801

Within 1 month of opening a UK establishment, an overseas company must send to Companies House a completed Form OS IN01 together with a registration fee.

If the company is registering its **first UK establishment**, it must also deliver the following documents to Companies House:
– a certified copy of the company's statutory documents (Memorandum etc) with a certified English translation; and
– a copy of the company's latest set of accounts (with a certified translation in English if necessary) where the company is required to prepare and deliver accounts in its country of residence.

A notification of the registration of a branch will be sent by Companies House to HMRC at the corporation tax office covering the registered office address in the UK, and that corporation tax office will normally be responsible for the tax affairs of the non-resident company.

Where the non-resident company is required to prepare audited **accounts**, these must be submitted to Companies House within 3 months of the deadline for disclosure in the overseas territory along with Form OS AA01. Otherwise, accounts which can comply with either

SI 2009/1801
regs 37 – 42

UK or overseas GAAP must be submitted to Companies House, along with certain other information. See *Company Law Memo* for further details.

Interaction with HMRC

92505 English accounts, comprising profit and loss accounts of both the branch and the non-resident company, along with the company's balance sheet, must be **submitted** along with a CTSA return.

ss 973–980
CTA 2010

Where **tax remains unpaid** for 6 months after its due date and HMRC have issued a notice see ¶69925.

92510 **Double tax treaty passport scheme** **Overseas corporate lenders**, who are resident in an overseas country that has a double tax treaty with the UK, which includes an article relating to interest and debt claims (as is the case with most treaties), can apply for double tax treaty passport status by completing Form DTTP1.

Where HMRC grant the treaty passport to the overseas company, it is entered in a public register and given a double tax treaty passport (DTTP) number. A potential UK corporate borrower can, therefore, check the status of any potential overseas corporate lender by consulting this register (which is available online).

Where a loan agreement is concluded with a UK borrower, the overseas lender can notify the UK borrower of their passport status and DTTP number, and the UK lender should notify HMRC on Form DTTP2 within 30 days of the passported loan, giving HMRC the necessary information to enable them to reach a decision. HMRC can then issue a direction to the UK borrower to deduct withholding tax from interest at the appropriate rate under the relevant double tax treaty.

For further details see flmemo.co.uk/ctm92510

92515 **Inward Investment Support (IIS)** Inward investment support is a service offered to non-resident businesses which have no prior relationship with HMRC, and which are making significant inward investments. Its aim is to give clarity and certainty by providing written confirmation (within 28 days) of how HMRC will apply UK tax law to specific transactions.

SP 2/12

Significant inward investments are generally regarded as investments of £30 million or more, but support is also provided where HMRC agree with the investor that an inward investment of less than £30 million is important to the national or regional economy, or is in the wider public interest.

On **applying** for support, businesses should supply as much information as possible about the proposed investment, including:
– the name, address and country of residence of the business;
– the nature and size of the projected transaction(s), the tax(es) involved and the chronology, or proposed chronology, of the transaction(s);
– the commercial background to the transaction(s);
– any specific legal points which are known or believed to arise, and, where appropriate, a copy of any written legal advice received; and
– the reasons why the investment is believed to be of importance to the national or regional economy.

> MEMO POINTS Applications should be **sent to**:
> Colin Miller,
> Inward Investment Support,
> HMRC CTIAA,
> Business International,
> 100 Parliament Street,
> London
> SW1A 2BQ

Subsidiary or branch?

A non-resident company must decide whether to incorporate a separate company in the UK or trade through a permanent establishment.

92565

Often, a branch will be established first (i.e. dipping a toe in the water), which can then be incorporated at a later date.

Comparison

The basic differences between a subsidiary and branch are summarised in the table below:

92570

Topic	Subsidiary	Branch
Corporation tax	Worldwide profits subject to UK tax unless double tax agreement states otherwise	Only activities undertaken in the UK subject to UK tax Not likely to be overridden by double tax agreement
Owning foreign interests	Double taxation agreement with UK would be beneficial	As no separate UK entity, double tax agreement would not involve UK
Payments of interest and royalties to non-resident company	Deductible	Not deductible
Start-up costs	Only relievable in the subsidiary itself or as losses	Can be set against non-resident company's profits
Trading losses	Carried forward against company's profits or available for group relief	Carried forward against branch profits or available for group relief (restricted where losses available for offset in non-resident company (¶66325))
Ceasing UK business	Sale of shares would be covered by exemption but potentially liable to stamp duty[1] If no sale, requires winding up, striking off or liquidation which would incur costs	Sale of assets would be taxable, and property is liable to stamp duty land tax[2]
Commercial implications	Certain companies prefer to trade with a UK company	Branch may find it harder to find trading partners
Accounts	Needs own accounts to be filed at Companies House, and may require an audit	Must file accounts of non-resident company with Companies House
Audit	UK audit may be required	No UK audit required

Note:
1. **Stamp duty** applies to any instrument used to transfer stock and marketable securities executed in the UK. The purchaser is liable to pay 0.5% stamp duty on the consideration for the transfer (inclusive of VAT). For further details, see *Tax Memo*.
2. **Stamp duty land tax (SDLT)** is charged as a percentage of the amount paid when land or property is bought or transferred. It applies to transactions involving land situated in the UK, regardless of where the transaction is executed, where the parties are located or whether the transfer is effected by a legal document or otherwise. Various rates apply depending on the value of the transaction. For further details, see *Tax Memo*.

Transfer of trade

A UK permanent establishment can be subsequently converted into a UK subsidiary, or vice versa, without any **UK tax charge** arising provided that there is no change of ownership of the trade (i.e. the same 75% group (¶65055+) owns the trade before and after the transfer). Briefly:

92575

– assets are transferred at tax written down value for capital allowances purposes;
– trading losses are retained; and
– assets are transferred at no gain/no loss between members of a capital gains group (¶65415+).

For further details see ¶79600+.

Obviously, any **overseas tax ramifications** must also be considered.

European companies

Since 8 October 2004, it has been possible to form a European Company, also known as a Societas Europaea or SE. The objective was to create a separate European corporate entity, with its own framework for company statutes and other management and administrative matters. This would enable companies situated in different EU member states to merge, or to form a holding company of a joint subsidiary, without having to overcome the administrative obstacles that are presented by the different legal systems and company laws in the member states. This would, therefore, allow groups to operate throughout the EU using a single corporate entity, and enable genuine corporate mobility for the first time.

93000
EC Directive
2157/2001

SECTION 1

Formation

1. What can become an SE?

There are four methods of forming an SE:

93050
EC Directive
2157/2001 art 2

Method	Outline (assuming two companies are subject to tax rules in two member states[1] and wish to create an SE)
Form a holding company	Set up an SE which holds shares in both companies
Merge	By acquisition i.e. one or more companies are wound up, and all of their assets and liabilities are transferred to the SE (which is an existing company) in exchange for shares in the SE (and a cash payment not exceeding 10% of the nominal value of the shares)
	Companies are dissolved without liquidation, and transfer all their assets to the newly formed SE which issues shares to the shareholders of both original companies The shareholders can also receive a cash payment of up to 10% of the nominal value of the shares As a result, the SE holds all the assets of the original companies, and the shareholders of both companies hold the shares in the SE

Method	Outline (assuming two companies are subject to tax rules in two member states [1] and wish to create an SE)
Form a joint subsidiary	Set up a new company in which both other companies hold shares
Existing company	Must have had a subsidiary company in another member state for at least 2 years
Note: 1. For these purposes, a company is **subject to tax** in a member state as a resident, and cannot be treated under a double tax treaty as being resident outside the European Union.	

Holding companies and joint subsidiaries

93055

Formation of an SE holding company is **available to** public and private companies with registered offices in different member states, or that have subsidiaries or branches in member states other than the state where their registered office is situated.

EC Directive
2157/2001 art 3

An SE can itself set up its own SE subsidiaries.

Mergers

93060

The formation of an SE by merger is available only where the **public limited companies** involved in the merger are **located** in different member states.

---

2. Requirements

Registered office

93090
EC Directive
2157/2001 art 7

The registered office must be **located** where the SE has its central administration. The SE must be registered in the state where it has its registered office, in the register that applies under the national law of the state.

EC Directive
2157/2001 art 8

An advantage of the SE is that it can **transfer** its registered office from one member state to another – where the true centre of administration of the SE is in that other state – without having to dissolve the company in one state, or form a new company in the other state.

Capital

93095
EC Directive
2157/2001 art 4

The SE must have a **minimum** capital of €120,000.

If a member state, in its **domestic legislation**, has a requirement for a larger minimum capital in the case of companies exercising a certain type of activity, that requirement will also apply to an SE that has its registered office in that member state.

Management

93100
EC Directive
2157/2001 art 38

The SE must provide, in its company statutes, for a general meeting of shareholders and either:
– a management board and supervisory board (two-tier system); or
– an administrative board (single-tier system).

Under the **two-tier system**, the management board is responsible for the management of the SE, and members of the board report to the SE in dealings with third parties. The supervisory board can appoint and remove members of the management board.

Employee participation

93105

Employees must be able to participate **in** the supervision and strategic development of the SE, but it is not required that they are involved in day to day management decisions.

Employee participation may be **carried out** by workers forming part of the supervisory board or administrative board, or by a separate body representing employees, or by an alternative method.

Insolvency etc

Matters relating to insolvency and liquidation of an SE will generally be **regulated by** the national law of the member state where its registered office is situated. If an SE transfers its registered office outside the EU, it must be wound up following an application by any person or competent authority concerned in the matter.

93110
EC Directive
2157/2001 art 63

SECTION 2

Consequences

Basically, an SE is subject to the same domestic corporation tax rules as any other type of company in the particular member state. However, it has been necessary to introduce measures to ensure that there are no tax obstacles to forming an SE (and also that there are no unfair tax advantages). This ensures that a decision to form an SE is not driven by tax considerations.

93160

---

1. Formation via merger

Where an SE is formed by way of a merger of two or more companies, which are resident in different member states, the transfer of assets etc is tax neutral, **provided that** the merger is carried out for bona fide commercial reasons.

93190

This means the following are **transferred** with no tax charge on the transferor:
- assets subject to chargeable gains or capital allowances;
- intangible assets; and
- loan relationships and derivatives.

Provided that the assets, etc remain within the scope of UK corporation tax, it is irrelevant in **which entity** they are held, as they will be taxed when realised or sold by the SE.

> MEMO POINTS 1. **Bona fide** basically means that the avoidance of tax was not the main purpose of the transaction. Tax in this case includes income tax, corporation tax and capital gains tax.
> 2. Anti-avoidance provisions ensure that where the merger or transfer of business is **part of a scheme or arrangement of which tax avoidance is one of the main purposes**, the tax neutrality rules will not apply. A company can apply to HMRC for clearance before the transaction takes place, so that it will be sure that the merger is undertaken for bona fide commercial reasons.
> 3. The disposal of **shares** in the dissolved companies and the issue of shares by the SE are treated as a reorganisation of share capital (¶79840), so the new shares are deemed to stand in the shoes of the old shares, provided that the shares issued by the SE are issued in proportion to the existing holdings in the original companies.

s 140G TCGA 1992

Tangible assets

For a merger involving:
- a **UK trade**, where the transferor and the SE are either UK resident or carrying on a trade through a permanent UK establishment (¶92140+), any qualifying assets used in the trade are transferred on a no gain/no loss basis, and no balancing allowances or charges for capital allowance purposes will be triggered. The SE takes on the base cost and tax written down value of the transferor. Note that where the rules in ¶79825+ apply i.e. the usual reconstruction rules, these take precedence; or
- a **non-UK trade**, where the UK transferor is trading in another member state via a permanent establishment and the transfer involves the transfer of all the assets and liabilities of the permanent establishment to a non-UK resident transferee, the transfer will give rise to a single chargeable gain (equal to the excess of the aggregate of the gains over the aggregate of the

93195
s 140E TCGA 1992;
s 561A CAA 2001

s 140F TCGA 1992

losses). There will be credit for any local tax that should have been deducted were it not for the EU merger regulations. Broadly, these regulations prohibit member states from charging tax on such transactions.

Intangible assets

93200
ss 820–823
CTA 2009

If a merger involves the transfer of intangible assets, they are treated as being transferred on a no gain/no loss basis, **provided** the asset concerned was both a qualifying intangible asset for the purposes of the intangibles regime (¶28135+) in the hands of the:
– transferor before the merger; and
– transferee after the merger.

If, however, these **conditions are not met** because the transferor is trading in another member state through a PE, then the transferor can claim double tax relief for the tax which would have arisen if the EU merger regulations did not apply (¶93195).

Loan relationships and derivatives

93205
ss 431–439
CTA 2009

If the merger involves the transfer of loan relationships and, immediately after the merger, the SE is either a UK resident company or PE, then the loan relationship is to be disregarded, **unless** the transferor is using fair value accounting (¶16200).

However, the following **must be accounted for irrespective** of the above rule:
– exchange gains and losses; and
– determining in which company debits and credits unrelated to the merger are brought into account (e.g. periodic payments under a swap).

CFM34160

It is possible to apply for **clearance** from HMRC that they agree that the transaction is bona fide and the above rules will therefore apply.

> ⌐MEMO POINTS⌐   The same rules apply in respect of **derivatives**.

Groups

93210

In a group situation, where the principal member of any group becomes an SE (or a subsidiary of an SE), the original group and the new group are to be **treated as the same group** for the purposes of the following provisions:
– transfers of chargeable assets (¶67080+), including intangible fixed assets (¶69180+);
– transfers of trading stock (¶67130+);
– reliefs on replacement of business assets (¶67315+);
– pre-entry capital gains and losses (¶67835+);
– depreciatory transactions (¶67625+); and
– dividend stripping (¶32370+).

---

2. Ongoing activities

93240

For most UK tax purposes, an SE based in the UK is treated like a UK plc, and will fit within the existing corporation tax regime and other regimes relating to UK companies.

Transfer of registered office

93245

The basic rule is that a transfer of registered office does not give rise to any tax charge on the SE's assets, provided that they remain liable to UK corporation tax i.e. remain effectively **connected with a UK permanent establishment** of the SE.

However, where this is not the case, exit charges will apply.

European co-operative societies

The rules which introduced European co-operative societies (also known as Societas Cooperative Europaea or SCE) were aimed at facilitating the cross-border activities of co-operative societies situated in EU member states, so that persons or legal entities situated in different EU member states can form an SCE.

93250
EC Directive
1435/2003

It is also possible for co-operatives situated in different member states to merge and form an SCE. For UK purposes, one of them would need to be registered under the Industrial and Provident Societies Act 1965.

MEMO POINTS   1. An SCE has a **minimum capital** of €30,000, divided into shares like a company.
2. The **registered office** of an SCE may be transferred from one EU member state to another, without the necessity for winding up the SCE.

UK overview

An SCE is UK resident for the purposes of taxation from the time of its registration in the UK. Similar rules apply as for SEs, i.e. the formation is tax neutral, and the transfer of the registered office should not result in exit charges.

93255

CHAPTER 4

Arbitrage

94000   The term arbitrage is used generally to **refer to** the exploitation of an asymmetrical situation in different markets or countries.

In a tax context, arbitrage refers to a scheme that exploits the differences between tax regimes in different countries, with the result of lowering the amount of taxation paid overall by a multinational group. Jurisdictions tend to diverge on the:
– definition of debt and equity i.e. where a deduction is given for interest payable in one jurisdiction, but the corresponding receipt is treated as a dividend in the other, and therefore non-taxable; and
– entities which are deemed to have corporate characteristics, and therefore are taxed as a separate person, and transparent entities which are looked through for tax purposes.

Any particular tax scheme involving arbitrage might aim to obtain:
– a tax deduction for interest or expenses without a corresponding tax receipt;
– a double deduction for interest or other expenses; or
– loss relief twice (in two different jurisdictions).

SECTION 1

Scope

94050
s 231 TIOPA 2010

Upon the issue of an HMRC notice to the company, the arbitrage **legislation applies** to contrived schemes involving deductions or receipts which exploit differences between, or within, the various tax codes of multiple jurisdictions, and this affects the UK tax position of the company.

In response, the **company must amend** its CTSA return to comply with the notice i.e. either:
– limiting the tax deductions, to ensure that any decrease in UK tax resulting from the scheme is cancelled out; or
– taxing an otherwise non-taxable receipt.

Exclusions

The arbitrage rules do not apply to:
– charities; or
– those companies and groups where the scheme has no effect on UK tax.

94055

Hybrid instruments

A hybrid instrument may aim to exploit differences in the definition, and tax treatment, of debt and equity.

94060

Tax systems normally give a tax deduction for **interest paid** on debt instruments, whilst there is no deduction for **dividends paid**, and there may be favourable treatment for dividends received (either no taxation, or sheltering any tax charge with double tax relief).

A hybrid instrument may be so constructed as to fall within the definition of interest in the jurisdiction where the interest is paid, whilst being regarded as equity (and the payment as a distribution/dividend) in the jurisdiction where the payment is received by a related company. A tax deduction could then be obtained in one country without any corresponding taxable income (from a group point of view) in the other jurisdiction.

Typical instruments where these issues arise are perpetual debt, deeply subordinated debt, and convertible debt.

Hybrid entities

A hybrid entity could also be used to gain a tax advantage through arbitrage.

94065

The entity may be seen as a **tax transparent** partnership in one jurisdiction, but as a **limited company** in another jurisdiction. This gives opportunities for enabling a double deduction in respect of the same interest payment. This is frequently encountered in respect of US companies who "check-the-box" (¶94160).

However, controlled foreign companies (¶90555+) are not considered to be hybrid entities solely because their profits are attributed to another company.

SECTION 2

Deduction schemes

The deductions rules aim to counter a situation where a scheme using a hybrid instrument, or a hybrid entity, increases UK tax deductions to more than they would have been without the scheme.

94115

---

1. When do the rules apply?

Companies within the charge to UK corporation tax i.e. either UK resident companies, or overseas companies with a UK permanent establishment, are potentially liable to the deductions rules which apply where the following **four conditions** are met:

94145
s 233 TIOPA 2010

a. the transaction involving the company is part of a qualifying scheme;
b. the company can claim a corporation tax deduction in relation to the transaction, or offset against profits an amount relating to the transaction;
c. the purpose or the main purpose should be to achieve a UK tax advantage; and
d. that tax advantage should be more than minimal. HMRC would normally consider the tax advantage to be minimal if all the UK tax deductions resulting from the scheme are less than £50,000.

Qualifying scheme

94150   The categories of qualifying scheme all **involve the use** of a hybrid entity (¶94065) or a hybrid instrument (¶94060), which result in either:
– two deductions relating to the same expense (known as double dipping); or
– a deduction without any corresponding taxable receipt.

Where there is a **funding arrangement** involving a hybrid entity or instrument, the qualifying scheme refers to the whole of the funding structure, including all the entities through which the funds are flowing.

94155   **Categories**   A scheme is a qualifying scheme if it:
ss 236–242 TIOPA   **a.** involves a **hybrid entity** (¶94065). This will include, for example, a limited partnership;
2010   **b.** contains a **hybrid instrument** (¶94060) that:
– has an alterable characteristic (i.e. one of the parties to the transaction can, by way of an election, alter the instrument such that the tax treatment of it will change);
– contains shares that can be converted to debt, or securities that can be converted to shares, on the occurrence of some event and there was a reasonable expectation that they would be so converted at the time of issue (or when the conversion right was created); or
– contains debt instruments treated as equity under GAAP;
c. includes the **issue of shares** to a connected party (¶31375) that does not confer on the holder a relevant proportion of profits and assets on a winding up; or
d. includes the **transfer of the right** to receive income or gains from a security to a connected party (¶31375).

> ⌐MEMO POINTS⌐   1. A scheme **may relate to** a single transaction, a series of related transactions, or any other arrangement or understanding, including the establishment of a particular capital structure.
> 2. Whether a transaction is part of a **series of related transactions** is a question of fact, but this would certainly be the case where one transaction would not occur without the other transaction, or where it would have been arranged on different terms if the other transaction had not taken place.
> 3. The UK does not recognise a **limited partnership** as existing independently of its partners, but many other tax codes treat limited partnerships as separate taxable entities.

94160   **HMRC guidance**   HMRC suggest the **following situations as examples** where the arbitrage
INTM597520   rules may potentially apply:
– the existence of members of the group which are companies registered in countries where a consolidation regime applies, such as the US check-the-box regime;
– the inclusion of foreign partnerships (with UK partners) that are treated as a separate entity and opaque for tax purposes in their country of residence, rather than tax transparent as they are treated in the UK;
– a large debt relationship;
– a group setting up a new holding company after a reorganisation;
– a deferred share consideration scheme;
– finance branches; or
– long term debt.

INTM597530   If some of the features are present which might indicate that arbitrage rules may apply, **factors** to take into account when considering if an arbitrage scheme exists include the following:
– whether debt has been pushed down into overseas subsidiaries e.g. if the overseas subsidiary is making an acquisition, normally it is that company which would incur the debt to fund the acquisition. However, where the local tax code makes this uncommercial, the debt may be placed in the UK parent company for sound business reasons;
– terms for repayment of the debt principal, which HMRC would normally expect to see wholly repaid during the term of the loan;
– levels of leverage in the worldwide group i.e. the reason a debt has been placed in the UK company is to equalise the leverage between all the members of the group. HMRC will

particularly challenge any conversion of equity into debt which is undertaken in order to accomplish this;
– mixture of debt and equity funding normally used by the group to fund acquisition vehicles when making third party acquisitions (especially when no hybrid entities are used); or
– in respect of an internal reorganisation, whether intra-group debt has increased as a consequence of the scheme, and whether this reflects genuine commercial need.

> ☐ MEMO POINTS   1. Various aspects of the **US check-the-box system** could result in a hybrid effect. The subsidiary of a US parent could effectively be treated as if it were a branch of its parent, with the result that loans between the subsidiary and its parent are disregarded. Neither a deduction nor a receipt would apply for US tax purposes, whereas the subsidiary would be treated as a legal entity for UK tax purposes.
> 2. Where a **UK parent is financing an overseas company** in order for it to acquire an overseas target, HMRC look at the amount the overseas company could borrow on commercial terms from a third party. Any shortfall is then deemed to be required funding from the UK parent company, and so a deduction reflecting this amount would be available.

Purpose is to achieve a tax advantage

There are various **reasons** why a group might include a hybrid instrument or entity in the funding structure, and these reasons are not necessarily connected with UK tax. For example, an overseas parent company of a UK group might use a hybrid entity for purposes connected with taxation in its own jurisdiction (i.e. to obtain a tax benefit overseas) rather than in the UK. If the main purpose of the arrangement is not to achieve a UK tax advantage, the arbitrage rules will not apply.

94165
INTM595070

Considerations to take into account are whether without the hybrid entity or instrument:
– the transaction resulting in the deduction would have taken place at all;
– it would have been of the same amount; and
– it would have been made under the same terms and conditions.

The scheme has achieved a UK tax advantage if, **as a result of** the operation of the scheme, the company has obtained higher tax relief (or tax credits), an increased tax repayment, or reduction of a tax charge.

> ☐ EXAMPLE
> 1. A foreign group of companies lends money to its UK subgroup, without using any hybrid entities or instruments. A number of years after this loan is set up, the debt is restructured using a scheme which involves a hybrid entity, and the interest paid abroad from the UK subgroup is no longer subject to tax in the foreign jurisdiction where it is received. The restructuring has not changed the amount of debt in the UK subgroup or the terms or conditions of the loans.
> When the original loan was made, the group did not have any intention of later setting up the hybrid structure. The decision to incur the interest expense at that time was not related to the possibility of any opportunity to be gained from arbitrage.
> When considering the purpose of the hybrid scheme, the question to be answered is whether the deductions for UK tax for the interest payments in the UK would still have been received if the interest receipts had been subject to tax in the overseas territory. In this example, it is clear that the interest deductions would still be received, because the tax deductions for interest did apply before the hybrid arrangement was set up. The use of a hybrid entity had not yet been considered at that point, and the decision to make the original loan was, therefore, not influenced by this consideration.
> Therefore, the arbitrage provisions do not apply.
>
> 2. A foreign group makes a loan to its UK subgroup. The loan is routed through a hybrid entity in a way that results in tax deductions for the loan, both in the UK and in a foreign jurisdiction. The loan enables the UK holding company to pay a dividend to the foreign parent company. The UK subgroup is funded by equity that represents retained profits.
> The effect of the loan to the UK subgroup (which has a 10 year repayment term), and of the dividend paid from the UK holding company to the foreign parent, is that part of the UK equity is replaced by debt. The scheme involving the hybrid does not create any new funds for investment. The size of the dividend, which represents several years of profit of the UK subgroup, is unusual compared to the usual policy of the UK subgroup. These profits are retained in the parent company, and are mostly not paid on to the ultimate shareholders of the group.
> The facts would suggest that the main purpose of the scheme was to increase UK tax deductions for interest, rather than, for example, to relieve a short term cash flow problem in the UK subgroup.

2. Interaction with other taxes

94195

The application of the arbitrage provisions is not dependent on other provisions, such as those relating to loan relationships, transfer pricing, thin capitalisation, or CFC legislation.

HMRC Brief 1/09

Where a company has made an arbitrage clearance application and an **advance thin capitalisation agreement** (ATCA) application (¶70805), so that the company is asking HMRC to consider the same set of transactions from both perspectives, HMRC will attempt to deal with this in a co-ordinated way.

The **worldwide debt cap rules** (¶70530+) apply to the financing expenses and income after the adjustments have been made under the arbitrage legislation.

3. Receiving a notice

Issue of notice

94215
INTM596510

A notice may be issued under the arbitrage rules either before or after a CTSA return is submitted by the company. A notice **applies in respect** of particular transactions in a specified period, and HMRC state that it is irrelevant whether the scheme, or the effect of the transactions, remains at the time that the notice is issued.

Where a notice is issued:

s 255 TIOPA 2010

– **before a tax return has been submitted**, the company must take into consideration the effect of the arbitrage rules when preparing the tax return. If it does not do so, the return will be regarded by HMRC as an incorrect return; or

s 256 TIOPA 2010

– **after the tax return is submitted**, this must form part of an enquiry. It might also be possible, exceptionally, for a notice to be issued under the discovery rules after an enquiry is closed. In any event, the company is given 90 days to amend its tax return so as to give effect to the arbitrage rules, and no penalty can be raised in this period. The amended return will then be regarded as an incorrect return if it does not properly adjust for the arbitrage rules.

If **HMRC and the company disagree** about the applicability of the arbitrage legislation, this dispute should be settled in the normal way in the course of the self-assessment enquiry procedures. If they are unable to reach agreement, the dispute can be referred to the First-tier Tribunal in the usual way. A referral to the Upper Tribunal is possible on a point of principle to determine to what extent the arbitrage rules apply.

INTM596540

Penalties in respect of an **incorrect return** arise only where there has been fraudulent or negligent conduct on the part of the company. HMRC state very clearly that where a company believed that the arbitrage rules did not apply, and this view resulted from a reasonable and tenable view of the law, then there would be no possibility of a penalty.

s 235 TIOPA 2010

MEMO POINTS 1. The notice will contain the following **information**:
– the name of the company;
– the period to which the notice relates;
– the transactions to which the notice relates; and
– an indication of how the notice affects the company's tax position.

INTM596520

2. A **dispute** could arise where:
– in the opinion of the company, the conditions required for the application of the arbitrage rules are not met;
– the effect of the arbitrage rules differs from that set out by HMRC in the notice; or
– there is disagreement about the amount of a disclaimer under the deductions rules.

INTM596530

3. The **discovery** rules (¶50600+) will only by available to HMRC where either:
– the absence of a notice was due to fraudulent or negligent conduct; or
– HMRC could not have been reasonably expected to realise that a notice should have been issued on the basis of information supplied before the enquiry period had lapsed.

Disclaiming

94220

After HMRC have issued a notice, the **company may choose** to disclaim the amount of tax deduction that arose as a result of using the arbitrage scheme. This prevents any further operation of the arbitrage legislation.

The company should disclaim an **amount** equal to the increase in UK tax deductions (or reduced UK tax) which has resulted from the scheme. The disclaimer can be made at any **time** between the issue of a notice under the arbitrage rules, and the time at which the assessment becomes final.

The company may make a **clearance** application in relation to the amount of the disclaimer (such as to obtain certainty that the company is not vulnerable to further action under the arbitrage rules), in which case the following information should be included in any application:
– the amount being disclaimed;
– the method by which it was calculated; and
– how the disclaimer relates to the purpose of the scheme in respect of obtaining a UK tax advantage.

INTM596560

The company can disallow deductions in relation to the scheme which:
– have been **deducted more than once**. This includes corporation tax, income tax and similar overseas tax deductions. It does not include indirect taxes. (This rule applies even if the non-UK territory has a similar rule to the UK arbitrage provisions. Consequently a deduction may be disallowed twice); or
– are **not taxed on the recipient** company. If the recipient company is only exempt from tax on a proportion of the receipt, the same proportion will be disallowed for the payer. The exempt receipt need not be in respect of the same payment that gave rise to the UK tax deduction, but it must arise out of the same transaction.

94225

---

4. Avoiding a notice

HMRC can give advice as to whether the arbitrage legislation will apply to proposed transactions that could constitute a scheme under the arbitrage rules, and can give their decision as to whether any notice would be issued with regard to disclosed transactions.

94255

This will give a company and its group certainty about whether HMRC agree that the arbitrage rules do not apply.

Clearance application

The application for clearance should include **details** of:
– scheme participants;
– the scheme; and
– its purpose, including its commercial rationale.

For further guidance see ¶94265.

94260
INTM596550

The exact information and supporting material will obviously depend on the particular circumstances. **HMRC** state that diagrammatic charts and step by step details of the transactions are particularly useful, along with an explanation of the purposes of the scheme and reconciliation of how funds are used.

The company should identify a **suitable comparison** to demonstrate that, in the absence of the hybrid, the amount of the transaction and the tax deduction (including the relevant terms and conditions) would have been the same, or to clarify the amount of the additional tax deduction arising under the scheme.

> <u>MEMO POINTS</u> The clearance application should be **sent to**:
> Margaret Kayser,
> HMRC,
> CTIAA, Business International,
> 3rd Floor,
> 100 Parliament Street,
> London,
> SW1A 2BQ.

94265
INTM596560

HMRC give the following **guidance** as to the nature of the information which should be provided:

Topic	Detail	Information
Scheme participants	Company claiming deduction	Name of company (and details of any branches including those in the UK)
		Name of ultimate UK parent (if member of a group)
		Nature of the business of company
		Territory of residence
		UK tax office and reference number
		Connection (if any) to recipient and other participants
		Copy of most recent accounts
	Recipient of payment for deduction claimed	Name of company (and details of any branches including those in the UK)
		Name of ultimate UK parent (if member of a group)
		Nature of the business of company
		Territory of residence
		UK tax office and reference number (where applicable)
		Connection (if any) to company and other participants
	Other participants	Name of each company (and details of any branches including those in the UK)
		Name of ultimate UK parent of each company (if member of a group)
		Nature of the business of each company
		Territory of residence of each company
		UK tax office and reference number of each company (where applicable)
		Connection (if any) to other participants
Details of the scheme	Outline description of the proposed scheme	Identification and explanation of the hybrid entities/instruments involved in the scheme
		Identification and explanation of the arbitrage(s) arising from the scheme
		Nature and amount(s) of the transaction(s) for which the deduction(s) is/are to be claimed
		Details of the UK tax advantage(s) arising from the scheme
		Estimate of effect on UK tax had the scheme not taken place
		Description of the flow of money within the scheme, including its sources and final destinations
	Details of the purpose of the scheme	Explanation of the purpose(s) of the scheme, including its commercial rationale
		Explanation of the purpose(s) of the transaction(s) in question, and other transactions, for which deduction(s) is/are to be claimed, including the commercial rationale for each
		Reasons, if any, why the transactions could not be carried out without the use of the hybrid and arbitrage
		Identification of a suitable comparison to show either that without the hybrid and arbitrage the result would be the same or the amount of the additional deduction

Response from HMRC

HMRC aim to work to a 28 day turnaround target from receipt of the application, provided all relevant information is included.

94270
INTM596550

If the company has a **particular need** for a clearance decision to be given **by a specific date**, it must specify this in the application.

Comment   Companies should allow as long as possible for the clearance procedure to reach its conclusion (certainly at least 2 months), as further information is often requested by HMRC before they reach a decision.

When **clearance cannot be given**, HMRC will state the reasons why. Where the company disagrees with HMRC's reasons, it is entitled to submit a tax return in accordance with its own view of the position. If a notice is subsequently issued by HMRC, the company can appeal in the normal way (¶54125+) against the amendments that HMRC want to make to the tax return.

94275

Any **clearance given** by HMRC will state the **terms** under which it is given, and the **period** for which it applies (particularly in respect of outbound transactions), provided that the facts and circumstances do not change.

94280
INTM596550

HMRC will consider themselves **bound** by the clearance given, provided that:
– all the relevant facts of the situation have been given accurately by the company; and
– in the case of advance clearance, that the transactions are subsequently carried out in accordance with the company's proposals.

HMRC may review the continued application of the clearance to ensure that the facts remain the same. Where there is a **change in the facts and circumstances**, the company should notify this to HMRC, otherwise penalties could apply if a return is submitted on the basis of a clearance which could no longer apply given the turn of events.

SECTION 3

Receipts schemes

In contrast to the deductions rules, the receipts rules are far more restricted in their application. However, there is no requirement for the arrangements to involve a qualifying scheme (¶94150+) i.e. use a hybrid entity or instrument.

94330

When do the rules apply?

In order for HMRC to issue a notice (which must identify the payment and accounting period concerned), all of the following **conditions** must be satisfied:
– a company has entered into a scheme under which it receives an amount that is not taxable in the UK;
– that amount is deductible in the hands of the payer;
– the mismatch in the tax treatment is a reasonable expectation of the parties to the transaction (i.e. they were aware of it); and
– the payment constitutes a contribution to the capital of the recipient company, which therefore excludes any loan arrangement.

94335
ss 249, 250 TIOPA
2010

> MEMO POINTS   A **contribution to the capital** is broadly any payment that directly increases the company's shareholder value and is untaxed.

Receiving a notice

If HMRC issue a notice, the company has 90 days in which to amend its tax return to treat the receipts identified as miscellaneous income.

94340
s 254 TIOPA 2010

For further detail of what happens when a notice is issued see ¶94215+.

Obtaining clearance

94345 The same procedure as set out in ¶94255+ applies, although the information required is slightly different.

94350
INTM596570

HMRC give the following **guidance** as to the extent of information which should be provided:

Topic	Detail	Information
Scheme participants	Company claiming deduction	Name of company (and details of any branches including those in the UK)
		Name of ultimate UK parent (if member of a group)
		Nature of the business of company
		Territory of residence
		UK tax office and reference number
		Connection (if any) to paying party and other participants
		Copy of most recent accounts
	Paying party	Name of company (and details of any branches including those in the UK)
		Name of ultimate UK parent (if member of a group)
		Nature of the business of company
		Territory of residence
		UK tax office and reference number (where applicable)
		Connection (if any) to company and other participants
	Other participants	Name of each company (and details of any branches including those in the UK)
		Name of ultimate UK parent of each company (if member of a group)
		Nature of the business of each company
		Territory of residence of each company
		UK tax office and reference number of each company (where applicable)
		Connection (if any) to other participants
Details of the scheme		Description of the proposed scheme
		Nature and amount(s) of all relevant transaction(s)
		Details of the tax deduction(s), or other relief(s)/allowance(s), available to the paying party and the territory in which each is available
		Explanation as to why the payment is not brought into account under the disguised interest rules (¶16120)
		Explanation as to why the payment is not otherwise brought into account as income or gains

Appendix

Finance Acts

95000

Year	Budget	Royal Assent
2013	20 March 2013	17 July 2013
2012	21 March 2012	17 July 2012
2011	23 March 2011	19 July 2011
2010 (No.3)	22 June 2010	16 December 2010
2010 (No.2)	22 June 2010	27 July 2010
2010	24 March 2010	8 April 2010
2009	22 April 2009	21 July 2009
2008	12 March 2008	21 July 2008
2007	21 March 2007	19 July 2007
2006	22 March 2006	19 July 2006

Corporation tax rates

95020

Financial year starting on 1 April	Full rate	Small profits rate	Lower limit of profits (£)	Upper limit of profits (£)	Marginal relief fraction	Marginal rate of tax
2014	21%	TBA	TBA	TBA	TBA	TBA
2013	23%	20%	300,000	1,500,000	3/400	23.75%
2012	24%	20%	300,000	1,500,000	1/100	25.00%
2011	26%	20%	300,000	1,500,000	3/200	27.50%
2010	28%	21%	300,000	1,500,000	7/400	29.75%
2009	28%	21%	300,000	1,500,000	7/400	29.75%
2008	30%	21%	300,000	1,500,000	7/400	29.75%
2007	30%	20%	300,000	1,500,000	1/40	32.50%
2006	30%	19%	300,000	1,500,000	11/400	32.75%

Capital allowances

95040   **Plant and machinery**   All WDA are given on a reducing balance basis.

From 1 April 2008, where the residue in either the main pool or special rate pool is **less than or equal to** £1,000 (after accounting for disposals and acquisitions), the company can claim the full amount of the residue as a writing down allowance (¶26055).

General

Qualifying item	Subcategory	Type of allowance	Pool	Rate
Environmentally friendly assets	Environmentally beneficial plant and machinery	First year (and repayable tax credit if makes a loss)	Main	100%
	Energy-saving plant and machinery			
	Gas refuelling stations	First year		100%
	Zero-emissions goods vehicles			
Assets with longer life	Thermal insulation	Writing down	Special rate	8%
	Integral features			
	Long life assets (useful economic life over 25 years)		Own pool	
Cars	Cars with carbon dioxide emissions not exceeding 95g/km [1]	First year	Main	100%
	Cars with carbon dioxide emissions > 130g/km [2]	Writing down	Special rate	8%
	Pre April 2009 purchases which cost > £12,000	Writing down	Separate pool	18% up to £3,000 p.a.
Short life assets		Writing down	Short life asset pool	18%
Fixtures		Writing down	Main or special rate	18% or 8% [3]
Ships		Writing down	Separate ship pool	18% or 8%

Qualifying item	Subcategory	Type of allowance	Pool	Rate
Assets leased out	Long funding leases	Writing down	Main	18%
	Other leases where asset used for trade	Writing down[4]	Main	18%
	Other leases where asset not used for trade	Writing down	Separate pool	18%
	Assets leased overseas where lease finalised before 1 April 2006:	Writing down	Depends on type of lease	
	Protected lease			18%
	Other lease			10%

Note
1. This limit was 110g/km for expenditure incurred prior to 1 April 2013.
2. This limit was 160g/km for expenditure incurred prior to 1 April 2013.
3. Depends on whether the asset is placed in a special rate pool: see ¶26230.
4. Unless of a type which attracts a first year allowance: see ¶82520

Rates and amounts

Type of allowance	Financial year beginning 1 April						
	2007	2008	2009	2010	2011	2012[1]	2013[1]
Annual investment	n/a	£50,000	£50,000	£100,000	£100,000	£25,000	£250,000
Writing down - main pool	25%	20%	20%	20%	20%	18%	18%
Writing down - special rate pool	n/a	10%	10%	10%	10%	8%	8%
First year allowance generally	n/a	n/a	40%	n/a	n/a	n/a	n/a
FYA for medium sized companies[2]	40%	n/a	n/a	n/a	n/a	n/a	n/a
FYA for small companies[2]	50%	n/a	n/a	n/a	n/a	n/a	n/a
FYA on green technologies	100%	100%	100%	100%	100%	100%	100%

Note:
1. A temporary increase in the AIA has been made for the period from 1 January 2013 to 31 December 2014. For this period the AIA is set at £250,000.
2. For the definition of small and medium sized companies see ¶95140

Other   All WDA are given on a straight line basis unless marked as RB (reducing balance):   **95060**

Qualifying item	Subcategory	Type of allowance	Rate
Enterprise zone assets	Located in assisted areas[1]	First year	100%
Business premises renovation	Maximum expenditure €20 million	First year	100%
Flat conversions	Expenditure up to 31 March 2013	First year	100%
Dredging		Writing down	4%
Mineral extraction	Exploration and access - RB	Writing down	25%
	Acquisition of assets - RB	Writing down	10%
Intellectual property[2]	Expenditure before 1 April 2002 - RB	Writing down	25%

Note
1. The former system of capital allowances for enterprise zones ended on 31 March 2011.
2. Includes patent rights, computer software and industrial know-how.
3. The former systems of allowances for industrial and agricultural buildings were phased out in 2007-11 and ended on 31 March 2011.

Land remediation relief

95080   The original qualifying expenditure plus an additional 50% is allowed as a deduction.

A qualifying land remediation loss can be surrendered in return for a tax credit payment of 16% of the amount surrendered.

Research and development

95100   The following reliefs are available for R & D expenditure:

Category	Financial years beginning 1 April						
	2007	2008	2009	2010	2011	2012	2013
SMEs (¶95120) - deduction[1]	150%	150%[1]	175%	175%	200%	225%	225%
Large companies - deduction[1,2]	125%	125%	130%	130%	130%	130%	130%
Rate of tax credit relief for SMEs[1]	16%	16%[2]	14%	14%	12.5%	12.5%	11%
Capital allowances on capital expenditure	100%	100%	100%	100%	100%	100%	100%

Note:
1. Prior to 1 April 2012 there was an annual expenditure threshold of £10,000 for these allowances.
2. For expenditure incurred on or after 1 April 2013 a system of tax credits has also been added. The rate of this has been set at 10%. For details see ¶78490.

Definition of SMEs

95120   **Research and development purposes**   The table below shows the maximum limits applying to a company that wants to claim the various types of R & D reliefs (¶78000). In each case, it must satisfy the headcount condition and then either the turnover or balance sheet condition to qualify (taking into account the staff, income and assets of linked or partnership enterprises).

Limits from 1 August 2008

Category	Larger SME	Medium	Small[1]	Micro
Headcount	<500	<250	<50	<10
Turnover	€100 million	€50 million	€10 million	€2 million
Balance sheet total	€86 million	€43 million	€10 million	€2 million

Note:
1. These limits also define a small company for the purposes of the distribution exemption (¶18385).

From 1 January 2005 **to 31 July 2008**, an SME was defined as having:
– a headcount of less than 250;
– turnover up to €50 million; and
– a balance sheet total of up to €43 million.

95140   **Capital allowances purposes**   The definition of a SME was pertinent up until 31 March 2008 (¶95040). The table below shows the maximum limits. Two of the conditions had to be satisfied in each accounting period in order to qualify as a small or medium sized business.

Category	Small	Medium
Turnover	£5.6 million	£22.8 million
Balance sheet assets	£2.8 million	£11.4 million
Number of employees	50	250

Retail prices index

	Jan	Feb	Mar	Apr	May	June	July	Aug	Sept	Oct	Nov	Dec
1965	14.47	14.47	14.52	14.80	14.85	14.90	14.90	14.93	14.93	14.96	15.01	15.08
1966	15.11	15.11	15.13	15.34	15.44	15.49	15.41	15.51	15.49	15.51	15.61	15.64
1967	15.67	15.67	15.67	15.79	15.79	15.84	15.74	15.72	15.69	15.86	15.92	16.02
1968	16.07	16.15	16.20	16.50	16.50	16.58	16.58	16.60	16.63	16.70	16.76	16.96
1969	17.06	17.16	17.21	17.41	17.39	17.47	17.47	17.41	17.47	17.59	17.64	17.77
1970	17.90	18.00	18.10	18.38	18.43	18.48	18.63	18.61	18.71	18.91	19.04	19.16
1971	19.42	19.54	19.70	20.13	20.25	20.38	20.51	20.53	20.56	20.66	20.79	20.89
1972	21.01	21.12	21.19	21.39	21.50	21.62	21.70	21.88	22.00	22.31	22.38	22.48
1973	22.64	22.79	22.92	23.35	23.52	23.65	23.75	23.83	24.03	24.51	24.69	24.87
1974	25.35	25.78	26.01	26.89	27.28	27.55	27.81	27.83	28.14	28.69	29.20	29.63
1975	30.39	30.90	31.51	32.72	34.09	34.75	35.11	35.31	35.61	36.12	36.55	37.01
1976	37.49	37.97	38.17	38.91	39.34	39.54	39.62	40.18	40.71	41.44	42.03	42.59
1977	43.70	44.24	44.56	45.70	46.06	46.54	46.59	46.82	47.07	47.28	47.50	47.76
1978	48.04	48.31	48.62	49.33	49.61	49.99	50.22	50.54	50.75	50.98	51.33	51.76
1979	52.52	52.95	53.38	54.30	54.73	55.67	58.07	58.53	59.11	59.72	60.25	60.68
1980	62.18	63.07	63.93	66.11	66.72	67.35	67.91	68.06	68.49	68.92	69.48	69.86
1981	70.29	70.93	71.99	74.07	74.55	74.98	75.31	75.87	76.30	76.98	77.78	78.28
1982	78.73	78.76	79.44	81.04	81.62	81.85	81.88	81.90	81.85	82.26	82.66	82.51
1983	82.61	82.97	83.12	84.28	84.64	84.84	85.30	85.68	86.06	86.36	86.67	86.89
1984	86.84	87.20	87.48	88.64	88.97	89.20	89.10	89.94	90.11	90.67	90.95	90.87
1985	91.20	91.94	92.80	94.78	95.21	95.41	95.23	95.49	95.44	95.59	95.92	96.05
1986	96.25	96.60	96.73	97.67	97.85	97.79	97.52	97.82	98.30	98.45	99.29	99.62
1987	100.00	100.40	100.60	101.80	101.90	101.90	101.80	102.10	102.40	102.90	103.40	103.30
1988	103.30	103.70	104.10	105.80	106.20	106.60	106.70	107.90	108.40	109.50	110.00	110.30
1989	111.00	111.80	112.30	114.30	115.00	115.40	115.50	115.80	116.60	117.50	118.50	118.80
1990	119.50	120.20	121.40	125.10	126.20	126.70	126.80	128.10	129.30	130.30	130.00	129.90
1991	130.20	130.90	131.40	133.10	133.50	134.10	133.80	134.10	134.60	135.10	135.60	135.70
1992	135.60	136.30	136.70	138.80	139.30	139.30	138.80	138.90	139.40	139.90	139.70	139.20
1993	137.90	138.80	139.30	140.60	141.10	141.00	140.70	141.30	141.90	141.80	141.60	141.90
1994	141.30	142.10	142.50	144.20	144.70	144.70	144.00	144.70	145.00	145.20	145.30	146.00
1995	146.00	146.90	147.50	149.00	149.60	149.80	149.10	149.90	150.60	149.80	149.80	150.70
1996	150.20	150.90	151.50	152.60	152.90	153.00	152.40	153.10	153.80	153.00	153.90	154.40
1997	154.40	155.00	155.40	156.30	156.90	157.50	157.50	158.50	159.30	159.50	159.60	160.00
1998	159.50	160.30	160.80	162.60	163.50	163.40	163.00	163.70	164.40	164.50	164.40	164.40
1999	163.40	163.70	164.10	165.20	165.60	165.60	165.10	165.50	166.20	166.50	166.70	167.30
2000	166.60	167.50	168.40	170.10	170.70	171.10	170.50	170.50	171.70	171.60	172.10	172.20
2001	171.10	172.00	172.20	173.10	174.20	174.40	173.30	174.00	174.60	174.30	173.60	173.40
2002	173.30	173.80	174.50	175.70	176.20	176.20	175.90	176.40	177.60	177.90	178.20	178.50
2003	178.40	179.30	179.90	181.20	181.50	181.30	181.30	181.60	182.50	182.60	182.70	183.50
2004	183.10	183.80	184.60	185.70	186.50	186.80	186.80	187.40	188.10	188.60	189.00	189.90
2005	188.90	189.60	190.50	191.60	192.00	192.20	192.20	192.60	193.10	193.30	193.60	194.10
2006	193.40	194.20	195.00	196.50	197.70	198.50	198.50	199.20	200.10	200.40	201.10	202.70
2007	201.60	203.10	204.40	205.40	206.20	207.30	206.10	207.30	208.00	208.90	209.70	210.90
2008	209.80	211.40	212.10	214.00	215.10	216.80	216.50	218.40	217.20	217.70	216.00	212.90
2009	210.10	211.40	211.30	211.50	212.80	213.40	213.40	214.40	215.30	216.00	216.60	218.00
2010	218.00	219.20	220.70	222.80	223.60	224.10	223.60	224.50	225.30	225.80	226.80	228.40
2011	229.00	231.30	232.50	234.40	235.20	235.20	234.70	236.10	237.90	238.00	238.50	239.40
2012	238.00	239.90	240.80	242.50	242.40	241.80	242.10	243.00	244.20	245.60	245.60	246.80
2013	245.80	247.60	248.70	249.50	250.00	249.70	249.70					

Short leases

95180

Short lease depreciation factors					
Years	%	Years	%	Years	%
50 (or more)	100	33	90.280	16	64.116
49	99.657	32	89.354	15	61.617
48	99.289	31	88.371	14	58.971
47	98.902	30	87.330	13	56.167
46	98.490	29	86.226	12	53.191
45	98.059	28	85.053	11	50.038
44	97.595	27	83.816	10	46.695
43	97.107	26	82.496	9	43.154
42	96.593	25	81.100	8	39.399
41	96.041	24	79.622	7	35.414
40	95.457	23	78.055	6	31.195
39	94.842	22	76.399	5	26.722
38	94.189	21	74.635	4	21.983
37	93.497	20	72.770	3	16.959
36	92.761	19	70.791	2	11.629
35	91.981	18	68.697	1	5.983
34	91.156	17	66.470	0	0

Filing deadlines

95220

Length of period of account	Filing deadline for CT600
12 months or less	On the later of the following dates: – 12 months after the end of the period of account; or – where a notice to file a return is received, 3 months after the date of receipt (which is deemed to be 4 days after the date of its issue). Where notice to file period does not match the accounting period see ¶46110
Greater than 12 months	Filing deadline is still based on the end of the period of account, even where more than one accounting period involved For periods of account longer than 18 months (which will be rare), the filing deadline is: – 30 months after the start of the period for which accounts are prepared; or – where a notice to file a return is received, 3 months after the date of receipt (which is deemed to be 4 days after the date of its issue). Where notice to file period does not match the accounting period see ¶46110

Payment due dates

95240

Liability	Detail	Due dates
Mainstream corporation tax of non-large company		9 months and 1 day after end of each accounting period
Mainstream corporation tax of large company (i.e. broadly taxable profits exceed £1.5 million[1] and liability exceeds £10,000[2])	Instalments (based on company's estimated profits)	For 12-month accounting period - 14th day of Months 7, 10, 13 and 16

Liability	Detail	Due dates
Income tax on interest, annual payments etc		14 days after end of return period
Tax on loan to close company participator	Non-large company	9 months and 1 day after end of the accounting period in which loan made
	Large company	Along with instalment payments

Note:
1. This threshold is pro-rated for the number of associated companies, and also where accounting period is less than 12 months.
2. As reduced for accounting periods of less than 12 months long.

Interest on late tax payments

Rates of interest on unpaid corporation tax for accounting periods ending after 30 June 1999 for payments **other than instalment payments**.   **95260**

Period of application	Rate %
From 29 September 2009	3.00
24 March 2009 to 28 September 2009	2.50
27 January 2009 to 23 March 2009	3.50
6 January 2009 to 26 January 2009	4.50
6 December 2008 to 5 January 2009	5.50
6 November 2008 to 5 December 2008	6.50
6 January 2008 to 5 November 2008	7.50
6 August 2007 to 5 January 2008	8.50
6 September 2006 to 5 August 2007	7.50
6 September 2005 to 5 September 2006	6.50

Rates of interest on unpaid corporation tax **instalments** for accounting periods ending after 30 June 1999.

Period of application	Rate %
From 16 March 2009	1.50
16 February 2009 to 15 March 2009	2.00
19 January 2009 to 15 February 2009	2.50
15 December 2008 to 18 January 2009	3.00
17 November 2008 to 14 December 2008	4.00
20 October 2008 to 16 November 2008	5.50
21 April 2008 to 19 October 2008	6.00
18 February 2008 to 20 April 2008	6.25
17 December 2007 to 17 February 2008	6.50
16 July 2007 to 16 December 2007	6.75
21 May 2007 to 15 July 2007	6.50
22 January 2007 to 20 May 2007	6.25
20 November 2006 to 21 January 2007	6.00
14 August 2006 to 19 November 2006	5.75
15 August 2005 to 13 August 2006	5.50

Interest on overpaid tax

95280

Rates of interest on overpaid corporation tax for accounting periods ending after 30 June 1999 for payments **other than** instalment payments and tax paid early. (Interest runs from normal due date.)

Period of application	Rate %
From 29 September 2009	0.5
27 January 2009 to 28 September 2009	0
6 January 2009 to 26 January 2009	1
6 December 2008 to 5 January 2009	2
6 November 2008 to 5 December 2008	3
6 January 2008 to 5 November 2008	4
6 August 2007 to 5 January 2008	5
6 September 2006 to 5 August 2007	4
6 September 2005 to 5 September 2006	3

Rates of interest on overpaid corporation tax for accounting periods ending after 30 June 1999 for **instalment payments and on corporation tax paid early** (interest period runs until normal due date).

Period of application	Rate %
From 21 September 2009	0.5
16 March 2009 to 20 September 2009	0.25
16 February 2009 to 15 March 2009	0.75
19 January 2009 to 15 February 2009	1.25
15 December 2008 to 18 January 2009	1.75
17 November 2008 to 14 December 2008	2.75
20 October 2008 to 16 November 2008	4.25
21 April 2008 to 19 October 2008	4.75
18 February 2008 to 20 April 2008	5.00
17 December 2007 to 17 February 2008	5.25
16 July 2007 to 16 December 2007	5.50
21 May 2007 to 15 July 2007	5.25
22 January 2007 to 20 May 2007	5.00
20 November 2006 to 21 January 2007	4.75
14 August 2006 to 19 November 2006	4.50
15 August 2005 to 13 August 2006	4.25

Accounting standards

95300

Topic area	Applicable accounting standards	
	Reference	Name
Accounting generally	FRS 3	Reporting financial performance
	FRS 12	Provisions, contingent liabilities and contingent assets
	FRS 18	Accounting policies
	FRS 21	Events after the balance sheet date
	FRS 28	Corresponding amounts
	SSAP 4	Accounting for government grants
	SSAP 5	Accounting for value added tax
	FRSSE	Financial Reporting Standard for Smaller Entities

Topic area	Applicable accounting standards	
	Reference	Name
Financial transactions	FRS 4	Capital instruments
	FRS 5	Reporting the substance of transactions
	FRS 13	Derivatives and other financial instruments: disclosures
	FRS 25	Financial instruments: disclosure and presentation
	FRS 26	Financial instruments: measurement
	FRS 29	Financial instruments: disclosures
	UITF Abstract 42	Reassessment of embedded derivatives
Foreign currency	FRS 23	The effects of changes in foreign exchange rates
	SSAP 20	Foreign currency translation
	FRS 24	Financial reporting in hyper-inflationary economies
	UITF Abstract 9	Accounting for operations in hyper-inflationary economies
	UITF Abstract 19	Tax on gains and losses on foreign currency borrowings that hedge an investment in a foreign enterprise
Leasing	SSAP 21	Accounting for leases and hire purchase contracts
	FRS 5	Reporting the substance of transactions
	UITF Abstract 28	Operating lease incentives
Intangibles	FRS 10	Goodwill and intangible assets
	FRS 11	Impairment of fixed assets and goodwill
	UITF Abstract 27	Revision to estimates of the useful economic life of goodwill and intangible assets
Tangibles	FRS 15	Tangible fixed assets
	FRS 11	Impairment of fixed assets and goodwill
Stock	SSAP 9	Stocks and long term contracts
	FRS 5	Reporting the substance of transactions
	UITF Abstract 5	Transfers from current assets to fixed assets
	UITF Abstract 40	Revenue recognition and service contracts
Groups	FRS 2	Accounting for subsidiary undertakings
	FRS 6	Acquisitions and mergers
	FRS 7	Fair values in acquisition accounting
	FRS 9	Associates and joint ventures
	UITF Abstract 31	Exchanges of businesses or other non-monetary assets for an interest in a subsidiary, joint venture or associate
Research and development	SSAP 13	Accounting for research and development
Pensions	FRS 17	Retirement benefits
	UITF Abstract 6	Accounting for post-retirement benefits other than pensions
	UITF Abstract 35	Death-in-service and incapacity benefits
	UITF Abstract 37	Accounting implications of the replacement of the retail prices index with the consumer prices index for retirement benefits
Share remuneration	FRS 20	Share-based payment
	UITF Abstract 41	Scope of FRS 20
	UITF Abstract 17	Employee share schemes
	UITF Abstract 32	Employee benefit trusts and other intermediate payment arrangements
	UITF Abstract 38	Accounting for ESOP trusts

Topic area	Applicable accounting standards	
	Reference	Name
Taxation	FRS 16	Current tax
	FRS 19	Deferred tax

Recognised stock exchanges

95320   A recognised stock exchange is one which has been so designated by HMRC. The following is a list of countries with exchanges that have been designated as recognised stock exchanges. Unless otherwise specified, any stock exchange (or options exchange) in a country listed below is a recognised stock exchange for these purposes, provided it is recognised under the law of the country concerned relating to stock exchanges.

Country	Effective date
Australia	
Australian Stock Exchange and its stock exchange subsidiaries	22 September 1988
Austria[1]	22 October 1970
Bahamas	
Bahamas International Securities Exchange	19 April 2010
Belgium[1]	22 October 1970
Bermuda	4 December 2007
Brazil	
Rio De Janeiro Stock Exchange	17 August 1995
Sao Paulo Stock Exchange	11 December 1995
Canada	
Any stock exchange prescribed for the purposes of the Canadian Income Tax Act	22 October 1970
Cayman Islands	4 March 2004
China	
Hong Kong - Any stock exchange recognised under Section 2A(1) of the Hong Kong Companies Ordinance	26 February 1971
Cyprus	
Cyprus Stock Exchange	22 June 2009
Denmark	
Copenhagen Stock Exchange	22 October 1970
GXG Official list	16 May 2013
Estonia	
NASDAQ OMX Tallinn	5 May 2010
Finland	
Helsinki Stock Exchange	22 October 1970
France[1]	22 October 1970
Germany[1]	5 August 1971
Greece	
Athens Stock Exchange	14 June 1993
Guernsey[1]	10 December 2002
Iceland	31 March 2006
Irish Republic[1]	22 October 1970
Italy[1]	3 May 1972
Japan[1]	22 October 1970
Lithuania	

Country	Effective date
NASDAQ QMX Vilnius	12 March 2012
Luxembourg [1]	21 February 1972
Malaysia	
Kuala Lumpur Stock Exchange	10 October 1994
Malta	
Whole of market	29 December 2005
European Wholesale Securities Market	17 January 2013
Mauritius Stock Exchange	
Official Market of the Stock Exchange of Mauritius	31 January 2011
Global Board of Trade	13 January 2013
Mexico	10 October 1994
Netherlands [1]	22 October 1970
New Zealand	22 September 1988
Norway [1]	22 October 1970
Poland	
Warsaw Stock Exchange	25 February 2010
Portugal [1]	21 February 1972
Russia	
MICEX Stock Exchange	5 January 2011
Singapore	30 June 1977
South Africa	
Johannesburg Stock Exchange	22 October 1970
The Bond Exchange of South Africa	16 April 2008
South Korea	10 October 1994
Spain [1]	5 August 1971
Sri Lanka	
Colombo Stock Exchange	21 February 1972
Sweden	
Stockholm Stock Exchange	16 July 1985
Switzerland	
Swiss Stock Exchange	12 May 1997
Thailand	10 October 1994
United Kingdom	
LIFFE Administration and Management	26 September 2011
London Stock Exchange	6 April 1965
ICAP Securities and Derivatives Exchange Ltd	25 April 2013
United States	
Any stock exchange registered with the Securities and Exchange Commission as a national securities exchange [2]	22 October 1970
NASDAQ Stock Market [3]	10 March 1992

Note:
1. Any stock exchange that is a stock exchange within the meaning of the law of the country concerned relating to stock exchanges.
2. The term "national securities exchange" does not include any local exchanges registered with the Securities and Exchange Commission.
3. As maintained through the facilities of the National Association of Securities Dealers Inc and its subsidiaries.

95340 **Alternative finance stock exchanges** The following stock exchanges are designated as recognised stock exchanges for the purposes of alternative finance arrangements only.

For alternative finance investment bonds to be treated as qualifying alternative finance arrangements, they must be listed on one of these exchanges.

Country	Exchange
United Arab Emirates	Abu Dhabi Stock Exchange
United Arab Emirates	Dubai Financial Market
United Arab Emirates	NASDAQ Dubai (formerly Dubai International Financial Exchange)
Bahrain	Bahrain Stock Exchange
Malaysia	Labuan International Financial Exchange
Saudi Arabia	Saudi Stock Exchange (Tadawul)
Indonesia	Surabaya Stock Exchange

Recognised futures exchanges

95360

Country	Effective date
Australia	
Sydney Futures Exchange	13 October 1988
Canada	
Montreal Exchange	29 July 1987
China	
Hong Kong Futures Exchange	15 December 1987
Sweden	
OM Stockholm	18 March 1992
United Kingdom	
International Petroleum Exchange of London	6 August 1985
London Gold Market	12 December 1985
London International Financial Futures and Options Exchange (LIFFE)	22 March 1992
London Metal Exchange	6 August 1985
London Rubber Market	6 August 1985
London Silver Market	12 December 1985
OMLX	18 March 1992
United States	
Chicago Board of Trade	29 July 1987
Chicago Mercantile Exchange (CME)	19 December 1986
Commodity Exchange (COMEX)	25 August 1988
Mid America Commodity Exchange	29 July 1987
New York Board of Trade	10 June 2004
New York Mercantile Exchange	19 December 1986
Philadelphia Board of Trade	19 December 1986

Contact details for HMRC

95380 Most queries and issues can be dealt with by contacting the usual HMRC office where the company submits its CTSA returns. If the company does not know the contact details of its HMRC office, these can be found at flmemo.co.uk/ctm95380-office.

Other contact details can be found in the table below:

Issue	Detail	Contact	Address
Payments	Actual corporation tax payments to be submitted to	HMRC Accounts Office	Bradford BD98 1YY
	Enquiries about payments	HMRC Corporation Tax Unit 01236 785057	Accounts Office St Mungo's Road Cumbernauld Glasgow G67 1YZ
	Group payments	01236 785499	
	Income tax payments	01236 785498	
	Business payment support service for companies in financial difficulties	0845 302 1435	
Appeals	Appeal must first be lodged with HMRC (at usual tax office) If company still dissatisfied, appeal can be made to First-tier Tribunal	The Tribunals Service: Tax Appeal forms can be downloaded from flmemo.co.uk/ctm95380-appeals	2nd floor 54 Hagley Road Birmingham B16 8PE 0845 223 8080 taxappeals@tribunals.gsi.gov.uk
Ordering forms	CTSA return, guide and supplementary pages	0845 300 6555	
Statutory clearances[1]	Demergers	Clearance and Counteraction Team: Anti-avoidance group	SO258 PO Box 194 Bootle L69 9AA
	Share exchanges		
	Intangible fixed assets		
	Purchase of own shares		
	Transactions in securities		
	Enterprise investment scheme - acquisition of shares by new company		
Non-statutory clearances	Issue is commercially significant, and there is material uncertainty	Normal client relationship manager (for large companies)	
		For smaller companies: HMRC Clearance Team	Alexander House 21 Victoria Avenue Southend-on-Sea Essex SS99 1BD
Investment schemes clearance	That qualifies as an EIS company	Small Company Enterprise Centre	1st Floor Ferrers House Castle Meadow Road Nottingham NG2 1BB
	That qualifies as a VCT issuing company		
	That qualifies as a CVS issuing company		
Cross border	Company migration	Neil Nagle Business International Transfer pricing team	100 Parliament St London SW1A 2BQ
	Advance pricing agreements	Ian Wood Business International	
	Controlled foreign companies	CTIAA, Outward Investment Team Registry (Controlled Foreign Company Clearances)	
	Arbitrage clearance	Margaret Kayser CTIAA, Business International	
	Inward investments of £250 million or more	Business International: Advance Agreements Unit	
	Double tax treaty passport scheme	flmemo.co.uk/ctm95380-passport	

Issue	Detail	Contact	Address
Research and development, and vaccine research	Enquiries about claims	Normal client relationship manager (for large companies)	
		For smaller companies, specialist HMRC unit can be found by using a post code search at flmemo.co.uk/ctm95380-R&D	
CASCs or charities	General enquiries	Charities helpline: 0845 302 0203 Email: charities@hmrc.gov.uk	HMRC Charities St Johns House Merton Road Liverpool L75 1BB
Charitable donations	Gift aid and transfers of assets	flmemo.co.uk/ctm95380-donations	
Members clubs	To be treated as dormant	flmemo.co.uk/ctm95380-clubs	
Share values	Negligible value quoted shares	flmemo.co.uk/ctm95380-negligible	
Non-resident landlords scheme	To receive rents gross	flmemo.co.uk/ctm95380-nrl	
Offshore funds	Details of reporting funds	flmemo.co.uk/ctm95380-offshore	
Employee share schemes		HMRC Employee Shares and Securities Unit	Room G52 100 Parliament St London SW1A 2BQ

Note:
1. Clearances under any of these headings can be amalgamated into one clearance letter. Sensitive information should be addressed to the Team Leader, who should be contacted on 020 7438 7215 before sending such information via email or fax. Clearances can be emailed to reconstructions@hmrc.gsi.gov.uk, or faxed on 020 7438 4409.

Official information

95400 The latest version of all official publications and online information can be obtained from the following website addresses:

Source	Website address
HMRC	flmemo.co.uk/ctm95400-leaflets
Details of environmentally beneficial technologies	flmemo.co.uk/ctm95400-eca
Department of Energy and Climate Change	flmemo.co.uk/ctm95400-decc
Environment Agency	flmemo.co.uk/ctm95400-ea
Department for Environment, Food and Rural Affairs	flmemo.co.uk/ctm95400-defra
Department of Work and Pensions	flmemo.co.uk/ctm95400-dwp
Department for Business, Innovation and Skills	flmemo.co.uk/ctm95400-bis
Adjudicator's office	flmemo.co.uk/ctm95400-ao
Parliamentary and Health Service Ombudsman	flmemo.co.uk/ctm95400-ombudsman
Vehicle Certification Agency	flmemo.co.uk/ctm95400-vca
OECD	flmemo.co.uk/ctm95400-oecd

Table of cases

A list of cases mentioned in *Corporation Tax Memo* is detailed below, in alphabetical order, together with the year of the case and the paragraph where the case is mentioned.

95420

Case name	Year	¶¶
A W Chapman Ltd v Hennessey	1982	¶66210
Alexander Drew and Sons Ltd v CIR	1932	¶75415
Alianza Company Ltd v Bell	1905	¶14095
American Leaf Blending Co Sdn Bhd v Director-General of Inland Revenue	1978	¶7105
American Thread Co v Joyce	1913	¶2045
Anchor International Limited v IRC	2003	¶25370
Ansell Computer Services Ltd v Richardson	2004	¶77240
Associated Restaurants Ltd v Warland	1989	¶25370
Attwood v Anduff car wash	1997	¶25375
Bamford v ATA Advertising Ltd	1972	¶14585
Barnett v Brabyn	1996	¶77230
Bayfine UK v HMRC	2010	¶90490
Beauchamp v FW Woolworth plc	1989	¶13060
Ben-Odeco Ltd v Powlson	1978	¶25450
Benson v Yard Arm Club Ltd	1979	¶25370
Bestway (Holdings) Ltd. v Luff	1998	
Birmingham & District Cattle By-products Ltd v CIR	1919	¶60185
Bolam v Regent Oil Co Ltd	1956	¶13280
Boughey	[2012]	¶52810
Brennan v The Deanby Investment Company Ltd	2001	¶75670
Bricom Holdings v CIR	1997	¶90985
British Insulated and Helsby Cables Ltd v Atherton	1925	¶13225
Brown v Burnley Football & Athletic Co Ltd	1980	¶13310, ¶25370
BSC Footwear Ltd v Ridgway	1971	¶11060
Buckingham v Securitas Properties Ltd	1980	
Burdge v Pyne	1968	¶5495
Burmah Steamship Co Ltd v CIR	1922	¶13150
Cadbury Schweppes v HMRC	2006	¶91005
Caillebotte v Quinn	1975	¶14550
Californian Copper Syndicate (Limited and Reduced) v Harris	1904	¶5295
Canada Safeway v IRC	1973	¶75315
Cannon Industries Ltd v Edwards	1965	¶36155
Cape Brandy Syndicate v CIR	1921	¶5255
Castle Construction (Chesterfield) Ltd v HMRC	2008	¶77220
Carlisle & Silloth Golf Club v Smith	1913	¶5435
Carpet Agencies Ltd v CIR	1958	¶6210
Celtic Football and Athletic Club Ltd v C & E	1983	¶14585
CIR v Alexander von Glehn & Co Ltd	1920	¶14585

Case name	Year	¶¶
CIR v Anglo Brewing Co Ltd	1925	¶14940
CIR v Barclay Curle and Co Ltd	1969	¶25420
CIR v Fraser	1942	¶5050, ¶5145, ¶5210, ¶5285, ¶5415
CIR v Gardner Mountain & D' Abrumenil Ltd	1947	¶11060
CIR v Livingston and Others	1926	¶5210, ¶5250, ¶5285
CIR v Marine Steam Turbine Co Ltd	1919	¶6125, ¶7100
CIR v Nchanga Copper Mines	1964	¶13280
CIR v Park Investments Ltd	1964	¶75415
CIR v The Korean Syndicate Ltd	1921	¶6125, ¶7100
CIR v The Stonehaven Recreation Ground Trustees	1929	¶5335
CIR v Tring Investments Ltd	1939	¶75415
CIR v Tyre Investment Trust Ltd	1924	¶6120
CIR v Scottish & Newcastle Breweries Ltd	1982	¶25335, ¶25420
Clark v IRC	1978	¶21455
Coates v Arndale Properties Ltd	1984	¶67160
Cole Brothers Ltd v Phillips	1980	¶25375
Collins v Addies	1992	¶75790
Collins v The Firth-Brearley Stainless Steel Syndicate Ltd	1925	¶14085
Conservative & Unionist Central Office v Burrell	1982	¶2000
Cooke v Beach Station Caravans Ltd	1974	¶25420
Cooke v Haddock	1960	¶5150
Creed v H & M Levinson Ltd	1981	¶14300
Crusabridge Investments Ltd v Casings International Ltd	1979	
Crusader v HMRC	2007	¶30360
Cyril Lord Carpets Limited v Schofield	1966	¶25185
De Beers Consolidated Mines Ltd v Howe	1906	¶2040
Dixon v Fitch's Garage Ltd	1976	¶25370
Donald Fisher (Ealing) Ltd v Spencer	1989	¶13265, ¶14300
Down v Compston	1937	¶5495
DSG Retail v HMRC	2009	¶70155
E Y L Trading Co Ltd v CIR	1962	¶6210
Earl Howe v CIR	1919	¶14715
ECC Quarries Ltd v Watkis	1975	¶13210
Edwards v Bairstow & Harrison	1955	¶5255
Elson v Price Taylors Ltd	1962	¶14330
Evans Medical Supplies Ltd v Moriarty	1957	¶29180
Express and Echo Publications v Tanton	1999	¶77235
Family Golf Centres Ltd v Thorne	1998	¶25420
FPH Finance Trust Ltd v CIR	1944	¶6085
G H Chambers (Northiam Farms) Ltd v Watmough	1956	¶26170
Gallagher v Jones	1994	¶11055, ¶11070, ¶11075
Gaspet Ltd v Ellis	1987	¶78670
Girobank plc v Clarke	1998	
Glenboig Union Fireclay Co Ltd v CIR	1930	¶13150

Case name	Year	¶¶
Golden Horse Shoe (New) Ltd v Thurgood	1934	¶14095
Gordon & Blair v IRC	1962	¶36155, ¶61050
Graham v Green	1925	¶5490
Grays v Seymours Garden Centre (Horticulture)	1993	¶25420
Greenbank Holidays Ltd v HMRC	2011	¶28290
Greenberg v IRC	1972	¶21490
Grove v YMCA	1903	¶5335
Hall v Lorimer	1994	¶77215
Hampton v Fortes Autogrill Ltd	1980	¶25410
Harvey v Caulcott	1952	¶5395
Heather v P E Consulting Group Ltd	1972	¶13220, ¶15040
Herbert Smith v Honour	1999	¶11915
Higgs v Olivier	1952	¶13130
HMRC v Charlton and others	2012	¶50610
HMRC v Collins	2008	¶30360
HMRC v Household Estate Agents Ltd	2007	¶50625
HMRC v Lansdowne Partners Ltd	2010	¶50615
HMRC v Marks & Spencer plc	2013	¶66380
HMRC v Salaried Persons Postal Loans Ltd	2006	¶7105, ¶40190
HMRC v Taylor and another	2011	¶80095
HMRC v William Grant & Sons Distillers Ltd	2007	¶11705
Hughes de Lasteyrie du Saillant v Ministere de l'Economie, des Finances et de l'Industrie	2004	¶91435
Humphries (George) & Co v Cook	1934	¶36155
Hunt v Henry Quick	1992	¶25420
ICI v Colmer	1999	¶65110
IRC v Aken	1990	¶5500
IRC v Brebner	1967	¶21455
IRC v Reid's Trustees	1949	¶18125
IRC v Saxone, Lilley and Skinner (Holdings) Ltd	1967	
IRC v Wiggin	1979	¶21495
J Bolson & Son Ltd v Farrelly	1953	¶14090
J D Wetherspoon plc v HMRC	2012	¶25370, ¶25450
J P Harrison (Watford) Ltd v Griffiths	1962	¶5500
J & R O'Kane & Co v CIR	1922	¶60180, ¶61050
James Snook & Co Ltd v Blasdale	1952	¶14645
Jarrold v John Good & Sons Ltd	1963	¶25420
John M Harris (Design Partnership) Ltd v Lee	1997	¶7105
Johnson v CIR	1996	¶50200
Johnston v Britannia Airways	1994	¶11070
Johnston v Heath	1970	¶5190
Johnston Publishing (North) Limited v HMRC	2008	¶79500
Jones v Nuttall	1926	¶84060
Jowett v O'Neill and Brennan Construction Ltd	1998	¶7110, ¶40190
Kawthar Consulting Ltd v Revenue and Customs Commissioners	2005	¶36155
Kelsall Parsons & Co v CIR	1938	¶13155
King v Brindisco	1992	¶25420

Case name	Year	¶¶
Laerstate BV	2009	¶2040
Lagunas Nitrate Co Ltd v Schroeder & Co and Schmidt	1901	¶18130
Land Management Ltd v Fox	2002	¶7105, ¶40190
Law Shipping Co Ltd v CIR	1923	¶13315
Leach v Pogson	1962	¶5220
Lean & Dickson v Ball	1925	¶84060
Leeds Permanent Building Society v Proctor	1982	¶25420
Lewis Emmanuel v White	1965	¶5160
Lindsay, Woodward & Hiscox v CIR	1932	¶5500
Lingfield Park 1991 Ltd v Shove	2004	¶25370
Liverpool Corn Trade Association Ltd v Monks	1926	¶5435
Lowe v J W Ashmore Ltd	1970	¶84060
MacDonald v Dextra Accessories Ltd	2005	¶15035
Macfarlane v Glasgow City Council	2001	¶77235
MacKinlay v Arthur Young McClelland Moores & Co	1989	¶14550
MacNiven v Westmoreland Investments Ltd	1997	¶6085
Maidment v Kibby	1993	¶36155
Mallalieu v Drummond	1983	¶14550
Mallett v Staveley Coal & Iron Co Ltd	1928	¶13270
Mann v Nash	1932	¶5500
Market Investigations Ltd v Minister of Social Security	1969	¶77225
Marks & Spencer plc v Halsey	2008	¶66365
Marren v Ingles	1980	¶16105, ¶30375, ¶31165
Marriot v Lane	1996	¶61050
Marshall Hus & Partners Ltd v Bolton	1981	¶3065, ¶85225
Marson v Morton and Others	1986	¶5190, ¶5415
Martin v Lowry	1926	¶5290
Mawsley Machinery Ltd v Robinson	1998	¶15045
McGowan v Brown & Cousins	1977	¶14295
McKnight v Sheppard	1999	¶14555
MEPC Holding Ltd v Taylor	2002	¶66150
Meat Traders Ltd v Cushing	1997	¶11915
Medway Housing Society Ltd v Cook	1996	¶6120
Minsham Properties Ltd v Price	1990	¶75800
Mitchell Bros v Tomlinson	1957	¶5300
Mitchell v B W Noble Ltd	1927	¶14585, ¶14635
Morgan v Tate and Lyle Ltd	1954	¶14585
Morley v Tattersall	1938	¶14330
Murray v Goodhews	1978	¶14295
Murray v Imperial Chemical Industries Ltd	1967	¶29180
Napier v Griffiths	1990	¶60180
Netlogic Consulting Ltd v HMRC	2005	¶14585
New Angel Court v Adam	2004	¶5345
Nuclear Electric plc v Bradley	1996	¶16300, ¶36150
Odeon Associated Theatres Ltd v Jones	1971	¶13315
O'Grady v Bullcroft Main Collieries Ltd	1932	¶13310

Case name	Year	¶¶
O'Keefe v Southport Printers Ltd	1984	¶14940
Ostime v Duple Motor Bodies	1961	¶11745
Overseas Containers (Finance) Ltd v Stoker	1989	¶5340, ¶5345
Owen v Southern Railway of Peru Ltd	1956	¶11060
Page v Lowther	1983	¶19495
Partridge v Mallandine	1886	¶5500
Pearce v Woodall Duckham Ltd	1978	¶11705
Pertemps Recruitment Partnership Ltd v HMRC	2011	¶14330
Peter Reid v CIR	1947	¶84060
Philips Electronics UK Ltd v HMRC	2009	¶66325, ¶66380
Pickford v Quirke	1927	¶5215
Potel v IRC	1971	¶18130
Powerlaunch Ltd v HMRC	2012	¶75705
Protec International Ltd v HMRC	2010	¶14540
R v CIR (ex parte Newfields Developments Ltd)	2001	¶75310
R (oao Prudential plc and another) v Special Commissioner of Income Tax and another	2013	¶50160
Ransom v Higgs	1974	¶5050, ¶60180
Re Euro Hotel (Belgravia) Ltd	1975	¶16250
Re Severn and Wye and Severn Bridge Rly Co	1896	¶18130
Ready Mixed Concrete (South East) Ltd v Minister of Pensions and National Insurance	1968	¶77215
Reed v Nova Securities Ltd	1985	¶67160
Robroyston Brickworks Ltd v CIR	1976	¶61050
Rolfe v Wimpey Waste Management Ltd	1989	¶13270
RTZ Oil & Gas Ltd v Elliss	1987	¶11910
Rutledge v CIR	1929	¶5145, ¶5210, ¶5330
Ryan v Crabtree Denims Ltd	1987	¶13160
Salt v Chamberlain	1979	¶5330
Salt v Golding	1996	¶78670
Samuel Jones & Co (Devondale) Ltd v CIR	1951	¶13010
Schofield v R & H Hall Ltd	1975	¶25420
Seaham Harbour Company v Crook	1931	¶16250
Shelfside (Holdings) Ltd	2012	¶52810
Shepherd v Law Land plc	1990	¶65295
Simpson v Reynolds & Co (Insurances) Ltd	1975	¶14295
Small (Inspector of Taxes) v Mars UK Ltd	2007	¶11705
Smart v Lincolnshire Sugar Ltd	1937	¶16105
Smidth & Co v Greenwood	1921	¶92110
Smith Barry v Cordy	1946	¶5050
Smith's Potato Estates Ltd v Bolland	1948	¶14540
St John's School v Ward	1974	¶25420
Steele v EVC International NV	1996	¶75310
Stott and Ingham v Trehearne	1924	¶14620
Strand Options & Futures Ltd v Vojak	2004	¶18360
Strick v Regent Oil Co Ltd	1965	¶13280
Strong & Co of Romsey Ltd v Woodifield	1906	¶14540

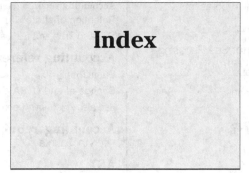

Index

Using the index

The numbers cross-refer to the paragraphs, and the plus sign (+) indicates that the entry covers a number of paragraphs. A list of abbreviations used in the index is given below.

ACT	Advance corporation tax	**DTR**	Double tax relief
BPRA	Business property renovation allowance	**EIS**	Enterprise investment scheme
CASC	Community amateur sports club	**FII**	Franked investment income
CFC	Controlled foreign company	**FYA**	First year allowance
CIHC	Close investment holding company	**OECD**	Organisation for Economic Co-operation and Development
CITR	Community investment tax relief	**PCTCT**	Profits chargeable to corporation tax
CT	Corporation tax	**R&D**	Research and development
CTSA	Corporation tax self-assessment	**SEIS**	Seed enterprise investment scheme
CUP	Comparable uncontrolled price	**SSE**	Substantial shareholding exemption
CVS	Corporate venturing scheme	**VCT**	Venture capital trust
DOTAS	Disclosure of tax avoidance schemes	**WDA**	Writing down allowance

N

Negligence:
Careless error: 52580

Negligible value:
Main entry: 31720+
Disposal of unquoted shares: 37230

No gain/no loss:
Chargeable gains - groups: 67080+
Transfer of UK trade between EU resident companies: 61205

Non-charitable expenditure:
Restriction of reliefs: 86185+

Non-commercial trade:
Losses: 36010

Non-profit making venture: See Trade

Non-qualifying distributions: See Distributions

Non-qualifying territories: See Residence

Non-resident company:
Close company rules: 75080
UK income: 92105+
UK participator: 76040+

Non-resident landlords:
Main entry: 19435+
See also Property

Non-sterling currency: See Foreign currency, Foreign exchange

Non-UK trade:
Transfer to EU resident company: 61210+

Notice to file a return:
Notice received late: 45205
Where notice period differs from accounting period: 46110

Notifiable scheme:
DOTAS: 46515+

Notification:
Coming within the charge to corporation tax: 60050+

Notional intra-group transfers: See Chargeable gains

Nuclear sites: See Contaminated land

O

OECD Model Tax Convention:
Main entry: 92285+
Attribution rules: 90140, 90175
See also Double tax agreements

Office:
Definition: 25740

Offshore funds:
Main entry: 21675+

Oil:
Exploration/exploitation: 14150
R&D: 78640

Oilseed support scheme:
Main entry: 84345

Operating lease:
Definition: 82085
Accounting treatment: 82130
Amount of capital expenditure: 82400
Disposal value: 82425+

Option:
Chargeable gains: 31415+

Ordinary share capital:
Change in ownership of company: 60250

Overseas:
Income - main entry: 90000+
Controlled foreign companies: 90555+
Double tax agreements: 90055
Intangible assets: 28775+
Letting of overseas properties: 90345
Liability to tax of overseas branch: 90110+
Loan relationships: 90345
Partnerships: 85530+
Residence: 90050+
Trading losses: 36000, 66085
UK resident company with foreign income: 90260+

Overseas government:
Close company rules: 75190

P

Parent:
Arbitrage: 94160
Issue of HMRC information notice: 50105

Vehicle:

HMRC power to inspect: 50345

See also Car, Commercial vehicles

Venture capital trust (VCT):

Main entry: 80355+

Qualifying subsidiary: 80450

Qualifying trade: 80445

W

Waste disposal:

Main entry: 14820+

Wasting assests:

Main entry: 31605+

Welfare:

For staff - whether deductible expenditure: 14625

Winding up:

Available assets in groups on winding up: 65205+

Distribution on - shadow ACT: 79500+,

Material interest on winding up for close company: 75645

Notional winding up for close company tests: 75485+

See also Liquidation

Woodlands:

Income from: 14145, 30195

Worldwide debt cap:

Main entry: 70530+

CFC: 91015

Writing down allowance (WDA):

Main entry: 26035+

See also Capital allowances

Typeset by NORD COMPO
Printed October 2013 by L.E.G.O. S.p.A, Lavis (TN)